American Studies

A CONCEPTUAL APPROACH

(Revised 1980)

Irving L. Gordon

Author of:
Review Text in American History
Review Text in World History
World History, Second Edition

Dedicated to serving

AMSCO

our nation's youth

When ordering this book, please specify:
either **R 167 P** *or*
AMERICAN STUDIES, **Paperback**

AMSCO SCHOOL PUBLICATIONS, INC.
315 Hudson Street New York, N.Y. 10013

To my dear ones
Who make everything worthwhile
Lois
My wife and companion
And our children
Meryl, Jesse, Reena

ISBN 0–87720–603–1

Preface

We Americans today expect the study of our nation's history to yield significant benefits.

In terms of content, we want subject matter that will explain our past history and shed light on our recent problems. Such subject matter includes—in addition to traditional areas—two new fields of inquiry: (a) American people—who are we? where did we come from? why did we come? how did we become Americanized? and (b) American civilization—what are our ideals and values? where did these ideals and values originate and how did they develop? what contributions have we made to science, culture, and civilized living?

In terms of teaching, Americans want history to emphasize, not the accumulation of irrelevant data, but the learning of basic concepts. Such concepts have value not only for understanding the past and present but also for anticipating the future.

American Studies: A Conceptual Approach has been designed to meet these new needs—fresh subject matter and emphasis upon concepts. It is meant for use as a basic text in courses in American studies. It may be supplemented, as the teacher sees fit and as the needs of the students require, by other materials such as primary sources, readings, and audio-visual aids.

American Studies: A Conceptual Approach provides the following features:

1. It presents the traditional topics—government, economy, and foreign policy—but with new perspectives and insights. It also provides extensive treatment of new topics: American people and American civilization. Through its wide-ranging discussion of ethnic groups and women, the book highlights the pluralism of American society. Through its presentation of American ideals, education, science, and arts, the book invites consideration of our cultural values.

2. The text focuses attention upon significant developments and concepts. In presenting concepts, the text makes considerable use of the case study approach, which leads students to read carefully, absorb historical knowledge, and think analytically. The case study approach seeks to have students arrive at intelligent but tentative conclusions which are subject to further examination and, if necessary, revision.

3. The text draws upon the latest historical scholarship. It does not, however, neglect traditional scholarship but seeks to present differing points of view fairly. This approach is meant to enrich the subject matter and to stimulate student interest.

4. To facilitate understanding, every effort has been made to provide crisp and clear language. The text nevertheless conveys the complexity of our historical development. It is mature, not simplistic.

5. The text contains much illustrative material. Maps relate geographic factors to historical events. Cartoons illuminate and comment upon current problems. Charts provide data for analyzing recent economic and social trends. Photographs illustrate the discussions of architecture, sculpture, and painting.

6. The book includes ample test material, consisting of a variety of short-answer and essay questions, arranged by topic and placed after the appropriate chapters. The questions probe significant information and measure the student's mastery of content and concept. Many questions require logical reasoning and mature understanding—major objectives of social studies teaching.

Contents

UNIT III. AMERICAN ECONOMIC LIFE

UNIT I. THE AMERICAN PEOPLE

Part 1. The Americans: A Diverse People in a Pluralistic Society

1. An Overview

ORIGINS OF THE AMERICAN PEOPLE

We Americans are all of immigrant origins: a small number are recent immigrants and the overwhelming majority are the descendants of earlier arrivals in the New World as follows:

1. Migrating Peoples. Long before the European discovery of the New World (1492), migratory peoples came here in cohesive groups. *Asian nomads*, thousands of years ago, traveled from northeastern Asia into the unpeopled Western Hemisphere. Their descendants became known as *Indians* and *Eskimos*. Other Asian peoples migrated from southeast Asia to the south and central Pacific islands. Their descendants became known as *Polynesians* (from the Greek word meaning "many islands"). Eventually, some Polynesians reached Hawaii and their descendants became known as *Hawaiians*.

2. Immigrants. After Columbus stumbled upon the New World (1492), immigrants began coming here to settle permanently. Many immigrants were attracted to the English colonies along the Atlantic seaboard. After these colonies won their independence from England (1783), immigrants came in even greater numbers. From 1783 until today immigrants coming from every part of the world to the United States have totaled more than 45 million persons.

3. Involuntary Immigrants. Negroes were forcibly uprooted from West Africa and transferred in captivity chiefly to be slaves on plantations in the New World.

4. Occupants of Territories Annexed by the United States. These peoples include (*a*) the descendants of earlier migratory groups—Indians in mainland United States, Indians and Eskimos in Alaska, and Hawaiians; (*b*) French

1

settlers at New Orleans acquired with the 1803 Louisiana Purchase; *(c)* Spanish settlers acquired with the 1819 Florida Purchase; *(d)* Mexicans acquired with the 1845 annexation of Texas and the 1848 Mexican Cession; and *(e)* Puerto Ricans acquired with the 1898 annexation of their Caribbean island home.

SIGNIFICANCE OF IMMIGRATION

In a broad sense, immigration refers to all persons who came to America —regardless of when and how they came. Consequently the United States is frequently referred to as a *nation of immigrants* and therefore, because of its diverse population, as a *pluralistic society.*

Oscar Handlin, an historian specializing in immigration, explained in his study *The Uprooted:* "Once I thought to write a history of the immigrants in America. Then I discovered that the immigrants *were* American history."

DIVERSITY OF THE AMERICAN PEOPLE TODAY

In 1967 the United States population topped the 200 million mark. These 200 million Americans were not *homogeneous,* or all alike; rather they were *heterogeneous,* or different from each other as follows:

1. Racial Identity

a. Meaning of Race. Most scholars agree that (1) a race consists of persons of similar physical characteristics transmitted by heredity from parents to children, (2) no race is "pure" or superior or inferior to any other race, and (3) the three primary racial groups are *Caucasoid,* or white, *Negroid,* or black, and *Mongoloid,* or yellow, brown, and red.

b. Races in America. Of the 200 million Americans in 1967 (1) 88 percent were Caucasoid, (2) almost 11 percent were Negroid, and (3) a little over 1 percent were Mongoloid.

2. Originating Areas.
In tracing their ancestors, white Americans are led back to the nations of Europe; yellow and brown Americans to the nations of Asia. These Americans whose ancestors originated from established nations are identified by the term *national origins.*

The ancestors of most black Americans were brought here from the west coast of Africa years before the establishment of modern African nations. Afro-Americans today, consequently, are identified by the term *continental origins.*

3. Native-Born or Foreign-Born.
Some 191 million of our 1967 population were native Americans—born in this country. All native-born Americans are citizens of the United States and of the state wherein they reside.

Some 9 million of our 1967 population were immigrants born in foreign countries. Of these foreign-born, a number have become citizens through the process of *naturalization;* the others reside here as *aliens.*

4. Religious Affiliation.
Some 126 million people were formally affiliated with religious groups—the largest ones being: various Protestant sects—67 million; Roman Catholics—47 million; Jews—5.6 million; Eastern Orthodox—4.1 mil-

lion; and Mormons—2.5 million. Some 74 million people were reported as having no formal religious affiliation.

5. Ethnic Groups

a. Meaning. *Ethnic groups* refers to the subdivisions among the American people based upon such factors as race, religion, originating area, history, culture, and common problems. Each ethnic group constitutes a recognizable *community of interest.*

b. Typical Ethnic Groups. (1) *White Anglo-Saxon Protestants* (the so-called WASPS), our largest ethnic group, represent an English-oriented culture and for many years dominated America's development. (2) *Black Americans* face the common problems of improving their social, economic, and political status. These same problems are shared by at least two other disadvantaged ethnic groups: *Mexican-Americans* and *Puerto Ricans.* (3) *Other Ethnic Groups.* These include *Jewish-Americans, Irish-Americans, Italian-Americans, Polish-Americans, German-Americans,* and *Greek-Americans.*

2. The Earliest Americans Were the Migratory Peoples

INDIANS

1. **Legendary Origins.** Many thousands of years ago, the first people to enter the Western Hemisphere came from Siberia in Asia into Alaska in North America. At that time, these two regions were probably connected by a land bridge where today are found the waters of the Bering Strait. These people over long periods of time spread out over the two American continents. By 1492, when Columbus discovered the New World, its population was between 15 and 20 million people.

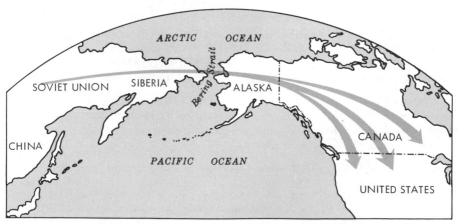

Routes of the Earliest Migrants to the New World

2. Named "Indians." Columbus believed, wrongly as we know, that he had reached the Indies off the coast of Asia. He consequently named the reddish-skinned natives "Indians." Later explorers used this name for most other natives of the New World.

3. Complex Pre-Columbian Indian Civilizations. The Indians living below the Rio Grande created three highly developed civilizations: (a) The *Mayas* of Central America (A.D. 4th to 10th centuries) devised a system of hieroglyphic writing, constructed buildings of stone, and calculated astronomical data including an accurate calendar. (b) The *Incas* of Peru (A.D. 13th to 16th centuries) conquered a 2500-mile empire along the west coast of South America. The Incas built roads, bridges, public buildings, and irrigation systems; they wove fine textiles and shaped elaborate gold and silver pieces. The Inca empire was overthrown in 1532 by the Spanish *conquistadors* (conquerors) under *Francisco Pizarro.* (c) The *Aztecs* of Mexico (A.D. 14th to 16th centuries) conquered a sizable empire and extorted heavy tribute. The Aztecs built irrigation systems, pyramids, temples, and palaces of stone. Aztec rule was ended in 1510 by the Spanish conquistadors under *Hernando Cortez.*

4. Simpler Pre-Columbian Indian Civilizations. Indians living above the Rio Grande consisted of many separate tribes. Each tribe was headed by a chieftain who usually was advised by the warriors, the elders, and the religious leader —the "shaman" or "medicine man." Some tribes settled in villages and lived mainly from farming; other tribes were nomadic and depended mainly on hunting. Many tribes glorified warfare.

CASE STUDY—A SIMPLER INDIAN CIVILIZATION: THE IROQUOIS OF NEW YORK STATE

1. Background. The Iroquois were a group of tribes living in the Northeast and speaking related languages. They lived in villages and used tree poles and bark to construct their "long houses." The Iroquois secured the necessities of life through both hunting and farming. They also were fierce warriors.

2. Iroquois Tribal Organization. The best-known Iroquois tribes resided in central New York. They were the Mohawks, Oneidas, Onondagas, Cayugas, Senecas, and Tuscaroras. Known as the *Six Nations*, they dealt with common problems through a confederacy, the *League of the Iroquois.*

3. Status of Women. Iroquois society, to some extent, was *matriarchal.* Family descent was traced through the mother. Women headed the family groups that made up the clans; women helped choose the men who served on the tribal councils and at the League of the Iroquois.

4. In the American Revolution and Afterwards. The Iroquois League split apart as two tribes sided with the colonists and four tribes with the British. *Joseph Brant,* a Mohawk chief, led the pro-British Iroquois in massacres of colonists at Cherry Valley, New York, and Wyoming, Pennsylvania.

In 1779 Brant's forces of Loyalists and Indians were decisively defeated by an American expedition under General *John Sullivan.* After the war, Brant led his people into Canada; *Cornplanter*, a Seneca chief, led those Iroquois who remained in New York State.

Indian Contributions

1. Domestication of Plants: maize (corn), potato, pumpkin, banana, cotton, tobacco
2. Domestication of Animals: duck, turkey
3. Use of Medicinals: cocaine, quinine, atropine, witch hazel
4. Practical Inventions: tepee, hammock, canoe, simple products of rubber
5. Decorative Arts: pottery, rugs, masks, totem poles
6. Ecology: man must live in harmony with nature
7. Words: moccasin, wigwam, powwow, squaw

ESKIMOS

1. Origins. Over 2000 years ago, Asian immigrants crossed the Bering Strait by boat to North America. Later they spread across the Arctic region eastward as far as Greenland. Their descendants became known as *Eskimos*.

2. Eskimo Life. The Eskimos had no tribes and no formal government; their basic unit of society was the family. They secured the necessities of life by fishing and hunting. The Eskimos used *(a)* harpoons and bows and arrows for hunting, *(b)* kayaks (skin-covered canoes) and dogsleds for traveling, *(c)* goggles to protect their eyes against snow glare, and *(d)* ivory and bone to carve distinctive works of art.

3. Eskimos in Alaska Today. Of Alaska's 300,000 people, the Eskimos number about 20,000. Most Eskimos speak English, live in villages, and a number work at fish canneries and airfields. The Eskimos face communal problems: improving their living standards, bettering their education, developing pride in their own heritage, and gaining the respect of white Alaskans.

POLYNESIANS IN HAWAII

1. Hawaiian Life. When Captain *James Cook*, the English explorer, discovered Hawaii in 1778, the natives lived in a semifeudal society. The ruling class consisted of the nobles who held the land and the priests who directed the pagan religion of idols and human sacrifice. The lower class consisted of fishermen and farmers.

2. Impact of the Americans on Hawaii. The coming of the Americans transformed the Hawaiian islands as *(a)* missionaries converted the natives to Christianity, *(b)* investors purchased land for sugar and pineapple plantations, *(c)* mainland diseases decimated the islanders so that plantation owners brought in workers especially from China, Japan, and the Philippines, and *(d)* in 1898 the United States finally annexed Hawaii.

3. Hawaii Today. *(a) Population.* Of more than 750,000 people: the Hawaiians of full or part native ancestry constitute 20 percent; Japanese—30 percent;

Filipinos—10 percent; Chinese—5 percent; Europeans and Americans—30 percent. About one-third of the population has mixed ancestry. *(b) Grievances of Native Hawaiians.* (1) They are a minority in their own homeland. (2) They generally do not own land. (3) They fear that their native culture is being overwhelmed by the civilization of mainland America.

MULTIPLE-CHOICE QUESTIONS

Select the number of the item that best completes the statement or answers the question.

1. The United States is known as a pluralistic society because of its diverse (1) governments (2) geographic features (3) peoples (4) news media.
2. The earliest known people in the New World were (1) natives who originated here (2) migratory groups who came from northeastern Asia (3) voluntary immigrants from northwestern Europe (4) seafaring groups from Hawaii.
3. Which one of the following is *not* a primary racial group? (1) Caucasoid (2) Negroid (3) WASP (4) Mongoloid
4. In regard to people, the word *homogeneous* means (1) diverse (2) all men and women (3) all alike (4) heterogeneous.
5. The largest ethnic group in America consists of (1) Irish-Americans (2) White Anglo-Saxon Protestants (3) German-Americans (4) Polish-Americans.
6. Complex Indian civilizations in the New World did *not* include the (1) Aztecs (2) Incas (3) Mayas (4) Iroquois.
7. Iroquois society was to some extent matriarchal, meaning that an influential role was played by (1) men (2) women (3) tribal elders—both men and women (4) tribal warriors.
8. During the American Revolution, the League of the Iroquois (1) supported the British (2) supported the Americans (3) was neutral (4) split apart, with two of the six tribes supporting the Americans.
9. The European explorer who discovered Hawaii was (1) Hernando Cortez (2) James Cook (3) Joseph Brant (4) John Sullivan.
10. The early Eskimos were known for (1) building pyramids (2) shaping elaborate pieces of gold (3) traveling by kayaks (4) weaving fine textiles.
11. Hawaiians of full- or part-native ancestry today (1) constitute a majority of the population of the Hawaiian islands (2) are mainly farmers who own their own land (3) have rejected the white settlers' religion (4) fear the disappearance of their native culture.
12. Oscar Handlin is best known as (1) an historian of immigration (2) an anthropologist of Indian culture (3) a geographer of the Bering Strait region (4) an economist of the modern African nations.

ESSAY QUESTIONS

1. Americans are a diverse people. *(a)* Discuss *three* evidences that support this statement. *(b)* Is population diversity a strength or a weakness? Defend your answer.
2. American history and culture began long before the European discovery of the New World. For any *two* of the following groups—Indians, Eskimos, and Hawaiians—show how their early history and culture are related to modern America.
3. Name *one* ethnic group to which you belong or with which you are familiar. Discuss any *three* factors to prove that the members of this ethnic group have a recognizable *community of interest.*

3. Many Different Peoples Settled in the Thirteen Colonies

The Thirteen Colonies by 1775: A Pluralistic Population

Ethnic Origins			Percent
English settlers		1,500,000	57
Other settlers from the British Isles (mainly Scotch-Irish; also some Irish, Scots, and Welsh)		370,000	14
Settlers from Continental Europe			
Germans	200,000		
Dutch	67,500		
Swiss	25,000	330,000	12
Swedes and Finns	20,000		
French	15,000		
Spanish and Portuguese Jews	2,500		
Blacks from Africa			
Slaves		400,000	15
Free Men		50,000	2
Totals		2,650,000	100

ENGLISH SETTLERS

(1) Religious Motives. As *Anglicanism* during the 16th century became the official religion of England, other religions suffered discrimination and persecution. Some non-Anglicans left for the colonies. *(a)* The *Pilgrims*, a small group of Puritans, in 1620 sailed on the *Mayflower* and settled at Plymouth in Massachusetts. *Puritans* in greater numbers in 1630 founded Massachusetts Bay Colony. *(b) Roman Catholics* in 1634 settled in Maryland, founded as a Catholic refuge by *Lord Baltimore*. *(c) Quakers*, also known as the *Society of Friends*, settled in 1681 in Pennsylvania, founded by *William Penn*. (2) Political Motives. For most of the 17th century, England was torn by political strife between its absolutist Stuart kings and its Parliament, which finally triumphed by the 1688–1689 "Glorious Revolution." Many English, however, fled to the colonies to escape political unrest and civil war. (3) Economic Motives. Landless peasants, unemployed city dwellers, persons convicted of minor crimes, and debtors—all looked to start life anew in the colonies.

OTHER SETTLERS FROM THE BRITISH ISLES

1. **Scotch-Irish and Irish.** The Scotch-Irish *(a)* were of Scottish ancestry, *(b)* were Protestants (Presbyterians), and *(c)* lived in Ireland's northern province, *Ulster*. In the 18th century, as English markets were closed to Ulster's foodstuffs and textiles and as English absentee landlords raised rents, many Scotch-Irish left for the New World. From southern Ireland, some Irish Catholics also left for colonial America.

2. **Scots.** From the "Highlands" or mountainous regions of Scotland, some few Scots migrated to the colonies to escape poor soil and high land rents.

3. Welsh. In small groups, Welsh Quakers went to Pennsylvania in search of religious freedom and fertile soil.

SETTLERS FROM CONTINENTAL EUROPE

1. German Settlers. Motives. *(a) Religious.* By the treaty ending the Thirty Years' War (1618–1648), Catholic, Lutheran, and Calvinist rulers in the Germanies gained the right to determine their subjects' religion. Members of dissenting Protestant sects—Quakers, Mennonites (Amish), and Baptists (Dunkers)—fled to America to escape persecution and maintain their own faith. *(b) Warfare.* Inhabitants of the Palatinate, a Rhineland area, fled to escape the death and destruction of religious and dynastic wars. *(c) Economic.* Farmers fled high rents and heavy taxes. Many Germans settled in Pennsylvania colony. They were among the ancestors of today's *Pennsylvania Dutch.*

2. Dutch Settlers. In the New Netherland colony, Dutch farmers and fur traders occupied Manhattan Island, eastern Long Island, and the Hudson River Valley—all in New York—and also northern New Jersey. In 1664 New Netherland surrendered to the English navy and came under English rule.

3. Spanish and Portuguese Jews. After living in the Iberian Peninsula for hundreds of years, these *Sephardic Jews,* or *Sephardim* (from the Hebrew word meaning "Spain"), were driven out—in 1492 from Spain and in 1496 from Portugal. With great difficulty, some Sephardic Jews reached more tolerant lands in North Africa and Europe. Mainly from Holland, some few Jews came to colonial America. In 1654 *Asher Levy* led the first group of 23 Jews to settle in New Amsterdam (later New York). They were refugees from a Dutch settlement in Brazil captured by Portuguese forces. Other Jewish communities developed in Philadelphia, Savannah, Charleston, and Newport.

4. Other Continental European Settlers. *(a) Swiss,* mainly Protestant and German-speaking, settled in Pennsylvania. They too were among the ancestors of today's Pennsylvania Dutch. *(b) Swedes* and *Finns,* seeking better farmlands, settled in Delaware. Eventually their colony came under English rule. *(c) French Huguenots* (Protestants) fled Catholic France after 1685, when King Louis XIV ended religious tolerance. A number of French settled in South Carolina.

WORKERS TO OVERCOME THE COLONIAL LABOR SHORTAGE

1. The Problem. In the English colonies labor was scarce. Newcomers were unwilling to work for others when they easily could acquire land and themselves become independent farmers.

2. The Solutions. *(a) Indentured Servants From the British Isles.* Impoverished persons, who lacked funds to pay for their transportation to America, included poor and landless farmers, unemployed and low-paid workers, debtors unable to repay loans and therefore facing prison, orphans, and paupers. These would-be immigrants signed *indentures,* or contracts agreeing to work, from four to seven years, in exchange for passage to the New World. *(b) Redemptioners From*

Continental Europe. Impoverished German and Swiss immigrants agreed that their services be sold in the New World to *redeem* their debt to the ship's captain for their transportation. Together known as *bonded servants,* the indentured workers and redemptioners totaled over half of all white immigrants to colonial America. *(c) Forced Negro Migrations.* In 1619, 20 Africans brought to Jamestown, Virginia, were the first Negroes in colonial America. Although originally considered as indentured servants, by the 1660's most blacks were legally held as slaves. By 1775 the colonies contained some 400,000 Negro slaves, of whom three-fourths were in the South.

4. The United States Is a Nation of Immigrants

From the Birth of the Nation to the Close of the Frontier (1783–1890)

STATISTICAL DATA ON IMMIGRATION

1. **Estimated by Historians.** From 1783 to 1820: 250,000.

2. **Provided by Government Records**

Decade	Number	Decade	Number
1821–1830	143,000	1861–1870	2,300,000
1831–1840	600,000	1871–1880	2,800,000
1841–1850	1,700,000	1881–1890	5,200,000
1851–1860	2,600,000		

IMMIGRANTS FROM EUROPE TO 1890

1. **Irish.** *(a) Motives.* Irish nationalists resented English rule over Ireland; Irish Catholics resented English taxes to support the Anglican Church in Ireland; Irish tenant farmers resented English absentee landlords who charged high rents. *(b) Peak Immigration.* With the great *potato famine* of the 1840's, Irish immigration swelled into a tremendous wave. From 1840 to 1860, nearly 2 million Irish came to the United States. *(c) Urban Dwellers.* The Irish settled in cities, notably Boston and New York. They lacked money to buy farmland and, as Roman Catholics, desired to remain close together. They found work in factories, mills, mines, and in construction gangs building canals and railroads.

2. **Germans.** *(a) Motives.* German peasants could not compete with grain grown on large estates of the nobles. German artisans could not compete with machine-made goods. German liberals were discontented with despotic governments. *(b) Peak Migration.* From 1830 to 1890, some 4.5 million Germans came to our shores. Liberal Germans, who came after the failure of the pro-democratic revolutions of 1848, were called *Forty-Eighters. (c) Areas of Settlement.* The Germans settled chiefly in the Midwest, both on farms and in cities (Cincinnati, St. Louis, and Milwaukee). Germans became prominent in making watches, optical equipment, pianos, beer, and pharmaceuticals.

"It seems to me the majority of people in this country belong to some minority group!" (*Gerard in the Wall Street Journal*)

3. Scandinavians. *(a) Motives.* Swedish, Norwegian and Danish farmers, workers, and small businessmen migrated to better their economic conditions. Also religious minorities feared the policies of the official Lutheran churches. *(b) Peak Migration.* Scandinavian immigrants started coming in the 1840's but they reached their peak—over 500,000—in the 1880's. *(c) Areas of Settlement.* Scandinavians settled chiefly in the upper Mississippi Valley region. Some became farmers, others lumberjacks, and still others carpenters and machinists.

4. Other European Immigrants. These included considerable numbers of English and lesser numbers of Scots, Welsh, French, Dutch, and Swiss.

5. "Old Immigrants"—Meaning. Historians have traditionally referred to the European peoples coming before 1890 as "old immigrants." They originated mainly from northern and western Europe: chiefly Great Britain, Ireland, Germany, Holland, France, Switzerland, and the Scandinavian countries. They arrived while the frontier was still open, and many settled on farms in the West. It has been claimed that, since these "old immigrants" possessed customs and traditions similar to those of native Americans, they were easily assimilated into American life.

PEOPLES FROM OTHER CONTINENTS

1. Blacks From Africa. In 1808, the first year permitted by the Constitution, Congress outlawed the importation of slaves into the United States. Since this law was enforced inadequately and since Southern plantation owners needed additional workers, the slave trade continued illegally. By 1860 an estimated 250,000 slaves had been smuggled into the Southern states.

2. Chinese From Asia. To escape from famine, oppressive government, and civil war, and to benefit from the discovery of gold in California (1848) and relatively high wages, some 300,000 Chinese, by the 1880's, migrated to our West Coast. Mainly peasants without families, they worked as cooks, laundrymen, miners, and railroad construction laborers. By the white majority, the Chinese were derogatively called *coolies*.

3. Canadians From North America. By 1890 some 1 million Canadians resided chiefly in the northern United States. The *British-Canadians,* in the Midwest, became farmers and skilled workers; they blended easily into the American population. The *French-Canadians,* in northern New York and New England, worked as farm laborers, lumberjacks, and textile millhands. Being Catholics and speaking a French dialect, the French-Canadians remained distinct from the American population.

From the Close of the Frontier to the
End of the World War I Decade (1890–1920)

STATISTICAL DATA ON IMMIGRATION

Decade	Number
1891–1900	3,700,000
1901–1910	8,800,000
1911–1920	5,700,000

Comment. More immigrants came than in the previous 100 years. Travel had become easier, and news of America had reached southern and eastern Europe and Japan.

IMMIGRANTS FROM EUROPE—TO 1920

1. Italians. *(a) Motives.* Peasants, overwhelmingly from southern Italy and Sicily, fled poor soil, small farms, and high land rents. Italian citrus growers, facing competition from Florida and California orange growers, gradually lost their American markets. Italian artisans and small shopkeepers achieved only a bare existence. *(b) Peak Immigration.* From 1890 to 1920, some 4.5 million Italians arrived at American ports. Most landed at New York City; some came to other Atlantic Coast cities and to New Orleans. *(c) Urban Dwellers.* Too poor to buy farms and accustomed to village life, the Italians formed ethnic enclaves called "Little Italies" in most sizable American cities from Boston to New Orleans. They found work in highway and railroad construction, in the building industry, and in the garment trades.

2. Greeks. *(a) Motives.* Greek peasants, mainly tenants who paid high interest on loans and heavy taxes, suffered in the 1890's from the price drop of currants, their chief export crop. They came to America to escape grinding poverty. Greeks living as a subject nationality outside Greece left to escape foreign rule. *(b) Peak Immigration.* From 1890 to 1920, some 500,000 Greeks entered the United States. At first the men came; later they sent for their families. *(c) Urban Dwellers.* Most Greeks settled in cities of the Northeast. Some worked in mines and on railroads; others opened small retail businesses —tobacco and candy stores, flower shops, and restaurants.

3. Poles. *(a) Motives.* From 1795 to 1920, Poland did not exist as an independent nation; its people and territory were held partly by Austria and Prussia but mainly by Russia. Three times in the mid-19th century, Polish nationalists rebelled for independence from Russia but were easily suppressed. Polish nationalists resented "Russification" and after 1870 "Germanization." Both programs sought to destroy Polish culture, including adherence to the Roman Catholic faith. Polish peasants, who owned small farms or labored on the nobles' estates, earned a scant living. *(b) Peak Immigration.* From 1890 to 1920, Polish immigrants numbered 1.5 million. Of all Slavic-speaking immigrants to the United States, the Poles were most numerous. *(c) Urban Dwellers.* Settling mainly in major cities of the Northeast, the Poles formed ethnic enclaves called "Little Polands." They provided unskilled labor for meat-packing plants, steel mills, coal mines, and textile factories.

4. Other Peoples From East European Empires. *(a) Austro-Hungarian Empire.* Slavic-speaking peoples—Czechs, Slovaks, and Yugoslavs—were *subject nationalities*. They lacked their own governments and were subject to autocratic rule by the Austrians and Hungarians. In addition to alien rule, these Slavic-speaking peoples fled economic distress. *(b) Russian Empire.* Russian peasants lacked sufficient land; Russian workers received low wages; Russian liberals feared Czarist political tyranny. Subject nationalities in Russia—such as Catholic Lithuanians and Lutheran Finns—faced religious and cultural persecution.

Jews in large numbers also fled these two empires.

5. Jews

a. Brief History. Jews have been considered as a religious group—united by the religion and culture of Judaism, and also as a nationality—the descendants of a people who had lived in a Jewish national state in Palestine. When a Jewish revolt against Roman rule was crushed in the 1st century A.D., most Jews were driven out of their Palestine homeland and became scattered, especially in the Middle East, North Africa, and Europe. From the Middle Ages onward, Jews in Christian Europe faced (1) religious persecution—as they resisted conversion to Christianity, (2) economic discrimination—as they were prohibited from owning

"The Steerage," a 1911 photograph by Alfred Stieglitz (*Philadelphia Museum of Art: Given by Carl Zigrosser*)

land and entering many professions so that they were driven to become moneylenders (an occupation prohibited to Christians by the medieval Church as usury) and merchants (considered a demeaning occupation), (3) social discrimination—as they were required to live in special city quarters later called *ghettos*, and (4) violence and oppression—by mobs seeking to loot and murder and by governments treating the Jews as *scapegoats*. Although innocent and powerless, Jews were blamed for any evils that befell the various countries.

b. Early Jewish Migrations to America. The first Jews to come to America were the relatively few Sephardim of colonial times. The second group to come to America were the *Ashkenazic Jews* or *Ashkenazim* (from the Hebrew word meaning "Germany"). They came by the thousands in the mid-19th century, mainly from Germany. A number became peddlers or owners of small shops —from which evolved several of today's notable department stores. By 1880 some 250,000 Jews lived in the United States.

c. Motives for Leaving East Europe. The East European Jews were also Ashkenazim. They fled Czarist Russia and Russian Poland to escape discrimination and oppression—they had been compelled to live in a special area called the *Pale of Settlement*, kept from owning land, barred from most professions, restricted by *quotas* from schools of higher learning, and victimized by Czarist government-inspired outbursts of violence called *pogroms*. In Rumania and in the Austro-Hungarian Empire, Jews were subjected to similar indignities and oppressions.

d. Peak Immigration. Beginning in the 1880's, many East European Jews fled. Some, inspired by *Zionism*, went to Turkish-controlled Palestine to rebuild a Jewish national homeland, but most came to the United States. From 1900 to 1920, this third and largest wave of Jewish immigrants totaled over 1.5 million.

e. Urban Dwellers. These Jews settled in the Northeast, forming ethnic enclaves in major cities—New York, Philadelphia, Boston, and Chicago. Many found work in the needle trades, some becoming owners but most remaining workers, and helped to create the first garment trades labor unions. Jews also pioneered in the new motion picture and radio industries. Jewish parents encouraged their children to seek higher education and to enter the professions.

6. Other European Immigrants. Other East European immigrants to America included Rumanians and Hungarians. Also some 3 million "old immigrants" continued to arrive from Scandinavia, Germany, Ireland, and Great Britain.

7. "New Immigrants"—Meaning. Historians have traditionally referred to European peoples coming after 1890 as the "new immigrants." Unlike the "old immigrants," the "new immigrants" originated chiefly in southern and eastern Europe: Italy, Greece, Austria-Hungary, Rumania, Russian Poland, and Russia. They arrived when the frontier was closed and therefore settled chiefly in the cities. It has been claimed that, since the "new immigrants" possessed customs and traditions different from those of Americans, they experienced difficulty in adjusting to American ways of life.

PEOPLES FROM NON-EUROPEAN COUNTRIES—TO 1920

1. Japanese. After the Japanese government lifted its ban on emigration in 1885, some Japanese workers left their homeland in search of work or better pay. Many went to Hawaii and worked on sugar plantations; others came to the continental United States. By 1907 about 100,000 Japanese lived along our Pacific Coast, especially in California. Although some worked in the fishing and canning industries, most turned to agriculture—first as hired hands and later as truck farm owners.

2. Mexicans. *(a) By Annexation of Territory.* In 1845 the United States admitted Texas to the Union and in 1848, by winning the Mexican War, acquired California and the American Southwest—together called the *Mexican Cession.* Some 100,000 Mexicans thusly came under American rule. *(b) By Immigration.* Driven by poor living standards, from 1900 to 1920, some 270,000 Mexicans migrated into the Southwest—chiefly Texas, Arizona, and California. Most became migratory farmworkers, going from one large farm to another and picking crops—citrus fruits, grapes, berries, sugar cane, and cotton. (Check the Index for "Mexican-Americans.")

3. Other Peoples. *(a)* Canadians totaling about 1 million, from 1890 to 1920 crossed the border into the United States. *(b)* West Indian Negroes left their Caribbean island homes and, by 1920, some 200,000 resided in our Atlantic seaboard cities. Those who spoke English adjusted more easily to American life than did those whose native tongues were Spanish or French.

From the End of the World War I Decade to the Present (1920–   )

DECLINING NUMBER OF IMMIGRANTS—REASONS

(1) The United States in the 1920's and afterwards enacted immigration laws severely curtailing the entry of immigrants. (2) European dictators, unwilling to lose workers and soldiers, opposed emigration. (3) During the years of the Great Depression, beginning in 1929, the United States was not a land of economic opportunity. (4) World War II (1939–1945) made travel difficult.

After 1945 the United States somewhat eased its immigration restrictions.

STATISTICAL DATA ON IMMIGRATION

Half Decade	Number	Half Decade	Number
1921–1925	2,639,000	1951–1955	1,088,000
1926–1930	1,468,000	1956–1960	1,428,000
1931–1935	220,000	1961–1965	1,450,000
1936–1940	308,000	1966–1970	1,871,000
1941–1945	171,000	1971–1975	1,936,000
1946–1950	864,000		

IMMIGRANTS FROM EUROPE FLEEING DICTATORSHIP

1. Before America's Entrance Into World War II (1941). In part due to World War I, many European nations were beset by economic and political troubles and came under the rule of dictators. Among such tyrannies were several smaller nations and three major powers: Russia became a Communist dictatorship first

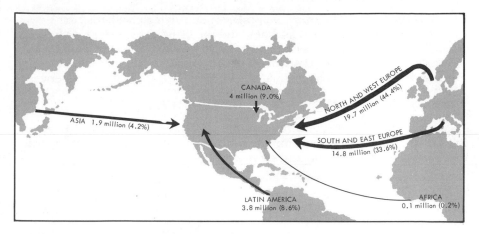

CANADA
4 million (9.0%)

NORTH AND WEST EUROPE
19.7 million (44.4%)

ASIA 1.9 million (4.2%)

SOUTH AND EAST EUROPE
14.8 million (33.6%)

LATIN AMERICA
3.8 million (8.6%)

AFRICA
0.1 million (0.2%)

Sources of Immigration to the United States

under Lenin and then under Stalin; Italy became a Fascist dictatorship under Mussolini, and Germany became a Nazi dictatorship under Hitler. The rise of the dictators brought persecution of political opponents, economic or class enemies, subject nationalities, religious minorities—especially Catholics and Jews—and intellectuals.

From 1917 to 1941, some 300,000 refugees fled for their lives from European dictatorships to the United States. Among them were a large percentage of *Illustrious Immigrants*—to use the title of the book by Laura Fermi—as follows: orchestra conductors *Arturo Toscanini* from Italy and *Bruno Walter* from Germany; pianists *Artur Schnabel* from Germany and *Vladimir Horowitz* from Russia; writers *Thomas Mann* and *Erich Remarque* from Germany; aviation pioneers *Alexander de Seversky* and *Igor Sikorsky* from Russia; atomic scientists *Albert Einstein* from Germany, *Edward Teller* from Hungary, and *Enrico Fermi* from Italy.

2. After World War II Ended (1945). *Refugees* and *displaced persons* (DP's), totaling several million in Europe, included *(a)* the few survivors of the German concentration camps—some Jews and anti-Nazis of various nationalities, *(b)* slave laborers, chiefly East Europeans, who had been forced to work in Germany during the war and who refused to return home to Communist rule, and *(c)* escapees from Communist rule in eastern Europe, such as a considerable number of Hungarians who fled their homeland when their 1956 revolt against Soviet domination was brutally suppressed by Russian forces.

Of these refugees and displaced persons, over half a million were allowed into the United States above the yearly immigration quotas by the provisions of special *Displaced Persons Acts*.

THE "BRAIN DRAIN"

Since World War II, the United States has attracted a considerable number of highly trained and educated immigrants—engineers, doctors, nurses, scientists, scholars—a population flow termed the "Brain Drain." They came because of employment opportunities, high salaries and living standards, the newest research equipment, cultural facilities, and the climate of freedom. At first, the highly educated immigrants came mainly from developed countries—Canada, Japan, and West European nations—but starting in the 1960's increasing numbers came from the developing nations of Asia, Africa, and Latin America.

PEOPLES FROM THE WESTERN HEMISPHERE

Not restricted by the American immigration laws of the 1920's, these peoples, coming chiefly for economic reasons, constituted an increasing proportion of the post-World War I immigration to the United States.

1. Canadians. In the 1920 decade, almost 1 million Canadians came to the United States. Thereafter, Canadian immigration decreased sharply—in the 1930's due to the depression; during and after World War II due to Canada's booming economy.

2. Mexicans. *(a) Legal Immigration.* In the 1920 decade, Mexican immigration was substantial but in the depression decade of the 1930's, it declined sharply. During the World War II years, by special arrangement between the United States and Mexican governments, many Mexicans were admitted as temporary "contract laborers" to offset American manpower shortages in industry, railroad transportation, and agriculture. *(b) Illegal Immigration.* Millions of Mexicans entered the United States illegally. They were known as "wetbacks." (Check the Index for "Mexican-Americans.")

3. Immigrants From the Caribbean Islands. *(a) Blacks From the British West Indies.* Until 1952, when the immigration law was revised to halt the admission of British West Indies blacks under the large British quota, they came in considerable numbers. They settled along the Atlantic seaboard in major cities and found employment as unskilled workers, as skilled needle trades operators, and some well-educated professionals as lawyers, dentists, and doctors. They felt themselves to be set apart from the American blacks since the West Indians represented British not American culture, often were better educated, and believed

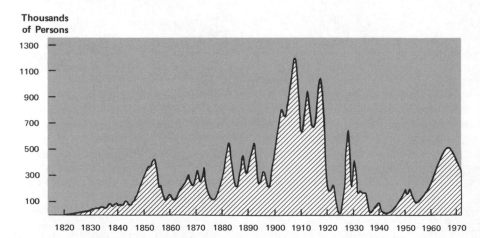

Total Immigration to the United States, 1820–1970

that they were more ambitious and maintained stronger family ties. Between the West Indian and American black communities, there developed considerable friction. *(b) Refugees From Cuba.* In 1959 Fidel Castro seized control of Cuba and thereafter established a totalitarian Communist regime. Some half a million Cubans—including democratic adherents, devout Catholics, professionals, merchants, and businessmen—fled to other Western Hemisphere nations, mostly to the United States. They settled chiefly in Florida, especially in Tampa and Miami. Workers found employment in the construction and tourist industries; professionals continued their careers as engineers, technicians, dentists, and doctors; merchants opened retail stores; businessmen started cigar-making, shoe manufacturing, and banking companies. *(c) American Citizens From Puerto Rico.* As American citizens, Puerto Ricans could freely move to the mainland. During World War II and the postwar boom, they came in large numbers, chiefly to East Coast cities. (Check the Index for "Puerto Ricans.")

REFUGEES FROM INDO-CHINA (SINCE 1975)

Following the Communist takeovers in Cambodia, Laos, and South Vietnam, over 1 million Indo-Chinese fled their homelands. Some feared imprisonment or execution for having opposed the Communists; others fled renewed warfare in Cambodia between rival Communist factions; still others fled Communist tyranny and harsh living conditions. By 1980 over 220,000 of these homeless human beings had been admitted into the United States. (For details, check the Index for Refugees, Indo-Chinese.)

TIME-LINE QUESTIONS

The letters *A-F* represent time intervals as indicated. For *each* event listed below, select the *letter* that indicates the time interval within which the event occurred.

1. Irish immigration to America reached its peak.
2. Fleeing Communist rule, Hungarian and Cuban refugees came to the United States.
3. A group of Sephardic Jews, refugees from a Dutch settlement in Brazil captured by the Portuguese, landed in New Amsterdam.
4. Scandinavian immigration to America reached its peak.
5. "Brain drain" immigrants began coming to the United States.
6. Some 250,000 slaves had been smuggled into the United States illegally.
7. Seeking religious freedom, the Pilgrims sailed on the *Mayflower* to the New World.
8. Italian immigration to America reached its peak.
9. The United States government did not collect any data on immigration.
10. Japanese immigration to America reached its peak.

MULTIPLE-CHOICE QUESTIONS

1. The settlers who constituted the largest ethnic group in the colonies were the (1) Irish (2) Dutch (3) English (4) Swedes.
2. The English colony founded as a refuge for Roman Catholics was (1) Maryland (2) Rhode Island (3) South Carolina (4) Massachusetts.
3. The English colony founded as a refuge for Quakers was (1) Delaware (2) Virginia (3) Pennsylvania (4) Connecticut.
4. The Scotch-Irish who settled in colonial America came directly from (1) Scotland (2) Wales (3) the Palatinate (4) Ulster.

5. Which event had the *most* immediate effect upon immigration to the United States? (1) the defeat of Mexico by the United States in 1848 (2) the potato famine in Ireland in the 1840's (3) the Communist seizure of power in Russia in 1917 (4) the independence by Belgium, recognized in 1839

6. Which was an important cause of immigration to the United States in the 1840's? (1) the Napoleonic wars (2) changes in our immigration policy (3) revolutions in Europe (4) failure of the citrus crop in Sicily

7. The immigrants who worked in the New England textile mills toward the end of the 19th century were (1) French-Canadians (2) British-Canadians (3) Jews (4) Irish.

8. Today's Pennsylvania Dutch trace their ancestry to (1) Germans and Irish (2) Germans and Swiss (3) Dutch and French (4) Dutch and Welsh.

9. Of all the white immigrants to colonial America, bonded servants totaled what percent? (1) 10 (2) 30 (3) 50 (4) 90

10. Which immigrant group furthered the manufacture of optical equipment and pianos in 19th-century America? (1) Germans (2) Greeks (3) Italians (4) Japanese

11. Of all Slavic-speaking immigrants to America, the *most* numerous were the (1) Czechs (2) Poles (3) Russians (4) Yugoslavs.

12. A scapegoat refers to a person who (1) commits a crime but escapes punishment (2) is innocent but blamed for the misfortune of others (3) follows a strong leader unquestioningly (4) has no sense of responsibility.

13. Jews in Czarist Russia suffered from government-inspired outbursts of violence known as (1) pogroms (2) quotas (3) Soviets (4) ghettos.

14. In the early 20th century, immigrants from southern Europe settled chiefly (1) in the cities of the Far West (2) in the cities along the East Coast (3) on the farmlands in the Midwest (4) on the farmlands of the Far West.

15. In which period did the *largest* number of immigrants enter the United States? (1) 1789–1810 (2) 1841–1860 (3) 1871–1890 (4) 1891–1910

16. Members of which immigrant group in mid-19th-century America set the foundations for many modern department stores? (1) Russian Jews (2) Greeks (3) Irish (4) German Jews

17. In which decade did the *smallest* number of immigrants enter the United States? (1) 1861–1870 (2) 1911–1920 (3) 1931–1940 (4) 1951–1960

ESSAY QUESTIONS

1. By 1775 the 13 American colonies contained a *pluralistic population.* (*a*) Explain the italicized term. (*b*) Discuss *two* examples to prove the statement. (*c*) Over the past 200 years, has the American population become *more* pluralistic or *less* pluralistic? Present *two* arguments to support your answer.

2. Compare immigrants to colonial America with immigrants to 20th-century America so as to show that their reasons for migrating here were (*a*) in *two* ways similar and (*b*) in *two* ways different.

3. Some historians have classified the European peoples coming to America into two groups: "old immigrants" and "new immigrants." For these two groups describe (*a*) *three* ways in which they were different and (*b*) *three* ways in which they were similar.

4. When considering immigration into the United States, *most* Americans think of immigrants from Europe. (*a*) Explain *one* reason why most Americans usually think of immigrants from Europe. (*b*) Name any *two* non-European immigrants to the United States and describe *from where, when,* and *why* they came. (*c*) Are the reasons for coming of non-European immigrants similar to or different from those of European immigrants? Defend your answer. (*d*) State *one* generalization regarding the reasons why all immigrants came to America. Indicate briefly what evidence you would need to support your generalizations.

5. American Attitudes and Policies Toward Immigration Have Changed With the Times

AMERICANS WELCOME IMMIGRATION—NEARLY TO THE END OF THE 19TH CENTURY

1. Reasons for Welcome. Immigrants represented (a) workers to construct canals and railroads and to labor in mines and factories, (b) settlers to join the westward movement and farm the Western lands, (c) consumers to purchase the products of agriculture and industry, (d) soldiers to increase the nation's military power, and (e) men of special abilities, talents, and skills. Furthermore, Americans took pride in the humanitarian tradition of the United States as a haven for the downtrodden and oppressed.

2. Evidences of Welcome. (a) American mine, mill, and factory owners sent agents especially to Great Britain to recruit skilled coal, iron and steel, and textile workers. (b) From the 1850's onward, American (and European) steamship companies maintained agents and distributed circulars and posters to encourage immigration to America so as to sell transportation tickets. (c) Railroads that had received land grants from the federal government advertised and sent agents to European countries and to Atlantic port cities to attract settlers to their lands. (d) The *Homestead Act of 1862* offered 160 acres of land free not only to American citizens but also to aliens who declared their intention to become citizens. (e) Many Midwestern states and, after the Civil War, Southern states maintained bureaus of immigration to attract newcomers to their borders. (f) Earlier immigrants, in letters sent to their kinsmen at home, overwhelmingly praised conditions in America. Throughout European communities, these "American Letters" stirred up the "America fever." (g) In 1886 the Statue of Liberty, a gift from the French to the American people, was officially dedicated in New York Harbor. It stood as a symbol of freedom and as a welcome to immigrants. On its base was inscribed the poem "The New Colossus," by *Emma Lazarus*, saying in part, "Give me your tired, your poor, your huddled masses yearning to breathe free."

AMERICANS OPPOSE IMMIGRATION—MAINLY FROM THE END OF THE 19TH CENTURY

1. Reasons for Opposition. (a) With the frontier closed, immigrants no longer could secure free or cheap land. (b) American industry, it was claimed, was no longer expanding and had no need of additional immigrant workers. Since they were willing to work for low pay, immigrants took jobs away from native Americans and depressed American living standards. (c) The "new immigrants" from southern and eastern Europe were difficult to remold into the American "image." They had little education. They settled in large cities, creating ethnic enclaves, where they resisted assimilation into the dominant American culture. Their ghetto areas became breeding places of disease and crime. (d) The "new immigrants," some people argued, were physically and mentally inferior to the "old immigrants." Since the "old immigrants" had come from northern and western Europe, whose people were reputed to be of the "Nordic race," this assumption of their superiority became known as the *Theory of Nordic Supremacy.*

2. Evidences of Opposition. *(a)* In 1882 the United States passed the *Chinese Exclusion Act* prohibiting Chinese immigration for a ten-year period—the first restrictive immigration act. *(b)* In 1892 the *Knights of Labor,* an early labor organization, came out for a general restriction on immigration. The *American Federation of Labor* (A.F. of L.), meanwhile, with its many foreign-born members, was bitterly divided on the issue of immigration. In 1897, however, the A.F. of L. convention adopted a resolution endorsing a literacy test as a method of limiting immigration. *(c)* In 1907 Congress established the investigative *Immigration Commission* under Senator *William Dillingham.* Reporting in 1911, the *Dillingham Commission* stressed that the "new immigrants" were racially inferior to the "old immigrants" and were uneducated, unskilled, and difficult to assimilate. The commission urged adoption of a literacy test as a "method of restricting undesirable immigration." *(d)* In 1915 the *Ku Klux Klan,* a terrorist organization, was revived in Georgia and spread especially in the South and Midwest. It proclaimed as its goals 100 percent Americanism and protection of the racial purity of "Anglo-Saxon" Protestant America. The Klan was anti-Catholic, anti-Negro, anti-Jewish, and anti-immigrant. *(e)* In 1916 anthropologist *Madison Grant* published a plea for "racial purity" in his book *The Passing of the Great Race in America.* Grant asserted that the "new immigrants" were filling "our jails, insane asylums, and almshouses" because, he went on to claim, "they belonged to inferior—Alpine, Mediterranean, and Jewish—races." He warned that, unless "new immigrants" were kept from entering America, they would imperil its Nordic stock—the "great race" that had built the nation.

3. Arguments in Defense of the "New Immigrants." *(a)* The Dillingham Commission report, according to many social scientists, was inaccurate and unfair. Historian *Michael Kraus* in his book *Immigration, the American Mosaic* stated that the commission members "pretending to be scientific . . . had already arrived at conclusions they wished to prove" and that their report contained "assumptions, unscientific investigations, and distorted statistics." *(b)* The "new immigrants" assimilated as well as had the Irish and German "old immigrants." The Germans had clung to their native tongue; the Irish had been impoverished and uneducated; and both groups had been accused of being clannish and of not assimilating quickly into the American Protestant society. *(c)* The "new immigrants" who flocked to the cities were joined by native-born Americans who moved in from the farms. Both groups contributed to the emerging urban problems of slums, disease, and crime. *(d)* The "new immigrants" provided the additional workers needed by our expanding industry. Furthermore, by enlarging the domestic market for goods, they stimulated industrial growth and raised living standards. *(e)* Reputable scientists such as anthropologist *Margaret Mead* asserted that "pure races" do not exist and they rejected the "racist theory" of "Nordic supremacy" as false. *(f)* The "new immigrants" contributed greatly to American life. *Adam Dan,* the Danish immigrant poet, spoke for all immigrants when he said proudly, "We came not empty-handed here but brought a rich inheritance."

CASE STUDIES—"NATIVIST" HOSTILITY TO NEWCOMERS

1. "Know-Nothing" Opposition to Irish and Germans—Before the Civil War. The policy of favoring native-born Americans and opposing immigrants became known as *nativism*. In the mid-19th century, nativism was urged by several minor groups, the most influential being the *American party*, popularly known as the *Know-Nothing party*. It was so called because its members, pledged to secrecy, answered "I know nothing" when asked about the party's activities. The Know-Nothings condemned the Irish and German immigrants for taking jobs away from native Americans, for being clannish and failing to assimilate into American society, and especially for being Roman Catholic. The Know-Nothings purported to defend Protestantism against Catholicism; they sought to limit office-holding to native-born Americans; to require 21 years for naturalization, and to restrict immigration. In the 1850's, the party died out.

2. Pacific Coast Opposition to Orientals—After the Civil War to the 1920's

a. Anti-Chinese Agitation. Although Chinese immigrants had been reliable workers and orderly residents, Pacific Coast nativists aroused widespread anti-Chinese feeling. They accused the Chinese of being cheap "coolie" labor, serving as strikebreakers, following strange customs that were sweepingly condemned, and of being unassimilable into American society. In 1877 *Denis Kearney*, a recently naturalized citizen of Irish birth, founded the *Workingman's party* in California and harangued crowds, especially in San Francisco, with the slogan "The Chinese must go." The nativists secured passage of state and local laws discriminating against Chinese workers and shopkeepers; nativists also employed sporadic mob violence, business boycotts, and property destruction—all to terrorize the Chinese communities. In 1882 Congress passed the *Chinese Exclusion Act.* Thereafter, as some Chinese returned to their Asian homeland and others moved eastward, anti-Chinese agitation subsided in the Pacific Coast area.

b. Anti-Japanese Agitation. As more Japanese immigrants came to the Pacific Coast at the turn of the 20th century, nativists aroused fury against these Orientals. Agitators and newspapers, pointing to Japan's victory in war against Russia (1904–1905), portrayed the Japanese immigrants as the "Yellow Peril" endangering America. San Francisco labor unions accused them of threatening the living standards of American workers; mobs rioted; state and local governments passed discriminatory laws. In 1906 the San Francisco School Board ordered all Orientals to attend a segregated school. When the Japanese government protested to Washington, President Theodore Roosevelt pressured the San Francisco School Board to rescind the segregation order and also negotiated the 1907 *Gentlemen's Agreement* by which Japan agreed to deny passports for America to Japanese laborers. Although Japanese immigration was so curtailed, anti-Japanese agitation continued. In 1913 California passed a law forbidding Japanese from purchasing land—an example followed by other Western and several Southern states. In 1924 Congress *unilaterally* (by itself) ended the Gentlemen's Agreement by prohibiting all Japanese immigration to the United States.

3. Opposition to Minority Religious Groups—From the Late 19th Century Into the Early 20th Century

a. Anti-Catholic Agitation. Nativists were perturbed that many of the "new immigrants"—from Italy, Poland, and Hungary—were Catholics. Agitators berated Catholic parents for sending their children to Catholic parochial schools; condemned Catholic spokesmen for demanding public tax monies to support these schools; called attention to growing Catholic political power as Irish politicians gained influence over many East Coast city governments; and warned against a "papal conquest" of the United States. In 1887 *Henry F. Bowers,* a nativist, founded the *American Protective Association.* It became the largest of the secret anti-Catholic societies, reaching its peak membership during the depression years of the 1890's but then disintegrating. After 1915 the theme of anti-Catholicism was circulated by the revived Ku Klux Klan.

b. Anti-Jewish Agitation. The nativists were also *anti-Semites*—persons who are prejudiced against Jews as a group and therefore support discrimination and even persecution of Jewish people. The nativists were perturbed that many of the "new immigrants"—from Eastern Europe—were Jews. Agitators stressed that Jews observed strange and different customs; they labeled them as ambitious, greedy, and materialistic; they charged them with being wealthy international bankers conspiring to rule the world; and, with no logic or sense, charged them also with being impoverished radicals fomenting revolution. In the 1890's, serious anti-Semitic demonstrations took place in several Northern towns and in the rural South. In the 1920's, anti-Semitism increased: Employers rejected qualified Jewish job applicants; colleges set quotas restricting the admission of Jewish students; social clubs and real estate agents practiced discrimination. In the rural South and Middle West, the Ku Klux Klan stressed anti-Semitism. In 1920 the *Dearborn Independent,* a magazine published by auto magnate *Henry Ford,* began a series of abusive and false anti-Semitic articles. The articles were condemned by the *Federal Council of Churches of Christ* and by leading American statesmen, including *William Howard Taft* and *Woodrow Wilson.* In 1927 Ford admitted the injustice of his anti-Semitic charges, made a complete retraction, and extended a public apology.

4. "Racist" Opposition to Blacks and Latin Americans. (Check the Index for "Blacks," "Mexican-Americans," and "Puerto Ricans.")

CASE STUDIES—IN TIME OF WAR, HOSTILITY TO CITIZENS AND ALIENS RELATED TO THE ENEMY

1. World War I (1914–1918)—Hostility to German-Americans

a. Before United States Entry Into the War. For almost three years, while the Allies and Central Powers were at war, the United States was officially neutral. Except for two ethnic groups, most Americans sympathized with the Allies, especially Britain and France. However, Americans of Irish descent were traditionally anti-British, and Americans of German descent favored the Central Powers of Austria-Hungary and Germany.

German-Americans contributed funds for the German Red Cross and purchased German war bonds; the German-language newspapers defended the German invasion of Belgium; the German-American Alliance demanded an embargo on the shipment of war goods to the Allies and denounced the Wilson administration as being pro-British.

As the American people perceived the persistence of Old World ties, many accused German-Americans of "divided loyalties" and called for "100 percent Americanism." Former President *Theodore Roosevelt* attacked "hyphenated-Americans" in general and especially those German-Americans who "spiritually remain foreigners in whole or in part."

b. Following United States Entry Into the War. After Congress declared war on Germany in April 1917, most German-Americans loyally supported the American cause. Nevertheless, anti-German hysteria swept the nation and nativists acted to obliterate every aspect of German culture in the United States. In many instances, concert groups ceased performing German music and opera; town officials removed German names from streets and buildings; schools dropped the teaching of the German language; newsstands refused to carry German-language papers; superpatriots renamed "sauerkraut" as "liberty cabbage" and "hamburgers" became "Salisbury steaks." The public heard rumors of German-American spies and saboteurs—acting as "agents of the Kaiser." Congress passed: (1) the *Espionage Act* (1917) to punish persons for spying and obstructing the war effort and to ban use of the mails to antiwar materials; and (2) the *Sedition Act* (1918) to punish persons who spoke or wrote against the American form of government or the American war effort. Using these two laws, the government arrested some 1500 pacifists, socialists, and pro-Germans. With the Allied victory and the end of World War I, anti-German agitation ceased.

2. World War II (1939–1945)—Hostility to Japanese-Americans

a. Background. World War II was a struggle of the Axis powers—Nazi Germany under Hitler, Fascist Italy under Mussolini, and Imperial Japan under the military—against the Allies. In Europe the Nazi military machine overran many Allied nations, including Poland, Denmark, Norway, Holland, Belgium, France, Yugoslavia, and Greece. The Axis powers eventually met defeat with the brunt of the fighting being carried by three Allied nations: Britain and later Russia and the United States.

b. Before United States Entry Into the War. For more than two years, the United States was officially neutral but increasingly supplied equipment to the Allies. Except for two ethnic groups, most Americans sympathized with the Allies, especially Britain and the Nazi-occupied European nations. Some Italian-Americans and German-Americans, however, favored the Axis powers. Italian-Americans retained an attachment to Italy although seemingly they were indifferent to the political and economic philosophy of Fascism. German-Americans identified emotionally with their original "Fatherland," and a considerable vocal minority supported the pro-Nazi activities in America of *Fritz Kuhn* and his *German-American Bund.* Both ethnic groups urged strict American isolation and condemned the *Franklin D. Roosevelt* administration for favoring the Allies.

c. Following United States Entry Into the War. With the Japanese attack upon Pearl Harbor (1941), the American people experienced a surge of national unity and a determination to win the war against Italy, Germany, and Japan. Possibly because the American people considered the war issues not national but ideological—fascism versus democracy—they did not treat the Italian-Americans and the German-Americans with suspicion. With few exceptions, these two groups demonstrated loyalty to America.

Equally loyal, but less fortunate in their treatment by the American people, were the Japanese-Americans. They consisted of (1) immigrants, who were then ineligible for American citizenship by naturalization and therefore were aliens, and (2) *Nisei*, who were children born in America to Japanese parents, and therefore American citizens by birth. Living mainly on the Pacific Coast, especially in California, the Japanese-Americans had long been viewed with animosity. After Pearl Harbor, the Japanese-Americans were wildly rumored to be a "fifth column" engaged in espionage and sabotage on behalf of the Japanese emperor. Although these rumors were false, they were widely accepted by many Americans—the more so as early Japanese victories in the Pacific stirred West Coast residents to hysteria.

In early 1942, General. *John L. De Witt,* commander of our Western Defense, citing military necessity, began the removal of the Japanese from the Pacific Coast into the interior. Over 110,000 Japanese-Americans, of whom 70,000 were American citizens, were removed from their homes and jobs. Placed in inhospitable *relocation centers,* they were kept behind barbed wire and under armed guard. This removal program had the sanction of legislation by Congress, of an executive order by President Franklin D. Roosevelt, and of a decision by the Supreme Court in *Korematsu vs. United States* (1944) upholding the exclusion order on grounds of military necessity. (Although Hawaii was closer to the war zone than the Pacific Coast, its Japanese-Americans were not evacuated or relocated. Throughout the war, no Japanese-American—in Hawaii or on the mainland—was found guilty of espionage or sabotage.)

The mainland Japanese-Americans were dismayed by their treatment at the hands of the United States government. Whereas some bitterly renounced their American citizenship and after the war moved to Japan, the overwhelming majority determined to prove their loyalty to America. They gave blood to the American Red Cross, purchased United States war bonds, and taught the Japanese language to army interpreters. Some 12,000 Nisei served in army combat units in Europe. Many Nisei units suffered heavy casualties and won numerous decorations.

After the war, although a majority of Japanese-Americans returned to the Pacific Coast, many established residence elsewhere in the United States. They also diversified from small-scale farming into other occupations. The Japanese-Americans now found less discrimination and greater acceptance by their fellow Americans.

REGULATIONS AFFECTING THE FLOW OF IMMIGRATION

1. Early Steps Restricting Immigration

    a. The Chinese Exclusion Act (1882). (Check the Index.)

    b. The Gentlemen's Agreement (1907). (Check the Index.)

    c. The Literacy Test Act (1917) required immigrants to be able to read English or their own language before entering the United States. Four times from 1896 to 1917 such a measure had been vetoed by a President: first by Cleveland, then by Taft, and finally by Wilson. In support of these vetoes, each President had employed similar reasoning: that (1) the measure departed from America's tradition of asylum for oppressed peoples, and (2) literacy indicated not mental ability, but merely the opportunity to go to school. In 1917, just two months before America entered World War I, Congress overrode a second veto by President Wilson and passed the *Literacy Test Act.*

2. Further Immigration Restrictions Following World War I—Reasons

    a. Political Reasons. (1) With the Communist seizure of Russia (1917), many Americans opposed immigration for fear that foreign radicals would infiltrate the United States. (2) Disillusioned with the results of World War I, many Americans reverted to our traditional foreign policy of isolation. This came also to mean opposition to immigration.

    b. Economic Reasons. (1) With the end of war-spurred overtime and the beginning of the depression of 1920–1921, workers received smaller paychecks and feared unemployment. Labor unions insisted that immigrants threatened jobs and living standards of American workers. (2) Employers too favored immigration restrictions for fear of foreign radicals who might spur labor unrest.

    c. Social Reasons. (1) As World War I demonstrated the persistence of Old World ties, many Americans wondered how long it would take to transform immigrants into loyal Americans. (2) The literacy test proved ineffective to limit immigration. Between 1918 and 1921, of 1.5 million immigrants, those excluded because they failed the literacy test numbered only 6000.

3. Restrictive Immigration Laws Following World War I

    a. Two Emergency Immigration Acts, in 1921 and in 1924, began the sharp curtailment of immigration from outside the Western Hemisphere. The 1924 act also contained the more permanent regulations constituting the 1929 national origins system.

    b. The National Origins System of 1929 (1) permitted no more than 150,000 immigrants from outside the Western Hemisphere to enter the United States per year, (2) allotted each country a quota in proportion to the number of persons in the United States having that national origin according to the census of 1920, (3) granted each eligible nation at least 100 immigrants per year, (4) placed no restrictions on immigration from the Western Hemisphere, and (5) prohibited all immigration from Asian countries.

    c. Effects of Post-World War I Immigration Laws. (1) The restrictive immigration laws of the 1920's, coupled with the depression of 1929, sharply curtailed immigration from Europe. Most quotas allotted to northern and western European countries remained unfilled, and the annual immigration from Europe remained far below quota limits. (2) With fewer European immigrants arriving to join their fellow countrymen, the immigrant communities already here experienced a weakening of ties to the "old country," a decline of immigrant institutions—foreign-language press and theatre and ethnic fraternal organizations. This weakening of "old country" ties resulted in a more rapid process of Americanization. (3) Of the total number of immigrants, a greater proportion now came from the Western Hemisphere, especially Canada, Mexico, and the West Indies. (4) During and after World War II, the labor needs of industry were met, not as before by European immigrants, but by the entrance of Puerto Ricans and Mexicans and by the movement of poor whites and blacks out of the South.

4. Immigration Laws Following World War II

a. Displaced Persons Acts. (Check the Index for "Displaced persons.")

b. The McCarran-Walter Immigration and Nationality Act of 1952

(1) *Internal Security Provisions.* Enacted during the cold war era, this law attempted to preserve our internal security against Communist infiltration. It provided for careful screening of immigrants, for revoking the citizenship of recently naturalized persons who joined pro-Communist organizations, and for deporting undesirable aliens.

(2) *Immigration Provisions.* The new law (a) restated the national origins system by setting a limit of 154,000 immigrants per year and by granting each country a quota based on the 1920 census, (b) allowed each Asian country a quota, usually 100 immigrants per year.

(3) *Arguments for the Immigration Provisions.* (a) The total of 154,000 admissions per year from outside the Western Hemisphere prevented the flooding of the United States with immigrants. (b) The use of the national origins system preserved the "nationality makeup" of our population. (c) The law rejected any racial bias by admitting immigrants from Asian countries.

(4) *Arguments Against the Immigration Provisions.* (a) The United States, with its relatively low population density, could absorb a larger number of immigrants per year. (b) The use of national origins quotas discriminated against immigrants from eastern and southern Europe and from Asia. The law assigned a quota of 109,000 out of a total of 154,000 to three countries: Great Britain, Germany, and Ireland. Unused quotas could not be transferred to nations that had already filled their quotas.

President Truman vetoed the McCarran-Walter bill as "repressive and inhumane," but Congress overrode the veto. Subsequently, Presidents Eisenhower, Kennedy, and Johnson all requested a revision of our immigration laws.

c. The Immigration Act of 1965—Signed by President Johnson at the Statue of Liberty

(1) *Provisions.* For countries outside the Western Hemisphere, the law (a) abolished the national origins system, (b) established a quota of 170,000 immigrants per year, (c) set a limit of 20,000 immigrants per year from any one nation, and (d) provided standards for admitting immigrants according to the following preferences: close relatives of United States residents; scientists, artists, professional people, and skilled and unskilled workers needed to fill labor shortages; and refugees from Communist rule and from natural calamity.

President Lyndon Johnson about to sign the 1965 immigration act at the Statue of Liberty, in New York Harbor. (*Wide World Photos*)

For countries within the Western Hemisphere, the law introduced for the first time a quota, set at 120,000 immigrants per year, but did not set any quotas for individual countries or any system of preferences. It allowed a first-come, first-served basis. (In 1976 the law was revised, retaining the 120,000 annual quota for Western Hemisphere immigrants but subjecting them to the same provisions as other immigrants—a limit of 20,000 per year from any one nation and standards of admission according to the preference system.)

(2) *Significant Changes*. (*a*) The new law replaced the national origins system, stressing race and nationality, with a preference system emphasizing family relationship, value to the United States, and motive for migrating. (*b*) It ended the favored position of northern and western European nations, and placed them on an equal footing with other countries. As a result, fewer immigrants have come from Great Britain, Ireland, and Germany. (*c*) It permitted an increase in the number of immigrants from Asia, Africa, and southern and eastern Europe. As a result more immigrants have come from Taiwan, the Philippines, Italy, Greece, and Portugal. (*d*) The law reduced the number of Western Hemisphere immigrants from about 150,000 legal entrants in 1965 to a quota maximum of 120,000. (*e*) The 1976 revision was expected to reduce Mexican immigration, which had been averaging 40,000 people a year, to the legal limit of 20,000, to spur illegal Mexican immigration, and to increase legal immigration from the Caribbean and Central America.

MULTIPLE-CHOICE QUESTIONS

1. No significant restrictions were placed on immigration to the United States before the 1880's because   (1) most immigrants in the early 19th century came from southern Europe   (2) the birthrate in the United States was low   (3) the American economy needed additional workers   (4) prosperous times in Europe discouraged immigration.

2. Where can an expression of the philosophy of the United States concerning immigration be found?   (1) in Washington's Farewell Address   (2) on the base of the Statue of Liberty   (3) in the Homestead Act   (4) in Lincoln's Gettysburg Address

3. Which is the *most* valid generalization pertaining to the concept of nativism?   (1) Nativism stems in part from economic fears.   (2) Nativism is essentially sectional in character.   (3) Nativist movements are present only in free democratic societies.   (4) Racial prejudice is the strongest factor in explaining nativism.

4. The charge made by nativist groups in the United States that Italian immigrants sent their children to parochial schools *most* clearly supports the idea that   (1) nativist activity was restricted to the Eastern cities   (2) all immigrants have faced opposition from nativists   (3) immigrants refused low wages in order to avoid criticism   (4) nativism was based, in part, on religious bias.

5. In the latter part of the 19th century, a liberal immigration policy was generally opposed by   (1) Eastern manufacturers   (2) land speculators   (3) labor unions   (4) railroad companies.

6. Which statement is true of the immigration policy of the United States in the late 19th century?   (1) Restrictions were placed on Mexican agricultural workers.   (2) Quotas were assigned to European countries.   (3) Chinese immigration was prohibited.   (4) Japanese immigration was limited.

7. From 1920 to 1965, immigration to the United States was influenced by laws based on the "national origins" principle. This principle was widely criticized, however, because it   (1) permitted unlimited entry to Orientals   (2) favored migration from northern and western Europe   (3) gave large quotas to immigrants from Latin America   (4) restricted the admission of French-Canadians.

8. Which of the following differed in purpose from the other three?   (1) Gentlemen's Agreement   (2) National Origins Plan   (3) Displaced Persons Acts   (4) Chinese Exclusion Act

9. Which was true of the McCarran-Walter Act?   (1) The quota for Asians was lowered.   (2) All literate persons could enter the country and become citizens.   (3) Aliens could be deported if they were found to have Communist affiliations.   (4) The quota system for Latin America was revised.

10. The United States immigration laws of the 1920's differed from previous immigration laws in that the immigration laws of the 1920's   (1) were considered too liberal   (2) encouraged immigration from eastern and southern Europe   (3) established broad general restrictions upon most immigration   (4) brought about improved relations between the United States and Asian nations.

11. The Immigration Act of 1965 provided that the United States   (1) retain the national origins system   (2) prohibit immigrants from the Western Hemisphere   (3) admit more Irish immigrants   (4) give high priority to needed professional people.

12. Country Z advertises: "We Want You! Government-Assisted Passage. Unlimited Opportunities. Latest Information Available." Country Z is *most* probably running this advertisement because it   (1) needs workers   (2) is a land of freedom   (3) has a surplus of agricultural products   (4) has wages that are very low.

13. If one assumes that immigration to Country Z will parallel United States' immigration history, it would be most logical to conclude that in time Country Z will   (1) become a world power   (2) suffer from overcrowding   (3) adopt restrictive immigration laws   (4) compel the majority of immigrants to return to their native lands.

14. Which statement concerning immigration to the United States is *best* supported by historical evidence? (1) Industrial growth led to a decreased demand for cheap labor. (2) Organized labor generally favored unrestricted immigration. (3) The quota laws were designed to prevent discrimination in immigration. (4) The diversity of the immigrant population created a pluralistic society.

IDENTIFICATION QUESTIONS: WHO AM I?

For each description below, write the name of the person to whom the description best applies, making your selection from the following list:

William Dillingham	Denis Kearney	Franklin D. Roosevelt
Henry Ford	Fritz Kuhn	Theodore Roosevelt
Madison Grant	Emma Lazarus	Harry Truman
Lyndon Johnson	Margaret Mead	Woodrow Wilson

1. While President, I worked to overcome resentment caused by a racist segregation order of the San Francisco School Board.
2. A newly naturalized American citizen myself, I aroused nativist opposition against Oriental workers and shopkeepers.
3. Although I vetoed the Literacy Test Act, it became a law as Congress overrode my veto.
4. An anthropologist, I attributed America's greatness to the "Nordic race" and urged that "inferior races" be kept from entering the country.
5. An anthropologist, I found no evidence of "superior" or "inferior" races and I rejected the theory of "Nordic supremacy."
6. I expressed compassion and understanding for immigrants in my poem "The New Colossus."
7. A Senator, I headed a commission investigating immigration. The commission's report stressed that "new immigrants" were undesirable.
8. Although I vetoed the McCarran-Walter Act as "inhumane," it became a law as Congress overrode my veto.

ESSAY QUESTIONS

1. In the 19th century, Americans generally welcomed immigration, but in the 20th century their attitude changed and Americans generally supported severe limitations on immigration. Discuss *one* economic, *one* political, and *one* social factor that caused Americans to change their attitude toward immigration.
2. The immigration policy of the United States has reflected trends in both the development and the problems of our country. (a) State our policy in relation to immigration during each of the following periods: (1) 1789–1870 (2) 1880–1910 (3) 1920–1960 (4) 1965 to the present. (b) Explain *one* factor that influenced our policy in *each* case.
3. Nativist groups in the past have agitated against Catholic and Jewish immigrants. (a) State a hypothesis to explain the reasons for such agitation. (b) Present a community program to combat anti-Catholic and anti-Jewish agitation. Explain *why* and *how* you would use each of *three* major agencies. Also state *three* major arguments that you would seek to convey to the community.
4. In regard to the Immigration Act of 1965, (a) state *three* of its major provisions and (b) for *each* provision stated, explain fully why you approve or disapprove of it.
5. (a) Which group was treated more harshly: German-Americans during World War I or Japanese-Americans during World War II? Present *two* arguments to support your opinion. (b) In no more than *two* sentences, provide a generalization regarding the effect of war upon minority-majority relations. Be careful not to make too sweeping a statement.

6. The Immigrant Experience Has Been Both Bitter and Sweet

HARDSHIPS BESETTING EUROPEAN IMMIGRANTS—19TH AND EARLY 20TH CENTURIES

1. Hardships of the Journey. *Oscar Handlin,* historian of immigration, described the human aspects of migration in his study *The Uprooted.* The immigrants were the uprooted, having left their relatives, friends, and native lands. Being poor, many made their way on foot to European seaports where they awaited ocean transportation. Until the 1850's the immigrants boarded sailing vessels for crossings that lasted one to three months; thereafter they came on steamships that made the trip in ten days. Traveling on lowest-fare tickets which they purchased themselves or received from kinsmen in America, most immigrants came via *steerage.* This was the least desirable section of the ship where conditions were usually crowded and unsanitary.

2. Hardships Upon Debarkation. Upon arrival in American ports, the immigrants were bewildered by sights and procedures strange to them. The fortunate newcomers were met by relatives, friends, and agents of some few ethnic benevolent organizations; others often were victimized by greedy and dishonest individuals, especially *runners* working for disreputable boarding houses and fraudulent inland transportation offices. New York led the seaboard states in providing some protection: setting aside hospital facilities for immigrants who were ill; establishing an immigrant employment exchange; and in 1855 designating an immigrant reception center in lower Manhattan at *Castle Garden* where immigrants could receive reputable advice regarding lodgings, railroad tickets, and jobs. (In 1892 Castle Garden was replaced by a federal debarkation center in New York Harbor at *Ellis Island.*)

3. Hardships in Adjustment. Many immigrants, lacking funds and occupational skills, were forced to remain in the port cities, to accept low-paying jobs or seek public welfare, and to occupy cheap living quarters. Those with funds could open small shops or could travel inland and secure farms. Immigrant farmers faced problems in adjusting to American agriculture. The climate, the soil, the farm size, and the tools were all quite different from the "Old World" experience, as was the emphasis upon commercial instead of subsistence farming.

Most immigrants at first felt strange and insecure in the American environment. In the cities, they congregated close to each other, thereby forming voluntary ethnic ghettos; in the rural areas, they purchased farms adjacent to each other, thereby creating distinct ethnic settlements. Immigrants supported their own foreign-language newspapers and theatres; attended their own houses of worship; and formed their own fraternal organizations—mutual aid societies that provided advice, sick benefits, funeral expenses, and, most important, companionship with their kinsmen and a link to the "old country."

FROM IMMIGRANT TO AMERICAN: THE GENERAL PATTERN OF CHANGE

1. At First—Discrimination

a. Examples. Most immigrants experienced discrimination from the native-born Americans—the descendants of earlier immigrants—who considered themselves representative of the majority groups. Newcomers were belittled by word of mouth and in newspapers and books. They were hired last, advanced least, and fired first. They were excluded from better residential areas, hotels, restaurants, and clubs, and faced restrictive admission quotas at institutions of higher learning.

b. Causes. Discrimination is largely rooted in the fears and suspicions of the in-groups against outsiders, as follows: (1) Physical Differences. The newcomers were different in the color of their skin, the slant of their eyes, or the shape of their heads. (2) Competition. The newcomers meant more competition for jobs, business opportunities, college admissions, and political offices. (3) Social and Psychological. The newcomers observed strange customs, worshipped God in unfamiliar ways, and maintained a different "life-style." To fearful and prejudiced eyes, they were not individuals, each with personal weaknesses and strengths, but rather faceless "strangers" all exhibiting the same alien traits. Such distorted representations—based on exaggeration, ignorance, and error and reinforced by repetition—are known as *stereotypes.*

2. Then—Acculturation.
Most immigrants adapted to American cultural patterns through their own deliberate actions and through the pressures of living in American society. They learned to speak and read the English language. They secured an understanding of American history and government. They became citizens through naturalization, and took part in American politics. They acquired the customs and traditions of America—its foods, songs, sports, and holidays. Acculturation for the immigrants was the process of *Americanization.*

3. Finally—Assimilation.
At some hard-to-define point in the process of Americanization, the immigrants figuratively "crossed over" from their old culture and became part of the American way of life. They had achieved assimilation. First-generation immigrants found assimilation a difficult and emotional experience; usually they achieved only a mixture of both cultures. Their children and grandchildren, although perhaps retaining aspects of the old culture, assimilated much more easily. In recent years, descendants of immigrants have experienced a resurgence of "ethnic pride" and a desire to preserve some aspects of their original cultural heritage.

a. Factors Speeding Americanization. (1) Schools. As a result of compulsory education laws, immigrant children were compelled to attend school—parochial or public. They were taught to speak, read, and write the English language and were instructed in American history, government, and ideals. The knowledge the children so acquired they transmitted to their elders at home. (2) Immigrant Press. Although preserving a link with the "old country," foreign-language newspapers also helped Americanize their readers by providing news, advertisements, and articles about American life. The immigrant press included the German *Staats-Zeitung,* the Jewish *Daily Forward,* the Czech *Denni Hlasatel,* and the Italian *Il Progresso.* (3) Immigrant Organizations. Founded along ethnic and religious lines, benevolent societies arose to aid the immigrants. Among their purposes, these societies proclaimed, was to instill in the immigrants a knowledge of American ideals, history, and institutions. Typical immigrant organizations included the Irish Emigrant Society, Polish National Alliance, Sons of Italy, Lithuanian National Society, and Hebrew Immigrant Aid Society, or HIAS. (4) Naturalization. Congress set the requirements for naturalization —the legal process by which aliens could acquire American citizenship—and in 1906 established the *Bureau of Immigration and Naturalization*. Immigrants over 18 years of age were required to file a declaration of intention to seek American citizenship, to reside here at least five years, to be able to speak and read English, to have witnesses certify as to "good moral character," and to pass a simple examination on the United States Constitution, history, and government. To prepare for citizenship, immigrants in large cities attended Americanization classes conducted by public schools and by naturalization clubs. (5) Other Factors. Civic and patriotic societies, political parties, churches, and business organizations—all promoted Americanization of immigrants.

b. Typical Groups Assimilating Easily. These included the Scotch-Irish, the English, and the British-Canadians. All three groups had the advantages of speaking English, being familiar with the British concepts of democracy and government, and worshipping as Protestants. In addition: the Scotch-Irish in colonial times settled the little populated frontier region and became Indian fighters helping to guard the older settlements; the English and British-Canadians possessed funds with which to purchase farmland and vocational skills valuable to American mining and industry.

c. Typical Groups Assimilating With Difficulty. These included the Irish, Chinese, Jews, Mexicans, Puerto Ricans, French-Canadians, Japanese, Poles, Italians, American Indians, and blacks. Can you discern reasons why each of these groups experienced difficulty in assimilating into American society?

DIFFERING CONCEPTS OF AMERICANIZATION

1. Anglo-Conformity. This earliest concept of Americanization held that our predominantly Anglo-Saxon or British stock, of colonial times and the early days of the republic, had molded a fixed, homogeneous American culture. It was rooted in the English language, English political institutions (as modified by the American experience), and English social patterns. To achieve Americanization, immigrants were expected to divest themselves of their native cultures and to conform to Anglo-American ways. This Anglo-conformity concept helps explain the easy assimilation of many colonial settlers and many 19th-century "old immigrants"—especially those stemming from a white, Anglo-Saxon, Protestant heritage. Anglo-conformity also found expression during World War I in anger against "hyphenated-Americans" and from 1929 to 1965 in the national origins system.

2. Melting Pot. This later concept of Americanization held that all immigrants to America have contributed to "God's crucible, the great Melting Pot" from which has emerged a remarkable and homogeneous—but constantly changing —American culture. In the late 18th century, this melting pot concept was expressed by the French writer *St. John de Crevecoeur* who, in his *Letters From* *an American Farmer*, said that "individuals of all nations are melted into a new race of men"—the Americans. In the early 20th century, this concept was popularized by the Jewish-English writer *Israel Zangwill* in his play *The Melting Pot*. The melting-pot concept found strong support among the "new immigrants" coming after 1890 as properly recognizing their contributions to the American way of life.

3. Cultural Pluralism. This most recent concept of Americanization held that all immigrants should absorb those aspects of a uniform culture essential for the functioning of our democratic society, but that they may preserve certain facets of their own heritages. American culture therefore should consist of a homogeneous center—of English language, political ideals, and economic institutions—surrounded by heterogeneous ethnic patterns, especially in social and intellectual life. Each immigrant group thusly should take pride in its own cultural heritage, but all should live together in harmony and contribute to an American society described variously as a *mixing bowl*, a *cultural mosaic*, or a *symphony of cultures*. This cultural pluralism concept was expressed in 1915 by the Jewish-American philosopher *Horace Kallen* in two magazine articles entitled "Democracy Versus the Melting Pot." Since World War II, as minority groups have asserted their own "identities" and have sought full integration into American life, the concept of cultural pluralism has received increasing support.

IMMIGRANT IMPACT UPON AMERICAN LIFE

Although specific ethnic groups have become identified with particular developments in American life, immigrants from all nations have had their impact upon the United States.

1. Economic. *(a) In Agriculture.* In colonial times, most settlers cleared the wilderness and became farmers. In the 19th century, Negroes raised cotton, at first on Southern plantations and later as sharecroppers; German, Scandinavian, and British-Canadian farmers settled the Midwest and the Great Plains. In the 20th century, Mexicans in labor gangs harvested the crops of the Southwest; Japanese and Italians engaged in intensive truck farming. *(b) In Transportation.* The Irish helped build the Erie Canal and other Eastern canals. The Irish, Italians, and Slavs constructed many bridges and railroads. In the Far West, the Chinese built the Union Pacific Railroad. *(c) In Mining and Industry.* The Welsh worked in the coal mines, as did the Poles, other Slavic peoples, and Hungarians. These latter three groups also mined iron ore and labored in the steel mills. The English helped establish the New England textile mills, which later utilized Irish and French-Canadian workers. The Germans were occupied in the optical, piano construction, beer brewing, and chemical industries. The Jews, followed by Italians and then Puerto Ricans, helped develop the garment industry. Jews also played a major role in beginning the radio and movie industries. To American mining and industry, immigrant groups brought organizing ability, enterprise, and inventiveness. *(d) As Consumers and Workers.* Immigrants increased the demand for the products of agriculture and industry, thereby further encouraging American economic growth. Also, by coming in great numbers, especially during times of business expansion, immigrants served to prevent any shortage of labor.

2. Political. *(a) On Political Machines.* Strangers in a new land, the urban immigrants welcomed assistance—a basket of food, a place to live, a job— arranged by a political leader and, upon being naturalized, they repaid him with their votes. Thus the immigrants were used by political bosses and party machines—both Republican and Democratic—in many American cities. However, as the immigrants Americanized, learned to value their vote, and turned increasingly to the government for welfare services, their support of political machines sharply waned. *(b) In State and National Affairs.* That newly naturalized citizens vote as a "bloc" is a myth. Depending upon the issues, immigrant groups may differ one from the other and even within the same group. Further, as newcomers, immigrants probably are swayed less by party loyalty and more by the issues. Nevertheless, reflecting their ties to the "old country" and their economic status in American society, immigrant groups have voted in major part along predictable lines. *(c) Case Studies.* (1) In the Presidential election of 1884, a Republican orator in New York labeled the Democrats as the party of "Rum, Romanism, and Rebellion." This prejudiced attack, most historians believe, rallied Irish and other Roman Catholics to the Democratic candidate, Grover Cleveland. He carried New York State by slightly more than 1000 out of 1.1 million votes and won the election narrowly. (2) In the Presidential election of 1920, ratification of the Treaty of Versailles was urged by the Democratic candidate, James Cox. The treaty, however, was opposed by many ethnic groups: it failed to provide independence for Ireland, said Irish-Americans; it was too harsh upon Germany, said German-Americans; it did not grant Italy her territorial demands, said Italian-Americans. Such opposition to the treaty helped build an overwhelming election victory for Republican Warren Harding. (3) In mid-20th-century New York City and State elections, the major parties often have appealed for the ethnic and religious vote by arranging "balanced tickets." For the top three positions, candidates have been so chosen as to include a Protestant, a Catholic, and a Jew.

3. Cultural. Immigrants to America brought their native cultural heritages. With time certain features of these heritages died out while other features survived and became part of American life. In foods, we eat hamburgers and frankfurters named after German cities, English muffins, Irish stew, Hungarian goulash, Chinese chop suey, Jewish delicatessen, and Danish pastry. In music, we listen to Italian operas, German symphonies, Negro spirituals, Spanish tangos, Rumanian dances, and Polish mazurkas. In literature, we read the plays of England's Shakespeare and Norway's Ibsen, the poetry of England's Browning and Germany's Goethe, and the novels of France's Hugo and Russia's Tolstoi. In sports, we follow football developed from England's rugby, jai alai popularized in Latin America, bowling introduced by the Dutch, and ice hockey developed in Canada. Our language contains words from tongues spoken throughout the world. Our art, social studies, philosophy, ethics, and science have borrowed from the great men of all ages and all places. "We are the heirs of all time," wrote the American novelist Herman Melville, "and with all nations we divide our inheritance." Perhaps our most important inheritance, an outgrowth of the diversity of our immigrant background, is the American spirit of toleration and fair play.

SOME OUTSTANDING IMMIGRANTS

1. **British.** Inventor of the telephone *Alexander Graham Bell;* steel magnate and philanthropist *Andrew Carnegie;* physician and surgeon *William W. Mayo;* labor leader *Philip Murray;* writer *Thomas Paine,* whose pamphlet *Common Sense* aroused colonial support for the Declaration of Independence; chemist *Joseph Priestley;* textile machinery builder *Samuel Slater,* who became known as "father of the American factory system."

2. **Canadian.** Economist and statesman *John Kenneth Galbraith;* Food and Drug Administration medical officer *Frances Kelsey,* who kept a dangerous drug from being prescribed and sold; actor and theatrical producer *Raymond Massey,* famed for his stage and screen portrayals of Abraham Lincoln.

3. **Chinese.** Cinematographer *James Wong Howe;* architect *Ieoh Ming Pei;* financial investment expert *Gerald Tsai;* theoretical physicists and Nobel Prize winners *Chen Ning Yang* and *Tsung Dao Lee;* writer *Lin Yutang.*

4. **Dutch.** Editor and philanthropist *Edward Bok,* who entitled his autobiography *The Americanization of Edward Bok;* symphony orchestra conductor *Hans Kindler;* writer and historian *Hendrik Van Loon* noted for his ever-popular *Story of Mankind.*

5. **French.** Gunpowder manufacturer *Eleuthère Irénée Du Pont,* whose company evolved into today's giant chemical concern; architect *Pierre Charles L'Enfant,* who provided the basic design for the city of Washington, D.C.; opera star *Lily Pons.*

6. **German.** Governor *John Peter Altgeld* of Illinois; optical equipment manufacturers *John J. Bausch* and *Henry Lomb;* piano manufacturers *Valentine Knabe* and *Henry Steinway;* political cartoonist *Thomas Nast,* who devised the donkey and elephant symbols for the Democratic and Republican parties respectively; engineer and designer of the Brooklyn Bridge *John Roebling;* civil service reformer *Carl Schurz;* electrical engineer *Charles Steinmetz;* symphony orchestra conductor *Bruno Walter;* colonial New York newspaper publisher *John Peter Zenger,* who helped establish the principle of freedom of the press in America.

7. **Greek.** Educator and philanthropist *Michael Anagnos,* who headed the *Perkins Institution for the Blind* in Boston; symphony orchestra conductor *Dimitri Mitropoulos;* motion picture executive *Spyros Skouras.*

8. **Irish.** Magazine publisher *Peter F. Collier;* meat packing industrialist *Michael Cudahy;* light-opera composer *Victor Herbert;* inventor *John P. Holland,* who devised the first practical submarine; educator *Thomas Hunter;* sculptor *Augustus Saint-Gaudens,* noted for his statue of the standing Abraham Lincoln in Chicago.

9. **Italian.** Airplane designer *Giuseppe Bellanca;* artist *Constantino Brumidi,* who painted the frescoes in the Capitol building in Washington, D.C.; *Mother Frances X. Cabrini* (later sainted), founder of orphanages and hospitals; atomic scientist and Nobel Prize winner *Enrico Fermi;* opera composer and lyricist *Gian-Carlo Menotti;* symphony orchestra conductor *Arturo Toscanini.*

10. Japanese. Painter *Yasuo Kuniyoshi*, who combined American and Oriental art forms; medical scientist *Hideyo Noguchi*, who developed a preventative vaccine for yellow fever.

11. Jewish. From Austria—Supreme Court Justice *Felix Frankfurter;* musical comedy composer *Frederick Loewe;* nuclear physicist and Nobel Prize winner *Isador Rabi*. From England—labor leader *Samuel Gompers*. From Germany —physician and surgeon *Simon Baruch;* theoretical physicist and Nobel Prize winner *Albert Einstein;* department store merchant *Nathan Straus,* who as a philanthropist established public health stations and distributed free milk to infants in New York City. From Hungary—pediatric physician *Bela Schick,* who devised a test for diphtheria; atomic scientist *Edward Teller*. From Portugal —colonial settler *Asher Levy,* who wrested citizenship rights from the reluctant Dutch governor of New Amsterdam; merchant *Aaron Lopez* who aided the American Revolution with ships and funds. From Russia—musical comedy composer *Irving Berlin;* radio and television executive *David Sarnoff;* microbiologist *Selman Waksman,* discoverer of antibiotics; motion picture producer *Harry Warner*.

12. Polish. Biochemist and vitamin researcher *Casimir Funk;* engineer and bridge construction specialist *Ralph Modjeski;* military leader *Casimir Pulaski,* who gave his life in 1779 fighting for American independence.

13. Russian. Choreographer *George Balanchine*, director of the New York City Ballet; airplane designer and manufacturer *Igor Sikorsky,* who invented the helicopter; composer *Igor Stravinsky*.

14. Scandinavian. From Denmark—automobile magnate *William Knudsen,* President of General Motors; writer and social reformer *Jacob Riis,* who deplored slum conditions in his book *How the Other Half Lives*. From Norway —football coach *Knute Rockne;* novelist *Ole Rölvaag* who wrote of pioneer life in America in his *Giants in the Earth*. From Sweden—engineer *John Ericsson,* designer of the ironclad warship *Monitor;* geologist *John Udden,* who uncovered the Texas oil fields.

15. Swiss. Scientist *Louis Agassiz,* naturalist, geologist, and teacher; statesman *Albert Gallatin,* who served as Secretary of the Treasury under Presidents Jefferson and Madison.

16. Yugoslavian. Author *Louis Adamic,* who wrote on immigrant themes; scientist and inventor *Michael Pupin;* symphony orchestra conductor *Artur Rodzinski*.

(For outstanding individuals of other ethnic groups, discussed at greater length, check the Index for "American Indians," "Blacks," "Mexican-Americans," and "Puerto Ricans.")

MATCHING QUESTIONS

Select the *letter* of the item in Column B that best matches the item in Column A.

Column A—*Immigrants*	Column B—*Achievements*
1. Irving Berlin	a. Founder of orphanages and hospitals
2. Igor Sikorsky	b. Opera composer
3. John Roebling	c. Educator
4. Frances Cabrini	d. Motion picture producer
5. Thomas Hunter	e. Symphony orchestra conductor
6. Ieoh Ming Pei	f. Medical officer
7. Albert Einstein	g. Choreographer
8. Thomas Nast	h. Political cartoonist
9. Arturo Toscanini	i. Inventor of helicopter
10. Frances Kelsey	j. Musical comedy composer
	k. Architect
	l. Theoretical physicist
	m. Designer of Brooklyn Bridge

MULTIPLE-CHOICE QUESTIONS

1. Which is the *most* valid statement pertaining to the experiences of immigrant groups in United States history? (1) All groups have met the same problems. (2) Most groups solved their problems unassisted. (3) Some groups had no problems adjusting to the new society. (4) All groups faced problems; some similar, others very different.
2. One problem common to most groups that emigrated to the United States was that they were (1) resented by earlier immigrants (2) denied the right to own property (3) persecuted because of their religious views (4) denied admission to the public schools.
3. By naming European immigrants to America as "the uprooted," historian Oscar Handlin implied that these immigrants (1) had no ties to Europe (2) were stereotypes lacking any individuality (3) had strong ties to Europe broken only with much personal anguish (4) did not put down roots in the United States.
4. Imagine a Polish immigrant family arriving at New York in 1905. The family consisted of four members: husband, age 43; wife, age 37; son, age 19; and daughter, age 8. Which family member probably assimilated most easily into the American way of life? (1) husband (2) wife (3) son (4) daughter
5. The immigrant who came to an American city at the turn of this century was *more* likely to have had what advantage over the migrant of today? (1) familiarity with the English language (2) eligibility for welfare assistance (3) availability of jobs for unskilled labor (4) existence of integrated housing patterns
6. The melting-pot theory of Americanization holds that American culture (1) is homogeneous, with contributions of all immigrant groups blended together (2) is inferior to British culture (3) is heterogeneous, with each ethnic group preserving its own individuality (4) contains almost no aspects attributable to Anglo-Saxon immigrants.
7. An indication that recently arrived immigrants to the United States were involved in the process of assimilation would be (1) use of their native language at home (2) conformity to ethnic customs of their native land (3) attendance at an English-language class (4) marriage to other members of the same nationality.
8. Which statement related to immigration to the United States is *most* difficult to support by fact? (1) The ancestry of citizens of the United States can be traced to

countries in all parts of the world. (2) Immigrant groups have enriched the culture of the United States. (3) The United States has often been called a melting pot. (4) Native-born Americans are better citizens than foreign-born Americans.

9. Immigration to the United States has been beneficial chiefly because immigrants have (1) brought over much-needed investment capital (2) been an important factor in our recent population growth (3) provided willing tenants for our cities' apartment dwellings (4) contributed to our social and economic development.

10. In the 1750's, a person of English origin born in the colony of Pennsylvania made the following comment on the increase of Germans in Pennsylvania: "Why should [they] be suffered to swarm into our settlements, and, by herding together, establish their language and manners, to the exclusion of ours?" This statement might be considered as an early example of (1) racial integration (2) nativism (3) compulsory segregation (4) class distinction.

11. To become an American citizen by naturalization, an immigrant did *not* have to fulfill which requirement? (1) five years' residence in the United States (2) membership in a major political party (3) ability to speak English (4) satisfactory knowledge of American history

ESSAY QUESTIONS

1. America owes its greatness, in part, to its liberal immigration policy of the 19th and early 20th centuries. (a) Discuss *three* ways in which immigrants contributed to America's greatness. (b) Explain *two* problems that the liberal immigration policy posed for the United States.

2. At many times during the history of the United States, immigrants have faced serious difficulties in adjusting to American life and in being accepted by other Americans. Using an ethnic or a national immigrant grouping as a model, illustrate some of the difficulties faced by immigrants in *each* of the following situations: (a) unfamiliarity with surrounding cultural patterns (b) relationships with the political system (c) adjusting to the American economy.

3. Describe the immigrant impact upon American life—with reference to an outstanding immigrant or a specific immigrant group—in the following areas: (a) fine arts (b) literature (c) science and invention (d) political affairs (e) economic activity (f) social life.

4. *Agree* or *disagree*, presenting *two* arguments to support your opinion, with *each* of the following statements: (a) The diversity of the American people has strengthened our democracy. (b) The melting-pot theory provides a more accurate explanation of American culture today than does cultural pluralism. (c) Although the immigrant experience has been both bitter and sweet, in the long run the sweet has far exceeded the bitter. (d) As immigrants in 19th-century America, British-Canadians assimilated far more easily than did French-Canadians.

5. In 19th- and early 20th-century America, members of each immigrant group settled close to one another, thereby forming distinct rural and urban ethnic enclaves. Discuss this pattern of settlement, explaining (a) *two* reasons why newly arrived immigrants tended to do so and (b) *two* reasons why native-born Americans whose families had been here for several generations criticized this practice.

Part 2. The Growth and Variety of American Cultural Patterns

Meaning of Culture. The term *culture*, as generally accepted, means the total of human achievements and activities that are learned and passed on from one generation to the next. Culture includes (1) human institutions such as family, religion, education, government, and economy; (2) technological matters such as tools, utensils, weapons, and machines; and (3) language and art such as word concepts, literature, legends and myths, painting, and music. All cultures grow and change, and many become complex.

7. The American People Have Developed a Complex Culture

The American people, coming from diverse backgrounds, share a culture composed of many interrelated elements and therefore quite *complex.* (1) It is in part *derivative*—reflecting our debt to European, African, Asian, and Latin American cultures brought here by the many peoples of our pluralistic society —and in part *original*—reflecting modifications of these imported cultures by creative new responses to American conditions. (2) The American culture is in part *fixed*—reflecting the permanence of American customs, ideals, and institutions, and in part *changing*—reflecting the infusion of additional cultural elements by more recent immigrants and by more recent responses to the American environment. (3) It is in part *uniform:* a *dominant* or *mass culture*—reflecting the broad general similarity of American life, and in part *diverse*—reflecting the existence of many subcultures.

AMERICANS ADOPT AND ADAPT EUROPEAN SOCIETAL PATTERNS

1. American Family Patterns

a. The European Heritage. Mirroring West European family life, colonial families performed the same major functions—bearing and rearing children; providing them with an education—especially religious instruction, good citizenship, and occupational training; and organizing the family members to work together in a predominantly agricultural economy. Colonial families were *patrilineal*—the wife and children took the father's family name and the children traced their family line or *genealogy* through the father. Colonial families also

39

were *patriarchal:* the father ruled the family, made its important decisions, and exercised full authority over its members. The mother ran the household —cleaning, cooking, sewing, and caring for the children. In rural families, the mother also assisted with the farmwork and the many children were an economic asset performing necessary chores. Especially among the middle- and upper-class colonial families, marriages were arranged by the father or at least with his consent. In the patriarchal family, the father had authority over the children and control of the family's "worldly goods" from which he could provide a dowry for a daughter or an inheritance for a son.

In the Southern colonies, the well-to-do planters resembled the English landed aristocracy in that they possessed sizable estates and lived in spacious homes, thereby enabling them to maintain large families. The planter, wife, and children constituted the *nuclear family;* the grandparents and other close relatives living with them made up the *extended form.* When all these related persons live together, the family may be described as the *nuclear extended form.*

b. Colonial Changes in Family Patterns. Since the New England colonies featured family-size farms and comparatively small farmhouses, New England farmers rarely maintained nuclear extended families. With land easily available and jobs plentiful, newly married couples left the paternal household and set up their own small homes. Also within the patriarchal family, colonial women bettered their status as compared to their European sisters. Colonial women were highly valued: they were relatively scarce among the early settlers, and in rural households they were considered to be *economic assets.*

c. American Families Today. As the United States changed from a rural-agricultural to an urban-industrial society, the American family also changed. (1) Today's family no longer functions as a self-contained economic unit. The father goes to work at the office or factory; the mother takes care of the home or, in many cases, secures outside employment; the children may be in a day care center and later in school. The family further has lost some of its educational functions to schools, churches, labor unions, and other societal agencies. On the other hand, with industrialization providing additional leisure, family members have more time that they may spend with each other, thereby being able to develop a sense of *togetherness.* (2) The colonial patriarchal family has given way to the *equalitarian family*—wherein mother and father share in making family decisions, children possess a good deal of freedom to develop as individuals, and parents exercise authority within a democratic framework. Modern families are small, averaging less than two children per family, and the cost of rearing and educating children is high—estimated at over $60,000 per child from birth through four years of college. Young people select their own marriage partners, usually on the basis of "romantic love," and the practice of giving a dowry has largely disappeared. With household work reduced by small families and labor-saving appliances, over 35 percent of all married women work outside the home and have a measure of financial independence. (3) In our industrialized society, with its small urban apartments and high living costs, the parents and unmarried children live together as the typical nuclear family. Newlyweds almost immediately set up their own households. Elderly family members—grandparents, uncles, aunts—generally live by themselves or reside in *senior citizens' homes* or in *retirement communities.*

2. American Religious Practices

a. The European Heritage. Following Old World practices, most colonies set up an *official* or *established church.* It was supported by government funds raised through taxes and, especially in the 17th century, church membership was required for voting and office holding. In the Southern colonies and New York, the official church was the *Anglican Church*—an extension of the Church of England. (After the American Revolution, the Anglican Church in America was disestablished and became known as the Protestant Episcopal Church.) In the New England colonies, except for Rhode Island, the official church was the *Puritan* or *Congregational Church.*

Also following Old World practices, the colonial Anglican and Puritan establishments were intolerant of and often persecuted Catholics and Protestant dissenters. In Massachusetts, the early Puritan leaders punished and exiled any religious nonconformists.

b. Colonial Changes in Religious Practices

(1) *Factors Promoting Tolerance. (a) Many Religious Groups.* Colonial settlers represented a great number of religions—overwhelmingly Protestant sects (Puritan, Anglican, Quaker, Presbyterian, Dutch Reformed, Baptist, and Lutheran), but also some Roman Catholics and a small number of Jews. The settlers realized that, if their own religion was to survive, they had to tolerate all other religions. *(b) Need for Settlers.* Settlers in colonial America, who could provide labor, purchase land, and produce goods, were an asset. Settlers could be more easily attracted, colonial governments realized, by overlooking religious differences. *(c) Frontier Conditions.* Faced with the difficulties of securing a living and safeguarding the settlement, frontier settlers were not disposed to engage in theological disputes or to question the religion of their neighbors. *(d) Splits Within Existing Churches.* The *Great Awakening*, a religious movement beginning in the 1730's, stressed the emotional aspects of religion. In mass revival meetings, *itinerant* (traveling) ministers emphasized fear of Hell and love of God. The Great Awakening caused *schisms* (splits) in the existing churches, thereby promoting religious diversity and in the long run furthering religious tolerance.

(2) *Steps Toward Tolerance. (a) Rhode Island. Roger Williams* and his followers—dissenters from Puritan beliefs and practices—were expelled from Massachusetts in 1636 and settled in Rhode Island. Under Williams' leadership, the Rhode Island government provided complete religious freedom. It rejected any established church, meaning no public funds for religious purposes, no compulsory church membership, and no religious qualifications for voting. This idea of *separation of church and state* was later incorporated into the First Amendment to the United States Constitution. *(b) Maryland.* Lord Baltimore founded Maryland as a haven for Catholics, but the colony soon attracted a majority of Protestants. To protect the Catholic minority and to prevent religious strife, Lord Baltimore in 1649 secured from the colonial assembly the *Maryland Toleration Act.* It granted religious freedom to all Christians. *(c) Pennsylvania.* William Penn founded Pennsylvania as a haven for Quakers but opposed setting up any established church. In 1682 he granted religious freedom to all settlers, no matter what their religion, as long as they believed in God. *(d) Other*

Colonies. New Jersey and South Carolina took limited but significant steps toward religious tolerance.

c. Religious Trends in America Today

(1) *A Protestant Majority.* The United States remains chiefly Protestant but not, as in colonial times, overwhelmingly so. Of total religious membership reported recently, Protestants constituted 58 percent, Catholics 37 percent, and Jews 5 percent. The increase in the non-Protestant proportion of our population reflects, for Catholics, their high birthrate and their heavy immigration from Ireland, Italy, Poland, Canada, and Latin America, and, for Jews, their heavy immigration from eastern Europe.

(2) *Religion and Marriage.* Within America's three major religions, each has demonstrated a tendency toward blurring of lines of internal division. Protestants tend to marry Protestants regardless of denomination or nationality. Catholics tend to marry within their religion but across Irish, Polish, and Italian nationality lines. Jews tend to marry Jews regardless of national origin and orthodox, conservative, or reform religious beliefs. (A small but growing number of marriages, however, have been between persons of different religions, that is, *interfaith marriages.*)

(3) *Interfaith Cooperation.* Among the three major religions, efforts have been made to achieve understanding and cooperation. The *National Conference of Christians and Jews,* founded in 1928, combats religious prejudice and seeks to improve intergroup relations. It sponsors observance of an annual *Brotherhood Week.* Vatican Council II, which concluded its work in 1965, strongly influenced the Catholic Church in America toward *ecumenism*—the movement toward Christian unity through dialogue, understanding, and cooperation between Catholics and non-Catholics.

(4) *The Judeo-Christian Heritage.* While not overlooking doctrinal differences that divide them, religious leaders of all three faiths have stressed their unifying Judeo-Christian heritage: beliefs that a single God is Father of all human beings who therefore are brothers and sisters; that each individual is a person of worth, entitled to respect and dignity; that relations among persons should be guided by ethical conduct—*negatively,* not to steal and not to lie—*positively,* to honor parents, to give charity, and to provide social justice, especially for the widow, the orphan, and the oppressed; that all persons should observe the *Golden Rule,* "Do unto others as you would have others do unto you"; and finally that a better world can be achieved, and worthy persons will be rewarded in this world or in the afterlife. To implement this Judeo-Christian heritage, many religious leaders have expressed concern and taken action regarding vital social problems—minority civil rights, discrimination, and poverty.

(5) *Church-State Relations and Schools.* The First Amendment to the Constitution decrees separation of church and state by providing that "Congress shall make no law respecting an establishment of religion, or prohibiting the free exercise thereof." In recent years, the Supreme Court has upheld indirect and limited government aid to parochial schools, such aid as bus transportation, school lunches, and secular textbooks. The Supreme Court, however, has rejected state laws providing direct financial aid to parochial schools as causing "excessive entanglement" of church and state. In general, Protestants and Jews are opposed to government aid to church schools, whereas Catholics, with their

extensive parochial school system, are in favor of such aid. Catholic spokesmen further warn that, in these inflationary times, unless government aid is forthcoming, the Catholic parochial schools may be compelled, by finances, to further closings—thereby placing the entire burden of educating all Catholic children upon the public schools. From 1965 to 1971, the number of Catholic schools decreased by 20 percent. (Check the Index for "Parochial schools.")

3. American Social Structure

a. The European Heritage. As in the Old World, colonial society was divided into three classes: (1) The *upper class* or aristocracy consisted of the large landowners (the well-to-do planters in the South and the Dutch patroons in the Hudson Valley of New York); the leading merchants of Northern towns who owned ships, warehouses, and real estate; the major government officials; and notable professionals such as clergymen and lawyers. (2) The *middle class,* which was most numerous, consisted of small landowning farmers; lesser merchants; skilled workmen and master artisans who owned tools and shops; managerial employees such as plantation overseers and ship captains; less important government officials; and many professionals. (3) The *lower class* consisted of propertyless city workers, farm laborers, sailors, indentured servants, and slaves.

As in Europe, the upper class in colonial America was keenly aware of its superior social status. In the South, the well-to-do planters consciously imitated the English aristocracy—with large mansions, elaborate household furnishings, ostentatious dress, and conspicuous leisure-time activities such as hunting and horse racing. In New England, Harvard College arranged its student register, not in alphabetical order, but by family social status.

b. Colonial Changes in Social Structure. (1) Self-Made Aristocracy. The nobles in Europe, having inherited their titles and estates as a birthright, constituted an hereditary class. In contrast, the colonial planter and merchant aristocracy, measured by recently acquired wealth, was largely a self-made aristocracy. (2) Land Availability. Land in Europe was limited in supply, held almost entirely in large estates of the nobility, and was the basis of their wealth and power. In contrast, land in colonial America seemed limitless and was easily available to all settlers. Although a form of colonial wealth, land could not provide the basis for an exclusive aristocracy. (3) Social Mobility. Social positions in Europe were determined by birth and maintained by sharp class distinctions. In contrast, colonial classes were not hereditary, except for the slaves, and colonists moved easily up and down the social ladder. Such *social mobility*—movement from one status to another within the social structure—was a unique American development. (4) Slavery. Although the peasants in Europe were impoverished economically, unrepresented in government, and inferior socially, they were not slaves and Europe had no slave class. In contrast the Southern colonies, faced with a shortage of labor for their large plantations, came to depend upon Negro slaves. They constituted an hereditary laboring class.

c. American Social Structure Today. Except for the abolition of slavery, American society today retains the major colonial characteristics—three broad classes but no sharp dividing lines, an aversion to an hereditary aristocracy reinforced by the Constitutional provision against granting any "title of nobility," and an open-class society with considerable social mobility. Historically, Americans have experienced an upward mobility, made possible by our political freedom, educational opportunity, economic growth, and popular acceptance of the *Protestant ethic*—that ambition, hard work, and material success are virtues. As newer immigrant groups arrived and occupied the bottom social rungs, the earlier groups moved up the social ladder. With immigration sharply curtailed since the 1920's, will our disadvantaged groups be able to continue the historic pattern of upward mobility?

Other aspects of American culture could be analyzed in terms of the European heritage, the colonial adaptions, and the current situation. (Check the Index for "Architecture," "Education," "Literature," "Music," "Painting," "Science," and "Technology.")

SUBCULTURES: VARIATIONS WITHIN THE AMERICAN CULTURE

Meaning of Subculture. Within the American culture, specific groups exist who share the total culture but who, in addition, exhibit traits peculiar to the group. Such a group is said to constitute a *subculture*. The group members display a certain unity—of historical background, common problems, and future aspirations, and maintain a sense of in-group belonging. Three subcultures, discussed below, are based upon urban-rural divisions and upon an age group.

CASE STUDIES OF SUBCULTURES

Meaning of Urban and Rural. The United States Census Bureau reported that our population in 1970 was 73.5 percent *urban*—defined as living in communities with 2500 or more inhabitants—and 26.5 percent *rural*—defined as living in communities of fewer than 2500 people. These definitions hide considerable internal variations. Despite obvious differences, Ithaca, a town of 30,000 people in central New York State, and New York City, a metropolitan area of 12 million inhabitants, are both classified as "urban." Similarly, a Maine potato farmer, a Georgia sharecropper, and a Montana sheep herder are all classified as "rural."

1. Urban Subculture

a. People. Urbanites are a heterogeneous people representing different religions, national origins, and ethnic groups. Because their community is a large or mass society, the members cannot know all the others personally. To overcome the feeling of personal isolation, urbanites are joiners—of political clubs, social organizations, and adult education classes.

b. Economic Activities. Urbanites are highly specialized workers representing a complex division of labor. They depend upon each other for goods and services so that, for example, a transit strike in New York City can disrupt the entire metropolitan area. They also depend upon other regions to buy their manufactured goods, to use their banking, shipping, and cultural services, and to supply them with raw materials and foodstuffs. Urbanites live in an *interdependent* economy and many maintain a better than average standard of living.

c. City Life-Styles. Urbanites find that life is continuously changing or *dynamic*. They live at a fast tempo and with considerable mobility. They utilize personal and, where available, mass-transportation facilities to go to work, to school, to friends, and to cultural and recreational events. Urbanites are *cosmopolitan*, that is, interested in happenings in the rest of the nation and the world. To keep up to date, they read varied newspapers and magazines, listen to radio and television broadcasts, and attend lectures and meetings. Frequently, they have business dealings with persons from distant areas. Also they are concerned with their own community and seek solutions to urban problems. Urbanites are *sophisticated*, that is, worldly wise. They patronize the creative arts, appreciate the value of education, and many have achieved a good level of educational attainment. Urbanites tend to be *open-minded*, that is, receptive to new ideas and new ways of doing things.

d. Urban Problems and the Flight to the Suburbs. In recent years urban problems—such as mass transportation, education, crime, drugs, and pollution—have been intensified by conflicts between the well-to-do and the poor city residents, usually minority groups. Many well-to-do have fled the central cities for the surrounding areas, the suburbs.

2. Rural Subculture

a. People. Within most rural areas, except for the South, the inhabitants tend to be rather homogeneous. In small communities where the same families have resided for generations, the people often know each other personally and have a strong in-group feeling.

b. Economic Activities. The small farmer tends to be a multiskilled worker, that is, a *jack-of-all-trades*. He farms the land but also performs other tasks such as tending animals, overhauling machinery, and repairing farm buildings. The rural family usually remains an economic unit under strong patriarchal control with each member assigned chores. In villages and small towns, tradesmen may cultivate their own garden plots. Rural inhabitants tend to be more *self-sufficient* economically but their living standards often fall below the national average.

c. Rural Life-Styles. Rural people find that life remains more or less the same or *static*. They live at a slow tempo and stay mainly within their own area— visiting friends, exchanging news, attending church, going on picnics. They claim to have greater peace of mind or *contentment*. Rural inhabitants live in self-imposed *isolation*. Their interests seem limited to their own immediate vicinity, that is, *local*. Rural dwellers may appear *unsophisticated*, that is un-worldly, but the automobile, radio, and television have considerably expanded their horizons. They tend to place less value on formal education and, since rural communities have a small tax base, they spend less on school facilities. (In some rural areas, consolidated schools—serving several districts—provide quality education for rural youth.) Many rural inhabitants have a low level of educational attainment. Rural people tend to find satisfaction in a slow-paced life and prefer to follow familiar and time-tested ways of doing things.

3. An Age-Group Subculture.
Teenagers can be said to constitute a distinct subculture cutting across regional, socioeconomic, and ethnic lines. Many teenagers claim an in-group feeling based on such factors as school environment; slang; readiness to experiment with clothing and hair styles, with current music, and in other areas; idealism not tempered by practical experience; and depen-dence upon their parents while at the same time asserting independence and rebelling against numerous adult values.

4. Other Subcultures. Other types of subcultures that could be examined include (a) geographic regions such as the Northeast, South, Midwest, Southwest, and Pacific Coast; (b) ethnic minorities such as blacks, Mexicans, Puerto Ricans, Indians, French-Canadians, Jews, and Italians; and (c) occupational groups such as "hard-hat" construction workers, doctors, and teachers.

FACTORS PROMOTING CULTURAL UNIFORMITY

Many factors operate in American society to counter the diversity of subcultures and to further an awareness of and conformity with the national culture : (1) The *national government* comes in contact with all Americans. It requires them to obey federal laws, encourages them to partake in national affairs through voting, and compels them to support national objectives through paying taxes. (2) The *national economy* is interdependent. Regardless of subculture, Americans do not live in isolation economically but depend upon one another. (3) The *military services* take young people from their homes and familiar activities; intermingle them, thereby widening their personal contacts; subject them to a standardized training; and assign them to posts throughout the nation and in foreign countries. (4) The *mobility of population*, long an American trait, in recent years has been spurred by the automobile and the airplane. Historically, Americans have been moving out of the rural areas and into the cities; they also have been moving from the Eastern seaboard into the West. Retired people especially have relocated in the warmer climates of Florida, Arizona, New Mexico, and southern California. With workers securing longer vacations, many Americans have spent their leisure time in travel—"seeing America first." Such population mobility has encouraged a national cultural uniformity. (5) The *schools*, public and private, reach all of our children. They foster an American patriotism as they teach about national events, heroes, and holidays. Textbooks and other teaching materials have nationwide distribution. Even in farm areas, some children are attending, not the isolated rural schoolhouse, but the more modern consolidated or central school. (6) The *mass-communications media*—radio, television, newspapers, news-gathering services, magazines, and even book clubs—encourage a national uniformity of speech, thought, dress, and outlook on life.

MULTIPLE-CHOICE QUESTIONS

1. In its *broadest* sense, the term "culture" is *best* defined as (1) a high level of technological achievement (2) the ideals and hopes of a nation (3) a people's total way of living (4) all of the fine arts, such as painting, sculpture, and music.
2. In general, the societal pattern of the early English colonists in the New World was primarily (1) an original pattern born of necessity (2) an adaptation of the American Indian tribal form (3) an adaptation based on European culture (4) a pattern identical to that of English society.
3. In the patriarchal family, major decisions are made (1) after discussion and with approval of all nuclear family members (2) by the father (3) by the mother (4) by the grandparents as the elders in the nuclear extended family.
4. "Culture in colonial America was largely European in origin." Which best supports this statement? (1) development of public schools (2) creation of established churches (3) practice of religious freedom (4) establishment of universal suffrage

5. "My sermons demanded freedom of worship for all and just payment to the Indians for land. The authorities forced me to flee." This statement could have been made by (1) Roger Williams (2) William Penn (3) Thomas Paine (4) Asser Levy.

6. By the early 18th century, religious developments in the 13 English colonies indicated that the (1) Anglican Church was the established church in most colonies (2) religious leaders were generally the civil administrators (3) principle of religious toleration had made significant headway (4) separation of church and state was the policy in most colonies.

7. Which factor contributed *most* to the development of religious freedom in the United States? (1) the rise of nativist movements (2) the traditions of Puritanism (3) the European tradition of religious toleration (4) the variety of religious beliefs

8. Which *best* describes the major religions in the United States today? (1) They are supported by government funds. (2) They have little influence on the nation's cultural development. (3) They have some basic beliefs in common. (4) They remain apart from national and international politics.

9. The term *ecumenism* refers to a movement to (1) establish more parochial schools (2) achieve better understanding between Catholics and non-Catholics (3) prohibit interfaith cooperation (4) involve religious leaders in our political processes.

10. The *Protestant ethic* encourages people to (1) work hard and seek material success (2) live in idleness (3) convert to Protestantism (4) contemplate ethical issues and achieve spiritual contentment.

11. In an outline, which would be the main topic that includes the other three as subtopics? (1) nuclear families (2) ethnic groups (3) social mobility (4) social structure

12. Which *best* illustrates the concept of social mobility? (1) A farmer moves from the South to a Northern city. (2) A skilled construction worker moves from one job to another. (3) The son or daughter of an immigrant laborer is appointed to the presidency of a major university. (4) A young executive is transferred from corporate headquarters in Long Island to a subsidiary company in California.

13. After a study of life in an *urban* area and life in a *rural* area of the United States, it would be valid to conclude that (1) different cultural patterns exist (2) racial groups have been assimilated (3) cultural patterns are the same everywhere (4) about the same number of immigrants settled in all sections.

14. Which is the *most* valid statement concerning cultural patterns in the United States during the 20th century? (1) Extended families are common in the suburbs. (2) Cultural standards are determined solely by the federal government. (3) The family has come to play a more important role in maintaining social control. (4) Regional cultural differences have been reduced because of the influence of mass media.

ESSAY QUESTIONS

1. American culture has been described by the following pairs of terms: (a) derivative and original (b) fixed and changing (c) uniform and diverse. Select *one* term from *each* of these pairs and discuss an aspect of our culture today that illustrates the term.

2. (a) Explain how *each* of *three* factors has furthered cultural uniformity in the United States. (b) Select *one* subculture in the United States and explain how it has been able to survive despite pressures for cultural uniformity. (c) Do you approve or disapprove of the existence of subcultures? Present *one* argument to support your opinion.

3. American culture from colonial times to the present has followed the technique of *adopt and adapt*. Select any *three* of the following areas: (a) family (b) religion (c) social classes (d) science and technology (e) government. For *each* area selected discuss *one* factor that American culture has adopted from the rest of the world and *one* factor that American culture has adapted to our needs and realities.

Part 3. Population Growth: Its Effects Upon Humanity

8. The World Faces Problems Resulting From the Population Explosion

RELATIONSHIP OF POPULATION TO NECESSITIES OF LIFE

We human beings are all passengers traveling through space on the space-craft called "earth." We depend for survival on the relation between our numbers and the earth's resources essential for providing the necessities of life. We depend also on the wise use of these resources.

Today the rapid and uncontrolled increase in world population threatens to outstrip man's capacity to secure from the earth the necessities of life. *Demographers*—population experts—view such an imbalance, with numbers of people overwhelming resources, as creating the basic population problem. To redress such imbalance, demographers suggest three approaches: (1) Man can work to increase the supply of food and other necessities—but how and to what extent? (2) Man can endeavor to slow down the growth of population—but how and to what extent? (3) Man can reduce his demands on the earth's resources by accepting a lower living standard deliberately—but will he and to what extent?

THE MALTHUSIAN THEORY OF POPULATION

In 1803 *Thomas Malthus,* a British economist, published his revised *Essay on the Principle of Population.* His main ideas, which earned Malthus the reputation of outstanding population theorist, were as follows: (1) Population tends to increase more rapidly than food supply. (This generalization replaced Malthus' previous statement that population increases in geometric ratio—1, 2, 4, 8, 16, 32—whereas food supply increases in arithmetic ratio—1, 2, 3, 4, 5, 6.) (2) As population growth crowds upon food supply, the effect is to depress living standards. (3) In the past, population growth has been limited by such accidental factors as famine, disease, natural catastrophe, and war. (4) Malthus urged that population growth should be curtailed by deliberate human effort. Malthus advised the British government to abolish welfare for the poor since it enabled them to survive, marry, and have children. He advised individuals to practice "moral restraint" by postponing marriage and limiting family size.

This *Malthusian theory* has stirred great controversy. *Critics* claim that Malthus underestimated man's ability to increase sharply the production of food

48

and other necessities and man's willingness to limit family size so as to achieve higher levels of living. *Supporters* insist that Malthus was correct and point to the tremendous population growth of the 19th-century United States and to the current worldwide *population explosion.*

THE POPULATION EXPLOSION: A WORLDWIDE PHENOMENON

1. Tremendous Recent Growth of World Population. Since the end of World War II, the population of the world has increased tremendously. In 1950 world population totaled 2.5 billion; in 1971 it was 3.7 billion. If the current unprecedented 2 percent annual growth rate continues, world population will double in 35 years; by the year 2000, it will be over 6 billion. This astounding and recent growth of the number of people inhabiting the earth is referred to as the population explosion.

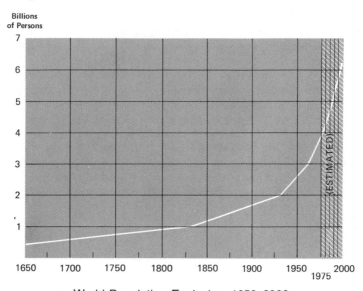

World Population Explosion, 1650–2000

2. Greatest Percentage Growth in Underdeveloped Nations

a. Statistical Data (1945–1947 to 1965). Population during these two decades increased:

(1) *For Developed Countries.* The United States, 36 percent; Great Britain, 13 percent; France, 20 percent.

(2) *For Underdeveloped Countries.* Egypt, 56 percent; India, 62 percent; Mexico, 78 percent; Nigeria, 170 percent.

b. Reasons for the Population Explosion in Underdeveloped Nations. Well past the mid-20th century the underdeveloped nations—of Latin America, Africa, and Asia—remained producers of agricultural and other raw materials; their peoples had extremely low living standards and were mostly illiterate, but at the same time, they maintained their traditionally high birthrates of 40 to 50 per 1000 of population.

In the post-World War II years, these underdeveloped nations received the full impact of Western advances in public health and modern science, brought by private agencies such as the *Rockefeller Foundation,* by foreign aid programs of industrialized countries, and by the United Nations' specialized agency, the *World Health Organization* (WHO). With pesticides combating mosquitoes carrying malaria, antibiotics treating communicable diseases, vaccinations immunizing against smallpox, and water purification inhibiting the spread of germs—the underdeveloped nations experienced a sharp drop in death rates. Consequently, their *natural increase rate* (the difference between birthrate and deathrate) became extremely high and their population growth reached explosive proportions.

3. Problems Arising From the Population Explosion in Underdeveloped Nations

a. Depressed Living Standards. In many underdeveloped nations, the rapid population growth has outdistanced a rise in gross national product (GNP)—a measure of the money value of all goods and services. The result has been that income per capita (per person) has fallen and living standards have further declined.

b. Increased Burden on Older People. With infant mortality rates sharply down in underdeveloped nations, younger people have constituted a greater proportion of the total population. This increased number of dependent infants and children has placed additional burdens upon the older generations for providing food, clothing, and shelter.

c. Drain on Food Supplies and Mineral Resources. Many underdeveloped nations have been unable to provide sufficient food to keep their people from starvation. India, Red China, and several African nations have depended upon

The human race
(*Morris for Wide World Photos*)

substantial shipments of wheat from America to feed their hungry masses. In considering mineral resources, even at current consumption rates, the world faces shortages of silver, mercury, tin, and cobalt.

d. Widened Gulf Between "Have" and "Have-Not" Nations. With underdeveloped nations making little, if any, economic progress, while developed nations have moved steadily ahead, the gulf between the "have" and the "have-not" nations has widened. Understandably, impoverished nations have tended to develop attitudes of envy, resentment, and hostility toward their more affluent neighbors.

EFFORTS TO CONTROL WORLD POPULATION GROWTH

1. By International Organizations. The United Nations *General Assembly* and *Economic and Social Council* approved UN agency programs to reduce population growth in countries requesting such programs. The *World Health Organization* (WHO), one UN agency, plans programs of birth control research and information. The *World Bank,* another UN agency, offers grants to nations to finance family-planning programs.

2. By Government Programs

a. The United States. The *Agency for International Development* (AID), which administers the American foreign aid program, provides considerable sums for population research and family-planning programs to countries requesting such assistance.

b. Other Governments. (1) In some 30 underdeveloped nations, the governments are actively pursuing programs to educate their peoples to the need for and methods of birth control. In this group are India, Turkey, Taiwan, South Korea, the Philippines, Morocco, Tunisia, Kenya, and several Latin American countries. (2) Some 30 other developing nations have no programs of their own but are cooperating somewhat with private family-planning agencies. (3) Although Communist theoreticians asserted that the population explosion threatened living standards only in capitalist nations, Communist China undertook programs to limit family size.

3. By Private Agencies

Private agencies, chiefly American, seek to "defuse the population time bomb" by varied efforts: *(a)* educational—pamphlets, newspaper advertisements, television programs, films, and conferences; *(b)* financial—funds for demographic studies, birth control and family-planning research, and family-planning clinics; and *(c)* political—to spur government action.

The major private agencies include the following: *International Planned Parenthood Federation, Ford Foundation, Rockefeller Foundation,* the *Population Reference Bureau, Population Council,* and *Zero Population Growth* (ZPG).

FACTORS COMPLICATING POPULATION CONTROL EFFORTS

1. Illiteracy and Poverty. *(a)* Unable to read and write, illiterate peoples remain relatively unaware of population problems and of modern birth control methods.

(b) Impoverished peoples, primarily concerned with securing the necessities of life, remain unwilling to spend monies for birth control devices and drugs.

Illiteracy and poverty, many demographers claim, help explain why underdeveloped countries maintain higher birthrates than developed countries and why low-income groups raise larger families than middle- and upper-income groups.

2. Rural Economies. In rural economies, typical of most underdeveloped countries, parents consider children as economic assets. When young, children work on the farm; when children reach adulthood, they take care of their aged parents.

3. Religious Factors. Roman Catholic teaching approves natural methods of birth control while rejecting, as immoral, artificial or manmade methods. Many Hindus believe that each father requires at least two sons to perform the traditional religious rites at the time of his death.

4. Other Cultural Factors. (a) In many underdeveloped countries, people marry at a young age, thereby increasing the child-bearing years of marriage. For example, in India the average age of girls at time of marriage in 1900 was 13 and today is 16. (b) In Latin American countries, fathers want large families as proof of their *machismo*, that is, their masculinity.

EFFORTS TO INCREASE SUPPLIES OF FOOD AND OTHER NECESSITIES

1. Efforts to Increase Food Supplies

a. Export the Agricultural Revolution to Underdeveloped Nations. *Agronomists,* who are agricultural experts, believe that underdeveloped countries could increase crop yields dramatically if they utilized modern agricultural methods—artificial fertilizers, farm machinery, and improved seed strains. The change from subsistence to commercial farming, however, will severely disrupt the traditional agricultural practices and the way of life of the native farmers.

b. Scientific Advances. Scientists continually develop new and improved strains of grain. *Norman Borlaug,* an American agronomist working for the Rockefeller Foundation, received the 1970 Nobel Peace Prize for his leadership in the *"Green Revolution"*—the effort to improve agriculture by developing strains of wheat and rice that are disease-resistant, have a high protein content, and provide a higher yield per acre. Borlaug's work has helped farmers improve crop output in India, Mexico, and Pakistan. Agricultural scientists also have been experimenting with growing plants not in soil but in nutrient-enriched water—a method called *hydroponics.*

c. Desalinization. By devising methods of low-cost, large-scale desalinization, or desalting, of ocean waters, scientists hope to provide society with large quantities of usable pure water. Society could then use these waters to irrigate and bring under cultivation lands presently arid.

d. "Farming" the Ocean. Scientists look to the oceans to increase food supply (1) by increasing fish catches, (2) by cultivating crops of *algae* that are high in protein and are already being used for food in parts of the world, and (3) by discovering human uses for *plankton*—the masses of microscopic animal and plant life found floating in oceans and eaten by fish.

e. Controlling Pollution. The pollution of our food-producing land, river, and ocean areas has raised mounting concern. Ecologically sensitive citizens and scientists are alerting the public to the need of preventing pollutants from destroying irreplaceable food sources. The 1972 *UN Conference on Human Environment,* held at Stockholm (Sweden) and attended by delegates of over 100 nations, (1) acknowledged the existence of a worldwide environmental emergency and (2) requested nations to cooperate in international programs to prevent further environmental deterioration.

f. Changes in Food Habits. Nutritionists believe that man can be educated to expand his diet to include new and strange foods. Such changes, however, will not be brought about easily. For example, religious prohibitions deter Jews and Moslems from eating pork and Hindus from eating beef; cultural aversions deter Americans from eating insects.

2. Agencies Seeking to Increase World Food Supplies. Public agencies include the *Food and Agriculture Organization* (FAO), a specialized UN agency, and the *Agency for International Development* (AID), which administers the United States foreign aid program. Private groups include the *Ford Foundation* and the *Rockefeller Foundation.* In general, both public and private organizations provide funds to further research, to send technical assistance to underdeveloped lands, and to maintain experimental and demonstration farms.

The 1974 *UN World Food Conference,* held at Rome (Italy) and attended by delegates of 130 nations, (1) short range—acknowledged that 500 million people, especially in India, Bangladesh, Pakistan, and the sub-Saharan African nations, faced immediate starvation, but the delegates provided no solution to meet this emergency; and (2) long range—proposed an international system of grain reserves to meet future emergency needs and called for creation of a *UN World Food Council* which would coordinate the efforts of all UN agencies dealing with food, spur increased food production, and channel future food supplies to hungry nations.

3. Efforts to Increase Supplies of Other Necessities. *(a) Chemists* have produced artificial or synthetic products—fibers, rubber, and leather for making shoes and clothing, and plastics with a wide range of uses. *(b) Nuclear scientists* have learned to utilize atomic energy—a new source of power for propelling ships and for producing electricity. *(c) Geologists* have uncovered new deposits of minerals and petroleum such as the 1968 find of a large oil field on the north slope of Alaska.

9. American Population Trends Affect Our Society

SURVEY OF AMERICAN POPULATION GROWTH

1. The Census Reports of Population

a. 1790 to 1900. Every ten years, starting with 1790, the United States government has taken a population count, called a *census.* In 1790 the United States contained almost 4 million people; in 1800—over 5 million; in 1850—23 million; in 1860—31 million; and by 1900—76 million. From 1790 to 1860 our population increase per decade averaged almost 35 percent. From 1860 to 1900 the increase per decade averaged almost 25 percent.

b. 1900 to the Present

Year	Population in Millions	Increase Over Preceding Census	
		In Millions	In Percent
1900	76	13	21
1910	92	16	21
1920	106	14	15
1930	123	17	16
1940	132	9	7
1950	151	19	15
1960	179	28	19
1970	203	24	13

2. Factors Promoting American Population Growth

a. Heavy Immigration. Immigration has augmented the American population by some 45 million people.

b. Relatively High Natality, or Birthrate

(1) *Statistical Data.* In 1800 the birthrate in the United States was estimated at 55 per 1000 of population. This figure, demographers explained, represented humanity's highest known reproduction rate. It meant that American mothers in the early 1800's had an average of over eight children. Throughout the 19th century, the American birthrate declined gradually but still remained at a high level: in 1900 it was 32 per 1000 of population. In the 20th century, the American birthrate continued to drop so that by 1972 it had fallen to 15 per 1000 of population.

(2) *Reasons for Our Relatively High Birthrate.* (*a*) In rural America, children were an economic asset. (*b*) American farmers were able to increase the output of food tremendously. Cultivating previously untilled tracts of fertile land, they utilized scientific farming methods and agricultural machinery—both major aspects of the *Agricultural Revolution.* (*c*) To provide other necessities of life, the United States utilized its tremendous natural resources such as forests, iron ore, and coal. (*d*) American industrialists sped the output of essential goods—shoes,

clothing, household equipment—by use of machinery and mass production, both aspects of the *Industrial Revolution*. *(e)* To meet expanding demands for energy, American scientists utilized new sources of power: electricity, petroleum, natural gas, and the atom. They also created a wide range of new synthetic products: rubber, fibers, and plastics. *(f)* Americans were brought up in the Judeo-Christian tradition which includes the Biblical injunction to "be fruitful, and multiply." *(g)* Having overwhelmingly experienced rising standards of living, Americans were confident that their children too would have comfortable lives.

c. Declining Mortality, or Deathrate

(1) *Statistical Data.* In 1800 the deathrate in the United States was estimated at 25 per 1000 of population. Throughout our history, the deathrate has continued to fall gradually: in 1900 it was 17 per 1000 of population; by 1970 it had declined to 9.5.

The declining deathrate has meant a tremendous increase in life expectancy: in 1800 Americans had an average life span of 35 years; in 1850—41 years; in 1900—47 years. Today Americans have an average life span of over 70 years.

(2) *Reasons for Our Declining Deathrate: Public Health and Medical Advances.* *(a)* Local governments have expanded facilities for sanitation, water purification, and control of communicable diseases. *(b)* People have been educated to follow nutritionally balanced diets, to recognize symptoms of illness, and to avail themselves of medical and hospital facilities. Americans today have an average of one physician for about 700 people—one of the best doctor-population ratios of any country. *(c)* Medical scientists have conquered many diseases. Typhoid fever, tuberculosis, and certain childhood diseases—all major killers in

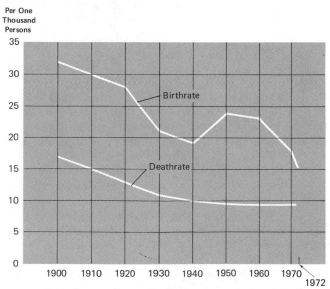

United States Birthrates and Deathrates, 1900–1972

1900—have almost disappeared today. Infant mortality has fallen sharply from 1900, when it was 125 per 1000 newborn babies, to fewer than 20 today.

3. Factors Restraining American Population Growth

a. Emigration. Throughout our history, 12 to 13 million people left the United States. Some returned to their native homelands in Europe, Latin America, Africa, and Asia; others moved on to still newer countries such as Australia and Canada.

b. Natural and Man-Made Catastrophes. Fires, floods, hurricanes, tornadoes, and earthquakes—all have taken considerable numbers of American lives. Also, as more Americans acquired automobiles and drove them at high speeds, the number of auto accidents mounted tremendously. In 1971 over 55,000 Americans lost their lives in motor vehicle accidents.

c. Disease. With childhood and other diseases having been brought under control, the major diseases causing death today are heart (cardiovascular) disease and cancer—chiefly afflicting older people.

d. Wars. By taking the lives of young men in military service, wars have retarded population growth. Wars also caused young people to postpone getting married and having children.

e. Economic Depression. Facing difficult economic times, young people postpone marriage and existing families remain small. During the 1930's depression decade, the rate of population increase fell sharply to the lowest point of any decade in our history.

f. Family Planning. In recent years, many American parents have purposely limited their family size. The number of families with two or three children has increased greatly and become typical; the number with six or more children has decreased sharply. This trend toward smaller families has been most evident among the well-to-do, educated, higher- and middle-income families; it has been least evident among the disadvantaged minorities.

4. Differing Views on American Population Growth

a. Approval. For most of our history, Americans have looked with satisfaction on our rapid population growth. They viewed expanding population as an asset: more settlers; more workers; more consumers; more soldiers; more talented individuals.

b. Recent Concern. In messages to Congress, President Nixon pointed out that Americans took 300 years (to 1917) to number 100 million; they took 50 years (to 1967) to achieve the second 100 million, and if the present growth rate continues, they will reach the third 100 million within 35 years. Nixon recommended increased funds for research in methods of birth control, expanded family-planning services to persons desiring such information, and the creation of an investigatory *Commission on Population Growth and the American Future.* In 1972 the commission submitted a report on population growth, concluding that (1) "neither crisis nor complacency are in order," (2) "no substantial benefits would result from continued growth of the nation's population," and therefore (3) it would be advisable that America slow—and gradually stop—the growth of her population.

OUR YOUTHFUL POPULATION: GROWING NUMBER OF PERSONS UNDER 30

1. Statistical Data (1950–1970)

Year	Total Population in Millions	Persons Under 30	
		Millions	Percent
1950	151	75.3	49.8
1970	203	105.0	52.5

2. Analysis. From 1950 to 1970, the under-30 population gradually increased and constituted more than half the total population. Because of the post-World War II "baby boom," the 20–29-year age bracket is projected to be, for the decade to 1980, our fastest growing group.

3. Impact of Our Under-30 Population

a. Special Wants. (1) For consumer goods: convenience foods, highly styled clothing, flashy cars, rock and roll music, records and tapes, youth-oriented movies, television programs, and magazines; and, upon marriage: homes, home furnishings, and appliances. (2) For educational facilities: technical, college, and graduate facilities. From 1960 to 1970, the number of college students more than doubled—from 3.5 million to 7.5 million, and by 1980 their number is expected to be 11 million. (3) For employment: additional jobs for younger people, who traditionally have a higher unemployment rate than older persons. The federal government, under its antipoverty programs, has provided youths with job training and occupational education. Unions have gained shorter workweeks, making possible more jobs for youths. Social Security has permitted earlier retirement—at age 62 instead of 65—thereby opening up additional jobs.

b. Political Influence. Beginning in the 1960's, the under-30 group —especially college students—showed greater interest in political affairs. Many were outspoken against the war in Vietnam, for justice and equality for blacks, and for protection of the environment against pollution. Many took an active part in politics—supporting Presidential candidates and lobbying among Congress members. In 1971 youths at age 18 received the right to vote in all elections— federal, state, and local—by the Twenty-Sixth Amendment.

OUR SENIOR POPULATION: INCREASING NUMBER OF PERSONS OVER 65

1. Statistical Data

Year	Total Population in Millions	Persons Over 65	
		in Millions	in Percent
1850	23	.6	2.6
1900	76	3.1	4.1
1950	151	12.2	8.1
1960	179	16.5	9.2
1970	203	20.0	9.9

"I know less now than I did thirty years ago. I suppose that's maturity."
(*Drawing by Weber;* © *1968 The New Yorker Magazine, Inc.*)

2. Reasons. The steady increase in the percentage of persons over 65 is due to
(*a*) improvements in general welfare: better food, housing, sanitation facilities,
and working conditions, and (*b*) improvements in medical science: new drugs,
advanced surgical techniques, additional medical facilities, and the development
of *geriatrics*—a special branch of medicine concerned with older people.

3. Problems Facing Our Senior Citizens

a. Forced Retirement—Previously at Age 65. Many 65-year-old workers, in
good health and with a life expectancy of 14 more years, dreaded the change from
purposeful activity to idleness. Their complaints led some corporations to try
flexible retirement—judging each individual worker's health and outlook—or
gradual retirement—reducing the work load gradually for workers past 65.

In 1978 Congress passed and President Carter signed a Retirement Age
measure prohibiting mandatory retirement for most workers in private industry
before age 70.

Social insecurity (*Hesse in the
St. Louis Globe-Democrat*)

b. Use of Leisure Time. Retired workers may keep occupied by engaging in a part-time business or job, doing charity work, pursuing a hobby, taking courses, and joining *golden age* or *sixty-plus* clubs.

c. Housing. Older people need small, low-cost housing with features to prevent accidents: such as ramps instead of stairways and hand grips at the bathtubs. Since the 1950's Congress has passed housing acts with provisions to benefit older persons.

d. Income. Most retired persons face a problem of "making ends meet." Although retired workers have lower living expenses, they no longer receive a salary. They must now depend upon their pensions, savings and investments, and Social Security. Since World War II, the United States has been in a period of *inflation*, a continual increase in prices and decrease in the purchasing power of the dollar, thereby raising the cost of living. Congress therefore has regularly increased Social Security benefits and in 1972 provided that benefits be increased automatically with rises in the *Consumer Price Index* (CPI). (Check the Index for "Consumer Price Index.")

e. Medical Care. Americans over 65, as a group, possess limited finances, suffer disproportionately more from illness and therefore are most burdened by high medical costs. In 1965 Congress enacted a bill providing *Medicare*—medical benefits for persons over 65. The law provides for hospital and nursing home insurance financed through the Social Security tax, and for voluntary medical insurance covering physicians' and surgeons' services financed by a monthly premium paid by the enrollee and matched by the government. (Check the Index for "Medicare.")

OUR URBAN POPULATION: GROWING URBANIZATION OF THE AMERICAN PEOPLE

1. Statistical Data

Year	Total Population in Millions	Distribution by Percent Urban*	Rural	Cities over 1 million Population	Cities of 100,000 to 1 million Population
1790	4	5.1	94.9	0	0
1850	23	15.3	84.7	0	6
1900	76	39.7	60.3	3	35
1950	151	64.0	36.0	5	101
1960	179	69.9	30.1	5	125
1970	203	73.5	26.5	6	147

* An urban area is defined by the Census Bureau as a place with 2,500 or more inhabitants.

2. Urbanization by States and Cities. The most highly urbanized states, with over 80 percent of their populations living in urban areas, are New Jersey, Rhode Island, California, New York, Massachusetts, and Illinois. The most rural states, with over 60 percent of their populations still living in rural areas, are North Dakota, Mississippi, West Virginia, Vermont, South Dakota, and North Carolina.

Our six most populous cities are New York, Chicago, Los Angeles, Philadelphia, Detroit, and Houston.

3. Reasons for the Growth of Cities

a. Industrial Revolution. As industries arose, workers congregated about the factories. These workers added to existing city populations or created new cities. Because urban dwellers needed food, clothing, entertainment, and professional services, still more people came to the cities.

b. Social and Cultural Attractions. Many people were attracted to cities by social and cultural facilities: colleges and universities, theatres and movies, symphonies, libraries, and lecture forums.

c. Improved Transportation and Communication. The railroads, telegraph lines, and telephones enabled city dwellers to (1) obtain foodstuffs and other essentials, (2) distribute the products of city factories throughout the land, and (3) conduct business transactions quickly and efficiently from central offices.

d. Decreasing Farm Population. Farmers were driven from the countryside by the (1) drabness and hardships of farm life, (2) low agricultural prices and difficult times, especially following the Civil War and again following World War I, and (3) increased mechanization and growth of commercial farming.

e. Immigration From Europe. Some "old immigrants," and almost all "new immigrants" coming after 1890, settled in cities, creating many ethnic ghettos.

f. Migrations of Blacks, Puerto Ricans, and Mexicans. (1) Black Migrants. In the 20th century, millions of blacks left the rural areas of the South for urban centers. Some blacks moved to cities in the South, but more moved to cities in the West and North. (2) Puerto Rican and Mexican Migrants. In the 1940's, Puerto Ricans began coming to the United States mainland to seek wartime jobs. They settled mostly in New York; by 1970 the city's Puerto Rican population had swelled to 1 million. By 1970 Mexicans totaling about 5 million persons resided in the United States, four-fifths of them in California and Texas. Mexicans inhabited ghettos in Los Angeles, Houston, and other cities throughout the Southwest.

PROBLEMS FACING CITIES AND URBAN POPULATIONS

1. Public Health. Since city dwellers live close together, diseases may spread easily and become epidemics. Consequently, cities maintain public health services such as hospitals, clinics, and visiting nurses. In addition, cities insure a pure water supply and proper sewage disposal and enforce sanitation laws. In recent years, cities have also taken steps to combat air and water pollution.

2. Crime Prevention. The crime rate in cities is high. *(a)* Cities contain many people and much wealth. *(b)* Impoverished slum inhabitants are tempted into crime. *(c)* Members of youth gangs lack jobs, guidance, and recreational facilities. *(d)* Some youths have turned to illegal and habit-forming drugs. Since such drugs are expensive, these youths may become criminals to secure the monies necessary to support a drug habit.

Cities have tried to deter crime by maintaining police forces to apprehend criminals and municipal courts to try them and impose jail sentences. Cities also have tried to deal with drug abuses by providing youth guidance counselors, by offering schools films and lectures on the danger of drugs, and by maintaining rehabilitation centers for drug addicts.

3. Mass Transit. Cities are being "choked to death" by the ever-increasing number of motor vehicles, private and commercial. Streets are too narrow, parking facilities inadequate. Cities have attempted to meet these problems by improving mass transit services, building expressways around and through the city, and constructing parking areas at the city's outskirts, where commuters can leave their autos and take public transportation. The federal government and some state governments have provided funds to help cities expand mass transit facilities.

4. Education. Cities administer their own educational systems, although these are financed in part by state and federal funds and are subject to state supervision. Cities have faced demands for (*a*) more education: prekindergarten classes, adult education courses, and two- and four-year community colleges; (*b*) better education: new buildings, more teachers, and up-to-date teaching materials such as language laboratories, modern science equipment, and recently published textbooks; and (*c*) school integration—since the 1954 Supreme Court decision in *Brown vs. Board of Education of Topeka*. (Check the Index.)

5. Slum Clearance and Housing

a. The Problem. Many cities contain slum areas, today chiefly inhabited by disadvantaged black, Puerto Rican, and Mexican minorities. City authorities have acted to eradicate slums by razing *tenement houses*—buildings that are filthy, run-down, poorly ventilated and heated, and inadequately protected against fires—and replacing them with low-rent public housing projects. For such *urban renewal*, cities have used their own funds and secured loans and outright subsidies from their states and especially the federal government.

b. Observations. Although many low-rent public housing projects have been built, the slums remain: (1) Seemingly, funds provided for slum clearance —although substantial amounts—were insufficient to do the job of urban renewal. (2) Taxpayers resented the seemingly endless demand for funds for urban renewal. In notable instances, they voted down proposals to extend state public housing programs for low-income families. (3) Minority group families, relocated in low-rental apartments, resented the barracks-like appearance and strict management of the housing projects. (4) Social reformers realized that better housing, by itself, had failed to eradicate juvenile delinquency and crime among project tenants.

6. Need for More City Services. City inhabitants need more and better services, especially in slum areas. As a result, cities have expanded their facilities in recreation, education, housing, transportation, welfare assistance, and public health; and city budgets have soared.

7. Flight to the Suburbs and Its Effect on Cities. Since the end of World War II, many middle- and upper-class families, especially whites, have left the cities for the suburbs. They reasoned that they would be escaping the city's crowded living, racial and other problems, and taxes, and yet would be living near enough to the city to work there and utilize its social and cultural facilities. Businesses too fled the major cities to escape the many urban problems and to escape what

"We want to know why people are leaving cities." (*Shanks in the Buffalo Evening News*)

businessmen called city "nuisance" taxes. The flight to the suburbs has had a twofold effect:

a. Decrease in the City Tax Base. The outflow from large cities of businesses and affluent white families decreased the *tax base*—the businesses and people providing a city with its major tax monies. Cities felt compelled to raise the rates of existing taxes, to increase transportation fares, and to impose new taxes, including a city income tax.

b. Increase in Proportion of Minorities to Total City Population. While white families have moved out, minority group members have moved into the cities. As a result, the central cities have grown but slightly in total population whereas the suburbs have increased substantially. Also minority groups have come to constitute a greater proportion of the population of central cities. From 1950 to 1970 the percentage of blacks has risen sharply in our six largest cities. If this trend continues, urban society may face increasing "polarization" between minority-inhabited inner cities and an outer ring of white-dominated suburbs.

FAIR REPRESENTATION FOR CITIES: LEGISLATIVE REAPPORTIONMENT

1. Background: Rural Overrepresentation. With the rapid growth of cities, from the late 19th century to the early 1960's, rural voters were overrepresented at the expense of urban voters in the federal House of Representatives and in almost all state legislatures. As population shifted from rural to urban and suburban areas, state legislators failed to reapportion seats because of inertia, political disagreement regarding new election district boundaries, or deliberate intent to maintain rural control of the state legislature. For example, in Tennessee a rural district of 3500 people and an urban district of 78,000 people each elected one legislator.

2. Supreme Court Decisions: More Representation for Urban Areas. In 1964 the Supreme Court ruled *(a)* in *Wesberry vs. Sanders* that election districts for the House of Representatives must be equal "as nearly as is practicable" and *(b)* in *Reynolds vs. Sims* that the "one-man, one-vote" principle requires election districts for both houses of state legislatures to be approximately equal in population.

3. Effects of the Decisions. Most states have acted to reapportion election districts on a more equitable basis. The result has been increased representation for cities and suburbs in both houses of state legislatures and in the federal House of Representatives. City officials hope that this change will mean greater attention by legislatures to urban problems.

MULTIPLE-CHOICE QUESTIONS

1. If world population trends from 1945 to 1965 continue, they will most likely result in the (1) decline in agricultural productivity (2) need for high-speed transportation (3) reduction of infant mortality (4) threat of world famine.
2. Which statement tends to support the Malthusian theory of population? (1) The population increase in Nigeria has been accompanied by a corresponding rise in living standards. (2) A majority of the population of Mexico is engaged in manufacturing. (3) Food production in India is lagging behind her population growth. (4) As world population increases, nations will observe higher ethical standards.
3. Which prediction is advanced as being the *most* serious result of the worldwide population explosion? (1) Nations showing the highest population growth rate will greatly increase their political power. (2) The more advanced nations will have the highest population growth and will dominate the less developed nations. (3) The economic gap between prosperous and less prosperous peoples will broaden. (4) The number of member nations in the United Nations will automatically increase.
4. In a nation in which population is increasing at a faster rate than production, it is also *most* likely that (1) average living standards are declining (2) industrialization is taking place (3) people are moving from urban to farming areas (4) taxes and government spending are increasing.
   To answer questions 5 and 6, refer to the cartoon "The human race" on page 50.
5. Which conclusion may *best* be drawn from the cartoon? (1) The world's food supply can easily support the increasing world population. (2) The increase in world population is outstripping the world food supply. (3) World population and available food supplies are still in balance. (4) The increased food supply is responsible for the increase in world population.
6. This cartoon describes a concern that became obvious during which period? (1) 1890–1900 (2) 1910–1920 (3) 1930–1940 (4) 1960–1970
7. A major factor in explaining the population explosion in developing countries since 1945 is that these countries (1) gained independence after World War II (2) received the full benefit of Western medical and public health knowledge (3) had an increase in infant mortality (4) were unaware of population problems.
8. Norman Borlaug is *best* known for his work in (1) increasing agricultural yields (2) combating pollution (3) discovering new oil fields (4) developing synthetics to replace scarce natural products.
9. At the present time, the population of the United States is (1) stationary (2) declining (3) increasing at a lower rate than in the 19th century (4) increasing at a higher rate than in the 19th century.

10. In 1970 the population of the United States reached about   (1) 60 million   (2) 75 million   (3) 160 million   (4) 203 million.

11. Which has been a 20th-century American population trend?   (1) an increasing natality rate   (2) an increasing mortality rate   (3) a stationary infant mortality rate   (4) an increasing number of families with no more than three children.

12. The expression "Don't trust anyone over 30" is *most* closely related to the   (1) conflict between age groups in American society   (2) strong opposition by civil rights groups to national political leaders   (3) basis for conflict between college faculty and the college president   (4) criticism of law-enforcement officers for lenient treatment of law violators.

13. In the United States, an important effect of the population shifts from East to West and from rural to urban areas has been to   (1) decrease the need for governmental services   (2) reduce the food supply   (3) weaken regional differences   (4) increase traffic hazards.

14. The "generation under 30" in the United States has had an impact in many areas of our society. This impact has been *most* directly evident in its effect on   (1) patterns of fashion and taste   (2) demands made by organized labor   (3) advancement of technology in business and industry   (4) the federal government's farm policy.

15. The addition of medical insurance provisions to Social Security reflects concern with the   (1) hazards of industrial employment   (2) rising proportion of young people in our population   (3) retirement problems of an increasingly large number of elderly persons   (4) decline in job opportunities in economically depressed areas.

16. A period of inflation would probably have the *most* unfavorable effect on   (1) the owner of a small business   (2) a retired person living on a pension   (3) an industrial laborer who is a union member   (4) a doctor in general practice in a large city.

17. The *most* densely populated area in the United States is the   (1) South   (2) Far West   (3) Rocky Mountain region   (4) Northeast.

18. City governments do *not* deal with the problem of   (1) immigration regulations   (2) fire protection   (3) public health   (4) education.

19. To take advantage of population trends in the United States since 1945, a retail merchant would be *most* likely to establish a new store in   (1) a suburban shopping center   (2) the central area of a large city   (3) a small town in a farming region   (4) a community where there is one major employer.

20. Which is an important result of the movement of people from the cities to the suburbs?   (1) increase in the proportion of low-income families in the cities   (2) decline in the urban crime rate   (3) decline in urban renewal and planning   (4) decline in the cost of public transportation in the cities

21. Which is true of population trends in the United States?   (1) The closing of the frontier marked an end of major population shifts.   (2) The population of the United States is characterized by immobility.   (3) Population shifts have political effects.   (4) Economic development has had little effect on population trends.

22. The Supreme Court decision on reapportionment in *Reynolds vs. Sims* has helped bring about   (1) a shift in political power from rural to urban areas   (2) an increase in Republican party strength in state legislatures   (3) better representation of farm interests in state legislatures   (4) an increased representation in Congress for states with growing populations.

23. The table on page 59 strongly supports which statement regarding the general trend of urban population?   (1) Population in urban areas will probably continue to increase.   (2) Increased demands for food by city dwellers will probably encourage a back-to-the-farm movement.   (3) Decreasing immigration will reduce the proportion of the population living in the cities.   (4) The problems of pollution will reverse the present trend.

24. Which is the *most* valid conclusion that may be drawn from a study of the population shift in the United States from the city to the suburbs? (1) The middle class is moving to the suburbs because of the loss of federal aid to the city. (2) Metropolitan governments are being created that are able to solve financial problems through regional planning. (3) City leaders are better able to deal with urban problems because growth in suburban areas widens the tax base. (4) The urban situation is becoming more critical because of the reduction of the tax base.

ESSAY QUESTIONS

1. To answer this question, refer to the line graph "World Population Explosion" on page 49. (a) Give *one* explanation as to why the graph is entitled "World Population Explosion." (b) Discuss *two* reasons for the growth in world population after 1800. (c) Identify *two* problems that have resulted from the growth in world population and discuss a different solution for each problem.
2. In regard to efforts to control the population explosion, describe (a) the work of any *one* government agency (b) the work of any *one* private agency (c) *two* factors that operate against efforts at population control.
3. Discuss how *each* of the following population factors has had a significant effect on life in the United States: (a) numerical increase of "youth" (b) increase in the number of aged and retired persons (c) mobility of the population (d) concentration of population in urban areas.
4. Much attention is being given to the plight of urban areas in the United States today. (a) Name and describe any *two* aspects of the urban crisis. (b) Show that the urban crisis has significance for those living in nonurban areas.
5. Read the following paired phrases about urban living:

    (1) Respect for civic law/Freedom to do exactly what I want
    (2) A city that's easy to walk around in/A city that's easy to drive around in
    (3) Varied neighborhoods/Neighbors who are just like me
    (4) Cleaner, faster subways and buses/Lower bus and subway fares

    (a) State a valid generalization based on *all* the paired phrases. (b) Select *two* sets of paired phrases and for *each* pair selected, explain the basic issue involved. (c) For *one* of the pairs selected in answer to (b), describe a different, workable process that *two* of the following persons might use in attempting to solve the issue: (1) the mayor (2) a citizen who is a civic leader (3) a local business person.
6. According to the *Statistical Abstract of the United States*, approximately 50 percent of the people in the United States are under the age of 30. Show how this distribution of population has influenced *each* of the following: (a) consumer goods (b) political campaigns (c) mass media (d) educational facilities (e) employment opportunities.
7. (a) Discuss *two* reasons why the percentage of persons over 65 in our population has more than doubled since 1900. (b) State *two* problems that face our senior citizens. (c) For *each* problem stated, discuss *one* effort that can be made either by the individual or by the government to provide a solution.

Part 4. Some Disadvantaged Groups in the American Population

10. American Indians Seek to Improve Their Condition

WHITE SETTLERS VS. INDIANS: A DIFFERENCE IN LIFE-STYLES

1. Differences Regarding Land Ownership. With the discovery and exploration of the New World, various European rulers claimed ownership and sovereignty over the vast lands. In Britain, the Crown granted these lands to royal favorites such as John Berkeley and George Carteret (New Jersey), to proprietors such as George Calvert (Maryland) and William Penn (Pennsylvania), and to joint-stock companies such as the Virginia Company and the Massachusetts Bay Company. In turn these grantees assigned their lands as the personal property of white settlers who cleared forests for farmland and built towns.

The Indians had long occupied the open lands so freely claimed by the European settlers. Indians lacked the Western concept of private land ownership and the buying and selling of lands. They viewed the land as belonging to the entire tribe—an inalienable community property—available for hunting and farming by all tribal members.

From colonial times onward, the white settlers pressed continuously to transfer lands from Indian tribal ownership to white private ownership.

2. Cultural Differences. In addition to physical differences, the white settlers and the Indians differed as to language, religious concepts, view of nature, and way of life. The white settlers considered themselves to be civilized and superior; most viewed the Indians as savages and inferior. Although scientifically indefensible, this widely accepted view of the Indians was used (*a*) to the late 19th century by some whites to justify cheating and decimating the Indians, and (*b*) to the present, by many whites to justify pressuring the Indians to abandon their own culture and assimilate into the whites' "superior" civilization.

3. Advantages of the White Settlers. (*a*) *Weapons.* White settlers had weapons—firearms and gunpowder—that were far more powerful than the Indians' spears and bows and arrows. (*b*) *Agricultural Output.* White settlers, using improved agricultural methods, were able to increase output and support more people. By 1700 the 250,000 settlers in the British colonies probably outnumbered the region's Indian population. (*c*) *Manufactured Goods.* White settlers had available a variety of manufactured goods and knew their value to the

66

Indians. White traders were able to take advantage of the Indians by bartering insignificant amounts of goods for valuable lands—as, for example, the reputed $24 in goods exchanged for Manhattan Island. *(d) Immunity to Certain Diseases.* White settlers had developed immunity to certain diseases—such as measles, smallpox, and influenza—that they brought to the New World. The Indians, having had no previous contact with such diseases, had no such immunity. Whole Indian tribes were decimated upon exposure to these diseases. *(e) Political Organizations.* White settlers were organized, under colonial governments and British rule, to deal with the Indians. By contrast, the Indians were separated into numerous tribes, many with long histories of intertribal rivalries and conflicts. With few and temporary exceptions, the Indians proved unable to unite against the whites. Indian disunity enabled the whites to pursue successfully the policy of "divide and conquer."

WHITE SETTLERS VS. INDIANS: TO THE END OF THE 19TH CENTURY

1. Indian Response to Colonial Settlement

a. Initial Friendliness. In notable cases, the Indians showed friendship to the first white settlers. In Virginia, Massachusetts, and New York, the Indians provided the settlers with food and helped them survive the early difficult years. In Pennsylvania the Indians signed a treaty with *William Penn* who, although he held a land grant from the British Crown, insisted that the Indians be paid for their lands.

b. Subsequent Hostility. With time, European settlers became more numerous; they began to cheat and mistreat the Indians and to pressure them for additional lands. In Massachusetts the preacher and social reformer *Roger Williams* condemned colonial seizures of land without paying the Indians and insisted that the Indians, not the British Crown, were the rightful owners.

Along the North Atlantic Coast, settlers and Indians fought each other in numerous "Indian wars" in which both sides committed atrocities and brutalities. The settlers, sometimes aided by friendly Indians, proved victorious. They decimated the hostile Indians and drove out the remnants, usually westward toward and beyond the Appalachian Mountains.

2. British Policy Toward the Indians: Proclamation of 1763.

The British government announced an Indian policy following two military events: *(a)* By 1763 Britain had defeated France in the French and Indian War and acquired Canada and all French territory from the Appalachians to the Mississippi (except for New Orleans); *(b)* Later in 1763 the British suppressed an uprising in the upper Ohio Valley by pro-French Indians led by the Ottawa chieftain *Pontiac.*

By the *Proclamation of 1763*, the British *(a)* reserved the region west of the Appalachians for the Indians, *(b)* prohibited colonists from settling there, and *(c)* ordered colonists already there to withdraw eastward. Britain hoped that this proclamation would remove causes for Indian uprisings, protect the fur trade, and prevent colonial settlements beyond the reach of British authorities.

The British lacked the power to enforce this proclamation. Colonial settlers—notably the frontiersman *Daniel Boone*—pushed westward across the

Appalachians and battled the Indians for the fertile lands of Kentucky and the upper Ohio Valley.

3. Early United States Indian Policy: The Northwest Ordinance of 1787. For settlers in the *Northwest Territory*—the area bounded by the Ohio and Mississippi Rivers and the Great Lakes—the *Northwest Ordinance of 1787* provided civil liberties, territorial government, and eventual statehood. For Indians in the Northwest Territory, the ordinance called for them to be treated with the "utmost good faith" and specified that "their lands and property shall never be taken from them without their consent." These provisions, intended to protect the Indians, soon proved meaningless.

As settlers pushed into the territory, they occupied lands claimed by the Indians and received military protection against Indian attacks. *William Henry Harrison*, as governor of the Indiana Territory, often employed questionable methods—including threats, bribes, and liquor—to induce the Indians to cede substantial land areas. Harrison was opposed by *Tecumseh*, a Shawnee chief, who denied that any tribe could cede lands, insisted that all the tribes together owned the lands, and united certain tribes to oppose the whites. In 1811 Harrison defeated Tecumseh's forces at the battle of *Tippecanoe*. In the War of 1812, the Americans fought the Northwest Indians who had allied themselves with the British; after that war, the Americans drove the remaining Indians out of the Northwest Territory and westward across the Mississippi.

4. The Seminole Indians and the Purchase of Florida (1819). From colonial days onward, some Indians of the American Southeast had fled into Florida where, together with the native Indians and some runaway slaves, they formed a new tribe, the *Seminoles*. With Spanish authorities in Florida too weak to restrain them, the Seminoles raided American settlements in the Southeast and then retreated to safety across the international border.

In 1818 *Andrew Jackson* led an American military force into Florida, captured two Spanish forts, and crushed the Seminole Indians. Spain, having already lost West Florida to the United States, now feared the loss of the rest of Florida. Consequently, in 1819 Spain sold Florida to the United States. Thereafter, the American government temporarily moved the Seminole Indians to a reservation in the Florida interior.

5. Later United States Indian Policy: Removal West of the Mississippi

a. Indian Removal Act of 1830. This act authorized the President to negotiate treaties to remove the remaining Eastern Indians to lands west of the Mississippi. Under President *Andrew Jackson,* himself an Indian fighter, and under his successor President *Martin Van Buren,* federal agents vigorously acted—often by threats, bribes, and the use of liquor—to secure Indian consent to removal treaties. The federal government removed thousands of Indians, some in chains, on a trip marked by hunger, disease, and death so that the Indians named it the "trail of tears." Also the army suppressed uprisings by Indians who refused to be removed—such as the Sac and Fox in Illinois under Chief *Black Hawk* and the Seminoles in Florida under Chief *Osceola*. By the late 1840's, almost all Indians had been removed west of the Mississippi.

b. The Cherokees and the Supreme Court. Residing in northwestern Georgia under treaty with the federal government, the Cherokees had adopted the white settlers' civilization and became known as a "civilized tribe." They lived in peace, working as farmers, building houses and roads, publishing a newspaper printed in both English and Cherokee. Their bilingual newspaper was made possible by the work of Chief *Sequoyah,* who devised the symbols for printing the Cherokee language. In 1828 gold was discovered on Cherokee lands, whereupon white settlers moved in, and the state of Georgia claimed jurisdiction (authority) over the Cherokees and their lands. To confirm their independence from Georgia, the Cherokees appealed to the Supreme Court, and Chief Justice *John Marshall,* speaking for the majority, in the case of the *Cherokee Nation vs. Georgia,* decided in favor of the Indians. Disagreeing with the decision, President Jackson is reputed to have said, "John Marshall has made his decision. Now let him enforce it." Instead, the federal government pushed the removal of the Cherokees, and by 1838 most had been relocated to lands in Oklahoma.

6. Indians of the Last Frontier—The Great Plains: To the 1890's

a. Indian Hostility. On the Great Plains west of the Mississippi, the Indians—such as Comanches, Cheyennes, and Sioux—were nomadic, horse-riding peoples. From the huge buffalo herds roaming the Plains, the Indians secured meat for food and hides for clothing and shelter.

The Plains Indians resented (1) white settlers for taking their lands for farms, (2) white hunters for wantonly slaying buffalo for pelts and for sport, (3) white communities for upsetting the traditional migratory paths of buffalo herds and the region's ecological balance, and (4) white traders and government officials for cheating, stealing, and breaking promises.

b. Indian Wars (To About 1890). For over 25 years the Plains Indians battled wagon trains, settlers, and federal troops in savage guerrilla warfare. In 1876, after white men invaded an area in South Dakota assigned to the Indians, the Sioux, led by Chief *Sitting Bull,* overwhelmed General *George A. Custer* in his "last stand" at the *Battle of the Little Big Horn.* Despite this and lesser victories, the Indian cause was doomed. The Indians lacked manpower, organization, equipment, and—with the extermination of the buffalo herds—food. The last battle—the Indians call it a massacre—took place in 1890 when federal troops wiped out a Sioux band under Chief *Big Foot* at *Wounded Knee* (South Dakota).

c. Indian Reservations. By the 1880's most Indians were confined to specific, usually undesirable, lands called *reservations.* No longer a free and independent people, they received from the federal government food, clothing, and shelter and were treated as legal dependents or *wards.* Their way of life, indeed their very existence, was under the control of federal Indian agents, many of whom were corrupt and most unsympathetic to Indian needs.

MORE HUMANE TREATMENT OF THE INDIAN—SINCE THE END OF THE 19TH CENTURY

In 1877 President *Rutherford B. Hayes* in a message to Congress said, "Many, if not most, of our Indian wars have had their origin in broken promises and acts of injustice on our part." In 1881 *Helen Hunt Jackson* further helped awaken white Americans to their shameful treatment of the Indians through her book *A Century of Dishonor.*

The nation attempted to make amends toward the Indian by new legislation—which proved only partially successful.

1. Dawes General Allotment Act (1887). This act provided that (1) each Indian family head be allotted a 160-acre farm out of reservation lands, (2) each allottee who abandoned tribal practices and adopted the "habits of civilized life" be granted American citizenship, and (3) "surplus" reservation lands remaining after the allotments be available for sale to white settlers.

The Dawes Act, although well intentioned by its leading Congressional supporters, did not benefit the Indians. Since most Indians were unfamiliar with farming and were assigned poor lands, they were often unable to secure a living, and many became paupers. Also many Indians did not wish to become "civilized" as reflected in the white culture but sought to retain their own tribal cultures. Finally, chiefly as a result of the "surplus" land provision, the Indians by the 1930's had lost some 90 million out of 140 million acres of their former reservation lands.

2. Snyder Indian Citizenship Act (1924). In recognition of the many Indians who volunteered for military service during World War I, this act granted American citizenship to all Indians born in the United States. (It applied to about one-third of the Indian population who had not yet acquired citizenship.)

3. Wheeler-Howard Indian Reorganization Act (1934). This act (1) ended land allotments, restored unsold "surplus" lands to tribal ownership, and began the repurchase of lands for Indian use, (2) authorized the tribes to form corporations with power to launch tribal business enterprises, and (3) provided for elected tribal councils with significant powers over their people. The act marked a reversal of previous federal policies by restoring the tribe as the center of Indian culture and life.

TERMINATION POLICY

In 1953 Congress announced a new, sharply different Indian policy which became known as the *termination policy*. Termination meant (a) dividing the tribal property among the tribe's members, to be held by each Indian individually or through a corporation and, in either case, subject to taxes, (b) curtailing tribal self-government and relocating Indians from the reservations to cities where jobs were available, and (c) ending federal responsibility and social services—education, health, and welfare—to the Indians.

1. Arguments for Termination. Supporters argued that termination would (a) get the government "out of the Indian business" and reduce costs to the taxpayer, (b) "free the Indians from the reservations," thereby ending their segregation, and (c) break down the remaining tribal bonds, thereby hastening Indian assimilation into American society. These latter arguments accorded with the prevailing 1950's mood against segregation.

2. Indian Opposition to Termination. Indians vehemently opposed termination, arguing that they (a) would lose rights pledged by the federal government in treaties, such as the right to hold land free of taxes, (b) would still need social services but that the burden would fall upon uninterested states and municipalities, *(c)* were not segregated on reservations since they were free to come and go, *(d)* wanted to maintain their tribal organizations, and *(e)* lacked the education and experience to manage their own business enterprises without federal assistance.

By the 1960's, the termination policy was abandoned in practice.

THE INDIANS TODAY: A DISADVANTAGED MINORITY

1. Indian Population. In 1492 Indians residing in what is now the United States were estimated to number 850,000. By 1890, after four centuries of contact with the white man, the Indian population was estimated at fewer than 300,000. Today the Indian population is sharply up, although estimates vary. One Indian author claims that there are 500,000 Indians living in the cities, 100,000 in scattered Eastern bands, and 400,000 on the reservations.

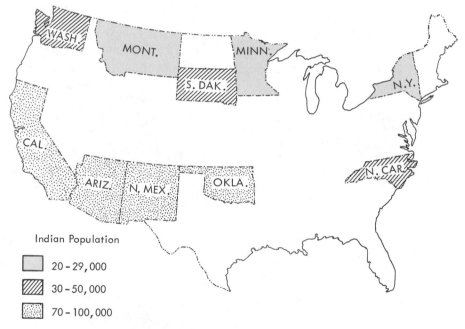

Indian Population

[ ] 20 - 29,000

[////] 30 - 50,000

[....] 70 - 100,000

Where the American Indians Live Today

2. Problems Facing the Indians. *(a) Poor Health.* In infant mortality, malnutrition, and infectious diseases, Indian rates are much above the national average; the reservation Indian has a life span of about 50 years compared to the national average of about 70 years. *(b) Poor Education.* Many Indians are illiterate; Indian children average only five years of schooling; their school dropout rate is almost double the national figure; very few have gone on to colleges and graduate schools. *(c) Poverty.* Many Indians occupy substandard dwellings; city and reservation Indians lack training to hold down decent jobs and experience heavy unemployment; three-quarters of Indian families earn less than $3000 a year as compared to the national average of over $8000.

3. Indians and the "War on Poverty." President *Lyndon Johnson* was eager that his "war on poverty" improve the conditions of the Indian, especially on the reservations. Antipoverty and other funds for Indians were used to upgrade educational facilities, offer adult occupational training, provide part-time jobs, construct houses, and locate factories on the reservations. In 1968 President Johnson sent Congress a special message, devoted entirely to helping the Indian, whom he called "the Forgotten American"; Congress responded by voting the largest sums ever allocated for Indian-aid programs. Conditions on Indian reservations have improved slowly.

4. Indian Moods and Organizations. Indians today are no longer willing to accept passively an inferior status. They have become more vocal and more aggressive in pressing their demands for justice and equality. They speak of "Indian power" and inform whites that "Indians discovered America." To further their goals, they have created a number of organizations: *(a)* The *National Congress of American Indians* represents 90 tribes with a membership of 300,000. It publicizes Indian problems, furthers economic aid programs, serves as an Indian lobby with Congress, and maintains liaison with the federal Bureau of Indian Affairs. *(b)* The *National Indian Youth Council* organizes Indian youth to demonstrate for Indian rights and recognition. *(c)* The *National Traditionalist Movement* seeks a return to the traditional Indian culture, especially the Indian religious outlook. *(d)* The *United Native Americans*, a small and militantly antiwhite group, emphasizes Indian kinship with the poor and oppressed peoples of the "third world."

5. What Do the Indians Want?

    a. Acceptance as Indians. Indians demand that society accept and respect them as Indians both in the individual and in the tribal sense. They want to cherish and preserve their Indian identity, heritage, and culture. They insist that they can be Americans—part of the larger society—and at the same time Indians

Onondaga (Iroquois) Indians demonstrate outside the New York State Capitol in Albany. (*United Press International*)

within their social groupings. This Indian demand reflects the concept, applied to the immigrant experience, of cultural pluralism.

b. Social and Economic Improvement. Indian spokesmen demand massive aid, including grants, long-term loans, and technical assistance, such as the United States has extended to underdeveloped foreign nations. The reservation Indians want more and better social services—health clinics, sanitary facilities, housing programs, and schools for general and occupational education. They want technical assistance in utilizing their land resources and funds to attract industries to the reservations. Indians seek to raise their health, educational, and living levels to those of other Americans.

c. Control of Their Own Lives. Indians demand that they, just as other American citizens, have the right to make the basic decisions affecting their lives, property, and life-styles. They insist that the federal government honor the provisions of treaties made with Indians. They want the "great white father" in Washington to cease setting Indian policy in a paternalistic and unilateral fashion. Responding to such demands, the federal government has named Indians to head its Bureau of Indian Affairs.

SOME OUTSTANDING INDIANS—IN THE NATIONAL CULTURE

Vine Deloria, of Sioux ancestry, was formerly Executive Director of the National Congress of American Indians. He is an active worker for Indian rights. To enable the white man to comprehend the Indian viewpoint, he wrote the powerful book *Custer Died for Your Sins.*

Charles Eastman, a Sioux Indian, was educated as a physician at Boston University and was the first Indian to serve as doctor on Indian reservations. He also wrote books on Indian themes.

Francis La Flesche, the son of an Omaha chief, was a well-known anthropologist who wrote an autobiographical account of his school days and undertook Indian ethnic studies for the Smithsonian Institution. Also a lawyer, La Flesche actively worked to protect Indian rights.

Arthur Parker, of Seneca ancestry, majored in anthropology at Harvard. He is known for his anthropological studies of the Indians of New York State and as director of the Rochester Museum of Arts and Sciences.

Will Rogers, in part Cherokee, was an actor, writer, and humorist best known for his homespun philosophical comments on national and world events.

Buffy Sainte-Marie, a full-blooded American Indian of Cree parents, is a popular folk singer. Her songs tell about the plight of the American Indian, as do her lectures and writings.

Maria Tallchief, daughter of an Osage chief, became one of America's great classic ballet dancers. For many years, she was prima ballerina with the famed New York City Ballet.

Jim Thorpe, more than half Sac, Fox, and other Indian ancestry, was an outstanding football star at Carlisle Indian School and as a professional. He also was the 1912 Olympic winner of both the pentathlon and decathlon, and a major league baseball player. In 1950 Thorpe was named in an Associated Press poll as the greatest all-round athlete in the first half of the century.

IDENTIFICATION QUESTIONS: WHO AM I?

Big Foot	Helen Hunt Jackson	Buffy Sainte-Marie
Black Hawk	Osceola	Sequoyah
George Calvert	Arthur Parker	Sitting Bull
Vine Deloria	William Penn	Maria Tallchief
William Henry Harrison	Will Rogers	Jim Thorpe

1. I wrote the book *A Century of Dishonor*, protesting the white man's treatment of the Indians.
2. Although I received a British land grant, I insisted upon paying the Indians for their lands.
3. Of Seneca ancestry, I published anthropological studies of the Indians of New York State.
4. As governor of the Indiana Territory, I led the territorial forces that defeated the Indians at the Battle of Tippecanoe.
5. Part Cherokee, I won fame as an actor, writer, and humorist.
6. I led the Seminole Indian uprising against removal from Florida.
7. A popular folk singer, I used my songs to call attention to the problems of the Indians.
8. I devised the symbols that made possible the printing of the Cherokee language.
9. My exploits—in football, baseball, and the Olympics—won me the title of outstanding athlete of the first half of the 20th century.
10. A Sioux warrior, I overwhelmed General Custer's forces at the Battle of the Little Big Horn.

MODIFIED TRUE-FALSE QUESTIONS

If the statement is correct, write the word *true*. If the statement is incorrect, substitute a word or phrase for the italicized term to make the statement correct.

1. In the Indian culture, land belonged to the *entire tribe*.
2. By the Proclamation of 1763, the British government reserved for the Indians the region west of the *Mississippi*.
3. The Supreme Court decision, in the case of the *Cherokee Nation vs. Georgia*, was *supported* by President Andrew Jackson.
4. Wounded Knee in South Dakota was the site of a 19th-century Indian military *victory*.
5. For Indians residing within the United States area, their number today is *slightly above* their estimated number in 1492.
6. The Indians' desire today to retain their Indian identity and heritage reflects the concept of *the melting pot*.

ESSAY QUESTIONS

1. For *each* of the following government policies affecting Indians, (*a*) present *one* government argument to show that the policy was intended to benefit the Indians and (*b*) present *one* Indian argument to show that the policy was not beneficial: (1) Northwest Ordinance of 1787 (2) Dawes General Allotment Act of 1887 (3) Termination Policy of 1953.
2. Indians today claim that they are a disadvantaged minority in the American population. (*a*) Discuss *two* arguments to support this claim. (*b*) Name *one* Indian organization and describe its activities on behalf of the Indians. (*c*) To better their social and economic conditions most rapidly, should Indians remain on or leave the reservations? Present *one* argument to defend your answer.

11. Americans of Spanish Origin Seek to Improve
Their Condition

1. Names. Americans whose backgrounds reflect the Spanish culture have been known by the following terms: (*a*) Persons of Spanish origin—as reported by them to the 1970 census takers. (*b*) Persons with Spanish surnames (family or last names); this term may include some non-Spanish persons such as women of other ethnic backgrounds who married Spanish men. (*c*) Hispanic-Americans—the word "Hispanic" means Spanish. (*d*) Latin-Americans—the word "Latin" reflects the Roman origins of the Spanish culture.

2. Number and Residence. In the early 1970's, persons of Spanish origin numbered 9.2 million, placing them after blacks as our second largest minority. Of the 9.2 million people (*a*) Mexican-Americans totaled 5.3 million, or 57 percent. They resided overwhelmingly in our five Southwestern states: Arizona, California, Colorado, New Mexico, and Texas. Less than half the Mexican-Americans lived in the central cities. (*b*) Puerto Ricans totaled 1.5 million, or 17 percent. They lived mainly in the major cities of the New York and New Jersey areas. (*c*) Cubans, most of whom had fled from their island home after Fidel Castro seized power and established a Communist state, numbered 600,000, or 7 percent. They lived mainly in Florida, especially in the Miami area. (*d*) Persons from Central and South America and others of Spanish origin totaled 1.8 million, or 19 percent.

Where Americans of Spanish Origin Live Today

3. **Vital Statistics.** In the early 1970's, Americans of Spanish origin had larger families but in other respects lagged behind the American average.

	Americans of Spanish Origin	All Americans
Family size: four or more members	60%	40%
Education: four years of high school or more	33%	60%
Unemployment	6%	3.5 %
Employment: in white-collar jobs	23%	44%
Median income: by family	$7,500	$10,300

THE SPANISH HERITAGE OF THE UNITED STATES

Spain financed the 1492 expedition of Columbus that discovered the New World. Spanish explorers were the first white men to traverse the southern region of what is today the United States. *Ponce de León,* searching for a legendary "Fountain of Youth," in 1513 discovered Florida. *Coronado,* seeking rumored cities of gold between 1540 and 1542, explored the American Southwest. *De Soto,* also seeking gold, traveled westward from Florida, and in 1541 discovered the lower Mississippi River. The Spanish established the first colonies in territory that is today part of the United States. In Florida in 1565, the Spanish founded St. Augustine, the oldest city in the United States. In New Mexico in 1605, they founded Santa Fe, the second oldest city in the United States. They also made other settlements throughout Florida, New Mexico, Arizona, Texas, and California.

First to reach the New World, the Spanish introduced horses and cattle. Based on these two animals, the Spanish began, in northern Mexico and the Southwestern United States, the ranch system and the cattle industry. The Mexicans were the earliest cowboys and much of the distinctive cowboy vocabulary—bronco, chaparajos or chaps, lariat, lasso, mustang, and sombrero—derives from the Spanish language. The Spanish also began sheepherding in the American Southwest. In other ways, the Spanish contributed to American culture in the Southwest: Spanish law regarding land titles, water rights, and mining rights; Spanish architecture in building homes, churches, and missions; and Spanish foods, music, clothes, and art.

Persons of Spanish origin came under American rule by annexation—a small number in 1819 with the purchase of Florida; a large number in the 1840's with our annexation of Texas, California, and the rest of the American Southwest; and another large number in 1898 with our annexation of Puerto Rico.

The Mexican-American Experience

MEXICANS COME UNDER AMERICAN RULE

1. **By Annexation of Territory (mid-19th century).** The first Mexicans to come under American rule were the inhabitants of territories annexed by the United States. In 1836 American settlers in Texas, then a Mexican province, revolted and won independence. In 1845, when Texas was admitted to the Union, several thousand Mexicans lived there. The admission of Texas was resented by Mexico

and helped bring about the Mexican War. The United States was victorious and in 1848 acquired California and the American Southwest—together called the *Mexican Cession*. In 1853 the United States purchased from Mexico a small strip of land, now part of southern New Mexico and southern Arizona. This strip of land, containing a railroad pass through the mountains to California, was known as the *Gadsden Purchase*.

By these territorial acquisitions, about 100,000 Mexicans came under American rule and became American citizens. At first known as Mexican-Americans, they later were called *Chicanos* (a contraction of the word "Mexicanos"). With time and the building of railroads, large numbers of American settlers of European background entered the region. Called "Anglos" by the Mexican-Americans, these newcomers soon outnumbered the Mexican-Americans, thereby making them a minority.

As inhabitants of the United States, these Mexican-Americans faced many difficulties. Scorned by the Anglos, the Chicanos were stereotyped as lazy, cowardly, and dishonest. The Chicanos further were easily identifiable and different. Most were *mestizos* of mixed Spanish and Indian ancestry; all spoke Spanish, worshipped as Roman Catholics, and identified with Spanish culture. Many Mexicans claimed ownership of lands based on old Spanish and Mexican grants, which documents were in many cases lost or destroyed. Many Mexican land claims, consequently, were invalidated by the American authorities and the lands assigned to newly arrived Anglo claimants.

2. By Immigration

a. Early 20th Century. Mexicans were prompted to migrate to the United States by poor economic and harsh living conditions in Mexico. In addition, many were freed from *peonage*—the status of semislave laborers on large agricultural estates—by the Mexican Revolution of 1911. From 1900 to 1920, some 270,000 Mexican immigrants came to the Southwest, chiefly into Texas, Arizona, and California. While some helped build railroads or worked in mines, most became migratory farmhands. At harvesttime, they went from one large farm to another, picking crops—citrus fruits, berries, vegetables, sugarcane, and cotton. Unskilled laborers, and not then organized into unions, they received poor housing and low wages. Constantly on the move and working in crews with other Mexicans, they had little contact with Americans. Out of work during the off-season, they huddled together in ghettos or "shantytowns," called *barrios*, on the outskirts of such large cities as San Antonio and Los Angeles. Consequently these Mexican immigrants were slow to put down roots and adopt the ways of the dominant "American culture."

b. Since World War I

(1) *Legal Immigration.* In the 1920's decade, 459,000 Mexicans entered the United States, chiefly in the Southwest where they worked as migratory farmhands. In the depression decade of the 1930's, Mexican immigration declined sharply. During the World War II years, Mexican workers were needed to offset manpower shortages in American industry, railroad transportation, and agriculture. By special arrangement between the United States and Mexican governments, more than 300,000 Mexicans were admitted on a temporary or short-term basis as "contract laborers," or *braceros*. In the years since World War II, the

number of Mexican immigrants increased; by the early 1960's, they averaged over 50,000 per year.

(2) *Illegal Immigration—The "Wetbacks."* Large numbers of Mexicans—in some years as many as 1 million—have entered the United States illegally. These illegal immigrants possibly were unaware that they were exempted from quota restrictions, perhaps felt they could not pass the literacy test requirement of reading a language or could not meet the health standards, or wished to avoid the expense and delay of securing American *visas* (entry permits). Since some illegal Mexican immigrants entered the United States by crossing the Rio Grande —some swimming across it—they all became known as "wetbacks."

Most illegal immigrants did not remain permanently in the United States. Some, after working for a while and accumulating money, voluntarily returned to Mexico. Others were eventually caught and deported to Mexico by the Border Patrol of the *United States Immigration and Naturalization Service.* During a five-year period in the 1950's, the number deported back to Mexico reached the staggering total of 3.8 million.

MEXICAN-AMERICAN MOODS AND ORGANIZATIONS

Since World War II, Mexican-Americans increasingly have expressed dissatisfaction with their status in American society and have sought reforms. In the 1940's, Mexican-American youths in Los Angeles rioted to protest discrimination—the so-called "zoot suit" riots. During the war, almost half a million Mexican-Americans served in the armed forces. Learning skilled trades and seeing that people outside the barrios lived better lives, many Mexican-American servicemen returned home determined to improve conditions for themselves and their communities. Mexican-Americans increasingly spoke of *la Raza*—which narrowly translated means *the race* but broadly understood refers to the Mexican-American sense of ethnic unity and pride.

In California former servicemen of Mexican-American origin helped form the *Community Service Organization* (CSO). The CSO sought to activate the Mexican-American community to political activity so as to improve conditions and secure equal rights for all members of *la Raza*. In Texas, Dr. *Hector Garcia,* a physician and World War II hero, acted, after a funeral home refused to bury a Mexican-American war veteran, to found the *G.I. Forum.* It served to arouse the Mexican-American community to political activity—register and vote. Two other political organizations—in California the *Mexican-American Political Association* (MAPA) and in Texas the *Political Association of Spanish-Speaking Organizations* (PASSO)—endeavored to get Mexican-Americans elected or appointed to political office.

In 1963 *Reies Lopez Tijerina* formed a more radical political group known by its original name as the *Alianza* or Alliance, or more generally as the *Chicano movement.* Tijerina charged that after 1848 the Anglos had seized Chicano lands illegally, demanded the return of these lands to the Mexican-American community, and extolled the culture and history of *la Raza.* To further his goals, Tijerina employed militancy, including the raiding of a New Mexico courthouse to free members of his organization being held there and attacking rangers of the United States Forest Service. In 1969 Tijerina was sentenced to three years in jail. In

Denver, Colorado, *Rodolfo (Corky) González* led the Chicano movement seeking city action to improve Mexican-American conditions.

WHAT DO THE MEXICAN-AMERICANS WANT?

1. In Education. Mexican-American children have fared poorly in the public schools. Their scholastic achievements have been low, their dropout rate high, and at least until the 1954 Supreme Court decision in *Brown vs. Board of Education of Topeka* they were kept in de facto segregated schools with inferior facilities. Chicano leaders demand upgrading of facilities for Mexican-American children, the employment of bilingual teachers who can provide instruction in Spanish, the teaching of English as a second language, and the introduction of courses in Chicano history and culture.

2. In Employment. Mexican-Americans, being mainly unskilled and semi-skilled workers, earn low wages. (Illegal Mexican immigrants—the wetbacks—often work for less than the minimum wage.) In 1970 almost one-third of all Chicano families had incomes that fell below the federally determined poverty level. Mexican-Americans have a higher than average unemployment rate, which in agriculture is in part caused by the increasing use of farm machines. In 1965 *César Chávez*, head of the United Farm Workers—an AFL-CIO union —began a drive to organize California's grape pickers. *La Huelga* (the strike) became the rallying cry for the Chicano farmworkers. Chávez received widespread support from influential Anglo political, religious, and labor figures and he urged a nationwide boycott of nonunion table grapes. After five years of bitter struggle, Chávez won contracts from the grape growers which provided for union recognition, higher wages, and health and welfare benefits. Chávez then turned his attention to organizing Arizona and California lettuce workers. (Recently, Chávez's representation of migratory farmworkers has been challenged by a

César Chávez leads a demonstration by Chicano farmworkers.
(*George Ballis for Black Star*)

rival labor group, the Teamsters Union.) In cities Chicano workers were aided by President Johnson's "war on poverty" as the Office of Economic Opportunity provided many with vocational training and jobs. In the early 1970's, the Amalgamated Clothing Workers Union (AFL-CIO) succeeded in organizing low-paid Chicano workers in the Texas garment industry.

3. In Housing. Mexican-Americans in the barrios reside in run-down, dilapidated buildings. They demand that these structures be torn down and replaced by low-rent public housing units.

4. In Health. As compared to the Anglos, the Mexican-Americans have an infant mortality rate that is three times higher and a life expectancy that is some ten years lower. They demand more and improved public health services for both Chicano farmworkers and barrio residents.

5. Treatment by Law-Enforcement Agencies. Mexican-Americans are bitter regarding their treatment by law-enforcement agencies—the various city and state police departments and the Border Patrol of the Immigration Service. They claim that the law-enforcement personnel—overwhelmingly Anglos and constantly looking for illegal Mexican wetbacks—are unnecessarily hostile and prone to violence against persons of Spanish origin. Chicano leaders demand that these agencies instruct their personnel to respect the civil rights of all suspects and to spur the hiring of qualified Chicano personnel.

6. Voice in Government. Chicano leaders have been prodding their followers to take an active part in politics—joining political parties, attending meetings, registering, and voting. In this way Mexican-Americans can make government—city, state, and federal—more responsive to their needs.

7. Acceptance as Mexican-Americans. Chicanos demand that the Anglos accept them as equals and respect their Spanish and Indian culture. Chicanos want to enter into the mainstream of American life—enjoying its benefits and contributing to its well-being. They insist that they can preserve their ethnic heritage and yet be good Americans—which belief is central to the concept of cultural pluralism.

SOME OUTSTANDING MEXICAN-AMERICANS

César Chávez was born in Arizona into a migrant farm family. With his family constantly on the move, he did not receive a formal school education beyond the seventh grade before he began working full time in the fields. During World War II Chávez served in the Navy and thereafter devoted himself to helping impoverished Mexican-Americans. He headed the United Farm Workers and became the first labor leader to successfully organize migratory farmhands.

Dennis Chávez, born in New Mexico, left school at the age of 13 to help support his family. Returning to school, he secured a law degree from Georgetown University in 1920 and then practiced law and entered into New Mexico politics. Appointed to fill a vacancy as United States Senator from New Mexico, he was elected to four successive terms. As Senator, Chávez helped originate the Good Neighbor Policy toward Latin America and furthered measures to aid disadvantaged minorities—Indians, Puerto Ricans, and Chicanos.

Dr. Julian Nava, born in California, secured a doctorate in history from Harvard University. He has served as professor of history in several California colleges, encouraged the study of Latin-American history, and in 1967 became the sole Mexican-American member of the Los Angeles Board of Education.

George I. Sánchez, born in New Mexico, secured in 1934 a doctorate in education from the University of California. Sánchez has taught history and philosophy of education at various southwestern schools of higher learning. He also has served as consultant to various federal agencies regarding Indian affairs and Latin America, especially Mexico. He has written numerous books and magazine articles about Latin America.

Lee Trevino was born in Texas, the son of a Mexican immigrant gravedigger. He worked as a caddie on various golf courses and soon excelled at the sport. In 1971 Trevino won four major golf championships and was named Professional Golfer of the Year. He laughingly calls himself "Super Mex."

Vincent Ximenes, born in Texas, was educated as an economist at the University of New Mexico. He entered into politics in New Mexico and there founded a branch of the G.I. Forum. He served as chairman, beginning in 1967, of the federal Inter-Agency Committee on Mexican-American Affairs to find solutions to Chicano problems; later he was appointed a member of the federal Equal Employment Opportunity Commission to end discrimination in employment.

The Puerto Rican Experience

POLITICAL EVOLUTION OF PUERTO RICO: FROM COLONY TO COMMONWEALTH

In 1898 the United States defeated Spain in the Spanish-American War and annexed Puerto Rico. This annexation ended tyrannical Spanish rule over the island that had endured almost four centuries.

Under the United States, Puerto Rico evolved politically as follows:

1. Foraker Act (1900). Congress provided that the President of the United States appoint the Island's governor and the upper house of the Puerto Rican legislature but that the Puerto Ricans elect the lower house. Thus began Puerto Rico's training into the workings of democracy.

2. Jones Act (1917). Congress granted the Puerto Ricans American citizenship and the right to elect both houses of the Puerto Rican legislature.

3. Elected Governor (1948). Congress passed a law to permit the Puerto Ricans to elect their own governor. They chose, as their first elected governor, *Luis Muñoz Marín.* Winning four consecutive terms until he retired in 1965, Muñoz Marín helped shape modern Puerto Rico. He furthered economic progress through "Operation Bootstrap" and gained the island Commonwealth status.

4. Commonwealth Status (Since 1952). Congress empowered the Puerto Ricans to draw up their own constitution. Under Muñoz Marín's leadership, the islanders overwhelmingly chose to become freely associated with the United States as a self-governing *Commonwealth. (a)* Puerto Ricans elect their own legislators, who pass local laws, and their own governor, who enforces them. *(b)* Puerto Ricans are American citizens. However, as long as they reside in Puerto Rico, they do not vote in Presidential elections and do not elect Congressmen. They do, however, send a Resident Commissioner to Washington with power to speak, but not to vote, in the House of Representatives. *(c)* Puerto Ricans are subject to most federal laws. They serve in the American armed forces, and their products enter the mainland free of tariff duties. However, individuals and corporations on the island are exempt from federal income taxes.

5. Political Developments. Until recently, a majority of Puerto Rican voters approved of the Commonwealth status, very few desired independence, and a large minority favored statehood—which would mean voting in federal elections but also paying federal income taxes. In 1976, the Puerto Ricans narrowly elected as governor *Carlos Romero Barcelo,* an advocate of statehood. This surprising result, probably reflecting economic discontent, spurred interest in statehood, and Romero Barcelo pledged a plebiscite on that issue.

In 1979 President Carter, citing "humane considerations," freed from American prisons four Puerto Rican independence nationalists—one who in 1950 had attempted to assassinate President Truman and three who in 1954 had sprayed gunfire into the House of Representatives and wounded five Congressmen. The nationalists' unconditional release was opposed by Puerto Rico's governor Romero Barcelo as encouraging terrorism and menacing public safety.

ECONOMIC DEVELOPMENTS IN PUERTO RICO

1. Problem of Poverty. Despite the fertile soil, a favorable climate, and good crops of sugar and tobacco, the Puerto Ricans subsisted for a long time at minimal living standards. *(a)* The island lacked sufficient area to support its rapidly growing population in agriculture. In contrast to a population density of 51 inhabitants per square mile for the United States, Puerto Rico had a population density of over 750. *(b)* Most Puerto Rican land was held by American corporations. Eighty percent of the islanders were landless. *(c)* The island's economy depended upon sugar. A drop in world sugar prices meant depression.

2. Operation Bootstrap: Efforts to Improve Conditions. In the early 1940's, the Puerto Rican government initiated a program of economic improvement. Since Puerto Rico was trying "to lift itself by its own bootstraps," the project became known as "Operation Bootstrap." *(a) Limits on Landholdings.* Puerto Rico began enforcing a law, passed in 1900, limiting corporate land ownership to 500 acres. The government bought up the excess holdings and distributed the land to agricultural cooperatives and individual farmers. *(b) Tourism.* The Puerto Rican government encouraged the building of hotels and developed the island as a resort area. Beaches, gambling casinos, the *Pablo Casals Music Festival,* and touches of Spanish culture all attracted American vacationers. *(c) Social Welfare Projects.* The Puerto Rican government paved roads, built hydroelectric plants, provided public health facilities, constructed low-income housing projects, and substantially increased educational expenditures. Instruction is in Spanish; the chief second language studied is English. Literacy has risen to over 90 percent of the population. *(d) Industrialization.* "Operation Bootstrap" especially emphasized attracting American capital and industry. The Puerto Rican government offered new factories, easy credit, and vocational training of workers. Most

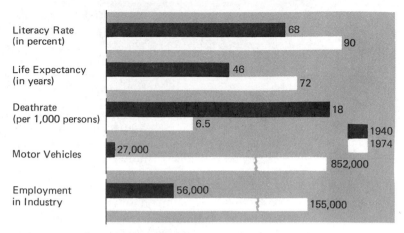

Progress in Puerto Rico, 1940 and 1974

important, corporations in Puerto Rico are exempt from federal income taxes. Since corporate income taxes on earnings above $25,000 had started at about 50 percent, this exemption represented a considerable savings and a tremendous incentive. Over 1000 new enterprises—manufacturing textiles, electrical equipment, plastics, chemicals, and many other products—were set up on the island and provided many jobs.

3. Results. Today Puerto Rico's income from manufacturing exceeds that from agriculture. The people's standard of living has risen substantially; it is among the highest in Latin America. On the other hand, the unemployment rate in Puerto Rico is above 10 percent, and the per capita income of Puerto Ricans remains considerably below that of Americans on the mainland.

THE PUERTO RICAN IMMIGRANT

1. Emigration From Puerto Rico to the Mainland. As American citizens Puerto Ricans may move freely to the mainland. Until 1940 Puerto Ricans here totaled fewer than 70,000—a comparatively small number. Starting in the early 1940's, they came in large numbers. They learned about the mainland from Puerto Rican servicemen of World War II and from the mass media; they were attracted by jobs in industry during wartime and the postwar boom; beginning in 1945, they were transported quickly and cheaply—for $50 or less—by airplane from San Juan to New York City. By 1960, 1 million Puerto Ricans resided in and about New York City. They created ethnic enclaves, called *barrios*, in such areas as Brooklyn, the south Bronx, and Manhattan's East Harlem.

They provided the unskilled and semiskilled labor, previously performed by European immigrants who, curtailed by restrictive laws, were now a mere trickle. The Puerto Ricans secured jobs in the garment trades; the transport industry; hotels, hospitals, and restaurants; and small consumer goods factories. Some were unable to secure work and reluctantly went on *public welfare*. They, however, constituted a far smaller number than popularly believed.

2. Was the Puerto Rican an Immigrant? Cultural and Economic Problems.
Can Puerto Ricans who left for the American mainland be considered immigrants? Legally *no*, since they came from American territory and possessed American citizenship. Also they were familiar with American ideals and institutions. Culturally and economically *yes*, since they faced problems similar to those of European and other immigrants. The Puerto Ricans *(a)* were of mixed white (Hispanic), Indian, and black ancestry and therefore ethnically different from mainland Americans, both white and black, *(b)* were brought up in a Latin culture far different from mainland America, *(c)* spoke Spanish as their native tongue, which complicated the education of their children, *(d)* came from a rural economy dependent on a single crop—sugar—into an urban, industrialized society, *(e)* came for economic reasons—most were impoverished, few owned land, many had no work, and the island was overpopulated, *(f)* lacked vocational skills, which left them no choice but low-paying jobs and considerable unemployment, and *(g)* encountered considerable discrimination in employment and housing. Those who were dark-complexioned suffered the most.

3. Return to the Island. Starting in the early 1960's, the number of Puerto Ricans returning to the island roughly equaled those coming to the mainland. The returnees were motivated by *(a)* discrimination and unemployment on the mainland, *(b)* improved living standards, educational and health facilities, and job opportunities on the island, and *(c)* a desire to bring up their children within the Latin culture.

PUERTO RICAN MOODS AND ORGANIZATIONS

The Puerto Ricans on the mainland want to be considered as equals, treated with dignity, and permitted to enjoy the benefits of American life. To further their goals, the Puerto Ricans have a number of organizations: (1) The Migration Division of the *Puerto Rican Department of Labor* helps Puerto Ricans adjust to mainland life, finds them jobs, and helps organize Puerto Rican communities politically. It also supplies mainland Americans with information about Puerto Rico. (2) The *Puerto Rican Forum* seeks to help mainland Puerto Ricans adjust culturally and succeed economically. It provides job training for unskilled workers, assistance to businessmen, and language classes for non-English-speaking Puerto Ricans. It also founded *Aspira* to encourage capable Puerto Rican students to continue their education into college and graduate work. (3) The *Council of Puerto Rican and Hispanic Organizations* encourages Puerto Ricans to be active politically by joining clubs, registering, and voting. (4) The *Puerto Rican Legal Defense and Education Fund* maintains a staff of lawyers to defend Puerto Rican rights in the courts.

Puerto Ricans have also been assisted by various state, federal, and city efforts as follows: (1) The *New York State Division of Human Rights* combats discrimination in housing and jobs. (2) The federal *Equal Employment Opportunity Commission* acts to prevent discrimination in employment. (3) The *Voting Rights Act of 1965* declared that a sixth grade education in Spanish in Puerto Rico was evidence of literacy for voting purposes. In 1966, in *Katzenbach vs. Morgan*, the Supreme Court upheld this provision. In 1973 a federal district court ordered the New York City Board of Elections to print all election materials in Spanish as well as English so as to prevent "irreparable damage" to Puerto Rican voters. (4) In 1970 New York City instituted its college plan of *open admissions*. The plan guaranteed all high school graduates admission to one of the city's two- or four-year colleges, with remedial classes to make up for any educational deficiencies. Within one year, the number of Puerto Rican college students doubled.

More fortunate than earlier immigrants in this respect, the Puerto Ricans have had substantial government assistance in combating discrimination in housing and jobs and in progressing in education.

WHAT DO THE MAINLAND PUERTO RICANS WANT?

1. In Education. Teaching and instructional materials in Spanish; teaching English as a second language; more bilingual, especially Puerto Rican, teachers; courses in the history and culture of Puerto Rico.

2. In Employment. More vocational training programs; opening up of apprenticeship programs by the building trades unions to Puerto Ricans; and ending to discrimination in employment and advancement.

3. In Housing. More low-rental public housing projects; an end to discrimination in the rental and sale of private housing.

4. In Health. More public health centers and hospital clinics available at little or no cost.

5. In Politics. A greater voice in government so as to make it more responsive to Puerto Rican needs.

6. As Human Beings. Treatment as equals; the right to maintain their Latin heritage within the predominant American culture: that is, cultural pluralism.

Puerto Ricans demonstrate in New York City for education to meet their children's needs. (*United Press International*)

SOME OUTSTANDING PUERTO RICANS

1. In Government Service. *Luis Muñoz Marín* was the first elected governor of Puerto Rico. He began Operation Bootstrap and achieved Commonwealth status for the island. *Herman Badillo* was elected Borough President of the Bronx and in 1970 to the federal House of Representatives. *Teodoro Mascoso* served as Coordinator of the Alliance for Progress, a Latin-American aid program begun during the Kennedy administration. *Horacio Rivero, Jr.,* rose to become an admiral in the United States Navy.

2. In Literature. *Luis Palés Matos* was a respected poet. *Piri Thomas* employed English to write his autobiography *Down These Mean Streets*.

3. In the Performing Arts. *Pablo Casals* left Spain in 1939 because of his opposition to the Franco dictatorship and settled in Puerto Rico, the birthplace of his mother. He was world famous as an orchestra leader and cellist. *Julio de Arteago* is known for his musical compositions and organ recitals. *Tito Puente* and *Noro Morales* were orchestra leaders of popular music, especially Latin American rhythms. *José María Sanroma*, a classical pianist, performed with many symphony orchestras. *Olga San Juan* and *Rita Moreno* won fame as motion picture stars. *José Ferrer*, a great Shakespearian actor, was also famed for his portrayal of Cyrano de Bergerac.

4. In Sports. *José Torres* and *Sixto Escobar* were well known to boxing fans. *Roberto Clemente, Felix Mantilla,* and *Orlando Cepeda* won recognition as baseball stars.

MULTIPLE-CHOICE QUESTIONS

1. Among Americans of Spanish origin, the *largest* group is composed of (1) Cubans (2) Puerto Ricans (3) Mexican-Americans (4) South Americans.
2. The Spanish heritage is *most* evident in which American economic activity? (1) growing cotton (2) raising cattle (3) drilling for oil (4) manufacturing shoes
3. Spanish settlers founded the oldest city in the United States. This city is (1) Miami (2) Santa Fe (3) Los Angeles (4) St. Augustine.
4. Illegal Mexican immigrants coming into the United States frequently are known as (1) barrios (2) visas (3) braceros (4) wetbacks.
5. César Chávez is *best* known as a (1) labor leader (2) member of the United States Senate (3) professor of history (4) clothing manufacturer.
6. Lee Trevino won fame as an athlete in (1) basketball (2) boxing (3) golf (4) tennis.
7. The history of Americans of Spanish origin shows that (1) a democratic government insures equality for all (2) a tribal form of society is best for minority groups (3) prejudice against minority groups is an obstacle to their development (4) public education insures equal opportunity for minority groups.
8. Which term describes Puerto Rico's relationship to the United States today? (1) colony (2) state (3) trust territory (4) Commonwealth
9. Operation Bootstrap, for Puerto Rico, did *not* include (1) limiting land ownership (2) attracting tourists (3) seeking independence (4) offering corporations exemption from federal income taxes.
10. Most Puerto Ricans coming to the United States mainland faced all the following problems *except* (1) learning the English language (2) gaining American citizenship (3) securing a job (4) adjusting to urban life.

11. *Aspira* encourages capable Puerto Rican students to (1) go on to college (2) return to the island (3) pursue vocational training (4) join revolutionary groups protesting against the establishment.

12. Luis Muñoz Marín was *best* known as (1) the first elected governor of Puerto Rico (2) a member of the House of Representatives (3) an admiral in the United States Navy (4) a poet.

13. Pablo Casals, who for many years lived in Puerto Rico, was a famed (1) actor (2) baseball player (3) cellist (4) architect.

ESSAY QUESTIONS

1. Similarities and differences often exist between present and past situations. For Mexican-Americans in the United States today and any one European immigrant group in 19th-century America, compare their conditions so as to show (a) *two* similarities and (b) *two* differences.
(a) In the 1940's Puerto Ricans in large numbers began leaving the island and coming to the mainland. Describe *two* conditions on the island that explain this outbound migration. (b) By the 1960's, Puerto Ricans in considerable numbers were returning to the island. Discuss *two* reasons for their return, including the influence of (1) Commonwealth status and (2) Operation Bootstrap.

3. For *each* of the following fields, discuss an individual or organization to prove that Americans of Spanish origin have made valuable contributions to our nation: (a) government service (b) literature, music, or art (c) sports (d) economic life.

12. *American Women Change Their Role and Status*

WOMEN IN THE COLONIAL PERIOD AND INTO THE 19TH CENTURY

1. Women's Status—Inferior to Men. In the patriarchal family and agricultural economy, typical of the colonial period and early 19th century, women occupied a place in society subordinate to men. In America women (a) were under the legal authority of their husbands or fathers; (b) could own property under certain circumstances, but upon marriage women surrendered control of their property to their husbands; (c) were restricted economically to household and farm activities and denied equal opportunity in business and the professions; (d) received little schooling, limited to household tasks and moral training, or none at all, and were restricted in access to higher and professional education; and (e) were denied the right to vote and otherwise participate in political affairs.

2. Women's Contributions to Early American Life: As Workers and Mothers. Living in isolated settlements and mainly in a self-sufficient agricultural economy, women worked hard. They cleaned house; prepared meals; wove cloth; made, mended, and ironed clothing; and made many other household items. In addition, they assisted in farmwork. They also faced the dangers of too many and too closely spaced childbirths. These burdens—harsh living conditions, heavy work, and too closely spaced births—all contributed to the high female deathrate at an early age.

3. Outstanding Women in the Colonial Period

Anne Hutchinson, in Massachusetts colony, held weekly meetings where she preached to a following of men and women. She challenged both Puritan religious orthodoxy and male dominance. In 1637 she was exiled and thereafter went to Rhode Island, the more religiously tolerant colony founded by Roger Williams.

Abigail Adams, whose husband and son were both to become Presidents of the United States, was an early advocate of education and suffrage for women. She insisted that, if sons were to become men of stature, they needed mothers who were learned women. In 1776 Abigail wrote to her husband John in Philadelphia, at the Second Continental Congress, asking that the "code of laws" for the new nation "be more generous" to ladies by not putting "unlimited power in the hands of husbands" and warning that "we ladies will not hold ourselves bound to obey the laws in which we have no voice or representation."

THE WOMEN'S RIGHTS MOVEMENT—PART OF THE HUMANITARIAN IMPULSE OF THE JACKSONIAN ERA

1. Humanitarianism: Meaning and American Origins. Humanitarians feel deep concern for and seek to improve the welfare of unfortunate or disadvantaged human beings. The earliest humanitarian movements in the United States emerged strongly during the Jacksonian Era (1828–1840) as movements for social reform: improved treatment of the insane and criminals; care for the physically handicapped, war casualties, and peacetime disaster victims; child welfare; and women's rights. For women the goal of humanitarian reform has been to be treated as equal human beings.

2. Factors Strengthening the Women's Rights Movement

a. Democratic Atmosphere. By teaching respect for each individual, democracy encouraged Americans to concern themselves with removing the disadvantages imposed upon women.

b. Industrialization. By opening up jobs, the Industrial Revolution enabled women to secure considerable employment outside the home. Able to earn their own living, women were less economically dependent on fathers and husbands.

c. Leadership. The *women's rights movement* developed vigorous, determined leaders, chiefly women from the Northeastern states, who were persistent and united in their goals. They benefited from the wealth created by the Industrial Revolution that provided them with time and money to promote their cause. Also they benefited from inventions of the Industrial Revolution that made possible printing their messages inexpensively in newspapers and pamphlets and traveling rapidly to meetings and rallies.

WOMEN'S RIGHTS IN EDUCATION

1. Elementary and Secondary Education for Girls

a. The Colonial Period and Into the Early 19th Century. In the early years, most children received little or no formal education. Young girls of well-to-do families could attend private schools specially designed to provide instruction in morals, housekeeping practices, and social graces. Also young ladies who could meet the tuition payments usually were permitted to enroll in town academies. Quite numerous in Massachusetts and New York, town academies were founded by civic-minded citizens and concerned parents primarily to prepare young men for admission to college. Howe /er, "young ladies" in attendance received a sufficient knowledge of basic subjects to enable them to secure employment as elementary school teachers.

b. The Jacksonian Era and Afterwards. On the elementary school level, all children benefited from the educational awakening, part of the humanitarian impulse of the Jacksonian Era. *Horace Mann* of Massachusetts, who insisted that "in a republic, ignorance is a crime," helped lead the movement for free elementary schools for both boys and girls. By 1860 the tax-supported public elementary school had become a Northern institution.

c. Starting in the Latter 19th Century. With the development of free public high schools in the latter part of the 19th century, young girls were able to secure a secondary level education preparing them for citizenship and home-making as well as an occupation or admission to institutions of higher learning.

2. Higher Education for Women

a. Pioneers in Higher Education for Women

Emma Willard supplemented some formal schooling with self-instruction and became a teacher. In 1821 she founded in New York State the *Troy Female Seminary,* later renamed the *Emma Willard School.* Enrolling young women on a tuition basis, the school offered formal instruction in the "household arts" and in addition subjects of higher learning—notably mathematics, science, history, and training for teaching careers.

Catherine Beecher attended a private school for instruction in the social graces, and thereafter by independent study mastered subjects of higher learning such as mathematics, Latin, and philosophy. She devoted her life to seeking for women an equal opportunity with men for higher education. Her methods were to arouse public opinion by writing and lecturing and to establish a number of women's schools of higher learning. In 1824 Catherine Beecher founded a young ladies' school at Hartford, Connecticut; in 1832 she began the *Western Female Institute* at Cincinnati, Ohio; and thereafter organized "female colleges" in Midwestern cities in Illinois, Iowa, and Wisconsin.

Mary Lyon, educated in an academy in Massachusetts, became a teacher. With difficulty she raised funds from many small contributors and in 1837 established *Mount Holyoke Seminary* in Massachusetts, which school later became the first full-fledged women's college. Although Mount Holyoke charged tuition, Mary Lyon sought to keep the fees reasonable by having the students themselves undertake various school maintenance chores. In this way she sought to attract young women of intellectual ability but of moderate means. Mount Holyoke offered a general college-level program and also prepared many women to become teachers. It set the pattern for the establishment of other Northeastern women's colleges such as *Barnard, Bryn Mawr, Radcliffe, Smith, Vassar,* and *Wellesley.*

Emma Willard, Catherine Beecher, and Mary Lyon all urged higher education for women so as to prepare them for responsibilities as wives, mothers, and teachers. Perhaps because they drew their students from middle- and upper-income families, these educational leaders did not support the suffrage movement to secure for women the right to vote.

b. Coeducation. In the 1830's, *Oberlin College* in Ohio became the first coeducational college. Oberlin's example, of admitting women as well as men students, was soon followed by other Midwestern institutions: *Antioch College* in Ohio and *Iowa State* and *Wisconsin State* Universities. After the Civil War, many schools of higher learning throughout the nation, except for the South, began to admit women students.

In recent years, the trend toward coeducation on the college level has accelerated. Women's colleges such as Hunter, Vassar, and Skidmore have begun to enroll men; also men's colleges such as Yale and Princeton have opened their facilities to women.

c. Land-Grant Colleges. The *Morrill Act* of 1862 granted federal lands to states to support colleges and universities teaching "agriculture and the mechanic arts." This act helped increase the number of such state institutions with enrollment open to both men and women. With time the land-grant institutions interpreted the term "agriculture and the mechanic arts" to mean courses in home economics and domestic science. The first land-grant college to offer a degree in domestic science was the *University of Illinois;* other outstanding land-grant colleges offering courses in home economics were the *University of Wisconsin* and, in New York, *Cornell University.*

d. Higher Education Today. In recent years, the federal government has been a powerful force combating sex discrimination by institutions of higher learning. The 1964 *Civil Rights Act* prohibited discriminatory practices by employers against women. Using this provision, the Department of Health, Education, and Welfare has pressured colleges and universities to take "affirmative action" regarding the hiring and promoting of women faculty members. The 1972 *Higher Education Act* prohibited public colleges and universities and all graduate schools—together constituting the overwhelming number of institutions of higher learning—from discriminating against women in school admission policies. Any higher learning institution subject to this prohibition but violating it faces the loss of federal aid funds.

Today, despite minor complaints, women generally have achieved equal access with men to higher educational opportunities.

WOMEN'S RIGHTS IN ECONOMIC MATTERS

1. The Industrial Revolution Spurs Employment Outside the Home

a. Earliest Employment Opportunities

At the start of the 19th century, New England textile mill owners, confronted by a labor shortage, recruited women workers by a program known after the original "company towns" as the *Waltham* or *Lowell System.* The mill owners attracted young girls from the farms by offering a combination of: relatively good wages; room and board in strictly chaperoned company-owned houses; religious guidance; educational facilities, and literary opportunities. Although the girls worked long—about 70 hours in a six-day week—they had some leisure time; many considered themselves fortunate to be economically independent of male relatives and to be able to earn money so as to return home with a "nest egg." British visitors, aware of the poor conditions in their country's mill towns, often spoke of the New England mill towns as the "Working Girls' Paradise." In the 1840's, with the heavy inflow of Irish immigrants, labor was in plentiful supply in New England, and working conditions in the mill towns deteriorated.

In the Northeastern United States, women found part-time or seasonal employment in food-processing factories. Also, skilled seamstresses worked at home, sewing gloves, shirts, and other items of apparel and were paid by "piecework."

b. Later Employment Opportunities and Problems

(1) *In Industry.* Women found many more jobs, often requiring minimal physical exertion, as a result of several important inventions—the sewing machine (invented 1846) opened up employment for women as machine operators in the clothing industry; the typewriter (1867) pointed the way for women to become typists and secretaries; the telephone (1876) created positions for women as switchboard operators. From the later half of the 19th century onward, the number of working women sharply increased.

As more women joined the labor force and worked long hours for poor pay, they sought better conditions by joining labor unions. In 1911 about 150 workers, mostly women, died as a result of a fire and the lack of safety facilities, at the Triangle Shirtwaist Company in New York City. This shocking event led to state laws regulating wages, hours, and factory conditions—especially for women and children—and led also to both men and women garment workers, in considerable numbers, joining the *International Ladies Garment Workers Union* (ILGWU).

(2) *In the Professions.* Women, long accepted as teachers of young children, began to overcome obstacles keeping them from other professions. *Elizabeth Blackwell* was rejected by eight medical schools before being accepted, as a joke, by vote of the student body, at the Geneva, New York, College of Medicine. She graduated in 1849 at the head of her class but was ostracized by the medical profession and ridiculed by the general public. Dr. Blackwell persevered. In 1857 she helped establish the *New York Infirmary for Women and Children,* which institution later opened a nurses' training school and a women's medical college. Dr. Elizabeth Blackwell helped overcome prejudice against women doctors. Her sister-in-law, *Antoinette Louisa Blackwell,* became the first fully ordained female minister in the United States when in 1852 she took the pulpit of the Congregational Church at South Butler, New York. *Ellen H. Richards,* the first woman admitted to the Massachusetts Institute of Technology, graduated with a degree in chemistry. In 1894 in Boston, she began the first school lunch programs, thereby enabling mothers to hold jobs without having to worry about the midday feeding of their school-age children. Ellen Richards spurred the teaching of home economics.

c. Employment During Wartime.

In wartime more women have secured employment to replace men who have gone off to fight and to increase goods and services for war needs. During the Civil War, women filled newly created factory jobs and many served as volunteer nurses, hospital aides, and welfare workers. *Clara Barton,* who had served as a nurse and medical aide during the Civil War, founded in 1881 the *American Red Cross*. For 23 years—until 1904—she headed that organization and expanded its activities also to victims of peacetime disasters. During World War I, women in great numbers contributed to the war effort and won public support for the Nineteenth Amendment, which guaranteed women the right to vote. During World War II, women enlisted in newly created women's military noncombat units: Army Wacs, Navy Waves, and Women Marines. Also with so many men in military service, women worked on assembly lines, especially in defense industries. Their efforts were lauded in a popular song "Rosie the Riveter."

2. Women as Workers in the Economy Today

a. In the Total Labor Force: A Sharp Increase

Year	Working Population			
	In Millions		In Percent	
	Women	Men	Women	Men
1900	5	24	17	83
1940	14	41	25	75
1970	30	49	38	62

Of the working women, about two out of five were single, widowed, or divorced, usually supporting themselves, and three out of five were married and working to raise family incomes.

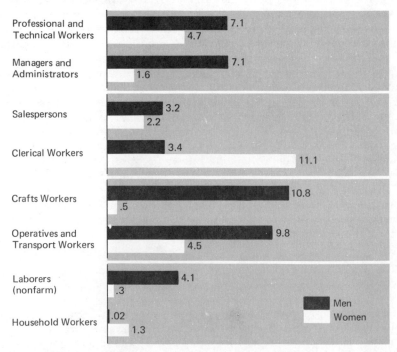

Employed Men and Women, by Occupational Groups (Millions of Persons)

b. By Major Occupation Groups. Of the total number of employed women (1) one of every three (33 percent) does clerical and office work; (2) one of every six (16 percent) is a service worker in hospitals, restaurants, and beauty parlors; (3) one of every six (16 percent) works as an operator in textile and clothing factories; (4) one of every six (16 percent) is a professional such as an accountant, doctor, lawyer, or teacher; (5) less than one of every ten (less than 10 percent) is a sales worker; and (6) less than one of every ten (less than 10 percent) is a private household worker.

By comparison with working men: a greater percentage of all women are employed as clerical, office, household, and service workers; a roughly equal percentage of women and men are employed as professional workers and sales-persons; a smaller percentage of women are employed as managers, officials, crafts workers, supervisors, and laborers.

c. Preponderance in Office Jobs. Why do such a large percentage of working women hold clerical and other office jobs? Many young women think of employment as a temporary stage that will end when they marry and begin raising families. Therefore they seek jobs that do not require lengthy preparation, are willing to accept lower wages and to forego opportunities for advancement —characteristics typical of most clerical positions. Also when their children are grown up, an increasing number of women plan to return to work. They find that they can "brush-up" quickly on their clerical skills and qualify for many available office positions.

d. Women Earn Less Than Men. In 1972 the average income of women was $6,100, which figure was 60 percent of the $10,500 average income for men. Earning less than $3,000 per year were 12 percent of the women as compared to only 5 percent of the men. Earning more than $10,000 per year were 7 percent of the women as compared to 40 percent of the men. Among salespersons, women's earnings were 40 percent of those of men; in the professions, women's earnings were 65 percent of those of men.

What factors explain why women earn on average so much less than men? (1) A greater percentage of women are concentrated in the lower-paying clerical, household, and service jobs; a smaller percentage are in the higher-paying managerial and skilled crafts positions. (2) Among salespersons, women gener-ally do not remain in the job as long as men, thereby losing seniority and missing out on the accompanying pay raises. (3) Among service workers, women are more likely to hold the lower-paying jobs of cooks and waitresses, while men are more likely to hold the higher-paying jobs of police officers and fire fighters. (4) Within the educational system, fewer women than men are promoted from classroom teachers to the higher-paying supervisory and administrative posi-tions. (5) Women have faced discrimination based on sex both from the general public and from employers.

3. Government Protection for Women in Employment.

Benefiting from gen-eral worker-protection laws—such as minimum wage, Social Security, and fac-tory inspection—women workers also benefit from special laws designed to protect them. Many states have laws limiting women's working hours per day and per week and prohibiting women's employment in "hazardous occupations" and at night. New York and some other states have laws requiring employers to give women and men "equal pay for equal work." The federal government, by the *Civil Rights Act of 1964*, bars employers, employment agencies, and labor

Professional and Technical Workers	$13,800	
	$9,000	
Managers and Administrators	$14,000	
	$7,300	
Clerical Workers	$10,000	
	$6,200	
Crafts Workers	$10,700	
	$5,900	
Factory Workers	$8,900	
	$5,100	
Salespersons	$11,900	
	$4,700	
Service Workers	$8,100	Men
	$4,700	Women

Median Annual Income of Men and Women, by Occupational Groups

unions from discriminating against women in hiring and salary offers, in job referral, and in apprenticeship programs. To investigate complaints of discrimination and seek remedies, the act established a federal *Equal Employment Opportunity Commission*. As a result of federal (and state) laws, many companies seeking help specify that they are "Equal Opportunity Employers" and their newspaper "help-wanted" ads no longer specify male or female.

4. Women as Consumers and Property Owners

a. Consumers. Constituting 51 percent of the population, women do the overwhelming amount of the country's total retail purchasing. They represent the mass market for producers of consumer goods and suppliers of services. For women, clothing articles are styled, convenience foods are prepared, household appliances are produced, furniture pieces are crafted, cars are designed, and entertainment and vacation plans are geared. They receive appeals for financial aid from philanthropic and social reform movements. They are the objects of advertising campaigns—the soap operas on television, jingles on radio, and the attractive layouts especially in women's magazines.

b. Property Owners. Women constitute more than half of the individual stockholders in all major corporations and half of the number of millionaires. With women today being statistically three years younger than their husbands and living seven years longer, women are beneficiaries of their husbands' estates and have inherited much property. Also working women have used their earnings to purchase property. To attract women depositors and investors, banks and stock brokerage firms have utilized special advertising and employed women personnel.

Neither as consumers nor as property owners have women organized to use the power inherently theirs to promote women's causes.

5. Items of Unfinished Economic Business. To achieve economic equality with male workers, women seek the following: (a) They want to overcome bias—by some unions against admitting women members, by some banks and lending institutions against granting mortgages and other forms of credit to women, and by some employers against hiring and promoting women. For example, despite the many women stockholders, few women have held top management positions or membership on the boards of directors of major corporations. Women may combat some, but not all, economic bias by filing complaints with state and federal equal employment opportunity commissions. (b) Women want to overcome prejudice by the general public against women in certain occupations such as driving taxicabs, piloting airplanes, or preparing prescriptions. Women may combat such prejudice by seeking to change their "image" in the mass media. Militant feminists of the Women's Liberation Movement protest advertisements that portray women as deferring to and living only to please men and as belonging in the home attending to domestic chores. (c) Women want all states to adopt "equal pay for equal work" laws and to repeal laws that discriminate against women in the guise of protecting them. For example, some states prohibit women waitresses from working during the "high-tip" night hours on the grounds of health, yet permit cleaning women to work at night. Women may seek favorable legislation by organizing politically and lobbying effectively— activities that are promoted by the *League of Women Voters.*

6. One Further Item of Unfinished Business—Legal and Economic Equality With Men. Women themselves are divided regarding the advisability of one further reform—a Constitutional amendment prohibiting discrimination between men and women. In 1972 Congress overwhelmingly proposed an Equal Rights Amendment (ERA) stating that "equality of rights under the law shall not be denied or abridged by the United States or by any state on account of sex."

Feminists, who had fought for almost 50 years to get Congress to propose this amendment, were jubilant. They argued that this amendment would assure women equal treatment with men in conducting a business, in receiving payment for similar types of work, in setting the age for attaining legal adulthood, and in gaining admission to tax-supported educational institutions.

Opponents of the amendment, including some women, were fearful. They argued that the amendment would end the preference usually given mothers in child-custody cases arising out of divorces, would make women eligible for all types of military duty, and would prohibit state laws extending protections to women—forbidding them to work on night shifts or in hazardous occupations.

ERA required ratification within seven years, by three-fourths, or 38, of the states. By early 1979, with the seven-year deadline at hand, ERA had only 35 ratifications. Congress therefore, by majority vote, extended the deadline 39 months to June 1982. This unprecedented extension and the action of several states rescinding their ratifications both mean that ERA—if it gains the additional three states—will be subject to considerable legal dispute.

WOMEN'S RIGHTS IN POLITICAL MATTERS

1. The Struggle for Women's Suffrage

a. Leading Suffragettes. Those women who militantly sought to gain for women the right to vote were known as *suffragettes.*

Susan B. Anthony was the outstanding 19th-century suffragette leader. Born in Massachusetts, she devoted her life—writing, lecturing, organizing, and agitating—in the cause of women's suffrage. After the Civil War, as Congress was considering the wording of the Fourteenth and Fifteenth Amendments to guarantee civil and voting rights to Negroes, Susan B. Anthony pleaded that these amendments also guarantee women the vote, but Congress did not heed her pleas. In 1872, claiming that she was a "citizen" and "person" within the meaning of these amendments, she attempted to vote so as to force a legal test case. Arrested and fined, she refused to pay the fine, but her case was dropped. Thereafter she worked to arouse public support for a women's suffrage amendment. In 1920, some 14 years after her death, the nation ratified such an amendment—the Nineteenth—and in her honor popularly called it the *Susan B. Anthony Amendment.*

Lucretia Mott and *Elizabeth Cady Stanton* issued the call for and directed the first women's rights convention held in 1848 at Seneca Falls (New York). *Lucy Stone,* who graduated from Oberlin College in 1847, later married Henry Blackwell (brother of Elizabeth Blackwell), but insisted upon retaining her maiden name and being known as Mrs. Stone. (Today women, usually in the professional field, who, after marriage, continue to use their original names are known as "Lucy Stoners.") *Amelia Bloomer* for a time edited a newspaper supporting temperance, abolition of slavery, and women's rights. She is best remembered, however, for her wearing of "sensible" clothing—a short dress and loose trousers gathered at the ankle—which trousers became known popularly as "bloomers" and were worn by many of her followers.

b. Support From Men. Although most men at first ridiculed and opposed the women's suffrage movement, the early suffragette leaders had some masculine support (1) from their husbands, especially *James Mott, Henry Stanton,* and *Henry Blackwell,* and (2) from other humanitarian reformers, notably abolitionists such as Frederick Douglass, Wendell Phillips, Horace Greeley, and William Lloyd Garrison.

c. Later Suffragettes. The leaders who carried on the fight for women's rights into the early 20th century were *Anna Howard Shaw* and *Carrie Chapman Catt.*

2. Major Events in the Struggle for Women's Suffrage.
In 1848 the *Women's Rights Convention,* held at Seneca Falls, New York, drafted a declaration that paraphrased the Declaration of Independence by stating that "all men and women are created equal," listing women's grievances against a man-dominated society, and demanding for women opportunities in education, the business world, and professions as well as rights regarding property, child guardianship, and voting. In 1869 the Territory of Wyoming granted the vote to women. By 1900 four Western states permitted women to vote, and by 1914 twelve other states had so acted. By 1920, in recognition of the contribution of women to the American effort in World War I, the states quickly ratified the Nineteenth

Amendment prohibiting the states and the federal government from denying the right to vote to citizens "on account of sex."

3. Notable Women in Political Life. Women have been elected to the House of Representatives and to the Senate; they have also been appointed to top-level administrative positions, even to Cabinet and ambassadorial posts. A few women have become state governors, usually to complete the terms of husbands who died in office. Increasingly women have been elected and appointed to important state and local offices.

In 1916 *Jeanette Rankin* of Montana became the first woman ever elected to the House of Representatives. She voted against two American declarations of war: in 1917 upon Germany and in 1941 upon Japan. *Frances Perkins*, Secretary of Labor under President Franklin D. Roosevelt, was the first woman Cabinet member. *Eleanor Roosevelt*, wife of Franklin D. Roosevelt, lectured and wrote to help promote social and economic legislation benefiting disadvantaged groups. Later, as first chairman of the United Nations *Human Rights Commission*, she played a major role in the writing and adopting of the UN *Declaration of Human Rights*. In recent years, *Shirley Chisholm* of Brooklyn became the first black woman ever elected to the United States House of Representatives; *Bess Myerson*, a former Miss America, was appointed Commissioner of Consumer Affairs for New York City; *Virginia H. Knauer* was named Special Assistant to President Nixon for Consumer Affairs; *Margaret Chase Smith* of Maine won respect and fame as a member of the United States Senate; *Marina Whitman* was the first woman appointed to the President's *Council of Economic Advisers*; and *Ella Grasso* won election as first woman governor of Connecticut.

4. Other Political Gains by Women. The right to vote has been a powerful force in gaining additional political recognition. In federal and many state courts,

"Founding Fathers! How come no Founding Mothers?"
(*Drawing by Dana Fradon;* © *1972 The New Yorker Magazine, Inc.*)

women have served as jurors and as judges. Women also are represented on the governing committees—local, state, and national—of our major political parties.

The *League of Women Voters*, organized in 1920, is a nonpartisan organization that seeks to promote political responsibility by all citizens. The league provides accurate information regarding candidates and issues as essential to the democratic process; and it seeks to influence legislators to pass worthwhile legislation for world peace, economic prosperity, and social progress.

5. Items of Unfinished Political Business. Despite their considerable gains politically, women still face certain inequalities: (a) In some states women have only a limited right to serve on juries or, unlike men, are required to file a special request to be eligible for jury duty. (b) Although women have equal representation with men on most political party committees, they do not always exercise equal authority with their male counterparts. (c) Some women still feel that politics is a "man's world" and are reluctant to undertake political activity. (d) Both women and men cling consciously or subconsciously to the belief that women are unfit—emotionally, intellectually, and biologically—to hold political positions of great authority. For example, our major parties have never seriously considered a woman candidate for the Presidency. Democrats and Republicans have been uninfluenced by the examples of women prime ministers in other countries: *Golda Meir* of Israel, *Indira Gandhi* of India, and *Margaret Thatcher* of Britain.

WOMEN'S LEGAL RIGHTS IN FAMILY MATTERS

1. Legal Disabilities of Married Women: In Early America. According to 18th-century English legal theory from which was derived early American law, a woman upon marriage became a "chattel" or property of her husband and completely dependent on him. Married women were classified with minors and mental defectives as not legally responsible; they could not sue or be sued except through their husbands; they surrendered control of any property to their husbands; if they worked, their wages belonged to their husbands; any children resulting from the marriage belonged to the husband.

In early America, because of the shortage of women and their economic value, wives sometimes were not strictly subject to the above legal theory. Some were permitted to manage business and acquire land.

2. Gains Made by Women in Family Law. Since the laws concerning marriage and divorce are powers reserved to the states under the Constitution, women had to seek legal reforms through state legislatures. In New York State, Elizabeth Cady Stanton, the suffragette, and *Ernestine Rose*, a Jewish immigrant originally from Poland, led the legal reform movement. Throughout New York State, Stanton and Rose made speeches, circulated petitions, and lobbied for action by the state legislature. Their efforts were supported by well-to-do New Yorkers who wanted to safeguard their daughters' dowries and inheritances. In 1848, after a 12-year campaign, the state legislature passed the *Married Women's Property Act,* which allowed the property of the wife at the time of marriage to remain under her control and not be subject to seizure to pay debts of her husband. In 1860 New York State enacted further laws giving women the right to sue and be sued, to control their own wages and personal property, and to exercise joint guardianship of minor children.

New York's example in liberal property and child guardianship laws was followed by most states in the North and West. Today, women in most states have achieved legal equality with men and, in cases of divorce, are considered the preferred guardians of minor children.

3. Items of Unfinished Business in Family Matters. In some few states, women's legal rights as wives, property owners, and mothers are still restricted or unrecognized. In these states, a wife may not control real or personal property independently of her husband; has no claim, other than to income for sufficient support, to her husband's earnings and property; faces restrictions if she seeks to engage in business separate from her husband; and is not considered the preferred legal guardian of minor children.

THE WOMEN'S LIBERATION MOVEMENT TODAY

1. Brief History and Organizations. The struggle for women's rights *(a)* languished temporarily following the adoption in 1920 of the Nineteenth Amendment guaranteeing women the right to vote, *(b)* revived in the post-World War II years, under stimulus of the black civil rights movement and the concern for the rights of the individual, and *(c)* burst into full public view in the 1960's with an outpouring of college courses, lectures, magazine articles, books, and organizations. The struggle for women's rights now became known as the *Women's Liberation Movement,* or popularly as *Women's Lib.* Its active participants became known as *feminists* or sometimes as *militant feminists.*

Women's Lib speaks through many voices and hundreds of organizations ranging from small radical groups that seek to overthrow our existing culture and society to more influential reformist groups that seek to improve conditions for women within the existing societal framework. The oldest and largest feminist group, founded in 1966 by *Betty Friedan,* is the *National Organization for Women* (NOW). By the early 1970's, NOW had about 100 chapters throughout the nation and some 10,000 members, mainly white, middle-class, professional women. NOW is a reformist organization seeking to gain "full equality for women in America in a truly equal partnership with men."

2. Women's Lib: Criticisms of Women's Role in Our Culture

a. No "Weaker Sex." Women's Lib advocates deny that women are the "weaker sex." They claim that women bear pain better than men and point out that women live longer than men. They assert that women are more sensitive, more artistic, and more imaginative than men. They insist that women have been limited in opportunity for physical exercise by cultural taboos: girls are encouraged to play with dolls, boys to play baseball.

b. No Exclusive Care of Children and Home. Women's Lib advocates assert that, although women bear children, women must not necessarily raise the children and keep house. "Liberated" women insist on an equal partnership of the parents—that men as fathers must accept a vital role in rearing children and in performing household tasks.

c. No Inequality With Men. Women's Lib advocates admit that women and men are different but insist they are equal. They demand that this equality be demonstrated in our society in every aspect. They want women to be treated, not as women, but as human beings.

3. Women's Lib: Reform Demands. Women's Lib advocates have demanded *(a)* the end of sex segregation that permits male-only restaurants, clubs, and social events and allows help-wanted ads to specify that the job applicant be male or female; *(b)* the end of advertising that uses women as "sex symbols" to sell products for manufacturers and retailers; also the end of "beauty contests"; *(c)* the end of the cultural stereotype of women as seeking only the goal of marriage and motherhood; also the establishing by government of child care centers so that mothers, who so wish, may be free to pursue business and professional careers; *(d)* the use of the title Ms. (in place of both Miss and Mrs.) for women as comparable to Mr. for men—neither title indicating marital status; and *(e)* full equality for women with men in employment, education, and before the law.

Women today demonstrate for equal rights. (*U.S. News and World Report*)

4. Women's Liberation Leaders

Betty Friedan graduated from Smith College with highest honors and with a major in psychology. Thereafter she pursued graduate study at the University of California at Berkeley. In personal life she was twice divorced and had three children—which experiences helped form the basis of her well-known 1963 book, *The Feminine Mystique.* She wrote that raising children and taking care of a home results in a "sense of emptiness and lack of identity." Betty Friedan insisted that women want to be more than wives and mothers, that they want careers and other forms of self-fulfillment as individuals. In 1966 she formed

NOW and served as its first president till 1970, when she resigned to devote her time to lecturing and writing.

Aileen Hernandez, a black woman, won a scholarship to Howard University and graduated with highest honors and with majors in sociology and political science. She held a number of interesting positions: with the ILGWU on the Pacific Coast as public relations and education director, with the California *Fair Employment Practices Commission,* and in 1965 and 1966 with the federal *Equal Employment Opportunity Commission.* Thereafter she established her own management consultant agency to advise business, labor, and government on programs for employing minority groups and women. In 1970 Aileen Hernandez became the second president of NOW. She vowed to change the organization's "middle-class image" saying, "I'm much more interested in the problems of the mass women than the professional."

Gloria Steinem graduated from Smith College with highest honors and a major in government. She became a magazine editor and writer, contributing articles on Women's Lib to many widely read magazines. Using a calm approach in her articles, Gloria Steinem has appealed to many men and women who have been offended by the more impassioned advocates of the new feminism. She has presented the positive philosophy that "if Women's Lib wins, perhaps we all do." In 1972 she founded a Women's Lib monthly magazine, *Ms.*

Wilma Soss studied journalism at Columbia University, became a reporter, and then a public relations counselor. Becoming aware that women stockholders in major American corporations outnumber men, she battled to gain women a greater voice in economic matters. In 1947 she founded the *Federation of Women Shareholders in American Business.* Attending the annual meetings of major corporations, Wilma Soss spoke out demanding reforms: simpler annual statements, more accessible locations for holding annual meetings, and, most importantly, more women on the corporate boards of directors. Her efforts have received considerable publicity in business circles and have led some few corporations to elect women directors.

SOME OUTSTANDING CONTRIBUTIONS OF AMERICAN WOMEN

1. Women Poets. In the 19th century, *Emily Dickinson* wrote wryly observant, often profound poems about people and nature. Her many poems, published only after her death, have taken their place in the world's great literature. Also in the 19th century, *Emma Lazarus* wrote her famed poem, "The New Colossus." She portrayed the Statue of Liberty, then just erected in New York harbor, as a symbol of welcome to immigrants entering America—the land of freedom.

In the 20th century, many women contributed to American poetry. *Amy Lowell,* an eccentric individual who scorned convention, protested against tradition, and introduced new experimental poetry to America. Her best-known poems reflected themes of her native New England. *Marianne Moore* employed wit and satire in poems of everyday objects such as plants, animals, and antiques. *Edna St. Vincent Millay* expressed the rebellious spirit of the post-World War I years and later the social consciousness of the World War II era. She condemned Nazi inhumanity in her poem "The Murder of Lidice."

Two black women have made outstanding contributions to modern poetry.

Gwendolyn Brooks, whose earliest poems were published in a black newspaper in Chicago, became in 1950 the first black to win the Pulitzer Prize for poetry. *Nikki Giovanni*, a young and talented poet, has drawn themes from her personal life. Her poems (and other works) are popular among the younger generation.

2. Women Novelists and Short Story Writers. *Willa Cather* wrote stories of pioneer life and problems in the Midwest and Southwest. In *My Antonia*, her famed novel, she described the struggles of an immigrant family to survive on the Nebraska prairie. *Katherine Anne Porter* used her knowledge of the Southwest, Mexico, and pre-World War II Europe as background for many short stories. *Ship of Fools*, her first novel, exposed the follies and failures of humanity. *Pearl Buck*, the daughter of missionaries who spent many years in China, tried to interpret Chinese civilization for Westerners. She described the struggle of a Chinese peasant to acquire land in her famed novel *The Good Earth*. She was the first American woman to receive the Nobel Prize in literature. *Marjorie Rawlings* was a "Florida regionalist" who employed local customs and speech in her writings. *The Yearling*, her novel of a young boy and his pet fawn, has become a juvenile classic. *Edna Ferber* wrote novels and short stories of American life in its historical setting. Three of her novels are *So Big*—about a woman who triumphed against odds to become a successful truck farmer; *Show Boat*—about a theatrical family performing on a Mississippi River boat; and *Cimarron*—about the Oklahoma land rush.

3. Women Dramatists. *Lillian Hellman* wrote dramas of powerful personal conflict, such as among members of a well-to-do Southern family in *The Little Foxes*. Also she warned the American people against the dangers of Nazism in her play *Watch on the Rhine*. *Mary Chase* won acclaim for her play about a drunkard whose friend was an invisible six-foot-tall rabbit named *Harvey*. *Lorraine Hansberry*, a black playwright whose life was cut short by cancer, portrayed blacks realistically in her moving drama *A Raisin in the Sun*.

4. Women Nonfiction Writers. At the beginning of the 20th century, *Ida Tarbell*, a muckraker, wrote a series of magazine articles that were later published as a book, *History of the Standard Oil Company*. She criticized this giant monopoly for its ruthless practices against competitors and consumers. More recently, *Barbara Tuchman* has written on various historical events. Her best-known work, describing how World War I began, is entitled *The Guns of August*.

5. Women Artists. *Anna Mary (Grandma) Moses*, in her seventies, when unable to continue with farmwork, began painting farm scenes and landscapes of rural New York. She expressed the hope that her paintings—which totaled over 1000—would enable people to "see how we used to live." *Malvina Hoffman*, a sculptor, is known chiefly for 101 figures of ethnic types located in the Hall of Man in the Chicago Museum of Natural History. *Georgia O'Keeffe*, a painter, took as her subject natural objects—such as rocks, bones, flowers, and clouds—and applied abstract painting techniques. *Margaret Bourke-White*, a photographer (and journalist) of the mid-20th century, took vivid pictures in the United States, Communist Russia, World War II, and India after independence.

6. Women Social Service Leaders. In the mid-19th century, *Dorothea Dix* labored to secure better treatment for the insane, to abolish imprisonment for debt, and to improve prison conditions for criminals. Toward the end of the 19th century, *Jane Addams* established *Hull-House* in Chicago, and *Lillian Wald* established the *Henry Street Settlement* in New York City. These settlement houses, located in slum areas, provided playgrounds, meeting rooms, and libraries, and offered classes at every level from nursery school to adult education.

7. Women Scientists. *Karen Horney*, a psychiatrist, who was born and educated in Germany, came to the United States in 1932 and later became an American citizen. Here she helped direct attention to psychiatric problems, and in 1941 she helped found the *American Institute for Psychoanalysis*. *Margaret Mead*, an anthropologist, gained her reputation by studies of the primitive peoples of the South Pacific islands. She became curator of ethnology of the American Museum of Natural History in New York City and later professor of anthropology at Columbia University. She employed her knowledge and prestige to combat the unscientific and erroneous theories associated with racism. *Maria Goeppert Mayer*, a physicist, who was born and educated in Germany, came to the United States in 1930 and became an American citizen. For her research upon the structure of the atom's nucleus, she shared the 1963 Nobel Prize in physics—the second woman in history to be so honored. (The first woman who, 60 years earlier, won the 1903 Nobel Prize in physics, was Marie Curie of France.) *Rachel Carson*, marine biologist, wrote several books combining scientific knowledge and poetic descriptions of the sea—including the widely acclaimed book *The Sea Around Us*. In 1962 she wrote the book *Silent Spring* warning humanity of the dangers to wildlife and food supply from the indiscriminate use of pesticides. *Frances Kelsey*, a physician, who was born and educated in Canada, moved to the United States and became an American citizen. Working with the Food and Drug Administration, she refused permission for the marketing of the drug thalidomide, which had been introduced in several European countries as a sleeping pill. Her judgment was vindicated when European mothers who had taken thalidomide gave birth to severely deformed babies.

MULTIPLE-CHOICE QUESTIONS

1. Which is the *best* example of the inferior role assigned to women in a patriarchal society? (1) a pioneer woman during the westward movement (2) a New England woman in the early 1800's (3) an Iroquois woman in the 1600's (4) a working mother in the 1970's.
2. The inferior status of women in colonial times reflected (1) a continuation of the European tradition (2) the lack of work for women in an agricultural economy (3) women's disinterest in political affairs (4) the scarcity of women in a frontier society.
3. Under the Morrill Act of 1862, land grants to colleges spurred the enrollment of women for programs in (1) agriculture (2) teaching (3) home economics (4) law.
4. The Waltham System was a program for (1) giving women the right to vote (2) training women for careers in education (3) appointing more women to college faculties (4) hiring young women in New England textile mills.
5. Which invention resulted in a large increase in the number of women workers? (1) steam locomotive (2) typewriter (3) electric light bulb (4) automatic elevator
6. The women's rights movement in the United States has been *least* successful in achieving the right of women to (1) register and vote (2) own property (3) have equal job opportunity (4) dress as they choose.

7. The Equal Employment Opportunity Commission would *not* be concerned with (1) a labor union refusing membership to a woman worker (2) a passenger airline employing women only as flight attendants (3) a company hiring a woman clerk at a wage 25 percent less than the wages of other clerks hired three years ago (4) an employment agency advertising for a male engineer with five years of experience.

8. Which has had the *least* effect on increasing the employment of women in the post-World War II era? (1) increase in the number of clerical and office jobs (2) increase in the number of service occupations (3) passage of minimum wage laws requiring higher hourly rates (4) passage of laws forbidding discrimination against women in employment

9. A recent study indicates that women face serious inequities in employment. Evidence to support this finding includes the fact that most women are (1) failing to complete high school (2) unwilling to assume the responsibilities of administrative positions (3) able to accept only part-time employment at low wages (4) employed at jobs that offer few chances for advancement.

10. Which *best* explains the progress of women in the United States toward social and economic equality? (1) Women found new educational and employment opportunities outside the home. (2) Churches provided the needed leadership in the drive for women's rights. (3) Both major political parties demanded voting privileges for women. (4) European nations provided an example for the United States to follow.

11. The Women's Liberation movement (1) has raised public awareness of both subtle and obvious discriminations against women (2) arose immediately after World War I (3) considers women better qualified than men to bring up children (4) speaks with one voice for all women.

12. An analysis of women's outstanding contributions indicates that women have (1) avoided the field of science (2) in literature, dealt mainly with frivolous themes (3) a varied and extensive list of achievements (4) been making important contributions only in the 20th century.

IDENTIFICATION QUESTIONS: WHO AM I?

Abigail Adams	Betty Friedan	Eleanor Roosevelt
Susan B. Anthony	Ella Grasso	Elizabeth Cady Stanton
Rachel Carson	Anne Hutchinson	Gloria Steinem
Shirley Chisholm	Mary Lyon	Lucy Stone
Edna Ferber	Anna Mary (Grandma) Moses	Barbara Tuchman

1. To provide women with higher education, I founded Mount Holyoke.
2. I was the leading advocate of women's right to vote. An amendment to the Constitution has been "named" for me.
3. An historian, I am known for my study *The Guns of August*, detailing the beginnings of World War I.
4. A moderate in the Women's Liberation movement, I founded the magazine *Ms*.
5. I was the first black woman elected to the House of Representatives.
6. Unable to continue with farmwork, I began painting scenes of farmlife in rural New York State.
7. Wife of one American President and mother of another, I advocated women's rights years before there was such a movement.
8. I wrote *Show Boat* and other novels depicting major episodes in American history.
9. A prominent public figure in the 1930's, I later headed the UN Human Rights Commission.
10. A marine biologist, I wrote several books about the sea. I also wrote the book *Silent Spring*, warning against the dangers of pesticides.

ESSAY QUESTIONS

1. For over 150 years, women in America have struggled to overcome disadvantages imposed upon them and to secure equal rights. (*a*) Discuss *three* evidences to prove that women, in the early 19th century, were a disadvantaged group. (*b*) Explain *one* way in which the status of women has been altered by each of the following: (1) the democratic atmosphere of the Jacksonian Era (2) the Industrial Revolution as it developed toward the latter part of the 19th century (3) the civil rights ferment of the post-World War II years (4) the need for workers during major wars.

2. The table gives some statistics about the status of men and women in the United States.

Percent of	Men	Women	Percent of	Men	Women
Population	49	51	Elementary school teachers	10	90
Jobs held	62	38	Elementary school principals	80	20
Doctors	93	7	Senators	99	1
Lawyers	97	3	Representatives	98	2
Engineers	99	1	Presiding judges	96	4

(*a*) Using only the information presented in the table, what would be the *best* general statement that you could make concerning the relative status of women in the United States today? (*b*) Discuss other information you already possess that supports or modifies this generalization. (*c*) In order to support or revise the generalization you stated in (*a*), what additional statistics or information would you need? (*d*) What sources or methods would you use to obtain this additional information?

3. Agree or disagree with *each* of the following statements and present *two* arguments to support your opinion: (*a*) Women are basically unwilling to assume positions of leadership in the business world. (*b*) The Equal Rights Amendment deserves the support of all men and women. (*c*) Since men generally become the family breadwinners, they should receive preference over women in regard to college and professional school admissions. (*d*) American voters would support a woman of ability and proven political experience as a candidate for the Presidency. (*e*) Today, the women's rights movement still has a number of items of unfinished business.

13. American Blacks Progress From Slavery to Legal Freedom and on Toward Equality

A Brief Historical Survey: From African Origins to the End of Reconstruction (1877)

1. African Origins. From the early 17th into the mid-19th century, some 14 million blacks were forcibly removed from West Africa and transported to the New World. Only about half survived the barbarous trans-Atlantic voyage, called the *Middle Passage*. Sold into slavery and subjected to white rule, the blacks nevertheless retained parts of their native African culture: songs, brightly colored clothing, words, and foods.

2. Blacks and the Revolutionary War Era. (*a*) *The Declaration of Independence (1776).* In regard to slavery, the Declaration of Independence was silent.

Jefferson's original statement condemning the slave trade and slavery was removed by the Continental Congress. Since the Congress required unanimous approval for the Declaration, the removal of any condemnation of slavery secured the support of New England, whose shipowners engaged in the slave trade, and of the South, whose plantation owners used slave workers. *(b) Military Matters.* In 1770 *Crispus Attucks,* a black, was one of five men killed when British soldiers fired upon a hostile crowd—an event the colonists called the *Boston Massacre.* During the Revolutionary War, of some 300,000 American soldiers, 5000 were Negroes. Best known to us were two Bunker Hill battle heroes, *Peter Salem* and *Salem Poor.*

3. Earliest Steps Against Slavery. The *Northwest Ordinance* of 1787, providing for the government of the Northwest Territory, closed that area to slavery. By 1804 all Northern states were committed to the abolition of slavery. In the South a number of planters left wills freeing their slaves. Southerners and Northerners favoring the transport of free Negroes back to West Africa founded the *American Colonization Society.* Although few Negroes were willing to return to their ancestral continent, the society in the 1820's founded the West African nation of *Liberia.*

The original Constitution provided that Congress, after 20 years, could prohibit the importing of slaves. In 1808 Congress did so, but the law was poorly enforced.

4. The Cotton Gin: Its Effect Upon the South and Slavery. The cotton gin, a machine invented in 1793 by *Eli Whitney,* provided an inexpensive method of separating the cotton seeds from the fibers. With cotton production now extremely profitable, Southern plantations grew rapidly and increasingly became dependent upon slave labor. Southern whites began to defend slavery, not as a necessary evil, but as a positive good.

5. Opposition to Slavery. *(a) Slave Uprisings. Gabriel Prosser* in 1800, *Denmark Vesey* in 1822, and *Nat Turner* in 1831—each led a major Southern slave uprising. These and other resistance efforts were sternly suppressed. *(b) Abolitionist Movement.* Arising in the 1830's chiefly in the North, the abolitionists denounced slavery as a moral evil and demanded the immediate freeing of slaves without compensation to their owners. Leading abolitionists included: *William Lloyd Garrison,* who edited the foremost abolitionist newspaper, *The Liberator; Harriet Tubman,* a former slave who worked on the *Underground Railroad,* leading runaway Southern slaves to freedom in the North and Canada; and *Harriet Beecher Stowe,* who swayed Northern emotions against slavery with her novel *Uncle Tom's Cabin.* Even in the North, the abolitionists had only a limited following.

6. Slavery and Sectionalism. The North and the South struggled bitterly for control of the federal government so as to use its powers to further their sectional interests. This struggle frequently centered upon the status of slavery in new states seeking admission to the Union. The North wanted more free states; the South sought more slave states.

(a) The North and South agreed upon the *Missouri Compromise of 1820* admitting Maine as a free state and Missouri as a slave state and prohibiting

slavery in most of the Louisiana Territory. *(b)* The North delayed the *admission of Texas* to 1845—nine years after it had gained its independence from Mexico—because Texas would strengthen the Southern slave bloc. *(c)* The North and South agreed upon the *Compromise of 1850* dealing mainly with the status of slavery in the *Mexican Cession*—the territories acquired as a result of the Mexican War. *(d)* The North and South battled over Kansas when the *Kansas-Nebraska Act* of 1854 opened the status of slavery in those two territories to determination by the territory residents—a policy called *squatter-sovereignty.* *(e)* The North denounced and the South applauded the Supreme Court decision in the *Dred Scott* case (1857): that slaves were property and might be taken into all federal territories. *(f)* The North honored and the South despised *John Brown,* who was caught raiding the arsenal at *Harpers Ferry* (1859) for guns to arm Negroes in a slave rebellion.

7. Election of 1860 and the Civil War. *Abraham Lincoln,* the Republican candidate, opposed the extension of slavery, carried the North and West solidly, and was elected President. Considering Lincoln a "black Republican," seven Southern states seceded from the Union and founded the *Confederate States of America.* They were later joined by four more states. Declaring secession illegal, Lincoln fought the Civil War to "preserve the Union."

What were the causes of the Civil War? Slavery, as a moral issue most clearly distinguishing North from South, was a major cause. Other causes were economic—Northern industry vs. Southern agriculture; political—Northern belief in a strong central government vs. Southern support of states rights; and social—Northern democratic society vs. Southern planter-dominated aristocracy.

In 1863, during the Civil War, Lincoln acted to weaken the Confederacy by issuing the *Emancipation Proclamation.* It declared free those slaves under Confederate control. Thereafter Union armies accepted Negroes as fighting men—they were called the United States Colored Troops. Over 180,000 Negroes saw military service and played a part in the Union victory.

8. Reconstruction Era (1865–1877). *(a) Meaning. Reconstruction* refers to the process of restoring the Southern states to the Union and of granting rights to Negroes. *(b) Negro Gains.* (1) The Thirteenth Amendment prohibited slavery throughout the United States, the Fourteenth Amendment granted citizenship to Negroes, and the Fifteenth Amendment prohibited states from denying Negroes the right to vote. (2) Northern philanthropists established schools of higher learning for Negroes: such as *Howard University, Hampton Institute,* and *Fisk University.* (3) Negroes played a role in the Southern state Reconstruction governments, supporting universal male suffrage and free public education for all children. Fourteen blacks served in the House of Representatives and two blacks—*Hiram Revels* and *Blanche Bruce*—were elected from Mississippi to the Senate. *(c) Southern Whites Regain Control of Their State Governments.* Southern whites were enabled to regain control by employing secret terrorist societies such as the *Ku Klux Klan,* by the waning of Northern interest in Negro problems, and by the withdrawal in 1877 of federal troops in the South by President Hayes. Reconstruction was over.

From Reconstruction to the 1929 Depression—
Problems of Legal Freedom

SOUTHERN NEGROES: TO WORLD WAR I

1. Target of Racism. As the Southern whites regained control of their state governments, they found ways to evade the Fourteenth and Fifteenth Amendments so as to "put the Negro in his place," that of a subordinate and inferior person.

a. Politically. (1) Southern states required payment of a poll tax which discouraged blacks, mostly poor, as well as impoverished whites from voting. (2) Southern states established difficult and unfair literacy requirements, which effectively barred blacks, mostly little educated, from voting. (3) To preserve the vote for illiterate whites, some states enacted a *grandfather clause*, exempting from literacy requirements persons whose grandfathers had been eligible to vote before the Civil War. (4) The Democratic party in the South denied membership to blacks and thus kept them from voting in party primaries. This had the effect of disenfranchising blacks, since the Democratic nomination in the South, until well into the 20th century, was equivalent to election. By 1900 most Southern blacks did not vote and had negligible political influence.

b. Economically. Many blacks had hoped that with freedom from slavery they would also receive the basis of economic independence, namely "forty acres and a mule." But this was not so. Having received no land with their freedom, black farmers became *sharecroppers*. From a landowner, former slaves secured the use of a few acres of land and perhaps a cabin, a mule, and tools in exchange for a 50 percent or larger share of the crop. Often the sharecroppers also pledged an additional share of the crop to the local merchant to secure credit to buy foodstuffs, seeds, and tools. The sharecroppers worked with crude equipment, employed little or no fertilizer, and depleted the soil of its minerals by continuous planting of a single cash crop, such as tobacco or cotton. Owing the landowner and merchant a large portion of the crop, sharecroppers found themselves entrapped in mounting debt and practically bound to the land. In the cities, black workers were barred from labor unions and relegated to the lowest-paid occupations, usually domestic service, unskilled work, and nonunion occupations—the so-called "Negro jobs." Whether as sharecroppers or as city workers, most Southern blacks remained economically dependent upon whites and lived in poverty.

c. Socially. By "Jim Crow" laws which mandated segregation, blacks were legally required to be separated from whites in railroads, restaurants, beaches, and schools. Facilities provided for blacks were almost always inferior to those for whites. By 1900 "Jim Crow" ruled the South.

2. Contrasting Views of Post-Reconstruction Black Leaders

a. Remain in or Leave the South?

Frederick Douglass, an acknowledged leader of his people, recorded his myriad activities in his autobiography *The Life and Times of Frederick Douglass*. In pre-Civil War days, Douglass had been a runaway slave; editor of the abolitionist newspaper *The North Star* in Rochester, New York; and an underground railroad worker. During the war, he helped recruit black soldiers for the Union; and during Reconstruction, he supported federal efforts to assist Southern blacks. With Reconstruction over, Douglass advised his people to remain in the South. He argued that blacks would find no remedy for their problems by running away and that regardless of where they lived they were entitled to federal protection. Further he believed that by remaining in large numbers in the South, blacks someday would there achieve considerable political power.

Richard T. Greener, who in 1870 became the first black man to graduate from Harvard, taught philosophy at the University of South Carolina until forced out at the end of Reconstruction. He then taught law at a Negro school, Howard University. He disagreed with Douglass and advised Afro-Americans to flee from discrimination by leaving the South. Greener argued that blacks would find greater economic and educational opportunities outside the South and that by leaving in great numbers they would reduce that region's labor supply, thereby improving conditions for the remaining Southern blacks.

The Douglass-Greener debate probably had little practical effect upon the decisions of Southern blacks regarding migration. Whether through lack of financial resources, without hope for better conditions, sheer inertia, or personal preference, the overwhelming number of Negroes remained in the South until the World War I era.

b. Economic Progress or Social and Political Equality: Which Priority for Blacks?

Booker T. Washington, the outstanding leader of his people in the decades following Reconstruction, expounded on his life and philosophy in his autobiography *Up From Slavery.* Raised in poverty but determined to gain an education, Washington worked to support himself through Hampton Institute. From 1881 until his death in 1915, Washington founded, expanded, and won prestige for an advanced technical training center, *Tuskegee Institute,* which offered vocational education to blacks. Washington counseled that blacks should first concentrate on making economic progress and therefore he emphasized the dignity of labor and the importance of vocational education. As blacks improved their economic conditions, Washington reasoned, they would win the respect of the white community and eventually would achieve social integration and political equality. He therefore advised that blacks temporarily accept segregation and forgo agitation in pursuing the ballot, confident that they would move forward in these directions through *gradualism.* Washington's philosophy of race relations, summarized in his famous speech at Atlanta in 1895, became known as the *Atlanta Compromise.* His views were hailed by the white community, South and North, and for many years accepted by most black Americans.

William E. B. DuBois, black historian and educator, was born in Massachusetts after the Civil War. He received his Doctor of Philosophy (Ph.D.) degree at Harvard in 1895 after submitting his original study on "The Suppression of the African Slave Trade." After 1901 DuBois shifted his views regarding black priorities from agreement with Booker T. Washington to sharp disagreement. DuBois deplored Washington's emphasis on vocational training as a narrow education for blacks that would retard their intellectual development and prevent them from attaining economic power through filling professional and managerial positions. DuBois rejected Washington's temporary acceptance of voting discrimination, claiming that blacks could not progress economically without first exercising their right to vote. DuBois expressed impatience with "gradualism"; he urged blacks to resist social and political inequality, to assert their self-respect, and to struggle militantly for full civil rights.

To carry on this struggle, DuBois led a group of black intellectuals in 1905 to form the *Niagara Movement*. With the support of white reformers this movement in 1909 evolved into the biracial *National Association for the Advancement of Colored People (NAACP)*. For many years DuBois was a leading spirit in the NAACP and editor of its monthly periodical *The Crisis*. (In the last years of his long life, DuBois joined the Communist party, moved to Ghana where he became a citizen, and in 1963 died there.)

Until Washington died in 1915, his views prevailed among most black Americans and, according to many observers, probably represented the most practical and realistic advice for blacks. Starting in the 1930's, however, as public opinion became concerned with economic reform and minority rights, DuBois' views gained increasing acceptance among American blacks.

EXPANDING BLACK HORIZONS: DURING AND AFTER WORLD WAR I

1. Blacks in the Armed Forces. During World War I, almost 400,000 blacks served in the armed forces. Barred from the Marines and assigned only to menial tasks in the Navy, most black recruits ended up in the Army. Trained in army camps throughout the nation, many black recruits encountered considerable discrimination from whites—both in civilian and military life—and the resulting frictions led to a number of riots.

Some 100,000 blacks were shipped overseas to France, half in service and half in fighting units. Black fighting units achieved commendable records, and many individual blacks won citations for bravery. Black soldiers generally ignored German propaganda that they were treated as "second-class citizens" in America. Both overseas and at home, blacks were moved by President Wilson's talk of making the world "safe for democracy." They hoped that, in the postwar years, America would set a top priority on expanding democracy to its black citizens. Instead, in the 1920's, America moved, in the words of President Harding, to "return to normalcy," that is, the status quo of the late 19th century.

2. Migration to Northern Cities. During World War I, a third of a million blacks, lured by jobs in war industries, moved from the South to Northern (and Western) cities. After the war, they continued to move northward, as expanding industries hired black workers. In securing jobs, blacks benefited unexpectedly from the restrictive immigration laws of the 1920's which sharply curtailed the admission of white European workers. From 1910 to 1930, the black population in the North more than doubled.

3. Northern Discrimination. Northern blacks freely exercised their right to vote, but they encountered other forms of discrimination. *(a) Socially.* Many blacks were crowded into slum areas, or ghettos, where they inhabited run-down, unsanitary housing for which they paid high rents. Their children attended neighborhood schools that were segregated not by law, or *de jure*, but in fact, or *de facto*, because of residential patterns. Such segregated black schools were often inferior to schools in white neighborhoods. *(b) Economically*. Blacks got the lowest-paying jobs, had little opportunity to advance, and were still barred from most labor unions and professional organizations.

4. Marcus Garvey and the "Back to Africa" Movement. A talented public speaker and magnetic leader, *Marcus Garvey* was born in Jamaica, British West Indies, and raised there in poverty. In 1914 he founded the *Universal Negro Improvement Association* to promote Negro betterment, and in 1916 he moved to New York City. In the early 1920's, at the height of his influence, Garvey claimed that his organization had over 2 million members. To further trade among black-inhabited areas of the world, Garvey established the Black Star Steamship Company.

Garvey appealed to the black masses on the basis of racial pride. Emphasizing that "black is beautiful," he preached that blacks belong to "a gifted race with a proud past and a great future." However, since white America was imbued with racial prejudice and injustice, Garvey insisted that American blacks must return to Africa and create their own civilization in their own homeland. To further this end, Garvey proclaimed himself the "provisional President of Africa."

Garvey was opposed by most other black leaders, especially NAACP leader DuBois and labor leader *A. Philip Randolph*. Garvey's critics claimed that he was bombastic, insincere, and impractical, and that his "back to Africa" solution for the problems of American blacks was a delusion. Although Garvey was hailed by the black masses for extolling black pride, they did not follow his "back to Africa" advice, preferring instead to remain in the United States.

In 1923 Garvey was brought to trial for using the mails to defraud investors in his steamship company, was found guilty, imprisoned for two years, then pardoned by President Coolidge, and deported to Jamaica as an "undesirable alien." Some years afterwards, he died relatively unknown in London.

5. Effect of the 1929 Depression. Since they were generally unskilled and poorly paid, Northern blacks were particularly hard hit by the depression of 1929. In 1932 they overwhelmingly voted for Franklin D. Roosevelt and his promise of a "New Deal." Under Roosevelt the status of the Negro improved, as New Dealers fought the depression and provided jobs and housing for blacks as well as for whites.

From the World War II Era to the Present—Toward Equality

GAINS DURING WORLD WAR II

1. Reawakening of Public Concern. As the United States fought to destroy German Nazism with its racist ideas, many Americans realized that *(a)* racial discrimination at home was morally unjust, and *(b)* black soldiers who serve their country in battle deserved equality for themselves and their families. Americans were also influenced by the publication in 1944 of a monumental study of the American black written by the Swedish sociologist *Gunnar Myrdal*. Entitling his work *An American Dilemma*, Myrdal pointed out to Americans the contradiction between their belief in the principles of democracy and their treatment of blacks. American public opinion became concerned with improving conditions of blacks so as to narrow the gap between idealism and reality.

2. In the Armed Forces. During World War II about 1 million blacks were part of the American military force. Although not treated fully as equals, they found conditions had improved as compared to World War I. The black servicemen of World War II *(a)* were admitted to the Marine Corps, *(b)* were trained for more skilled tasks and received higher ratings in the Navy, *(c)* experienced less discrimination in the Army, and *(d)* participated in fewer serious riots growing out of racism.

Half a million blacks served overseas both in service and fighting units. Many black units as well as individuals were cited for distinguished action.

The first black promoted to the rank of Army brigadier general was *Benjamin O. Davis*. His son *Benjamin O. Davis, Jr.*, a West Point graduate, was an Air Force pilot who flew many World War II missions and won a number of citations. After the war, Benjamin O. Davis, Jr., was promoted to Air Force major general.

3. In Employment. A. Philip Randolph, the black labor leader who headed the Brotherhood of Sleeping Car Porters, planned a mass march of blacks in Washington in 1941 to protest defense plant discrimination against hiring black workers. To ward off such a demonstration and to combat hiring discrimination, President Franklin D. Roosevelt established a temporary *Fair Employment Practices Committee* (FEPC). It sought to prevent discrimination by defense industries against workers because of "race, creed, color, or national origin." From 1941 to 1945 the number of black workers in war plants quadrupled, and many blacks advanced to more skilled and better paying jobs.

GAINS SINCE WORLD WAR II

1. State Antidiscrimination Laws. In 1945 New York State passed the first law against discrimination in employment, the *Ives-Quinn Act*. Subsequently, New York State prohibited discrimination in housing and places of public accommodation and in admission to educational institutions. The *New York State Division of Human Rights* investigates complaints of discriminatory practices and tries to end discrimination by persuasion, conciliation, mediation, and, if necessary, by orders enforceable in state courts.

Today about 30 states in the North and West have fair employment practices laws. About ten states have laws requiring fair practices in the rental and sale of housing units. Also a number of cities have local antidiscrimination ordinances.

2. Private Efforts Against Discrimination. Many corporations have sought qualified blacks for skilled factory, clerical, and managerial positions. They have also offered blacks on-the-job training. Industrial unions have extended membership to blacks. Major league baseball dropped its unwritten color bar in 1947 and admitted the first black ballplayer, *Jackie Robinson*. After his brilliant baseball career ended, Robinson was employed by a fast-service restaurant chain, becoming one of the first blacks to attain a managerial position. Movie producers have stopped portraying blacks as happy-go-lucky stereotypes and have started presenting them as well-rounded human beings with their fair share of human strengths and weaknesses. Advertising agencies have begun including blacks in their magazine and television displays. Insurance companies have pledged to invest funds to stimulate building projects and new businesses in inner-city areas.

3. **Federal Efforts on Civil Rights.** President Truman prohibited discrimination in federal employment, began the integration of servicemen in the armed forces, and repeatedly—but unsuccessfully—requested that Congress enact civil rights legislation. Truman's actions elevated civil rights into a major national issue.

Thereafter, all three branches of the federal government became increasingly involved in civil rights matters—as discussed in the following pages.

PROBLEM OF SEGREGATION IN EDUCATION

1. **Background.** Because the Fourteenth Amendment guarantees all citizens "equal protection of the laws," the constitutionality of state and local segregation laws has often been challenged before the Supreme Court. In 1896, in *Plessy vs. Ferguson*, which involved a Louisiana law segregating railroad passengers, the Supreme Court declared Constitutional state laws giving Negroes *separate but equal* facilities. Thus fortified, the South pressed forward its program of segregation. However, facilities for blacks were almost always inferior to those for whites. In education black schools were poorly constructed and equipped and black teachers and administrators were poorly paid.

2. **The Supreme Court Establishes a New Doctrine That "Separate Educational Facilities Are Inherently Unequal" (1954)**

a. Supreme Court Decision. In 1954, in *Brown vs. Board of Education of Topeka* (Kansas), the Supreme Court unanimously decided that segregation of black children in public schools violates the Fourteenth Amendment. Chief Justice *Earl Warren* pointed out that (1) education plays a vital role in training children for citizenship, employment, and use of leisure, (2) separating black children from others solely on the basis of race "generates a feeling of inferiority" that may affect them "in a way unlikely ever to be undone," and (3) therefore, "separate educational facilities are inherently unequal."

In 1955 the Supreme Court empowered federal district courts to supervise plans of state and local authorities for achieving school desegregation with "all deliberate speed."

b. Support for the Decision. In the North the Supreme Court decision was praised for upholding American democratic beliefs in human dignity and equality of opportunity. In the South it was (1) accepted by a minority of whites, who urged obedience to the law, (2) praised by many religious leaders, who condemned segregation as morally wrong, and (3) hailed by blacks, who felt that segregation meant second-class citizenship.

c. Opposition to the Decision. (1) *Southern White Groups.* The White Citizens Councils and the Ku Klux Klan defended segregation as part of the Southern way of life. These groups used publicity, economic pressure, threats, and sometimes violence against advocates of integration. (2) *Southern State Legislatures.* Several legislatures approved *interposition resolutions*, defying the desegregation decision on the ground that the federal government has no Constitutional power over education. Some Southern legislatures also appropriated funds for private school systems, thus permitting localities to shut down public schools. Such techniques for evading the Supreme Court decision also were held unconstitutional.

3. Crisis in Little Rock. In 1957 Governor *Orval Faubus* used the Arkansas National Guard to prevent nine black children from entering an all-white school in Little Rock. After a meeting with President Eisenhower, Faubus obeyed a court order to withdraw the National Guard. When a mob kept the black children from the school, Eisenhower ordered United States army units to Little Rock to restore order. Under federal protection the nine blacks attended the previously all-white high school.

4. Developments on the Educational Front in the South

   a. Substantial Acceptance. Six states with small black populations Delaware, Kentucky, Maryland, Missouri, Oklahoma, and West Virginia— faced little public opposition to desegregation. The District of Columbia, with its black majority, also achieved desegregation.

   b. Token Acceptance. The 11 states of the former Confederacy resisted the Supreme Court decision. In 1963–1964 only 2 percent of their black students attended desegregated schools. In the Deep South states, where the black population is largest, white opposition to integration was strongest.

   c. Federal Pressure for Integration. The 1964 *Civil Rights Act* allowed the federal government to deny financial aid to state programs practicing discrimination. The 1965 *Elementary and Secondary Education Act* authorized federal funds for distribution to local school districts. Thereupon, the United States *Office of Education,* in the Department of Health, Education, and Welfare, required Southern school districts desiring federal aid to satisfy certain "guidelines." They were required to submit and begin implementing plans for the desegregation of school faculties and pupils. In 1969 the Supreme Court, now under its new Chief Justice, *Warren Burger,* unanimously held that all districts must "terminate dual school systems at once."

   d. Further Integration in the South. For the 1970–1971 school year, black enrollment in integrated schools in the 11 states of the former Confederacy had risen from 2 percent (1963–1964) to 39 percent. For the 1971–1972 school year, the Nixon administration claimed that over 90 percent of Southern black children were attending desegregated schools. Critics claimed that this figure reflected only the end of dual school systems, whereas many black children were still segregated within unitary school systems and only 38 percent were actually integrated. Meanwhile over 400,000, or almost 7 percent, of Southern white students left the public schools for makeshift, underfinanced, understaffed, underequipped, but all-white private schools.

5. Developments on the Educational Front in the North

   a. Toward School Integration. Most Northern cities contain black ghettos and these cause school segregation not by law but in fact. Public schools in black areas have tended to be more crowded and to have poorer facilities than schools in white areas. Since 1963 several Northern communities have experienced mass demonstrations, picket lines, and school boycotts by black groups protesting such de facto school segregation. Many school boards thereupon took steps to integrate "fringe area" schools and to permit open enrollment by black students in underpopulated white schools.

These steps failed to satisfy some civil rights groups. They demanded that all schools achieve racial balance, by mass busing of both black and white pupils if necessary. As some black groups insisted upon total integration, some white parents formed groups to defend the *neighborhood school* policy.

b. Toward "Quality Education." Many school boards made efforts to improve facilities in ghetto schools and provide "quality education." They assigned additional teachers, reduced class sizes, scheduled special classes, and made available more textbooks and other instructional materials.

c. Toward School Decentralization. Some civil rights groups, realizing that substantial integration of school systems in large cities would take many years, have demanded school decentralization. These groups seek to control the de facto segregated schools of the ghettos. They wish to replace the centralized school administration, which they claim is bureaucratic and dominated by whites, with local school boards. They argue that black community school boards could best provide for the education of black children.

Opponents of decentralization fear that local control would result in a lowering of educational standards. Furthermore, they argue, it might enable extremist groups to dominate ghetto schools, to harass the teaching staff, and to introduce questionable courses of study.

6. The Busing Issue. In 1971, in *Swann vs. Board of Education of Charlotte-Mecklenburg* (North Carolina), the Supreme Court unanimously upheld the busing of children as a proper means of overcoming deliberate Southern state-imposed school segregation. Thereafter lower federal courts ordered extensive busing to overcome *de jure* school racial imbalance in the South and also *de facto* imbalance in cities of the Midwest and the Far West. These latter busing orders aroused much public resentment.

In 1974 Congress approved a provision that limited busing. Except where necessary to protect the Constitutional rights of minority group children, the law barred federal courts from ordering busing beyond the school closest or next closest to the child's home. Also in 1974 the Supreme Court, in *Milliken vs. Bradley*, decided by 5 to 4 that children should not be bused across school district lines. The decision prohibited the cross-busing of black children in the urban Detroit school district with white children in the suburban Detroit school districts. The Court majority held that, unless the districts involved had deliberately practiced discrimination, the Constitution did not require interdistrict busing.

In 1979 in cases involving two Northern cities (Columbus and Dayton, Ohio), the Supreme Court found that the school boards had deliberately pursued segregationist policies in the past and ordered the school boards to "eliminate the effects of past discrimination" by undertaking extensive busing programs. These decisions were expected to spur further efforts for busing to achieve school desegregation in Northern and Western cities.

7. Affirmative Action in Education: The Bakke Case—1978. The 1964 Civil Rights Act prohibited discrimination based on race by any educational institution receiving federal funds. Citing this provision, the Office of Education urged college and university admissions offices to redress past discrimination by programs that would benefit minority groups—programs known as *affirmative* *action.* At the Davis Medical School of the University of California, the admissions office set aside 16 out of 100 positions in the freshman class for members of minority groups—blacks, Chicanos, and Asians.

Allan Bakke, a white engineer who had served with the Marines in Vietnam, determined to become a doctor. He twice applied to the Davis Medical School and was twice rejected—although his medical aptitude test scores were higher than those of some minority group applicants who gained acceptance. Bakke felt that he was a victim of the Davis admissions program of minority *quotas* and *reverse discrimination.* He took legal action, claiming that he was being denied his Constitutional rights under the "equal protection" clause of the Fourteenth Amendment and was being subjected to racial discrimination, for being white, in violation of the 1964 Civil Rights Act.

In 1978, the Supreme Court, by a 5-to-4 vote, handed down a complex decision of two major parts: *(a)* Bakke must be admitted to the Davis Medical School, and the Davis affirmative action program with its set quota for minority students is invalid because it is biased against nonminority applicants. (This part of the decision appealed to persons opposed to quotas and in favor of merit selection of applicants.) *(b)* Race and ethnic origins may be considered as one of many factors in establishing programs of college admissions. (This part of the decision appealed to persons who supported affirmative action programs to assist the victims of past discrimination.)

Many observers held that the Supreme Court decision was ambiguous and confusing, that most affirmative action programs (in education and employment) would continue as is or as revised, and that further lawsuits would be brought to challenge affirmative action programs.

(For affirmative action in employment, check the Index for the Weber Case.)

CIVIL RIGHTS PROBLEMS IN VOTING, EMPLOYMENT, AND PLACES OF PUBLIC ACCOMMODATION

1. **Two Civil Rights Acts,** in 1957 and 1960, spurred federal efforts on behalf of citizens denied the right to vote. To protect voting rights, these acts required court procedures, which proved to be cumbersome and time-consuming.

These two laws helped increase the number of black voters, but slowly. Civil rights leaders demanded further laws against discrimination.

2. **Continuing Struggle for Civil Rights**

   a. Nonviolent Protests by Blacks. In 1955–1956 in Montgomery, Alabama, blacks boycotted the city's bus system for almost a year before the buses were desegregated. From 1960 to 1963 Southern black "sit-ins" at "for whites only" lunch counters and "ride-ins" on segregated buses furthered desegregation.

   b. March on Washington. In 1963 some 200,000 blacks and whites demanded new civil rights legislation by participating in an orderly and peaceful "March on Washington." They heard the Reverend Martin Luther King, head of the Southern Christian Leadership Conference, cry out eloquently, "I have a dream" of equality, of brotherhood, and of freedom and justice.

   c. Violence Against Blacks and Civil Rights Workers. Although black leaders stressed nonviolence, the surge of demonstrations aroused violence by white segregationists. In the South black demonstrators were subjected to strong-arm tactics by police: clubbings, fire hoses, and mass arrests. Blacks also experienced threats and violence from private individuals. Blacks' houses and churches were

Martin Luther King delivers his
"I have a dream" speech.
(Pictorial Parade)

damaged by "hate bombings." Black and white civil rights workers were assaulted, and several were murdered. In the North blacks faced heckling, fistfights, and counterdemonstrations. "The fury of bigots and bullies," President Johnson said, "served to strengthen the will of the American people that justice be done." In 1964 he secured passage of a comprehensive civil rights measure.

3. Civil Rights Act of 1964. *(a) Voting.* The law prohibited election officials from applying different standards to black and white voting applicants and declared, as evidence of literacy, a sixth grade education. *(b) Public Accommodations.* The law forbade discrimination in most places of public accommodation: hotels, motels, restaurants, lunch counters, retail stores, gas stations, theatres, and sports arenas. *(c) Public Facilities.* The law prohibited discrimination in government-owned or -operated facilities such as parks, swimming pools, and libraries. *(d) Federally Assisted Programs.* The law authorized the federal government to withhold financial aid from state and local programs involving discrimination. *(e) Employment.* The law prohibited discriminatory practices by most employers, employment agencies, and labor unions. To promote voluntary compliance, the law created an *Equal Employment Opportunity Commission.*

4. The Twenty-Fourth Amendment (1964) prohibited the use of a poll tax as a requirement for voting in elections for federal officials. It affected the five southern states that still had poll taxes.

5. Voting Rights Act of 1965

a. Background. Amidst much publicity, Southern officials thwarted a Negro voter registration drive at Selma, Alabama. There, out of 15,000 eligible blacks, the number registered was only 335. Blacks thereupon marched through Alabama from Selma to Montgomery to focus the nation's attention upon Southern racial barriers to voting. The violence with which blacks and civil rights workers were treated shocked the nation. Identifying the Ku Klux Klan as a source of the violence, President Johnson denounced its members as a "hooded band of bigots" and insisted that "every American citizen must have an equal right to vote." Congress quickly enacted the *Voting Rights Act of 1965*.

b. Provisions. (1) In any state or county where less than half of the voting-age population was registered or had voted in 1964, all literacy and other qualification tests were suspended. This provision applied immediately to five Southern states and parts of two others. (2) The Attorney General was empowered to send federal examiners to any county practicing voting discrimination. These registrars were authorized to register all would-be voters who met the state's age and residency requirements. This provision replaced the time-consuming court processes required by previous laws. (3) The Attorney General was empowered to file suits challenging the constitutionality of state poll taxes. This provision affected four Southern states.

c. Developments. The Supreme Court almost unanimously held Constitutional the key provisions of the 1965 Voting Rights Act. This law, Chief Justice Warren wrote, was an appropriate means for enforcing the Fifteenth Amendment and wiping out racial discrimination in voting.

In another decision, the Supreme Court struck down Virginia's state poll tax. The court declared that any poll tax was a burden irrelevant to voting qualifications and in violation of the Fourteenth Amendment.

6. Overview: Increase of Southern Black Voters

In 1957 the proportion of eligible Southern blacks registered to vote was 25 percent. Thereafter, additional black voters enrolled. They were aided by federal voting laws, federal court decisions, drives by civil rights organizations, cooperation of some Southern registrars, and the efforts of federal examiners who set up registration offices in counties practicing discrimination. By 1972 the proportion of eligible Southern blacks registered had risen to 65 percent.

Beginning in the late 1960's, blacks increasingly were elected to legislative and local offices even in the Deep South, and white candidates increasingly appealed for black votes.

ORGANIZATIONS TO IMPROVE THE STATUS OF BLACKS: DIFFERENCES IN METHODS AND GOALS

1. Civil Rights Organizations: Lawful Efforts to Achieve Black Integration Into American Life

a. The National Association for the Advancement of Colored People (NAACP), a biracial group founded in 1909, is the largest and best known of the civil rights organizations. It has worked to put an end to lynchings, to promote school integration, and to secure laws for fair practices in employment and housing. The NAACP has employed publicity, lobbying, and legal action which achieved its greatest triumph in the 1954 Supreme Court decision against public school segregation. *Roy Wilkins*, as Executive Secretary, ably presented the NAACP viewpoint: that blacks want to live as free and equal Americans. (In 1977 Wilkins retired and was succeeded by *Benjamin L. Hooks*.)

b. The National Urban League, a biracial group founded in 1910, has assisted Negroes, who in growing numbers were leaving the rural South, to adjust especially to Northern city life. It has endeavored to better facilities for blacks in health, housing, employment, and recreation. The Urban League has utilized studies of Negro conditions, lobbying of legislators for equal-opportunity laws, and persuasion of industrial and labor leaders to open job opportunities for blacks. In charge of the league's work is its executive director, a position filled since 1971 by *Vernon Jordan*.

c. **The Southern Christian Leadership Conference (SCLC)**, founded in 1957 by a group of Southern Negro leaders, has opposed discrimination in the use of public facilities, in employment, and in voting. The leading spirit and first president of SCLC was the Reverend *Martin Luther King*. Inspired by Henry Thoreau's essay "Civil Disobedience" and by Mahatma Gandhi's use of passive resistance against British rule in India, King followed in their path. As the most effective weapon in the black struggle against racial injustice, King urged demonstrations of nonviolent resistance. King effectively used nonviolent methods many times, starting in 1955–1956 with an economic boycott that compelled Montgomery, Alabama, to desegregate the city buses. In 1964 King was awarded the Nobel Peace Prize, which he accepted as honoring all people of goodwill who supported nonviolent resistance to injustice. In 1968, however, when King went to lead a protest march for striking sanitation workers, mainly black, in Memphis, Tennessee, he was assassinated by a white man. Despite King's tragic death, the SCLC reaffirmed its belief in his philosophy of nonviolence, named his widow *Coretta King* to its board of directors, and chose as its new head King's friend and co-worker, the Reverend *Ralph D. Abernathy*. (In 1973 Abernathy resigned as SCLC president. The current head is the Reverend *Joseph E. Lowery*.)

In summary, these three groups have stood for operating within the law, employing nonviolence, and seeking black equality and integration into American society. They have supported a policy of "gradualism" in contrast with other groups, next discussed, that demand "instant" progress and thus are considered "militants."

2. The Black Muslims: A Black Nationalist Group to Achieve Black Separation.
The Black Muslims are both a religious sect and a nationalist group. Their Muslim religion teaches them to practice hard work, maintain close family bonds, observe personal habits of clean living, and especially to refrain from alcohol, tobacco, and drugs. They reject Christianity as the "white man's religion" and reject their Americanized names as remnants of their enslavement. They held that the white man is evil and not to be trusted and therefore sought complete separation from the white world. In some American cities, the Black Muslims maintain their own schools and temples (mosques), and have become an economic force in the black community by owning retail businesses and small manufacturing concerns. The Black Muslims demanded that, as long-overdue "back wages," a considerable portion of the United States be turned over to them for creation of a separate black state. Although the Black Muslims claimed to oppose violence, they were uncompromisingly militant and maintained a trained paramilitary corps, the *Fruit of Islam*.

Elijah Muhammad, the Black Muslim founder, was born in the South and at an early age moved to the Midwest. In 1929 he claimed to have met "Allah on earth" and thereafter called himself "Allah's messenger." Muhammad attracted a considerable following. (He died in 1975 and his place as Black Muslim head was taken by his son *Wallace Muhammad*.)

Malcolm X, who became a Black Muslim while serving a jail sentence for burglary, was for many years Elijah Muhammad's top aide. His *Autobiography of Malcolm X* provides a fascinating view of his life and ideas. In 1963 Malcolm X and Elijah Muhammad had a falling-out and Malcolm X formed his own splinter group. Assassinated in 1965 by three Black Muslim gunmen, Malcolm X has become an heroic symbol for black militants.

In the mid-1970's, the Black Muslims eased their antiwhite stand and turned away from militancy.

3. The Black Panthers: A Revolutionary Organization to Overthrow the Existing System and Achieve Black Liberation. Organized in 1966 in Oakland, California, the Black Panther party stated its purpose: to protect the ghetto blacks against "police harassment." Claiming to be against violence but for "self-defense," the Black Panthers affected a paramilitary stance, wearing similar attire and prominently displaying guns. They dismissed the question of black integration or separation as irrelevant; instead they called for a revolutionary struggle of all oppressed peoples, black and white, to overthrow the existing American system, which they labeled as "racist, fascist, and imperialist." They predicted a successful revolution and the establishment of a "democratic socialist society" free of racism and controlled by the people. By conducting community programs such as antidrug clinics and children's breakfasts, the Black Panthers spread their ideas and influence among black ghetto inhabitants.

Many times the Black Panthers came into conflict with the law. This statement applies both to ordinary members and to party leaders, especially minister of information *Eldridge Cleaver*. While in prison for assault, Cleaver wrote a series of personal and political articles published as *Soul on Ice*. Released on parole, Cleaver later was ordered rejailed as a parole violator, but he fled the United States to refuge in leftist nations. (In 1975, having abandoned his radical views, Cleaver voluntarily returned to face charges in the United States.)

In the 1970's, the Black Panthers moderated their radicalism and placed greater emphasis upon community programs and political action.

RECENT DEVELOPMENTS IN THE BLACK CIVIL RIGHTS MOVEMENT

1. Unfinished Business: Reasons for Continued Discontent. Despite some improvement in their conditions, many blacks remain discontented. They assert that not enough is being done to dispel white-majority racial prejudice: blacks are frustrated by white *ethnocentrism,* or the emotional attitude that whites are superior to black people; blacks also are frustrated by white *xenophobia,* or the fear of black people as strange and different. Blacks also complain that communities are making slow progress in integrating schools and in enrolling black voters. Finally, they protest that in every phase of life blacks are in an inferior position to whites. *(a) Education.* Proportionately fewer black than white students gain high school and college educations. *(b) Jobs and Wages.* Blacks are concentrated in low-wage occupations. A disproportionately large number of blacks work as unskilled laborers and service workers. *(c) Unemployment.* Blacks suffer twice the unemployment rate of white workers. *(d) Housing.* Many blacks are confined to slum areas and have no access to decent housing in better neighborhoods. *(e) Health.* Blacks have an average life expectancy of 64 years as compared to 71 years for whites.

2. Destructive Protest in Black Ghettos (1964–1967). "Long hot summers" in Northern and Western cities witnessed bloody and destructive riots. The riots expressed the blacks' discontent with their status. The most violent riots came in the Harlem section of New York, in the Watts section of Los Angeles, in the Central Ward of Newark, and in Detroit. Mobs wantonly destroyed property —belonging to blacks as well as to whites—and maintained a reign of terror leading to many injuries and deaths. Several cities called upon National Guardsmen to restore law and order. The riots perturbed many Americans who supported the civil rights movement but who expected blacks to behave responsibly. President Johnson cautioned blacks that violence and discord would retard the movement for social justice. Also, President Johnson appointed an Advisory Commission on Civil Disorders.

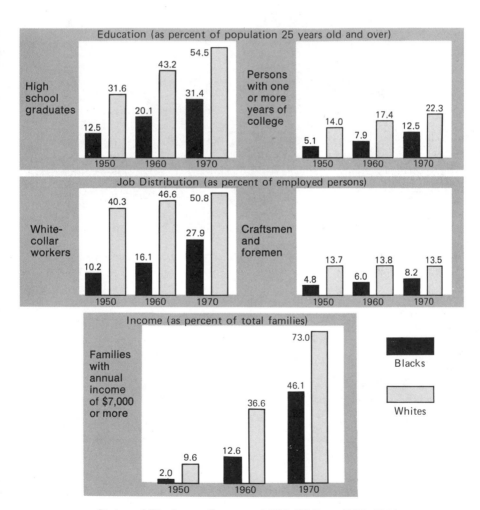

Status of Blacks as Compared With Whites, 1950–1970

3. Report of the Kerner Commission (1968). Governor *Otto Kerner* of Illinois was chairman of the *Advisory Commission on Civil Disorders*. Its 11 members were drawn from major groups in American life: Democrats and Republicans, labor and industry, North and South, white and black. Its two black members were Roy Wilkins, head of the NAACP, and Edward Brooke, Senator from Massachusetts. In 1968 the commission issued a unanimous report.

a. General Conclusions. "Our nation is moving toward two societies, one black, one white—separate and unequal." This trend threatens our "basic democratic values."

b. Riot Findings. The commission found that the riots were not the result of an organized conspiracy, although it acknowledged that calls for violence by militant black leaders contributed to a climate conducive to rioting. The commission placed the chief blame for the urban riots on conditions resulting from "white racism." This racism, the commission wrote, leads to discrimination in employment, education, and housing, and it implants in many blacks a sense of degradation, misery, and hopelessness.

c. Goals. The commission opposed racial separatism as leading to a permanently inferior status for blacks and a permanently divided country. It favored immediate enrichment of ghetto life and long-range integration of blacks into society outside the ghetto.

d. Recommendations. (1) Creation of additional jobs, half by governments and half by private industries. (2) On-the-job training, partly subsidized by the federal government, for the chronically, or "hard-core" unemployed. (3) Sharply increased efforts to eliminate de facto school segregation and to improve schools serving disadvantaged children. (4) Improvement of the public welfare system through massive federal financial aid making possible increased payments to the needy and through measures designed to keep black families together. (5) Construction of additional housing for low- and moderate-income families.

e. Reactions to the Report. Civil rights leaders approved the report as a strong document and hailed its conclusion that the riots ought to be blamed on "white racism." Critics generally did not reject the entire report but condemned it for (1) not sufficiently pointing out black progress since World War II, (2) excusing black participants of any blame for the riots, and (3) raising black expectations by recommendations that cannot be implemented because they require many billions of dollars not now available.

4. Civil Rights Act of 1968

a. Background. Despite President Johnson's urging, Congress for two years failed to pass a bill outlawing discrimination in the rental and sale of housing. Southern Congressmen, still opposed to civil rights legislation, received support from some Northern Congressmen, whose constituents feared that the influx of blacks into a white neighborhood would lower property values and destroy the character of the community.

In early 1968 the Senate narrowly voted cloture to prevent any filibuster, easily approved an "open housing" bill, and sent it to the House where opponents were able to delay its consideration.

b. Passage of the Civil Rights Bill. While the bill was stalled, Martin Luther

King, in Memphis, Tennessee, was assassinated by a white man. His death, mourned by both whites and blacks, created an emotional atmosphere that spurred quick House approval of the open housing bill. President Johnson hailed the bill as evidence that "America does move forward."

c. Provisions. (1) The law bars discrimination in the rental and sale of 80 percent of the nation's housing. (2) The law provides stiff penalties for persons guilty of intimidating or injuring civil rights workers. (3) It provides penalties for persons who travel from one state to another with intent to incite a riot and for persons who provide firearms meant for use in a riot.

5. Voting Rights Acts of 1970 and 1975. These laws together extended to 1982 the provisions of the 1965 act protecting Southern black voters. The 1970 law also *(a)* suspended all literacy tests as a voting qualification, and *(b)* set a 30-day residency requirement for voting in Presidential elections. The 1975 law also required—in voting districts where less than half of the voting-age population had registered or voted in 1972 and where more than 5 percent belong to a single language minority—that election materials be printed, in addition to English, in the minority language.

6. Affirmative Action in Employment: The Weber Case—1979. The Kaiser Corporation and the United Steel Workers Union agreed to establish a voluntary affirmative action plan. This voluntary plan called for special programs to train workers for skilled craft jobs, available to blacks and whites on a 50-50 basis. Brian Weber, a white, worked at the Kaiser plant in Louisiana where the training program had 13 openings. Weber lacked sufficient seniority to secure one of the six places reserved for whites, but he had more seniority than two of the blacks accepted for the program. Weber brought suit charging "reverse discrimination"

There's a long, long trail a-winding—(*Shanks in the Buffalo Evening News*)

in violation of the 1964 Civil Rights Act, which prohibits racial discrimination by employers and unions.

The Supreme Court, by a 5-to-2 vote, decided against Weber and held that the Kaiser plan—with its numerical quota giving special preference to black workers—was legal. The Court majority claimed that the Kaiser plan was within the spirit of the 1964 Civil Rights Act—"to improve the lot of those who had been excluded from the American dream for so long." The Court minority deplored the decision as a misreading of the plain language of the 1964 Civil Rights Act.

Civil rights groups hailed the Weber decision as a go-ahead signal for extensive affirmative action programs. The Supreme Court majority, however, had emphasized that its decision was a narrow one—applying only to a voluntary plan adopted by private parties and not involving any government action. Observers predicted that the Supreme Court would be called upon to decide further cases involving affirmative action programs.

"NEGRO" OR "BLACK" OR "AFRO-AMERICAN" REVOLUTION

1. Meaning. The three terms above have been used interchangeably to encompass the entire post-World War II civil rights movement and the improvement in the status of black people in America.

2. Signs of Progress. Black problems were brought to the attention of the public and became a national issue. Blacks were emboldened to speak up and act in their own behalf. As one result, Southern blacks made considerable progress in exercising their right to vote. Progress also was made in desegregating public schools and places of public accommodation, and in gaining for blacks union membership and better employment opportunities. Many blacks entered into the middle class and a few into the upper class. Most significantly, the civil rights movement convinced most Americans that discrimination is morally wrong.

3. Criticisms and Responses. Some whites have opposed, in part or in whole, the black civil rights movement. In the South many whites feel that black aspirations threaten the traditional Southern way of life. In the North some whites in cities and suburbs feel that black aspirations threaten their jobs and neighborhoods. This hostile reaction among whites, evidenced by demonstrations against civil rights activities and by votes against candidates favoring civil rights, has been called the "white backlash."

Criticisms of the "Black Revolution" together with the responses of its defenders include the following:

a. Criticism. Blacks are demanding too much too soon. They have made considerable gains since World War II. Now, instead of making additional demands, they should learn to use their gains, extend them to all blacks, and give the white community time to adjust to new conditions.

a. Response. Blacks were guaranteed their freedom and their political and civil rights by the Reconstruction Amendments. They have waited over 100 years for these guarantees to be honored. Blacks demand no more than equality with whites and will accept no less.

b. Criticism. Blacks are not making sufficient efforts to lift themselves out of poverty and ghetto life. They demand that the government do for them what they should be doing for themselves. After all, white immigrants faced similar handicaps. But white immigrants worked hard and escaped from the ghetto by their own efforts.

b. Response. Blacks are seeking to improve themselves, but they are deliberately kept down by discrimination, especially in employment and housing. Therefore, they need government help to outlaw discrimination. Also, when the white immigrants arrived, industry needed their unskilled labor; but when blacks came to the cities, industry had become more mechanized and had few jobs for unskilled workers.

c. Criticism. Blacks have rioted in our cities, destroyed property, looted stores, started fires, battled the police, caused injuries and deaths, and fomented disrespect for authority. They must not be permitted to destroy "law and order."

c. Response. Blacks have rioted out of a sense of misery and frustration. They had appealed peacefully to the "white power structure" for help in overcoming their problems—but to little avail. "Law and order" should mean not repression but equality and opportunity.

SOME OUTSTANDING BLACK CONTRIBUTIONS TO AMERICAN LIFE

1. In Government Service. As blacks moved heavily into Northern cities, starting in the World War I era, they began to exert influence upon Northern politics. In recent years blacks have been elected to the office of mayor, to lesser local posts, to state legislatures, and to the United States Congress. In 1966 *Edward Brooke* of Massachusetts was elected to the United States Senate, the first black Senator since Reconstruction days. In 1968 *Shirley Chisholm,* from Brooklyn's Bedford-Stuyvesant black ghetto district, was elected to the House of Representatives. She was the first black woman ever to be a member of Congress.

Blacks have also been appointed to high positions in the federal government. *Thurgood Marshall,* the NAACP lawyer who won the Supreme Court decision on school desegregation in 1954, later became the first black appointed as a Supreme Court Justice. *Carl T. Rowan* served as United States ambassador to Finland and later headed the United States Information Agency. *Andrew F. Brimmer,* an economist, was the first black member of the Federal Reserve Board. *Robert Weaver,* first head of the Department of Housing and Urban Development, was the first black Cabinet member.

In the international field, *Ralph Bunche* served the United Nations as mediator of the 1949 Arab-Israeli dispute and as Undersecretary for Special Political Affairs.

2. In the Academic World. In recent years black scholars have filled positions on college and university faculties. Among them have been the mathematician *David Blackwell,* the psychologist *Kenneth Clark,* and the historian *John Hope Franklin.* In 1968 Robert Weaver, the first black Cabinet member, was named president of the Bernard Baruch College, a liberal arts school in New York City.

3. In Sports. Competing on the basis of equality with other athletes, blacks have demonstrated outstanding ability and have won many awards and great public acclaim. In the 1930's, two black athletes helped refute the Nazi racist doctrine that Germans were a master race superior to all other peoples. In 1936 at the

Olympic Games held in Berlin, *Jesse Owens* set new world records in winning three track events. In spite of these achievements, Owens was publicly snubbed by the Nazi dictator, Adolf Hitler. In 1938 *Joe Louis* defended his boxing title as world heavyweight champion by a first-round knockout of a German challenger.

Other famous black athletes include the following: *Jimmy Brown*—football star; *Wilt Chamberlain*—basketball star; *Althea Gibson*—women's international tennis champion; *Wilma Rudolph*—track star; *Willie Mays* and *Henry "Hank" Aaron*—baseball stars.

4. In the Performing Arts. Blacks have enriched American music. *W. C. Handy*, a composer, won acclaim for his "St. Louis Blues." *Marian Anderson*, world-famed for the beauty of her voice, was a singer of spirituals and operatic arias. *Leontyne Price* has sung in the world's great concert halls and opera houses. Other well-known Negroes in music have included *Louis Armstrong* and *Duke Ellington*—jazz musicians; *Harry Belafonte*—folk ballad singer; *Ella Fitzgerald, Lena Horne,* and *Leslie Uggams*—singers of popular music.

In the movies, *Sidney Poitier* is an established star and a leading box-office attraction. In 1964 Poitier received the highly prized Academy Award ("Oscar") as best actor. In television *Diahann Carroll, Bill Cosby, Sammy Davis,* and *Flip Wilson* have all provided entertainment for millions of Americans.

5. In Literature. In the post-Reconstruction era, *Paul Laurence Dunbar*, the son of former slaves, wrote dialect poems describing Negro life. In more recent times, there has been a great outpouring of works by black writers. *Richard Wright* was the author of *Native Son*, a novel portraying black urban life, and *Black Boy*, an autobiographical work about his Southern childhood. *James Baldwin*, essayist, playwright, and novelist, wrote *The Fire Next Time*, an essay on the American black. Other well-known blacks in the field of literature include *Gwendolyn Brooks*—poet and novelist, and first black to win the Pulitzer Prize for poetry; *Countee Cullen*—lyric poet; *Langston Hughes*—poet, novelist, and short story writer; *Ralph Ellison*—who drew upon personal experience for his novel *Invisible Man*.

6. In Science and Invention. *Benjamin Banneker*, a free Negro born in colonial Maryland, became an accomplished mathematician and astronomer. For many years, he published an almanac, which was highly praised by Thomas Jefferson. Banneker also worked as a surveyor with Pierre L'Enfant in designing the city of Washington, D.C. *Jan E. Matzeliger*, who came to the United States from South America, substantially decreased the cost of manufacturing shoes by his invention in 1883 of a shoe lasting machine. *Daniel Hale Williams*, a surgeon, did pioneer work in the 1890's in heart operations. *George Washington Carver*, who in 1896 joined the staff of Tuskegee Institute, was a botanist and chemist. To end the dependence of Southern Negro farmers on the cotton crop, Carver studied and discovered many commercial uses for the peanut. More recently, *Percy L. Julian*, a chemist and industrialist, did research on hormones and other aspects of organic chemistry. *Charles R. Drew*, a surgeon, devised procedures for the preservation of blood plasma. During World War II, he directed the American Red Cross blood program in New York City.

7. In the Economic World. About 2 million blacks are members of labor unions, and blacks have occupied various positions of leadership in the labor movement.

Cleveland Robinson was president of the Afro-American Labor Council, established to protect the interests of black unionists. *A. Philip Randolph* was head of the Brotherhood of Sleeping Car Porters and Vice President of the AFL-CIO.

Also, blacks are increasingly filling important executive and technical posts with large corporations and are entering the professions, becoming doctors, dentists, lawyers, and architects. In addition many blacks have gone into business for themselves in such fields as insurance, banking, and real estate. Generally black businessmen specialize in serving the black community, and a number have become affluent. Several hundred blacks have amassed fortunes in the range of $250,000 to $500,000; about 35 are millionaires. *John H. Johnson*, a highly successful black businessman, is the publisher and editor of *Black World, Ebony, Tan,* and *Jet*—magazines that present topics of interest to black readers. Johnson is also on the board of directors of several financial institutions and has represented the United States government in its dealings with the new African nations.

MULTIPLE-CHOICE QUESTIONS

1. "If you put a chain around the neck of a slave, the other end fastens itself around your own." This statement refers to the idea that   (1) absentee ownership of plantations was not wise   (2) slavery was an economically costly institution   (3) slavery degraded both master and slave   (4) slavery should accompany settlers going West.
2. Which is the *most* valid statement concerning slavery in 19th-century United States?   (1) Although slaves deeply resented their status, they did not openly protest.   (2) There were individual protests and collective rebellions by slaves.   (3) Many laws were enacted to protect the slaves from cruel treatment.   (4) Most slaves accepted their status and did not want to obtain their freedom.
3. Which was a result of the other three?   (1) strong Southern support of slavery   (2) invention of the cotton gin   (3) Industrial Revolution in England   (4) abundant supply of good land in this country
4. The territorial expansion of the United States before the Civil War became a matter for furious political debate because   (1) the South would send no troops to acquire free territory   (2) Northerners were opposed to any expansion   (3) additional states would tend to upset the sectional balance in the Senate   (4) no new territory could be admitted until the Texas controversy was settled.
5. The significance of the Dred Scott decision was that   (1) Congress could not prohibit slavery in the territories   (2) only Congress could prohibit slavery in any part of the United States   (3) the people of a territory could, by popular sovereignty, outlaw slavery   (4) the Emancipation Proclamation was illegal.
6. The *chief* reason for the opposition of the South to the election of Abraham Lincoln in 1860 was his   (1) support for the development of industry   (2) demand for the immediate abolition of slavery   (3) hostility to the extension of slavery   (4) insistence on equal education for Negroes and whites.
7. Which one of the following statements is *most* valid?   (1) The evils of slavery have been greatly exaggerated.   (2) Prior to the 1960's, cooperation between blacks and whites was almost totally lacking.   (3) The Reconstruction Era provided many illustrations of black progress and achievement.   (4) The Northwest Ordinance prohibited slavery in Missouri.
8. After the Civil War, which was *not* a method used to keep Negroes from voting?   (1) Fifteenth Amendment   (2) poll tax   (3) literacy test   (4) activities of the Ku Klux Klan

9. The first major surge of Negro migration to Northern and Western cities took place during (1) the Civil War (2) Reconstruction (3) the New Deal (4) World War I.
10. The first post-World War II President who focused the nation's attention upon the problem of civil rights for blacks was (1) Truman (2) Franklin D. Roosevelt (3) Kennedy (4) Eisenhower.
11. In 1954 the Supreme Court handed down its decision in the case of *Brown vs. Board of Education of Topeka*. This decision (1) reversed the "separate but equal" doctrine (2) reaffirmed the "separate but equal" doctrine (3) left questions of segregation up to the states (4) gave the federal government control over all private schools.
12. On which part of the federal Constitution did the United States Supreme Court base its 1954 decision concerning desegregation of the public schools? (1) "general welfare" clause (2) Congressional power to regulate interstate commerce (3) "necessary and proper" clause (4) "equal protection of the laws" clause of the 14th Amendment.
13. After 1964, which factor *most* sped integration in public schools in the Deep South? (1) Southern white opinion shifted in favor of integration. (2) Southern blacks participated in demonstrations. (3) Southern school districts complied with Office of Education "guidelines" in order to qualify for federal funds. (4) Most Southern legislators supported school integration to gain black votes.
14. The problem of de facto segregation faces many large city school districts *primarily* because (1) specific local laws forbid integrated schools (2) whites are a minority group in most cities (3) integrated schools are opposed by many community groups (4) segregated schools have resulted from housing patterns.
15. Since the Civil Rights Act of 1964, a motel owner may legally deny a black person's request for a room if (1) there is a local "Jim Crow" ordinance (2) the motel is not directly engaged in interstate commerce (3) the black person is not an American citizen (4) there are no vacancies.
16. Which way of protecting black voters was *first* provided in the Voting Rights Act of 1965? (1) the suspension of literacy tests in certain states (2) court injunctions to prevent unfair voting practices (3) reduction of the number of Representatives of a state that limits black voting (4) use of federal troops on election day
17. The surge of the civil rights movement following 1945 *best* illustrates the idea that (1) the most effective leadership comes from state legislators (2) laws are more effective when backed by constructive action of individuals and organizations (3) militancy is the result of Communist conspiracies (4) the courts will not become involved in social issues.
18. In the civil rights movement, Martin Luther King was *most* closely identified with (1) practicing nonviolent direct action (2) undermining the NAACP (3) investigating the "black power" movement (4) demanding creation of a federal Civil Rights Commission.
19. The existence of such groups as the Ku Klux Klan and the Black Panthers clearly shows that (1) some groups feel compelled to resort to extremism in pursuit of goals (2) constitutions do not generally support the principle of equal rights (3) most radical groups are founded by aliens (4) radical groups have found widespread public acceptance.
20. James Baldwin, the black author, has stated that an Afro-American has "a feeling of no past, no present, and no future." This statement is *best* interpreted to mean that in American society black people feel that they have been denied (1) a sense of identity (2) equal economic opportunity (3) political equality (4) the right to protest.
21. Which is the *most* valid statement regarding the post-World War II civil rights movement? (1) Most black leaders advocated similar methods for reaching their

goals. (2) The civil rights movement accomplished very little. (3) Black militancy inspired other minority groups to organize and to strive for equal rights. (4) The civil rights movement concentrated on political institutions but ignored economic institutions.

MATCHING QUESTIONS

Column A	*Column B*
1. Founder of Tuskegee Institute	a. A. Philip Randolph
2. Leader of raid at Harper's Ferry	b. Nat Turner
3. Editor of *The Liberator*	c. Abraham Lincoln
4. Negro leader of slave insurrection	d. Booker T. Washington
5. Advocate of a "Back to Africa" movement	e. Harriet Beecher Stowe
6. Author of *An American Dilemma*	f. John Brown
7. Labor union and civil rights leader	g. Benjamin O. Davis
8. Organizer of the NAACP	h. Frederick Douglass
9. Negro editor of abolitionist newspaper	i. William Lloyd Garrison
10. Author of *Uncle Tom's Cabin*	j. Marcus Garvey
	k. Gunnar Myrdal
	l. William E.B. DuBois
	m. Harriet Tubman

DISCUSSION ANALYSIS QUESTIONS

Base your answers to the following questions on the quotations from the writings of Afro-American Authors *A, B, C,* and *D* and on your knowledge of American studies.

Author A: "The Negro must have a country, and a nation of his own. . . . Don't encourage them to believe that they will become social equals and leaders of the whites in America, without first on their own account proving to the world that they are capable of evolving a civilization of their own."

Author B: "Our greatest danger is that, in the great leap from slavery to freedom, we may overlook the fact that the masses of us are to live by the production of our hands and fail to keep in mind that we shall prosper in proportion as we learn to dignify and glorify common labor and put brains and skill into the common occupations of life."

Author C: "We went in for agitation. We pushed our way into the courts. We demanded the right to vote. We urged and pushed our children into college. We encouraged Negro art and literature. We studied African history and in season and out of season we declared that the colored races were destined at least to share in the heritage of the earth."

Author D: "Many white men fear retaliation. The job of the Negro is to show them that they have nothing to fear, that the Negro understands and forgives and is ready to forget the past. He must convince the white man that all he seeks is justice, for both himself and the white man."

1. Which author believes that the first step in the black man's economic advancement must be similar to that taken by immigrant groups who came to the United States in the 19th century? (1) *A* (2) *B* (3) *C* (4) *D*
2. Which author *most* clearly assumes that under present conditions the status of the blacks in the United States will *not* improve? (1) *A* (2) *B* (3) *C* (4) *D*
3. Twentieth-century black nationalist leaders would probably agree *most* strongly with the statements of Authors (1) *A* and *B* (2) *A* and *C* (3) *B* and *D* (4) *C* and *D.*
4. Which measure would a person sharing the views of Author *B* probably consider *least* important in gaining civil rights for blacks today? (1) integration of public high

schools, as prescribed by the Supreme Court   (2) training of youth for some occupational skill, such as the Job Corps program   (3) increasing job opportunities in the
skilled trades   (4) scholarships and grants for use in technical and agricultural colleges
5. Which *best* explains why there are differences among the authors regarding the
problem of how to gain equal rights?   (1) Only better-educated black leaders have
attempted to solve the problem.   (2) Improvements in transportation have caused the
development of highly individual approaches to the problem.   (3) Third parties have
consistently supported the advancement of equal rights.   (4) Black leaders have
developed varied approaches to meet changing social and economic conditions.

ESSAY QUESTIONS

1. For more than 100 years the issue of civil rights has frequently played a significant role
in the United States. Describe *two* ways in which *each* of the following has affected the
cause of civil rights: (*a*) Presidents (*b*) Congress (*c*) the Supreme Court (*d*) state
legislatures (*e*) organizations of private citizens.
2. The following is a list of chapter titles in a book that deals with the history of black
Americans. Choose *three* of these chapter titles. For *each* one chosen, discuss *two*
historical events which you would expect to find included in that chapter. (*a*) The Role
of Negroes in Early America (1619–1783) (*b*) The Negro Struggle for Freedom
(1800–1860) (*c*) The Negro in the Civil War and Reconstruction (1860–1877) (*d*)
Dilemmas Facing Black Leaders in the Post-Reconstruction Years (1877–1914) (*e*) The
Black as a Second-Class Citizen (1877–1945) (*f*) The Black Revolution (1945–1970)
3. For *each* of the following fields, name *one* black person and discuss the contribution: (*a*)
sports (*b*) literature (*c*) economic life (*d*) government (*e*) science (*f*) music.
4. Using *two* facts, agree *or* disagree with *each* of the following statements: (*a*) Blacks in
the United States were greatly affected by World War II. (*b*) In their efforts to secure
equal rights, blacks have had little help from the United States Constitution. (*c*) Blacks
in the North face problems different from the problems of blacks in the South. (*d*)
Blacks will find their efforts toward improving their conditions hindered by rioting and
violence. (*e*) Today, many blacks can improve conditions for themselves and their
families through their own efforts. (*f*) The post-World War II civil rights movement was
weakened because it was divided into many factions with varying methods and goals.
5. Base your answer to this question on your analysis of the data in the table and on your
knowledge of American studies.

US Distribution of Whites and Blacks, by Residence, 1970
(*in percentage of total residents*)

	Whites	Blacks
Central cities	25	55
Suburbs	39	16
Nonmetropolitan areas	36	29

(*a*) Identify a problem indicated by the data presented in the chart. (*b*) Discuss the
issues and forces involved in the problem you identified. (*c*) Discuss a proposal that you
think would help solve the problem.

UNIT II. THE AMERICAN GOVERNMENT
Our Complex and Diverse
Democratic System

Part 1. Introduction to Government

1. Why People Need Government

Meaning of Government. The word *government* denotes a man-made institution or way of doing things whereby a small number of people exercise authority over the entire community or society. In its broad sense—the exercise of authority—government may refer to (1) a mother setting rules of conduct for her children; (2) a corporation establishing regulations for its employees; (3) a religion promulgating ethical principles for its members; and (4) a college requiring standards of behavior and achievement for its students. In its narrow sense—of an institution—government refers to the agencies that make, enforce, and interpret the laws of society.

ORIGINS OF GOVERNMENT: CASE STUDIES

1. In Prehistoric Times. A primitive tribe, dependent upon hunting for food, often faced questions essential for survival: shall we migrate to new hunting grounds? what route shall we take? how shall we protect ourselves against attack while on the way? To supply answers for the entire tribe, the members might look possibly to the "ancient one" because of his wisdom and experience, or to the "powerful one" because of his hunting and fighting prowess, or to a council of elders and warriors—in other words, to a common leadership or government.

2. In Ancient Egypt. More than 5000 years ago, the people dwelling in the Nile Valley saw the possibility of growing abundant crops if only they could control the Nile River. They needed dikes and reservoirs to prevent the annual floods; they needed irrigation canals to water the farmlands. These major projects required group effort which led to local government, usually chiefdoms. Through war and marriage, these chiefdoms eventually combined so that by 3100 B.C. they were part of a single government—the kingdom of Egypt.

131

3. In Colonial Virginia. The first English settlers who founded Jamestown in 1607 included too few farmers and artisans and too many impractical "gentlemen" fortune hunters. The latter began to search for gold instead of undertaking the tasks necessary for survival of the colony. Thereupon, *John Smith*, a practical-minded soldier, forced his way into control. He compelled the settlers to abandon the search for gold and instead to plant food crops, stock firewood, and build fortifications. Smith provided the Virginia colony with effective leadership—a government.

DIFFERENT FORMS OF GOVERNMENT

1. Absolute Monarchy. The absolute monarch or autocrat concentrated in his hands all powers of government. He ruled without formal checks upon his authority and demanded absolute obedience from his subjects. His claim to such rule usually rested upon (a) hereditary right—he was the legitimate heir of the previous ruler and (b) divine right—he was a demigod or at least God's representative on earth. With variations, the absolute monarchy existed from ancient times until the early 20th century. The best known of the absolute monarchs were—in ancient times: certain pharaohs of Egypt and certain emperors of Rome; during the transition from medieval to modern times: Louis XIV of France, Frederick the Great of Prussia, and Peter the Great of Russia; and in the early 20th century: Kaiser William II, the last hereditary ruler of Germany, and Czar Nicholas II, the last hereditary ruler of Russia.

2. Dictatorship. The dictator, the modern counterpart of the absolute monarch, likewise controlled every aspect of government. Usually, the dictator came to power by means of intrigue and force. In the 20th century, the best known dictators were Stalin in Communist Russia and Hitler in Fascist Germany. Although Communism and Fascism differed significantly in origins, supporters, economic doctrines, and goals, they revealed marked similarities in political matters. As dictatorships, both held to the following beliefs: (a) The interests of the state are *paramount* (supreme) and the people exist to serve the state. (b) The state denies the people civil liberties, uses secret police to ferret out those it considers enemies, and punishes them without regard for elementary human decencies. (c) The state permits only one political party to exist and holds elections in which people vote but without having any choice. (d) The state molds the thinking of the people through propaganda spread by the educational system and the mass media and through censorship to exclude "dangerous" ideas. (e) Since the ordinary people are presumed to lack the intelligence and ability to conduct their own affairs, the state controls every aspect of human activity, thus constituting a *totalitarian regime.*

3. Oligarchy or Aristocracy. A few persons, known together as an *oligarchy*, exercised full power as the government. If the term *aristocracy* was used, it implied that these few persons were the "best" citizens—by virtue of their social position, wealth, military prowess, or education. The oligarchy historically has not been a lasting form of government: its ability to rule was weakened by internal disputes and by the desire of any powerful member to seize personal control. Examples of oligarchies include the warrior aristocracy that ruled the ancient Greek city-state of Sparta and the merchant aristocracy that ruled the 14th-century Italian city-state of Venice. In modern times, an example of an attempt to rule by oligarchy was in the Soviet Union where, after the ouster of dictator Nikita Khrushchev in 1964, control was exercised by party Secretary Leonid Brezhnev and Premier Aleksei Kosygin but in the name of the "collective leadership" of the Communist party Politburo—a small group of top Communist leaders. By the 1970's, however, Brezhnev dominated the party's "collective leadership" and emerged as the Soviet Union's chief spokesman.

4. Democracy. The word *"democracy,"* derived from the Greek language, means the rule of the people. Democracy rests upon the political principle that government is created by, derives its powers from, and exists to serve the people. In practice today, political democracy means a system of government characterized as follows: *(a)* Governmental powers are limited by a written constitution or by basic laws and historic traditions. *(b)* Governmental officials, chosen by secret ballot in free and frequently held elections, are responsible to the people. *(c)* The legislators debate issues, arrive at compromises, and, by majority vote, pass laws. *(d)* More than one political party exists, each free to present its views in seeking to become the majority party. *(e)* Minority groups, regardless of race, color, religion, or national origin, have the right to full and free existence. *(f)* The people are protected against possible governmental tyranny by guarantees of basic civil liberties, especially (1) freedom of speech, press, religion, and assembly, and (2) the right to bail, impartial trial, and equal treatment under the law.

The democratic form of government appeared first in the ancient Greek city-states and the Roman republic and then disappeared for many centuries. It reappeared as a result of the 17th-century English Revolution and the 18th-century American and French Revolutions, and developed into the political systems of many Western nations today, especially France, Great Britain, and the United States.

VARIATIONS IN THE DEMOCRATIC FORM OF GOVERNMENT: GREAT BRITAIN VS. THE UNITED STATES

1. Limited Monarchy vs. Republic. *Great Britain* is a limited monarchy since it is headed by a hereditary ruler—a King or Queen who is a figurehead without power but who serves as a symbol of unity. The *United States* is a republic since it is headed by an elected President—the chief executive who exercises great power.

2. Unwritten vs. Written Constitution. *Great Britain* has no single formal written plan of government prepared at one time. Rather its fundamental principles are contained in historic precedents, major documents, and basic laws—together known as an unwritten constitution. The *United States* has a formal written constitution, drawn up at Philadelphia in 1787, which established the fundamental structure and principles of government.

3. Parliamentary Supremacy vs. Separation of Powers. *Great Britain* concentrates so many powers in Parliament, the law-making body or legislature, that it stands supreme in British government—above the judicial and executive branches. Parliament enacts laws which may not be declared invalid by any court. Parliament determines who shall be Prime Minister and how long he remains in office since the Prime Minister must control a majority in the House of Commons. The *United States* separates the powers of government among the three branches: legislature, judiciary, and executive. Each branch may "check and balance" the other two branches. Congress enacts laws but the Supreme Court may "throw out" any act it considers unconstitutional. Aside from extraordinary circumstances, Congress does not determine who shall be President or how long he remains in office.

4. Unitary vs. Federal. *Great Britain* has a unitary system wherein powers are concentrated in the national government. Local governmental bodies exist as its agencies. The *United States* has a federal system wherein powers are divided between the states and the national government. The states are independent and, in matters of local government, usually supreme.

(Also democratic in theory is the *confederate* system wherein powers are concentrated in the member states while the central body, exercising little or no power, serves as their agency. In practice the confederacy—as seen in the Articles of Confederation [1781–1789], the Southern Confederacy during the Civil War, and the United Nations today—is so weak and ineffective as to raise doubts whether it really constitutes a form of government.)

FUNCTIONS OF THE AMERICAN GOVERNMENT

The Preamble to the United States Constitution outlines the purposes of our democratic government: (1) form a more perfect union—by establishing national institutions to bring the people and the states closely together and create a sense of "oneness," (2) insure domestic tranquility—by providing law-enforcement agencies to maintain "law and order" so that people may go about their everyday routines in safety and without fear of violence, (3) establish justice—by creating fair legal procedures and courts to protect the innocent, punish lawbreakers, and enforce valid contracts, (4) provide for the common defense—by raising military forces to protect the people and promote the "national interest" against foreign threats, (5) promote the general welfare—by enacting laws and creating agencies to further the economic and social well-being of the people, and (6) secure the blessings of liberty—by restraining the powers of government and guaranteeing civil liberties so that people may live in freedom.

In simple language, Abraham Lincoln explained clearly that the purpose of government is "to do for the people what needs to be done, but which they cannot, by individual effort, do at all, or do so well, for themselves." By this definition, Lincoln drew a line between what the people should do for themselves and what the government should do for them.

MULTIPLE-CHOICE QUESTIONS

1. Generally speaking, *most* governments depend *primarily* for their existence upon (1) consent and force (2) constitution and laws (3) natural resources and trade (4) education and free elections.

2. The *most* logical explanation for the origins of government is the   (1) effort of men to dominate women   (2) effort of the warrior class to live in comfort at the expense of farmers and city workers   (3) need of society for leadership to solve common problems   (4) need of society for a scapegoat to blame in case of disasters.

3. Which is a *basic* characteristic of a totalitarian state?   (1) a representative parliament   (2) restrictions on civil liberties   (3) existence of many political parties   (4) a balance of power among executive, legislative, and judicial branches

4. In practice, communism and fascism *differ* in their attitude toward   (1) ownership of the means of production   (2) supremacy of the state   (3) safeguarding civil liberties   (4) functions of a political party.

5. The oligarchy as a form of government   (1) has never been tried   (2) is exemplified today by the United Nations   (3) was developed first in the Soviet Union   (4) has rarely lasted long because of disputes among its members.

6. Which would be considered a necessity in *most* definitions of a democratic society?   (1) a detailed, written constitution   (2) free and honest elections of government officials   (3) a one-party system   (4) a system of free public education

7. The *main* reason for having a written constitution is to   (1) fulfill the requirements of international law   (2) inform the public about the laws of government   (3) define and provide a structure for a government's powers, duties, and limits   (4) encourage official recognition of new governments by other nations.

8. The functions of a democratic government include all the following *except* to   (1) assure cultural uniformity   (2) establish justice   (3) provide for the common defense   (4) maintain law and order.

9. During the transition from medieval to modern times, in general the governments of continental western Europe can *best* be described as   (1) absolute monarchies   (2) constitutional monarchies   (3) totalitarian dictatorships   (4) democratic republics.

10. In a totalitarian society, the group in power uses the press, the arts, education, and science *chiefly* to   (1) put world interests ahead of national interests   (2) provide for experimentation with new ideas   (3) support the prevailing political system   (4) call the attention of the people to weaknesses in the existing order.

ESSAY QUESTIONS

1. It is customary for totalitarian countries to attempt to disguise themselves as democracies. (*a*) Describe *three* democratic features of life in the United States that do *not* exist in the Soviet Union. (*b*) Discuss *two* devices used by the Soviet Union to give the impression that it is democratic.

2. Compare the British with the American system of government so as to explain (*a*) *two* ways in which they are similar (*b*) *two* ways in which they are different (*c*) *one* reason why, despite these differences, both governments are considered democratic.

Part 2. The Constitution: Background and Principles

2. The Constitution Combines Western Tradition and American Experience

As it nears its 200th birthday, the United States Constitution is the world's oldest functioning written plan of government. During its history, countless constitutions and governments in other countries have come and gone—unable to adjust to the changes affecting industry and society.

The survival of the American Constitution has been attributed to the following factors: (1) The *Founding Fathers*—the 55 delegates who met in Philadelphia in 1787—were men of exceptional ability and highly qualified to draw up the new Constitution. (2) The delegates were well educated and widely read in history, government, and law. They were able to utilize their knowledge of government from the ancient world of Athens and Rome to the English experience in guaranteeing civil liberties and asserting Parliamentary supremacy over the King. They were also able to draw upon the writings of the 17th- and 18th-century political philosophers—the leaders of the *Intellectual Revolution* and the *Age of Reason*. (3) The delegates had considerable practical experience in politics, many having served in the colonial and postcolonial periods as governors, judges, and legislators. (4) Without sacrificing their basic principles, the Founding Fathers were able to agree on details for the Constitution by utilizing the *democratic process of compromise*. They cleverly diffused power by the federal system of division of powers between the central and state governments and by the separation of powers within the central government. They denied power by restrictions upon both the state and central governments so as to protect the rights of the people. Also they provided for the Constitution to change with time: by a formal amending process and by use of language —deliberately or accidentally vague—which could be reinterpreted to meet new conditions. By these features of the Constitution the delegates reflected 18th-century rationalism—the belief that, by applying logic and reason, human intelligence could devise a more perfect society.

DEMOCRATIC ROOTS IN ANCIENT TIMES

1. **Athens.** In the ancient world, where most governments remained autocracies, Athens and a number of other Greek city-states evolved from autocracy

toward democracy. From the 7th to the 5th centuries B.C., Athens led the way and Athenian democracy reached its height during the *Age of Pericles* (461–429 B.C.). Thereafter, torn by internal dissension, exhausted by a losing war against Sparta (431–404 B.C.), and conquered by King Philip of Macedon (338 B.C.), Athens gradually lost its democratic institutions.

Athenian democracy left the Western world a heritage of: *(a)* a *republic* wherein the executive head was the leader of a board of ten military generals or *strategoi,* each elected by the male citizens, *(b)* *direct democracy* wherein all male citizens themselves were members of the Athenian legislature, the Assembly, *(c)* a *jury system* wherein male citizens chosen in large numbers by lot from eligible lists served as jurors to try cases, and *(d)* *salaries for public officials,* thereby enabling poor citizens to accept jury duty and other governmental service.

(As we understand the term "democracy" today, Athens was undemocratic in that its male citizens constituted a minority as compared to the disenfranchised majority—women who had no political rights and slaves and aliens who were denied citizenship.)

2. Rome. Evolving as had Athens previously, Rome from the 5th to the 3rd centuries B.C. changed from a monarchy into a republic with many democratic features. Thereafter Rome conquered a Mediterranean empire (by the 1st century B.C.), but the Roman armies changed from citizen-soldiers loyal to the state to professional soldiers loyal to their own commanders. Rome experienced a series of civil wars which ended the republic and began the Roman Empire—a long era of military dictatorship (27 B.C.–A.D. 476).

Rome left to the Western world a great political heritage with democratic peoples especially interested in the following: *(a) The veto.* Tribunes elected by the common people or *plebeians* could *veto,* or forbid, laws passed by the hereditary Senate representing the upper classes or *patricians.* *(b) The danger of military power independent of civilian control.* With the rise of professional armies not subject to state control, power shifted from the political institutions of the Roman republic to army commanders and was one cause for the rise of military dictatorship. *(c) Roman law.* The Romans developed bodies of law on business matters, family relationships, individual rights, and international affairs. By order of the Roman Emperor *Justinian* at Constantinople (A.D. 527–565), Roman law was arranged systematically as the *Justinian Code.* It has influenced the legal systems of Western Europe and, less directly, the United States. Unlike the harsh legal codes of most other ancient peoples, Roman law was intended to be consistent but flexible, impartial toward all men, and humane. Two of its principles of justice were: (i) All persons are equal before the law. (ii) Accused persons are guaranteed legal protection. For example, confessions obtained by force are invalid.

DEMOCRATIC ROOTS IN THE ENGLISH EXPERIENCE

In a number of royal charters authorizing the establishment of English colonies, the settlers in the New World were assured their "rights and privileges as Englishmen." These rights and privileges rested upon four major landmarks in English history:

1. Magna Carta (1215). King John was compelled by the feudal nobles to sign the *Great Charter*, or *Magna Carta*. Originally, Magna Carta was meant to protect the feudal nobility against the king; in time, the charter's protections were extended to all Englishmen. Magna Carta came to mean that *(a)* the king is not an absolute ruler but is subject to the laws, *(b)* all persons are guaranteed trial by a jury of their *peers*, or equals, and *(c)* Parliament alone may levy taxes.

2. Evolution of Parliament. By the 14th century, Parliament had split into two houses: the higher clergy and nobility constituted the hereditary *House of Lords;* representatives of the wealthy middle class constituted the elected *House of Commons*. Also, by threatening to withhold tax laws, Parliament compelled English kings to accept its legislation, not only on taxes, but also on all other matters.

3. English Common Law. By the 14th century, English courts had established the practice of referring to similar past cases and following the previous decisions of judges. These legal precedents collectively formed a body of judge-made law, called the *common law*. Its principles, some of which in time were enacted by Parliament and became *statute law*, helped protect the individual against governmental tyranny. By the end of the 17th century, common and statute law assured the English people certain basic rights: *(a)* Life, liberty, and property could not be taken away arbitrarily. *(b)* If arrested, a person was entitled to a writ of *habeas corpus* (providing for a statement of charges and a speedy trial) and to a trial by jury. *(c)* A man's home was considered his "castle." Government officials could not search a private home without first securing from a court a search warrant specifically stating the goods being sought.

4. English Bill of Rights (1689). As part of the *Glorious Revolution,* which deposed James II and placed William and Mary on the throne of England, Parliament passed the Bill of Rights. It provided that *(a)* the king may not make or suspend laws, levy taxes, or maintain an army without the consent of Parliament, *(b)* the king may not interfere with Parliamentary elections and debates, and *(c)* the people are guaranteed basic rights to petition the government; to an impartial and speedy jury trial; to protection against excessive fines and bails, and against cruel and unusual punishments.

DEMOCRATIC ROOTS IN THE COLONIAL EXPERIENCE

Although the colonies were far from being democratic, as we understand the term today, they were significantly more democratic than Continental Europe and, in some ways, even England. The American colonists introduced the following institutions:

1. Virginia House of Burgesses (1619). The Virginia Company gave the colonists of Virginia the right to elect representatives to a colonial legislature, the *House of Burgesses*. In the New World, this was the first elected legislature and the first institution of representative government. Other colonies followed Virginia's pattern in establishing similar lawmaking bodies.

2. Mayflower Compact (1620). Before disembarking from their ship, the *Mayflower*, the Pilgrims made plans for self-government in their new home at

Plymouth, Massachusetts. In a compact to further the general good of the colony, they pledged to enact and obey just and equal laws. The Mayflower Compact was an example of *(a) direct democracy,* wherein the citizens themselves, not their representatives, were the lawmakers, *(b)* acceptance of majority rule, and *(c)* the principle that laws should treat all persons fairly.

3. New England Town Meetings. The Pilgrims began the practice, which became typical of colonial New England, of building towns with farms at the outskirts and a church meetinghouse at the center. Town life concentrated around the church. The freemen, originally only men who owned property and belonged to the town church, conducted town affairs and enacted local ordinances in *town meetings.* They also elected town representatives to serve in the colonial assembly. The town meeting, an example of direct democracy and possible only in a small community, provided the colonists with training in self-government.

4. Fundamental Orders of Connecticut (1639). The Connecticut settlers drew up this first written constitution of modern times. It permitted all loyal citizens to elect a legislative assembly, which in turn would choose a governor. The Fundamental Orders implied that government rests upon the consent of the governed and that it should express the will of the majority.

5. Religious Tolerance. Check the Index for "Religion, in colonies."

COLONIAL GOVERNMENT BY THE 1750'S: A SUMMARY

1. Undemocratic Aspects. In 11 of the 13 colonies, the colonists had little voice in the selection of a governor. He was appointed by the English Crown or by the owner of the colony, the *proprietor.* The governor was empowered to veto laws passed by the colonial legislature and to appoint lesser colonial officials. Furthermore, the English Crown claimed the power to review and reject any law passed in the colonies.

In many colonies, voters had to meet religious qualifications. In all colonies, landless urban dwellers could not satisfy property qualifications for voting. Frontier settlers, living in danger and isolation, found it difficult to vote and were under-represented in the colonial assemblies. Finally, membership in the assembly was restricted to the well-to-do by the high property qualifications for officeholding.

2. Democratic Features. The legal rights of the colonists were protected by colonial judges, who followed English common law. The colonists were also protected against tyranny by the separation of governmental powers. With power divided between an appointed governor representing the Crown or proprietor and a colonial assembly representing the settlers, neither branch of government could become all-powerful.

The colonial assembly was elected by the qualified voters, and its consent was necessary to enact laws, such as to levy taxes and dispense funds. Often, the assembly was able to bend the governor to its will by withholding funds for his salary or for running the government. Such use of a legislature's financial power has been named the *power of the purse.*

THE DECLARATION OF INDEPENDENCE—A DEMOCRATIC DOCUMENT

In April 1775 colonial Minutemen and British troops clashed in battles at Lexington and Concord, thereby starting the American Revolution. During the first year of active warfare, the colonists were not certain whether they were fighting for their rights as Englishmen within the Empire or for complete freedom. By the summer of 1776, the colonists had decided that this was a war for independence.

AUTHORSHIP AND ORIGINS OF THE DECLARATION

On July 4, 1776, the Second Continental Congress, speaking for the American colonies, formally adopted the Declaration of Independence. Although Benjamin Franklin and John Adams made some contributions, the Declaration was written chiefly by *Thomas Jefferson*. Claiming no originality, Jefferson asserted that he merely placed on paper the political beliefs widespread among the American people. In so doing Jefferson drew heavily upon the ideas of the 17th-century English philosopher John Locke and was familiar with the writings of the 18th-century French philosopher Jean Jacques Rousseau.

John Locke had justified England's Glorious Revolution of 1689 in his work *Two Treatises of Government*. He had affirmed the democratic political theory that *(a)* the people possess *natural rights* to life, liberty, and property, *(b)* the people, by means of a *social contract* among themselves or with their rulers, create and grant authority to government for the purpose of protecting their rights, and *(c)* the people may replace a government that fails in this purpose, if necessary by revolution.

Jean Jacques Rousseau had expanded upon Locke's ideas and popularized them on the European continent. Rousseau's major political work, appearing in 1762, was entitled *The Social Contract*.

BASIC IDEAS OF THE DECLARATION

1. **Introduction.** Jefferson introduced the Declaration by explaining that "when in the course of human events," the colonists declare their independence from Britain, they should show "a decent respect to the opinions of mankind" by declaring "the causes which impel them to separation."

2. **Democratic Philosophy of Government.** In simple yet eloquent language, Jefferson declared: *(a)* "All men are created equal" and "are endowed by their Creator with certain unalienable rights," including "life, liberty, and the pursuit of happiness." *(b)* "To secure these rights, governments are instituted [started] among men, deriving their just powers from the consent of the governed." *(c)* "Whenever any form of government becomes destructive of these ends, it is the right of the people to alter or to abolish it, and to institute new government." *(d)* However, "governments long established should not be changed for light and transient [temporary] causes."

3. **List of Grievances.** To prove that the colonists had sufficient cause, the

Declaration enumerated the many "injuries and usurpations" committed against them by Britain's King George III.

4. Conclusion. Jefferson concluded that "these united colonies are, and of right ought to be, free and independent states."

SIGNIFICANCE OF THE DECLARATION

1. Proclamation of New Ideas. The Declaration affirmed political concepts that, for its time, were revolutionary. To a world long accustomed to sharp and hereditary class distinctions, it stated that "all men are created equal" and are endowed with "unalienable rights." To a world long accustomed to absolute monarchs ruling by "divine right," it proclaimed that governments rule by "consent of the governed." To a world long accustomed to the mother country ruling her colonies strictly, it announced that colonists have the right to overthrow such despotism and to "institute new government."

2. Effects Upon the American Revolution. The Declaration elevated the colonial struggle against the English armies into a war for independence. It encouraged France and Spain to assist the colonists.

3. Long-Term Effects Throughout the World. To peoples throughout the world, the Declaration became a source of inspiration. It inspired the French revolutionaries, who in 1789 rebelled against the old order or regime and adopted the *Declaration of the Rights of Man*. It encouraged Latin American leaders, in the early 19th century, to fight for independence from Spain. It inspired Asian and African nationalists, in the 20th century, to oppose imperialist control and to achieve national independence.

4. Long-Term Effects Within the United States. Although not part of the formal government of the United States, the Declaration reflected the views of many of the Founding Fathers of our Constitution and influenced certain Constitutional provisions. Further, by providing Americans with a basic democratic philosophy, the Declaration has inspired movements for social and democratic reforms, such as the abolition of slavery, equal rights for women, and full civil rights for blacks.

THE AMERICAN EXPERIENCE UNDER THE ARTICLES OF CONFEDERATION (1781–1789)

1. Establishing the Articles of Confederation. During the Revolutionary War, the Continental Congress realized that the 13 American states had to be kept together by some binding form of union. Congress leaders, however, (1) held that the American people gave primary loyalty to their individual states and (2) feared that a strong central government might—as Britain had—infringe upon civil liberties and economic freedoms. In 1777 the Continental Congress proposed the Articles of Confederation which went into effect in 1781 following ratification by all the states.

Proclaiming that "each state retains its sovereignty, freedom and independence," the Articles constituted for these states a "perpetual Union" but only as "a firm league of friendship"—in other words a confederation or weak central government.

2. A "Critical Period." The Articles sought to govern during times of great difficulty: *(a) Economic Distress.* With the Revolutionary War over, American merchants were excluded from the British West Indies and lost their favored position in English markets. Farmers and planters saw agricultural prices decline, city workers experienced unemployment, and soldiers went unpaid for wartime service. *(b) Political Disunity.* With the Revolutionary War over, the states no longer faced a common enemy. With this unifying factor removed, the people tended to emphasize not national but state loyalty.

Beset by these problems, the United States experienced a "critical period" which was made worse by the weaknesses of the Articles.

WEAKNESSES OF THE ARTICLES OF CONFEDERATION

1. Defects in Governmental Structure. *(a)* The Articles established a central government consisting only of a Congress—a one-house legislature of delegates from the 13 states, each state casting one vote. The Articles contained no provision for a chief executive to enforce the laws and no provision for courts to handle disputes between citizens of different states. *(b)* For Congress to enact laws, the Articles required, not a simple majority, but a "yes" vote of *nine* out of the 13 states. With delegates from more than ten states rarely present at any one time, Congress practically was unable to legislate. *(c)* To add an amendment, the Articles required the approval of all 13 states—that is, a *unanimous vote.*

2. Lack of Essential Legislative Powers. *(a)* Congress could not tax the people directly; it could only request the states to supply funds—which requests were mainly ignored. *(b)* Congress could issue money, but it could not prevent each state from issuing its own currency. Some states printed huge quantities of paper money unbacked by metal, thereby causing the value of money to fall and prices to rise. This *cheap money* pleased the debtor class of small farmers and city workers because it enabled them to repay their mortgages and other loans easily. Other states refused to cheapen the value of their money, thus pleasing the creditor class of bankers and merchants. Without a nationwide uniform currency, merchants were reluctant to do business outside their own states. *(c)* Congress could not directly recruit men for an army; it could only request the states to supply troops. The states, however, were reluctant to provide men, and the central government remained militarily helpless. *(d)* Congress could not control commerce between the states, that is, interstate commerce. Each state established its own commercial regulations. New York taxed farm products from Connecticut and New Jersey, and these states retaliated by taxing goods from New York. Maryland and Virginia each claimed control of navigation on the Potomac, an interstate river. Such disputes disrupted trade between the states. *(e)* Congress could not control foreign commerce, and each state maintained its own tariffs on imports. Britain refused to enter into a commercial treaty with the United States, realizing that Congress could not enforce such a treaty. Furthermore, Britain closed her West Indies ports to American merchant ships and Spain closed the lower Mississippi and New Orleans port to American shipping of Western farm produce. Both nations realized that the American government lacked the power to retaliate.

3. Groups Most Dissatisfied. The failings of the Confederation most dejected the propertied and business groups: merchants, shippers, bankers and other creditors, lawyers, manufacturers, and large landowners. Also dissatisfied were Western farmers and national patriots.

ACHIEVEMENTS UNDER THE ARTICLES OF CONFEDERATION

Congress (1) successfully concluded the Revolutionary War and achieved the advantageous 1783 Treaty of Paris, (2) kept the states united in name, if not always in fact, through a period of great difficulty, (3) passed the *Land Ordinance of 1785* which provided for the survey and sale of Western lands and which set aside the income from one section of land in every township (of 36 sections) for the support of public education, and (4) passed the *Northwest Ordinance of 1787* which applied to the area bounded by the Mississippi and Ohio Rivers and the Great Lakes—the *Northwest Territory.* The Ordinance prohibited slavery, guaranteed civil liberties, encouraged education, and fostered the admission to the union of new states. Any territory, upon achieving 60,000 inhabitants, could adopt a constitution and apply for statehood "on an equal footing with the original states in all respects whatever." The Northwest Ordinance provided a model for the democratic treatment of colonies. (See map of Northwest Territory, page 517.)

Groups Most Satisfied. The weak Articles of Confederation pleased many small farmers, frontiersmen, and city workers. They held this government least likely to threaten their rights and liberties. Also pleased were debtors, who enjoyed the prevalence of cheap money, and the advocates of state loyalty.

CONSTITUTIONAL CONVENTION AT PHILADELPHIA (1787)

1. Background. With dissatisfaction mounting against the Articles, Congress in 1787 reluctantly issued a call for a convention at Philadelphia for the "sole and express purpose of revising the Articles of Confederation."

2. Absentees. The Philadelphia Convention included scarcely any representatives of over 90 percent of the country's population: small farmers, city workers, and frontiersmen. Also, several leaders of the Revolutionary period were absent: Patrick Henry, opposing a stronger central government, refused to attend; John Adams and Thomas Jefferson were stationed as our ministers in London and Paris.

3. Delegates. The Philadelphia Convention consisted of 55 delegates from all the states except Rhode Island. Since they were mainly lawyers, large landowners, bankers, and merchants, they reflected propertied and business interests. They were well-educated men with considerable political experience.

Several outstanding leaders exercised great influence over the convention: (a) *George Washington* presided over the convention with dignity and fairness. (b) *James Madison*, a scholar of government, took detailed notes of the proceedings. Since the delegates conferred in secret to facilitate agreement, Madison's notes are our chief source of information about the convention. Madison played a major role in the proceedings and has been called "father of the Constitution." (c) *Alexander Hamilton,* a lawyer and son-in-law of a large New York landowner, was an effective spokesman for the propertied interests. (d) *Benjamin Franklin* employed his wisdom and prestige to bring about agreement on crucial issues.

4. Points of Agreement: Lessons Learned From Experience Under the Articles. (a) Agreeing that the Articles of Confederation were entirely inadequate, the delegates at Philadelphia proceeded to draw up a new Constitution, thus turning the meeting into a Constitutional Convention. Its members have become known as the *Founding Fathers.* (b) The delegates wanted a government strong enough to govern effectively at home and to command respect abroad, yet not so strong as to become a tyranny, threatening the liberty and property of the people. (c) The delegates believed that such a government must have a visible executive head and an independent judiciary as well as a legislature. (d) The delegates believed that the central government had to have the power to levy taxes, control interstate and foreign commerce, raise an army, and protect property, and the sole power to coin money. Furthermore, it had to be able to exercise its powers directly on the people, not indirectly through the states.

THE CONSTITUTION AS A "BUNDLE OF COMPROMISES"

1. Representation. The more populous states supported the Virginia Plan, that representation in the national legislature be based on population. The less populous states supported the New Jersey Plan, that each state have equal representation. This issue, the most serious one dividing the delegates, was settled by the *Great Compromise,* or *Connecticut Compromise.* The legislature was to consist of two houses: (a) a House of Representatives, where representation was to be based on population, and (b) a Senate, where each state was to have equal representation.

2. Slavery. The Southern states, which contained many Negro slaves, proposed that (a) slaves be counted as part of the population for purposes of representation, thus increasing the number of Southerners in the House of Representatives, and (b) slaves not be counted as part of the population for purposes of direct taxation, thus decreasing the Southern tax burden. The Northern states, in which slavery was fast dying out, supported the opposite positions. The issue was settled by the *Three-Fifths Compromise:* five slaves were to be counted as three free persons for purposes of both representation and direct taxation.

By another compromise on slavery, Congress was forbidden for 20 years (until 1808) to interfere with the importation of slaves into the country.

3. Tariffs. The Southern states opposed giving the central government the power to levy tariffs. Since they were chiefly agricultural, they feared that Congress would pass a tariff on their exports of indigo, rice, and tobacco. The Northern states, being highly commercial, wanted the central government to have the power to establish uniform regulations on commerce with foreign nations. The issue was settled by granting Congress the power to control foreign commerce and to levy tariffs on imports but not on exports.

4. Presidency. The delegates disagreed over the term of office of the President and over the method of choosing him. Suggestions for his term of office ranged from three years to life. Some delegates wanted the President elected directly by the people. Others, fearing too much democracy, suggested that he be elected by Congress. The issues were settled *(a)* by authorizing a tenure of four years, and *(b)* by establishing a complex procedure for electing the President through an Electoral College. (Check the Index for "Electoral College.") By this procedure, the delegates meant to allow the people only an indirect voice in choosing the President.

ADOPTION OF THE CONSTITUTION

1. Method of Ratification. The Founding Fathers provided that the new Constitution go into effect when ratified by conventions in nine of the thirteen states. Thus they disregarded the Articles of Confederation, which had specified that changes must be approved unanimously.

2. Debate Over Ratification. The *Federalists*, supporters of the Constitution, consisted of men with business and property interests, and of others who considered the nation more important than their state. They argued that the Constitution would provide a stable government capable of maintaining law and order, furthering economic prosperity, and commanding respect abroad. The *Anti-Federalists*, opponents of the Constitution, consisted of farmers, city workers, and others who gave their chief loyalty to their state or community. They argued that the Constitution served the propertied classes, threatened the powers of the states, and left the people unprotected against federal encroachment upon their civil liberties. Acknowledging the last argument, the Federalists pledged to add a Bill of Rights to the Constitution.

3. Process of Ratification. Each state held its own Constitutional convention to consider ratification. The less populous states of Delaware, New Jersey, and Georgia quickly and overwhelmingly gave their approval. The more populous states approved ratification more slowly and by narrow margins. In Massachusetts, the sixth state to ratify, the convention voted 187 to 168. In Virginia, the tenth state, the convention vote was 89 to 79. In New York, the eleventh state, the convention voted 30 to 27.

After George Washington was inaugurated as first President of the new government, the Constitution was ratified by the last two states, North Carolina and then Rhode Island. The 13 states were now bound together in a strong federal union.

4. Reasons for the Success of the Federalists

a. Effective Organization. A well-organized group, the Federalists expended much energy and money toward achieving ratification. At various state ratifying conventions, the Federalists won the support of doubtful delegates and delayed the voting until they were assured a majority. The Anti-Federalists could not compare with them in funds, organization, and effectiveness.

b. Voting Qualifications. Most supporters of ratification could satisfy state property qualifications for voting and could therefore vote for convention delegates. The Anti-Federalist urban workers and poorer people, probably one-third of the population, lacked property and were denied the vote.

c. *The Federalist Papers.* Alexander Hamilton, James Madison, and John Jay argued persuasively for the new Constitution by writing a series of articles for New York newspapers. These learned essays helped swing New York public opinion in favor of ratification. The articles were later collected and published under the title *The Federalist.* Read to this day, *The Federalist* provides insights into the political thinking of the Founding Fathers and into the principles of the Constitution.

d. *Influential Supporters.* The Federalists enjoyed the support of two highly respected men: Benjamin Franklin and George Washington. Their approval of the Constitution influenced many doubters.

MULTIPLE-CHOICE QUESTIONS

1. One democratic idea traceable to the Greek city state of Athens is to (1) give women the vote (2) allow foreigners to become naturalized citizens (3) prohibit slavery (4) provide for jury trials.

2. Roman law may be considered democratic in that it (1) was never written down (2) prohibited the use of the veto (3) considered all persons equal before the law (4) permitted torture to secure confessions.

3. Which was a result of the signing of Magna Carta? (1) The king lost the power to impose taxes by himself. (2) All classes were represented in Parliament. (3) No freeman could serve on a jury. (4) Parliament could pass laws for the colonies.

4. The Mayflower Compact was an important step in the growth of democracy because it (1) guaranteed trial by jury to the Pilgrims (2) indicated that the people were the proper source of political authority (3) freed the indentured servants on the *Mayflower* (4) guaranteed religious freedom to all settlers.

5. The House of Burgesses and the New England town meetings were *similar* in that both (1) originated in the New England states (2) were free from vetoes by colonial governors (3) were initially established by the English Parliament (4) represented colonial participation in the government.

6. Which was the *most* common feature of government in the 13 colonies? (1) a legislature with an elected lower house (2) a legislature appointed by the king (3) a governor elected by the people (4) a governor and council appointed by the established church

7. Although *most* of the 13 colonies required property qualifications for voting, the majority of adult white males in 1750 could vote because (1) suffrage laws were strictly enforced (2) ownership of land was easily attained (3) Great Britain followed a policy of hereditary rights (4) the colonists accepted the principle of "virtual" representation.

8. In the 18th century, the colonial assemblies frequently used the "power of the purse" to (1) obtain the royal governor's assent to laws (2) encourage political union among the colonies (3) promote economic dependence on England (4) extend suffrage on the frontier regions.

9. The principles of the Declaration of Independence can be described as (1) part of America's debt to European thought (2) Roger Williams' contribution to political philosophy (3) concepts of government applicable only to an agrarian society (4) a defense of the Articles of Confederation.

10. According to the Declaration of Independence, the purpose of government is to (1) secure the people in their natural rights (2) equalize opportunities for all citizens (3) provide for the common defense (4) establish a system of free public schools.

11. The *chief* significance of the Declaration of Independence is that it (1) expressed for the first time the right of a people to self-government (2) furnished a body of ideals

for future generations   (3) listed colonial grievances against King George III   (4) provided a framework for a new government.

12. During the period of the Articles of Confederation, the lack of adequate central authority to deal with national problems can *best* be explained by the   (1) fear of the kind of rule experienced under the British   (2) lack of concern for these national problems   (3) absence of any feeling of American nationalism   (4) failure to develop competent statesmen.

13. Which was a weakness of the government under the Articles of Confederation?   (1) ease with which laws could be passed in Congress   (2) dictatorial power of the executive   (3) the amount of power held by the federal courts   (4) Congressional power to request, not demand, an army from the states

14. Which *best* explains the dissatisfaction of the merchant class with the Articles of Confederation?   (1) The power of Congress to tax was unlimited.   (2) Individual states lacked the power to regulate commerce.   (3) The President's treaty-making power was unchecked.   (4) There was no provision for a uniform currency.

15. The Northwest Ordinance has been regarded as nonimperialistic because it provided for the   (1) establishment of public education in the territories   (2) defense of the inhabitants from Indian attacks   (3) permanent abolition of slavery in the territories   (4) preparation of a territory for statehood.

16. Which provision of the Northwest Ordinance was based upon an established practice followed in Great Britain?   (1) prohibition of slavery   (2) admission of new states on an equal footing with the original states   (3) guarantee of habeas corpus and trial by jury   (4) encouragement of public education

17. Which group was largely unrepresented at the Constitutional Convention?   (1) lawyers   (2) small farmers   (3) large landowners   (4) wealthy merchants

18. The Great Compromise and the Three-Fifths Compromise at the Constitutional Convention were both concerned with   (1) regulation of interstate commerce   (2) representation in the Congress of the United States   (3) admission of new states into the Union   (4) the future of slavery in the United States.

19. Which decision reached at the Constitutional Convention represented a concession to the South?   (1) Tariffs on exports were prohibited.   (2) The President was to be chosen by an Electoral College.   (3) Revenue bills must originate in the House of Representatives.   (4) Congress was given control of interstate commerce.

20. The Constitution was an improvement over the Articles of Confederation in that the Constitution   (1) provided for a federal legislature   (2) delegated to Congress the power to declare war   (3) gave the national government control over United States territories   (4) enabled the national government to deal directly with the people in regard to collecting taxes and raising an army.

21. The original reason for adding the Bill of Rights to the Constitution was to   (1) prevent any one branch of the government from becoming too powerful   (2) prohibit the federal government from depriving individuals of certain basic rights   (3) exclude the states from exercising any authority over civil rights   (4) restrict the states from challenging the Constitution as the supreme law of the land.

22. *The Federalist*, a series of political essays, was written to urge   (1) ratification of the Constitution   (2) rejection of the Constitution   (3) election of George Washington as President   (4) adoption of the Northwest Ordinance.

MODIFIED TRUE-FALSE QUESTIONS

If the statement is correct, write the word *true*. If the statement is incorrect, substitute a word or phrase for the italicized term to make the statement correct.

1. The author of the Declaration of Independence was *John Locke*.
2. Under the Articles of Confederation, the states were *sovereign*.

3. Amendments to the Articles of Confederation required the approval of *three-quarters* of the states.
4. The issuance of huge quantities of paper money caused the value of money to *rise*.
5. *Alexander Hamilton* was president of the Constitutional Convention.
6. In New York State, the Constitution was ratified by *an overwhelming* majority.
7. *Rhode Island* did not ratify the Constitution until after the new government had been organized.
8. The Great Compromise at the Constitutional Convention was sponsored by the state of *New Jersey*.
9. The Constitutional Convention provided that the Constitution go into effect when ratified by *seven* of the 13 states.
10. The "father of the Constitution," who kept detailed notes of the proceedings of the Constitutional Convention, was *Benjamin Franklin*.

ESSAY QUESTIONS

1. One justification for the study of history is that we can learn from the past—learn to adopt past good features and to avoid past mistakes. (*a*) Prove that American democracy today has adopted *one* good feature and avoided *one* mistake of ancient Athens. (*b*) Do the same for American democracy and ancient Rome.
2. Show in *one* way how the 13 colonies were influenced by their English heritage with respect to *each* of the following: (*a*) law and court procedures (*b*) individual rights (*c*) structure of government (*d*) religious beliefs.
3. (*a*) State *two* principles of the Declaration of Independence that challenged previously held political views. (*b*) Describe *two* ways in which the United States has tried since the adoption of the federal Constitution to carry out each of these principles. (*c*) Giving specific illustrations, show how *one* foreign government pursues policies contrary to the principles of the Declaration of Independence.
4. The United Nations has often been compared to the American government under the Articles of Confederation. (*a*) Show *three* ways in which this comparison is justified. (*b*) Show *two* ways in which the situations are *different*.
5. (*a*) Show how the Constitutional Convention of 1787 settled a dispute that arose over *each* of the following: (1) control of commerce (2) importation of slaves (3) representation of the states in Congress. (*b*) State *two* ways in which the organization of the government under the federal Constitution differed from its organization under the Articles of Confederation. (*c*) For a book on the Constitutional Convention of 1787, would you approve the title *Miracle at Philadelphia*? Give *two* reasons to support your opinion.

3. The Constitution Divides, Separates, and Limits the Powers of Government

CONSTITUTIONAL PHILOSOPHY UNDERLYING THE GRANTING AND LIMITING OF POWER

The Founding Fathers were concerned with establishing a government that would maintain a balance between power and liberty. James Madison, "father of the Constitution," claimed "the truth was that all men having power ought to be distrusted to a certain degree." Expanding on this theme Madison observed, "In framing a government which is to be administered by men over men, the great difficulty lies in this: you must first enable the government to control the governed; and in the next place oblige it to control itself."

To preserve liberty for the people and to prevent tyranny by government, the Founding Fathers provided for the distribution of power among many hands with each expected to resist encroachment of the others. As Madison said, "Ambition must be made to counteract ambition." The Founding Fathers also denied powers to various governments. These two factors—the distribution of power and the denial of power—underlie the framework of government provided by the Constitution.

Federal System: Division of Powers Between the Central Government and the States

The Constitution set up a system of *federalism*, a dual system of government whereby powers are divided between the state governments and the central (also known as the national or federal) government. The Constitution limits the federal government to *delegated*, or *enumerated*, powers. These are powers specifically listed in the Constitution as being granted to the federal government. Powers not given to the federal government and not denied to the states are reserved to the states or to the people. These are called *reserved*, or *residual*, powers. Certain powers, called *concurrent* powers, may be exercised by both the federal government and state governments.

Under the federal system each government is supreme within its own sphere. Every American is a citizen both of the United States and of the state in which the citizen resides.

DELEGATED, OR ENUMERATED, POWERS (Article I, Section 8)

The following powers are specifically granted to Congress. They are the delegated, or enumerated, powers of the federal government.

1. Financial. To levy and collect taxes; borrow money; coin money and regulate its value; punish counterfeiters.

2. Commercial. To regulate interstate and foreign commerce; establish rules for bankruptcy; establish post offices and post roads; grant patents and copyrights.

3. Military. To declare war; raise, support, and make rules for an army and navy; call up the state militia to enforce federal laws; suppress insurrections and repel invasions; punish piracy.

4. Miscellaneous. To establish rules for the naturalization of aliens; provide for courts below the Supreme Court; control the seat of government (Washington, D.C.) and all federal property.

ELASTIC CLAUSE (Article I, Section 8, Clause 18)

1. Statement. Concluding the list of delegated powers, the Constitution grants Congress the power "to make all laws which shall be necessary and proper for carrying into execution the foregoing powers." Because this statement enables Congress to expand its delegated or foregoing powers, it is known as the *elastic clause*.

2. Applications: The Elastic Clause and Implied Powers. *(a)* Congress in 1791 authorized a national bank although the Constitution nowhere specifically grants this power. Nevertheless, Congress considered the law "necessary and proper" for carrying out its delegated powers to collect taxes, coin and borrow money, and regulate its value. *(b)* Congress, beginning in 1877, passed legislation to regulate railroad fares, although, when the Constitution was written, the railroad had not been invented. Since railroads go from state to state, such federal control is based upon the elastic clause together with the delegated power "to regulate commerce among the states."

Such powers, each derived from the elastic clause plus one or more of the foregoing delegated powers, are not specifically stated in the Constitution but are hinted at or can be inferred. Consequently, they are called *implied* powers.

3. Controversy Regarding the Use of the Elastic Clause. Throughout our history, Americans have debated the extent to which the federal government should use the elastic clause.

    a. Strict Construction or Interpretation. Some Americans have held that the Constitution should be interpreted strictly and that Congress should be limited to its specific delegated powers. These people advocate restraints on the federal government so that the states may exercise more power. Their attitude is called "states' rights." Although states' righters have been found in all sections of the nation, they have been most numerous and influential in the South.

    b. Loose Construction or Interpretation. Other Americans have held that the Constitution should be interpreted broadly and that Congress should exercise many powers not specifically given to it, but merely implied. These people, champions of a powerful federal government, have usually been in the majority.

4. Historic Trend Toward Loose Construction. Over the years, the central government has greatly increased the scope of its functions by using its implied powers. Today, the federal government utilizes the elastic clause: *(a)* together with the clause giving Congress control of interstate commerce, to regulate such matters as interstate transportation, communication, business practices, the sale of securities, labor unions, and minimum wages, *(b)* together with the power to tax for the general welfare, to maintain Social Security and Medicare, and *(c)* together with the power to raise and support armies, to further atomic research and development for peaceful as well as military purposes.

RESERVED, OR RESIDUAL, POWERS (Amendment X)

Adopted in 1791, the Tenth Amendment to the Constitution states: "The powers not delegated to the United States by the Constitution, nor prohibited by it to the states, are reserved to the states respectively, or to the people." The states consequently have retained control over such matters as education, *intrastate* (within the state) commerce, most intrastate crimes, traffic laws, marriage, and divorce. State powers directly concerned with protecting the health, welfare, safety, and morals of the people are called *police powers*.

CONCURRENT POWERS

Concurrent powers are exercised by both the federal government and the states. Concurrent powers include levying taxes, borrowing money, building roads, and maintaining courts.

POWERS DENIED THE FEDERAL GOVERNMENT

1. Article I, Section 9. The original Constitution specifically prohibits the federal government from *(a)* passing any commerce or revenue law favoring one state at the expense of another, *(b)* granting any title of nobility, *(c)* levying any tax on exports, *(d)* levying any direct tax not based on population, *(e)* spending money without an appropriation authorized by law, and *(f)* encroaching upon the civil liberties of the people by suspending the right of habeas corpus (except in time of rebellion or invasion) or passing a bill of attainder or an ex post facto law. (Check the Index for "Bill of Attainder" and for "Ex post facto law.")

2. Amendments to the Constitution. The first ten amendments, together known as the *Bill of Rights,* deny the federal government the power to interfere with various civil liberties of the people and assign the reserved powers to the states or people. (Check the Index for "Bill of Rights.")

Four later amendments—the Fifteenth, Nineteenth, Twenty-Fourth, and Twenty-Sixth—prohibit the federal government (and the states) from denying voting rights of citizens on account of "race, color, or previous condition of servitude," "sex," "failure to pay any poll tax" in the election of federal officials, and "age" if the citizen is at least 18 years old. (Check the Index for these four amendments.)

POWERS DENIED THE STATES

1. Article I, Section 10. The original Constitution also denies certain powers to the states. *(a)* States may not coin money, enter into foreign treaties, or impair (lessen) obligations of contract. *(b)* Without the consent of Congress, states may not levy import or export duties, enter into agreements with each other, maintain troops in peacetime, or engage in war. *(c)* Like the federal government, the states may not grant titles of nobility or pass bills of attainder or ex post facto laws.

2. The 14th, 15th, 19th, 24th, and 26th Amendments. The Fourteenth Amendment prohibited states from abridging the privileges of citizens or depriving "any person of life, liberty or property without due process of law" or denying any person "equal protection of the laws." The other four amendments prohibit the states (and the federal government) from denying voting rights of citizens.

Federal System: Intergovernmental Relationships

Federal Obligations to the States (Article IV, Sections 3 and 4). The Constitution empowers Congress to admit new states into the Union. It also requires the federal government to assure each state (1) a republican form of government, (2) protection against invasion, and (3) upon request of the state, protection against domestic violence.

FEDERAL-STATE DISPUTES TO 1865

Basic Issue: States' Rights and Nullification vs. Federal Supremacy. From the adoption of the Constitution, Americans disputed regarding the nature of the federal union. States' righters argued that (1) the states had entered into a compact creating the federal government to serve as their agent, (2) the states remained independent and sovereign entities with power to declare federal laws null and void and (3) as a last resort the states could withdraw from the federal union, that is, the right of *secession*. National patriots insisted that (1) the people had created the federal government with full right to exercise its delegated and implied powers, (2) the Supreme Court was the only agency empowered to determine the constitutionality of federal laws, and (3) no state has the right to secede lest the union be, in Daniel Webster's words, a "rope of sand." This dispute of states' rights versus federal supremacy was at the heart of several historic confrontations.

1. Alien and Sedition Acts (1798)

a. Political Background. While the United States was engaged in an undeclared naval war against France, Federalist party partisans in Congress passed the *Alien and Sedition Acts*. Although the Federalists claimed that these laws were meant to protect the United States against alien agitators, many Americans held that the chief purpose of these laws was to weaken the opposition Democratic-Republican party. The laws (1) lengthened the naturalization process from 5 to 14 years, since most immigrants upon becoming citizens voted for Democratic-Republican candidates, (2) gave the President the power to deport any alien whom he considered dangerous to the United States, and (3) provided fines and imprisonment for any person guilty of sedition by uttering or writing "false, scandalous and malicious" statements against Congress or the President. This last provision was used to convict ten Democratic-Republican printers and editors.

b. The Dispute. The Democratic-Republican leaders, to gain votes in the forthcoming 1800 elections, attacked the Alien and Sedition laws as a threat to the people's civil liberties. At the urging of *James Madison* and *Thomas Jefferson*, the state legislatures of Virginia and Kentucky passed resolutions condemning these acts as unconstitutional. The *Virginia and Kentucky Resolutions* constituted the first formal expression of states' rights and *nullification*.

c. Outcome. Following the election in 1800 of Jefferson as President and of a Congress controlled by Democratic-Republicans, the federal government moved to annul the Alien and Sedition Acts by: restoring the five-year period for naturalization; permitting most other provisions to expire; and pardoning persons convicted of sedition. The issue of states' rights and nullification, however, was left unresolved.

2. The Tariff Issue (1828–1833)

a. Sectional Background. The Northeast, by now an industrial section producing textiles, iron implements, and machinery, favored a protective tariff to help its manufacturers and workers against foreign, especially British, competition. The West, an agricultural section of small family-size farms raising wheat, corn, and meat, generally supported the Northeast on a protective tariff. Although Western farmers disliked higher prices on manufactures, they wanted a prosperous Northeastern market for their foodstuffs. The South, an agricultural section of large plantations using slave labor and raising tobacco, rice, sugar, and, most important, cotton, was dominated by a small but wealthy planter class. The South opposed a protective tariff because it increased the prices of manufactured goods Southerners bought and because it aroused fears that Britain might retaliate by curtailing purchases of Southern cotton.

b. The Dispute. In 1828 Congress approved a very high protective tariff which Southerners promptly dubbed as hateful, the *Tariff of Abominations.* *John Calhoun* of South Carolina, the leading Southern spokesman, protested the 1828 tariff and secretly wrote the *South Carolina Exposition and Protest.* In this document, patterned after the Virginia and Kentucky Resolutions, Calhoun presented the states' rights doctrine, including nullification and secession. In the United States Senate in 1830, Calhoun's arguments were voiced by *Robert Hayne* of South Carolina who was answered by the leading Northern spokesman, *Daniel Webster* of Massachusetts. In this *Webster-Hayne debate*, Webster appealed to nationalist sentiment by dramatically calling for "Liberty and Union, now and forever, one and inseparable." In 1832 Congress passed a new tariff that provided only modest relief from the rates of the Tariff of Abominations. South Carolina thereupon passed an *Ordinance of Nullification*, declaring the new tariff null and void within South Carolina's borders. President *Andrew Jackson* warned that nullification is "incompatible with the existence of the Union" and pledged to enforce the nation's tariff law in South Carolina by utilizing the army and navy if necessary.

c. Outcome. With all sections seeking to avoid an armed clash, Congress passed the *Compromise Tariff of 1833*, introduced by *Henry Clay* of Kentucky, which provided for a gradual but significant reduction of tariff rates. South Carolina withdrew its Ordinance of Nullification, thus averting an armed clash. As a defiant gesture, however, South Carolina reasserted its right to nullify federal laws. Henry Clay's Compromise thusly settled the tariff issue but did not resolve the more basic issue of states' rights and nullification.

3. The Secession Issue (1860–1865)

a. Political Background. With the 1860 election of *Abraham Lincoln* as President, the Southern states reacted sharply. They considered Lincoln a "black Republican" hostile to slavery and ignored his pledge not to interfere with slavery in the states where it already existed. South Carolina passed an *Ordinance of Secession* declaring dissolved the "union between South Carolina and the other states under the name of the United States of America." South Carolina soon was joined by six other Southern states and after the outbreak of hostilities by four Southern border states.

b. As a Cause of the Civil War. The dispute over the nature of the federal union has always been listed high among the causes of the Civil War. Southern leaders insisted that any state had the right to secede from the Union. Speaking for the federal government, Lincoln labeled secession as illegal and proclaimed that the primary object of the war was not to abolish slavery but to preserve the Union. In its constitution, the Southern Confederacy affirmed that each state was sovereign and independent and implied that each state had the right to secede. During the Civil War, the Confederacy was hampered by state leaders who upheld states' rights even against the Confederate government.

   c. *Outcome.* The Union victory in the Civil War marked the triumph of nationalism over sectionalism. Never again has a state threatened to secede. The United States emerged as one nation, indivisible and indissoluble.

REASONS FOR THE EXPANSION OF FEDERAL POWER: ESPECIALLY SINCE 1865

Following the Civil War, the American nation entered upon an unprecedented era of economic growth and social change. This transformation brought about an increase in the responsibilities and powers of both the federal government and the states. Federal power, however, expanded far more rapidly than state power. This expansion of federal power, given impetus by the nationalist triumph in the Civil War, was further spurred by the following factors:

1. Geography. Great rivers as well as mountain ranges of America extend over many states. The mighty Mississippi River flows 2300 miles through ten states from Minnesota to Louisiana. It can be kept from flooding only by coordinated effort which requires federal action. Appalachia, a mountainous area, extends over 11 states from Pennsylvania to Alabama. It has become a poverty-stricken region whose inhabitants, regardless of the states in which they live, all face similar problems: poor soil, loss of coal-mining jobs due to automation, and inadequate health facilities. The area's problems call for an overall or national approach.

2. Industrialization. The growth of American industry brought problems such as prevention of monopoly, unemployment, democracy in labor unions, discrimination in hiring, and disposal of industrial wastes. Since industry was now nationwide, its problems could no longer be regulated effectively by state action but required the attention of the federal government.

3. Improvements in Technology. The development of modern means of transportation—the railroad, truck, auto, and airplane—and of communication—telephone, radio, and television—all have tended to obliterate state lines. The products that people buy, the news they hear, the sport teams they follow—almost all involve interstate commerce and therefore are subject to federal supervision. Also, as people have become more mobile, moving easily from one part of the United States to another, they think of themselves, not as state partisans, but as Americans.

With the arrival of the "atomic age" and the "space age," the federal government has assumed the major role in developing nuclear power and in pursuing space exploration.

4. Urbanization: Growth of Metropolitan Areas. With our population increasing substantially and also moving from rural areas to cities and suburbs, the nation has experienced the growth of huge metropolitan areas. As defined by the Census Bureau, a metropolitan area consists of a central city of at least 50,000 population plus the surrounding areas or "suburban rings" economically and socially tied to the central city. Of our more than 200 metropolitan areas, many overlap state boundaries. For example, the New York City metropolitan area includes parts of three states: New York, New Jersey, and Connecticut. Metropolitan areas face problems such as mass transportation, pollution control, and low-rent housing, but since many metropolitan areas encompass more than one state, their problems call for federal initiative.

5. National Crises: World Wars and Economic Depressions. With two world wars requiring total national involvement, the federal government increased its powers: conscripting and training men for military service, directing the economy toward war production, settling labor-management disputes, combating inflation, and developing new weapons. Also economic depressions, especially the great 1929 depression, have been national in scope. Since 1933 the federal government has assumed the responsibility of combating depressions by aiding the unemployed, spurring industrial and agricultural recovery, and instituting basic economic reforms.

6. Federal Income Tax. With the adoption of the Sixteenth Amendment, the federal government was empowered to levy a tax on incomes. By the World War II years, the federal government had raised income tax rates to such high levels as to effectively preempt this form of taxation. States and cities could levy an income tax but only at low rates, and their real estate, sales, and other taxes brought in relatively limited revenue. With states and cities facing mounting costs for education, welfare, housing, and mass transit, they were forced to look to Washington for federal aid.

FEDERAL-STATE DISPUTES IN THE 20TH CENTURY

Basic Issue: States' Reserved Powers vs. the 14th and 15th Amendments. Conflicts have arisen regarding the manner in which states have employed certain reserved powers. In such areas as education, voting requirements, and election district boundaries, states' righters have argued that the authority of the state is practically without limit. National patriots have insisted that the state may exercise its authority only within the limits set by the *Fourteenth Amendment: not* to abridge the privileges of citizens; *not* to deprive "any person of life, liberty, or property without due process of law"; *not* to deny any person "equal protection of the laws"; and by the *Fifteenth Amendment: not* to deny voting rights on account of "race, color, or previous condition of servitude." Consequently, certain state and local laws have been challenged before the Supreme Court as to their constitutionality. Some state and local laws have been declared unconstitutional; others have been superseded by federal laws.

1. Education. A Kansas law had required that the state keep Negro children apart from white students in public schools by maintaining separate educational systems. In 1954, in *Brown vs. Board of Education of Topeka,* the Supreme Court declared such segregation of Negro children a denial of the Fourteenth Amendment guarantee of "equal protection of the laws" and therefore held the state law unconstitutional. This decision was protested by several Southern state legislatures on the ground that the federal government has no Constitutional power over education. Despite such protests, the Supreme Court decision has been enforced by federal district courts and by the United States Office of

Education. (Check the Index for "Education, desegregation.") The states still control education, as a reserved power, but in so doing, the states must provide all public school children with "equal protection of the laws."

2. Voting Qualifications. A number of states, North and South, had required proof of literacy as a qualification for voting. In the South, however, white officials frequently used literacy tests as one device for keeping blacks from voting. For many blacks, who had little schooling, the tests were too difficult. For educated blacks, the tests often were administered unfairly. In 1957 the proportion of eligible Southern blacks registered to vote was only 25 percent.

The federal government should act, civil rights and black leaders demanded, to guarantee all citizens the right to vote. Congress responded with a series of laws: notably the *Civil Rights Act of 1964* which prohibited election officials from applying different standards to black and white voting applicants and declared a sixth grade education as evidence of literacy; the *Voting Rights Act of 1965* which suspended all literacy and other qualification tests in any state or county where less than half of the voting-age population was registered or had voted in 1964; and the *Voting Rights Act of 1970* which forbade all states from requiring literacy as a requirement for voting. In part as a result of such legislation, the proportion of eligible Southern blacks registered to vote has risen to 65 percent.

The Supreme Court has held Constitutional federal legislation limiting and then prohibiting the use of literacy tests as a voting qualification. These laws, the Court held, were appropriate means of enforcing the Fifteenth Amendment and wiping out racial discrimination in voting. In other decisions regarding the 1970 Voting Rights Act, the Court held that Congress had the power to set a uniform 30-day residency requirement for Presidential elections and to grant the vote to 18-year-olds in federal elections.

As a result of federal laws and Supreme Court decisions, the reserved power of the states over voting qualifications has been whittled away. The states retain control over some qualifications for state and local elections, but in exercising such control, the states must provide all citizens with "equal protection of the laws" and must not discriminate on the basis of "race or color." Further, as a practical matter, many states voluntarily adopted federal residency standards so as to avoid keeping separate federal and state registration records and separate voting machines.

3. Election District Boundaries: Legislative Reapportionment. The states historically have drawn the district boundaries for electing members of the federal House of Representatives and members of the state legislatures. For Representatives, the states are empowered by Article I, Section 4 of the Constitution to prescribe "the times, places and manner of holding elections" but state regulations may be altered by laws of Congress. For state legislators, the states' authority is derived from the reserved powers of the Tenth Amendment.

From the late 19th century onward, as our population increasingly shifted from rural to urban and suburban areas, most state legislatures refused to redraw election district boundary lines. As a result rural voters were overrepresented at the expense of urban and suburban voters.

For many years the Supreme Court held that legislative reapportionment was not a matter for the courts but a political issue to be decided by Congress, state legislatures, and the people. In 1962 the Supreme Court shifted its position by declaring, in *Baker vs. Carr*, that some election districts may be so "arbitrary and capricious" as to violate the "equal protection" clause of the Fourteenth Amendment. Shortly thereafter the Supreme Court held: in *Wesberry vs. Sanders* (1964) that in electing Representatives the Constitution requires that one man's vote "be worth as much as another's"; and in *Reynolds vs. Sims* (1964) that in electing state legislators the "equal protection" clause of the Fourteenth Amendment requires election districts roughly equal in population—that is, "one man, one vote."

As a result of these Supreme Court decisions, most states have reapportioned election districts on a more equitable population basis. The states retain control over the drawing of election district boundaries, but in so doing they cannot violate the Fourteenth Amendment guarantee of "equal protection of the laws."

FEDERAL-STATE COOPERATION IN THE 20TH CENTURY

Reasons. Whereas a federal-state dispute often is dramatic and makes the headlines, federal-state cooperation usually is commonplace and attracts little public attention. Nevertheless, the central government and the 50 state governments consistently work together, thereby (1) making possible the smooth operation and survival of our system of federalism and (2) furthering their shared goal of providing for the needs of the people. Such a federal-state partnership is sometimes referred to as *cooperative federalism*.

EXAMPLES OF COOPERATION

1. **By Government Agencies and Employees.** (a) The *Federal Bureau of Investigation* (FBI) assists state and local law-enforcement officers by providing data from its crime laboratory and fingerprint files and by offering criminal-investigation training courses. FBI agents work together with state and local police in apprehending persons wanted by the law. (b) The federal *Bureau of the Census* assists state and local agencies—concerned with public health, city planning, and business prospects—in establishing statistically sound methods of gathering and interpreting local population data. (c) The federal *Public Health Service* advises state and local officials on methods of preventing and controlling disease. Federal and state agencies conduct research on cancer, heart disease, the common cold, and dental decay; they exchange findings and sometimes coordinate their research efforts.

2. **By Regionalism.** To deal with regional problems that extend beyond state lines, the national government has devised the technique of a federal regional agency that cooperates with and coordinates the efforts of the states involved. The *Tennessee Valley Authority* (TVA), established in 1933, pioneered in this regional approach. (Check the Index for "Tennessee Valley Authority.") Another example of the regional approach is the *Appalachian Regional Commission*. Established by the federal government, this commission consists of the governor of each state in the region and a federal representative appointed by the President. The commission plans, coordinates, and supervises federal and state efforts to improve conditions for the people of Appalachia.

3. By Grants-in-Aid. *(a) Meaning.* Federal grants-in-aid are cash payments made by the central government to the states to finance specific state-run programs. Grants have supported some 1400 detailed programs, mostly classified under such broad categories as education; low-cost public housing; public health; aid to the aged, the physically handicapped, and dependent children; unemployment insurance payments; and highway and airport construction. *(b) Conditions.* To qualify for any specific grant-in-aid, the states must agree to (1) set up and administer the program, (2) maintain minimum standards as set by the federal government, (3) accept federal supervision of the program, and (4) supplement federal funds, which may range from 50 percent to 90 percent of the cost, with state funds to provide the balance. The states are free to accept or reject any specific grant. They are, however, under considerable pressure to accept, since rejection means the loss of federal monies. *(c) Amounts.* The amounts provided under federal grant-in-aid programs have increased tremendously. In recent years, such grants have totaled over 10 percent of the federal government's expenditures and have provided the state governments with 25 percent of their revenues. For a recent fiscal year, federal grants-in-aid to states and localities amounted to almost $33 billion.

PRESIDENT NIXON'S PROPOSALS FOR REVENUE SHARING

1. The Proposals. In 1971 President Nixon proposed a new plan of federal revenue sharing with the states and localities. He urged Congress to provide the states and localities with funds not restricted as to use or limited only into broad categories such as urban development, rural development, education, transportation, job training, and law enforcement. These revenue-sharing funds would replace many grants-in-aid previously earmarked by the federal government for specific programs.

2. Arguments For. President Nixon insisted that the time had come to reverse the flow of power, which historically has been toward Washington, by sending power back to the states and localities. He further claimed that his revenue-sharing plans would strengthen the state and local governments by *(a)* entrusting them with a greater share of the responsibility for the people's welfare, *(b)* freeing them from federal interference, *(c)* allowing them more initiative and greater flexibility in spending monies, and *(d)* rescuing them from financial crisis, thereby easing the pressures for ever higher real estate and sales taxes.

3. Arguments Against. Opponents of President Nixon's revenue-sharing plan insisted that the federal government *(a)* collects the tax revenues and therefore should determine the uses of the funds, *(b)* must exercise controls over the state and local governments to insure that the monies are spent honestly, efficiently, and for worthwhile purposes, *(c)* will be compelled to maintain high income tax rates and perhaps to impose additional taxes so as to raise revenue-sharing funds, *(d)* cannot afford an expanded revenue-sharing program in view of federal budget deficits and huge debt, and *(e)* can better aid the states financially by such ways as lowering federal income tax rates so that the states can raise theirs or by assuming the total financial burden of welfare.

"Pinch me . . . I must be dreaming!"
*(Eldon Pletcher in The
New Orleans Times-Picayune)*

4. The Revenue Sharing Act of 1972. This act provided for the distribution, over a five-year period, of $30.2 billion of federal monies: one-third to the states and two-thirds to the local governments. These monies are unrestricted as to use. (In 1976 the revenue sharing program was extended to 1980.)

Relations Among the States

States' Obligations to Each Other (Article IV, Sections 1 and 2). The Constitution specifies that each state shall (1) give "full faith and credit" to the legal actions of the other states (a couple married in New York is still considered married even though they move to California), (2) extend to citizens of other states the privileges of local citizenship, such as the right to own property and engage in business, and (3) honor requests from other states for *extradition,* that is, the return of a fugitive charged with committing a crime.

REASONS FOR GROWING STATE COOPERATION

Unlike in 1789, the states today have many contacts with each other and cooperate on many matters. This change toward greater state cooperation has resulted from the following: (1) growth of big corporations with headquarters in one state but owning factories, securing raw materials, and selling merchandise in many states, (2) improved transportation facilities making possible greater mobility of people and products across state lines, (3) growth of densely populated metropolitan areas encompassing several states, and (4) improved technology making possible better control and utilization of rivers, harbors, and other natural resources shared by several states.

EXAMPLES OF STATE COOPERATION

1. **Interstate Compacts.** "No state shall," in the words of the Constitution (Article I, Section 10), "enter into any agreement or compact with another state" without the consent of Congress. States have secured Congressional approval for interstate compacts dealing with port facilities, water resources, fishing rights, oil conservation, economic development of metropolitan areas, and reciprocal supervision of parolees and probationers. (a) The *Port of New York Authority*, established by New York and New Jersey, has planned the unified development of the metropolitan harbor area. The authority has constructed and maintained piers, bridges, tunnels, airports, and recently World Trade Center buildings. (b) The *St. Louis Bi-State Agency*, of Missouri and Illinois, has encouraged the economic development of the metropolitan St. Louis area. (c) The *Ohio River Valley Sanitation Compact*, of eight states, has sought to halt water pollution and prevent floods of the Ohio River. (d) The *Interstate Compact for the Supervision of Parolees and Probationers*, adhered to by all 50 states, has permitted a lawbreaker on parole or probation to move to another state and be under its supervision.

2. **Efforts for Uniform State Laws.** The *National Conference of Commissioners on Uniform State Laws*, begun in 1892, consists of representatives from each state and meets regularly. It draws up model laws which it urges the states to adopt. Many states have uniform laws regarding business records, narcotics, and criminal extradition procedures. Conference efforts, however, have been far from successful, for the states still maintain diverse laws in major areas such as business incorporation, consumer protection, marriage and divorce, motor vehicle regulations, education, welfare, and taxation.

3. **Interstate Organizations and Meetings.** The *Governors' Conference, National Association of Attorneys General, National Association of State Budget Directors*, and other similar organizations—all enable officials of the 50 states to meet regularly, discuss common problems, seek uniform solutions, and thereby further interstate cooperation. The *Council of State Governments* serves as an information center for data on state problems. It also publishes a magazine, *State Government*, and a reference work, *The Book of the States*.

EXAMPLES OF STATE DISPUTES AND COMPETITION

1. **State Disputes.** States have quarreled with each other over such issues as boundaries, fishing rights, and ownership of water. For example, Arizona and California long disputed the division of Colorado River waters. In 1963 this dispute was settled, in favor of Arizona, by the United States Supreme Court.

2. **State Competition.** States have competed with each other to attract tourists, secure business enterprises, and assist local industries: (a) Nevada offers an "easy" divorce law so that persons seeking divorce come to the state and spend money there while meeting the minimal residence requirements. Other states, however, have denied "full faith and credit" and have rejected the validity of Nevada "quickie" divorces on the ground that the out-of-state persons submitting to the jurisdiction of the Nevada court were only temporary, not "bona fide," or genuine residents of that state. (b) Delaware has long been known for its

"easy" corporation charters which place few restrictions upon the business managers. Delaware benefits by collecting incorporation fees and by requiring the corporation to maintain headquarters, even if only token, within the state. The Delaware-chartered corporation benefits from the Constitution's "full faith and credit" clause and may do business in all the 50 states. (c) The states compete with each other to attract business concerns that will provide jobs for local residents. The states have offered to provide land sites and low-cost loans for constructing factories, to train local workers to meet company needs, and to grant exemptions from state and local taxes. (d) Some states have required that buyers for state agencies give preference to local products. Some states have barred out-of-state fruits and vegetables, supposedly to keep out agricultural diseases but thereby increasing the in-state market for local farmers. Other states have passed retaliatory laws, in effect erecting state barriers to interstate trade.

FEDERAL AND STATE RELATIONS WITH CITIES

1. **Federal-City Relations.** The federal government occasionally has bypassed the states and dealt directly with city and other local officials in providing grants-in-aid for such programs as mass transit, urban renewal, low-cost public housing, pollution control, and education. It is not unusual for Washington, D.C., to be visited by delegations of city mayors seeking increased federal funds.

2. **State-City Relations.** The states grant the charters under which cities are established as legal entities with limited governmental powers and subject to state supervision and control. The states provide *state aid* or funds to cities for such local purposes as public health, education, and welfare. City officials frequently have complained that the states (1) deny sufficient *home rule* so they cannot effectively deal with city problems and (2) deny them sufficient state aid so they cannot adequately provide needed services. In these days of public resistance to heavy taxation and public demand for more services, state-city relationships are far from harmonious.

EVALUATION OF FEDERALISM: STRENGTHS AND WEAKNESSES

1. **Strengths.** (a) The federal government can best handle matters of national interest. State governments, being closer to the people, are best aware of local conditions and are best qualified to handle local problems. (b) By dividing powers between the federal government and a group of independent states jealously guarding their authority, federalism prevents complete centralization, which might lead to tyranny. Democracy survives best, it is argued, when powers are divided, not concentrated. (c) By preserving independent states, federalism prevents sole reliance upon national authority, provides a training ground for government officials, and encourages people to exercise local initiative and civic responsibility. (d) A state may serve as a laboratory for reform without involving the entire nation. For example, Wyoming experimented with woman suffrage and Wisconsin with unemployment insurance before these measures were adopted by the national government.

2. **Weaknesses.** (a) Conflicts arise between the federal government and the

states because the Constitutional provisions dividing their powers have proved vague and subject to differing interpretations. For example, advocates of states' rights consider education an area reserved for the states. Nevertheless, the federal government has legislated on education, claiming that scientific knowledge is essential for national defense. (b) On matters reserved to the states, laws have varied considerably from state to state. For example, Nevada permits gambling casinos, whereas other states do not; New Jersey requires a minimum age of 17 for an auto driver's license whereas most states set a minimum age of 16 and some six states grant a license at age 15. (c) Federalism results in inefficiency, waste, and overlapping administration. For example, duplicate federal and state agencies exist in such areas as housing, agriculture, and law enforcement.

Within the Federal Government: Separation of Powers

Three Branches of Government. The Founding Fathers separated the powers of the federal government among three distinct branches: (1) The *executive branch*, headed by the President, administers, or carries out, the laws. (2) The *legislative branch*, Congress, enacts, or makes, the laws. (3) The *judicial branch*, the court system, interprets the laws, that is, it settles disputes regarding the meaning of the laws.

The Constitution further provides that no member of Congress may serve, at the same time, in another branch of the federal government. Thus, before John Kennedy took office as President, he was compelled to resign his position as Senator from Massachusetts. Nor, by tradition, may a person simultaneously serve in the executive and judicial branches.

The three branches of government, however, are not separated rigidly as to powers, and to some extent their powers overlap. President, Congress, and the courts are not independent of each other but rather are interconnected. For the federal government to function smoothly, the three branches must work together with a considerable degree of harmony.

CHECKS AND BALANCES

The Constitution enables each branch of the federal government to brake and counteract the powers of the other two branches through a system of checks and balances.

1. Executive. (a) The President may check Congress by vetoing legislation. He may exert influence on Congress also by calling it into special session and by recommending legislation. (b) The President may check the federal courts by nominating judges, by granting pardons and reprieves (except in cases of impeachment), and by refusing to enforce court orders.

2. Legislative. (a) Congress may check the President by refusing to pass legislation and to appropriate funds, and by overriding the President's veto (a two-thirds vote of each house). In addition, the Senate may check the President by refusing to approve his appointments (a majority vote) and refusing to ratify treaties (a two-thirds vote). The House of Representatives may bring impeachment charges of "high crimes and misdemeanors," against the President, and the Senate, acting as the jury, may find the President guilty (a two-thirds vote) and remove him from office. *(b)* Congress may check the Supreme Court by passing a somewhat altered law to replace a law held unconstitutional, by initiating an amendment to the Constitution, by impeaching and convicting judges of "high crimes and misdemeanors," and by increasing the number of judges on the Supreme Court. The Senate also has the power to refuse to approve men nominated by the President for judgeships. *(c)* The House of Representatives and the Senate may check each other, since approval of both houses is necessary to pass laws.

3. Judicial. *(a)* The Supreme Court may check the President by declaring actions of the executive branch unconstitutional. *(b)* The Supreme Court may check Congress by declaring laws unconstitutional.

EVALUATION OF CHECKS AND BALANCES: STRENGTHS AND WEAKNESSES

1. Strengths

a. Checks and balances prevent any branch of government from becoming too powerful and establishing a dictatorship. The Founding Fathers greatly feared the danger of tyranny. They derived the idea of checks and balances from (1) the political theory of the *Baron de Montesquieu,* the French philosopher, who in his book *The Spirit of the Laws* urged a three-part division of governmental powers to protect liberty, and (2) the experiences of the colonial legislatures that had fought the royal governors.

b. Hasty, ill-considered action by any one branch of government is discouraged, since each branch is aware that its action is subject to checks by the other two.

c. In national emergencies, the branches temporarily and voluntarily suspend their powers of check and balance in order to work together quickly and efficiently. In 1933, to combat the depression, President *Franklin D. Roosevelt* requested a considerable number of major New Deal laws, which Congress passed within a 100-day period. On December 7, 1941, Japan attacked Pearl Harbor; on December 8, President Roosevelt requested a declaration of war, which Congress passed the same day. In these two instances, Congress abbreviated its usual procedures of debating, criticizing, and deliberating so as to accede quickly to executive requests.

2. Weaknesses

a. Checks and balances may paralyze the workings of government, especially if one party controls Congress and another the executive. For example, in 1947–1948, when President *Harry Truman,* a Democrat, and Congress, controlled by Republicans, disagreed on most domestic matters, they accomplished little toward meeting the nation's domestic needs.

b. In case of an executive-legislative deadlock, no provision exists for calling a special election so that the voters may end the deadlock. Instead, the nation must await the next regular election.

 c. Checks and balances may cause delay and uncertainty. For example, a law passed by Congress and signed by the President may be declared unconstitutional by the Supreme Court after an interval of several years.

MULTIPLE-CHOICE QUESTIONS

1. James Madison's statement that "ambition must be made to counteract ambition" means that (1) ambitious men would seek federal office (2) men without ambition should not be trusted (3) by distributing governmental powers, no one ambitious man could become too strong (4) ambition could spur a counteraction in favor of the Articles of Confederation.

2. Which illustrates the fact that the United States has a federal system of government? (1) Congress passes laws, but the President enforces them. (2) The President appoints Cabinet members, but the Senate must approve them. (3) The Supreme Court has the power to declare laws of Congress unconstitutional. (4) The national government regulates interstate commerce, but state governments regulate commerce within the states.

3. The powers of Congress were limited by the Constitution, *chiefly* because the (1) advocates of states' rights wanted state powers specified in detail (2) representatives of the states feared too powerful a central government (3) defenders of the federal government planned a strong role for the states in the use of enumerated powers (4) supporters of a strong central government planned to make widespread use of the reserved powers.

4. Local, state, and national governments *all* have the power to (1) set tariffs and issue patents (2) enact rules of naturalization and imprison criminals (3) establish post offices and build roads (4) levy taxes and borrow money.

5. The powers of Congress derived from the provision "to make all laws which shall be necessary and proper for carrying into execution the foregoing powers" are said to be (1) concurrent (2) implied (3) residual (4) enumerated.

6. The *most* frequent basis for legislation expanding the role of the federal government in our economy has been the elastic clause together with the delegated power of Congress to (1) coin money (2) issue patents and copyrights (3) promote the progress of science (4) regulate interstate commerce.

7. Which action by a state legislature would be permissible under the Constitution? (1) imposing a tariff on imported products which compete with local industry (2) establishing a quota for immigrants to reside in that state (3) licensing a merchant ship engaged in transporting goods from New York to Boston (4) lowering the voting age requirement in that state

8. Which is an example of a power denied both to the federal government and to the states? (1) enactment of ex post facto legislation (2) impeachment of judges (3) levying of tariffs (4) coining of money

9. According to the doctrine of nullification, the right to determine the constitutionality of an act of Congress resides in (1) Congress itself (2) the states (3) the United States Supreme Court only (4) the executive branch of the federal government.

10. The Democratic-Republican party used the Alien and Sedition Acts to (1) unite the country for possible war against Great Britain (2) advance arguments for a strong central government (3) indicate approval for war against France (4) influence voters against the Federalists.

11. An advocate of states' rights would have *opposed* the (1) Tenth Amendment to the Constitution (2) Kentucky and Virginia Resolutions (3) South Carolina Ordinance of Secession (4) Fourteenth Amendment to the Constitution.

12. Before the Civil War, the South objected to high tariffs because they (1) kept the price of cotton low (2) increased the cost of slaves (3) increased the prices of manufactured goods (4) helped Western farmers at the planters' expense.

13. According to the *South Carolina Exposition and Protest*, a federal law could be nullified by a state because the federal government was (1) dependent on the states for taxes (2) created by the states (3) composed of men elected or appointed from the states (4) limited in its use of power by the Bill of Rights.

14. President Jackson's action in the nullification controversy (1) antagonized the North (2) was challenged before the Supreme Court (3) won him the support of Calhoun (4) strengthened the power of the national government.

15. Which is a reason why federal power has grown at the expense of the power of state governments? (1) State governments have shown little interest in solving their own problems. (2) State governments want the federal government to control state activities. (3) The federal government attracts leading political figures. (4) Many modern problems require solutions that cut across state lines.

16. The rapid expansion of metropolitan areas in the United States has resulted in (1) the need for greater intergovernmental cooperation (2) a reduction in the amount of federal aid needed by the cities (3) the disappearance of local government boundary lines (4) an increase in the power of city governments.

17. After World War II, which issue contributed *most* to the growth of sectionalism in the United States? (1) population growth of California (2) civil rights (3) foreign policy toward Soviet Russia (4) legislative reapportionment

18. The Constitutional argument advocated by some sections of the South against federal action for integration in education is based upon (1) delegated powers (2) reserved powers (3) the system of checks and balances (4) the elastic clause.

19. Which Constitutional principle was involved in the Supreme Court decision on reapportionment in *Baker vs. Carr?* (1) separation of church and state (2) separation of powers (3) "separate but equal" (4) equal protection of the laws

20. In contrast to federal grants-in-aid, the federal revenue-sharing program (1) costs the federal government nothing (2) sets no restrictions on the states regarding use of the monies (3) maintains strict federal supervision of state programs (4) requires states and localities to lower real estate tax rates.

21. Which of the following could be considered a weakness of federalism? (1) State laws vary greatly on such matters as divorce and minimum age for auto drivers' licenses. (2) A state-chartered corporation can do business only in that state. (3) State law-enforcement agencies are denied assistance by the FBI. (4) No facilities exist for settling disputes between states.

22. The system of checks and balances set up by the Founding Fathers showed (1) a rejection of unrestricted immigration (2) a fear of concentrated political power (3) an abandonment of the principle of separation of powers (4) reliance on the House of Representatives to restrain popular influence.

23. In adopting the principle of separation of powers, the framers of the Constitution were *most* influenced by the writings of (1) Jefferson (2) Rousseau (3) Hamilton (4) Montesquieu.

24. Which is an illustration of the system of checks and balances? (1) An individual pays an income tax to both the United States and New York State. (2) New York State requires at least 180 school days per year. (3) The Senate approves a President's nominee to the Supreme Court. (4) The United States Senate censures one of its members.

25. Which has been an important result of the expansion of metropolitan areas in the United States? (1) The white middle class has tended to move from the suburbs to the central city. (2) Industries have been attracted to urban core areas. (3) City governments have become less complex in recent years. (4) The federal government has assumed increasing responsibility for problems in urban areas.
26. A criminal suspect wanted in Georgia is found in New York. To have the suspect arrested in New York and returned to Georgia, the Georgia governor can (1) authorize the Georgia police to do so (2) require the FBI to do so (3) request New York authorities to do so (4) appeal to the Supreme Court for a certificate of arrest and return.

ESSAY QUESTIONS

1. (a) By giving two examples, prove that the Constitution divided powers between the states and the national government. (b) Give two examples of the increase in power of the national government in the 20th century. (c) Give one argument for or one argument against the increase in power of the national government at the present time.
2. Choose one federal-state controversy in the 19th century and one in the 20th century. (a) For each explain (1) the issue in the controversy and (2) the outcome. (b) For the two controversies you have chosen, discuss one similarity and one difference.
3. Agree or disagree with each of the following statements and present two arguments to support your opinion. (a) For federalism to succeed, the central government and the states must seek cooperation and avoid conflict. (b) In giving funds to states and localities, the federal government should allot the monies for specific programs and should exercise strict supervision over the programs. (c) In the 20th century the federal government has shown increasing concern for public welfare. (d) Social and economic developments in the United States since the Civil War have brought about the expansion of federal power.
4. (a) Giving two examples, illustrate the operation of the system of checks and balances in our federal government. (b) State one reason for including this system in our Constitution. (c) Explain one advantage and one disadvantage of the system of checks and balances. (d) Giving one example, illustrate the workings of this system during the last ten years.
5. To answer this question, refer to the text of the Constitution: Article I, Section 9, for powers denied to the federal government, and to Article I, Section 10, for powers denied to the states (see pages 693–694). (a) Show the extent to which information in these two sections supports the following hypotheses: (1) The Constitution is basically an economic document. (2) Problems involving trade prompted the writing of a new Constitution in 1787. (3) There was considerable distrust among the various states at the time of the adoption of the Constitution. (b) For one of the hypotheses in (a), describe the kinds of additional information you would need in order to prove or disprove the hypothesis.

Part 3. The Three Branches of Government

4. The President Is the Chief Executive and Serves as Leader of the Nation

At the Constitutional Convention, the Founding Fathers had two opposing fears regarding the office of the Presidency: making it too powerful might lead to a tyranny such as King George III had attempted to impose upon the colonies; making it too weak might repeat the mistakes of the Articles of Confederation. In their decisions regarding the Presidency, the Founding Fathers were swayed by the thought that the farsighted George Washington, who sought no personal rule, would shape the office as first President. They created an independent executive with definite and important powers and also with limitations upon those powers. They left unsaid, whether deliberately or accidentally, many details regarding the Presidential office. Evolving out of practical experience, such details now constitute our Presidential traditions and customs.

Over the years, the Presidency has grown in power, gained in prestige, and become the paramount branch of our national government. Clinton Rossiter, the noted political scientist, in his book *The American Presidency* concluded that the Presidency is "one of the few truly successful institutions created by men in their endless quest for the blessings of free government."

Selection of Presidential Candidates

CONSTITUTIONAL REQUIREMENTS

The Constitution requires that a candidate for the Presidency be a "natural-born" citizen of the United States, at least 35 years of age, and for 14 years a resident within the United States.

BRIEF HISTORY OF NOMINATING PROCEDURES

The Constitution is silent regarding the nominating of Presidential candidates. This task was assumed, early in our history, by political parties.

1. **Caucus System (To 1828).** A *caucus*, or meeting of a small group of influential party leaders, mostly Congressmen, selected the party candidate for the Presidency. Because the rank-and-file party members had no voice in this process, *King Caucus* was condemned as undemocratic.

167

2. Nominating Convention (Since 1832). Spurred by the democratic spirit of the *Jacksonian Era*—the period of Andrew Jackson's ascendancy in American life —political parties began selecting their Presidential candidates by a new method, the *nominating convention*. Since a large group of party members attended the convention, it was a democratic advance over the caucus.

NATIONAL NOMINATING CONVENTION SYSTEM TODAY

1. Selection of National Convention Delegates

a. By District and State Conventions. In about one-quarter of the states, delegates are chosen by the political parties through district and state conventions. These procedures, operating within the party machinery, usually are controlled by local and state party leaders.

Evaluation. These procedures have been criticized as being undemocratic and enabling the party "bosses" to dominate the national convention; they have been defended as being practical and enabling informed political leaders to exercise their best judgment.

b. By Presidential Primaries. In about three-quarters of the states, the party members vote for delegates in preliminary elections, called *primaries*. The party members may have a choice of different slates of delegates, each supporting its own candidate. Usually, delegates pledge to vote for their candidate at least on the first ballot of the national convention. In recent years the number of Presidential primaries has increased sharply.

Evaluation. Presidential primaries have been hailed as a democratic advance over district and state conventions, since primaries reflect the wishes not of a few party leaders, but of the many party members. However, the primaries have been criticized because they (1) generally attract a low voter turnout, so that an active minority of party members may gain delegates for their candidate while the majority of party members may remain apathetic, (2) involve considerable expense, thereby favoring the candidate with the greater campaign funds, and (3) tend to discourage qualified candidates who lack the money and time from actively seeking the Presidency.

In recent years, political parties have insisted that national convention delegates—regardless of how chosen—include more women, youths, and ethnic minorities. In this way the parties hope that the convention delegates will more accurately reflect the interests of all their members.

2. National Convention. Held some two to three months before Election Day, the convention—full of noise, motion, and color, and broadcast over radio and television—has been called a "political circus." It serves to center public attention upon the party, to enthuse rank-and-file party workers, to reconcile differing party views and unite delegates on a statement of party policy or *party platform*, and to nominate the party candidates for President and Vice President.

3. Qualifications Considered in Selecting a Candidate

a. Party Criteria. Each party seeks to nominate a candidate who can win. Such a person, party leaders generally believe, should (1) possess great personal popularity and have few enemies, (2) reflect moderate views on controversial issues, and (3) come from a heavily populated and *doubtful state*, that is, a state that has not consistently voted for one major party. Since the Civil War, a large number of candidates have come from such populous and "doubtful" states as New York, Ohio, Illinois, and California.

b. Personal and Professional Backgrounds of Presidents (Since 1865). The major political parties have chosen their Presidential candidates from the wide spectrum of American life. Of the candidates who gained the Presidency since the Civil War, two men—Grant and Eisenhower—advanced through military careers; all the others came from civilian life. More than half were lawyers; Wilson was an educator and historian; Harding, a newspaper editor; Hoover, a mining engineer; Truman, a farmer and later a small men's-clothing-store owner. Some Presidents—Cleveland, Truman, Eisenhower, and Nixon—traced their origins to hard-working lower-class and middle-class families; whereas others—Theodore Roosevelt, Franklin D. Roosevelt, and John Kennedy—came from wealthy and aristocratic families. Educated at prestigious colleges were: both Roosevelts and Kennedy at Harvard, Taft at Yale, Wilson at Princeton, and Hoover at Stanford; only two Presidents—Cleveland and Truman—had no formal college training. In climbing the political ladder to the Presidency, some men—T. Roosevelt, Coolidge, Truman, and both Johnsons—were Vice Presidents who inherited the office upon the death of the President; others —Cleveland, Wilson, and F. D. Roosevelt—advanced from state governorships; still others—Harding and Kennedy—moved up from the Senate.

In conclusion, although Presidential hopefuls might consider as assets a college education, a civilian career especially as a lawyer, and residence in a politically "doubtful" state, no one knows any sure road to the Presidency.

c. Disadvantaged Persons. For the Presidency, no major political party has ever nominated a black, a Jew, or a woman. Twice only, the Democrats have nominated Catholics—in 1928 Alfred Smith, who lost the election, and in 1960 the victorious John Kennedy. With these two exceptions, the candidates of the major parties have been white, Protestant, and male.

4. The Convention Selects the Party Ticket

a. Presidential Candidate. The names presented to the convention include those of (1) *active candidates*, who have previously declared their intention to seek the nomination and possibly have won the support of delegates in various states through Presidential primaries and political arrangements, and (2) *favorite sons*, who are state leaders honored by their delegations on the basis of state loyalty even though they may not be actively seeking the Presidency. To gain the nomination, a candidate requires a majority of the votes. If repeated balloting fails to give any candidate a majority, the convention is deadlocked and may unite behind a compromise choice, usually a person not previously considered and therefore called a *dark horse*.

Of course, if the President is seeking a second term, the convention usually loses the sense of battle and becomes "cut-and-dried" as it grants him the nomination.

b. Vice Presidential Candidate. After the Presidential candidate is nominated, the convention selects the Vice Presidential candidate. Usually, the convention respects the wishes of the Presidential nominee as to his running mate. The Vice Presidential candidate is expected to bring strength to the ticket by attracting voters indifferent to the Presidential nominee. For example, the two candidates may come from different sections of the country and may be identified with different economic interests. The Vice Presidential candidate is said, therefore, to *balance the ticket*.

Since nine Vice Presidents—five in the present century—have moved into the Presidency, political scientists criticize national conventions for their "balance-the-ticket" motives and casualness in selecting the Vice Presidential candidate. (Of all Vice Presidents who moved into the Presidency, Gerald Ford was the only one who had not been nominated by a national convention but became Vice President under the provisions of the Twenty-Fifth Amendment.)

Election of the President

ELECTION CAMPAIGN

1. Appeal to the Voters. For eight to ten weeks, the Presidential and Vice Presidential candidates "go to the people." They present their philosophies of government and their views on current issues. They employ sizable organizing and publicity staffs, travel extensively, deliver major addresses and brief talks, and appear on radio and television.

Evaluation. Some political scientists question the need of such long campaigns today. They argue that (a) the candidates actually engage in two campaigns—for the nomination and for the election; (b) by means of radio, television, and airplane, candidates today reach more voters in less time than ever before; (c) in Great Britain, national election campaigns last about three weeks; and (d) shorter campaigns would make possible reduced expenditures.

2. Campaign Finances. Presidential campaigns are expensive. In 1972 the Democrats spent $27 million and the Republicans spent $45 million. The major political parties have sought funds through small contributions from their many members, but this approach has produced only insignificant sums. Their main source of funds, however, has been well-to-do contributors.

a. **Federal Campaign Regulations.** To prevent political parties from being unduly indebted to large contributors, Congress passed several "corrupt practices" laws—none really effective. One provision still in force prohibits corporations or unions from contributing campaign funds. However, corporate officials may contribute as individuals; union members may also contribute voluntarily to labor's *Committee on Political Education* (COPE).

b. **The 1974 Federal Campaign Reform Act.** The Senate Committee on Presidential Campaign Activities, under *Sam Ervin*, investigated the 1972 election and uncovered two major weaknesses: (1) A number of corporations and milk cooperatives had made large and illegal campaign contributions, mostly to the Committee to Reelect the President [Richard Nixon]. (2) The Justice Department lacked the personnel to handle all election law violation cases. To remedy such weaknesses, Congress enacted the 1974 *Federal Campaign Reform Act*.

(1) The law limited spending and provided federal funds for Presidential elections. For Presidential primaries, each candidate who raises $100,000 in private contributions of $250 or less from at least 20 states is eligible for federal funds. These funds are to match all private contributions of $250 or less up to a

maximum of $5 million, thereby limiting the spending of each candidate in the primaries to $10 million. For the national nominating convention, each major party is to receive federal funds of $2 million. For the Presidential general election, each major party candidate is to receive and be limited to federal funds of $20 million. (A minor party may be eligible for federal election funds in proportion to its votes in the previous election.) Those federal funds are to come from individual income tax payers—some 80 million—who since 1972 have had the right to check off or assign $1 of taxes for election campaign purposes.

The law provided that, in future years, certain of these monetary limits were to be revised in keeping with the Consumer Price Index.

(2) The law provided no federal funds for but limited spending by Senate and House candidates.

(3) The law limited contributions by individuals and political organizations. For a single federal candidate, an individual is limited to a contribution of $1000 for the primaries and $1000 for the general election, making a total of $2000. Political organizations—such as labor union committees and public interest groups—may contribute to a Presidential candidate no more than $5000. Contributions of over $100 may not be in cash. Presidential candidates may spend on their own behalf no more than $50,000.

(4) The law established a *Federal Elections Commission* of six members— two named by the President and four by Congress. The Commission is to receive reports from candidates of receipts and expenditures, to investigate suspicious contributions, and to institute civil suits against suspected campaign law violators. Candidates who violate the law may be barred for a number of years from running again for federal office. All violators may be fined up to $50,000.

c. The 1976 Supreme Court Decision on the Campaign Reform Act. (1) The Court held unconstitutional the spending limits on Presidential candidates for themselves and on Senate and House candidates. Such limits, the Court reasoned, violated the First Amendment guarantee of free speech. (2) The Court ordered the restructuring of the Federal Elections Commission to have all six members named by the President. The Commission, the Court held, is an

Fat cat (*Hesse in the St. Louis Globe-Democrat*)

"Just give me your credit card." (*Hesse in the St. Louis Globe-Democrat*)

executive agency and must conform to the principle of separation of powers. (By law, the Commission was so restructured.) (3) The Court upheld *(a)* limits on individual and group contributions to political candidates as only a "marginal" restraint on free speech, outweighed by the need to insure the "integrity" of the election process; *(b)* requirements that political candidates provide detailed reports of contributions and expenditures; and *(c)* public financing of Presidential candidates. In upholding these provisions, the Court cited the need to avoid the "actuality and appearance of corruption" in federal elections.

3. Election Day. On the first Tuesday after the first Monday in November each leap year, the voters go to the polls. They vote their choice of candidate not directly, but through a group of relatively unknown persons called *electors.*

ELECTORAL SYSTEM

1. Number of Electors. According to the Constitution, the *Electoral College*—the term for all electors as a group—chooses the President and Vice President. For each state, the number of electors equals the total of the state's Representatives and Senators in Congress. Although the District of Columbia is not a state, according to the Twenty-Third Amendment, it is currently entitled to three electors. Since the number of Representatives equals 435, the number of Senators equals 100, and the District of Columbia has 3 electors, the Electoral College today totals 538.

2. Election Procedures. On the ballot, the voters see the phrase "electors for" followed by the names of the Presidential and Vice Presidential candidates. Thus, the voters actually choose from among several slates of electors, each slate being pledged in advance to support its party's candidates. The winning slate receives either *(a)* a *majority*—more than half the popular votes cast in the state, or *(b)* a *plurality*—the largest number of popular votes, though less than half, as may happen if more than two slates are contesting the election.

The Presidential and Vice Presidential candidates of the winning slate in each state receive that state's total electoral votes—the *winner-takes-all* principle. For election to the Presidency or Vice Presidency, a candidate must secure a majority in the Electoral College, now 270 votes.

3. Appeals From an Electoral College Deadlock

a. Constitutional Provisions (Article II, Section 1, revised in 1804 by the Twelfth Amendment). If the Electoral College does not give any candidate the necessary majority, the House of Representatives chooses the President from among the top three candidates in electoral votes. In such a situation the House votes by states, with each state having one vote. To be elected President, a candidate must receive the votes of a majority of the states. For the Vice Presidency, if no candidate receives a majority in the Electoral College, the Senate selects a Vice President from the top two candidates.

b. Case Studies. Twice the Electoral College has failed to elect a President and has thrown the election into the House of Representatives. (1) In 1800 Thomas Jefferson and Aaron Burr, meant to be respectively the Presidential and Vice Presidential candidates of the Democratic-Republican party, defeated the

Federalist contenders. As each Democratic-Republican elector cast two ballots, unmarked as to office, Jefferson and Burr were tied in electoral votes. The House of Representatives, controlled by its Federalist members, took 36 ballots before choosing Jefferson. This election crisis led to the adoption of the Twelfth Amendment, requiring electors to cast separate ballots for President and Vice President. (2) In 1824 Andrew Jackson led the other candidates—respectively Adams, Crawford, and Clay—but lacked a majority in electoral votes. The House of Representatives, authorized to choose from among the top three candidates and influenced by Henry Clay, named as President John Quincy Adams. When Adams later appointed Clay as Secretary of State, Jackson's supporters shouted "corrupt bargain."

4. From Undemocratic Intent to "Rubber Stamp." The Founding Fathers devised the electoral system so as to reduce the voice of the people in electing the President. They intended that the electors express their own judgment. Since 1796, however, political parties have overcome this undemocratic intent by naming electors who were pledged in advance to vote for the party's Presidential candidate. Thus, the people vote for the Presidential candidate they desire by voting for his group of electors, and the Electoral College reflects the people's wishes. It has become a "rubber stamp."

5. Effects of the Electoral College System

a. The electoral vote distorts the public voice as registered in the popular vote. In 1960 John Kennedy defeated Richard Nixon by a very narrow margin in the popular vote, 34,227,000 to 34,109,000, but the electoral vote of 303 to 219 indicated a ratio of almost 3 to 2.

b. A candidate may lose the small states overwhelmingly in the popular vote while carrying the large states by narrow margins. The electoral votes of the large states may then give the candidate a victory in the Electoral College though his opponent had more popular votes. In 1888, although Grover Cleveland outdrew Benjamin Harrison by 100,000 popular votes, Harrison received a majority of the electoral votes and was elected President.

c. Most minor parties are discouraged by the electoral system, since they rarely poll enough popular votes to capture any electoral votes. People often feel that a vote for a minor party candidate is a "wasted" vote.

d. In most states, electors are not legally bound to honor their pledges to vote for their party's candidates. In a few recent instances, electors have broken their pledges.

e. Candidates tend to campaign little in small states and rural areas. They concentrate upon the industrial states, and upon heavily populated cities and suburbs, aiming to win the states with the most electoral votes.

f. To carry closely contested or *doubtful* states, especially in the North, candidates seek to satisfy minority groups whose numbers could determine, that is, *swing* the electoral vote of an entire state.

g. When more than two strong candidates are running, the Electoral College may convert a popular plurality into an electoral majority and so prevent a deadlock. In 1968 Republican Richard Nixon led with 43.4 percent of the popular vote to 42.7 percent for Democrat Hubert Humphrey and 13.4 percent for the states' rights candidate George Wallace. Although Nixon lacked a nationwide popular majority, he carried 32 states with 301 electoral votes—a clear electoral majority—and was elected President.

6. Proposed Changes. The 1968 Presidential election, with three forceful candidates, aroused the nation to the possibility of an Electoral College deadlock. Although this deadlock did not then materialize, the House of Representatives in 1969 proposed a Constitutional amendment that would (*a*) abolish the Electoral College, (*b*) base the election upon the popular vote, (*c*) require the top pair of candidates for President and Vice President to secure at least 40 percent of the popular vote, and (*d*) if no pair secured this minimum, provide for a runoff election between the top two pairs. This proposal still requires a two-thirds vote in the Senate and ratification by 38 states.

a. Arguments For. This proposed amendment (1) is more democratic since the people themselves will directly elect the President, (2) would encourage candidates not to campaign mainly in the populous states but more evenly throughout the country, (3) would eliminate "faithless" electors who violate their voting pledges, (4) would avoid the political intrigues that have occurred in past elections thrown into the House of Representatives, and (5) provides a method for resolving election deadlocks quickly so that, in these times of crisis, the nation will not long be without a President.

b. Arguments Against. This proposed amendment (1) in a close election could enable dishonest voting practices in a single state to determine the national outcome whereas under the present system such dishonest voting practices could affect only that state's electoral vote, (2) with candidates campaigning throughout the country, would cause campaign costs to rise, (3) is not necessary to remedy so obvious a weakness as compelling electors to honor their pledges, (4) would shift the major party Presidential nominations from moderate, "middle-of-the-road" candidates of "doubtful" states who can win the support of minority groups to more conservative candidates from "one-party" states who can attract a large popular state and sectional vote, and (5) by eliminating the "winner-takes-all" principle, would weaken the two-party system and encourage the growth of splinter parties, making divisive class, ethnic, or sectional appeals and hoping to compel a runoff election in which they could bargain votes in exchange for influence.

PRESIDENTIAL INAUGURATION

On the 20th of January following the election, the President takes office. In a solemn and impressive ceremony, he takes an oath or affirmation to "preserve, protect, and defend the Constitution of the United States."

Presidential Tenure and Succession

TERM OF PRESIDENTIAL OFFICE

1. Two-Term Tradition. The Constitution sets the term of office at four years. George Washington, our first President, originated the tradition of serving no more than two terms.

2. Breaking the Two-Term Tradition. In 1940 Franklin D. Roosevelt broke the two-term tradition when he was nominated for and elected to a third term. His supporters argued that the people (a) needed an experienced statesman to deal with the critical problems of World War II, and (b) had made and therefore could unmake traditions. His opponents insisted that the people (a) should not consider any one man indispensable, and (b) needed the two-term tradition as a safeguard against dictatorship.

3. Twenty-Second Amendment (1951): Two-Term Limitation. Passed after Roosevelt's breaking of the two-term tradition, this amendment prohibits any one person from being elected President for more than two terms. A person who has served more than two years of another person's term may be elected for only one additional term.

SUCCESSION TO THE PRESIDENCY

1. Original Constitution (Article II, Section 1). In case of the death, resignation, or removal of the President, the Constitution provides that he be succeeded by the Vice President.

2. Presidential Succession Act of 1947. In the event of a vacancy in both the Presidency and the Vice Presidency, the *Presidential Succession Act of 1947* provides the following order of succession to the Presidency: first the Speaker of the House of Representatives, then the President pro tempore of the Senate, and finally the Cabinet members, starting with the Secretary of State.

3. Problems of Presidential Disability and Succession. Until the 1960's, Congress failed to deal with the problem of Presidential disability. For example, in 1919–1920 President Wilson was bedridden with a stroke, and, for much of this time, the executive branch remained leaderless. Wilson's Vice President, Thomas Marshall, made little effort to assume the President's responsibilities. Also, from 1955 to 1957, President Eisenhower suffered three serious illnesses. Eisenhower's Vice President, Richard Nixon, took an active part in maintaining the administration, but did not become Acting President—a position not foreseen by the Founding Fathers.

Still another problem: the Vice Presidency has often been vacant. In 1963, following President Kennedy's assassination, Lyndon Johnson succeeded to the office of President, and the Vice Presidency remained vacant for over a year. This event and Eisenhower's illnesses turned the nation's attention to the problem of Presidential disability and succession.

4. Twenty-Fifth Amendment (1967): Presidential Disability and Succession

a. In case the office of Vice President is vacant, the President shall nominate a new Vice President, subject to approval by a majority vote of both houses of Congress.

b. In case of Presidential disability, the President himself or—if he does not or cannot—the Vice President, with a majority of the Cabinet members, may so inform Congress. Thereupon, the Vice President shall serve as Acting President.

c. When the President informs Congress that his disability no longer exists, he shall resume the duties of his office. In case the Vice President and a majority of the Cabinet officers dispute the President's ability to resume office, the President may be declared still disabled and kept from office by a two-thirds vote of Congress. The Vice President then continues as Acting President.

5. First Applications of the Twenty-Fifth Amendment. Resigning as Vice President of the United States in 1973, *Spiro Agnew* also pleaded "no contest" to a charge of income tax evasion—that, while Baltimore County executive and Maryland governor, he had diverted political contributions to personal use without reporting the money as income. Sentenced to three years' probation and a fine, Agnew was the first Vice President ever to be forced from that office because of criminal charges. Acting under the Twenty-Fifth Amendment, President Richard Nixon nominated his choice for the Vice Presidency—the Republican minority leader of the House of Representatives, *Gerald Ford.* After extensive Congressional investigations of Ford's personal and political life, the nomination was overwhelmingly approved by Congress. In December 1973, Ford took the oath of office as Vice President.

In August 1974, Richard Nixon resigned as President. His resignation, the first by any American President, followed investigations into White House involvement in the 1972 Watergate burglary and subsequent "cover-up" efforts, impeachment charges voted against the President by the House Judiciary Committee, and the erosion of support for Nixon in Congress. (Check the Index for "Richard Nixon, resignation of.") Gerald Ford was sworn in as President.

With the Vice Presidency again vacant, Ford moved promptly to nominate his choice—oil millionaire and former New York governor *Nelson Rockefeller.* After intensive committee hearings, both houses of Congress, in December 1974, overwhelmingly approved the nomination of Rockefeller as Vice President.

6. The Vice Presidency

a. Constitutional Requirements. The Constitution requires that the Vice President (1) have the same qualifications as does the President—35 years of age, a native-born citizen, and 14 years United States residence, (2) be elected by a majority vote of the Electoral College, and (3) if no candidate secures an electoral majority, be selected by the Senate from the two top candidates.

b. Powers. The Vice President is empowered by the Constitution (1) to serve as presiding officer of the Senate and (2) to vote in the Senate only if "they be equally divided." Neither of these two powers is particularly significant. Excluded from Senate committees, debates, and voting—except in the rare case of a tie, the Vice President has little Senate influence. He usually absents himself from Senate sessions, and his place as presiding officer is occupied by a Senate-elected "president pro tempore."

The Vice President is also empowered by the Constitution to assume the office of the Presidency upon the resignation, removal, or death of the President. Thus, the Vice President is the "heir apparent" who will become powerful if he succeeds to the Presidency but in the meantime is powerless—dependent on Congress and the President for assignments and responsibilities.

c. Early Disdain for the Vice Presidency. John Adams, our first Vice President, described the position as "the most insignificant office that ever the invention of man contrived or his imagination conceived." Other early leaders reinforced this critical appraisal by referring to the Vice President as "His Superfluous Excellency." *John Calhoun*, elected Vice President in 1828 on the ticket with Andrew Jackson, resigned in 1832 to become Senator from South Carolina. As Senator, Calhoun felt he could more decisively influence the events of the then raging states' rights and nullification controversy. *Theodore Roosevelt* in 1900 reluctantly accepted the Vice Presidential nomination on the Republican ticket with McKinley. Roosevelt's nomination had been engineered by political bosses who disliked Roosevelt and hoped to stifle his career by "kicking him upstairs" into the Vice Presidency. Roosevelt himself observed that "I would a great deal rather be anybody, say a professor of history, than Vice President."

d. Growing Respect for the Vice Presidency— In the 20th Century

(1) *Succession to the Presidency.* In this century, five Vice Presidents have succeeded to the Presidency: Theodore Roosevelt in 1901 upon the assassination of McKinley; Calvin Coolidge in 1923 upon the death from illness of Harding; Harry Truman in 1945 when a massive stroke ended the life of Franklin D. Roosevelt; Lyndon Johnson upon the assassination of Kennedy; and Gerald Ford upon the resignation of Nixon. These latter three successions, occurring since World War II, made the American people realize that the Vice President stands but one step away from the nation's most powerful political office.

(2) *Vice Presidential Assignments by Congress.* By law Congress has assigned the Vice President to serve as a member of the National Security Council and as chairman of the National Aeronautics and Space Council.

(3) *Vice Presidential Assignments by the President.* With the burdens of the Presidency becoming more onerous in our modern complex world, recent Presidents have delegated certain duties to, and thus provided training for, their Vice Presidents. President Truman employed his "Veep," *Alben Barkley*, as liaison man between the White House and Congress. President Eisenhower kept his Vice President, Richard Nixon, busy attending Cabinet meetings, serving on various government committees, welcoming distinguished visitors, undertaking foreign trips, campaigning in the midterm elections, and strengthening relations with Congress. Subsequent Presidents have continued this practice of training and utilizing their respective Vice Presidents. However, the President retains full power to decide if and to what extent he will employ his Vice President.

The Presidency: A Study of Powers, Their Growth and Limitations

POWERS OF THE PRESIDENT

The President of the United States is the most powerful democratically elected official in the world. His powers are derived fundamentally from the Constitution and also, evolving from or related to these Constitutional powers, are other powers based upon custom and tradition.

1. **Executive Powers.** (*a*) The President enforces the Constitution and the laws passed by Congress. For these purposes, he may issue executive orders. (*b*) He appoints all important government officials, including Cabinet officers and

members of administrative agencies. (c) He is the chief of state, or ceremonial head of the government and symbol of national unity.

2. Legislative Powers. (a) In his "State of the Union" message, required by the Constitution, and in other messages, the President may request that Congress pass specific legislation. (b) If Congress adjourns without passing the requested legislation or if an emergency arises, the President may recall Congress into special session. (c) He may veto legislation of which he disapproves. (d) As head of his political party, the President may often influence the votes of the members of his party in Congress. He may also use his power of *patronage;* that is, he may offer political jobs for distribution by those members of Congress who vote as he wishes. (e) In radio and television talks and through press conferences, the President may inform the people on public issues and appeal for their support.

3. Judicial Powers. (a) The President may grant pardons and reprieves in cases involving federal crimes, except in cases of impeachment. (b) He appoints all federal judges. (c) He enforces or may refuse to enforce federal court decisions.

4. Powers Over Foreign Affairs. (a) The President determines the foreign policy of the nation and is responsible for the conduct of foreign affairs. Today, he is also considered the leader of the free nations of the world. (b) He appoints officials to assist him in foreign affairs: the Secretary of State, ambassadors, consuls, and ministers. (c) He directs diplomatic matters and negotiates treaties with foreign countries. (d) He receives foreign ambassadors, and he may therefore recognize or refuse to recognize foreign governments.

5. Military Powers. (a) The President is commander in chief of the armed forces, thereby maintaining civilian control over the military. (b) He appoints the top military commanders, may offer them military advice, and also may remove them from their commands. (c) He may order the armed forces into action in case of disturbances within the United States and in foreign countries.

Clinton Rossiter, the noted authority on American government, has entitled the original or Constitutional powers of the President as: chief of state, chief executive, commander in chief, chief diplomat, and chief legislator; he has entitled the additional Presidential powers arising out of custom, tradition, and experience as: chief of (political) party, voice of the people, protector of the (internal) peace, manager of (economic) prosperity, and world leader. The President may find that certain powers reenforce each other: the commander in chief strengthening the chief diplomat; whereas other powers conflict with each other: the national voice of the people clashing with the partisan chief of party.

LIMITATIONS ON PRESIDENTIAL POWERS

1. Executive Powers. The *executive* powers of the President are limited: (a) his appointments of important government officials require approval by a majority of the Senate; (b) his executive orders may be challenged in the courts and reviewed as to their constitutionality; (c) his chief assistants may be called to testify, regarding executive policies and actions, before critical Congressional investigating committees.

2. Legislative Powers. The *legislative* powers of the President are limited: (a) his requests for legislation need not be passed by Congress either in regular or special session; (b) his veto may be overriden by a two-thirds vote of each House of Congress; (c) his party members may refuse to back his programs especially, analysts believe, if the President is in his second and last term; (d) his public appeals for support may go unheeded if many citizens disapprove of his views and actions.

3. **Judicial Powers.** The *judicial* powers of the President are limited: (a) his appointments of federal judges require the approval of a majority of the Senate; (b) federal judges have life tenure and decide cases independent of Presidential wishes or judgment; (c) his power to grant pardons for federal offenses does not extend to cases of impeachment.

4. **Powers Over Foreign Affairs.** The *foreign affairs* powers of the President are limited: (a) his appointments of major foreign affairs officials require the consent of a majority of the Senate; (b) treaties negotiated with foreign countries go into effect only if ratified by two-thirds of the Senate; (c) his foreign policies may be examined and criticized by the House Foreign Affairs Committee and the Senate Foreign Relations Committee.

5. **Military Powers.** The *military powers* of the President are limited in that (a) his authority does *not* extend to declaring war, for that power resides exclusively in Congress; (b) his management of the military depends upon Congressional legislation authorizing such programs as conscription of men and development of weapons; (c) his funds to pay for military expenditures require Congressional appropriations of money.

In 1973 Congress limited the Presidential military power by enacting, over President Nixon's veto, the *War-Powers Resolution*. It provides that, if the President commits American troops to combat abroad for more than 90 days, he must secure the approval of Congress or else terminate the military action. This resolution grew out of the Vietnam struggle in which American troops fought by orders of three successive Presidents—Kennedy, Johnson, and Nixon—without any Congressional declaration of war. (Check the Index for "War-Powers Resolution.")

6. **Impeachment Power of Congress.** The impeachment power of Congress provides an extreme check upon the President. The House of Representatives by majority vote may bring impeachment charges against the President for "treason, bribery, or other high crimes and misdemeanors." The Senate, with the Chief Justice of the Supreme Court presiding, acts as the jury and hears the charges. The Senate requires a two-thirds vote to declare the President guilty and remove him from office.

a. *The Impeachment of Andrew Johnson (1868).* For the election of 1864 held during the Civil War, the Republicans adopted the name Union party, renominated Abraham Lincoln for President, and in a gesture of national unity, selected for Vice President a pro-Union Democrat, Andrew Johnson. The Lincoln-Johnson ticket swept the election. Following Lincoln's assassination in 1865, Johnson became President.

Johnson retained Lincoln's Cabinet, including Secretary of War Edwin Stanton, a radical Republican who demanded harsh Reconstruction of the South.

Johnson, favoring lenient treatment of the South, soon broke sharply with the radical Republicans who controlled Congress. Johnson's vetoes of harsh Reconstruction measures were overridden, and he was hemmed in by the *Tenure of Office Act* (1867) which prohibited him from discharging any major government official without consent of the Senate. To test this law, which he considered unconstitutional, and to rid himself of a radical Republican in his Cabinet, Johnson fired Stanton. Thereupon, Johnson was impeached by the House of Representatives on charges of "high crimes and misdemeanors"—the only President ever to be so impeached. Tried before the Senate, Johnson was declared not guilty by a one-vote margin. (Johnson's view of the Tenure of Office Act was upheld in 1887 when Cleveland secured its repeal and again in 1926 when the Supreme Court affirmed the President's power to dismiss Cabinet officials.)

b. The Resignation of Richard Nixon (1974). Overwhelmingly reelected President in 1972, Richard Nixon was plagued in his second term by *Watergate*—a word that meant (1) in general—a series of political scandals, and (2) specifically—the June 1972 break-in at Democratic national headquarters in Washington at the Watergate apartments to steal documents and "bug" the offices, and the subsequent efforts to hide involvement of top administration officials by a cover-up—all criminal offenses. Publicized by the newspapers, Watergate was investigated beginning in 1973 by a Senate committee and by an independent special prosecutor.

President Nixon claimed that he had no knowledge of the Watergate break-in before it occurred and no knowledge of the cover-up until nine months later. The President reluctantly gave the special prosecutor some tapes of White House conversations but then refused his request for additional tapes on the ground of *executive privilege*—the right of the President to maintain the confidentiality of his records and to defend executive power against encroachment. In July 1974, under order of the Supreme Court, the President turned over the additional tapes—one of which revealed that Nixon had known of the Watergate break-in immediately after it had occurred. This revelation destroyed Nixon's credibility and eroded his support in Congress.

Meanwhile the House Judiciary Committee voted to recommend to the full House two major articles of impeachment: the first charging the President with obstructing justice in the Watergate cover-up; the second charging Nixon with abusing Presidential power for personal purposes. These two articles had strong bipartisan support in the committee and were passed by wide margins. Advised that the House would approve and the Senate sustain the impeachment charges overwhelmingly, Richard Nixon in August 1974 resigned—the first President ever to do so.

HISTORIC TREND TOWARD AN INCREASE IN PRESIDENTIAL POWERS

The Presidency today is a more powerful office than it was in the days of George Washington. It has grown tremendously in its functions and personnel; it has become much more involved in solving the nation's problems and therefore much closer to the people; it has attained greater esteem and prestige.

This growth of Presidential powers has not been uninterrupted but has been

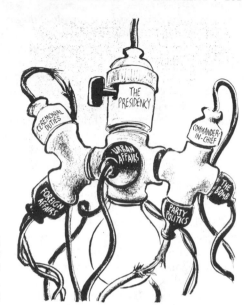

Overload
(*Copyright* © *1969*
the Chicago Sun-Times. Reproduced
by courtesy of Wil-Jo Associates, Inc.
and Bill Mauldin.)

marked by an "ebb-and-flow" pattern. Strong Presidents who have expanded their powers and vitalized the executive office have been followed frequently by weak ones who through inability or indifference have constricted Presidential powers. Each strong President, however, has built upon the traditions of the earlier strong ones, and the historic trend has been toward greater Presidential powers. This trend began in the first administration of George Washington; it gained momentum in the 19th century, but the greatest growth of Presidential powers has taken place in our present 20th century.

1. Reasons for the Growth of Presidential Powers

   a. Economic and Social Change. As the United States has evolved from a small agricultural and rural society into a large industrial and urbanized nation, it has faced complex new problems—many beyond the reach of solution by individuals or states acting separately. Federal effort to deal with such problems has focused on the President as chief executive, able to act quickly and decisively. (1) In 1902, with the coal miners on strike and winter approaching, President Theodore Roosevelt summoned the mine owners and union leaders to the White House. At first, the mine owners refused to arbitrate the strike issues, but when the President threatened to seize the mines, they agreed to accept the decisions of a Presidential arbitration commission. (2) In 1957, with an unruly mob keeping nine black children from attending a previously all-white school, President Eisenhower sent army units to Little Rock, Arkansas, to end mob rule and enforce court-ordered school integration.

   b. Foreign Affairs. Foreign affairs always have been of major concern to the United States. This concern inevitably has strengthened the leadership of the President who, with his constitutionally granted powers, is predominant in foreign matters. (Check the Index for "President, role in foreign affairs.")

c. *Change in Public Attitude Toward Government.* In early America, the people generally held, as said by Thomas Jefferson, that "that government is best which governs least." However, as economic and social problems became more complex, the American people began to demand that their government accept responsibility and take action. Historically, that branch of government which responded most vigorously was the executive.

d. *The Presidency as the Focal Point of Governmental Responsibility and Action.* A single person, the President, is better able to accept responsibility and take action than (1) a two-house Congress consisting of several hundred legislators of varied opinions, or (2) a Supreme Court operating under time-consuming legal processes and lacking means to enforce its own decisions. The President's advantages are many: (1) He is one person, able to secure information rapidly, make decisions swiftly, and act effectively. (2) He holds the constitutionally granted powers as commander in chief and chief executive. (3) His authority expands every time Congress enacts legislation, for each new law requires enforcement by the executive. (4) He derives prestige as ceremonial head of state and additional leverage as head of his political party. (5) He fulfills the public need for a specific and visible leader who can be held accountable for his actions.

e. *Rise of the Democratic Presidency.* Between the administration of George Washington, our first President, and the administration of Andrew Jackson, our seventh President, the Presidency was transformed from a staid, distant post into a democratic office with its occupant the people's chief spokesman and protector. This transformation resulted largely from the rise of political parties, the recasting of the electoral system into a "rubber stamp," and the achieving of universal male suffrage, which enabled the popular will to be expressed in Presidential elections. Andrew Jackson proclaimed that "the President is the direct representative of the American people . . . and it is his especial duty to protect the liberties and rights of the people and the integrity of the Constitution against the Senate, or the House of Representatives, or both together."

f. *Domestic and Foreign Emergencies.* During crises, such as war and economic depression, the people have looked to the President for leadership. In response strong Presidents have acted with speed and decision, stretched their authority, and exercised almost dictatorial power. Usually, they have received cooperation from the Congress which, during crises, voluntarily has suspended its powers to check the President. (1) For Presidential leadership in response to the crisis of Southern secession in 1861, check the Index for "Abraham Lincoln." (2) In 1917, before the United States entered World War I, unarmed American merchant ships were threatened by unrestricted German submarine warfare. President Wilson requested Congress to authorize the arming of American merchant ships, but a "little group of willful men"—so named by Wilson --filibustered the bill to death in the Senate. Thereupon, Wilson discovered an 1819 statute on piracy and, citing its provisions, ordered the arming of American merchant ships. (3) For Presidential leadership in response to the crisis of the 1929 economic depression, check the Index for "Franklin D. Roosevelt."

2. Evaluation of the Growth of Presidential Powers

a. *Is a Strong President Necessarily a Good President?* (1) When faced by crises, the nation needs and expects powerful leadership and therefore would consider a strong President to be a good one. (2) Strong Presidents frequently have been followed by weak ones—as Jackson by Martin Van Buren or Wilson by Warren Harding. This pattern, reflecting a change in the national mood with the absence of crisis, probably means that the nation does not always consider a strong President to be a good one.

b. Does the Growth of Presidential Powers Threaten Our Democracy?

The 1964 Republican Presidential candidate, *Barry Goldwater*, expressed dismay over the trend toward a strong Presidency. He warned that it could upset our traditional separation of powers and eventually could lead to the wiping out of all opposition and to the instituting of a totalitarian rule. His Democratic opponent Lyndon Johnson argued for a strong Presidency. By giving Johnson an overwhelming victory, the voters seemed to dismiss Goldwater's warning and to endorse the modern strong Presidency.

In so doing, the voters instinctively or explicitly reflected our national experience. Our strong Presidents have used power not for their personal aggrandizement, but to cope with national crises. When crises have subsided, our strong Presidents have been subjected to effective "checks and balances" by the other governmental branches. No rabble-rouser or demagogue has ever come close to gaining the Presidency. The conclusion to date would seem to be that the strong Presidency does *not* threaten our democracy.

The Nature of the American Presidency: Variations and Contrasts

THE PRESIDENTIAL "RATING GAME"

Historians have long enjoyed the parlor game "rating the Presidents." Although differences of opinion exist, historians generally are agreed—on the basis of Presidential record *only*—to the following ratings:

Great Presidents: Washington, Jackson, Lincoln, Theodore Roosevelt, Wilson, Franklin D. Roosevelt.

Near-greats: John Adams, Jefferson, Polk, Hayes, Cleveland, Truman.

At the bottom: Pierce, Buchanan, Grant, Harding.

(This listing omits Presidents since 1953 since their administrations are too recent for valid objective judgment; it also omits other Presidents who rate somewhere in the wide area between "near-greats" and "at the bottom.")

The major factors that determine the performance record of the "man in the White House" are (1) the man himself—his personality and outlook, (2) the times during which he serves as President, and (3) his advisers and assistants.

THE MAN IN THE WHITE HOUSE: HIS PERSONALITY

The personal qualities that make for a successful President, according to Clinton Rossiter in his study, *The American Presidency*, are as follows: (1) *bounce*—that extra energy necessary to manage and thrive in the world's toughest political office; (2) *affability*—that concern about the welfare of the people which underlies basic democratic instincts; (3) *political skill*—that wizardry to secure support for his programs from both the general public and the politicians;

(4) *cunning*—that knack to attract and utilize the best men to serve in his administration; (5) *sense of history*—that awareness of his position as heir to the nation's past and trustee for its future; (6) *newspaper habit*—that curiosity to know, in truth, what people are thinking and saying about his administration; (7) *sense of humor*—that ability to laugh at the world and see himself in perspective; and (8) *other intangibles*—that include intelligence, moderation in views, friendliness, eloquence, achievement, and the look of a winner.

THE MAN IN THE WHITE HOUSE: HIS PHILOSOPHY REGARDING THE USE OF PRESIDENTIAL POWERS

Each President has had substantially the same powers, but the extent to which each has used these powers has varied greatly.

1. Limited Use of Presidential Powers. This type of President sees himself as a purely administrative officer. He follows Congressional initiative and uses Presidential powers sparingly.

2. Moderate Use of Presidential Powers. This type of President sees himself as an administrative officer and as a defender of executive power and public welfare against Congressional encroachment. He uses Presidential powers moderately. One exponent of this philosophy was Grover Cleveland.

3. Dynamic Use of Presidential Powers. This type of President sees himself as a forceful national leader. He advocates a legislative program, rallies public opinion, and battles to secure Congressional enactment. He tries to anticipate the needs of the nation and uses Presidential powers to the utmost. The earliest exponent of this philosophy was Andrew Jackson. (Check the Index for "Andrew Jackson.")

CASE STUDIES OF PRESIDENTS EXEMPLIFYING LIMITED USE OF POWERS

1. James Buchanan (1857–1861). In the four months between Lincoln's election and his inauguration, Buchanan remained President and faced a major crisis—the declared secession of seven Southern states. Buchanan denied the right of any state to secede but also disclaimed his power to prevent secession. He stated, "It is beyond the power of any President . . . to restore peace and harmony among the States. Wisely limited and restrained as is his power under our Constitution and laws, he alone can accomplish but little for good or for evil on such a momentous question. . . . After all, he is no more than the chief executive officer of the Government. His province is not to make but to execute the laws."

2. Calvin Coolidge (1923–1929). President during the prosperous years of the 1920's, Coolidge held the following views. On Government: "If the Federal Government should go out of existence the common run of people would not detect the difference . . . for a considerable length of time." On Political Activity: "Four-fifths of all our troubles in this life would disappear if we would only sit down and keep still." On Presidential Powers: "I have never felt that it was my duty to attempt to coerce Senators or Representatives. . . . The people sent them to Washington. . . . It seems to me public administrators would get along better if they would restrain the impulse to butt in or be dragged into trouble."

CASE STUDIES OF PRESIDENTS EXEMPLIFYING DYNAMIC USE OF POWERS

1. **Abraham Lincoln (1861–1865).** Whereas Buchanan had disclaimed authority to move against the seceding Southern states, Lincoln held far different views of his Constitutional responsibilities and, following his inauguration, acted accordingly. Lincoln expanded the regular army, called for army volunteers, spent funds not yet appropriated—explaining that when Congress met in special session, it would approve these actions. Stretching his war powers as commander in chief, Lincoln ordered a naval blockade of Southern ports, substituted martial law for civil law in various states, thereby suspending the writ of habeas corpus and keeping Southern sympathizers in jail, and in 1863 issued the Emancipation Proclamation declaring free all slaves in the Confederacy so as to weaken the Southern war effort. Lincoln reasoned: "It became necessary for me to choose whether, using only the existing means, agencies, and processes which Congress had provided, I should let the Government fall at once into ruin or whether, availing myself of the broader powers conferred by the Constitution in cases of insurrection, I would make an effort to save it, with all its blessings, for the present age and posterity."

2. **Theodore Roosevelt (1901–1909).** Presiding over the nation in relatively crisis-free times, Roosevelt nevertheless acted vigorously. In foreign affairs, he aided Panama to gain independence from Colombia, thereby speeding a treaty allowing America to construct the Panama Canal. In domestic affairs, Roosevelt pursued policies of curbing "bad" trusts, promoting conservation of natural resources, and protecting the consumer. Roosevelt rallied public support for his leadership and called the White House a "bully pulpit." He theorized: "My view was that . . . every executive officer in high position was a steward of the people. . . . I declined to adopt the view that what was imperatively necessary for the Nation could not be done by the President unless he could find some specific authorization to do it. My belief was that it was not only his right but his duty to do anything that the needs of the Nation demanded unless such action was forbidden by the Constitution or the laws. . . . I did not usurp power, but I did greatly broaden the use of executive power." This Roosevelt statement on the Presidency has become known as the *stewardship theory*.

3. **Franklin D. Roosevelt (1933–1945).** Taking office during the worst year of the Great Depression, Roosevelt revived public confidence by his Inaugural Address, explaining "the only thing we have to fear is fear itself," and declaring "this nation asks for action and action now." Roosevelt acted swiftly: proclaiming a bank holiday which closed the nation's banks so as to halt a run on the banks by fearful depositors demanding their money, and subsequently permitting the reopening of those banks in sound financial condition; calling Congress into special session and, in a hundred-day period, securing an amazing number of New Deal laws designed to lift the nation out of the depression. Roosevelt stated his views: "The Presidency is not merely an administrative office. That is the

least of it. . . . It is pre-eminently a place of moral leadership. . . . All of our great Presidents were leaders of thought at times when certain historic ideas in the life of the nation had to be clarified. . . . Without leadership alert and sensitive to change we are bogged up or lose our way."

The Man in the White House: His Times

The record of each President depends in part upon the nature of the times. Some men have presided during times of great crisis; others during difficult but not crisis times; and still others in relatively untroubled times. Those men who have faced and surmounted crises have been rated as our strong Presidents; those men who have turned away or left little imprint upon crises have been rated as less successful. But what of those men who have presided in crisis-free times? They still had ample opportunity for leadership because the nation has always faced problems that required solutions.

CASE STUDIES: PRESIDENTIAL LEADERSHIP IN DOMESTIC MATTERS

1. George Washington and the Setting of Precedents. As first President, George Washington was keenly aware that his actions would provide future Presidents with precedents. Washington began the practice of calling together the heads of his executive departments for consultation as a group, thereby creating our first Cabinet. Although Washington himself generally refrained from influencing the legislature, he approved the efforts of his Secretary of the Treasury, *Alexander Hamilton,* to secure enactment of a comprehensive financial program. Thus, the Washington administration set the precedent of executive pressure to secure legislation from Congress. Washington signed the bill providing for the establishment of the National Bank, thereby giving his assent to loose construction of the Constitution and wide use of the elastic clause. Washington enforced the authority of the new government when western Pennsylvania farmers refused to pay the excise tax on whisky and resisted federal tax collectors. Washington recruited 15,000 troops and crushed the so-called *Whisky Rebellion.*

2. Andrew Jackson and Nullification. Jackson faced the problem of the South's dissatisfaction with tariff laws it considered too high, which led South Carolina to declare the 1832 tariff null and void within its borders. Jackson made his position clear: declaring nullification "incompatible with the existence of the Union," asserting "Our Federal Union: it must be preserved," and securing from Congress the *Force Bill* empowering him to use the military if necessary to enforce the nation's tariff laws within South Carolina. Although an armed clash was averted by agreement to lower rates by the *Compromise Tariff of 1833,* Andrew Jackson set precedents that would be vital later to Abraham Lincoln.

3. Lyndon Johnson and Civil Rights. Assuming office at the time of a strong movement to achieve equal rights for black Americans, Johnson gave leadership to this movement. He rallied public opinion, by means of television speeches and messages to Congress, against "bigots and bullies" who hate-bombed black homes and churches and assaulted black and white civil rights workers. He secured Congressional passage of three major civil rights laws: in 1964 prohibiting discrimination in employment and in places of public accommodation; in 1965 protecting the right of all Americans to register and vote; in 1968 outlawing discrimination in the rental and sale of most housing. Johnson's achievements made him a major figure in the furtherance of American civil rights.

CASE STUDIES: PRESIDENTIAL LEADERSHIP IN FOREIGN AFFAIRS

1. Thomas Jefferson and the Louisiana Purchase (1803). Check the Index for "Thomas Jefferson."

2. James Polk and the Mexican War (1846–1848). Polk was elected President in 1844 on a program calling for the "reannexation of Texas" and further territorial expansion to the Pacific Coast. Polk's election strengthened those Congressmen who favored territorial expansion. Just before Polk took office, Congress ended nine years of delay and admitted Texas to the Union. Texas' southern boundary, however, was in dispute, as Mexico claimed that the boundary was the Nueces River and the United States claimed the Rio Grande.

In 1845 Polk sent James Slidell as his special envoy to Mexico to secure the Rio Grande boundary and to purchase the California and New Mexico territories. Slidell was not even received by the Mexican government—a new nationalist regime pledged to protect Mexico's territory. Meanwhile, Polk as commander in chief ordered American troops into the disputed Texas border area where in 1846 they fought a minor skirmish with Mexican forces. Polk thereupon informed Congress that "Mexico has invaded our territory and shed American blood upon American soil" and secured a declaration of war.

With Polk himself planning the military operations, the American forces won an easy victory over Mexico. Polk's representative negotiated the 1848 *Treaty of Guadalupe Hidalgo* by which the United States gained the Rio Grande boundary and the *Mexican Cession*—the California and New Mexico territories. These acquisitions closely paralleled Polk's proposals which Mexico had refused to hear from Slidell before the war.

Polk's actions toward Mexico showed how a determined President may use his many powers to achieve his foreign policy objectives.

3. Harry Truman and the Cold War Policy of Containment (Beginning by 1946). Truman became President in 1945 as World War II ended and as the United States and the Soviet Union ceased their wartime cooperation only to enter upon a worldwide struggle for power and influence—the *Cold War*. This struggle was so named because it was fought by propaganda, diplomacy, espionage, scientific and economic competition, and localized military action—but not all-out war.

As the Soviet Union declared the spread of communism essential for her security and propped up a number of Communist nations in Central Europe and Asia, President Truman abandoned his verbal efforts to get the Kremlin to stop its aggressive expansion and countered with a *policy of containment*. To contain the Soviet Union within its existing territories and spheres of influence, Truman instituted many major foreign policy measures. (a) The *Truman Doctrine* (1947) began economic and military aid for Greece and Turkey to help them resist Communist pressures. (b) The *Marshall Plan* (1947) was an unprecedented and generous program of economic aid to further recovery in non-Communist Europe. (c) The *Berlin Airlift* (1948–1949) supplied West Berlin with the necessities of life, thereby thwarting Communist efforts to drive us from that city by a blockade of surface transport routes. (d) The *Point Four Program* (1949) offered technical assistance to underdeveloped countries in Latin America, Africa, and Asia. (e) The *North Atlantic Pact* (1949), overwhelmingly ratified by the Senate, provided for United States membership in the *North Atlantic Treaty Organization* (NATO), our first peacetime military alliance. It was designed to defend its members against Communist aggression. (f) American troops were committed, under the United Nations banner, to help South Korea defend itself against the 1950 North Korean Communist invasion. These measures all reflected the Truman viewpoint expressed in his statement, "I make American foreign policy." By using his powers decisively, Truman enhanced the Presidential office and provided American leadership in world affairs.

4. John Kennedy and the Cuban Missile Base Crisis (1962). Check the Index for "John Kennedy."

The Man in the White House: His Advisers and Assistants

A single person carrying heavy and diverse responsibilities, the President must recruit and rely upon many people for advice and assistance. They serve the President in the following ways: (1) gathering and organizing information, (2) undertaking special missions and conducting negotiations, (3) expressing opinions and providing new ideas, (4) administering government laws and policies and handling routine details, and (5) presenting the administration viewpoint to the American people. The record of each President reflects, to a significant degree, the quality of his advisers and assistants.

THE EXECUTIVE DEPARTMENTS

1. Number and Work. As our nation has grown in size and complexity, the number of executive departments has increased—from three in the administration of George Washington to 13 today. Each department enforces the laws and furthers the programs that fall within its jurisdiction as follows:

(a) *State*—furthers our foreign policies, (b) *Treasury*—manages the nation's finances, (c) *Defense*—provides military protection, (d) *Justice*—handles the legal work of the federal government, (e) *Interior*—conserves the nation's natural resources, (f) *Agriculture*—aids farmers, (g) *Commerce*—aids businessmen engaged in domestic and foreign trade, (h) *Labor*—aids workers, (i) *Health and Human Resources* (formerly Health, Education, and Welfare)—directs social welfare programs, (j) *Housing and Urban Development* (HUD)—encourages housing construction and slum clearance projects, (k) *Transportation*—supervises our transportation systems, (l) *Energy*—deals with the regulation and conservation of energy, and (m) *Education*—coordinates and directs education programs.

2. Department Heads. The President with the consent of the Senate appoints the heads of executive departments. In selecting these administrative assistants, the President must consider various factors. His appointments *(a)* may be used to repay political debts such as support in the Presidential election, *(b)* may represent the various factions in the President's political party, *(c)* must satisfy the interested economic and geographic groups, such as farm organizations and Midwestern Congressmen concerned about the person to be Secretary of Agriculture, *(d)* occasionally may be a man from the opposing political party in the hope of gaining bipartisan support for administration plans, and *(e)* should *not* be weak and indecisive individuals who may discredit the administration, nor should they be strong, determined individuals who may cause dissension within the administration.

In view of these political, economic, and personal factors, the President appoints as executive department heads relatively few of his closest supporters and intimate friends. Nevertheless, these department heads together constitute the group of top-level Presidential advisers called the *Cabinet*.

THE PRESIDENT'S CABINET

1. Origins. The original Constitution mentions executive departments, but it says nothing about the Cabinet. (The first Constitutional reference to the Cabinet came in 1967 with the adoption of the Twenty-Fifth Amendment on Presidential disability and succession.)

The Cabinet, as a group of executive department heads and other top advisers meeting together with the President, was begun by George Washington. It became an American governmental tradition.

2. The President and the Cabinet. The President calls Cabinet meetings, frequently or infrequently, according to his wishes. In addition to the executive department heads, the President may invite to Cabinet meetings personal advisers, the Vice President, the American Ambassador to the United Nations, and other top officials. The President may use the Cabinet to *(a)* demonstrate administration unity and dramatize policy on public issues, *(b)* enable departmental heads to exchange information and to coordinate their work, and *(c)* propose, discuss, and evaluate new ideas and policies. As the final authority, the President may accept, modify, or reject any Cabinet recommendations.

CASE STUDIES: VARYING RELATIONSHIPS OF THE PRESIDENT TO HIS CABINET MEMBERS

1. George Washington Supports the Views of His Treasury Secretary. Washington began our tradition of Cabinet meetings by consulting as a group his Attorney General and the heads of his three executive departments—War, Treasury, and State. With his major advisers—Secretary of State Thomas Jefferson and Secretary of the Treasury Alexander Hamilton—in considerable disagreement, Washington consistently sided with Hamilton. Washington *(a)* supported Hamilton's financial plans and signed the bill establishing the National Bank, thereby endorsing loose construction of the Constitution; *(b)* recruited militiamen and crushed the Whisky Rebellion; and *(c)* maintained peace with Britain by securing Senate ratification of the unpopular Jay Treaty —all measures reflecting Hamilton's advice. Washington's administration thusly illustrates that a brilliant Cabinet member, such as Hamilton, may wield tremendous influence.

2. Abraham Lincoln Dominates His Cabinet. Lincoln, faced with the Civil War, assembled a Cabinet of strong and ambitious men, none being his personal friends. Often considered the most capable Cabinet ever, its outstanding members were Secretary of State *William Seward*, Secretary of the Treasury *Salmon Chase*, and Secretary of War *Edwin Stanton*. Lincoln exercised considerable patience and political skill in keeping his Cabinet working together under his leadership and mastery. On one issue, when all the Cabinet members were opposed to a Lincoln proposal, Lincoln announced the vote result, with tongue-in-cheek, as "seven nays, one aye—the ayes have it."

3. Andrew Johnson Dismisses His War Secretary and Faces Impeachment. (Check the Index for "Andrew Johnson.")

4. Woodrow Wilson Overrules His Secretary of State. Wilson secured the 1912 Democratic Presidential nomination with the considerable help of the influential party leader, *William Jennings Bryan*. Elected President, Wilson repaid Bryan by appointing him Secretary of State. The Wilson administration soon faced the problem of maintaining American neutral rights as European nations began World War I. In 1915 a German submarine sank the British passenger ship *Lusitania* with a loss of over 1000 lives, including more than 100 Americans. Wilson drafted a vigorous note protesting unrestricted German submarine warfare and destruction of American lives—which note Bryan considered too strong but signed reluctantly. The German reply was evasive, Wilson felt, so he drafted a second and stronger protest note. Bryan refused to sign this second note and instead resigned his position. Wilson appointed a more amenable Secretary of State, *Robert Lansing*, who approved and dispatched the second *Lusitania* note.

CASE STUDIES OF PRESIDENTIAL ADVISERS OTHER THAN CABINET MEMBERS

Most Presidents look to their close personal associates, who rarely occupy Cabinet positions, for advice, companionship, and loyalty. These friends of the President, possibly holding non-Cabinet government positions or none at all, have exercised considerable influence in past administrations.

1. President Jackson and the "Kitchen Cabinet." Choosing his Cabinet members mainly to reward political support, Jackson named to the Cabinet only one personal friend, *Martin Van Buren*, as Secretary of State. In his early Presidential years, Jackson rarely held Cabinet meetings but sought the advice of a group of close friends which his opponents dubbed the *Kitchen Cabinet*. Although membership in this group varied, its outstanding figures were Van Buren, a strong political leader; *Amos Kendall*, a former newspaperman appointed to a minor Treasury post who helped Jackson prepare his major messages; and *Francis Blair*, an editor of a Democratic newspaper.

2. President Wilson and Colonel House. In 1911 Wilson met Colonel *Edward House*, a successful Texas businessman, a shrewd political analyst, and a personable individual. They became close friends. After Wilson became President, he employed House as his unofficial adviser. House served as Wilson's personal representative in secret and unsuccessful negotiations to end World War I by mediation; after America entered the war in 1917, House coordinated United States and Allied war efforts; he advised Wilson in formulating his war aims, the *Fourteen Points*, and in planning a charter for the *League of Nations;* he accompanied Wilson to Paris in 1918 and helped draw up the *Treaty of Versailles.* In 1919 Wilson rejected House's advice to compromise with the Senate so as to secure ratification of the treaty. Thereafter the two men ceased their friendship although House for many years remained influential in Democratic party affairs.

3. President Franklin D. Roosevelt and the "Brain Trust." In gaining the Presidency and in his early years in office, Roosevelt relied heavily upon the advice of a group of college professors soon dubbed by the newspapers as the *brain trust.* Roosevelt respected academic scholarship and, from the clash of ideas among his advisers, derived new governmental policies. Reflecting the nation's concern with the depression, the earliest members of Roosevelt's brain trust were economists *Adolf Berle, Raymond Moley,* and *Rexford Tugwell.*

THE EXECUTIVE OFFICE OF THE PRESIDENT

In 1939, with the consent of Congress, President Roosevelt reorganized much of the executive branch into the new *Executive Office of the President.* It assists the President by keeping him informed, advising him on future programs, presenting him with matters that call for his decision while directing lesser matters elsewhere, conserving his time and energy, and following up programs to assure that subordinates comply with the President's policies.

This 1939 reorganization set the broad outlines for much of the executive branch as it exists today.

1. White House Office. Members of the White House Office are in close and intimate contact with the President. They constitute the President's "home team" and include the following: *(a) Assistants to the President* specialize in various problem areas such as domestic affairs, national security affairs, and Congressional relations. *(b) Press Secretary,* in charge of public relations, must arrange just the "right amount" of presidential exposure to the news media. This secretary prepares press conferences, distributes news releases to reporters, and plans radio and television broadcasts. *(c) Appointments Secretary* budgets the President's time by scheduling only important people to see the Chief Executive. *(d) Speech writers* translate the President's views into written form for messages to Congress and public addresses. They seek to express ideas clearly and to coin "catchy" phrases. *(e) Other members* of the White House Office include a correspondence secretary, advisers on such matters as urban affairs, consumer problems, and science, and diplomatic and military aides.

2. Major Agencies. Major agencies within the Executive Office which work under and report directly to the President include the following: *(a)* The *Council* *of Economic Advisers* studies our economy, gathers data, and proposes government economic policies. *(b)* The *Office of Management and Budget* prepares the annual estimate of federal income and expenditures and seeks efficient government operations. *(c)* The *Council on Environmental Quality* develops policies to deal with problems of environmental protection. *(d)* The *Central Intelligence Agency* (CIA) evaluates intelligence data and directs undercover missions relating to national security. *(e)* The *National Security Council* advises in regard to "domestic, foreign, and military policies" that affect the nation's security.

INDEPENDENT REGULATORY AGENCIES

1. Meaning. The independent regulatory agencies administer laws that deal with complicated economic or technical problems. They thereby are assisting the President and exercising *executive powers*. They issue detailed rules and regulations, thereby exercising *quasi-legislative powers*. Many agencies also investigate charges of violations, hold hearings, and hand down decisions, thereby exercising *quasi-judicial powers*. However, an individual or corporation found guilty before an independent agency may appeal the case to the federal courts.

2. Agency Members and the President. The members of the independent regulatory agencies are appointed by the President, with the consent of the Senate, for fixed and overlapping terms. To provide a bipartisan approach, these officials, by law, often must be selected from both major political parties. Once in office, these officials exercise their own judgment regardless of Presidential wishes. They may *not* be removed by the President for failure to conform to his policies.

3. Typical Agencies. As our society has become more complex, the number of independent agencies has increased. Among the typical agencies today are the following: *(a)* The *Interstate Commerce Commission* (ICC) regulates rail, bus, truck, and pipeline transportation in interstate commerce. *(b)* The *Federal Reserve Board* ("the Fed") regulates the credit, currency, and major banks of the nation. *(c)* The *Federal Trade Commission* (FTC) regulates business to prevent unfair competition and to protect the consumer. *(d)* The *Securities and Exchange Commission* (SEC) regulates transactions on stock exchanges and the issuance of new securities. *(e)* The *National Labor Relations Board* (NLRB) regulates the process of collective bargaining between labor unions and management. *(f)* The *Federal Communications Commission* (FCC) licenses radio and television stations, assigns broadcast wave lengths, and encourages a variety and choice of programs.

MULTIPLE-CHOICE QUESTIONS

1. Which statement concerning the national nominating conventions for the Presidency is true? (1) They are provided for in the federal Constitution. (2) They preceded the Congressional caucus as a nominating procedure. (3) They have been the basic Presidential nominating procedure since the early 1830's. (4) They are not held when a President seeks reelection.
2. A governor of New York State is likely to be a candidate for the Presidential

nomination because   (1) he is a "dark horse"   (2) New Yorkers are well known nationally   (3) New York is a "doubtful" state with a large number of electoral votes   (4) New York is the most rapidly growing state in the nation.

3. In 1972 political parties obtained *most* of their campaign funds from   (1) contributions of individuals and organizations   (2) appropriations voted by Congress   (3) state and local taxes   (4) the personal wealth of their candidates.

4. The 1974 Federal Campaign Reform Act   (1) for the first time prohibited corporations from contributing campaign funds   (2) failed to provide for a commission to enforce the law   (3) for the first time provided for federal funds for Presidential candidates   (4) prohibited labor union members from contributing campaign funds.

5. A voter in a Presidential election casts his ballot for   (1) his candidate directly   (2) a slate of electors   (3) a candidate selected by a Congressional caucus   (4) the state party committee.

6. The practice that Presidential electors vote for the candidate nominated by their political party is based upon   (1) the Constitution   (2) custom and tradition   (3) a law of Congress   (4) a decision of the Supreme Court.

7. As a result of the election of 1968, Nixon was a "minority" President. This means that he   (1) received less than 50 percent of the popular vote   (2) received less than 50 percent of the electoral vote   (3) was elected by running on the tickets of two parties   (4) was elected by the House of Representatives.

8. The election of a President is decided by the House of Representatives when   (1) the Senate is unable to decide on a candidate   (2) no candidate receives a majority of the electoral vote   (3) no candidate receives a majority of the popular vote   (4) the President-elect dies before January 20.

9. Because of the Electoral College system, the two major-party Presidential candidates   (1) find it necessary to campaign in all 50 states   (2) spend much of their time campaigning in states with large populations   (3) use much of their time appealing to the electors, rather than to the people   (4) make an effort to campaign chiefly in those states containing disadvantaged minorities.

10. Under the Presidential election system in the United States, which might a third-party candidate *most* likely be able to accomplish?   (1) win a majority of the popular vote by capturing the rural states   (2) gain an electoral majority by winning in ten urban states   (3) force a major party candidate to name him Vice President   (4) prevent either major party candidate from gaining a majority in the Electoral College

11. The limitation on the number of terms a President may serve is based upon   (1) a law of Congress   (2) a Constitutional amendment   (3) an agreement between the two major political parties   (4) a decision of the Supreme Court.

12. In case the office of Vice President is vacant, the Twenty-Fifth Amendment provides that a new Vice President be nominated by   (1) the President   (2) a special meeting of the Electoral College   (3) the Senate   (4) the President's Cabinet.

13. The growing importance of recent Vice Presidents is *most* clearly shown by their   (1) expanded roles as spokesmen in behalf of administration policies   (2) increased influence in the United States Senate   (3) positions as national chairmen of the political party in power   (4) decisive voices in determining foreign policy.

14. The President has power to influence legislation by   (1) appointing ministers to negotiate treaties with foreign nations   (2) making changes in the qualifications of members of Congress   (3) requesting measures in his messages to Congress   (4) requiring the Supreme Court to declare specific laws unconstitutional.

15. To secure Congressional support for his legislative program, the President may make use of his power   (1) to dismiss Cabinet members   (2) to protect the public health and safety   (3) over patronage   (4) over gerrymandering.

16. President Franklin D. Roosevelt's recognition of the Soviet Union in 1933 was based primarily on his Constitutional power to   (1) sign or veto bills   (2) receive

ambassadors and other public ministers   (3) be commander in chief of the armed forces   (4) inform Congress on the "State of the Union."

17. As commander in chief of the armed forces, the President can   (1) declare war   (2) lower the age for drafting men and women into the armed forces   (3) establish a treaty of peace   (4) order the Marines into foreign countries to protect American interests.

18. A President of the United States exercises political leadership without using a specific or implied Constitutional power when he   (1) appoints a new chairman of the Joint Chiefs of Staff   (2) suggests a new national chairman for his party   (3) appoints an ambassador to another nation   (4) nominates a Justice for the United States Supreme Court.

19. A major check on Presidential control of foreign policy is   (1) Congress's power regarding appropriations   (2) the power of the House of Representatives to reject treaties   (3) the existence of immigration laws   (4) Congress's power to appoint ambassadors.

20. In general, Presidents considered by historians to have been outstanding leaders are those who   (1) had complete control of the judicial and legislative branches of government   (2) distributed government jobs to members of their political party only   (3) initiated new programs and new directions in government policy   (4) were elected by an overwhelming majority of the people.

IDENTIFICATION QUESTIONS: WHO AM I?

James Buchanan	Thomas Jefferson	Franklin D. Roosevelt
Grover Cleveland	Andrew Johnson	Theodore Roosevelt
Calvin Coolidge	Lyndon Johnson	Harry Truman
Gerald Ford	Abraham Lincoln	George Washington
Andrew Jackson	Richard Nixon	Woodrow Wilson

1. My election as President was thrown into the House of Representatives and led to the adoption of the Twelfth Amendment to the Constitution.

2. I was the first person to become Vice President under the terms of the Twenty-Fifth Amendment, and soon thereafter I was sworn in as President.

3. As President I fired my Secretary of War, which action helped bring about my impeachment by the House of Representatives. I was declared not guilty by the Senate.

4. During my administration, seven Southern states seceded but I held that the Constitution gave me no power to deal with this crisis.

5. Although President in relatively crisis-free times, I spurred conservation and consumer protection. I proclaimed the stewardship theory of the Presidency.

6. Becoming President during the Great Depression, I gave the nation "action and action now" and revived public confidence in our democratic institutions.

7. I became President following a career as historian and educator. Concerned chiefly with war in Europe, I consulted a trusted but unofficial adviser—Colonel Edward House—regarding my policies.

8. Upon the death of my predecessor, I became President and served in relatively prosperous times. I believed that the existence of the federal government made little difference to the common people.

9. As President, I was keenly aware that my actions would set precedents for future occupants of that office. I depended heavily upon the advice of my Treasury Secretary, Alexander Hamilton.

10. Faced with Soviet expansion in the immediate post-World War II years, I originated a series of foreign policy measures for the containment of communism.

ESSAY QUESTIONS

1. Agree or disagree with *each* of the following statements regarding the process of Presidential elections. In *each* case support your opinion with two facts. (*a*) The system of primary elections serves a useful purpose. (*b*) The personal qualities and/or public image of the candidate have a greater impact on election outcomes than do issues. (*c*) An incumbent running for office has great advantages over his opponent. (*d*) Candidates must appeal to ethnic groups and their interests in order to win elections. (*e*) The national nominating convention system should be reformed. (*f*) Federal financing of Presidential candidates, as provided in the 1974 Federal Campaign Reform Act, is a well-thought-out and worthwhile reform.
2. Discuss *two* facts to prove *each* of the following statements concerning the Presidency of the United States: (*a*) Amendments to the federal Constitution have affected the Presidency. (*b*) The process of electing the President encourages candidates to concentrate much campaign activity in certain states. (*c*) The Electoral College reform, proposed by the House of Representatives in 1969, could create new problems and could have undesirable effects. (*d*) To fulfill his many responsibilities, the President is assisted by a number of individuals and agencies. (*e*) A President may be considered either strong or weak not according to the powers available to him, but according to his use of these powers.
3. The problem of Presidential succession has received considerable attention. (*a*) Discuss *two* criticisms that have been voiced concerning the factors that at present help to determine the selection of a party's Vice Presidential nominee. (*b*) Discuss *one* argument for *and one* argument against the Presidential Succession Act of 1947. (*c*) State *one* provision of the Twenty-Fifth Amendment and explain whether or not you approve of this provision.
4. Discuss *two* powers by which the President may accomplish *each* of the following: (*a*) influencing Congress (*b*) enforcing laws (*c*) controlling his own political party (*d*) determining foreign policy. For *each* power discussed, indicate whether it is stated in the Constitution or derived from custom and tradition.
5. The nature of the American Presidency is determined by such factors as (*a*) Constitutional provisions, (*b*) the President's attitude toward his office, and (*c*) the times in which he serves. Select *one* President's administration and show how his term of office was affected by *each* of factors *a*, *b*, and *c* above.

5. The Congress Is the Legislature and Enacts the Nation's Laws

The Founding Fathers, who wrote our Constitution, believed firmly that the preeminent, or leading, branch of government would be the legislature. They based this belief upon the history of England, whose Parliament (1) twice had overthrown Stuart Kings, ending absolute rule, and (2) had served as the arena for great orators, brilliant thinkers, and decisive men of action. The Founding Fathers further knew of, and some had taken part in, resistance by colonial legislatures against royal governors.

The Founding Fathers, consequently, expected that the Congress would be the governmental branch most clearly expressing the public will and most effectively furthering the public welfare. Their expectations did not prove wholly correct. Over the years the Congress has taken much criticism, fallen in public esteem, and been surpassed as spokesman for the people by the executive.

Congress nevertheless constitutes an essential and significant branch of our American government.

Organization of Congress. The Congress consists of a *bicameral* or two-house legislature: the House of Representatives represents the people by population and the Senate represents them by state.

HOUSE OF REPRESENTATIVES

1. Requirements for Office. The Constitution requires that a Representative be at least 25 years of age, a citizen of the United States for seven years, and an inhabitant of the state electing him to the House.

2. Apportionment of House Seats. As the American population grew, the number of Representatives increased from 65 in 1789–1790 to 435 in the early 20th century. If House membership had continued to increase with population growth, political scientists feared, then the House would become too large to conduct its business efficiently. Congress consequently by a 1929 law fixed House membership at 435. These seats are apportioned as follows:

a. Among the States. The number of Representatives for each state is calculated by the ratio of the state population to the national population. To provide population data, the Constitution directed the taking of an "enumeration" or census every ten years. The first such census was taken in 1790.

The 1970 census disclosed a national population of 203 million which when divided by 435 House seats meant one Representative for about 465,000 persons. The 1970 census also required a shift of 11 House seats among the states: the largest gainers being California—five more, and Florida—three more; the largest losers being Pennsylvania and New York—each with two less. In the case of New York, its population for the 1960–1970 decade increased from 16.4 to 18.2 million, but this 8 percent increase was below the 13 percent national increase and therefore the state lost two seats, dropping from 41 to 39 Representatives.

b. Within Each State

(1) *Political Considerations in Drawing Boundaries.* The state legislatures, practically unchecked by Congress, assumed the task of drawing state boundaries for Congressional districts. In many states, the legislatures created inequitable or unfair districts as follows: *(a) Gerrymandering.* The political party in control of the state often drew district boundaries so as to concentrate its opponent's strength in a few districts while spreading its own strength in order to give itself a majority in many districts. This practice, used in 1812 by Governor *Elbridge Gerry* of Massachusetts, became known as *gerrymandering. (b) Rural Overrepresentation.* Until the early 1960's, state legislatures dominated by rural members failed to redraw election district boundaries so as to reapportion or redistribute Congressional (and state legislative) seats as population shifted from rural to urban and suburban areas. Rural people consequently were overrepresented at the expense of urban and suburban dwellers. State legislative failure to reapportion was due to inertia, disagreement on new election district boundaries, or most often deliberate intent to maintain rural dominance.

(2) *More Equitable Election Districts.* In 1964, in *Wesberry vs. Sanders*, the Supreme Court decided that "as nearly as is practicable, one man's vote in a

Congressional election is to be worth as much as another's." The Constitution, the Court held, established the principle of equal representation in the House for equal numbers of people. In 1965 Congress legislated (a) against gerrymandering by requiring Congressional election districts to be contiguous and compact and (b) against rural overrepresentation by requiring Congressional election districts to have a population that was not above or below the average by more than 15 percent.

3. **Term of Office.** Each Representative serves a two-year term and the entire House membership is elected every two years. Theoretically, therefore, the entire House membership may be drastically altered in a single election. In reality, however, this is not so. In over 300 Congressional districts, political support is heavily weighted for one or the other of the two major parties so that, barring a landslide election, these districts are "safe" for the incumbents. In about 125 Congressional districts, political support is closely divided so that these districts are doubtful and their seats are really contested.

4. **Presiding Officer.** The *Speaker of the House* serves as its presiding officer. Named for this office by the majority party in the House, he is elected by the Representatives voting along strict party lines. The Speaker therefore is always a member of the majority party.

THE SENATE

1. **Requirements for Office.** The Constitution requires that a Senator be at least 30 years of age, a citizen of the United States for nine years, and an inhabitant of the state electing him to the Senate.

2. **Membership.** The Senate has 100 members, with each of the 50 states, regardless of population, entitled to two Senators.

3. **Term of Office.** Senators are elected for a six-year term, but elections are staggered so that only one-third of the members of the Senate are chosen every two years. Senate membership, consequently, cannot be drastically altered by any one election, and the Senate functions as a continuing body.

4. **Presiding Officer.** According to the Constitution, the Vice President serves as the presiding officer of the Senate but otherwise has no part in Senate work and has no vote except in case of a tie. Having such a minor role in the Senate, the Vice President frequently does not attend sessions and the presiding officer is the *President pro tempore* (President for the time being). He is chosen by the Senate majority party and elected by the Senators voting along strict party lines.

SPECIAL PRIVILEGES OF MEMBERS OF CONGRESS

1. **Remuneration.** Members of Congress receive fixed and substantial salaries, membership in a pension system (to which they contribute); travel allowances from home to Washington and back; special tax exemption for expenses while living away from home; free office space in Washington and in their home districts or states; funds for office expenses including supplies, telephones, clerical help, and administrative assistants; and the right to send official mail free of postage, called the *franking privilege*.

2. Senatorial Courtesy. A Senator of the same political party as the President expects to be heeded on important federal appointments (district attorneys, judges, revenue collectors) within his state. If the Senator objects to the President's nominee as "personally obnoxious," then the Senate will show "courtesy" to its member by not approving the appointment.

3. Immunities Granted to Congressmen (Article I, Section 6)

a. Freedom From Arrest. While attending sessions, Congressmen are free from arrest on civil charges and misdemeanors (but not on charges of treason or major crimes). Congressmen thusly are protected against petty and undue interference with their legislative duties.

b. Freedom From Suits for Libel and Slander. For any speech on the floor of Congress, Congressmen "shall not be questioned in any other place," that is, they shall be immune, or exempted, from lawsuits for libel and slander. Congressmen thusly are free to speak and debate in Congress and to have their remarks printed in the official journal of proceedings, the *Congressional Record.* (Congressmen occasionally abuse this immunity from libel suits and malign individuals by making personal attacks and unsupported charges.)

SESSIONS OF CONGRESS

Each Congress exists for a two-year term. By custom, beginning with our first Congress of 1789–1790, Congresses have been numbered consecutively.

Each Congress meets in two regular sessions, each session convening, in accordance with the Twentieth Amendment, on or soon after January 3. Congress remains in session as long as its members feel that they have important work to do. As our society has grown more complex, Congressional sessions have increased in length. In recent years, most sessions have run into late autumn.

GENERAL POWERS OF CONGRESS

Congress has the general powers to (1) regulate itself, especially judging its members and determining its procedures, (2) enact laws, legislating upon those matters specifically enumerated in the Constitution and implied by the elastic clause, and (3) hold hearings and conduct investigations.

SPECIAL POWERS OF THE HOUSE OF REPRESENTATIVES

The House has the sole power to (1) start all revenue (tax) bills (which the Senate later may amend), (2) bring charges of impeachment against federal officials, including the President, and (3) elect the President if the Electoral College fails to give any one candidate a majority.

SPECIAL POWERS OF THE SENATE

The Senate has the sole power (1) to ratify treaties negotiated by the President (two-thirds vote), (2) when the House brings charges of impeachment, to sit as a jury and decide the guilt of the impeached person (two-thirds vote), (3) to approve Presidential appointments (majority vote), and (4) to elect the Vice President if the Electoral College is deadlocked (majority vote).

CONGRESS REGULATES ITSELF

1. Ethical Conduct of Members. According to the Constitution (Article 1, Section 5), each house of Congress shall judge "the elections, returns, and qualifications of its own members," may punish its members for disorderly behavior, and by a two-thirds vote may "expel a member."

a. Case Studies of Congressional Self-Regulation. (1) *Victor Berger*, a Socialist and opponent of World War I, was elected to the House in 1919 from a Milwaukee, Wisconsin district. He was denied his seat on the ground that he had been convicted of obstructing the war effort—a violation of the 1917 Espionage Act. Berger's conviction was reversed by the Supreme Court and, after his 1921 reelection, he was permitted to take his House seat. (2) *William Vare*, elected Senator from Pennsylvania in 1926, was denied his seat on the ground that he had "bought" the election by excessive and unethical use of campaign funds. (3) *Joseph McCarthy*, Senator from Wisconsin. (Check the Index for "Joseph McCarthy.") (4) *Adam Clayton Powell*, long-time Representative from the Harlem district in New York City, was denied his seat in 1967 on the grounds of misusing public funds and defying New York court orders. Reelected by his constituents, Powell was later seated but with a loss of seniority. (5) *Charles Diggs, Jr.*, Representative from Michigan, convicted in court of misusing government funds, was censured in 1979 by the House. (6) *Herman Talmadge*, Senator from Georgia, was "denounced" in 1979 by the Senate, which charged that he "either knew or should have known" of financial misconduct—diverting campaign funds to his personal use and submitting false office expense accounts. (Talmadge claimed that the Senate's failure to censure, expel, or strip him of seniority was a "personal victory.")

b. Ethical Codes. In 1968 the House and the Senate adopted "ethical codes" and in 1977, while voting a substantial Congressional pay raise, made these codes more stringent: broadening financial disclosure requirements, prohibiting acceptance of expensive gifts, restricting the use of franked (postage-free) mail, and limiting outside earned income to 15 percent of the Congressional salary. The codes were hailed as evidencing Congressional concern with maintaining ethical standards. They were criticized for containing loopholes and lacking adequate enforcement.

In 1979 the Senate by voice vote postponed to 1983 the effective date of limits on outside earnings. Also the Senate and the House voted to ease the required annual financial disclosure statements.

2. Lawmaking Procedures. The Constitution states that in order to conduct its business, each house shall require the presence of a majority of its members—a minimum number called a *quorum*. In most other procedural matters, the Constitution permits each house to determine "the rules of its proceedings." The House and the Senate each has developed its own detailed procedures.

HOW CONGRESS MAKES LAWS: THE COMMITTEE SYSTEM

1. Introduction of the Bill. Except for money bills, which must originate (start) in the House, any bill may be introduced by any Congressman. The bill may reflect the thinking of the Congressman, of a special interest group, or of the executive branch. In the case of a bill requested by the President, its provisions may be drawn up by the executive branch, but the bill must be *sponsored,* or formally presented, by a Congressman for legislative consideration. In the Senate the bill is announced orally; in the House of Representatives the bill is placed in a basket, called the *hopper.*

2. Referral to Committee. Thousands of bills on many subjects are introduced during each session of Congress. These are classified as *public bills* that deal with national problems or as *private bills* that deal with an individual person or place. Each bill is given a number that is preceded by the letters "HR" or "S" (depending on the originating house), its sponsors are listed, and it is printed.

Since neither house acting as a whole can adequately consider all these bills, each house is divided into small legislative bodies, called *committees.* In each house, the presiding officer refers each bill to the appropriate committee.

3. Number and Organization of Committees. The House of Representatives and the Senate each has about 20 standing or regular committees. Among the House committees are Agriculture, Armed Services, Banking and Currency, Education and Labor, International Relations, Interstate and Foreign Commerce, Judiciary, Rules, Science and Technology, and Ways and Means (finance). Among the Senate committees are Agriculture and Forestry, Armed Services, Commerce, Energy and Natural Resources, Environment and Public Works, Human Resources, Judiciary, and Foreign Relations.

Committee members are chosen from both political parties. House committees average about 30 members, Senate committees about 15. On each committee, the majority of the members belong to the majority party, which thereby controls the committee. Committee members are expected to become experts in their respective fields. Committee chairmen, always of the majority party, are usually chosen on the basis of length of service, or *seniority.*

4. Committee Proceedings. The committee disposes of most bills by *pigeonholing* them, that is, deferring consideration indefinitely. Some 90 percent of all bills introduced in Congress are *killed in committee.*

On a major bill the committee usually conducts research, holds hearings, and considers arguments for and against the measure. Then the committee, by majority vote, may approve the bill as it was introduced, approve an amended version of the bill, or reject the bill.

If a House committee delays action on a vital bill, a majority of the House membership can move the bill from the committee onto the House floor by signing a *discharge petition.* This rarely occurs.

5. Action in the Originating House. If approved by the committee, the bill is scheduled for consideration by the entire house by being placed on the calendar. (In the House of Representatives, this function is performed by the powerful *Rules Committee.* It also sets the rules for House consideration of the bill: regulating debate and restricting or permitting amendments from the floor.) The originating house debates the bill, possibly amends it, and finally takes a vote. The *majority leader,* assisted by the *majority whip,* works to secure votes for his party's bills. The *minority leader* and the *minority whip* direct the activity of the opposition party. If a majority votes against the bill, it is dead. If a majority approves, the bill goes to the other house.

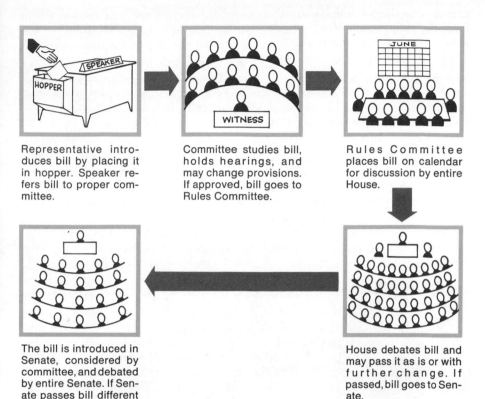

Representative intro-
duces bill by placing it
in hopper. Speaker re-
fers bill to proper com-
mittee.

Committee studies bill,
holds hearings, and
may change provisions.
If approved, bill goes to
Rules Committee.

Rules Committee
places bill on calendar
for discussion by entire
House.

The bill is introduced in
Senate, considered by
committee, and debated
by entire Senate. If Sen-
ate passes bill different
from House version, bill
goes to conference
committee.

House debates bill and
may pass it as is or with
further change. If
passed, bill goes to Sen-
ate.

If conference commit-
tee, of House and Sen-
ate members, resolves
differences, compro-
mise bill is submitted to
both House and Senate.

If both House and Sen-
ate pass compromise
bill, it goes to President
for signature.

If President signs, bill
becomes law; if he ve-
toes, Congress may
override veto by two-
thirds vote of both
House and Senate.

How a Bill Becomes a Law
When the Bill Originates in the House

6. Action in the Second House. Here the bill follows a similar path: introduction, referral to committee, consideration in committee, referral to the entire body, and decision.

7. Conference Committee. A bill is often approved by the two houses in versions that differ as to details. To adjust these differences, members designated by the presiding officer of each house meet as a temporary *conference committee*. Usually, they arrive at a *compromise bill*, and this bill is then submitted to each house for approval.

8. Presidential Action. After passage by Congress, the bill goes to the President for his decision. There are four possibilities: *(a)* If the President signs the bill within ten days, it becomes a law. *(b)* If the President holds the bill for ten days without signing it and Congress is still in session, the bill becomes a law without his signature. *(c)* If the President holds the bill for ten days without signing it and Congress is *not* in session, the bill is automatically killed. This is known as a *pocket veto*. *(d)* If the President *vetoes* the bill, he returns it to the originating house together with a statement of reasons for his veto. Congress may override the Presidential veto by a two-thirds vote in each house.

EVALUATION OF CONGRESSIONAL LAWMAKING PROCEDURES

1. Committee System. *(a) Merits.* The committee system provides a sensible way of handling the great number of bills proposed in Congress. It enables bills to receive a thorough and careful consideration. Committee hearings permit interested parties to express their views. *(b) Criticisms.* The committee system is time-consuming and complex. It involves needless duplication, as House and Senate committees cover essentially the same ground. The committee system prevents most bills from ever being considered by Congress. In killing some 90 percent of the bills proposed in Congress, the committees do not necessarily reflect the views of Congress or of the people.

2. Seniority and Committee Chairmen. *(a) Merits.* Chosen by seniority, committee chairmen are men of legislative experience. They are capable of exercising strong control so that their committees function smoothly. *(b) Criticisms.* Seniority does not necessarily mean ability. Committee chairmen usually represent "safe" districts and states, such as the Democratic South and the Republican states in the Midwest, where voters consistently support the same party. They rarely come from "doubtful" districts and states, where voters often switch support, thus making it difficult for their Congressmen to acquire sufficient seniority. Since chairmen owe their positions to continuous reelection, not to assignment by their party, seniority weakens party authority over its members. Furthermore, chairmen exercise too much power over their respective committees. They hire secretarial and research staffs, call or postpone committee meetings, and determine the *agenda*—the list of matters to be discussed.

In the 1975–1976 Congress, the Democrats, with a 2-to-1 majority in the House of Representatives, responded to popular demand for reform of the seniority system. This effort was spearheaded by 75 "freshmen" Democratic Representatives, characterized as young, liberal, and reform-minded. After considerable political in-fighting, the House Democratic *caucus*—consisting of

"Enter and kneel."
—Copyright 1971
by Herblock in the Washington Post

"It's grown a lot of barnacles over the years." (McLeod in the Buffalo Evening News)

all Democratic Representatives—voted to oust three veteran committee chairmen. These three chairmen, products of the seniority system, were Southerners and were all considered out of step with the thinking of the Democratic majority. The Democratic caucus also voted to assign the three vacated chairmanships to younger men with less seniority, two from the Midwest and one from the Far West, all considered more in harmony with the views of the Democratic majority.

The rejection of seniority in these three cases was labeled a revolution, an upheaval, and a break with a 65-year-old House tradition. It was interpreted as a warning to all House committee chairmen that they owe their positions, no longer to seniority alone, but also to election by the party caucus; therefore, if they desire to retain their chairmanships in subsequent Congresses, they must be responsive to the will of the party majority.

3. **Rules Committee in the House of Representatives.** (a) *Merits*. The Rules Committee arranges the orderly flow of bills for consideration by the entire House. It serves as a "traffic director." (b) *Criticisms*. Composed of senior Congressmen, the Rules Committee does not reflect necessarily the views of the House membership but tends to be conservative and to resist new programs. If the Rules Committee opposes a bill approved by a standing committee, the Rules Committee may prevent consideration by the entire House. It may serve as a "roadblock."

RULES ON DEBATE

The House maintains strict rules limiting debate. These House rules enable the Representatives to discuss bills and reach decisions without deliberate delay through debate. The Senate, however, usually permits its members the privilege of unlimited debate. This makes possible the *filibuster*.

FILIBUSTER IN THE SENATE

1. Purpose. A filibuster is a deliberate attempt sometimes used by a minority group of Senators (or a single Senator) to talk continuously so as to consume time and prevent a favorable vote on a bill. The filibuster members hope to compel the Senate leaders, concerned about the regular work schedule of the Senate, to return the disputed bill to committee probably to be pigeonholed. In the post-World War II years Southern Senators used the filibuster to stall voting on civil rights legislation.

2. Cloture. A filibuster may be halted by *cloture*, a special vote to close debate. *Senate Rule 22*, adopted in 1917, permitted cloture by a two-thirds vote of the Senators present. Cloture was infrequently used because (*a*) Southern Senators are opposed and often have mustered enough votes to block cloture, and (*b*) many Senators are unwilling to employ cloture against others for fear that, at some future time, it may be used against themselves.

In 1975 the Senate moved to ease its cloture rule. While still requiring a two-thirds vote of all Senators present for any further change in its cloture rule, the Senate adopted a new regulation permitting cloture on all other issues by a vote of three-fifths of its total membership. This new regulation reduces from as many as 67 to 60 the number of votes needed to invoke cloture.

Scholars pointed out that from 1917 to 1975, of 103 cloture attempts only 24 were successful— of which 16 occurred in the past five years. If the new Senate rule had been in effect since 1917, the number of successful cloture attempts would have increased only by four.

3. Evaluation of the Filibuster. (*a*) *Merits.* A filibuster against a specific bill (1) permits thorough discussion and free expression of ideas, (2) allows time for the public to become informed and to make known its views, and (3) protects the rights and interests of the minority. (*b*) *Criticisms.* A filibuster (1) prevents meaningful discussion on a bill when filibustering Senators "talk a bill to death," by reading such extraneous materials as telephone directories and novels, (2) frustrates the will of the majority, and (3) wastes time and prevents the Senate from functioning. (For 83 days, in 1964, Southern Senators filibustered against a civil rights bill before the Senate voted cloture.) Critics of the filibuster point out that the rights of minorities are adequately safeguarded by the Constitution and that minorities have the opportunity to appeal to the voters to elect Senators favorable to their viewpoint.

PRESSURES UPON THE CONGRESSMAN

1. From Constituents. The Congressman is a politician who has won election. To remain in office he must continue to win elections, which means that he must retain and strengthen support among his constituents. To this end the typical Congressman proceeds as follows:

a. He keeps in close contact with his home district or state by maintaining an office there, attending local functions, answering letters, informing the voters of his many activities, greeting constituents who visit Washington for social or business reasons, and assisting them in their dealings with the government.

"Not so fast—one at a time, please . . ." (*LeCocq—Rothco Cartoons*)

b. He builds a legislative record. (1) He supports special-interest legislation favored by powerful groups—such as veterans, ethnic minorities, workers, and manufacturers—in his home district or state. (2) He supports bills to provide his home district or state with public works—such as new post offices, better highways, and river and harbor improvements. In this way he proves to the "folks back home" that he is looking out for their interests. If such bills provide public works regardless of need, they are called *pork-barrel* legislation. These bills are usually passed by means of *log-rolling*. This term refers to the trading of votes between Congressmen who, regardless of shortcomings of their respective bills, agree with each other, "If you vote for my bill, I'll vote for yours." (3) The Congressman seeks an active role in the passage of major legislation. In voting on a major bill, the Congressman has no problem when his convictions and those of his constituents are similar. However, if their views are dissimilar, what does the Congressman owe to his constituency: to vote its views or to vote according to his best judgment?

2. From Political Leaders. The Congressman is indebted to the local party leaders who supported his nomination, worked for his election, and who now help maintain a local organization for future contests. He seeks to provide them with *patronage* which means government jobs and also to grant them personal and political favors. To his national party organization the Congressman has few ties since it probably played little if any role in his election. However, he usually cooperates with the veteran leaders of his party in Congress who will influence his committee assignments, the fate of his "pet" measures, and in general his legislative standing. He indicates to the party leaders that they may count on his support and vote on major issues. Finally, the Congressman, especially if he is a member of the President's party, may be invited to gatherings at the White House and be urged directly or indirectly to support measures favored by the President.

The Congressman, however, retains the full right to vote as he sees fit. He knows that if he opposes the national party organization, it has negligible powers to discipline him. Congressmen at times display little hesitation in voting across party lines.

3. From Lobbyists. The Congressman receives the attention of special-interest groups who make their influence felt through their agents, called *lobbyists*.

LOBBYING

1. Special-Interest Groups. To secure the passage of laws they desire or to defeat laws unfavorable to their interests, many economic and social organizations try to "pressure" members of Congress. Typical large, nationwide pressure groups include the National Association of Manufacturers (NAM), American Federation of Labor and Congress of Industrial Organizations (AFL-CIO), American Farm Bureau Federation, American Medical Association (AMA), and American Legion. Typical smaller, more specialized pressure groups represent interests such as postal clerks, chiropodists, teachers, cotton growers, dairy farmers, home builders, petroleum producers, and tobacco manufacturers.

2. Meaning and Methods of Lobbyists. Lobbyists are politically experienced persons—many being attorneys, public relations experts, and former Congressmen—employed to further the purposes of special-interest groups. The name, "lobbyists," was derived from the practice originally of such persons buttonholing Congressmen in the lobbies just outside the legislative chambers.

Lobbyists seek to influence Congressmen by (*a*) drafting bills, testifying at hearings, and supplying data carefully selected to support their views, (*b*) cultivating personal contacts with Congressmen—arranging parties, granting favors, and providing campaign funds, (*c*) preparing for special-interest delegations to visit and chat with Congressmen, and (*d*) urging the public to deluge Congress with postcards, letters, and telegrams. Sometimes the work of one lobby, such as a businessmen's organization, is offset by the work of another lobby, such as a labor organization. Lobbyists also seek to influence the members of executive agencies and regulatory commissions.

3. Arguments in Favor of Lobbies. (*a*) Lobbying is in accord with the Constitutional guarantee that the people have the right to petition the government. (*b*) Lobbying enables special groups to make their views known. (*c*) Lobbyists may call attention to the need for laws. (*d*) Lobbyists may provide Congressmen with valuable information.

4. Arguments Against Lobbies. (*a*) Lobbyists sometimes utilize questionable methods, including the giving of lavish gifts and campaign contributions. (*b*) Lobbying gives well-organized groups, such as industry and labor, an advantage over poorly organized groups, such as consumers. (*c*) Lobbying may foster laws that benefit special-interest groups. (*d*) Lobbyists may provide information that is incomplete and one-sided.

5. Federal Regulation. By the *Regulation of Lobbying Act* (1946), Congress defined lobbyists as persons directly seeking to influence legislation and required that they (*a*) register with Congress and provide the names and addresses of their employers, (b) identify current legislation they support or oppose, and (c) file quarterly statements regarding the sources of their funds and the nature of their expenditures. Since passage of this law, some 4000 lobbyists have so registered. (This law has served as a model for many states to regulate lobbying in state capitals.)

6. Weaknesses of Federal Regulation. Although providing publicity for lobbying activities, the law has many weaknesses: (a) It defines lobbying in a limited way. Some lobbyists have claimed that their chief work is not to influence legislation but to educate the public and that they therefore need not register. (b) It sets no bounds on the activities and expenditures of lobbyists. (c) It lacks adequate enforcement powers, especially to compel the filing of reports and to check upon their accuracy.

CONGRESSIONAL COMMITTEES CONDUCT INVESTIGATIONS

1. Purposes. To assist Congress in its major functions, House and Senate committees hold hearings and conduct investigations. The committees may be the regular standing committees or their subcommittees engaged in normal legislative routines; they also may be specially created investigating committees. Investigating committees—both regular and special—seek to (a) determine the effectiveness of existing laws, (b) measure the performance of the executive branch in enforcing existing laws, and (c) assess the need for Congressional action, especially the passage of new laws. In many cases, the committee members are aware in advance of what their investigation will reveal, but they use the hearings to gain publicity and arouse support for Congressional action.

2. The Hearings. Committees may hold hearings anywhere in the country, but usually they are held in Washington, D.C. The hearings may be in executive or closed session but usually they are open to the public and press and sometimes may be broadcast on radio and television.

The committee has its legal counsel and staff assistants do the preparatory work, especially providing a list of witnesses and indicating the nature of their testimony. The committee may request the appearance of any executive official from Cabinet officer down to clerk. The committee also may hear private individuals—experts, lobbyists, and other interested persons—most of whom are willing to testify.

In some investigations, the committee may want to question persons who are not willing to testify. The committee may use the *subpoena*—a legal document ordering a person to appear for questioning. If a witness refuses to appear or refuses to answer legitimate questions pertaining to the investigation and not infringing upon the witness' civil rights, then the committee may have the witness cited for *contempt of Congress* and face the possibility of a jail sentence.

3. Criticisms of Investigating Committees. In the post-World War II years, Congressional committees investigating "sensitive areas," such as organized crime, labor racketeering, and especially Communist activities, were subjected to considerable criticism. These committees, critics charged, were (a) merely looking for publicity, (b) engaging in "fishing expeditions," that is, not seeking any specific information and not having any legislative purpose, and (c) accusing witnesses on the basis of hearsay evidence and "trying" them in the newspapers without permitting courtroom legal safeguards: such as the right to counsel, cross examine hostile witnesses, and produce friendly witnesses. Supporters argued that these committees had served to alert the nation to serious problems and that questionable committee procedures could be remedied.

4. Limitations Upon Investigating Committees

a. The Fifth Amendment. A number of witnesses called before Congressional committees investigating "sensitive areas" refused to answer questions. They pleaded the Fifth Amendment, which contains the "witness clause" stating that no person "shall be compelled in any criminal case to be a witness against himself." Witnesses who "take the Fifth," some observers claimed, must have something to hide and therefore must be guilty of illegal activity. On the other hand, the federal courts held that witnesses employing the privilege against self-incrimination have the legal right to do so and without any inference of guilt.

To compel reluctant witnesses to testify in national security cases, Congress in 1954 passed the *Compulsory Testimony Act*. It empowered federal courts to grant a witness *immunity* (exemption) from prosecution based upon his testimony. If a witness so granted immunity still refuses to testify, he is subject to contempt of court charges punishable by jail.

b. House Rules for Investigations. To guide its investigating committees, the House in 1955 adopted the following rules: witnesses must be informed of the purpose of the investigation; also they may have counsel and may make brief sworn statements; the committee must hear defamatory evidence in closed session and then decide if such testimony is to be made public. (The Senate did not follow this House example but permitted each Senate investigating committee to set its own rules.)

c. Watkins vs. United States (1957). John Watkins, a witness before the *House Un-American Activities Committee,* refused to name former Communist party members. He claimed that such information was not pertinent to the committee's investigation of labor unions. Found guilty of contempt of Congress by the lower court, Watkins appealed to the Supreme Court and won his case. The Supreme Court held that, in questioning witnesses, Congressional committees (1) must respect the individual's rights guaranteed in the First Amendment, (2) must clearly indicate the purpose of the investigation, and (3) must not demand information to "expose for the sake of exposure."

5. Case Studies of Investigating Committees

a. The Truman Committee. The special *Senate War Investigating Committee,* established in 1941 and headed by Senator *Harry Truman* of Missouri, energetically scrutinized government expenditures for World War II military equipment. The committee helped to save the government considerable sums on war contracts, to eliminate production bottlenecks and speed output, and to improve the work of wartime executive agencies. The committee received much favorable comment, and Harry Truman gained national prominence. In 1944 he was nominated as Democratic Vice-Presidential candidate and in 1945, upon Franklin D. Roosevelt's death, Truman became President.

b. House Un-American Activities Committee (HUAC). Established as a special committee in 1938 with Representative *Martin Dies* of Texas as first chairman, the *House Un-American Activities Committee* in 1945 became a regular committee. Under several chairmen and with changing membership, HUAC has had a long and tumultuous existence. To uncover un-American or subversive activities, the committee investigated the German-American or *Nazi Bunds* in the late 1930's and the Ku Klux Klan in the mid-1960's, but the committee's work mostly has centered upon Communist activities. To this end, HUAC investigated in such diverse areas as labor unions, the entertainment world, and government employees. The committee's work has been praised for alerting the nation to the internal Communist danger and for helping to draft internal security bills. The committee's work has been condemned for conducting "fishing expeditions" and for bullying and defaming witnesses. A HUAC member who first gained national prominence in the Communist investigations was Richard Nixon.

    c. The McCarthy Committee. The *Senate Subcommittee on Investigations* (part of the standing committee on Government Operations) was headed by Senator *Joseph McCarthy* of Wisconsin. He made newspaper headlines in 1950 by charging that the State Department contained a large number of Communists. McCarthy's charges, investigated by a special Senate committee, were found to be half-truths and untruths. Undaunted, McCarthy continued his attack, charging the Democratic administrations with "twenty years of treason." McCarthy's supporters praised his efforts to alert the nation to the danger of Communist subversion. McCarthy's detractors labeled him a demagogue whose wild and reckless charges divided the nation and fanned public hysteria. Later, McCarthy directed his "treason" charges against the Republican administration of President *Dwight D. Eisenhower.* In 1954 McCarthy was censured by the Senate for "unbecoming conduct" and thereafter lost influence.

    d. The McClellan Committee. Check the Index for "McClellan Committee."

Portraits of Outstanding Congressmen

REPRESENTATIVES

1. Thomas Reed (1839–1902) for over 20 years was elected by a Republican district in Maine to the House. Reed served as a member of the powerful Rules Committee and in 1889 was chosen Speaker. To end the delay of House business by a minority, Reed enforced new rules that strengthened the Speaker's powers. He recorded Representatives who did not respond to the roll call as "present and refusing to vote," thereby securing a quorum, and he refused to consider motions he held to be only dilatory or time-wasting. Reed's opponents labeled him a "Czar," but his supporters insisted that he transformed the House into an effective legislative body.

2. Joseph Cannon (1836–1926) almost continuously for over 40 years was a Representative from Illinois. Nicknamed "Uncle Joe," Cannon from 1903 to 1911 served as Speaker. A conservative Republican, Cannon used his tremendous powers, inherited from "Czar Reed," to block legislation desired by progressive Republicans and Democrats. In 1910–1911 his opponents gained sufficient votes to amend the House rules and reduce the powers of the Speaker. No longer could he appoint the members and chairmen of committees and no longer could he serve on the Rules Committee. Thereafter Cannon left the Speakership although till 1923 he remained a member of the House.

3. Samuel Rayburn (1882–1961), Democrat from Texas, from 1912 onward won 25 consecutive elections to the House. With two interruptions when his party lacked a House majority, Rayburn served as Speaker for a record of 17 years. Rayburn was instrumental in guiding much legislation through the House. Called "Mr. Sam," he was an informal and popular man who built lasting friendships with members of both major parties. A strong and capable leader, Rayburn proved that the Speaker could exercise his great powers honestly, fairly, and tactfully.

4. Other Representatives. Other Representatives who may be considered outstanding include *Thaddeus Stevens, James Beauchamp ("Champ") Clark, Nicholas Longworth,* and *John McCormack.*

SENATORS SELECTED FOR THE SENATE HALL OF FAME

The following five "outstanding Senators of the past" were selected in 1959 by the Senate for its "Hall of Fame." They were chosen for "overall statesmenship" during the most significant periods of Senate history, for bringing "distinction to the Senate," and for leaving a "permanent mark on our nation's history."

1. Henry Clay (1777–1852), from the border state of Kentucky, was an early 19th century American statesman whose career included service as Speaker of the House of Representatives, three unsuccessful tries for the Presidency, a term as Secretary of State, and many years in the Senate. While in the House, Clay won national fame as a "war hawk" in favor of the War of 1812 against Britain; as an advocate of national economic self-sufficiency; and as the *Great Pacificator* or *Great Compromiser* between North and South who arranged the 1820 *Missouri Compromise.* In the Senate, Clay together with *John Calhoun* and *Daniel Webster* formed the *great triumvirate* of the pre-Civil War days. As Senator, Clay continued his efforts to moderate sectional disputes by sponsoring the 1833 *Tariff Compromise* and the slavery *Compromise of 1850.* Warm, enthusiastic, and esteemed by his colleagues, Clay was a man of principle who said "I would rather be right than President," and "I know no North—no South—no East—no West."

2. John Calhoun (1782–1850) of South Carolina, a man of great talent, occupied many important government positions: Representative, Secretary of War, Vice President, Secretary of State, and for 17 years Senator. In his years in the House (1811–1817), Calhoun was a nationalist, being a "war hawk" and supporting a protective tariff. By the 1820's Calhoun had become a sectionalist, a champion of slavery and the South, who in his document *South Carolina Exposition and Protest* opposed the protective tariff and defended "state rights," nullification, and secession. As Senator, Calhoun accepted Clay's 1833 Tariff Compromise but spurned the slavery Compromise of 1850. A logical thinker, Calhoun foresaw the coming of the Civil War. On his deathbed in 1850, Calhoun's last words were "the South, the poor South."

3. Daniel Webster (1782–1852) of Massachusetts won fame as an orator, as a lawyer, Representative, Secretary of State, and, for nearly 20 years, Senator. Toward the end of the 1810 decade Webster became a nationalist, advocating a protective tariff, national bank, and strong central government. As a Constitutional lawyer before the Supreme Court, he presented the nationalist position and won two major cases: the *Dartmouth College Case* (1819) and *McCulloch vs. Maryland* (1819). (Check the Index for these cases.) In the 1830 debate with Senator Robert Hayne of South Carolina, Webster delivered a speech often considered the greatest ever in Senate history. Webster rebutted Calhoun's states' rights arguments, presented the Union viewpoint, and concluded "Liberty and Union, now and forever, one and inseparable." By supporting the slavery Compromise of 1850, Webster alienated many Northern antislavery men, but Webster insisted that he was right in speaking "not as a Northern man but as an American."

4. Robert M. La Follette (1855–1925) of Wisconsin was a progressive Republican who, in the early 20th century, battled for domestic reforms. Opposing the regular state Republican leadership allied with railroad and lumber interests, La Follette was elected three times as governor of Wisconsin; he secured state legislation to regulate railroads, curb lobbying, begin civil service reform, and provide more equitable taxation. Elected Senator in 1906, La Follette remained outside the regular Republican establishment as "the lonely man of the Senate." Nevertheless, he fought vigorously for railroad regulation, lower tariffs, and other progressive laws. During the World War I era, La Follette was a strict isolationist opposing American entrance into the war and membership in the League of Nations. In the 1924 elections, dismayed by the conservative Republican program and candidate, La Follette ran for President on the Progressive party ticket. Although he lost the election, La Follette polled almost 5 million votes, more than polled by any previous third-party candidate.

5. Robert A. Taft (1889–1953) of Ohio, son of President William Howard Taft, gained experience in the state legislature, and from 1938 to his death in 1953 served as United States Senator. During these years, with the Senate Republicans usually in the minority, Taft became their spokesman and earned the title of "Mr. Republican." Considered a conservative, Taft opposed most Democratic legislation of the "New Deal" and the "Fair Deal." As chairman of the *Senate Labor Committee,* he pushed through the 1947 *Taft-Hartley Act* to curb the power of labor unions. Taft himself insisted that he was a middle-of-the-roader, pointing to his advocacy of such measures as federal aid to education, medical care, and low-income housing. In foreign affairs, Taft was an isolationist before World War II but thereafter endorsed American membership in the United Nations and other measures for international cooperation. Supported by the conservative "Old Guard" Republicans, Taft tried and failed three times to secure his party's Presidential nomination. Friend and foe alike, however, respected Taft for his honesty, courage, and devotion to principle.

6. Other Senators. Other Senators who may be considered outstanding include *Thomas Hart Benton, Edmund Ross, Henry Cabot Lodge, Sr., George Norris,* and *Robert Wagner, Sr.*

CONSIDERATIONS REGARDING CONGRESSIONAL REFORMS

1. Criticisms of Congress. The American people, according to public opinion polls, view Congress with considerable dissatisfaction. They criticize Congress for *(a)* working too slowly, *(b)* following inefficient and duplicatory procedures, *(c)* failing to cooperate with the President, and *(d)* passing unsatisfactory laws and neglecting vital legislation. To what extent are such criticisms justified?

2. Defense of Congress. Supporters claim that criticisms of Congress are vastly overdone. They point out that Congress is easy to criticize because *(a)* more than the other two governmental branches, Congress works in the public spotlight, *(b)* by its investigative and legislative functions, Congress is a center of controversy, and *(c)* with 535 Congressmen each free to act as he wishes, Congress has little control over its members but is held to blame for any individual misdeeds.

Supporters further point out that the value of Congress is measured *not* by the speed with which it works and *not* by the extent to which it cooperates with the President. The true measure of the value of Congress, supporters assert, is what Congress contributes to the well-being of our democratic society by *(a)* serving to check and counterbalance the powers of the other two governmental branches, *(b)* arousing public concern over vital issues, *(c)* reflecting diverse political, economic, and social interests in the nation, *(d)* arriving at satisfactory compromises between such diverse interests, and so *(e)* enacting legislation that is workable and rooted in public acceptance. However, even supporters of Congress admit that its procedures can be improved.

3. Congressional Reforms Already Achieved

a. The Legislative Reorganization Act of 1946 (1) reduced the number of standing committees in each house, (2) authorized committees to employ additional research and professional help, (3) enlarged the Legislative Reference Service at the Library of Congress, and (4) required lobbyists to register and disclose their activities.

b. The Legislative Reform Act of 1970 (1) established a new Senate *Committee on Veterans Affairs* (paralleling a similar House committee), (2) provided for radio and television broadcasting of House committee proceedings (as already allowed for Senate committee proceedings), (3) empowered a majority of the members of any House or Senate committee to call a meeting if the committee chairman refuses to do so, and (4) upon the request of 20 Representatives, required the House to record how each member voted on amendments to bills as well as on the final bills (as already practiced in the Senate). For House members, this provision meant that all their votes would be fully disclosed to the public.

c. Other reforms already achieved and discussed in the preceding pages are legislative reapportionment, codes of ethical conduct, the discharge petition in the House, cloture in the Senate, regulation of lobbying, and House rules for investigating committees.

4. Possible Further Reforms

a. Stronger Party Discipline. In the two major political parties, reformers urge that each national organization exercise effective control over the party members in Congress and assure votes for party programs. To achieve this goal, each national party organization would have to (1) take part in and finance Congressional election campaigns, (2) control the committee assignments of Congressmen and name committee chairmen, if necessary without regard for seniority, and (3) be able to expel persistently nonconforming members. At present, such powers appear beyond the ambition or reach of the national party organizations. Further party conformity would make impossible political insurgency such as typified the career of Robert M. La Follette.

b. Four-Year Term for Representatives. In 1966 President Lyndon Johnson urged Congress to propose a Constitutional amendment extending the term of office for Representatives to four years. The longer term would enable Representatives to devote more time to their legislative duties and less to "politicking" and campaigning. On the other hand, it would enable Representatives to be less responsive to the wishes of their constituencies. To date the proposal has few supporters.

c. Joint House-Senate Committees. By holding hearings and conducting research jointly, reformers claim, similar House and Senate committees could avoid needless duplication and speed up their work. On the other hand, each legislative chamber is jealous of its own powers and, by having committees function separately, each serves to check upon the other.

d. Improved Relations With the Executive Branch. Reformers have made various proposals to coordinate Congressional and executive efforts in regard to legislation such as by (1) establishing a legislative council to meet regularly with the President and (2) setting aside a definite time, perhaps once a week, when legislators could question executive officials. These proposals have gained little support.

e. Item Veto. Congress has, at times, added to a vital bill an unrelated provision called a *rider*. Although this provision may be objectionable to the President, he has no power to veto a single item but must approve the entire bill

"Isn't that an awfully long leash?"
(*Goodwin in the Columbus Dispatch*)

including the rider. Reformers have proposed that the President be granted the power to veto single items, thereby checking pork-barrel provisions in appropriation bills and riders added to vital measures. Congress, however, is reluctant to increase the powers of the President.

f. Other Proposed Reforms. (1) For cloture to halt filibuster in the Senate, reduce the vote needed from 60 to a simple majority of the Senators present, (2) for a discharge petition to move a bill out of a House committee, reduce the number of signatures needed from 218 to 150 Representatives, (3) further limit the power of the House Rules Committee to delay bills, (4) strengthen disclosure requirements for lobbyists, and (5) in selecting committee chairmen, consider in addition to seniority such factors as ability and adherence to party programs. Although this last reform was begun in 1975 by House Democrats, observers question whether or not it will survive in future Congresses.

MULTIPLE-CHOICE QUESTIONS

1. The framers of the Constitution *best* expressed their faith in the people by the provision for choosing the (1) Justices of the Supreme Court (2) President and Vice President (3) Speaker of the House of Representatives (4) members of the House of Representatives.
2. The increasing influence of California in national politics is *best* explained by that state's (1) outstanding political leaders (2) increase in population (3) increased number of primary contests (4) peaceful campus life.
3. The term "gerrymandering" refers to the (1) unequal distribution of campaign contributions (2) unfair system of apportionment of districts for election purposes (3) unusual power of the Southern states in Congress (4) unjust practice of dismissing officeholders for political reasons.
4. One argument for the election of Representatives biennially rather than every four years is to (1) secure more state electors for Presidential elections (2) make legislators more accountable to the people they represent (3) insure that legislators have adequate time to study bills (4) have all legislative elections coincide with the Presidential elections.
5. What is the *smallest* number of members of Congress that a state, regardless of its population, may have? (1) five (2) two (3) three (4) four
6. By its *most* recent rule on debate, the Senate (1) outlawed filibusters (2) required a two-thirds vote of the Senators present and voting to end a filibuster (3) extended the right of unlimited debate to the House of Representatives (4) required the vote of 60 Senators to limit debate on any measure except a proposed Senate rules change.
7. Filibustering is *most* likely to be used by a (1) lobbyist favoring a new federal law (2) majority attempting to override a Presidential veto (3) minority seeking to delay a vote (4) Congressional committee chairman attempting to kill a bill.
8. Which action of the Senate requires a simple majority vote? (1) ratification of a treaty (2) approval of an appointment (3) passage of a bill vetoed by the President (4) conviction of an impeached official
9. According to the Constitution, Congress is required to meet (1) twice a year (2) annually (3) once every two years (4) only when called into session by the President.
10. According to the Constitution, which of the following must originate in the House of Representatives? (1) a bill to levy an excise tax on television sets (2) a proposed amendment to require a referendum for a declaration of war (3) a contempt of court order against a witness refusing to answer questions of a Congressional investigating committee (4) approval of appointment of a new Attorney General

11. Congressional immunity prevents (1) taxation of a Congressman's salary by the federal government (2) a libel suit against a Congressman for remarks made in Congress (3) expulsion of a member of Congress (4) arrest of a Congressman by a foreign power.

12. Although many Southern Democratic Representatives and Senators have in recent years voted against their party's program, most have remained within the Democratic party *chiefly* because (1) the Republican party is hostile to Southerners (2) the system of gerrymandering forces them to do so (3) they would lose their seniority rights on Congressional committees (4) they would lose their representation on the Supreme Court.

13. No bill may become a law without the approval of (1) the Supreme Court (2) the President (3) a two-thirds vote of the Senate (4) both houses of Congress.

14. Usually, after a bill has been introduced into either house of Congress, it is first (1) signed by the presiding officer of that house (2) debated by members of that house (3) referred to a committee of that house (4) considered by a joint committee representing both houses.

15. The Rules Committee of the House of Representatives is important because it (1) acts as a liaison between the House and the President (2) functions as an independent legislative body (3) censures members who are out of order (4) determines the order in which bills are to be put before the House.

16. In the legislative process, a conference committee is usually appointed (1) when Congress desires to investigate corrupt practices in government (2) when the President wishes to call Congress into special session (3) after the President has vetoed an act of Congress (4) after the Senate and the House have passed different versions of the same bill.

17. Which statement *best* supports the contention that lobbyists perform a useful and needed function in the legislative process? (1) They have a national, not a sectional, background. (2) They are recognized in the federal Constitution. (3) They provide information that might not ordinarily be available. (4) They usually reflect majority opinion.

18. The major role of Congressional investigating committees is to provide (1) factual information for the enactment of legislation (2) public exposure of subversive activities (3) opportunities for the news media to expose corrupt government practices (4) data on criminal activities for use by the FBI.

ANALYSIS QUESTIONS: SENATORIAL ACTIVITY

Base your answers to the following questions on the activities of the United States Senators described below and on your knowledge of American studies.

Senator A is talking with a representative of the AFL-CIO concerning a labor bill about to be introduced.

Senator B has been speaking on the floor of the Senate for several hours in an effort to prevent a vote on a bill he opposes.

Senator C is attending committee hearings on a treaty about to be submitted to the Senate for ratification.

Senator D is drafting a bill that will provide for a federal flood-control project in his home state.

1. Which Senator would be most opposed to cloture? (1) A (2) B (3) C (4) D
2. Which Senator is most likely to be involved with pork-barrel legislation? (1) A (2) B (3) C (4) D
3. Which Senator appears to be most directly involved with a lobbyist? (1) A (2) B (3) C (4) D

4. Which pair of Senators is engaged in activities that might also be typical of those carried on by members of the House of Representatives? (1) *A* and *B* (2) *A* and *C* (3) *A* and *D* (4) *B* and *D*
5. In the post-World War II years, Senator *B* would *most* likely represent which section of the country? (1) Northeast (2) South (3) Midwest (4) Pacific Coast
6. If Senator *C* opposed the treaty under consideration, what minimum number of votes in the Senate would he need to defeat its ratification? (1) one-third (2) one-third plus one (3) one-half (4) one-half plus one
7. In regard to the measures under consideration above, how many of these four Senators might consider the use of log-rolling? (1) one (2) two (3) three (4) four
8. The AFL-CIO representative talking with Senator *A* might be expected to talk with all of the following *except* (1) the Speaker of the House of Representatives (2) the Secretary of Labor (3) a Justice of the Supreme Court (4) the chairman of the Senate Education and Labor Committee.

IDENTIFICATION QUESTIONS: WHO AM I?

Victor Berger	Robert La Follette	Thomas Reed
John Calhoun	Joseph McCarthy	Robert Taft
Joseph Cannon	Adam Clayton Powell	Harry Truman
Henry Clay	Samuel Rayburn	Daniel Webster

1. A leading spokesman for the planter aristocracy, I wrote the *South Carolina Exposition and Protest.* As Senator, I defended states' rights, nullification, and secession.
2. I exercised the powers of Speaker of the House fairly and tactfully. A Democrat, I was popular with members of both political parties.
3. A progressive Republican from Wisconsin, I battled for domestic reforms but against American membership in the League of Nations. In 1924 I ran as a third-party candidate for the Presidency.
4. A socialist, I was elected to the House of Representatives by a Milwaukee, Wisconsin district. The House at first denied me my seat because I had vigorously opposed American participation in World War I.
5. A New Englander, I won two major cases before the Supreme Court. In a famous Senate debate, I presented the nationalist viewpoint of the Constitution and called for "Liberty and Union."
6. As Speaker of the House, I enforced new rules to enable legislative work to proceed efficiently. My opponents called me a "czar."
7. A Representative from a Harlem district in New York City, I was denied my seat in the House on various charges of misconduct but was eventually seated with a loss of seniority.
8. A Westerner and a "war hawk" in favor of the War of 1812, I later made three unsuccessful tries for the Presidency. By arranging major laws to calm sectional disputes, I earned the title of Great Compromiser.

ESSAY QUESTIONS

1. President Kennedy is said to have remarked, "It is very easy to defeat a bill in Congress. It is much more difficult to pass one." (*a*) Discuss *two* specific features of Congressional organization and procedures to support President Kennedy's point of view. (*b*) Explain *one* way in which the legislative process is affected by each of the following: (1) the President (2) public opinion (3) special-interest groups (4) the Congressman's desire to be reelected.

2. Present *one* argument to support *or one* argument to oppose *each* of the following statements: (*a*) Congress remains in session too long. (*b*) The requirements for members of Congress should include a college education. (*c*) The filibuster is undemocratic. (*d*) A majority vote of both houses of Congress should be required to ratify treaties. (*e*) The committee system of Congress is a sensible way of handling legislation. (*f*) Congress should outlaw all lobbying in Washington, D.C. (*g*) Congressional investigating committees perform a worthwhile task. (*h*) The national party organization should exercise strict discipline over party members in Congress.
3. The practices of Congress have been both vigorously defended and vigorously attacked. (*a*) Discuss *two* Congressional practices to show why *each* has been defended. (*b*) Discuss *two* other Congressional practices to show why *each* has come under attack. (*c*) Explain *one* remedy proposed for *each* of these attacked Congressional practices. (*d*) Has criticism of Congress been overdone? Defend your answer.
4. Assume that you are considering a career as a member of Congress. (*a*) Discuss *one* advantage and *one* disadvantage of such a career. (*b*) How would you prepare yourself for such a career? (*c*) Explain how any *three* of the following items might further your Congressional career (where possible, provide examples of past Congressmen): (1) oratorical ability (2) tact (3) determination (4) devotion to a cause (5) luck (6) ability to reconcile conflicting interests.

6. The Federal Courts Are the Judiciary and Interpret the Nation's Laws

Of the Founding Fathers who drew up the Constitution, half were lawyers and many others, experienced in business and government, possessed strong legal backgrounds. Well read in the turbulent history of 17th-century England, they approved of the efforts of Parliament to make the Stuart kings rule "within the law" and respect the legal "rights of Englishmen." The Founding Fathers were aware of, and many had taken part in, colonial protests against English laws and actions which, they held, deprived them of the "rights of Englishmen." Further they knew that, in defending America's right to nationhood, the Declaration of Independence cited the British king for committing many legal "injuries and usurpations." During the Articles of Confederation, they had been dismayed by the conflict and confusion resulting from the existence of 13 independent state legal systems and the lack of any unifying national judiciary.

The Founding Fathers were determined to "establish justice" by creating a government not of men but of laws. True, men would make, enforce, and interpret the laws, but in so doing they would treat all persons equally and impartially. The Founding Fathers were aware that each state would maintain its own court system, but they were determined to create some measure of national legal uniformity. For this purpose, they declared that the Constitution "shall be the supreme Law of the Land" (Article VI) and they provided for a national judiciary (Article III).

JURISDICTION OF THE FEDERAL COURTS

The federal courts have *jurisdiction*, or authority, over cases as follows:

1. By Matters Involved. *(a)* Determining Constitutional issues, which means the constitutionality of federal and state laws and executive actions; *(b)* interpreting federal laws and treaties, including maritime law; and *(c)* ascertaining treason, the only crime specifically defined in the Constitution—"levying war" against the United States, or giving "aid and comfort" to its enemies.

(The federal courts have *no* power to issue *advisory opinions* in advance of the enactment or enforcement of laws. They consider legal matters only when involved in actual disputes that become court cases.)

2. By Parties Involved. *(a)* Ambassadors and other representatives of foreign nations, *(b)* the United States government itself, *(c)* two or more states, *(d)* citizens of different states, and *(e)* American citizens or states in dispute with foreign citizens or nations. All other cases, not included within the jurisdiction of the federal courts, are reserved for the state and local court systems.

FEDERAL COURT SYSTEM

The Constitution (Article III, Section 1) specifically provides for one Supreme Court and empowers Congress to establish *inferior* (lower) courts. Accordingly, Congress passed the *Judiciary Act of 1789* setting the broad outlines of our federal court system. Today it consists as follows:

1. About Ninety District Courts

a. Jurisdiction. These lowest courts in the federal system have *original jurisdiction;* that is, they hear and decide most cases first. They hear *civil cases* in which two or more persons usually dispute each other such as (1) one corporation suing others on claim of infringement of trademark rights—a matter of federal law, and (2) a manufacturer in one state suing for payment for goods sold to a retailer in another state—an interstate matter. District courts also hear *criminal cases* in which the government accuses persons of violating federal law such as by (1) robbing the mails or using them for fraudulent schemes, (2) making or passing counterfeit money, (3) entering the United States illegally, and (4) destroying the records of a selective service board. In total annually, the district courts handle over 100,000 cases, of which two-thirds are civil and one-third criminal cases. In most civil and all criminal cases, the district courts provide trial by jury.

b. Procedures. The federal district court judge presides over the selection of the jury and over the trial. Attorneys represent each party to a legal dispute —one side is known in both civil and criminal cases as the *defendant;* the other side is known in civil cases as the *plaintiff* and in criminal cases as the *prosecutor.* A federal *district attorney*, an official of the Justice Department, represents the government in prosecuting criminal cases.

With the judge in charge of the proceedings, attorneys for each side (1) question members of a large jury panel so as to select 12 "impartial" trial jurors, (2) place witnesses on the stand, (3) question and cross examine witnesses, (4) raise objections to testimony and pose legal issues, and (5) conclude by summing up their best arguments in oratorical addresses to the jury.

c. Possible Jury Findings. After receiving instructions from the judge, the jury retires to consider the evidence and reach a decision—which must be *unanimous.* (1) If the jury declares the defendant innocent, he is set free. (2) If the jury is unable to arrive at a unanimous decision despite lengthy deliberation, then the judge may declare a *mistrial* and dismiss the deadlocked or *hung jury.* Usually the case is retired with a new jury. (3) If the jury declares the defendant guilty, he is sentenced by the judge. In a civil case the sentence may be to pay a fine compensating for damages, and in a criminal case to pay a fine and to serve a prison term.

If a party to the case claims legal grounds for dissatisfaction with the district court trial or verdict, then that party's attorney may file an appeal to a higher court—as happens on average in one out of every 20 cases.

2. Eleven Circuit Courts of Appeals. These intermediate courts have *appellate jurisdiction;* that is, they hear cases on appeal from the district courts. The appeals court has no jury and hears no witnesses; it does not retry the case. The appeals court reviews the record to determine whether *(a)* the district court trial revealed any irregularities such as prejudice by the court, use of illegal evidence, or other violations of Constitutional rights, and *(b)* the law that the defendant violated is Constitutional. The circuit court may confirm or void the lower court judgment. Its decisions are made by a panel of three or more judges. In most cases, circuit court decisions are accepted as final, thereby ending the case. Some cases, however, may be further appealed to the Supreme Court.

3. One Supreme Court

a. Appellate Jurisdiction. The Supreme Court, the highest federal judicial authority, has appellate jurisdiction over cases coming from lower federal courts and from the highest state courts. The Supreme Court is not required to hear all cases appealed to it; of 2000 cases annually appealed to it, the Supreme Court hears on average about 200—one out of every ten cases. Usually, it considers only cases involving new or important legal principles. If an appeal is rejected by the Supreme Court, the decision of the preceding court remains in effect.

b. Original Jurisdiction. The Supreme Court also has original jurisdiction in cases involving a state and in cases involving ambassadors, foreign ministers, and consuls.

c. Procedures. The Supreme Court "sits," or is in session, usually from October into June. It divides its work into alternating periods: two weeks to hear cases—in public—and two weeks to study the evidence, arrive at decisions, and write opinions—in private. In the public hearings, the Supreme Court Justices sit on the bench, the attorneys make their oral presentations limited to one hour for each side, and the Justices may interrupt to ask questions. The Justices also have available previously submitted written briefs, presenting the attorneys' detailed arguments. In private contemplation, the Justices, assisted by their law clerks, review the case record from the state or lower federal courts and search for related past legal cases as *precedents.* Supreme Court decisions are usually made public on Mondays.

d. Decisions. The Supreme Court today consists of one Chief Justice and eight Associate Justices, totaling nine judges. Decisions are made by a majority vote. One Justice of the majority writes an explanation of the decision, the *majority opinion* or the *opinion of the Court.* A Justice who agrees with the Court's decision but disagrees with its reasoning may write a *concurring opinion.* A Justice who disagrees with the Court's decision may write a *dissenting opinion.* Supreme Court decisions are final.

4. Special Courts. The Court of Claims handles claims against the government of the United States. The Customs Court handles questions of tariffs on imports. The Court of Customs and Patent Appeals handles appeals from the Customs Court and the Patent Office.

FEDERAL JUDGES

1. Appointment and Tenure. Federal judges are *not* required to meet any Constitutional qualifications: neither age nor residence, neither education nor experience. They are nominated by the President who, to secure the names of suitable nominees, usually consults advisers—the Attorney General, friends, judges, political leaders, and bar associations. After being named by the President, the federal court nominees must secure the consent of a majority of the Senate. They serve "during good behavior," meaning usually for life. Protected by life tenure, federal judges can render impartial decisions free from unwarranted pressures.

2. Removal From Office: Impeachment. Federal judges may be removed for "treason, bribery, or other high crimes and misdemeanors" through the process of impeachment. Of thousands of federal judges, only four ever have been impeached by the House of Representatives and found guilty by the Senate. Of all Supreme Court Justices, only one—*Samuel Chase,* in 1805—faced impeachment charges and he was declared *not* guilty.

3. Presidential Considerations in Making Judicial Appointments

   a. General Fitness. The President seeks men of favorable reputation and broad legal experience. For federal district courts, Presidents have chosen some state judges and mostly practicing attorneys. For the Supreme Court, in addition to these groups, Presidents also have chosen from among lower federal court judges, university law professors, and men of outstanding public service.

   b. Political Patronage. The President may use judicial nominations, especially below the Supreme Court level, to pay political debts and to strengthen his political party.

   c. Senate Approval. Since judicial nominees must be approved by the Senate, the President must consider Senate sensibilities. If a district court judgeship is open in a state whose Senators (one or both) are of the same political party as the President, then in view of the practice of Senatorial courtesy, the President must secure their approval in advance for his nominee. Because of Senatorial courtesy, recent Democratic Presidents have had to nominate, for federal district courts in the South, men acceptable to Southern Democratic Senators who were mainly opposed to civil rights laws.

   In the case of Supreme Court Justices, the Senate almost always accepts Presidential nominees. Only three times in the 20th century has the Senate rejected Supreme Court nominees on the broad grounds of unethical conduct and prejudiced judicial outlook. Two of these three rejections were nominees of President Nixon when he attempted to move a "Southern judge" from the federal Court of Appeals to the Supreme Court.

d. General Philosophy. Especially in regard to Supreme Court nominees, the President wants men who reflect his own views as to the powers of government and the Constitution. No President, however, can be certain as to how his nominee, once on the bench, will decide in specific cases.

Theodore Roosevelt, the progressive Republican "trust-buster," placed *Oliver Wendell Holmes* on the Supreme Court in 1902; two years later Holmes angered Roosevelt by deciding against the government in the vital *Northern Securities Railroad* antitrust case. President Franklin D. Roosevelt's nomination of *Felix Frankfurter* won Senate approval in 1939 only after strong opposition protesting the nominee's alleged liberalism; once on the Supreme Court Frankfurter became the leading spokesman for its conservative wing. President Eisenhower named *Earl Warren* as Chief Justice in 1953 and later was rumored to be displeased by the Warren Court's liberal trend.

4. Philosophies Regarding the Use of Judicial Power. In deciding Constitutional issues, Supreme Court Justices, although not always individually consistent, have advocated two contrasting judicial philosophies.

a. Judicial Self-Restraint. Justices who advocate *judicial self-restraint* insist that the chief responsibility for setting public policy rests with the national and state legislatures and executives—all elected by the people. In deciding Constitutional issues, these Justices hold that they should set aside their own preferences and achieve objectivity, respect the Constitutional views of the other branches of government, and avoid broad, sweeping opinions in favor of narrow, limited decisions only on the specific issue so as not to create new public policy. To keep the Supreme Court from expanding its power and influence, these Justices urge the exercise of judicial self-restraint.

b. Judicial Activism. Justices who advocate *judicial activism* assert that the Supreme Court has the right to initiate public policy and to bring about constitutionally sanctioned changes. They deny that Supreme Court Justices can, or even should, achieve total objectivity. They insist that, with the ultimate responsibility of interpreting the Constitution, the Supreme Court must make political decisions that will help us move toward our national goals. In our earliest history, judicial activism was illustrated by Chief Justice *John Marshall*, notably in assuming for the Supreme Court the power of judicial review.

THE SUPREME COURT AND JUDICIAL REVIEW

1. Meaning. *Judicial review* refers to the power of courts, especially the Supreme Court (*a*) to determine whether or not laws are in harmony with the provisions of the Constitution and (*b*) for such laws as are in conflict with the Constitution, to declare them invalid, void, and unconstitutional.

2. Implied in the Constitution. The Constitution implies but nowhere specifically grants the power of judicial review. The Founding Fathers, many scholars believe, expected the Supreme Court to exercise judicial review certainly over state legislation and probably over federal laws.

3. Assumed by the Supreme Court Under John Marshall: Case of *Marbury vs. Madison* (1803)

a. Issue. William Marbury, a Federalist, was appointed justice of the peace for Washington, D.C. by outgoing President John Adams in 1801, but was denied his official papers, or commission, by James Madison, the incoming Democratic-Republican Secretary of State. In accordance with the Judiciary Act of 1789, Marbury went *directly* to the Supreme Court for an order, called a *writ of mandamus*, to compel Madison to deliver the commission.

b. Decision. Speaking for a unanimous Court, Marshall declared that, although Madison was wrong in withholding the commission, the Court could not grant Marbury the requested writ. Marshall explained that the section of the 1789 Judiciary Act expanding the Supreme Court's original jurisdiction to include the issuing of writs of mandamus violated the Constitution. Marshall reasoned that (1) the Constitution is the supreme law of the land, (2) the Supreme Court is the final interpreter of the Constitution, and therefore (3) the Supreme Court may declare unconstitutional and inoperative any law contrary to the Constitution. Acting boldly and confidently, Marshall thus established the precedent of *judicial review*.

4. In Subsequent Years. During Marshall's tenure (1801–1835), the Supreme Court did not invalidate another federal law but did declare several state laws unconstitutional. To 1975, the Supreme Court has held some 80 federal laws (out of 40,000 laws passed) and some 1000 state and local laws unconstitutional. Among democratic nations this power of the Supreme Court remains unique.

SUBSEQUENT CASES OF JUDICIAL REVIEW: DECLARING FEDERAL LAWS AND ACTIONS UNCONSTITUTIONAL

1. Dred Scott vs. Sanford (1857)

a. Issue. Dred Scott, a Negro slave, had been taken by his master into the Minnesota region, which according to the 1820 Missouri Compromise was free territory. He was then brought back to Missouri, a slave state. To create a test case, the abolitionists had Dred Scott sue for his freedom on the grounds that his residence in free territory had made him a free man.

b. Decision. Speaking for the Court majority, Chief Justice *Roger Taney* stated that Dred Scott, a Negro slave, was not a citizen and therefore could not bring suit for his freedom in a federal court. This statement would have sufficed to conclude the case if Taney had adhered to his life-long philosophy of judicial self-restraint. Taney, however, made an exception in this case, hoping to end the slavery controversy by a judicial pronouncement. Assuming an activist stance, Taney stated further conclusions that *(a)* slaves are property, *(b)* Congress may not deprive any person of the right to take property into federal territories, and consequently *(c)* the Missouri Compromise, which prohibited slavery in part of the Louisiana Territory, was unconstitutional.

The dissenting Justices in the Dred Scott case pointed out that free Negroes had been considered as citizens in some states and that the Constitution granted Congress the power to make "all needful rules and regulations" for federal territories.

Taney's decision was the second instance of judicial review being used to hold a federal law unconstitutional. Needless to say, Taney's effort to settle the slavery controversy by a Supreme Court decision proved futile.

2. Schechter Poultry Corporation vs. United States (1935)

a. Issue. To help business recover from the 1929 depression, President Franklin D. Roosevelt in 1933 secured Congressional passage of the *National Industrial Recovery Act* (NIRA). This New Deal measure (1) established the *National Recovery Administration* (NRA), (2) empowered the NRA to supervise industry in drawing up "codes of fair competition" providing for minimum wages, maximum hours, price-fixing, and production controls. In the district court, the Schechter brothers were found guilty of violating the NRA's *Live Poultry Code*. The case was appealed to the Supreme Court.

b. Decision. Speaking for a unanimous Court, Chief Justice *Charles Evans Hughes* declared the NIRA unconstitutional. He explained: (1) Congress may *not* delegate its lawmaking powers to an executive agency. The NRA codes, therefore, were illegal since they were laws not enacted by Congress. (2) Although the Schechters received poultry from other states, their business—of slaughtering and selling chicken—was conducted entirely within New York State. The federal government has no Constitutional right to regulate intrastate commerce. Hughes further noted that although the NRA was enacted to counter a national emergency—the depression—"extraordinary conditions do not create or enlarge constitutional power." The conviction of the Schechter brothers was set aside.

3. United States vs. Butler (1936)

a. Issue. To help agriculture recover from the 1929 depression, President Franklin D. Roosevelt secured Congressional passage of the *Agricultural Adjustment Act* (AAA) of 1933. To raise farm prices, this New Deal measure called for curtailing output through the reduction of acreage under cultivation. It provided for (1) farmers voluntarily to reduce their acreage in basic crops and to receive cash bounties for such land left idle, and (2) processors of farm products to pay a tax that would provide funds for the cash bounties. *William Butler*, acting for the *Hoosac Mills Corporation*, a Massachusetts cotton mill, refused to pay the processing tax on cotton.

b. Decision. With the Supreme Court split 6 to 3, Justice *Owen J. Roberts* wrote the majority opinion declaring the law unconstitutional. He explained that (1) the processing tax was invalid since its purpose was not to raise funds but to regulate agricultural production, and (2) agriculture, being intrastate, was not subject to federal regulation. In a vigorous dissent, Justice *Harlan Stone* upheld the government's right to levy the processing tax and spend its funds for cash bounties; he warned his brethren on the bench that "courts are not the only agency of government that must be assumed to have the capacity to govern."

To circumvent the majority decision Congress in 1936 passed the *Soil Conservation and Domestic Allotment Act* which provided that farmers (1) plant soil-conserving crops such as clover and alfalfa on a part of their acreage, thereby curtailing production, and (2) receive cash bounties paid from the federal Treasury. This law the Supreme Court held Constitutional since its purpose was conservation, a legitimate federal power, and the funds for cash bounties came from the general treasury and were a legitimate government expenditure.

4. Youngstown Sheet and Tube Company vs. Sawyer (1952)

a. Issue. In 1952, after lengthy negotiations between the *United Steelworkers Union* and the steel companies failed to achieve a new labor contract, the union scheduled a strike. To forestall a halt in steel production, President Harry Truman ordered his Secretary of Commerce, *Charles Sawyer,* to seize the steel mills. The steel companies appealed to the Supreme Court, challenging the seizure of their property because it (1) was not authorized by the Constitution or any federal law and (2) violated the Fifth Amendment, which prohibits the federal government from taking property without "due process of law." Government attorneys defended the seizure claiming that (1) the Constitution grants the President the *inherent* or implied power to protect the national well-being, and (2) any interruption of steel production would imperil the Korean War effort.

b. Decision. With the Supreme Court divided 6 to 3, Justice *Hugo Black* delivered the majority opinion holding the seizure unconstitutional. He denied that seizure was a proper exercise of the President's power as commander in chief and explained that the President's power "must stem either from an act of Congress or from the Constitution itself" but that in this case neither authorization existed. By this decision the Supreme Court placed a check upon the powers of the executive branch.

President Truman immediately returned the mills to private ownership and the steelworkers went out on strike. After a two-month strike, the union and the steel companies agreed upon a new labor contract.

SIGNIFICANT CASES OF JUDICIAL REVIEW: DECLARING STATE LAWS AND ACTIONS UNCONSTITUTIONAL

The first three cases herein discussed were decided by the Marshall Court. (Check the Index for "John Marshall, Supreme Court under.")

1. Dartmouth College vs. Woodward (1819)

a. Issue. Without the consent of the board of trustees (governing body) of Dartmouth College, a New Hampshire law revised the college's original charter of incorporation, placed the college under state control, and created a new board of trustees. The "old" trustees objected and brought suit against *William Woodward,* secretary of the new board, to recover possession of the college records. The "old" board lost in the state court but appealed to the Supreme Court where its case was argued by a famed Dartmouth alumnus, *Daniel Webster.*

b. Decision. Speaking for a 6 to 1 court majority, Marshall held: (1) Dartmouth's charter was a contract protected by the Constitutional provision that states may not pass any "law impairing the obligation of contracts." This part of the decision assured not only colleges, but also business interests, that charters, once granted, were fixed and not changeable according to the fancy of state legislatures. (2) The state law revising the Dartmouth charter was therefore unconstitutional. Marshall thus employed the Supreme Court's power of judicial review against both a state court decision and a state law.

2. McCulloch vs. Maryland (1819)

a. Issue. Maryland's legislators, hostile toward the Bank of the United States operating under a federal charter, placed a heavy tax upon the Bank's Baltimore branch. When *James McCulloch*, a Bank official, refused to pay the tax, Maryland sued him and won in the state court. The case, however, was appealed by the Bank to the Supreme Court.

b. Decision. Speaking for a unanimous Court, Marshall declared the Maryland bank tax unconstitutional. He (1) denied the power of a state to tax an agency chartered by the federal government, declaring that "the power to tax involves the power to destroy," and (2) upheld the constitutionality of the United States Bank, thus supporting the doctrines of loose construction and implied powers.

3. Gibbons vs. Ogden (1824)

a. Issue. *Aaron Ogden*, operating under a New York State monopoly grant, ran a ferry on the Hudson River between New York and New Jersey. *Thomas Gibbons* ran a competing line under a federal license. Ogden sued to halt Gibbons and won in the New York State court, but the case was appealed to the Supreme Court.

b. Decision. The Supreme Court unanimously declared that New York's grant of a Hudson River monopoly to Ogden was invalid. Marshall held that this grant violated the Constitution's delegation of interstate commerce to federal control. Further, he defined commerce in the broadest possible terms. Marshall thus prepared the way for federal regulation of railroads, buses, airlines, radio and television broadcasting, business organizations, and labor unions—when engaged in interstate commerce.

The following three cases reflected economic and social issues since the late 19th century.

4. Wabash, St. Louis, and Pacific Railway Company vs. Illinois (1886)

a. Issue. Heeding farmers' complaints of unfair prices by railroads, the Illinois legislature passed a law prohibiting railroads from charging more for a short haul than for a long haul. When the Wabash line violated the law, the state brought suit and the case eventually went to the Supreme Court.

b. Decision. With the Court split 6 to 3, Justice *Samuel Miller* wrote the majority opinion declaring the Illinois law unconstitutional. He explained that the railroad, passing through many states, was engaged in interstate commerce and therefore, according to the Constitution, subject exclusively to federal control. (The following year, Congress began federal regulation of railroads by passing the *Interstate Commerce Act*.)

5. Lochner vs. New York State (1905)

a. Issue. To protect the health of bakery workers and thus indirectly to protect the consumer by keeping sick men from handling baked goods, the New York State legislature passed a law limiting employment in bakeries to ten hours a day and 60 hours a week. The state based its right to pass this law on its police powers—to protect the health and safety of the people. *Joseph Lochner*, a bakery owner, violated the law, was found guilty in a state court, and appealed the case to the Supreme Court.

b. Decision. The Court split sharply 5 to 4, and Justice *Rufus Peckham* delivered the majority opinion holding the New York State law unconstitutional. He insisted that the law violated the "due process" clause of the Fourteenth Amendment because it interfered with the right of contract of workers to sell their labor for more than 10 hours a day and more than 60 hours a week. Further, he held that the law was an unwarranted exercise of the state's police powers.

In his classic dissent Justice *Oliver Wendell Holmes* declared the regulation of bakery hours a reasonable exercise of the state's police powers "on the score of health"; he pointed out that other state regulatory laws—affecting schooling, taxation, and health—had been held legal; he affirmed that "this case is decided upon an economic theory" and he lectured the majority that "the Constitution is not intended to embody a particular economic theory, whether of paternalism . . . or of laissez-faire." Finally, Holmes predicted that the New York State law, herein declared unconstitutional, would be only "a first install-ment of a general regulation of the hours of work."

6. Brown vs. Board of Education of Topeka (1954). Check the Index.

THE SUPREME COURT SOMETIMES REVERSES ITSELF

1. Case Studies of Reversals

a. Segregation of Races. (1) In *Plessy vs. Ferguson* (1896), the Supreme Court, by 8 to 1, held Constitutional a Louisiana law requiring segregation by race of railroad passengers. The Court held that such segregation did not violate the "equal protection of the laws" clause in the Fourteenth Amendment, pro-vided that facilities were *separate but equal.* (The lone dissenter, Justice *John Marshall Harlan*, declared that the arbitrary separation of citizens on the basis of race is inconsistent with equality before the law, condemned the Louisiana segregation measure for treating colored citizens as "inferior and degraded," and affirmed "our Constitution is color-blind, and neither knows nor tolerates classes among citizens.") (2) In *Brown vs. Board of Education of Topeka* (1954), the Supreme Court unanimously held that racial segregation in public schools violated the Fourteenth Amendment. (Check the Index for this case.)

b. Prohibition of Child Labor. (1) In *Hammer vs. Dagenhart* (1918), the Supreme Court, by 5 to 4, held invalid the Child Labor Act by which Congress prohibited the interstate shipment of goods produced with child labor. The Court majority declared that the law regulated the production of goods, not their shipment in interstate commerce. (The dissenting opinion, written by Justice *Oliver Wendell Holmes*, insisted that the Constitution's "interstate commerce" clause be given the broadest possible interpretation.) (2) In *United States vs. Darby* (1941), the Supreme Court unanimously overruled the Hammer decision and adopted the Holmes meaning of interstate commerce. The Court upheld the 1938 *Fair Labor Standards Act* which prohibited goods produced with child labor from entering into interstate commerce.

c. Legislative Reapportionment. (1) In *Colegrove vs. Green* (1943), the Su-preme Court, by 4 to 3, refused to consider a case dealing with the failure of the Illinois legislature to reapportion seats since 1901, thereby maintaining the overrepresentation of downstate rural voters at the expense of Chicago urban residents. In his majority opinion, Justice *Felix Frankfurter* held the issue to be "of a peculiarly political nature," and therefore not suited for "judicial determination"; he further warned against involving "the judiciary in the politics of the people." (2) In *Baker vs. Carr* (1962) the Supreme Court, by 6 to 2, held that federal courts may consider issues of legislative reapportionment because some districts may be so "arbitrary and capricious" as to violate the "equal protection of the laws" clause in the Fourteenth Amendment. (Justice Frankfurter filed a dissenting opinion.) Following this decision, the Court in two 1964 cases established the principle of "one man, one vote" for both Congressional and state legislative districts.

2. Reasons for Such Reversals. (a) The membership of the Supreme Court changed as "old" judges left the bench and were replaced by "new" men. The replacement of one or two justices often sufficed to change a previous court minority into a majority. (b) The expansion of man's knowledge provided the Supreme Court with new evidence on which to base decisions. The Court's reversal of the Plessy decision by the Brown Case undoubtedly reflected man's increased knowledge of human psychology, notably that segregation "generates a feeling of inferiority." (c) The failure of other governmental branches to remedy obvious injustices spurred the Supreme Court to action. The Court's reversal on the question of the legislative reapportionment undoubtedly reflected six decades of inaction by state legislatures to end underrepresentation of urban and suburban voters. (d) Changes in public opinion strengthened the Supreme Court's ability to give new interpretations to Constitutional provisions. The Court's reversal on the question of federal regulation of child labor undoubtedly reflected public acceptance of a broad interpretation of the "interstate commerce" clause and of greater intervention by the federal government in economic affairs.

Does the Supreme Court follow the election returns? In a narrow and immediate sense, the answer is *no*. In many instances, Court decisions have outraged considerable portions of public opinion. In a broad and long-range sense, the answer is *yes*. As Professor *James MacGregor Burns* aptly stated: "But ultimately the Constitution is what the people want it to be. The Supreme Court is able to make its decisions effective only to the extent that these decisions are supported by a considerable portion of the electorate."

THE SUPREME COURT AND DISSENTING OPINIONS

1. Majority and Dissenting Opinions. In deciding cases, the Supreme Court sometimes reaches unanimous decisions but more often the decisions are split. In split decisions, the court usually presents not only the *majority opinion* or *opinion of the Court* but also the *minority* or *dissenting opinion*. Both opinions are fully documented and often, implicitly or directly, attack each other as to reasoning, precedents cited, and conclusions. By this practice of presenting both majority and minority opinions, the Court (a) acknowledges that interpretations of the Constitution and various laws are subjective matters on which honorable and learned men may be expected to differ, (b) shows respect for the democratic process, for while the majority opinion becomes the law of the land, the minority opinion is heard, and (c) recognizes that with time certain minority opinions may seem more cogent and may win sufficient legal and public support to become majority opinions.

2. The Great Dissenters. The following Supreme Court justices were considered "great dissenters" not only because they filed a large number of dissenting opinions but also because they dissented with such logic, persuasiveness, and foresight that certain of their dissents became the basis of later majority opinions.

a. John Marshall Harlan (1833–1911) was born in the border state of Kentucky into a politically prominent family that owned slaves. Educated as a lawyer, Harlan in 1858 won election as a local judge. At this time Harlan was strongly anti-abolitionist and anti-Republican, mildly proslavery and ardently pronationalist, and devoted to preserving the Union. With the outbreak of the Civil War, Harlan labored to keep Kentucky in the Union and then led a volunteer Kentucky battle regiment. He, however, opposed Lincoln's Emancipation Proclamation as altering the purpose of the Civil War from preserving the Union to freeing the slaves. After the war, Harlan's views gradually changed: he publicly admitted that he had been wrong in his proslavery stance and he joined the Republican party. In 1877 he was appointed by President Hayes to the Supreme Court, where he served for almost 34 years. Harlan wrote over 800 majority and concurring opinions, but as an independent thinker and man of moral courage, he dissented more than 350 times. With great foresight, Harlan was willing to uphold regulation of the economy by the federal government under its interstate commerce power and by the states under their police powers; he also favored broad interpretation of the Fourteenth Amendment to protect civil rights. Harlan's outstanding dissents occurred in the *Lochner Case,* in which he berated the Court majority for holding unconstitutional the New York State ten-hour bakery law, and in the *Plessy Case,* in which Harlan alone opposed the "separate but equal" racial facilities doctrine.

b. Oliver Wendell Holmes (1841–1935) was born into an aristocratic Boston family, the son of a well-known physician and poet. With the outbreak of the Civil War, Holmes joined the Massachusetts Volunteers and served with distinction. Thereafter, he completed Harvard Law School and in 1881 published *The Common Law,* a study presenting Holmes' philosophy that the law is not immutable but changes with the times. He said, "The life of the law has not been logic: it has been experience. . . . In order to know what it is, we must know what it has been, and what it tends to become." Widely acclaimed for his legal thinking, Holmes served for 20 years on the Massachusetts Supreme Court.

In 1902, at the age of 61, Holmes was named by President Theodore Roosevelt to the United States Supreme Court. Holmes served for over 30 years, until 1933, siding with the majority in the overwhelming number of cases but winning a reputation for his dissents. More than most of his colleagues, Holmes was willing to uphold legislative experiments by laws regulating social and economic conditions—not because he necessarily approved of the laws but because he believed in judicial self-restraint and legal adaptation to changing times. Holmes' outstanding dissents occurred in the *Lochner Case* in which he voted to uphold New York State's law regulating bakery workers' hours; in the *Hammer Case* in which Holmes voted to uphold the federal law against child labor by broadly interpreting the interstate commerce clause; and in certain First Amendment cases in which Holmes felt that the Court majority placed unwarranted limits on freedom of speech and press. (Holmes also won fame for his majority opinion in the *Schenck Case,* establishing the "clear and present danger" measuring rod for First Amendment freedoms. Check the Index for the "Schenck Case.")

c. *Louis D. Brandeis* (1856–1941) was born in Kentucky to Jewish immigrants who had fled from Central Europe after the failure of the 1848 liberal revolutions. Graduating from Harvard Law School, Brandeis eventually established a prosperous legal practice in Boston. Because of his willingness to defend, without fee, the interests of consumers, workers, and investors, Brandeis became known as a liberal crusader, the "people's attorney." In 1908, before the Supreme Court, he defended an Oregon State ten-hour law for women workers by presenting, in addition to legal arguments, sociological and economic data: statistics, historical records, factory inspection reports, and expert opinions. Brandeis won a unanimous decision and approval of his pioneering use of socioeconomic facts which the Court said, "may not be technically speaking authorities, . . . yet they are significant." In 1914 he published *Other People's Money,* a book analyzing the influence of bankers over the American economy and people.

In 1916, Brandeis was nominated by President Wilson for the Supreme Court and was approved by the Senate only after a bitter four-month struggle —in part because he was Jewish and in part because he was a liberal. Brandeis served for 23 years, until 1939, applying his philosophy of reform, that "the law must keep pace with the rapid development of the political, economic and social ideals." Of his more than 500 written opinions, Brandeis spoke for the Court majority in 90 percent of the cases, but he nevertheless became known for the quality and vigor of his dissents. *Holmes and Brandeis dissenting* soon became a familiar Court phrase. Brandeis joined with Holmes in dissents in the *Hammer Case* and in certain First Amendment cases; after Holmes retired, Brandeis continued his dissents, most notably in the *Butler Case,* in which he defended the processing tax on agricultural produce.

THE SUPREME COURT: CENTER OF CONTROVERSY

At various times the Supreme Court, by virtue of the leadership of its Chief Justice and its decisions upon vital public issues, has been at the center of stormy controversy.

1. Marshall Court (1801–1835)

a. *The Chief Justice.* John Marshall was born in 1755 in Virginia, fought for American independence in the Revolutionary War and thereafter became a lawyer. A leading Federalist, he deplored the weaknesses of the Articles of Confederation, supported the new Constitution, and helped secure its ratification in Virginia. In 1801 Marshall was appointed by President John Adams as Chief Justice of the Supreme Court—the fourth Chief Justice. In 12 years his three predecessors had done little to enhance the status of the Court. Not so Marshall.

b. *Direction and Decisions.* For 34 years, Marshall dominated the Supreme Court and made it into a coequal branch of the federal government. Possessing a logical mind and great legal ability, Marshall converted to his views many Justices appointed by Democratic-Republican Presidents. Reflecting an activist legal philosophy, Marshall (1) strengthened the Supreme Court at the expense of the other federal branches by assuming the power of judicial review (*Marbury vs. Madison*), (2) expanded federal power at the expense of states by declaring state laws unconstitutional (*Dartmouth College*), by denying a state the right to tax a federal agency (*McCulloch vs. Maryland*), and by upholding a broad interpretation of interstate commerce (*Gibbons vs. Ogden*), (3) protected the terms of business contracts against impairment by state law (*Dartmouth College*), and (4) upheld the loose interpretation of the Constitution's elastic clause (*McCulloch vs. Maryland*).

    c. Center of Controversy. The Marshall Court, with its nationalist outlook, faced considerable opposition as the Democratic-Republicans, who favored states' rights, gained control of the executive and legislative branches. Commenting on Marshall's decisions weakening states' powers, Jefferson wrote bitterly, "The Constitution is a mere thing of wax in the hands of the judiciary, which they may twist and shape into any form they please." States' rights supporters spoke of placing limits upon the powers of the Supreme Court, but they did not do so.

2. Taney Court (1835–1864)

    a. The Chief Justice. Roger Taney, born in 1777 into an aristocratic slave-holding Maryland family, gained a reputation as a lawyer. Eventually, he joined the Democratic party and became a close friend of Andrew Jackson. With Jackson in the Presidency, Taney served as Attorney-General and then as Treasury Secretary. In 1835 Taney was named by President Jackson to replace the deceased John Marshall as Chief Justice of the Supreme Court.

    b. Direction and Decisions. Differing from the Marshall Court, the Taney Court (1) practiced greater judicial self-restraint and (2) favored more states' rights. The Taney Court, however, maintained Marshall's broad assertion of Court powers and in 1857 used judicial review to hold the Missouri Compromise unconstitutional in the famed *Dred Scott Case.* Although Taney the man had freed his own slaves, Taney the judge held that slaves were property and could not be excluded from federal territories.

    c. Center of Controversy. Instead of settling the slavery issue, as the 80-year-old Taney had hoped, the Dred Scott decision intensified sectional passions. The South was elated while the North heaped verbal abuse upon the Taney Court. Northern newspapers said that the Dred Scott decision "is the Moral Assassination of a Race and Cannot be Obeyed." Republican party spokesmen urged various proposals to curb the Court's powers.

    The Dred Scott decision (1) blackened Taney's reputation for many years, (2) did not prevent the Civil War, and (3) temporarily weakened but did not permanently destroy the power and prestige of the Supreme Court.

3. Hughes Court (1930–1941)

    a. The Chief Justice. Charles Evans Hughes was born in 1862 in upstate New York, graduated at the top of his class from Columbia Law School, and became a prosperous corporation lawyer. As counsel to two New York State commissions investigating gas, electric, and insurance companies, he helped bring down utility rates and end insurance abuses. Acclaimed by the public, Hughes entered upon a political career: a reform governor of New York (1906–1910), Associate Justice of the United States Supreme Court (1910–1916), Republican candidate for President in 1916 but defeated in a close election by Woodrow Wilson, and Secretary of State (1921–1925) under Presidents Harding and Coolidge. In 1930 Hughes was nominated by President Herbert Hoover as Chief Justice of the Supreme Court.

   b. Direction and Decisions. The Hughes Court served during the period of the Great Depression and Franklin D. Roosevelt's New Deal administration. In 1935–1936, the Hughes Court held unconstitutional several major New Deal laws, notably the National Industrial Recovery Act to help industry (*Schechter Case*) and the Agricultural Adjustment Act (*Butler Case*).

   c. Center of Controversy. Roosevelt complained that the Supreme Court was living in the "horse and buggy" age, and he feared for the fate of other New Deal laws. Roosevelt consequently proposed a Court reorganization plan that would have permitted him to appoint up to six additional Supreme Court Justices. Roosevelt's enemies labeled his plan *Court packing*, and Hughes wrote a letter opposing the reorganization plan. Eventually, the Court bill was defeated in Congress.

   Meanwhile, on the bench, Hughes and one other middle-of-the-road Justice swung definitely to the liberal position, making the liberals the Court majority. In 1937, by 5 to 4, the Court held Constitutional two major New Deal laws: the National Labor Relations Act, to guarantee collective bargaining, and the Social Security Act. Thereafter, a conservative Justice resigned, enabling Roosevelt to appoint a New Dealer to the Court—the first of several such appointments. Roosevelt later claimed that he had lost the battle but won the war. Hughes, however, had helped to save the Court from political tinkering and to preserve its role in our governmental system.

4. Warren Court (1953–1969)

   a. The Chief Justice. Earl Warren was born in 1891 in California, graduated from the University of California with a law degree, became State Attorney-General and then for three terms (1942–1953) Governor of California. In 1953 he was appointed by President Dwight Eisenhower as Chief Justice of the Supreme Court.

   b. Direction and Decisions. The Warren Court served during an era of democratic progress, especially rights for minority groups and for individuals. Reflecting those times, the Warren Court pursued a liberal and activist course especially in three major areas. (1) In the *Brown Case*, the Warren Court unanimously held racial segregation in schools unconstitutional, thereby contributing to the movement for black civil rights. (2) In the *Baker Case,* the Warren Court held legislative reapportionment to be a judicial matter, thereby furthering democracy through more equitable election districts. Warren considered this ruling to be the most important of his 16 years on the Court for, with equal representation in government, he said, the people can solve their problems "through the political process rather than through the courts." (3) In several cases affecting persons accused of crime, the Warren Court insisted upon protection of their rights to a lawyer and against self-incrimination.

Over the barrel (*By Dan Dowling, Courtesy of Field Newspaper Syndicate*)

c. Center of Controversy. The Warren Court was condemned by its opponents for violating precedents, delivering politically minded rather than legally justified decisions, and usurping powers of other bodies of government. President Eisenhower is reputed to have called his appointment of Warren the "biggest damfool mistake I ever made."

The Warren Court was hailed by its supporters for upholding the Constitution, protecting the rights of the people against governmental tyranny, and furthering democracy. President Lyndon Johnson labeled Warren "the greatest Chief Justice of them all."

5. Burger Court (1969–   )

a. The Chief Justice. Warren Burger was born in 1907 in Minnesota, worked his way through law school, and for 22 years combined a private legal practice with teaching law. In 1953 he became Assistant Attorney General in the Eisenhower Administration and in 1956 a judge of the United States Court of Appeals. In 1969 Burger was nominated by President Nixon to become the fifteenth Chief Justice of the Supreme Court.

b. Direction and Decisions. The choice of Warren Burger reflected Nixon's campaign pledge to appoint judges who would "interpret the law—not make the law" and "interpret the Constitution strictly and fairly and objectively." Burger rejected the view that the Supreme Court should or can solve the problems of American society, and he supported the philosophy of judicial self-restraint. A believer in "law and order," he urged "fair," not "perfect," trials for accused persons and criticized Warren Court rulings in criminal cases. At the same time, Burger held a moderate view on civil rights.

The Burger Court now consists of four Warren Court holdovers, four Nixon appointees, and one Ford appointee. The Burger Court has moved somewhat to the right of its predecessor, and its decisions have reflected a conservative Court majority opposed to judicial activism. The Burger Court upheld busing to remedy *de jure* school segregation; however, in the absence of deliberate discrimination, it struck down interdistrict school busing; it tended to limit the protection of accused persons in criminal cases; it granted broad discretion to trial judges to close criminal pretrial hearings to the press and public; it was ambiguous regarding affirmative action programs to aid minority students but supported a voluntary affirmative action program in employment. Has the Burger Court accurately reflected the mood of the American people, or will it also become a center of controversy?

In 1974 the Burger Court ruled that, when arresting a motorist for a traffic violation, the police do not need a warrant to search the motorist and the auto.

"Mister, the Supreme Court says if you drive with a burnt-out tail light, you belong to us." (*Copyright © 1974 the Chicago Sun-Times. Reproduced by courtesy of Wil-Jo Associates, Inc. and Bill Mauldin.*)

Unhandcuffed
(*Arthur A. Henrikson in the Rockford Morning Star*)

PROPOSALS TO LIMIT THE SUPREME COURT: NONE ADOPTED

Opponents of the Supreme Court claimed that the traditional checks upon judicial powers are insufficient. They therefore proposed other checks:

1. Increase the Number of Supreme Court Justices. The number of Supreme Court judges is not fixed by the Constitution, and court membership has varied from a low of five judges (1801–1807) to a high of ten (1863–1867). In 1937 President Roosevelt requested Congress to permit him to appoint additional Supreme Court members, but Congress refused to pass such legislation.

2. Limit the Supreme Court's Appellate Jurisdiction and Voting Regulations. Congress is empowered by the Constitution (Article III, Section 2) to control the appellate jurisdiction of the Supreme Court by making "exceptions" and "regulations." Court opponents have urged Congress to limit the Supreme Court's appellate jurisdiction, especially denying it the right to consider matters involving national security. Opponents also have urged Congress to prohibit the Supreme Court from declaring a law unconstitutional by a bare majority, and to require a vote of at least 6 to 3 or of 7 to 2.

3. Permit Congress to Override an Adverse Supreme Court Decision. Court opponents also have urged a Constitutional amendment to permit Congress, by a two-thirds vote, to override a Supreme Court decision holding a federal law unconstitutional. They argue that Congressmen are as competent as Supreme Court Justices to determine constitutionality.

4. Expand the Reasons for Impeachment of Supreme Court Justices. Court opponents have urged Congress to utilize its impeachment power over Justices more freely. They insist that Congress remove Justices not only for "high crimes and misdemeanors" but also for views contradicting Congressional and popular opinion.

MULTIPLE-CHOICE QUESTIONS

1. Congress is empowered by the Constitution to establish "inferior courts," meaning courts that (1) hear cases only of persons of low income (2) have no appellate jurisdiction (3) do not provide for trial by jury (4) are below the Supreme Court.

2. The power of the Supreme Court to declare acts of Congress unconstitutional was (1) assumed by the Court itself (2) granted by President Washington (3) granted by Congress in 1789 (4) secured by a Constitutional amendment.

3. The term *judicial review* refers to the (1) review of court decisions by the President (2) confirmation of judicial appointments by the Senate (3) requirement for a unanimous vote in Supreme Court decisions (4) power of the Supreme Court to decide the constitutionality of laws.

4. The Supreme Court decides on the constitutionality of a federal law when (1) the measure is introduced into either house of Congress (2) the measure has been passed by both houses of Congress (3) the bill has been signed into law by the President (4) a case involving the law is brought to the Supreme Court from a lower court.

5. In which instance would the Supreme Court have original jurisdiction? (1) New York State suing New Jersey over navigation on the Hudson River (2) the robbing of a national bank (3) violation by a citizen of the federal income tax law (4) violation of a citizen's civil rights

6. A Supreme Court decision that declares an act of Congress unconstitutional requires (1) at least a simple majority vote (2) at least a two-thirds vote (3) at least a three-fourths vote (4) a unanimous vote.

7. In the 20th-century United States, the principle of judicial review has been *most* closely associated with cases that (1) expand civil rights (2) limit freedom of movement (3) advance the economic interests of the working class (4) discourage the activities of lobbyists.

8. A decision of the Supreme Court declaring a law unconstitutional can be reversed by (1) a Presidential veto (2) a vote of the legislatures of three-fourths of the states (3) an amendment to the Constitution (4) a two-thirds vote of Congress.

9. Supreme Court judges are (1) elected by the people (2) chosen by Congress in a joint session (3) nominated by the President (4) chosen by the Electoral College.

10. Federal judges hold office for life *chiefly* to (1) lessen political interference in judicial decisions (2) allow them time to gain experience in their jobs (3) reward political supporters with secure jobs (4) save expenses caused by frequent changes in office.
11. The number of Justices on the Supreme Court is determined by (1) its own membership (2) a law of Congress (3) a Constitutional provision (4) the President.
12. The decisions of the Supreme Court under the leadership of Chief Justice John Marshall (1) supported the doctrine of states' rights (2) strengthened the power of the federal government at the expense of the states (3) were based on Court principles established under previous Chief Justices (4) supported Thomas Jefferson's views on the division of powers.
13. The Taney Supreme Court is *best* remembered for its decision declaring that (1) the Southern states could secede legally (2) the federal government must protect the Cherokee Indians against the state of Georgia (3) slaves are not citizens and cannot sue in federal courts (4) the Supreme Court lacks the power of judicial review.
14. The Warren Court handed down important decisions on all of the following issues *except* (1) segregation in public schools (2) rights of accused persons in criminal cases (3) legislative reapportionment (4) Presidential power to withhold from Congress tapes of White House discussions.
15. Which two Justices, who for a time served together on the Supreme Court, were famous for their dissenting opinions? (1) Holmes and Hughes (2) Holmes and Brandeis (3) Brandeis and Warren (4) Black and Frankfurter

IDENTIFICATION QUESTIONS: SUPREME COURT CASES

Baker vs. Carr	Gibbons vs. Ogden	Schechter Poultry
Brown vs. Board	Hammer vs. Dagenhart	United States vs. Butler
of Education	Lochner vs. New York	Youngstown Sheet
Colegrove vs. Green	Marbury vs. Madison	and Tube
Dartmouth College	McCulloch vs. Maryland	Wabash vs. Illinois
Dred Scott	Plessy vs. Ferguson	

1. This decision established the right of the Supreme Court to judicial review.
2. This decision of the Marshall Court adopted a broad interpretation of the Constitution's interstate commerce clause.
3. By upholding the constitutionality of the Bank of the United States, this decision endorsed a loose construction of the Constitution's elastic clause.
4. By declaring that a state could not regulate a railroad going from state to state, this decision hastened federal regulation of railroads.
5. This decision of the Hughes Court held that agriculture is an intrastate activity and therefore not subject to federal regulation.
6. By declaring unconstitutional a state law regulating the working hours of bakers, this decision restricted state police powers.
7. This decision held that "separate but equal" facilities met the requirements of the Fourteenth Amendment.
8. This decision reverted to a narrow interpretation of interstate commerce to declare illegal federal prohibition of child labor.
9. This decision ordered the executive branch to return the steel mills to their owners even though a strike would take place and curtail production essential for the Korean War effort.
10. This decision held that a state legislature could not change the terms of a charter because such change violated the "obligation of contracts."

ESSAY QUESTIONS

1. (a) For an imaginary or a real case involving the Constitution, explain the *two* conflicting points of view regarding the Constitutional issue. (b) Trace the case through the federal court system to explain the roles of the district court, the circuit court, and the Supreme Court.
2. (a) Explain how the power of judicial review was established by the Supreme Court. (b) Discuss *one* reason *for* limiting the power of the Supreme Court and *one* reason *against* limiting its power. (c) Evaluate *one* proposal for limiting the power of the Supreme Court.
3. The decisions of the Supreme Court in the 19th century gained for the Court the reputation of being a conservative body; the Supreme Court in the 20th century has become known as a body that has hastened change. Discuss this statement, giving *two* examples from *each* of these two centuries.
4. The Supreme Court has often been at the center of controversy. For any *one* of the following Supreme Court eras (a) prove the preceding statement to be true and (b) evaluate the impact of the decision(s) of the Court upon American life: (1) Marshall Court (2) Taney Court (3) Hughes Court (4) Warren Court.
5. Supreme Court Justice Louis Brandeis stated that "the law must keep pace with the rapid development of the political, economic, and social ideals." Apply this statement to *one* of the following issues: (1) racial segregation (2) child labor (3) legislative reapportionment. (a) For the issue chosen, describe *two* cases to prove that the Supreme Court has kept pace with changing conditions in American life. (b) Which philosophy of judicial power—self-restraint or activism—would be more likely to respond to changing conditions? Defend your answer.

7. The Courts Interpret the Constitution to Protect— Within Limits—Rights and Liberties

PROTECTION OF RIGHTS AND LIBERTIES: ORIGINAL CONSTITUTION (ARTICLE I, SECTIONS 9 AND 10)

At the Constitutional Convention, the Founding Fathers, recalling colonial experience as well as cases from English history, sought to protect the individual against possible governmental tyranny. They consequently included in the original Constitution the following restrictions on the powers of government:

1. Protection of Writ of Habeas Corpus. Except during rebellion or invasion, the federal government may not suspend the privilege of the *writ of habeas corpus*. This document, issued by a judge upon the request of a defense attorney, protects an arrested individual. It requires the police to bring the prisoner before the judge and to provide a statement of charges. If the judge determines that the prisoner is being held illegally, he is freed. If he is being held legally, the prisoner may be released on bail or returned to jail pending a speedy trial.

2. Prohibition of Bill of Attainder. Neither the federal nor the state legislatures may pass a *bill of attainder*. Such a law would punish individuals without granting them a trial in court.

3. **Prohibition of Ex Post Facto Law.** Neither the federal nor the state legislatures may pass an *ex post facto law*. Such a law would punish persons for acts that were not criminal at the time the act was committed.

4. **Protection of Property Rights.** *(a)* No state may declare as acceptable for payment of debts anything but gold and silver coin. This provision protects creditors from being compelled to accept paper money of little or no value for repayment of loans. *(b)* No state may pass a law impairing the obligation of contracts. This means that no state law may alter the terms of a valid business contract.

PROTECTION OF RIGHTS AND LIBERTIES: BILL OF RIGHTS (AMENDMENTS I THROUGH X)

1. **Historic Background.** In the original Constitution, the Founding Fathers did not include a *bill of rights*. They held that a federal bill of rights was superfluous in a Constitution of limited and specific powers; that it was unnecessary since each state constitution already contained a bill of rights to protect the people against possible state governmental tyranny; and that it was unwise for fear that rights not listed might be considered as denied.

During the struggle over ratification, the anti-Federalists who opposed the Constitution argued effectively that the lack of a bill of rights left the people inadequately protected against the federal government. To win popular support, the Federalists pledged to add a bill of rights to the Constitution. In his first Inaugural Address, President Washington urged Congress to give this matter its prompt attention. Congress proposed a series of amendments and by 1791 the states ratified ten of them, constituting our *Bill of Rights*.

2. **Applicability to the States.** Originally, the Bill of Rights was intended to protect individual liberties against encroachment by the federal government. With the adoption of the Fourteenth Amendment after the Civil War, however, much of the federal Bill of Rights was made applicable to laws and actions of the states. The Fourteenth Amendment prohibited states from depriving "any person of life, liberty, or property without due process of law." According to subsequent Supreme Court decisions, many safeguards of individual liberties listed in the federal Bill of Rights apply to the states under the "due process of law" clause.

3. **The First Ten Amendments—The Bill of Rights**

The *First Amendment* prohibits Congress from abridging freedom of speech, press, and religion, and from abridging the right to assembly peaceably and to petition the government. By prohibiting any established religion, it signifies the separation of church and state.

The *Second Amendment* declares that, a state militia being necessary, the right of the people to bear arms shall not be infringed.

The *Third Amendment* forbids the quartering of soldiers in private homes in peacetime except with the owner's consent.

The *Fourth Amendment* prohibits the unreasonable search and seizure of persons and property, and requires that warrants for search or arrest be issued upon probable cause and be specific as to the place to be searched and the persons or things to be seized.

The *Fifth Amendment* provides that a person accused of a crime may not be tried twice for the same offense, meaning no *double jeopardy;* that he may not be compelled to be a witness against himself, meaning no *self-incrimination;* and that no person may "be deprived of life, liberty, or property, without *due process of law,*" meaning proper legal procedures. It further provides that the government may take private property for public use, that is, exercise the power of *eminent domain,* but the government must pay just compensation.

The *Sixth Amendment* gives an accused person in a criminal case certain basic rights: to a speedy trial, an impartial jury, defense counsel; and to know the charges against him, confront hostile witnesses, and obtain friendly witnesses.

The *Seventh Amendment* guarantees a jury trial in most civil cases.

The *Eighth Amendment* prohibits excessive fines and bails and cruel and unusual punishments.

The *Ninth Amendment* states that the rights of the people enumerated in the first eight amendments shall not be construed to deny or disparage their other rights.

The *Tenth Amendment* declares that all powers not prohibited to the states or given to the federal government are reserved to the states or the people. These are known as *reserved powers.*

PROTECTION OF RIGHTS AND LIBERTIES: THE 14TH AND 15TH AMENDMENTS

The *Fourteenth Amendment* declares that all persons born or naturalized in the United States are citizens; provides that no state shall abridge the privileges of citizens nor deprive any person of life, liberty, or property without due process of law nor deny any person the equal protection of the laws.

The *Fifteenth Amendment* provides that neither the United States nor any state shall abridge the right of citizens to vote on account of race, color, or previous condition of servitude.

DUE PROCESS CLAUSE: THE 5TH AND 14TH AMENDMENTS

The Fifth Amendment prohibits the federal government, and the Fourteenth Amendment prohibits the states, from depriving any person of "life, liberty, or property without due process of law." The due process clause serves to protect the people's civil liberties and property rights. Many federal and state laws affecting life, liberty, or property have been challenged in the courts for denying due process.

RIGHTS AND LIBERTIES IMPLY DUTIES

Our rights and liberties as Americans carry with them certain duties. Freedom of speech implies the duty to speak honestly and with a full knowledge of the facts. Freedom of religion implies the duty to respect the freedom of others whose religion differs from our own. The right to vote implies the duty to know the candidates and the issues in an election. The right to trial by jury implies the duty to respond willingly when called for jury service.

INDIVIDUAL RIGHTS VS. THE NEEDS OF SOCIETY

Democratic peoples constantly face the problem of adjusting the rights of the individual to the needs of society. What is the correct balance between personal liberty and *social control*—that is, between individual freedom and governmental restraint in the public interest? May the individual exercise freedom of speech even if his words cause a riot? May he exercise freedom of the press even if his writings obstruct the nation's war effort? Such questions arising out of specific cases have been answered by the Supreme Court.

In general, the Court has held that *individual rights are not absolute but relative*, depending upon specific circumstances: what, where, when, and how.

SELECTED CASES INVOLVING RIGHTS AND LIBERTIES

1. Freedom of Speech and Press

a. Schenck vs. United States (1919)—Issue: Freedom of the Press. Charles *Schenck*, general secretary of the Socialist party, published pamphlets urging World War I draftees to resist conscription. Convicted of obstructing the war effort—a violation of the 1917 *Federal Espionage Act*—Schenck appealed the case, claiming that the law violated freedom of the press. Justice Oliver Wendell Holmes, speaking for a unanimous Supreme Court, held that "free speech would not protect a man falsely shouting fire in a theater and causing a panic" and that Schenck's writings in wartime created a "clear and present danger" to the American government and people. Schenck's conviction was upheld.

The "clear-and-present-danger" doctrine, first stated in this case, became the yardstick for subsequent cases involving the freedoms protected by the First Amendment.

b. Feiner vs. New York (1951)—Issue: Freedom of Speech. Irving Feiner, a university student speaking from a box on the sidewalk in Syracuse to a crowd, urged Negoes to "rise up in arms and fight for their rights." His speech made the crowd restless and belligerent, but there was no riot. Requested by the police to stop speaking, Feiner refused and was arrested. Feiner appealed his conviction for disorderly conduct as a violation of his freedom of speech. By a 6 to 3 decision, the Supreme Court upheld the conviction.

Speaking for the majority, Chief Justice *Fred Vinson* declared that Feiner had attempted "incitement to riot" and had created a clear danger of public disorder. In his dissenting opinion, Justice *Hugo Black* claimed that Feiner had been sentenced "for the unpopular views he expressed" and condemned the majority for making "a mockery of the free speech guarantees" in the Constitution.

c. Dennis vs. United States (1951)—Issue: Freedom of Speech. Eugene Dennis and ten other American Communist party leaders were charged with violating the *Smith Act*. This 1940 federal law prohibited teaching or advocating "the overthrow or destruction of any government in the United States by force or violence." Found guilty by a District Court jury, the Communist party leaders appealed to the Supreme Court. They claimed that the Smith Act violated the First Amendment protection of free speech. By 6 to 2, the Court upheld the law and affirmed the convictions.

For the majority, Chief Justice Fred Vinson wrote that, in this era of the Cold

War struggle between Russia and the United States, the American Communist leaders were not merely explaining "an abstract doctrine" of overthrowing the government by force and violence but were seeking to incite people to such action "as speedily as circumstances would permit" and consequently constituted a "clear and present danger." In his dissent, Justice *William Douglas* pointed out that the Communist leaders were not charged with any overt acts, declared that free speech should not be denied to these "miserable merchants of unwanted ideas," and accused the Court majority of misusing the "clear-and-present-danger" yardstick.

2. Freedom of Religion and Separation of Church and State

a. West Virginia State Board of Education vs. Barnette (1943)—Issue: Freedom of Religion. The Jehovah's Witnesses, a religious sect, consider saluting the flag a form of idolatry. Their children therefore refuse to give the flag salute in the public schools. Since such refusal violated a West Virginia statute, the children were threatened with expulsion and their parents with prosecution. *Walter Barnette* and other Jehovah's Witnesses brought suit to restrain enforcement of this statute as a violation of freedom of religion. By a 6 to 3 decision, the Supreme Court declared the West Virginia flag-salute law in violation of the First Amendment and therefore unconstitutional.

For the majority, Justice *Robert Jackson* pointed out that refusal to salute the flag does not infringe upon the rights of others and does not constitute a "clear and present danger." In his dissenting opinion, Justice *Felix Frankfurter* claimed that the Court must not consider "the wisdom or evil of a law" but solely if the legislature had the Constitutional right to enact it. He concluded that West Virginia had the right to require the flag salute for "the promotion of good citizenship."

b. Prince vs. Massachusetts (1944)—Issue: Freedom of Religion. Sarah *Prince*, a Jehovah's Witness, permitted her nine-year-old niece—her legal ward—to sell the sect's magazine on the streets. Convicted of violating a Massachusetts law that prohibited a guardian from allowing such child labor, Prince appealed the case eventually to the Supreme Court, claiming that the law interfered with freedom of religion. The Supreme Court decided that the law was a proper exercise of the state's police powers and upheld the conviction.

Delivering the opinion of the Court, Justice *Wiley Rutledge* explained that "a democratic society rests, for its continuance, upon the healthy well-rounded growth of young people" and therefore the states may legislate against evils such as "the crippling effects of child employment, especially in public places." In his lone dissent, Justice *Frank Murphy* insisted that, in selling the sect's magazine, the child "was engaged in a genuine religious, rather than commercial, activity" and therefore the Court should have sustained her freedom of religion.

c. Engel vs. Vitale (1962)—Issue: Separation of Church and State. Steven *Engel* and four other parents, representing various religious views, sued to stop the New Hyde Park, New York, school board from requiring their children to recite a short, nondenominational prayer. The parents claimed that, by the so-called "Regents' Prayer," New York State was "establishing" a religion. For the school board, *William Vitale* replied that the prayer itself was a generalized statement, affirming dependence upon God and asking for His blessings, and that the school children could participate or abstain—as they wished—during the prayer recital. The Supreme Court, by 6 to 1, held the "Regents' Prayer" unconstitutional.

Speaking for the Warren Court majority, Justice *Hugo Black* said that the "Regents' Prayer" was a religious activity sponsored by New York State and that while not "a total establishment of one particular religious sect to the exclusion of all others," it was a dangerous step in violation of the First Amendment.

Justice *Potter Stewart*, the lone dissenter, pointed out that New York State had not "interfered with the free exercise of anybody's religion," that our government has invoked the name of God in many cases—the pledge of allegiance, the Star-Spangled Banner, the imprint on our coins—without violating the First Amendment, and that, as within this category, the "Regents' Prayer" should have been upheld.

d. *Robinson vs. Dicenso (1971)—Issue: Separation of Church and State.* To attract competent teachers and improve the quality of education in religious and other private elementary schools, the Rhode Island legislature in 1969 enacted the *Salary Supplement Act.* It provided that the state could add a 15 percent supplement to the salaries of parochial school teachers who taught nonreligious subjects and who utilized "only teaching materials which are used in the public schools." Of 250 teachers who applied for the salary supplement, all were employed by Roman Catholic schools. To challenge this law, a suit was instituted technically against the Associate State Commissioner of Education, *William P. Robinson*, and eventually reached the Supreme Court. By 8 to 1, the Burger Court held the Rhode Island law a violation of the First Amendment and therefore invalid.

For the majority, Chief Justice *Warren Burger* pointed out that, although previous Court decisions since 1947 had upheld indirect government aid to parochial schools—such as bus transportation, school lunches, and secular textbooks—this supplemental salary law involved "excessive entanglement." It would, for example, require the state to keep the parochial schools under surveillance "to insure that state aid supports only secular education." It would therefore breach the wall of separation between church and state. Further, the Chief Justice stated that such state-aid programs have a "divisive political potential," dividing the community along religious lines, and that this "was one of the principal evils against which the First Amendment was intended to protect." In a concurring opinion Justice *William Brennan*, the Court's lone Roman Catholic member, joined the majority and emphasized that the religious and secular aspects of teaching cannot be separated. (Roman Catholic leaders, whose schools contain about 90 percent of the parochial school students in the United States, expressed the hope that other approaches for state aid to parochial schools would be found and held Constitutional.)

3. Rights of Accused Persons

a. *Rochin vs. California (1952)—Issue: Due Process of Law and Self-Incrimination.* Antonio Rochin, a narcotics suspect facing arrest by state police, swallowed two morphine capsules. Forcibly subjected to a stomach pump, he vomited the capsules, which were later used as evidence to convict him. Rochin appealed his conviction. With Justice *Felix Frankfurter* delivering the opinion, the Supreme Court unanimously held that the police methods, involving "conduct that shocks the conscience," had denied Rochin his due process of law. The Court further held that forcibly taking evidence from the defendant had compelled him to be a witness against himself. The conviction was overturned.

b. Gideon vs. Wainwright (1963)—Issue: Due Process of Law and Right to Counsel. *Clarence Gideon*, charged with burglary, was tried in a Florida state court. Too poor to afford a lawyer, Gideon requested free legal counsel, but the state refused his request on the ground that he was not being tried for a capital offense punishable by death. Found guilty and imprisoned, Gideon appealed to the Supreme Court, which unanimously overturned his conviction.

With Justice *Hugo Black* delivering the opinion, the Warren Court held that Florida had denied Gideon his "due process" under the Fourteenth Amendment which, the Court reasoned, requires that the state fulfill the Sixth Amendment guarantee of "assistance of counsel" for the indigent even in noncapital cases. Subsequently assisted by a lawyer in a new trial in Florida, Gideon was acquitted of the original burglary charge.

c. Escobedo vs. Illinois (1964)—Issue: Self-Incrimination and Right to Counsel. *Danny Escobedo* was arrested as a murder suspect. The police told him that they had a "pretty tight" case and subjected him to a continuous barrage of questioning. The police refused Escobedo's repeated demands to see his lawyer and failed to inform him that he had a right to remain silent. Escobedo eventually made incriminating statements that were used against him in state court to secure a verdict of "guilty." Escobedo appealed the case, and the Supreme Court, by 5 to 4, reversed the conviction.

Delivering the majority opinion for the Warren Court, Justice *Arthur Goldberg* explained that the police, while interrogating the accused, had denied him his Constitutional rights to speak to his counsel and to be informed of his privilege against self-incrimination. The dissenting Justices, notably *Byron White*, held that the ruling was "wholly unworkable . . . unless police cars are equipped with public defenders" and claimed that it would cripple law enforcement.

d. Miranda vs. Arizona (1966)—Issue: Self-Incrimination and Right to Counsel. *Ernesto Miranda* was picked up by the police for questioning about kidnapping and assaulting a young woman. Placed in a police lineup, Miranda

"How many times have I told you to blurt out a confession before they inform you of your Constitutional rights?" (*Kaufman in the Wall Street Journal*)

was identified by the victim, whereupon he confessed his guilt. His confession was used in court and helped to convict him. This case was appealed on the ground that the police had denied the suspect his Constitutional protection against self-incrimination. In a 5 to 4 decision, the Warren Court expanded the Escobedo Case doctrine and overturned the conviction.

Chief Justice *Earl Warren* wrote the majority opinion that, before questioning, the police must inform the suspect of his rights to remain silent and to legal counsel, must offer to provide counsel if the suspect is indigent, and must warn him that his remarks may be used against him. The dissenting judges, who wrote three separate opinions, attacked the majority for being unsound legally, complicating the job of law enforcement, and enabling criminals to gain freedom on technicalities. In a second trial, Miranda was convicted by a jury after his common-law wife testified that he had told her of his guilt.

MULTIPLE-CHOICE QUESTIONS

1. A lawyer would probably seek a writ of habeas corpus for a person who has been (1) charged with a crime and who cannot afford bail (2) imprisoned without being charged with a crime (3) tried and convicted (4) tried twice for the same crime.

2. In 1920 a man committed a murder in State X. In 1921 the penalty for murder in State X was changed from life imprisonment to death. In 1922 this man was convicted of this crime in a state court and sentenced to death. On what Constitutional grounds might he appeal to a federal court? (1) "due process of law"—Fourteenth Amendment (2) double jeopardy (3) bill of attainder (4) ex post facto

3. Most of the federal Bill of Rights now applies also to the states because of the (1) due process of law clause—Fifth Amendment (2) reserved powers—Tenth Amendment (3) due process of law clause—Fourteenth Amendment (4) no voting discrimination based on race or color—Fifteenth Amendment.

4. Why has the Fifth Amendment of the Constitution frequently been invoked in Congressional committee hearings? (1) It guarantees each person Congressional immunity. (2) It assures the accused the right to a trial by an impartial jury. (3) It prevents a person from being held without an indictment by the grand jury. (4) It protects a person from being compelled to be a witness against himself.

5. The right of the government to take private property for public use, providing just compensation is made, is known as (1) bill of attainder (2) eminent domain (3) habeas corpus (4) ex post facto.

6. When a judge tells an accused person that he is charged with armed robbery and that he may have legal counsel and a jury trial, the accused is being (1) indicted by a grand jury (2) denied due process of law (3) granted a writ of habeas corpus (4) informed of his Constitutional rights.

7. The "double jeopardy" clause of the Constitution protects the legal rights of the individual by (1) requiring the testimony of two witnesses to the same criminal act in order to convict the defendant (2) prohibiting the placing of legal penalties on innocent members of a criminal's family (3) exempting a person from having to testify without adequate counsel (4) freeing an acquitted defendant from facing another trial based on the identical criminal charge.

8. Which conclusion can be drawn from the statement, "Peace demonstrations may be regulated by local ordinances"? (1) Freedom of assembly is no longer a right of Americans. (2) Freedoms guaranteed by the Bill of Rights have been limited by judicial action. (3) "Freedom" is a relative rather than an absolute right. (4) Police powers of local governments are too strong.

9. Which part of the Constitution has been the basis of controversies over federal censorship and federal aid to religious schools? (1) Preamble (2) First Amendment (3) Thirteenth Amendment (4) powers denied to Congress

10. In *Engel vs. Vitale*, the Warren Court held that the New York State "Regents' Prayer" was (1) approved by the three major religious groups and therefore Constitutional (2) too general a statement to have any meaning (3) a dangerous step toward state religious activity and therefore unconstitutional (4) not to be printed in a magazine and sold on the streets.

11. In *Robinson vs. Dicenso*, the Burger Court held the Rhode Island Salary Supplement Act unconstitutional. Which argument did the Court *not* use against this Rhode Island act? (1) It would involve excessive entanglement of church and state. (2) It would divide the community along religious lines. (3) Religious and secular aspects of teaching cannot be separated. (4) Parochial schools in Rhode Island draw their students mainly from wealthy families and therefore have no need of supplemental state funds.

12. The "clear and present danger" rule for cases involving freedom of speech was first stated in (1) the original Constitution (2) the Bill of Rights (3) an opinion written by John Marshall (4) an opinion written by Oliver Wendell Holmes.

13. One criticism that some law-enforcement officers have leveled at Warren Court decisions is concerned with the (1) right of a defendant to counsel in pretrial questioning (2) expansion of federal police power (3) lenient attitude toward civil rights demonstrators (4) elimination of capital punishment for major crimes.

14. Which statement about the Supreme Court is *best* classified as an opinion? (1) Supreme Court decisions are responsible for the recent decline in law and order. (2) Supreme Court decisions have affected the apportionment of state legislatures. (3) A dissenting view in one Supreme Court can become the majority view of a later Court. (4) The Supreme Court has broadened the interpretation of the "equal protection of the laws" clause.

DISCUSSION ANALYSIS QUESTIONS: RIGHTS OF ACCUSED PERSONS

Speakers *A, B, C,* and *D* have been accused of violating a law, and they are attempting to protect their rights. Base your answers to the following questions on their statements and on your knowledge of the Constitution and Supreme Court decisions.

Speaker A: I was found guilty of a serious crime in a federal district court. My conviction was based largely on the testimony of anonymous witnesses whose identities were concealed by the prosecution so as "to insure their safety."

Speaker B: I was indicted in a state court for the crime of murder. At the conclusion of the trial the jury was unable to reach a verdict. As a result, I was retried for the same offense.

Speaker C: I was arrested on suspicion of arson and questioned by the police for several days. During that time I confessed in order to get some rest. The police never told me I had a right to call a lawyer, but I wouldn't have been able to pay one, anyway.

Speaker D: I was arrested for giving a talk on a street corner. The police said I was inciting to riot. A police judge convicted and fined me on the grounds that I was creating a "clear and present danger." I maintained that my freedom of speech was violated.

1. Which speaker is trying to plead double jeopardy? (1) *A* (2) *B* (3) *C* (4) *D*

2. Will the plea of double jeopardy, in this case, be (1) upheld by the state court (2) denied by the state court (3) heard by the Supreme Court (4) used to compel the jury to reconsider the case?

3. The right of the accused to confront his accusers has been violated in the case of Speaker   (1) *A*   (2) *B*   (3) *C*   (4) *D*.

4. The Constitutional provision that a person shall not be compelled to be a witness against himself has been violated in the case of Speaker   (1) *A*   (2) *B*   (3) *C*   (4) *D*.

5. In cases similar to that of Speaker *C*, the United States Supreme Court has ruled that the accused   (1) has no right to break the continuity of questioning by confessing   (2) has a right to refuse to answer questions unless a lawyer, supplied by the state if necessary, is present   (3) should not have been arrested solely on suspicion of arson   (4) should have been furnished with a public defender after confessing.

6. A Supreme Court case similar to that of Speaker *C* was   (1) *Escobedo vs. Illinois*   (2) *Schenck vs. United States*   (3) *Dennis vs. United States*   (4) *Prince vs. Massachusetts*.

7. In previous cases like that of Speaker *D*, the United States Supreme Court has ruled that   (1) the accused cannot plead the First Amendment when charged with violating local laws   (2) the accused should have been tried in a federal court on the riot charge   (3) freedom of speech does not include the right to endanger public safety   (4) freedom of speech does not include the right to make speeches in public in support of a religious belief.

8. A Supreme Court case similar to that of Speaker *D* was   (1) *Rochin vs. California*   (2) *Dartmouth College*   (3) *Feiner vs. New York*   (4) *Miranda vs. Arizona*.

9. In which case did the Supreme Court decide that the state must provide impoverished accused persons with a lawyer—even in noncapital charges?   (1) *West Virginia State Board of Education vs. Barnette*   (2) *Dred Scott*   (3) *Prince vs. Massachusetts*   (4) *Gideon vs. Wainwright*

10. The lawyer for Speaker *A* would appeal his client's conviction to   (1) another federal district court   (2) a federal circuit court   (3) the state court of appeals   (4) the local bar association.

ESSAY QUESTIONS

1. (*a*) Describe the historical circumstances under which the Bill of Rights became a part of the Constitution. (*b*) Several amendments in the federal Bill of Rights safeguard the rights of individuals before the courts. Give *three* provisions of these amendments relating to court procedures and show how *each* provision protects the individual against an unjust practice followed in totalitarian countries.

2. At times the rights of the individual may conflict with the needs of society. (*a*) What is the attitude toward such conflict in (1) a totalitarian society (2) a democratic society? (*b*) Select any *one* Supreme Court case involving either freedom of speech, freedom of the press, freedom of religion, or the rights of accused persons. For the case you have selected (1) show that it illustrates a conflict between the individual and society, (2) state the Supreme Court decision in the case, and (3) explain why you agree or disagree with the decision.

3. To answer this question, refer to the two cartoons placed side by side on page 233. (*a*) State *one* present-day issue in the United States with which the cartoonists are concerned. (*b*) List and explain *two* actions that the law-enforcement officers have the legal right to take in this situation as indicated by the 1975 Supreme Court decision. (*c*) List and explain *two* legal rights that the private citizen retains in this situation under the Constitution. (*d*) Identify the point of view expressed by one of the cartoonists and explain why you *either* agree *or* disagree with this viewpoint.

Part 4. The Living Constitution

8. *The Constitution Couples Stability With Flexibility*

In 1787, when the Constitution was written, the United States consisted of 13 states with a total population of 4 million people, over 90 percent occupied in agriculture. As yet unknown were the giant machines, the large factories, the huge cities, and the rapid means of transportation and communication that are commonplace today. How has it been possible for this Constitution, drawn up in a small and simple agricultural society, to function in today's huge and complex industrial civilization?

Our Constitution couples stability with flexibility. It is a stable Constitution in its expression of the purposes of government, its protection of the rights and liberties of the people, and its broad outlines of the structure of government. It is a flexible Constitution in its ability to redirect and expand the powers of government to serve the needs of the nation. This flexibility has enabled the Constitution to survive periods of great crisis: the Civil War, World War I, the 1929 economic depression, and World War II. President Franklin D. Roosevelt said in 1933, "Our Constitution is so simple and practical that it is possible always to meet extraordinary needs by changes in emphasis and arrangement without loss of essential form. That is why our constitutional system has proved itself the most superbly enduring political mechanism the modern world has produced."

The flexibility of our Constitution has been based upon (1) the elastic clause and other general or vague terminology used in the Constitution, (2) judicial interpretation of the Constitution to reflect changing times, (3) the adoption of amendments, and (4) the growth of governmental traditions and practices, called the *unwritten Constitution.*

GENERAL TERMINOLOGY IN THE CONSTITUTION

1. Elastic Clause. By the elastic clause, Congress received the power to pass all laws "necessary and proper" for its delegated powers. Interpreting the term "necessary and proper" in its broadest sense, Congress has utilized implied powers and has adopted a loose construction of the Constitution. Congressional legislation, consequently, has been able to keep pace with the changing times. (Check the Index for "Elastic clause.")

2. Other Terminology Susceptible to Reinterpretation. Among its delegated powers, Congress may collect taxes for the "general welfare" and may "regulate

246

commerce . . . among the several states." As our society has evolved, Congress has accepted new meanings for such ambiguous or vague terms so as to deal with current problems. Among other terms, found in the amendments to the Constitution, that have changed meaning with the times are "due process of law," "unreasonable searches and seizures," "impartial jury," and "equal protection of the laws."

JUDICIAL INTERPRETATION

The Supreme Court has played a major role in assuring flexibility in the Constitution. *(a)* By the decisions of John Marshall, the Supreme Court established the precedents of *judicial review* of federal and state laws, *loose construction* of the Constitution, and *broad interpretation* of the interstate commerce clause. *(b)* Over the years, the Supreme Court has proved willing to reverse itself with its newer decisions in many cases reflecting more modern interpretations of the vague terminology in the Constitution.

Woodrow Wilson, who was both a political scholar and President, once asserted that "the Supreme Court is a constitutional convention in continuous session."

LAW COMPARED WITH AMENDMENT

1. Law. A federal law must be based upon a specific power granted in the Constitution. For example, acting on its Constitutional power to establish "inferior" courts, Congress passed laws authorizing district and circuit courts.

2. Amendment. To change the Constitution an amendment is necessary. *(a)* Some amendments add to or subtract from the existing Constitutional powers of the federal government. For example, the Sixteenth Amendment gave Congress the added power to levy income taxes. *(b)* Other amendments limit the powers of the states. For example, the Fourteenth Amendment prohibited the states from denying any person the equal protection of the laws. *(c)* Still other amendments alter the election processes or the federal government structure. For example, the Seventeenth Amendment transferred the power to elect United States Senators from the state legislatures to the people.

PROCESS OF AMENDMENT

An amendment to the Constitution must be proposed and ratified as follows:

Proposed by	Ratified by
1. A two-thirds vote of each house of Congress.	1. The legislatures of three-fourths of the states.
or	*or*
2. A national convention called by Congress upon the request of two-thirds of the states. (This method has never been used.)	2. Special conventions called by three-fourths of the states. (This method has been used only once—for the Twenty-First Amendment.)

EVALUATION OF THE PROCESS OF AMENDMENT

1. **Merits.** (a) By requiring the approval of many legislatures, the amending process may prevent hasty and ill-considered changes in the Constitution. (b) By requiring an "extraordinary" majority, the amending process may prevent any "temporary" majority, arising out of momentary excitement, from tampering with our governmental system or revoking basic civil liberties. A difficult amending process seeks to place our Constitution beyond the reach of any "ordinary" majority. (c) Members of special state conventions, which may be called to ratify a proposed amendment, are elected by the voters on that single issue. The state convention, a method used only once, reflects public opinion.

2. **Criticisms.** (a) The amending process, necessitating action by many legislative bodies, may be cumbersome and time-consuming. (b) Since the amending process requires far more than a simple majority, few amendments are passed, and the process may thwart the will of the people. Of thousands of amendments introduced in Congress, very few have become part of the Constitution. (c) State legislators, who are empowered to ratify proposed amendments, may have been elected on other issues. Lacking a formal expression of the public will, they may vote their personal preference.

BRIEF SUMMARY OF AMENDMENTS

First Ten Amendments (1791). The first ten amendments, listing the rights and liberties of the people, are known as the Bill of Rights. (Check the Index.)

Background. The supporters of the original Constitution promised these amendments to secure votes for ratification.

Eleventh Amendment (1798). Federal courts shall have no power to hear suits against a state begun by a citizen of another state or by a citizen of a foreign country.

Background. In *Chisholm vs. Georgia* (1793), the Supreme Court had affirmed the right of a citizen of South Carolina to sue Georgia without that state's consent. Georgia denied the authority of the federal court in this matter and rejected the decision. To protect state sovereignty, the states secured adoption of the Eleventh Amendment.

Twelfth Amendment (1804). Electors (members of the Electoral College) shall cast separate ballots for President and Vice President.

Background. According to the original Constitution each elector voted for two persons. The candidate with the most votes became President, provided that he had a majority of the electoral vote. The runner-up became Vice President. In 1800 the Democratic-Republican party nominated Thomas Jefferson for President and Aaron Burr for Vice President, and the party won a majority in the Electoral College. The Democratic-Republican electors cast an equal number of votes for Jefferson and Burr, thereby creating a tie and throwing the election into the House of Representatives. On the thirty-sixth ballot Jefferson was chosen President. The Twelfth Amendment prevents a repetition of such a tie between a Presidential and a Vice Presidential candidate.

Thirteenth Amendment (1865). No slavery shall exist within the United States.

Background. During the Civil War, President Lincoln issued the Emancipation Proclamation (1863) declaring free the slaves in the states still in rebellion. The Proclamation did not apply to slaves in Confederate territories occupied by Union armies and in border slave states loyal to the Union. The Thirteenth Amendment, the first Civil War amendment, prohibited slavery throughout the country.

Fourteenth Amendment (1868). *(a)* All persons born or naturalized in the United States are citizens of the United States and of their state. *(b)* No state shall abridge the privileges of citizens, or deprive "any person of life, liberty, or property without due process of law," or deny to any person "equal protection of the laws." *(c)* Leading Confederate officials shall be disqualified from holding any federal or state office. *(d)* The Confederate debt shall be void.

Background. This second Civil War amendment, passed during the Reconstruction Era, was intended to prevent states from infringing upon the rights of Negroes and to punish leaders and bondholders of the Confederacy.

Fifteenth Amendment (1870). The right of citizens to vote "shall not be abridged by the United States or any state on account of race, color, or previous condition of servitude."

Background. This third Civil War amendment was intended to assure the voting rights of Negroes.

Sixteenth Amendment (1913). Congress shall have the power to levy a tax on incomes.

Background. To supplement federal revenue from tariffs, Congress in 1894 authorized a 2 percent tax on certain incomes. In *Pollock vs. The Farmers' Loan and Trust Company* (1895), the Supreme Court held the income tax to be a direct tax not levied among the states in proportion to population and therefore in violation of the Constitution. The Sixteenth Amendment overcame this Supreme Court ruling. The income tax, on individuals and corporations, has become the main source of federal revenue.

Seventeenth Amendment (1913). Senators shall be elected directly by the people.

Background. The Seventeenth Amendment ended the election of Senators by state legislatures. It was a democratic reform.

Eighteenth Amendment (1919). The manufacture, sale, or transportation of intoxicating beverages was prohibited.

Background. For years, temperance groups—most notably the Anti-Saloon League and the Woman's Christian Temperance Union—had agitated for prohibition so as to protect the people against the evils of intoxicating beverages. Starting in Maine in the mid-19th century, some form of prohibition was adopted in about half the states. During World War I, to conserve grain, which is used in manufacturing liquor, Congress authorized *prohibition* as a wartime measure and submitted to the states the Eighteenth Amendment.

Nineteenth Amendment (1920). The right of citizens to vote shall not be denied by the United States or by any state on account of sex.

Background. For years, suffragettes had demanded that women be given the right to vote. Some states, chiefly in the West, gradually permitted woman suffrage. In recognition of women's services during World War I, the nation adopted the Nineteenth Amendment.

Twentieth Amendment (1933). Congress shall meet annually on January 3, and a new President shall take office on January 20 following his election.

Background. The Twentieth Amendment recognized advances in communication and transportation by moving up the dates for taking office. Previously, the new Congress, elected in November, did not meet until 13 months later. The old Congress, which met in December immediately following the election, contained some defeated Congressmen, called *lame ducks.* The "lame duck" Congress rarely proved to be a productive legislative session. Also, before this amendment, a new President waited an additional six weeks before taking office on March 4.

Twenty-First Amendment (1933). The Eighteenth (Prohibition) Amendment was repealed.

Background. The Eighteenth Amendment, attempting to legislate moral standards and change personal habits, aroused widespread opposition. It gave rise to an era of gangsters, bootleggers, speakeasies, and public disrespect for the law. Its repeal, quickly ratified by special state conventions, returned liquor control primarily to the states.

Twenty-Second Amendment (1951). No person shall be elected President for more than two terms.

Background. The two-term tradition, established by George Washington, had been broken in 1940 by Franklin D. Roosevelt. The Twenty-Second Amendment transformed a tradition into a Constitutional provision.

Twenty-Third Amendment (1961). Residents of the District of Columbia shall have the right to vote for the President. The District's electoral vote shall be no greater than that of the least populous state (currently Alaska with three electoral votes).

Background. Since the District of Columbia is not a state and has no representation in Congress, its residents previously had no vote in Presidential elections.

Twenty-Fourth Amendment (1964). The right of citizens to vote in primaries and general elections for federal officials—President, Vice President, Senators, and Representatives—shall not be denied by the United States or by any state because of failure to pay a poll tax.

Background. The poll tax had been used chiefly in the South to keep poor whites and blacks from voting. The amendment affected five remaining Southern poll-tax states.

Twenty-Fifth Amendment (1967). In case the office of Vice President is vacant, the President shall select a new Vice President subject to Congressional approval. In case of Presidential disability, the Vice President may serve as Acting President until the President is able to resume his duties.

Background. The public worried over (1) Presidential disability—President Eisenhower suffered three major illnesses, and (2) Presidential succession—the Vice Presidency was vacant for 14 months after President Kennedy was assassinated and Vice President Johnson became President.

Twenty-Sixth Amendment (1971). The right of citizens 18 years or older to vote shall not be denied by the United States or by any state on account of age.

Background. The Supreme Court ruled that a 1970 federal law granting the vote to 18-year-olds was valid for federal elections but not state and local elections. This amendment gave 18-year-olds the vote in all elections.

Old enough to drive
(*Liederman in the*
Long Island Press, N.Y.)

THE UNWRITTEN CONSTITUTION

The *unwritten Constitution* consists of the American governmental practices and institutions not specifically set down in the Constitution but based upon custom and tradition. Examples are (1) judicial review by the Supreme Court, (2) the committee system in Congress, (3) the Cabinet as an advisory group to the President, (4) pledges by Presidential electors to vote for specific candidates, and (5) political parties.

The "unwritten Constitution" may be changed or broken easily. (Check the Index for the "Two-term tradition" and "Amendments to the Constitution, Twenty-Second.")

Individual and Group Influence Upon the Government

INFLUENCE THROUGH POLITICAL PARTIES

1. **Purpose.** In a democracy a political party consists of people with similar interests and ideas who have banded together to advance their program by peacefully influencing and gaining control of the government. The active party members are motivated, in varying degrees, by the desire to enact their program, to exercise the powers of government, and to occupy elective and appointive political offices.

2. **Brief Survey of the Major American Political Parties**

   a. Origins and Development. Political parties were not mentioned in the Constitution and they were condemned for "baneful effects" in the "Farewell Address" of our first President, George Washington. Nevertheless, two distinct parties arose during Washington's administration and evolved as follows:

   (1) The *Federalists* were led by John Adams and Alexander Hamilton. They drew strong support from the wealthier people: merchants, bankers, and large landowners. The Federalists favored, among other things, a loose interpretation of the Constitution, considerable federal involvement in economic matters, and a strong central government. After the War of 1812, the Federalist party disappeared, but many of its supporters, economic principles, and Constitutional views emerged in the short-lived mid-19th century Whig party and thereafter in the more durable Republican party.

   (2) The *Democratic-Republicans* were led by James Madison and Thomas Jefferson. They drew strong support from the common people: farmers, small shopkeepers, and city workers. The Democratic-Republicans favored, among other things, a strict interpretation of the Constitution, limited federal involvement in economic matters, and strong states' rights. Emerging from the War of 1812 as the only major political party, the Democratic-Republicans split after 1824 into two parts: one becoming the Whig party and the other, which held to many of the original Jeffersonian principles, becoming the Democratic party.

   b. The Two-Party System Today. The Republican and Democratic parties today comprise our traditional *two-party system*. Although both parties have supporters from all social, ethnic, and economic backgrounds, each party has traditionally been identified with certain segments of our population. Also both parties have differed, sometimes slightly and sometimes considerably, on broad economic and Constitutional principles.

   (1) The *Republican party,* true to its Federalist ancestry, has drawn strong support from businessmen and well-to-do farmers. Unlike the original Federalists, however, today's Republicans have veered to favor less federal involvement in the economy, more states' rights, and a less powerful central government.

   (2) The *Democratic party,* like its Democratic-Republican predecessor, has drawn strong support from among minority groups, workers, and poor farmers. Unlike the original Democratic-Republicans, however, today's Democrats have veered to favor greater federal involvement in economic matters, less states' rights, and a more powerful central government.

c. "Broad-Spectrum" Parties. Since control of the government depends upon gaining the support of a majority of the American electorate, our major parties today usually avoid narrow regional or class appeals. Each is a *broad-spectrum* party, containing spokesmen of divergent political views —liberal, moderate, and conservative. Each party, however, usually adopts moderate positions so as to gain the widest possible public support.

d. Factional or Intraparty Strife. With each of our major political parties not tied to any one ideology but including a broad spectrum of political views, each party has been torn by bitter factional strife. Conservative Republicans oppose liberal Republicans; conservative Democrats oppose liberal Democrats. Such divisions, which run deep within each party, often surface during Presidential election years. Each faction struggles to secure the party's Presidential nomination for its candidate. After the candidate is nominated, the party divisions may be glossed over in a "unity appeal," or the defeated faction may "sit on its hands," extending little assistance to the party candidate, or the defeated faction may even run its own candidate on a third-party ticket.

For example: (1) In 1912, after conservative *William Howard Taft* won the Republican nomination over liberal Theodore Roosevelt, the liberal Republicans nominated Roosevelt as candidate of the hastily formed Progressive or "Bull Moose" party. The Republican split made victory possible for the Democratic candidate, Woodrow Wilson. (2) In 1952 *Robert A. Taft,* candidate of the more conservative and isolationist "Old Guard" Republicans, lost the party nomination to General Dwight Eisenhower, who was supported by the party's liberal and internationalist wing. Thereafter, Taft and Eisenhower conferred and issued an appeal for party unity which helped bring about the Republican election victory. (3) In 1964 the conservative Republicans won the party nomination for *Barry Goldwater.* He received only lukewarm support, if any, from many liberal Republicans and was overwhelmingly defeated by the Democratic candidate, *Lyndon Johnson.*

3. Role of Minor or "Third" Parties. With one exception, minor or *"third" parties* have attracted little support from the American electorate. Such parties usually have advocated limited objectives, have appealed to limited groups —economic, regional, or racial—and sometimes have revolved about a single individual. Usually, they have been short-lived. *(a)* The *Free-Soil* party before the Civil War opposed the extension of slavery. *(b)* The *Populist* party of the 1890's appealed to farmers with a program calling for cheap money and other reforms such as direct election of Senators and government control of railroads. *(c)* The *Progressive,* or *Bull Moose,* party, organized in 1912, was an unsuccessful effort to win the Presidential election for Theodore Roosevelt on a broad program of reform. *(d)* The *Socialist* party, created in 1900, advocated many social and economic reforms but appealed only to a relatively small number of voters. Its best-known leaders were: *Eugene V. Debs,* leader of the 1895 Pullman Railroad strike, who from 1900 to 1920 ran five times as Socialist candidate for President, and *Norman Thomas,* articulate spokesman for democratic Socialism, who in each Presidential election from 1928 to 1948 was his party's candidate. *(e)* The *American Independent* party in 1968 ran George Wallace, an advocate of segregation and states' rights. Wallace polled almost 10 million votes, half in the South. His popular vote was the greatest ever received by a "third-party" candidate, but as a percentage of the total vote it was far lower than the percentage of the 1912 vote for "Bull Moose" candidate Theodore Roosevelt.

The Republican party, which started in 1854, has been the only minor party to become a major party. Its initial success was due, in part, to its broad appeal—not only to antislavery groups, but also to businessmen, farmers, Western settlers, and supporters of a strong national government.

Minor parties have made contributions to our government, chiefly by presenting the people with new ideas, such as the income tax, direct election of Senators, and Social Security. In time the major parties have adopted and enacted into law such new ideas as were practicable and in keeping with American tradition.

4. Services of Political Parties. Political parties are essential to American democracy. They hold conventions, draw up political platforms, reconcile conflicting interests, nominate candidates for public office, and conduct campaigns. Thus they crystallize campaign issues, educate the public, and offer the voters a choice of ideas and candidates. Parties also keep check on each other, since each party is eager to uncover and publicize the other's mistakes.

The party candidate for President automatically is considered head of his political party. If victorious in the election, he draws upon his party members for appointments to key governmental positions; he expects cooperation from his party members in Congress and in state offices, thereby harmonizing executive-legislative and federal-state relations; he depends upon his party to explain and praise his administration to the voters.

The unsuccessful candidate remains nominal head of his party, although his grip is weakened by his defeat and lack of power and patronage. His leadership may also be challenged by rivals for party control. The defeated party assumes the role of opposition, in most instances criticizing the administration and presenting alternative proposals for solving problems—in the hope of gaining sufficient public support to win the next Presidential election.

5. Dangers of Political Parties

, **a. Dependence Upon Large Contributors.** Parties raise funds chiefly from well-to-do persons and organizations. Such contributors may want favors in return: appointments to office or passage of special legislation. By various laws, the federal government regulates contributions to reduce the political influence of large contributors. The 1974 Federal Campaign Reform Act also provides for extensive federal funding of Presidential elections. This law, however, leaves the funding of Congressional races entirely to private contributors. (Check the Index for the "Federal Campaign Reform Act of 1974.")

b. Partisanship. Since the party out of power seeks to unseat the party in control of the government, the "outs" often denounce the "ins" unfairly. They may oppose worthwhile measures, becloud issues, misinform the nation, raise irrelevant objections, and seek partisan advantage at the expense of the public welfare.

c. Party Machines. Especially on the local level, political parties may be controlled undemocratically by a small group of insiders, called a "party machine." These insiders are professional politicians who devote their lives to politics, usually as a means of earning a living. They are generally led by a "party

"Who stole the people's money? IT WAS HIM!" (*A cartoon of the Tweed Ring, by Thomas Nast. Wide World Photos*)

boss." The political machine remains in power as long as it is able to crush opposition, control votes, and win elections. Many party machines have become infamous for graft, corruption, and disregard of public welfare. These have included the *Pendergast Machine* in Missouri, the *Vare Machine* in Pennsylvania, and the *Tweed Ring*, which controlled Tammany Hall in New York City.

d. Public Apathy. The average citizen, having little contact with or knowledge of political parties, generally restricts his political activities to reading a newspaper and to voting in general elections. Usually, he is content to permit the politicians to control his government.

The "man in the street" remains indifferent, even for long periods, to rule by party machine. Only when machine rule becomes flagrant and a fighting reform leader appears may the average citizen become aroused. He may then become active in seeking to awaken the community to go to the polls and "throw the rascals out."

6. The People and Political Parties. Political parties have been called a bridge between the people and their government. The more the people are involved with political parties, the greater is their influence on the government; and, conversely, the less involved politically, the less influence they exert. In a democracy, the kind of government the people get depends, in considerable measure, upon their own political involvement.

a. The American Voter. Voters may be classified as follows: (1) *independents*, who have no party affiliation and vote without regard to party labels; (2) *informal party supporters*, who consider themselves generally loyal to one party but have never bothered formally to declare themselves; and (3) *registered party members* who have formally indicated their party preference.

Such registered party membership is a minimal step—merely a matter of public record that involves no obligations: no dues to pay, no attendance at meetings, and no legal compulsion to vote for party candidates. Registered party

members, however, are listed on the party roster, usually receive party literature, and may vote in the party primaries.

b. More Active Party Members. To be more active in party affairs, average citizens may join the local political club, pay the nominal dues, attend
general meetings, and do volunteer work. Such work includes (1) at the
clubhouse—typing, answering the telephone, addressing and mailing en-
velopes, (2) in fund raising—planning picnics, dinners, and theatre parties
and soliciting contributions, and (3) at election time—canvassing for votes
by ringing doorbells, handing out circulars, and making speeches at rallies and
by watching at the polls to assure an honest vote.

For such expenditure of time and energy, active party members may reap
the following benefits: (1) They come in direct contact with the political leaders
whose power base is the local clubhouse. (2) They take part in clubhouse
councils, help formulate party programs, and learn politics from the inside. (3)
Eventually, they may be chosen as delegates to state and national party conventions and perhaps be considered for elective or appointive public offices. (4) They
may derive personal satisfaction from the knowledge that they are helping to
"make democracy work."

INFLUENCE THROUGH VOTING

1. Democracy and the Right to Vote

Democratically minded peoples, historically, have struggled to extend the
suffrage to more citizens and to remove unfair restrictions upon voting. Over the
years Americans have achieved much: the states eliminated property and religious qualifications for voting; Constitutional amendments guaranteed the vote
to all citizens regardless of race, color, or sex, and to 18-year-olds; amendments
also provided for the direct election of Senators and outlawed the poll tax in
federal elections; political parties and tradition turned the Electoral College into
a "rubber stamp"; and the Supreme Court ordered legislative reapportionment
to provide more equitable districts reflecting the "one-man, one-vote" principle.

Armed with the ballot and offered a choice of candidates in honest elections,
American citizens can place in public office those candidates who they hope will
best further the public interest. American citizens, further, can scrutinize the
doings of their elected officials and subsequently reelect those who have performed satisfactorily and retire from public life those whose performances have
been disappointing. Through the ballot, the American people can exercise their
greatest influence upon their government.

2. American Voting Patterns

Despite the importance of the ballot, millions of Americans fail to vote. *(a) In
Presidential Elections.* The greatest number of voters turn out for Presidential
elections, but as a percentage of total voting population in recent years, they
have constituted only slightly more than 60 percent. This means that the number
of nonvoters has been almost 40 percent. *(b) In Congressional Elections.* Fewer
citizens vote in Congressional elections. In a Presidential election year, from 3 to
5 percent of those who go to the polls and vote for President do not vote for
members of Congress. In a non-Presidential or off-year election, the number

going to the polls has dropped sharply—below 50 percent of the total voting population. *(c) In State and Local Elections.* Still fewer citizens vote in purely state and local elections.

Voters go to the polls in greater numbers, studies indicate, when the offices to be filled are more important, when the candidates are exciting personalities and differ sharply over the issues, and when the contest is close, with the outcome in doubt.

As a percentage of total voting population, fewer American citizens go to the polls than do the citizens of other democratic nations—notably Canada, Australia, Israel, and the democracies of western Europe.

3. Nonvoting: Reasons and Remedies

a. Deliberate Obstructions of the Right to Vote. Especially in the South and before the 1960's, blacks and poor whites were kept from voting by poll taxes, unfair literacy tests, and threats of economic reprisals and physical violence.

Remedies. In 1964 the Twenty-Fourth Amendment prohibited the poll tax in federal elections; in 1965 the *Voting Rights Act* suspended all literacy and other qualifying tests in areas suspected of deliberate denial of voting rights; and in 1970 the Voting Rights Act suspended literacy tests across the nation as a qualification for voting. Civil rights groups also have been active, encouraging blacks and poor whites to register and vote.

b. Residency Requirements. Voters in all states had to satisfy state residency requirements—ranging from six months to two years with the norm being one year before election time. This requirement disenfranchised many citizens who had moved from state to state. Also disenfranchised were citizens who had moved within a state and could not meet the county and district residency requirements before the election deadline.

Remedy. The 1970 *Federal Voting Rights Act* set a 30-day state residency requirement for voting in federal elections. Many states are adopting this requirement for state and local elections, in part to avoid the need of keeping two sets of voter registration records.

c. Personal Reasons. Many potential voters have not gone to the polls for personal reasons: (1) aged citizens were infirm or ill, (2) small storekeepers feared the loss of business and workers feared a deduction in wages for the time spent in voting, (3) housewives were busy with young children and housekeeping chores, and (4) college students, vacationers, and traveling salespersons were away from their homes.

Suggested remedies. Political scientists have suggested making election day a national holiday so that storekeepers and workers would not have to go to work, simplifying absentee ballot procedures so that sick persons, travelers, and college students away from home could vote by mail, and providing babysitters so that busy housewives could get to the polls.

d. Disinterest. Some 10 percent of the potential voters have claimed that they have no interest in the government, find no candidates worth voting for, and are "fed up with politics."

Possible Remedy: Compulsory Voting? Belgium and Australia have a system, which they claim works well, of compulsory voting under which citizens who fail to perform this civic duty must pay a fine. Should the United States adopt

Let's count our blessings. (*Goodwin in the Columbus Dispatch*)

compulsory voting? Supporters claim it would further democracy by increasing the number of voters. Opponents insist it would harm democracy, for such voters would be resentful and indifferent rather than proud and concerned citizens.

INFLUENCE OF THE MASS MEDIA

1. Mass Media and the Government. In the long run, democratic government must respond to the "will of the people." Elected officials eventually will not be reelected if, on major issues, they continually resist public opinion. Consequently, government leaders are concerned with the molders of public opinion—notably the mass media.

The mass media serve to interest, inform, and influence the American people in regard to their government. Newspapers and magazines report, comment, and editorialize upon political happenings, as do radio and television. Although the influence of the mass media on public opinion cannot be measured accurately, political scientists believe that it is considerable.

The mass media also keep a close and critical watch upon the activities of governmental leaders. Reporters are assigned to cover the news at Washington, D.C, and some travel with the President on his national and international trips. Reporters attend and ask questions at Presidential press conferences and at White House briefings conducted by the President's press secretary; they interview lesser governmental figures both officially and off the record; finally they may receive confidential data from informants and friends in government service. Television commentators also frequently interview and question government officials.

In summary, by helping to mold public opinion and by keeping check upon the government, the mass media in a democratic society exert a powerful political influence.

2. Mass Media and the Individual. The individual may influence newspapers by writing letters to the editor. Many such letters, either critical or laudatory of newspaper policies, are printed by the paper and help indicate the community's thoughts and emotions. The individual also may subscribe to those newspapers he feels are doing an honest job of reporting in their news columns and are in tune with his thinking in their editorials. An individual who is displeased with one newspaper may switch to another. If enough people stop reading any given newspaper, its circulation will drop and its sale of advertising space—its chief source of revenue—will fall off, thereby compelling the paper to rethink its policies or go out of business. The ability of readers to switch from one paper to another, however, is limited by the fact that many communities contain only one newspaper.

The individual also may influence television broadcasts by writing letters to the station and by "tuning out" programs. If enough people "tune out" a station, they will cause a decline in the station's viewer ratings and eventually in its advertising income.

INFLUENCE THROUGH OTHER METHODS

Individuals and groups may attempt to influence the government by (1) writing letters and sending petitions to the President, the members of Congress, and other governmental officials, (2) themselves lobbying or employing lobbyists, (3) demonstrating peacefully by means of picketing, marches, rallies, and mass turnouts at government hearings, and (4) deliberately violating laws that they consider "immoral."

Do individuals have the right to defy a law on the ground that they consider it "immoral" and that they must follow their own "conscience"? Those who answer *no* argue that the laws have been legally and democratically enacted; that such laws may be opposed—if necessary—within our legal and democratic framework; and finally that if laws are to be obeyed or disobeyed according to each person's "conscience," the result would be anarchy. Those who answer *yes* argue that by defying an "immoral" law they publicize its evils and speed the democratic process for its repeal; that they are willing to pay the penalty required by society for such lawbreaking; and finally that they must place their sense of morality above the nation's statutes—that is, follow a "higher law."

Some individuals and small groups who deliberately resisted laws and actions they considered "immoral" were as follows:

(1) *Henry Thoreau,* the New England social critic and individualist, refused in 1846 to pay the Massachusetts poll tax on the ground that it would help finance the "immoral" and proslavery Mexican War. Thoreau spent the night in jail until his fine was paid by his friends. In his essay "Civil Disobedience," written subsequently, Thoreau expounded his views regarding *passive resistance*—that the individual must obey his moral conscience even to the extent of disobeying, by peaceful resistance, "immoral" governmental policies. Thoreau's views later influenced India's freedom leader *Mahatma Gandhi* and America's black civil rights leader *Martin Luther King.*

(2) In the pre-Civil War days, *Harriet Tubman* and other Abolitionists working on the Underground Railroad helped Negroes escape from slavery in

the South to freedom in Canada. These Abolitionists violated laws that required the return of fugitive slaves to their owners.

(3) During World War I, *Eugene V. Debs, Charles Schenck*, and other pacifists spoke out against American involvement in the war, were found guilty of violating the 1917 *Espionage Act* or the 1918 *Sedition Act*, and served prison sentences.

(4) In the black civil rights movement of the post-World War II era, civil rights partisans deliberately violated Southern state laws requiring segregation on buses and at lunch counters. Many were arrested and imprisoned. In 1956 Martin Luther King led a nonviolent boycott of the Montgomery, Alabama, buses which compelled the bus company to allow integrated seating. These nonviolent protests spurred the federal government to pass the 1964 *Civil Rights Act* prohibiting discrimination in most places of public accommodation.

MULTIPLE-CHOICE QUESTIONS

1. Flexibility is provided in the Constitution by the   (1) Preamble and Bill of Rights   (2) amending process and elastic clause   (3) division of federal and state powers   (4) Electoral College system and enumerated powers of Congress.
2. Loose construction of the elastic clause has contributed to the fact that   (1) a committee system has developed in Congress   (2) the Constitution has met the needs of changing times   (3) the principle of checks and balances is generally accepted   (4) gerrymandering has become an established practice.
3. In authorizing a space-exploration program, Congress used   (1) an implied power   (2) a police power   (3) a concurrent power   (4) a delegated power.
4. Which of these facts about the Supreme Court *best* illustrates the flexibility of the Constitution?   (1) Past decisions are sometimes reversed by the Court.   (2) Dissenting opinions are often given greater publicity than majority opinions.   (3) Supreme Court Justices are appointed by the President with the approval of the Senate.   (4) The Supreme Court has been frequently criticized for resistance to change.
5. The Constitution provides that amendments may be proposed by   (1) a two-thirds vote of Congress   (2) the President   (3) the governors of three-fourths of the states   (4) a two-thirds vote of the Senate.
6. An amendment to the Constitution needs to be ratified by   (1) the President and Congress   (2) a majority of the Supreme Court Justices   (3) legislatures or conventions in three-fourths of the states   (4) a majority of the eligible voters.
7. The process of amending the Constitution requires much more than a simple majority. This statement could be used to prove that   (1) laws are more important than amendments   (2) the Founding Fathers did not understand the meaning of democracy   (3) true democracy sometimes requires a check upon hasty and ill-considered action by any simple majority   (4) methods other than amendment are more desirable to achieve flexibility in our federal government.
8. Since the adoption of the Twentieth Amendment, Congress convenes every year on or about   (1) December 10   (2) January 3   (3) January 20   (4) March 4.
9. Citizens living in the District of Columbia   (1) elect voting Representatives to Congress   (2) do not pay personal income taxes   (3) are ineligible for civil service positions   (4) vote for Presidential electors.
10. Of thousands of suggested amendments, relatively few have been added to the Constitution. This is evidence that the   (1) amendments reflect vital and basic changes   (2) amendments tend to favor the needs of a rural society   (3) Constitution

needs only minor changes to keep it up to date   (4) original Constitution was written by lawyers who lacked experience in self-government.

11. Which one of the following would require a Constitutional amendment?   (1) eliminating the Electoral College system   (2) raising the minimum wage   (3) increasing the number of Supreme Court Justices   (4) terminating American membership in the United Nations

12. Of the Constitutional amendments adopted since the Civil War, the largest number have dealt with the   (1) prohibition of intoxicating beverages   (2) succession to the Presidency   (3) voting rights of American citizens   (4) federal powers to levy taxes.

13. Which has changed from "unwritten" to written Constitution?   (1) provision for judicial review by the Supreme Court   (2) provision for the committee system in Congress   (3) formation of political parties   (4) limiting the number of terms for any one President

14. The President makes use of the "unwritten Constitution" when he   (1) vetoes a Congressional bill   (2) appoints an ambassador to a foreign country   (3) calls a special session of Congress   (4) summons his Cabinet to meet with him.

15. The *main* reason why major political parties present a party platform is to   (1) contradict the other party's platform   (2) explain to the voters the reasons why they should support the party   (3) compile a list of issues prior to the nominating convention   (4) publicize the party's achievements during the last administration.

16. Each of our major political parties has usually   (1) eliminated differences among its members   (2) financed its activities without difficulty   (3) represented a cross section of interest groups   (4) differed radically from its opposition party on basic principles.

17. Which was a *leading* cause for the rise of our earliest political parties?   (1) provision for their creation under the Constitution   (2) need for some structure for groups with common economic and political interests   (3) controversy over the selection of the person to succeed George Washington after he retired from the Presidency   (4) personality conflicts between Hamilton and Jefferson

18. Members of a political party are given a ballot on which they may choose a candidate from among three members of that party—*A*, *B*, or *C*. This situation is typical of   (1) an uncontested election   (2) a machine-controlled district   (3) a primary election   (4) a gerrymandered district.

19. The *most* important reason why a person should enroll in a political party is to be able to   (1) help influence the choice of party candidates and policies   (2) attend party rallies and dinners   (3) vote in local elections   (4) petition the state legislature.

20. Which is the *most* valid statement regarding minor political parties in the United States?   (1) They usually have evolved into major parties.   (2) They usually have been started by wealthy individuals who have desired political power.   (3) They have presented new ideas, some of which have been adopted by our major parties.   (4) They have served no useful function in our society.

21. The federal government has acted to increase the number of citizens who vote in Presidential elections by all of the following *except*   (1) prohibiting a poll tax   (2) setting a 30-day residency requirement   (3) suspending literacy tests as a voting qualification   (4) placing a penalty tax upon any qualified citizen who failed to vote.

22. Voters in the United States have the *most* direct voice in the selection of   (1) the President   (2) their United States Senator   (3) the Chief Justice of the United States Supreme Court   (4) their local postmaster.

23. Which statement *best* expresses the idea of civil disobedience?   (1) The people have a moral and religious duty to obey the law.   (2) A nation without an effective government is an awful spectacle.   (3) We must apply for a permit to hold our demonstration in front of city hall.   (4) I will break a law that my conscience tells me is unjust and will pay the penalty—even if it means going to jail.

24. Why have relatively few amendments been added to the Constitution? (1) Necessary changes have been brought about through a broad interpretation of the Constitution. (2) The sole initiative for the amending process resides in the federal government. (3) The federal government has restricted state activity in the amending process. (4) The need for changes has been met by the states.

25. Which statement *most* accurately describes the history of political parties? (1) The victorious party in the national election always controls the three branches of government. (2) The same political parties have remained in existence throughout our history. (3) Within each major party, there is a wide variety of political opinion. (4) Third parties have not been needed since the major parties have shown sufficient flexibility in dealing with controversial issues.

26. Which is a result of the fact that, in our political system, each major party must appeal to a wide variety of viewpoints? (1) Positions taken by major parties on issues usually are compromises. (2) Elections are likely to produce sharp disagreement on major issues. (3) Minority parties are likely to succeed in national elections. (4) Minority groups have too much influence on national nominating conventions.

ESSAY QUESTIONS

1. For over 175 years the Constitution has been able to survive in a rapidly changing civilization. Giving *one* specific example for *each*, show how the original Constitution has been expanded by the following: (*a*) amendments (*b*) laws of Congress (*c*) custom and usage.

2. The United States Constitution is a living document. Describe a circumstance that led to the adoption of *one* amendment to the Constitution in each of the following periods: (*a*) 1789–1815 (*b*) 1860–1875 (*c*) 1900–1930 (*d*) 1930 to the present.

3. "The cure for the ills of democracy is not more democracy but more intelligence." (*a*) Give *one* argument for *or* one argument against this statement. (*b*) Discuss *two* attempts to cure the ills of democracy by more democracy.

4. Agree or disagree with each of the following statements and provide *two* arguments to support your opinion. (*a*) The general terminology used in the Constitution has turned out to be a blessing in disguise. (*b*) The method of amending the Constitution should be changed. (*c*) Citizens could improve the workings of our democracy if they involved themselves actively in political party affairs. (*d*) Third-party movements have been an important factor in the democratic process. (*e*) Civil disobedience is not a practical way of achieving change in our democratic society.

5. Over the years government in the United States has become more truly representative of all the people. (*a*) Show how *each* of the following has furthered this goal: (1) an amendment to the Constitution (2) a decision of the Supreme Court (3) a state or federal law (4) an action within political parties. (*b*) Describe *two* proposals that could lead to increased participation by citizens in government.

UNIT III. AMERICAN ECONOMIC LIFE

Part 1. Introduction to Economics

1. What Problems Affect Economic Life?

Some Vocabulary of Economics. The word *economics* was coined by the ancient Greeks and originally meant the *management of a household*. Economics has come a long way since ancient times and today covers a broad range of human activity. No brief definition can provide any full explanation—but it can provide a starting point. Economics is the study of the activities of individuals, groups, and governments as they use available *resources* in the production and distribution of goods and services. This definition calls attention to (1) *activities*—of individuals such as workers, farmers, and businessmen; of groups such as labor unions, farm cooperatives, business organizations, and families; and of local, state, and national governments; (2) *production*—the process of using resources to turn out desirable goods and services; and (3) *distribution*—the process of dividing up these goods and services among the various segments of society.

In all societies, people become accustomed to doing things in specific ways—called *institutions*. When these ways of doing things relate to economic matters, they are called *economic institutions*. We are familiar with many economic institutions such as shopping malls for suburban consumers, banks for savers and borrowers of money, and private ownership of property for businessmen and home buyers. Taken together, the economic institutions of any given society deal with economic matters in an organized way and constitute an *economic system* or an *economy*.

Economists are people who specialize in the study of economics and economic systems. They may be employed as teachers in high schools and universities; also they may be engaged in research for universities, business corporations, banks, labor unions, and government agencies. Research economists are usually writers who present their findings to interested special groups and to the general public.

In writing textbooks many economists begin their analysis by pointing out that we are all consumers with unlimited wants living in a world of limited resources and therefore we face problems of scarcity.

Consumers' Wants and the Problems of Scarcity

Consumers All. We are all *consumers individually* as persons who want and use goods and services. At the time of birth we become consumers of goods such as special foods, blankets, and cribs; and of services such as those of doctors and nurses. Thereafter, we continue as consumers of goods such as food, clothing, shelter, toys, and athletic equipment; and of services such as those of doctors, dentists, and teachers. Throughout our entire lives, we remain consumers —wanting and using goods, needing and securing services.

We are all *consumers collectively* as members of our society—usually considered in terms of government. Acting on our behalf, the government uses goods for such purposes as building highways, constructing post offices, producing guns and military weapons, and sending spacecraft on journeys to other planets. The government also provides services such as those of highway police, letter carriers, young men in the armed forces, and space scientists.

Consumer Wants and Scarcity. Economists believe that, regardless of the type of economic system, consumer wants for goods and services far exceed the available resources of materials and labor. Although the desire of a single consumer for a specific good may be satiated—such as a young girl's liking for ice cream sodas may be fully gratified by her sixth consecutive soda—yet her desire for other goods remains unquenched. Likewise, the desires of all consumers, taken in total or aggregate for all goods and services, remain boundless. In other words, human wants are virtually unlimited, whereas the resources to satisfy such wants are limited.

All economic systems consequently must cope with the problems of *scarcity*.

SCARCITY IN PREHISTORIC AND ANCIENT TIMES: A MOTIVATING FORCE FOR CHANGE

The scarcity of resources has existed throughout human history and has been a strong force making for change.

1. Prehistoric Days. Living in tribal groups, people depended for food upon the hunting of wild game and the gathering of wild fruits and cereal grains. The supply of wild game, however, proved undependable—as animals were decimated by hunters, fled to safer areas, and became scarce during the winter months. The supply of wild fruit and cereal grain likewise proved undependable—and ofttimes tribes faced hunger and famine. To overcome the scarcity of food: hunters began to domesticate food-providing animals and became shepherds of sheep and cattle flocks; food gatherers gave up a nomadic existence and became farmers, settling down to tend orchards and raise grain crops.

2. Ancient Times. The ancient Greeks inhabited a mountainous terrain on which they tended olive tree orchards and grape vineyards, producing a surplus of olive oil and wine. Lacking fertile farmlands, the ancient Greeks faced a scarcity of cereal grain foodstuffs. They therefore became traders whose merchant ships exchanged their surpluses of olive oil and wine for foodstuffs of Egypt and other North African countries.

SCARCITY AS A MOTIVATING FORCE IN AMERICAN HISTORY

1. Discovery of America: Scarcity of Spices in Western Europe. In the later Middle Ages, West European peoples faced a scarcity of Far Eastern goods such as precious stones, drugs, dyes, cottons, silks, sugar, and especially spices. To preserve meats and to vary monotonous diets, the West European peoples treasured Far Eastern pepper, cloves, cinnamon, and nutmeg.

The profitable trade of importing Far Eastern goods became the monopoly of *(a)* Asian middlemen who brought the goods overland to east Mediterranean seaports, especially Alexandria and Constantinople, and *(b)* Italian merchants from city-states such as Genoa and Venice whose ships controlled the Mediterranean trade routes and transported the Far Eastern products to western Europe. Because the goods were scarce and each middleman tacked on the cost of his services, the Far Eastern goods remained high in price.

To break the Italian city-states' import monopoly, Portugal and Spain each sought an alternative trade route—all-water—to the Far East. Portuguese sea captains pushed southward along the Atlantic coast of Africa until in 1497–1498 Vasco da Gama rounded the southern tip of Africa and sailed on to India. His return, with a cargo of spices worth 60 times the cost of the voyage, excited western Europe. In 1492, meanwhile, Spain financed an expedition led by the Italian navigator *Christopher Columbus.* Convinced that the earth was round, Columbus planned to reach the Far East by sailing westward across the Atlantic. After a two-month voyage, Columbus found his way blocked by a land mass hitherto unknown to Europe. Columbus had stumbled across a *new world* whose two continents subsequently were named *North America* and *South America.* The discovery of America therefore resulted directly from western Europe's scarcity of spices.

2. Colonial Times

a. Scarcity of Land in Western Europe. In 17th-century western Europe, the monarchs, nobles, and churches owned almost all the land. Although some peasants possessed small farms, most common people labored on the upper-class estates almost as serfs paying feudal dues, or as tenant farmers paying rents. They eked out a meager existence. In England especially, many peasants were driven from the land by powerful landowners who enclosed or "fenced in" open-field strips and the village commons—a practice legalized by *Enclosure Acts.* Beset by the scarcity of land and the constant struggle to survive, many impoverished peasants and landless farmers in western Europe emigrated to New World colonies where land was plentiful, fertile, and easily obtainable.

b. Scarcity of Labor in the Colonies. In the English colonies, land was plentiful but labor was scarce. Settlers were unwilling to work for others when they could easily acquire land and themselves become independent farmers. To overcome the labor shortage, colonial farmers and planters turned to indentured servants and Negro slaves. (Check the Index for "Indentured servants" and "Slavery.")

3. Nineteenth Century: Scarcity of Land for Cotton Cultivation. Planters in the Southeastern states raised the same cotton crop year after year and depleted the soil of its fertility. As fertile soil became scarce in the Southeastern states, planters acquired landholdings to the Southwest, eventually within the Louisiana Purchase territory. There Southern planters repeated the process of "mining" the soil and consuming its fertility. They then looked for land beyond the borders of the United States—to Mexican territory. Thus the scarcity of fertile soil for additional cotton cultivation was one factor—of many—leading the United States to annex Texas and wage the Mexican War. (Check the Index.)

4. **Twentieth Century.** (a) Close of the Frontier: Scarcity of Resources. With the close of the frontier by the end of the 19th century, Americans became aware that the nation's material resources are not boundless. They began efforts at conservation. (Check the Index for "Conservation.") (b) Scarcity of Labor. During World War II, as war needs siphoned off tremendous numbers of workers, industry faced a severe shortage or scarcity of labor. One solution to this problem was automation, the use of automatic devices, chiefly electronic, to replace human labor in the operation of machines. (Check the Index for "Automation.") (c) Scarcity of Energy. In 1973, as the Arab nations instituted an oil boycott, the United States as well as the world's other industrialized nations were shocked into realizing the scarcity of world energy resources. To meet the oil-energy crisis, the United States undertook: to reduce oil consumption by using smaller automobiles and driving them less and by lowering thermostats to reduce heat in homes, offices, and factories; to intensify exploration, drilling, and development of non-Arab oil fields; and to spur greater use of other energy resources such as coal and uranium for generating electric power.

Problems of Opportunity or Alternative Cost

Meaning of Opportunity or Alternative Cost. Since material and labor resources, in any economic system, are scarce, individual consumers and the government must decide how best to utilize the scarce resources. What are the individual's competing desires and the government's competing goals? What are their *priorities*, that is, the order of importance they assign to their desires and goals? Which comes first and must be satisfied, and which comes last and can be postponed or neglected?

When individual consumers and the government choose a specific good or service, their choice compels them to sacrifice some other good or service which for them has a lower priority. In other words, they obtain one thing only by giving up the possibility of having another. This sacrifice of other desired goods or services is called the *opportunity* or *alternative cost*.

OPPORTUNITY COST APPLIED TO INDIVIDUALS

(1) A high school student receives a $25 birthday gift. With summer approaching, the student desires athletic equipment: either a baseball catcher's mitt or a tennis racquet. He must establish his priorities and make a choice. If he decides to buy the tennis racquet, he gives up the catcher's mitt—which thusly becomes his opportunity or alternative cost. (2) A family plans a vacation. Should they take a car trip or stay at a resort hotel or perhaps forego a vacation so as to splurge next year on a cruise? Whatever the family decides, the discarded alternatives represent the opportunity cost.

OPPORTUNITY COST APPLIED TO GOVERNMENT

Governments too must set their goals, establish their priorities, and make their decisions. (1) In prehistoric times, the tribal chief concerned over the approach of winter may have ordered all the young people to work at building new huts, repairing old ones, and gathering firewood. So engaged, the young people could not hunt and bring in additional food supplies, which loss represented the tribe's opportunity or alternative cost. (2) In the Soviet Union, the government's decision to allot labor and steel to the production of military weapons meant that these resources were not available for the production of automobiles, refrigerators, and other consumer goods—this sacrifice being the Soviet Union's opportunity or alternative cost. (3) In the United States during the 1960's, the government gave high priority to sending a man to the moon and back—a space goal achieved in 1969. By expending the labor of scientists, engineers, and mass-production workers and consuming raw materials of steel, copper, and energy fuels on this space goal, the government could not use these resources, for example, to improve urban mass-transit systems. This sacrifice represented America's opportunity or alternative cost.

Problems of Types of Economic Systems

BASIC QUESTIONS CONFRONTING ANY ECONOMIC SYSTEM

Paul Samuelson, the noted economist and Nobel Prize winner, states in his textbook *Economics* that "any society, whether it consists of a totally collectivized communistic state, a tribe of South Sea Islanders, a capitalistic industrial nation, a Swiss Family Robinson, or Robinson Crusoe—or, one might almost add, a colony of bees—must somehow confront three fundamental and interdependent problems." These problems or basic questions are as follows:

1. **What Goods Shall Be Produced?** This question has various aspects. Shall society give precedence to military weapons or foodstuffs—that is, guns or butter? To heavy industry or consumer goods—that is, electric power plants or shoes? In what quantities shall each good be produced?

2. **How Shall Goods Be Produced?** This question also has various aspects. In what proportions shall society combine the available resources, usually thought of as four factors of production: (*a*) land, including raw materials, (*b*) labor, (*c*) capital, usually thought of as investment funds for the purchase of buildings and machinery, and (*d*) management? Shall wheat farming be *intensive*—that is, use less land but more labor and machinery per acre? Or *extensive*—that is, use more land but less labor and machinery per acre? Shall electricity be generated by waterpower, coal, oil, or nuclear energy?

3. **For Whom Shall Goods Be Produced?** This question too has various aspects. What proportion of the goods produced shall go to the government and what proportion to individuals and their families? Shall the goods going to individuals and their families be divided more or less equally? If yes, how? Or shall these goods be divided unequally—to a few rich and many poor? Or to a few rich, many in moderate circumstances, and a few poor? Shall society set a minimum on the amount of goods going to the poor?

The three basic questions herein just posed are answered differently by different economic systems.

THREE TYPES OF ECONOMIC SYSTEMS

Using history, sociology, and psychology, in addition to their own subject, economists have concluded that economic systems may be classified into three types. Economists warn, however, that in today's world each one of these three systems may have, to a limited extent, aspects of the other two, and that none are "pure." The three types of economic systems are as follows:

1. **Traditional Economy.** This economy was found in primitive societies such as among South Sea Islanders and Arctic Eskimos and in simple agricultural societies such as in western Europe during the height of feudalism (9th to 11th centuries). This economy answered the three basic questions—what, how, and for whom to produce—by referring to tradition. The present generation followed the policies and practices of preceding generations. In effect: "What was good enough for my forefathers is good enough for me." Two examples: (a) Among the Arctic Eskimos who faced a constant struggle for food, some groups made no effort to hunt the numerous caribou (a variety of reindeer that could provide meat and hides) because it had never been done. (b) In feudal western Europe, the serfs followed the time-honored *three-field system*, leaving one-third of the land uncultivated each year so as to restore soil fertility. They made no effort to discover and practice more advantageous methods of restoring soil fertility such as rotation of crops and use of fertilizer.

2. **Command Economy.** This economy was found in 17th-century France under King Louis XIV and in early 20th-century Fascist Italy and Nazi Germany; currently it is found in the Communist nations of Asia and Europe, notably the Soviet Union. In the command economy, the answers to the three basic questions—what, how, and for whom to produce—are provided by the government. Political leaders and state planning agencies make the basic decisions and hand down their commands which are enforced by the full power of the government. The command economy illustrates *centralized decision-making* with its advantages and disadvantages. The interests of the state are paramount; those of the individual are secondary. Two examples: (a) Nazi Germany, determined to become a supreme military power and dominate Europe, embarked in peacetime upon a total war economy. The Hitler regime established agencies that exercised complete economic control: over management—telling them what and how much to produce and at what price; over labor—setting wages and working conditions and prohibiting strikes; over foreign trade and capital investment —reducing imports to a minimum and constructing factories to produce synthetic products so that Germany would be self-sufficient and able to withstand any wartime blockade. With its secret police and concentration camps, this all-powerful state vigorously crushed any protest or opposition. Within six years, Nazi Germany was fully rearmed and ready for war. (b) In the Soviet Union beginning in 1928, the Communist regime instituted centralized economic planning to achieve master Five-Year Plans. This all-powerful state

owned or controlled all the factors of production: land and natural resources, labor, management, and capital investment. The Communists transformed Russia from a backward agricultural nation into a major industrial power, second only to the United States. Russian industrial output increased over twentyfold. On the other hand, Soviet centralized planning resulted in bureaucratic errors, waste of materials and manpower, high costs of production, poor quality of many goods, a housing shortage, and a scarcity of consumer goods.

3. Market (Private-Enterprise) or Free-Enterprise Economy: Capitalism. This economy began to emerge in 17th-century England and in 18th-century West European continental nations, notably France and Holland; currently it is found in the developing nation of Canada and in the world's major industrial nations, especially West Germany, Japan, and the United States. In the free-enterprise economy, the answers to the three basic questions—what, how, and for whom to produce—are provided by the interaction in the marketplace of millions of individual buyers and sellers. Their decisions do not reflect any conscious effort to resolve the three basic questions but are made on the basis of self-interest. As these myriad decisions interact, they determine market price and provide a largely self-regulatory economy. The market economy illustrates *decentralized decision-making* with its advantages and disadvantages.

For example: New York City requires a constant flow of foodstuffs and unfinished materials into the city so as to feed and provide work for the people, and a constant flow of manufactured goods to markets out of the city. This constant flow into and out of the city takes place without coercion or centralized planning or conscious policy, but by the automatic self-regulation of supply and demand determining price in the marketplace. Take bananas. If the supply of bananas coming into the city exceeds the demand, the price of bananas will fall, automatically discouraging their inflow. At such time as the demand for bananas exceeds the supply, the price will rise, automatically encouraging their inflow. Of course bananas may temporarily be in oversupply or in undersupply. However imperfectly, the market economy works and the 8 million people of New York City take for granted that their economic needs will be met by the workings of the free-enterprise system.

The market or private-enterprise system, which has guided the economic development of America, from colonial beginnings to the present, is more frequently known as *capitalism.*

MODERN CAPITALISM

1. Emergence. The Industrial Revolution, which began in 18th-century England, introduced new methods of production—in the factory not the home, by machines using water and steam power not by hand labor of workers, and in anticipation of sales not after receipt of orders. These new methods required capital—economic wealth, usually thought of as money. Capital was necessary to build factories, purchase machines, secure raw materials, and pay workers—all before any goods were sold. Consequently, the capitalist, who risked his money by investing in business, controlled the entire process of production. This economic system, based on private capital, is known as *capitalism.*

2. Basic Institutions of Capitalism. *(a) Private Ownership.* Individual persons and corporations own the means of production and control the distribution of goods. *(b) Free Enterprise.* Individuals are free to engage in any business and run it as they wish. *(c) Profit Motive.* Businessmen direct their affairs to avoid loss and make a profit. *(d) Competition.* To outstrip his rivals, each producer strives to improve the quality and lower the cost of his goods. *(e) Market Price.* Supply and demand, operating under conditions of free competition, determine the price of goods.

3. Role of Government. Within a capitalist economy, the role of government has evolved as follows: *(a) Almost Complete Laissez-Faire.* Adam Smith, the Scottish economist and author of *The Wealth of Nations* (1776), urged government to follow a policy of *laissez-faire*—that is, leave business alone and avoid interference in economic matters. Smith reasoned that free competition would lower prices, increase the variety and improve the quality of goods, provide new business opportunities, and in general further the best interests of society. Laissez-faire was practiced in 18th- and early 19th-century Britain, and to a major extent in 19th-century United States. *(b) Moderate Interference.* As the laissez-faire economy demonstrated abuses, especially the exploitation of disadvantaged groups, democratic governments began *moderate interference* in the economy. In 19th-century Britain, the government passed laws limiting child and women labor in factories, prohibiting their labor in mines, and requiring standards of factory safety and sanitation. Britain's factory and mine legislation set an example followed by most industrialized nations, especially Germany and the United States. *(c) Strong Interference.* In the 20th century, democratic governments began *strong interference* in the economy. Such policy was in response to many pressures: (1) universal suffrage, which gave the average citizen more say in the government, (2) the Great Depression of 1929, which brought untold economic hardship upon entire peoples, and (3) popular acceptance of government responsibility for the national economic well-being. Britain, by passing social security and health service laws, exemplified *regulated capitalism* and became known as the *welfare state*. After World War II, Britain also nationalized the electric power, coal, and steel industries, thereby moving toward a *mixed economy* of private and public enterprise. In the United States, the *New Deal* administration of President *Franklin D. Roosevelt*, beginning in 1933, marked America's transition to regulated capitalism. The United States too reflected some aspects of a mixed economy: The federal government maintained the Postal Service, which delivers the mails, and created the Tennessee Valley Authority, which produces electricity and nitrates. Other nations today that have regulated capitalism with varying degrees of a mixed economy are Norway, Sweden, Denmark, Holland, Belgium, France, Italy, West Germany, and Japan.

4. Philosophy of Interdependence. Democratic capitalist nations today acknowledge the interdependence of capital, labor, and government. Capital provides the means of production and the managerial skills; labor provides the work; government provides law and order, protects the people against economic abuses, and seeks to maintain minimum standards of economic well-being.

CAPITALISM: A DYNAMIC AND EVOLVING ECONOMIC SYSTEM

Appealing to man's self-interest to better himself and thereby, according to Adam Smith, automatically working to improve society, capitalism has encouraged change: New technologies of machines, energy sources, and production processes; new industries; and new institutions for conducting business enterprise. As the economy has changed, so too has capitalism. *Louis Hacker*, the American economic historian, in his study *The Triumph of American Capitalism*, traced the evolution of capitalism through four overlapping but distinct stages as follows:

1. **Mercantile Capitalism.** Mercantile capitalists appeared before and during the 17th century—in the early years of the Industrial Revolution. They were engaged to a limited extent in the production of goods but mainly in banking and trade. As producers, mercantile capitalists wanted goods for purposes of trade. They did not own any workshops but rather used the "putting-out" or domestic system. They provided the raw materials to the workers at home and paid them for the finished goods on a piece-work basis. To speed output and lower costs, the mercantile capitalists broke away from medieval guild restrictions: such as limiting output of goods, setting hours and wages of labor, and mandating a fixed or *just price*. As bankers, mercantile capitalists loaned "risk" capital and charged interest; in trade, they owned warehouses and merchant ships, bought and sold goods at wholesale, transported goods to and from markets, and maintained agents in various cities. They developed a system of double-entry bookkeeping which analyzed business transactions so as to determine costs and to measure profits. Their awareness of costs and profits was fundamental to the emergence of modern capitalism.

In American history, mercantile capitalism was associated with the founding, growth, and discontent of the 13 American colonies. Thereafter, up to the 1840's, mercantile capitalism existed in America but grew less important with the rise of industrial capitalism.

2. **Industrial Capitalism.** Industrial capitalists appeared during the latter 18th century and into the 19th century; they coexisted with the heyday of laissez-faire. Industrial capitalists were engaged primarily in the production of goods under private enterprise and in the distribution of these goods through the market economy. They built factories, equipped them with machines, and produced vast quantities of goods that they sold in domestic and foreign markets. As their form of business organization, industrial capitalists utilized mainly individual ownerships (also known as single proprietorships) and partnerships, but some few, engaged in large enterprises such as canal and railroad building, formed corporations.

In American history, industrial capitalism was associated with developments from the beginnings of the new nation until the post-Civil War years, when it gave way to finance capitalism.

3. **Finance Capitalism.** Finance capitalists appeared during the later 19th century and, until after World War I, exercised great economic power. They were engaged in banking and related financial activities. Although removed from direct involvement in industrial production, finance capitalists exercised consid-

erable control by providing the capital necessary for huge mass-production factories and for tremendous business consolidations. They also provided the capital for investment and economic development in far-flung parts of the world, usually referred to as overseas *imperialism*. In economically backward regions they gained cheap and certain supplies of raw materials, markets reserved for the home country's manufactured goods, and investment opportunities for surplus capital.

In American history, finance capitalism was associated with the developments from the post-Civil War years to the Great Depression of the 1930's. The era of finance capitalism was marked by the growth of big business and the protests of small business, farm, labor, and consumer groups. Their protests eventually led to government intervention in the economy, making for the next stage—a regulated or state capitalism.

4. State or Regulated Capitalism. The era of state or regulated capitalism arose in Europe after World War I as the state was called upon to use its power to reform capitalism. The state began to control the economy by regulating production, labor-management relations, standards for consumer goods, and capital investment. The state also built new enterprises and removed others from the private domain, creating a mixed economy. As the state intervened in economic matters, it created a powerful bureaucracy—an army of government officials or bureaucrats whose activities limited the freedom of capitalist enterprise.

In American history, state capitalism has been associated with developments from the Great Depression of the 1930's until today. Beginning with the New Deal of President Franklin D. Roosevelt, state capitalism has operated within our democratic environment. It has moved the American economy away from laissez-faire and into government intervention, creating a regulated capitalism.

MULTIPLE-CHOICE QUESTIONS

1. Economics is basically a study of (1) meeting human wants and needs with available resources (2) markets and their relation to prices (3) money and how it is used as capital (4) the relationship between labor and management in a free-enterprise system.
2. A basic problem that must be solved by every economic system is that of (1) equal sharing of the wealth of the nation (2) scarcity of resources and unlimited wants (3) establishment of fair wages and working conditions (4) encouraging trade to foster international cooperation.
3. The discovery of America may be attributed, in part, to the scarcity in Western Europe of (1) fur-bearing animals (2) rubber (3) spices (4) cereal grains.
4. Which argument for sharply curtailing American foreign aid to underdeveloped nations represents the concept of opportunity costs? (1) Our aid is wasted on useless projects. (2) The nations aided do not support American foreign policies. (3) The aid does not benefit the impoverished masses—only the government officials. (4) The money could be better used to help solve our domestic problems.
5. In a market economy, the answer to the question "What shall be produced?" is supposedly determined by (1) government (2) manufacturers (3) consumers (4) retailers.
6. Skilled tool and die machinists are assigned to work on armaments, not refrigerators. This situation would be typical in which type of economy? (1) traditional (2) command (3) free enterprise (4) barter

7. As a result of the Industrial Revolution, the power of the capitalist class was (1) transferred to the landed aristocracy (2) increased tremendously (3) weakened slightly (4) transferred to the working class.
8. *Not* a principle of capitalist economy is (1) the profit motive (2) competition (3) free enterprise (4) government ownership of major industries.
9. Adam Smith pointed out the advantages of (1) rule by divine right of kings (2) separation of governmental powers (3) price regulation by the laws of supply and demand (4) mercantilist regulations of trade.
10. Laissez-faire is the economic theory that government should (1) regulate all business strictly (2) not interfere in business (3) own the railroads (4) give the public lands free to the people.
11. In the 18th century, an evidence of the growth of mercantile capitalism in Great Britain was the (1) decline of banking (2) rise of the guild system (3) steady commerce in raw cotton from South America (4) development of the domestic system of production.
12. Government ownership and operation of the railroad systems in both France and Great Britain is an indication that some western European countries have (1) accepted certain aspects of a traditional economy (2) adopted certain elements of a command economy (3) made the free-enterprise system illegal (4) adopted the Soviet economic system.
13. In the United States, a "mixed economy" means that the government (1) owns most business enterprises but permits operation by private management (2) places agriculture under strict regulation but leaves industry to private management (3) makes redistribution of income a major objective of taxation (4) affects the economy through regulations and spending but leaves most industry to private management.
14. The success of an economic system is *best* measured by (1) its ability to control monopolies (2) its ability to satisfy human wants (3) the extent to which it depends upon the profit motive (4) the extent to which basic economic decisions must be made by the government.

ESSAY QUESTIONS

1. According to many economists, economic systems are classified into three types: traditional, command, and market. (*a*) Of these three types, which *one best* describes our present American economy? Present *two* arguments to support your opinion. (*b*) For *each* of the types you rejected in answer to (*a*), describe *one* aspect of our present American economy that might be considered typical of it. (*c*) How do you account for the fact that our present American economy contains elements of all three types of economic systems?
2. Scarcity has been a motivating force in American history. Prove this statement by (*a*) identifying *one* factor in scarce supply and (*b*) showing its effect upon American history for *each* of the following periods: (1) 1450–1750 (2) 1800–1900 (3) 1900–1950 (4) 1950–present.
3. Capitalism has been defined as a dynamic and evolving system. (*a*) Explain the meaning of this statement. (*b*) Compare American capitalism of today with *either* mercantile capitalism of colonial times *or* industrial capitalism of the early 19th century to show (1) *two* ways in which they differ and (2) *two* ways in which they are the same. (*c*) Has American capitalism of the last 50 years ceased to be dynamic and evolving? Give *one* argument to support your opinion.

Part 2. The Eras of Mercantile Capitalism and Industrial Capitalism: Colonial Times to the Post-Civil War Years

2. The American Colonies Develop Under But Eventually Overthrow English Rule

Mercantilism and the Founding of the American Colonies

Theories of Mercantilism. Economists in Europe by the 17th century had developed a cohesive set of economic principles constituting *mercantilism*. To further the national power and prosperity, mercantilists argued, the government must intervene actively in economic matters. The nation must (1) attract the maximum amount of gold and silver, since wealth is measured in these metals, (2) export more than it imports, thereby achieving a favorable balance of trade and receiving payment for the difference in gold and silver, (3) increase exports by stimulating domestic industries with bounties (subsidies), (4) discourage imports of foreign manufactures by levying tariffs, (5) acquire colonies to assure markets for manufactured goods and to guarantee sources of raw materials, (6) restrict colonial manufacturing, and (7) forbid colonies to trade with any country except the mother country. Mercantilists held that colonies exist for the benefit of the mother country.

THE ENGLISH GOVERNMENT PURSUES MERCANTILISM IN COLONIZING NORTH AMERICA

Like other European regimes, the English government accepted the mercantilist doctrine that colonies serve to enrich the mother country—to assure raw materials and markets for English manufacturers, trade for English merchants, and revenues for the English treasury.

England founded ten colonies along the north Atlantic seaboard and, in 1664, having driven the Dutch from New Netherland, the English divided that territory into three colonies, making a total of 13 English colonies.

In founding colonies, the English government sought to maximize the economic strength and glory of the nation but to minimize the cost. To these ends, England authorized colonization efforts by joint-stock companies and by proprietors.

THE EARLIEST TWO COLONIES: FOUNDED BY JOINT-STOCK COMPANIES

1. The Joint-Stock Company. This form of business organization arose in 16th-century England (and later in Holland and France) to seek profits from trade and colonization opportunities that developed with the finding of all-water routes to the Far East and the discovery of America. The joint-stock company received a charter from the English Crown granting it, for a period of years and a specific area, a monopoly over trade and colonization. In return the company was to give the Crown a share of the profits earned and the precious metals acquired. The joint-stock company sold stock to numerous investors, thereby raising the needed capital and also sharing the business risks. If the company made a profit, the stockholder would benefit by receiving dividends in proportion to his investment. If the company failed, however, the stockholder would lose, at least, his investment. The individual stockholder did not have to take an active role in the company's operations, but his stock gave him the right to vote for company officials, notably the members of a policy-making committee similar to a board of directors. The joint-stock company as a form of business organization was the predecessor of the present-day corporation.

2. Virginia Colony

a. The London Company. Spurred by the knowledge of the English East India Company's profits and Spain's wealth gathered from her American colonies, a group of London merchants organized a joint-stock company, the *Virginia Company of London*, also called the *London Company*. The company secured a charter from King James I granting it, over the Virginia area, a monopoly of trade and colonization. In return the company agreed to colonize the area and pay the king one-fifth of all the gold and silver it acquired. The company raised capital by selling stock entitling the stockholders to dividends —if profits were earned—and to a land parcel in the colony. The money so raised was used to send settlers to Virginia as company employees. After seven years, these employees were to be free to work for themselves.

b. The Company Founds Jamestown (1607). The company sent a first group of over 100 settlers and in 1607 founded Jamestown. The company mistakenly intended the colony to engage in trade with the Indians and to explore for gold and silver—not to be an agricultural settlement. But the Indians had few goods for trade, and the area contained no gold or silver. The company had included, among the original settlers, too few farmers and artisans and too many "gentlemen" unaccustomed to work. *John Smith*, a practical-minded soldier, seized control and forced the colonists to undertake tasks necessary for survival: building fortifications, planting food crops, and stocking firewood. Nevertheless, fewer than half the settlers survived the early years.

c. The Company Offers Land to Attract Settlers. In London the company officials were distressed by the lack of profits, but they decided to sell more stock and use the additional capital to make the colony profitable. The company now offered each settler who completed seven years of work as its employee 50 acres of land. In 1610 the company sent new settlers and supplies to Jamestown, thereby saving the colony from abandonment. As news from the colony remained unfavorable, the company resorted to a lottery—the winners to receive company stock—so as to raise capital. Also, the company offered 100 acres of land to settlers who would pay their own transportation costs to the colony.

d. *The Company Fails But Virginia Colony Survives.* Gradually, Virginia became an agricultural settlement as colonists took possession of their own lands and raised tobacco, introduced from the West Indies by *John Rolfe*. Tobacco was a crop suitable to Virginia's soil and commanded a good price in Europe. The company, however, still did not realize any profits. In 1624 the company was dissolved, its stockholders in England received nothing for their investment, and Virginia became a royal colony. As a mercantile capitalist business venture, Virginia was a failure; as an English colony, Virginia was a success, surviving many hardships and setting an example for further English settlements in the New World.

3. Massachusetts Colony

a. *Plymouth (1620).* The Pilgrims were a small group of Protestant dissenters who had been persecuted in England by the dominant Anglicans. Determined to escape persecution by establishing a New World colony, the Pilgrims organized a joint-stock company. They sold stock to a group of London merchants who hoped to make a profit; also they gave stock to each person who himself "adventured" or became a colonist. For seven years, the colonists were to contribute all the wealth they produced into a "common storehouse" which would be used to repay the London merchants and thereafter be divided equally among the colonists.

In contrast with the first settlers in Virginia, the Pilgrim colonists had a far better arrangement: they were stockholders, not merely company employees; they were governed by officials they elected, not by officials chosen by the company and sent from England; and they eventually would share in the land and in the profits of the "common storehouse," not merely receive their freedom from company service.

The Pilgrims received permission from the Virginia Company of London to settle within its territory, but their ship, the *Mayflower*, was blown northward off course and the Pilgrims landed instead at *Plymouth*. Beset by cold, hunger, and disease, only half the group lived through the first winter. However, under the leadership of *William Bradford* and with the help of friendly Indians, the colony farmed, fished, traded for furs, and survived. In the fall of 1621, the Pilgrims held a celebration to give thanks to God for His bounty and blessings—the origin of our Thanksgiving Day. In 1623 the Pilgrims, resenting the "common storehouse" as a hindrance to individual enterprise, abolished it, divided up its goods, and instituted private ownership of land. In 1627 the Pilgrims arranged to buy up, at a nominal price, the interests of the London merchant stockholders, using chiefly the profits made in the fur trade. Plymouth did not attract many settlers and finally was absorbed by the Massachusetts Bay Colony.

b. *Massachusetts Bay (1630).* The Puritans, so named because they wished to "purify" the Anglican Church of practices remindful of Roman Catholicism, suffered discrimination at the hands of Anglican churchmen and King Charles I. Nevertheless, a Puritan group, organized as the Massachusetts Bay Company, managed to secure a royal charter for a joint-stock company as a business enterprise. The leading Puritans, many being wealthy merchants, bought up the stock of the company; they made plans themselves to emigrate, to take the company charter with them, and to establish company headquarters in the colony. The joint-stock company thus was converted from a profit-seeking business enterprise into a religious haven with significant powers of self-government.

In 1630, led by *John Winthrop*, 1000 Puritans settled in the Massachusetts Bay area, most of them at *Salem, Cambridge,* and *Boston.* Having learned from the experiences of Jamestown and Plymouth, these settlers were well equipped with food, tools, and valuable skills, and the colony prospered almost immediately. During the 1630's, as Puritans in England suffered greater persecution and as England moved toward civil war, additional Puritans emigrated. By 1640 the Massachusetts Bay Colony had grown to 20,000 inhabitants.

The colonial government strongly supported the Puritan church and did not tolerate disagreement with Puritan beliefs and practices. Massachusetts settlers, some seeking greater religious tolerance and some seeking better farmlands, left the Bay Colony and founded three new colonies: Rhode Island (1636), Connecticut (1636), and New Hampshire (1638).

From the experiences of the Virginia and Massachusetts colonies, English mercantile capitalists concluded that no quick profits—if any—could be realized from investing in joint-stock companies planning New World settlements. Subsequent English colonization efforts, therefore, were undertaken almost entirely by individuals called *proprietors.*

PROPRIETARY COLONIES

1. Proprietors as Mercantile Capitalists. The proprietors were wealthy men, usually friends or relatives of the king, who received royal grants of New World lands to colonize and rule. The major restriction upon the proprietors was the requirement, contained in the royal grants, that the laws for the colony must be made "by and with the consent of the freemen," that is, a colonial legislature. The proprietors faced financial risks to bring settlers to the colony, but they expected to make substantial profits from the sale of land; from tenants required to make an annual payment of *quitrents*—a payment in lieu of feudal services; and from the crops raised on their own estates. The proprietors, however, were unable to collect any sizable sums because they *(a)* had too much land to be able to charge high prices and *(b)* were too far away and too weak to prevent settlers from squatting on the land and refusing to pay quitrents. Since the proprietors took risks and sought profits, they are considered mercantile capitalists.

2. Colonies Under Proprietary Control. *(a)* The first proprietary colony, planned by *George Calvert*, the first *Lord Baltimore*, was *Maryland.* Baltimore viewed Maryland not only as a real estate speculation but also as a place of refuge for his persecuted co-religionists, the English Catholics. His son, the second Lord Baltimore, in 1634 sent the first group of settlers to the colony. Eager to rent and sell land, Baltimore permitted Protestant as well as Catholic settlers, and the Protestants soon became the majority. To safeguard the Catholic minority, Baltimore secured from the colonial assembly the *Maryland Toleration Act*, granting religious freedom to all Christians. *(b)* The next proprietary colonies, founded by a group of proprietors seeking real estate profits, were *North Carolina* and *South Carolina* (1663). The proprietors proved unable to control the settlers who were unwilling to pay quitrents and were demanding more self-government. The proprietors finally surrendered their charter and the Carolinas became royal colonies (1729). *(c)* The last proprietary colony founded by England was *Pennsylvania* (1681). *William Penn*, the proprietor, envisioned the colony not only as a business venture but also as a place of refuge for his persecuted co-religionists, the *Quakers*. Under Penn's direction, the colony became known for religious freedom, a popularly elected legislature, and fair treatment of the Indians. Although Penn himself encountered serious financial difficulties, including a term in debtors' prison, his colony grew strong and prosperous. *(d)* As a result of war with Holland, England seized the New Netherland colony which had been founded and developed by a joint-stock company, the *Dutch West India Company*. England divided New Netherland into three proprietary colonies: (1) *New York* was given by King Charles II to his brother *James*, then *Duke of York*. When James became king in 1685, New York became a royal colony. (2) *New Jersey* was granted by James to two of his friends, *Lord John Berkeley* and *Sir George Carteret*. (3) *Delaware* was assigned to William Penn.

Economic Life in the Colonies

COLONISTS SUPPORT CAPITALIST PRINCIPLES

The colonial settlers adjusted their thinking to the American economic environment: an abundance of land, timber, fish, and fur-bearing animals; a scarcity of labor, managerial skills, and capital. In their everyday living, the colonists demonstrated support for capitalist principles: *(a)* In Virginia the first settlers sent by the London Company had the status of company employees. To attract additional settlers, the company felt compelled to offer grants of land—an appeal to private ownership. *(b)* In Plymouth the colonists soon abandoned the "common storehouse"—a cooperative concept—in favor of each individual disposing, as he saw fit, of any surplus output—an aspect of private enterprise. *(c)* On the frontier, colonists faced risks of hostile Indians, natural calamities, and poor transportation facilities so as to acquire fertile lands and build an independent economic existence. The frontiersmen took risks in the hope of reaping profits. *(d)* In Massachusetts Bay, the colonial government attempted to enforce medieval European guild concepts: of a fixed wage for workers, a just price for consumers, and trade regulations for merchants—but these attempts failed. With labor scarce, workers secured higher wages; with manufactured goods scarce, small-scale colonial producers secured higher prices. Both colonial workers and producers subscribed to the capitalist theory that price should be set by supply and demand. Colonial merchants secured an end of trade regulations by colonial governments. In the profitable overseas trade, they insisted that all merchants be able to compete freely.

GEOGRAPHIC CONDITIONS INFLUENCE COLONIAL OCCUPATIONS

1. New England Colonies

a. Economic Activities. The rocky, inhospitable soil and the cold climate discouraged agriculture. Farms were small and produced little beyond the needs of the farmer and his family. On the other hand, the abundant forests, swift-flowing streams, and fine natural harbors—such as Portsmouth, Boston, and Providence—turned New Englanders to lumbering, shipbuilding, whaling, fishing for cod and mackerel, and trade.

b. Triangular Trade. New England merchants developed various overseas trade routes, several involving a *triangular trade.* One profitable route took fish, grain, and lumber from the colonies to the West Indies for sugar and molasses, which, in turn, were exchanged in England for manufactured goods needed in the colonies. On another profitable trade route, New Englanders took rum to Africa and exchanged it for Negro slaves. The slaves were sold in the West Indies for sugar and molasses, and these products were shipped back to New England and distilled into rum.

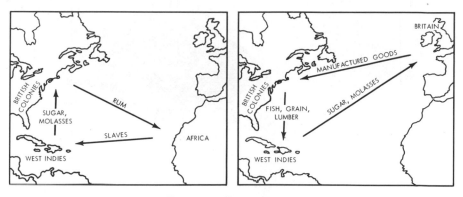

Triangular Trade Routes

New England's merchants made substantial profits, but they also faced great obstacles: the hazards of the sea, the dangers of pirate attack, and the mercantilist policy of England.

c. English Mercantilist Laws. In accordance with mercantilist principles, England enacted a series of *Navigation Acts,* designed to keep colonial ships trading with England and the British West Indies rather than with the European Continent and the French and Spanish West Indies. For example, the *Molasses Act* of 1733 required the colonists to pay a high duty on sugar and molasses if they were secured from any place but the British West Indies. This act was resented by colonial merchants because the British West Indies did not produce enough sugar and molasses to meet the needs of the colonies and the high duty would raise prices for colonial consumers. The act was widely violated.

2. Middle Colonies.

Fertile, level land and a favorable climate encouraged family-size farms, which produced surplus grain (wheat, corn, and oats) for export to the other colonies and to England. The Middle Colonies soon became known as the *bread colonies*. Long, navigable rivers—such as the Hudson, Susquehanna, and Delaware—promoted trade with the Indians for furs. First-class harbors, such as at New York and Philadelphia, stimulated trade with other colonies, England, and the European Continent.

3. Southern Colonies

a. Economic Activities. Forests yielded pitch and tar, sticky substances known as *naval stores*. These were vital to preserve the wooden hulls of English and colonial ships. Fertile soil and a warm climate resulted in a plantation economy that raised indigo, rice, and tobacco. These products were shipped mainly to England in return for manufactured goods.

The Thirteen English Colonies in 1763

b. *Planter Domination.* As the planters became wealthy, they steadily added new lands to their plantations, in part because tobacco-raising quickly exhausted the soil. They dominated Southern colonial society and sought to imitate the ways of the English aristocracy. The planters' lives contrasted sharply with those of the small Southern farmers and of the frontiersmen struggling in the back country.

In summary, throughout the 13 colonies, the settlers were overwhelmingly engaged in *extractive occupations:* obtaining furs, fish, and lumber and raising farm produce. The abundance of raw materials and the shortage of manufactured goods led to a considerable overseas trade.

COLONIAL INDUSTRIES

1. **Beginnings of Colonial Manufacturing.** The colonists also engaged in certain basic manufactures: weaving cloth and sewing clothes, tanning leather and making shoes, trimming lumber and making furniture, forging iron and shaping implements. These activities were at first performed on the farm or plantation as household industries.

As the colonial population grew and as manufactured goods came into greater demand, craftsmen began founding small local shops. In time textiles, iron implements, and beaver hats became somewhat larger industries, and manufacturers sought to expand beyond local markets. The most important manufacturing activity, centered in New England, was shipbuilding.

2. **Obstacles to Colonial Industrialization**

a. *Scarcities.* Colonial manufacturing remained limited because of the (1) lack of capital, (2) lack of skilled workmen and experienced managers, (3) lack of adequate inland transportation facilities for the distribution of goods, and (4) opposition from England.

b. *English Mercantilist Laws.* England passed laws in accordance with the mercantile theory: that colonies should produce raw materials and exchange them for manufactured goods from the mother country. The *Woolen Act* (1699) and the *Hat Act* (1732) prohibited any colony from exporting these manufactured goods to any other colony or overseas. The *Iron Act* (1750) encouraged the shipment of crude iron to England but prohibited the colonists from making finished iron products.

Economic Factors as One Cause for Revolt by the American Colonies

ENGLAND'S COLONIAL POLICY OF SALUTARY NEGLECT (BEFORE 1763)

Beset by internal strife which culminated in the Glorious Revolution of 1689 and thereafter engaged in three indecisive wars with France, England for many years had neglected her American colonies. They exercised considerable self-government and they disregarded English mercantilist laws considered harmful to colonial interests. Governing themselves and prospering economically, the colonists labeled English policy as beneficial or *salutary neglect.*

FRENCH AND INDIAN WAR (1754–1763)

1. Britain Victorious. Although the first three wars between Britain and France were indecisive, the fourth war—the *Seven Years' War* in Europe and India and its American phase, the *French and Indian War*—brought victory to Britain. British forces supplemented by colonial militia eventually drove the French from the Ohio Valley and seized control of Canada. These British victories in North America were paralleled by British triumphs in India and by the success of Britain's ally, Prussia, in Europe. France was completely defeated.

The *Treaty of Paris* (1763) eliminated France as a colonial power in North America. France ceded (*a*) to Spain: all French territory west of the Mississippi, as well as the city of New Orleans, and (*b*) to Britain: Canada and all French territory east of the Mississippi, except New Orleans.

2. Impact of the War. In analyzing the impact of the French and Indian War upon the colonies, the British government concluded that (*a*) the colonies had not helped the mother country sufficiently with men and supplies, but (*b*) the colonies had gained greatly for, by removing the French from North America, the British victory lessened the danger of Indian attacks upon colonial frontier settlements, and therefore (*c*) the colonies should pay their part of the cost of the war and of maintaining the British Empire.

BRITAIN'S NEW COLONIAL POLICY: STRICT CONTROL

Starting in 1763 the British government adopted a new colonial policy seeking to (1) place the colonies under strict British political and economic control, (2) compel the colonists to respect and obey British mercantilist laws, and (3) tax the colonists, with the revenues going mainly into the British treasury.

1. Strict Enforcement of Existing Laws

a. Navigation Acts. Reflecting mercantilist doctrine, these laws required the colonists to (1) transport their goods only in British (and colonial) ships (although Dutch freighters offered lower rates), (2) export certain *enumerated articles,* such as tobacco, sugar, indigo, and furs, only to Britain (although Continental European markets offered higher prices), and (3) purchase their imports from Britain or, when colonial ships secured goods from the European Continent, to stop at a British port and pay duties. These laws sought to benefit British (and also colonial) shipbuilders, British merchants, and British manufacturers. Beginning in 1763, *George Grenville,* British Prime Minister, sent to the colonies an increasing number of customs collectors, royal inspectors, and naval patrols to enforce the laws.

b. Writs of Assistance. These general search warrants were court orders authorizing British officials to search colonial homes, buildings, and ships for smuggled goods. Unlike a search warrant in the United States today, which authorizes an officer to search only a particular place for specified goods, a writ of assistance permitted an official to search any place and seize any smuggled goods.

2. New Taxes

a. Sugar Act (1764). This act reduced the existing duties on colonial imports of sugar and molasses from the Spanish and French West Indies, but called for strict enforcement.

b. Stamp Act (1765). This was the first *internal tax* (as contrasted with import and export duties) levied on the colonies. It required the purchase of stamps that were to be put on printed materials such as wills, mortgages, almanacs, pamphlets, and newspapers. It mostly affected influential groups such as lawyers, clergymen, and printers.

c. Townshend Acts (1767). At the suggestion of Chancellor of the Exchequer *Charles Townshend,* Parliament levied new taxes on colonial imports of paper, glass, paint, and tea.

Colonists accused of violating the British tax laws were tried in Admiralty (military) Courts, where they were denied a jury trial. The colonists very likely would have found more sympathy from a jury in a colonial court.

3. Western Land Policy: Proclamation of 1763. This royal decree prohibited colonists from settling west of the Appalachian Mountains. By reserving this region for the Indians, King George III sought to protect the fur trade and remove a cause of Indian uprisings. The proclamation also sought to prevent colonial settlements beyond the reach of British authorities.

4. Stationing of Soldiers: Quartering Act of 1765. This act, considered a form of taxation by the colonists, required them to provide food and living quarters for British soldiers. Supposedly, the soldiers were to protect the colonists from the Indians. However, the soldiers were mostly stationed not in frontier settlements, but in populous coastal cities, such as New York and Boston.

COLONIAL OPPOSITION

1. Violations of British Laws. Merchants and shipowners continued to smuggle goods into the colonies to avoid import duties. Frontiersmen and Southern planters continued to settle the fertile lands beyond the Appalachians.

2. Protests Against Writs of Assistance. Lawyers and writers protested the writs of assistance as illegal invasions of colonial homes. In a Boston court, *James Otis* eloquently but unsuccessfully denounced the writs for violating the English common law principle that "a man's home is his castle."

3. Stamp Act Congress of 1765. At the urging of the Massachusetts assembly, delegates from nine colonies met in New York City to plan united action against the Stamp Act. The delegates asserted that the colonists possessed all the rights of Englishmen and could be taxed only by colonial legislatures, not by Parliament. They also began a boycott of British goods.

4. Mass Action: Boycotts and Defiance. The delegates to the Stamp Act Congress urged colonial merchants to sign *nonimportation agreements.* These were pledges not to import British goods until the repeal of the Stamp Act. In addition, resistance throughout the colonies prevented distribution of the tax stamps.

Parliament repealed the Stamp Act but passed the *Declaratory Act* (1766), reaffirming its power to tax the colonies.

When Parliament enacted the Townshend taxes (1767), colonial consumers again boycotted British goods. The colonists hoped that British businessmen would pressure Parliament into repealing the hated tax laws. In 1770 Britain yielded to the colonists and repealed all the Townshend import duties except on tea.

BOSTON TEA PARTY (1773)

Parliament passed the *Tea Act* (1773), exempting the East India Company from paying taxes in Britain on tea shipped to the colonies. By this act, Parliament offered the colonists the cheapest tea ever. Nevertheless, the colonists resented the Tea Act. (1) Colonial merchants, who had smuggled tea from Holland to avoid paying the import duty, would be undersold by the inexpensive tea of the East India Company. (2) The colonists would still have to pay the Townshend import duty. In New York and Philadelphia, colonists turned back the British tea ships with their full cargoes. In Boston, colonists disguised as Indians boarded the British ships and dumped the tea into the harbor. This action, defying British authority and destroying British property, was named the *Boston Tea Party*.

"INTOLERABLE" ACTS (1774)

Determined to punish Massachusetts and assert British authority, Parliament passed a series of acts that the colonists termed "intolerable." These acts (1) closed Boston harbor until the colonists paid for the destroyed tea, (2) authorized the quartering of troops in any colonial town, (3) permitted British officials accused of crimes in Massachusetts to stand trial in Britain, and (4) severely curtailed self-government in Massachusetts. By their severity, these acts solidified colonial support for Massachusetts.

FIRST CONTINENTAL CONGRESS (1774)

To present unified colonial resistance to the Intolerable Acts, delegates of twelve colonies met at Philadelphia as the *First Continental Congress*. They addressed a "Declaration of Rights and Grievances" to King George III, asking for a redress (correction) of wrongs, especially for repeal of the Intolerable Acts. Meanwhile, they voted to impose a boycott on British goods.

In Virginia, *Patrick Henry* acclaimed the work of the Continental Congress in a famous speech, concluding with: "Give me liberty, or give me death." Realizing that liberty might require defense, colonial patriots began training militiamen and storing military supplies.

OUTBREAK OF THE AMERICAN REVOLUTION (APRIL 1775)

In Massachusetts the British General Thomas Gage ordered a detachment of troops to seize colonial military supplies at Concord and to arrest the colonial leaders John Hancock and Samuel Adams, believed to be at Lexington.

Forewarned by Paul Revere, *Minutemen*, who were Massachusetts militiamen pledged to be ready at a minute's notice, were waiting to resist the British troops. Fighting broke out. As the poet Ralph Waldo Emerson later said, "Here once the embattled farmers stood and fired the shot heard round the world." Thus started the American Revolution.

ECONOMIC CAUSES OF THE AMERICAN REVOLUTION

Colonial manufacturers and merchants were indignant over British mercantilist laws, which hampered their industry and trade. They rejected the doctrine that colonies exist only to enrich the mother country. Plantation owners and frontiersmen, eager for new land, disliked the prohibition against westward expansion. Professional people opposed the stamp tax on printed matter, such as newspapers, pamphlets, and legal documents. Consumers resented import taxes, which raised living costs. The colonists were determined to free themselves from restrictions and exploitation by the mother country.

The British argued that Britain's mercantilist laws assigned the colonies their proper role in the economy of the British Empire as producers of raw materials. They further pointed out that mercantilist laws encouraged colonial shipbuilding, provided bounties for colonial producers of essential products such as naval stores, permitted colonial merchants to trade freely with Britain and the British West Indies, and helped colonial planters by requiring British merchants to buy tobacco only from the British colonies. Finally, Britain claimed that her armed might protected colonial shipping and frontier settlements.

OTHER CAUSES OF THE AMERICAN REVOLUTION

Other causes include: (1) Political—the colonists held that they were being denied their "rights as Englishmen," (2) Social—the colonists of British stock had been transformed into Americans, and many non-British colonists came from countries hostile to Britain, (3) Misunderstandings—the colonists were separated from Britain by 3000 miles of Atlantic Ocean waters bridged only by slow-moving ships, and extremists on both sides hampered efforts to resolve disagreements by compromise.

THE COLONIES GAIN INDEPENDENCE

In the course of eight long years of warfare (1775–1783), the American colonies issued the Declaration of Independence (1776), were assisted by France and later by Spain and Holland, thereby transforming the revolution into a major European war, and with French help won the decisive battle at Yorktown (1781). By the *Treaty of Paris* (1783), the 13 colonies won British recognition of their independence.

ECONOMIC RESULTS OF THE AMERICAN REVOLUTION

1. **Gains.** The American Revolution resulted in (a) the end of British mercantilist restrictions on American trade and industry, and consequently the growth of an American merchant marine and American manufacturing, especially in muni-

tions and consumer products, *(b)* the end of British restrictions on migration across the Appalachians and consequently the movement of land-hungry settlers westward, *(c)* the breakup of large estates, especially those taken from the Tories—colonists who had remained loyal to Britain, and consequently an increase in the number of small, independent farmers, and *(d)* the end of primogeniture, the legal right of the oldest son to inherit the entire estate of his deceased father and consequently ending the superior status of the oldest son over his younger brothers.

2. Problems. The end of the Revolution also brought economic problems. American merchants were excluded from the British West Indies and lost their favored position in British markets. With the wartime demand for goods ended, American farmers and planters saw agricultural prices decline, and city workers faced unemployment. The new nation was plagued by two other economic problems: how to curtail inflation and how to repay the large public debt incurred in waging the Revolutionary War.

MULTIPLE-CHOICE QUESTIONS

1. An important aim of mercantilism as practiced by European countries during the 17th and 18th centuries was to (1) further national power by economic self-sufficiency (2) acquire naval bases (3) destroy the Italian trade monopoly in the Mediterranean (4) achieve free trade.
2. The *primary* purpose of the English mercantile system was to (1) encourage trade among the 13 American colonies (2) stimulate individual initiative in colonial industries (3) promote English investments in colonial industries (4) provide England with a source of raw materials and a market for manufactured goods.
3. According to mercantilism, a world power should (1) not seek colonies (2) seek only colonies rich in gold (3) permit colonial self-government (4) regulate colonies so as to enrich the mother country.
4. Early English settlements in the New World were *largely* financed by (1) the royal family (2) military leaders (3) joint-stock companies and individuals (4) the Anglican Church.
5. Proprietors did *not* found which one of the following colonies? (1) Virginia (2) Pennsylvania (3) Maryland (4) North Carolina
6. Which is the *most* valid statement regarding the joint-stock companies that founded the earliest English colonies in America? These joint-stock companies (1) made tremendous profits (2) sold out their interests to proprietors (3) made settlements without permission of the English king (4) showed that risky investments sometimes lead to losses.
7. The geography of a region will have the *most* direct influence on its people's (1) means of support (2) form of worship (3) system of education (4) system of government.
8. The *chief* occupation of most American colonists was (1) farming (2) manufacturing (3) shipping and shipbuilding (4) fishing.
9. In colonial times in America, the so-called triangular trade routes involved commerce in (1) sugar and molasses with the West Indies (2) silks and spices with China (3) gold and silver with Central America (4) furs and lumber with Canada.
10. In 1700 the *most* important export of Virginia was (1) cotton (2) tobacco (3) wheat (4) fish.
11. Before 1763 *most* colonial farmers wore clothing that was (1) imported from

Europe   (2) made in American factories   (3) made by tailors in their shops   (4) made by housewives in their homes.

12. The French and Indian War increased tension between Britain and the American colonies because the   (1) colonists had not been allowed to participate in that war   (2) colonists had hoped to win independence   (3) British pressed the colonists to settle in Canada   (4) British insisted that the colonists share the expenses of the war.

13. Immediately following the French and Indian War, the colonists opposed the British policy of   (1) stricter enforcement of mercantilism   (2) stricter adherence to "salutary neglect"   (3) prohibition of emigration to the colonies   (4) greater attention to new possessions in India and Canada.

14. The purpose of the Navigation Acts was to protect   (1) New England merchants   (2) the economic interests of the British Empire   (3) colonial trade with the West Indies   (4) the slave trade between England and the colonies.

15. The *primary* reason why the British Parliament repealed some of the laws to which their American colonists objected was that   (1) the colonists used economic sanctions which hurt the merchants of Great Britain   (2) the colonists were strongly represented in the Parliament   (3) Great Britain feared the military power of the colonies   (4) colonial petitions were generally well written and therefore effective.

16. The British government felt that a policy of mercantilism also helped her American colonies because it   (1) assured the American colonists a secure English market for their products   (2) stimulated colonial manufacturing and self-sufficiency   (3) encouraged colonial trade with the rest of the world   (4) guaranteed the American colonists a favorable balance of trade.

17. Which action of the British government *most* directly affected the people on the frontier?   (1) "Intolerable" Acts   (2) Stamp Act   (3) Proclamation of 1763   (4) Townshend Acts.

18. The American Revolution resulted in all of the following *except* the   (1) breakup of large estates   (2) increase of American trade with the British West Indies   (3) end of primogeniture   (4) increase in number of settlers moving westward across the Appalachians.

19. A major reason why Americans regarded the American Revolution as of worldwide importance was that it   (1) was led by men of recognized ability   (2) was successful after eight years of fighting   (3) ended European imperialism in the Western Hemisphere   (4) marked the emergence of a new nation free to experiment with new political and economic institutions.

20. Theodore Roosevelt once remarked that the American Revolution broke out because "England failed to recognize an emerging nation when she saw one." Which statement *best* supports this point of view?   (1) England had not allowed colonial legislatures to develop.   (2) England had failed to cope with the growing power of France in the New World.   (3) England's policies had attempted to keep the colonies in a state of perpetual economic dependence.   (4) England's power was declining and the colonists did not want to support her quest for an empire.

ESSAY QUESTIONS

1. Mercantilism was a major factor in American history from colonial beginnings through to the gaining of independence. (*a*) State *two* theories of mercantilism; for *each* indicate whether you agree or disagree and why. (*b*) Show *one* way in which mercantilism encouraged colonial settlement. (*c*) Discuss *one* way in which English mercantilist policy benefited the colonies. (*d*) Discuss *two* ways in which English mercantilist policy led the colonies to revolution.

2. In discussing the English colonies, we must distinguish between the motives of the settlers and the motives of the government. (*a*) Discuss *two* motives that led English-men to settle in the New World. (*b*) Discuss *two* motives that led the English government to encourage such settlement.

3. The 13 English colonies usually are considered as three groups—(*a*) New England (*b*) Middle (*c*) Southern—chiefly because each group had its own distinctive geographic features. For *each* group-of colonies (1) describe *two* of its distinctive geographic features and (2) show how these features influenced the way its colonists earned a living.

4. Show *one* way in which *each* of the following contributed to the revolt of the American colonies against Britain: (*a*) geography (*b*) "rights of Englishmen" (*c*) Proclamation of 1763 (*d*) "Intolerable" Acts (*e*) French and Indian War.

3. *The New Nation Overcomes Difficulties and Prospers*

Toward a Strong Central Government. Business and propertied groups were most dissatisfied under the Articles of Confederation. Not only had the Articles established an incomplete governmental structure, but they had also failed to provide powers to further economic stability and growth. Business and proper-tied groups played major roles in convening the Constitutional Convention at Philadelphia in 1787, and in drawing up and securing the adoption of the Constitution. (Check the Index for "Articles of Confederation" and for "Constitutional Convention.")

CONSTITUTIONAL PROVISIONS AFFECTING ECONOMIC MATTERS

To safeguard property rights and to permit laws promoting the free-enterprise economy, the Constitution contains the following provisions:

1. Interstate Commerce. "The Congress shall have power to regulate com-merce . . . among the several States." This provision has made possible the movement of goods throughout the nation without any state-imposed tariff barriers. (Check the Index for the Supreme Court decision in *Gibbons vs. Ogden.*)

2. Foreign Commerce. "The Congress shall have power to regulate commerce with foreign nations," and furthermore, "no State shall, without the consent of Congress, lay any imposts or duties on imports or exports." These provisions gave Congress exclusive control over foreign commerce and made possible the levying of uniform tariffs on imports to protect domestic industry and agriculture against foreign competition.

3. Coinage of Money. "The Congress shall have power to coin money [and] regulate the value thereof," and furthermore, "no State shall . . . coin money." By giving Congress the exclusive power to coin money, these provisions made possible a uniform currency, thereby encouraging nationwide business enterprise.

4. Patents. "The Congress shall have power to promote the progress of science and useful arts by securing for limited times to authors and inventors the exclusive right to their respective writings and discoveries." This provision encouraged individuals and corporations to engage in research seeking new industrial processes and new inventions. (Check the Index for "Science" and "Inventions.")

5. Private Property. "Nor shall private property be taken for public use, without just compensation." (Check the Index for the "Fifth Amendment" and the right of "Eminent domain.")

6. Sanctity of Contracts. "No State shall pass any law impairing the obligation of contracts." This provision means that no state may alter the terms of a valid business contract. (Check the Index for the Supreme Court decision in *Dartmouth College vs. Woodward.*)

7. Due Process of Law. Neither the federal government nor the states shall deprive "any person of . . . property without due process of law." (Check the Index for "Amendments to the Constitution," "fifth and fourteenth," each containing the "due process of law" clause.)

The New Government: Under George Washington

As first President, George Washington concentrated upon achieving major goals: fostering national unity, developing respect for the new government, and promoting economic prosperity. To assist in his administration, Washington appointed a number of capable officials.

Two appointees—men of talent and leadership—held directly opposing views on major economic and political issues. Thomas Jefferson, who became Secretary of State, favored an agricultural society of small independent farmers, believed in democracy, urged government by capable leaders protecting the interests of the common people, wanted to limit the role of government, and consequently supported strict interpretation of the Constitution. Alexander Hamilton, who became Secretary of the Treasury, envisioned the United States becoming an industrialized society, feared the "excesses of democracy," urged government by and for the "rich, well-born and able," wanted the government to take an active role in economic matters, and consequently favored loose interpretation of the Constitution. Of all Washington's assistants, the one who exercised the greatest influence upon him was Alexander Hamilton. (Check the Index for "Alexander Hamilton, Washington supports.")

HAMILTON'S FINANCIAL PROGRAM

The new government faced a most urgent problem: organizing its finances. Hamilton urged Congress to enact the following program:

1. Payment of Debts. According to the Constitution (Article VI, Section 1), the new government assumed responsibility for all debts contracted by the central government during the Revolutionary War and Confederation periods. Hamilton recommended: (a) Full payment of the domestic debt—government bonds and certificates held by Americans. Hamilton proposed that this debt be "funded," that is, that all old bonds and certificates be exchanged for new bonds to be issued by the government. (b) Full payment of the foreign debt—loans extended by our Revolutionary War allies: France, Spain, and the Netherlands. (c) Assumption of state debts by the federal government, since these debts were incurred in fighting the Revolutionary War.

Such repayments, Hamilton argued, would firmly establish the credit of the United States at home and abroad.

2. Excise Tax. To raise funds, Hamilton proposed an excise tax on various commodities, notably on distilled liquors.

3. Protective Tariff. Congress had already passed a low tariff on imports to provide revenue for the new government. In 1791 Hamilton sent his *Report on Manufactures* to Congress, arguing that the government should take measures to encourage industrial enterprise. He recommended a protective tariff to discourage imports of foreign manufactured goods, bounties to encourage new American industries, and government programs to stimulate inventions and train skilled workers. Hamilton's protective tariff proposal was opposed by farmers who feared higher prices for manufactured goods and by merchants who feared disruption of foreign trade. Congress rejected Hamilton's recommendations for spurring industrial enterprise although it raised tariff rates slightly for revenue purposes.

4. National Bank for Money Management. Hamilton urged the chartering of a *National Bank*, or Bank of the United States. This would be a private institution with a capital stock of $10 million, of which private investors would own 80 percent and the government 20 percent. The Bank would serve the government as its financial agent, holding government monies, assisting in tax collections, and selling government bonds. Also, the Bank would issue bank notes, or paper money, but with a sufficient backing of specie (gold and silver) to constitute a stable currency. Finally, the Bank would enable investors to buy its stock, would provide loans for manufacturing and other business ventures and would facilitate financial transactions throughout the nation.

5. Overall Objectives. Hamilton's program—to establish the national credit, encourage manufacturing, and provide a sound currency—favored men of wealth and enterprise: creditors, bankers, merchants, and industrial entrepreneurs. By giving these groups an economic stake in the new government, Hamilton believed that he was assuring its success.

ADOPTION OF HAMILTON'S PROGRAM DESPITE BITTER OPPOSITION

1. Repayment of the Domestic Debt. Speculators had purchased government bonds from their original owners at prices far below face value. The original owners now protested that repaying the domestic debt in full would enrich the speculators. Hamilton argued that the measure was necessary to establish the nation's credit. Hamilton won, and in 1790 Congress passed the Funding Bill.

2. Assumption of State Debts. Hamilton's opponents argued that this proposal was unfair to those states, chiefly in the South, that had paid off their indebtedness themselves. Hamilton won adoption of the proposal by logrolling. In exchange for Southern votes, he promised to support the establishment of the nation's permanent capital in the South—on the banks of the Potomac between Maryland and Virginia.

3. Excise Taxes. Congress passed Hamilton's excise taxes. The excise tax on whisky chiefly affected farmers on the Western frontier, who were converting much of their bulky, low-priced grain into less bulky and higher-priced liquor for shipment to the East.

When a group of farmers in western Pennsylvania forcibly resisted paying the tax, Hamilton prevailed upon Washington to send troops, thereby crushing the Whisky Rebellion.

4. Bank of the United States. Opponents of the Bank argued for a strict interpretation of the Constitution. Thomas Jefferson pointed out that Congress was not specifically granted the power to establish a National Bank. Hamilton replied that the Bank was "necessary and proper" for carrying out the delegated power to "coin money" and "regulate the value thereof." Hamilton's loose interpretation was accepted by George Washington, who signed the bill chartering the Bank.

RESULTS OF HAMILTON'S FINANCIAL PROGRAM

The bitter struggle over Hamilton's program resulted in the formation of our earliest political parties. The *Federalists*, led by John Adams and Alexander Hamilton, represented the well-to-do classes. The *Anti-Federalists* (also known as *Democratic-Republicans*), led by James Madison and Thomas Jefferson, represented the common people.

The full repayment and funding of the national debt established the credit of the United States government as excellent, enabled its bonds to sell at face value, and allowed the speculators in the old bonds to reap great profits. The new government, having its own sources of revenue and demonstrating ability to enforce its laws, appeared strong and secure. The nation's economy was facilitated by the uniform and relatively stable currency and entered upon a period of prosperity. The nation, however, remained overwhelmingly agricultural. At that time industrial enterprise did not expand markedly but was stimulated two decades later during the era of the War of 1812.

The Era of the War of 1812 and Afterwards

THE WAR OF 1812

Check the Index for a discussion of the war, including the background events, their impact upon the New England mercantile capitalists, the causes of the war, and the historians' debate regarding the primary cause (maritime rights or territorial ambitions), the major military events, and the peace treaty of Ghent.

ECONOMIC DEVELOPMENTS FOLLOWING THE WAR OF 1812

1. Population Trends

a. Rapid Growth. With the close of the Napoleonic Wars (1815), Europeans seeking to migrate to the United States could travel with greater safety. Also, with the development of the ocean-crossing steamboat, they could travel with greater comfort and speed. Immigrants now came to America in rapidly rising numbers. (Check the Index for "Immigration.")

In addition to more immigrants, the United States experienced a high native birthrate. The result was a soaring American population: from 9.6 million in 1820 to 31.4 million in 1860.

b. Westward Migration. After the War of 1812, Americans in growing numbers began moving westward. Several war battles had destroyed hostile Indian forces and made the West safer for settlement. The war had shut down the shipping industry, so New Englanders who had lost their jobs moved westward. The federal government in 1820 offered settlers cheap land—as little as 80 acres at $1.25 per acre. Finally various Western territories and states adopted policies to attract settlers.

Between 1810 and 1820, settlers west of the Appalachian Mountains more than doubled in number, and by 1850 almost half the American population lived there. Between 1816 and 1821 five Western territories achieved sufficient population to be admitted to the Union as states, and between 1836 and 1859 eight more Western territories became states.

c. Impact of Population Trends. The growth and westward movement of the American population had a major impact upon American economic life. More people meant more farmers to help raise agricultural surpluses; more workers to build transportation facilities and to labor in factories; more consumers to purchase foodstuffs and manufactured goods; more urban dwellers to crowd into old cities and start new ones. One further impact was the need for new and improved methods of transportation.

2. New and Improved Transportation Facilities to the West

a. Early Turnpikes and Public Roads. (1) Even before the War of 1812, settlers were traveling the *Lancaster Turnpike*, a toll road built by a private company, which linked Philadelphia to Lancaster. These settlers then crossed the Appalachian Mountains and reached Pittsburgh by taking the *Pennsylvania State Road*, built by a private company and in part financed by the state. At Pittsburgh they transferred their goods to flatboats and floated down the Ohio River. (2) Settlers also crossed the Appalachians by following the *National* or *Cumberland Road*. In 1818 this road, which started at Cumberland, Maryland, reached Wheeling on the Ohio River. By 1852 the road was extended to Vandalia in Illinois. This road was financed partly by federal funds derived from the sale of land. (3) Farther to the south, settlers traversed Appalachian mountain passes by following state roads such as the *Wilderness Road*. This road went through the *Cumberland Gap*, an often-traveled mountain pass running from North Carolina into Tennessee and Kentucky.

b. Steamboats. In 1807 Robert Fulton built the *Clermont*, the first successful steamboat, thereby making river transportation quicker and cheaper. By the

1820's steamboats carrying settlers and cargoes were plying the Mississippi and Ohio Rivers. Cincinnati and Louisville on the Ohio and St. Louis on the Mississippi became thriving river cities. New Orleans, at the mouth of the Mississippi, served both West and South, and became a major commercial center.

Major Roads and Waterways to the West

c. **Canals.** The Erie Canal, financed by New York State and completed in 1825, proved an immediate success. Settlers going west from New York City could travel up the Hudson River to Albany, and then westward on the Erie Canal to Buffalo on Lake Erie. With this all-water route between the Great Lakes and the Atlantic Ocean, Western farmers could ship their produce eastward at greatly reduced cost—as much as 85 percent less than before. Cities on the Great Lakes—such as Rochester, Buffalo, and Cleveland—prospered from trade in grain, hides, iron ore, and lumber. New York City, at the junction of the Hudson River and the Atlantic Ocean, became the nation's leading commercial center.

The success of the Erie Canal spurred an era of canal building, most notably by (1) Philadelphia, which wanted to partake of the Western trade, and (2) Ohio and Indiana, which built canals to connect Lake Erie with the Ohio River and its tributaries.

d. **Railroads.** The invention of the steam locomotive in 1814 by the Englishman *George Stephenson* spurred Americans to railroad building. *Peter Cooper* built *Tom Thumb*, a locomotive that in 1830 traversed the 14 miles of track of America's first railroad, the *Baltimore and Ohio*. Track mileage steadily increased to 30,000 by 1860, almost all east of the Mississippi and north of the

Ohio. In the main, railroads linked the cities of the Northeastern seaboard with cities in the Northwestern interior.

e. Sources of Capital. From whence came the money—the capital—needed to build turnpikes, canals, steamboats, and railroads? (1) Private Capital. Foreign investors, mainly from Britain, were willing to speculate that American transportation facilities would prove profitable. New England mercantile capitalists, confronted by the decline of shipping, had funds available for investment. Merchants and farmers located along proposed transportation routes often invested, expecting the new facilities to bring more business and to increase land values. Speculators who had reaped profits from government bonds (funded at face value by Hamilton) and from rising land values also provided investment funds. (These same sources of private capital were available for investment in industry.) (2) Public Capital. Various Eastern and Midwestern states themselves built or provided loans to private companies for the construction of turnpikes, canals, and railroads. So did a number of cities which hoped to benefit from new transit facilities. The federal government, beginning in 1850, granted public lands, lying in alternate sections along projected railroad routes, to states that transferred these lands to railroads. By selling land to settlers, the railroads raised money for construction and gained customers to use their facilities.

f. Impact of New and Improved Transportation Facilities. The building of turnpikes, steamboats, canals, and railroads hastened the settlement of the West, reduced substantially the cost of transporting farm products and manufactured goods, tied together the economic interests of the Northeast and the Northwest, and provided an outlet for the investment of capital. Also, the construction work, which employed men and used lumber, iron, and varied equipment, stimulated the development of American industry.

3. Development of American Industry

a. Early Years and Slow Beginnings. Despite "Yankee ingenuity" and the domestic market for manufactured goods, the young nation moved toward industry slowly. The Northeast began industrialization. *Samuel Slater*, an immigrant from England, in 1790 in Rhode Island, constructed the nation's first cotton-spinning mill. Since England forbade textile workers to emigrate, Slater had left in disguise and built his machines in America from memory. Slater became known as the "father of the American factory system." *Eli Whitney*, a Yankee mechanical genius, in 1798 in Connecticut, began to mass produce guns by assembling them out of interchangeable parts. Whitney later applied his mass-production methods to the manufacture of inexpensive clocks. *Francis Cabot Lowell*, an inventor and wealthy Boston merchant, in 1813 in Massachusetts built the nation's first textile factory to combine all steps from raw material to finished product—processing the raw cotton, spinning thread, and weaving cloth.

The early industrial capitalists faced difficulties: (1) British imports, undeterred by low tariff rates, provided severe competition. (2) Household industries, often sustained by merchant capitalists who "put out" goods to be worked at home, produced competing products. (3) Markets were limited, generally to the immediate vicinity, by the lack of adequate inland transportation facilities. (4) Workers, especially skilled workers, were scarce. Most men preferred to secure land and become independent farmers. Skilled workers in Britain were prohibited from emigrating. (5) American mercantile capitalists were reluctant to invest in industry when, they believed, they could make fortunes in land speculation and trans-Atlantic trade. British capitalists likewise preferred to invest in land and transportation facilities.

b. War of 1812 Era. The interference with and then stoppage of American commerce during the War of 1812 era encouraged Americans to develop industry. New England mercantile capitalists, faced by the decline of shipping, now looked to invest in industry. American consumers, unable to secure imports of British goods, constituted a "sure" market. To profit from these conditions, many new industrial enterprises arose—especially textiles and leather goods in New England and iron products in New Jersey and Pennsylvania.

c. After the War of 1812: Difficult Times. With the end of the war, the "infant" American industries faced difficult times: (1) The British deliberately "dumped" low-priced goods here to stifle American manufacturing which, a member of the British Parliament said, "the war has forced into existence, contrary to the natural course of things." British competition was somewhat lessened by the higher rates, especially on textiles, of the 1816 tariff. (2) The Panic of 1819—a financial crisis—drove the nation into an economic depression. The weaker industrial enterprises failed; the surviving enterprises were the more efficient in terms of adequate capital, capable management, superior production facilities, and effective marketing techniques.

d. Industrialization Assured. After the mid-1820's, American industry again began to grow and become firmly established. Its growth was aided by protective tariffs passed from 1824 to 1832 to keep out foreign manufactures, by the improvements in transportation to make available nationwide markets, by the increasing population to provide both consumers and workers, and by the greater use of capital and machinery. From 1820 to 1840, capital invested in American factories rose to $250 million—a fivefold increase. After 1840 industry continued to grow; during the Civil War it expanded rapidly in the North, satisfying civilian and military needs and making possible the victory of the Union.

e. Impact of Industrialization. The growth of industry brought significant changes to American life: existing cities expanded and new ones arose; factories flourished, especially in New England textile mill towns; urban workers became completely dependent for a livelihood upon their employers; some workers sought to improve wages and working conditions by forming the first labor unions; industrial capitalists made greater use of the corporate form of business organization; and industrial capitalists became major figures in the American economy.

Sectional Disputes and Civil War

FROM NATIONALISM TO SECTIONALISM

After the War of 1812, Americans developed strong feelings of *nationalism*. They gave their primary loyalty to the nation and considered problems from a national viewpoint. By the mid-1820's, however, nationalism gave way to a growing spirit of *sectionalism*. Americans now gave their primary loyalty to their state or section, and considered problems from a sectional viewpoint.

Southerners sought to protect their sectional interests by supporting states' rights and opposing federal power. Northerners and Westerners argued that what was good for their section was good for the nation and sought to further their interests by using federal power. The struggle between sectionalism and nationalism eventually resulted in the Civil War and, ultimately, in the triumph of nationalism.

ECONOMIC BASIS OF SECTIONALISM: REGIONAL SPECIALIZATION

1. Industrial Northeast. Consisting of New England and the Middle Atlantic states, the Northeast pursued shipping, fishing, lumbering, and farming—and industrialized significantly. By the mid-1840's, the Northeast contained a powerful class of industrial capitalists and was the nation's manufacturing region. Its leading industrial state was Massachusetts. The Northeast's chief manufactures were textiles, leather goods, iron implements, utensils, and machinery.

Industrialization in the Northeast was aided by the following factors: *(a)* Shipbuilding and foreign commerce had declined during the War of 1812 era, and workers and capital were available for the new industries. *(b)* Waterpower was readily available from swift-flowing streams, and steampower from Appalachian coal. *(c)* Factory hands could easily be recruited from farm families discouraged by New England's rocky soil, as well as from among immigrants. *(d)* As the nation's banking center, the Northeast possessed investment capital. *(e)* The South and the West represented a growing market for the Northeast's manufactured goods.

2. Plantation South. Consisting of the South Atlantic and Southwestern states, the South contained many small subsistence farmers but was dominated by a small number of wealthy and influential plantation owners. They were planter capitalists whose money was invested in land and slaves. They specialized in raising cash crops for the market: tobacco, rice, sugar, and, most important, cotton. From 1790 to 1826 cotton production increased from 2 million to 330 million pounds annually.

The rise of *King Cotton* was aided by the following factors: *(a)* Cheap, fertile land was plentiful. As the soil became exhausted by the continuous cultivation of a single crop, planters gradually moved from the South Atlantic states into the fertile lands of the Southwest. *(b)* The cotton gin, invented by Eli Whitney in 1793, provided a simple and inexpensive method of separating the cotton fiber from the seed. *(c)* Cotton-growing was a simple and year-round activity. Negro slaves could therefore be trained easily and kept occupied continuously. *(d)* Northern and English factories provided a growing market for the South's raw cotton.

3. Small-Farm West. Consisting of the Central and Northwestern states, the West specialized in agriculture on the small, family-size farm. Western settlers were competent farmers who, with an eye to the marketplace, raised tremendous surpluses of wheat, rye, corn, and meat. In producing abundant harvests, Westerners were aided by the following factors: *(a)* Fertile lands were plentiful. *(b)* The federal government sold the Western lands at very liberal prices—after

1820 at $1.25 per acre. *(c)* Free men worked hard on their own farms, seeking larger crops so as to better their economic status. *(d)* Northern and English cities represented an ever-growing demand for foodstuffs.

SECTIONAL ISSUES

By the mid-1820's the sections held differing viewpoints, notably on the following economic issues:

1. Protective Tariff. The *Northeast* strongly favored a protective tariff in order to protect factory owners and workers against foreign competition. The *South* opposed a protective tariff in order to buy manufactured goods at lower prices. Also, the planters feared that Britain might retaliate by curtailing purchases of Southern cotton. The *West* generally supported the North on this issue. Although Western farmers disliked the higher prices on manufactures, they wanted a prosperous Northeastern market for their foodstuffs.

2. The Bank of the United States. The *Northeast* strongly supported the Bank, since manufacturers and bankers benefited from available investment capital and stable currency. The *South* and the *West* both opposed the Bank. Planters, farmers, and debtors generally preferred state banks, since these would bring easy credit, cheap money, and high agricultural prices.

3. Internal Improvements at Federal Expense. The *West* favored such projects; farmers needed roads and canals to send their agricultural products to Northeastern markets and seaports. The *South* opposed these federal expenses; planters had satisfactory water routes to Northeastern and English markets and had little need of routes to the West. The *Northeast* generally supported the West on this issue; manufacturers desired improved routes to Western markets. However, many Northeasterners preferred internal improvements through private enterprise or at the expense of the states.

SECTIONAL DISPUTES

1. On Economic Issues

a. The Tariff Issue. Check the Index for "Tariffs, as sectional issue."
b. The Bank Issue. President Andrew Jackson, who led the fight against the Bank, opposed it in part because it exercised undue political influence but mainly because it enabled a few private individuals—the Bank's officers and directors—to maintain a monopoly over the nation's credit and currency. Jackson vetoed the bill to recharter the Bank, won overwhelming victory in the 1832 Presidential election in which the Bank was the main issue, and then withdrew government funds on deposit in the Bank, placing them in state banks. With the National Bank so enfeebled, state banks, especially in the West, pursued imprudent banking practices. Nicknamed *wildcat banks*, they made unwise loans—not backed by adequate collateral and used for land speculation. They also printed more paper bank notes (used as money) than were justified by their specie reserves. The nation experienced a financial crisis, known as the Panic of 1837, and thereafter several years of depression.

2. On Slavery and the Admission of New States. Check the Index for "Slavery."

3. On the Presidential Election of 1860 and Secession. Check the Index for "Secession."

CAUSES OF THE CIVIL WAR

1. Overview. Historians have long disputed regarding the causes—especially the primary cause—of the Civil War. Some have insisted that the primary cause was slavery as a moral issue. Others have focused attention elsewhere: *(a)* on the Constitutional issue—do states have the right to secede or are we one nation indivisible, *(b)* on political developments—the South's realization that eventually the North with Western support would secure control of the central government, *(c)* on fanaticism by extremists of both sides and on blundering leadership, *(d)* on differences in civilization between a static South dominated by a planter aristocracy and a dynamic North reflecting democratic values, and *(e)* on economic differences between the South and the North.

2. Economic Differences. Because of geographic conditions, the South had become agricultural and the North industrial. These economic differences led to bitter sectional rivalry on such issues as slavery, the protective tariff, and the National Bank. The aristocratic Southern planters were determined to resist domination by the Northern industrialists and to advance the interests of the South's agrarian economy.

Charles and *Mary Beard*, the authors of *The Rise of American Civilization*, advanced the argument that economic differences—between an agricultural society and an industrial society—were paramount in bringing about the Civil War. The Beards stated that, although the "forces which produced the irrepress-

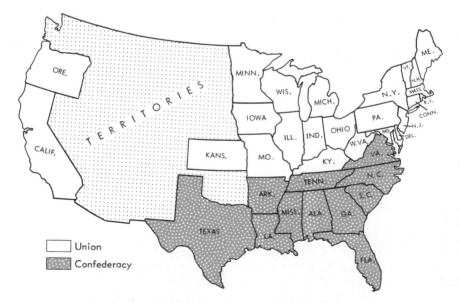

The Divided Nation: the Union and the Confederacy

ible conflict were very complex," the root of the controversy lay "in social grouping founded on differences in climate, soil, industries, and labor systems" and therefore the "civil war was in reality a Second American Revolution" which resulted in "the undisputed triumph of a new combination of power: Northern capitalists and free farmers."

Critics of the Beard thesis pointed out that the interests of Northern industrial capitalists and Southern planter capitalists often did not conflict but rather coincided. Northern textile factories purchased Southern cotton, wove it into cloth, and made it into garments, which were sold in Southern markets. Other Northern manufactures, such as leather goods and iron products, also were sold in Southern markets. Again, if the Beard thesis were correct, critics claimed, then the agricultural West should have sided with the agricultural South, not with the industrial North.

ECONOMIC ADVANTAGES OF THE NORTH

The North had a population of 22 million, far greater than the South's 9 million, of whom 3 ½ million were slaves. Of the entire United States, the North contained 90 percent of the industry, 75 percent of the financial resources, and 70 percent of the railroad mileage. These economic advantages of the North, in the long run, far outweighed the South's advantages of fighting a defensive war, retaining the loyalty of outstanding military leaders, and having men, accustomed to riding and hunting, better prepared for military life.

William T. Sherman, who in 1864 was to lead his Union army on a "march through Georgia," warned Southerners before the outbreak of the war as follows:

> The northern people not only greatly outnumber the whites [of] the South, but they are a mechanical people with manufactures of every kind, while you are only agriculturalists . . . and in all history no nation of mere agriculturalists ever made successful war against a nation of mechanics. . . . The North can make a steam engine, locomotive or railway car; hardly a yard of cloth or a pair of shoes can you make. . . . You are bound to fail. . . .

Economic Effects of the Civil War

ON THE SOUTH

1. Physical and Economic Devastation. The South was physically ruined by the war. Its lands were devastated, its railroads demolished, and its cities ravaged by the military campaigns waged on its soil. The Southern economy was destroyed as the war (a) kept Southern cotton from Northern and European markets, (b) exhausted Southern wealth for war needs, and (c) resulted in freeing the slaves without payment to the owners.

2. Revival of Southern Agriculture

a. Sharecropping. At the close of the Civil War, Southern plantation owners had land but no labor, and the newly freed slaves had no land but needed work. This situation led to the rise of *sharecropping.* (Check the Index.)

b. Diversified Agriculture. To end dependence upon a single crop and to halt soil depletion, Southern farmers near the end of the century turned to diversified agriculture. Today, the South raises varied crops, including fruits, vegetables, soybeans, and peanuts.

3. Development of Industry: The "New South." Learning from their experience in the Civil War, Southerners realized the importance of establishing industries. The South had cheap labor, a plentiful water supply, valuable minerals, and agricultural products. Iron and coal gave rise to steel mills; tobacco to cigarette factories; cotton to textile mills; timber to paper mills and furniture plants; oil to refineries and chemical works. Despite low wages and poor working conditions, Southerners left the countryside and flocked to the new factory towns. Birmingham, Alabama, developed into a steel center and became known as the *Pittsburgh of the South*. To describe the industrialization of the South, historians use the term the *New South*.

ON THE WEST

Western farmers prospered as the war increased the demand for foodstuffs. To overcome labor shortages, farmers purchased improved farm machinery, especially more efficient plows and reapers. Western agriculture was furthered by federal laws such as the *Homestead Act* (1862), which gave 160 acres free to any head of a family who cultivated the land for five years; the *Morrill Act* (1862), which encouraged agricultural education by providing for the endowment of land-grant colleges; and laws providing land grants to encourage the building of transcontinental railroads. Free homesteads and improved transportation, in addition to the natural resources of the West, attracted many settlers after the Civil War, and the population of the West increased rapidly.

ON THE NORTH

1. Republican Control. During the war and for many years afterwards, the Republican party, largely favorable to Northern business interests, dominated the federal government. Republican legislators furthered business interests by laws providing high tariffs, a system of nationally chartered banks, and land grants for railroads.

2. Economic Prosperity. During the war, Northern industrialists operated their factories at full capacity and even built new factories to meet the unprecedented demand. They overcame labor shortages by rapidly introducing new machinery. Given impetus by the war years, captains of industry soon created tremendous empires in meat-packing, flour-milling, oil-refining, and steel production. The United States entered an age of enterprise.

MULTIPLE-CHOICE QUESTIONS

1. Historians who claim that the authors of the United States Constitution were motivated by economic interests could *best* support their position by pointing to the fact that (1) capitalism was introduced immediately before the writing of the Constitution (2) bankers controlled government offices in the early days of the United States (3) commercial businesses flourished under the policies of the new government established by the Constitution (4) consumer protection was denied in the original Constitution.

2. Thomas Jefferson believed that democracy would be promoted by (1) encouraging the development of corporations (2) creating a national banking system (3) fostering a society of small farmers (4) supporting a loose interpretation of the Constitution.

3. Which powers did Congress use to charter the Bank of the United States in 1791? (1) concurrent powers (2) unlimited powers (3) implied powers (4) reserved powers

4. Alexander Hamilton based much of his financial program on his belief that (1) the success of the new government required the support of the propertied classes (2) the states should be discouraged from depending on the federal government (3) speculation in government securities had to be prevented (4) land was the most important source of wealth.

5. A *major* purpose achieved by Hamilton's financial program was to (1) protect the interests of the farmers (2) provide for more trade through lower tariffs (3) assure the states an equal share in tax revenue (4) strengthen the credit and increase the prestige of the national government.

6. Political parties appeared in the United States shortly after the adoption of the Constitution because (1) Washington disliked Jefferson (2) the Constitution provides for the two-party system (3) Great Britain had a two-party system (4) differences arose over political and economic issues.

7. During most of the 19th century the development of industrial capitalism in the United States was characterized by (1) a decrease in sectional economic interdependence (2) the effective conservation of natural resources (3) extensive capital investment in foreign countries (4) a minimum of government intervention in economic affairs.

8. During the period of 1830–1860, which was *most* significant in stimulating the growth of nationwide markets in the United States? (1) stability of the national banking system (2) development of nationwide advertising (3) improvement in transportation facilities (4) increase in the variety of banknotes in circulation

9. Which contributed to the development of the Industrial Revolution in the United States during most of the 19th century? (1) adoption of a bimetallic standard by Congress (2) restrictions on immigration from eastern Europe (3) decline in government control of the economy (4) availability of investment capital from Europe.

10. An important result of the War of 1812 was that it (1) discouraged the South from growing cotton (2) stimulated American maritime commerce (3) encouraged the migration of Americans to Canada (4) encouraged manufacturing in the United States.

11. Between 1825 and 1860, which of the following would probably have received support from *both* a New England factory owner and a Western farmer? (1) a policy of selling land at low prices (2) a national banking system (3) restrictions on immigration (4) a national program of building roads and canals

12. Samuel Slater is *best* known as the (1) builder of the Erie Canal (2) inventor of the steamboat (3) inventor of the railway locomotive (4) father of the American factory system.

13. Andrew Jackson *most* clearly demonstrated the Westerner's point of view in his (1) request for passage of the Force Bill (2) selection of his successor to the Presidency (3) attitude toward the Bank of the United States (4) acceptance of advice from his "Kitchen Cabinet."

14. The history of the tariff between 1800 and 1860 shows that (1) President Jackson supported the South in its stand on the tariff (2) the North consistently opposed a protective tariff (3) the tariff issue contributed to the conflict between North and South over states' rights (4) the tariff restored American industry destroyed during the War of 1812.

15. President Jackson claimed that the Bank of the United States (1) was supported by the plantation aristocracy (2) was responsible for the Panic of 1837 (3) gave private

interests a monopoly over the nation's credit and currency (4) had become unprofit-able.

16. During the period 1830–1860, which is the *best* example of a minority that exercised great political power within a section? (1) planter class in the South (2) unionized workers in Northern cities (3) farmers in the Northeast (4) shipbuilders in New England

17. In 1860, 19 million bushels of corn went East over the railroads while 4.8 million bushels went South over the Mississippi–Ohio River system. This statement helps to explain the (1) victory of canals over railroads (2) sympathy of the West for the South in the secession movement (3) dislike of Southern cotton farmers for the West (4) support given the North by the West in the Civil War.

18. Which was a *major* cause for the secession of the Southern states? (1) Northern demands that slave states get out of the Union (2) failure of Congress to support the principle of popular sovereignty in the territories (3) President Buchanan's forceful attack on the doctrine of nullification and secession (4) belief that Southern interests could be better advanced outside the federal Union

19. Which advantage did the North *lack* in fighting the Civil War? (1) large population (2) more industry (3) greater financial resources (4) interior lines of communications in a defensive war

20. Which section of the United States was *most* directly affected by the Homestead Act? (1) South (2) New England (3) West (4) Central Atlantic states

21. Since the Civil War, the expression "New South" has often been used to refer to the (1) importance of cotton cultivation in Southern agriculture (2) gradual indus-trialization of the South (3) revival of the plantation system in the South (4) changed attitude on the part of the Southern states toward Negroes.

22. Since the early 1900's, United States Senators from the South have reversed their attitude toward protective tariffs *chiefly* because they have wanted to (1) insure a favorable balance of payments (2) show their opposition to other administration programs (3) express the development of a new feeling of nationalism (4) protect new industries that had developed in the South.

ESSAY QUESTIONS

1. Show *two* ways in which *each* of the following met a pressing domestic need of its time: (*a*) the Constitution of the United States (1788) (*b*) Hamilton's financial program (1789–1791) (*c*) the Erie Canal (1825) (*d*) the Compromise Tariff of 1833 (*e*) the "New South" (1865–1900).

2. It has been said that the principles of Hamilton and Jefferson are still very much alive. (*a*) Discuss briefly a difference of opinion between Hamilton and Jefferson concerning *two* of the following issues of their day: (1) federal taxation (2) protective tariff (3) national control of banking (4) national debt. (*b*) Select *two* issues listed in part (*a*) and show why *each* has been an important problem in the United States during the 20th century.

3. Students of American history continue to argue about the fundamental causes of the Civil War. (*a*) Explain fully *two* arguments advanced by some historians that economic differences were the primary cause of the Civil War. (*b*) To what extent do you agree with this economic interpretation? Defend your answer. (*c*) State briefly *two* other fundamental causes for the Civil War that have been advanced by historians.

4. Show how the growth of American industry was affected in *one* way by *each* of the following: (*a*) the War of 1812 (*b*) westward expansion (1815–1860) (*c*) the era of rail-road building (1830–1860) (*d*) the faith of British investors in America (1815–1860) (*e*) the Civil War (1860–1865).

Part 3. The Eras of Finance Capitalism and State Capitalism: The Post-Civil War Years to the Present

4. Big Business Becomes the Dominant Influence in Our Economy

FACTORS ENCOURAGING INDUSTRIAL GROWTH (IN THE LATER 19th CENTURY)

1. **Natural Resources.** Nature endowed the United States with a wealth of natural resources: *(a)* raw materials: coal, oil, iron, copper, gold, silver, and lumber; *(b)* fertile soil for raising foodstuffs, cotton, and tobacco; *(c)* swift-running streams for waterpower.

2. **Government Policies.** From the Civil War to the end of the 19th century, the government spurred the growth of business by *(a)* granting land and cash subsidies to railroad builders, *(b)* levying high tariffs to protect manufacturers, *(c)* establishing a national banking system to provide a uniform and stable currency, and *(d)* in most other matters, maintaining a policy of laissez-faire —leaving business alone and letting the economy regulate itself.

3. **Growing Population.** Because of a high birthrate and considerable immigration, the American population in the later 19th century increased tremendously: from 31 million in 1860 to 76 million in 1900. This steady increase meant sufficient workers for industry and expanding markets for goods.

4. **New Sources of Power**

   a. Electricity. After the Englishman *Michael Faraday* discovered the principle of electromagnetic induction (1831), scientists developed the *dynamo*—an electric generator that converts mechanical energy into electric energy. At first electricity was used mainly for communication, in the telegraph and the telephone. Later it was used for lighting and for driving motors.

   b. Petroleum. In 1859 *Edwin Drake* in Pennsylvania drilled the first successful oil well. At first, oil was used for lubrication and lighting. Late in the 19th century, two petroleum products—gasoline and diesel oil—were first used in internal combustion engines, the basis of modern transportation.

5. **American Inventors and Inventions.** The American people displayed a genius for invention, as follows: *(a) Charles Goodyear*—the process of

vulcanizing, or hardening, rubber, *(b) Elias Howe*—the sewing machine, *(c) Elisha Otis*—the safety elevator, *(d) Gordon McKay*—a machine for sewing shoes, *(e) Christopher Sholes* (with Carlos Glidden and Samuel Soulé)—the modern typewriter, *(f) Ottmar Mergenthaler*—a typesetting machine, *(g) William Burroughs*—a key-operated calculating machine, and *(h) Thomas A. Edison*—the phonograph, the electric light bulb, and a motion picture machine. (Check the Index for "Scientists, American applied.")

6. Improved Means of Transportation and Communication

a. Transportation. Following the Civil War, America stepped up its railroad building. In 1900 the country had five transcontinental railroads and nearly 200,000 miles of track—more than the total trackage in all of Europe. Safety and comfort were increased by using iron and then steel in place of wood for rails and bridges, and by making heavier roadbeds. *George Pullman* invented the sleeping car, and *George Westinghouse* the air brake.

Railroads helped the growth of industry by bringing foodstuffs to city markets, raw materials to factories, and manufactures to consumers throughout the land.

b. Communication. (1) In 1844 *Samuel F. B. Morse* proved the practicability of the telegraph. Later, to provide telegraph service nationally, several telegraph companies merged to form *Western Union*. (2) In 1876 *Alexander Graham Bell* exhibited a successful telephone. His work led to the formation of what is today the world's largest communications company, *American Telephone and Telegraph*.

Rapid communications enabled businessmen to direct their salesmen, contact customers, and take orders quickly and efficiently.

7. Effect of Wars.
Industrialization in America was encouraged by wars. *(a)* Because the government needed war materials, industry prospered. *(b)* Because farmers and city workers had more money to spend, consumer goods were in greater demand. *(c)* Because the military services drained men from factories and farms, industrialists and farmers turned to labor-saving machines. In particular, the growth of industry was promoted by the Civil War.

RESULTS OF INDUSTRIAL GROWTH

1. New Industrial Products and Services. Manufacturers displaced hand- and home-made products with machine- and factory-made products. Investors financed new industries to provide new services and goods: railroad transportation, telegraph and telephone communication, steel, and oil.

2. Higher Standard of Living. Our industrial economy produced a greater volume and variety of goods at lower cost than ever before. The average American enjoyed an ever-increasing array of material comforts.

3. Great Fortunes. Industrial and finance capitalists accumulated great wealth, exercised tremendous economic power, and exerted considerable influence upon the government. Some men of wealth returned part of their fortunes to society by financing various philanthropies. In noteworthy instances, members of wealthy families devoted their lives to public service.

4. Growth of Cities. Many people flocked to the cities, some to find jobs, others to be near to urban society and culture. Cities faced many problems: clearing slums, constructing housing, preventing fire and crime, providing education, expanding mass transit, and assuring efficient local government.

5. Increased World Trade and Imperialism. Manufacturers looked abroad for markets and raw materials. American trade with the rest of the world increased. Toward the end of the 19th century, the United States moved away from its foreign policy of isolation and embarked on a policy of imperialism.

6. Serious Economic Problems. The growth of industry gave rise to major domestic problems: preventing monopoly, protecting consumers and small businessmen, conserving resources and protecting the environment, improving the living standards of workers, maintaining an effective banking system, levying fair taxes, and leveling out the business cycle.

Corporations and Business Consolidation

INADEQUACIES OF THE OLD FORMS OF BUSINESS ORGANIZATION

Single proprietorships and *partnerships* proved inadequate, in the post-Civil War era, to meet the needs of large-scale business. Weaknesses were the (1) inability to raise large sums of money, (2) unlimited financial responsibility of the owners, extending even to their personal assets, for claims against the business, and (3) disruption of the business upon death of the owner or partner. To overcome these weaknesses, businessmen turned increasingly to another form of business organization, the *corporation*.

MEANING OF CORPORATION

A corporation is a form of business organization usually created by the grant of a state *charter*. The corporation enables a group of individuals to operate as a single "artificial legal person." The corporation can sue and be sued, hire and fire, buy and sell, manufacture and trade.

ADVANTAGES OF INCORPORATION

1. Securing of Capital. By selling stocks and bonds to the public, the corporation can raise large sums of money. Stockholders are part owners of the corporation and share in the profits, which they receive as dividends. Bondholders are creditors who lend money to the corporation and receive interest.

2. Limited Liability. The personal assets of the part owners, or stockholders, cannot be seized in order to satisfy claims against the corporation. Even if the corporation goes bankrupt, the most that the part owners can lose is the money they had paid for the stock.

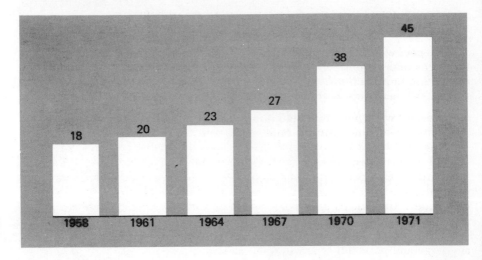

Capital Invested per Production Worker in Manufacturing (Thousands of Dollars)

3. Transferability of Shares. Investors may withdraw from the corporation simply by selling their shares of stock.

4. Perpetual Life. The life of the corporation is not affected by the death of any one of the part owners. The shares of the deceased person are transferred to the heirs, who thus become the new part owners.

DISADVANTAGES OF INCORPORATION

1. As a state-created entity, the corporation must make public its business and financial records by filing periodic reports.

2. As an "artificial legal person," the corporation is subject to taxes on its profits in addition to taxes paid by its individual part owners on their dividends. This is called "double taxation."

3. Most of our nation's corporations are small, but the corporate form has made possible the growth of business giants. There is no personal contact between the large corporation and its workers and customers.

TURN TO MONOPOLY

Following the Civil War, business leaders increasingly moved to combine competing corporations in order to control prices, production, and sales territory. Such control would enable them to eliminate competition, thereby approaching full control or *monopoly*. A company then could set high prices and increase profits at the expense of the consumer. In practice, corporations almost never achieved perfect monopoly.

MONOPOLISTIC PRACTICES IN THE 19TH CENTURY: ILLEGAL TODAY

1. The *pool* was an agreement, usually secret, among competing companies to fix prices and output, or to divide sales territory. In the 1870's and 1880's competing railroad lines often formed pools. By the Interstate Commerce Act (1887), railroad pools were declared illegal.

2. The *trust* was a more permanent consolidation than the pool. Stockholders of competing companies turned their stock over to a board of trustees and in exchange received trust certificates. In this way, the board of trustees gained full control and managed the member companies so as to eliminate competition. The Standard Oil Company (the forebear of several of today's leading oil companies) originated the trust arrangement with success, and it was imitated by other giant companies. After the passage of the Sherman Antitrust Act (1890), businessmen abandoned the trust and turned to other forms of consolidation.

The word "trust," however, remained part of our vocabulary, referring to any large and powerful business combination or corporation.

FORMS OF BUSINESS CONSOLIDATION IN THE 20TH CENTURY: LEGAL WITHIN LIMITS

1. The *holding company* buys sufficient voting stock in different companies, called *subsidiaries*, to be able to control them. Some complex forms of the holding company have been declared illegal, but many holding companies legally exist today.

2. The *interlocking directorate* is an arrangement in which one or more men serve on the boards of directors of several companies. Interlocking directorates are legal unless they tend to lessen competition.

3. The *merger* is the consolidation of two or more companies into a single corporation. The merger is legal unless it causes an unreasonable restraint of trade. It is the most common form of business consolidation today, as corporations try to achieve economy and diversify their interests. Giant corporations that have used the merger to branch out into unrelated fields are called *conglomerates*.

EXAMPLES OF BUSINESS CONSOLIDATION

1. Railroads

a. Cornelius Vanderbilt acquired the nickname "Commodore" and a fortune in steamboating, and then turned to railroads. He built the *New York Central* and by 1869 had combined a group of small lines into one railroad system running from New York City to Chicago. Vanderbilt improved the safety, comfort, and service of his railroad. However, he was disdainful of the public interest and of government regulations, once proclaiming, "What do I care for law? Hain't I got the power?"

b. James J. Hill built the *Great Northern Railway* westward from Minnesota. In 1893, after a series of mergers, his railroad reached the Pacific Coast. Hill did not receive any federal land grant or cash subsidies. To attract settlers to Great Northern territory, Hill farsightedly provided free transportation from the East, easy credit, and expert agricultural advice.

Later Hill battled another railroad magnate, *Edward Harriman*, for control of a competing road, the *Northern Pacific*. Hill was backed by the Morgan banking interests and Harriman by the Rockefeller banking interests. After a costly fight, the contestants agreed to compromise. They formed the *Northern Securities Company*, a holding company, to control the *Great Northern*, the *Northern Pacific*, and the *Chicago, Burlington, and Quincy*, a road that provided an entrance from the West into Chicago. In 1904 the Supreme Court ordered the Northern Securities Company dissolved as a violation of the Sherman Antitrust Act.

2. Oil. *John D. Rockefeller*, a food merchant, entered the oil-refining business and in 1870 formed the *Standard Oil Company of Ohio*. Rockefeller accumulated strong cash reserves, fought successful price wars, received secret railroad rebates on oil shipments, and, aided by the depression of 1873, ruthlessly drove out or bought out many competitors. By 1879 the Standard Oil Company controlled over 90 percent of the country's oil refineries. Rockefeller improved his product and distributed it efficiently.

In 1882 Rockefeller combined his various holdings into the *Standard Oil Trust*, but in 1890 it was ordered dissolved by the Ohio Supreme Court. Reorganized as a holding company, it was ordered dissolved in 1911 by the United States Supreme Court, which ruled that the 34 member companies had to function as separate units.

3. Steel. *Andrew Carnegie*, a railroad executive and an outstanding salesman, entered the steel business. He built a company that owned iron ore deposits in the Mesabi Range (Minnesota) near Lake Superior, steamships on the Great Lakes, and steel mills in Pittsburgh. He pioneered the use of the Bessemer process for making steel and improved the quality of steel. He undersold competitors and drove them out of business. By 1900 the *Carnegie Steel Company* was producing one-fourth of the country's steel.

To reduce competition, other steel companies planned to form a huge monopoly. *J. P. Morgan*, the investment banker, handled the project. He bought out Carnegie's interests for $500 million and in 1901 combined the various steel companies under a single holding company, the *United States Steel Corporation*. This first billion-dollar corporation in the United States controlled 60 percent of the nation's steel production.

4. Other Industries. Business leaders who formed consolidations in other industries were: *Gustavus Swift* and *Philip D. Armour*—meat-packing; *Charles A. Pillsbury*—flour-milling; *James B. Duke*—cigarette-manufacturing; *Andrew W. Mellon*—aluminum.

5. Evaluation and Comment. The business leaders of the post-Civil War era have been both praised and condemned. For destroying small companies, charging high prices, exploiting workers, manipulating stock, and corrupting government officials, they have been called "robber barons." For organizing new industries, providing better services, improving the quality of their products, supporting philanthropies, and hastening industrialization, they have been called "captains of industry."

Robert Heilbroner, the economist, in his engrossing study *The Making of Economic Society*, comments on the almost imperceptible process by which the captains of industry began to assume the functions of finance capitalists. He writes:

> The American captains of industry were not typically men whose leadership rested on inventive or engineering skills. With the growth of large-scale production, the engineering functions became the province of salaried production experts, of second-echelon plant managers. What was required now was the master touch in guiding industrial strategy, in making or breaking alliances, choosing salients for advance, or overseeing the logistics of the whole operation. More and more the great entrepreneurs were concerned with the strategy of finance, of competition, of sales, rather than with the cold technics of production itself.

ADVANTAGES OF BIG BUSINESS

1. Mass Production. Giant corporations reduced their fixed, or overhead, cost per unit by producing goods in large quantities. They introduced the most modern machinery, purchased raw materials in bulk at low prices, and utilized by-products. Most important they applied mass-production methods: *(a) Division of Labor.* The worker does not make the entire product but performs one small operation only. He can be trained for his job quickly. However, he never achieves varied skills and often finds his work monotonous. *(b) Standardization.* The various parts that go into making the finished product are standardized or *interchangeable.* This standardization enables workers easily to assemble the components into the finished product. *(c) Assembly Line.* The worker takes a position alongside a moving or conveyor belt which brings him the product being processed. The worker performs his small task as the belt moves the product to the next man for the next operation. The belt moves, at a steady pace, from worker to worker until the product is completely assembled. In the automobile industry, at the end of the assembly line, the completed cars are "gassed up" and driven away.

2. Wide Distribution. Large corporations increased their profits by using large-scale advertising and by selling their products throughout the nation. Their efforts to achieve wide product distribution have been assisted by new advertising media—radio and television, and by new transport facilities—steamboats, railroads, motor trucks, and freight airplanes.

3. Efficient Management. Large corporations could hire capable executives, maintain costly research laboratories, and raise capital for expansion.

ABUSES BY BIG BUSINESS

1. Elimination of Competition. Large corporations could afford local price wars and use other methods of "cutthroat competition" to drive out small businesses.

The mere fact that large corporations could sell at a lower price and even offer a superior product has had the effect of destroying the small businessman.

2. Power Over the Consumer. Once a large company achieved a degree of monopoly, it could force the consumer to pay high prices and accept inferior quality.

3. Exploitation of Workers. By achieving control of the labor market in some communities, large companies were in a position to pay low wages and keep workers from forming unions.

4. Influence Over the Government. Some unscrupulous businessmen have degraded the government by bribing politicians and buying the votes of legislators. By their great concentration of wealth, large corporations have exercised great influence over government policy.

Government and Big Business

GOVERNMENT POLICIES TOWARD BUSINESS

1. Freedom From Government Regulation (To the End of the 19th Century). The government followed a policy of fostering but not regulating business. The government maintained protective tariffs and provided business subsidies but otherwise practiced Adam Smith's laissez-faire policy—leaving business alone.

2. Regulation in the Interests of Society (Since the End of the 19th Century). In the post-Civil War period, giant corporations arose and restrained the free competition that was supposed to regulate the economy automatically and thereby benefit society. Big business gained dominance over the economy and committed abuses threatening the public health and welfare, and harming the interests of farmers, laborers, and small businessmen. An aroused people demanded government regulation of industry, a policy that was adopted gradually and that persists in increased measure to this day.

RAILROADS: THE FIRST REGULATED INDUSTRY

1. Railroad Abuses (In the Latter 19th Century)

  a. High Rates. (1) Each railroad, having a virtual monopoly over transportation in its territory, charged "what the traffic would bear." (2) Many railroads issued *watered stock* (stock in excess of the actual worth of the company) and charged high rates in order to pay dividends on their watered stock. (3) Railroads frequently entered into *pooling agreements* to divide business and raise rates. Since no other means of transportation could compete with railroads, shippers had to pay what the railroads charged.

  b. Discrimination Regarding Rates. (1) Railroads granted large shippers *rebates*, whereas small shippers—farmers and small businessmen—paid the full rate. (2) Railroads charged lower rates for freight hauled between big cities, where they faced competing lines, than for freight hauled to or from rural areas, where they faced no competition. As a result, a long haul often cost less than a short haul.

c. Political Corruption. Railroads unduly influenced state and federal politics by the bribery of legislators, campaign contributions to political parties, and free railroad passes to influential people.

Farmers, small merchants, small businessmen, and the general public protested these abuses. The Grange, an organization of farmers, secured several state regulatory laws. In 1886, in *Wabash vs. Illinois*, the Supreme Court declared state regulation of interstate railroads unconstitutional. (Check the Index for this case.)

2. Beginning of Federal Regulation: Interstate Commerce Act (1887)

a. Provisions. This act (1) forbade discrimination between persons in the form of special rates or rebates, (2) prohibited railroads from charging more for a short haul than for a long haul, (3) prohibited pooling, (4) ordered a ten-day notice and public posting of new railroad rates, (5) declared that railroad rates should be "reasonable and just," and (6) established an enforcement agency, the *Interstate Commerce Commission* (ICC).

b. Weaknesses. The ICC originally was handicapped by (1) the vague language of the law, (2) the complexity of the railroad business, (3) the shortage of qualified personnel to work for the commission, and (4) its inability to enforce its decisions without appealing to the courts, which tended to be sympathetic toward the railroads.

c. Significance. Nevertheless, the Interstate Commerce Act established the precedent of government regulation of private interstate business and paved the way for subsequent and stronger legislation.

3. Subsequent Regulation.
The ICC was strengthened by *(a)* the *Elkins Act* (1903), enabling the ICC to punish shippers as well as railroads engaged in rebating, *(b)* the *Hepburn Act* (1906), empowering it to set maximum railroad rates, and *(c)* the *Physical Valuation Act* (1913), empowering it to determine the value of railroad property as a basis for setting fair rates.

To meet the emergency of World War I, the government operated the railroads, coordinating service and eliminating duplication.

The *Transportation Act (Esch-Cummins Act)* of 1920 returned the railroads to private operation. It also empowered the ICC to *(a)* fix minimum as well as maximum rates, and *(b)* approve railroad pools and consolidations. Since many railroads were in financial trouble, the ICC was now concerned with the welfare not only of the shippers but also of the railroads.

4. Railroads Today.
Railroads no longer have a virtual monopoly, but face fierce competition from bus lines, trucking companies, and airlines. To meet such competition, railroads have requested that the ICC grant them greater flexibility in setting their own rates. Also, railroads have tried to improve their lines by purchasing fast, low-cost diesel engines as well as flatcars for carrying loaded trailers "piggyback."

To cut costs, many railroads have obtained permission from the ICC to abandon unprofitable lines, chiefly short-run commuter hauls. To eliminate duplication, various railroads have applied for ICC approval of mergers. The New York Central and Pennsylvania Railroads, with ICC approval, merged in 1968 but in 1970 went into bankruptcy.

To assure service between heavily populated cities, especially in the Northeast, Congress in the 1970's created and provided funds for the *National Railroad Passenger Corporation*, or *Amtrak*, and the *Consolidated Rail Corporation*, or *Conrail*.

REGULATION OF BIG BUSINESS

1. Sherman Antitrust Act (1890)

a. Provisions. To break up existing monopolies and compel competition, this law (1) declared illegal "every contract, combination in the form of trust or otherwise, or conspiracy, in restraint of trade," and (2) provided penalties for corporations and individuals that violated the act.

b. Weaknesses. In enforcing the law, the Department of Justice was handicapped by (1) the vague language of the law, (2) the ability of business leaders to use forms of combination other than the trust, (3) the lack of sufficient funds, personnel, and executive determination for enforcement, and (4) interpretations by the Supreme Court favoring big business. The Supreme Court held illegal only "unreasonable" restraint of trade, thereby establishing a loophole, called the *rule of reason.*

2. Theodore Roosevelt: "Trust Buster" (1901–1909).
Theodore Roosevelt, who pledged a *Square Deal* for all the people, was the first President who vigorously enforced the Sherman Act. Roosevelt believed that the growth of big business was inevitable. He approved "good" trusts, but he sought to destroy "bad" trusts. Roosevelt instituted over 40 antitrust cases. He won his most famous victory, by a 5-to-4 Supreme Court decision, against the *Northern Securities Company*, a railroad holding company that threatened to monopolize railroad service in the Northwest.

Roosevelt's successor, William Howard Taft, stepped up the government's trust busting by instituting some 90 antitrust suits.

3. Publicity: Muckrakers.
The trust-busting campaigns of Roosevelt and Taft were aided by a group of writers called *muckrakers*. To arouse the American people to demand reforms, they exposed the evils of big business.

Author	Major Work	Theme
Ida M. Tarbell	*History of the Standard Oil Company*	Ruthless practices of a gigantic monopoly
Frank Norris	*The Octopus*	Struggle of wheat farmers against the railroad
Gustavus Myers	*History of the Great American Fortunes*	Corruption and exploitation as practiced by leaders of big business
Ray Stannard Baker	*Railroads on Trial*	Railroad evils and abuses
Upton Sinclair	*The Jungle*	Disgusting practices of the meat-packing industry

The Jungle in particular aroused public opinion. In 1906 Congress inaugurated government protection of the consumer: *(a)* The *Meat Inspection Act* set up sanitary regulations for meat packers and provided for federal inspection of meat-packing plants. *(b)* The *Pure Food and Drug Act* forbade the manufacture, transportation, and sale of adulterated and poisonous foods and drugs.

4. Woodrow Wilson and Business Regulation. Woodrow Wilson, who pledged the American people a *New Freedom*, secured Congressional enactment of the following business reform laws:

a. Clayton Antitrust Act (1914). This law attempted to strengthen the Sherman Antitrust Act by listing specific illegal practices and combinations: (1) price discrimination toward purchasers, (2) "tie-in" contracts by which a merchant could buy goods from a company only on condition that he would not handle the products of that company's competitors, and (3) certain types of holding companies and interlocking directorates. The law declared these practices and combinations unlawful if they tended "to lessen competition or create a monopoly." This proviso limited the effectiveness of the Clayton Act. As with the Sherman Act, the Supreme Court held illegal only restraint of trade considered "unreasonable." (The Clayton Act prohibited the use of antitrust laws against farm cooperatives and labor unions.)

b. Federal Trade Commission Act (1914). This act established the Federal Trade Commission (FTC) to receive reports from and make investigations of business firms. The FTC enforces the Clayton Act prohibitions of certain business practices and seeks to prevent other unfair methods of competition.

The FTC ruled the following practices as unfair: (1) misbranding and adulteration of goods, (2) false and misleading advertising, (3) spying and bribery to secure trade secrets, and (4) closely imitating a competitor's product. To halt such practices, the FTC issues *cease and desist* orders. FTC orders may be challenged by the firm involved and subjected to court review.

Industrial Growth and Problems Since World War I

BUSINESS FOLLOWING WORLD WAR I: FROM BOOM TO BUST

1. Boom Conditions (To 1929)

a. Continued Growth of Big Business. During the war and in the prosperous postwar years, business leaders modernized their plants and utilized the newest techniques of production. They promoted business consolidations at a rapid pace by instituting mergers and forming holding companies, thereby further concentrating industrial and financial wealth. The government ignored this process of consolidation by failing to initiate new antitrust suits.

b. Scientific Management. Inspired by the work of industrial engineer *Frederick Taylor*, corporate executives applied the ideas of scientific management: efficient plant organization and time-and-motion studies. Factories lowered production costs per unit and increased productivity per worker.

c. Age of the Automobile. Just prior to World War I, Henry Ford revolutionized the automobile industry by applying the methods of mass production. Ford's efficiency in production permitted him to reduce the price of his cars so that they could be bought by millions of Americans. After the war, the American people found that a car was a necessity, and auto production mounted rapidly.

The growth of the automobile industry had widespread effects. Automobile factories required raw materials: rubber, steel, aluminum, glass, and plastics. New enterprises appeared: gasoline and repair stations, garages and parking lots. The popularity of the automobile led to the construction of a vast system of new and improved highways.

d. **New Industries.** When chemicals from Germany were cut off during World War I, American industrialists expanded the domestic chemical industry. After the war, the government assigned confiscated German patents to American chemical companies and set high tariffs against chemical imports, both measures aiding the growth of the American chemical industry.

Entertainment-seeking Americans delighted in the growth of movies (first "silents" and then "talkies") and radio. Travelers took to a new and faster means of transportation, the airplane. Invented by *Wilbur* and *Orville Wright* in 1903, the airplane was still in the early stages of commercial development. Homeowners used more electricity to power new inventions: refrigerator, radio, phonograph, vacuum cleaner, and toaster.

2. Bust: The Great Depression. In 1929 the American economy entered its most severe depression. By 1933 American business had reached its lowest ebb. (Check the Index for "Great Depression.") This depression sapped the belief in a self-regulating economic system and strengthened the trend toward regulated capitalism.

THE NEW DEAL AND BUSINESS

1. Background. In the 1932 Presidential election, *Franklin D. Roosevelt*, the Democratic candidate, ran against the incumbent Herbert Hoover. The two men disagreed basically regarding the government's role in the economy. Roosevelt insisted that the government should take firm steps to insure the well-being of the people. He believed that the government must accept social responsibility. Hoover argued for only limited government interference in the economy. Hoover credited America's greatness to free enterprise and "rugged individualism." He feared that excessive government interference would disrupt the market economy, endanger recovery from the depression, and threaten personal liberty. Roosevelt won the election overwhelmingly and carried his party into control of Congress.

2. Philosophy of the New Deal. Roosevelt expressed his concern for the "forgotten man at the bottom of the economic pyramid" and pledged the American people a "new deal." Roosevelt favored bold experimentation: "Above all, try something." He adopted the pragmatic or practical approach of trial and error. Roosevelt summarized *New Deal* goals in three words: (1) *relief*—to assist distressed persons, (2) *recovery*—to lift the nation out of the depression, and (3) *reform*—to eliminate abuses in the economy.

The New Deal marked two significant changes in the relationship of the government to the economy: (1) By committing the government to an ever-increasing role in the economy, the New Deal completed the transition from laissez-faire to regulated capitalism. (2) By hiring many people to enforce complex economic laws and to staff numerous existing and new government agencies, the New Deal created a powerful and influential bureaucracy.

3. National Industrial Recovery Act (1933). *(a) Provisions.* The *National Industrial Recovery Act* (NIRA) (1) established the *National Recovery Administration* (NRA), (2) empowered the NRA to supervise industry in drawing up "codes of fair competition" providing for minimum wages, maximum hours, price-fixing, production controls, and fair methods of competition, and (3) exempted agreements made under the NIRA from the Sherman and Clayton Antitrust Acts. Thus the NIRA allowed monopolistic practices but kept them subject to government control. *(b) Business Response.* The NIRA was at first welcomed enthusiastically, but it soon drew much criticism. While small businessmen complained that the codes favored the large corporations, large businessmen complained about government "regimentation." *(c) Held Unconstitutional.* In 1935 the NIRA was declared unconstitutional by the Supreme Court in the *Schechter Case.* (Check the Index for this case.) The Antitrust Division of the Department of Justice thereafter renewed enforcement of the Sherman and Clayton Acts.

4. Other New Deal Efforts Affecting Business. *(a) Unemployment.* Three agencies—*Civilian Conservation Corps* (CCC), *Public Works Administration* (PWA), and *Works Progress Administration* (WPA)—provided unemployed persons with work on government projects. *(b) Electric Power.* The *Tennessee Valley Authority* (TVA) was created as a government corporation to generate and sell hydroelectric power. The *Rural Electrification Administration* (REA) provided municipal and cooperative utility companies with loans to bring electric power to rural areas not served by private utilities. *(c) Banking and Finance.* The *Federal Deposit Insurance Corporation* (FDIC) guaranteed depositors against loss, up to a maximum amount, in case of bank failure. The *Securities and Exchange Commission* (SEC) regulated the issuing and trading of stocks and bonds. *(d) Labor.* The *National Labor Relations Board* (NLRB) guaranteed labor the right of collective bargaining. The *Fair Labor Standards Act* set minimum wages and maximum hours of labor. *(e) Consumer.* The *Food, Drug, and Cosmetic Act* strengthened government regulation of product labeling and advertising. (Check the Index for these agencies and laws.)

BIG BUSINESS AND WORLD WAR II (1939–1945)

1. "Miracle of Production." With the onset of World War II in 1939 and the fall of France to the Germans in 1940, many Americans realized our shocking military unpreparedness. Congress authorized tremendous expenditures for the production of military equipment. When the Japanese attacked Pearl Harbor in 1941, America was drawn actively into the war. American industrialists, displaying great managerial ability and drawing upon the pool of unemployed workers, fulfilled the nation's war needs. From 1940 to 1945 industry almost doubled the production of manufactured goods, thereby supplying our military forces and providing huge quantities of equipment for our allies. American industry significantly helped win the war.

2. Increased Government Control. To mobilize and coordinate American industry, the government established the following agencies: (*a*) The *War Production Board* (WPB) directed the conversion of industry to wartime production, granted essential industries priorities on raw materials, and brought about the construction of new factories. These new plants increased the production of aluminum, steel, airplanes, and ships, and initiated the production of synthetic rubber and of materials for atomic research. (*b*) The *Office of Price Administration* (OPA) combatted price rises and inflation by setting price ceilings and by rationing scarce goods. (*c*) The *War Manpower Commission* (WMC) directed labor to essential war industries. (*d*) The *War Labor Board* (WLB) settled labor-management disputes.

3. Evaluation. Credit for America's "miracle of production" in World War II has been given to the managerial ability of private industry as well as to the centralized planning and controls exercised by government agencies. The American people regained their faith, severely shaken by the depression of 1929, in American industrial leadership.

Industrial Growth and Problems Since World War II

CONTINUED ECONOMIC CONCENTRATION

Since World War II, the trend toward bigness has continued as corporations have actively pursued mergers. While permitting most mergers, the government has enforced the antitrust laws against unreasonable restraint of trade.

Large American companies have acquired or established subsidiaries in foreign countries and have become known as *multinational corporations.*

CONTINUED TECHNOLOGICAL PROGRESS

1. Electronics Industry and Automation. During the war the electronics industry developed many significant new products, such as high-fidelity sound reproduction equipment and television sets. Manufacturing and mining firms employed *automation,* the use of automatic devices, chiefly electronic, to

There seems to be no letup
(*Partymiller in the Gazette and Daily, York, Pa.*)

operate machines. Many businesses employed *computers* to perform routine clerical and mathematical tasks. (Check the Index for "Automation.")

2. Other Industries. Chemical manufacturers produced many new synthetic fibers and plastics. Airlines employing modern jets provided faster, more comfortable service, and attracted large numbers of passengers. Drug companies developed radioactive isotopes to diagnose body ills. Public utilities turned increasingly to the newest source of energy, atomic power.

CONTINUED ECONOMIC GROWTH: AS MEASURED BY GNP

1. Gross National Product (GNP)

a. Meaning. To analyze the health of our economic system, economists have devised various statistical tools. *Gross national product* (GNP), one such tool, measures the output of goods produced and services rendered each year in total money value. Computed by the Department of Commerce, GNP includes the purchases of goods and services by the consumer, by industry, and by governmental units as well as net exports of goods and services to foreign countries.

b. Limitations. (1) Since GNP is a measure of money value, rising prices due to inflation may cause an increase in GNP in terms of current dollars without any corresponding increase in output. To offset this limitation, economists may measure the current GNP in terms of prices that prevailed in a base year, the result being known as the GNP in *constant dollars.* (2) GNP may increase as a result of rising population, which provides more workers to produce goods and

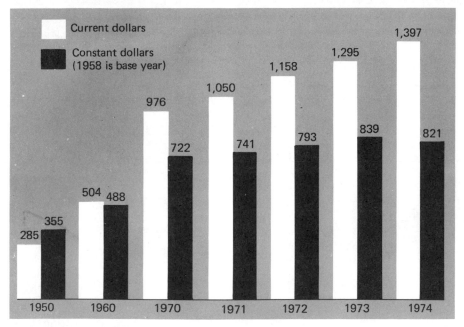

Gross National Product, in Current Dollars and Constant Dollars, 1950–1974
(In Billions)

services. To offset this limitation, economists divide total GNP by the national population and arrive at a figure known as GNP *per capita*, or per person. (3) GNP fails to measure many important factors: (a) social desirability of goods —GNP deals only with the monetary weight of a machine gun used for destruction and a bicycle used for pleasure, (b) quality of goods—GNP does not differentiate between shoddy goods and quality products, (c) for whom the goods are intended—GNP does not indicate if goods are distributed inequitably: too much to a small group of rich people and too little to a large group of impoverished people; or too much for military purposes and too little for consumer needs, (d) non-economic goods—GNP does not measure the value of leisure time, of a beautiful sunset, or of a swim in a clean lake, and (e) the social costs—GNP includes the money value of automobiles produced but neglects the cost in terms of air pollution that will result from the gasoline fumes.

2. GNP and Post-World War II Economic Growth. Subject to these limitations, GNP has been used to measure the post-World War II behavior of our economy. From 1950 to 1974, the GNP increased from $212 billion to $1,397 billion, or almost six-fold; in terms of constant dollars with 1958 the base year, the GNP increased from $355 billion to $821 billion, or more than double.

Business prospered, profits rose, and production increased. Industry provided jobs for more workers, and unemployment remained relatively low. Business downturns, or recessions, were comparatively short-lived and mild.

CONSUMER PROTECTION

1. Role of Consumers. According to market economy theory, "consumers rule." They are the ultimate judges of the goods produced and the services offered. Every time consumers make purchases, they are voting in favor of the selected products and against competing choices. By not purchasing a new car offered by a major auto manufacturer in the post-World War II years, consumers voted their disapproval, causing the company to withdraw the car from the market and to absorb many millions of dollars of financial losses. Conversely, by purchasing a new orange juice product that had a better taste than others on the market, consumers assured the success of the new producing company.

In contrast to the above description, many economists hold that "consumers are bewildered." They are bewildered by a barrage of advertising that often appeals to personal emotions regarding health, beauty, and popularity and utilizes endorsements, largely irrelevant, of leading sports and movie figures. They are bewildered by a multiplicity of fabrics—cotton, wool, orlon, nylon, polyester, dacron, acrilan—not knowing the advantages and disadvantages of each fabric. They are bewildered by the complexity of products and are unable to distinguish between superior and inferior merchandise. They are bewildered by the fine print in warranties, often so tiny as to be hard to read and inexplicable when read. In this state of bewilderment, consumers have made purchases forewarned only by the saying "Let the buyer beware." Until recently, consumers have lacked any powerful organization or "political clout" to secure government action for their protection.

LET THE
BUYER
BEWARE

NUTRITION

BIOCHEMISTRY

HOME REPAIRS

PRACTICAL ENGINEERING

POLLUTANTS

INTERNAL COMBUSTION ENGINE

What every young girl
should know
(*Crawford. Reprinted by
permission of Newspaper
Enterprise Association*)

2. Efforts at Consumer Protection

a. Private, Local, and State Action. Help for consumers has come from private efforts: (1) *Consumers Union* tests and rates products, which data are published in its own monthly magazine, (2) *Better Business Bureaus* advise consumers regarding the reliability of local business concerns and investigate complaints, and (3) *Ralph Nader,* a lawyer and self-appointed crusader for consumers, has investigated various products and used publicity to spur government action to help the consumer. Nader has been assisted in his efforts by volunteer college students, sometimes called *Nader's Raiders.*

Help for consumers has also come from local and state governments through laws and agencies: requiring honest weights and measures, the proper dating and grading of milk, and sanitary inspection of restaurants.

b. Early Federal Action. The first federal law to protect consumers, passed during the Theodore Roosevelt administration, was the *Pure Food and Drug Act* (1906). It was not strengthened for over 30 years. During the New Deal, Congress passed the *Food, Drug, and Cosmetic Act* (1938) empowering government agencies to (*a*) prevent adulteration, misbranding, and false advertising, (*b*) require manufacturers to list the ingredients of their products, (*c*) regulate cosmetics as well as food and drugs, and (*d*) require adequate testing of new drugs. The *Drug Industry Act* (1962) gave the Food and Drug Administration (FDA) more power over testing, advertising, and prescribing of new drugs. This law was passed amidst publicity caused by the FDA ban on the sale of a new sleeping pill, thalidomide, and the subsequent birth of deformed babies to European mothers who had taken thalidomide.

"What are you going to do about this wheel nut?" (*Crockett in the Washington Star*)

3. **Recent Federal Action.** In recent years, the federal government has acted vigorously to protect consumers. The *Truth in Packaging Act* (1966) outlawed deceptive containers, required simple and easily read labels stating weight or volume, and set standards for such words as "small," "large," and "family-size." The government agency empowered to enforce this law was the Federal Trade Commission (FTC). The *Traffic Safety Act* (1966) created a *National Traffic Safety Agency* to establish and enforce minimum safety standards in the design and equipment of new automobiles. This law was passed after Ralph Nader published *Unsafe at Any Speed*, a book that attacked the automobile industry for emphasizing style, power, and speed while ignoring economy and safety. The *Meat Inspection Act* (1967) offered federal funds to the states to improve their inspection of intrastate meat packers. It empowered federal agents to inspect packing plants in states not complying with federal standards. The *Truth in Lending Act* (1968) required retailers and lenders to inform most consumers of the true cost of credit in dollars and in annual interest rates. The *Wholesome Poultry Act* (1968) authorized the Agriculture Department to help the states set and enforce poultry inspection standards.

In 1971 President Nixon established the *Office of Consumer Affairs* to handle consumer complaints, further consumer education, and press for consumer legislation. The *Consumer Products Safety Act* (1972) created the Consumer Products Safety Commission to enforce safety standards for household items such as ladders, power tools, electric heaters, pressure cookers, and toys.

In 1976 the Supreme Court declared void—a violation of free speech—state regulations prohibiting pharmacists from advertising prescription prices. Subsequent Supreme Court and Federal Trade Commission rulings have allowed other professionals—lawyers, engineers, dentists, and doctors—to advertise their services.

SOCIAL ROLE OF BUSINESS

Business executives increasingly showed concern not only for corporations and stockholders, but for all American society. A considerable number encouraged their corporations to provide grants to institutions of higher learning. They also supported retraining programs for displaced workers, participated in studies on the effects of automation, and advanced civil rights by hiring members of minority groups. Businessmen cooperated with the government to further economic and social progress. The leaders of industry realized that our capitalist economy must eliminate such problems as ignorance and poverty.

MULTIPLE-CHOICE QUESTIONS

1. Which factor had *least* to do with the industrialization of the United States in the 19th century?   (1) inventions   (2) foreign demand for American manufactures   (3) abundant natural resources   (4) Constitutional protection of private property
2. In the United States, which was a result of the Industrial Revolution?   (1) elimination of class distinctions   (2) movement of people from the cities to rural areas   (3) fewer booms and busts in the business cycle   (4) increased production of consumer goods
3. Which has been a significant change brought about by industrialization?   (1) The family unit was strengthened.   (2) The urban-rural population balance was changed.   (3) Commerce ceased to be important.   (4) The number of new products decreased.
4. "In our economic system, specialization in industry serves an important function." The *best* argument to support this statement is that specialization   (1) utilizes all the available labor supply   (2) promotes individual pride in accomplishment   (3) encourages efficient production through division of labor   (4) causes the cost of production to rise in the long run.
5. Which characterized big business during the period 1850–1890?   (1) demand for government action to end immigration   (2) use of organizational power to control prices and eliminate competition   (3) pressure on the government for action to prevent inflation   (4) opposition to the introduction of labor-saving devices
6. Industrial leaders contributed to economic growth during the last half of the 19th century by their willingness to   (1) support low-tariff legislation in order to expand exports   (2) accept legislation designed to increase competition   (3) bargain collectively with elected representatives of their employees   (4) reinvest profits in expansion.
7. The *primary* purpose of the Interstate Commerce Act was to   (1) grant land to the railroads   (2) regulate railroad rates   (3) establish government ownership of railroads   (4) supervise interstate truck and bus lines.
8. Which pairs an industrial leader with his industry?   (1) Cornelius Vanderbilt—railroads   (2) Andrew Carnegie—meat-packing   (3) Andrew Mellon—automobiles   (4) Philip Armour—steel
9. The *most* important purpose of the Sherman Antitrust Act (1890) was to   (1) encourage competition in business   (2) improve relations between big business and the government   (3) improve working conditions in factories   (4) prevent business from becoming more powerful than labor.
10. An important effect of the Sherman Antitrust Act was that it   (1) restored active competition   (2) led to the passage of the National Banking Act   (3) corrected the weaknesses of the Clayton Antitrust Act   (4) caused a change in the forms and techniques of business consolidation.
11. The attitude of Theodore Roosevelt toward business was that the federal government should   (1) own public utilities   (2) follow a policy of laissez-faire   (3) eliminate bad business practices   (4) leave the regulation of railroads to the states.

12. Which action was hastened *largely* because public opinion was aroused by a contemporary novel? (1) ratification of the Sixteenth (Income Tax) Amendment (2) establishment of the Interstate Commerce Commission (3) passage of the Sherman Antitrust Act (4) enactment of the Meat Inspection Act of 1906

13. By the "rule of reason," the Supreme Court affected the powers of Congress by (1) making a distinction between commerce and manufacturing (2) declaring that any reasonable regulation was Constitutional (3) increasing the powers of the federal regulatory commissions (4) assuming the power to decide whether or not a business combination was legal.

14. The Clayton Antitrust Act strengthened the Sherman Antitrust Act by (1) forbidding corporate mergers (2) placing greater restrictions on labor unions (3) listing specific illegal methods of competition (4) prohibiting false advertising.

15. According to the Federal Trade Commission, which is an example of an unfair business practice? (1) creating a subsidiary corporation (2) lowering prices to meet competition (3) incorporating in one state and doing business in another (4) closely imitating goods sold by a competitor

16. Which was an important reason why President Herbert Hoover was slow to apply relief measures in the Great Depression? He was (1) preoccupied with foreign affairs (2) unable to achieve currency reform (3) reluctant to use the surplus in the Treasury (4) of the opinion that government interference in the economy would prolong the depression.

17. According to its supporters, one of the greatest contributions of the New Deal was that it (1) retained the principle of the balanced budget (2) weakened the power of the federal government (3) preserved the capitalistic system by making necessary reforms (4) prohibited speculation in corporate stocks and bonds.

18. Opponents of Franklin D. Roosevelt criticized his New Deal program on the grounds that it (1) created a powerful federal bureaucracy (2) weakened the power of the Chief Executive (3) failed to include labor legislation (4) promoted the ideas of laissez-faire economics.

19. The New Deal confirmed a change in American political thinking because it advanced the principle that (1) a public office is a public trust (2) government intervention in business should be kept to a minimum (3) the government should play a significant part in solving social and economic problems (4) the government should not become involved in building hydroelectric power plants.

20. Which philosophy could *best* be used to support the role of our national government in economic affairs since 1930? (1) Marxist philosophy of government control over basic economic decisions (2) laissez-faire philosophy of no government interference in economic affairs (3) Jeffersonian philosophy of little government participation in economic affairs (4) Hamiltonian philosophy of government participation in economic and fiscal affairs

21. The gross national product (GNP) of the United States is a measure of the (1) total annual production of our mines and factories (2) increase in the number of people living in cities (3) extent to which natural resources have been used up (4) total money value of all the goods and services produced in a year.

22. In order to interpret the significance of the gross national product (GNP), economists must take into consideration the (1) changes in price levels (2) interest charges on the national debt (3) total amount collected in taxes (4) type of economic system.

23. If a country's population increases at the same rate as its GNP, the net effect is to (1) nullify any benefits from gains in production (2) decrease the standard of living of the population (3) increase the standard of living of the population (4) increase productivity because of a larger market.

24. The role of Ralph Nader in the consumer movement today is *most* similar to the career of (1) John D. Rockefeller (2) Ida Tarbell (3) Woodrow Wilson (4) Thomas Edison.

25. Which statement regarding consumers is *most* valid? (1) Since consumers can always refuse to buy, they have no need of government protection. (2) Before World War II, the federal government had not passed any consumer protection laws. (3) In the 1960's, the federal government passed laws to require truth in packaging and in lending. (4) Federal safety standards for automobiles are unnecessary as long as the price of gasoline remains high.

26. "When one devotes his property to a use in which the public has an interest, he . . . must submit [it] to be controlled by the public." This quotation can be cited in support of (1) taxes on real estate (2) income taxes (3) the right of eminent domain (4) the right to regulate railroads.

27. "The less government interferes with private pursuits, the better for the general prosperity." The author of this statement would *most* likely have favored the (1) economic policies of the "welfare state" (2) antitrust legislation of the United States (3) mercantilist doctrine of Great Britain (4) philosophy of "rugged individualism."

28. An increase in the Gross National Product indicates an increase in (1) real income (2) per capita income (3) the value of goods and services produced (4) the production of civilian rather than military goods.

ESSAY QUESTIONS

1. Various factors have influenced economic growth in the United States. Show in *one* way how *each* of the following factors *either* stimulated *or* retarded economic growth in the United States: (a) an important invention or discovery (b) a specific condition in Europe (c) a policy of the United States government (d) a religious attitude held by a group of Americans (e) a policy of a captain of industry (f) a specific war.

2. Give *one* reason to explain why you agree *or* disagree with *each* of the following statements relating to the United States economy: (a) The small businessman must inevitably disappear. (b) The Sherman and Clayton antitrust laws have proved effective. (c) Since consumers benefit from a competition among corporations, consumers do not need the protection of the government. (d) Corporation executives today are showing concern for the overall welfare of American society. (e) Railroads today must be prevented from consolidating and compelled to compete. (f) Gross national product (GNP) is a valid measure of the people's standard of living.

3. The policy of the federal government toward business has varied from one period in American history to another. (a) Describe *two* ways in which the federal government aided the growth of business during the period 1865–1890. (b) Explain how *one* federal law passed during the 20th century attempted to regulate business. (c) Discuss *two* basic reasons for the change by the federal government from a policy of aiding the growth of business to a policy of regulating business. (d) Show *two* ways in which business has helped the United States assume a position of leadership in world affairs.

4. To answer this question, refer to the cartoon "What every young girl should know" on page 319. (a) Identify the problem depicted in this cartoon. (b) What is the attitude of the cartoonist regarding this problem? (c) The reaction to this cartoon of a consumer advocate would probably differ from that of a corporation president. For *either one*, describe what you believe would be the reaction and why. (d) Discuss *two* ways in which the federal government has attempted to deal with the problem depicted in the cartoon.

5. The United States now has the highest standard of living ever attained by any society. Giving *two* specific examples, explain how *each* of the following has helped to bring about this high standard of living: (a) labor supply (b) inventions (c) government policies (d) natural resources (e) techniques of mass production.

5. Farmers Struggle for an Increased Share of the National Income

The Agricultural Revolution

BEFORE THE AGRICULTURAL REVOLUTION: COLONIAL FARMERS

Colonial farmers employed primitive implements and methods. They had only a few simple, crudely constructed tools: the rake, hoe, scythe, and wooden plow. They cultivated their farms inefficiently because they (1) had little knowledge of proper soil care, and (2) could secure additional fertile land at low cost. Although they worked long hours, usually at exhausting tasks, their harvests remained relatively small; productivity, or output per worker, was low. Agricultural methods changed little from parent to child.

AGRICULTURAL REVOLUTION: BRIEF DESCRIPTION

1. Meaning. The term *Agricultural Revolution* refers to the change from primitive to modern farming methods: the use of farm machinery and scientific agriculture. In the United States, the Agricultural Revolution began early in the 19th century and continues, at a rapid pace, to this very day.

2. Farm Machinery. For centuries the farmer's basic tool had been the wooden plow. In 1797 *Charles Newbold* invented a cast-iron plow. In 1814 *Jethro Wood* designed a cast-iron plow that turned soil more easily and more deeply than any plow used before. Still more advanced plows were designed by *John Deere*, who in 1837 invented the self-cleaning steel plow, and *James Oliver*, who in 1877 perfected a plow made from chilled iron.

A pioneer in devising other farm machinery was *Cyrus McCormick*. In 1831 he invented a reaper that cut grain many times faster than a scythe. Other agricultural inventions included the thresher to separate grain from the stalk; the harvester to cut and bind the grain; the combine to cut, thresh, and sack the grain; the tractor to pull equipment through the field; the corn planter; the potato digger; the electric milker; and the cotton picker.

3. Scientific Agriculture. Agricultural research led to *(a)* the rotation of crops and the use of artificial fertilizer to renew soil fertility, *(b)* contour plowing to prevent soil erosion, *(c)* the drainage of swamps and the irrigation of dry land to change useless land to land suitable for crops, *(d)* insecticides and germicides to combat insect pests and plant diseases, *(e)* breeding of plants and animals to produce better offspring, *(f)* new uses for agricultural products, and *(g)* processing of canned, frozen, and powdered foods.

EFFECTS OF THE AGRICULTURAL REVOLUTION

1. Proportional Decrease in Farm Population. In proportion to the entire nation, our farm population decreased from 80 percent in 1860 to 40 percent in

1900. Nevertheless, farmers produced enough to feed our growing population and, in addition, provided surpluses for export.

2. Increased Production. Farmers increased their output tremendously, in terms of both output per worker and total output. From 1860 to 1900, total cotton production rose almost threefold and total wheat production fourfold.

3. Increased Mechanization. As machines took over the heavy, back-breaking tasks, farmers' work became less wearisome, but they had to learn the mechanical skills of operating and maintaining their machines.

4. End of Farm Isolation. With the invention of the telephone and the automobile, farmers came into closer contact with the world around them. They no longer lived in isolation.

5. Shift From Self-Sufficient to Commercial Farming. Until the middle of the 19th century, most farmers were self-sufficient, or subsistence, farmers. Using family labor, they raised the food for their own tables, and produced their own clothes, furniture, and implements. Many farmers also raised crops for sale. Increasingly after the Civil War, farmers became less self-sufficient and more commercial. They raised large quantities of a few staple crops—such as corn, cotton, or wheat. They sold their crops either to middlemen or directly to industrial enterprises; and from industry or retail distributors, they purchased needed supplies.

6. Problems Facing Commercial Farmers as Businessmen. *(a) Credit.* Farmers often needed long-term loans to purchase land, livestock, and machinery, and short-term loans to sustain them until harvesttime. *(b) Labor.* Farmers employed full-time hired hands and, at peak seasons, migratory labor. *(c) Production.* Farmers sought maximum harvests at minimum cost. Since they hired workers and used expensive machinery, farmers achieved greater efficiency by operating large farms. The number of small farms, consequently, steadily decreased. *(d) Prices.* Farmers experienced good or bad times depending upon the price their products commanded in the marketplace. *(e) Supplies.* Farmers relied upon industry for manufactured goods and upon other farmers for foodstuffs.

Agriculture From the Civil War to World War I

AGRICULTURAL PROSPERITY DURING THE CIVIL WAR

Northern and Western farmers experienced heavy demand for foodstuffs for the Union armed forces and for the thriving industrial cities. Farmers brought increased acreage under cultivation, employed more machines, and enjoyed relatively high agricultural prices.

COMPLAINTS OF FARMERS FOLLOWING THE CIVIL WAR

1. Low Agricultural Prices. After the Civil War the demand for agricultural produce declined and prices fell. American farmers also faced increased competition in world markets from newly plowed lands in Argentina, Australia, and

Canada. Nevertheless, American farmers continued to bring more land under cultivation and to expand their output.

Wheat farmers in 1866 received more than $1.50 per bushel, but in 1894 received less than $.70. Corn and cotton farmers suffered similar sharp price declines. With low prices, farmers had great difficulty earning a living.

2. Insufficient and Expensive Credit. Since farmers were considered poor credit risks, banks were reluctant to grant them loans. Despite state laws prohibiting usury, farmers often had to pay excessive interest rates, as high as 25 percent per year. Farmers unable to meet their mortgage payments lost their homes and farms.

3. High Rates Charged by Middlemen. Farmers complained that they received only about half the price that city consumers paid for agricultural produce. Farmers blamed this situation on the high rates charged by middlemen: grain storage elevators, packinghouses, insurance companies, wholesale distributors, and especially the railroads. Since each railroad had a virtual monopoly over the transportation of crops from the small farm-towns along its tracks, farmers endured poor service and exorbitant rates. The rule that guided railroads in determining their rates was "what the traffic will bear."

4. High Industrial Prices. While farmers received low agricultural prices, they paid dearly for manufactured goods. The farmers blamed high industrial prices upon (a) high tariff rates, which kept out many foreign goods and thus protected American manufacturers from foreign competition, and (b) the growth of business monopoly, which curtailed domestic competition.

AGRARIAN CRUSADE (1865 to 1900)

To improve their economic conditions, farmers undertook an *agrarian crusade.* They joined in organizations—the Grange and the Populist party—to demand help from the state and federal governments. These movements signaled the beginning of a significant change in the thinking of American farmers: away from the doctrine of laissez-faire and toward the doctrine of government responsibility for the economic well-being of the people.

GRANGER MOVEMENT

1. Granger Laws. The Patrons of Husbandry, or *National Grange*, founded by *Oliver H. Kelley* in 1867, was an organization of local farmers' clubs. As farmers became discontented with their economic conditions, they joined their local Granges, and these became active in state politics. Farmers elected Granger spokesmen to state legislatures, and several Midwestern states passed *Granger laws* regulating the rates and practices of grain elevators and railroads. However, in *Wabash vs. Illinois* (1886), the Supreme Court ruled that, since railroads were engaged in interstate commerce, they were not subject to regulation by the states.

2. Granger Cooperatives. To eliminate the profits of middlemen, the Grangers established *cooperatives*, or *"co-ops."* Owned and operated by the farmers, these organizations were to do the middleman's work: grading, packing,. selling, and shipping crops, and buying farm equipment and other goods at wholesale prices. The profits that the cooperatives earned were to be distributed to their farmer owners. These early "co-ops" failed, in part because of insufficient capital and inexperienced management.

3. Lasting Contributions. The Grange *(a)* taught farmers to work together to solve their common problems, *(b)* hastened federal railroad regulation, which started in 1887 with the Interstate Commerce Act, *(c)* stimulated the development of mail-order houses, such as Montgomery Ward and Sears Roebuck, to compete with local merchants, *(d)* paved the way for the successful present-day farm cooperatives, and *(e)* still serves rural communities today by providing social activities—meetings, lectures, picnics—and by lobbying in behalf of farmers.

FARMERS DEMAND INFLATION

To arrest the downward trend in agricultural prices after the Civil War, farmers demanded cheap money, or inflation. Cheapening the value of money would increase prices and ease the repayment of debt. For example, if wheat sold at $1 per bushel, a farmer would need 5000 bushels to pay off a $5000 mortgage debt. However, at an inflated price of $2 per bushel, he would need only 2500 bushels—half the amount—to pay off the same debt. True, the farmer would have to pay more for his manufactured goods, but he would benefit overall. For, while he received higher prices for his agricultural produce, the amount of his debt remained fixed. Since cheap money could best be attained by having the government increase the amount of currency in circulation, the farmers supported the movement for the free coinage of silver.

SILVER MOVEMENT

1. Crime of '73. For years the federal government used two metals, silver and gold, for coinage—a monetary practice called *bimetallism*. The government set the ratio between silver and gold at 16 to 1; that is, the government considered 16 ounces of silver to be worth 1 ounce of gold. Since private silversmiths needed silver commercially and offered a slightly higher price, the government received very little silver for coinage. So Congress passed the *Coinage Act* in 1873, ending the coinage of silver money, that is, *demonetizing* silver. Shortly afterwards, when miners discovered rich deposits of silver in Nevada and Colorado, the market price of silver fell sharply. Silver interests, which now wanted to sell their silver to the government, vigorously denounced the demonetization of silver as the *Crime of '73*.

2. Silver Purchase Acts (1878, 1890). Silver interests demanded that the government resume the coinage of silver at the ratio of 16 to 1, and their demand received the support of the nation's farmers. The political alliance of farmers and silver interests mustered sufficient strength in Congress to pass the *Bland-Allison Act* (1878). This law required the government to purchase and coin silver in limited quantities. The law did little to relieve the money shortage, and farmers and silver interests agitated for a further expansion of silver coinage.

Congress passed the *Sherman Silver Purchase Act* (1890), which increased the amount of silver that the government was required to buy. Like the Bland-Allison Act, it did not halt the decline of agricultural prices.

3. Effects of Silver Purchases on Currency. So much silver was now being mined that its value rapidly declined. It was now advantageous to redeem silver coin and paper money for gold. By 1893 these redemptions reduced the government's gold reserves to a bare minimum. Many people believed that the Treasury would soon be unable to redeem silver currency for gold and that the country would have to go off the gold standard.

CLEVELAND PROTECTS THE GOLD STANDARD

In 1893, the United States suffered a severe depression. President Grover Cleveland, a conservative Eastern Democrat, blamed the depression as well as gold reserve losses upon a single cause: the government's purchase of silver. He claimed that, by paying out gold for silver, the nation had drained its gold reserve and that this had caused the depression. Cleveland (1) secured Congressional repeal of the Sherman Silver Purchase Act, and (2) authorized the Treasury to obtain gold by selling bonds. He permitted the largest sale of bonds to be handled directly through the Wall Street banking house of J. Pierpont Morgan.

Cleveland's actions preserved the gold standard but did little to improve economic conditions. Cleveland was hailed by banking and business interests, which opposed inflation and favored sound money. He was condemned as a "tool of Wall Street" by the silver interests and farmers.

POPULIST PARTY

1. Origin. Farmers came to believe that Eastern industrialists and bankers controlled both the Democratic and Republican parties. Exhorted by agrarian spokesmen to "raise less corn and more hell," farmers in the 1880's established *Farmers' Alliances.* These politically minded organizations evolved into the *People's* or *Populist party.*

2. Program. Meeting in convention at Omaha, Nebraska, in 1892, the Populists adopted the following program: *(a)* Free and unlimited coinage of silver at the ratio of 16 to 1. Populists expected this proposal to increase the amount of money in circulation, from $20 to at least $50 per person. *(b)* A graduated income tax. Such a tax would bear more heavily on wealthy persons than on farmers and workers, and would provide the federal government with a source of revenue to replace the tariff. *(c)* Government ownership of telephone, telegraph, and railroad systems. Farmers looked to government ownership as a remedy for the abuses of private enterprise in the communication and transportation industries. *(d)* The secret ballot and direct election of Senators. These proposals would provide greater democracy.

To achieve a farmer-labor alliance, the Populists also endorsed prolabor planks: shorter working hours and restrictions on immigration.

3. Early Vote-Getting Successes. In the 1892 Presidential election, the Populist candidate, General James B. Weaver, received more than one million popular votes and 22 electoral votes, all from Western states. In the 1894 Congressional elections, the Populists increased their voting strength. Elated, they looked forward confidently to the 1896 Presidential election.

PRESIDENTIAL ELECTION OF 1896

1. Candidates

a. William Jennings Bryan. Farmers and silver interests gained control of the Democratic nominating convention. They cheered William Jennings Bryan, the "silver-tongued orator" from Nebraska who delivered an emotional attack upon the gold standard in his famous "Cross of Gold" speech, concluding: "You shall not crucify mankind upon a cross of gold." Bryan became the Democratic candidate. He also won the Populist nomination.

b. William McKinley. Conservative Eastern industrial and banking interests controlled the Republican convention. They nominated the skillful Ohio politician William McKinley, who opposed free silver, supported the gold standard, and advocated high protective tariffs.

2. Campaign. Traveling extensively and speaking frequently, Bryan demanded reforms to help the farmer. In a larger sense, however, Bryan crusaded for social and economic justice. McKinley stayed at home, content to issue carefully prepared campaign statements. His campaign was managed by the astute Marcus Hanna. This wealthy Ohio industrialist and banker alerted his friends to warn workers and mortgagors that, if Bryan were elected, they would lose their jobs and farms. Hanna received campaign contributions of many millions of dollars, at least ten times the amount available to Bryan. McKinley also benefited from the almost unanimous support of the press, which ridiculed Bryan as a radical, irresponsible "boy orator."

The election offered clear-cut issues: McKinley stood for the gold standard, high tariffs, and government noninterference with business. Bryan stood for free coinage of silver, lower tariffs, and government responsibility for the economic well-being of the people. McKinley drew his greatest support from bankers and industrialists; Bryan, from silver miners and farmers. McKinley's strength lay in the North and the East; Bryan's, in the South and the West.

3. Results. McKinley carried all industrial states and even won the older agrarian states. With 271 electoral votes to Bryan's 176, McKinley won the election. Shortly afterwards, the Populist party disappeared.

TEMPORARY AGRICULTURAL PROSPERITY

Unexpectedly, after 1896, American farmers entered upon better times. (1) New goldfields were discovered in South Africa, Australia, and Alaska, and methods of gold mining were improved. The considerable increase in the supply of gold permitted an increase in the amount of money in circulation. (2) Crop failures in Europe and India led to increased foreign demand for American agricultural products. (3) Heavy immigration to the United States caused the domestic market to consume more agricultural products.

Farmers, cheered by rising agricultural prices, abandoned their interest in free silver. They offered little opposition when Congress in 1900 passed the *Gold Standard Act*. This act declared that the United States was on the gold standard and made all paper money redeemable in gold.

Farmers considered the pre-World War I years from 1900 to 1914 as the *golden age of American agriculture*.

Agriculture From World War I to the Present

WORLD WAR I AND AGRICULTURE

1. Immediate Effect: Favorable. During World War I, farmers experienced a tremendous demand for agricultural produce for domestic, military, and export use. They enjoyed high prices; for example, wheat, which had sold for less than $.70 per bushel in 1894, now sold at over $2.

2. Long-Range Effect: Unfavorable. To meet the increased demand, farmers sought to increase output by purchasing more land and more farm machinery, paying inflated wartime prices. Since most farmers lacked funds, they borrowed money, often at high interest rates. After the war, the demand for produce declined and prices fell. Desperate, farmers could not afford to allow their land and machines to lie idle, so they continued to produce huge surpluses, which had the effect of driving farm prices still farther downward. Many farmers, unable to meet payments on their mortgages, lost their farms through foreclosure. Having no other home or occupation, they frequently remained on the land as tenants of the new owners, usually banks and life insurance companies.

DEVELOPMENTS AFTER WORLD WAR I

1. Cooperative Movement. Farmers again turned to cooperatives. *Marketing co-ops* graded, stored, packed, sold, and shipped the produce of their members. *Purchasing co-ops* bought supplies for resale to members. Co-ops performed the functions of middlemen and distributed their profits to their members. They benefited from federal and state laws offering them loans and allowing them special tax exemptions. Today, with a membership of several million, co-ops are an essential aspect of American agriculture.

2. Agricultural Marketing Act (1929). To tackle the problem of surpluses, President *Herbert Hoover* requested Congress to pass the Agricultural Marketing Act. It created a *Federal Farm Board* with $500 million to lend to farm organizations. They would purchase and store surplus agricultural products until the surpluses could be resold in time of scarcity. The act failed because it made no attempt to limit production, and the Federal Farm Board soon exhausted its funds.

3. Farmers and the Great Depression (Starting in 1929). With the onset of the depression of 1929, farmers were especially hard hit. From 1929 to 1932 wheat fell from $1.00 to $.38 a bushel; cotton fell from $.16 to $.06 a pound; average farm prices fell more than 50 percent; average cash income per farmer fell about 70 percent. Farmers could not keep up their mortgage payments or buy the necessities of life. Angry and desperate, farmers demanded federal action.

THE NEW DEAL AND THE PROBLEM OF FARM SURPLUSES

Promising the nation a *New Deal*, Franklin D. Roosevelt won the 1932 Presidential election and thereafter involved the federal government actively in assisting the farmer.

1. Agricultural Adjustment Act (1933). The objective of the AAA of 1933 was to raise agricultural prices in relation to industrial prices so that the farmer would regain the purchasing power he had enjoyed in the prosperous years of 1909–1914. This level of farm prices was called *parity*. If, for example, the price of wheat and the price level of industrial goods were both four times their 1909–1914 average, then wheat was said to be selling at *100 percent of parity*. However, if the price of wheat had only tripled while the price level of industrial goods had quadrupled, then wheat was said to be selling at *75 percent of parity*.

The law tried to raise farm prices by reducing acreage under cultivation and thereby preventing the production of surpluses. It provided for *(a) voluntary curtailment* of production of basic commodities, such as tobacco, corn, cotton, and wheat; *(b) cash bounties*, or *bonus payments*, to those farmers who left a percentage of their land idle; and *(c) processing taxes*—to be levied on wheat millers, cotton spinners, and meat packers—to raise funds for bonus payments. In 1936 the Supreme Court declared the AAA unconstitutional. (Check the Index for the Butler Case.)

2. Soil Conservation and Domestic Allotment Act (1936). To replace the defunct AAA, Congress passed the SCDAA. It provided that farmers be paid a bounty for planting a percentage of their land with soil-conserving crops such as clover and alfalfa. Indirectly, this law worked to curtail production of basic agricultural crops. The Supreme Court held the SCDAA constitutional. (Check the Index for the Butler Case.)

3. Agricultural Adjustment Act (1938). Drawing upon its experience with the two previous laws, the New Deal enacted the extensive AAA of 1938.

a. The government established *acreage quotas* for basic commodities, and paid the farmers bounties for planting soil-conserving crops on acreage withheld from production.

b. If, despite acreage quotas, farmers raised surplus crops, the government could establish *marketing quotas* with the consent of two-thirds of the farmers producing the commodity. These quotas limited the amount that the farmers could sell.

c. Farmers stored surplus crops under government seal. With the crops in storage as security, the government granted farmers *price supports* through *commodity loans*. The government set the price support or loan value for each commodity at slightly below parity. In good harvest years, to prevent falling prices, farmers placed surplus crops in storage and accepted commodity loans. In bad harvest years, they could take advantage of rising prices by taking surpluses out of storage, selling the commodities, and paying off the loans. This idea was called the *ever-normal granary plan*.

d. Also to bring prices up to the 1909–1914 levels, the government gave the farmers direct subsidies, called *parity payments*.

4. Evaluation of New Deal Farm Surplus Laws

a. In Favor. (1) The New Deal farm laws helped farmers secure higher prices. Between 1932 and 1940 farm income rose from less than $5 billion to over $9 billion. (2) Farmers enjoyed a fairer share of the national income. From 1932 to 1936 the parity ratio of agricultural to industrial prices rose from 55 to 90. (3) The entire nation's economy was lifted, as farmers now had the money to purchase more manufactured goods. (4) Soil conservation was widely practiced. (5) Farmers learned to follow the example of industry and adjust production to demand. (6) The farmer's confidence in the federal government and the nation was restored.

b. Against. (1) The New Deal farm laws forced domestic consumers to pay higher prices. (2) Agricultural prices above world levels caused American farmers to lose foreign markets. (3) Taxpayers were burdened with the cost of financing government spending for agriculture. (4) Complex government regulation reduced the farmer's individual initiative. (5) The farm laws proved unable to decrease output sufficiently. Even though farmers cultivated less land, they were able to increase total output by sharply raising productivity per acre. Farmers retired the least fertile lands from cultivation, practiced intensive farming, and expanded the use of fertilizer. From 1930 to 1940 wheat productivity rose from 11 to 15 bushels per acre. (6) The laws brought little benefit to the tenant farmer, the sharecropper, and the migratory worker. In some cases, tenant farmers and sharecroppers were driven off their farms by the landowners, who wanted to withdraw land from production and thus qualify for bounties. (7) The laws tried to curtail agricultural production at a time when many people throughout the world were hungry.

OTHER NEW DEAL FARM MEASURES

1. **Credit.** The *Farm Credit Administration*, established in 1933, furnished long-term, low-interest loans to farmers to refinance existing mortgages and prevent foreclosures.

2. **Electrification.** The *Rural Electrification Administration* (REA), established in 1935, provided low-interest loans to cooperatives for generators and power lines to supply electricity to rural areas not served by private utilities. The REA enabled many farmers and their families to enjoy the convenience of modern electrical appliances.

3. **Aid to Tenants and Other Poor Farmers**

a. Disadvantages of Tenancy. Of our farm population in the early 1930's, sharecroppers and tenant farmers comprised over 40 percent. They constituted most of the rural poor. Tenants and sharecroppers (1) received the poorest lands to farm, (2) took poor care of the property since it was not theirs, (3) earned extremely low incomes, often less than $250 in cash per year, and (4) worked their children on the farms instead of sending them to school.

b. Federal Programs. The *Bankhead-Jones Farm Tenant Act* (1937) established the *Farm Security Administration* (FSA) to assist needy farm families. The FSA provided loans to sharecroppers, tenant farmers, and farm laborers for the purchase of land, equipment, and supplies. Loans were made for as long as 40 years and at the low interest rate of 3 percent. (In 1946 the FSA was replaced by a new agency, the *Farmers Home Administration*.)

 c. Results. Sharecropping and tenancy were reduced by *(a)* these government efforts, *(b)* the flight of poorer farmers to the city, and *(c)* farm prosperity during World War II. Of our farm population in 1969, sharecroppers and tenant farmers comprised only 13 percent, a substantial decrease from 40 percent in the 1930's.

AGRICULTURE DURING WORLD WAR II AND AFTERWARDS

 With World War II, American farmers again enjoyed a period of prosperity generated by war. The demand for farm produce increased, and prices rose to new highs. To stimulate production, the government (1) removed all restrictions on output, (2) gave special draft deferments to farmers and farm laborers, and (3) guaranteed the farmers 90 percent of parity for two years following the war. Many farmers used their increased earnings to reduce debts, replace equipment, and acquire acreage.

 For several years following the war, foodstuffs from the United States were used to help feed the war-torn countries of the world, and demand for American farm goods remained high. In 1949, however, as relief needs overseas tapered off, agricultural prices turned downward.

 A series of laws—providing acreage quotas, marketing quotas, price supports through commodity loans, and transfer of substantial acreage from commercial production to conservation uses—all proved ineffective. From 1947 to 1960 farmers' total income fell from $17 billion to $11 billion, a decrease of 35 percent. From 1952 to 1960 agricultural prices fell 25 percent while industrial prices rose 10 percent. Despite government programs, farmers still produced surpluses as they offset decreased acreage by increased productivity per acre.

AGRICULTURE TODAY: THE TECHNOLOGICAL SPEEDUP

 For more than 100 years the Agricultural Revolution has been changing American farming, but since World War II at a quicker pace than ever before. Farmers have utilized the latest technological advances: complex machines, improved fertilizers, pesticides, weedkillers, and better seed varieties. Since 1940, the record has been startling.

1. Increase in Productivity per Acre. The per acre output of wheat increased from 15 to 30 bushels, of cotton from 262 to 454 pounds. Overall crop production per acre rose 66 percent. This sharply increased output per acre has been called the *green revolution*.

2. Increase in Output per Worker. The number of worker-hours needed to produce one bale of cotton fell from 200 to 47. Whereas one farmer used to produce enough goods to meet the needs of 12 other persons, today one farmer can meet the needs of 47.

3. Decrease in Farm Population. The ratio of farm population to total population decreased from 23 to 5 percent. Some 21 million people left agriculture.

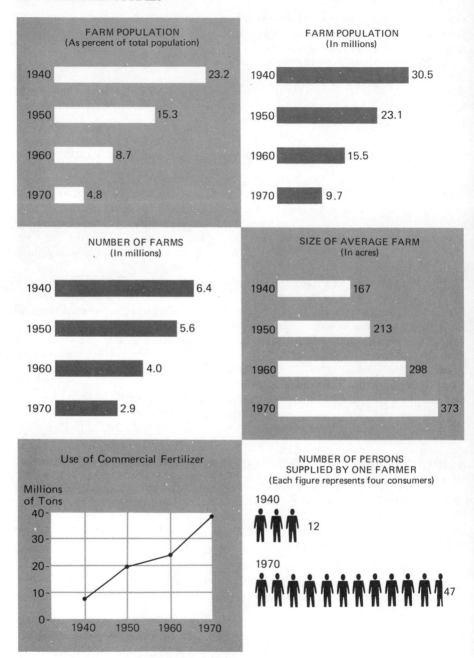

FARM POPULATION
(As percent of total population)

1940   23.2
1950   15.3
1960   8.7
1970   4.8

FARM POPULATION
(In millions)

1940   30.5
1950   23.1
1960   15.5
1970   9.7

NUMBER OF FARMS
(In millions)

1940   6.4
1950   5.6
1960   4.0
1970   2.9

SIZE OF AVERAGE FARM
(In acres)

1940   167
1950   213
1960   298
1970   373

Use of Commercial Fertilizer

Millions
of Tons
40 -
30 -
20 -
10 -
0 -
  1940   1950   1960   1970

NUMBER OF PERSONS
SUPPLIED BY ONE FARMER
(Each figure represents four consumers)

1940   12

1970   47

Trends in Agriculture, 1940–1970

These were mostly (a) poor farmers who lacked sufficient land and capital, and (b) farm laborers and migratory workers who were replaced by machines. Most of these people migrated to the cities.

4. Decrease in Number of Farms. The number of farms declined from 6.4 million to 2.9 million. The decrease was due to the abandonment of many subsistence farms and the merging of other farms.

5. Increase in Farm Size. The size of the average farm increased from 167 to over 373 acres. By using modern machines, the larger farm achieved greater efficiency. The worth of the average farm in land, livestock, equipment, and buildings rose from $7000 to $76,000.

6. Growing Importance of the Large Farm. Of total farm produce, the amount sold by (a) small, or subsistence, farms has decreased from 28 to less than 10 percent, (b) medium-sized farms has remained at about 50 percent, and (c) large farms has increased from 22 to over 40 percent. Large commercial scientifically run farms are known as *factories in the field, corporate farms, agribusiness,* or *agricorporations.*

AGRICULTURE TODAY: RECENT TRENDS

1. Dwindling Food Surpluses. Government-held food surpluses have declined to, and in some cases below, the levels of necessary reserves. The drop in farm surpluses came about as follows: (a) Acreage quotas have restrained the growth of farm output. (b) Domestic consumption has increased because of a growth in population, *food-stamp plans* for the poor, and food-distribution programs for schoolchildren. (c) Demand has risen from prosperous foreign countries, such as Japan and the nations of western Europe. (d) Demand has also increased from most developing countries in Asia, Africa, and Latin America, which have a small agricultural output and an "explosive" population growth. Many of these countries obtain surplus crops from the United States under the *Food for Peace* program. (e) The Soviet Union and Communist China, both experiencing insufficient harvests to meet the food needs of their people, purchased substantial quantities of American grain.

With increased domestic and foreign demand for farm products, American farmers were urged to expand output.

2. New Emphases in Farm Legislation

a. Direct Subsidy Payments. The *Agricultural Act of 1965* sharply reduced government price supports for wheat, corn, and cotton. To protect farmers against lower market prices, the act authorized direct cash, or subsidy, payments.

b. Subsidy Limitations. The *Agricultural Act of 1970* generally extended the 1965 reduced price supports and also limited subsidy payments to $55,000 a year for any one farmer for each of three basic crops: feed grains, wheat, and cotton. Of over 2 million farmers receiving subsidies, this provision affected only 1100 large individual and corporate farmers, who in 1969 had been paid in excess of the $55,000 limitation.

c. Continued Subsidy Payments and Limitations. The *Agricultural Act of 1973* established a four-year program of "target prices" for basic crops: wheat, corn, and cotton. If market prices as set by supply and demand should fall below the "target prices," the government would make up the difference by crop loans or cash subsidies, limited to a maximum payment per farmer of $20,000. Supporters pointed out that the 1973 law (1) does away with the New Deal approaches of "parity price" and complex farm regulation, (2) is simple to administer, (3) encourages increased farm acreage and output—both essential to bringing down high farm prices, which in turn helps the consumer and enables farmers to compete in world markets, (4) protects farmers by assuring them a "floor" under their income based on "target prices," and (5) costs the taxpayer and the government nothing as long as market prices exceed "target prices." Critics warned that (1) in case market prices fell sharply below "target prices," the government would be obligated to make heavy loans or payments and (2) farmers would lobby for higher "target prices."

The *Food and Agriculture Act of 1977* (1) raised "target prices" and provided that they be geared to production costs, (2) empowered the Secretary of Agriculture—in case an excessive basic crop surplus seemed likely—to institute acreage set-aside programs, (3) required farmers to accept the acreage cuts in order to be eligible for crop loans or subsidy payments, and (4) established a grain-reserve system to store surplus crops on farms.

This 1977 law was enacted during a period of farmer discontent caused by declining world prices of basic crops and by rising costs: of taxes, interest, wages, seed, fuel, machinery, and fertilizer. As farmers faced a squeeze on earnings, they protested loudly and demonstrated for additional government assistance.

In 1978–1979 farmers continued to produce crops at record levels, but they were cheered by higher farm prices, increased agricultural exports, and an improvement in their financial condition.

The farmer as a businessman: Rising farm costs diminish profits. (*Borgstedt in the Philadelphia Bulletin*)

3. Problem of the Poor in Rural Areas

a. Impoverished Farmers. Two million farmers are unable to earn a decent living in agriculture. Their average income, including home-grown food and government benefits, is less than $3000 per year. Eventually, some will achieve profitable farm operations. Others will combine farming with part-time employment in industry. Most will leave the soil.

The government has assisted these farmers by two laws: (1) The *Rural Areas Development Act* (1961) provided loans for low-income farmers to expand their landholdings to an adequate size; created new rural jobs by community projects, such as home repairs and water-system construction; encouraged new industry in rural areas; and granted funds for occupational retraining of farmers. (2) The *Economic Opportunity Act* (1964), to wage "war on poverty," encouraged rural communities to undertake job-creating projects and offered farm youths further education, new work experience, and vocational training.

b. Migratory Workers. These workers total possibly a quarter million. They travel from region to region and find employment chiefly on large commercial farms at peak periods such as harvesttime. Working about 140 days a year and earning about $1000 a year, they live in extreme poverty. Until the 1960's their plight evoked little government concern, and their efforts to form unions were blocked by the commercial farmers.

In 1964 the migratory workers benefited when Congress prohibited the importation of temporary Mexican farm laborers. In 1965 California migratory workers, mainly *Chicanos*, went on strike for recognition of their AFL-CIO union, the United Farm Workers (UFW), led by *César Chávez.* They won union contracts from the major grape and lettuce growers. In 1977 Chávez reached agreement with the Teamsters Union to end their jurisdictional struggle over representation of farm workers. The UFW was to organize workers mainly engaged in growing and harvesting farm produce; the Teamsters were to organize workers chiefly engaged in processing and transporting farm produce. Any dispute between the two unions was to be submitted to binding arbitration.

MULTIPLE-CHOICE QUESTIONS

1. A *major* difference between farmers and industrial producers is the (1) use of expensive machinery on large farms (2) need for credit by farmers (3) need for skilled labor in factories (4) farmers' difficulty in adjusting production to meet market demand.
2. Following the Civil War, what effect did the decline of prices have upon the Western farmers? (1) It helped them by lowering the prices of manufactured goods. (2) It helped them by creating a greater demand for their crops. (3) It hurt them by forcing them to pay back a more valuable dollar than they had borrowed. (4) It had no important effect upon them.
3. During the late 19th century, Western farmers demanded that Congress enact laws to (1) restrict farm production (2) establish and maintain a gold standard (3) assure fair transportation rates and practices (4) tax agricultural exports to other nations.
4. A major problem confronting American farmers in the period 1865–1900 was (1) unavailability of agricultural machinery (2) severe inflation in the United States (3) selling in world markets in competition with farmers of foreign countries (4) limited amount of arable land.

5. In the 1890's, the Populist party supported (1) removal of immigration restrictions (2) abolition of income taxes (3) repeal of the Sherman Antitrust Act (4) proposals to raise farm prices by increasing the amount of currency in circulation.

6. Which statement concerning the Populist party of the United States is *most* valid? (1) It obtained most of its support from the East. (2) It succeeded in getting its Presidential candidates elected in the 1890's. (3) It succeeded in influencing other political parties. (4) It failed to influence reforms in government.

7. During World War I, farmers helped create some of their later problems by (1) limiting production to raise prices (2) forming cooperatives to market their products (3) borrowing to expand production (4) urging the defeat of the Agricultural Marketing Act.

8. In the early 1930's, a fundamental problem of the farmer was the (1) increase in price of agricultural products (2) production of surplus crops (3) scarcity of fertile land (4) shortage of farm equipment.

9. The New Deal administration attempted to solve the farm problem *primarily* by (1) purchasing one-half of all farm products (2) sponsoring the cooperative movement (3) increasing the tariff on farm products (4) inducing farmers to curtail production.

10. In applying the principle of parity to farm prices, the government tried to (1) fix prices on farm products (2) provide farmers a purchasing power equivalent to their spending power in a base period (3) establish price levels agreed upon at commodity exchanges (4) reduce imports from low-wage-paying nations.

11. In which area was the New Deal farm program *least* successful? (1) encouraging soil conservation (2) preventing farm surpluses (3) keeping farm surpluses from the market (4) giving stability to farm prices.

12. Which has been the *basic* cause of the decline in the number of agricultural workers in the United States since 1945? (1) decline in the rural birthrate (2) high cost of the price-support program (3) reduced consumption of agricultural production (4) increased mechanization of agricultural production

13. In the United States, agriculture has posed a persistent problem since the end of the Civil War *chiefly* because (1) consumers have been buying fewer farm products (2) the federal government has done little to aid the farmer (3) the technological revolution in farming required major social and economic adjustments (4) there generally has been insufficient money in circulation.

TIME-LINE QUESTIONS

On the time line the letters *A–F* represent time intervals as indicated. For *each* event listed below, select the *letter* that indicates the time interval within which the event occurred.

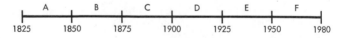

1. The Supreme Court decision in *Wabash vs. Illinois* led, the next year, to federal regulation of railroads.

2. The government offered aid to rural communities through "war on poverty" programs.

3. Cyrus McCormick patented the mechanical reaper, which helped to revolutionize agriculture.

4. The Rural Electrification Administration was established to bring electricity to neglected farm areas.

5. Most farmers were still using only a few simple tools.
6. An Agricultural Act set a "floor" under farm income by establishing "target prices."
7. Cleveland purchased gold bullion and preserved the gold standard.
8. An Agricultural Adjustment Act provided for acreage and marketing quotas.
9. The National Grange was founded to organize farmers for political action.
10. Farmers enjoyed prosperous years that later were used as the base period for determining parity prices.
11. Migratory grape pickers in California gained recognition of their union.
12. William Jennings Bryan was the Presidential candidate of both the Democratic and the Populist parties.

ESSAY QUESTIONS

1. (a) Discuss briefly two major problems that the farmer faces because of the nature of his business. (b) Describe two attempts that were made by the farmers before 1900 to solve their problems. (c) Describe two attempts made by the government since 1930 to help farmers.
2. Discuss each of the following statements, giving two specific facts to support or two specific facts to refute each statement: (a) The Industrial Revolution has greatly influenced the life of the farmer. (b) Wars have had important effects on the farmer. (c) The farmer has always been a "rugged individualist" in that he has made few demands for assistance from the government. (d) The farm problem is an important political issue today. (e) The surplus of American farm products has been a factor in our foreign relations since World War II.
3. (a) Using one specific law dealing with agriculture, explain the effect of the law upon each of the following groups: (1) farmers (2) industrial workers (3) businessmen (4) consumers (5) taxpayers. (b) On the basis of your answer to part (a), would you agree or disagree with the statement "When the farmer prospers, the nation prospers"? Defend your answer.
4. To answer this question refer to the six-part bar graph, "Trends in Agriculture" on page 334. Select either the three white graphs or the three tinted graphs and for each (a) state the trend indicated by the graph (b) explain one reason for this trend (c) explain one effect of this trend.

6. Workers Struggle for an Increased Share of the National Income

THE INDUSTRIAL REVOLUTION CREATES LABOR PROBLEMS

With the development of the factory system, workers could no longer labor in their own homes or in small shops. They therefore became dependent upon factory owners for their livelihood. In the early years of the Industrial Revolution, employers took advantage and (1) paid workers low wages for long hours, (2) employed women and children, (3) introduced machines that permitted employers to hire unskilled workers and that made the work monotonous, (4) compelled workers to conform to the speed of the machines, and (5) maintained unsafe, unsanitary, and badly lighted factories.

WORKERS TURN TO UNIONS: COLLECTIVE BARGAINING

Poor conditions aroused widespread dissatisfaction among workers. The worker soon found that by *individual bargaining*, that is, by appealing singly to the employer for better wages and better working conditions, he could not very well improve his lot. Under individual bargaining, he did not have the means to compel the employer to meet his demands, and the employer could discharge him without seriously affecting production.

Workers came to realize that they would be in a stronger position by *collective bargaining*, that is, by uniting as a group to make demands upon the employer. Under collective bargaining, workers could threaten to strike, thereby halting production and hurting the employer. In order to bargain collectively with the employer, workers formed labor unions.

LABOR UNIONS AFTER THE CIVIL WAR

After 1865, labor unions entered a period of growth in membership and power. They were aided by the following factors: (1) The emergence of large corporations destroyed personal contact between the employer and the employees, and made workers realize the necessity of organizing to deal with their employer. (2) The establishment of huge mills and factories drew the workers together and enabled them to discuss their common problems. (3) The courts developed a more favorable attitude toward unions. In the case of *Commonwealth vs. Hunt* (1842), the Supreme Court of Massachusetts ruled that unions were not unlawful conspiracies. After a long struggle, this precedent was finally accepted by the courts of most states. (4) Labor leaders gained experience. (5) By the end of the 19th century, the frontier was closed and workers could no longer look to the West for free fertile lands.

Post-Civil War workers faced powerful corporations controlling millions of dollars of assets, thousands of workers, and factories throughout the nation. To win concessions from these powerful employers, workers formed nationwide labor organizations and engaged in strikes.

KNIGHTS OF LABOR

1. **Structure and Early Successes.** Organized by *Uriah S. Stephens* in 1869, the Knights of Labor admitted all workers, both skilled and unskilled, regardless of race or national origin. Despite differences in occupation and craft, all workers in an area became members of the same local chapter.

Under *Terence V. Powderly* as "Grand Master Workman," the Knights in the 1880's urged an eight-hour day, the abolition of child labor, and the establishment of cooperatives. Although Powderly personally frowned upon strikes, members of the Knights of Labor won several important industrial battles. By 1886 the Knights reached their peak membership of over 700,000. Thereafter, the Knights declined in power and disappeared by 1895.

2. **Reasons for Decline**

a. *Unsuccessful Strikes.* Beginning in 1886 the Knights lost several strikes. These had been called without sufficient preparation and without sufficient financial resources.

b. Admission of Unskilled Workers. Unskilled members of the Knights of Labor who went on strike could be replaced easily. Also, workers in local chapters lacked common economic interests, and skilled members were unwilling to strike in support of the unskilled.

c. Failure of Cooperatives. The consumer and producer cooperatives run by the Knights lost money.

d. Haymarket Affair (1886). When Chicago strikers, demonstrating for an eight-hour day, were brutally treated by the police, the workers organized a protest meeting in Haymarket Square. Someone, unidentified to this day, threw a bomb at the police, killing seven people and wounding more than 60. In an emotionally charged atmosphere, eight radicals were arrested, tried, and found guilty of murder. The Haymarket Affair helped arouse public opinion against organized labor. Although the Knights of Labor condemned the Haymarket Square bombing, public opinion wrongly identified the Knights with violence.

(In 1893 *John P. Altgeld,* newly elected Governor of Illinois, reviewed the case. He pardoned the three convicted men still alive, believing that their trial had been unfair and that the evidence pointed to their innocence.)

AMERICAN FEDERATION OF LABOR

1. Aims and Structure. Organized by *Samuel Gompers* in 1881, the American Federation of Labor shunned political crusades and cooperatives. It emphasized "bread and butter" unionism: the furthering of the economic well-being of its members by means of strong unions.

Gompers' organizational policies made the A.F. of L. more successful than the Knights of Labor. *(a)* The A.F. of L. admitted mostly skilled workers. They could strike with greater hope of success than could the unskilled members of the Knights of Labor. *(b)* The A.F. of L. organized workers into separate *craft unions.* A craft, or trade, union is limited to workers of a particular skill; for example, a carpenter and a plumber would belong to different unions even though they both worked for the same construction company. By combining workers with the same economic interests, A.F. of L. craft unions could serve their members better than the Knights' local chapters.

2. Significant Early Strikes

a. Homestead Steel Strike (1892). Workers at the plant of the Carnegie Steel Company in Homestead, Pennsylvania, were members of an A.F. of L. union. They went out on strike to protest a reduction in wages. The workers fought a bloody battle and drove off 300 Pinkerton detectives hired by the company to guard the plant and help break the strike. To prevent further violence, the governor of Pennsylvania sent in the state militia. Eventually, the union's resources were exhausted, and the strike collapsed.

b. Anthracite Coal Strike (1902). The United Mine Workers, an A.F. of L. union, went on strike for union recognition, shorter hours, and higher wages. As winter approached, President Theodore Roosevelt summoned both sides to the White House, but the mine owners stubbornly rejected the union's offer to have the dispute arbitrated. The President then threatened to seize the mines, whereupon the owners agreed to accept a Presidential arbitration commission.

The commission awarded the workers a wage increase and a nine-hour day, but denied them union recognition.

3. Growth. Despite occasional setbacks the A.F. of L. prospered. Its membership increased from 100,000 in 1890 to 4 million in 1920 and almost 11 million in 1955. The A.F. of L. faced difficult times during the prosperous 1920's and the early years of the 1929 depression. It experienced great growth during World War I, the New Deal Era, and World War II. In the 1950's the A.F. of L. consisted of over 100 member unions. Almost all were craft unions such as the International Association of Machinists, United Brotherhood of Carpenters and Joiners, and American Federation of Musicians.

4. Leaders. Samuel Gompers, an immigrant from England and a member of the Cigar Makers' Union, organized the A.F. of L. and served as its president for some 40 years. A practical man who rejected radicalism, Gompers urged labor to benefit from a capitalist economy by forming strong unions and gaining high wages. His successor, *William Green*, who served from 1924 to 1952, continued Gompers' emphasis on craft unionism. Green was succeeded by *George Meany*, who later merged the A.F. of L. with the Congress of Industrial Organizations.

CONGRESS OF INDUSTRIAL ORGANIZATIONS

1. Industrial Unionism. An *industrial* union consists of all workers—skilled, semiskilled, and unskilled—in a given industry. In 1935 a small group of A.F. of L. leaders, who headed not craft but industrial unions, urged the expansion of industrial unionism. Notable among these leaders were *John L. Lewis* of the United Mine Workers, *David Dubinsky* of the International Ladies Garment Workers, and *Sidney Hillman* of the Amalgamated Clothing Workers. These leaders condemned the A.F. of L. for its emphasis on craft unions and its consequent neglect of the many semiskilled and unskilled workers in the expanding mass-production industries.

2. Development of a New Nationwide Organization. Supporters of industrial unionism formed the *Committee for Industrial Organization* and unionized the workers at leading mass-production companies such as General Motors, Chrysler, and United States Steel. To organize the workers, the C.I.O. utilized a new weapon, the sit-down strike. The employees not only refused to work, but in addition refused to leave the factories, thereby preventing the companies from operating with strikebreakers. By 1939, when the Supreme Court declared the sit-down strike illegal, C.I.O. unions had won recognition in the automobile, steel, rubber, oil-refining, textile, and shipbuilding industries.

The C.I.O., with its large voting power, represented a threat to the craft unions' control of the A.F. of L. Consequently, the A.F. of L. suspended the industrial unions and ordered the dissolution of their committee. Instead, in 1938 the industrial unions established their own nationwide organization, the *Congress of Industrial Organizations*.

3. Growth. The C.I.O. grew in membership from 3.6 million in 1940 to almost 5 million in 1955. In the 1950's the C.I.O. consisted of over 40 member unions, mostly industrial unions, such as the Textile Workers Union of America, the United Steel Workers, and the United Automobile Workers.

4. Leaders. The first president of the C.I.O. was *John L. Lewis.* An energetic and determined leader, Lewis spurred organizational drives and fought to keep the C.I.O. free of Communist influence. Lewis stepped down in 1940, but his policies were continued by both subsequent heads of the C.I.O.: *Philip Murray* (1940–1952) and *Walter Reuther* (1952–1955).

AMERICAN FEDERATION OF LABOR AND CONGRESS OF INDUSTRIAL ORGANIZATIONS

1. Reasons for Unity. In 1955 the A.F. of L. and the C.I.O. merged to form a single organization, thereby ending the 20-year split in the labor movement. This merger was the work chiefly of a new generation of labor leaders, especially George Meany, President of the A.F. of L., and Walter Reuther, President of the C.I.O. These labor leaders expected that a unified labor movement would *(a)* strengthen labor's influence in political and economic matters, and *(b)* spur union harmony by preventing membership raids and jurisdictional strikes.

2. Structure. *(a)* The AFL-CIO consists of about 120 affiliated unions with a total membership of 16 million workers. *(b)* It is governed by an executive council composed of the AFL-CIO president, a secretary-treasurer, and 27 vice presidents. *(c)* It finances its activities by taxing each affiliated union on the basis of membership.

3. Leaders. George Meany was unanimously elected first President of the AFL-CIO. In 1979, after twenty-four years as "Mr. Labor," Meany retired because of age. *Lane Kirkland,* formerly the secretary-treasurer, was unanimously elected second AFL-CIO President. He immediately called upon all nonmember unions to join the labor federation.

INDEPENDENT UNIONS NOT AFFILIATED WITH THE AFL-CIO

(1) A few *railroad brotherhoods,* including the locomotive engineers and the conductors and brakemen, remain independent. The railroad brotherhoods are among the nation's oldest unions. For many years the brotherhoods, loosely united among themselves and benefiting from favorable federal legislation, felt no need of national affiliation. Today, however, most railroad brotherhoods —including firemen and enginemen, trainmen, carmen, and maintenance-of-way employees—belong to the AFL-CIO. (2) The *United Mine Workers,* originally affiliated with the A.F. of L., helped form the C.I.O., then returned to the A.F. of L., and later became independent. (3) The *United Electrical Workers* and several smaller unions were expelled from the C.I.O in 1949–1950 on the charge of Communist domination. (4) The *International Brotherhood of Teamsters* was expelled from the AFL-CIO in 1957 on the ground of corruption and domination by gangsters. (5) The *United Automobile Workers* left the AFL-CIO in 1968, claiming that the federation had failed to act vigorously to achieve labor goals. (Check the Index for the "Teamsters" and the "United Auto Workers.") These and lesser known independent unions have a total membership of 5 million.

UNORGANIZED WORKERS: THE GREAT MAJORITY

1. **Extent.** The American civilian labor force contains 90 million workers, and of these only 21 million are union members. Hence, unorganized workers total 69 million, or 77 percent of the American labor force.

2. **Reasons**

   a. Occupational Factors. Self-employed workers, such as small storekeepers and many repairmen, are both workers and owners. Government employees enjoy civil service status, which provides job security, regular pay increases, sick leave, and retirement benefits. Agricultural laborers and household domestics are often transient workers who go from one employer to the next. Professionals, such as doctors, lawyers, accountants, and engineers, are highly trained, well-paid workers who generally consider unions unbecoming to professional dignity. Many professional groups have societies capable of serving functions similar to those of unions.

   b. Satisfactory Conditions. Workers feel no need of unions when they have high wages and good working conditions. Often, they owe such good conditions to general economic prosperity, to the spread of union-won benefits to nonunion workers, and to the deliberate policy followed by certain employers to keep

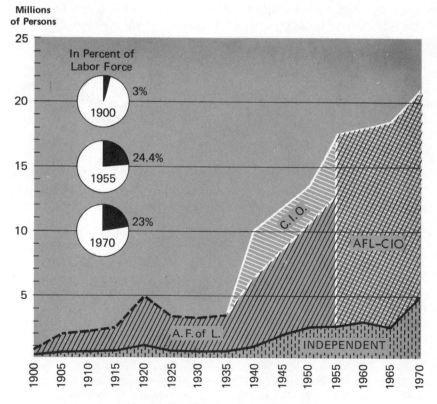

Labor Union Membership, 1900–1970

workers from joining unions. An employer may try to discourage unionization by granting the workers benefits such as profit-sharing plans, medical and hospital care, pensions, and recreational facilities. This policy is called *welfare capitalism.*

    c. Antiunion Sentiment. Some employers are strongly opposed to unions and vigorously combat union organizational drives. This attitude prevails among large commercial farmers in the West and among industrialists in the Deep South.

    d. Restrictive Union Practices. To assure employment and decent wages to their present members, some unions severely restrict the admittance of new members. The "father-and-son" unions, especially in the building and printing trades, limit new admissions to close relatives of present members.

GOALS OF MANAGEMENT AND LABOR

1. Common Goals. To make possible higher dividends for stockholders and higher wages for workers, management and labor both favor *(a)* a prosperous company with increasing productivity, *(b)* an expanding economy with rising living standards, and *(c)* our system of free enterprise under government regulation. Unlike European labor unions, which have frequently supported Socialist and Communist policies, organized American labor has remained true to Gompers' teachings that labor should benefit from capitalism. Most American workers have rejected anticapitalist organizations, notably the Industrial Workers of the World (IWW) in the early 1900's and, more recently, the Communist party in America.

2. Goals of Management. Industrialists have consistently aimed at *(a)* managing their companies with as little interference from unions as possible, *(b)* increasing productivity by instituting more efficient methods and utilizing labor-saving machinery, *(c)* requiring unions and workers to live up to the terms of their labor contract, *(d)* hiring, promoting, and firing workers as required by company needs, and *(e)* maintaining an *open shop.* In theory an open shop permits an employer to hire both union and nonunion workers; in practice, most open-shop companies hire nonunion workers only.

3. Goals of Labor Unions

    a. Traditional Goals. Unions have worked to secure (1) recognition of the union as the sole bargaining agent of the workers, (2) higher wages and shorter hours, (3) good working conditions, including safety devices on machinery and well-lighted, well-ventilated, sanitary factories, (4) job security, including seniority to enable older workers to gain promotions and avoid layoffs, and also including a union voice regarding the introduction of laborsaving machinery, (5) a *union label* to identify union-made products, thus enabling consumers to support unions by buying only goods with this label, (6) the *checkoff* system, which requires an employer to deduct union dues from the workers' pay and forward the lump sum to the union, and (7) union security, through either the *union shop* or the *closed shop.* In a union shop the employer may hire union or nonunion workers, but all workers must join the union within a specified time or lose their jobs. In a closed shop the employer may hire only workers who are already union members. (The closed shop was outlawed by the Taft-Hartley Act.)

b. More Recent Goals. In recent years unions have also sought to secure (1) the *guaranteed annual wage* (GAW), assuring each worker 52 weekly paychecks a year regardless of whether the employer can provide a full year's work, and (2) *fringe benefits*, including paid vacations and holidays, pay for sick leave, hospital and medical care, group life insurance, and retirement pensions.

PEACEFUL METHODS OF SETTLING LABOR-MANAGEMENT DISPUTES

The overwhelming number of labor-management disputes are settled peacefully, and with little publicity, by the following methods:

1. Collective Bargaining. Employer and union representatives meet, negotiate directly, settle the issues, and complete a labor contract. Sometimes the major employers in a given industry, such as steel, rubber, or clothing, negotiate as a group with the union for contract terms covering the entire industry. Such negotiations are called *industrywide bargaining.*

2. Mediation. A disinterested third party, who has the confidence of both the employer and the union, brings about an acceptable agreement by inducing each side to make concessions. A staff of trained mediators is available through the *Federal Mediation and Conciliation Service.*

3. Arbitration. The employer and the union together agree on a neutral third party to hear the dispute and hand down a decision, or *award.* The parties agree in advance to accept the arbitrator's award.

4. Fact-Finding Board. In strikes affecting the welfare of the nation, the President may appoint a fact-finding board to hear the dispute and hand down a recommendation. Although the board's recommendation is not binding, the disputing parties usually accept it for fear of adverse public opinion. (The fact-finding method is sometimes used by governors and mayors to settle local labor disputes.)

COSTS OF INDUSTRIAL WARFARE

A small minority of labor-management disputes erupt into industrial battles, frequently accompanied by much publicity. Industrial warfare causes hardship. (1) Employers suffer halted production, decreased profits, and unfavorable publicity. (2) Workers suffer unemployment and loss of income. (3) Consumers endure a shortage of products or a loss of services. (4) The government experiences loss of tax revenues and sometimes a scarcity of goods or services essential to the national welfare.

WEAPONS OF UNIONS

(1) Strike. Employees refuse to work until the employer yields to union demands. (2) Strike Fund. This fund serves to sustain union members and pay for

Nonprofit enterprise (*Morris for Wide World Photos*)

union activities during a strike. (3) Picketing. Workers parade outside the strikebound premises. They seek to enlist public support and to deter strikebreakers from taking their jobs. (4) Boycott. Workers request consumers not to patronize the strikebound company. (5) Publicity. Unions appeal for public support through mass demonstrations, newspapers, radio, and television.

WEAPONS OF EMPLOYERS

(1) Strikebreakers. To fill the jobs of strikers, the employer hires other workers, called strikebreakers or *scabs*. (2) Financial Resources. When a strike halts production and curtails business income, most corporations have sufficient financial reserves to meet their overhead costs and to continue paying dividends to stockholders. (3) Lockout. The employer keeps the workers from their jobs until the union accepts his terms. (4) Injunction. Upon the request of either a company or the federal government, a court may issue an order, called an injunction, forbidding the union to strike, picket, or boycott, on the ground that such union action may damage the employer unfairly or harm the national welfare. Violators of the injunction are liable to fine or imprisonment, or both, for *contempt of court*. The use of the injunction by the employer was severely limited in 1932 by the Norris-La Guardia Act, but its use by the federal government was expanded in 1947 by the Taft-Hartley Act. (Check the Index for "Injunctions," in labor disputes.) (5) Publicity. The employer presents his case to the public through mass communications media.

LABOR AND POLITICAL ACTION

1. Early Efforts

a. *Unsuccessful Attempts to Build a Labor Party.* In the 1830's and again in the 1870's, unions, small and newly organized, tried to form a labor party or to join in a political party with farmers. These efforts failed.

b. *Gompers' Advice.* In the 1880's Samuel Gompers urged members of the A.F. of L. to work within the two major parties by punishing enemies and rewarding friends. A.F. of L. leaders and organizations followed Gompers' advice by endorsing prolabor candidates regardless of party label. However, once elected, these candidates did little to help unions. They owed their nomination and election chiefly to political leaders and therefore felt little obligation to organized labor.

2. Labor Disputes Spur Political Activity

a. *Pullman Strike (1894).* Workers at the Pullman car plant near Chicago went on strike to protest a wage cut up to 40 percent, unaccompanied by any rent reduction in the company-owned town. These workers belonged to the industry-wide American Railway Union, led by *Eugene V. Debs.* To support the strikers, railroad employees refused to handle any trains with Pullman cars. Most railroad transportaion out of Chicago halted.

Attorney General *Richard Olney*, formerly a railroad lawyer, acted to break the strike. Using the Sherman Antitrust Act, he secured an injunction against the union as a "conspiracy in restraint of trade." When Debs violated the injunction by continuing the strike, he was arrested and jailed for contempt of court. President Cleveland meanwhile sent federal troops to Chicago, ostensibly to assure delivery of the United States mail. Cleveland's action was protested as unnecessary by Illinois Governor Altgeld. The arrival of federal troops led to protests by mobs and to violence. With troops on the scene and Debs in jail, the Pullman strike collapsed. It marked the first effective use of the injunction against a labor union.

b. *Danbury Hatters' Strike (1902).* Striking workers of the Loewe Hat Company in Danbury, Connecticut, organized a successful boycott of the company's products. The union and its members were sued by the company, which claimed that the boycott was a "conspiracy in restraint of trade" violating the Sherman Antitrust Act. In a Supreme Court decision in 1908, the union and its members were found guilty and fined heavy cash damages.

c. *Results.* The Pullman and the Danbury Hatters' strikes convinced labor leaders that they had to secure legislation to keep the injunction and the antitrust law from being used against labor unions. Labor became increasingly active in political campaigns and in 1912 helped elect Woodrow Wilson as President and also a number of prolabor Congressmen. During the Wilson administration, Congress passed the Clayton Antitrust Act (see page 349).

3. More Recently: Considerable Political Activity.
Following the formation of the C.I.O., labor took a more active part in politics. In 1943 the C.I.O. organized the *Political Action Committee* (P.A.C.). The P.A.C. not only endorsed candidates but fought to secure nominations for friends of labor and contributed funds

to campaigns. The P.A.C. also engaged in the hard work of politics: ringing doorbells, printing literature, holding rallies, providing speakers, and getting out the prolabor vote. The success of the P.A.C. encouraged the A.F. of L. to become more active in politics. Following the merger of the A.F. of L. and the C.I.O. in 1955, the AFL-CIO assigned its political efforts to its *Committee on Political Education* (COPE).

FEDERAL LEGISLATION AIDS LABOR: EARLY 20TH CENTURY

1. Clayton Antitrust Act (1914). In addition to strengthening the power of the government in fighting monopolistic business practices, this act stated that labor is not a commodity and, therefore, legitimate union activities are not subject to antitrust laws. Thus, it sought to outlaw suits against unions as combinations or conspiracies in restraint of trade, as in the Danbury Hatters' case.

This act also prohibited the use of federal injunctions in labor disputes "unless necessary to prevent irreparable injury." Thus, it sought to prevent federal courts from issuing injunctions indiscriminately. Furthermore, the act guaranteed a trial by jury to persons accused of contempt of court for violating an injunction.

Samuel Gompers hailed the Clayton Act, for its intended help to labor, as the workingman's "Magna Carta." In practice, the law helped unions very little. The courts applied the "irreparable injury" clause to grant injunctions halting many strikes and boycotts.

2. Adamson Act (1916). To head off a threatened railroad strike, this act legislated an eight-hour day for railroad employees.

3. Norris–La Guardia Act (1932). *(a)* This act prohibited federal courts from granting injunctions against workers who engaged in strikes, boycotts, or peaceful picketing. *(b)* It made *yellow-dog contracts* unenforceable. Under such a contract, workers seeking employment had been required to state that they were not members of a union and would not join a union during the term of their employment.

FEDERAL LEGISLATION AIDS LABOR: THE NEW DEAL

Under the New Deal, labor began an era of great gains. Having strongly supported Franklin D. Roosevelt for President, unions now enjoyed his support and encouragement. Also, as a result of the depression, public opinion was increasingly sympathetic to the workers' needs. Labor and political leaders sensed that the time was ripe for favorable labor laws.

1. National Industrial Recovery Act (NIRA) (1933). Section 7a of the NIRA guaranteed workers the right to "organize and bargain collectively through representatives of their own choosing." To evade Section 7a, however, many employers established *company unions*. These were unions sponsored and dominated by employers. The employer coerced the workers into joining the company union and thus deterred them from joining a union of their own choice. In 1935 the Supreme Court declared the NIRA unconstitutional.

2. Wagner (National Labor Relations) Act (1935). This act replaced the defunct Section 7a of the NIRA. The Wagner Act prohibited employers in interstate commerce from committing unfair labor practices relating to collective bargaining. It forbade employers to *(a)* interfere with labor's right to organize, *(b)* interfere in the operation of unions, *(c)* use *blacklists*, which contained the names of active union members to be denied jobs as "trouble-makers," *(d)* hire *labor spies* to infiltrate unions and secure confidential information about their membership and plans, *(e)* organize company unions, *(f)* discriminate against union members, and *(g)* refuse to bargain collectively with employees. It created a *National Labor Relations Board* (NLRB) to enforce these prohibitions and to hold elections among the workers to determine their choice of a union, if any, to represent them. (Similar "little Wagner Acts" were passed by most industrial states to regulate labor relations in intrastate commerce.)

By guaranteeing collective bargaining, the Wagner Act was largely responsible for the subsequent growth in legitimate union membership. Within six years, over 300 company unions were dissolved, and the number of workers in genuine unions grew from under 4 million to over 10 million. Employer groups, led by the National Association of Manufacturers, condemned the Wagner Act for giving too much power to labor. (Its provisions were severely modified in 1947 by the Taft-Hartley Act. Check the Index for this act.)

3. Social Security Act (1935). This act began a modest insurance program to combat economic insecurity due to unemployment and old age. Proponents of Social Security argued that it was self-financing and humanitarian, and that it protected individuals against hazards over which they had little control. Opponents argued that it was "socialistic," that it substituted government financial assistance for private initiative, and that it weakened the individual's will to work.

With time, as Social Security became accepted overwhelmingly, the original law was amended many times to extend coverage, increase benefits, and expand into the area of medical care for the aged.

a. Old-Age and Survivors Insurance (OASI)

(1) *Coverage.* OASI coverage now includes almost the entire working population. *Compulsory* coverage has been extended to most self-employed persons (such as farmowners, shopkeepers, accountants, engineers, lawyers, and doctors), most domestic help, most farmworkers, and all members of the armed forces. *Voluntary* coverage has been provided for employees of state and local governments, and for clergymen and other employees of nonprofit organizations. These workers may be covered if they and their employers agree to pay Social Security taxes.

Still *excluded* from coverage are federal civil service employees.

(2) *Benefits.* Social Security provides *old-age insurance.* Upon retirement at the age of 65, an insured worker is entitled to monthly benefits determined according to salary, years at work, and number of dependents. Social Security also provides *survivors insurance;* upon the death of the insured, benefits may be paid to the following: widow or widower, dependent children, and other dependents.

Benefits have been increased to keep pace with the rising cost of living. Lower benefits are paid to workers who choose to retire at age 62. Full benefits are paid to totally disabled workers regardless of age. Since 1975 benefits have been tied to increases in the Consumer Price Index.

(3) *Financing the Plan.* Employee and employer contribute equally. The tax rate, increased many times, now pays for old-age and survivors insurance as well as for hospital insurance. In 1977 the tax rate was 5.85 percent on the maximum salary base of $16,500.

In 1977, aware that benefit payments were outrunning the system's income, Congress sharply increased Social Security taxes. In 1980 employer and employee will each pay at the rate of 6.13 percent on the first $25,900 of the employee's annual salary. By 1987 the rate will rise to 7.15 percent on the base pay of $42,600. These increases led to strong taxpayer protests.

b. Unemployment Insurance. The Social Security Act of 1935 encouraged the states to establish their own unemployment insurance systems. The act authorized the federal government to levy a payroll tax on employers (of four or more workers) and to grant each state 90 percent of the money collected within its borders, provided that the state establish a satisfactory unemployment insurance system. Within two years every state had done so.

Systems of unemployment insurance vary from state to state. They cover few workers in agriculture but most workers in industry. In general, the state systems grant an unemployed worker a weekly benefit, calculated according to previous earnings and limited to a certain number of weeks. The worker must report regularly to a State Employment Office, which lists job openings and helps the unemployed person find suitable work.

c. Medicare for the Aged

(1) *Background.* First officially proposed in 1945 by President Truman, health insurance under Social Security for persons over 65 won the support of liberals and labor unions. Advocates argued that *Medicare* was necessary for Americans over 65 because, as a group, they possessed limited finances, suffered disproportionately more from illness, and were therefore most burdened by high medical costs. Medicare was opposed by conservatives and doctors' groups led by the *American Medical Association.* They argued that Medicare for the aged was unnecessary in view of existing private health insurance plans and of state aid programs. Further, the AMA feared Medicare as the opening wedge that might lead to government control of all medical care, or *socialized medicine.*

(2) *Provisions.* In 1965 President Johnson requested and Congress passed a "Medicare" bill. Revised several times since, "Medicare" now offers the following to persons over 65:

(a) Basic Hospital Insurance Plan. This plan provides (1) hospitalization up to 60 days for each illness, after the first $180, (2) nursing home care, fully paid up to 20 days, (3) post-hospital nursing visits at home, up to 100 visits, and (4) 80 percent of the cost, after the first $60, for hospital outpatient services. This plan is financed through the Social Security Tax.

(b) Voluntary Medical Insurance Plan. This plan provides for 80 percent of the cost, after the first $60, for (1) services of physicians and surgeons, and (2) surgical dressings and appliances, diagnostic tests, and other medical services.

This voluntary plan is financed by a small monthly premium paid by the enrollee and matched by the federal government.

Both plans permit the patient free choice of hospitals, nursing homes, and doctors.

4. Fair Labor Standards (Wages and Hours) Act (1938). For most workers in interstate commerce, this act *(a)* established a minimum wage of 40 cents per hour and a standard workweek of 40 hours, *(b)* required payment for overtime (beyond 40 hours) at the rate of time and a half, and *(c)* prohibited most child labor.

This act has been revised many times to keep up with the rising cost of living. The 1977 revision raised the hourly minimum for 1978 to $2.65 with further increases for 1979 to $2.90, for 1980 to $3.10, and for 1981 to $3.35. What effect may these minimum wages have on the hiring of unskilled workers?

STATE LEGISLATION AIDS LABOR

Most industrial states improved the conditions of labor by laws that provided (1) *workmen's compensation*, requiring the employer to take out insurance covering his workers in case of occupational disease or job accident, (2) *factory inspection*, requiring the employer to maintain proper sanitation, sufficient lighting, and safety devices on dangerous machinery, (3) *protection of women and children*, limiting their hours of work and prohibiting their employment in hazardous occupations, and (4) *compulsory education*, keeping children in school and out of the labor market.

LABOR AND WORLD WAR II

1. Gains During the War. Labor realized that the war would be fought not only abroad on battlefields but also at home in mines and factories. Victory depended upon an ever-increasing supply of the implements of war: ships, tanks, guns, planes, ammunition. To maintain maximum production, both the A.F. of L. and the C.I.O. pledged a policy of no strikes. To settle labor disputes peacefully, the government established the *War Labor Board* (WLB). During the war the loss in worker-hours due to walkouts, mostly unauthorized by union leaders, was less than one percent.

The demands of the armed services for personnel and of industry for workers resulted in labor shortages. The government established the *War Manpower Commission* (WMC) to shift workers from nonessential to essential industries, to "freeze" workers in their jobs in essential industries, and to train new workers, especially women, for jobs in defense industries.

Between 1941 and 1945 labor unions increased their membership from 10 million to 14 million.

2. Strikes in the Immediate Postwar Era. Now free of their no-strike pledge, labor unions began walkouts for higher wages. Workers justified their demands because *(a)* take-home pay was sharply reduced by the loss of overtime pay, *(b)* the purchasing power of the dollar was cut by the soaring cost of living, and *(c)* business profits were at an all-time high.

Long and bitter strikes took place in the automobile, steel, coal, and electrical equipment industries. By these strikes, labor unions aroused public resentment. Unions were blamed for delaying the production of long-awaited consumer goods, feeding the forces of inflation, and accepting the leadership of "power-hungry labor bosses."

CRITICISMS OF UNIONS IN THE POST-WORLD WAR II ERA

1. Limits Upon Union Membership. Some unions sharply restricted the number of new members, often admitting only relatives of present members, and charged high initiation fees. Also, some unions deliberately excluded blacks and other minority groups. These practices prevented new workers from competing with union members for jobs in closed-shop industries.

2. Opposition to Laborsaving Machinery. Many unions fought the introduction of laborsaving machinery. Although these technological advances reduced the employer's expenses and permitted the consumer more and cheaper goods, unions opposed such machines because they would decrease the number of jobs.

3. Featherbedding. To prevent technological unemployment, some unions forced employers to retain unneeded help. For example, the railroad brotherhoods compelled the keeping of coal-stoking firemen even though no coal was used in the newer oil-burning diesel locomotives.

4. Lack of Union Responsibility. Some unions failed to keep their members from violating the union's contract with the employer. One such contract violation was the *wildcat strike*—a spontaneous walkout by workers without the formal approval of their union.

5. Lack of Financial Statements. A number of unions did not publish financial statements. Their members and the general public had no knowledge of the unions' income and expenditures.

6. Lack of Union Democracy. Some unions were controlled by small groups of insiders. Rank-and-file members, sometimes through indifference and sometimes through fear, had little say in union affairs. Their union resembled a dictatorship rather than a democracy.

7. Racketeer Influence. Racketeers gained control of some few unions and used them for corrupt purposes. They treated union funds as their own and paid themselves excessive salaries. They employed strong-arm methods to suppress critics within the union and to force the union upon employers. In return for monetary "gifts" and other personal favors, they granted employers lenient terms in "sweetheart" labor contracts.

8. Communist Influence. During the depression years of the 1930's, Communists worked hard to gain control of the American labor movement as a means of overthrowing our capitalist economy and democratic government. However, only a few unions fell under Communist leadership.

9. Jurisdictional Strikes. Such a strike came about when two unions competed for control of the same workers. For example, the carpenters' union and the stagehands' union each claimed jurisdiction over workers building movie sets. In the ensuing strike the employer was caught in the middle and suffered from the interruption of production.

TAFT-HARTLEY (LABOR-MANAGEMENT RELATIONS) ACT (1947)

Partly because of the criticisms leveled at labor unions, the Republican-controlled Congress in 1947 passed the *Taft-Hartley Act*. President Truman vetoed the bill, but a combination of Republicans and Southern Democrats overrode the veto. The Taft-Hartley Act provided as follows:

1. Reaffirmed Collective Bargaining. The law reaffirmed the right of workers to organize and bargain collectively.

2. Outlawed the Closed Shop. The law prohibited the closed shop but permitted the union shop, unless it was contrary to state regulations. Section 14b of the Taft-Hartley Act authorized states to bar even the union shop by passing "right-to-work" laws.

3. Prohibited Unfair Union Practices. The law prohibited unions from (a) refusing to bargain collectively with employers, (b) engaging in a jurisdictional strike, (c) engaging in a *secondary boycott*, an action against a businessman dealing with a firm involved in a labor dispute (as, for example, when a union requests the public not to buy from a retail establishment that sells goods of a manufacturer whose workers are on strike), (d) protecting jobs by certain forms of featherbedding, (e) charging new members excessive initiation fees, (f) contributing funds to candidates for federal office, and (g) denying responsibility for contract violations by their members, especially wildcat strikes.

4. Established Requirements for Unions. The law required each union to file with the government (a) annual financial reports and details about the operation of the union, and (b) affidavits that union officials were not members of the Communist party.

5. Established New Regulations for Strikes. (a) *Sixty-Day "Cooling-Off" Period*. The law required unions to notify employers of intent to strike and then to wait 60 days. (b) *Eighty-Day Temporary Injunction*. In strikes affecting the national welfare, the federal government was empowered to secure a temporary injunction restraining the union from striking for an additional 80 days. During both the 60-day and 80-day periods, labor and management could seek peaceful settlement of their dispute.

CONTROVERSY REGARDING THE TAFT-HARTLEY ACT

1. Opposition by Unions. Most union leaders condemned the Taft-Hartley Act as a "slave-labor" law. In particular, they opposed the (a) abolition of the closed shop, since, under the union shop, the union had no power over hiring, (b) right granted to the states to bar even the union shop, (c) use of a temporary injunction, which revived fears of "government by injunction," and (d) anti-Communist oath, which union leaders considered an insult, since it was not required of any other segment of American society.

2. Approval by Major Corporations. Most corporate leaders hailed the Taft-Hartley Act for *(a)* prohibiting unfair practices by unions, just as the Wagner Act had prohibited unfair practices by employers, *(b)* outlawing the closed shop and thus giving employers the right to hire anyone they wanted, *(c)* providing a cooling-off period to encourage peaceful collective bargaining, and *(d)* insisting that unions force their members to honor their labor contracts.

3. Observations. *(a)* Despite labor's fears, unions made further gains, growing in membership from 14 million in 1947 to 17 million in 1957 and winning higher wages and many fringe benefits. *(b)* Some 20 states, most of them in the South, have "right-to-work" laws, outlawing the union shop. These laws, union leaders claimed, hampered unions in organizing workers. *(c)* Organized labor stepped up its efforts to rid itself of Communist influence. Today, in organized labor, Communist influence is at an all-time low. *(d)* Employers gained some relief from unfair labor practices.

In general, the Taft-Hartley Act brought little change into the power relationship between unions and employers.

LANDRUM-GRIFFIN (LABOR-MANAGEMENT REPORTING AND DISCLOSURE) ACT (1959)

1. Background: McClellan Senate Investigating Committee. Investigating corruption in labor unions, the McClellan Committee concentrated upon the huge and powerful truckers' union, the *International Brotherhood of Teamsters*. The investigators found Teamster officials to be reluctant witnesses. Nevertheless, the hearings disclosed a shocking picture of racketeering, misuse of union funds, and abuse of union power for personal advantage.

2. AFL-CIO and the Teamsters Union. Following disclosures before the McClellan Committee in 1957, the AFL-CIO acted to enforce its *Ethical Practices Code*. Its executive council *(a)* charged that *James Hoffa*, a vice president of the Teamsters, as well as other officials of the union, associated with gangsters and used the union for personal profit, and *(b)* ordered the Teamsters to clean house by getting rid of their corrupt leaders. The Teamsters defied the AFL-CIO by overwhelmingly electing Hoffa as president. Thereupon the AFL-CIO expelled the Teamsters. Expulsion failed to weaken or to bring about basic reforms in the Teamsters Union.

3. Landrum-Griffin Act. To combat the corrupt union practices uncovered by the McClellan Committee and to assure democracy in union affairs, Congress passed the Landrum-Griffin Act, providing as follows:

a. Union Elections. Union officials must be elected by secret ballot. Elections must be held at least every three years for local offices and every five years for national offices. To insure an honest vote, each candidate must be permitted to inspect the membership lists and have observers at the polls. Criminals convicted of serious offenses may not serve as union officials until five years after being released from prison. Communist party members may not serve as union officials until five years after leaving the party.

b. Bill of Rights. To protect rank-and-file members against coercion by union officials, this "bill of rights" guarantees union members freedom of speech and assembly, and the right to participate in union matters. No union member may be subject to disciplinary action by union leaders without a written statement of charges, time to prepare a defense, and a fair hearing. If these rights are violated, a union member may seek a federal court injunction against the officials of his union.

c. Financial Reports. Unions must file with the Secretary of Labor detailed reports disclosing the handling of union funds, including salaries of union officials, loans to union officials, and loans to business concerns. Union officials must report any monetary benefits received from an employer. Employers must report any loan or payment made to a union or to union officials. Persons filing reports must keep their records for five years.

Supporters hailed this law as an effort to curb racketeering and safeguard the rights of union members. Many labor leaders, however, condemned this law, arguing that *(a)* its "bill of rights" would enable disgruntled members to obstruct legitimate union activities, and *(b)* it would have no effect on Hoffa's Teamsters Union. (From 1967 to 1971, Hoffa was imprisoned for jury tampering and mail fraud. Since 1967, the Teamsters' president has been Frank E. Fitzsimmons.)

4. The United Mine Workers Elections (1969, 1972). Insurgent rank-and-file miners, whose leader Joseph Yablonski had been murdered, challenged the 1969 reelection of W. A. (Tony) Boyle as president of the United Mine Workers. They charged fraud and other election irregularities in violation of the Landrum-Griffin Act. Their charges were upheld by a federal court which ordered a new union election. It was held in 1972 under strict supervision of the Labor Department. The insurgents gained enough votes to oust Boyle and elect their candidate, Arnold Miller. (In 1974 Boyle was found guilty of instigating the murder of Yablonski. In 1977 Boyle won a new trial on the ground that the 1974 trial had not heard vital defense testimony. In 1978 he was again found guilty.)

RECENT LABOR TRENDS AND PROBLEMS

1. Weaknesses of the AFL-CIO

a. Internal Dissension. Despite the merger of the A. F. of L. and the C. I. O. in 1955, labor has not achieved internal harmony. The leaders of the AFL-CIO remain divided into two camps, as personality clashes have heightened policy differences. The former A.F. of L. leaders are generally conservative and favor craft unionism. The former C.I.O. leaders are generally more progressive and favor industrial unionism.

In 1967 Walter Reuther, president of the United Automobile Workers, dramatized his dissatisfaction with the AFL-CIO by resigning from its Executive Council. Reuther angrily condemned the AFL-CIO for failing to organize the many industrial, farm, and white-collar workers. In 1968 the United Automobile Workers disaffiliated and, although Reuther died in 1970, the union has remained outside the AFL-CIO.

b. Failure to Expand Membership. In 1956 the combined membership of the AFL-CIO and independent unions reached a peak of 17 million persons, or 25 percent of the labor force of 68 million. By the mid-1970's, union membership was 21 million. Meanwhile, the labor force had increased to 90 million persons, and union membership now represented only 23 percent of the total.

Despite the expulsion of the Teamsters and the withdrawal of the Auto Workers—two large unions, the AFL-CIO increased its membership slightly from 15½ million in 1955 to about 16 million in the mid-1970's. Nevertheless, the AFL-CIO has proved unable to organize the vast majority of workers.

2. Right-to-Work Laws. Section 14b of the Taft-Hartley Act permitted states to pass laws to prohibit the union shop. Some 20 states, mostly Southern, have "right-to-work" laws which prohibit compulsory union membership by stating that no worker can be compelled to join a union in order to hold a job.

Supporters argue that "right-to-work" laws (a) protect the democratic right of workers to join or not join a union, and (b) encourage honest unions, since workers may resign from corrupt unions without losing their jobs.

Opponents argue that "right-to-work" laws (a) weaken unionism by limiting a union's control over its members, (b) deny the democratic principle of majority rule, since a minority of workers may remain outside a union approved by a majority, and (c) enable nonunion workers to benefit from the union's efforts without paying a fair share of union costs.

Labor's efforts to secure repeal of Section 14b have so far failed.

3. Civil Rights and Labor Unions. Supporting full civil rights for American blacks, top AFL-CIO leaders have exerted pressure upon unions to eliminate discrimination in admitting apprentices and new members. They approved the *Civil Rights Act of 1964*, which prohibited discrimination by either employers or unions and provided for investigation of complaints by an *Equal Employment Opportunity Commission.*

Since most industrial unions did not practice discrimination, the law chiefly affected craft unions. Some unions, especially in the building trades, obeyed the law by little more than "token" integration. Traditionally father-and-son organizations, the building trades unions used difficult apprenticeship tests to keep out most blacks. At construction sites in major cities, these unions were the target of mass demonstrations seeking to publicize discriminatory practices and to compel the unions to admit qualified blacks.

4. Problems of Wages

a. Money Wages vs. Real Wages. Unions realize that an increase in *money wages*, that is, wages measured in dollars, is often offset by rising prices, which reduce *real wages*, that is, wages measured in purchasing power. For example, if over a three-year period a worker has received a wage increase of 5 percent and if the cost of living has risen 10 percent, the worker is worse off than before. Since World War II, the cost of living has been steadily rising. Some unions consequently had their labor contracts include an *escalator clause*. This clause provides for an adjustment in wages, up or down, according to changes in the cost of living as indicated by the Bureau of Labor Statistics of the Department of Labor in its *Consumer Price Index.*

b. Consumer Price Index (CPI). The CPI measures the change in the prices of goods and services as compared to prices in the base year. The CPI currently

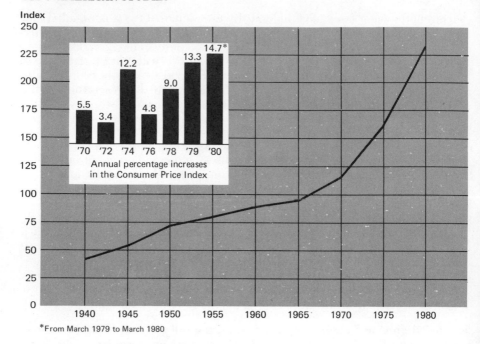

Consumer Price Index, 1940–1980 (1967 = 100)

measures the prices of 400 goods and services commonly purchased by urban wage earners. The 400 goods and services constitute the *market basket;* each item is weighted to reflect its relative importance in the consumer's budget. Obviously, milk, which is purchased every day, has a greater weight than a man's haircut, which is needed only once in several weeks. The CPI is not foolproof, for over the years: (1) a higher price may reflect an improved quality of goods, and (2) the typical market basket may neglect significant changes in the consumer's purchasing habits. The CPI, nevertheless, remains a highly regarded measure of change in the value of the dollar or, stated differently, in the "cost of living."

The current CPI uses 1967 as the base year, with an index of 100. Since this base year, the CPI has recorded an almost continuous process of inflation—the dollar declining in value and the cost of living going up. By early 1980 the CPI was at 233. This meant that the amount of goods bought for $1.00 in 1967 now costs $2.33, indicating that the purchasing power of the dollar had fallen considerably.

c. Guaranteed Annual Wage. In 1955 the United Auto Workers secured labor contracts that provided a modified form of the guaranteed annual wage, called *supplementary unemployment benefits.* During periods of layoff, a worker receives, for a limited time, company payments as well as state unemployment insurance benefits.

This modified guaranteed annual wage (1) provides the worker with a livable income during periods of layoff, (2) stimulates management to find ways of providing year-round employment, and (3) helps maintain consumer demand for goods, thereby moderating a recession.

5. Automation. Following World War II, labor became greatly concerned over automation. Unions knew that automation increased productivity, that is, output per worker, and that it enabled workers to receive higher wages. But unions feared that automation would displace large numbers of workers. For example, the automation of coal mining has increased productivity and permitted an increase in the average hourly wage, but it has greatly decreased jobs.

In 1964 Congress established a *National Commission on Technology, Automation, and Economic Progress.* The commission recommended that the government *(a)* encourage faster growth of the economy so as to provide additional business opportunities and jobs, *(b)* expand free public education to include at least two years of college so as to meet the need for skilled and professional workers in automated industries, and *(c)* increase efforts to retrain and relocate technologically unemployed workers, most of them semiskilled or unskilled, and, if necessary, provide them with jobs through a permanent government-financed employment program.

6. Problem of Strikes Affecting the Public Welfare. Following World War II, the government became increasingly concerned over labor-management disputes affecting national security and public welfare. These included strikes by steelworkers, longshoremen, airline ground service crews, and railroad employees. The government employed the 80-day Taft-Hartley injunction, but it was of questionable effectiveness in settling labor-management disputes.

Some Congressmen proposed legislation that would *(a)* outlaw industry-wide strikes and compel unions to deal with only one employer at a time, or *(b)* require labor and management to accept compulsory arbitration, or *(c)* permit the government to seize an essential industry involved in a strike and to operate it pending a labor contract.

"Come any further and I'll strike!" (*Eric in the Atlanta Journal*)

Unions opposed all these proposals as restrictions on their economic power. Management feared compulsory arbitration as an opening wedge for government price-fixing and suspected that government arbitration would favor unions with their large blocs of votes. Management furthermore considered government seizure of plants as a threat to private ownership.

While such proposals remain in the talking stage, the basic problem remains: How should a democratic society provide for the settlement of labor-management disputes affecting the national welfare?

MULTIPLE-CHOICE QUESTIONS

1. Which statement *best* describes a 19th-century laissez-faire attitude of factory owners toward laborers? (1) Workers should be in control of the state. (2) Workers should achieve gains through their individual efforts. (3) Social insurance should protect workers from economic hazards. (4) Labor unions should bargain collectively for workers.

2. An important reason for the decline of the Knights of Labor was the (1) organization of the Socialist party (2) high cost of membership (3) conflict between skilled and unskilled workers (4) passage of antilabor laws by the federal government.

3. At its beginning, the A.F. of L. aimed to (1) unite skilled and unskilled workers into one union (2) establish industrial unions (3) form craft unions of skilled workers (4) campaign actively for the election of its members to public office.

4. The organizational principles of the Congress of Industrial Organizations reflected the (1) increased need for skilled workers (2) rise of mass-production industries (3) opposition by many labor leaders to the political involvement of the A.F. of L. (4) decline in union membership during the New Deal.

5. In the 1930's which issue caused a split within the A. F. of L. and led to the formation of an independent C.I.O.? (1) the sit-down strike (2) the reelection of Franklin D. Roosevelt (3) industrial unionism (4) the National Labor Relations Act

6. Which statement about organized labor is true? (1) All large unions are affiliated with the AFL-CIO. (2) The 1950's saw the most rapid membership increase in labor's history. (3) Less than one-third of the labor force belongs to unions. (4) Craft-industrial union rivalry ceased to be a problem with the merger of the AFL-CIO.

7. A system under which an employer, by agreement with the union, deducts union dues from the wages of his employees and turns them over to the union is known as (1) checkoff (2) collective bargaining (3) processing tax (4) transfer payment.

8. The introduction of the newest machinery into a factory could benefit both labor and management by (1) decreasing the number of workers needed (2) increasing borrowing costs to pay for the machinery (3) increasing worker output per man-hour (4) selling the old machinery at a profit.

9. A graph shows that output per man-hour has increased from 100 in the base period of 1957–1959 to 130 by 1968. A labor union in 1968 could *best* use these data to support (1) an increase in membership dues (2) a campaign against racial discrimination in employment (3) an expansion of its apprenticeship program (4) a drive for a shorter workweek.

10. The increase in the power of labor unions during the 1930's was due *mainly* to the (1) passage of legislation guaranteeing workers' rights to organize and bargain collectively (2) support of the workers by newspapers and other mass media (3) attitude of the farmers toward the organized labor movement (4) cooperation of employers with labor union organizers.

11. The purpose of Social Security is to (1) provide cheap life insurance (2) curtail

employers' profits   (3) help relieve workers from the fear of destitution   (4) provide more business for the big insurance companies.

12. By law, funds for unemployment insurance come from   (1) appropriations by Congress   (2) appropriations by the state legislature   (3) contributions by the employees   (4) payments by the employers.

13. Over the years, the Social Security tax has   (1) gone up   (2) gone down   (3) been paid entirely by the employer   (4) remained fixed at the present level.

14. Which statement is *not* correct regarding Social Security benefits?   (1) They are paid to an insured worker upon retirement at age 65.   (2) They are paid to the widow of an insured worker who died before retirement.   (3) Since 1975, the amount of benefits has been tied to increases in the Consumer Price Index.   (4) The amount of benefits is reduced during periods of heavy unemployment.

15. The Senate committee investigating labor racketeering acted within the Constitution by seeking to   (1) destroy the principle of collective bargaining   (2) provide evidence for criminal action against labor racketeers   (3) provide Congress with information on which to base corrective legislation   (4) force the AFL-CIO to expel the Teamsters.

16. A major purpose of the Landrum-Griffin Act was to   (1) reestablish the closed shop   (2) replace the injunction provisions of the Taft-Hartley Act   (3) strengthen the position of the AFL-CIO   (4) promote democratic operation within labor unions.

17. A successful New England woolen manufacturer found himself forced to deal with a strong industrial union among his workers and was forbidden to fire them for membership or to restrict their union activities with injunctions. This probably occurred   (1) before the Clayton Antitrust Act was enacted   (2) after the Clayton Act but before the Norris–La Guardia Act   (3) after the Norris–La Guardia Act but before the Wagner National Labor Relations Act   (4) after the Wagner National Labor Relations Act but before the Taft-Hartley Act.

18. Which two practices are now forbidden?   (1) lockouts and injunctions   (2) yellow-dog contracts and secondary boycotts   (3) secondary boycotts and strikes   (4) blacklists and injunctions

19. An action against an employer who uses or sells products from an establishment where the workers are on strike is called a   (1) lockout   (2) general strike   (3) jurisdictional strike   (4) secondary boycott.

20. The author of the statement, "Railroads would have fewer financial difficulties if unions would permit them to eliminate unnecessary jobs," believes that   (1) unions are blocking automation   (2) the closed shop is a valuable protection for labor   (3) many railroads are owned by labor unions   (4) featherbedding is expensive.

21. The author of the quotation, "Confronted with a contracting number of unionized jobs in an expanding labor force, unions have fought one another for control of work opportunities," is probably trying to prove that   (1) unemployment has decreased union strength   (2) the A.F. of L. and C.I.O. should again split   (3) jurisdictional strife is a major labor problem   (4) unions are fighting for an expanded labor force.

22. "The American worker is primarily interested in real wages." This statement is valid because real wages represent the   (1) minimum wages that the unions are demanding   (2) amount of money the worker receives as a regular weekly wage   (3) amount of money the worker takes home after taxes have been deducted   (4) amount of goods and services the worker's dollars will buy.

23. The *principal* problem created in the United States as a result of the increasing pace of automation is   (1) lack of governmental interest in preserving natural resources   (2) widespread shortage of manufactured products   (3) unemployment among unskilled workers   (4) prohibitive costs of essential consumer goods.

24. The *most* reliable basis for measuring changes in the cost of living is the   (1) Consumer Price Index of the Bureau of Labor Statistics   (2) summary of replies to a

public opinion poll   (3) list of quotations on the stock market   (4) unemployment rate reported by the Labor Department.

25. An escalator clause in a labor-management contract is *usually* designed to   (1) protect the seniority rights of workers in the event of unemployment   (2) provide for a periodic increase in pension benefits   (3) keep real wages reasonably stable   (4) protect collective bargaining rights not guaranteed by state or federal laws.

26. Organized labor opposes "right-to-work" laws because these laws   (1) are contrary to the Taft-Hartley Act   (2) prohibit the union shop   (3) limit unemployment insurance benefits   (4) restrict the right to strike.

27. A union leader who speaks against "the hourly wage system from which so much of the worker's insecurity stems" *most* probably supports   (1) a piecework wage system   (2) a higher federal minimum wage   (3) a guaranteed annual wage   (4) longer paid vacations.

28. Which act would the President probably use as a basis for intervening in a strike that might endanger the national health or the safety of the United States?   (1) Clayton Antitrust Act   (2) Taft-Hartley Act   (3) Norris–La Guardia Anti-Injunction Act   (4) Wagner National Labor Relations Act

29. One provision of the Clayton Act concerning labor resulted from the   (1) opposition of the A. F. of L. to the Taft-Hartley Act   (2) failure of the Landrum-Griffin Act to end union racketeering   (3) Supreme Court decision declaring the National Industrial Recovery Act unconstitutional   (4) injunctions issued against labor unions under the Sherman Antitrust Act.

30. During the 20th century, federal legislation in the area of labor-management relations has most frequently been based on the Constitutional power of Congress to   (1) enforce the Fourteenth Amendment   (2) levy and collect taxes   (3) establish lower courts   (4) regulate interstate commerce.

MATCHING QUESTIONS

Column A

1. Founder of A. F. of L.
2. Senator who sponsored a law to curtail abuses by labor unions
3. Labor leader arrested during Pullman strike
4. Senator who sponsored New Deal law guaranteeing collective bargaining
5. Head of Teamsters Union when expelled from AFL-CIO
6. First head of merged AFL-CIO
7. Head of United Mine Workers and first president of the C.I.O.
8. Reform candidate elected in 1972 as head of United Mine Workers
9. Founder of Knights of Labor
10. President who helped settle coal strike of 1902

Column B

a. Grover Cleveland
b. Arnold Miller
c. George Meany
d. Tony Boyle
e. Robert A. Taft
f. Theodore Roosevelt
g. Franklin D. Roosevelt
h. Robert F. Wagner, Sr.
i. Samuel Gompers
j. Uriah S. Stephens
k. Eugene V. Debs
l. James Hoffa
m. John L. Lewis

ESSAY QUESTIONS

1. In 1955 the American Federation of Labor and the Congress of Industrial Organizations merged. (*a*) Describe *two* circumstances that led to the formation of the A.F. of L. (*b*) Discuss *two* factors that led to the growth of the C.I.O. (*c*) Discuss *two* reasons for the merging of the A.F. of L. and the C.I.O. (*d*) Has the merger of the A.F. of L. and the C.I.O. strengthened the labor movement? Defend your answer by presenting *two* arguments.

2. Show how *each* of the following has been a problem for organized labor: (*a*) large numbers of unorganized workers (*b*) jurisdictional disputes (*c*) racketeering (*d*) "right-to-work" laws (*e*) the civil rights movement (*f*) inflation.

3. Discuss *each* of the following, giving *two* specific facts to support *or* to refute each statement: (*a*) During the 19th century, labor experienced difficulties in organizing. (*b*) Changed conditions contributed to the rapid rise in union membership after 1933. (*c*) The Taft-Hartley Act marked a change in the government's policy toward labor organizations. (*d*) Good labor-management relations are essential to the welfare of the United States. (*e*) As automation increases, the result will be mass unemployment. (*f*) Minimum wage laws are beneficial to workers with low skills.

4. A dockworkers' union objects to the use of automated loading machines on the docks. The shipping companies consider the machines necessary and need some men to run the machines. (*a*) Identify the *two* groups in conflict and briefly state *one* argument of *each* to support its position. (*b*) Describe in detail a process by which the groups involved might settle this conflict. (*c*) List *two* provisions of such a settlement and explain why you consider *each* provision to be a fair compromise.

5. To answer this question refer to the graph "Labor Union Membership, 1900–1970," on page 344. Explain *one* reason to account for the data on union membership for *each* of the following periods: (*a*) 1900–1920 (*b*) 1920–1935 (*c*) 1935–1960 (*d*) 1960–present.

6. The federal government has, through legislation, court decisions, and intervention by the executive department, frequently exerted a strong influence on the relations between labor and management. (*a*) Discuss *two* actions by the federal government that exerted a strong influence on the relations between labor and management during the period 1865–1900. (*b*) Discuss *two* actions by the federal government that exerted a strong influence on the relations between labor and management during the period 1945 to the present.

Part 4. The Era of Regulated Capitalism: Recent Government Involvement in American Life

7. The Government Furthers Conservation to Protect Resources and Environment

WASTE: AN AMERICAN TRADITION

Blessed with an abundance of natural resources, the American people used them wastefully. Their squandering habits were encouraged by the federal government, which disposed of land at little or no cost. (1) Farmers and planters cultivated their lands improperly and exhausted the soil's fertility. (2) Farmers cleared their lands by chopping down or burning trees wantonly. (3) Lumber companies leveled vast forests without sparing unripe trees and without reforesting the cutover areas. (4) By destroying trees whose roots had served to bind the soil, farmers and lumbermen invited floods and erosion of the rich topsoil. (5) Hunters depleted wildlife, almost completely destroying the vast herds of buffalo. (6) Oil drillers who struck successful wells burned the escaping natural gas and made little attempt to cap gushers to stop the initial flow of oil from new wells. (7) Coal-mining companies dug shafts to reach the richest seams and neglected the rest. (8) Cities and factories dumped sewage and wastes into nearby streams and lakes, thereby polluting the waters and killing the fish.

By such wasteful actions, Americans speeded the day when they had to face problems of scarcity. (Check the Index for "Scarcity, problems of.") One response Americans adopted for problems of scarcity was *conservation*.

BEGINNINGS OF THE CONSERVATION MOVEMENT

In the late 19th century, as the frontier was drawing to a close, the American people became aware that the nation's resources, although great, were not limitless. Agricultural scientists, forestry experts, nature lovers, and other public-spirited citizens awakened interest in conservation—the proper care and wise use of our natural resources.

THEODORE ROOSEVELT AND CONSERVATION

More than any other man, Theodore Roosevelt awakened the American people to the need for conservation. An outdoorsman and nature lover, Roosevelt had lived in the West and had personally seen the waste and destruction of our natural resources. During his Presidency (1901–1909) Roosevelt promoted the following conservation measures:

1. **Land Reserves.** Roosevelt withdrew from sale about 150 million acres of forest land, 80 million acres of coal land, and 1½ million acres of potential waterpower sites. Under government control, these lands were to be saved from reckless exploitation and used wisely for the national welfare.

2. **Newlands Reclamation Act (1902).** This act provided that the federal government use the proceeds from the sale of lands in 16 Western states to finance irrigation projects. It inaugurated a program of government construction of huge dams, the earliest important ones being the *Shoshone Dam* in Wyoming and the *Roosevelt Dam* in Arizona.

3. **Forest Service.** At Roosevelt's urging, Congress strengthened the *Forest Service*, headed by Roosevelt's friend *Gifford Pinchot*. An ardent conservationist, Pinchot had studied forestry in conservation-minded Europe. Using his increased funds and expanded powers, Pinchot built the Forest Service into a major force for conservation. Rangers of the Forest Service patrol the national forest reserves, fight fires, and replant cutover areas.

4. **Governors' Conference.** In 1908 Roosevelt invited the state governors and other interested persons to confer with him regarding further efforts for conservation. The conference led to the establishment of *(a)* 41 state conservation commissions, and *(b)* a *National Conservation Commission* to make an inventory of the nation's resources and to suggest plans for their wise utilization.

OPPOSITION TO CONSERVATION

Theodore Roosevelt's conservation efforts aroused considerable opposition. Coal and lumber companies wanted to take over the government's land reserves. Privately owned utility companies were hostile to the government's dam-building program because they feared competition from government hydroelectric power. Anticonservationists hoped that, after Roosevelt retired, the public would again become apathetic about conservation.

THE NEW DEAL AND CONSERVATION

1. **Background.** In 1933 *Franklin D. Roosevelt* became President and faced *(a)* the Great Depression, with 13 million persons unemployed, and *(b)* a series of natural disasters: droughts, dust storms, and floods. A strong supporter of conservation, Roosevelt sponsored a dual-purpose program to provide work for the unemployed and to protect our natural resources.

2. **Major Undertakings**

   a. Civilian Conservation Corps. The CCC, from 1933 to 1942, provided employment for 2 million young men in conservation work. They constructed reservoirs, planted trees, cut forest trails, dug drainage ditches, fought plant diseases, and established forest-fire control systems.

   b. Public Works Administration. The PWA, from 1933 to 1939, spent several billion dollars, a considerable portion going for conservation programs. The PWA provided work directly for half a million unemployed on projects involving hydroelectric power, sewage treatment, and flood control.

   c. Soil Conservation. The New Deal farm laws (SCDAA of 1936 and AAA of

1938) granted bounties to farmers for planting soil-conserving crops. The Soil Conservation Service educated farmers in methods of preventing and halting soil erosion.

d. Multipurpose Dam Projects. The New Deal completed construction, begun during the Hoover administration, of the *Hoover (Boulder) Dam* on the Colorado River. The dam provides electric power, irrigation, and flood control. To utilize other Far Western waterpower sites, the New Deal completed the *Fort Peck Dam* on the upper Missouri River and the *Bonneville Dam* and *Grand Coulee Dam* on the Columbia River.

e. Tennessee Valley Authority (TVA). Because of its great importance, the TVA is discussed at length below.

TVA: CASE STUDY OF AN ALL-INCLUSIVE REGIONAL APPROACH

1. Background. The Tennessee River Valley, encompassing parts of seven states, was a region of impoverished farmers, eroded soil, cutover forests, and floods. Its rural areas had almost no electricity. But the region contained the valuable waterpower site at *Muscle Shoals*, Alabama.

During World War I the federal government began construction at Muscle Shoals of a project for producing nitrates and electricity. Completed in the 1920's, the project caused considerable dispute between public power and private power interests. Three times Congress passed bills providing for federal ownership and operation. The first bill was vetoed by President Coolidge; the second bill, by President Hoover. The third bill, passed in 1933, met with the hearty approval of President Roosevelt.

2. Organization and Services. The TVA is a government corporation empowered to plan for the "economic and social well-being of the people" in the Tennessee Valley. It provides a *regional approach* and, in many of its activities, TVA cooperates closely with and delegates responsibilities to various state and local agencies. Physically, TVA consists of a series of dams, reservoirs, nitrate factories, power plants, and electric transmission lines.

A multipurpose project, the TVA *(a)* controls the Tennessee River to prevent floods and permit navigation, *(b)* encourages reforestation and soil conservation, *(c)* produces nitrates for cheap fertilizer, *(d)* maintains agricultural experiment stations, and *(e)* generates electricity, at first by waterpower and later also by coal and nuclear power. The TVA sells its power primarily to municipal and cooperative utility companies that resell the electricity to the public, generally at rates below those of private utilities. Many persons have urged that TVA rates be used as a *yardstick* to measure the fairness of private utility rates.

3. Achievements. The TVA greatly improved the standard of living of the inhabitants of the Tennessee Valley. Farmers diversified their crops, used more fertilizer for higher yields, and enjoyed rising incomes. Their homes were brightened by low-cost electricity. Foresters replanted cutover areas. Aluminum and chemical companies, attracted by plentiful low-cost electric power, established plants in the valley and created new jobs. During World War II the TVA produced nitrates for explosives and furnished electric power for the atomic bomb project at Oak Ridge, Tennessee.

4. Opposition. Fearing the competition of the TVA, private utility companies tried to overturn the TVA by legal action. They failed, as the Supreme Court, in a series of cases, upheld the constitutionality of the TVA and its right to sell electricity. Spokesmen fearful of "big government" have also attacked the TVA. President Eisenhower called the TVA an example of "creeping socialism"; Senator Barry Goldwater, the Republican Presidential candidate in 1964, proposed that the TVA be sold to private interests.

The TVA has weathered all opposition, but its enemies have proved sufficiently strong to prevent establishment of other all-inclusive regional projects on the Columbia, Missouri, and St. Lawrence Rivers.

DISPUTE OVER PUBLIC DEVELOPMENT OF HYDROELECTRIC POWER

1. Arguments For. (a) Being able to borrow large sums of money at low interest rates, the government can undertake projects too expensive for private enterprise. (b) The government does not seek to make a profit and therefore can charge lower rates. (c) Government-owned utility companies provide a yardstick for measuring the fairness of private utility rates. (d) Multipurpose dams not only provide electric power but also further irrigation, navigation, and flood control. (e) Federal projects, such as Hoover Dam, Grand Coulee Dam, and the TVA, have proved successful in practice.

2. Arguments Against. (a) By competing with private industry, the government is violating our tradition of free enterprise. (b) The "big government" resulting from the army of federal officeholders, or *bureaucracy*, threatens our freedom. (c) Taxpayers throughout the nation should not have to pay to benefit inhabitants of specific regions.

Private utility companies also claim that government power projects provide an unfair yardstick of rates because the projects pay no federal income taxes and can produce hydroelectric power more cheaply than private utilities can produce steam-generated power.

ST. LAWRENCE RIVER PROJECT

1. Background. Proposed early in the 20th century, this project called for the construction of (a) hydroelectric power dams on the St. Lawrence River, and (b) a seaway that would enable oceangoing vessels to sail from the Atlantic Ocean up the St. Lawrence and into the Great Lakes. The project met opposition. (a) Railroads feared the loss of freight business. (b) Private utilities feared competition from public power. (c) Atlantic ports, from Maryland to Maine, feared loss of trade to Canadian and American ports on the Great Lakes. The project was urged repeatedly by Canada but turned down repeatedly by our Congress.

2. Construction of the Project (1954–1959). President Eisenhower recognized the importance of the St. Lawrence project for national defense and economic well-being, but he rejected an all-inclusive regional approach. He authorized New York State to proceed, with the Province of Ontario, in building dams for hydroelectric power. He secured Congressional approval for the United States to cooperate with Canada in dredging the river and building canals for the seaway. By 1959 both the seaway and the power projects were completed.

The seaway charges tolls to ships using its facilities. It has substantially increased the amount of cargo carried on the St. Lawrence River and the Great

Lakes, made possible low transport rates, and facilitated the economic growth of the Great Lakes area. The New York State Power Authority sells its St. Lawrence power to municipal and cooperative electric systems as well as to private manufacturing and utility companies.

RECENT FACTORS SPURRING PUBLIC INTEREST IN CONSERVATION

1. **Postwar Prosperity.** Following World War II, affluent Americans had more time and money for recreational purposes. However, the number of campers overwhelmed the limited facilities of national and state parks.

2. **Growing Population.** From 1940 to 1970 the American population multiplied from 132 million to 203 million, an increase of over 50 percent. More people meant greater demands upon our shrinking natural resources.

3. **Floods.** Dwellers along the Mississippi and Missouri Rivers have suffered severe floods, with much property damage and loss of life.

4. **Water Pollution.** As cities and factories continued to dump sewage and industrial wastes into nearby waters, magnificent rivers (such as the Hudson and the Potomac) and beautiful lakes (such as Lake Erie and Lake Michigan) became polluted, disease-ridden, and ugly. Bathers found beaches closed, and fishermen found fish dying out.

5. **Air Pollution.** Exhaust fumes from automobiles and the smoking chimneys of factories, apartment houses, and private homes have polluted the urban air. Dwellers in heavily populated metropolitan areas breathe this polluted air, which is often called *smog*. As a result of air pollution, urban dwellers suffer eye and nose irritations, many respiratory ailments, and heart trouble.

6. **Education.** After World War II, conservationists redoubled their educational efforts. They encouraged schools to teach students about conservation, usually as part of biology, geography, or history. They produced specialized films and published popular articles and books. Fairfield Osborn wrote the book *Our Plundered Planet*, warning that the human race can survive only if it stops wasting the earth's resources. Rachel Carson wrote the book *Silent Spring*, warning that the irresponsible use of pesticides and other chemicals harms birds and other wildlife, and contaminates our food supply.

In recent years, the conservation movement has emphasized the relationship of man to his surroundings and has become known as *environmental protection*.

RECENT PRIVATE EFFORTS IN ENVIRONMENTAL PROTECTION

(1) Large-scale commercial farmers have been employing the latest scientific methods of soil conservation. (2) Timber companies have undertaken extensive reforestation programs. They have managed their land as *tree farms*, with annual harvests and with replantings to assure further harvests. (3) Iron and steel companies, having almost exhausted our deposits of high-grade iron ore, have devised techniques for mining and utilizing low-grade *taconite* ore. (4) Oil companies have improved refining techniques to extract more usable products

from crude petroleum. (5) Electric utility companies, until recently dependent upon coal, gas, and oil to fuel their generators, have turned to atomic energy. They were encouraged as nuclear fuel became competitive in cost with conventional fuels. By 1978 some 70 nuclear power plants were providing the nation with 13 percent of its electricity. (For opposition to nuclear power, see page 426.)

RECENT STATE AND LOCAL EFFORTS IN ENVIRONMENTAL PROTECTION

Many state and local governments undertook diverse conservation activities. They expanded parks, playgrounds, and wildlife preserves; encouraged good forestry; built improved sewage treatment plants; and combated air pollution. Specific illustrations include the following: (1) California required that all new cars sold in the state contain exhaust-control devices. (2) New York City adopted stringent controls to reduce air pollution, requiring soot-control devices on chimneys, and ordering refuse compressors in place of incinerators in new buildings. (3) Pennsylvania, Illinois, Florida, and California all provided stiff fines for polluters. (4) Oregon reduced litter by requiring a deposit on all beverage bottles and cans so as to spur consumers to return the empties.

RECENT FEDERAL EFFORTS IN ENVIRONMENTAL PROTECTION

1. **Environmental Protection Laws.** (a) The *Wildnerness Act* (1964) established a National Wilderness Preservation System of 9 million acres of national forest lands. Its purpose is to preserve "an enduring resource of wilderness" as recreational sites for public enjoyment. (b) The *Highway Beautification Act* (1965) assigned federal funds for the removal of billboards and junkyards from alongside interstate and primary highways. (c) The *Water Quality Act* (1965) and the *Clean Rivers Restoration Act* (1966) empowered the government to set standards of water quality and provided funds for federal and state programs to construct sewage treatment plants and to combat water pollution. (d) The *Water Quality*

"The Pollutant"
(*Crawford. Reprinted by permission of Newspaper Enterprise Association*)

Improvement Act (1970) sharply increased penalties against companies responsible for oil spills in United States waters. *(e)* The *Resource Recovery Act* (1970) provided funds for states and cities to build solid waste disposal systems and to develop methods of recycling salvageable materials such as aluminum cans. *(f)* The *Clean Air Act* (1970) required the automobile industry to develop an engine that would eliminate 90 percent of auto fumes.

2. New Agencies. Two new agencies were created: *(a)* the *Council on Environmental Quality*, within the Executive Office, to advise the President, and*(b)* the *Environmental Protection Agency* (EPA), to enforce laws regarding conservation, environment, antipollution, and *ecology*—the relationship between people and other living things and their surroundings.

ENVIRONMENTAL PROTECTION: BENEFITS AND COSTS

With the 1973 Arab oil embargo against the United States, the American people became aware of their energy crisis. They began to consider environmental benefits in relation to energy and monetary costs. They asked: (1) Which goal should the nation seek first—energy self-sufficiency or environmental protection? (2) Which standards should environmental protection seek—"absolute" or "reasonable"? These problems are illustrated as follows:

1. Alaska Pipeline. With the 1968 discovery of oil in the Prudhoe Bay area of Alaska's North Slope, oil companies planned to construct an 800-mile pipeline to bring the oil southward to Alaska's ice-free port at Valdez. (From there tankers are to carry the oil to West Coast refineries.) The pipeline was delayed for several years by conservation groups—notably the *Sierra Club* and the *Environmental Defense Fund*—which brought court suits claiming that the pipeline would damage the Alaskan environment. In 1973 Congress overwhelmingly approved legislation authorizing construction of the pipeline by private enterprise. Congress thus expressed its view of American priorities: The need for Alaskan oil far outweighed any possible damage to the Alaskan environment. (In 1977 the Alaska pipeline was completed.)

2. Strip-Mining of Coal. Private utility companies have looked to our Western lands—both government reserves and private holdings—for clean, low-sulfur coal that can be dug out by surface or strip-mining. Conservation groups claimed that strip-mining will scar the land permanently unless costly standards are imposed for restoring the mined land to good condition. In 1974 Congress enacted a strip-mining bill that imposed strict environmental safeguards. By a pocket veto, President Ford withheld his approval, claiming that the measure would reduce coal production "when the nation can ill afford significant losses from this critical energy source."

In 1977 Congress enacted another strip-mining bill that *(a)* required coal companies to restore strip-mined land to its original shape, to replant grass and trees, and to prevent the pollution of nearby waters, *(b)* prohibited strip-mining on prime farmland, and *(c)* placed a tonnage fee on both strip-mined and underground coal to provide funds for restoring land left damaged by previous strip-mining. In signing this bill, President Carter claimed that it would encourage the "much-needed production of coal and also assuage the fears that the beautiful areas where coal is produced were being destroyed."

3. Auto Exhaust Fumes. Automobile manufacturing companies were granted a delay—to 1979 by Congress—in meeting auto exhaust standards set by the 1970 Clean Air Act and intended to be achieved by 1975. The auto manufacturers claimed that these standards were unrealistic and could not be met over so short a time. They further claimed that these standards will raise the cost of cars and impair auto operating efficiency. The Public Interest Research Group, a Ralph Nader organization, attacked the postponement and accused the auto manufacturers of "environmental blackmail."

THE COMPREHENSIVE NATIONAL ENERGY ACT OF 1978

In 1977 President Carter asked Congress to enact a comprehensive energy bill as necessary for the nation's well-being and as the "moral equivalent of war."

The President's proposals, complex and controversial, were intently scrutinized by Congress over a period of 18 months. The final bill bore only a faint resemblance to Carter's original proposals, but the President hailed it as declaring to the world "our intent to control our use of energy and thereby to control our own destiny as a nation."

The major provisions of the law were to: (1) permit the price of newly discovered natural gas to rise gradually until controls are removed in 1985, (2) require new electric utility plants to install boilers using coal—not oil or gas, (3) require existing electric utility plants using oil or gas to switch to coal by 1990, (4) provide tax benefits to business firms and homeowners who save energy by use of insulation and solar-energy equipment, (5) provide tax benefits to business firms who voluntarily switch from the use of oil and gas to coal, (6) require manufacturers of household appliances to meet fuel efficiency standards, (7) tax gas-guzzling cars beginning with the 1980 models.

What results may be expected of this legislation? (1) The rise in natural gas prices may mean higher bills for consumers but may also spur increased exploration and production of natural gas. (2) Electric utility rates may rise as power companies expend large sums to convert their facilities from oil and gas to coal.

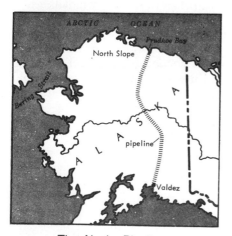

The Alaska Pipeline

"It's necessary—but I'll make it as easy to live with as possible!" (*Crockett in the Washington Star*)

(3) The greater use of coal may intensify the environmental problems of air pollution. (4) The increased use of natural gas and coal may enable the United States to decrease its imports of oil.

PRESIDENT CARTER PROPOSES FURTHER ENERGY MEASURES

By 1979 the United States was dependent upon foreign imports for 50 percent of its oil needs. The United States consequently was severely affected when revolution in Iran sharply curtailed that country's oil exports and when the OPEC cartel raised oil prices by about 60 percent above the previous year's high levels. American motorists endured long lines at service stations and paid over $1 a gallon for gasoline.

To deal with the recurring energy crisis, President Carter moved to mobilize public opinion. He told the American people they faced a "crisis of confidence" that threatened "to destroy the social and political fabric of America." He asked the American people to forego narrow interests, to rebuild national unity, and to support further measures to deal with the energy problem.

President Carter proposed that Congress enact the following energy legislation: (1) Grant the President authority to institute gasoline rationing—if necessary. (2) Establish an Energy Security Corporation (ESC), with massive funds, to develop a synthetic fuel industry. The ESC will spur the production of "*synfuels*"—synthetic fuels made from such sources as coal and oil shale, so as to replace 2.5 million barrels of imported oil per day by the year 1990. (3) Establish a Solar Bank to spur the use of solar power so as to provide 20 percent of our energy needs by the year 2000. (4) Establish an Energy Mobilization Board with broad powers to cut through red tape and override environmental and regulatory delays so as to speed key energy projects. (5) Assign additional funds to improve mass-transportation facilities and to aid needy Americans to cope with rising energy costs. (6) To provide the enormous funds needed for the previous proposals, enact a "windfall-profits tax"—an additional levy on the extra profits that oil companies are expected to make as the government, by September 1981, removes price controls on domestic oil and its price rises. This "windfall tax" is expected to provide a multi-billion-dollar fund within ten years.

President Carter's proposals were subjected to considerable criticism: (1) The "synfuels" program would be in the hands of a government bureaucracy rather than under private initiative. The synthetic fuels so produced would be costly. (2) In speeding energy projects, the Energy Mobilization Board might override essential safeguards for the environment. (3) The "windfall-profits tax" would deprive oil companies of funds that could be used to uncover new energy supplies. (4) The major proposals set long-range goals; they do not deal with current energy problems.

By early 1980 Congress had enacted two of President Carter's energy proposals: (1) A law authorizing the President to prepare a standby gasoline-rationing plan that could be put into operation in case of a gasoline shortage. This law provided that the President's plan and its enforcement both be subject to a Congressional veto. (2) A law placing a "windfall-profits tax" on the domestic oil companies, which tax is estimated to raise $227.3 billion over the next ten years.

Meanwhile Congress was actively considering President Carter's other energy proposals.

MULTIPLE-CHOICE QUESTIONS

1. Many Americans did not awaken to the necessity of conserving natural resources until (1) the frontier had disappeared (2) immigration quotas were enacted (3) slavery was abolished (4) the Civilian Conservation Corps was established.
2. A major stimulus for President Franklin D. Roosevelt's interest in conservation was his desire to (1) set aside land as an oil reserve for the navy (2) find work for millions of unemployed young men (3) follow the tradition established by Theodore Roosevelt (4) reward the Western states for their support in the election of 1932.
3. The Tennessee Valley Authority has (1) tended to raise the standard of living in the region that it serves (2) established widespread irrigation projects (3) been declared unconstitutional (4) been ineffective in controlling floods.
4. The New Deal's concern for conservation is *best* illustrated by the (1) passage of the Homestead Act (2) building of the St. Lawrence Seaway (3) free distribution of the book *Silent Spring* (4) creation of the Tennessee Valley Authority.
5. The St. Lawrence Seaway officially was built to (1) increase trade between the United States and Canada (2) strengthen the defenses of the United States and Canada (3) increase the prestige of New York State (4) bring more world trade to the Great Lakes region.
6. The economic concept of the yardstick is *most* frequently associated with (1) minimum wages (2) income taxes (3) public utility rates (4) Social Security payments.
7. Which of these is a pressing conservation problem in the United States today? (1) location of new sources of timber (2) control of predatory animals near inhabited areas (3) search for new sources of gold to stem the gold bullion drain (4) shortage of fresh water and the contamination of existing sources
8. One major conservation problem of the United States today is the result of (1) radiation in the atmosphere (2) air pollution from smoking chimneys and auto exhaust fumes (3) soil erosion from experiments with atomic fertilizers (4) depletion of coal resources from the application of automation to mining.
9. Environmental protection groups opposed the Alaska pipeline on the ground that the (1) United States did not need the oil from Alaska's North Slope (2) Alaskan oil was of a poor quality (3) pipeline would damage the Alaskan natural habitat (4) pipeline would take too long to build.

ESSAY QUESTIONS

1. (a) Discuss *two* reasons why the conservation of natural resources is more important today than it was 100 years ago. (b) Discuss briefly *two* ways in which the federal government *or* state governments have promoted conservation. (c) Explain *two* ways in which corporations and individuals can promote conservation.
2. The future development of the natural resources of the United States will come not so much from discovery as from advances in science and from skill in the utilization of our resources. (a) Why can we no longer depend upon discovery as a means of substantially increasing our supply of natural resources? (b) Indicate how *each* of *three* natural resources has been needlessly wasted. (c) Show how *each* method—advances in science, skill in utilization—has been used to expand or conserve our raw materials.
3. Environmental pollution is as much a result of what people do as it is a result of what they fail to do. Giving *two* specific evidences, show how the above statement applies to *each* of the following: (a) the producer (b) the consumer (c) the government.
4. To answer this question, refer to the cartoon, "Sacrificial altar" on page 372. (a) State the problem depicted in this cartoon. (b) What is the attitude of the cartoonist to this problem? Explain. (c) Do you agree or disagree with the cartoonist's attitude in regard to each of the following: (1) Alaska pipeline (2) strip-mining of coal (3) auto exhaust fumes? For each case, give *two* reasons to support your position.

8. The Government Pursues Policies for Economic Well-Being

Business Cycle

PHASES OF THE BUSINESS CYCLE

1. Prosperity: a great output of goods, extensive factory expansion, high prices and profits, easy bank credit, full employment, good wages, and a general feeling of optimism.

2. Recession: a falling off of demand for goods, decreased production, falling prices and profits, the calling in of bank loans, decreasing employment, falling wages, and a general feeling of caution and worry.

3. Depression: low production, low prices, little or no profits, widespread business failures, few bank loans, heavy unemployment, low wages, and a general feeling of pessimism.

4. Recovery: increasing production, rising prices and profits, extension of bank loans, increasing employment, rising wages, and a general feeling of hopefulness.

CAUSES OF BUSINESS CONTRACTION

1. Overproduction. Factory owners and merchants overestimate demand and build up excessive inventories of goods. Eventually, retailers curtail orders, and factory owners reduce production, thereby causing a downturn in business.

2. Underconsumption. Workers and farmers find their incomes insufficient to purchase industry's output of goods. Eventually, this disproportion of industrial supply to consumer demand becomes too great, and the economy slows down.

3. Imbalance Between Savings and Investment. People who save money instead of spending it decrease the demand for consumer goods. They are, however, accumulating capital, which is essential for economic growth. Their savings are invested in securities or deposited in banks. A sizable proportion of the bank deposits is invested in mortgage loans for the construction of homes and buildings, and in business loans for the purchase of materials and machinery. However, not all savings are invested, since banks may desire to increase their cash reserves or may lack sufficient demand for loans. When a large proportion of savings is not invested, the total demand for goods falls off, and the economy turns downward.

4. Psychological Causes. When pessimism sets in, consumers refrain from buying, businessmen limit expansion, and bankers restrict loans. All these responses cause the economy to worsen and pessimism to deepen.

Economists believe that recessions are not caused by any one factor but by the interaction of several factors. Many economists are convinced, furthermore, that the business cycle is man-made and can be controlled by intelligent human effort.

MAJOR DEPRESSIONS SINCE THE CIVIL WAR

1. The Depression of 1873 was caused by the overexpansion of railroads and industry; the granting of unsound bank loans; insufficient farm purchasing power because of low agricultural prices; and economic distress in Europe. The immediate cause was the failure of Jay Cooke and Company, a leading banking house.

2. The Depression of 1893 was caused by the overexpansion of railroads and industry; continued low agricultural prices; and fear among businessmen for the stability of our currency, due to the shrinking of the gold reserve and the battle for free silver.

3. The Depression of 1929

a. Causes. (1) American industry overexpanded its production facilities. (2) Consumers lacked sufficient income to purchase the total output of industry. Farmers in particular had low incomes following World War I because of the agricultural depression. Workers' wages failed to keep pace with increased productivity. (3) Bankers made unsound loans, and these ultimately resulted in bank failures that wiped out the savings of many depositors. (4) "Get-rich-quick" speculators bid up the price of real estate and stocks to unrealistic levels. (5) International trade declined because World War I had hurt Europe's economy and had lessened Europe's ability to purchase goods. Also, high protective tariffs interfered with the flow of goods between countries. (6) The immediate cause was the severe stock market crash starting in October 1929.

b. Differences From Earlier Depressions. The 1929 depression was the most severe in American history because (1) Americans no longer had the frontier with its economic opportunities, (2) the economy had become primarily industrial, and more Americans were affected by business variations, and (3) the depression was not limited to the United States but was worldwide.

c. Depth of the Depression. By 1932 production, prices, and profits were substantially down, business bankruptcies were numerous, 5000 banks had failed, wages had been slashed, and some 13 million workers, or 25 percent of the labor force, were unemployed.

d. New Deal. In 1933 Franklin D. Roosevelt took office as President and began a concerted attack against the depression. His New Deal included the following approaches:

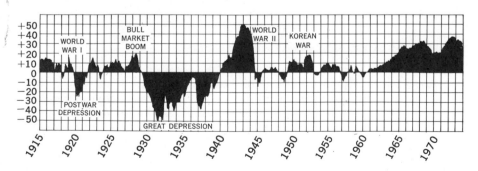

Business Cycles, 1915–1974 (*Cleveland Trust*)

(1) *Deficit Budgeting and Public Works.* Roosevelt incurred deficit budgets by heavy government borrowing. He used government funds to provide direct relief for the unemployed and, in addition, to stimulate business and create jobs. The *Public Works Administration* let out contracts to construction companies for massive programs of public works, which in turn stimulated businesses throughout the economy. The *Works Progress Administration* spent government funds on such programs as statistical surveys, art and theater projects, and some construction work. By thus pumping funds into the economy, the New Deal attempted to invigorate business.

(2) *Banking Reforms.* The New Deal restored public confidence in the banks by insuring depositors' money in case of bank failure and by strengthening the powers of the Federal Reserve Board. To spur loans for business purposes, the Federal Reserve followed an easy-money policy.

(3) *Investment Reforms.* To restore investor confidence in the securities markets and thusly to stimulate the investment of capital essential for business growth, the New Deal established the Securities and Exchange Commission (SEC). The SEC requires corporations offering new securities for sale to register the issue with the SEC and to provide potential investors with full data regarding the corporation in a statement called a *prospectus*. The SEC also regulates stock exchanges to prevent fraud and price manipulations.

(4) *Production Controls.* To avoid overproduction, New Deal laws encouraged farmers to reduce output and temporarily suspended the antitrust laws so that businessmen could establish industrywide production controls.

(5) *Encouragement of Consumption.* To promote mass purchasing power, the New Deal legislated minimum wage standards, encouraged the states to establish unemployment insurance systems, and fostered labor unions by guaranteeing the right of collective bargaining. To preserve the purchasing power of older citizens in the future, the New Deal began the program of Social Security.

(6) *Optimism.* Roosevelt instilled confidence into the people by asserting that the nation was basically sound. His optimism proved contagious.

By 1939 people had regained confidence in our economy, and business had achieved a partial recovery. Unemployment, however, although it had decreased, was still a substantial 17 percent of the labor force, over 8 million persons being out of work. The depression was not fully wiped out until the economy was spurred by the national defense program and American participation in World War II.

BUSINESS CYCLE SINCE WORLD WAR II

1. **Less Extreme Variations.** The American people experienced six post-World War II recessions. The first five were of short duration and comparatively mild. As measured by the gross national product (GNP), business activity recorded a pause or slight downward turn. The stock market fell, but there was no panic. Bank failures remained few. Unemployment rose, but not above 7 percent of the labor force. The people remained confident in our economic future.

The sixth recession, 1973 into 1975, was the most severe of the post-World War II economic downturns. It lasted the longest, the GNP dropped the

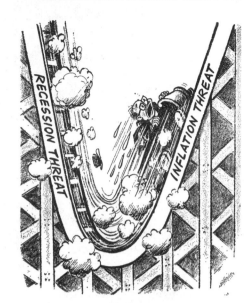

Never a dull moment
(*Shanks in the Buffalo Evening News*)

sharpest, the stock market declined the steepest, and the unemployment rate climbed above 9 percent. This sixth post-World War II recession was complicated because it occurred during a period of inflation. Whereas a recession usually brings falling prices, this recession was accompanied by rising prices caused, in part, by the (*a*) increased world demand that drove up prices of raw materials and foodstuffs and (*b*) monopolistic action of the Arab and other oil-producing countries, joined together as the *Organization of Petroleum Exporting Countries* (OPEC), which quadrupled oil prices. Some economists blamed the steepness of this "inflationary recession" upon the rampant inflation.

In 1975 the United States began to emerge from this sixth recession. The recovery, however, was uneven: GNP went up as did employment, but unemployment remained above 6 percent and inflation persisted—becoming, according to public opinion polls, the nation's most severe economic problem.

2. Measures to Level Out Extremes of the Business Cycle

a. Nongovernmental Efforts. (1) Strong labor unions kept wage levels steady even during periods of recession. They divided the available work to keep workers from being laid off, and kept down unemployment due to the introduction of new machines. Unions also sought to assure their members 52 paychecks a year by securing the guaranteed annual wage. (2) Responsible business leaders geared their corporate policies to maintain steady employment and capital investment even during recessions.

During prosperity both unions and management have been urged by the government to exercise restraint regarding wage and price increases.

b. Employment Act of 1946. This law affirmed the "policy and responsibility of the federal government to promote maximum employment, production, and purchasing power." It authorized the President to furnish Congress with economic reports covering current economic conditions and foreseeable future trends, and including, if necessary, recommendations for federal action to halt any extreme swings in the business cycle. To assist the President in these responsibilities, the law established a three-man *Council of Economic Advisers.*

c. *Government Tax Policies.* In 1968 Congress moved to curb serious inflation by extending excise taxes on new automobile purchases and telephone service, and by approving a 10 percent surcharge on individual and corporate income taxes. In 1971, to spur the economy, Congress slightly reduced income taxes of individuals, granted businessmen a tax credit for buying new equipment, and ended the excise tax on new automobiles. In 1975, again to spur the economy, Congress passed a complex tax bill whose major provisions were as follows: (1) to assist individuals—a rebate, up to a maximum of $200, against 1974 income tax payments; a personal tax credit of $30 for the taxpayer and each dependent against 1975 income taxes; and, for taxpayers who do not itemize deductions, a larger standard deduction against 1975 income taxes; (2) to stimulate the home-building industry—a direct credit against 1975 income taxes, up to a maximum $2000 for each taxpayer buying a newly built home before the end of 1975; and (3) to assist corporations—a substantial increase in the tax credit for new investments in plant and equipment, and a decrease in the 1975 income tax rate on the first $50,000 of earnings. This, the biggest tax cut in history, amounting to almost $23 billion, was intended to help the nation climb out of its most severe post-World War II recession.

d. *Built-in or Automatic Stabilizers.* Since 1933 the government has enacted significant laws that serve to stabilize the economy once it turns downward. To maintain consumer purchasing power, these laws provided: unemployment insurance for laid-off workers, Social Security payments to retired workers, price supports and subsidies for farmers, and minimum wages. Another type of built-in stabilizer is the Federal Deposit Insurance Corporation. The FDIC now guarantees every depositor up to $100,000 per account in case of bank failure. FDIC protection helped restore confidence in our banking system and drastically reduced the number of bank failures.

e. *Public Works Programs.* During recession periods, the federal government and the states increased the funds spent for public works. Such increased spending pumped more money into the economy and helped reverse the cyclical downtrend. For example, in 1974 Congress approved substantial federal funds for states and localities to create 100,000 public service jobs.

f. *Use of Federal Reserve Powers.* The Federal Reserve Board used its bank and credit powers to prevent extremes in the business cycle. A discussion of the Federal Reserve System follows.

Banking (Monetary Policy)

FEDERAL RESERVE SYSTEM

Established by Congress in 1913 and strengthened during the 1930's, the *Federal Reserve System* serves as our centralized banking system.

1. **Purposes.** The Federal Reserve (a) supervises banks and helps them serve the general public and the business community, (b) serves as the fiscal and

banking agent of the federal government by holding government funds, selling government securities, and issuing currency (Federal Reserve Notes, which are our paper money), and *(c)* encourages the healthy growth of the national economy by acting to prevent business extremes: runaway prosperity and inflation, as well as serious recession and deflation.

2. Twelve Federal Reserve Banks. The United States is divided into 12 Federal Reserve Districts, each served by its own Federal Reserve Bank. Since the Federal Reserve Banks do business not with individuals or corporations, but only with member banks, they are called "bankers' banks."

3. Member Banks. Banks chartered by the federal government must join the Federal Reserve System. Banks chartered by a state may do so if they wish. (State-chartered banks are regulated by state agencies.) Today approximately 5000 federally chartered and 2000 (out of 9000) state-chartered banks, doing over 80 percent of the nation's commercial banking, are Federal Reserve members. They provide the capital for the 12 Federal Reserve Banks. All Federal Reserve members must (and other banks may) join the *Federal Deposit Insurance Corporation*.

4. Board of Governors. The Federal Reserve System is controlled by its Board of Governors. The Board consists of a chairman and six other members, each appointed for a 14-year term by the President with the consent of the Senate. The Board of Governors, however, is independent of the President and the Senate. It exercises its own best judgment regarding the use of its powers over credit and banking.

FEDERAL RESERVE POWERS

1. Setting the Reserve Ratio. Each business day, a bank pays out and receives money. Because on some days it may pay out more money than it receives, it must keep a reserve. The Federal Reserve Board of Governors determines the size of this reserve by setting the *reserve ratio* (the proportion of reserves to deposits).

By raising the reserve ratio, the Federal Reserve Board forces its member banks to increase their reserves. They have less money to lend, which should lead to fewer loans and therefore a decline in business expansion. Conversely, the Board can encourage business expansion by lowering the reserve ratio and thus permitting member banks to lend more money.

2. Setting the Discount Rate. If a member bank wants more money, it can borrow from a Federal Reserve Bank. The interest rate charged by the Federal Reserve is called the *discount rate* (or *rediscount rate*). When the Federal Reserve Board raises the discount rate, the member banks in turn raise their interest rate to their customers, and business expansion is slowed down. The Federal Reserve Board can achieve the opposite effect by lowering its discount rate.

3. Engaging in Open-Market Operations. The Federal Reserve Banks buy and sell government securities by dealing with individuals and corporations in the open market. When they sell government securities, the Federal Reserve Banks receive payment in checks drawn on the member banks. By cashing these checks, the Federal Reserve Banks decrease the cash reserves of their member banks and thereby reduce the ability of the member banks to make loans. Conversely, by buying government securities, the Federal Reserve Banks increase the cash reserves of their member banks, thus pumping money into the economy. The Federal Reserve Board directs open-market operations.

4. Setting the Margin Requirement. When an investor buys stock on *margin*, he pays for the securities in part with his own cash and borrows the remainder from his broker. The Federal Reserve Board fixes the margin requirement at a percentage of the dollar amount of the purchase.

When the economy is depressed, the Federal Reserve Board reduces the margin requirement in order to encourage investment. When the economy is expanding too rapidly, the Board increases the margin requirement in order to discourage overspeculation.

5. Regulating Installment Buying. In emergency situations, such as World War II and the Korean War, the Federal Reserve Board received temporary powers to regulate installment buying. By requiring a large down payment and giving the buyer little time to complete his payments, the Federal Reserve Board discouraged installment buying and slowed down inflation.

Taxation (Fiscal Policy)

GOVERNMENT EXPENDITURES

1. Local governments spend money to provide schools, libraries, hospitals, public welfare for the unfortunate, police and fire protection, courts of justice, sanitation, local roads and streets, and parks.

2. State governments spend vast sums to provide state police, courts, highways, hospitals, and parks. States also provide *grants-in-aid*, or *state aid*, to local governments for public welfare and education.

3. The federal government spends the greatest part of its budget for national security, including the maintenance of the armed forces and the development of nuclear and other weapons. It also spends money for foreign aid; space exploration; aid to veterans, farmers, workers, and businessmen; interstate highways; national parks; and grants-in-aid to state and local governments for roadbuilding, education, conservation, housing, and anti-poverty programs. Also, the federal government spends a considerable sum in interest payments on the national debt.

REASONS FOR THE TREND TOWARD INCREASING GOVERNMENT EXPENDITURES

1. Increasing Population. As the population of the United States has increased, federal, state, and local governments have had to provide services for many more people. As the percentage of the population over 65 and under 21 has increased, governments at all levels have had to increase their spending for aid to the aged and for education.

2. Government Responsibility for Social Welfare. The depression of 1929 led the various governments to accept greater responsibility for the people's welfare. The federal government provided aid sometimes directly, as to the farmer, and sometimes indirectly through grants-in-aid to state and local governments. Also, as more persons moved into cities, governments have been forced to spend more money to deal with the problems of urbanization.

3. Cold War. Following World War II the United States became the leader of the free nations in their efforts to contain aggressive communism. The federal government sharply increased its expenditures for national defense, foreign aid, and localized conflicts, as in Korea and Vietnam.

4. Improvements in Technology. To improve our national defenses, the federal government has faced great costs for the development of new weapons. The federal government has also assumed the major role in space exploration. Technological progress has led to an increased number of government agencies to regulate transportation and communication, and certain industries, such as drug manufacturers. Finally, all levels of government have spent vast sums to provide roads and highways for the ever-increasing number of automobiles and trucks.

GOVERNMENT REVENUES

1. Theories of Taxation. (a) *Ability to Pay.* By this theory the government should tax individuals according to their income. The person with the greater income has the greater ability to pay and should bear a greater part of the tax burden. This theory underlies the income tax. (b) *Benefit.* By this theory the government should tax the people according to benefits, or gains, they receive. This theory underlies the gasoline tax in those states in which the funds received from the tax are used for road-building.

2. Tax Rates as Percentages of Income. (a) *Progressive.* The federal income tax is an example of a progressive, or graduated, tax. A person earning a greater income pays taxes at a higher percentage. For example, in 1974 the federal income tax rate for single taxpayers started at 14 percent on taxable income up to $500 and went up to 70 percent on taxable income over $100,000. (b) *Proportional.* An example of a proportional tax would be an income tax that taxed everyone at the same rate. (c) *Regressive.* A regressive tax requires a person earning a smaller income to pay a higher percentage of his income for the tax than does a person with a larger income. A cigarette tax is an example of a regressive tax. The laborer who smokes a pack of cigarettes a day pays as much tax as a millionaire who also smokes a pack a day. The laborer is therefore being taxed at a much higher rate in proportion to his income than the millionaire. By applying this reasoning, economists consider the general sales tax as a regressive tax.

3. Other Criteria of Taxation. Economists believe that a good tax should (a) be fair—treating all taxpayers in the same category equally and not penalizing any segment of the population or region of the country, (b) be easy and convenient to collect—keeping the expense of collection, the red tape, small in relationship to the revenue collected, (c) be difficult to evade—keeping fraud and tax evasion to a minimum, (d) yield sufficient revenue—making the collection of the tax worthwhile, and (e) *not* discourage individual and business enterprise—allowing the individual and the corporation to retain enough of their earnings so as to spur hard work and economic growth.

4. Major Sources of Revenue

a. Local Sources. Local governments generally secure their largest revenue from the property tax, chiefly on real estate. They may also derive income from the sales tax, minor business taxes, transit fares, water service fees, traffic fines, and special assessments. In addition, they receive considerable sums in state and federal aid. New York City and a number of other cities impose an income tax on residents and a payroll tax on commuters working in the city.

b. State Sources. Most state governments secure their largest revenues from the income tax and commodity taxes. The latter include general sales taxes and taxes on specific items such as gasoline, alcohol, and cigarettes. States also receive revenue from licenses, minor business taxes, and the inheritance, or estate, tax. In addition, they receive grants of federal aid.

c. Federal Sources. The federal government secures most of its revenue from the individual income tax, the corporate income tax, and the Social Security, or payroll tax. The federal government also levies excise taxes on gasoline, alcohol, tobacco, telephone service, and new car purchases; tariffs on imports; and an inheritance, or estate, tax.

"Taxes," according to Supreme Court Justice Oliver Wendell Holmes, "are what we pay for civilized society."

5. Government Use of Taxation for Social and Regulatory Purposes. The power of taxation may be used to bring about certain social and economic goals:

a. To further housing construction and attract new industries, local governments sometimes offer limited exemptions from the property tax.

b. To encourage philanthropy, the federal government and the states permit charitable contributions, within limits, to be deducted from taxable income.

c. To aid the elderly, the federal government and some states favor persons

"Now you must do your duty . . . spend it!" (*Berryman;* © *the Washington Star*)

over 65 by permitting them to take a double personal exemption from their income taxes.

d. In part to discourage the consumption of liquor and tobacco, both of which may be harmful to the individual, the federal government and most states levy heavy excise taxes on these products.

e. To overcome recession and spur economic growth, Congress in 1975 passed a complex tax bill. By providing individuals with 1974 tax rebates and 1975 lower income taxes, Congress was encouraging consumers to buy more goods and services. By providing corporations with lower 1975 tax rates on the first $50,000 of earnings and with increased tax credits for new plants and equipment, Congress was encouraging corporations to increase dividends to stockholders and to expand their capital investment programs.

In theory, the government can also use its tax powers in the reverse manner, raising taxes to reduce consumer and corporate spending and thus to help check runaway inflation. Political considerations, however, sometimes may prevent this theory from working out in practice. Congress finds it easier to spur economic growth by reducing taxes—a move that wins taxpayer approval; it is more difficult politically for Congress to check inflation by raising taxes—a move that creates taxpayer resentment.

MULTIPLE-CHOICE QUESTIONS

1. Which is *not* a characteristic of business depressions? (1) decline in employment (2) increase in government spending for relief (3) increase in bank loans (4) decline in imports
2. Which was an important factor contributing to the Great Depression of 1929? (1) unsound expansion of credit (2) large military expenditures (3) increased importation of foreign goods (4) government restrictions on business activity
3. The decline in the relative purchasing power of farmers and industrial workers in the 1920's contributed to the depression of 1929 because this decline (1) led to strikes and farm agitation (2) led to a decline in the debtor class (3) kept a close balance between production and consumption (4) limited the domestic market for industry's products.
4. Which was a significant result of the depression of 1929? (1) elimination of the business cycle (2) establishment by the federal government of certain safeguards against depression (3) failure of the Republican party to win the Presidency since then (4) sharp increase in the proportion of Americans engaged in agriculture
5. The President's Council of Economic Advisers is responsible for (1) preparing the budget (2) analyzing business trends (3) reviewing the work of the independent agencies (4) improving the efficiency of government operations.
6. The term "built-in stabilizers" refers to government programs designed to (1) reduce the possibility of an economic crisis (2) increase government control over banks (3) maintain a balanced budget (4) equalize the tax burden.
7. The Federal Reserve System helps to stabilize the economy of the United States by (1) preparing the federal budget (2) insuring deposits in savings banks (3) chartering new banks (4) controlling the credit activities of member banks.
8. If the Federal Reserve System wished to cut down on the loans made by member banks, it could (1) lower the margin requirement (2) lower the rediscount rate (3) raise the reserve ratio (4) order all loans stopped.
9. The term "open-market operations" refers mainly to the (1) speculation in stocks

and bonds by members of the stock exchange   (2) Federal Reserve purchase and sale of government securities   (3) Federal Reserve loans to its member banks   (4) Federal Reserve regulation of the margin requirement.

10. Which pairs the major source of revenue of the federal government with the *major* source of revenue of local governments in the United States?   (1) excise taxes—sales taxes   (2) tariffs—inheritance taxes   (3) employment taxes—corporation taxes   (4) income taxes—property taxes

11. There is widespread criticism of the sales tax as a means of raising revenue because it   (1) takes little heed of the people's ability to pay   (2) is primarily a progressive form of taxation   (3) tends to "soak the rich" and expect nothing of the poor   (4) is hidden from the people by being concealed in the price of the product.

12. An economic change from prosperity to recession is likely to be reflected *most* accurately in a state's income from   (1) sales taxes   (2) real estate taxes   (3) customs duties   (4) inheritance taxes.

13. Which action would probably push prices up and therefore be inflationary?   (1) a tight-money policy by the Federal Reserve   (2) sale of savings bonds to industrial workers   (3) a reduction in government spending   (4) wage increases without increased productivity

14. Which is likely to be the *most* effective use of federal power to reduce inflation?   (1) increasing personal income taxes   (2) decreasing FHA interest rates   (3) repealing the surtax on corporate income taxes   (4) increasing Medicare payments

15. In an attempt to relieve a continuing problem of unemployment, the federal government would be *most* likely to use the policy of   (1) granting tax credits to corporations that invest in new production capacity   (2) reducing government spending   (3) increasing the interest rates charged by the Federal Reserve banks   (4) increasing taxes on personal incomes.

16. Which is a *major* reason why the federal government reduced its income taxes in 1975?   (1) The Treasury's annual surplus was running above normal.   (2) Lower federal expenditures made high tax collections unnecessary.   (3) Lower tax rates gave the people more income for spending and investing.   (4) Foreign nations were paying their debts to the United States at an increasing rate.

ESSAY QUESTIONS

1. The following have been used by our federal government to help prevent or control economic depression: (a) public works projects (b) minimum wage laws (c) parity payments to farmers (d) the Federal Reserve Board's control over money and credit (e) unemployment insurance (f) lower income taxes. For *each* item (1) state which cause of depression it is designed to prevent or control and (2) explain how it may work.

2. Give *one* reason to explain why you would agree *or* disagree with *each* of the following statements: (a) The expenditures of a local government generally reflect the economic and social goals of the community. (b) Cuts in personal income taxes will increase the gross national product. (c) The increase in government expenditures—federal, state, and local—must come to a halt. (d) All state banks should be compelled to join the Federal Reserve System. (e) The automatic stabilizers built into our economic system since 1933 will prevent a severe depression. (f) Government efforts to halt a recession are much more popular than government efforts to halt runaway inflation.

3. Inflation has become a major economic problem in the United States. (a) Explain what is meant by the term *inflation*. (b) During which phase of the business cycle is inflation most likely to occur? Defend your answer. (c) Select *one* item from each of the three following groups. For each item selected, discuss how it could play a role in the struggle to control inflation: (1) strong labor unions or large corporations (2) defense expenditures or social welfare programs (3) government tax policy or Federal Reserve credit policy.

UNIT IV. AMERICAN CIVILIZATION IN HISTORICAL PERSPECTIVE

Part 1. American Ideals and Values

1. Americans Derive Their Ideals and Values From Many Sources

Characteristics of the "Average American." American and foreign observers have attempted, throughout our history, to identify "typical American traits." Their conclusions have been based upon subjective and intuitive reactions to the American scene—not upon measurable data and scientific examination. Each trait in the following list consequently should be subjected to critical analysis. Why was the trait singled out? Is it true of Americans in the 19th century? in the 20th century? in both centuries? in neither century? For Americans today, what traits should be omitted? What ones added? By coming to grips with such questions, students should deepen their understanding of the American national character.

Americans have been described as possessing the following traits: (1) hard working, materialistic, and practical, (2) adventuresome and optimistic, (3) impatient and inclined toward violence, (4) patriotic and nationalistic, (5) supporters of humanitarian and idealistic goals, and (6) believers in fair play, equality of opportunity, and individual responsibility.

Sources of American Ideals and Values

EUROPEAN SOURCES

Since most settlers in America came from Europe, they brought European ideals and values that greatly influenced the American way of life.

1. Religious

a. "Judeo-Christian Heritage." The Bible consists of two parts: the *Old Testament*, containing the history, religious beliefs, and moral values of the Hebrews; and the *New Testament*, containing the life and teachings of Jesus and his earliest followers. The Old Testament and New Testament together provide a code of ethical living—the *Judeo-Christian heritage.* (Check the Index for the "Judeo-Christian heritage.")

b. Puritan Ethic. With the split in European Christendom in the 16th century by the Protestant Reformation, *John Calvin,* a French religious reformer, became a leading Protestant spokesman. His religious teaching became known as Calvinism. In England, Calvinism became the religion of the *Puritans,* a group so-named because they wished to "purify" the official Anglican Church of England of practices remindful of Catholicism. In the 17th century, Puritan groups migrated to Massachusetts, where they established the Calvinist *Congregational Church.* Later they expanded throughout New England and into the Middle Colonies, bringing with them the *Puritan Ethic* which stressed the following beliefs: that those elected beforehand by God would achieve eternal salvation; that those so elected for salvation could be recognized by how they lived on earth; that they would shun idleness, extravagance, and vanity; that they would avoid frivolous pastimes such as dancing, card-playing, and theatre-going; that they would read the Bible regularly for religious and moral guidance; and that they would devote their lives to working hard, being thrifty, achieving business success, and accumulating material wealth. In recent years Americans have referred to the Puritan ethic as the "work ethic."

2. Political. Many of our political ideals came from the experiences of ancient Greece and Rome, from developments in England, and from the writings of English and French political scientists. (Check the Index for these subjects.)

3. Economic. Many of our economic ideals derived from European economists: first mercantilists and later advocates of laissez-faire. (Check the Index for "Mercantilism" and "Laissez-faire.")

"Religious freedom is my immediate goal,
but my long-range plan is to go into real estate."
(Drawing by Donald Reilly,
© *1974 The New Yorker Magazine, Inc.)*

NON-EUROPEAN SOURCES

A minority of Americans trace their origins, not to Europe, but to Africa, Latin America, and Asia. These peoples—blacks, Hispanic-Americans, and Orientals—have contributed to our American values and way of life. So too have contributions been made by the first inhabitants of the land, the American Indians. (Check the Index for contributions of these peoples.)

AMERICAN SOURCES

In this and following chapters of this unit, we discuss various American sources of our ideals and values—starting with the frontier and continuing with education, science and technology, creativity in the fine arts, and the mass media.

THE FRONTIER IN AMERICAN HISTORY

Meaning of the Frontier. The *frontier* in American history refers to the furthermost region of settlement—an imaginary line dividing civilization from wilderness. The United States Census Bureau defined the frontier as that area having less than six but more than two persons per square mile.

For almost 300 years, the frontier was part of the American environment. In 1650 the frontier ran along the Atlantic Coast. By 1750 it spread to the foothills of the Appalachian Mountains. By 1840 it reached the Mississippi River. By 1890 the West was sufficiently populated for the Census Bureau to consider the frontier as closed.

INFLUENCE OF THE FRONTIER

Frederick Jackson Turner, a famous American historian, himself born on the agricultural frontier of Wisconsin in 1861, wrote the perceptive essay *The Significance of the Frontier in American History.* Turner stated: "The true point of view in the history of this nation is not the Atlantic coast, it is the Great West." He argued that the frontier was the chief influence in shaping a distinctive American way of life.

1. **Social Equality.** The frontier offered free or cheap land, so that no person had to work for another. The individual's survival and progress on the frontier depended on the ability to hunt, fight, and farm. Frontier conditions prevented the rise of class distinctions and promoted the ideal of equality. The West judged people not by ancestors, race, religion, or national origin, but by deeds.

2. **Growth of Political Democracy.** Frontier settlers believed in political equality, hated special privilege, and considered the government as their servant. The West originated such democratic reforms as universal manhood suffrage, woman suffrage, and direct election of Senators. Turner claimed that democracy in the United States resulted from frontier conditions.

3. **Nationalism.** Frontier settlers were nationalistic because they depended on the federal government for cheap land, acquisition of new territories, and protection against the Indians.

4. **Faith in the Future.** Inspired by the resources of the West, the frontier

settlers looked to the future optimistically. This optimism was reflected in the boast that "the difficult we do immediately; the impossible takes a little longer."

5. Economic Independence. The frontier reduced America's economic dependence upon Europe by *(a)* providing raw materials and foodstuffs for the industrial cities, *(b)* providing a market for goods manufactured in the East, and *(c)* serving as a place for investment of surplus capital. Such economic independence enabled 19th-century America to follow a foreign policy of isolation.

6. Safety Valve for Factory Workers. Knowing that workers could leave their jobs and migrate westward, employers in the East offered good wages and working conditions. Labor in the 19th century seldom sought the protection of unions. Workers had a simpler solution to their problems: going to the frontier—the "safety valve."

7. Invention. The frontier encouraged the invention of new machinery. As westward migration drained labor out of the East, factory owners turned to new labor-saving machines. Labor was also scarce in the West. Farmers therefore needed new farm machinery.

8. Wasteful Agriculture. Since land was so easily available, frontier settlers were not mindful of the need for conservation. They cut down trees senselessly and cultivated the soil unwisely, damaging its fertility.

EFFECTS OF THE CLOSE OF THE FRONTIER: AFTER 1890

Turner stated that the close of the frontier, ending the era of cheap or free land, caused many of the problems that face us today.

1. Labor. Discontented factory workers no longer had the "safety valve" of easily available land in the West. These workers therefore remained in the industrial East and turned to labor unions to improve their conditions. This intensified the struggle between capital and labor.

2. Immigration. Immigrants could no longer easily acquire farms. More of them now crowded into the cities and competed for jobs in the factories. Americans began to demand restrictions upon immigration.

3. Conservation. The American people awakened to the need for conservation. (Check the Index for "Conservation.")

4. Imperialism. American capitalists, who had looked to the frontier for raw materials, markets, and investment opportunities, now began to look elsewhere. The United States embarked on a program of imperialism in the Caribbean, Central and South America, and the Far East.

CRITICISM OF TURNER'S FRONTIER THEORY

Many historians believe that Turner exaggerated the importance of the frontier. They claim that Turner ignored the following facts: (1) American democracy was fostered by our democratic heritage from England and by the demands of workers in the cities of the industrial East for a voice in government. (2) England developed a democratic form of government without the existence of a frontier. (3) The Southwestern frontier, settled by cotton planters, developed neither democracy nor nationalism. (4) The frontier did not serve as a "safety valve" for many Eastern factory workers. They lacked a knowledge of farming. They lacked the funds necessary to transport their families and to equip farms in the West. (5) The frontier itself was the result of industrial expansion in Europe and in the Northeastern United States. The demand from industrial areas for raw materials and agricultural produce encouraged Western settlement. (6) Despite the frontier, 19th-century America was never economically independent. It always depended on Europe for markets for its agricultural produce and for capital with which to build up American industry.

Most historians agree that many factors, including (1) European ideals and influences, (2) industrialism and the factory system, and (3) agriculture and the frontier—all have helped shape modern America.

THE FRONTIER AND AMERICAN ARTISTIC EXPRESSION

The frontier inspired American writers and painters to record the Western scene for posterity.

1. Writers

Mark Twain (1835–1910), the pen name of Samuel Clemens, was a great writer of satire and humor. Born in frontier Missouri, in a small town on the banks of the Mississippi River, Twain drew upon his boyhood experiences for two novels: *The Adventures of Tom Sawyer* and *The Adventures of Huckleberry Finn*. In *Huck Finn*, Twain viewed society through teenage eyes and satirized slavery and hypocrisy. Twain's years as a Mississippi River steamboat pilot formed the basis of his autobiographical *Life on the Mississippi*. During the Civil War, Twain went west to the mining frontier in Nevada and California. He depicted his Western trip and mining camp life in *Roughing It;* he also penned a classic Western "tall tale" of humor and exaggeration in a short story, "The Celebrated Jumping Frog of Calaveras County." Shortly after the Civil War, Twain went on a European tour and wrote his impressions in *The Innocents Abroad*. From his Western democratic and egalitarian viewpoint, Twain satirized Old World society, manners, and pretenses.

Bret Harte (1836–1902), born in New York State, went to California in 1854 as a teenager. For 17 years, to 1871, he lived there, absorbing impressions of the young, rough, and vigorous mining frontier. Harte worked as a typesetter, journalist, and magazine editor, and eventually won fame as a "local-color" writer. His short stories of the mining camps portrayed them with humor, sentiment and striking characters, such as in "The Luck of Roaring Camp." Harte expressed the Westerners' resentment of Chinese immigrants in his popular poem, first known as "Plain Language From Truthful James" but later entitled "The Heathen Chinee."

Hamlin Garland (1860–1940), born on the Wisconsin agricultural frontier, lived his first 24 years in various frontier communities. In his early writings, Garland portrayed frontier farm life with bitter realism: the hard work, sweat, drudgery, dust, monotony, and loneliness. His first, most realistic, and perhaps best collection of short stories was *Main-Travelled Roads*. Much later in life, with time having dulled his bitter memories, Garland wrote nostalgic stories of his youth in two books, *A Son of the Middle Border* and *A Daughter of the Middle Border*.

Willa Cather (1873–1947), born in Virginia, moved at the age of ten to the Nebraska frontier prairie. There she learned of the farmers' love of the land and of the European immigrant settlers' strong family ties. These themes she wove into two realistic novels: the story of a Swedish woman in *O Pioneers*, and the story of a Czech girl in *My Antonia*.

Ole Rölvaag (1876–1931), born in Norway, emigrated at age 20 to America and worked on his uncle's farm in South Dakota. After attending college, Rölvaag became a professor of literature and a novelist. *Giants in the Earth*, his best-known novel, describes the hardships, loneliness, and courage of the Norwegian immigrant settlers in the South Dakota region.

2. Painters

Frederic Remington (1861–1909) was born in New York State, studied fine art at Yale, and later moved to the Great Plains. He became the West's outstanding illustrator, producing almost 3000 paintings and hundreds of magazine drawings. His pictures are realistic, accurate, and colorful. They excel in portraying action: a cavalry charge, cowboys riding, a stagecoach fleeing Indians. Remington also sculpted a number of small statuettes depicting Western action: a cowboy broncobuster, an explorer on horseback descending a mountain.

The following three painters—Thomas Hart Benton, Grant Wood, and John Curry—have much in common. They were all born in the Midwest, lived at about the same time, drew inspiration from American history, from the ordinary farm people of the Midwest and from their everyday activities. These three artists are known as "American scene" painters and as "regionalist" painters.

Thomas Hart Benton (1889–1975), born in Missouri, was famed for his paintings, especially murals, which are paintings usually done on a building's interior walls. His paintings are dramatic, expressive, and realistic. Some notable works deal with the history of Indiana, the early history and folklore of Missouri including a scene of Jesse James robbing a train, and farmers hand-cutting July hay.

Grant Wood (1892–1942), born in Iowa, became a painter known for his bright colors, realistic subjects, and a highly formalized style. His most famous work, of a serious, middle-aged farm couple whose faces reflect hard work and determination, is *American Gothic*.

John Curry (1897–1946), born in Kansas, became known for paintings and murals of Midwestern rural life. One art critic claimed that Curry's works reflected the loneliness and courage of the pioneer. His mural in the Interior Building in Washington, D.C., has one section showing homesteaders building a barbed wire fence. His paintings include *Tornado* and *Baptism in Kansas*.

THE FRONTIER AND POPULAR AMERICAN CULTURE

1. Frontier Myth. The development of movies, pulp magazines, and television created a tremendous demand for stories that would be simple to comprehend, spiced with interesting characters, and full of action and excitement—a surefire recipe for success. Writers created stories embodying the frontier myth—(a) that frontier people were sharply delineated into "good guys" and "bad guys"

Thomas Hart Benton: "Arts of the West" (*The New Britain Museum of American Art* [Harriet Russell Stanley Fund])

such as the white settlers against the Indians, the homesteaders against the cattle ranchers, the honest sheriff against the rustlers; (*b*) that the frontier contained interesting, sometimes eccentric, people such as the town drunk, the gambling casino girl with the heart of gold, the Indian giving his life for his white friend; (*c*) that frontier life was exciting, filled with escapes from jail, long chases, fisticuffs, and gun battles.

The movies presented the frontier myth in many movies, most notably *The Plainsman*, with Gary Cooper, and *Chisholm*, with John Wayne. The outstanding "good guy" of movie "Westerns," Wayne always triumphed at the end—as

Frederic Remington: "Cavalry Charge on the Southern Plains"
(*The Metropolitan Museum of Art, Gift of Several Gentlemen, 1911*)

required by the frontier myth. Radio gave us the Lone Ranger, who, with his faithful Indian friend Tonto, always brought the lawbreakers to justice. Television presented the frontier myth in serials such as "Gunsmoke" and "Bonanza."

2. Debunking the Frontier Myth. *(a) By Satire.* More recently, writers have created Westerns poking fun, in a good-natured way, at the frontier myth. The movies presented *Support Your Local Sheriff*, in which an impoverished stranger takes the job of sheriff in order to earn some money and, by a series of improbable but hilarious events, restores law and order. Television presented "F Troop," featuring a bumbling army captain who is, nevertheless, always successful and a nearby tribe of Indians who are cowardly and businesslike. *(b) By Realism.* Hollywood produced *High Noon*, which although fanciful in its ending—as the sheriff almost single-handedly wiped out a gang of five outlaws—yet was realistic—in portraying the motives of the townspeople for refusing to assist the sheriff. A Swedish production, *The Immigrants*, showed settlers facing everyday problems as they sought to secure the necessities of life and build homes in the American West.

MULTIPLE-CHOICE QUESTIONS

1. Which of the following is the *most* valid statement regarding the Puritan ethic? (1) It applied almost entirely to an agricultural economy. (2) It emphasized eat, drink, and be merry. (3) It provided a religious basis for the hard work necessary in establishing the New England settlements. (4) Its principles have no value for American society today.

2. During most of the 19th century, the *greatest* shift in United States population was from (1) West to East (2) North to South (3) East to West (4) South to North.

3. What is the *best* definition of the term "American frontier"? (1) a fixed boundary line (2) the Atlantic or Pacific coastline (3) a shifting area where pioneer settlement ended (4) the dividing line between French and English settlements

4. What is the generally accepted date for the disappearance of the frontier in American history? (1) 1860 (2) 1890 (3) 1910 (4) 1940

5. The government's land policy in the West before 1890 did *not* (1) promote wise use of the land (2) lead to the development of transportation facilities (3) permit most settlers to own farms (4) encourage settlers to develop a spirit of independence.

6. Frederick Jackson Turner contributed *most* to American history by (1) discovering the frontier (2) distinguishing between the mining and agricultural frontiers (3) making the frontier central to an interpretation of the American experience (4) explaining how the frontier brought about the Civil War.

7. The Western frontier contributed to American democracy by (1) establishing the first public elementary schools (2) serving as a symbol of economic opportunity and political equality (3) supporting the establishment of Indian reservations (4) opposing government involvement in internal improvements.

8. An important influence of the expanding frontier on American life was that it *decreased* (1) our dependence on Europe (2) the growth of nationalism (3) our concern over the slavery controversy (4) our interest in manufacturing.

9. The disappearance of the frontier (1) brought new social and economic problems to the United States (2) decreased American investments abroad (3) discouraged American workers from joining unions (4) made conservation unnecessary.

10. Which one of the following characterizes *all* movements to the frontier? (1) search for religious freedom (2) greed (3) escape from political persecution (4) hardship

11. Which characteristic of the American frontier is still an important part of American life? (1) established churches in some states (2) self-sufficient farming (3) a predominantly industrial economy (4) absence of a rigid class system

IDENTIFICATION QUESTIONS: WHO AM I?

Thomas Hart Benton	Hamlin Garland	Ole Rölvaag
Willa Cather	Bret Harte	Mark Twain
John Curry	Frederic Remington	Grant Wood

1. A painter, magazine illustrator, and sculptor, I portrayed the romantic West, full of excitement and action.
2. A humorist and satirist, I wrote many works but am best known for relating the adventures of two interesting youths, Tom Sawyer and Huck Finn.
3. In two realistic novels with women as the central characters, I described the immigrant experience on the agricultural frontier.
4. A realist, I wrote short stories of the agricultural frontier, emphasizing the hard work, drudgery, and loneliness of frontier farm life.
5. I completed a number of murals dealing with the early history of the Midwest, notably the states of Indiana and Missouri.
6. I lived on the mining frontier and depicted its rough and vigorous ways in many "local color" short stories.

ESSAY QUESTIONS

1. American ideals and values have been greatly affected by European developments. Describe *one* way in which Americans have been affected by European developments in *each* of the following fields: (a) religion (b) economics (c) government.
2. "Go West, young man" has been important advice for the American people. (a) Show *two* different ways in which the westward movement affected life in the Eastern seaboard states. (b) Describe *three* effects of the closing frontier upon American life. (c) What is meant by the statement that there are still frontiers in American life?
3. Giving *one* specific fact, show how *each* of the following was *either* a cause *or* a result of the westward movement in the 19th century: (a) the growth of democracy (b) internal improvements (c) immigration from Europe (d) nationalism (e) the growth of labor unions (f) the development of industry (g) the conservation movement.
4. The frontier has influenced our nation in several ways. Give *two* facts to prove *each* of the following statements: (a) The frontier has helped the growth of democracy. (b) The frontier has led to conflicts. (c) The frontier has helped the nation to achieve greater economic self-sufficiency. (d) The frontier has inspired a considerable amount of American literary and artistic expression. (e) The frontier myth has expressed worthwhile American ideals.

2. Americans Esteem Education as a Cornerstone of Democracy

IMPORTANCE OF EDUCATION

Education serves Americans in many ways: By teaching basic skills, especially reading, writing, and arithmetic; training for employment; encouraging constructive—not wasteful—use of leisure time; and explaining complex world affairs and other cultures. Two further services of education are as follows:

1. Upward Social Mobility. Education enables Americans to improve their status in our society—that is, upward mobility. By learning to speak properly, to observe good manners, and to qualify for better occupations, educated individuals have moved up the social ladder. *(a)* The relationship between education and upward social mobility was apparent to immigrant groups. While immigrants often became unskilled and semiskilled workers, many insisted that their children attend school and qualify for managerial and professional positions. *(b)* This relationship was also apparent to black leaders. In 1847 Frederick Douglass, the Negro abolitionist, in his first editorial in the newspaper *North Star*, advised his "oppressed countrymen" to seek education, saying that "we shall be the advocates of learning from the very want of it" and shall respect "those who have labored hardest, and overcame most, in the praiseworthy pursuit of knowledge." In the post-Civil War years, Booker T. Washington, the head of Tuskegee Institute, urged blacks to secure an industrial or a vocational education, to prosper "as we learn to dignify and glorify common labour," to learn that "there is as much dignity in tilling a field as in writing a poem." *(c)* More recently, leaders of other disadvantaged minorities—Puerto Ricans, Mexican-Americans, and Indians—have urged their people to pursue education as the major highway for improving their status in society.

2. Citizenship in a Democracy. Education prepares individuals for the duties and responsibilities of American citizenship. Education links past generations to the present by transmitting our democratic heritage. Education trains individuals to understand local and national problems, to distinguish among candidates for public office and to vote intelligently, and to evaluate governmental actions.

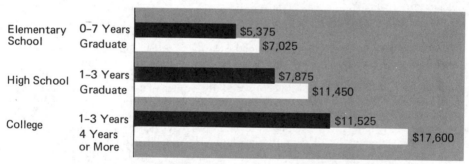

Average Yearly Income of Males, as Related to Years of Schooling

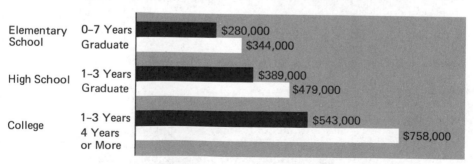

Average Lifetime Income of Males, as Related to Years of Schooling

Being a citizen in a democracy has always been more difficult than being a citizen in a dictatorship. The individual in a dictatorship does not have to understand national problems—merely to accept the official position; does not have to vote intelligently—merely to approve a single slate of candidates; does not have to evaluate governmental actions—merely to applaud the official policy.

This relationship between education and the responsibilities of democratic citizenship was apparent to our earliest leaders.

a. George Washington, in his 1796 Farewell Address, advised his countrymen to "promote, then, as an object of primary importance, institutions for the general diffusion of knowledge. In proportion as the structure of a government gives force to public opinion, it is essential that public opinion should be enlightened." In his last will and testament, Washington expressed regret that American youths were sent for education to foreign countries, where they learned "principles unfriendly to republican government and to the true and genuine liberties of mankind," and he urged establishment in the United States of a national university "to do away with local attachments and State prejudices" in educating "youths of fortune and talents."

b. Thomas Jefferson realized the need for an educated citizenry to assure wise legislation and to prevent governmental tyranny. In 1779, while Americans were still fighting for independence, Jefferson proposed that the Virginia Assembly enact a bill "For the More General Diffusion of Knowledge." The bill offered three years of elementary education at public expense to all free children, and secondary and college education at public expense for the most capable students. Too far ahead of the time, Jefferson's proposals were not enacted. In 1819 Jefferson established a free secular school of higher education, the University of Virginia.

c. James Madison was deeply interested in public education as a bulwark of democracy. He argued that "a people who mean to be their own Governors must arm themselves with the power which knowledge gives."

EDUCATION IN COLONIAL TIMES

1. Elementary Education

a. In New England. These colonists, overwhelmingly Congregationalist and intensely religious, believed that each individual should be able to read the Bible and therefore favored teaching children to read. They settled in towns so that schools could be located within walking distance. Massachusetts Colony led the way with its 1642 law requiring parents to enable their children "to read and understand the principles of religion" and with its 1647 law requiring each town of 50 families or more to maintain an elementary school to teach children to read and write—thereby furthering knowledge of the Scriptures and thwarting "that old deluder, Satan." Although poorly enforced, this and similar laws in other New England colonies reflected religious influence and established the principle that the community is responsible for the education of the children.

b. In the Middle Colonies. These colonists lived together in towns or farm communities. They belonged to many different Protestant sects, most of which provided elementary education in church schools. Children attending such schools paid tuition, although some poor children were admitted free. Other poor children may have received some education at home from their parents.

c. In the South. These colonists, belonging to diverse religious groups, were discouraged from establishing church schools by the great distances separating plantations. Children of well-to-do planters were taught by private tutors or in small private schools, whereas poorer children received little formal education.

d. On the Frontier. Children of frontier families received the least formal education but were often taught at home by their parents.

Throughout colonial America, elementary schools followed the European curriculum—the three R's, proper behavior, and religious instruction. American colonists as a group were better educated than the people of England and continental Europe. By the time of the Revolutionary War, over half the white colonial population probably could read and write.

2. Secondary Schools and Colleges. Children from well-to-do families prepared for professional careers through secondary and higher education. Young "gentlemen" attended secondary or Latin grammar schools, received instruction in Greek and Latin, and read the works of the ancient Roman authors. Having mastered these intellectual disciplines, they were ready for college. Various Protestant groups, in order to train ministers, established eight colonial colleges: Congregationalists—Harvard, Yale, Dartmouth; Anglicans—William and Mary, Columbia; Presbyterians—Princeton; Baptists—Brown; and Dutch Reformed—Rutgers. College students studied Latin, Greek, Hebrew, rhetoric (oratory and debating), ethics, and philosophy. While many students trained for the ministry, others prepared for careers in law, medicine, commerce, and government.

After 1750 the traditional Latin grammar school began to give way to the more democratic and more practical academy. Although the academy offered Greek and Latin, it emphasized English, history, politics, mathematics, and natural science. The Academy at Philadelphia, perhaps the first such school (1751), was inspired by Benjamin Franklin's Proposals Relating to the Education of Youth in Pennsylvania. Franklin, a printer and a self-educated man, urged that students be taught "those things that are likely to be most useful" with a view to professional careers. Franklin's academy evolved into the University of Pennsylvania—the first nondenominational liberal arts college in America.

DEVELOPMENT OF THE FREE PUBLIC SCHOOL: ELEMENTARY AND SECONDARY EDUCATION

1. Education as a State Function: Constitutional Provisions. Although the Founding Fathers were well aware of its importance, they made no mention of education in the Constitution. Perhaps they were too concerned with other matters: the Federalists with securing a strong central government and the anti-Federalists with protecting the people's civil liberties. Most likely the Founding Fathers were influenced also by the colonial school experience and considered education to be, not a federal concern, but a function of the various religious groups and of local or state governments.

The Tenth Amendment to the Constitution declares that all powers not given to the federal government nor prohibited to the states are reserved to the states or to the people. Education consequently became a "reserved" power.

2. Educational Currents in the Young Nation (To the 1820's)

a. Continuation of Colonial Educational Patterns. The states, preoccupied with recovering from the destruction and dislocation of the Revolutionary War, were content generally to leave education—as in colonial times—to towns and to religious and other private groups. Children of well-to-do families that could afford the tuition fees went to private schools. Some children of poorer families attended religious schools or, especially in New England, public primary schools maintained by towns. Most children, however, attended no school at all.

b. Major Educational Developments. (1) A number of states began giving limited financial aid to private and philanthropic schools providing elementary education to poorer children. (2) Public-spirited citizens in large Eastern cities founded free school societies. In 1805 New York City citizens organized a Free School Society. For half a century, it solicited private contributions, maintained schools, and gave instruction to half a million poorer children. In the public mind, however, pupils attending such free schools were viewed as "paupers." (3) In secondary education, the number of academies—private and church-controlled—grew sharply. Charging tuition, they attracted middle- and upper-class children—some preparing for the business world, others for college.

c. Progress in New York State. Exercising leadership in education, New York State enacted two laws—limited in immediate impact but significant in pointing the way toward state control of education—as follows: (1) In 1784 the state legislature established the University of the State of New York, an educational body, headed by the Board of Regents, to supervise secondary and higher education. (2) In 1812 the state legislature passed the New York Common School Act creating, for the first time in the United States, the position of state superintendent of elementary schools, and empowering him to plan a state system of common schools to be financed by local and state funds and supplemented by tuition fees. These tuition fees, levied upon parents who could afford to pay for their children's schooling, were known as *rate bills.* Parents unable to pay could be excused, but their children faced the charge of "pauperism." (In 1821 the position of state superintendent of schools was abolished, not to be restored until the 1850's.)

3. The Educational Awakening (From the Jacksonian Era Through the Civil War Era: 1820's–1860's)

a. Education Influenced by National Developments. The principle of free, tax-supported public elementary schools, available to all children without stigma of pauperism, became widely accepted and firmly established. The victory of this principle was made possible by major national developments: politically—the extension of the right to vote to all men, and the spirit of Jacksonian democracy; economically—the development of industrial capitalism, which resulted in the growth of cities and the formation of labor unions; and socially—the separation of church and state, the upsurge of American nationalism in the Northeastern and Northwestern states, and the rise of humanitarian concern for the welfare of children.

b. Opposition to Free Public Schools. The victory of the free public school movement was achieved only after long and bitter struggles against determined opposition, as follows: Wealthy persons claimed that taxing them to provide education for the children of the poor was unjust. Some upper-class persons argued that children of the poor did not need and could not benefit from an education. Private school spokesmen feared the loss of pupils, even those able to pay tuition, to free public schools. Religious leaders warned that secular public schools would not provide moral instruction and would encourage "godlessness."

c. Support for Free Public Schools. The principle of free public education had many supporters, as follows: Democratically minded persons insisted that all children receive an equal opportunity for education to develop their own potentials and to preserve our democratic way of life. Nationalists wanted all children educated regarding our nation's history, heroes, and holidays so as to foster patriotism. City workingmen demanded free public schools so as to educate their children and to remove children from the labor market. Nonsectarian leaders explained that free public schools were necessary to maintain separation of church and state. Humanitarians sought to remove the "pauper" stigma from children attending free schools and to lessen child labor. Educators envisioned the free public schools as the best way to provide children with civic, vocational, and moral training. Two outstanding educators who played major roles in this public school movement were Horace Mann and Henry Barnard.

Horace Mann was selected in 1837 to be the secretary of the newly founded Massachusetts Board of Education. Serving in this office for 11 years, Mann *(a)* aroused the public to the need for free, tax-supported, nonsectarian schools, *(b)* raised professional standards by establishing the first state-supported teacher-training school, and *(c)* introduced compulsory attendance, less rigid discipline, and a more varied curriculum. He expressed his philosophy of life in the statement "Be ashamed to die until you have won some victory for humanity." Horace Mann is known as the "father of the American public school."

Henry Barnard greatly improved the public school systems in Connecticut and Rhode Island. In 1867 he was appointed the first United States Commissioner of Education.

d. In New York State. By the 1860's the free public elementary school had become prevalent, especially in the Northeast. Typical were the developments in New York State. In 1834 the state began to support a teacher-training program by providing funds to academies to maintain special classes dealing with teaching methods and problems. In 1842 the state legislature prohibited the giving of tax money to schools teaching "any sectarian doctrine or tenet." In the 1850's New York restored the position of state superintendent of elementary schools. In 1867, by the *New York Free School Act,* the legislature abolished all tuition payments for common schools, leaving the system financed entirely by local and state taxes.

4. To the Present. In the past hundred years, educators and political leaders have greatly expanded free public school systems by *(a)* providing elementary schools throughout the nation, *(b)* developing public high schools and gradually raising the age for compulsory education to 16, and, in a few states, to 17 or 18 (whereas in 1900 only 11 percent of youths 14 to 17 years old attended high school, today the comparable figure is 93 percent), *(c)* equipping schools with facilities such as libraries, science laboratories, museums, gymnasiums, vocational shops, and homemaking and business-machine rooms, *(d)* enlarging the scope of the high school to include—in addition to the traditional preparation for college—training for citizenship, for the use of leisure time, and for gainful employment, and *(e)* offering students greater attention to their individual needs, a wider selection of courses, and a more democratic school atmosphere.

Many 20th-century developments in education were influenced by the noted educational philsopher *John Dewey*. At the turn of the century, Dewey presented his ideas in a series of books, most notably *School and Society* and *Democracy and Education*. Dewey advanced the theory that education was not merely the acquisition of academic knowledge but was part of living. He urged new methods of teaching that would appeal to the interests of pupils and would encourage them to learn by doing. Dewey insisted that American education must transmit to students a moral commitment to the democratic way of life.

Today more than 45 million pupils between the ages of five and 17 are enrolled in the public school systems, seeking to prepare themselves for life through education.

PRIVATE ELEMENTARY AND SECONDARY EDUCATION

Despite the great expansion in free public education, a significant role remains for private elementary and secondary schools. Supported largely by tuition payments, these schools enroll some 10 percent of the student population, or about 4.5 million pupils. These schools are of three types: (1) schools for special children—physically handicapped, mentally retarded, or exceptionally bright, (2) "prep" and other exclusive schools for upper-class children—often providing them with intensive preparation for college, and (3) the largest number—private religious or parochial schools. Of the parochial schools, 10 percent are maintained by Protestant and Jewish groups, 90 percent by the Roman Catholic Church. Like the public schools, the private and parochial schools must meet the educational standards set by state boards of education.

The upsurge in Catholic parochial schools was due to (1) the large increase in America's Catholic population resulting from the annexation in the 1840's of Texas, California, and other territories containing Mexican Catholics, the heavy immigration in the mid-19th century of Irish and German Catholics and at the turn of the 20th century of Italian and Polish Catholics, and the high birthrate among American Catholic families; (2) the desire of many Catholic parents that their children receive a Catholic-oriented education, including religious instruction; and (3) the efforts of Catholic religious leaders to establish a church-controlled school system.

Supporters claimed that private and parochial schools could better provide for children's special needs, more easily introduce educational innovations, allow teachers greater freedom, and preserve America's cultural diversity. Opponents claimed the private and parochial schools could engender feelings of separation in students and create "class" and religious divisions undercutting efforts to develop a uniquely American sense of values.

In recent years, as the costs of education have soared, especially due to inflation, some Catholic parochial schools have been forced to close and Catholic

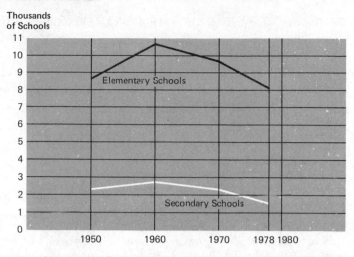

Number of Catholic Parochial Schools, 1950–1978

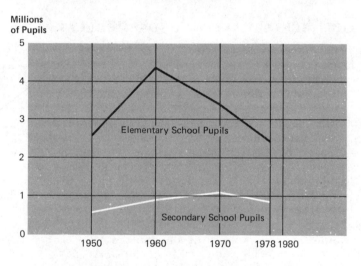

Enrollment in Catholic Parochial Schools, 1950–1978

spokesmen have requested state and federal funds for parochial schools. They point out that (1) Catholic parents whose children attend parochial schools are paying tuition in addition to taxes supporting public education, (2) the parochial schools relieve the public schools of a heavy financial burden and educational responsibility, and (3) the parochial schools meet state standards and provide a moral education rooted in American values. Opponents of providing public funds for parochial schools include most Protestant and Jewish groups and most public school educators. They insist that the First Amendment to the Constitution, separating church and state, prohibits the granting of public funds for church-controlled schools. (Check the Index for "Supreme Court, on financing public education.")

EDUCATION AS A CONCERN OF THE CENTRAL GOVERNMENT

1. Under the Articles of Confederation. Congress passed two Western land ordinances affecting education as follows: *(a)* The *Land Ordinance* of 1785 provided that (1) the Western lands be surveyed and divided into square townships of 36 sections each, a section being one square mile (640 acres), and (2) one section within each township be reserved for "the maintenance of public schools." The section reserved for education could be the site of a school building or it could be rented or sold with the resulting income going for public education. *(b)* The *Northwest Ordinance* of 1787 provided for government in the Northwest Territory and confirmed the previous policy of reserving one section in each township for education. The ordinance proclaimed that "religion, morality, and knowledge, being necessary to good government and the happiness of mankind, schools and the means of education shall forever be encouraged." The provisions of these ordinances were reenacted by Congress following the adoption of the Constitution.

2. The Federal Government and Education: Constitutional Provisions. Although the Tenth Amendment made education a power reserved to the states or people, the Constitution did not prohibit the federal government from encouraging, financing, and guiding education. By granting Congress the power to dispose of territory belonging to the United States, the Constitution enabled Congress to designate lands for the use of public education. By granting Congress the power to collect taxes for the "general welfare of the United States," the Constitution enabled Congress to declare education part of "general welfare" and therefore to appropriate money for educational purposes. By granting Congress the powers to "support armies" and "maintain a navy," the Constitution enabled Congress, in recent years, to declare education essential to national defense and therefore to provide money to strengthen the teaching of science, mathematics, foreign languages, English, and history.

3. Major Federal Legislation Pertaining to Education

a. The Morrill Land-Grant Act (1862) provided federal lands to states to spur the teaching of agriculture and mechanic arts. (Check the Index.)

b. The Office of Education Act (1867) provided for the establishment of the United States Office of Education (originally called a Department). Headed by a commissioner of education, this office has collected data regarding the condition of American education, has diffused information regarding school systems and teaching methods, and has otherwise promoted the cause of education. Lacking direct control over schools, the Office of Education has provided leadership by issuing reports, publishing bulletins, stimulating research, and recently setting desegregation "guidelines." In 1953 the Office of Education became part of the Cabinet-level Department of Health, Education, and Welfare.

c. Three Agricultural Education Acts provided federal funds under the (1) Hatch Act (1887) for agricultural experiment stations affiliated with land-grant colleges, (2) Smith-Lever Act (1914) for county agents to bring agricultural information directly to farmers, and (3) Smith-Hughes Act (1917) for high schools to give courses in agriculture.

d. The Servicemen's Readjustment Act (1944), popularly known as the *G.I. Bill of Rights*, provided financial assistance to World War II veterans seeking a college education. Subsequent laws offered similar benefits to veterans of the Korean and Vietnamese wars.

e. The National Defense Education Act (1958) began a program of federal aid to schools in the interests of national defense. (Check the Index.)

f. The Elementary and Secondary Education Act (1965) began a comprehensive program of direct and unrestricted federal aid to schools. (Check the Index.)

g. Various Laws, passed since World War II, provided (1) grants to subsidize school lunches for needy children, to aid the education of disadvantaged children, and to encourage construction of college classrooms, (2) federal guarantees of private loans to college students, and (3) federal scholarships, called "educational opportunity grants," for needy college students.

BRIEF SURVEY OF HIGHER EDUCATION

1. To the Civil War. Before 1860 various religious groups founded about 200 colleges. Originally, these schools prepared students for the ministry and taught Latin, Greek, grammar, and philosophy. Later, as they began preparing students for other vocations, they expanded their courses of study. Also, a few states, such as Georgia and Virginia in the South, Vermont in New England, and Michigan in the Midwest, founded state universities, which offered courses in the liberal arts and in various professional subjects.

2. Developments to the Present. Since 1860 American colleges and universities have grown in number and broadened their scope. *(a)* The *Morrill Land-Grant Act* (1862) granted federal lands to states to support colleges teaching agriculture and mechanic arts. This act helped increase the number of state colleges and universities. Furthermore, it stimulated the movement toward more practical subjects such as agricultural science, veterinary medicine, and engineering. Among the well-known land-grant colleges today are the state universities of Wisconsin, Illinois, Texas, and California. The University of California, which has campuses throughout the state and enrolls over 100,000 full-time students, is one of the largest institutions of higher learning in the world. *(b) Technical schools,* usually privately endowed, were founded and have maintained high standards in training chemists, physicists, architects, and engineers. One example is the Massachusetts Institute of Technology.

3. Higher Education Today. The United States today contains over 2000 colleges and universities. They may be classified as follows: *(a)* Slightly more than one-third are church-controlled institutions, mostly Protestant and Roman Catholic. *(b)* Slightly less than one-third are privately controlled. *(c)* One-third are publicly controlled—by states, cities, or school districts. Among the largest is the State University of New York, consisting of a number of colleges throughout the state with a total enrollment of over 340,000.

American colleges and universities may also be classified according to their programs: *(a)* Slightly more than two-thirds offer a four-year course, and many of these institutions offer graduate work. *(b)* Slightly less than one-third are community, or junior, colleges. These schools, which grew rapidly after World War II, offer a two-year course, enabling students to prepare for a technical career or to transfer to a four-year college.

The number of students in today's colleges and universities totals about 12 million. Whereas in 1900 only 4 percent of youths 18 to 21 years old were enrolled in college, today the comparable figure is about 40 percent.

In 1976, with all colleges facing sharply rising costs from inflation, the City University of New York abandoned its 125-year tradition of free higher education and imposed tuition.

EDUCATION THROUGH INFORMAL MEANS

1. Education: A Perspective. In its broadest sense, education is a solitary or individual attainment in which the learner is influenced by both formal means —the classroom and laboratory—and informal means. Informal education is derived from life itself, for individuals learn from the very process of living.

Certainly, a number of our outstanding early leaders had little formal education. Andrew Jackson lived on the frontier where his schooling was scant and sporadic, yet he learned to read and write, served in a lawyer's office, studied law by himself, and at age 20 was admitted to the bar; later he became an attorney-general and a judge. Abraham Lincoln, a frontier farmboy, had about one year of formal schooling, but he learned to read, write, and do arithmetic; he eagerly read whatever books he found, including the Bible, Shakespeare, and a life of Washington. At age 25, Lincoln began studying law; he borrowed law books from an attorney friend, was soon admitted to the bar, and became a successful lawyer.

2. Multiple Sources of Informal Education. In the course of daily living, individuals come in contact with many sources from which they learn. Such sources include: *(a)* parents—who set patterns of intrafamily behavior and express family values, *(b)* the home—which constitutes the immediate and most direct environment, *(c)* church—which proclaims standards of ethical and moral behavior, *(d)* friends or peers—who influence each other and together arrive at group opinions, *(e)* travel—which provides examples of different patterns of living and standards of value, and *(f)* mass media, including books, magazines, newspapers, radio and television programs, and movies.

All individuals learn from these sources. For most, such learning is not a conscious process but results automatically from repeated contacts and examples. For others who have a keen sense of observation and awareness, such learning may be a more deliberate process—accepting and discarding.

3. Facilities for Informal Education

a. Chautauqua Movement. Begun in 1874, this program of adult education was designed originally for Sunday school teachers on summer vacation, but it proved so successful that it was opened to the general public. The movement took its name from Lake Chautauqua in western New York, the site of the original and most successful program. Chautauqua combined summer relaxation with a rich cultural program—of lectures, discussion groups, concerts, readings, and plays. The success of the original Chautauqua led, in the late 19th century, to the establishment of other Chautauquas throughout the country. In the 20th century, however, with the coming of airplanes, movies, radio, and television, the Chautauqua movement declined. The original Chautauqua still thrives, attracting each summer thousands of people who seek a purposeful vacation.

b. Public Libraries. In 1731 Benjamin Franklin founded in Philadelphia the first subscription library society. Each member contributed funds for the purchase of books and could borrow from the collection. Other colonial cities soon established their own library societies. In 1800 Congress established the *Library of Congress* to serve legislative needs, and the institution has become a national public library. In the mid-19th century, towns and states began appropriating tax funds for free public libraries. Further expansion of free public libraries was aided by contributions of private philanthropists, the best-known one being *Andrew Carnegie*. Starting in the 1880's, he provided $31 million to construct library buildings in 1700 towns on condition that the town officials agree to use public funds to purchase books, hire personnel, and maintain library services. Today Americans have access to thousands of free public libraries. In addition to lending books, magazines, and phonograph records, many libraries conduct educational programs—discussion groups, lectures, and movies—of interest to members of the community.

c. Other Facilities. (1) Museums, under government or private control, are usually open to the public free or for a nominal charge. Museums are organized generally around themes such as natural history, fine art, modern art, Indian lore, an ethnic group, and local history. Museums have been reaching out to attract visitors by offering guided tours, special exhibits, lectures, and movies. (2) National parks, historic sites, and historic monuments are maintained by the federal government through the National Park Service. These areas are visited by some 80 million Americans annually. National parks—such as Yellowstone (Wyoming), Acadia (Maine), and Shenandoah (Virginia)—offer visitors the opportunity to use recreational facilities and to observe the natural scenery. National historic sites—such as the Saratoga (New York) battlefield, the Gettysburg (Pennsylvania) battlefield, the Booker T. Washington birthplace (Virginia) and the Franklin D. Roosevelt home (New York)—offer visitors the opportunity better to understand our history. Other parks and historic sites are maintained by various states. (3) Concerts and plays, usually free or at low cost, are sponsored by federal agencies and local recreation departments. (4) Lecture series and discussion sessions are offered by labor unions, management groups, churches, and other community-minded organizations.

EDUCATIONAL ISSUES AND PROBLEMS TODAY

1. Integration of Public Schools, Including Related Subsidiary Problems. (Check the Index for "Education, desegregation of.")

2. Various School Policies

a. Remedial Classes for Underprivileged Children. As part of a massive effort to teach underprivileged children to read, write, and do arithmetic, many schools have spent considerable sums for special teachers, small classes, and expensive instructional materials. Educators are divided as to the effectiveness of such programs. Supporters claim that the programs have been of great educational value. Critics claim that the programs have had little educational impact and that children's academic progress is determined more by home environment and socioeconomic status than by the school itself.

b. Homogeneous Grouping. In the upper elementary grades and high schools of large cities, students frequently are separated on the basis of academic ability as determined by reading tests and class marks. Especially in the high schools, students are placed in one of three tracks—the bright in honors classes, the average in regular classes, and the poorest achievers in modified classes. This arrangement, placing together students of similar ability, is known as *homogeneous grouping.* The alternative arrangement, providing random or unplanned selection, so that students of diverse abilities are placed in the same class, is known as *heterogeneous grouping.*

Supporters claim that homogeneous grouping permits each class to work at its own pace and avoids frustrations that result when "bright" and "slow" pupils are in the same class. Critics claim that slow learners placed in modified classes are stigmatized as "dumb." Critics also complain that in large integrated city high schools, homogeneous grouping results in segregated classes—with whites assigned to the bright and average classes, whereas blacks, who are often educationally disadvantaged, fill the modified classes.

c. Teaching Ethnic Group History. Since World War II, Americans have become aware that we constitute a pluralistic society of different ethnic backgrounds. This awareness has spilled over, especially into the large city high schools, where Social Studies departments have offered new ethnic history courses and English departments have offered ethnic literature courses. Supporters claim that such courses fill in neglected areas of our history and literature and enable ethnic minority children to learn of their own heritage and to develop self-respect. Critics claim that such courses become lost in trivia and that they serve to divide one ethnic group from the other instead of achieving the American ideal of "e pluribus unum," meaning "out of many, one."

d. Open Enrollment in New York City Colleges. In the late 1960's, New York City pioneered an educational innovation known as *open enrollment.* The city guaranteed every graduate from a city high school a place in one of the city's two-year community colleges or in one of the city's four-year regular colleges. Supporters praised this innovation for opening higher education to disadvantaged minority children, especially blacks and Puerto Ricans, and for furthering the democratic goal of education for all. Critics condemned this innovation for burdening the colleges with more students than their facilities could handle, compelling the colleges to offer remedial courses in reading and arithmetic, lowering standards of achievement in regular courses, and leading to a large dropout rate. Critics also pointed out that our society has many worthwhile and well-paying occupations that do not require a college education and therefore not every high school graduate needs to go to college.

3. Need for Adult Education. Adults have increasingly shown interest in courses to improve their written and spoken English, to learn new vocational skills, and to broaden their cultural horizons. Their interest has resulted in additional night schools, college extension courses, forums, lectures, and study groups. Still more facilities are planned for the future.

4. Education for National Defense: Challenge of Soviet Russia. Americans were startled by Russia's early leadership in the space race when, in 1957, Russia launched the world's first artificial satellite, Sputnik I. Americans began to reexamine their educational system. Many observers made the following conclusions: (*a*) In science, mathematics, and technical subjects, Russian high school graduates, after ten years of study, were far ahead of American graduates after

12 years. (b) Communist society channeled the ablest Russian students into the fields of science, mathematics, and engineering by offering incentives of higher pay, better living conditions, and community approval. American society did not provide comparable incentives, and many American students preferred non-technical occupations.

Congress passed the *National Defense Education Act* (1958) providing for (a) grants to states for the purchase of textbooks and other materials needed to strengthen the teaching of science, mathematics, and foreign languages, (b) grants to states for programs to locate and encourage gifted students, and (c) loans and graduate fellowships for college students, especially for those interested in teaching. (The act has been extended several times and expanded to include grants to states for instructional materials for English and history.)

5. Finances for Elementary and Secondary Schools

a. State and Local Support. Public education has been financed overwhelmingly by state and local taxes. In the late 1970's the average annual expenditure for public education was over $1,800 per pupil. This average figure, however, hid wide variations from state to state. Relatively wealthy industrial states spent considerably more than other states. New York spent over $2,600 per pupil, New Jersey about $2,300. The poorer, rural Southern states of Kentucky, Mississippi, and Arkansas each spent just over $1,200. The Southern states as a group lagged behind the rest of the nation in educational spending.

b. Debate Over Federal Aid

(1) *Supporters.* Especially since World War II many educators and political leaders have urged that federal funds be used for the overall improvement of

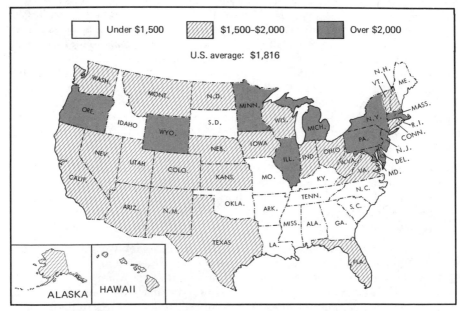

Per Pupil Public Education Expenditure by the States

public education. They argued that federal funds are necessary to improve education generally and to raise the level of education in the poorer states.

(2) *Opponents.* Advocates of states' rights feared that federal aid might lead to federal control of education, thereby further reducing the powers of the states. Roman Catholic leaders opposed any federal program that omitted funds for parochial schools.

c. Elementary and Secondary Education Act (1965). By gearing federal education aid to the "war on poverty" and adopting a new approach to the parochial school issue, President Lyndon Johnson gained quick Congressional passage of this law. It provided for (1) grants to the nation's public school districts based on their number of children from families whose annual incomes were below $2000 (the school districts may use these funds to hire more teachers, raise teachers' salaries, construct new buildings, and provide special courses), (2) grants to states for the purchase of textbooks, library books, and audiovisual aids to be used by public, private, and parochial school students, and (3) grants to create public education centers for special instruction on a "shared-time" basis for public, private, and parochial school students.

This act (1) satisfied Roman Catholic leaders by providing instructional materials and educational centers for parochial students, (2) satisfied advocates of separation of church and state by giving public officials control of the shared resources and by granting aid to parochial students rather than to parochial schools, and (3) established a precedent of direct federal aid for overall improvement of the public schools. (This act continues to be funded by renewed federal appropriations.)

d. Recent Financial Developments. (1) In *Robinson vs. Dicenso* (1971), the Supreme Court declared unconstitutional the Rhode Island law that provided state funds to help pay salaries of parochial school teachers of nonreligious subjects. (2) In 1971 several lower courts held unconstitutional the reliance chiefly upon local property taxes for financing public education. Within a state, poor districts obtained much less money per child for education than did rich

Shaky position
(*Englehardt in the*
St. Louis Post-Dispatch)

districts. In *Rodriguez vs. San Antonio School District* (1973) the Supreme Court, by a 5 to 4 vote, upheld the property tax as a method of financing public school systems. The majority opinion held that the "equal protection" clause of the 14th Amendment did not require "absolute equality" and that education is not listed in the Constitution as a fundamental right. The majority opinion further stated that the need for reform in financing public education was clear but that such reform should come, not from the Supreme Court, but from the states. The minority opinion attacked the decision as a "retreat from an historic commitment to equality of educational opportunity." The battle for more equitable public school financing is now expected to shift to the various state courts and legislatures.

MULTIPLE-CHOICE QUESTIONS

1. Historically, free public education in the United States has been urged as necessary (1) for the effective functioning of a democracy (2) for promotion of the arts (3) to instill moral qualities in the citizenry (4) for scientific advancement.
2. Statistics show that, as a group, persons with more education will earn higher incomes than those with less education. This information leads to the conclusion that (1) educators control the job market in the United States (2) a poorly educated person has no hope of earning a good living (3) education is a major route for disadvantaged groups to improve their status in our society (4) college-educated persons need have no fear of unemployment.
3. The early leaders of Massachusetts Colony emphasized education because they desired to encourage (1) democracy in government (2) an enlightened public opinion (3) the reading of the Bible (4) religious toleration.
4. In the New England colonies, elementary schools were generally maintained by the (1) towns (2) English government (3) Anglican Church (4) colonial legislatures.
5. The first colleges in New England were organized primarily to (1) teach medicine and law (2) teach the practical arts and sciences (3) prepare persons for the ministry (4) train gentlemen-farmers.
6. During the period 1825–1860, which was an important factor in the movement for a tax-supported public school system? (1) unpopularity of religious schools (2) heritage of state-supported schools brought from Europe (3) leadership of wealthy groups who believed in equal opportunity for all (4) influence of the wage-earning class in the cities
7. Which statement is *not* true of the career of Horace Mann? (1) He served as secretary to the Massachusetts Board of Education. (2) He established the first state-supported teacher-training school. (3) He introduced compulsory school attendance and a more varied curriculum. (4) He served as first president of Harvard College.
8. An upsurge in elementary parochial schools in the United States in the latter 19th century resulted from (1) heavy Catholic immigration to the United States (2) heavy Jewish immigration to the United States (3) the availability of federal funds for private schools (4) federal land grants for private elementary schools.
9. Under the Articles of Confederation, the central government encouraged education by (1) establishing the United States Office of Education (2) setting aside one section of land in each township for public education (3) providing funds for agricultural experiment states (4) providing funds for Revolutionary War veterans to go to college.

10. The Morrill Act of 1862 aided education by giving (1) to each state the right to control its own schools (2) to colleges funds for research (3) to each state public land, the income from which was to be used for agricultural colleges (4) to the federal government a grant of money to set up an office of education.

11. Which event spurred Congress to pass the National Defense Education Act of 1958? (1) the Soviet launching of Sputnik I (2) China's explosion of her first atomic bomb (3) the seizure of power in Cuba by Fidel Castro (4) French expulsion from Vietnam

12. Beginning in the 1950's, the federal government has aided college education by all of the following *except* (1) loans for construction of college classrooms (2) grants for purchase of equipment (3) special tax exemptions for parents supporting children at college (4) scholarships for needy students.

13. In the United States, which *best* explains why the federal government played a minor role in education until recent years? (1) Historically, education has been regarded primarily as the responsibility of the individual localities and states. (2) Until recently, parents have been financially responsible for their children's education. (3) The federal government could not afford to provide aid until after World War II. (4) All Presidents, until after World War II, opposed federal aid to education.

14. Which statement *best* describes the role of the federal government in education in the United States since World War II? (1) Federal funds for education have greatly increased. (2) Federal legislation has abolished school segregation. (3) Many states have refused aid from the federal government. (4) Local and state control of education has been taken over by the federal government.

15. A basic reason for federal expenditures for education in the United States is the (1) attempt to centralize education under a single agency (2) concern for the full development of the nation's human resources (3) desire to eliminate the existing dual system of private and public education (4) need to justify the high federal income tax rates.

16. Expanded public library facilities throughout the United States are primarily a reflection of the increasing (1) rate of illiteracy (2) value of informal education (3) responsibilities of citizenship (4) inadequacy of the public school system.

17. Which statement regarding the Elementary and Secondary Education Act of 1965 is *not* true? (1) It was related to the "war on poverty." (2) It granted money to states for the purchase of instructional materials to be used by parochial school students. (3) It began federal aid to public education. (4) It provided federal aid directly to school districts.

18. Today, public education in the United States is supported by (1) local governments only (2) state governments only (3) the national government only (4) local, state, and national governments.

19. Today, most policy decisions affecting public schools in the United States are made by (1) federal courts (2) Congress (3) local boards of education (4) the Secretary of Health, Education, and Welfare.

20. Which is a valid statement about education in the United States in the 1970's? (1) The number of high school graduates is declining. (2) The federal government is spending a larger amount of money in support of education than all state and local governments combined. (3) The public school system is under considerable criticism. (4) Private schools are gradually replacing public schools.

ESSAY QUESTIONS

1. Throughout the history of the United States, our practices and policies in the field of education have been influenced by our national ideals and by historical developments.

Give *two* specific examples to prove the truth of this statement for *each* of the following periods: (*a*) 1829–1860 (*b*) 1860–1945 (*c*) 1945–present.

2. The United States today faces the problem of equalizing educational opportunities for all Americans. (*a*) Show in *two* ways how this problem arose out of conditions in American life. (*b*) Describe in *one* way how this problem affects the welfare of the American people as a whole. (*c*) Illustrate *two* ways by which this problem is being tackled by the federal government.

3. Agree or disagree with *each* of the following statements and present *two* reasons to support your opinion: (*a*) Religious factors, from colonial times onward, have influenced the development of education in America. (*b*) Informal means of education can supplement but not replace formal schooling. (*c*) In large city high schools, homogeneous grouping—the placing of pupils of similar ability in the same classes—provides for better learning. (*d*) Regardless of academic achievement, every high school graduate should be guaranteed admission to college. (*e*) The granting of federal funds for public education will eventually lead to federal control of public education. (*f*) The local property tax, as a major source of funds for public schools, has many disadvantages. (*g*) The American educational system reflects both the strengths and weaknesses of diversity.

4. In your high school, you are currently receiving an education. (*a*) Describe *two* ways in which this education has been of benefit to you. (*b*) Discuss *two* ways in which this education could be improved. Support your opinion with facts.

Part 2. American Culture:
Rich and Varied

3. *Americans Excel at Science and Technology*

Definition of Terms

(1) *Science* is an intellectual and creative pursuit seeking to understand the world of nature: man, matter, and the universe. This definition emphasizes science as an experimental method of accumulating and interpreting data. Science is also a body of organized knowledge relating to the world of nature. The second definition emphasizes science as a collection of data. To arrange scientific knowledge logically, science is divided into branches such as chemistry, physics, geology, biology, medicine, and astronomy. Frequently, scientific branches overlap, creating interesting and exciting areas of study, such as biochemistry and astrophysics.

(2) *Pure*, or *basic*, *science* is primarily concerned with gathering new knowledge for its own sake without direct regard for its use. Pure scientists strive for knowledge to better understand the world of nature, not for any immediate practical value.

(3) *Practical*, or *applied*, *science* is concerned with utilizing the discoveries of pure science to meet specific, down-to-earth purposes. Applied scientists seek the causes and cures of disease, the invention of new machines, the introduction of new processes, and the development of new products.

(4) *Technology*, which includes engineering, is the study of the industrial arts for their practical value. Technologists work in industry seeking to achieve the most efficient methods of production and the highest quality of product. Technologists may depend upon the work of applied scientists or may themselves be applied scientists. In the general sense, technology and applied science are considered synonymous and are used interchangeably.

AMERICAN SCIENCE: FROM COLONIAL TIMES TO THE MID-20TH CENTURY

1. American Dependence Upon European Pure Science. Until recently Americans relied largely on European scientists for the fundamental concepts of pure science: such as the law of gravitation, laws of heredity, theory of evolution and structure of the atom. For pure science, Europeans had the advantages of established universities, research facilities, scientific associations, and financial resources. (In addition to pure science, Europeans also made major contributions to applied science—as evidenced by the numerous inventions that ushered in the Industrial Revolution in England.)

2. American Emphasis Upon Applied Science. Meanwhile American scientists excelled in applied science. Americans were concerned with solving practical problems: such as separating the seed from the cotton fiber, cultivating large farms in a labor-scarce society, and binding together a nation whose size was greater than all Europe from the Atlantic coast to the Russian border. Americans became known for their originality, resourcefulness, and inventiveness—traits encompassed by the term "*Yankee ingenuity.*"

CASE STUDIES: EUROPEAN PURE SCIENCE AND AMERICAN APPLIED SCIENCE

1. In Electricity: A Branch of Physics

European Pure Scientists

Michael Faraday (1791–1867), an English chemist and physicist, discovered the principle of electromagnetic induction; utilizing a magnet, he caused an electric current to flow in a wire. This principle later made possible the *dynamo* and *generator* for producing electricity.

James Clerk Maxwell (1831–1870), a Scottish physicist and mathematician, built upon Faraday's work to state mathematically the laws of electromagnetic fields. These laws became the foundation of electrical and radio science.

American Applied Scientists

Benjamin Franklin (1706–1790) was a man of many talents—printer, author, diplomat, and scientist. By his famed kite experiment during a thunderstorm, he identified lightning as electricity. To keep lightning from damaging houses, barns, and other buildings, Franklin devised a *lightning rod* which conducts lightning harmlessly into the ground. (Franklin also devised two other practical inventions: bifocal lenses and a fuel-conserving iron stove.)

Joseph Henry (1797–1878), born in Albany, New York, was a physicist who utilized his fundamental understanding of electromagnetism for practical purposes. By insulating wire, Henry was able to wind wire in many layers around an electromagnet and thereby increase its strength. (Henry's improvement —insulated wire—aided Faraday in his discovery of electromagnetic induction.) Henry also devised other practical equipment: an electric motor; the first electromagnetic telegraph, which served as a model for subsequent commercial telegraphy; and the electromagnetic relay, which amplifies electric impulses sent through wire and thereby increases the distance over which telegraphic messages could be sent.

Samuel F. B. Morse (1791–1872) demonstrated the first long-distance telegraph and devised the Morse code; *Alexander Graham Bell* (1847–1922) invented the telephone; *Thomas Edison* (1847–1931) invented the phonograph, electric light bulb, and motion picture machine.

2. In Biological Sciences

European Pure Scientists

Charles Darwin (1809–1882), an English naturalist, in his book *The Origin of Species*, stated his *theory of evolution*. Darwin held that, during vast intervals of time, man and other complex forms of life evolved from simpler forms by the process of *natural selection* or *survival of the fittest*.

Gregor Mendel (1822–1884), an Austrian monk and botanist, experimented with the crossbreeding of pea plants and developed the *laws of heredity*. "Mendelianism" gave impetus to scientific breeding of plants and animals.

American Applied Scientists

Luther Burbank (1849–1926), a horticulturalist and plant breeder, applied Darwin's principle of selection and Mendel's laws of heredity to breed over 800 new and improved varieties of grasses, flowers, vegetables, and fruits. Burbank originated the edible spineless cactus, the "plumcot"—a crossbreeding of plum and apricot—and the Burbank or *Idaho potato*. Burbank also raised new and improved varieties of plums, apples, peaches, and nectarines.

George Washington Carver (1864–1943), a Negro, was a botanist, chemist, and scientific agriculturalist associated with Tuskegee Institute. He worked to help Southern farmers—many being black—end their dependence on cotton and diversify their crops. Carver discovered new commercial uses for sweet potatoes, soybeans, pecans, and peanuts. From the peanut and the sweet potato, Carver derived over 300 different products, including plastics, dyes, oils, medicines, and fertilizer. Carver also experimented with crossbreeding to produce an improved cotton plant and better vegetables. Carver's efforts vitally transformed Southern agriculture.

Percy Julian (1899–   ), a black chemist and industrialist, worked especially on hormones and sterols—which are vital chemical substances found in plants and animals. For many years, Julian was director of soybean research at a large agricultural processing corporation and thereafter he established his own specialized chemical company. Julian's investigations resulted in a synthetic drug used in treating glaucoma—an eye disease, an aerofoam fire extinguisher product used by the United States Navy in World War II, and another synthetic drug, *cortisone*, used to help sufferers from arthritis.

3. In Atomic Science

European Pure Scientists

John Dalton (1766–1844), an English chemist and physicist, explained the structure of matter by his *atomic theory*. He held that all matter is composed of tiny, invisible particles called *atoms*.

Ernest Rutherford (1871–1937), a British physicist, discovered that the atom is composed largely of empty space with almost all of its mass concentrated in its center, or nucleus.

Albert Einstein (1879–1955), a Jew born in Germany, has been hailed as perhaps the outstanding theoretical physicist of all time. He expressed the complex relationship of matter, space, motion, and time in his *theory of relativity*. Einstein predicted that a small amount of matter could be converted into a tremendous quantity of energy according to the formula $E = mc^2$ (energy equals mass multiplied by the speed of light—186,000 miles per second—squared). Einstein fled his native land because of Nazi religious persecution, became a naturalized American citizen, and in 1939 informed President Franklin D. Roosevelt that an atomic bomb could be built and that Nazi scientists were working to that end. Einstein advised the President to initiate an American atomic-bomb project and his advice was heeded.

Niels Bohr (1885–1962), a Danish physicist, described the atom as a miniature solar system. A refugee from Nazi-occupied Europe during World War II, Bohr worked on the American atomic-bomb project.

Enrico Fermi (1901–1954), an Italian physicist, employed slow-speed neutrons to split the nucleus of the uranium atom. He fled in 1938 from Fascist Italy, became a naturalized American citizen, and served with the United States atomic-bomb research team. In 1942 at Chicago, Fermi achieved the first man-made nuclear chain reaction.

American Applied Scientists

Vannevar Bush (1890–1974), engineer and administrator, believed that military strength was essential for the preservation of American democracy. In 1940 Bush convinced President Roosevelt of the importance of mobilizing American scientists and technologists for war. Bush became head of a federal defense research committee which evolved into the Office of Scientific Research and Development. From this post Bush had overall responsibility for developing sophisticated new weapons such as radar, amphibious vehicles, antisubmarine devices, and, most important, the atomic bomb. Even before Fermi in 1942 achieved the first atomic chain reaction, Bush took a calculated risk to save time and ordered construction of plants to process the uranium fuel for atomic bombs. After the war Bush urged heavy federal support for basic scientific research.

Leslie R. Groves (1896–1970), born in Albany, New York, was an army engineer and general. In 1943 Groves assumed overall responsibility for building the atomic bomb. Since Groves headed the army's Manhattan Engineer District, the atomic bomb project became known as the *Manhattan Project*. While Bush continued to advise the program, Groves supervised the creation and operation of atomic research and production facilities.

J. Robert Oppenheimer (1904–1967), a nuclear physicist, devoted his early career to teaching and pure research. From 1943 to 1945, he was in charge of the *Los Alamos, New Mexico*, laboratory—a part of the Manhattan Project. Oppenheimer headed the group of scientists and engineers who built the first atomic bomb. From 1947 to 1966, he was director of the *Institute for Advanced Study* at Princeton, New Jersey, an outstanding American center for pure or theoretical physics.

AMERICAN SCIENCE IN RECENT TIMES

Especially since the World War II era, American scientists have continued with practical research but have begun also to delve deeply into basic research. This new emphasis probably reflected the following factors: (1) American scientists have become increasingly aware that discoveries in basic research are essential prerequisites for progress in technology. (2) Because World War II had brought so much destruction to Europe, Americans could no longer depend upon European scientists for basic research discoveries. (3) America emerged from World War II with an undamaged homeland and tremendous financial resources. America had the advantages of research facilities and funds to finance studies in basic science. (4) Because of its high standard of living, excellent research facilities, and atmosphere of freedom, America attracted to its shores many European and other foreign scientists—the "brain drain." Among prominent "brain drain" scientists who came to America were *Wernher von Braun*, the rocket engineer and space flight expert from Germany, and *Jean Mayer*, the physiologist and nutrition specialist from France. (5) More aware than ever before of the importance of science in coping with national problems, the federal government began appropriating tremendous sums for scientific research. These sums—in the billions of dollars—went mainly for applied research, but increasingly substantial amounts, over 10 percent, supported basic research.

RECENT AMERICAN SCIENCE: AREAS OF RESEARCH

American scientists are engaged in basic and applied research in many areas, as follows:

1. **Solar energy** deals with the study of the sun—the fiery center of our solar system—and its radiation of heat and light. Although the earth receives only a minute portion of the sun's radiation—one part in two billion—it suffices to warm the earth, affect our weather, and make possible plant growth. In studying solar energy, pure scientists have been seeking answers to basic research questions such as: By what process does the sun emit radiation? What is the physical nature of such radiation? Can more solar radiation be directed toward the earth? How does the earth's dense atmosphere affect the passage through it of solar radiation? To what extent is solar energy dissipated and why? American solar-energy scientists have received invaluable data and gained important insights from our space program.

With the Arab oil boycott in 1973, Americans abruptly realized that our nation faced an energy crisis. We were using too much fossil fuels such as oil and gas and were becoming too dependent for supplies upon foreign nations. American attention focused upon alternative sources of energy—one obvious possibility being the sun. The federal government, through its *National Science Foundation*, made grants to major corporations for applied research—to determine the feasibility of solar heating and to develop the necessary hardware, especially radiation collectors. These corporations have reported making substantial progress toward harnessing solar energy. They have also predicted that solar energy would be competitive in cost with fossil fuels by 1985–1990 beginning in the sun-drenched West and Southwest, and that by the next century solar energy would save the nation more gasoline than is presently being consumed by automobiles.

2. **Oceanography** deals with the study of the oceans—the great bodies of salt water that cover more than two-thirds of the earth's surface, provide a home for extensive plant and animal life, and contain varied mineral and other resources in the waters and on and below the ocean floor. Oceanography is not a single study but cuts across many scientific fields such as botany, biology, geology, mineralogy, and geography.

American scientists became increasingly interested in oceanography in the late 1950's, following a report by the prestigious science advisory body—the

National Academy of Sciences. Scientific interest was spurred in the 1960's as Congress established the *National Sea Grant Program* to encourage universities to develop and expand departments of oceanography. Pure scientists have been engaged in: exploring the plains, valleys, and mountains under the oceans; drilling holes in the ocean floor for data regarding the theory of continental drift—that millions of years ago the continents were joined together and then drifted apart to where they are now; analyzing the content and sources of *plankton*—that microscopic animal and plant life found in the oceans and eaten by fish; and cataloging marine flora and fauna.

Oceanographic research is expensive since it requires specially constructed ships and submarines containing complex scientific equipment. Oceanography also requires special research facilities such as those provided by the Rockefeller Foundation at its *Woods Hole Oceanographic Institution* on Cape Cod, Massachusetts, and by the University of California at its *Scripps Institute of Oceanography* at La Jolla, California.

The expense of oceanographic research has placed increasing emphasis upon achieving practical results. For "Effective Use of the Sea"—the title of a 1966 report by the President's Science Advisory Committee—many government grants and industry assignments have gone to technologists and applied scientists to: control coastal waters so as to prevent shoreline erosion; increase the supply of shrimp and other marine foods for human consumption; assist fishing boats by locating major schools of tuna; determine favorable locations for off-shore drilling for natural gas and oil; develop economical methods of scooping up from the ocean floor the nodules containing minerals such as manganese, iron, nickel, copper, and cobalt; and achieve a low-cost process for desalinization of seawater so as to provide fresh water for drinking and irrigation purposes.

3. Other areas in which American scientists are engaged in basic and applied research include biochemistry, nuclear physics, geophysics, and solid-state physics.

FINANCIAL SUPPORT FOR SCIENCE IN AMERICA

1. From Colonial Times Through the 19th Century

a. By Individual Scientists. American scientists generally supported themselves while engaged in the quest for invention and technological progress. The experiences of American scientists, previously discussed (pages 412–414), serve to illustrate this statement.

Benjamin Franklin started working at an early age as a printer's apprentice and eventually became the owner of a profitable printing business. At age 42, Franklin retired, turned the printing business over to a partner, and received an income that permitted him to live in comfort and to devote his time to other activities, especially public service and science. A few years after his business retirement, Franklin performed his kite experiment and devised the lightning rod.

Joseph Henry worked for a livelihood as an instructor in natural science at the Albany Academy and then at the College of New Jersey (now Princeton). During his teaching career, Henry made time for his scientific research, but his duties as a teacher took precedence over and interfered with his research activities. Some observers believe that Henry discovered the principle of electromagnetic induction before Faraday but that Henry lacked the time to write up and publish his findings so that Faraday received credit for being the original discoverer.

Samuel F. B. Morse worked on his long-distance telegraph while living on his salary as an art teacher at the University of the City of New York (now New York University). Morse's equipment interested Alfred Vail, a student and son of a prosperous iron manufacturer, who began providing Morse with financial assistance. Morse and Vail lobbied in Washington and eventually secured from Congress a $30,000 grant to build a telegraph line from Washington to Baltimore. In 1844 Morse sent over this line the first long-distance telegraphic message: "What hath God wrought!"

Alexander Graham Bell, while working on the telephone, taught vocal physiology at Boston University and privately tutored deaf children. From two parents—one a prosperous attorney and the other a successful merchant—of the deaf children he tutored, Bell received financial assistance, enabling him to complete his telephone invention. The following year, 1877, Bell married his pupil—the deaf daughter of the prosperous attorney who had assisted him.

Thomas Edison, who had little formal education, worked as a telegrapher and later as a supervisor at a stock-ticker firm. Edison enjoyed taking apart and reassembling mechanical devices and he made significant improvements on the stock-ticker machine. These improvements—among Edison's early inventions—he sold for $40,000 and used the money to set up research facilities in New Jersey at *Menlo Park*. Edison worked hard and gave the world many important inventions. Hailed as the "Wizard of Menlo Park," Edison replied that "genius is 1 percent inspiration and 99 percent perspiration."

b. By the Smithsonian Institution

(1) *Origins. James Smithson* (1765–1829), an English scientist interested in mineralogy and chemistry and lacking any close relatives, bequeathed his entire property to the United States of America. His estate amounted to over $500,000—a munificent sum in the early 19th century. Smithson directed that the money be used "to found at Washington, under the name of the Smithsonian Institution, an Establishment for the increase and diffusion of knowledge among men." After many years of delay, Congress eventually accepted Smithson's bequest and later in 1846 passed a law authorizing the establishment of the Smithsonian Institution.

(2) *Growth.* Joseph Henry became the first administrator or Secretary of the Smithsonian and set its guidelines: (*a*) Since Smithson and Henry both were scientists, the Institution emphasized science. (*b*) To increase knowledge, the Smithsonian made financial grants to assist scientists, especially in basic research. (*c*) To diffuse knowledge, the Smithsonian published reports and research findings which were distributed worldwide to scholars, libraries, and scientific institutions.

Over the years, the Smithsonian has grown tremendously and today consists of the following: (*a*) The original Smithsonian Institution building is now used for administrative purposes and lectures. (*b*) The United States National Museum exhibits the records and artifacts of American history and culture. It contains two branch museums: History and Technology and the science-oriented Natural

History. *(c)* The Bureau of American Ethnology encourages research on the American Indian and exhibits Indian artifacts. *(d)* The Astrophysical Observatory now has its headquarters in Cambridge, Massachusetts and cooperates closely with Harvard University scientists. *(e)* The National Zoological Park, a great zoo, contains an extensive collection of wildlife. *(f)* A number of art galleries are part of the Smithsonian. The National Gallery of Art, perhaps the best known, was established in 1935 by the Pittsburgh aluminum and banking millionaire *Andrew Mellon.* He gave his personal art collection, funds for an exhibit building, and an endowment for maintenance. *(g)* The National Air Museum contains exhibits of America's achievements in aviation and space. *(h)* The John F. Kennedy Center for the Performing Arts—the most recent major addition —expands the Smithsonian's interest into a new area—music, dance, and theatre.

(3) *Finances.* The Smithsonian today is supported by the income of the original Smithson endowment, by gifts and grants of private individuals, and by annual appropriations voted by Congress.

(4) *Influence.* The Smithsonian is visited annually by millions of people who cannot help but be impressed by its exhibits and work. Its publications are distributed worldwide and are of immeasurable influence. Its facilities and staff are available to assist in founding and maintaining museums elsewhere. Its research activities and grants further American science. Smithsonian research grants enabled *Robert Goddard* to continue his rocket experiments and in 1926 to demonstrate the first successful liquid-fuel rocket.

2. In the 20th Century. Science has benefited from the emergence of new and major sources of financial support.

a. By Large, Science-Oriented Corporations. In the 20th century, corporations have grown larger and a significant number have depended upon scientific progress to provide them with salable products. Recognizing this interdependence of science and industry, many American corporations have budgeted large sums for *R and D,* meaning *research and development.* These corporations have established their own research laboratories and have staffed them with scientists and technicians. Although they have sought salable products—the result of applied research and development—these corporations have recognized the dependence of applied research upon basic research and have permitted their scientific staffs, within reason, to engage in basic research.

Corporations most interested in supporting scientific research are in areas such as chemicals and chemical manufacturing, drugs and medicinals, communications, petroleum refining, metal refining, rubber processing, paper and pulp, and electronics. From corporate research laboratories have come such familiar products as artificial turf, or astroturf (Monsanto), nylon (Du Pont), and the solid-state transistor (Bell Telephone Laboratories).

b. By Foundations

(1) *Meaning and Brief History.* A foundation is a nongovernmental, nonprofit organization, managed by its own directors, endowed with funds by an original donor (or group of donors) to undertake activities to further the common welfare. More simply stated, a foundation is a private organization that receives private wealth to be utilized for the public welfare.

Although philanthropy has been known throughout history, the foundation as a philanthropic organization arose largely in 20th-century America. In the post-Civil War era, many American capitalists amassed tremendous fortunes. Andrew Carnegie, the steel millionaire, in 1900 published an essay on *The Gospel of Wealth*, challenging men of wealth to use their fortunes to aid the poor and to benefit the community. True to his essay, Carnegie from 1902 to 1910 endowed several foundations—to further scientific research, to improve teaching, and to achieve international peace. Carnegie's writing and example stimulated other donors. Their motives may have been both selfish and selfless: to satisfy a philanthropic urge, to perpetuate a name, to erase an unfavorable public image, and, in the era of very high income and estate taxes since the 1940's, to secure tax deductions for charitable contributions.

In the United States today, foundations number 22,000, they possess assets of over $20 billion, and they make grants of $1.5 billion annually. Of these foundations, 1500 each possess assets of over $1 million. The 13 largest foundations together control over one-third of all foundation assets. The single largest foundation, with assets of over $3 billion, is the *Ford Foundation*.

(2) *Major Foundations Aiding Science.* (a) The *Carnegie Institution of Washington* (established in 1902) seeks to promote knowledge so as to improve humanity. From current assets of over $100 million, it makes grants for high-level research in such areas as astronomy, biology, geophysics, and physics. (b) The *Rockefeller Foundation* (1913) seeks to promote the well-being of humanity through advancing and applying knowledge. From assets of over $800 million, it supports research in the social sciences, the humanities and the biological, medical, and agricultural sciences. Rockefeller Foundation grants played a major role in developing high-yield agricultural seed—the *Green Revolution*. (c) The *Charles F. Kettering Foundation* (1927), founded by the organizer and head of General Motors research laboratories, sponsors research and education in the natural sciences, especially on photosynthesis and cancer. Its assets are over $100 million. (d) The *John A. Hartford Foundation* (1929), founded by the head of the Great Atlantic and Pacific grocery chain, has assets of over $300 million. Although it claims broad interests, this foundation has supported intensive work in biomedical research such as use of the laser, cryosurgery (surgery performed at very low temperatures), and human organ transplants. (e) The *Alfred P. Sloan Foundation* (1934), endowed by a former president of General Motors, has assets of over $300 million. It supports research in a wide range of activities, including the physical sciences, especially on cancer. (f) The *Sloan-Kettering Institute for Cancer Research*, an outgrowth of two previously discussed foundations, works with Memorial Hospital in New York City. It trains medical scientists and conducts laboratory research seeking hopefully to prevent, control, and cure cancer. (g) The *Ford Foundation* (1936) seeks "to advance the public good" through solving major world problems. This largest of all foundations engages in a broad range of activities such as education, hospitals, culture, civil liberties, and international peace. In the sciences, it investigates problems of growth of population, use of resources, and protection of environment.

(3) *Conclusions.* In recent years, foundations have given millions for research in the life sciences and the physical sciences. In determining specific projects and making grants, foundations have worked largely through universities, colleges, research institutes, and learned societies—organizations that

contain persons of imagination and unusual competence. *Warren Weaver*, active for many years in foundation management, concluded in his study, *United States Philanthropic Foundations*, that foundations in the 20th century have been a "major force in establishing this country's present level of basic research in the physical, biological, and medical sciences."

c. By the Federal Government. In recent years, the federal government has been involved in almost every area of scientific research and development. On "R and D," it spends approximately 10 percent of the annual federal budget. It assigns some "R and D" to "in-house" or government scientists, but more frequently it gives grants and makes contracts for the work to be done by university and industry personnel.

The tremendous increase in federal support for scientific research has resulted from the high cost of research, the complexity of research (all the "easy" discoveries seemingly have been made) the importance of science to national defense, and the worldwide prestige accorded to nations providing scientific leadership.

The following list, which is not complete, indicates the extent of government involvement with science.

(1) *Within Cabinet Departments.* *(a) Agriculture.* The *Agriculture Research Service* seeks to provide the knowledge and technology to enable farmers to conserve the environment and to produce efficiently. It sponsors research to improve crop yields, develop superior livestock, and discover new uses for farm commodities. *(b) Commerce.* The *National Bureau of Standards* sets standards for weights and measures, conducts research on various materials, and tests automatic data-processing equipment. The *National Oceanic and Atmospheric Administration* seeks to explore the global oceans so as to assess their potential value to industry and the nation. It further warns against impending environmental hazards. It directs research under the *National Sea Grant Program.* *(c) Defense.* The army, navy, and air force each have an assistant secretary in charge of research and development. Military leaders today recognize the close relationship between scientific progress and weapons excellence. *(d) Health, Education, and Welfare.* The *Food and Drug Administration* conducts research on the purity, efficacy, and safety of foods, food additives, and cosmetics. It also studies the efficacy and safety of drugs. The *National Institutes of Health* conducts and supports research on major diseases afflicting humans: cancer, heart ailments, eye diseases, allergies, arthritis, and childhood diseases. *(e) Interior.* The *Geological Survey* conducts surveys and research of our American topography, geology, and mineral and water resources. The *Office of Coal Research* seeks more efficient methods of mining and using coal. The *Office of Water Resources Research* seeks to solve water-resource problems and to train hydrologists (water scientists) and engineers. *(f) Transportation.* The *National Highway Traffic Safety Administration* conducts a broad research program testing motor vehicles and their equipment so as to devise safety standards.

(2) *Independent Agencies.* *(a)* The *Energy Research and Development Administration* (ERDA), established in 1974, took over the research activities of the Atomic Energy Commission. ERDA spurs research to develop nuclear power and to find new energy sources. It grants contracts to industrial concerns and other institutions for basic and applied research in biological, medical,

physical, and engineering sciences. *(b)* The *Environmental Protection Agency* (EPA) seeks to control pollution and protect the environment. It supports research to set standards for air and water quality, use of pesticides, disposal of solid wastes, and safe levels of radiation. *(c)* The *National Aeronautics and Space Administration* (NASA) has charge of the nation's space effort. It conducts research, develops, and launches manned and unmanned space vehicles; it records, interprets, and makes available scientific data gathered by space flights. NASA sponsors a broad range of research—in the medical, biological, engineering, meteorological, and physical sciences. *(d)* The *National Science Foundation* (NSF) seeks to strengthen research and education in American science. It awards grants and contracts to universities and research organizations for basic research in various sciences. It encourages the educational system to provide trained scientific and technical personnel to meet the nation's needs. It seeks to increase nongovernmental investment in research and to speed the application of research findings to practical use. In 1968 the NSF was directed by Congress to give greater support to social and behavioral sciences and also to applied science and engineering.

3. Recent Costs of Scientific Research and Development. In the 1970's the costs of scientific research and development in America approximated an annual figure of $51.6 billion. This cost is shown in the illustration, below.

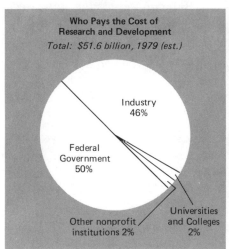

Who Pays the Cost of Research and Development
Total: $51.6 billion, 1979 (est.)

Industry 46%
Federal Government 50%
Other nonprofit institutions 2%
Universities and Colleges 2%

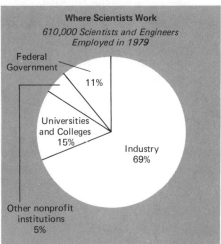

Where Scientists Work
610,000 Scientists and Engineers Employed in 1979

Federal Government 11%
Universities and Colleges 15%
Industry 69%
Other nonprofit institutions 5%

FROM 19TH-CENTURY INDIVIDUAL RESEARCH TO 20TH-CENTURY TEAM RESEARCH

Through the 19th century, creative individuals usually worked by themselves or with a few assistants and some achieved major scientific and technological discoveries. For the 20th century, especially since the World War II era, this previous statement does not hold true. Modern research problems are complex, often involving several scientific areas, so that no one person possesses complete "expertise." Modern research equipment is expensive. The big telescope to see deeply into the heavens, and the atomic smasher to peer deeply into the atom are both essential equipment costing many millions of dollars. Scientific progress has become too important to industry and government to leave to chance discoveries of individuals—no matter how creative.

With major support of research now coming from industry and government, the creative individual has given way to the creative scientific team. Under centralized supervision, each team member pursues experiments and contributes knowledge to enable the team to solve the overall research problem.

Examples of modern research teamwork: (1) The Manhattan Project consisted of a group of scientists and technicians who, working together under centralized leadership during World War II, produced the first atomic bomb. (2) The discovery of nylon resulted when a group of du Pont researchers, working together under the leadership of *Wallace Carothers,* synthesized this very strong and most useful product.

IMPACT OF SCIENCE AND TECHNOLOGY: A BRIEF ANALYSIS

1. Upon the Nation

a. Size. The United States was too large, said Frederick the Great of Prussia in the late 18th century, for one central government and could not possibly survive intact. This opinion may have been correct in the transportation era of the horse and the wind-blown sailing vessel. But with the coming of the steam locomotive and steamboat, the United States was bound together by rapid transportation. Its size was no longer an obstacle to centralized government. An American today can travel by airplane from coast to coast in less time than it took an 18th-century American on horseback to travel from New York City to Philadelphia.

b. Industrialization and Urbanization. In 1790 about 95 percent of Americans secured a living from agriculture, while 5 percent lived in cities. Today about 25 percent of our population is rural while 75 percent is urban. This drastic change resulted from the rise of factories which attracted workers to live nearby and led to urban growth. Large cities were able to survive because farmers mechanized their work so as to produce huge food surpluses and because the newer means of transportation brought these food surpluses to the cities, quickly and certainly.

c. Military Power. The United States today is probably the world's greatest military power. Our strength derives in part from the ability of our fighting men. But it also derives from the ability of our industry to convert from peacetime to war production and from the ability of our scientists to achieve new and more powerful weapons. During World War II, for example, American industry turned out tremendous quantities of aircraft, naval vessels, tanks, and other military goods. American scientists devised or adapted for war purposes various products such as radar and the atomic bomb.

d. Other Cases. Can you explain the impact of science and technology in the following cases: (1) the cotton gin upon the South (2) the Erie Canal upon New York City (3) the steamboat upon immigration to the United States (4) the air conditioner upon the American Southwest?

2. Upon the Family. Check the Index for "Family patterns."

3. Upon the Individual. Science and technology have brought individual Americans tremendous changes: *(a)* Workers have much more leisure time. For the use of leisure, they are surfeited by suggestions ranging from inexpensive movies and ballgames to costly cruises and vacation cottages. *(b)* Americans are healthier and live longer. The average life span has increased, and senior citizens have become a political and economic force. *(c)* Americans today enjoy more physical comforts than did the monarchs of old. Americans tend to take for granted comforts such as elevators, running water, dishwashers, steam heat, buses, cars, radio, and television.

SCIENCE AND TECHNOLOGY: RECENT ISSUES AND PROBLEMS

1. Is federal financial support of science desirable?

a. Yes. Only the federal government is able to provide funds sufficiently large for worthwhile research. Federal support enhances the prestige of science and assures that scientific research is in the national interest. Federal patronage of creative people in science, some observers claim, is proof of the "maturing of American civilization."

b. No. Federal funds may be cut off for political considerations, thereby abruptly terminating scientific projects. Federal funds may be channeled heavily into one popular or "glamor" area, thereby diverting talented people from other important but less glamorous areas. Scientists may come under bureaucratic domination and be compelled to seek specific practical goals rather than be allowed to investigate freely.

2. Does science further international cooperation?

a. Yes. Science knows no boundaries of race, religion, or nationality. All scientists share a common heritage rooted in the scientific method and in the search for knowledge. Science consequently has served to bring people together. The International Geophysical Year (1957–1958), which led to the first space flights, saw many nations cooperate to increase humanity's knowledge of the physical environment. United Nations specialized agencies seek to raise world health, food, educational, and scientific standards through international cooperation. The Rockefeller Foundation sponsored research in Mexico by the American agricultural scientist Norman Borlaug, who brought forth high-yield cereal seeds vital to underdeveloped nations. Russia and the United States cooperated in a 1975 joint Soviet-American manned space flight.

b. No. Science is subject to political control and therefore has served as an additional and vital aspect of international competition. During World War II, American scientists, aided by many refugee scientists from Nazi-held Europe, outraced German scientists and produced the first atom bomb. In the early cold war years, Russia defeated efforts to establish international control over atomic energy, in part so that its scientists could end the "American monopoly" which they did in 1949 by producing a Soviet atom bomb. In 1957, when Russia orbited man's first space vehicle, Soviet leaders claimed that this achievement proved the superiority of communism over capitalism. The American response was an effort to beat the Russians in sending a man to the moon and back—which Americans achieved in 1969 with the Apollo 11 flight. Even today, the two superpowers and several other nations are competing scientifically to devise more effective weapons of mass destruction.

3. Does automation represent a threat or benefit to humanity?

a. Meaning. Automation refers to (1) the use of complex machines which receive information through a process called *feedback* and are able to use this information to control other machines as well as entire production processes and (2) the use of computers which utilize *memory banks* to store vast amounts of data and are able to utilize these data to perform routine clerical tasks and to solve problems. Automation is sometimes known as the study of complex electronic calculating machines or *cybernetics.*

b. Examples of Automation

(1) *Automation and You.* Automation touches our lives in many ways. In homes heated by oil, automation is a thermostat set to maintain the temperature—say at 70 degrees—by controlling the furnace. When the temperature drops below 70 degrees, the thermostat receives this information as feedback from the temperature gauge and starts the furnace. Conversely when the temperature goes above 70 degrees, the thermostat shuts down the furnace. In schools using automation, computers prepare student programs, enter attendance, fill out report cards, schedule examinations, and retrieve (call back) information regarding a student's record. Traffic control uses automation to regulate the flow of motor vehicles by varying the operation of traffic lights. Banks use automation to record deposits and withdrawals, to compute interest, and to sort checks. Airports use automation to space incoming and outgoing planes. The federal Internal Revenue Service uses automation to check the accuracy and completeness of income tax returns.

(2) *Automation and Industry.* At a Ford Motor Company plant, an automatic control panel moves a rough casting through 42 machines linked together so that the casting emerges as a finished engine block. This automated process takes 15 minutes as compared to the conventional process time of nine hours. In other industries—such as chemical manufacturing, oil refining, electric power generating, and bread baking—automation uses systems of control instruments to operate the entire production process from raw materials to finished product. For our daily newspapers, automation is able to set the printed page by use of machines obeying instructions on tape.

c. Automation: A Threat to Humanity. (1) Automation causes unemployment, particularly among semiskilled and unskilled workers in the service industries. This burden of unemployment falls most heavily upon young people and members of minority groups. For example, in New York City alone, automatic elevators in skyscrapers have replaced some 40,000 elevator operators. (2) Automation causes individuals to feel a "loss of identity." People tend to resent machines that outperform them at work, that identify them not as individuals but as numbers in a computer memory bank, and that thwart them when they try to correct errors in a bank statement or a department store charge account.

d. Automation: A Benefit to Humanity. (1) Automation lowers production costs, speeds output, and increases productivity per worker. It also helps in

"Don't forget—I'm the boss!"
(*Crockett in the Washington Star*)

decision-making by quickly providing full information. (2) Automation frees workers from routine service and clerical jobs while providing more skilled positions in the manufacturing, servicing and programming of automatic equipment. (3) Automation enables individuals to "discover their identity" by providing more interesting work and by making possible more leisure time. This time, the individuals can use creatively by doing volunteer work in community agencies and by pursuing artistic, literary, and industrial arts hobbies. (4) Automation is a special boon to the scientist and engineer for, by digesting data speedily, it makes possible new and previously unattainable goals.

4. Does the Public Readily Accept or Resist New Scientific Discoveries? The answer to this question depends upon the nature of the new discovery, its effect upon the lives of the people, and its impact upon traditional beliefs and habits.

a. Acceptance. (1) In 1945 the American air force dropped upon *Hiroshima* in Japan the first atom bomb used in warfare. The American people accepted the reality of the bomb—after all, it worked—and many approved its use against Japan for hastening the end of the war and avoiding countless American and Japanese casualties that would have resulted from a seaborne invasion of the Japanese homeland. (2) In 1953 *Jonas Salk,* basing his work upon the efforts of scientists of the past 50 years, prepared the first vaccine, given by injection, against *infantile paralysis,* or *polio.* Shortly afterwards, *Albert Sabin* devised a second polio vaccine, which is taken by mouth. In the initial years, the demand for these vaccines outran the available supply, and priorities were established to assure treatment of the most susceptible groups. (3) In 1957 the Soviets ushered in space flight by orbiting Sputnik I, the first man-made satellite, and by 1969 the Americans, through the Apollo 11 mission, landed the first men on the moon and brought them back safely to earth. At first the American people accepted space flight with interest and enthusiasm, and supported government policies to make the United States first in space. After all, space flight was a reality, proved our scientific and technological ability, and opened up a new frontier. By 1972, with the sixth successful American lunar landing mission, the American people continued to accept space flight but with waning interest and enthusiasm.

b. Resistance

(1) Although fully aware of the reality of nuclear power, many American people have opposed the building of nuclear power plants. Community spokesmen fear the danger of an accidental nuclear explosion and accidental discharge of radioactive wastes; environmental groups fear the effect of the plants' discharge of heated water upon the ecology of nearby rivers and lakes. These groups have maintained their opposition despite the reassuring statements of knowledgeable scientists and despite the stringent requirements for a plant license set by the *Nuclear Regulatory Commission.*

In 1979 nuclear power received a severe setback because of an accident at the Three Mile Island (Pennsylvania) nuclear power plant. Although causing considerable damage to the plant, the accident seemingly caused negligible harm to people and the environment. Nevertheless, the accident aroused public concern and spurred mass antinuclear demonstrations. Opponents charge that nuclear power is not safe, endangers the environment, and lacks facilities for the proper disposal of nuclear waste materials. Nuclear advocates deny these charges, insisting that nuclear power poses less danger to people and the environment than coal or hydroelectric power, and that scientists have solved the problem of nuclear waste disposal. President Carter asserted that, for the foreseeable future, the United States cannot "abandon the nuclear supply of energy." This view was upheld by the President's commission investigating the Three Mile Island accident. After recommending a new regulatory setup and improvements in licensing procedures and safety standards, the commission concluded that, by keeping nuclear risks "within tolerable limits," the country could if it wished continue to develop nuclear power.

In another sense most peoples and nations throughout the world have rejected the cultural implications of atomic power. *Robert MacIver,* professor of philosophy at Columbia University, stated that atomic power "renders obsolete age-old traditions concerning war and sovereignty." In an age when nuclear war between nations probably means their mutual suicide, peoples still insist upon complete national sovereignty and nations refuse to accept minimal international controls and to reduce—not set limits upon—nuclear weapons.

(2) In the 1960's, after detailed computer analysis of statistics, the United States Public Health Service concluded that cigarette smoking contributes to cancer. Subsequently, cigarette advertising was banned from television where it might be seen by impressionable youths, and cigarette advertising in newspapers and magazines had to carry the warning, "The Surgeon General Has Determined That Cigarette Smoking Is Dangerous to Your Health." Although some smokers heeded the warning, most rejected it and continued smoking. They found the habit too pleasing and too powerful to break. Cigarette sales slumped briefly, but after the initial warning wore off, sales rose and reached new highs. In recent years, over 70 million Americans smoked cigarettes.

(3) In the 1930's, the United States Public Health Service, after conducting

research and analyzing statistics, concluded that in communities whose water supply contained naturally occurring *fluorides*—chemical compounds—the children had far fewer dental cavities than children in communities whose water supply lacked fluorides. The Public Health Service advised *fluoridation*—that communities should add fluorides to their water supplies to protect the teeth of their children. Starting in 1945, some 5000 communities, including the largest American cities, began fluoridation. Thereupon, a number of groups arose to fight fluoridation on various grounds: that it is "compulsory medicine," introduces into the body a poison—fluorides—that may cause cancer and bone and kidney diseases, violates the beliefs of certain religious sects, and infringes upon individual liberties. In response to these arguments, supporters of fluoridation quote statements by leading health organizations—American Medical Association, American Dental Association, and World Health Organization—that fluoridation is safe and effective; also they quote decisions in state court cases that "fluoridation does not infringe on the rights of the individual"; and finally they point out that health care manufacturers have added fluorides to their toothpastes. The opponents of fluoridation, however, have not abandoned their cause.

(4) You might investigate the validity of public opposition in the following cases involving science: opposition to Darwin's theory of evolution as applied to the origins of mankind; opposition to the government's ban on the pesticide DDT because it harms wildlife and contaminates food supplies; opposition to the government ban on cyclamates—synthetic substances replacing sugar in diet foods and drinks—because in huge quantities they may cause cancer.

5. What factors complicate evaluating the influence of scientists upon public opinion?

a. Scientists Speak Out. Especially since World War II, scientists have begun to speak out on public issues. Scientists have realized that in many cases their contributions are related to or have created public issues: such as the extent of atomic arsenals, peaceful uses of nuclear power, and the impact of automation. By expressing opinions and seeking to exert leadership, scientists have discredited the previously popular notion that they were recluses—oblivious to the implications of their discoveries and living in an *ivory tower*.

b. Scientists Differ. Scientists do not speak with a single voice. Depending upon their upbringing, education, and outlook on life, they frequently differ among themselves. After World War II, *J. Robert Oppenheimer*, who had directed the Los Alamos atomic bomb project, advised against building the more destructive hydrogen bomb. He based his opposition on both technical and humanitarian grounds. *Edward Teller*, the atomic scientist who had fled from Nazi German universities to the United States, urged building the hydrogen bomb. In 1949 President Truman rejected Oppenheimer's advice. With Teller in charge of the project, the United States soon produced a hydrogen bomb. In the 1970's search for alternatives to oil and gas energy, Professor *Hans Bethe*, the Nobel Prize-winning physicist of Cornell University, urged nuclear power, but Professor *Barry Commoner*, environmentalist at Washington University, St. Louis, urged solar energy.

c. Scientists Talk on Scientific Matters. When scientists deal with matters directly related to their areas of "expertise," they speak with prestige, command a large audience, and receive a respectful hearing. *Vannevar Bush*, who headed the wartime Office of Scientific Research and Development, prepared a report, "Science, the Endless Frontier," urging heavy federal support for basic scientific research. Bush's prestige and the logic of his arguments led eventually to the establishment of the *National Science Foundation*.

   d. Scientists Talk on Nonscientific Matters. When scientists deal with matters unrelated to their areas of expertise, they are speaking as citizens —intelligent and concerned—but not as experts. They are entitled to a respectful hearing not because they are prestigious scientists, but because they are members of our democratic society. Many scientists opposed American participation in the Vietnamese War. Most notable were *Benjamin Spock*, the famed pediatrician and author of *Baby and Child Care*, and *Noam Chomsky*, the professor of linguistics and linguistics theory, the science of languages. Spock and Chomsky spoke loudly against the Vietnamese War, calling it "illegal" and "criminal." However, since the causes, constitutionality, and results of the Vietnamese War were not related to child care or to linguistics, Spock and Chomsky spoke not as scientists but as citizens.

SCIENCE: GOOD OR EVIL?

   It is impossible to state whether science is a force for good or evil. Science is a body of knowledge and a method of acquiring such knowledge. Consequently, science is merely the servant of humanity. More properly, the question that should be asked is whether humanity is a force for good or evil.

   Humanity has used science for good purposes: to build labor-saving devices, to provide more leisure, to further human comfort and well-being, to extend the average life span, to wipe out disease, and to employ natural resources more efficiently. But humanity has also used science for evil purposes: to wage war, to torture innocent people, to kill, to bomb and destroy cities, and to seek world domination. What does the future hold? That answer lies not with science but within humanity itself.

MULTIPLE-CHOICE QUESTIONS

1. The pure scientist would be *most* concerned with   (1) purifying gasoline so as to achieve more miles per gallon   (2) producing complex computers   (3) writing technical manuals for operating nuclear generators   (4) studying the basic truths of our universe.
2. The practical scientist   (1) seeks knowledge for its own sake   (2) usually disregards the findings of pure science   (3) searches for new and useful products   (4) has contributed little to the American standard of living.
3. Which is the *most* valid statement regarding 19th-century American science?   (1) It was almost nonexistent.   (2) It concentrated upon solving practical problems.   (3) It was completely isolated from European scientific developments.   (4) It made valuable contributions to basic research.
4. Michael Faraday and James Clerk Maxwell both made important contributions in the field of   (1) heredity   (2) electromagnetism   (3) atomic structure   (4) evolution.
5. I was an American applied scientist whose work was *most* closely related to that of Michael Faraday. My name is.   (1) Benjamin Franklin   (2) Charles Darwin   (3) Joseph Henry   (4) Niels Bohr.

6. The lightning rod and bifocal lenses were practical inventions of (1) Benjamin Franklin (2) John Dalton (3) Thomas Edison (4) Samuel Morse.

7. Luther Burbank, the American horticulturalist, based his work on the findings of the European scientist Gregor Mendel in the field of (1) artificial fertilizer (2) radioactivity (3) heredity (4) irrigation.

8. The careers of *both* George Washington Carver and Percy Julian prove that (1) Americans made important contributions to pure research (2) wars stimulate scientific research (3) scientific achievement knows no boundaries of race (4) Southern farmers should raise more peanuts and less cotton.

9. Which statement is true of Albert Einstein, Niels Bohr, and Enrico Fermi? (1) They all were Jews. (2) They all were Germans. (3) They all fled to America to escape Nazi and Fascist terror in Europe. (4) They all had no part in practical scientific work.

10. Which statement is *not* true regarding oceanographic research? (1) It requires expensive equipment. (2) It involves many scientific areas. (3) It seeks to increase the food supply for humanity. (4) It has received no encouragement from the federal government.

11. To finance his scientific activities, Thomas Edison depended upon (1) government grants (2) foundation grants (3) the income from his sale of an early invention (4) the Smithsonian Institution.

12. Since World War II, science in the United States has been characterized by (1) an increasing dependence on European concepts of pure science (2) an increased emphasis on basic research (3) inventions and discoveries by individuals rather than groups (4) almost total neglect by the federal government.

13. Which statement regarding the Smithsonian Institution is *not* true? (1) Its original establishment resulted from a bequest by an English scientist. (2) It attracts millions of visitors annually to its scientific and historical exhibits. (3) It receives no financial assistance from the federal government. (4) It includes the John F. Kennedy Center for the Performing Arts.

14. Which statement regarding philanthropic foundations is *not* true? (1) They provide funds for research in the sciences and humanities. (2) They outspend industry in furthering scientific research. (3) They were established mainly by American capitalists. (4) They seek to further the common welfare, not to make a profit.

15. Which best explains why, in the United States today, individuals are less likely to be credited with inventions, discoveries, and breakthroughs? (1) Individuals are less interested in public recognition. (2) Accomplishments are frequently the result of team effort. (3) Private investment for research has decreased sharply. (4) Governmental grants for research have been eliminated.

16. Leisure time presents a problem in present-day American society primarily because (1) increases in leisure time have caused a decline in production (2) participation in hobbies and other leisure-time activities is too costly (3) leisure time is available only to those who are unemployed or in the upper class (4) many people feel that they do not know how to use leisure time.

17. "Technology has developed to the point where most work which has been done by people with less than a high school education can now be done more cheaply by machines." The author of this quotation is probably trying to prove that (1) most machines have ability equivalent to a person with a high school education (2) most people without a high school education will have difficulty finding adequately paid employment (3) the need for skilled labor will disappear in the very near future (4) automation is "a real curse to society."

18. In the United States, which field of employment has been *least* influenced by automation? (1) domestic services (2) banking (3) baking industry (4) automobile industry

19. Which has been the *most* direct result of technological developments? (1) less emphasis on formal education (2) increased productivity per working man-hour (3) gradual decline in the growth of urban areas (4) rising prices of consumer goods

20. "When people allow machines and the machine-state to master their consciousness, they imperil not only their inner beings but also the world they inhabit. . . ." The author of the statement is *most* concerned with the (1) danger of political revolution (2) impersonal nature of technology (3) impact of the union movement on society (4) need to increase technological development.

21. Which is the *most* valid conclusion that may be drawn from the quotation? (1) Technology will ultimately create the "good" life. (2) People should utilize all of the available natural and human resources. (3) Serious social and ethical problems may be created by the extensive development of technology. (4) The environmental crisis can be lessened by the advent of newer technology.

22. Public rejection of the best scientific advice is *most* obvious in regard to (1) cigarette smoking (2) polio vaccine (3) high-yield cereal grain seeds (4) space flights.

23. Which can *best* be described as a reaction against the impersonal nature of a modern technological society? (1) the computerization of an assembly line (2) a strike for higher wages by an industrial union (3) the organization of a research team to solve a scientific problem (4) the movement of some families back to farm life and a more self-sufficient way of living

24. Which is the *most* accurate statement concerning scientific development? (1) The future of science is completely predictable. (2) Man must find a balance between the risks and the opportunities being created by scientific progress. (3) The interaction of science and society is less important today than in earlier ages. (4) Today's social structure is keeping pace with the invention of new machinery.

ESSAY QUESTIONS

1. Scientific and technological progress in America has been closely related to the needs of society. For *each* of the following periods in American history, (*a*) name *one* scientific or technological advance and (*b*) show how this advance met the needs of society at that time: (1) 1750–1850 (2) 1850–1900 (3) 1900–1950.

2. Scientific research and development today receive financial support from three major sources: (1) large, science-oriented corporations (2) the federal government and (3) philanthropic foundations. Explain *one* advantage and *one* disadvantage of *each* of these three sources of financial support for science.

3. Automation has been hailed as a boon to humanity and has been condemned as a curse to society. (*a*) Explain what is meant by automation. (*b*) For *each* of the following, discuss *one* possible effect of automation and indicate whether that effect is a "boon" or a "curse": (1) employment opportunities (2) leisure time (3) role of education (4) concern for individual identity.

4. Agree or disagree with *each* of the following statements and present *two* arguments to support your opinion: (*a*) Applied scientists and technologists in America owe a great debt to pure scientists in Europe. (*b*) The construction of the atom bomb during World War II proves that science knows no boundaries of religion or nationality. (*c*) In the near future Americans will concentrate scientific effort in the fields of solar energy and oceanography. (*d*) The federal government contains many agencies concerned with scientific matters. (*e*) The development of technology has improved the quality of human life. (*f*) Science has given humanity the power either to create a better world or to destroy civilization.

4. Americans Demonstrate Creativity
in Many Fields

Architecture

Architecture and Architects. Architecture is the science and art of creating buildings. Architecture is a *science* in that scientific principles underlie the construction of all buildings. The architect must know building material qualities, such as their strength, weight, and flexibility; structural principles, such as stresses and supports; and the status of building technology, such as tools and machines. Architecture also is a *visual art* since buildings are judged by the human eye as to their beauty. Of course, not all buildings are works of art. The skillful and imaginative architect is able to embody in a building an artistic unity and the spirit of the times. As tastes and times change, so too will the prevailing architectural trends change.

The architect is concerned with three factors regarding a building: (1) its purpose or use—is it to be a home? a library? a museum? a place for religious worship? an office? a legislative chamber? (2) its strength or durability—what materials are available? at what price? how will they withstand the climate and weather conditions? how long will they last? (3) its beauty or appeal—what is the existing artistic sense? what is the national mood? how can such esthetic and intangible values be expressed by the building?

In creating a building, the architect generally proceeds through the following steps: (1) secures a commission to undertake the work for a sponsor: usually a wealthy person, a corporation, or a public agency (because buildings need sponsors whose artistic tastes must be considered, architecture is less subject to change and experimentation than most other art forms), (2) prepares an overall design, (3) makes detailed drawings of each portion, (4) receives the approval of the sponsor, and (5) oversees the actual construction.

Architecture, in a larger sense, deals not only with buildings, but with planning and constructing entire neighborhoods and whole cities and with landscaping parks.

STAGES OF AMERICAN ARCHITECTURE

American architecture has been variously divided into distinct stages or time periods, each encompassing an historical era with its own distinctive architectural trends. The dates of each time period are approximate, not exact, for historical eras and architectural trends overlap, and each time period merges gradually into the next. We here shall consider American architecture as divided into the following five major stages: (1) Early America—Pre-Columbian times to the mid-17th century, (2) Colonial America—to the end of the American Revolution era, (3) The Young Nation—the first 100 years up to the 1880's, (4) America in Transition—to Urbanization and Industrialization—to the end of the World War I era, and (5) Modern America—to the present.

431

EARLY AMERICA: ARCHITECTURE OF THE NATIVE INDIANS AND THE FIRST WHITE SETTLERS

Before white settlers came to America, the Indians were here. They needed functional dwellings that would provide shelter from hostile tribes, from wild animals, and from the elements—the wind, rain, and snow, the cold of winter, and the heat of summer. With skill and ingenuity, considering their technology, the Indians utilized easily secured materials such as wood poles, tree bark, vines, clay, stone, grassy sod, and animal sinews and skins. The Indians possessed an artistic sense and sometimes decorated their dwellings.

1. Indians of the Eastern Woodlands. Using wood as their basic building material, the Winnebago Indians of Wisconsin fashioned the simple one-family *bark lodge* and the Iroquois of New York constructed the more elaborate multifamily dwelling, the *long house*. Both buildings consisted of wood pole frames covered with tree bark for side walls and topped by a simple pitched roof.

2. Indians of the Great Plains. When they followed a sedentary life, the Mandan Indians built entire villages of *earth lodges*, and the Navahos used this basic structure for a one-family dwelling, the *hogan*. Both buildings used wood pole frames that supported earth walls and domed roofs of sod. The use of sod as a building material reflected the scarcity on the Great Plains of trees and timber. After white settlers introduced the horse and the gun, the Plains Indians became nomadic, following the buffalo and engaging in warfare. They then developed an easily portable shelter, usually considered the typical Indian dwelling, the *tepee* or *wigwam*. It consisted of wood pole frames arranged in conelike shape and covered by animal skins. The Crow and other Plains Indians sometimes decorated the outsides of their tepees with geometric designs or with pictures of birds and animals. (The tepee was the forerunner of our modern portable tent.)

3. Indians of the Southwest. Using the natural openings in the stone cliffs of canyons, the Pueblo Indians long ago constructed great multiple-family units which we call *cliff dwellings*. The Pueblo Indians used the stone cliffs as walls and employed wooden beams and branches sealed with clay as floors and ceilings. They had wooden ladders to climb from one level to the next, and when the ladders were pulled up, the structure became a fortress. Later Pueblo Indians, such as the Zuni and Hopi, built on the plains near rivers fortified village communities called *pueblos* (from the Spanish word meaning villages). The Indians constructed the pueblos of stone and sun-dried clay brick called *adobe*. The pueblos usually consisted of a number of rectangular rooms, of varying height, with access to the higher levels provided, as in the cliff dwellings, by crude log ladders. In the community *kiva*, or religious chamber, the adobe brick walls were sometimes decorated with murals. As the adobe walls have crumbled, only fragments remain of the original decorations.

The first white settlers in America, needing shelter, burrowed into hillside caves or copied the early Indian dwellings. When these first settlers felt more securely established, they abandoned their primitive abodes and constructed more permanent buildings. In so doing, they imitated the architecture they had known in Europe, thereby setting the architectural pattern for colonial America.

COLONIAL AMERICA: IMITATION OF EUROPEAN ARCHITECTURAL STYLES

As the 13 English colonies along the North Atlantic seaboard prospered, the settlers constructed more permanent, comfortable, and impressive structures. With the axe and saw brought from Europe, the colonists cleared the forests and secured the basic building materials such as logs, beams, planks, and clapboard and shingles. In time they also used brick, plaster, and stone and replaced oil-soaked paper in windows with locally made glass. The major architectural trends of colonial America were as follows:

1. New England Colonial. In the 17th century, the New England colonists erected substantial dwellings patterned after the living quarters they had known in England. They built one- and two-story rectangular-shaped homes, using the plentiful wood to frame and brace the structures, and finishing the interiors with stone, brick, and plaster and the exteriors usually with clapboard. These homes had chimneys at first made of wood but later of stone and brick, and had high-pitched roofs usually covered with wood shingles. An example of the New England colonial building, erected in 1676, in Boston, Massachusetts, is the *Paul Revere House.*

Paul Revere House: a New England colonial home *(United Press International)*

2. The Georgian Style. In 18th-century America, impressive buildings were patterned on the fashionable English architectural style called *Georgian.* It was so named to honor the first three Georges, who reigned during most of the 18th century in England. Its outstanding characteristics were massive size, symmetry of exterior design, large windows of glass, and an elaborate center entrance. These characteristics permitted considerable variations among Georgian buildings. Details of Georgian design and structure were provided in many carpenters' handbooks, printed in England and widely circulated in America. Georgian buildings in the colonies coupled a restrained dignity with a sense of comfort and warmth.

a. Georgian-Style Private Houses. Wealthy Southern plantation owners and Northern merchants commissioned the building of impressive Georgian-style residences. In Virginia, William Byrd, a leading aristocrat, inherited a fortune derived from land, the Indian trade, and the slave trade. From 1730 to 1734, he built a stately brick mansion called *Westover.* In a suburb of Boston, Massachusetts, Isaac Royall, a Loyalist, inherited a fortune made in the triangular rum and slave trade. In the mid-18th century, he remodeled his house into a splendid wooden mansion called the *Royall House.*

b. Georgian-Style Public Buildings. In the 18th century, colonial officials approved the Georgian style in the construction of public buildings. For Williamsburg, which long served as capital of colonial Virginia, one royal governor—an amateur architect—designed the legislative building, or *Capitol.* It featured two huge, symmetrically placed, semicircular wings intended to house the colony's bicameral legislature. (With the assistance of John D. Rockefeller, Jr., Williamsburg has been restored to its 18th-century condition with its many Georgian-style buildings. It attracts numerous Americans interested in their colonial heritage.) For Philadelphia, the Pennsylvania colonial assembly authorized the building of a *state house.* It was designed in the Georgian style with a superb centrally placed tower. This building, in which the Declaration of Independence was adopted and the Constitution drawn up, is now known as *Independence Hall.*

Two examples of colonial architecture in the Georgian style
(left) Westover: a private mansion (*The Library of Congress*) (right) Independence Hall: a public building (*Bloom from Monkmeyer*)

3. Architectural Contributions of Other Than English Settlers. *(a)* The *Dutch*—who settled New Amsterdam (later called New York), the Hudson River Valley up to Albany, Long Island, northern New Jersey, and southern Connecticut—greatly influenced the region's architecture. The Dutch upper classes imitated the buildings of Holland. Patroons, or large rural landowners, favored long, low, one-story houses, whereas the city merchants built narrow two- and three-story dwellings. Their homes often featured walls built with brick of different colors—a status symbol considered superior to wood and stone, steep roofs ending in or interspersed with triangular decorative shapes called *gables*, and gaily colored tiles used for ornamental purposes. *(b)* The *Swedish* settlers in Delaware brought from their homeland an excellence in carpentry. With great skill, they carefully fitted together rough-cut rectangular logs to construct the earliest *log cabins*. In wooded frontier regions, the log cabin became the standard dwelling. Later in our national history, the log cabin became a political symbol signifying that the candidate running for office had originated as "one of the ordinary people."

THE YOUNG NATION: ADAPTATION OF PAST EUROPEAN ARCHITECTURAL STYLES

Americans won their independence from England politically, and then moved to express their independence of England architecturally by rejecting the Georgian style. As American statesmen had turned to the past for ideas in framing the Constitution, so too did American architects turn to the past for inspiration and models. They were not content, however, merely to imitate past styles but adapted them so as to employ new technological advances—such as the iron nail, cast iron, structural steel, and plate glass—and to express American sentiments—such as individual freedom, republican dignity, and national pride. With time American buildings more and more were designed by trained, dedicated, professional architects. The major architectural trends of the young nation were as follows:

1. The New Classicism (To the 1840's). Classicism refers to the cultural movement inspired by the civilizations of ancient Greece and Rome—the classical era of European history. In architecture, classical buildings employed the forms and shapes used by the ancient Greeks and Romans and expressed the classical ideals of emotional restraint, formality, symmetry, dignity, and grandeur.

a. Roman Revival: The Federal Style. During the early years of the young republic, as the federal government was established, the new classicism in architecture looked mainly to ancient Rome. The *Roman Revival* consequently became known as the *Federal style.* To plan the new capital city of Washington, D.C., the federal government first commissioned an engineer turned architect, *Pierre L'Enfant.* With the Capitol and White House to be at the center, L'Enfant proposed to have broad avenues radiating outward and intersected by spacious streets. He envisioned that the city would have magnificent buildings to house the government and many small parks with patriotic monuments to express the national spirit.

Thomas Jefferson—author, statesman, politician, scientist, educator, and architect—was the leading advocate of the Roman Revival. This architectural

 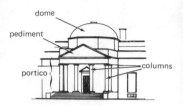

(left) Monticello: Jefferson's home in the Federal style (*Thomas Jefferson Memorial Foundation*)   (right) line drawing of Monticello with labels of major architectural features

style, he believed, best expressed American ideals as he had stated them in the Declaration of Independence, and best symbolized the American republic as successor to the ancient Roman republic. In remodeling *Monticello*, his home in Virginia, Jefferson utilized Roman shapes such as tall columns supporting a roof over an entrance porch or portico, a triangular gable or pediment over the entrance, and a low, centrally placed dome. In the interior Jefferson introduced practical features such as double doors opening and closing together and manually operated dumbwaiters. Monticello conveys a sense of pride, dignity, and comfortable living. Jefferson also used the Federal style in designing two major public buildings: the *Virginia State Capitol* at Richmond and the *central library*, or *Rotunda*, at the University of Virginia—which institution Jefferson had founded.

    b. Greek Revival. By the 1820's, the new classicism had shifted its emphasis from Roman to Greek architectural styles. Americans were reminded by the career of Napoleon Bonaparte, who had overthrown the French republic, that the Roman republic also had ended in a despotic empire. Americans furthermore sympathized with the Greek people, who were then struggling for independence against Turkey, and recalled that ancient Greece had been the original home of democracy. Although the Roman and Greek styles had certain similarities in the use of columns, entrance porches, and triangular pediments, *Greek Revival* architecture lacked domes, rejected ornamentation, and was more severe. Many American cities established in this era adopted Greek names—such as Athens, Ithaca, and Homer—and usually constructed their public buildings in the Greek Revival style. The more settled Eastern communities contained two major examples of the Greek style: the National Bank building in Philadelphia and the nearby home of Nicholas Biddle, the bank's most prominent president.

2. Romanticism (From the 1840's Into the Post-Civil War Era). *Romanticism* refers to the cultural movement that rebelled against the classical tradition. In architecture, classicism had emphasized symmetry, formality, restraint, dignity, and grandeur. Now romanticism proposed irregularity, informality, exuberance and imagination in decoration, and free reign for emotion. Americans now held that, in architecture, romanticism would best express the growing spirit of democracy.

a. Gothic Revival. Romanticism in architecture first looked to medieval European cathedrals built in the *Gothic style*. This style utilized flying buttresses (wall supports), tall windows of stained glass, pointed arches, tall spires, towers, turrets, and ribbed vaulting for interior ceilings. Two outstanding buildings in the *Gothic Revival style* are in New York City: *St. Patrick's Cathedral*, on fashionable Fifth Avenue, and *Trinity Church* in the Wall Street area—both now surrounded by modern skyscrapers.

b. Romanesque Revival. In the post-Civil War era, romanticism in architecture began emphasizing another medieval European style called *Romanesque*. This style featured thick walls, few windows, rounded arches, and substantial columns. In America the Romanesque style became associated with the architect *Henry Richardson* (1838–1886).

Although Richardson borrowed ideas from other styles, he used the Romanesque to express the buoyant energy and massive strength of America. He also incorporated his own original ideas into his designs. Richardson used Romanesque features in constructing a number of buildings, including the *New York State Capitol* at Albany. In 1872 Richardson won the competition for the design of *Trinity Church* in Boston. When the church—a massive and dramatic building—was completed, Richardson was recognized as a great architect.

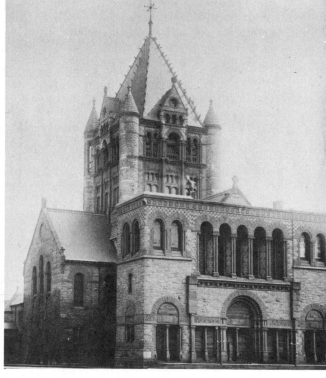

Two examples of 19th-century architecture in the romantic style
(left) St. Patrick's Cathedral: Gothic Revival   (right) Henry Richardson—Trinity Church in Boston: Romanesque Revival (*Brown Brothers*)

Richardson is noteworthy for two other reasons: (1) He was a professionally trained architect who, in the era of industrial capitalism, organized an architectural corporation. As commissions came in, Richardson would divide the work among his staff so as to speed the projects and produce distinctive buildings. (2) In 1885 Richardson began construction of a massive, seven-story warehouse in stone for the Marshall Field department store in Chicago. By designing this building to be strictly utilitarian, Richardson provided the prototype, or forerunner, of the soon-to-be-born architectural form—the modern skyscraper.

c. *Romanticism in Planning Parks.* In planning parks to provide recreational facilities for large city populations, romantic architects rejected classical symmetry and restraint upon nature. They favored working with nature so as to preserve the landscape's natural beauty such as the sloping terrain, the curved walks, and the intermixture of trees, shrubs, and grass. The outstanding 19th-century landscape architect in the romantic tradition was *Frederick Law Olmstead* (1822–1903). He planned several fine parks for our major cities, especially Central Park and Prospect Park (Brooklyn), both in New York City.

AMERICA IN TRANSITION TO URBANIZATION AND INDUSTRIALIZATION: OLD AND NEW ARCHITECTURAL STYLES

The United States changed from a largely rural and agricultural way of life to an urban and industrial one. Industrial and financial capitalists established large enterprises and amassed tremendous fortunes. These developments affected American architecture as follows:

1. **Homes for the Wealthy: In European Architectural Styles.** Having made their fortunes, the "new rich" in America wanted to impress the world by spending their money conspicuously. They toured Europe and saw the homes of the European nobility—Italian villas, French châteaux, and English mansions. Since the "new rich" considered themselves the American nobility, they desired similar dwellings and commissioned the services of several Eastern architectural firms, most notably *McKim, Mead, and White.* This firm, headed by three talented and trained architects, was eclectic—that is, willing to utilize any past styles such as Italian Renaissance, colonial Georgian, and classical Roman and Greek Revival. McKim, Mead, and White built private homes for the wealthy and also a number of notable public buildings. They employed the classical Roman style in designing the *Columbia University Library* and the Italian Renaissance style in designing the *Villard Houses*—both in New York City.

2. **The Skyscraper: Louis Sullivan.** As corporations grew, businessmen wanted to locate their offices and showrooms in desirable city areas. Such city land, however, was both scarce and expensive so that the only way to increase usable space was to build upward. By this time the multistoried building had been made possible by new technological advances such as low-cost, high-strength steel beams for construction, electric elevators, large-size plate glass for windows, as well as the telephone, electric light, and modern plumbing and heating.

Louis Sullivan emerged as the forward-looking and inventive architect of the modern skyscraper. A master of design, Sullivan held that *"form follows function,"* meaning that a building must be viewed in its entirety as to its purpose so as to determine its form or shape. In 1890 in St. Louis, Sullivan constructed the

Louis Sullivan—Wainwright Building: the first modern skyscraper (*Hedrich-Blessing*)

Wainwright Building. He borrowed none of the forms of traditional architecture but instead used sharp edges and geometric shapes to convey the sense of a technological society. The Wainwright Building has been acclaimed for its lightness and loftiness, for soaring into the sky, and for setting the overall pattern of the modern skyscraper.

3. The World's Fair Columbian Exposition in Chicago (1893). In planning its buildings, this World's Fair, commemorating Columbus' discovery of America, looked to the past. It selected the classical Roman style and gave commissions to several Eastern architectual firms, typified by McKim, Mead, and White. The major concession to progressive or forward-looking architecture was a single commission to the local Chicago firm of Louis Sullivan. To display the newest railroad cars and engines, Sullivan designed the *Transportation Building*—a long, low depot with a geometrically ornamented series of colored arches highlighting the entrance. The American people came to the Fair and were impressed—not by the modernity of Sullivan's building—but by the grandeur of the classical revival style. For many decades thereafter, classicism dominated American architecture.

Sullivan, meanwhile, received fewer commissions—mainly for small-town Midwestern banks—and devoted himself more to lecturing and writing on his philosophy of architecture. He died in poverty in 1924 but with the knowledge that his book, *Autobiography of an Idea*, was published and that he had inspired many disciples, especially *Frank Lloyd Wright*.

A contrast in architectural styles at the 1893 Chicago World's Fair
(left) Louis Sullivan—Transportation Building: forward looking   (right) McKim, Mead,
and White—Agricultural Building: classical Roman (*Brown Brothers*)

MODERN AMERICA—EXPERIMENTATION, INNOVATION, AND AN INDIGENOUS (NATIVE) ARCHITECTURE

Americans during the past half-century have undergone dramatic experiences: the 1929 depression, the Nazi challenge to democracy, World War II, the cold war with its threat of nuclear weapons, and the progress of the civil rights movement in America. Life in America, meanwhile, became increasingly dominated by technology and machines. Americans came to realize that there were no easy answers to present-day problems, either by turning to the past or by looking to the future, and that humanity's progress was slow, uncertain, and dependent upon trial and error.

These experiences and their implications affected American architecture. American public opinion agreed—mostly but not entirely—that it was absurd to construct railroad stations looking like ancient Roman bathhouses and department stores looking like medieval palaces. Thus public opinion swung in favor of forward-looking or *modern* architecture.

Modern architecture utilizes all kinds of materials—traditional and new—to achieve its major goals: buildings that are *functional*, meaning able to serve the needs of the people; that express a sense of freedom from tradition through clean lines and rational structures; and that mirror the beauty inherent in our scientific, mechanized, and technological age. Modern architecture does not require a single style but permits each architect to express his own originality and inventiveness. Modern architecture is exemplified by the works of its leading proponents, as follows:

Frank Lloyd Wright (1869–1959), often considered the greatest architect of the 20th century, was a founder of modern architecture. Although he worked for a while under Louis Sullivan and designed some large buildings, Wright concentrated on private homes. He believed that (*a*) a building should harmonize with its environment or surroundings—a home should not be built on a hill but should grow out of the hill; *(b)* the interior of a home should not be rigidly divided into boxlike rooms but, using walls of mobile screens and partitions, rooms should flow into each other; *(c)* the interior and exterior of a house also should flow into each other by use of mobile glass partitions as walls and an overhanging roof to shield the exterior area; *(d)* large cities with their congestion and slums should be replaced by planned, smaller, and self-sufficient communities; and *(e)* architecture should provide the best, or most practical, new building forms "suited to democratic life."

Wright's career falls into three major periods: *(a)* Between 1900 and 1910, he designed numerous "prairie"-style homes for upper middle-class businessmen and professionals in the Chicago area. He gained an international reputation as a bold, imaginative, and forward-looking architect. *(b)* For over two decades into the 1930's, Wright was not active in construction. He used these years to reappraise his architectural philosophy, to write his *Autobiography*, and to establish at his home in Wisconsin an architectural training school, *Taliesin Fellowship*. *(c)* From the mid-1930's onward, Wright attained new heights in achievement. He designed numerous important buildings, especially the Kaufman *"Falling Water" House* in Pennsylvania, hailed as "a matchless fusion of fantasy and engineering"; the *Johnson Wax Company Building* in Wisconsin, which has glass ceilings and walls permitting light to enter; and his final creation, the *Guggenheim Museum* in New York City, which features an interior spiral ramp that keeps visitors moving and provides continuous gallery space.

Raymond Hood (1881–1934) achieved a simplicity and machine-like precision in designing, alone and with others, several New York City skyscrapers: the *Daily News Building* and the cluster of buildings constituting *Rockefeller Center*.

Two examples of architecture in the modern style
(left) Raymond Hood and others—Rockefeller Center (*Rockefeller Center, Inc.*)
(right) Frank Lloyd Wright—Guggenheim Museum (*Pictorial Parade, photo by Alan Clifton, Camera Press, London*)

Buckminster Fuller (1895–   ), mathematician, inventor, and philosopher, has designed automobiles, buildings, and cities. Since World War II, he has concentrated on *geodesic domes*. These are large, lightweight, prefabricated structures of nearly spherical shape whose transparent plastic skin is enframed by many-sided steel shapes giving the appearance of a huge spider web. For the *United States Pavilion* at the Montreal World's Fair—Expo 67—Fuller designed a most impressive geodesic dome. These domes have also been used for military shelters, convention halls, and an enclosed all-weather sports arena in Houston, Texas—the Astrodome.

Edward Durell Stone (1902–1978) changed from an early severe and restrained architectural style to a later one of more warmth and decoration. For columns and exterior walls, he has used concrete blocks shaped into geometric patterns, which permit light to pass through and form flickering and changing designs. Stone's later works include the series of buildings constituting the *New York State University at Albany* and the *John F. Kennedy Center for the Performing Arts* in Washington, D.C.

Eero Saarinen (1910–1961) as a young boy emigrated from Finland to the United States and became an architect. He designed the *Trans World Airlines Building* at Kennedy Airport in New York City—using concrete to create curved and flowing lines that give the impression of a giant bird about to take flight. Saarinen gave free reign to his imagination in designing the *Gateway Arch* for the Jefferson Westward Expansion Memorial in St. Louis. Using stainless steel, he created a huge curved arch, visible for many miles, and expressing humanity's freedom to soar into space and into new modes of living. (Saarinen also designed a highly popular chair, made of reinforced plastic, which rests on a single pedestal base and is both useful and beautiful.)

Three famed European architects, in the late 1930's, fled from Nazi Germany. Their modern architectural style—simple, rational, and international in scope—was incompatible with Nazism, which demanded that architecture be ostentatious, glorify the state, and extol German nationalism. These three men

Examples of architecture in the modern style (above and facing page)
(left) Buckminster Fuller—United States Pavilion at Expo 67, Montreal:
geodesic dome, a new architectural concept, at night (*Wide World Photos*)
(right) Edward Durell Stone—John F. Kennedy Center for the
Performing Arts, at night (*Paul Conklin from Monkmeyer*)

(left) Eero Saarinen—Trans World Airlines Building (*Ezra Stoler © ESTO*)
(right) Ludwig Mies van der Rohe—Crown Hall, Illinois Institute of Technology
(*Illinois Institute of Technology*)

came to the United States and enriched our nation with their talent, teaching, and work.

Walter Gropius (1883–1969), who became head of the department of architecture at Harvard, designed with assistants the *Harvard Graduate Center* in Massachusetts and the *Pan Am Building* in New York City. Gropius taught that modern architecture is the inevitable product of the "intellectual, social, technical conditions of our time."

Ludwig Mies van der Rohe (1886–1969), who became head of the department of architecture at the Illinois Institute of Technology, created the master plan for a series of buildings at the institute's new campus. Mies also (with an assistant) designed the bronze-covered *Seagram Building* in New York City. Mies favored functional buildings with a clear and uncluttered design because he believed that in architecture "less is more."

Marcel Breuer (1902–   ), who for a time taught architecture at Harvard, designed furniture of aluminum, plywood, and tubular steel. He designed the *Whitney Museum of Art* in New York City. He also planned a number of buildings for colleges such as the library for Hunter College in New York City and the faculty houses for the Institute for Advanced Study at Princeton, New Jersey.

Sculpture

FROM COLONIAL TIMES INTO THE EARLY 20TH CENTURY

1. Patriotism as a Major Theme. In colonial times, Americans neglected sculpture (except for wood carving) as an important art form. After the War for Independence, Americans turned to sculpture to commemorate their victory and honor their heroes. Since America contained no native sculptors of prestige, the earliest commissions went to European sculptors. Thereafter, as American sculptors received training—some in Italy, others in the United States—they secured commissions from governmental bodies for works dealing with Revolutionary War leaders; Civil War military and civilian figures; democratic virtues, such as justice and wisdom; state and local celebrities; and citizens who gave their lives in their country's wars. Sculptors also attempted other works, including scenes of American life such as an Indian hunter and men playing checkers at the farm.

Into the early 20th century, American sculptors largely maintained the same themes: American life, virtues, and heroes, constituting an expression of American patriotism.

2. Styles and Materials. To the Civil War, sculptors chiefly imitated the classical works of ancient Greece and Rome. Of the many statues of George Washington: he is shown variously as standing and resting his arm on the *fasces*—the Roman symbol of authority; as dressed in the garb of a Roman general; as seated on a throne with his body naked to the waist and draped below—in the manner of a Greek statue of the god Zeus; and astride a horse, in an equestrian statue of Roman tradition. After the Civil War, a number of American sculptors turned from classicism to an "American" style of detailed realism. This style suited the growing interest in sculpting scenes of American life. To the early 20th century, sculptors worked with a number of traditional materials such as marble, granite, wood, and bronze.

3. Outstanding American Sculptors

Augustus Saint-Gaudens (1848–1907), brought as an infant from Ireland to America, studied art here and in Paris, and for a quarter of a century to his death in 1907 dominated American sculpture. To his works, Saint-Gaudens brought

Two statues of George Washington in the classical style
(left) dressed as a Roman general, by William Rush (*Courtesy of Pennsylvania Academy of the Fine Arts*) (right) seated as the Greek god Zeus, by Horatio Greenough (*Courtesy of National Collection of Fine Arts, Smithsonian Institution*)

warmth, careful attention to details, and a realistic or lifelike quality, as he set high standards of excellence. Although he chose his subject matter chiefly from American history, in his style Saint-Gaudens reflected the influence of classical European and other past sculptural achievements.

Among his major public works, Saint-Gaudens is famed for sculptures of three Civil War Union leaders: (1) Located in Madison Square in New York City is a monument of the naval commander who captured New Orleans, Admiral David Farragut. (This work Saint-Gaudens did in collaboration with the architect *Stanford White*.) (2) Located at Central Park in New York City is a monument of the army commander who led Northern troops marching through Georgia, General William T. Sherman. (3) Located in Lincoln Park in Chicago is a statue of the *Standing Lincoln*.

Daniel Chester French (1850–1931), born in New Hampshire, studied sculpture in Boston and in various European cities. He achieved a simple realistic style that often reflected classical influences. Like Saint-Gaudens, French chose his subjects mainly from American history—statues of John Harvard and of the New England author Ralph Waldo Emerson, portrait figures of Civil War generals, and *Mourning Victory*, a memorial, now in the Metropolitan Museum of Art in New York City, to three brothers who gave their lives in the Civil War. French is most famous for two works: (1) the first at the beginning of his career—the *Minuteman* at Concord, Massachusetts (modeled in part after a classical statue of the mythical Greek god Apollo), and (2) the second—40 years later, at the end of his career—the *Seated Lincoln*, a powerful and impressive figure in the Lincoln Memorial in Washington, D.C.

Daniel Chester French—two statues on American themes
(left) The Minuteman at Concord (*United Press International*)
(right) The Seated Lincoln (*Monkmeyer Press Photo Service*)

Gutzon Borglum (1871–1941), born in Idaho, studied art in San Francisco and in European cities. Borglum executed traditional statues of persons from American history—Philip Sheridan, a Union general in the Civil War; James Smithson; and Abraham Lincoln. However, Borglum is best known for his "sculpture with dynamite." Under federal commission, he carved into the rock of Mount Rushmore, South Dakota, the likenesses of four great American Presidents —Washington, Jefferson, Lincoln, and Theodore Roosevelt. These huge sculpted faces—among the largest ever attempted—are part of the *Mount Rushmore Memorial.*

SCULPTURE IN MODERN AMERICA—THE PAST 50 YEARS

1. New Styles and New Materials. Modern American sculpture, like other art forms, has been affected by 20th-century historical forces and cultural movements.

The historical forces have included the success of the Western democracies in resisting totalitarian control; the renewed emphasis upon civil liberties and individual rights; the further growth of industrialization and technological innovation in our society; and the increasing complexities of modern life. The artist in modern sculpture has been encouraged to express individuality, to pursue inventiveness, to experiment with new styles, and to reflect the virtues and problems of our industrialized society. Sculpture has become eclectic: Some artists have studied the art of primitive man, of medieval times, and of the Orient; other artists have explored expressionist, surrealist, cubist, and other abstract modes; still other artists have turned to a vigorous realism and to a *kinetic* or moving sculpture. Sculptors have employed traditional materials but have turned increasingly to new materials such as stainless steel, aluminum, plywood, wire, metal tubing, and plastics. In summary, modern sculpture has been marked by great diversity.

2. Outstanding American Sculptors

Jo Davidson (1883–1952), born in New York City, studied art at home and in Paris, and became a noted portrait sculptor. Working in *terra cotta* (clay) and bronze, he achieved a vigorous, lifelike style and expressed the personality of his subject. Davidson sculpted busts of many world-famous people: literary figures Anatole France, Gertrude Stein, and George Bernard Shaw; scientist Albert Einstein; and political leaders Woodrow Wilson, Mahatma Gandhi, Charles de Gaulle, and Franklin D. Roosevelt.

Jacques Lipchitz (1891–1973), born in Lithuania, studied sculpture in Paris and lived there for many years. In 1941, to escape the Nazi German invasion of France, he fled to the United States and later became an American citizen. In his early period in France, Lipchitz sculpted abstract figures as part of his cubist approach. In the 1930's Lipchitz became concerned with problems of the depression and of Nazi tyranny and turned to a more naturalistic sculptural style that could more easily convey messages to his viewers. For the 1937 Paris World's Fair, Lipchitz sculpted a 30-foot statue of *Prometheus*—a symbol of freedom for humanity. In America Lipchitz sculpted *Mother and Child II*, in which the mutilated arms of a legless torso appealed, silently but eloquently, for an end of war, destruction, torture, and murder; he also did works on Biblical themes, such as the patriarch Abraham and his son Isaac in the *Sacrifice*.

Alexander Calder (1898–1976), born into an artistic American family, studied in New York and in Paris. He became a sculptor of *stabiles*—which are abstract, free-form, and stationary works, and of *mobiles*—which are abstract free-form works that move. Both stabiles and mobiles are made of discs, spheres, wires, rods, and sheet metal. The mobiles, which vary from small to very large, usually hang from a beam or a ceiling, and are set in motion by the slightest puff of air. They may represent animals, people, and familiar objects. The mobiles have been hailed for typifying our present era of dynamic change, for representing the "restless Yankee," for indicating a light and graceful attitude toward life, and for creating visual excitement.

Painting

BRIEF SURVEY OF AMERICAN PAINTING

1. In Colonial Times: Portraiture. As the first European colonists settled the Atlantic seaboard, they were concerned overwhelmingly with securing the necessities of life: food and shelter. Once secure in their new environment, the settlers turned their thoughts toward obtaining some refinements of civilized life, including portraits of family members. In the 17th century, middle- and upper-class colonists in New York and New England employed the services of *itinerant*—that is, traveling from town to town—portrait painters called *limners*. Generally anonymous (names unknown) these limners painted children, matriarchs, and entire families of leading colonists. Although their works vary in quality, in their best efforts the limners achieved accuracy of detail and good character expression.

Unknown 17th-century limner—Mrs. Elizabeth Freake and Baby Mary (*Worcester Art Museum, Worcester, Massachusetts*)

John Singleton Copley—
Paul Revere: a colonial
portrait (*Courtesy, Museum
of Fine Arts, Boston; gift of
Joseph W., William B., and
Edward H. R. Revere*)

In the 18th century, American colonists commissioned portraits from a number of foreign and native-born artists. In their works, these artists emphasized earnestness and simplicity. The outstanding colonial painter of the latter 18th century was *John Singleton Copley* (1738–1815).

Born in Boston and given some artistic training by his stepfather, Copley developed his own realistic and natural painting style. Up to the eve of the American Revolution, Copley produced some 300 portraits, some of New Yorkers and Philadelphians but mainly of Bostonians. Among his best-known portraits are those of Samuel Adams and Paul Revere. (Loyal to the King, Copley fled from Boston in 1774, settled in London, studied European painting styles, and for many years continued his career, but as a British painter. Although he retained an interest in America and assisted American artists who came to study in London, Copley never returned home.)

2. From Independence Into the Mid-19th Century

a. Artists Apply European Painting Styles to American Topics

With the end of the American Revolution, American painters increasingly traveled to Europe to observe the great original works of European art and to receive instruction in European painting techniques. The tradition of studying art abroad had begun during colonial times. Now American artists went to London, Paris, and Rome; studied under European masters; and returned home to apply their knowledge in the painting of American personages, scenes, and wildlife.

b. Portrait Painters

Charles Peale (1741–1827), born in Maryland colony, decided upon a painting career, studied art in London for two years, and returned to the colonies, eventually making his home in Philadelphia. A strong believer in freedom, Peale served with the American forces in the Revolutionary War. He painted portraits of American leaders, including Washington and Lafayette. At Valley Forge, Peale made miniature portraits of the soldiers for them to send home. In addition to portraits, Peale painted realistic, everyday scenes, such as his two sons ascending the stairs, in his 1795 work Stairway.

Also a naturalist and taxidermist interested in wildlife, Peale stuffed and mounted the skins of many wild animals. In Philadelphia he organized one of America's first museums displaying his collections of natural history and his portraits of great American leaders. To commemorate the museum, Peale at age 81 painted a canvas entitled Peale in His Museum. (Peale also influenced members of his immediate family to become painters. His son Rembrandt Peale (1778–1860) executed a highly popular and widely acclaimed portrait of the mature Thomas Jefferson.)

Gilbert Stuart (1755–1828), born in Rhode Island colony, went abroad while in his teens to study painting in Edinburgh and London, where he matured his artistic talents. Stuart specialized in portraits only, depicted face and head to the exclusion of all other details, and probed for fundamental character. After 17 years in the British Isles, Stuart in 1793 returned to America. Here he executed nearly 1000 commissions, including portraits of our first six Presidents. Stuart is best known for his portrait of George Washington, now in the Boston Museum of Fine Arts. Stuart shows Washington as strong, dignified, and humane; this portrait has become the nationally accepted likeness and the basis of the imprint on our $1 bill.

c. Landscape Painters: The Hudson River School

Throughout the 19th century in America, landscape painting had great appeal. It reflected many popular sentiments: romantic love of nature, religious awe of the Almighty's scenic wonders, scientific interest in natural history, resentment against society's growing industrialization and urbanization, and patriotic pride in the attractiveness of the American countryside. Landscape painters also were inspired by American writers dealing with American themes: Washington Irving relating the Hudson Valley legends and James Fenimore Cooper writing the Leatherstocking Tales. (Check the Index for these writers.)

Toward the mid-19th century, a group of painters began detailing scenes of the American landscape. Although these painters depicted landscapes of many areas throughout the Northeast, they are primarily associated with the Catskill Mountains and the Hudson Valley and are known as the Hudson River School. Thomas Cole (1801–1848), the leader of this school, is known for his landscape of a bend in the Connecticut River—a work called The Oxbow. George Inness (1825–1894), who worked a generation later, followed the Hudson River School of painting in his early works: Delaware Valley and Peace and Plenty.

d. Paintings of Birds

John J. Audubon (1785–1851) was born in Haiti and educated in France, where he also studied painting. At age 18 he came to America. Here he married, moved to the Kentucky frontier, and opened a general store. A failure in business, Audubon pursued his passion for painting the birds of America. He traveled the nation's vast wilderness land, observing and recording birds in their natural habitats and at ordinary activities. As an ornithologist, or bird specialist, Audubon achieved detailed accuracy and as an artist he produced colorful and dramatic drawings. When in need of money, Audubon headed for cities where he painted portraits and gave lessons in French, drawing, and dancing.

With more than 400 completed paintings, Audubon desired to publish them in a book. Unable to find a publisher in America, Audubon went to England where, acting as his own publisher, he found engravers to make the plates for printing and sold subscriptions to the forthcoming books. Between 1827 and 1839, Audubon published a four-volume *Birds of America* accompanied by a five-volume explanatory text, the *Ornithological Biography*. Audubon's work won him fame, fortune, and prestige.

3. From the Civil War Era Into the Early 20th Century

a. Artists Record the American Scene With Realism. Winslow Homer and Thomas Eakins, two outstanding American painters of this era, were in several ways similar. Both visited Europe but their works showed no European influences; both rejected the public's demand for sentimentality and affectation in painting; both chose their subjects from the American environment; and both painted with vigor and realism. Also, in many ways, they were quite different.

Winslow Homer (1836–1910), born in Boston, worked as an apprentice to a lithographer, preparing metal plates for printing, and then as a free-lance illustrator chiefly for the popular magazine *Harper's Weekly*. During the Civil War, Homer served as an artist-correspondent with the Union forces, and from his sketches, later painted several powerful war pictures such as *Prisoners From the Front*. Homer won artistic acclaim but his paintings sold slowly and he continued to work as a magazine illustrator. In 1883 Homer moved to Maine where he portrayed nature—the ocean and the rockbound coast—in conflict with the fisher folk. Among his vivid seascapes are *The Lifeline*, *Eight Bells*, and *The Herring Net*. Homer again won artistic acclaim but this time coupled with public realization of his talent and demand for his works.

Thomas Eakins (1844–1916), born in Philadelphia, studied art and anatomy, and produced portraits and paintings of everyday American life. Among Eakins' best-known works are his *Self-Portrait*; the portrait of the poet Walt Whitman; paintings of various athletic activities—boxing, wrestling, swimming, and boating; and his small painting, now in the Metropolitan Museum of Art, entitled *The Chess Players*.

Although possessing great talent and high principle, Eakins was blunt and tactless. He antagonized his fellow artists and withdrew from the Society of American Artists; he offended many portrait sitters by refusing to soften any physical blemishes; he shocked Philadelphia society by using nude live models in his classes and was dismissed as professor of painting at the Philadelphia Academy of Fine Arts; he submitted his surgery study, *The Gross Clinic*, for exhibition in the art section of the Philadelphia Centennial Exposition (1876), but it was rejected as unfit for public viewing and he was reviled as a "butcher." Eakins never tasted public approval and only after his death received recognition as one of America's great painters.

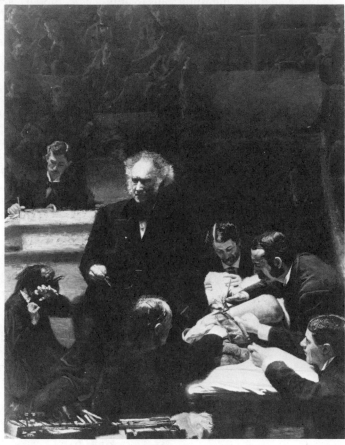

Realism in painting *(top)* Winslow Homer—"The Herring Net"
(Collection, The Art Institute of Chicago) *(above)* Thomas Eakins—
"The Gross Clinic" *(Property of the Jefferson Medical College
of Thomas Jefferson University, Philadelphia, Pa.)*

b. The New York Armory Show of 1913. Sponsored by a group of artists to exhibit modern works "usually neglected by current shows," this show was a major event in the artistic growth of America. It featured 1600 works—paintings, drawings, and sculptures—some by Americans but mainly by Europeans, executed in the style of "modern art"; abstractions, especially cubism; various schools of impressionism, a style in which the artist neglects details but emphasizes his overall impressions; and primitivism. The show was seen by an estimated 300,000 persons mainly in New York but also later while on tour in Chicago and Boston. Postcard reproductions of displayed works were seen by additional thousands.

The show astonished and shocked the American public, which had had little contact with and little preparation for "modern art." The show received an avalanche of newspaper and magazine publicity, which in the main was critical and uncomplimentary.

In its long-term effect, the Armory Show brought American art into a new era. In began educating Americans to appreciate "modern art"; it created a new market for "modern art" and sold American collectors some 200 works from the show; it encouraged American painters to experiment with new art forms; and finally it emboldened American artists to welcome diversity and to express individualism. The art of modern America, thusly, has become boundless and varied.

4. Painting in Modern America—The Past 50 Years: Representative Artists. For Midwest regional painters—such as "Thomas Hart Benton," "John Curry," "Frederic Remington," and "Grant Wood"—check the Index.

Anna Mary "Grandma" Moses (1860–1961) began painting in her seventies, without ever having had an art lesson. In gay colors she depicted scenes of farmlife and of the rural countryside such as *Out for Christmas Trees.* Her paintings, classified as in the primitive art style, were hailed as an expression of popular, or folk, art. Used frequently for Christmas cards and calendars, "Grandma" Moses' homespun scenes became widely known in America.

Grandma Moses—"It Snows, Oh It Snows": folk art
(copyright © 1969 Grandma Moses Properties Co., New York)

Edward Hopper (1882–1967), born in Nyack, New York, studied art in New York City and later in Paris. In his mature years, Hopper painted familiar scenes of New York City life—a gas station, movie house, night cafeteria, and ghetto area. With intense realism, Hopper portrayed urban living as lonely, empty, and monotonous. Among his best-known works are *From the Williamsburg Bridge, Nighthawks,* and *Early Sunday Morning.*

Ben Shahn (1898–1969), born in Lithuania and as a child brought to the United States, became at age 16 a lithographer's apprentice and later studied art in Europe. Returning here in 1929, Shahn portrayed America during the Great Depression, then at war with Fascism, and thereafter in the post-World War II years. Shahn was a socially conscious artist who painted realistic works protesting against evils of society. Shahn denounced what he believed to be a miscarriage of justice in his painting, *The Passion of Sacco and Vanzetti;* he did murals in the Bronx, New York, Post Office and the Social Security Building at Washington, D.C.; during World War II, he provided the Office of War Information with effective war posters, notably *This Is Nazi Brutality;* after the war and at the request of the State Department, he protested global starvation in his poster *Hunger.*

Jackson Pollock (1912–1956), born in Wyoming, studied art in New York, and developed into an abstract expressionist painter. A controversial artist, Pollock painted large canvases by laying them on the floor and, from cans, brushes, and sticks, dripping paint upon them. By this "drip" technique, he sought exciting patterns, varied textures, and interlaced colors—as in his work *Autumn Rhythm.* For the art world, Pollock became a symbol of innovation and freedom.

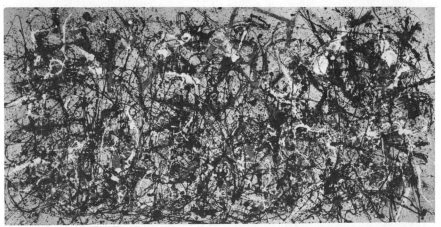

Jackson Pollock—"Autumn Rhythm": abstract art (*The Metropolitan Museum of Art, George A. Hearn Fund, 1957*)

Andrew Wyeth (1917–), born in Pennsylvania, the son of a noted book illustrator, received artistic training in his father's studio and began painting at an early age. A realist of great technical skill, Wyeth found his themes in everyday American life—its scenery and its people. His paintings were precise representations often expressing the loneliness of the individual and the beauty of nature, as in *Christina's World* (see page 454) and the *Scarecrow.*

Andrew Wyeth—"Christina's World" (1948). Tempera on gesso panel, 32¼ x 47¾"
(Collection, The Museum of Modern Art, New York)

Jacob Lawrence (1917–) as a youth lived in New York City near a settlement house where he was encouraged to pursue an artistic career. During the Great Depression Lawrence worked on WPA art projects. He developed his own painting style combining aspects of primitivism with cubism. A black, Lawrence used his art to extol black heroes, portray black history, and protest racial injustice. Among his best-known works are series of panels: *The Life of Frederick Douglass*, *The Life of Harriet Tubman*, and *The Migration of the Negro*.

VARIED PUBLIC ACCEPTANCE OF ARTISTS AND ART STYLES

In art the general public readily accepts that which is familiar and, conversely, least accepts or even rejects that which is strange. The public judges artistic works, as familiar or as strange, in accordance with the subject matter and the painting style. The public's attitude toward an artist may be affected by other factors such as the artist's personality and life-style, the opinions of art critics and the mass media, and the artist's status in a foreign country. These factors are illustrated in the following discussion:

1. Rapid Acceptance. Charles Peale won rapid public acceptance. As an American, he served with the colonial forces in the Revolutionary War. As an artist, he painted popular and patriotic portraits of American leaders; he also painted pleasant, realistic, and recognizable everyday scenes. As a naturalist, he mounted skins of wild animals and founded a museum, which activities accorded with the prevailing American interest in science. "Grandma" Moses also won rapid public acceptance. She was hailed as representing the ordinary people and admired for developing her painting talent at such an advanced age. Her works were acclaimed for their clear, simple style and their nostalgic subject matter.

2. Slow Acceptance. John J. Audubon was accepted by the American public but slowly. Considered an eccentric backwoodsman, Audubon was unable, in Philadelphia and New York, to secure a publisher for his bird paintings. He sailed to England, where he received an enthusiastic welcome and himself published his *Birds of America*. This work won him fame and fortune not only in England, but also, upon his return, in America. Winslow Homer also gained public acceptance but slowly. He painted Civil War scenes and later Maine seascapes, both with vivid realism. These realistic works disturbed the art public, which wanted paintings that were romantic and fanciful. Supporting himself in part as a magazine illustrator, Homer persevered and in his later years finally won public acceptance.

3. Long-Delayed Acceptance. Thomas Eakins did not gain public acceptance during his lifetime. Eakins painted realistic pictures for an era that wanted romantic works. In addition Eakins lacked tact; he antagonized his fellow artists, lost portrait commissions by refusing to heed requests of the sitters, and shocked society by using nude models and by painting medical operations with blood dripping from surgical knives. "Modern" art forms introduced by the 1913 Armory Show did not gain even partial public acceptance until some 30 to 40 years later. "Modern" art was derided by the mass media and then was relegated into the background by international and national developments: World War I, the conservative 1920's, the Great Depression starting in 1929, the threat of Fascism, and World War II. In the post-World War II years, the modernist Jackson Pollock did not gain general public acceptance. Many viewers considered his abstract paintings as difficult, if not impossible, to understand and his "drip" technique of painting as a hoax perpetrated on the general public.

In recent years, modern art has been brought "home" to the general public by the mass media—especially, television, movies, newspapers, and picture magazines such as *Look* and *Life*. Modern art consequently has become more familiar and has gained greater public acceptance.

FINANCIAL SUPPORT FOR THE ARTS

1. The General Pattern. From colonial times to the present, the art public has been the major source of *patronage*—that is, financial support for artists. In colonial times, wealthy upper-class persons gave commissions to well-known painters for portraits, while middle-class persons secured their portraits from lesser-known or itinerant limners. During the 19th and 20th centuries, well-to-do persons commissioned portraits and paintings; they also purchased artistic works they had not commissioned but which they found appealing. Better-known artists provided for the sale of their works, in major cities, through art dealers.

Between the Civil War and World War I, there came into existence many art museums—some private; some affiliated with prestigious universities, such as Yale and Cornell; one—the National Museum in Washington—with federal support; some with state support; and a number with municipal support, such as the Boston Museum of Fine Arts and the New York Metropolitan Museum of

Art. Eager to display worthwhile paintings, museums became an important outlet for artistic works. Also in the 20th century, art dealers opened small galleries and sometimes held "one-man" shows so that the art public could browse, enjoy, and perhaps even purchase the assembled paintings. To develop public taste and secure sales, lesser-known artists displayed their works in outdoor exhibitions such as those held in the Greenwich Village section of New York City.

2. The Post-Civil War Years: The Gilded Age. The post-Civil War years —marked by the growth of big business, the dominance of industrial and finance capitalists, and the philosophy of "get-rich-quick" materialism—are often known as the *Gilded Age*. (This term originated as the title of a novel set in those years written by Charles Warner and Mark Twain.)

During the Gilded Age, Andrew Carnegie, the steel magnate, Henry Frick, the coke (coal) king, and Andrew Mellon, the banker and aluminum king—to name but a few—used their tremendous wealth to buy major art works and create large private art collections. Eventually, such collections were donated to existing museums or were used to found new museums where the art works were available for public viewing and enjoyment.

3. The Depression of 1929: Works Progress Administration. During the Great Depression, as commercial art jobs dwindled and art commissions declined sharply as did art sales, artists were particularly hard hit. Under the New Deal in 1935, artists were offered government jobs by the *Federal Arts Project* of the *Works Progress Administration* (WPA). Until halted during World War II, the WPA employed some 5000 artists—traditionalists and modernists—who decorated public buildings with over 1000 murals and other paintings. Some WPA artists who later became well known were Jacob Lawrence, Ben Shahn, and Jackson Pollock.

Although the art produced under the WPA was, with rare exception, of mediocre quality, the WPA project had important results. It enabled artists to sustain themselves, to paint full time and develop their skills, and to share experiences as they worked together on major endeavors. Further, by its free art classes and exhibitions, the WPA project expanded awareness of the art world.

4. Recent Years: Government Support for the Creative Arts. The *New York State Council on the Arts* (established in 1960) and the *National Foundation on the Arts and Humanities* (established in 1965) both indicate renewed government interest in and financial support for the creative arts. These organizations provide funds for the wide spectrum of creative arts such as the communications arts (film, television, and literature), the performing arts (theatre, dance, and music) as well as the fine arts, especially painting. The *National Endowment for the Arts*—an agency of the National Foundation—provides fellowships for painters, art historians, and printmakers; it grants subsidies—usually to museums—to finance art exhibitions.

As with science, government interest in and financial support for the creative arts has been hailed, by some observers, as proof of the "maturing of American civilization." Such government activity, however, has been viewed with skepticism by other observers who raise many questions: Is government financial support for the creative arts a justifiable expenditure of the taxpayers' money? Will average citizens devote their increased leisure time to the creative arts or rather to other activities such as sports and travel? Will government support stifle independent development of and impose political domination upon the creative arts? On what basis will the government determine the allocation of funds to the various creative arts, and how will it measure artistic ability?

Lithography

BRIEF HISTORY

Devised in 1796, *lithography* is a process of printing from flat surfaces, usually metal plates, by which images are reproduced on paper or other materials. By using a separate metal plate for each color, lithography makes possible color reproductions. With time the lithography process, utilizing newer equipment and techniques, provided improved reproductions.

By the mid-19th century, lithography had made possible fine but inexpensive prints—ranging in price from 25 cents to $3. It met the public demand for pictures and enabled persons who could not afford original paintings to collect reproductions of works of major artists.

Currier and Ives: American Lithographers

Nathaniel Currier (1813–1888), a lithographer, and *James M. Ives* (1824–1895), an artist, established a business firm—officially by 1857—to produce and sell lithographic prints. They employed a number of artists to provide paintings of various aspects of American life—such as notable persons, farm scenes, frontier doings, sports events, catastrophes, patriotic themes, recreational activities, and transportation facilities (railroads, steamboats, and clipper ships). From these paintings, Currier and Ives made their lithographic reproductions. Their catalog of prints contained over 4000 separate items. Although rated by critics as mediocre art, the Currier and Ives prints were enjoyed by millions and reflected American life and interests of the latter 19th century. Among the best-known Currier and Ives prints are *Home to Thanksgiving*, *The Great East River Suspension Bridge* (Brooklyn), *Western Frontier Home*, and *Hudson River Craft*.

Currier and Ives—"Home to Thanksgiving": lithograph (*Museum of the City of New York, Harry T. Peters Collection*)

Photography

BRIEF HISTORY

Although people had long known of the effect of sunlight upon silver compounds, modern photography began only in the early 19th century. By 1839 *Louis Daguerre*, a French painter and inventor, developed a process for making permanent photographs, and for some years photographs were known as *daguerreotypes*. Over the years many persons worked to simplify and improve the process of photography. In the 1880's *George Eastman* devised flexible roll film and a simple roll film camera, which two products were produced in Rochester, New York, by the *Eastman Kodak Company*. Increasingly popular, Kodak film enabled the public to take pictures and to send the exposed film to special laboratories for developing negatives and making prints. In the 1930's, Kodak developed color film for popular use. In 1947 *Edwin Land* invented a camera, using special film, that would take a picture and almost immediately produce a finished print. The Land film and variety of cameras are both manufactured by the *Polaroid Corporation* of Cambridge, Massachusetts. Today, cameras equipped with special lenses and using many accessories can be quite expensive but can produce magnificent pictures.

OUTSTANDING AMERICAN PHOTOGRAPHERS

Is photography a creative art? Debated into the 20th century, this question seemingly has been answered by a "yes." Supporters of this viewpoint claim that photographers—by choosing subject matter, planning composition, and capturing facial expression—are truly artists. For further evidence, these supporters point to the work of outstanding photographers, as follows:

Mathew Brady (1823–1896), born in New York State, became a portrait photographer and won several prizes for his skillful daguerreotypes. In 1861 Brady, who viewed himself as an historian, determined to produce a photographic record of the Civil War. Brady and a group of assistants—whom he hired, trained, and equipped—accompanied the Union armies and made thousands of on-the-spot war pictures. Although forced into bankruptcy by the cost of this project, Brady's Civil War photographic history won him great fame. Among his best-known photographs are the *Ruins of Richmond, Virginia*, and his portrait of Lincoln, which is copied on our $5 bill.

Alfred Stieglitz (1864–1946), born in Hoboken, New Jersey, studied engineering in Germany, where he purchased a camera. Fascinated by photography, he abandoned engineering for a career in the arts. Following his return to the United States, Stieglitz devoted himself to taking photographs, founding and editing a photography magazine, *Camera Work*, and battling for recognition of photography as a creative art. He won fame for his realistic and artistic photographs of New York City such as those showing the street scene of *Winter, Fifth Avenue* and the arrival of poor, bewildered immigrants in *The Steerage* (see illustration, page 12).

From 1905 onward Stieglitz maintained art galleries in New York City, where he displayed photographs taken by himself and others and introduced paintings by European and some American modernists. Many of the modernists he championed were later recognized as among the great 20th-century painters.

Stieglitz has been hailed for holding a unique role in American artistic development and for being the "father of modern photography."

Edward Weston (1886–1958), born in Illinois, lived in and is usually associated with central California. At first he earned a living from portrait photography, but he later won fame by his interesting abstractions and realistic pictures of nature. Weston had the ability to perceive beauty in ordinary subjects and to photograph them in simple but effective compositions. Among his major works are those of nudes, vegetables, landscapes, and seascapes.

The Performing Arts

Meaning. The term *performing arts* encompasses three major arts: music, dance, and theatre. They exist mainly in live performances given by entertainers—musicians, dancers, and actors—usually from a stage and before an audience. These arts appeal, in varying degree, to the visual and auditory senses and to the intellect—that is, to the eye, ear, and brain.

With the average American having more leisure time, the performing arts have gained increasing attention. They receive some financial support from government agencies such as the New York State Council on the Arts and the National Foundation on the Arts and Humanities. They have led to the establishment of cultural clusters—buildings grouped together and utilized for the presentation of concerts, operas, dance recitals, and plays. Among such cultural clusters for the performing arts are the *Music Center of Los Angeles* (California), the *Saratoga Center* (New York), the *Lincoln Center* in New York City, and the *John F. Kennedy Center* in Washington, D.C.

Music

THE EUROPEAN INFLUENCE

From colonial times onward, Americans have enjoyed listening to music and singing songs. Their musical tastes, however, have reflected European influence. For many years Americans have borrowed from European music, have listened to European musical experts, and have sent native talent abroad to study and absorb European musical traditions. Americans were occupied with settling a continent, gaining independence, and preserving the Union; meanwhile, Europeans enjoyed and built upon a rich musical heritage—vocal, instrumental, symphonic, and operatic. European musicians benefited from patrons in the Church, royalty, and the nobility.

In the Gilded Age of the post-Civil War era, wealthy Americans became patrons of music. For example, they financially supported the opening in 1883 of the New York *Metropolitan Opera House* and they attended performances in part to "be seen"—as a symbol of social status. For many years, the Met's programs consisted only of operas by European composers.

AMERICAN CONTRIBUTIONS TO MUSIC

Despite European influence, Americans have made original contributions to music in at least four areas:

1. Folk Music. Often created by unknown composers, folk music has stirred Americans to listen, dance, march, and sing. Folk songs have ranged in mood from the mournfully beautiful "Down in the Valley" to the sprightly comical "Pop! Goes the Weasel." Lively folk music such as "Turkey in the Straw" has animated countless participants and callers at square dances. Folk songs have arisen out of wars, such as the Civil War marching song "John Brown's Body" and the modern antiwar song "Where Have All the Flowers Gone?" Some folk songs, identified with work activities, have been "Pick a Bale of Cotton," "The Last Roundup," and "I've Been Working on the Railroad." Leading personalities of the American folksong, in modern times, have included John and Alan Lomax who recorded over 10,000 folk songs throughout the United States, and the popular performers Pete Seeger, Bob Dylan, Woody Guthrie, and Burl Ives.

2. Negro Spirituals. Originated by slaves on Southern plantations, Negro spirituals are a type of folk song. They reflect in varying combinations African rhythms, Southern "local color," simple but intense religious belief, anguish over slavery, and hope for the future—here on earth or in afterlife. Well-known Negro spirituals include "Go Down, Moses," and "Nobody Knows the Trouble I've Seen." A well-known singer of spirituals (and other songs) was the black contralto *Marian Anderson*.

Closely related to Negro spirituals are the folk songs of the mid-19th-century composer *Stephen Foster* (1826–1864). Still sung to this day, his songs include "Oh! Susanna," "Way Down Upon the Swanee River," and "My Old Kentucky Home."

3. Jazz. Marked by strong rhythm and powerful beat, jazz is a kind of music that permits the players to improvise. Although jazz is definitely American, its origins are obscure. Most experts hold that jazz evolved from American folk music and Negro spirituals; that it was developed by musicians of little or no formal training; and that it appeared in the 1890's, most probably first in New Orleans. Jazz has taken varied forms: (*a*) the lively *ragtime*, as heard in Scott Joplin's "The Entertainer" and in Irving Berlin's "Alexander's Ragtime Band," and (*b*) the mournful *blues*, as heard in W. C. Handy's "St. Louis Blues." Outstanding jazz musicians have included the trumpeter *Louis Armstrong*, the clarinetist *Benny Goodman*, and the bandleader *Duke Ellington*. In the 1920's, *George Gershwin* successfully wedded jazz to classical music in his compositions *Rhapsody in Blue* and *An American in Paris*.

Jazz has also been blended with folk music and some Latin American musical elements to create modern rock 'n roll. American rock 'n roll bands, equipped with electronically amplified instruments and featuring vocalists such as Elvis Presley and Diana Ross, have been seen and heard on concert tours and televison programs. Rock 'n roll festivals such as the outdoor concerts held at Woodstock, New York, and Monterey, California, have attracted thousands of young people.

4. Musical Comedies and Musical Plays. These consist of (*a*) a story or book with a plausible plot that unfolds through the spoken word or dialog, (*b*) songs that maintain the mood of the story and utilize a wide range of musical expression —melodic, rhythmic, chorale, and recitative, (*c*) lyrics that are clever and further the story, and (*d*) dances or choreography that arise naturally from the story. Although various elements can be traced to earlier American and European works, the musical as a unified production first appeared in the post-World War I era and was an original American contribution.

Of the early musicals, the best known are the Mississippi River drama *Show Boat*, the political satire *Of Thee I Sing*, and the black folk opera *Porgy and Bess*. From the 1940's onward, the musical achieved increasing popularity, with many splendid productions including: four works by *Richard Rodgers* (composer) and *Oscar Hammerstein II* (lyricist)—*Oklahoma! Carousel, South Pacific*, and *The King and I*—and the remarkable work of *Alan Jay Lerner* (book and lyrics) and *Frederick Loewe* (music) in transforming George Bernard Shaw's play *Pygmalion* into the musical comedy *My Fair Lady*.

Dance

THE EUROPEAN PREDOMINANCE

The dance as a performing art presented before an audience flourished in Renaissance Europe and evolved into classical ballet. Supported by rich patrons—royalty, nobility, and the upper middle class—European composers created ballet music, and dance companies executed complex choreographic works. Within the last 100 years, Europe produced great ballet composers, including Russia's Peter Ilich Tchaikovsky and Igor Stravinsky, and established great dance companies including the Royal Danish Ballet, Russia's Ballets Russes and Bolshoi Ballet, and Britain's Royal (Sadlers Wells) Ballet.

Until well into the 20th century, ballet in America reflected European predominance. Americans saw ballet largely as presented by touring European companies, featuring European stars, and dancing to European music.

AMERICAN DEVELOPMENTS IN THE DANCE

1. **Ballet.** *George Balanchine*, a Russian who came to the United States in 1933 and soon became an American citizen, played a major role in the development of American ballet. Balanchine used his talent as a *choreographer* to arrange new and interesting dances; he helped found the *New York City Ballet;* he served as its artistic director, achieving the highest standards of classical ballet performance and winning himself and the company international fame. There were other important persons in the development of American ballet: the choreographer *Agnes de Mille* arranged the dances for the musical comedy *Oklahoma!;* and American composers began writing ballet music, such as Aaron Copland's Western saga of *Billy the Kid* and Leonard Bernstein's tale of sailors on shore leave, *Fancy Free*.

2. **Modern Dance and Other Dance Forms.** In the early 20th century, several dancers—especially Isadora Duncan and Martha Graham—rebelled against the classical formality of the ballet and presented a freer and more natural dance style. This innovation led to the development of *modern dance*—using the varied movements of the human body to express emotions and relate experiences. Americans also began to experiment with other dance forms: ballroom dancing, ethnic and other folk dances, jazz styles, primitive dances, Oriental techniques, and other innovative dance arrangements. Today several hundred dance companies offer programs of various dance forms for the entertainment of American audiences.

Theatre

BRIEF HISTORY

In colonial times, theatrical performances were not held in New England because they violated the severe moral code of Puritanism, but plays occasionally were presented elsewhere in large cities such as New York, Philadelphia, and Charleston. Such plays closely imitated the English stage.

In 19th-century America, the theatre flourished and, by the century's end, a playhouse existed in most sizable towns and cities. Touring companies visited these playhouses, often presenting a dramatic version of the popular *Uncle Tom's Cabin* and various plays by William Shakespeare. A noted Shakespearean actor of this era was *Edwin Booth*. Most American plays, however, lacked dramatic quality and intellectual challenge: some were hastily written for immediate presentation; some were vehicles designed to enable popular actors to display their talents; some were ordered by theatre managers to cater to public taste so as to assure box office success. Titles of representative 19th-century plays are *The Indian Princess, Rip van Winkle, The Heart of Maryland*, and *A Texas Steer*.

In the 20th century, and especially after World War I, the American theatre experienced great changes: (1) Improved Staging. Theatres utilized the newest technological developments, such as electric lighting, revolving stages, and more realistic props. (2) Experimental Theatres. In addition to theatres in the Broadway area of New York City—the Great White Way—and in the central districts of other major cities, numerous theatres appeared in heretofore unlikely areas. These were small, experimental theatres: "Off-Broadway" in New York City, "summer stock" in rural communities, and facilities at major universities. These theatres gave aspiring newcomers training in various theatrical skills and often produced plays of little-known writers.

MODERN PLAYWRIGHTS

No longer dominated by actors and theatre managers, American writers created works of literature possessing dramatic impact. They analyzed individual behavior; examined the social environment; and interpreted economic and political forces. Their works reflected realism and maturity. The first major American playwright, whose early works were presented by the experimental Provincetown (Massachusetts) Players, was *Eugene O'Neill* (1888–1953). He analyzed human character and asked the meaning of life in such plays as *The Emperor Jones* and *Long Day's Journey Into Night*; he also penned a charming domestic comedy, *Ah, Wilderness!*

THEMES OF MODERN PLAYWRIGHTS

Many themes, worthwhile for today, have appeared in the works of modern American playwrights, but such themes are far more numerous than can be presented in this brief survey. Two such themes, which should be of interest to history students, are the following: (1) By retelling the stories of important political figures, plays offer lessons of value. In *The Patriots*, playwright *Sidney Kingsley* indicated that Hamilton and Jefferson—although bitter political opponents and representatives of different economic classes and views on government—were both American patriots. In *Abe Lincoln in Illinois*, playwright *Robert Sherwood* portrayed the personal and political factors that went into the making of our sixteenth President. (2) By dissecting social conflict, plays offer valuable insights into the thinking of our society. In *Winterset*, based upon the Sacco-Vanzetti case, playwright *Maxwell Anderson* raised problems of determining guilt or innocence in trials held during times of high public emotion. In *The Crucible*, dramatist *Arthur Miller* focused on the 17th-century Salem witchcraft trials so as to condemn mass hysteria and defend the right of individual dissent. This play, written in the 1950's, was, many observers felt, an attack on the tactics used by Senator Joseph McCarthy in his search for Communist influence in the United States. (Check the Index for "Joseph McCarthy.")

Literature

American literature is presented in this section because it is a major area of creativity. American writers have created an enormous number of literary works: poetry and prose; novel and short story; and history and autobiography. They have presented plots, developed ideas, examined regional traits, analyzed individuals, and interpreted events. Varied and extensive, American literature is today a vast subject.

In this brief survey of American creativity, literature cannot be presented in any depth. This survey attempts to arouse the reader's interest by presenting a number of literary themes or concepts—an overview of some American writers.

LIMITATIONS OF THE LITERARY THEME APPROACH

In using only a few literary themes, our discussion must omit writers whose works relate to other themes and must exclude writers whose highly individualistic works do not fit into any thematic approach. Two major figures in mid-19th-century American literature, whose works are highly individualistic and defy classification, are the following: (1) *Edgar Allan Poe* (1809–1849) wrote highly rhythmic poems such as "The Raven" and "Annabel Lee." He also perfected the short story of mystery and horror such as "The Fall of the House of Usher." (2) *Herman Melville* (1819–1891) wrote the novel *Moby Dick*. On the surface it is an adventure story of whaling but, for most literary critics, it is an allegory symbolizing the struggle of humanity against the brute forces of nature. Melville is a prime literary example of a great talent who was denied public acceptance during his lifetime.

SOME AMERICAN LITERARY THEMES

1. Writers in the early 19th century drew inspiration from the American environment: (a) *Washington Irving* (1783–1859) wrote of the early Dutch settlers in his satirical *Knickerbocker's History of New York*. He also related the folklore of the Hudson River Valley in his *Legend of Sleepy Hollow* and *Rip van Winkle*. (b) *James Fenimore Cooper* (1789–1851) wrote adventure stories detailing the exploits of an heroic frontiersman, Natty Bumppo. *The Deerslayer* and *The Last of the Mohicans* are two of the five Natty Bumppo novels, which together are known as the *Leatherstocking Tales*.

2. Writers in the mid-19th century spoke out for individualism. *(a) Ralph Waldo Emerson* (1803–1882) was an essayist who dealt with the world of ideas. In essays on "Self-Reliance," "Experience," and "Fate," he expounds on the worth and dignity of the individual. In his essay on "Civilization," Emerson claimed that "the true test of civilization is, not the census, nor the size of cities, nor the crops—no, but the kind of man the country turns out." *(b) Henry Thoreau* (1817–1862) wrote the autobiographical work *Walden.* In it he described the two years that he spent alone in the woods, seeking to live free of the pressures of society and in accordance with his values as an individual. In his essay on "Civil Disobedience," Thoreau insisted that, in case of a conflict between the individual's conscience and the government's dictates, the individual must follow his conscience.

3. Writers throughout our history have been social critics, protesting against abuses and demanding justice.

a. Before the Civil War—Spokesmen Against Slavery. John Greenleaf Whittier (1807–1892) hated slavery and wrote many abolitionist poems. *James Russell Lowell* (1819–1891) condemned the Mexican War and slavery in his poems collected as the *Biglow Papers. Harriet Beecher Stowe* (1811–1896) aroused Northern passions against slavery with her melodramatic novel *Uncle Tom's Cabin.*

b. In the Late 19th Century—Spokesmen for Reform. In addition to the muckrakers (check the Index), other writers spoke out for economic and political reform. *Edward Bellamy* (1850–1898) contrasted what conditions were with what they could be in his utopian novel *Looking Backward. Theodore Dreiser* (1871–1945), in two novels, *The Financier* and *The Titan,* drew an unflattering portrait of the business methods and personal life of a finance capitalist.

c. During the Depression Years of the 1930's—A Spokesman for Economic Justice. John Steinbeck (1902–1968) described the plight of the "Okies," migratory farmworkers, in his powerful novel *The Grapes of Wrath.*

d. In the Post-World War II Years—Spokesmen Against Racial Prejudice and Discrimination. Check the Index for "Writers, black."

4. Writers during the World War II era warned Americans against totalitarianism. *(a) Sinclair Lewis* (1885–1951) described the causes and consequences of a supposed Fascist attempt to seize power in the United States in his novel *It Can't Happen Here. (b) Ernest Hemingway* (1898–1961) related the story of a man who gave his life in a futile attempt to halt the Fascist military machine in his novel *For Whom the Bell Tolls.*

5. Poets have rhapsodized in praise of democracy. *(a) Walt Whitman* (1819–1892) expressed optimistic individualism and pride in American democracy in poems published together as *Leaves of Grass.* Anguished by the assassination of Lincoln, Whitman penned a poetic tribute, "O Captain! My Captain." Whitman has been called the "poet of democracy." *(b) Carl Sandburg* (1878–1967), who won fame for his biography of Lincoln, was also an outstanding poet. Writing poems of the common man engaged in commonplace activities, Sandburg expressed his faith in American democracy. Two volumes of his poems are *Chicago Poems* and *The People, Yes.*

MULTIPLE-CHOICE QUESTIONS

1. The houses built by sedentary Indians of the American prairies and plains illustrated (1) the misuse of the timber resources of the West (2) a practical adaptation to the environment (3) the influence of Scandinavian immigrants (4) an early form of cliff dwellings.

2. The forerunner of our modern portable tent was the (1) Navaho hogan (2) Pueblo cliff dwelling (3) Iroquois long house (4) Crow tepee.

3. In colonial America, the Georgian style of architecture was employed in all of the following *except* (1) public buildings in Williamsburg, the colonial capital of Virginia (2) homes for New England farmers and artisans (3) homes for wealthy Southern aristocrats (4) homes for wealthy New England merchants.

4. The log cabin, the symbol of the early American frontier, was introduced by which group of settlers? (1) Scotch-Irish (2) Dutch (3) Swedish (4) English

5. In the early years of the American republic, many buildings were constructed in the *Federal style*. This style was derived mainly from the architecture found in which European city? (1) London (2) Athens (3) Paris (4) Rome

6. Late 19th-century United States architecture can *best* be described as (1) copied directly from the Greek classical period (2) simple and distinctively Dutch in origin (3) ornate and mixed in style (4) imitative of Oriental design.

7. Which is a *basic* reason for the construction of skyscrapers in the United States? (1) high land costs in urban areas (2) high liability insurance rates in urban areas (3) high cost of steel (4) cheap immigrant labor

8. Which statement *best* describes contemporary architecture in the United States? (1) It is more concerned with color than size. (2) It is similar to 19th-century European architecture. (3) It is limited to large structures in metropolitan centers. (4) It encourages individual expression in design and materials.

9. Which one of the following pairs is *incorrect?* (1) Buckminster Fuller—geodesic domes (2) Eero Saarinen—Trans World Airlines building at Kennedy Airport, in New York City (3) Ludwig Mies van der Rohe—uncluttered design because in architecture "less is more" (4) Raymond Hood—John F. Kennedy Center for the Performing Arts in Washington, D.C.

10. For an archeologist of the distant future, which would provide a most helpful clue to 20th-century American culture? (1) human skeleton (2) petrified forest (3) fish fossil (4) ruins of a skyscraper

11. In the 19th century, which was the *most* evident theme in sculpture in the United States? (1) patriotism (2) realism (3) religion (4) nativism

12. The Mount Rushmore Memorial, sculpted by Gutzon Borglum, honors (1) the pioneers who crossed the Great Plains (2) the soldiers who gave their lives in the Civil War (3) four outstanding American Presidents (4) the signers of the Declaration of Independence.

13. Which is the *least* valid statement regarding American sculpture in the 20th century? It has (1) used new materials such as aluminum, metal tubing, and plastics (2) rejected the use of the human face and body (3) devised stabiles and mobiles (4) used techniques of primitive, Medieval, and Oriental art.

14. In the 19th-century United States, the fine arts tended to (1) receive wide popular support (2) be dominated by religious groups in the United States (3) be financed by the federal government (4) be influenced by European forms and designs.

15. Landscape painting in 19th-century America appealed to all of the following *except* (1) scientific interest in nature (2) resentment against growing urbanization (3) respect for symmetry and formality (4) appreciation of natural beauty.

16. Which theme would 19th-century American artists of the realistic school have been *least* likely to use? (1) war prisoners being marched to captivity (2) the hard life of

fisher folk   (3) details of a surgical operation   (4) a sun-drenched farmhouse surrounded by fields of ripening grain

17. The Armory Show of 1913 was important in art history because it   (1) was the first art show to be financed by the federal government   (2) spurred American interest in modern art   (3) established New York City as the artistic capital of America   (4) excluded entirely the works of European artists.

18. Which one of the following pairs is *incorrect?*   (1) Jackson Pollock—devised drip technique of painting   (2) Grandma Moses—studied painting in Europe   (3) Ben Shahn—used his art to protest Nazi brutality, worldwide hunger, and other evils of society   (4) Jacob Laurence—concerned with black history and heroes.

19. Which of the following statements regarding financial support for the arts is *not* true?   (1) In the 19th century, better known artists received commissions to paint portraits of wealthy patrons.   (2) During the Gilded Age, industrial and finance capitalists amassed large art collections.   (3) During the 1929 depression, the Works Progress Administration provided work for many artists.   (4) In the 1960's, the costs of the Vietnam War prevented the federal government from giving any financial aid to the fine arts.

20. Which *best* describes a present-day trend in painting in the United States?   (1) an attempt to revive Renaissance themes   (2) a revival of the styles of classical antiquity   (3) a search for new techniques of expression   (4) a return to romanticism

21. Which is a basic problem faced by artists in our modern society?   (1) The public generally accepts artistic change very slowly.   (2) The government places limits on the artist's freedom of expression.   (3) The artist has no opportunity to enjoy material comforts.   (4) A democratic society will not tolerate radical artistic expression.

22. Currier and Ives contributed to American artistic expression by their   (1) lithographic prints of 19th-century American life   (2) realistic paintings of 20th-century America   (3) collection of American folk music   (4) lyrics and music for outstanding musical comedies.

23. For which form of musical expression is America *most* indebted to Europe?   (1) jazz   (2) opera   (3) musical comedy   (4) folk music

24. Which one of the following is *not* associated with American developments in the dance as a performing art?   (1) Eugene O'Neill   (2) Aaron Copland   (3) George Balanchine   (4) Martha Graham

25. A study of the paintings and music produced in the United States since World War II would *most* likely reveal   (1) a popular revival of the patriotic themes predominant in 19th-century America   (2) an increased emphasis on imitating the art of western Europe   (3) a persistent effort to continue the rules and forms of the classical tradition   (4) a strong desire to develop original ideas and styles.

26. Historians are interested in studying such things as the sculpture of Jacques Lipchitz, the music of Irving Berlin, and the writing of James Baldwin because artistic and intellectual developments often   (1) reflect the values of society   (2) reveal the political structure of society   (3) help explain the role of religion in society   (4) illustrate the economic progress of society.

27. Which has been an effect of technological change on American culture in the 20th century?   (1) Artists and writers have turned to romantic themes in a mood of escapism.   (2) There is a lessening of general interest in art and music on the part of the public.   (3) Cultural activity is increasingly being directed toward the mass market.   (4) Government support has caused political pressures on the cultural world.

28. Which has been the *greatest* obstacle to government support of cultural programs in recent years?   (1) priority of other social needs   (2) the public's reaction against modern music   (3) widespread influence of American authors   (4) evident lack of capable artists

29. The United States has had spectacular achievements in the arts and sciences in the past 50 years. Which statement *best* explains the reason for such achievements? (1) The successful completion of a war often inspires scientific achievement. (2) The availability of leisure and wealth often leads to cultural progress. (3) An autocratic government is indispensable to cultural achievement. (4) A period of repression is often followed by one of permissiveness in the arts.

MATCHING QUESTIONS: LITERATURE

Column A—Themes

Column B—Literary Works

1. Conditions of migratory farmworkers
2. Poetic satires against the Mexican War and slavery
3. Experiences of frontier settlers and Indians
4. Pursuit of a white whale
5. Poems in praise of democracy and individualism
6. Hamilton and Jefferson: both great Americans despite their conflicting views
7. Fascism anywhere as a threat to liberty everywhere
8. Account of an individual living alone for two years in the woods

a. *Moby Dick*
b. *Rip Van Winkle*
c. *For Whom the Bell Tolls*
d. *The Patriots*
e. *The Financier*
f. *Biglow Papers*
g. *The Last of the Mohicans*
h. *The Grapes of Wrath*
i. *Walden*
j. *Leaves of Grass*

IDENTIFICATION QUESTIONS: WHO AM I?

John Audubon
Mathew Brady
John Singleton Copley
Thomas Eakins
Daniel Chester French

Winslow Homer
Thomas Jefferson
Frederic Law Olmstead
Charles Peale
Henry Richardson

Augustus Saint-Gaudens
Alfred Stieglitz
Gilbert Stuart
Louis Sullivan
Frank Lloyd Wright

1. Viewing the newly independent American republic as successor to the ancient Roman republic, I advocated the Roman Revival style of architecture and employed same in remodeling my home, Monticello.
2. A forward-looking Chicago architect, I held that "form follows function." I sought to convey the sense of a technological society in my design of the Wainwright Building in St. Louis. I am often considered the "father of the modern skyscraper."
3. A sculptor, I chose my themes mainly from American history, but my style reflected classical influences. Two of my best-known works are the *Minuteman* at Concord and the *Seated Lincoln* in the Lincoln Memorial in Washington, D.C.
4. I was a well-known portrait painter who executed likenesses of our first six Presidents. My portrait of George Washington has served as the basis of his picture on our $1 bill.
5. Although posterity rated me as a great 19th-century painter, I never enjoyed public recognition during my lifetime. Because I would not compromise my principles, I was called blunt and tactless. Because my painting of an operation showed surgical instruments and blood, I was called a "butcher."
6. I abandoned engineering for a career in the fine arts. I founded a photography magazine, established art galleries, and battled to win recognition for photography as a creative art.
7. A painter and naturalist, I served with the American forces in the Revolutionary War. At Valley Forge, I painted portraits of soldiers for them to send home. Late in life, I painted a picture of myself and the museum which I had organized in Philadelphia.

8. I devoted my life to painting, with detail and color, the birds of America. My collection of bird paintings, however, was first published not in America but in England.

9. Often considered the greatest architect of the 20th century, I insisted that a building should harmonize with its surroundings. I established an architectural training school at my home in Wisconsin. My final creation was the Guggenheim Museum in New York City.

10. A famed colonial portrait painter, I fled from Boston to London on the eve of the American Revolution and never returned home.

11. A 19th-century landscape architect in the romantic tradition, I designed two famed New York City parks—Central Park in Manhattan and Prospect Park in Brooklyn.

12. In the latter half of the 19th century, I recorded the American scene with realism. I won fame for my Civil War paintings and later for my seascapes of the Maine coast.

ESSAY QUESTIONS

1. The history and values of the American people have often found expression in their various art forms—such as architecture, sculpture, painting, music, photography, and literature. Prove this statement by (a) providing one specific example of creative expression and (b) showing how it reflected the history or values of the American people in each of the following periods: (1) colonial America (2) 1789–1860 (3) 1860–1914 (4) 1914–1945 (5) 1945–present.

2. Creativity in America has been greatly and directly affected by artistic and political developments in Europe. Prove the truth of this statement by providing one specific example in each of the following areas: (a) architecture (b) sculpture (c) painting (d) music (e) the dance.

3. Wealth, whether in the hands of individuals or the government, has been an indispensable ingredient in the development of artistic creativity. Present one specific example to illustrate the relationship of wealthy individuals or the government with the artistic creativity indicated for each of the following periods: (a) colonial America—painting (b) the young republic—architecture (c) the Gilded Age of the post-Civil War era into the early 20th century—music or sculpture (d) the Great Depression era of the 1930's—painting (e) the present decade—the performing arts.

4. Among its many functions, literature may serve to help the reader escape from reality or to face the problems troubling society. (a) Indicate which function of literature you consider more important—escapism or social consciousness. Give one argument to support your opinion. (b) Name one literary work that you consider an example of escapism and provide one reason to support your opinion. (c) Name one literary work that you consider an example of social consciousness and provide one reason to support your opinion.

5. Agree or disagree with each of the following statements and provide two arguments to support your opinion: (a) The works of painters can be used as a source of historical understanding. (b) Photography deserves to be considered a creative art. (c) By use of varied themes, materials, and styles, modern architects and sculptors seek to express their individuality. (d) Financial support for the arts by the federal government is both good and bad. (e) Americans have been innovators in the arts. (f) There is greater creativity in the arts when a nation is troubled than when it is contented.

Part 3. American Thought: Influences and Issues

5. *Americans Ponder Over the Power of the Mass Media*

Meaning of Mass Media. The term *mass media* refers to the methods or channels of communication which, by use of the printed or spoken word, present information and ideas to large numbers of people. Unknown less than two centuries ago, today's leading mass media all developed out of relatively modern inventions: huge printing presses for the mass-circulation newspaper; wireless telegraphy for the radio; and electronic transmission of pictures for television.

Newspapers

AMERICAN NEWSPAPERS: COLONIAL TIMES INTO THE 20TH CENTURY

1. The Colonial Press. The first regular colonial newspaper, started in 1704, was the Boston *Weekly News-Letter.* Within 50 years, some 30 newspapers were published in all but two of the colonies. The colonial newspaper usually *(a)* was published by a printer-editor who also printed pamphlets and kept a general merchandise store, *(b)* was a weekly of four pages, expensively priced, and sold by annual subscription, *(c)* had few subscribers—about 1000—but was passed from hand to hand and widely read, and *(d)* contained news—of England, foreign countries, local and colonial events; some brief advertising; letters to the paper; and discussions of public affairs.

By the eve of the American Revolution, one-third of the colonial newspapers were Loyalist or neutral, and two-thirds supported the Patriots. Most colonial papers resented the Stamp Act of 1765, which required them to pay a special and relatively high tax. Most papers evaded the tax and carried articles to arouse the colonial public against British rule. The newspapers thus helped prepare the colonists to fight for independence.

2. The Early Republic: Newspaper Growth. The newspapers continued the colonial practices as to their size, price, and circulation, but in other respects they experienced great changes. Newspapers grew in number, totaling by the 1830's about 1200. They presented much more advertising, set like today's classified ads. They became spokesmen for political parties and often engaged in vituperative debate. The functions of editor and printer began to be separated, and the editor rose in esteem as the author of newspaper policy.

3. The Mid-19th Century: The Penny Press. In 1833 *Benjamin Day* launched the first successful penny newspaper, the New York *Sun*. Less expensive than other papers, the *Sun* also serialized popular stories and presented news in a lively manner. It was sold by subscription and, for the first time in America, by newsboys in the streets. The *Sun* expanded its circulation—to 40,000 within three years, increased its sale of advertising space, and became a very profitable enterprise.

Day's example was followed by other editors: (1) *James Gordon Bennett* in 1835 founded the New York *Herald*. He presented "spicy" news of sports, society, and crime; he did not wait for the stories to come to him but started the practice of employing staff reporters to get the news. (2) *Horace Greeley* in 1841 founded the New York *Tribune*. A liberal reformer, Greeley supported abolition, labor unions, prohibition of intoxicating beverages, and westward expansion, advising "go west, young man." His vigorous antislavery editorials greatly influenced Northern public opinion. (3) *Henry Raymond* in 1851 founded the *New York Times*. He set standards of well-balanced and accurately written news stories. During the Civil War, Raymond was a leading spokesman for the Lincoln administration.

4. Industrial Revolution and the Press. Newspapers in the 19th century were greatly affected by the Industrial Revolution as it spurred the following inventions: Morse's telegraph (1844) and Bell's telephone (1876) simplified the process of news-gathering. Richard Hoe's rotary press (1847) speeded the printing and reduced the cost of newspapers. Ottmar Mergenthaler's linotype machine (1884) eliminated the hand-setting of newspaper type and made possible the mass-circulation newspaper.

5. At the Turn of the Century

  a. Yellow Journalism. Joseph Pulitzer, a journalist and successful St. Louis newspaper owner, in 1883 bought the New York *World*. Pulitzer introduced sensational journalism—screaming headlines, bold print, pictures, comics, emphasis on stories of crime and passion, exposés of political corruption, and occasional news distortions—which together became known as *yellow journalism*. (This term was derived from a popular comic strip, "The Yellow Kid.") The circulation of the *World* climbed dramatically and the paper became most profitable. *William Randolph Hearst*, who had adopted the methods of yellow journalism for his San Francisco newspaper, decided to challenge Pulitzer in New York. In 1895 Hearst bought the New York *Journal*. For several years, the *World* and the *Journal* battled, with events in Cuba and the Spanish-American War providing great opportunity for yellow journalism, and each paper saw its daily circulation rise above 1 million. By the early 1900's, the methods of yellow journalism had spread to many American newspapers.

  b. Conservative Journalism. Yellow journalism, however, was not the only road to 20th-century newspaper success. *Adolph Ochs*, a capable and enterprising Tennessee newspaperman who rejected yellow journalism, in 1896 took control of the *New York Times*. He maintained high journalistic standards, avoided sensationalism, presented "all the news that's fit to print" in a dependable and accurate manner; by this responsible approach, Ochs made the *Times* into a respected and successful newspaper.

c. Tabloids. The tabloids were half-page-size newspapers that emphasized pictures, and fully employed the methods of yellow journalism. They appeared after World War I and achieved tremendous circulation. The best-known tabloid, whose daily circulation has risen to about 3 million, is the New York *Daily News.*

AMERICAN NEWSPAPERS: MAJOR 20TH-CENTURY TRENDS

1. Fewer Newspapers and Less Competition. From 1919 to 1945, the number of daily newspapers decreased sharply, from 2600 to 1750; since 1945 the number has remained relatively stable. (These numbers should be viewed against the perspective of America's population, which, from 1920 to today, has doubled.) Today, of our 50 most populous cities, half lack competing newspapers; in these cities, the inhabitants are denied different news presentations and different editorial viewpoints. New York City, which not too many years ago boasted more than ten English-language daily newspapers for the general public, today has only three: in the morning the *Times* and the tabloid *News*, and in the evening the tabloid *Post.*

The reasons for the decreased number of daily English-language newspapers include the following: *(a)* During the 1920's, newspaper owners completed mergers so as to reduce costs, increase circulation, and improve profits. *(b)* During the depression years of the 1930's, newspaper income fell sharply as advertising was cut by 50 percent. *(c)* During World War II, newspapers faced shortages of men and materials. *(d)* Although the total amount spent on advertising has increased sharply, the proportion going to newspapers has decreased significantly as a result of competition from radio and television. *(e)* In large cities, many well-to-do persons who read the daily English-language newspapers moved to the suburbs, whereas the incoming minorities—disadvantaged as to income and literacy in English—either bought a tabloid or no English-language newspaper at all. (Many Hispanic-Americans bought newspapers written in their native language.) *(f)* In recent years, newspapers have faced higher material costs, rising wages, and union opposition to the use of labor-saving machines.

2. Growth of Newspaper Chains. Newspaper mergers, which accelerated during the 1920's, brought further growth to newspaper chains. Each chain consisted of a group of newspapers, in different cities, belonging to a single corporation. Each chain exercised centralized control over its newspapers, although some chains permitted their local editors a measure of individual initiative. By the 1960's, some 100 newspaper chains owned 30 percent of the nation's newspapers. The largest and best known of the newspaper chains are the nationwide Hearst, Scripps-Howard, and Newhouse groups, and the somewhat smaller but still influential Knight and Gannett groups.

3. News Standardization: Wire Services and Syndicates

a. News-gathering or *wire service* agencies, increasingly important in the 20th century, have employed extensive staffs to gather national and international news. They have sold their services—news reports—to most newspapers, especially the smaller, independent ones that could not afford large news-gathering staffs. As wire service reports have become widely used, they have fostered a nationwide standardization of major news.

Although a number of news-gathering agencies exist today, the largest and most influential are the *Associated Press* (AP) and the *United Press International* (UPI). Each serves almost all of America's daily newspapers. (In addition, each serves most radio and television stations.)

b. Syndicates also have fostered newspaper standardization. These syndicates are agencies that sell newspapers special features such as cartoons, comics, and especially columns by well-known commentators. The columnists may deal with such topics as politics, international affairs, health, social life, and economics. Syndicated features have become part of most daily newspapers.

4. New Typesetting Technology and Labor-Management Problems. Since the 1950's, unionized printers—members of the *International Typographical Union*—and newspaper owners have battled over the issue of automated typesetting. The union, whose members used a hand-craft linotype process relatively unchanged over the past 100 years, had opposed the introduction of computers and electronic typesetting as threatening members' jobs and the union's existence. Newspaper owners have urged automated typesetting because it is faster, reduces errors, and would substantially lower labor costs. For example, during the 1974 printers strike at the New York *Daily News*, the newspaper kept publishing as 35 secretaries used automatic equipment and performed the work normally done by 900 printers. Also, by 1974 some 400 newspapers without unionized printers were using the new typesetting technology.

In 1974 the New York local of the typographical union concluded an historic pact with the *Times* and the *News*. The pact, to run for ten years, gave the newspaper owners a free hand to introduce automatic typesetting equipment but protected the union members involved—1400 workers, whose average age was 56—by guaranteeing them lifetime employment and offering liberal retirement benefits. This pact is expected to be a model for agreements with other unionized newspapers.

FREEDOM OF THE PRESS

1. Establishing the Principle

a. In Colonial Times. In the colonies (as in England), the press was subjected to licensing, censorship, and suppression by the authorities—mainly the royal colonial governors. These restrictions, applied with varying degrees of severity, were opposed by many colonial printer-editors, who achieved notable progress toward greater press freedom.

(1) *Franklin's Apology for Printers (1731).* As printer-editor and owner of the Pennsylvania *Gazette*, Benjamin Franklin wrote a spirited defense of press freedom in his *Apology for Printers*. He said that "Printers are educated in the Belief, that when Men differ in Opinion, both Sides ought equally to have the Advantage of being heard by the Publick; and that when Truth and Error have fair Play, the former is always an overmatch for the latter." Franklin's statement won widespread support among literate colonial peoples.

(2) *Zenger Trial (1735)*. *John Peter Zenger*, publisher of the New York *Weekly Journal*, was arrested for libel because he had printed articles criticizing New York's royal governor. Jailed without bail for nine months, Zenger was brought to trial before a hostile judge who declared Zenger's articles to be libel even if true and ordered the colonial jury to return a verdict of guilty. Zenger was defended by the colonies' outstanding lawyer, *Andrew Hamilton*. He urged the jury to support a new legal theory—that the truth could not constitute libel. Defying the judge, the colonial jury courageously declared Zenger not guilty. This decision received widespread colonial support and was a major step toward press freedom.

b. In the Constitution. The First Amendment states that Congress shall make no law abridging freedom of the press. (This amendment served as a model for similar provisions in state constitutions.) Thomas Jefferson, an ardent supporter of press freedom even though he was subjected to bitter press criticism, remarked that if he had to choose between "government without newspapers or newspapers without a government" he would prefer the latter, provided—he added—all men received and read the newspapers.

The First Amendment does *not* define freedom of the press, nor does it indicate if press freedom is absolute or may be limited in case of conflict with the needs of society. These issues remain open—on a case-by-case basis—to judicial consideration and decision.

2. Restricting the Press During Wartime

a. Undeclared Naval War Against France. Check the Index for the 1798 Alien and Sedition Acts.

b. Civil War Era. (1) Abolitionist Press. In general, Northern abolitionist newspapers were free to publish and circulate. There were, however, notable exceptions: Northern abolitionist literature mailed to Southern addresses was rarely delivered by the post office. In 1835 *William Lloyd Garrison*, militant editor of the antislavery paper the *Liberator*, was dragged through the streets of Boston by a hostile mob, but he was released and he continued to publish the paper. *Elijah Lovejoy*, a clergyman and antislavery editor of the *Observer* in southern Illinois, was attacked several times by hostile mobs who wrecked his presses and finally in 1837 killed him. (2) During the Civil War. The Northern press experienced a number of restrictions. To halt papers from printing news about troop strengths and movements—of military value to the Confederacy—the government first censored most telegraph messages and later required war correspondents to submit their copy for military approval. Several army commanders banished war correspondents and occasionally censored or suppressed newspapers. The post office sometimes denied mail service to papers deemed "subversive." The government, however, established no central censorship agency and its restrictive measures were enforced inadequately.

In general the Northern press published with considerable freedom and reported the war thoroughly. Many papers criticized Lincoln—often with personal abuse and venom—attacked his administration, and deplored his conduct of the war. The press freely took sides in the 1864 Presidential election and emerged from the war years with great influence.

c. World War I: Two Restrictive Laws. The *Espionage Act* (1917) banned the mails to any newspapers containing antiwar materials, and the *Sedition Act* (1918) provided fines and imprisonment for publications and persons writing against the American form of government. These laws were used against a number of individuals and more than 75 newspapers—socialist, pacifist, and German-American. The laws were held Constitutional by the Supreme Court, notably in the *Schenck Case*. (Check the Index.)

The overwhelming number of newspapers supported the war effort and accepted the voluntary censorship code of the government's Committee on Public Information. Newspapers thus pledged not to publish news of military value to the enemy but retained the freedom to criticize individual officials and the conduct of the war.

d. World War II: Voluntary Censorship. American newspapers agreed to the Code of Wartime Practices issued by the government's Office of Censorship. With patriotic fervor, the press pursued three objectives: to assist the American war effort, to deny any aid to the enemy, and to preserve our free institutions. While reporting the war with thoroughness and accuracy, American newspapers also proved that a free press could enforce and survive voluntary censorship.

3. Problems Concerning Freedom of the Press

a. Does freedom of the press protect a reporter from divulging his sources of information? The press claims that, if it is to be free to gather news of extremist doings and criminal activities, reporters must be able to keep their information sources confidential. If reporters are not free to maintain confidentiality, they will forfeit the trust of their sources and will be unable to secure information. The government insists that reporters, like all citizens, have the obligation to provide information requested by grand juries and other official investigations. This issue exploded when Earl Caldwell, a *New York Times* reporter, refused to testify before a grand jury regarding his articles on the Black Panthers. Caldwell was held guilty of contempt and his case reached the Supreme Court. In 1972, by a 5 to 4 vote, the Court denied Caldwell's claim to First Amendment protection and asserted that freedom of the press is not abridged when reporters are required to testify before grand juries, even about their news sources.

Critics of the decision urged Congress to pass a shield law—as half the states had done—permitting reporters to shield their sources of information. To date no such federal law has been enacted.

b. Does freedom of the press protect a newspaper against the charge of libel? The answer is no, for newspapers are held liable under the provisions of libel laws. Such laws define libel as any written material exposing persons to humiliation, hatred, ridicule, or contempt. The laws, however, exempt newspapers from libel provided that (1) the printed material is true and was published with good motives, and (2) in regard to public figures, the printed material constituted "fair comment and criticism" offered to inform the newspaper's readers. The laws thus create a fine dividing line between what is and is not permissible—to be decided on a case-by-case basis.

In two significant libel cases of the 1960's against the *New York Times*, the Supreme Court decided in favor of the newspaper. Both cases involved the handling of racial disturbances by Montgomery, Alabama, officials. The Court held that (1) accurate reporting did not constitute libel since the city officials had not proved the reports had been deliberately false, and (2) inaccuracies in a paid advertisement did *not* constitute libel since the city officials had not proved that the paper knew in advance of the inaccuracies and published them with malicious intent.

OTHER PROBLEMS CONCERNING THE MODERN NEWSPAPER

1. Does the Press Foster Cultural and Intellectual Mediocrity?

a. Yes. Since newspapers desire to boost circulation and increase advertising rates, they direct their appeal to the greatest possible number of readers. They therefore feature sensational stories of passion, crime, and violence; neglect subjects of lasting importance; deal in trivia; and "write down" to their readers. By seeking the lowest common denominator of mass appeal, newspapers foster mediocrity.

b. No. Although newspapers desire to boost circulation, they have acted to raise the level of popular taste. They set acceptable standards of spelling and writing, report on cultural events, and provide editorial opinions and special comments on vital issues, thereby stimulating their readers to think and understand.

2. How Much Influence Do Advertisers Exert on Newspaper Policies?

a. Much influence. Since advertisers provide two-thirds and more of newspaper revenues, they directly or indirectly influence newspaper policies. Being mainly corporate executives and successful businessmen, advertisers help shape newspaper policies toward defending the "status quo" and supporting the "establishment."

b. Little Influence. The advertisers who provide most newspaper revenues are mainly department stores, discount chains, food supermarkets, and other retail stores. These advertisers share a common purpose—to attract customers and increase sales, but they do not necessarily share a common view on public issues. As advertisers they are concerned not with the newspaper's policies but with its effectiveness in reaching consumers. Also, newspapers themselves are "big business" and, regardless of advertisers, they tend to support the "establishment."

3. Do Newspapers Deliberately Present Their Readers With Biased News?

a. Yes. Critics claim that newspapers are not believed by their readers—a mistrust termed the *credibility gap.* Mistrust arises because newspapers, according to these critics, deliberately present slanted, biased news. Newspapers show bias in such ways as the selection or omission of news items, the length and placement of stories in the paper, and the mixing of opinion with fact in the news columns. Newspapers slant the news, these critics charge, because they protect their advertisers, they are "big business," they belong to the "establishment," and they wield political power. Some few critics, such as former Vice President Spiro Agnew, charge the press with having a liberal, leftist bias, but most critics charge a conservative, rightist bias.

b. No. Defenders admit that newspapers are "big business," but insist that, to survive, newspapers must retain their readers' confidence. Newspapers are aware that the reading public can check their accuracy by referring to other news media. Most newspapers, these defenders claim, are reliable and mature; they present only facts in news articles; they voice opinions in editorials and columns of comment; they seek to avoid biased news that might mislead the public. Honest men may differ, according to these defenders, on matters of judgment —such as the selection, length, and placement of news items—without involving deliberate bias. In answer to the many critics who charge a conservative, rightist newspaper bias, these defenders point to influential newspapers that have vigorously criticized the government and supported significant reforms.

4. Should the Government Have the Right to Withhold Information From the Press?

a. Yes. Concerned with national security, engaged in diplomatic efforts, and beset by internal administrative differences in determining policy, government officials insist that they must have the right to withhold documents whose disclosure they consider unwise. Such documents are officially stamped "secret" or "confidential."

b. No. By withholding certain information while releasing other data, newspapers charge, the government is manipulating the news—a practice termed *managed news.* This does not give the American people a fair and full disclosure of the facts and therefore denies the public's right to know.

c. Freedom of Information Act (1967). This law permits a reporter denied government documents to take his request for specific information to the courts.

5. Does Newspaper Publicity in Major Criminal Cases Prevent Defendants From Receiving Fair Trials?

a. Yes. To boost circulation, newspapers give major criminal cases extensive publicity—details of the crimes, gossip about the defendants and their assumed motives, and various interpretive articles. By such pretrial publicity newspapers make it impossible to select a fair and impartial jury and to grant the defendants their due process of law. In 1954 Dr. Samuel Sheppard, a Cleveland osteopath, was accused of murdering his wife. With the newspapers giving this case prejudicial treatment and with the judge permitting a "carnival atmosphere" in the courtroom, the jury found Sheppard guilty. In 1966 the conviction of Sheppard was set aside by the Supreme Court on the ground that "massive, pervasive, and prejudicial publicity" had denied the defendant a fair trial. Retried in 1966 before another jury and in a strictly controlled courtroom, Sheppard was declared not guilty.

b. No. By providing coverage of major criminal cases, newspapers are exercising freedom of the press and performing their intended function—informing the public. Prospective jurors are not required to be ignorant of the cases to be heard; despite pretrial newspaper coverage, jurors can be impartial and reach decisions based on the evidence presented in court. In 1974 two former Nixon Cabinet members—John Mitchell and Maurice Stans—were charged with criminal conspiracy: accepting from a financier a $200,000 cash contribution for the 1972 Nixon reelection campaign in exchange for their efforts to impede an SEC investigation of the financier's activities. With the case having received considerable pretrial publicity, lawyers for the two defendants requested the judge to dismiss the case or remove it from New York on the ground that prejudicial publicity had precluded a fair trial. Adopting a "let's see" attitude, the judge proceeded with the selection of jurors and empaneled a jury satisfactory to both defense and prosecution. The judge took the further precaution of sequestering the jurors—that is, keeping them in isolation and away from news media reports on the case. After a 48-day trial, the jury decided that Mitchell and Stans were *not* guilty. This decision indicated that defendants could receive a fair trial despite extensive newspaper pretrial publicity.

   c. Supreme Court Decision (1979). In *Gannett Newspaper Company vs. De Pasquale,* the Supreme Court, by 5 to 4, upheld broad powers for trial judges to close pretrial criminal hearings to the press and public—if such pretrial publicity might damage the defendant's case. This decision indicated that the defendant's rights, under the 6th and 14th Amendments, came ahead of the press' right, under the 1st Amendment, to report the news.

6. Is Press Influence Decreasing With the Rise of Other Mass Media?
   a. Influence of the Press. The press has had a significant impact upon public opinion and thereby upon major American developments. Horace Greeley's editorials in the New York *Tribune* helped shape Northern opinion against slavery and helped move Lincoln to issue the Emancipation Proclamation. The *New York Times* and *Harper's Weekly,* the latter with its cartoons by *Thomas Nast,* helped rescue New York City from the corrupt Tweed Ring. The yellow journalism of the New York *World* and the New York *Journal* helped propel the United States into the Spanish-American War. By uncovering, dramatizing, and pursuing the ramifications of the Watergate affair, the Washington *Post* and the *New York Times* helped compel Richard Nixon to resign from the Presidency.

   b. Yes—Declining Influence. In recent years, newspaper circulation has barely kept up with the increase in reading population and has fallen below the increase in total population. People are turning more and more to radio newscasts, to television newscasts, and to television discussions of public issues.

   c. No—Not Declining. Although people are listening to radio and watching television, they still depend on the papers for their news information. Unlike radio and television news coverage, which is broadcast at set times and in "capsule" form, the newspaper provides extensive coverage, vital details such as reprints of speeches, and a permanent record available for reference.

Radio, Television, and Other Mass Media

RADIO AND TELEVISION: SIGNIFICANT DEVELOPMENTS

1. Brief History. The radio, based primarily on inventions by the Italian *Guglielmo Marconi* of wireless telegraphy (1896) and the American *Lee De Forest* of an improved vacuum tube (1907), became important following World War I. In 1920 the first scheduled radio broadcast, announcing the results of the Presidential election, emanated from Pittsburgh's station KDKA. Over the next 25 years, radio became a powerful medium—there were sharp increases in the number of broadcast stations and of receiving sets. Due to technological changes and mass-production methods, radio receiving sets were improved in quality and available to the public at low prices.

   Television was made practical by the work of *Vladimir Zworykin,* a naturalized American citizen, who in 1934 devised the iconoscope, an electronic picture-transmitting tube. Television grew tremendously following World War II. Its growth, too, was spurred by technological changes and mass-production techniques that improved quality and lowered the cost of television receiving sets. With the advent of television, radio programming was cut back mainly to spot news and music. Television, having the advantage of visual as well as aural appeal, featured spectacular shows, movies, plays, serialized stories, interviews with public figures, and panel discussions.

2. Role of Advertising. Since almost all American households possess receiving sets, radio and television programs reach tremendous audiences who do not directly pay any program costs. The costs are borne by advertisers who purchase spot time or sponsor entire programs so as to deliver their messages to the public. Advertising rates vary considerably according to the medium used—radio or television, the time of day, and the number of viewers—usually estimated by sampling procedures of rating services. In the mid-1970's, one minute of advertising time on television between 7 P.M. and 11 P.M.—considered *prime time* because it attracts the largest number of viewers—cost between $60,000 and $140,000. Annual revenues of the radio and television broadcast industries are $1 billion and $3 billion, respectively—definitely "big business."

3. Trend Toward Standardization. Throughout the United States today, the number of commercial broadcasting stations in radio totals 7000 and in television 700. As in the newspaper industry, however, the trend is toward standardization and consolidation. The television industry is dominated by three major networks: the *American Broadcasting Company* (ABC), the *Columbia Broadcasting System* (CBS), and the *National Broadcasting Company* (NBC). According to government regulations, each network may own no more than five television broadcasting stations, but each network may maintain special relationships with additional broadcasting stations as *affiliates*. The affiliates are independently owned stations, each cooperating with the network and utilizing a considerable proportion of the network's major shows. The three networks together encompass almost all the commercial broadcasting stations as affiliates. Again, according to government regulations, each television network may own no more than 14 radio stations, but here also network influence extends to the many radio stations that are network affiliates. Some radio and television stations are owned by newspapers, and almost all stations subscribe to the wire services—both situations making for standardization of news reports.

PROBLEMS CONCERNING RADIO AND TELEVISION

Like the newspaper, radio and television face many of the same problems. Two problems, however, deserve special emphasis.

1. Do Radio and Television Programs Constitute a "Vast Wasteland"?

a. Yes. Critics claim that this charge, of a "vast wasteland," voiced by the Federal Communications Commission (FCC) chairman in 1961, remains true today. They find fault with many programs, especially with game shows, quiz shows, low-grade movies, formula comedies about unbelievable families, Western and detective series, cartoons, disc jockeys, soap operas, and the endless commercials—"many screaming, cajoling, and offending." Critics also berate children's programs for violence, stupidity, and lack of imagination. Radio and television, the critics insist, can do better.

b. No. Radio and television spokesmen refute the charge of "vast wasteland" by pointing to the many worthwhile programs such as fine musical offerings, classical and other serious plays, documentaries on national problems, interviews with public figures, panel discussions, historical dramatizations, and extensive live coverage of significant current happenings. They also ask people to remember that radio and television programming faces many problems such as the demands of advertisers, the need for a mass audience, the competition for ratings, the high production costs, the rapid turnover of programs, and the public's preference for entertainment, not enlightenment.

c. *Public Broadcasting Act (1967)*. This act created a nonprofit *Public Broadcasting Corporation* to administer federal funds so as to encourage quality television programs. Such programs are to be noncommercial—that is, not sponsored by advertisers, thereby freeing their producers to concentrate on worthwhile presentations, not on mass-audience ratings. In 1968 the Public Broadcasting Corporation, together with other government agencies and the Ford and Carnegie foundations, provided funds for a highly innovative and successful children's program, *Sesame Street*. Aimed mainly at disadvantaged ghetto youngsters of preschool age, *Sesame Street*, combining learning with fun, reinforced the demand for more programs and stations devoted to educational television. In 1975 public broadcasting stations presented an outstanding series written and narrated by the distinguished scientist *Jacob Bronowski*. Tracing man's biological and cultural evolution, the series was called *The Ascent of Man*.

By the mid-1970's, noncommercial public television stations numbered over 200. They offered mainly educational, literary, artistic, and public affairs programs; they were financed by public contributions, foundation grants, corporation grants, and government funds; and they were affiliated with a network, the *Public Broadcasting Service* (PBS).

2. Does the Federal Communications Commission Have Too Much Power Over Radio and Television?

a. *Powers of the FCC*. Established in 1934 to regulate the broadcast communications industry, the FCC exercises the following powers: (1) It grants licenses, good for three years, to radio and television stations and assigns them broadcast wavelength bands or channels. It decides among competing applicants for licenses. After each three-year period, it grants or refuses to grant license renewals. (2) To assure the use of the airwaves "in the public interest, convenience and necessity," the FCC supervises the broadcast companies and reviews their programs. The FCC advises stations to limit the proportion of time devoted to commercials and to offer sufficient programs on public issues. (3) It enforces the *equal-time doctrine*—that stations must provide candidates for the same political office with equal time to speak to the public, and it enforces the *fairness doctrine*—that, if a broadcast commentator attacks a public figure or expresses a view on a public issue, the station must provide the attacked person or the supporters of the opposing viewpoint with the opportunity to respond on its airwaves. (4) The FCC receives and investigates complaints of the public regarding the broadcasting industry.

b. *Yes—Too much power*. Broadcast industry spokesmen argue that the FCC has too much power by reason of its authority to refuse to renew licenses. Critics claim that the FCC pressures stations to accept what it considers "good programming" and thereby is exercising censorship and denying freedom of speech and press. Because of the equal-time doctrine, radio and television stations assert, they are unwilling to offer free time to major-party candidates for fear that they will have to do the same for minor-party candidates. Because of the fairness doctrine, radio and television stations claim, they refuse to take stands on public issues so as not to have to donate free and valuable time for presentation of the opposing viewpoints. Broadcast spokesmen imply that government regulation should be kept to a minimum.

c. No—Not too much. The FCC, its supporters point out, has rarely refused to renew a license and such few refusals have been for compelling reasons. Further, FCC decisions, on license renewals and all other major matters, may be appealed for review by the courts. FCC spokesmen deny that broadcasting stations are entitled to the same freedom of speech and press as newspapers. Whereas anyone with the necessary funds may publish a paper, a broadcasting station requires one of a limited number of broadcast wavelengths and therefore must be licensed. Although admitting that FCC regulations should change and improve with the times, supporters assert the agency must vigilantly regulate radio and television "in the public interest."

OTHER MASS MEDIA

These include magazines—sold on newsstands and through subscriptions, and books, records and tapes—sold in stores and through special mail-order clubs.

The Information Explosion. The vast proliferation of mass media in recent years has sometimes been called the *information explosion.* More information is available to and directed at Americans than ever before. The mass media have achieved a major role in shaping American life—in some ways for the better and in other ways for the worse. How would you evaluate their impact?

MARSHALL McLUHAN: SPOKESMAN FOR THE MASS MEDIA OF THE ELECTRONIC AGE

Marshall McLuhan, of the University of Toronto (Canada), has dealt extensively with culture, technology, and the impact of the electronic mass media. His ideas may be summarized as follows: (1) Technology is the primary influence that shapes society. (2) Change in the technology of communication is the crucial factor determining change in society. McLuhan suggests that Johann Gutenberg's invention of movable type (about 1450) shaped the subsequent four centuries of West European history—notably the Protestant Reformation, the French Revolution, the Industrial Revolution, and nationalism. (3) In our times, the electronic mass media are reshaping our civilization. They make possible the "extensions of man" as television projected our eyes and ears to the moon to watch the *Apollo* module landing while our bodies remained at home. The electronic mass media, McLuhan claims, are transforming the world into a "global village." (4) McLuhan insists that the nature of the communications media shapes society more than the content of the communications. This idea he states more succinctly as *"the medium is the message."* He further divides media into two groups: hot and cool. The hot media—being well filled with data, requiring little audience interpretation or participation and exciting the audience—are the printed page, photography, painting, and radio. The cool media—giving little detailed information, requiring considerable audience participation and calming the audience—are cartoons, the telephone, and television.

McLuhan's ideas have been criticized for (1) neglecting factors other than technology, such as economics and religion, in explaining the evolution of Western society, (2) debasing the content of a message while elevating the importance of the medium through which it reaches the audience, and (3) making contradictory and worthless distinctions between so-called hot and cool media. McLuhan's ideas have been labeled, by some critics, as "pages of hokum" and "nonsense adulterated by sense." McLuhan's defenders admit that some of his ideas are difficult to understand and some may be wrong, but they claim that most of McLuhan's ideas are brilliant insights. What do you think?

MULTIPLE-CHOICE QUESTIONS

1. Which British act *most* directly affected colonial newspaper publishers? (1) sugar tax (2) stamp tax (3) prohibition of westward migration (4) quartering of soldiers
2. Which invention *least* directly affected the newspaper industry? (1) telegraph (2) telephone (3) sewing machine (4) linotype machine
3. Which publisher elevated the *New York Times* into a respected and influential newspaper? (1) Adolph Ochs (2) Horace Greeley (3) Benjamin Day (4) James Gordon Bennett
4. Which term is *not* applicable to the New York *Daily News* today? (1) tabloid (2) large circulation (3) penny press (4) yellow journalism
5. Which has been a significant 20th-century development in the newspaper industry? (1) an increase in the number of daily newspapers in cities (2) a movement to improve journalism by eliminating sensational news (3) a greater reliance on central news-gathering agencies that have standardized news reporting (4) less dependence on advertising as a source of revenue
6. Recent consolidation of newspapers has caused concern in the United States *chiefly* because such mergers may result in (1) the threat of government censorship (2) a loss of advertising revenue (3) a decrease in circulation (4) less diversity of opinion.
7. Which principle was promoted as a result of the Zenger trial? (1) A newspaper must publish the replies of its critics. (2) A provable statement may be published without fear of punishment. (3) A newspaper may print the testimony given in criminal trials. (4) Newspapers may be operated under private ownership.
8. Which amendment to the Constitution reinforced the principle established in the Zenger case? (1) First (2) Tenth (3) Thirteenth (4) Eighteenth
9. During which wartime period were American newspapers *least* subject to government restrictions? (1) undeclared naval war against France (2) Civil War (3) World War I (4) World War II
10. Which is the *most* accurate statement about the right of newspapers in the United States to print what they want? (1) It may conflict with the national interest. (2) It has never been challenged by the federal government. (3) It has never been restricted. (4) It has become less important as the number of newspapers has declined.
11. The fact that there are libel laws in the United States demonstrates that (1) this nation is not a democracy (2) newspapers are forbidden to print opinions (3) newspapers cannot openly criticize federal officials (4) the freedoms guaranteed by the first amendment are not absolute.

12. Which one of the following do advertisers look for *most* in a newspaper? (1) its editorials on foreign policy (2) its relations with the typographical union (3) its circulation figures (4) its use of syndicated features

13. Which is the *most* vital function of the news media in the United States? (1) to show the defects of society (2) to standardize ideas and thereby promote national unity (3) to enable minority groups to express their needs (4) to inform people so that they can participate in the democratic process

14. The reluctance of commercial television producers to deal with controversial topics on national networks is frequently attributed by critics to the producers' (1) unwillingness to risk alienating either of the major political parties (2) difficulty in selling such programs to advertisers (3) inability to examine the topics objectively (4) fear of censorship by the federal government.

15. One important effect of television on American politics has been to (1) lengthen political campaigns (2) increase the expense involved in running for public office (3) eliminate the importance of the national party conventions (4) strengthen loyalties to political parties.

16. The goal of federal funding for public broadcasting programs was to (1) weaken the monopoly held by one corporation in television broadcasting (2) reduce advertising rates for prime-time programs (3) encourage the production of programs without need of advertising sponsors (4) increase the number of movies shown on television.

17. Which statement is *most* closely associated with the views of Marshall McLuhan? (1) all the news that's fit to print (2) free speech would not protect a person who falsely shouted "Fire!" in a theatre (3) a reporter has the duty to protect sources of information (4) the medium is the message

18. The assertion that "a broader spectrum of national opinion should be represented among the commentators in the network news" tends to indicate that (1) free speech is being eliminated (2) the federal government is seeking powers of censorship (3) the mass media perform a significant role in American life (4) television and radio stations are not regulated by the federal government.

ESSAY QUESTIONS

1. Newspapers have played a significant role in shaping American thought and actions. Prove this statement by discussing *one* specific example for each of the following: (a) the Revolutionary War era (b) the antislavery crusade of the first half of the 19th century (c) the Spanish-American War at the end of the 19th century (d) any issue of domestic or foreign policy in recent decades.

2. The mass media—newspapers, radio, and television—have a considerable impact upon American life. (a) Discuss *two* ways in which the mass media have affected you personally. (b) Should federal licensing be required of newspaper owners as it now is of radio and television station owners? Give *one* reason to support your answer. (c) In terms of the functioning and future of our democratic society, has the impact of the mass media been good or bad? Present *two* arguments to support your opinion.

3. Agree or disagree with *each* of the following statements and provide *two* reasons to justify your stand: (a) To determine whether a society is democratic or undemocratic, examine the status of its newspapers. (b) A reporter should have the right to shield the source of his information. (c) The trends toward fewer newspapers and greater news standardization are inevitable but unfortunate. (d) Since the advent of radio and television, the influence of newspapers has declined. (e) Commercial television stations should concentrate more on providing educational programs and less on entertainment. (f) To protect the public interest, the Federal Communications Commission should exercise stricter controls over all aspects of television broadcasting.

6. Americans Uphold Democracy in Ideological Battles Against Extremism

DIFFERENCES OF OPINION: ONE MEASURE OF DEMOCRACY

1. Relevant Democratic Principles. Our democratic system—typified by two major political parties generating differences of opinion on public issues —operates as follows:

a. Rule by the Majority. The majority vote of the people determines which candidates are elected to political office. The majority vote of Congress determines which bills secure legislative approval. The majority vote of the Supreme Court determines which laws being challenged satisfy Constitutional requirements.

b. Rights of the Minority. The minority holds views on public matters which differ from those of the majority. The minority has the right to express its views, to sway voters to its opinions, and in subsequent elections to become the majority.

Democracy thus includes the right to disagree and guarantees all people —the minority as well as the majority—freedom of speech, press, and assembly.

2. Opportunities for Individual Expression. Americans fulfill many roles in the daily routines of life. As each role involves problems, individuals may express their opinions and make them count in the following ways: *(a) politically*—as citizens, voters, lobbyists, campaign fund contributors, and members of political parties; *(b) economically*—as members of labor unions, professional societies, and business associations; and *(c) socially*—as high school students in classes and at General Organization (GO) meetings, as newspaper readers and church members, and as members of Parent-Teachers Association (PTA) chapters.

EXTREMIST GROUPS IN OUR SOCIETY

1. Ideology of Extremist Groups. Extremist groups generally subscribe to an *ideology*—their doctrines and ways of thinking—that includes the following ideas:

a. Extremist groups, not being in the center or mainstream of American life, reject such traditional American values as democratic government, civil liberties, and equality of opportunity. In our society, they are found on the fringes or extremities—hence the name extremist groups.

b. Extremists despair of American society as it exists and demand severe or radical changes. They approve the use of publicity, agitation, mass action, force, and violence, some even to the extent of revolution. By such means they would mold society to their own liking.

The extreme-right groups—also known as reactionaries, ultraconservatives, and the radical right—generally extol the past and wish to return to and preserve past ways. The extreme-left groups—also known as radicals, ultraliberals, and the radical left—generally extol the virtues of and wish to create a new and relatively untried social order.

c. Extremists deny that the problems facing society are complex. They insist that most problems are caused by the plots of a relatively small number of evil persons who wield great power and deceive the masses of people. Known as the "conspiracy theory" of history, this extremist view is uncomplicated: it oversimplifies cause—blaming the problems of society on evil persons who become the scapegoats, and oversimplifies remedy—ending the power of the scapegoats.

d. Extremists assert that the masses can be easily manipulated by the few evil but powerful persons, and therefore extremists conclude that the people cannot be trusted to govern themselves. Instead, extremists hold, the masses must be ruled by a superior, knowledgeable group—an elite—that will protect the masses against evil persons and dangerous ideas. This extremist reasoning, of course, denies freedom of thought and justifies totalitarian rule.

2. Democracy and Extremist Groups. Through the Constitution, our democracy guarantees the civil rights and legal protection of all individuals—including extremists. Democratic peoples realize that these guarantees allow extremists to operate with considerable freedom, even though, if extremist groups ever gained control, they would deny others such freedoms.

Our democracy is not impotent or helpless but has various ways to defend itself against extremist groups. The mass media, major political parties, schools, and other institutions all serve to expose extremist groups to public light and to refute their simplistic arguments. The Congress and state legislatures may pass laws to restrain extremists. The Federal Bureau of Investigation (FBI) keeps extremist groups under surveillance, or observation. At times secret FBI agents infiltrate extremist groups so as to gain inside information of their doings. (In the mid-1970's, Congressional committees charged the FBI with harassing extremists and violating their rights by opening their mail, burglarizing their offices, causing them to lose their jobs, and inciting them to violence. Steps were taken to stop such illegal activities.)

Democratic peoples hold, in the words of Thomas Jefferson, that "error of opinion may be tolerated where reason is left free to combat it."

3. Cases of Extremism in American History. Although extremist groups have appeared throughout American history, in general they have attracted relatively few supporters, have prompted most Americans to react negatively—even with shame and disgust—to their ideas, and many of them have been short-lived. Some typical cases of extremism have been the following:

a. Two Nativist Groups. The *Know-Nothings* in the 1840's blamed the problems of society upon immigrants, especially Catholics. The *Ku Klux Klan* in the 1920's blamed the problems of society upon minority groups—foreigners, Negroes, Jews, and Catholics. Check the Index for these nativist groups.

b. The Extreme Right: John Birch Society. Named after an American soldier, previously a missionary, killed by the Chinese Communists, the *John Birch Society* was founded in 1958 by a wealthy retired candy manufacturer, *Robert Welch.* The society claimed to be an educational and agitational organization—to expose and oppose the "Communist conspiracy." To spread its views, the society published pamphlets, books, and a monthly magazine, maintained bookstores, sponsored a speakers' bureau, and urged its membership—estimated at 100,000 persons in 4000 local chapters—to become active at school boards, PTA groups, city councils, and major party clubhouses.

John Birch Society views, which strongly reflected those of its founder, included the following: (1) America was in "the grip of the Communist conspiracy," with Red agents or sympathizers—called fellow travelers—exercising powerful influence in our government, courts, schools, universities, churches, and press. (2) Agents of the "Communist conspiracy" have included many high-placed persons: Franklin D. Roosevelt, Dwight D. Eisenhower, who in Welch's words was a "dedicated conscious agent of the Communist conspiracy," former Supreme Court Chief Justice Earl Warren, and Nelson Rockefeller, who planned "to make the United States part of a one-world Socialist government." (3) Birchers were to awaken the American people to the dangers of the "Communist conspiracy." They were to be active in their communities and support the society's special committees or front groups battling for public approval on various issues: to oppose gun controls, prevent water fluoridation, resist forced integration in public schools, and "get the United States out of the UN."

Other extreme-right groups have included a political pressure group, the *Liberty Lobby;* a propagandist movement, the *Christian Anti-Communism Crusade;* the secret, militant *Minutemen*, whose members hoarded guns to combat an expected Communist takeover of the country; and the anti-black and anti-Semitic *American Nazi party.*

c. The Extreme Left: Students for a Democratic Society (SDS). Founded in the early 1960's, the *Students for a Democratic Society* expanded to some 400 college and university branches with an estimated membership of 35,000 (out of a total student enrollment of 7 million). SDS members held diverse, but leftist, ideas, and the society had no single official spokesman. The major SDS views nevertheless have been summarized as follows: (1) American society and institutions had failed the people—failed to end war, poverty, and racism. These failures were the fault of the "establishment" or the "power elite," sometimes further identified as capitalists, imperialists, government leaders, and educational officials. (2) The SDS sought "basic social change," a revolution that would overthrow the "establishment" and institute an undefined system of "participatory democracy." (3) SDS members sought confrontations with university officials and the police so as to arouse public opinion against the "establishment" and "radicalize the students." The SDS, therefore, encouraged sit-ins and teach-ins in school buildings, disruption of selected classes, and mass demonstrations that might become riots.

During the 1960's, the SDS battled with some success for university changes: to abolish ROTC (Reserve Officer Training Corps) classes on campus; to end university research for the military; and to give students a greater voice in university affairs. On the national scene, the SDS joined in the struggle for civil rights and spurred student activity against the Vietnam war.

By the early 1970's, however, the SDS had split into three factions, all favoring revolution but differing as to tactics and leadership. The most extreme faction—which advocated armed struggle, endorsed terrorism, conducted classes in sabotage, and prepared homemade bombs—was called the *Weathermen*. In the mid-1970's, using the name *Weather Underground*, such extremists claimed responsibility for the bombings of several government buildings in Washington, D.C.

Other extreme-left groups have included the *Black Panthers* (check the Index); the *Symbionese Liberation Army*, which in 1974 engaged in kidnapping and bank robbery before losing its leaders in a shootout with Los Angeles policemen; and the best-known extreme-left group—the American *Communist party*.

Communism: A Complex Challenge to Democracy

WHY UNDERSTAND COMMUNISM?

1. Communists have proclaimed themselves the enemies of our democratic capitalist society. They are determined to destroy our society by whatever means are available. Having surfaced in the World War I era, the Communists constitute a long-range, continuous threat.

2. Communists control the Soviet Union, a tremendous military power second only to the United States in industrial strength. They also control Cuba, a number of small European and Asian countries, and the world's most populous nation, China. Of the world's almost 4 billion people, the Communists directly rule one-third. (World communism today is not a single, centrally directed, monolithic movement. Check the Index for "Iron Curtain.")

3. Communists actively compete with us for influence in other nations. They have achieved considerable influence in the developing nations of Asia, Africa, and Latin America. They also have a sizable following in the West European democratic nations of France and Italy. They stand committed eventually to place the entire world under Communist rule.

4. The Communist threat directly affects the American people. Because of our immigrant origins, many Americans have relatives overseas who are living under communism or the threat of Communist rule. As taxpayers, Americans pay the bills for defense against communism, especially military strength and foreign aid. As soldiers, millions of Americans served, and over 100,000 gave their lives, in two American wars against Communist forces in Asia—Korea and Vietnam. In these wars, American servicemen captured by the Communists were subjected to intensive *brainwashing*—continuous enemy pressures to "wash out" or remove American democratic values from the prisoners' minds and to implant Communist views. Although most Americans held prisoner withstood Communist brainwashing, some few did not.

5. If as Americans we are to defend our way of life and respond intelligently to Communist propaganda, then we must understand communism both as a way of thinking or ideology and as an ongoing system typified by conditions in the Soviet Union.

COMMUNISM IN THEORY: THE MARXIAN ANALYSIS

The Communists base their ideology on the ideas of the mid-19th-century German writer and economist *Karl Marx*. This ideology, which uses the terms "communism" and "socialism" interchangeably, is known as *Marxism* or *Marxian socialism*.

1. Ideas of Marx. In two major works—the *Communist Manifesto*, a simple propagandist pamphlet (co-authored with *Friedrich Engels*), and *Das Kapital*, a detailed analysis of the capitalist system—Marx presented his basic ideas.

a. Economic Interpretation of History. Marx argued that economic conditions determine the course of history. The class that possesses the greatest economic power controls the government and social institutions. In an industrial society based on private ownership, the capitalist class rules.

b. Class Struggle. Marx viewed history as a struggle between conflicting economic classes: the "have-nots" against the "haves." In ancient Rome, plebeians battled patricians; in feudal society, serfs opposed lords; under private enterprise, workers, who are the *proletariat*, clash with capitalists. This "class struggle," Marx predicted, will continue until the workers triumph and establish a "classless" socialist society.

c. Surplus Value. Capitalists exploit workers by paying them just enough to keep them alive, that is, subsistence wages. The difference between the workers' wages and the price of the goods the workers produce Marx called *surplus value*. Although capitalists contribute nothing to production, according to Marx, they take the surplus value as profit. Consequently, workers lack sufficient income to purchase all the goods produced, and this in turn, Marx claimed, leads to economic depression.

d. Inevitability of Socialism. Marx predicted that capitalism would destroy itself as depressions became more and more serious. In time, he said, wealth would concentrate in fewer and fewer hands, while workers' conditions steadily deteriorated. Eventually, the workers would be driven to overthrow the capitalists and establish a socialist state. Since the goal of the working class is socialism, Marx explained, it will arise first in those countries having the largest and most oppressed proletariat—the highly industrialized nations.

2. Criticisms of Marxian Ideology. Opponents of Marxism have pointed out the following errors: *(a)* The economic interpretation of history neglects the vital role of noneconomic factors—for example, religion and nationalism. *(b)* The interests of capitalists and workers often coincide—for example, increased production makes possible both higher wages and greater profits. *(c)* Capitalists are entitled to profits, since they risk money and manage industry. *(d)* Under capitalism the conditions of workers have improved steadily, instead of worsening, as Marx expected. *(e)* Communism came first, not to an industrialized nation as Marx predicted, but to Russia, which in 1917 was an overwhelmingly agricultural country.

COMMUNISM IN PRACTICE: SINCE THE ESTABLISHMENT OF THE SOVIET UNION (1917)

As a Communist society has taken shape in the Soviet Union, opponents of socialism have pointed to the following defects: (1) With the profit motive forbidden and private ownership strictly limited to a few personal possessions, individuals have lost their incentive to work and progress. (2) The government, exercising economic as well as political power, is a dictatorship. Since it controls every phase of its citizens' lives, the dictatorship is *totalitarian*. (3) The Communists claim that the government is a *dictatorship of the proletariat*, but in reality it is a dictatorship of a relatively small but highly organized group, the

Communist party. The workers have a negligible say as to their economic conditions and their government. (4) The government places the needs of the state ahead of the needs of the people. (5) The government encounters great difficulty in managing a complex economic system and commits serious errors in planning. As a result, the Communist economy is burdened by a considerable degree of incompetence and inefficiency. (Check the Index for a comparison of the Soviet Union with the United States.)

THE COMMUNIST MOVEMENT WITHIN THE UNITED STATES

1. The American Communist Party. Founded by left-wing extremists in 1919 and modeled after its Russian counterpart, the American Communist party advocated the long-range goal of establishing a Communist regime here. In the meantime, the party proclaimed, it would expose the "evils of capitalism" and help the workers and oppressed minorities. To further its program, the Communist party held meetings and demonstrations, designated its candidates for political office and ran their campaigns, published a newspaper called the *Daily Worker*, instructed its members to infiltrate and seek control of labor unions and liberal movements, and organized various Communist-front groups. These front groups, intended to attract persons who would not knowingly support Communist leadership, purported such liberal programs as defense of civil liberties, help for tenants, protection of the foreign-born, and opposition to war.

Although party membership probably never reached as high as 100,000 persons, the Communists exerted considerable influence during two periods: (*a*) During the economic depression of the 1930's, the Communists found more people willing to listen to their attacks on the "evils of capitalism." They also attracted a number of intellectuals who believed Communist promises to build a better society. However, in the Presidential election of 1932, at the bottom of the depression, the Communist candidate polled—out of 40 million votes cast—only 103,000 votes. (*b*) During World War II, as the United States and Russia were allied against German Nazism, the Communist party here strongly supported the war effort and seemed to become more respectable.

With the outbreak of the cold war between the United States and Russia, the American Communist party lost influence, declined in membership, and again came under public suspicion.

2. The American Communist Party: An Agent of the Soviet Union? Although the Communists deny this charge, many Americans believe that the Communist party gives its loyalty to the Soviet Union and serves as an agent of Soviet policy. To support this opinion, many Americans would cite the following: (*a*) The American Communist party joined the organization of world Communist parties, called the *Third International*, or *Comintern*. Dominated by Russia, the Comintern directed the efforts of the individual Communist parties—including the American—to spread unrest and revolution in capitalistic nations. Although the Comintern was officially dissolved by Russia during World War II, American Communist leaders have remained faithful to a Moscow-directed international Communist movement. (*b*) The American Communist party stand on world issues has slavishly followed the Russian party line. Consider the following about-face. While the Stalin-Hitler nonagression pact of 1939 was in effect, American Communists insisted that World War II was an "imperialist conflict," claimed to see no perceptible difference between democratic Britain and Nazi Germany, and urged American isolation. After Hitler attacked the Soviet Union in 1941, American Communists abruptly changed their stand and "discovered" that World War II was a "people's war" against Fascism.

Some Americans further believe, although these beliefs are inferred but not substantiated, that the American Communist party has been financed at least partially by Soviet funds and has directed espionage to secure American national defense secrets for the Soviets.

3. American Defenses Against the Internal Communist Threat. During the height of the cold war, the United States acted vigorously against domestic Communists. American efforts, however, were contained within the framework of the legal protections and civil liberties guaranteed by the Constitution to all persons.

a. The Truman administration instituted a loyalty program to weed out of government service persons considered "national security risks." Of almost 3 million persons investigated, some 2000 resigned and 200 were dismissed.

b. The FBI infiltrated the Communist party and Communist-front organizations to secure inside information about Communist plans.

c. The Justice Department secured the conviction of 11 Communist leaders for violating the Smith Act by advocating the violent overthrow of the government. (Check the Index for the Dennis Case.)

d. House and Senate investigating committees held hearings to uncover Communists in government positions, defense plants, education, and the mass media. In the 1957 Watkins Case, the Supreme Court somewhat limited the scope of Congressional committee investigations. (Check the Index for the Watkins Case.)

e. The Taft-Hartley (Labor-Management Relations) Act of 1947 required union officials to file statements that they were not members of the Communist party. (Check the Index for this law.)

f. The McCarran Internal Security Act of 1950 created the *Subversive Activities Control Board* (SACB) to identify Communist and Communist-front organizations, which groups were then to register with and supply membership lists to the Department of Justice. In 1965, after lengthy litigation, the Supreme Court held that Communists could not be compelled to register because of the Constitutional protection against self-incrimination. By this decision negating the registration provision of the McCarran Act, the Supreme Court rendered futile the work of the SACB. In 1973 the SACB officially went out of existence.

With all the measures herein discussed, our nation's strongest defense against the internal Communist threat remains the American people. With common sense and knowledge, they should be able to evaluate the Communist danger, to understand Communist tactics and motives, to recognize Communist propaganda, and to refute Communist specious arguments. Convinced of the worth of our democratic capitalist system, the American people are determined to preserve its benefits, to remedy its defects, and to solve future problems in accordance with our proud American heritage.

4. Communist Party Influence Today. With left-wing extremists divided into pro-Soviet, pro-Tito, pro-Mao, and other factions, the Communist party is only one of several leftist groups. Its current membership is estimated at no more than 10,000 to 12,000 persons. Claiming lack of funds, it ceased publication of its daily newspaper. In the 1972 Presidential election, the Communist candidate, Gus Hall, polled only 25,000 votes. However, the nature and range of the Communist party's secret activities—if any—remain unknown.

How would you assess the extent of danger to American institutions posed by domestic Communists today?

7. Americans Seek Social Control Acceptable to a Democratic Society

Meaning of Social Control. Social control means that society exercises authority over its individual members to conform to rules of conduct and patterns of behavior that are considered normal and acceptable. Social control is reflected in society's long-observed traditions and customs—its *mores,* and in society's legal regulations—its *laws.* Sometimes, a tradition may be enacted into law: The New England colonial tradition of giving thanks to God for His bounty became the legal holiday of Thanksgiving. Social control has existed in all societies, from the simplest to the most complex.

AGENCIES OF SOCIAL CONTROL

From early childhood, the individual is trained to conform to society's acceptable behavior patterns and ethical standards by many agencies, or institutions, as follows: (1) The family teaches the individual to behave decently, accept responsibility, live peaceably with other family members and respect their rights, realize the complexity of society, consider a future career, and pursue worthwhile leisure activities. The stronger the family ties and the more concerned the parents, the better adjusted the individual should be to society. (2) Friends, both singly and in clubs or gangs, provide interpersonal relationships and peer group standards of ethics and behavior. How often have individuals in trouble with the law placed the blame on "bad friends"! (3) Neighborhoods set examples of home cleanliness, personal dress, and public behavior. (4) Religious institutions preach standards of morality including to respect others, act justly, assist unfortunate peoples, and pursue ethical living. (5) Schools teach the individual to accept responsibility, respect others, appreciate the national heritage, know the duties and rights of citizenship, develop worthwhile leisure-time activities, and prepare for future employment. (6) Governments regulate the individual so as to protect the health and well-being of society. Among their many concerns, governments prohibit excessive noise and littering, provide pure water, sanitation services, and consumer safeguards; set building codes and zoning regulations; require school attendance, car registration, and tax payments; define crimes and maintain law-enforcement bodies.

EFFECT OF AMERICAN GROWTH ON SOCIAL CONTROL

As the United States has developed from a rural, handicraft society into an urban, industrialized nation, social control has been exerted less by the traditional informal agencies and institutions and more by formal ones. In other words, the family and neighborhood have played a decreasing role, whereas greater importance has devolved upon school and government. This shift in responsibility is illustrated by the following examples: (1) In a small rural community where everybody knew everybody else, neighborhood pressures usually sufficed to have the individual conform to community standards. In a large metropolis, neighbors know less about each other, and the individual remains relatively unknown. Less subject to neighborhood pressures, the individual is molded more by school and governmental regulations. (2) In the patriarchal family, typical of early America, the father exerted strict control over the children. In today's equalitarian family, the father exercises far less authority and the children possess a good deal of freedom. With parental authority weakened, children are influenced more by school and governmental pressures. (3) In our preindustrial society, teenagers desiring to drive the family horse and buggy proved their ability to their fathers. Because the horse and buggy moved slowly, few serious accidents occurred. In our industrial society, teenagers desiring to drive their families' cars must prove their ability to a state examiner and obtain state drivers' licenses. Further, because heavy, rapidly moving cars may cause serious accidents, teenagers must know and obey state safety regulations, especially speed limits. (4) In earlier years few if any persons were concerned if a building chimney or a car exhaust emitted heavy black smoke into the atmosphere. In recent years society has become concerned with protecting the environment and keeping pure the air we breathe. Whereas no agency had previously exerted significant social control regarding the environment, recently the government has moved to assume this responsibility.

CRIME: A CHALLENGE TO SOCIAL CONTROL

If social control were completely effective, society would have no crime. The effectiveness of social control, therefore, can be measured, to some extent, by the nature and prevalence of crime.

1. Analysis of Crime. Simply stated, a crime is an act that society considers harmful. A crime today usually involves a violation of a law.

Crimes have been classified in many ways: (1) A crime may be an *act of commission*, such as committing a robbery, or it may be an *act of omission*, such as omitting to file an income tax return. (2) A crime may be against the government or society in general, such as stealing guns from an army supply depot; or against publicly accepted morality, such as illegal gambling; or against an individual, such as causing bodily harm—a violent crime, and stealing possessions —a property crime. (3) A crime may be premeditated, or planned in advance, such as a bank robbery; or due to momentary excitement, or unplanned, such as a bitter verbal debate leading to physical assault. (4) A crime may be committed by a teenager, or juvenile delinquent, usually a first offender, or by an adult, possibly a hardened criminal. (5) A crime also may be committed by an individual or by a temporary gang, or by an organized crime syndicate. (6) A crime may be of a minor nature, punishable by a small fine and/or less than a year in prison; it is called a *misdemeanor*. A crime may also be of a major nature, punishable by a large fine and/or more than a year in prison; it is called a *felony*.

2. Protection Against Crime: A Brief Survey. Throughout our history Americans have sought protection against crime by establishing law-enforcement agencies. *(a)* In colonial America, town watchmen and local officials provided protection. Criminals were often punished in public by being branded on the forehead, or flogged at a whipping post, or locked in the stocks—a heavy wooden frame confining the criminal by his wrists and ankles. *(b)* In frontier communities, settlers often took the law into their own hands, forming groups called *vigilantes*. Best known in the cattle country and mining camps, vigilante groups often whipped or hanged offenders without prior trial. As frontier communities became more settled, vigilantes gave way to federal marshals and local sheriffs.

For law enforcement today, cities, counties, and states maintain police forces. States also have available the National Guard which, except when called into federal service, is under the command of the state governor. The federal government also maintains several law-enforcement agencies. *(a)* The Justice Department contains the Federal Bureau of Investigation (FBI) and the Drug Enforcement Administration (which in 1973 absorbed the Bureau of Narcotics and Dangerous Drugs). The FBI investigates offenses against federal laws including matters such as espionage, sabotage and subversion, interstate kidnapping, robbery of banks affiliated with the Federal Reserve System, interstate transportation of stolen motor vehicles, and other interstate crimes. The FBI maintains an extensive fingerprint identification file and a modern crime-detection laboratory; it trains state and local law-enforcement agents and cooperates with them in apprehending criminals; and it gathers national crime data. The Drug Enforcement Administration enforces federal narcotics laws to "dry up" sources of illegal drugs and to stop "drug pushers." *(b)* The United States Postal Service maintains inspectors to combat mail frauds, thefts, and robberies and to keep the mails free of explosive devices such as "letter-bombs." *(c)* The Treasury Department contains the Secret Service—to protect the President and his family and to suppress counterfeiting; the Internal Revenue Service—to prevent and uncover fraud and negligence in the filing of federal income tax returns; and the Customs Service—to prevent smuggling.

3. Recent Trends: An Increase in Crime. Despite the many law-enforcement agencies, crime has continued to increase. The FBI through its Uniform Crime Reporting Program provided the data shown in the table below.

Year	Violent Crimes	Property Crimes	Total Crimes	Crimes per 100,000 of Population
1960	286,000	1,734,000	2,020,000	1126
1970	733,000	4,848,000	5,581,000	2747

"We're doing something wrong." (*Le Pelley in the Christian Science Monitor* © *1970 The Christian Science Publishing Society*)

To society, the costs of crime are staggering. For law-enforcement purposes, taxpayers spend over $1 billion annually. Nevertheless, criminals rob, steal, and damage property at costs estimated in the hundreds of millions; they cause bodily harm and death to hundreds of thousands; furthermore, they destroy society's confidence in its ability to maintain law and order and to protect its members. In major cities, storekeepers barricade their premises with iron gratings, bus drivers no longer carry change, and people are afraid to walk the streets after dark.

Why has crime increased so? Among the many factors suggested are the following: industrialization of society; growth of cities; poverty, poor education and lack of opportunity of ghetto inhabitants; racial disturbances; weakening of traditional agencies of social control; lack of religious affiliation of some 40 percent of the people; wars and the lowering of the moral standards of the people; political corruption; ready availability of guns and other weapons; television and radio stress on crime; inadequate law enforcement.

4. Organized Crime: A Menace to Society

a. The "Invisible Empire." Because organized crime demands secrecy of its members, instills fear among the public, and is a flourishing activity, it is often called the *invisible empire.* Our knowledge of organized crime remains fragmentary and disjointed, having been put together from various sources as follows: (1) government agents fighting organized crime; (2) defectors from the crime syndicate—the best-known one in the 1960's being Joseph Valachi; (3) news stories about organized crime, such as the 1957 meeting of crime bosses at the small central New York State town of Apalachin and the warfare in Brooklyn, New York since the 1950's between the rival Gallo and Profaci crime gangs; and (4) government investigating committees. In 1950–1951 *Estes Kefauver* headed a Senate committee investigating organized crime, which held televised hearings in major cities throughout the country. The committee called some 600 witnesses, many of whom refused to testify by claiming their rights under the Fifth Amendment protection against self-incrimination. After the 1957 Apalachin meeting of crime bosses, the New York State Investigation Commission checked into their records. In 1957 John McClellan headed a Senate committee investigating labor and management. Despite witnesses "taking the Fifth," the committee found evidence of organized racketeering in some labor unions and business enterprises.

b. Structure of Organized Crime. Organized crime refers to those individuals—estimated to number from 100,000 to 250,000 persons—who engage in crime as their business. They make crime pay. From illegal activities, organized crime secures an income estimated at $40 billion per year. It is definitely a profitable operation.

Originally, organized crime was known as the Mafia or Cosa Nostra (our family) because many early members were of Sicilian ancestry and knew these names as applying to secret societies in Sicily. Today, organized crime encompasses individuals of diverse nationalities, religions, and races and has many nicknames: the "Syndicate," the "Confederation," the "Organization," and the "Mob." Organized crime is structured into "families," each "family" controlling crime within its "turf" or territory. Each "family" is headed by its own boss—who may also be known as the "godfather," a term popularized by a 1960's book and subsequent movies. The boss exercises unquestioned control. He is advised by his counselor and assisted by his lieutenants. His orders are carried out by the "family" members called "soldiers."

c. Brief History and Activities. Organized crime became "big time" during the 1920's era of prohibition. With many citizens opposing prohibition and losing

Remote control (*Hesse in the St. Louis Globe-Democrat*)

respect for the law, organized crime arranged to smuggle liquor in from foreign countries or to distill and distribute it here, especially through "speakeasies" and gambling casinos. As illegal liquor became a multibillion dollar activity, organized crime expanded its control over gambling, vice, stolen stocks and bonds, loansharking, and, later, narcotics and racketeering. Crime bosses began major efforts to corrupt police and other law-enforcement officials and to establish understandings or alliances with local politicians. As monies continued to roll in, crime bosses invested in legitimate businesses, especially garment manufacturing, trucking, vending machines, and wholesale meat distribution. Here too its Syndicate employed threats, bombings, and shootings to compel use of its services and purchase of its products.

    d. Society's Defenses Against Organized Crime. (1) The Internal Revenue Service has charged several notorious crime bosses with failure to file tax returns and pay income taxes. This approach has had limited success. In 1931 the charge of income tax evasion led to the jailing of the "big" Chicago gangster Al Capone, but organized crime was little affected. Some crime bosses, however, have begun to file tax returns, declaring income without indicating its sources, and to pay taxes. (2) The Justice Department established a special *Organized Crime and Racketeering* unit (OCR). This unit's work has been facilitated by several laws declaring the crossing of state lines for illegal purposes—such as gambling, extortion, transporting slot machines, narcotics traffic, and prostitution—to be interstate or federal offenses. (3) The *Organized Crime Control Act* of 1970 declared the following to be federal offenses: operating an illegal gambling business; conspiring to obstruct enforcement of state and local antigambling laws; and placing in legitimate interstate businesses money obtained in organized crime activities. The law further established federal control over the interstate sale of explosives and authorized federal judges to impose extra sentences of up to 25 years on "dangerous special offenders" whose records show a pattern of continued criminal conduct.

    e. Additional Proposals for Combating Organized Crime. Crime fighters propose the following additional steps: (1) stricter local and state law enforcement, (2) additional federal involvement, (3) more severe punishment of organized crime members, (4) a law granting immunity from prosecution to organized crime members for testimony given at government investigations so that they cannot plead the Fifth Amendment but must give evidence or face jail, (5) legalization of gambling under government control so as to remove this source of profits from organized crime, (6) permission for wiretap evidence to be used in court against organized crime members, and finally (7) increased public involvement in the fight against organized crime. (For a discussion of proposals 5, 6, and 7, check the Index for "Social control, issues of.")

    The American people must realize that as long as our society tolerates the operations of the "invisible empire," then to that extent our society is not wholly free or democratic.

5. The Problem of Juvenile Delinquency

    a. Meaning and Extent. Juvenile delinquents are youngsters, usually defined as under 18 years of age, who have broken the law. Such juveniles are not considered criminals but rather as delinquents—children who have committed faults or misdeeds. In society's view, they are not fully responsible for their actions and, with proper social control, they will return to acceptable behavior patterns.

Juvenile delinquency has been increasing, according to many observers, at an alarming rate. From 1960 to the late 1970's (1) the number of youths arrested increased from slightly above a half million to 1.7 million, and (2) the number of cases handled by juvenile courts per 1000 of youthful population increased from 20 to 38. The major juvenile crimes were:assault, robbery, burglary, narcotics possession and use, drunkenness, disorderly conduct, larceny or general theft, and auto theft. Juvenile delinquents committed one out of every two auto thefts.

While boys arrested for juvenile delinquency far outnumbered girls, the number of female delinquents has been increasing at a more rapid rate than the number of male delinquents. Also, while white youths arrested outnumbered black and other minority youths, the white delinquents were a far smaller percentage of the total white juvenile population than were the minority group delinquents of the total minority juvenile population. Finally, far more urban youths were arrested for juvenile delinquency than were rural youths.

b. Causes. The causes of juvenile delinquency have been classified as follows: (1) the individual—personality and intelligence, (2) associates—friends and peer-group activities, (3) social and economic environment—poor housing, lack of recreational facilities, and inadequate schooling; racial discrimination and despair regarding any future career; poverty, unemployment, and boredom; no religious guidance; television and movie portrayal of crime as glamorous and exciting; and weakened family ties with little or no parental control. Many *criminologists* (experts on crime) blame juvenile delinquency primarily on the environment.

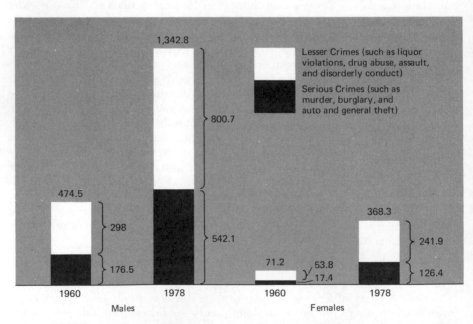

Arrests of Youths Under Eighteen Years of Age, 1960 and 1978 (In Thousands)

c. Preventive Measures. To prevent children from turning to delinquency, society has acted as follows: (1) Private groups—Boy Scouts, Girl Scouts, YMCA, and YWCA—have provided recreational facilities and have encouraged youngsters to expend their energies in worthwhile activities. (2) Cities and states have replaced slum dwellings with new housing projects, added to recreational facilities, established summer youth programs, provided more meaningful education, and increased opportunities for minority group members to advance to higher education. In some cities, the police work with youths in their own neighborhoods through *PAL*—the *Police Athletic League*. (3) The federal government has moved against racial discrimination in education, housing, and employment. Further, the federal government has battled to prevent juvenile delinquency through various programs: the *Job Corps* to provide unemployed out-of-school youths with remedial education and job training; the *Neighborhood Youth Corps* to provide underprivileged youths with summer and part-time community jobs; and *Operation Upward Bound* to provide remedial education so that disadvantaged youths can qualify for college.

d. Remedial Measures. If arrested, youthful offenders are brought before special juvenile courts. These courts seek to understand the problems of the offenders, to help them, and especially to rehabilitate—not punish—them. These courts have available the services of social workers and psychiatrists. Youthful offenders receive an informal hearing rather than formal trials with defense and prosecution attorneys; and they may be declared delinquents rather than found guilty. Depending on the specific case, delinquents may be (1) put on probation—that is, freed but subject to court restrictions on behavior and to supervision of a probation officer or (2) committed to a "training school," which is meant to be not a prison but rather a rehabilitation institution. Two well-known training schools are *Boys Town* in Nebraska and the *George Junior Republic* in central New York.

Critics have complained that juvenile courts carry too heavy a caseload, court officials often fail to understand and help youthful offenders, and "training schools" are indistinguishable from prisons. These critics received strong support from a 1967 Supreme Court decision. In the case of *In re Gault*, the majority opinion expressed considerable doubt regarding juvenile court procedures, questioned juvenile court effectiveness in achieving rehabilitation, and further held training schools to be little different from adult prisons. The Court therefore asserted that youthful offenders are entitled to the same Constitutional protections as adults: namely a statement of charges, no self-incrimination, a lawyer, and cross examination of witnesses. The lone dissenting Justice held that the decision would undermine the work of the juvenile courts and would be "a long step backwards."

ISSUES OF SOCIAL CONTROL

1. Does Society Benefit From Legalized Gambling?

a. Extent of Legalized Gambling. By the mid-1970's over 30 states permitted betting at racetracks, 13 states had lotteries, three states allowed offtrack betting, and one state—Nevada—sanctioned gambling casinos. In 1976 New Jersey voters approved casino gambling in Atlantic City.

b. Yes—Benefits. Legalized gambling dries up a source of profits for organized crime and thereby helps reduce the extent of police and political corruption. It provides the states with revenues to use for socially desirable purposes and lessens the need for additional taxes. Legalized gambling removes the stigma of crime from people who would gamble anyway—legal or not. Finally, legalized gambling enables the states to transfer their energies from upholding antigambling ordinances to enforcing more important anticrime laws.

c. No—Does Not Benefit. Legalized gambling has provided relatively little revenue to the states. It has been infiltrated by organized crime, especially at some racetracks and in some Nevada gambling casinos. Legalized gambling cannot compete with illegal bookmakers who take bets via telephone, extend credit, offer "action" not only on horse racing but on many other sports, and control the "numbers game," which is most popular with small bettors in ghetto areas. Most important, legalization makes gambling acceptable and weakens the moral fiber of society.

2. Should Law-Enforcement Agencies Be Permitted to Use Wiretapping Evidence in Criminal Cases?

a. Background. Subject to many state and federal laws and to varied court decisions, wiretapping in our society represents a most complicated problem. In general, the situation is as follows: Some states have permitted law-enforcement agents to use wiretapping with court approval in such cases as gambling, drug traffic, and larceny. Other states do not. Federal agents have employed wiretapping with court consent in "national security" cases. The *Omnibus Crime Control Act* of 1970 authorized federal and state law-enforcement agents to obtain court warrants allowing wiretapping in most criminal cases. State and federal court wiretap decisions have turned upon specific details and legal technicalities without establishing any broad, generally applicable principles.

b. Yes—Permit Wiretapping. Wiretapping can provide law-enforcement agents with information vital to pursuing and convicting criminals, especially members of organized crime. With organized crime so powerful and efficient, law-enforcement agents need the most modern detection devices. Wiretapping does not violate the Fourth Amendment protection against "unreasonable search" since in attaching an electronic device the government agent does not conduct a "search," and it does not violate the Fifth Amendment prohibition against "self-incrimination" since the suspect, unaware of the wiretap, is speaking freely but is *not* being compelled to testify. Frank Hogan, for many years District Attorney of New York County, called wiretapping the "single most valuable weapon in law enforcement's fight against organized crime."

c. No—Do Not Permit Wiretapping. Wiretapping denies individuals their "right to privacy," instills fear of surveillance in all citizens, and thereby smacks of the practices of totalitarian regimes. It violates the Fourth Amendment for, in attaching an electronic device, the government agent is trespassing, which can be considered an "unreasonable search"; and it violates the Fifth Amendment, since the suspect is being incriminated by his own words. Supreme Court Justice Oliver Wendell Holmes condemned wiretapping as "dirty business."

3. Should Citizens Accept Personal Responsibility to Assist in Law Enforcement Against Crime?

a. Public Fear and Apathy. Especially in large cities, the average citizen has been fearful of becoming personally involved in combating crime. In New York City subway riders have looked the other way while teenage gangs have maliciously destroyed property and have beaten and robbed defenseless persons. The city government has been compelled to increase the subway police force. In 1964 in Queens, New York, Kitty Genovese, a young woman, was brutally murdered while 38 persons saw her struggles and heard her screams but made no move to help her.

Some citizens have become involved in combating crime—because they were civic-minded, or hoped for a reward, or accidentally witnessed criminal acts. These citizens too frequently have suffered, at the least, loss of time from their work and daily routines and, at the most, bodily harm and death. In 1952 Arnold Schuster of Brooklyn, New York recognized Willie Sutton, a "most-wanted" bank robber, trailed him, and led the police to arrest Sutton. Three weeks later Schuster was shot to death—a still unsolved murder. In organized crime cases, witnesses have been threatened verbally, their cars and homes have been bombed, and some have been murdered—all to keep them from testifying in court.

b. Yes—The Citizen's Responsibility. All citizens bear the moral responsibility of helping to protect society against crime. Any citizen who witnesses a crime is morally obligated to assist the victim, cooperate with law-enforcement agents, and give testimony in court. Any citizen who does less is guilty of cowardice and, more important, is abandoning society to the domination of criminals. If all citizens join the fight against crime, some few may be hurt, but their combined efforts can lower the crime rate and achieve a decent society.

c. No—Not the Citizen's Responsibility. Citizens pay taxes so that society can hire, train, and equip sufficient law-enforcement agents. The citizen who by chance witnesses a crime usually does not realize what is happening and does not possess the strength and weapons to become involved. Citizens have been reluctant witnesses at trials because society does not compensate them for their loss of time and does not adequately protect them against harm. Fighting crime is not a game for the public; it is a serious business—the responsibility of the professional law-enforcement agent.

d. Laws to Encourage Public Responsibility Against Crime. New York and many other states have enacted so-called *Good Samaritan laws*. These laws state that doctors who provide emergency treatment to persons injured at the scene of an accident or a crime cannot be sued later on charges of improper or injurious treatment, known as *malpractice*. Sociologists have urged enactment of *civic-minded citizen laws* to compensate individuals for their time and effort in cooperating with law-enforcement agents.

4. Should the Federal Government Enact a Stricter Gun Control Law, Requiring Registration of Guns and Licensing of Owners?

a. Events Leading to Federal Gun Control Laws. In the 1960's, guns were used by assassins to murder three prominent Americans: in 1963 while in Dallas, Texas on a political tour—President John F. Kennedy; in 1968 while in Memphis, Tennessee to assist striking sanitation workers—the black civil rights leader Martin Luther King; and later in 1968 while in Los Angeles, California to campaign for the Democratic Presidential nomination—Senator Robert F. Kennedy. These murders focused public attention upon guns: the large number of people—estimated at 43 million—who possessed guns; the ease with which people obtained guns; the thousands of persons each year who were killed —accidentally and deliberately—by guns; and the lack of any federal controls over the possession and sale of guns.

Public opinion, as measured by polls and by newspaper editorials, overwhelmingly demanded strict gun controls. The *National Rifle Association*, speaking for some 1 million members and contending that it was an educational group not a "gun lobby," led the opposition. Under intense and conflicting pressures, Congress in 1968 passed the *Omnibus Crime Control Act* and the *Gun Control Act*. In regard to guns, these laws (1) banned the interstate mail-order sale of ammunition and of handguns, shotguns, and rifles; (2) forbade the sale of these guns to minors; and (3) prohibited possession of guns by illegal aliens and major criminals or felons. Although heartened by the passage of these laws, proponents of gun controls were not satisfied. They urged additional stricter federal controls, especially registration of guns and licensing of gun owners.

b. Yes—For Stricter Gun Controls. (1) Stricter controls have proved effective in reducing gun *homicides*—the use of guns in the accidental or deliberate killing of persons. In Britain, which requires gun registration, the gun homicide rate is far below that of the United States. In America, cities with strong gun regulations have gun homicide rates far below those of nonregulatory cities. New York City, with its Sullivan law requiring police permits for possession of pistols, has a gun murder rate far below the national rate. (2) Stricter

Bumper stickers for and against gun control
(*U.S. News and World Report*)

controls would not violate the Second Amendment, which guarantees "the right of the people to keep and bear arms." For comparison, the people's right to possess and drive cars has not been infringed by auto registration and driver licensing requirements. Furthermore, the Second Amendment right to bear arms relates not to the individual but to the need of the state for a "well-regulated militia." (3) Stricter gun controls would enable law-enforcement agents to arrest criminals for the illegal possession of guns rather than to arrest criminals after they have used the guns in committing violent crimes.

    c. No—Against Stricter Gun Controls. (1) Stricter controls would eventually destroy the sport of hunting, prevent farmers and ranchers from protecting their livestock against wild animals, and disarm law-abiding citizens, thereby denying them guns for self-protection. Stricter gun controls would be opposed by many Americans and would breed disrespect for the law—as did the prohibition of liquor. (2) Stricter controls would violate the Second Amendment by infringing upon the "right of the people to keep and bear arms." Stricter gun controls, therefore, would be unconstitutional. (3) Stricter controls would not disarm criminals. They would continue to obtain and use guns.

OTHER ISSUES OF SOCIAL CONTROL

    Students may be interested in researching and discussing other social control issues: *(a)* What has been the effect of Massachusetts' strict firearms control law of 1968—requiring licenses for gun ownership and permits for ammunition purchases? *(b)* Has New York State's tough drug law of 1973—requiring that convicted dealers in hard drugs receive mandatory life sentences but with provision for parole—proved effective against the narcotics traffic? *(c)* How effective are prisons in rehabilitating rather than merely punishing criminals? *(d)* Regardless of how serious the crime, should the death penalty be abolished? *(e)* For law-enforcement purposes, should the federal government require the fingerprinting of all inhabitants? *(f)* Has society been blamed too much and the individual not enough in weighing the factors that lead people to become criminals? *(g)* Do ethnic minority groups hold values and follow life-styles sufficiently different from the majority so as to complicate problems of social control?

SUMMARY: SOCIAL CONTROL IN A DEMOCRATIC SOCIETY

    Democratic peoples, who rule themselves through their elected representatives, face difficult choices in the managing of their society. They must choose between contending principles as follows: in civil liberties, the choices are defined as between the rights of the individual and the needs of society; in social control, the choices are similarly defined as between freedom for the individual and restraint in the interests of society. Too much freedom can result in anarchy, too much restraint in dictatorship.

    Between freedom and restraint: What is the correct balance? Where should the line be drawn? Democratic peoples seek to achieve a central or moderate position, thereby preserving both the blessings of liberty and the benefits of a decent and humane social order.

MULTIPLE-CHOICE QUESTIONS

1. Extremist groups generally (1) hold that the rights of all minorities must be respected (2) believe that the people have sufficient intelligence to decide upon national issues (3) insist that the cause and remedy of problems of society are simple (4) claim that our present system of government works satisfactorily.

2. Which statement would be most acceptable to persons who hold "extremist" views—both left and right? (1) We ought to go back to the "good old days." (2) Any methods are justified to get what we know is best. (3) Change comes through evolution, not revolution. (4) Any change is better than none.

3. Extremist groups have generally influenced United States political history by (1) offering Constitutional solutions to national problems (2) stimulating negative reactions to their ideas (3) endorsing legislation extending civil liberties to minority groups (4) changing basic principles of governmental organization.

4. An analysis of the doctrines of Karl Marx, in social studies classes of American high schools, would tend to (1) be inconsistent with democratic principles (2) increase awareness of the complex challenge of communism (3) indoctrinate the values and ideals of communism (4) explain the causes of student unrest.

5. Karl Marx was *most* accurate in stating that (1) communism would come first to the most highly industrialized nations (2) economic factors strongly affect historical events (3) communism would eliminate social problems (4) true value is determined by the amount of labor used in producing goods.

6. Which is *not* a belief of Karl Marx? (1) Capitalist countries will experience more and more serious depressions. (2) Workers' conditions will slowly improve under capitalism. (3) Labor is the most important factor in production. (4) Wealth in capitalistic countries will be concentrated in fewer and fewer hands.

7. Why would Karl Marx *not* have expected the Communist Revolution of 1917 to take place in Russia? (1) Russia was largely agricultural. (2) Most of Russia's leaders were moderates. (3) Russia retained many Oriental ideas. (4) Russia had a large population.

8. Which is a statement of opinion regarding the Communist party in the United States? (1) It was founded by left-wing extremists after World War I. (2) It polled relatively few votes in the Presidential election of 1932. (3) It has supported the Russian "party line" on world issues. (4) It represents a serious threat to the security of the United States today.

9. Which is a valid statement about mores, family life, and religion? (1) They are entirely individual matters. (2) They are all forms of social control. (3) They refuse to be changed by events in history. (4) Their purpose is to prevent social change.

10. The agency that exercises the *greatest* amount of social control today is the (1) family (2) religious institution (3) social club (4) government.

11. Which statement is correct regarding crime during the 1960–1970 decade? (1) There was a sharp decrease in the number of federal law-enforcement agencies. (2) The number of reported crimes, both violent and property, more than doubled. (3) Organized crime was almost completely wiped out. (4) Girls arrested for juvenile delinquency far outnumbered boys.

12. Maintaining social control in the United States has been a problem primarily because of the (1) indifference to crime by police forces (2) popular preference for a maximum of personal freedom (3) frequent return of immigrant groups to their homelands (4) lack of Constitutional provisions for police protection.

13. The assassinations, in the 1960's, of three prominent Americans—President John F. Kennedy, Senator Robert F. Kennedy, and civil rights leader Martin Luther King (1) supported the extremist belief in the conspiracy theory of history (2) showed the

power of organized crime   (3) led Congress to pass two laws that gun control advocates considered weak   (4) proved that federal laws cannot stop criminals from getting guns.

14. The need for maintaining social control and for increasing individual liberty gives rise to the dilemma of how to   (1) curb civil disorders and still suspend the writ of habeas corpus   (2) achieve the common good without anarchy   (3) control crime without ex post facto laws   (4) increase the number of policemen without increasing taxes.

15. The existence of social control in a democracy indicates that *most* of its citizens tend to   (1) act in full freedom without restraint   (2) conform to surrounding cultural practices and values   (3) favor concentration of responsibility in federal enforcement agencies   (4) be attracted to third-party candidates.

16. Which conclusion about social change in United States history is *most* valid?   (1) Reforms take place most rapidly in an agricultural economy.   (2) Most ideas for change have originated with public school educators.   (3) Changes have consistently occurred at a steady pace.   (4) Americans have seldom been receptive to sudden radical changes.

17. Generally, democratic forms of social control are *easiest* to maintain in areas in which   (1) there is an enlightened and concerned public   (2) the death penalty has been eliminated   (3) agriculture is the chief form of economic activity   (4) law-enforcement agencies do not adhere strictly to the legal codes.

ESSAY QUESTIONS

1. For *each* of the following problems facing the United States (a) analyze the problem as to possible causes and effects and (b) discuss a course of action to deal with the problem. Indicate if this course of action attacks the causes or effects of the problem: (1) right-wing extremism (2) left-wing extremism (3) deterioration of family life (4) organized crime (5) juvenile delinquency.

2. The phrase "law and order" has been used very frequently, but there is lack of agreement as to its meaning. (a) What is the relationship of "law and order" to the concept of social control? (b) Explain what the phrase "law and order" would *most* likely mean to *two* of the following individuals, and for *each* individual selected, show how training, position, *or* environment has influenced the person's attitude: (1) policeman (2) political candidate (3) resident of a black ghetto (4) high school student (5) widowed housewife living in a city apartment. (c) Describe *one* action of the federal government that has weakened *or* strengthened "law and order" in the United States.

3. Maintaining social control in a democracy is a particularly sensitive task, since democracy recognizes the right of dissent and the right of individual freedom. (a) Explain the meaning of this statement and illustrate by giving *two* examples. You may use both the United States and democratic European societies. (b) Identify *two* different types of nondemocratic societies and describe *two* methods by which they maintain social control.

4. Speakers X and Y below are discussing current problems.
    Speaker X: We have an obligation to protect society from the criminal elements that prey on it. Wiretapping cannot harm the innocent. It can only uncover the guilty and give law-enforcement officers the means of meeting their highest duty to society, prevention of crime.
    Speaker Y: When I was your age, I was earning my own living and paying board at home. I worked hard for every cent I had. We knew the value of a dollar in those days. Knew how to work, too. We didn't have time for all the tomfoolery that you youngsters fritter your time away with.

For *each* statement made, (*a*) discuss the possible values reflected by each speaker (*b*) for *each* speaker, write a statement a person holding an opposing point of view might make.

5. Agree or disagree with *each* of the following statements and present *two* arguments to support your opinion: (*a*) Neither the extreme right nor the extreme left represents a significant internal danger to our American way of life. (*b*) The best cure for extremism in America is not repressing the extremists but assuring all Americans economic security and social justice. (*c*) As it moves into legitimate businesses, organized crime will become even more difficult for the government to combat. (*d*) Legalized gambling—both as a method of raising government funds and as a method of combating organized crime—has been a failure. (*e*) The federal government should enact a strict gun control law requiring registration of all guns and licensing of all gun owners. (*f*) The average American citizen should take an active and more personal role in the battle against crime. (*g*) The balance between individual freedom and social control in America has varied according to the times.

UNIT V. THE UNITED STATES IN WORLD AFFAIRS

Part 1. An Introduction to
Foreign Policy

1. American Foreign Policy Results From the
Interaction of Many Factors

BACKGROUND: THE NATION-STATE OR NATIONAL STATE

1. Emergence Out of Medieval Europe. In western Europe during the later Middle Ages (11th to 14th centuries), people lived under a system of *feudalism*. Feudal life was typified *(a)* socially—by rigid class distinctions, *(b)* economically—by self-sufficient agricultural manors, and *(c)* politically—by local government and local military defense. With the central government or king unable to exercise authority beyond the royal domain (estate), the local nobles controlled their own territory and people. These nobles made laws, levied taxes, dispensed justice, and waged war, thereby providing decentralized or local government.

Over several hundred years, feudalism declined. The king extended his power over the local nobles, their territory and people; eventually he ruled a large, usually compact, area free from external religious or political control. In England, France, and Spain, the king united people of a common *nationality*—those sharing similar language, history, and customs. Imbued by *nationalism*—the feeling of patriotism toward one's own country—the people gradually transferred their loyalty from local lord and province to king and nation. In these countries, therefore, a strong monarch molded a unified *nation-state* or *national state*. (In Prussia and Austria, the king ruled diverse nationalities, although one predominated. These monarchs, therefore, established powerful *empires* but their peoples lacked a feeling of national unity.)

2. Case Studies: Foreign Policy of Emerging European Countries. By the 17th century in western Europe (except England), the king had become an *absolute* *monarch.* He claimed to rule by *divine right* and exercised unquestioned power over his people united in a national state or empire. The king set his foreign policy goals, assessed the country's strengths and weaknesses—geographic, economic, diplomatic, and military—available to pursue these goals, appointed government officials such as ambassadors and generals to assist him in foreign affairs, attended or sent his representatives to international conferences, and decided the vital questions of war or peace. (In England, after the Glorious Revolution of 1689, the English monarch ruled with the consent of Parliament. His government, nevertheless, was supreme in conducting foreign affairs.)

Foreign policy aspects typical of western Europe from the 17th century onward are illustrated in the following cases:

a. The Hapsburgs of Austria and the Thirty Years' War (1618–1648). The Hapsburgs were a large, devoutly Catholic royal family of western Europe whose leading branch ruled in Austria. In the early 17th century, the Hapsburg emperors of Austria set their foreign policy goals: to protect their family or *dynastic interests* by maintaining Hapsburg relatives on the thrones of lesser European states such as Bohemia (part of modern Czechoslovakia), to strengthen their control over the Germanies, and to defend Catholicism by stopping the spread of Protestantism. To achieve these goals, the Hapsburgs counted their strengths: Austria's strategic location in West-Central Europe, its prosperous economy able to support large armies and to provide funds for hiring mercenaries, its sizable and mainly Catholic population to provide men for military service, and, finally, the friendship and even active support of other Catholic rulers. The Hapsburgs also faced weaknesses: Austria's diverse nationalities —especially its Hungarian and Slavic peoples—might not be interested in Hapsburg dynastic and Germanic goals; some of Austria's people, notably the Czechs in Bohemia, were Protestants; the Hapsburgs would meet opposition from Protestant rulers in the Germanies and northern Europe, and, finally, as events proved, Austria would be opposed by the Bourbon rulers of France, who although Catholic, would seek to further their own national and dynastic interests. In 1618 Austria began a long and costly struggle known as the *Thirty Years' War.* It was fought almost entirely in the Germanies, involved many countries, and ended in 1648 with the *Treaty of Westphalia.* Although the Hapsburgs retained a family member on the throne of Bohemia, they failed to stop the spread of Protestantism in the Germanies and further were compelled to recognize the independence of two former Hapsburg possessions, now Protestant Switzerland and Protestant Holland.

(*Hugo Grotius,* a Dutch scholar, was shocked by the behavior of countries in resorting to and callously fighting the Thirty Years' War. He wrote *Law of War and Peace,* a book that called attention to the need for international regulations to govern wartime problems such as the status of noncombatants and the treatment of military prisoners. Grotius' work is considered the foundation of modern international law.)

b. Louis XIV and France's "Natural Boundaries." When Louis XIV, of the Bourbon family, became king in 1643, France was already a strong and populous nation-state with a powerful central government. Louis proclaimed his "divine right" to rule, exercised unlimited powers, built the magnificent Palace at Versailles, and became known as the *Sun King* or *Grand Monarch.* Louis XIV was ably served by his ministers: especially his finance minister, Colbert; his war minister, Louvois; and his generals Condé and Turenne. Louis XIV set his foreign policy goals: to further the dynastic interests of the Bourbon family, to make France supreme on the European continent, and to achieve France's natural boundaries—the Rhine River, the Alps, and the Pyrenees Mountains. Louis' ambitions to dominate Europe led most other continental countries and England to unite against him. Louis led France into four major wars which consumed French manpower, devoured French finances, and weakened the French economy. Although he placed a Bourbon relative on the throne of Spain, and acquired some minor territories, Louis failed to achieve France's natural boundaries. At Louis' death in 1715, France was the leading nation of Europe but did not dominate the continent. The French people, however, were weary of wars, heavy taxes, and despotism—and would eventually express their displeasure in the 1789 French Revolution.

    c. England and the "Balance of Power." By the early 16th century, England was a unified national state with a strong central government headed by a ruler of the Tudor family. Under Henry VIII (ruled 1509–1547), England broke with the Catholic Church and became a Protestant (Anglican) nation. England's economy—based then on agriculture, handicraft industry, and trade—was prosperous. Because England is an island separated from the European continent by at least 20 miles of English Channel waters, the English emphasized maritime activities. They built merchant ships for trade, established colonies throughout the world, and depended upon their navy for protection against invasion. Toward the continent of Europe, the English government pursued a fixed foreign policy goal—the *balance of power.* In accordance with this concept, England strove to prevent any one continental country from becoming all-powerful and dominating Europe. In a divided Europe, England could shift her support from one country to another and thereby wield the "balance of power."

    England's major wars resulted, at least in considerable part, from her adherence to the balance-of-power concept. In the latter 16th century, England fought Hapsburg Spain and defeated the Spanish Armada (1588) in part to prevent Hapsburg domination of Europe. In the 17th and early 18th centuries, England joined continental alliances and fought Louis XIV in part to prevent French domination of Europe. In the early 19th century, England joined continental alliances and fought Napoleon, in part again to prevent French domination of Europe. In two 20th-century wars, England joined in alliances with France and Russia in part to prevent German domination of Europe.

3. Implications for the United States. Out of the experiences of the European countries in foreign affairs, Americans deduced the following: (*a*) In international affairs, the nation exercises complete and independent authority, that is, *national sovereignty.* (*b*) In international affairs, each nation has complete control over its citizens and should speak with a single voice. (*c*) In setting foreign policy goals, the nation should realistically consider its strengths and weaknesses—geographic location, economy, population, ideology, and allies. (*d*) The nation should have sufficient power to achieve its foreign policy pledges or *commitments.* If commitments exceed the power of the nation to achieve them, then the foreign policy goals will not be reached. (*e*) The nation's foreign policy goals may conflict with those of another nation and sometimes lead to threats of war or war itself. In order to pursue its foreign policy successfully, the nation needs a strong military establishment. (*f*) With foreign policy conflicts inevitable, the nations of the world need the development of international organizations and law—in peacetime to settle disputes by reason, negotiation, and compromise; in wartime to prevent unnecessary cruelty and destruction.

GOALS OF AMERICAN FOREIGN POLICY

1. General Statement. The purpose of American foreign policy is to protect and preserve the *national interest*. What specifically constitutes the national interest?

2. Specific Goals

a. Political: To assure the survival of the United States as a free and independent nation; defend its territories and people; protect American citizens in foreign countries; further democracy throughout the world and view favorably any nation sharing our democratic outlook; disapprove of and, depending upon the circumstances, oppose any nation maligning democracy and advocating a conflicting governmental system such as military dictatorship, fascism, and communism.

b. Military: To maintain a strong military establishment; secure strategic military bases outside the United States; join in agreements and alliances for mutual protection, preferably with nations sharing our democratic philosophy; prevent any potentially hostile power from gaining military bases that could menace the United States; and, with the danger of nuclear war today between the United States and Communist Russia threatening near-total destruction of both nations, prevent misunderstandings and resolve issues peacefully so as to avoid an all-out nuclear war.

c. Economic: To assist American farmers and manufacturers who *export* products to foreign markets; assist American corporations that *import* raw materials, farm produce, and some manufactured goods from foreign nations; protect American workers and businessmen against competition of underpriced foreign-made goods produced by cheap labor; protect *foreign investments* of American individuals and corporations against harassment and *nationalization* (seizure) of their properties without payment of fair compensation by foreign governments; secure repayment of governmental and private loans made to foreign nations.

d. Idealism as a Goal. American national interests frequently have been expressed in terms of *high principles and idealism.* During World War I, President Wilson proclaimed America's goal *"to make the world safe for democracy."* During the 1930's, President Roosevelt urged American relations with the nations of Latin America to be based on the *"policy of the good neighbor."* These idealistic expressions were meant to present American foreign policy in its most favorable light, to gain the support of the American people, and to win world public opinion. These idealistic expressions were not meant to deny the existence of more realistic—political, military, and economic—foreign policy goals. The line separating idealistic from realistic foreign policy goals is difficult to determine. It would be inaccurate, however, to conclude that idealism has governed all foreign policy, as it would be inaccurate to claim that idealism has had no influence.

3. Relationship of Commitment to Power. In pursuit of its national interest, the United States has made implicit or explicit *commitments*. In making commitments, American leaders should be certain that the nation has the determination and the power to make good on its pledges. Obviously, if the nation undertakes a foreign policy commitment beyond its determination and power to support, then the nation will not achieve that foreign policy goal. Conversely, if the nation has sufficient determination and power to live up to its commitments, then the nation's foreign policy will be successful. (For American foreign policy commitments, check the Index for "Monroe Doctrine" and "Open Door Policy.")

CONSIDERATIONS REGARDING AMERICAN FOREIGN POLICY

1. International Cooperation and Foreign Policy. The United States has conducted its foreign policy as a free and independent nation exercising complete *national sovereignty*. Like other sovereign nations, the United States has been reluctant to yield any of its powers to regional or international organizations for fear of harming the national interest. National sovereignty, thusly, has been a major obstacle to the development of effective regional and international organizations.

In recent years, however, most nations have tended to join in regional and international agreements and organizations. The United States, for example, has joined in a grouping of Western Hemisphere nations—the *Organization of American States* (OAS), and has actively participated in the major international organization—the *United Nations* (UN). This trend is rooted in the belief that American national interest can in some ways be best furthered through international cooperation. American membership in the OAS may further the military protection of the Western Hemisphere and spur American economic interests in Latin America, and American activity in the UN may help to resolve international disputes peacefully and to reduce the risk of all-out nuclear war.

Supporters of international cooperation solemnly believe that if nations strictly adhere to their international obligations and strengthen international law, then they will speed the arrival of a peaceful world order. For the United States, these idealistically minded people urge that our foreign policy also contribute to international cooperation. Can the idealism of international cooperation be made to harmonize with the realities of the national interest?

2. Apparent Conflicts in Foreign Policy. The United States has pursued foreign policies that apparently are in conflict—but not really so. In each case, American leaders have had to decide among several foreign policy goals by setting *priorities*—that is, which goal is first and which goals are of lesser importance.

Although one American goal has been to further foreign trade, since 1960 the United States has maintained an embargo on trade with Communist Cuba—an apparent conflict. Not so, for American leaders have given priority to another goal: to stop the spread of Communist influence in the Western Hemisphere. By denying Cuba access to American markets to sell her raw materials and access to American industry to purchase machinery and replacement parts, American leaders have expected to weaken Cuba economically, thereby lessening her ability to influence other Latin American nations toward communism. The United States thus sacrificed the less important goal—trade—and opted for the more important one—stopping the spread of Communist influence.

Although another American foreign policy goal has been to further democracy, the United States has given substantial economic aid to Latin American military dictatorships—an apparent conflict. Not so, for American leaders have given priority to another foreign policy goal: to further hemispheric unity for mutual protection. American leaders further realize that we could not overthrow the military dictatorships and reshape the political life of these Latin American countries without intervening in their internal affairs—a course of action repugnant to American democracy.

3. Changes in Foreign Policy. In determining a foreign policy to protect the national interest, American leaders must consider three major factors: (a) *domestic conditions* such as the nation's economy, population, government, military strength, and internal problems; (b) *international affairs* such as the foreign policies of other nations, the existence of alliances and war, and public opinion regarding international problems; and (c) the *status of technology* as affecting transportation and weapons. As these factors change over the years, so too may change the nation's foreign policy.

An example: During the Washington administration (1789–1797), the young American nation had a new and untried government, a small population, and limited economic and military strength; witnessed the beginning of a 25-year period of warfare in Europe, the chief contestants being England and France; saw American public opinion sharply divided regarding this European war; and considered Europe far distant since sailing vessels required several weeks to travel the 3000 miles of the Atlantic Ocean. In viewing these factors, President Washington concluded that, to further the national interest, the United States should concentrate upon domestic problems, view Europe's quarrels as not our concern, and avoid entangling alliances and war. Washington consequently began a policy of neutrality which evolved into a policy of isolation.

Today, the modern American nation has a strong and stable government, a large population, a powerful industrial economy with worldwide interests, and enormous military strength; faces repeated challenges from a Russian Communist-led bloc of nations; sees American public opinion united to defend the democratic way of life; is involved in European affairs, as jet airplanes span the Atlantic Ocean in a few hours; and possesses—as does Russia—missiles with nuclear warheads capable of traveling at terrific speeds and causing tremendous destruction. In viewing these factors, American leaders today have concluded that, to further the national interest, the United States must provide leadership for the free world nations and yet seek understandings with Communist Russia that will preserve world peace. The United States, therefore, has pursued a policy of free world leadership.

A second example: Although it happens infrequently, a new Presidential administration may change the foreign policy of its predecessor. After World War I, both the Wilson and Harding administrations held that the national interest required peace. To move toward this goal, Wilson urged international cooperation and membership in the League of Nations; Harding advised a return toward isolation and rejected League membership.

4. Continuity of Foreign Policy. In most cases, succeeding Presidential administrations tend to follow the same foreign policies. In 1823 President Monroe issued the Monroe Doctrine declaring the Western Hemisphere closed to further European colonization. In 1867 President Andrew Johnson enforced the Monroe Doctrine by compelling France to withdraw her military forces from Mexico. In 1895 and again in 1902, Presidents Cleveland and Theodore Roosevelt respectively upheld the Monroe Doctrine.

MAKING OF FOREIGN POLICY TODAY

1. Preeminent Position of the President. The President determines and carries out American foreign policy. His authority derives from his Constitutional powers to receive ambassadors (and therefore to recognize or refuse to recognize foreign governments), to command the armed forces, to negotiate treaties, and to appoint officials concerned with foreign affairs.

The President also has extraconstitutional powers: to rally public opinion, to visit foreign countries, and to sign *executive agreements*. (Such agreements, between the President and the head of a foreign nation, do not have the status of treaties and therefore do not require Senate ratification. An example was the 1940 exchange of 50 American "over-age" destroyers for naval bases on British territory in the Western Hemisphere—an exchange known as the *Destroyer-Naval Base Deal*.)

2. The President's Assistants. The President receives assistance, information, and advice from many government officials appointed mostly by him. His two major assistants are his (*a*) assistant for national security affairs—a member of the White House office, and (*b*) Secretary of State—a member of the Cabinet. The national security assistant, an expert on foreign affairs, is the President's loyal supporter, confidant, and *personal adviser*. He directs a small staff to help him in analyzing and making recommendations regarding the national interest and foreign policy. The Secretary of State, usually a political appointment, is the President's *official adviser*. He has the time-consuming responsibility of administering the State Department with its myriad divisions, its many ambassadors and ministers stationed abroad, and its over 30,000 staff members. Both the national security assistant and the Secretary of State help implement the President's foreign policy decisions by undertaking foreign trips, negotiating with foreign leaders, and testifying before Congressional committees.

The President also receives information and advice from other top State Department personnel such as American ambassadors to foreign countries, American representatives to international organizations, and the head of the *Agency for International Development* (AID), which directs our foreign aid program; from the Secretary of Defense and the *Joint Chiefs of Staff* of the armed forces; from other Cabinet members whose departments affect or are affected by foreign developments; and from the director of the *Central Intelligence Agency* (CIA), which agency is charged with coordinating American intelligence activities as related to national security. The President and his key advisers on foreign policy and national defense together constitute the *National Security Council*.

The President, however, is the nation's chief spokesman on foreign affairs: he makes the final decisions and bears the final responsibility.

3. Role of Congress. The "advice and consent" of the Senate are necessary to approve Presidential appointments, including foreign service personnel, and to ratify treaties. Appointments require a majority vote; treaties, a two-thirds vote. Both houses of Congress must approve expenditures for military and foreign affairs. Both the Senate Foreign Relations Committee and the House International Relations Committee hold hearings, question witnesses, and make recommendations. Congress also has the power to regulate commerce with foreign nations, to voice its opinion upon foreign policy by means of a joint resolution, and, finally, to declare war.

Congress may respond to a President's foreign policy initiative in either *(a)* a *partisan* way, such as in 1919–1920, when generally Senate Republicans clashed with Senate Democrats and defeated President Wilson's treaty for American membership in the League of Nations, or *(b)* a *bipartisan* way, such as in 1945 when both major parties overwhelmingly approved President Truman's request for American membership in the United Nations. In notable instances since 1945, Congress and the President have sought to have "politics stop at the water's edge" and to make American foreign policy bipartisan.

4. Other Influences. The President may be influenced by *(a)* the policies of his predecessors, the views of our allies, the efforts of the United Nations; *(b)* the pressures of lobbyists representing domestic groups—such as business, labor, veterans, and ethnic minorities, and also of lobbyists representing foreign governments; and *(c)* the attitudes of the mass media, educational associations, and poll-taking organizations—which help shape and record public opinion. No matter how great his powers, no President has long maintained a foreign policy at sharp variance with public opinion.

Part 2. The Emerging Nation (From the War for Independence to the Monroe Doctrine)

2. Americans Employ Foreign Policy in Their War for Independence

Outbreak of the American Revolution. As Massachusetts militiamen clashed with British troops in April 1775 at Lexington and Concord, the American Revolution began. The Second Continental Congress, soon thereafter assembled at Philadelphia, took charge of the American war effort. Congress promptly adopted a resolution indicating that the colonies would look for foreign aid in their struggle against Britain.

EXPECTATIONS OF FOREIGN AID

Colonial leaders had high hopes of receiving foreign aid because many European nations, for their own reasons, were hostile to Britain. (1) *France* under Louis XIV had been kept from achieving its "natural boundaries" in major part because of British opposition. Later, in the Seven Years' War (1756–1763), France had been defeated by Britain and compelled to yield India and cede Canada to Britain. (2) *Spain* had been humbled by the British defeat of the Spanish Armada (1588), British raids upon Spanish colonies and treasure ships, and British seizure in 1704 of Gibraltar. (3) *Holland* had lost her New Amsterdam colony to Britain (1664) and resented British competition and interference with Dutch merchant ships. In early 1776, France and Spain agreed to aid the American colonists with money, munitions, and other supplies—but secretly so as not to provoke British reprisals.

THE DECLARATION OF INDEPENDENCE AND FOREIGN POLICY

On July 4, 1776, the Continental Congress declared the American determination to secede from the British Empire by unanimously adopting the Declaration of Independence. Colonial leaders hoped that the Declaration of Independence would enable the Americans to secure further assistance from foreign nations including diplomatic recognition, increased economic aid, and perhaps military assistance.

513

THE FRENCH ALLIANCE (1778)

In late 1776 the Continental Congress appointed a three-man mission to France, the most important member being *Benjamin Franklin*. Witty and unpretentious, Franklin captivated the French populace. He was, however, unable to move the French government to extend greater aid to the American cause —seemingly headed for military defeat. Then came the turning point of the war—the stunning American victory at the battle of *Saratoga* (1777). Franklin used this news with great diplomatic skill. By hinting that the Americans might now accept the generous British proposals for reconciliation, Franklin pressured the French government formally to recognize the independence of the United States and to enter into a treaty of alliance.

The *Franco-American Treaty of Alliance* provided that (1) both nations would fight as long as necessary to assure American independence, (2) neither nation would conclude a peace with Britain without the consent of the other, and (3) each nation would guarantee the American territories of the other forever. (France held small but valuable sugar-producing islands in the West Indies.)

OTHER FOREIGN ASSISTANCE AGAINST BRITAIN

(1) Spain. Spain was unwilling to recognize American independence but wanted to regain Gibraltar from Britain. In 1779 Spain joined France in the war against Britain, thereby indirectly helping the American cause militarily. Later Spain granted the Americans a small loan. (2) Holland. Dutch merchants had built up a profitable wartime trade with the Americans, much being in *contraband*—that is, goods destined for war use. To act against this trade, Britain in 1780 declared war on Holland. Thereafter, Holland formally recognized American independence and extended a sizable loan.

FRENCH MILITARY ASSISTANCE AND THE AMERICAN VICTORY AT YORKTOWN (1781)

In 1780 a French army of 5000 men under the Count *de Rochambeau* arrived in Rhode Island and later joined the American army of 9000 men in New York under General Washington. At the same time French Admiral *de Grasse* informed Washington that he was bringing his entire fleet from the West Indies for several months of operations along the Atlantic Coast.

With British General Cornwallis resting his 8000-man army at Yorktown, a Virginia seaport, Washington moved quickly. He and Rochambeau marched their troops southward into Virginia to besiege Cornwallis' forces on land while de Grasse brought the French fleet into Chesapeake Bay and cut off Cornwallis' escape route by sea. Cornwallis surrendered as the bands played "the world turned upside down." This victory marked the end of the war and assured American independence.

TREATY OF PARIS (1783)

Displaying considerable diplomatic skill, the American negotiators —Benjamin Franklin, John Jay, and John Adams—secured highly favorable terms from Britain and then maneuvered France to consent, as required by the

Franco-American alliance, to the formal treaty of peace. (1) Britain recognized the 13 United States as independent. The new nation was bounded (*a*) on the north by Canada and the Great Lakes, (*b*) on the south by Spanish-owned Florida, (*c*) on the east by the Atlantic Ocean, and (*d*) on the west by the Mississippi River. (See map, below.) (2) The Americans retained their previous rights to fish on the banks off Newfoundland. (3) The United States agreed to recommend to the various states the restoration of confiscated Loyalist properties and the payment of debts owed to British merchants. (This provision was little heeded by the state governments.)

The United States After the Treaty of Paris (1783)

Commenting on this treaty, historian Thomas Bailey in his *Diplomatic History of the American People* stated that the Americans could not "have received such generous terms if Britain had not been at war with three European powers" and further that "Europe's international distresses . . . spelled America's diplomatic successes."

3. The Articles of Confederation Prove Ineffectual in Foreign Affairs

Weaknesses of the Articles of Confederation Regarding Foreign Affairs. Under the Articles to 1789, the United States was unable to conduct a successful foreign policy, in considerable part because of governmental weaknesses. The Articles lacked a chief executive who could conduct foreign policy. Its Congress lacked several vital powers: to raise an army directly by recruiting men, to levy taxes directly upon the people, and to control foreign commerce. (For details of the weaknesses of the Articles of Confederation, check the Index.)

THE DISMAL RECORD IN FOREIGN AFFAIRS

1. British Refusal to Enter Into a Commercial Treaty. Britain refused American requests for a commercial treaty granting reciprocal trading privileges to British and American merchants. British merchants, dealing with the individual states, were already conducting a thriving business in America. Britain further realized that the American government could not enforce treaty provisions upon the 13 states.

2. British and Spanish Prohibitions Against American Shipping. To protect British merchants, Britain closed her West Indies ports to American ships. Spain, which controlled both banks of the lower Mississippi (see map, page 515), there forbade American shipping. Spain realized that American settlers on the Western frontier depended upon the lower Mississippi for transporting their agricultural produce. Spain hoped that the Western settlers would break away from the United States and accept Spanish rule.

3. British Retention of Posts in the Northwest Territory. In violation of the Treaty of Paris, the British retained their military and trading posts on American soil (see map, page 517). To justify their keeping these posts, the British argued that the United States was violating the Treaty of Paris by its failure to restore Loyalist estates and repay British merchants. The central government made no effort to oust the British from American territory.

By such open hostility and disdain for the United States, foreign nations helped Americans realize the weaknesses of the Articles of Confederation and drove them to adopt a stronger form of central government—under the Constitution.

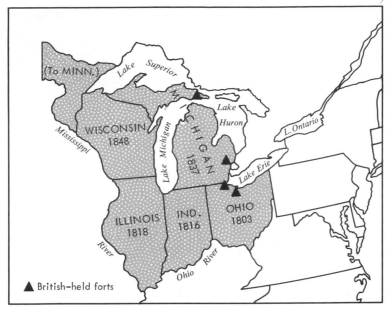

Northwest Territory

4. The Young and Relatively Weak Nation Seeks Neutrality and Isolation

FRENCH REVOLUTION OF 1789 STIRS AMERICA

Washington's inauguration as first President of the new nation coincided with the beginning of a 25-year period of revolution and warfare in Europe. In 1789 began the French Revolution, which led to the *Reign of Terror*—a short period of brutal suppression of all persons considered enemies of the Revolution—and to an armed struggle between France and a group of conservative European nations: Austria, Prussia, and Great Britain. (In 1799 France fell under the rule of the ambitious Napoleon Bonaparte, and until 1815 Europe experienced almost continuous warfare. The chief contestants were France and Britain. The prize was the domination of Europe.)

American public opinion sharply divided in regard to the early phase of the French Revolution and the outbreak of war in Europe.

1. Thomas Jefferson and his followers, who adhered to the Democratic-Republican party, were the liberals and pro-French. They sympathized with the French Revolution, contending that the French were fighting for democracy, and pointing to similarities between the French and American Revolutions. The French (*a*) had overthrown the authority of their king, (*b*) had issued the *Declaration of*

the Rights of Man, and *(c)* had proclaimed their democratic ideals as "liberty, equality, fraternity."

2. Alexander Hamilton and his followers, who backed the Federalist party, were the conservatives and pro-English. They favored the English government, which was dominated by the aristocratic upper classes, and they were hostile toward the French Revolution, pointing to the Reign of Terror as evidence of the "excesses of democracy."

WASHINGTON'S PROCLAMATION OF NEUTRALITY (1793)

President Washington deplored the violent division of American public opinion regarding the European war. He further feared that, in accordance with the 1778 Franco-American treaty of alliance, the French republic would call for American military assistance and would expect the use of American ports to outfit expeditions against British ships and colonies.

President Washington believed that for the young nation to become involved in the European war would be suicidal. His views were supported by Hamilton and Jefferson, both of whom urged neutrality. Washington issued a *Proclamation of Neutrality.* He declared the United States at peace with both Britain and France and urged Americans to be impartial toward the warring nations.

"CITIZEN" GENÊT AFFAIR (1793)

The French ambassador to the United States, "Citizen" Edmond Genêt, played upon the pro-French sentiments of many American citizens. Defying Washington's Proclamation of Neutrality, he outfitted privateers (privately owned armed ships) in American harbors and commissioned them to raid British ships and colonies.

Fearing that Genêt would involve the United States in a war against Great Britain, Washington ordered Genêt to halt these activities and, when this order was ignored, demanded Genêt's recall by the French government. Washington thus halted an attempt to breach our neutrality.

JAY TREATY WITH BRITAIN (1794–1795)

1. Background. Americans were aroused against Britain because: *(a)* The British navy was seizing American merchant ships bound for French ports. Such seizures violated *freedom of the seas:* the right of a neutral nation to trade with belligerents in *noncontraband*—that is, goods not intended for war use. *(b)* The British were impressing some American sailors into the British navy, claiming they were deserters. *(c)* The British were holding posts in the Northwest Territory. *(d)* The British, many Americans believed, were encouraging the Indians to raid American frontier settlements. To avoid war, Washington sent John Jay to London to settle the outstanding issues.

2. Provisions. England, confident that the United States would not go to war, made few concessions. The resulting *Jay Treaty* provided that *(a)* Great Britain withdraw its troops from the American Northwest, and *(b)* arbitration commissions settle financial claims of Americans against Britain and of the British against the United States.

3. American Reaction to the Treaty. The terms of the treaty further aroused American resentment. The treaty *(a)* did *not* provide for freedom of the seas, and *(b)* did *not* pledge England to halt the seizure of American ships or the impressment of American sailors. The treaty secured minimal Senate ratification only through the full influence of Hamilton and Washington. In spite of its failings, the Jay Treaty meant that the young, relatively weak nation would remain at peace with Britain.

PINCKNEY TREATY WITH SPAIN (1795)

Spain was alarmed by the Jay Treaty because she feared a secret Anglo-American alliance to seize her Florida and Louisiana territories. Spain therefore negotiated outstanding problems with the United States.

The resulting *Pinckney Treaty* (1) established the Mississippi as the western boundary and the 31st parallel as the southern boundary of the United States (see map, page 515), and (2) guaranteed Americans free navigation of the entire Mississippi and the *right of deposit* at New Orleans—the right to transfer goods from riverboats to oceangoing ships without payment of a Spanish tariff. The Pinckney Treaty was an American triumph.

WASHINGTON'S FAREWELL ADDRESS (1796)

Prior to his retirement as President, George Washington issued his *Farewell Address*. He advised the new nation regarding its future course. In foreign affairs, Washington urged developing commercial relations with all nations but avoiding political entanglements. He stated, "It is our true policy to steer clear of permanent alliances with any portion of the foreign world." He added, however, that the United States could "safely trust to temporary alliances for extraordinary emergencies."

The Farewell Address urged a policy of noninvolvement, not isolation—a significant but subtle distinction. In practical effect, Washington's words strongly influenced the United States toward remaining politically aloof from the rest of the world by following a foreign policy of *isolation*.

PRESIDENT ADAMS AND DIFFICULTIES WITH FRANCE (1797–1801)

1. French Hostility. French resentment against American foreign policy created serious problems for our second President, John Adams. The French government had been angered by *(a)* Washington's Proclamation of Neutrality and *(b)* Senate ratification of the Jay Treaty. French warships and privateers began attacking American merchant ships. Anti-French sentiment developed in the United States, and many Federalists demanded war.

2. XYZ Affair (1797). Seeking peace, President Adams sent a special negotiating mission to Paris. The delegation was insulted by French agents who demanded that, before talks begin, the Americans pay a large bribe. Adams, enraged, reported the episode to Congress, identifying the French agents only as X, Y, and Z. Hence the incident became known as the *XYZ Affair*. American public opinion reacted with an outburst of anti-French feeling illustrated by the slogan, "Millions for defense, but not one cent for tribute."

3. Undeclared Naval Warfare (1798–1800). Congress voted large military funds, especially to build up the navy, and in 1798 established a Cabinet-level Navy Department. American warships and privateers engaged in an undeclared war with France, capturing about 100 French vessels.

Although Hamilton wanted to expand the war, Adams steadfastly desired peace. In 1800 he sent a second mission to France, now controlled by Napoleon Bonaparte. Both countries agreed to end the naval conflict and to cancel the 1778 treaty of alliance. Adams lost popularity with prowar Federalists at home, but he ended the French treaty that had proved so troublesome to American foreign policy makers and, most important, he restored the peace.

PRESIDENT JEFFERSON AND THE PURCHASE OF LOUISIANA (1803)

1. Importance of the Mississippi River and New Orleans. At the beginning of the 19th century, the settlers west of the Appalachians found it difficult to send their bulky agricultural produce overland to Eastern markets and seaports. Instead, they depended for transportation upon the Mississippi River and the port of New Orleans. By the Pinckney Treaty with Spain (1795), the Americans had received the right of deposit at New Orleans.

2. Napoleon and the Louisiana Territory. In 1800 Napoleon Bonaparte secretly secured the vast Louisiana Territory from Spain. In 1802 the right of deposit was suspended. This action enraged the Western settlers and underlined the opinion of President Jefferson that the foreign nation possessing New Orleans "is our natural and habitual enemy." Jefferson quickly instructed Robert Livingston and James Monroe to negotiate with France for the purchase of New Orleans. Meanwhile, Napoleon decided to sell the entire territory. He (a) needed money to carry on his war against Britain, (b) could not defend the territory while the British navy controlled the seas, and (c) had abandoned plans for an American empire—in part because his armies had been unable to suppress a slave revolt in Santo Domingo begun by the Negro leader *Toussaint L'Ouverture.* Livingston and Monroe readily agreed to a purchase price of $15 million.

3. Constitutional Problem. Jefferson was disturbed by the agreement, for the Constitution did not specifically give the federal government the power to purchase territory. A "strict" interpreter of the Constitution, Jefferson suggested a Constitutional amendment to provide the necessary power. However, he was warned that delay might lead Napoleon to withdraw his offer. Jefferson consequently agreed to purchase Louisiana under the Presidential power to make treaties, thus adopting a loose interpretation of the Constitution.

4. Significance. The purchase of Louisiana (a) almost doubled the area and greatly increased the wealth of the United States, (b) gave the United States control of the entire Mississippi, (c) removed French influence in North America, (d) established a precedent for future purchases of territory, and (e) moved the Democratic-Republicans toward a loose interpretation of the Constitution.

MULTIPLE-CHOICE QUESTIONS

1. Which was typical of the feudal system?   (1) It advanced democracy by reducing the power of the kings.   (2) It promoted peace because of the weakness of national states.   (3) It encouraged the development of economic interdependence.   (4) It provided local or decentralized government.
2. Which factor *most* often contributes to a feeling of nationalism among a group of people?   (1) use of a common language   (2) low population density   (3) presence of a large peasant class   (4) agreement between major political parties
3. The balance of power concept explains all of England's wars *except* the war against   (1) Germany under Hitler   (2) France under Napoleon   (3) the 13 colonies under Washington   (4) Germany under the Kaiser.
4. The foreign policy of a nation is based *primarily* on that nation's interpretation of its   (1) moral commitments to others   (2) imperialist desires   (3) people's demands   (4) national interests.
5. Which characteristic of a nation-state has been *most* deeply questioned by supporters of international cooperation?   (1) national sovereignty   (2) democratic government   (3) a nationally supported religion   (4) public education for all
6. Which would probably promote the *greatest* degree of cooperation among the people of a nation?   (1) the election of a new national leader   (2) a threat to national security from an outside force   (3) the discovery of a new product that will improve the nation's economy   (4) the decision to join an international peacekeeping organization
7. Which is the *most* valid conclusion that may be drawn from a study of United States foreign policy?   (1) Each new administration initiates a new foreign policy.   (2) Foreign policy reflects what is presumed to be the self-interest of the nation.   (3) The Department of State is an autonomous agency.   (4) Pressure groups determine foreign policy.
8. Since the founding of the United States, the formulation of foreign policy has been the responsibility of the   (1) President   (2) diplomatic corps   (3) Cabinet   (4) Congress.
9. The official method by which the United States recognizes a foreign government is by   (1) an act of Congress   (2) an exchange of ambassadors   (3) a treaty of friendship   (4) a Presidential visit.
10. Which condition must exist in order to establish a bipartisan foreign policy in the United States?   (1) A new foreign policy must be created every two years.   (2) The Army and the Navy must be under one Defense Department.   (3) The President and Congress must be controlled by the same party.   (4) Both political parties must be in general agreement as to major foreign policy goals.
11. Which is an important check on the President's control of foreign policy?   (1) Congress must approve appropriations.   (2) The House of Representatives must approve Presidential appointments.   (3) The Senate can remove ambassadors.   (4) The Central Intelligence Agency must approve the admission of foreign diplomats to the United States.
12. Because of the treaty-making procedure provided in the Constitution, some Presidents have   (1) negotiated executive agreements instead of treaties   (2) vetoed proposed Constitutional amendments curbing the treaty power   (3) obtained advisory opinions from the Supreme Court before submitting treaties to the Senate   (4) referred treaties to the House of Representatives instead of to the Senate.
13. The primary motive behind French aid to the United States during the Revolutionary War was the French government's desire to   (1) regain Canada and Florida   (2) promote the principles of the French Revolution   (3) force British evacuation of

French islands in the West Indies (4) obtain revenge against Great Britain for previous French colonial losses.

14. Relations between France and the United States during the American Revolution were affected by all of the following *except* the (1) battle of Saratoga (2) diplomacy of Benjamin Franklin (3) "Citizen" Genêt affair (4) battle of Yorktown.

15. As a result of the Treaty of Paris (1783), the United States was bounded by all of the following *except* the (1) Atlantic Ocean (2) Great Lakes (3) Mississippi River (4) Gulf of Mexico.

16. The *chief* goal of President George Washington's foreign policy was to (1) persuade Spain to grant independence to her American colonies (2) maintain the neutrality of the United States (3) prohibit United States commercial contacts with Europe (4) extend the boundaries of the United States beyond the Mississippi River.

17. President Washington's reason for issuing the Proclamation of Neutrality was his desire to (1) fulfill our obligations to France (2) protect our interests in the Caribbean area (3) safeguard our newly won independence (4) unify the country on foreign policy.

18. The Jay Treaty was criticized for its failure to provide for (1) arbitration as a method of settling disputes (2) British withdrawal of troops in the Northwest (3) the prevention of impressment (4) trade with the British East Indies.

19. In his Farewell Address, Washington warned the United States against (1) expansion westward beyond the Mississippi (2) the imperialistic ideas of Napoleon (3) permanent alliances with foreign nations (4) quarrels with England over commerce.

20. The XYZ Affair showed that (1) Americans would not tolerate French seizure of Louisiana (2) Americans were developing a sense of national pride (3) our government was pursuing a policy of aggression (4) our government was still bound to its alliance with France.

21. "The moment France takes possession of New Orleans, we must marry ourselves to the British fleet and nation." This argument influenced the United States to (1) enter into a treaty of alliance with Spain (2) purchase the Louisiana Territory from France (3) become involved in a naval war with France (4) adopt neutrality legislation.

22. The primary reason for our purchase of the Louisiana Territory was to provide (1) people on the frontier with unrestricted use of the Mississippi River (2) Napoleon with money in return for French assistance during the American Revolution (3) New England manufacturers with a source of cheap raw materials (4) land for Indian reservations.

23. Which was a direct result of the purchase of the Louisiana Territory? (1) an amendment to the Constitution permitting the federal government to purchase land (2) the opening of a vast region for fur trading and land development (3) the loss of Canada by France (4) the elimination of Spain from the North American continent

ESSAY QUESTIONS

1. Foreign policy makers seek to protect and preserve the *national interest*. In so doing, they establish policies and often must set *priorities*. (*a*) Explain the meaning, in terms of foreign policy, of the italicized terms. (*b*) For the United States today, what would you consider to be *two* major aspects of the national interest? Defend your answer. (*c*) Suggest *three* foreign policies to further the national interests you have identified. (*d*) To which *one* of these foreign policies would you give top priority? Why?

2. Below are *three* groups of terms representing concepts of foreign policy. For *each* group (*a*) explain the meaning of the concepts and (*b*) explain if the paired concepts support or conflict with each other: (1) idealism—realism (2) commitment—power (3) national sovereignty—international cooperation.

3. Many individuals and groups have important roles in the making of American foreign policy. For *each* of the following pairs, *(a)* explain which *one* is more important in making American foreign policy and *(b)* give *two* reasons to support your opinion: (1) President *or* Congress (2) Senate *or* House of Representatives (3) White House assistant for national security affairs *or* Secretary of State (4) Central Intelligence Agency *or* National Security Council (5) newspapers *or* television.
4. For *each* of the following Presidents, *(a)* describe *one* foreign policy that was adopted *(b)* explain how that foreign policy was expected to protect and preserve the national interest and *(c)* evaluate the success or failure of that foreign policy: (1) George Washington (2) John Adams (3) Thomas Jefferson.

5. The Young Nation, Growing in Power, Asserts Itself in Foreign Affairs

After two decades, the United States had achieved a stable and effective government, a prosperous but chiefly agricultural economy, a population that had almost doubled, and a budding spirit of national loyalty. The government still adhered to the policy of isolation but it became more assertive of American national interest.

NAPOLEONIC WARS: FRANCE AGAINST GREAT BRITAIN (1803–1815)

In 1803 France and Britain renewed their conflict, and for the next 12 years they fought a life-and-death struggle for control of Europe. While, at first, France held supremacy on land, Britain dominated the seas. Their struggle is often referred to as the battle of "the tiger against the shark."

1. Economic Warfare. While military action was temporarily stalemated, the two countries endeavored to strike at each other economically. Napoleon issued the *Berlin* and *Milan Decrees* (1806–1807) restricting neutral trade with England. The British government issued *Orders in Council* (1806–1807) restricting neutral trade with the French-held continent. Since Britain had the stronger navy, her blockade of the European continent was far more successful than France's blockade of the British Isles.

2. Effect Upon the United States. In his Inaugural Address, Jefferson had reaffirmed Washington's foreign policy and had urged the United States to seek "peace, commerce, and honest friendship with all nations, entangling alliances with none." Now with Britain and France blockading each other, neutral American commerce was leading the United States not to "honest friendship," but to serious crises. American shippers, in large numbers, were carrying on a prosperous but risky trade with wartime Europe. If only one out of every three ships carrying foodstuffs and raw materials got through the blockades, its profits more than made up for the losses of ships caught. The greater damage to American commerce was inflicted by the British, who, in addition to seizing many

American ships, impressed several thousand American sailors into British service, claiming that they were deserters from the British navy.

3. Chesapeake-Leopard Affair (1807). Off the Virginia coast the captain of the *Leopard*, a British warship, demanded to search the American navy vessel *Chesapeake*. When the captain of the *Chesapeake* refused, the British fired on the *Chesapeake*, boarded her, and took off four seamen as deserters. Three were American citizens. This indignity inflamed the American public to demand that Jefferson take retaliatory action.

EMBARGO ACT AND ITS EFFECTS (1807–1809)

To avoid war, Jefferson secured from Congress the *Embargo Act* (1807), which forbade American ships to sail to foreign ports and prohibited American exports to all foreign countries. Jefferson believed that, by depriving Britain and France of our foodstuffs and raw materials, the United States could compel these nations to change their policies toward American shipping. However, the "peaceable coercion" of the Embargo did not sufficiently distress the warring nations.

In the maritime New England states, meanwhile, the Embargo brought considerable economic damage, almost completely destroying the region's commerce and causing widespread unemployment. Jefferson and the Embargo were roundly condemned by New England Federalists. The agricultural sections—South and West—were also somewhat distressed as they lost foreign markets for their farm produce. In 1809 Jefferson signed the *Non-Intercourse Act*, repealing the Embargo Act but continuing the prohibition on trade with Britain and France.

MADISON AND THE DRIFT TO WAR (1809–1812)

1. Efforts for Peace. James Madison, who succeeded Jefferson as President, tried for three years to protect American shipping by diplomatic negotiations, but he was unsuccessful. Meanwhile, the war spirit in America continued to grow.

2. "War Hawks." In 1810 Southern and Western voters elected to Congress a group of Democratic-Republicans called the "War Hawks." Led by *John Calhoun* of South Carolina and *Henry Clay* of Kentucky, they demanded war against Britain to acquire Canada and against Britain's ally, Spain, to acquire Florida. These acquisitions, they argued, would remove European powers from American borders and would open new lands for liberty-loving Americans.

In 1812 Madison surrendered to the war spirit and asked Congress for a declaration of war against Britain.

CAUSES OF THE WAR OF 1812

(1) Britain's seizure of American ships and impressment of American sailors. (Madison's war message emphasized these actions as violations of our "freedom of the seas.") (2) American resentment of Britain, dating back to Revolutionary

days. (3) American belief, probably correct, that the British in Canada were arming the Indians and inciting them to raid American settlements. (4) American ambitions to annex Canada and Florida.

Historians have long debated the primary cause of the war: maritime rights or territorial ambitions? The Congressional vote favoring war—by little more than a majority—showed that the Northeast, which was most directly concerned with maritime rights, was mainly opposed to the war. The South and West, which were most strongly for territorial expansion, were wholeheartedly in favor of the war.

MILITARY EVENTS OF THE WAR (1812–1815)

(1) American attempts to invade Canada all proved unsuccessful. (2) British attempts to invade the United States from Canada were thwarted when British naval squadrons were defeated on Lake Erie and on Lake Champlain. (3) On the high seas, American privateers and naval vessels—notably the warships *Constitution* (nicknamed "Old Ironsides") and *United States*—at first won great victories. In time, however, the British navy asserted its superiority and instituted a tight blockade of the American coast. (4) The British invaded the Chesapeake Bay area, captured Washington, D.C., burned many government buildings, and then advanced on Fort McHenry at Baltimore. Fort McHenry withstood the British bombardment, inspiring Francis Scott Key to write *The Star-Spangled Banner*. (5) The British attempted an invasion of the American Southwest but were decisively defeated at New Orleans. Andrew Jackson, the American commander, overnight became a national hero. (With modern methods of communication, this battle would not have been fought, since a peace treaty had already been signed in Europe.)

TREATY OF GHENT (1814)

At Ghent, Belgium, British and American negotiators arranged a treaty of peace that reestablished the prewar boundaries of the United States. The treaty did not mention the seizure of American ships and the impressment of American sailors. However, with the European war over, these issues were no longer crucial.

RESULTS OF THE WAR OF 1812

(1) Strengthening Isolation. Americans turned away from European affairs and concentrated upon domestic matters. (2) Spurring Westward Migration. Having lost maritime jobs, some New Englanders went westward. Their travels were safer since several war battles had destroyed hostile Indian forces. (3) Encouraging Industry. With British imports cut off, American capitalists increased domestic manufactures, especially textiles. (4) Inspiring Nationalism. Rejoicing in their military achievements, Americans felt greater pride in their country. The War of 1812, therefore, is often called the "Second War for American Independence."

AGREEMENTS REGARDING OUR NORTHERN BOUNDARY WITH CANADA

1. Rush-Bagot Agreement (1817). In this treaty, negotiated by Richard Rush for the United States and Charles Bagot for Great Britain, the two nations agreed to naval disarmament on the Great Lakes. Later, this agreement was extended to provide for disarmament along the land border between the United States and Canada. Today, the entire 3000-mile United States-Canadian border remains unfortified. The Rush-Bagot Agreement was significant in that Britain treated the United States as an equal.

2. Treaty Line of 1818. This treaty fixed the boundary line between the United States and Canada at the 49th parallel of latitude from Lake of the Woods (in northern Minnesota) to the Rocky Mountains. The treaty also provided that the United States and Britain jointly occupy the Oregon Country.

PURCHASE OF FLORIDA FROM SPAIN (1819)

1. Spanish-Owned Florida: A Trouble Spot. In the hands of Spain, Florida housed pirates, smugglers, runaway slaves, and Seminole Indians. With the Spanish authorities too weak to restrain them, the Indians raided American settlements in the Southeast and then retreated to safety across the Florida border.

In 1818 Andrew Jackson led an American military force into Florida, crushed the Seminole Indians, and captured two Spanish forts. Spain had already lost West Florida to the United States, and she now realized that unless she sold the rest of Florida she might lose it by force.

2. Adams-Onis Treaty. Secretary of State *John Quincy Adams* and Spanish minister *Luis de Onis* agreed that Spain sell Florida to the United States for $5 million. Also called the *Transcontinental Treaty*, this agreement provided that the United States give up claims to Texas and that Spain accept the 42nd parallel as the boundary between Spain's rebellious colony of Mexico and the Oregon Country.

Although the South gained the most, the entire country with nationalist fervor supported the purchase of Florida.

MONROE DOCTRINE (1823)

1. Latin American Independence. While Spain was entangled in the Napoleonic Wars, the inhabitants of Spain's colonies in Latin America revolted and began a series of wars for independence. (Brazil, meanwhile, threw off the rule of Portugal.) Spanish attempts to retain control were defeated by the colonists under the leadership of *José de San Martin, Bernardo O'Higgins*, and the "George Washington of South America," *Simón Bolívar.*

The United States hailed Latin American independence because *(a)* the American Revolution against Britain had helped inspire the Latin American colonists, *(b)* the United States preferred having weak independent republics to the south instead of the more powerful monarchical Spain, and *(c)* American merchants and shippers were building up a profitable trade with independent

Latin American countries. Such trade had previously been barred by Spain, whose mercantilist regulations required her colonies to trade only with the mother country.

2. Immediate Causes for Issuing the Doctrine. In 1823 President Monroe was faced with two threats of foreign intervention in the Western Hemisphere. *(a)* A reactionary European alliance of Austria, Prussia, France, and Russia—all opposed to revolution anywhere—was rumored planning to reconquer Latin America for Spain. *(b)* Russian expansion southward from Alaska toward Oregon and California constituted a threat to ultimate American expansion to the Pacific.

3. Rejection of the British Proposal for a Joint Declaration. Britain too opposed the restoration of Spanish control in Latin America, since British merchants had also built up a profitable trade with the new nations. *George Canning*, the British foreign minister, proposed that Britain and the United States issue a joint declaration warning Europe against any attempt to deny independence to Latin America.

John Quincy Adams, the American Secretary of State, vigorously opposed a joint declaration. He insisted that we act alone, as befits a proud, independent, nationalistic people. Adams did not want the United States to appear as a tiny boat coming "in the wake of the British man-of-war." Adams' point of view and much of his phrasing were accepted by Monroe. In his annual message to Congress, Monroe included a statement of Presidential foreign policy which became known as the *Monroe Doctrine*.

4. Basic Ideas of the Doctrine. *(a)* The Western Hemisphere was closed to further European colonization. *(b)* The United States would not interfere with the existing colonies of any European power. *(c)* The United States would not interfere in the internal affairs of any European power. *(d)* Any attempt by European powers to intervene in the Western Hemisphere would be regarded as "dangerous to our peace and safety." (This final statement did not commit the United States to a definite course of action in case of European intervention. Instead, it left the response, in terms of American national interest, to the discretion of the President.)

5. Significance and Some Results. The American people approved the Monroe Doctrine for *(a)* expressing the prevailing spirit of American nationalism, *(b)* evidencing America's importance in world affairs, and *(c)* attempting to isolate the entire Western Hemisphere from European affairs. Latin Americans generally welcomed the Monroe Doctrine as a friendly offer of assistance.

The Russians in 1824 agreed to halt their expansion by accepting the 54°40′ parallel as the southern boundary of Alaska. The European alliance did not pursue its rumored plans—if any—for the reconquest of Latin America. Its primary consideration was probably the power of Britain and the British navy. At that time, the United States hardly had the power to enforce the Monroe Doctrine. By 1862–1867, however, when the doctrine was challenged for the first time, the United States had grown powerful enough to force France to withdraw her army from Mexico. Maximilian, whom the French had installed as the puppet emperor of Mexico, remained and was executed by Mexican troops, thus concluding the *Maximilian Affair*.

Part 3. The Expanding Nation (From Manifest Destiny to Overseas Imperialism)

6. The Confident Nation Expands Across the Continent

MANIFEST DESTINY

Americans were satisfied temporarily by the relatively easy acquisitions of Louisiana and Florida. By the 1840's Americans had again become expansion-minded. They believed that their country had a "divine mission": It was destined to spread to the Pacific Coast, or perhaps over the entire North American continent. This belief became known as *manifest destiny*.

Manifest destiny was promoted by (1) land-hungry Americans who eyed tracts of rich but sparsely settled lands, (2) patriots who feared British designs upon such lands, (3) Eastern merchants whose ships trading with Asia needed ports on the Pacific Coast, (4) democratically minded people who believed that American territorial growth meant expanding the area of freedom, and (5) nationalists who sought American greatness.

EVENTS IN TEXAS

1. **Americans in Texas.** Americans were invited by newly independent Mexico in 1821 to settle in her northern province of Texas. *Stephen Austin* led the first group of land-hungry Americans. By 1835 some 30,000 whites with 5000 Negro slaves—all of American origin—resided in Texas. In the 1830's friction developed between the Mexican government and the American settlers, as Mexico attempted to (*a*) halt further American immigration into Texas, (*b*) free the Negro slaves, and (*c*) deprive Texas of local self-government.

2. **Texas Revolution (1836).** Claiming a parallel with the American Revolution against Britain, the Texans rebelled for independence. At the Alamo, a fortified church mission at San Antonio, a small Texan force was overwhelmed by a Mexican army under General Santa Anna. Inflamed by the bloody massacre of the Alamo defenders, the Texans raised the battle cry "Remember the Alamo!" Led by *Sam Houston*, the Texans won a great victory at the Battle of San Jacinto, capturing Santa Anna and driving his troops out of Texas. The settlers proclaimed the Republic of Texas (the Lone Star Republic), elected Sam Houston as President, and requested annexation by the United States.

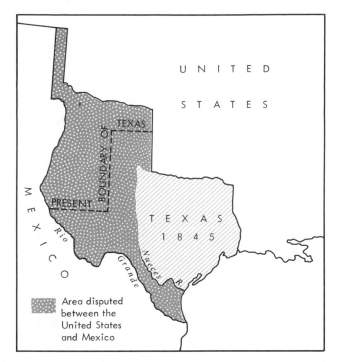

Annexation of Texas (1845)

ANNEXATION OF TEXAS

1. Delayed by Sectional Rivalry. While Southerners favored the annexation of Texas, Northeasterners opposed it. Northeasterners feared (a) the extension of slave territory, (b) increased Southern membership in the House of Representatives and the Senate, and (c) the possibility of war with Mexico. For nine years the United States delayed the annexation of Texas.

2. Achieved by Joint Resolution (1845). In the 1844 Presidential election, James Polk demanded the "reannexation of Texas," arguing that Texas had been part of the original Louisiana Purchase. Polk narrowly won the election. In 1845, just before Polk took office, Congress admitted Texas to the Union by means of a joint resolution. (Whereas a treaty requires a two-thirds vote in the Senate, a joint resolution requires only a majority vote, but in each house.)

WAR WITH MEXICO (1846–1848)

1. Causes. Mexican patriots resented the American (a) annexation of Texas, (b) claim that the southern boundary of Texas was the Rio Grande, rather than the Nueces River (see map, above), and (c) ambition to acquire additional Mexican territory. The unstable Mexican government, in response to public opinion, refused to receive the American negotiator, John Slidell, and refused to hear any American proposals. Mexican and United States troops meanwhile entered the disputed area between the Rio Grande and the Nueces River, and in 1846 a minor clash took place.

President Polk, infuriated, informed Congress that "Mexico has invaded our territory and shed American blood upon American soil." Polk secured an overwhelming declaration of war. Southern and Western Congressmen voted for the declaration, and their constituents welcomed the war. Most Northeastern Congressmen voted for the declaration, but many Northeasterners condemned the war as an imperialist plot against a weak neighbor to seize land and extend slavery.

Although some historians place primary responsibility for the war upon President Polk and American expansionists, other historians emphasize the inability or unwillingness of the Mexican government to settle outstanding disputes by peaceful negotiations.

2. Military Events. American volunteer armies soon demonstrated their military superiority. General Zachary Taylor won victory after victory in northern Mexico. General Winfield Scott captured Vera Cruz and Mexico City, the capital. In California, Captain John C. Frémont led American settlers to drive out the Mexican authorities and establish the temporary California (Bear Flag) Republic. Mexico's defeat was complete.

3. Treaty of Guadalupe Hidalgo (1848). Mexico (a) accepted the Rio Grande as the southern boundary of Texas, and (b) gave up California and the province of New Mexico, together called the *Mexican Cession*. (This area was eventually carved up into five states and parts of two others.) The United States agreed to

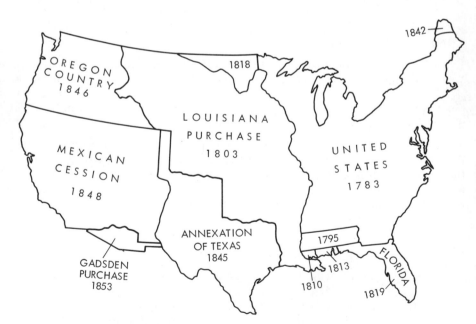

Territorial Growth of the United States (1783–1853)

pay Mexico $15 million and to assume the claims of American citizens against the Mexican government. (The terms of the treaty closely paralleled the American proposals that Mexico had refused to hear before the war.)

GADSDEN PURCHASE (1853)

Five years after purchasing the Mexican Cession for $15 million, the United States paid Mexico $10 million for a small strip of land in southern Arizona and New Mexico. *James Gadsden*, American minister to Mexico, negotiated the agreement and this land is called the *Gadsden Purchase*. It provided a favorable railroad route into California. Many Americans felt, however, that the large sum paid for this territory was "conscience money."

EXPANSION TO THE NORTH

1. Maine Boundary Dispute. Both the United States and Great Britain claimed a territory of 12,000 square miles lying between Maine in the United States and New Brunswick in Canada. Secretary of State Daniel Webster and British envoy Lord Ashburton negotiated a compromise boundary. The *Webster-Ashburton Treaty* of 1842 granted Canada 5000 square miles and gave the United States 7000 square miles, including the fertile Aroostook Valley.

2. Oregon Dispute

a. Conflicting Claims. Britain and the United States both claimed the Oregon Country, a huge area extending from the Rockies westward to the Pacific and from latitude 42° northward to 54° 40′. British claims were based upon the (1) 16th-century voyage of Sir Francis Drake, (2) 18th-century explorations of Captains Cook and Vancouver, and (3) subsequent fur-trading activities of the Hudson's Bay Company. American claims rested upon the (1) 1792 discovery of the Columbia River by Captain Robert Gray, (2) 1804–1806 explorations of Lewis and Clark, who after traversing the Louisiana Territory northward crossed the Rocky Mountains and descended the Columbia River to the Pacific, (3) subsequent fur-trading activities of the American Fur Company, owned by John Jacob Astor, and (4) 5000 Americans who had settled in the territory by 1845, many seeking the good climate and fertile land as reported by the American missionary to the Indians, *Marcus Whitman*. For many years the United States and Britain jointly occupied the territory.

b. Peaceful Settlement of the Dispute. In the Presidential campaign of 1844, James Polk demanded the "reoccupation of Oregon." His supporters chanted the slogan, "Fifty-four forty or fight." When he achieved the Presidency, however, Polk acted to compromise on the Oregon issue. In 1846 the United States and Britain agreed to divide the Oregon Country at the 49th parallel. This agreement extended the *Line of 1818* between the United States and Canada westward to the Pacific.

MULTIPLE-CHOICE QUESTIONS

1. The United States government has reacted strongly to interference with its commerce on the open seas *chiefly* because such interference (1) limits its naval power (2) hurts its balance of payments (3) violates its rights as a nation (4) violates the Monroe Doctrine.

2. During the administrations of Presidents Jefferson and Madison, the expression "British man-stealing" referred to (1) the sale of African slaves in British West Indian ports (2) the practice of forcibly enlisting United States seamen into the British Navy (3) England's incitement of Indian raids against frontier settlements (4) England's refusal to help the United States in the war against the Barbary pirates.

3. The Embargo and Non-Intercourse Acts illustrate the (1) unsuccessful attempt of the United States to isolate itself from a European conflict (2) success of the United States in obtaining recognition of its neutral rights (3) confiscation of British investments in America (4) overwhelming support given by Congress to President Jefferson's policy.

4. Which economic group *most* strongly protested the Embargo Act of 1807? (1) New England shippers (2) Southern cotton growers (3) frontier farmers (4) Northern factory workers

5. Why did the United States declare war on Great Britain rather than on France in 1812? (1) France had aided the United States during the American Revolution. (2) France's democratic revolutionary principles were similar to those of the United States. (3) New England merchants wanted revenge for shipping losses. (4) The "War Hawks" favored the conquest of Canada.

6. One reason why the United States was able to maintain its independence in *both* the Revolutionary War and the War of 1812 was that (1) American troops were better trained than British troops (2) American troops had the support of Indians in the Northwest Territory (3) Great Britain was fighting other enemies (4) the British navy avoided battles with American ships.

7. The Treaty of Ghent failed to prevent the Battle of New Orleans because (1) the United States was determined to destroy the British navy (2) the "War Hawks" continued to be important (3) Madison was eager to win a military reputation (4) communication at that time was slow.

8. By prohibiting trade and commerce with Europe, the Embargo Act of 1807 resulted in (1) gaining the support of New England citizens (2) upholding the principle of freedom of the seas (3) obtaining the approval of the Federalist party (4) stimulating manufacturing in New England.

9. Which illustrates the spirit of aggressive expansionism in the United States in the period following the War of 1812? (1) ratification of the Treaty of Ghent (2) negotiation of the Rush-Bagot Agreement (3) Andrew Jackson's action in the Florida Territory (4) John Quincy Adams' role in the issuance of the Monroe Doctrine

10. Spain sold Florida to the United States because Spain was (1) so ordered by Napoleon (2) in great need of funds (3) unable to control the Seminole Indians (4) afraid of losing the territory by force.

11. A fundamental reason for the issuance of the Monroe Doctrine was the belief that (1) it would justify increasing United States military forces (2) it would eliminate the threat of impending civil war (3) the policy of noninvolvement in European affairs no longer appealed to the American people (4) the defense of the United States depended upon limiting European influence in this hemisphere.

12. The original Monroe Doctrine was part of (1) an act of Congress (2) a treaty with England (3) a message to Congress (4) an agreement with Latin America.

13. The Monroe Doctrine declared that (1) the Western Hemisphere was no longer open to further European colonization (2) no European country could own territory in Latin America (3) there could be no trade agreements between Latin America and England (4) Spain should give up her possessions in the Western Hemisphere.
14. The reactionary alliance of European nations did *not* seriously threaten the Monroe Doctrine because (1) the United States was a great world power (2) Spain was willing to give up her colonies (3) Great Britain supported independence for Latin America (4) Russia had no interest in American affairs.
15. In 1823, Great Britain supported United States policy on Latin America *chiefly* because Great Britain (1) had agreed under the Jay Treaty to aid the United States (2) saw an opportunity to seize teritory in South America (3) wished to avoid war with France and Spain (4) feared a loss of profitable trade in Latin America.

MODIFIED TRUE-FALSE QUESTIONS

1. The belief of most Americans in the first half of the 19th century that the United States would expand to the Pacific Coast was known as *imperialism.*
2. Americans migrated to Mexico's northern province of Texas in order to get *cheap land.*
3. The battle at the Alamo resulted in a military victory for the *Texans.*
4. The section of the United States most opposed to the annexation of Texas was the *West.*
5. Texas was admitted to the Union by means of a *treaty.*
6. The Americans claimed that the southern boundary of Texas was the *Rio Grande.*
7. The American President who asked for a declaration of war against Mexico was *Andrew Jackson.*
8. An important result of the Mexican War was the annexation of *California.*
9. The *Gadsden Purchase* provided a railroad route into California.
10. The Oregon boundary dispute was settled by dividing the land at the *54° 40' parallel.*

ESSAY QUESTIONS

1. The United States from 1789 to 1815 was in a position similar to new African and Asian nations after 1945. (*a*) Prove this statement by discussing *two* similarities. (*b*) Why do newly emerging nations tend to favor a policy of nonalignment? (*c*) What is the distinction between nonalignment and isolation? (*d*) Give *one* argument for or against a United States policy of isolation today.
2. Some historians claim that the War of 1812 was "rash and unnecessary" for the United States. (*a*) Evaluate *two* causes of the war to show whether or not *each* supports the claim of "rash and unnecessary." (*b*) Discuss *two* results of the war to show whether or not *each* benefited the United States.
3. (*a*) Discuss *two* reasons why the United States in the 1820's opposed the restoration of Spanish control in Latin America. (*b*) Why did John Quincy Adams advise against a joint declaration with England? (*c*) State *two* provisions of the Monroe Doctrine. (*d*) How did the Monroe Doctrine protect and preserve the national interest?
4. (*a*) Explain *two* arguments used by Americans who opposed the Mexican War. (*b*) Explain *two* arguments of Americans who favored the Mexican War. (*c*) State *two* provisions of the treaty of peace ending the Mexican War.

7. The Industrialized and Powerful Nation Undertakes a Policy of Imperialism

REASONS FOR AMERICA'S TURN TO IMPERIALISM

Following the Civil War, and especially in the 1890's, the United States began to extend its control over "backward" or weaker areas. For the United States, the area of special concern became Latin America, which includes Mexico and the nations of the Caribbean, Central America, and South America. The United States also became interested in areas of the Central and Far Pacific. The following reasons help explain America's turn to imperialism:

1. Industrial Revolution. Spurred by Civil War needs, American industry continued to grow tremendously. Industrialists began to look abroad for *(a)* new sources of raw materials, *(b)* additional markets for manufactured goods, and *(c)* places to invest surplus capital. American merchants, whalers, and sugar planters, as well as missionaries, had already pioneered the way overseas.

2. Close of the Frontier. By 1890 the American West was sufficiently populated for the frontier to be considered closed. American manufacturers and investors began to look beyond our borders for economic opportunities.

3. Example of European Nations. Many European powers were engaged in imperialist ventures. Britain purchased control of the Suez Canal, established domination over Egypt, and planned a "Cape-to-Cairo" empire in Africa. France annexed Indo-China. Russia secured border territories from China. Such developments stimulated American interest in empire-building.

4. American Nationalism. American expansionists urged that the United States assume its rightful place as a great power by embarking upon a policy of imperialism. Most influential were the lectures and writings of Captain *Alfred Mahan*. In his book *The Influence of Sea Power Upon History*, Mahan urged the United States to "look outward": to expand foreign markets, construct a powerful navy, and acquire overseas bases. (Mahan had a notable admirer in Theodore Roosevelt.)

Some historians claim that overseas imperialism was a logical continuation of America's earlier pursuit of manifest destiny.

FIRST COLONIAL ACQUISITIONS

1. Alaska

a. Purchase from Russia (1867). Russia proposed to sell Alaska to the United States, and Secretary of State William Seward agreed to the purchase. Seward's reasons were (1) gratitude to Russia for her support of the Union during the Civil War, (2) a desire to reduce foreign possessions in North America, and (3) the belief that Alaska contained vast natural resources. Because many people thought the territory a "barren icebox," Alaska, costing $7.2 million, was called "Seward's Folly."

b. Importance. In 1959 Alaska was admitted to the Union as our 49th state. Alaska is important for (1) its natural resources of timber, fur, fish, coal, oil, and gold, and (2) its location, adjacent to Russian Siberia and also close to Northern

Europe and Asia via North Polar air routes. (See map, page 674.) Alaska contains major air force bases as well as several missile-warning systems.

2. Samoan Islands and Midway. The Samoan Islands in the South Pacific served American merchant ships as supply harbors and coaling stations. In 1899 several of the islands were annexed by the United States. Also annexed was the Central Pacific island of Midway.

3. Hawaii

a. Acquisition (1898). Hawaii consists of a group of islands in the Central Pacific, 2400 miles off the California coast. In 1893 revolutionists consisting mainly of American settlers overthrew the anti-American native Queen Liliuokalani, established a temporary republic, and asked for annexation by the United States. Annexation was delayed by President Cleveland who opposed American imperialism and believed that most native Hawaiians preferred independence. In 1898, however, with McKinley in the White House, the United States annexed Hawaii.

b. Importance. In 1959, Hawaii was admitted to the Union as our 50th state. Hawaii is important because it (1) produces sugar and pineapples, (2) attracts many tourists, and (3) contains the major American military installations in the Central Pacific, including the naval base at *Pearl Harbor*.

SPANISH-AMERICAN WAR (1898)

1. Cuban Background of the War

a. Early American Interest. Americans had long been interested in the Spanish colony of Cuba. They recognized Cuba's strategic location, within 90 miles of the Florida coast, and its importance as a key defense base in the Caribbean and at the entrance to the Gulf of Mexico. Americans feared for our security if Cuba passed from Spanish into stronger European hands.

b. Despotic Spanish Rule. Spain denied the Cubans civil liberties and political rights, levied heavy taxes, restricted foreign trade, and ruthlessly suppressed a number of rebellions. In 1895, as a depression hit the island, Spain faced another Cuban revolt for independence.

2. Causes of the Spanish-American War

a. Humanitarianism. Americans sympathized with the desire of the Cuban people for independence. Americans were outraged when Spain's General Valeriano Weyler placed Cuban civilians in concentration camps to prevent them from aiding the revolution. Some 200,000 concentration camp inmates, mainly women and children, died of hunger and disease.

b. Economic Interests. American merchants traded with Cuba to the amount of $100 million per year. American investors had placed $50 million in Cuban sugar and tobacco plantations. Our trade and investments suffered from unsettled conditions. (However, many American investors opposed war with Spain. They feared wartime destruction of their property and laws harmful to their enterprises if Cuba gained independence.)

c. "Yellow" Journalism. The "yellow" press—especially Hearst's New York *Journal* and Pulitzer's New York *World*—gave sensational treatment to news from Cuba. Journalists exaggerated stories of Spanish atrocities and falsified news pictures while playing down atrocities by the Cuban revolutionaries. The yellow press also publicized the *De Lome Letter*. Written by the Spanish minister in Washington to a friend in Cuba and stolen from the Havana post office, this private letter belittled President McKinley as a weak, incompetent politician. By such news stories, the yellow press enraged the American people against Spain.

　　d. Sinking of the "Maine." In 1898 the American battleship *Maine*, visiting in Havana, Cuba, was blown up with a loss of 260 American lives. The cause of the explosion remains unknown, but the American people placed the blame on Spain. They were goaded to do so by the yellow press, by jingoists, who boasted of American strength, and by imperialists, who wanted an overseas empire.

3. Outbreak of the War. President McKinley had sought to avert war and urged Americans to remain calm regarding Cuba. Now, with the sinking of the *Maine*, McKinley demanded that Spain proclaim an armistice, end the concentration camps, and negotiate with the rebels. Although Spain's reply was conciliatory, McKinley finally yielded to American public sentiment for war. At his request, Congress approved the use of American armed forces in Cuba. Congress also recognized the independence of Cuba and declared that the United States would not annex Cuba but would leave "control of the island to its people"—a self-denying declaration known as the *Teller Resolution*.

4. Conduct of the War. With "Remember the *Maine!*" as their battle cry, American forces swept quickly and easily to victory. In the Pacific, a fleet under Commodore *George Dewey* destroyed the Spanish fleet at Manila, the capital of the Philippines, and an American army took possession of the city. In the Caribbean, American naval forces destroyed the Spanish fleet at Santiago, Cuba. Meanwhile, American forces captured this city after a battle famed for the heroic dash up San Juan Hill by Theodore Roosevelt and his Rough Riders.

　　In this "splendid little war," so named by the American diplomat John Hay, more American soldiers died from tropical diseases, especially yellow fever, than from Spanish guns. (After the war, *Walter Reed*, an army surgeon, discovered that yellow fever is transmitted by a certain kind of mosquito. This discovery led to the wiping out of yellow fever.)

5. Treaty of Paris (1898). Spain agreed to the following peace terms: *(a)* Cuba was freed of Spanish control, *(b)* Puerto Rico, in the Caribbean, and Guam, in the Pacific, were ceded to the United States, and *(c)* the Philippine Islands, in the Pacific, were sold to the United States for $20 million.

6. Significance. The United States emerged from the Spanish-American War as a world power with colonies in the Caribbean and the Pacific. Anti-imperialists were alarmed. In the Presidential election of 1900, Democrat William Jennings Bryan warned that imperialism abroad would lead to despotism at home. Disregarding this warning, the people reelected William McKinley, who represented imperialism but who had campaigned on the issue of the "full dinner pail."

AMERICAN RELATIONS WITH CUBA

1. Temporary American Occupation. After the Spanish-American War, the United States temporarily took charge of Cuba, establishing schools, building roads, providing sanitation, and wiping out yellow fever. Americans also assisted the Cubans in drawing up a democratic constitution. In 1902 American forces withdrew from the island.

2. American Protectorate Over Cuba: The Platt Amendment. Under strong American pressure, the Cubans included in their constitution the *Platt Amendment*. It provided that Cuba would *(a)* not sign any foreign treaty that threatened her independence, *(b)* allow the United States to intervene to preserve Cuban independence and to protect life, liberty, and property, and *(c)* grant the United States naval bases. Under the last provision, Cuba leased to the United States the naval base at *Guantanamo Bay*.

The Cubans lacked political experience; for years their governments alternated between weak, inefficient regimes and tyrannical military dictatorships. The island abounded with corruption, fraud, violence, and revolt.

Using the Platt Amendment, the United States intervened four times to restore order in Cuba and safeguard American lives and investments. Our interventions aroused resentment among Cuban nationalists. In 1933, however, although Cuba was in the midst of another revolt, President Franklin D. Roosevelt did not intervene. Instead, in 1934, as part of his Good Neighbor Policy, he abrogated (abolished) the Platt Amendment. With Cuban consent, the United States retained the naval base at Guantanamo Bay.

3. Economic Ties. Although the Platt Amendment was ended, the United States continued to dominate the Cuban economy. Americans had over $1 billion invested in Cuban public utilities, railroads, iron and nickel mines, and sugar and tobacco plantations. The United States provided the chief market for Cuban agricultural and mineral exports, and was the chief source of Cuban imports of manufactured goods. American tourists flocked to Cuban vacation resorts.

The Cuban economy provided the people with no more than a very low living standard. Few farmers owned their own land, and farmworkers received low wages. Because Cuba was largely dependent upon the sugar crop, the entire economy frequently suffered from world competition and low prices.

4. Hostility (Since 1959). In 1959 *Fidel Castro*, leading Cuban rebels, overthrew the dictatorship of Fulgencio Batista and seized power. As Castro aligned himself with the Communist world, relations between Cuba and the United States deteriorated. (Check the Index for details.)

PUERTO RICO: AN AMERICAN SHOWCASE. Check the Index.

PANAMA CANAL

1. American Interest. Americans long desired a canal across the Isthmus of Panama to connect the Atlantic and Pacific Oceans. By eliminating the long voyage around South America, a canal would shorten the boat trip between our East and West coasts. The Spanish-American War pointed up the need for a canal *(a)* to provide greater mobility for our naval fleets, *(b)* to protect our new colonial empire, and *(c)* to further commerce with the Far East.

2. American Diplomatic Moves

a. With Great Britain. In the *Clayton-Bulwer Treaty* (1850) the United States and Great Britain agreed to share control of any canal across Central America. In 1901 Secretary of State John Hay negotiated the *Hay-Pauncefote Treaty*, by which Britain permitted the United States to go ahead without her in building and operating the canal.

b. **With the French Canal Company.** A private French company, under *Ferdinand de Lesseps*, builder of the Suez Canal, had attempted to construct a canal in Panama but had failed. The United States agreed to pay $40 million to the French company for its property and its franchise rights.

c. **With Colombia.** In 1903 Secretary Hay negotiated a treaty to pay Colombia $10 million and an annual rental of $250,000 for the right to build a canal across its province of Panama. The treaty was rejected by the Colombian Senate, which hoped for more money the following year when the French company's franchise would expire. Rejection of the treaty worried the French company, inflamed the people of Panama, and enraged President Theodore Roosevelt.

d. **Roosevelt and the Panama Revolution.** Roosevelt privately expressed the wish to see Panama independent of Colombia. Shortly afterwards, a revolt broke out. The United States openly aided the revolt as its naval vessels prevented Colombian troops from entering Panama. Later, Roosevelt boasted, "I took the Canal Zone." Roosevelt's actions earned us ill will in Latin America.

e. **Treaty With Panama.** Hay now negotiated a treaty with Panama, whose minister was the former French company official, *Philippe Bunau-Varilla*. The Hay–Bunau-Varilla Treaty (1903) provided for (1) American control, "in perpetuity," of the Canal Zone, a strip of land ten miles wide across the isthmus, (2) American intervention in Panama when necessary to preserve order, and (3) payment to Panama of $10 million and an annual rental of $250,000 for the Canal Zone. (The annual rental was increased several times up to $2.3 million.)

3. Building the Canal

a. **George W. Goethals,** an army engineer, had charge of building the canal. To solve the problem of the uneven terrain, Goethals built huge locks to raise and lower ships. In 1914 the 50-mile-long canal was opened to traffic.

b. **William C. Gorgas,** an army medical officer, wiped out malaria and yellow fever in the Canal Zone. By maintaining proper sanitation, Gorgas enabled the workers to complete the canal.

4. Protecting the Canal.
The United States (a) fortified the Canal Zone, (b) maintained military bases throughout the Caribbean, and (c) in 1917 purchased from Denmark an additional Caribbean base, the *Virgin Islands*.

5. Panamanian Nationalism and the Canal Zone.
By the 1960's, Panamanians strongly resented American control over the Canal Zone "in perpetuity" as well as the comfortable life of American personnel in contrast with the poverty of most Panamanians. In 1964 a Canal Zone incident involving the unauthorized flying of the American flag by American high school students sparked a series of anti-American riots. Thereafter the United States and Panama began negotiations to revise the status of the Canal Zone.

6. The 1977 Treaties.
After 13 years of intermittent talks spanning four American Presidential administrations, United States and Panama negotiators agreed to replace the 1903 Hay–Bunau-Varilla pact with two new treaties. The "Transfer of Ownership" treaty provided that (a) the United States transfer ownership and control of the canal to Panama by the year 2000, (b) until then the United States operate the canal but assign an increasing role to Panamanians, (c) soon after ratification, Panama assume control of most of the Canal Zone—those areas not essential for defense or operation of the canal, and (d) Panama receive $50 to $70

million annually out of canal tolls and also extensive American economic aid. The "Neutrality" treaty (a) guarantees the neutrality of the canal from the year 2000 onward and (b) gives the United States (as later spelled out) the right to intervene militarily to defend the canal's neutrality.

Although some Panamanians feared giving the United States the right to intervene militarily, the Panamanian voters strongly approved the treaties.

In the United States, President Carter exerted much political pressure to secure Senate ratification. A considerable number of Americans had strong doubts regarding the advisability of the treaties. The anti-treaty arguments included the following: (a) The United States had acquired its rights to the Panama Canal legitimately, had built the canal despite considerable hardship, and should not now surrender these rights. (b) Panama is not entitled to the huge sums to be paid out of canal tolls and extended as American economic aid. (c) Americans working on the canal will lose their jobs. (d) Panamanians lack the skill and ability to operate the canal. (e) The canal is vital to American security.

The Senate ratified the two treaties by identical votes of 68 to 32—one vote above the two-thirds required by the Constitution. President Carter hailed ratification, stating that these treaties "symbolize our determination to deal with the developing nations of the world . . . on the basis of mutual respect."

USE OF THE MONROE DOCTRINE TO DOMINATE THE CARIBBEAN

In 1823 the United States issued the Monroe Doctrine to keep European powers from extending their control in the Western Hemisphere. Beginning in 1895, the United States interpreted the Monroe Doctrine so as to justify its own political and economic domination of the Caribbean area.

1. Venezuela Boundary Dispute (1895). Great Britain and Venezuela had long disputed the boundary between Venezuela and British Guiana. The disputed area, its value heightened by the discovery of gold, extended north to the mouth of the Orinoco River. Britain had rejected proposals for arbitration.

Convenient screen
(*Poinier in the Detroit News*)

In 1895 *Richard Olney*, Secretary of State under President Cleveland, demanded that Britain submit to arbitration. Olney *(a)* claimed that British pressure on Venezuela violated the Monroe Doctrine, and *(b)* asserted that the United States may intervene in all Western Hemisphere affairs because "the United States is practically sovereign on this continent"—the *Olney Interpretation* of the Monroe Doctrine. Britain dismissed Olney's arguments, but, after Cleveland indicated that the United States was ready to use force, Britain agreed to arbitration. British Guiana was awarded most of the disputed territory, but Venezuela retained the mouth of the Orinoco River.

The Olney Interpretation greatly perturbed the Latin American nations, who foresaw intervention by the United States in their internal affairs.

2. Venezuela Debt Dispute (1902). Venezuela defaulted on debts owed to citizens of Italy, Great Britain, and Germany. The European powers sent warships to compel repayment of the debt by blockading Venezuelan ports. President Theodore Roosevelt feared that the naval display might lead to permanent occupation of Venezuela, in violation of the Monroe Doctrine. Roosevelt secured arbitration of the dispute and withdrawal of the warships.

3. Dominican Debt Default (1904–1905). The Dominican Republic (sometimes called Santo Domingo) failed to repay loans to European creditors. President Roosevelt opposed European intervention as a violation of the Monroe Doctrine, but he authorized intervention by the United States to protect the European creditors. In 1905 the United States took control of Dominican finances and initiated the repayment of Dominican debts.

Roosevelt generally advocated the "big stick" policy, a term derived from one of his favorite sayings, "Speak softly and carry a big stick." Roosevelt specifically justified his interference in Dominican affairs by asserting that, in case of "chronic wrongdoing" by any Western Hemisphere nation, the United States would exercise "international police power"—a statement known as the *Roosevelt Corollary* to the Monroe Doctrine. The Roosevelt Corollary pleased European and American investors, for it indicated that we would intervene, if necessary, to protect their investments. It enraged Latin Americans by implying that they needed help from the United States to manage their affairs.

4. "Dollar Diplomacy." President Taft endorsed the Roosevelt Corollary and expanded our role as "policeman" of the Western Hemisphere. Taft offered American businessmen in the Caribbean the full military and diplomatic support of the government, a policy called *dollar diplomacy*. Taft encouraged American bankers to expand their loans to Honduras, Haiti, and Nicaragua. After political disturbances broke out in Nicaragua, Taft in 1912 dispatched marines to that country to protect American lives and property, and to restore order.

President Wilson continued American intervention in Latin America. In 1915 he sent marines to occupy Haiti, and the United States took control of Haiti's finances. In 1916 he ordered marines to restore peace in the Dominican Republic. Wilson's greatest Latin American problem, however, was Mexico.

AMERICAN RELATIONS WITH MEXICO: AN UNEVEN RECORD

1. Relations in the 19th Century. Because of the annexation of Texas and the Mexican War (1846–1848), Mexicans had considerable ill-will toward the United

Caribbean Area

States. Mexican sentiments changed when the United States, from 1862 to 1867, invoked the Monroe Doctrine and helped overthrow a French protectorate in Mexico under the Emperor Maximilian.

2. Wilson's Policies Toward Mexico

a. "Watchful Waiting" (1913–1914). In 1913 General *Victoriano Huerta* seized control of Mexico. His dictatorial regime was opposed by reform-minded Mexicans under *Venustiano Carranza.* Mexico experienced civil war.

President Wilson refused to recognize the Huerta regime, claiming that it lacked the consent of the Mexican people. Wilson also resisted demands to send troops into Mexico to protect American lives and property. Instead, he applied various pressures against Huerta: ordering American forces to occupy the Mexican seaport of Vera Cruz so as to keep European arms from Huerta and permitting American arms to go to Carranza. Huerta finally fled from Mexico. Wilson's policy toward Mexico under Huerta became known as "watchful waiting."

b. Pursuit of Pancho Villa (1916–1917). After Wilson recognized the Carranza government, a rival Mexican leader, *Pancho Villa,* led several raids into the United States and murdered a number of Americans. Wilson ordered American forces under General John Pershing into northern Mexico to seize Villa, but he eluded capture.

3. Troubled Relations (Following 1917).

The Mexicans resented Wilson's military intervention at Vera Cruz and the pursuit of Villa into Mexican territory. They further feared "Yankee imperialism" and American economic power. For many years, Mexico remained unfriendly toward the United States.

In turn, many Americans disliked the actions of the Mexican government. American Catholics protested Mexico's seizure of Church lands and the supplanting of parochial schools by state-controlled schools. American oil interests objected to Mexico's nationalization in 1938 of all foreign oil properties.

President Franklin D. Roosevelt, as part of the Good Neighbor Policy, acknowledged Mexico's right to seize the oil properties but requested fair compensation for the foreign investors. Mexico complied with this request. The friendly conclusion to this dispute improved Mexican-American relations.

4. Recent Mexican-American Problems

a. Energy Supplies. In the 1970's Mexico uncovered huge deposits of natural gas and oil. These energy supplies, if sold to the United States, could reduce American dependence on the volatile Middle East oil-producing nations—Iran and various Arab states. Although Mexico is not a member of OPEC, its energy prices conform to the ever-rising OPEC price policies. The United States would like to see a halt to rising energy prices. In 1979 the two nations reached agreement on the price for Mexican natural gas to be sold to the United States.

b. Illegal Immigrants. The illegal Mexican immigrants (also known as "wet backs") in the United States are estimated to total 7 million. They are attracted primarily to the American Southwest by job opportunities and by wages higher than those paid in Mexico. If caught by the American authorities, these "illegals" face only deportation to Mexico. The United States holds that these illegal immigrants create problems: breaking our laws, perpetuating slums, depressing wage standards, and taking jobs away from American citizens. Mexico claims that the United States has made no serious effort to deal with this mass influx of human beings, that American employers exploit the "illegals" by paying substandard wages, and that American immigration authorities treat the "illegals" with unnecessary harshness.

c. Winter Vegetable Exports. Mexico exports large quantities of winter vegetables to the United States. American vegetable growers in Florida protest that the Mexicans are "dumping" their produce here at low prices, and they demand protection. If tariffs or other restrictions were imposed, American growers and their farmworkers would benefit, but other consequences might be: higher vegetable prices in the United States, fewer jobs for Mexican farmworkers, reduced Mexican imports of American goods, and more bitterness in Mexican-American relations. In 1980 the Commerce Department ruled that Mexico was not selling its winter produce here at unfairly low prices, and therefore no restrictions should be placed upon imports of Mexican winter vegetables.

8. The Good Neighbor Policy Replaces Imperialism in Inter-American Affairs

MOVEMENT FOR PAN-AMERICANISM

1. **Aims.** *Pan-Americanism* fosters cooperation among the nations of the Western Hemisphere to achieve common goals such as improved trade relations, greater political stability, military defense, and cultural interchange.

2. **Beginnings.** *Simón Bolívar*, the Latin American liberator, issued the call for the first Pan-American conference. Held in 1826, this first meeting was a failure, and interest in Pan-Americanism declined afterward.

3. **Revival (In the 1880's).** *James G. Blaine*, American Secretary of State, revived the idea of inter-American cooperation by calling for another Pan-

American conference. Convened in 1889, this meeting agreed to establish an information center, which later developed into the *Pan-American Union*.

4. Limited Accomplishment. To 1928 subsequent Pan-American conferences achieved little of practical value. The Latin American nations mistrusted the United States. They feared that our support of Pan-Americanism was designed to further American domination of the Western Hemisphere.

REASONS FOR LATIN AMERICAN MISTRUST OF THE UNITED STATES

The Latin American nations mistrusted the United States because of: (1) our annexation of Texas, (2) the Mexican War and our annexation of the Mexican Cession, (3) the Olney Interpretation of the Monroe Doctrine, (4) the Spanish-American War and our annexation of Puerto Rico, (5) the Platt Amendment, making Cuba a protectorate, (6) our role in the revolt of Panama against Colombia, (7) the Roosevelt Corollary to the Monroe Doctrine, and (8) our intervention in the Dominican Republic, Nicaragua, Haiti, and Mexico.

AMERICAN EFFORTS TO DISPEL MISTRUST

Under Herbert Hoover the United States moved to improve Latin American relations. As President-elect, Hoover made a goodwill tour of Latin America. His State Department disowned the Roosevelt Corollary. Despite revolutions and debt defaults by several Latin American nations, Hoover refused to intervene. In 1933 he withdrew American marines from Nicaragua.

GOOD NEIGHBOR POLICY (STARTING IN 1933): OBJECTIVES

President Franklin D. Roosevelt and his Secretary of State, Cordell Hull, labored to win Latin American goodwill by the "policy of the good neighbor." Their objectives were as follows: (1) Friendship. By respecting the rights of others, Americans hoped to overcome the hostility that many Latin Americans felt toward the United States. (2) Trade. With the United States in the midst of the Great Depression, Americans hoped to increase trade with Latin America and spur our economic recovery. (3) Defense. As the Nazis rose to power in Germany and as war clouds gathered over Europe and Asia, Americans wanted to strengthen hemispheric defenses. They sought to forestall Nazi influence in Latin America and to assure inter-American military cooperation.

GOOD NEIGHBOR POLICY IN PRACTICE

1. Retreat From Imperialism. (*a*) In 1934 American marines were withdrawn from Haiti, and the United States gave up its protectorate over Cuba by abrogating the Platt Amendment. (*b*) In 1936 the United States surrendered its right to intervene in the internal affairs of Panama. (*c*) In 1938 the United States acknowledged Mexico's right to expropriate American oil properties.

2. Pan-Americanization of the Monroe Doctrine. In 1933 the United States agreed that "no state has the right to intervene in the internal or external affairs of another," thereby formally abandoning the Roosevelt Corollary. In 1936 the American republics pledged to consult together in case of a threat to the peace of the Americas. In 1938 they further agreed that a threat to the peace of any one of them would be considered a threat to all. Thus the *unilateral* (one-nation) interpretation of the Monroe Doctrine was replaced by a *multilateral* (many-nation) interpretation. The Monroe Doctrine, henceforth to be interpreted and enforced not by the United States alone, but by all the American republics, became a Pan-American doctrine.

3. Strengthening Economic Ties. (a) In 1934 the United States created the Export-Import Bank. This agency granted low-cost, long-term loans to Latin American nations for building roads and developing natural resources. It also provided credit facilities to encourage inter-American trade. (b) In 1934 Congress passed the Reciprocal Trade Agreements Act. Hull negotiated trade agreements, providing for the mutual lowering of tariff barriers, with a number of Latin American nations.

4. Strengthening Social and Cultural Ties. The United States and Latin America used literature, art, music, science, education, radio, the press, movies, and goodwill tours to promote better understanding. In 1941 the United States established the *Office of Inter-American Affairs* to strengthen hemispheric bonds.

EFFECTIVENESS OF THE GOOD NEIGHBOR POLICY AS DEMONSTRATED DURING WORLD WAR II

With the major exception of Argentina, the nations of Latin America cooperated with the United States during World War II.

1. Upon the Outbreak of War (1939). At the Panama Conference the American republics declared their neutrality and forbade belligerents from entering a safety zone that ranged from 300 to 1200 miles off the coast of the Americas.

2. Following the Japanese Attack on Pearl Harbor (1941). At the Rio de Janeiro Conference the American republics declared the Axis powers a threat to the liberty and independence of the Americas, and recommended the severing of diplomatic relations. Thereafter, most Latin American nations gave assistance to the United States. They (a) severed diplomatic relations with Italy, Germany, and Japan, and declared war against them, (b) arrested Axis agents, seized Axis airplanes and ships, and prohibited Axis propaganda, (c) granted the United States military bases, and (d) increased the production of strategic raw materials. In addition, Mexico and Brazil sent troops to the fighting fronts.

For later developments, check the Index for "Latin America."

MULTIPLE-CHOICE QUESTIONS

1. Which pair of terms represents two major causes of imperialism in the 19th century? (1) industrialism and communism (2) communism and fascism (3) nationalism and industrialism (4) collectivism and missionary zeal
2. The United States had few foreign investments before 1890 because (1) Americans did not believe in imperialism (2) Congress had prohibited all loans to foreign countries (3) the development of the West offered a profitable field for the investment of capital (4) foreign countries did not need capital.
3. A *major* reason for United States empire-building at the turn of this century was the belief that colonies (1) could serve as an outlet for eventual surplus population (2) would help the United States to increase its trade and industrial development (3)

would provide the skilled labor needed in our industrial society   (4) would enable the United States to replace France as the major world power.

4. Since World War II, Alaska's strategic importance has increased because of   (1) the discovery of new gold mines   (2) the large-scale mining of uranium deposits   (3) the air routes across the north polar region   (4) her achievement of statehood.

5. The admission of Hawaii as our 50th state   (1) granted equality with the older states to an area with an Asian majority   (2) extended our defenses against Red China to the mid-Pacific   (3) eliminated the tariff on Hawaiian sugar   (4) permitted unlimited Hawaiian immigration to the mainland.

6. Which is the *most* valid conclusion that can be drawn concerning the territorial acquisitions of the United States?   (1) There was little interest in adding territory before the Civil War.   (2) Expansion frequently brought involvement with foreign nations.   (3) Peaceful means were always used to obtain additional territory.   (4) Desires for land were limited to the North American continent.

7. The United States declaration of war on Spain is an example of   (1) Presidential leadership in the face of Congressional disapproval   (2) army maneuvers making war inevitable   (3) the influence of the press on popular opinion   (4) the unanimous opinion of businessmen in favor of war.

8. A result of both the Mexican War and the Spanish-American War was that the United States   (1) established protectorates in Cuba and Mexico   (2) settled the question of neutrality in times of war   (3) acquired land belonging to another nation   (4) became a world power with overseas possessions.

9. The Platt Amendment provided that the United States   (1) annex Cuba   (2) maintain a protectorate over Cuba   (3) withdraw American investments from Cuba   (4) send an American to serve as president of Cuba.

10. A *major* reason why the United States built the Panama Canal was to   (1) improve the defense of the United States   (2) increase the prosperity of Central America   (3) force the reduction of railroad rates   (4) fulfill our treaty obligations with Great Britain.

11. Which idea was a corollary to the original Monroe Doctrine?   (1) The Western Hemisphere is closed to further colonization.   (2) The United States has the right to intervene in Latin America.   (3) The United States will not intervene in the affairs of Europe.   (4) The United States will respect European colonies already established in the New World.

12. The United States used the Roosevelt Corollary to justify   (1) intervention in Cuba's rebellion against Spain   (2) requests to Latin American countries to join in enforcing the Monroe Doctrine   (3) reversal of the policy followed in the Maximilian Affair   (4) intervention in the financial affairs of certain Caribbean republics.

13. Dollar diplomacy was used by both President Taft and President Wilson to   (1) provide aid for developing nations in Asia   (2) protect United States investments abroad   (3) promote an economic union of European nations   (4) encourage adoption of reciprocal tariff agreements.

14. Pan-Americanism is *chiefly* a movement to   (1) unite the countries of North America under one government   (2) strengthen our military bases in Canada   (3) bring about cooperation among the republics of the Western Hemisphere   (4) protect the Panama Canal.

15. When the United States grants specific import privileges to a foreign nation in return for similar privileges for the United States, the agreement is *generally* called a   (1) balance of payments   (2) common market   (3) protective tariff   (4) reciprocal trade pact.

16. The Good Neighbor Policy was promoted by the   (1) Platt Amendment   (2) "big stick" policy   (3) Roosevelt Corollary   (4) multilateral interpretation of the Monroe Doctrine.

17. A sharp contrast in our relations with Latin America is evident between   (1) dollar diplomacy and our intervention in Nicaragua   (2) the Roosevelt Corollary and our

intervention in Haiti (3) the Olney Interpretation and the Good Neighbor Policy (4) "watchful waiting" and nonrecognition of the Huerta government.

18. The present policy of the United States toward Latin America *differs* from that of the early 20th century insofar as it (1) is arrived at unilaterally (2) involves military aid primarily (3) recognizes more fully the sovereignty of most nations of the hemisphere (4) attempts to exclude by armed force any foreign influence.

IDENTIFICATION QUESTIONS—WHO AM I?

Grover Cleveland	Alfred Mahan	Franklin D. Roosevelt
Ferdinand de Lesseps	William McKinley	Theodore Roosevelt
George Goethals	Richard Olney	William Seward
John Hay	Walter Reed	Pancho Villa
Cordell Hull	Nelson Rockefeller	Woodrow Wilson

1. As President, I reluctantly asked Congress to authorize the use of American military forces to end Spanish rule in Cuba.
2. Although I won fame for building the Suez Canal, I failed in Panama.
3. I proclaimed American policy to intervene as "international police power" so as to correct "chronic wrongdoing" by any nation in the Western Hemisphere.
4. In my book *The Influence of Sea Power Upon History*, I urged the United States to build a powerful navy and expand overseas.
5. As an army doctor I conducted experiments to prove that a certain kind of mosquito transmits yellow fever.
6. To oppose a ruthless army general who seized control of Mexico, I instituted an American policy of "watchful waiting."
7. As Secretary of State during the Venezuelan boundary dispute, I declared that the "United States is practically sovereign on this continent."
8. I was the army engineer who constructed the Panama Canal.
9. As President, I applied the "policy of the good neighbor" to United States relations with Latin America.
10. I was the Secretary of State who handled the diplomatic negotiations with Britain, Colombia, and Panama—all regarding the building of the Panama Canal.

ESSAY QUESTIONS

1. Many historians believe that the war with Spain signaled America's turn to imperialism. (a) Explain *two* reasons why, in the latter 19th century, the United States turned toward imperialism. (b) Present *two* arguments to support the claim that, in the war with Spain, America's motives were imperialistic. (c) Present *two* arguments to disprove this claim. (d) Explain *two* effects of the war upon American foreign policy.
2. Giving *one* specific reason in each case, explain why *each* of the following either improved or worsened relations between Latin America and the United States: (a) Wilson's policy toward Mexico (b) Pan-Americanization of the Monroe Doctrine (c) reciprocal trade agreements (d) Venezuela boundary dispute (e) Theodore Roosevelt's policy toward Panama (f) plans for a second interoceanic canal.
3. The relations between the United States and Latin America are vital to the future welfare of the Western Hemisphere. (a) State specifically *two* policies of the United States toward Latin America as expressed in the Monroe Doctrine of 1823. (b) Discuss *two* actions of the United States in the period 1890–1930 that aroused ill-feeling in Latin America. (c) Describe *two* activities of the United States in the period 1930–1945 that fostered goodwill in Latin America. (d) Describe *two* reasons for the shift in our policies toward Latin America during the period 1930–1945.

4. "In the Venezuela boundary dispute, the United States helped protect the territory of Venezuela. In the Dominican debt dispute, the United States prevented European occupation of the Dominican Republic. The nations of Latin America should be grateful for American intervention in these disputes." (a) What conclusions could you draw from this statement regarding the nationality and foreign policy views of the speaker? Explain your reasoning. (b) What might you expect to be the nationality and foreign policy views of a speaker holding an opposing opinion? (c) For each of the two cases cited in the statement, present one argument to support an opposing opinion. (d) Do you approve or disapprove the statement that the "nations of Latin America should be grateful"? Give one reason to support your viewpoint.

9. The United States Pursues Its Interests in the Far East

AMERICAN INTERESTS IN THE FAR EAST

1. Economic Interests. In 1783, the year the American Revolution ended, an American sailing ship began the first successful voyage to China. Thereafter, American merchants created a small but thriving trade with the Far East, delivering furs and textiles, and bringing back tea, silk, and spices. Following the Civil War, as the United States became more industrialized, American manufacturers and investors looked to the Pacific area for markets, raw materials, and investment opportunities.

2. Religious Interests. American missionaries supplied Western medical, agricultural, and other knowledge to the Asian peoples and sought to convert them to Christianity.

3. Colonial Acquisitions. Between 1867 and 1899 the United States gathered a colonial empire in the Pacific: Alaska, Hawaii, Guam, the Philippines, Midway, Wake, and part of the Samoan Islands.

4. Defense. American military leaders utilized our possessions in the Pacific to establish army, navy, and air bases.

Philippines

PEOPLE AND ECONOMY

Located in the western Pacific, 7000 miles from California, the Philippines has a population of over 40 million. As a result of Spanish rule, the Filipinos are chiefly but not entirely Roman Catholic. The Filipinos have a standard of living low compared to Americans, but good compared to most Asians.

The Filipinos are engaged chiefly in agriculture, raising rice, manila hemp, tobacco, coconut oil, and sugar. The islands contain relatively undeveloped mineral deposits of gold, silver, copper, chromium, and iron. Their industrial plants are concerned chiefly with processing agricultural and forest products. The Philippines trades extensively with the United States.

AMERICAN ANNEXATION

1. Reasons. As a result of the Spanish-American War, the United States annexed the Philippines for *(a) economic reasons:* trade, raw materials, and investments, *(b) military reasons:* a strategic base in the Far East, and *(c) humanitarianism:* a desire, in the words of President McKinley, "to educate the Filipinos, and uplift and civilize and Christianize them."

2. Filipino Opposition. Many Filipinos had expected the United States to withdraw after 1898 and grant them independence. *Emilio Aguinaldo* led the embittered islanders in revolt against American rule. After three years of fighting and at great cost, American forces suppressed the Filipino rebels.

AMERICAN ACHIEVEMENT IN THE PHILIPPINES

1. Economic Development. American investors furthered the development of Filipino resources and processing industries. American authorities promoted extensive public works and helped peasants purchase small farms.

2. Conquest of Disease. American health officials started sanitation programs, wiped out cholera and smallpox, and built hospitals and health centers.

3. Education. By establishing free public schools, the United States substantially reduced illiteracy. Most Filipinos are able to read and write.

4. Gradual Self-Government. The United States trained the islanders for self-government. Beginning in 1907 the Filipinos elected the lower house of their legislature. By the *Jones Act of 1916*, they received the right to elect both houses of the legislature and were promised eventual independence.

AMERICAN SUPPORT FOR PHILIPPINE INDEPENDENCE

1. Reasons. Americans came to realize that most Filipinos desired independence. Also, American producers of sugar and edible oil wanted tariff protection against incoming Philippine sugar and coconut oil. American workers on the Pacific Coast wanted to halt the influx of Filipino immigrants. American taxpayers wanted to end federal spending in the Philippines. Finally, American military leaders, concerned by the distant location of the islands, wanted to end American responsibility for Philippine defense.

2. Tydings-McDuffie (Philippine Independence) Act (1934). This act offered the Filipinos independence after a transition period. The act permitted the gradual imposition of American tariffs and provided for sharp restrictions on Filipino immigration. It also empowered the Filipinos to write a constitution and establish a democratic government. The islanders agreed.

PHILIPPINES IN WORLD WAR II

In December 1941, immediately after bombing Pearl Harbor, Japan invaded the Philippines and quickly overran the islands. General *Douglas MacArthur*, the American commander in the Far East, fled to Australia but pledged, "I shall return." In 1944 MacArthur came back with a powerful military force and liberated the islands. Throughout the war the Filipino people resisted the Japanese occupation, and demonstrated their loyalty to the United States.

PHILIPPINES AS AN INDEPENDENT NATION

1. Independence. In 1946, at Manila, the Philippines formally received independence from the United States. It also received extensive postwar economic aid, as well as favorable tariff treatment for its exports.

2. Friendship for the United States. In 1947 the Philippines granted the United States military bases, and in 1951 the two nations signed a treaty of mutual defense. In 1954 the Philippines joined the Southeast Asia Treaty Organization (SEATO). To support the American effort in South Vietnam, the Philippine government sent a token force of troops, chiefly engineers.

3. Regime of Ferdinand E. Marcos (1965–   ). In control of the Filipino government since 1965, Marcos has acted as follows:
　　a. Foreign Policy Shifts. Marcos moved somewhat away from a pro-American and toward an independent foreign policy. He withdrew the Filipino troops from Vietnam. In 1975–1976, following the American setbacks in Indo-China, Marcos entered into diplomatic and trade agreements with the Soviet Union and Communist China. In 1979 Marcos secured a revised agreement regarding American military bases in the Philippines. While allowing the United States "unhampered" military use, the revised agreement acknowledged Filipino sovereignty over the bases.
　　b. Moves Against Moslem Guerrillas. Marcos has been unable to suppress a rebellion by a Moslem minority, allegedly aided by Libya, for their own separate state. Government troops have failed to crush the rebels.
　　c. Antidemocratic Actions. In 1972 Marcos imposed martial law. He initiated censorship of newspapers and radio and arrested many leaders of the political opposition. In 1973 Marcos proclaimed adoption of a new constitution, enabling him to increase his powers as head of government and to suspend meetings of the legislature. By 1980 Marcos faced growing opposition from college students protesting high tuition, from workers and farmers hurt by inflation, and from Catholic clergy fearing violence and asking for an end to martial law.

China

APPEAL TO IMPERIALISTS (FROM THE MID-19TH CENTURY)

China, a land occupying much of eastern Asia, attracted imperialist nations for several reasons: (1) China's huge population offered a tremendous market for manufactured goods and cheap labor for foreign-owned enterprises. (2) China's untapped mineral resources—coal, iron, and tin—attracted investors. (3) China's tea and silk found ready Western markets. (4) China's Manchu government was inefficient and lacked military power.

VICTIM OF MODERN IMPERIALISM

Britain, by the *Opium War* (1839–1842), compelled China to (1) allow imports of opium, a habit-forming narcotic, (2) open additional ports to British trade, (3) cede Hong Kong to Britain, and (4) grant British citizens the privilege of *extraterritoriality*. (This entitled an Englishman accused of a crime in China to be tried in a British court. Extraterritoriality, soon conceded to other foreign nations, offended Chinese justice and pride.) Britain later established a *sphere of influence* over the Yangtze River Valley. (A sphere of influence was a region over which an imperialist nation maintained an *economic monopoly:* licensing businesses, controlling tariff rates, and determining railroad and harbor fees.)

Other foreign nations secured trading and extraterritorial rights in China, annexed Chinese territory, and acquired spheres of influence. France gained a sphere of influence in southeastern China, as did Germany in the Shantung Peninsula. Russia annexed territory in northern China and established a sphere of influence over Manchuria. Japan annexed Taiwan (Formosa).

The imperialist nations seemed poised to annex their respective spheres of influence, thereby threatening further to dismember China.

AMERICAN RELATIONS WITH CHINA

The United States had long conducted a small but profitable trade with China. In 1844 *Caleb Cushing* negotiated a treaty with China securing for Americans the trading and extraterritorial privileges extended to other foreigners. However, unlike the imperialist nations in China, the United States annexed no territory and claimed no sphere of influence.

OPEN DOOR POLICY (1899)

By acquiring the Philippines in 1898, Americans anticipated an increase in our China trade. Such trade was threatened, however, by the existence of spheres of influence and by the prospect of China's dismemberment. *John Hay,* the American Secretary of State, therefore proposed equal trading rights in China for all nations—the Open Door Policy. Later, it also came to mean the preservation of China's independence and territory.

The "open door" was accepted by the imperialist nations in principle, but not in practice. However, it earned us China's goodwill and, for many years, served as the cornerstone of American policy toward the Far East.

(Some historians have contended that, by committing us to safeguard China's territorial integrity, the Open Door Policy was a long-range American blunder. They argue that America's trade with China was too small to justify our entanglement in Far Eastern affairs. They further point out that, once a single nation became dominant in the Far East, as Japan did, the United States had to face the choice of abandoning the Open Door Policy or fighting to uphold it. *Samuel Bemis,* in his *Diplomatic History of the United States,* claims that American diplomacy in the Far East made two great blunders: the first—acquisition of the Philippines, and the second—issuance of the Open Door Policy.)

BOXER REBELLION (1900)

The *Boxers*, a Chinese society encouraged by Manchu leaders, staged an uprising to drive out all foreigners and restore China to isolation. They wrecked foreign property and killed foreign citizens, chiefly missionaries, businessmen, and diplomatic officials. The Boxers were suppressed by an international military force of European, Japanese, and American troops.

When the foreign nations demanded damages from China, Secretary of State Hay urged that China pay not by surrendering territory, but by giving a monetary indemnity. The other nations agreed. (When the foreign powers imposed excessive indemnities, the United States returned half of its money to advance education in China and to enable Chinese students to attend American colleges.)

BRIEF SURVEY OF DEVELOPMENTS IN CHINA TO WORLD WAR II

In 1911–1912 the *Kuomintang*, or *Nationalist party*, under *Sun Yat-sen*, overthrew the feeble Manchu Dynasty and proclaimed a republic. Thereafter, the Nationalists struggled to subdue the local warlords. By 1928 General *Chiang Kai-shek* had led the Nationalist armies to victory over the warlords, but he now faced a greater threat, the Chinese Communists. Following a period of civil war, the Nationalists and Communists arranged a temporary truce to meet the challenge of Japanese imperialism.

Japan

OPENING OF JAPAN (1853–1854)

By the mid-17th century, feudal Japan had withdrawn into isolation, and for 200 years she remained unaffected by Western civilization.

In 1853–1854 Commodore *Matthew C. Perry*, heading an American naval squadron, convinced Japan to open certain ports to American trade. Soon afterwards, the leading European powers demanded and received similar trade rights. In 1857–1858 *Townsend Harris*, America's first consul to Japan, skillfully negotiated treaties expanding diplomatic and commercial relations between the two countries.

WESTERNIZATION OF JAPAN (STARTING IN 1867)

In 1864 European and American warships bombarded a Japanese seaport in retaliation against antiforeign outbreaks. Impressed by Western military might and fearful of foreign domination, the Japanese rapidly transformed their country from medieval feudalism to modern nationhood. In so doing, they demonstrated a talent for learning from the West and for adapting Western institutions to Japanese needs.

The Japanese (1) established a strong central government with a constitution that concentrated power in the hands of the emperor and the military leaders, (2) created a powerful army and navy, (3) ended serfdom and enabled many peasants to become landowners, and (4) encouraged a sweeping program of industrialization. Japan soon produced textiles, steel, machinery, and ships, and became a major trading and manufacturing nation.

JAPAN TURNS TO IMPERIALISM

1. Reasons. (a) Japanese industries needed imports of raw materials—especially cotton, iron ore, and oil—since Japan lacks mineral and oil resources and adequate farmland. They also needed markets for their manufactured goods. (b) Japanese nationalists sought honor for the emperor and glory for the military forces. They thought that colonies would raise Japan to the rank of a big power. (c) Densely populated, Japan wanted colonial outlets for her surplus population. (d) Japan's location placed her within easy reach of the underdeveloped nations of eastern Asia, especially China.

2. Sino-Japanese War (1894–1895). Japan overwhelmed China and acquired Taiwan and a sphere of influence in Korea. (In 1910 Japan annexed Korea.)

3. Russo-Japanese War (1904–1905). Caused by imperialist rivalries over Manchuria and Korea, this war was fought on Chinese territory and in the nearby Pacific waters. Japan, to the world's surprise, defeated Russia.

   a. Treaty of Portsmouth (New Hampshire). President Theodore Roosevelt brought the warring nations together to negotiate the *Treaty of Portsmouth.* Japan gained from Russia the southern half of Sakhalin Island, the lease of Port Arthur (in China), and the sphere of influence in southern Manchuria. Roosevelt was pleased that the treaty did not violate the Open Door Policy. (For his efforts, Roosevelt received the 1906 Nobel Peace Prize.)

   b. Significance. (1) Japanese militarists were cheered by their victory, the first in modern times of an Asian nation over a European power. They became determined to place eastern Asia under Japanese domination. (Later, they promised to bring a *New Order* to this *Co-Prosperity Sphere.*) (2) Japanese officials were satisfied with the treaty but many Japanese resented the lack of any war indemnity and were dissatisfied with their territorial gains. They blamed President Roosevelt and staged anti-American riots. (3) American government officials realized that Japan had become the major Far Eastern power. They feared for the safety of the Philippines and the maintenance of the Open Door Policy. To demonstrate American power, President Theodore Roosevelt sent the American navy on an around-the-world tour with a significant stop at Tokyo, where the navy received a friendly welcome. (4) The American people became aroused over what was loosely termed the *yellow peril.*

JAPAN AND THE UNITED STATES COME INTO CONFLICT

1. Japanese Resentment of American Immigration Policies. The Japanese government resented discriminatory actions by America against Japanese immigrants. (Check the Index for "Japanese-Americans.") These, however, were minor irritations when compared to the basic conflict of interests: American support of the Open Door Policy versus Japan's ambition to dominate China.

2. Japan's Twenty-One Demands Upon China (1915). During World War I, while the Western powers were preoccupied in Europe, Japan tried to turn China into a protectorate by making the *Twenty-One Demands*. Despite American protests, Japan compelled acceptance of most of these demands by weak, defenseless China.

After the war the United States called the *Washington Conference* (1921–1922) to discuss naval and Far Eastern problems. Under Western persuasion, Japan joined in the *Nine-Power Treaty*, pledging to respect the principles of the Open Door: *(a)* equal trade rights in China, and *(b)* China's territorial integrity and independence.

3. Japanese Invasion of Manchuria (1931). In violation of the Nine-Power Treaty, Japan invaded China's northern province of Manchuria, rich in coal, iron, and fertile soil. The *Lytton Commission*, investigating for the League of Nations, condemned Japan and recommended that she withdraw her troops. Instead, Japan withdrew from the League.

Henry L. Stimson, the United States Secretary of State, informed Japan that America disapproved of the aggression in Manchuria. He declared that the United States would recognize no seizure of territory by force—the *Stimson Doctrine*. As neither the League nor the United States took further action, Japan continued its aggression and by 1932 exercised full control over Manchuria. In violation of the Open Door Policy, the Japanese expelled foreign business interests and monopolized the region's economic development. They built railroads, developed hydroelectric power, and created a sizable iron and steel industry, thereby increasing Japan's economic and military power.

4. Japanese Invasion of China (1937). Japan invaded China proper, seeking to control the entire country. Initially, Japanese armies met with success and occupied most of coastal China. By 1939, however, their advance into the interior was slowed, often to a standstill, by Chinese guerrilla resistance. Meanwhile, the United States, in support of China, *(a)* extended loans for the purchase of war materials, *(b)* permitted American volunteer pilots to fight for China as the *Flying Tigers*, and *(c)* in 1940 embargoed the sale to Japan of scrap metal and aviation gasoline. Also, many American importers and consumers boycotted Japanese goods.

5. Japanese Attack on Pearl Harbor (December 7, 1941). Japanese leaders believed that they had to drive out Great Britain and the United States in order to dominate the Far East. In 1937 Japan joined the Axis alliance of Fascist Italy and Nazi Germany. When World War II began in 1939, Japanese leaders believed that their opportunity was at hand. Britain was at war against Germany; the United States was busy supplying military equipment to the Allied nations in Europe. On December 7, 1941, Japan staged a surprise attack against the American naval base at Pearl Harbor, Hawaii, and Japanese armies invaded the Philippines. (Check the Index for "Japan" and "World War II.")

MULTIPLE-CHOICE QUESTIONS

1. The American record in the Philippines includes all of the following *except* (1) training the Filipinos for self-government (2) developing a highly industrialized economy (3) reducing illiteracy (4) improving health conditions.
2. During the 1920's some Americans urged independence for the Philippines because (1) the Filipinos are brown-skinned (2) the Communists were very powerful in the islands (3) Filipino products were entering the United States without payment of any tariff (4) the islands had no need of American military protection.
3. Since independence, the Philippines generally has followed a foreign policy that (1) favors Communist China (2) opposes entangling alliances (3) supports the United States (4) seeks strict neutrality in the cold war.
4. A sphere of influence, in the history of China, was a region (1) annexed by a foreign power (2) ruled by foreign missionaries (3) nominally Chinese but controlled economically by a foreign power (4) lacking in Chinese courts.
5. The United States decided on its Open Door Policy at a time when China (1) was in danger of being partitioned by foreign nations (2) refused to trade with non-Asian powers (3) was engaged in a civil war between Communists and Nationalists (4) was undergoing rapid industrialization.
6. The Open Door Policy indicated that the United States was primarily interested in (1) acquiring a colonial empire in the Far East (2) protecting United States trade in China (3) applying the Monroe Doctrine to Asia (4) protecting United States bases in the Philippines.
7. The United States won the friendship of China immediately after the Boxer Rebellion by (1) encouraging Japanese expansion into Manchuria (2) returning a portion of the indemnity payments (3) allowing the admission of Chinese immigrants on a quota basis (4) refusing to recognize Chiang Kai-shek.
8. Commodore Perry's visit to Japan was made *primarily* to (1) open Japanese ports to American merchant ships (2) prevent Japanese domination of China (3) break the British monopoly of Japanese trade (4) settle the controversy over the seal fisheries.
9. Japanese imperialism in the 20th century (1) resulted from the desire for new trade routes (2) sought territory as indispensable for national power and prestige (3) was motivated by strong religious desires to convert peoples of developing nations (4) showed a willingness to share surplus products of the mother country with the less developed areas.
10. The *major* cause of Japanese-American tension during the 1930's was Japan's (1) violation of the Open Door Policy (2) expulsion of American missionaries from Japan (3) refusal to trade with the United States (4) military pact with Russia.
11. The Stimson Doctrine (1) had little effect on Japanese aggression in the 1930's (2) was issued when Japan annexed Formosa (3) placed an embargo on the sale of scrap metal to Japan (4) opposed efforts by the League of Nations regarding Manchuria.

MATCHING QUESTIONS

Column A	*Column B*
1. Commanded American army forces in the Far East	*a.* Ferdinand Marcos
	b. Theodore Roosevelt
2. Overthrew Manchu regime	*c.* Henry L. Stimson
3. Led Filipino revolt against United States	*d.* Douglas MacArthur
4. Formulated Open Door Policy	*e.* Emilio Aguinaldo
5. Received Nobel Peace Prize for efforts in ending Russo-Japanese War	*f.* Sun Yat-sen
	g. John Hay
6. Led Chinese Nationalists against warlords and then against Communists	*h.* Chiang Kai-shek
	i. Matthew C. Perry

DISCUSSION ANALYSIS QUESTIONS:
PHILIPPINE ISLANDS

Speakers A, B, C, D, and E are discussing the Philippine Islands. Base your answers to the following questions on their statements and on your knowledge of American studies.

Speaker A: "These poor, uncivilized, unchristianized people need our assistance if they are to be uplifted from their ignorance to a point at least approaching our level of civilization and accomplishment. The Philippines must be ours."

Speaker B: "These islands would certainly make excellent coaling stations for our great naval fleet, which is growing each year as Congress approves additional funds for the construction of new ships."

Speaker C: "The shipping interests really find the Philippines to be excellent trading centers. Furthermore, they can be used to develop our commerce with China and Japan. We can use the islands as stopover and storage points for our merchant fleets."

Speaker D: "We have no alternative but to accept the Philippines as our own. God would not forgive us if we rejected his obvious faith and trust in our nation. Democracy must be carried to the four corners of the globe."

Speaker E: "Were our economic rivals to obtain the Philippines, it would be a commercial disaster for our nation. We entered the race late, but we must not fall behind now."

1. Each statement made by the speakers could be used to justify   (1) imperialism   (2) containment   (3) coexistence   (4) genocide.
2. Speaker A would be willing to accept what the British called the   (1) defense of democracy   (2) appeasement policy   (3) lost cause   (4) white man's burden.
3. Which speaker's views are most in accord with an economic interpretation of history?   (1) A   (2) B   (3) C   (4) D
4. Speaker A's views are most similar to those of Speaker   (1) E   (2) B   (3) C   (4) D.
5. Which speaker *most* shows the influence of the writings of Captain Alfred Mahan?   (1) A   (2) B   (3) D   (4) E
6. Which speaker believes that the United States has been chosen to carry out a "divine mission"?   (1) B   (2) C   (3) D   (4) E
7. A Spanish cultural contribution to the Philippines disproves part of the statement made by Speaker   (1) A   (2) B   (3) C   (4) D.
8. When speaker E refers to "our economic rivals," he is *most* concerned about   (1) Canada   (2) Russia   (3) Britain   (4) Italy.

ESSAY QUESTIONS

1. As a result of the Spanish-American War, the United States acquired the Philippines. Discuss (a) *two* reasons why the United States annexed the Philippines (b) *two* problems that the Philippines posed for the United States after annexation (c) *two* reasons why the United States later offered the Philippines independence and (d) *one* way the Philippines was affected by World War II.
2. The United States championed the Open Door Policy with regard to China. (a) Briefly state the terms of the Open Door Policy. (b) Describe *one* circumstance that led to the issuance of the Open Door Policy. (c) Describe *one* incident in which Japan threatened the Open Door Policy during the period 1905–1945, and explain *one* action taken by the United States government to resist this threat.
3. Describe *one* action taken by the United States as a result of *each* of the following developments in the Far East: (a) emigration from the Far East to the United States between 1875 and 1929 (b) Boxer Rebellion (c) Russo-Japanese War (d) Twenty-One Demands (e) Japan's seizure of Manchuria (f) Japan's invasion of China proper.

Part 4. The Powerful Nation: Reluctance to Accept Responsibility (From World War I Through the Postwar Disillusionment)

10. The United States Seeks Neutrality But Becomes Involved in World War I

EUROPE GOES TO WAR (1914)

Divided into two hostile alliances, the major European nations had provoked each other in a series of international crises. They had turned Europe into a "powder keg" ready to explode into war. When in 1914 a Serb (Yugoslav) assassinated the heir to the Austro-Hungarian throne, World War I began. In the initial stage of the war, the conflicting nations were (1) the *Central Powers*—Germany and Austria-Hungary—against (2) the *Allies*—Great Britain, France, Russia, Serbia, and Belgium. (See map, page 557.)

FUNDAMENTAL CAUSES OF WORLD WAR I

1. Nationalism. (*a*) France was determined to recover from Germany the French-inhabited provinces of Alsace and Lorraine. (*b*) Subject nationalities sought independence. Yugoslavs, Czechs, and Slovaks sought freedom from Austria-Hungary. Poles, divided among Russia, Austria-Hungary, and Germany, longed to re-create a self-governing Polish state. (*c*) Intense patriotism assured popular support for warlike measures.

2. Imperialism. (*a*) France and Germany clashed over Morocco. (*b*) Russia and Austria-Hungary were rivals in the Balkans. (*c*) Britain and Germany competed for imperialist control in Africa and the Middle East, and for world markets.

3. Militarism. (*a*) By peacetime conscription, the continental European nations each sought military superiority. (*b*) Germany had a military tradition and extolled armed might. (*c*) Britain, relying heavily upon her navy for protection, felt threatened by Germany's huge naval building program.

4. International Anarchy. (*a*) No international organization existed with authority to compel nations to obey its decisions. (*b*) The *Hague Court of Arbitration*, a tribunal to settle international disputes, depended on voluntary acceptance of its authority and was ineffective.

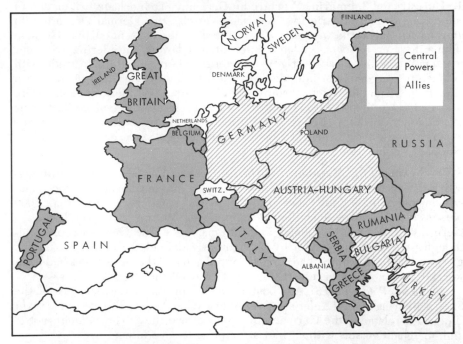

Europe: The Opposing Sides in World War I

OTHER NATIONS ENTER THE WAR

1. The Central Powers were joined by Turkey and Bulgaria.

2. The Allied Powers were joined by more than 25 nations. Most notable were (*a*) in 1914, Japan, which acted primarily to seize German territories in the Pacific, (*b*) in 1915, Italy, which had refused to honor her alliance with the Central Powers, now was won over to the Allies by a secret treaty promising her territorial gains, and (*c*) in 1917, the United States.

AMERICAN ENTRANCE INTO WORLD WAR I: REASONS

When war started in 1914, President Woodrow Wilson urged the American people to be "neutral in fact as well as in name" and issued a *Proclamation of Neutrality*. However, Americans could not help but take sides. Except for some Irish-Americans, who were traditionally anti-English, and some German-Americans, the people of the United States overwhelmingly sympathized with the Allies. In the administration, except for Secretary of State William Jennings Bryan, who resigned in 1915, Wilson and his chief advisers all favored the Allies.

Despite his pro-Allied leanings, Wilson desired peace for the United States and hoped to keep the nation neutral. In November 1916, Wilson narrowly won reelection with the slogan, "He kept us out of the war." In April 1917, only five months later, Wilson asked Congress to declare war on Germany. The main reasons, according to historians, were the following:

1. **Unrestricted Submarine Warfare by Germany.** To blockade Britain and to counteract British superiority in surface vessels, the Germans resorted to *unrestricted submarine warfare*. The United States contended that German submarines, or *U-boats*, violated international law by interfering with our *freedom of the seas: (a)* the right of American merchant ships to trade with belligerents in goods not intended for war use, and *(b)* the right of American citizens to sail on the merchant ships of belligerents. The American people were outraged as German U-boats violated our neutral rights and took an increasing toll of American lives. Before the United States entered the war, over 200 Americans, most traveling on Allied merchant ships, perished as a result of Germany's submarine warfare.

    a. Sinking of the "Lusitania" (1915). A German U-boat sank the *Lusitania*, a British passenger liner, without first searching for contraband war goods and without providing for the safety of the crew and passengers. More than 1000 persons lost their lives, including 100 Americans. Wilson sent several notes to Germany protesting this "illegal and inhuman act." The German replies, although regretting the loss of lives, vigorously defended the sinking on the grounds that the *Lusitania* had carried contraband and that Americans had been warned, by a newspaper advertisement, to stay off the ship.

    b. Sussex Pledge (1916). A U-boat torpedoed an unarmed French vessel, the *Sussex*, injuring several American passengers. When Wilson threatened to sever diplomatic relations, the German government gave the *Sussex Pledge*—not to sink merchant vessels without first attempting to save human lives.

    c. Unrestricted Submarine Warfare Again (1917). Believing that they now had enough U-boats to starve Britain, the German leaders took the risk of war with the United States and renewed their unrestricted submarine warfare. U-boats soon sank several unarmed American merchant ships. President Wilson ordered guns placed on our merchant ships and shortly afterwards asked Congress to declare war.

    (In spite of our protests, Britain blockaded our trade with the Central Powers, forced American ships into British ports to be searched, and intercepted American mail. However, Americans were less angered by British than by German acts, since British interference with our neutral rights did not endanger American lives.)

2. **Allied Propaganda.** Americans were receptive to Allied propaganda. *(a)* We felt a kinship for Britain, based upon a common language, culture, and belief in the democratic way of life. *(b)* Our friendship for France went back to French support of the colonial cause in the American Revolution.

3. **Hostility Toward Germany.** The American people became increasingly hostile toward Germany because the Germans *(a)* supported a thinly veiled dictatorship controlled by the military and the Kaiser, *(b)* invaded Belgium in violation of a treaty guaranteeing Belgian neutrality, *(c)* waged unrestricted submarine warfare, *(d)* attempted to sabotage American industries, and *(e)* plotted to draw Mexico into war against the United States, as evidenced by the *Zimmermann Note*.

    German Foreign Minister Zimmermann in early 1917 sent instructions to the German minister in Mexico. In the event of German-American hostilities, he

THE UNITED STATES IN WORLD AFFAIRS / 559

was to induce Mexico to declare war against the United States. Mexico might then regain Texas, New Mexico, and Arizona. Intercepted by the British, this secret German message inflamed American war sentiment.

4. American Economic Interests. Because Britain effectively blockaded the Central Powers, Americans sold foodstuffs, war materials, and other manufactured goods almost entirely to the Allies. Our manufacturers, workers, farmers, and exporters all shared in a period of prosperity. When the Allies exhausted their funds, American investors extended them substantial loans. Americans feared that, if Germany won the war, American loans to the Allies might never be repaid.

5. American Idealism. Americans felt that a better world would emerge if the Allied nations triumphed over the autocratic Central Powers. President Wilson called World War I the "war to end all wars" and proclaimed that "the world must be made safe for democracy."

6. American Security. Germany, if victorious, would have replaced democratic Britain as the dominant European power on the Atlantic. From this location, aggressive, militaristic Germany could have threatened the security of the United States.

AMERICA AT WAR: THE HOME FRONT

1. Increasing Presidential Powers. Wilson provided strong wartime leadership. He received from Congress emergency power to direct the economy and spur the war effort. Wilson commanded an array of government agencies representing a tremendous expansion of federal and executive power.

2. Mobilizing the Economy. The *War Industries Board* allocated raw materials, eliminated waste, and expanded war production. The *War Labor Board* mediated labor disputes so as to prevent work stoppages. The *Railroad Administration* took control of the railroads, unifying and improving their operations. The *Shipping Board* built a "bridge of ships" to transport men and materials to the European fighting fronts. The *Fuel Administration* stepped up the production of coal, gas, and oil, and combated wastefulness in their use. The *Food Administration* increased farm output and encouraged the public to observe "wheatless" and "meatless" days.

3. Punishing Espionage and Sedition. Check the Index for the "Espionage Act (1917)" and the "Sedition Act (1918)."

4. Financing the War. The government (a) raised income taxes and levied new and heavier excise taxes, securing $11 billion, or one-third of the cost of the war, and (b) borrowed from the American people by selling them *Liberty* and *Victory Bonds*, securing $21 billion, or two-thirds of the war's cost. The United States lent the Allies $10 billion to purchase war supplies.

5. Providing Military Manpower. Congress passed several *Selective Service Acts*. Our armed forces consisted of almost 3 million draftees and 2 million volunteers. The dispatch of army units to Europe was hastened by desperate Allied appeals for American manpower to turn the tide of battle.

MILITARY ASPECTS OF THE WAR

1. Worldwide Involvement. For the first time in history, all major nations throughout the world were involved in the same war.

2. New Weapons. The following devices were introduced into warfare: dirigibles, submarines, giant artillery guns, tanks, poison gas, and, most significant, the airplane. It was employed at first mainly for observation purposes but later for small-scale bombings and for attacks on ground forces.

3. Naval Warfare. The British navy, aided by the French, maintained control of the Atlantic shipping lanes, combated the German submarine menace, and effectively blockaded the Central Powers. In 1917 the American navy under Admiral *William Sims* bolstered the Allied fleets.

4. American Military Contribution in Europe. By early 1918, the military situation in Europe was as follows: *(a)* The *western front*, in France, was deadlocked. The opposing armies were dug into the ground for *trench warfare*. *(b)* The *eastern front* was no more. In 1917 Russia had experienced two revolutions and had come under Communist rule. In 1918 Russia withdrew from the war, freeing German forces for transfer to the western front.

The *American Expeditionary Force* (AEF), totaling 2 million men and led by General *John J. Pershing*, turned the tide of battle in France. In 1918 American soldiers helped halt a German offensive at *Château-Thierry* and *Belleau Wood*. Later they led the Allied end-the-war counteroffensive at *St. Mihiel* and in the *Argonne Forest*.

5. German Surrender. By late 1918 the German High Command under Generals *von Hindenburg* and *Ludendorff* realized that the German armies, although still fighting on foreign soil, had lost the war. Germany sued for peace and on November 11, 1918, ended hostilities by accepting an *armistice*.

PRESIDENT WILSON'S FOURTEEN POINTS

In early 1918, President Wilson addressed Congress on American war aims. His program, which evoked enthusiasm among peoples throughout the world, called for a lasting peace based upon *Fourteen Points:* (1) open covenants (treaties) of peace openly arrived at, (2) freedom of the seas, (3) removal of international trade barriers, (4) reduction of armaments, (5) impartial adjustment of colonial claims with due regard for the interests of the native peoples, (6–13) adjustment of European boundaries in accordance with the principle of *nationality*, that is, the right of any national group to self-determination regarding its own government and the formation of an independent national state, and (14) establishment of a League of Nations.

Allied statesmen approved Wilson's Fourteen Points only with significant reservations. In particular, each statesman upheld his nation's claims to territorial gains and to protection of vital national interests.

TREATY OF VERSAILLES WITH GERMANY (1919)

1. Different Allied Objectives. The "Big Four," the Allied leaders who dominated the peace conference, each sought different objectives. *(a) David Lloyd*

George, Prime Minister of Great Britain, sought to expand Britain's colonial empire, preserve her naval and industrial supremacy, and "make Germany pay for the war." (*b*) *Georges Clemenceau*, Premier of France, sought to make France safe against future German invasion and weaken Germany by imposing military limitations, financial payments, and territorial losses. (*c*) *Vittorio Orlando*, Premier of Italy, sought to enlarge Italy's territory in Europe and expand her empire overseas. (*d*) *Woodrow Wilson*, President of the United States, sought to provide a just peace and create a better world by implementing his Fourteen Points.

Out of these different and often conflicting objectives emerged the *Treaty of Versailles*, the result of months of struggle and compromise.

2. Major Treaty Provisions

a. Territorial Changes. Germany surrendered (1) Alsace-Lorraine to France; (2) minor border regions to Denmark and Belgium; (3) parts of Posen and West Prussia, including a corridor to the Baltic Sea, to the new nation of Poland (this "Polish Corridor" cut off East Prussia from the rest of Germany); (4) Danzig, a Baltic city, was placed under League of Nations authority to provide Poland with her only seaport.

Except for Danzig, predominantly German-inhabited, these territorial changes were in accord with the principle of nationality. The territory granted to Poland, however, contained a considerable German minority.

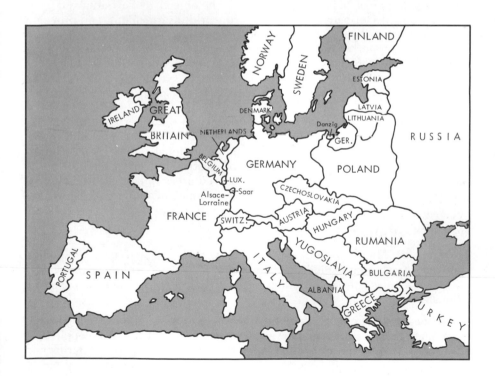

Europe Following World War I

b. Colonial Losses. Germany ceded all her colonies to the Allies, to be held as League of Nations mandates.

c. Disarmament. The German army was limited to 100,000 volunteers. Conscription was forbidden. The Rhineland, in western Germany, was demilitarized. The German navy was reduced to a few small ships. Submarines, military aircraft, and war industries were prohibited.

d. War Guilt and Reparations. Germany accepted sole responsibility for causing the war and agreed to pay reparations for war damages. (Germany later repudiated most of the debt.)

e. League of Nations. The first article of the treaty provided for the establishment of the League of Nations.

3. Differing Views of the Treaty

a. Arguments Against: A Harsh Treaty That Planted the Seeds of World War II. The treaty took German-inhabited territory away from Germany, forced Germany to give up all her colonies, and compelled her to accept sole "war guilt." It forced Germany to be unarmed while other nations remained armed, and it wounded German pride. Later, by attacking the treaty, the Nazi party gained the support of the German people, achieved power, and brought on World War II.

b. Arguments For: A Fair Treaty That Was Not Enforced. The treaty transferred German territory chiefly on the basis of nationality, assigned German colonies as League of Nations mandates with the objective of eventual independence, disarmed Germany as a start toward world disarmament, and provided for a League of Nations. The treaty alone cannot be blamed for the German people's later support of Nazism. Furthermore, if the military provisions of the treaty had been enforced, Nazi Germany would not have been able to wage war.

TREATIES WITH THE OTHER DEFEATED NATIONS

The Allies signed separate treaties with each of the other Central Powers. The treaties with Austria and Hungary broke up the Austro-Hungarian Empire. (1) Austria and Hungary became independent national states. (2) Czechoslovakia, a new republic, was created out of Austro-Hungarian territories. (3) Italy, Rumania, Poland, and Yugoslavia secured areas inhabited by their own nationals. (4) Also, Austria was forbidden *Anschluss*, or union with Germany.

RESULTS OF WORLD WAR I

1. Social. *(a)* Almost 10 million soldiers were killed and over 20 million wounded. *(b)* Millions of civilians died as a result of the hostilities, famine, and disease. *(c)* The world was left with a legacy of hatred, intolerance, and extreme nationalism.

2. Economic. *(a)* The total cost of the war was over $350 billion. Paying for the war brought heavy taxation and lower living standards to European peoples. *(b)* After the war, international trade suffered because nations raised tariffs and sought economic self-sufficiency. *(c)* In Russia, the Communists seized power and introduced a new economic system. *(d)* The United States changed from a debtor to a creditor nation. *(e)* Economic dislocations caused by the war helped bring on the Great Depression.

3. Political. *(a)* Three major European dynasties were dethroned: the Hohenzollerns of Germany, the Hapsburgs of Austria-Hungary, and the Romanovs of Russia. *(b)* New nations arose in Central Europe. Several contained minority groups (subject nationalities), such as the German-speaking populations of Poland and Czechoslovakia. *(c)* Beset by economic and political discontent, many European nations—notably Russia, Italy, and Germany—turned to dictatorship. *(d)* The League of Nations was established to solve international problems and advance world peace. *(e)* The United States emerged as a leading world power, though reluctant to assume international responsibilities.

MULTIPLE-CHOICE QUESTIONS

1. The division of the major European powers into two rival alliances in the years preceding 1914 resulted in a (1) reduction of world tensions (2) decline of imperialism (3) decrease in military expenditures (4) series of international crises.
2. The suppression of subject nationalities contributed to the outbreak of World War I. This statement can be illustrated by (1) Austro-Hungarian domination of part of present-day Yugoslavia (2) German domination of Danzig (3) French domination of Alsace and Lorraine (4) German and French domination of Morocco.
3. President Wilson's policy at the beginning of World War I was to (1) send lend-lease aid to nations attacked by Germany (2) declare war against the Central Powers (3) prohibit trade with warring nations (4) issue a Proclamation of Neutrality.
4. Immediately following the sinking of the *Lusitania*, President Wilson (1) signed a secret treaty to give aid to Britain (2) presented his Fourteen Points as a basis for promoting world peace (3) refused to be stampeded into any hasty act leading to war (4) prohibited Americans from traveling on ships of belligerents.
5. The immediate cause for the entry of the United States into World War I was Germany's (1) attempt to arrange an alliance with Mexico (2) invasion of Belgium (3) resumption of unrestricted submarine warfare (4) campaign of sabotage in the United States.
6. Which is *not* considered a factor that influenced the United States to enter World War I? (1) financial commitments to the Allies (2) desire to gain overseas possessions (3) desire to repay France for her assistance during our Revolutionary War (4) concern over the survival of democracy
7. One of the aims of the United States during World War I was (1) the defeat of Japan (2) the collection of indemnities (3) freedom of the seas (4) the division of Germany into two countries.
8. Which would be consistent with one of President Wilson's Fourteen Points? (1) the formation of new national states in Europe (2) the permanent separation of East Germany and West Germany (3) a secret military alliance between the United States and Japan (4) an increase in the United States tariff rates to keep out German goods
9. Which principle of Wilson's Fourteen Points was incorporated in the Treaty of Versailles? (1) open diplomacy (2) removal of economic barriers (3) limitation of armaments for all signers of the treaty (4) a League of Nations
10. An important result of World War I was that in many European nations (1) living standards rose (2) foreign trade increased (3) nationalism became less intense (4) dictators seized control.
11. Another result of World War I was that the United States (1) became a creditor na-

tion and world power   (2) abandoned its interests in the Caribbean area   (3) initiated a policy of imperialism in the Far East   (4) feared Germany's emergence as an
Atlantic power.

MODIFIED TRUE-FALSE QUESTIONS

1. The "Lusitania," sunk by a German submarine during World War I, was *an American*
   ship.
2. In winning the Presidential election of 1916, Woodrow Wilson was aided by the
   slogan, *"The world must be made safe for democracy."*
3. The Zimmermann Note called for a German offer of American territory to *Japan.*
4. Allied territorial claims, often in conflict with the principles of the Fourteen Points,
   were based upon *secret treaties.*
5. In returning Alsace and Lorraine to France, the Treaty of Versailles was *in accord with*
   the Fourteen Points.
6. The Treaty of Versailles limited Germany to an army of *1 million* men.

ESSAY QUESTIONS

1. (*a*) Briefly discuss *three* reasons why the United States entered World War I. (*b*)
   Evaluate these three reasons, explaining which one you consider *most* important and
   which one *least* important.
2. (*a*) List *five* important provisions of the Treaty of Versailles. (*b*) Discuss *two* reasons
   why Germany criticized this treaty. (*c*) Would you agree or disagree with *each* of the
   German criticisms? Defend your answer. (*d*) Did the Treaty of Versailles plant the
   seeds of World War II? Explain.
3. Describe *two* important results of World War I in *each* of the following areas: (a)
   social (*b*) economic (*c*) political.

11. The United States Is Torn Between Isolation and International Cooperation (1919–1939)

OPPOSING VIEWPOINTS ON AMERICAN FOREIGN POLICY

1. Isolation: The Predominant Sentiment

a. Disillusionment With World War I. Many Americans were disappointed
with the results of the war. It had proved costly in American lives and money.
Instead of making "the world safe for democracy," it had led to major European
dictatorships. Instead of being a "war to end all wars," it had apparently planted
the seeds for another world conflict.

b. American Tradition of Isolation. Isolationists claimed that, except for
World War I, the United States had successfully pursued a policy of isolation
since the days of George Washington. Now they demanded that the United
States return and strictly adhere to our traditional policy of isolation.

c. Peace Through Isolation. Isolationists argued that America could have
peace only by shutting herself off from the rest of the world. Let Uncle Sam "stay
on his side of the street" while Europe "stews in its own juice." Isolationist
sentiment was powerful during the 1920's as well as during the depression years,
when Americans concentrated upon domestic problems.

2. International Cooperation: The Minority View

a. Defense of World War I. Internationalists defended American entrance into World War I by emphasizing Wilsonian idealism and national security. They claimed that, by rejecting world leadership, the United States endangered its own security and lost the opportunity to assure world peace.

b. Failure of Isolation. Opponents of isolation insisted that isolation had not worked in the past, pointing to American involvement in the Napoleonic Wars (by the War of 1812) and World War I. Now that economic factors and scientific progress had made nations more dependent on each other than ever before, internationalists argued, isolation was unrealistic.

c. Peace Through International Cooperation. Internationalists argued that America could have peace only by cooperating with peace-loving nations against aggression. We cannot "stop the world and get off."

Sentiment for cooperation grew in the late 1930's, as Americans observed Fascist militarism and aggression. President Franklin D. Roosevelt, who had served under and admired Wilson, worked cautiously but deliberately to swing public opinion away from isolation. However, not until Britain stood alone in World War II did international cooperation achieve acceptance by a majority of Americans.

UNITED STATES REFUSAL TO JOIN THE LEAGUE OF NATIONS

1. Brief Survey of the League of Nations

a. Establishment. Woodrow Wilson believed that the single most important step toward world peace was the League of Nations. Wilson succeeded in placing the League Covenant (Charter) into the Treaty of Versailles.

b. Purposes. By international cooperation, the League proposed to (1) deal with economic and social problems, (2) encourage disarmament, and (3) settle disputes among nations peacefully. If an aggressor nation refused to submit to peaceful settlement, the League could advise its member nations to employ coercive measures, called *sanctions.* These might be withdrawing ambassadors; halting trade; and, finally, using military force.

2. Senate Defeat of the Treaty of Versailles and the League

a. Republican Opposition. In control of the Senate, the Republicans consisted of (1) a small group of extreme isolationists, notably *William Borah, Hiram Johnson,* and *Robert La Follette,* and (2) a large group of more moderate Senators, most of whom supported the chairman of the Foreign Relations Committee, *Henry Cabot Lodge,* Sr. Bitterly hostile to Wilson, Senator Lodge determined to humiliate the President, to "republicanize" the Treaty of Versailles, and to protect American sovereignty by altering the treaty through strong *reservations.* Lodge held lengthy committee hearings to delay action and win support from the public and the Senate.

b. Arguments Against the League. Lodge and his supporters offered the following arguments: (1) The League might involve the United States in a war, thereby violating the American Constitution, which gives Congress the exclusive power to declare war. (2) The League might interfere in domestic matters, such as tariff and immigration policies. (3) The League would be under the disproportionate influence of Great Britain, since Britain and each of her Commonwealth dominions had its own vote in the League Assembly. (4) League membership would involve us in world problems and thus violate America's traditional policy of isolation.

c. *Wilson's Countermoves.* Wilson denounced the Lodge reservations. To arouse the people and to bring pressure on the Senate, Wilson undertook an extensive speaking tour. His efforts ended abruptly when, overworked and exhausted, he suffered a paralytic stroke. From his sickbed, Wilson instructed the Democrats in the Senate to reject the Lodge reservations.

d. *The Senate Votes.* The Senate twice defeated the Treaty of Versailles with the Lodge reservations and once rejected the unamended treaty. (Later, the United States negotiated a peace treaty that ended the war with Germany but that did not provide for a League.)

e. *Who Defeated the Treaty and the League?* The Treaty of Versailles was defeated by (1) Lodge, by his insistence on reservations, (2) Wilson, by his refusal to compromise, and (3) the American people. At first, most people probably favored League membership, but they did not speak out with sufficient strength. As the League debate raged, Americans became confused, disillusioned, and unwilling to assume the burdens of world leadership.

3. Election of 1920 and the League. Appealing to the voters, Wilson asked that the 1920 Presidential election be a "great and solemn referendum" on the League. James M. Cox, the Democratic candidate, campaigned vigorously for the League. Warren G. Harding, the Republican candidate, urged a "return to normalcy" but took no definite stand on the League.

The voters were influenced by other factors, all working against the Democrats: falling farm prices; growing unemployment; disillusionment with the war; and the resentment of various ethnic groups who blamed Wilson for treating Germany harshly, denying territory to Italy, and failing to secure independence for Ireland. Harding won an overwhelming triumph. He interpreted the result to mean that Americans opposed League membership.

HISTORY OF THE LEAGUE: A FAILURE

1. Reasons for Failure

a. *Membership.* The League did not include all major nations. The United States never joined. Russia entered the League in 1934 but was expelled in 1939. Germany and Japan withdrew in 1933, as did Italy four years later.

b. *Voting.* League decisions required *unanimous* votes.

c. *Powers.* The League lacked the power to tax and to draft an army. Although the League could request money, men, and support from its members, each state was free to respond according to its own national interests. The League was not a world government, but a weak *confederation*.

2. Record of Failure. Although the League settled minor disputes between small nations, it failed in major crises to stop (*a*) the Japanese invasion of Manchuria, (*b*) the Italian conquest of Ethiopia, and (*c*) German rearmament in violation of the Versailles Treaty, and German territorial seizures.

In 1946 the League disbanded and transferred its properties to the new world organization, the United Nations.

LIMITED COOPERATION BY THE UNITED STATES

1. The United States Cooperates With the League. The United States cooperated with the League by (a) joining the *International Labor Organization* (ILO), a League agency to gather labor statistics and improve world labor conditions, (b) working with other League agencies to wipe out disease, suppress slavery, and establish standards in communication and transportation, and (c) supporting the League during the crisis over Manchuria. (Check the Index for "Stimson Doctrine.")

2. The United States Joins in Naval Disarmament

a. Early Agreements. To reduce the tax burden and to avoid a naval armaments race, which had helped cause World War I, the United States cooperated with other naval powers in seeking a reduction of naval forces.

(1) *Washington Conference (1921–1922).* The United States, Great Britain, Japan, France, and Italy agreed to stop building capital ships (large warships) for ten years and to maintain capital ships for each nation in a ratio of 5:5:3:1.67:1.67, respectively.

(2) *London Naval Conference (1930).* The United States, Great Britain, and Japan agreed to a ratio of approximately 10:10:7, for five years, for cruisers and destroyers as well as capital ships.

b. Eventual Failure. At the *London Conference* (1935), the United States and England faced a Japanese demand for a 10:10:10 ratio, or *parity*. The democracies refused on the ground that Japan had no need of such naval power unless for aggression. No agreement was reached; soon afterwards Japan started a new naval race.

3. The United States Joins in International Pacts

a. Nine-Power Treaty at the Washington Conference (1921–1922). The United States, Japan, Britain, France, and five smaller nations agreed to support equal trading rights in China and to respect China's independence, thus reaffirming the Open Door Policy.

b. Kellogg-Briand Pact (1928). *Frank Kellogg*, American secretary of state, and *Aristide Briand*, French foreign minister, proposed a pact to settle all disputes peacefully and to outlaw war "as an instrument of national policy." Most nations, including Germany, Japan, and Italy, signed this idealistic statement, also called the *Pact of Paris*.

c. Failure of International Pacts. In the 1930's militarist Japan, Fascist Italy, and Nazi Germany all violated the Kellogg-Briand Pact. Japan also violated the Nine-Power Treaty. Without provision for enforcement, these agreements proved worthless.

FURTHER EVIDENCES OF ISOLATION BY THE UNITED STATES

1. Refusal to Join the World Court. The World Court was established by the League to settle disputes between nations according to international law.

Despite the requests of four successive Presidents—Harding, Coolidge, Hoover, and Roosevelt—Senate isolationists managed to keep the United States from membership in the World Court. They insisted that the World Court would take us into the League through the "back door."

2. Immigration Restrictions. By a series of immigration laws in the 1920's drastically limiting admissions, Congress expressed its sentiment for fewer world contacts—an aspect of isolationism.

3. High Tariff Policy. Congress restored high import duties and in 1930 passed the highest rates ever. By such protectionism, Congress reflected the isolationist view in economic matters.

4. Insistence Upon Repayment of War Debts. During World War I the European Allies—mainly Britain, France, and Italy—had borrowed $10 billion from the United States, primarily for the purchase of American war materials. Thereafter, the Allies claimed that they could not repay these loans, especially since America's high tariffs made it difficult for them to sell goods here and secure dollars.

The United States refused to cancel the war debts. By 1934, as all debtor nations except Finland had ceased repayments, Congress passed the *Johnson Debt Default Act*. It prohibited public or private loans to any foreign government that had defaulted on debts in the United States.

5. American Neutrality Acts (1935, 1937). As Germany and Italy became more and more aggressive, Americans sensed that Europe was again headed toward war. Congress passed two *Neutrality Acts* which (a) prohibited the sale of war implements to belligerents, (b) prohibited loans to belligerents, (c) prohibited Americans from sailing on ships of belligerents, and (d) restricted the entry of American merchant ships into war zones.

These acts surrendered American claims to freedom of the seas. Congress hoped that neutrality would prevent the economic and emotional entanglements that, many believed, had involved the United States in World War I.

6. Unfavorable Response to President Roosevelt's "Quarantine" Speech (1937). After Japan's invasion of China proper, President Franklin D. Roosevelt braved isolationist sentiment by delivering his "quarantine" speech. Citing "the present reign of terror and international lawlessness," Roosevelt warned, "let no one imagine that America will escape . . . that this Western Hemisphere will not be attacked." He compared world lawlessness to an "epidemic of physical disease" and proposed that the aggressor nations be subjected to "quarantine." Deliberately vague, Roosevelt wanted to test the readiness of Americans to support efforts against the aggressors.

Public and press reaction to the speech was generally unfavorable. Americans still believed that they could avoid war by retreat into isolation. Extreme isolationists called Roosevelt a "warmonger."

Part 5. The Powerful Nation:
Global Commitment and Leadership
(From World War II to the Present)

12. *The Allies Defeat the Axis and Win World War II*

AXIS NATIONS: JAPAN, ITALY, AND GERMANY

Imperial Japan was controlled by the military, Fascist Italy was led by the dictator *Benito Mussolini*, and Nazi Germany was headed by the dictator *Adolf Hitler*. These nations (1) engaged in one act of aggression after another, thereby violating, without any effective opposition, the major international peace agreements: the Treaty of Versailles, the Covenant of the League of Nations, the Nine-Power Treaty, and the Kellogg-Briand Pact, (2) withdrew from membership in the League, and (3) joined together to form a military alliance, the *Rome-Berlin-Tokyo Axis*.

RECORD OF AXIS AGGRESSION

1. Manchuria. In 1931–1932 Japan invaded and conquered China's northern province of Manchuria. (Check the Index for "Manchuria.")

2. Ethiopia. In 1935 Italy invaded the African nation of Ethiopia. The League of Nations branded Italy an aggressor and voted minor economic sanctions but *not* an embargo on Italy's most essential import, oil. Undeterred by such feeble opposition, Mussolini conquered and annexed Ethiopia.

3. German Remilitarization. Nazi Germany violated the Versailles Treaty in 1935 by reintroducing conscription and in 1936 by remilitarizing the Rhineland. Hitler encountered no serious Allied effort to enforce the Versailles Treaty, although Germany's military strength was then still slight.

4. Spain. In 1936 General *Francisco Franco* began a revolt against the legally elected left-of-center government of Spain. The Loyalists, who supported the elected government, received limited aid from Russia; Franco received extensive support of troops and equipment from Italy and Germany. After three years of civil war, Franco won complete control and established a military dictatorship friendly to Germany and Italy. The Spanish civil war served Nazi Germany as a testing ground for new weapons and military tactics, such as dive-bombings and tank assaults, later used in World War II.

5. China. In 1937 Japanese forces from Manchuria invaded China proper. (Check the Index for "China.")

6. Austria. In 1938 Hitler invaded and annexed Austria on the ground that all German-speaking people belonged within one German nation. *Anschluss* (union) of Germany and Austria violated the World War I peace treaties. Anschluss furthermore was never approved by the Austrian people in an honest plebiscite.

7. Czechoslovakia

 a. Hitler Demands the Sudetenland. Later in 1938 Hitler claimed the *Sudetenland*, a region in Czechoslovakia bordering on Germany and inhabited by German-speaking people. Although the Sudeten people had not been op-pressed, Nazi propagandists manufactured stories of Czech "atrocities." The Czech government refused to yield. It counted on its alliances with Russia and France, and expected British support. However, Britain and France decided not to risk war but to appease Hitler.

 b. Munich Conference. British Prime Minister *Neville Chamberlain* and French Premier *Edouard Daladier*, meeting at Munich with Mussolini and Hitler, agreed to let Hitler annex the Sudetenland. Deserted by her friends, Czechoslovakia yielded. Chamberlain returned to England and proclaimed that he had preserved "peace in our time." Hitler promised that he would demand no more territory.

 c. Hitler Seizes the Rest of Czechoslovakia. Six months later, however, Hitler seized the Slavic-inhabited remainder of Czechoslovakia. In Britain the Chamberlain government at last realized that Hitler could not be trusted to keep his promises. Britain and France joined in a military alliance and guaranteed protection to Germany's next probable victim, Poland.

8. Albania. In 1939 Mussolini invaded and annexed the Balkan country of Albania, giving Italy control of the Adriatic Sea.

9. Poland

 a. Hitler's Demands. In 1939 Hitler demanded the return of Danzig and the Polish Corridor on the ground that they were inhabited by German-speaking people.

 b. Russo-German Nonaggression Pact. Before Poland responded, Nazi Germany and Communist Russia announced a ten-year *Nonaggression Pact*. The world was surprised because Hitler had always preached hatred of communism, and Joseph Stalin, the Russian dictator, had always condemned fascism. (1) The pact enabled Russia to avoid (for the time being) involvement in a major war and, by its secret clauses, gave Stalin a free hand over eastern Poland and the Baltic states of Estonia, Latvia, and Lithuania. (2) The pact protected Germany against a two-front war and promised Hitler foodstuffs and war supplies from Russia.

 c. Start of World War II. On September 1, 1939, German troops invaded Poland. Two days later, Britain and France honored their guarantee to Poland and declared war on Germany. World War II had started.

BASIC CAUSES OF WORLD WAR II: AXIS PHILOSOPHY AND AGGRESSION

1. Totalitarianism. The Axis nations—Germany, Italy, and Japan—were totalitarian dictatorships. They scorned the democratic ideals of civil liberties, of the dignity of the individual, and of world peace; and they openly declared their intent to destroy democracy.

2. Militarism. The Axis nations spent vast sums on armaments, devised new weapons and battle techniques, built huge military organizations, and psychologically prepared their peoples for war. They proclaimed war a glorious adventure and death for the Fatherland the highest honor.

3. Nationalism. Japanese Shinto teachings, Italian dreams of a revival of the Roman Empire, and German "master race" doctrines all fostered a narrow and bigoted nationalism. The Axis nations considered themselves superior and destined to rule over "lesser peoples."

4. Imperialism. The Axis powers embarked upon imperialism, claiming that they lacked land and resources and were *have-not* nations. Japan expanded into Manchuria and China proper. Italy enlarged her African empire and planned to make the Mediterranean an "Italian lake." Germany annexed Austria and Czechoslovakia as first steps toward domination of Europe and eventually, perhaps, of the world.

SUBSIDIARY CAUSES OF WORLD WAR II

1. Failure of Appeasement. Britain and France followed a policy of *appeasement*—that is, making concessions to the dictators in the hope that they would eventually be satisfied and stop their aggression. Anxious for peace, democratic peoples failed to understand that each concession strengthened the aggressors and emboldened them to make further demands. Neville Chamberlain of Britain was the chief advocate of appeasement, and its final application was the transfer of the Sudetenland to Germany by the Munich Conference.

2. Lack of Collective Security. Peace-loving nations, by coordinating their military strength and acting collectively, might have protected each other from aggression. However, the democratic peoples shrank from any kind of military action. The United States was determined to remain neutral. Britain and France delayed the formation of a firm alliance until 1939.

Communist Russia urged collective security because she feared attack by Nazi Germany. Democratic nations, however, were reluctant to enter into collective security pacts with the Soviet Union because they (a) doubted Russia's sincerity, (b) feared Communist plans for world revolution, and (c) were not eager to protect the Soviet Union. In 1939, however, Russia saw an opportunity to turn the Nazi war machine against Britain and France. Thereupon, Russia terminated her support of collective security and concluded the Stalin-Hitler Nonaggression Pact.

3. American Neutrality Legislation. By prohibiting loans and the sale of war implements to all belligerents, the Neutrality Acts actually favored the well-armed aggressor nations over their ill-equipped victims. Furthermore, these laws implied that Americans would not intervene to check Axis aggression in Asia and Europe.

WORLD WAR II (1939–1945)

1. Initial German Successes (1939–1940)

a. Conquest of Poland. German armies, employing massive air bombings and tank assaults, unleashed a "lightning war," or *blitzkrieg*, and destroyed all Polish resistance. Germany annexed western Poland. (As agreed in the Hitler-Stalin Pact, Russia seized eastern Poland and annexed the Baltic countries.)

b. Conquest of Denmark and Norway. Nazi armies next overran neutral Denmark and Norway. Germany thus gained valuable submarine bases on the Atlantic Ocean.

c. Conquest of France. Nazi armies invaded northern France in 1940 by going through the plains of neutral Holland and Belgium. By this route, the Germans bypassed the Franco-German border with its mountainous terrain and French defensive fortifications, the *Maginot Line*. Nazi armies easily defeated the Allied defenders. British troops were miraculously evacuated to England while the French forces fled southward. With Mussolini confident of victory, Italy entered the war. As the German forces continued their advance southward, France surrendered.

In Britain, General *Charles de Gaulle*, determined to liberate France, established the *Free French* movement.

2. Britain Stands Alone (1940–1941)

a. Leadership of Churchill. *Winston Churchill*, who had repeatedly opposed appeasement of the Nazis, succeeded Chamberlain as prime minister. Churchill inspired the British people to courage and determination as he called upon them to save the world from the "abyss of a new dark age." "I have nothing to offer," he said, "but blood, toil, tears, and sweat."

b. Battle of Britain. Hitler ordered his *Luftwaffe* (air force) to soften Britain for invasion. For three months Britain was subjected to devastating air attacks. The *Royal Air Force* (RAF), however, drove off the Luftwaffe. By maintaining control of the air, the RAF compelled the Nazis to shelve their invasion plans.

3. American Preparedness and Aid to the Allies (1939–1941)

a. Neutrality Act of 1939. Soon after World War II started, President Franklin D. Roosevelt requested Congress to pass the Neutrality Act of 1939. This law permitted belligerents to purchase war materials on condition that they pay cash and carry the goods away in their own vessels. *Cash and carry* was designed to give limited assistance to the Atlantic sea powers (France and Britain) and, at the same time, maintain American neutrality.

b. Changes in Public Opinion. President Roosevelt labored to awaken the American people to the threat to their national security. When France fell in 1940, Americans finally realized that Britain alone stood between them and a hostile Fascist world. For America's self-defense, Congress supported aid to Britain by *all measures short of war.*

c. Military Preparedness. Congress also supported a vast military buildup, approving a two-ocean navy, a huge air force, and the 1940 *Selective Service Act.* It provided for America's first peacetime conscription.

d. Destroyer-Naval Base Deal (1940). President Roosevelt traded 50 "over-age" destroyers to Britain in exchange for military bases on British territory in the Western Hemisphere from Newfoundland to British Guiana. Britain needed the destroyers to combat German submarines; the United States used the bases as defensive outposts. (Fearful of delay in the Senate, Roosevelt negotiated this exchange by an executive agreement rather than by a treaty, which would have required Senate approval.)

e. Lend-Lease Act (1941). Realizing that Britain's cash was almost exhausted, President Roosevelt requested new legislation to maintain the United States as the "arsenal of democracy." Congress passed the *Lend-Lease Act* authorizing the President to lend or lease goods to any nation whose defense he deemed necessary for the defense of the United States. Immediately, Roosevelt extended substantial aid to Britain; he later gave aid to other Allies, including Russia. (Total lend-lease amounted to $50 billion.) Also, Roosevelt ordered that merchant ships carrying lend-lease materials be convoyed by the United States Navy part way across the Atlantic. When convoys were attacked by German submarines, American warships responded with fire, thus beginning a limited naval war.

f. Embargo on Strategic Materials to Japan. The United States opposed Japanese aggression in eastern Asia. In 1940–1941 the United States protested Japanese occupation of French Indo-China. Since protests proved ineffective, President Roosevelt embargoed the sale of aviation gasoline and scrap iron to Japan and "froze" Japanese assets in the United States.

4. The Axis Makes Two Mistakes (1941)

a. German Attack Upon Russia (June 22, 1941). Despite the Russo-German Nonaggression Pact, Hitler ordered war against Russia. Hitler expected a quick victory, but Russia proved to be a formidable foe. The Nazis occupied much territory but were unable to crush the Soviet armies.

b. Japanese Attack Upon the United States (December 7, 1941). Japan staged a surprise attack upon the American naval base at *Pearl Harbor,* Hawaii, forcing the United States actively into the war. Under General *Hideki Tojo,* the Japanese government planned to humble the United States and assure Japanese domination of eastern Asia. Japan's Axis partners, Germany and Italy, immediately declared war on the United States.

5. The United States Organizes for Victory

a. Presidential Leadership. Franklin D. Roosevelt showed confidence and determination in directing the national war effort. As commander in chief he planned the overall war strategy: first beat Hitler, then Japan. He met with top Allied leaders in several wartime conferences. On the home front, Roosevelt established an array of government agencies to direct the economy toward winning the war.

b. Economic Mobilization. (1) The *War Production Board* (WPB) ordered military equipment, shifted peacetime plants to war production, set up priorities for raw materials, and built new plants, most notably to produce aluminum and synthetic rubber. (2) The *War Labor Board* (WLB) settled labor-management disputes, permitted limited wage increases, and endeavored to prevent strikes. With a few exceptions, unions adhered to their no-strike pledge. (3) The *War Manpower Commission* (WMC) trained workers and channeled them into essential industries, supervised the Selective Service system, and recruited new workers, including several million women. (4) The *Fair Employment Practices Committee* (FEPC) encouraged maximum use of labor by combating racial and religious discrimination in employment. (5) The *Office of Price Administration* (OPA) combated inflation by imposing price and rent ceilings and by rationing scarce consumer goods, such as sugar, meat, shoes, and gasoline.

c. Civil Liberties. Except for the forced removal of Japanese-Americans from the West Coast to interior relocation centers, civil liberties survived the war strains. Compared to World War I, the nation experienced less war hysteria. The press and the people remained free to criticize the government, and vigorous debate marked the Presidential election of 1944, in which Roosevelt won a fourth term.

d. Wartime Finances. The government greatly increased corporate and individual income tax rates and for the first time taxed individuals in the low-income brackets. The number of taxpayers rose from 8 million to 55 million. The government also raised and expanded excise taxes.

Of the total war cost of $330 billion, taxes provided one-third. The rest the government borrowed through the sale of *war bonds*. From 1940 to 1945 the federal debt rose from less than $50 billion to over $250 billion.

e. Military Personnel. With Selective Service draft boards providing most of the recruits, the armed forces enrolled 15 million men. At peak strength the army totalled 8½ million men, the navy 3½ million, and the marines half a million. To release men for frontline duty, women's branches—Army Wacs, Navy Waves, and Women Marines—took over necessary noncombat duties.

6. Victory in Europe

a. From North Africa to Italy. In October 1942 a British army under General *Bernard Montgomery* defeated the Germans and Italians at *El Alamein*, Egypt, and began pursuing them westward. In November 1942 an Anglo-Canadian-American army under General *Dwight D. Eisenhower* invaded French North Africa and moved eastward. By thus placing the enemy in a vise, the Allies destroyed the Axis African armies. In 1943 the Allies crossed the Mediterranean and invaded Sicily and southern Italy. Mussolini's Fascist government collapsed, and Italy surrendered unconditionally. To resist the Allied advance northward, Germany rushed troops into Italy.

b. Russian Counteroffensive. In early 1943, following a six-month battle, the Russians annihilated a 300,000-man Nazi army deep inside the Soviet Union at *Stalingrad*. Following this great victory Russian armies seized the initiative. The Communists drove the Nazis from Russia and pursued them through Rumania, Bulgaria, Yugoslavia, Hungary, Austria, Czechoslovakia, and Poland. In 1945 the Russians reached eastern Germany and stormed into Berlin.

c. Anglo-American Invasion of France. On June 6, 1944, American and British forces, led by General Eisenhower, crossed the English Channel and landed in *Normandy* in northern France. This greatest waterborne invasion in history established a major *second front.* The invading forces met a strong German army which, anticipating this attack, had been kept from the Russian front. Allied forces pushed back the Nazi army, recaptured Paris, and drove the Germans from France.

d. Surrender of Germany. In 1945 Anglo-American armies crossed the Rhine River in Germany and continued eastward to the Elbe River. Here they met the Russians driving in westward. After Hitler committed suicide, Germany surrendered unconditionally.

7. Victory in the Pacific

a. Initial Japanese Offensive. In 1941–1942 Japanese forces overran the Philippines, the Malay States, the Dutch East Indies, and part of New Guinea. Poised just north of Australia, they were halted by American naval victories in the *Coral Sea* and afterward in the central Pacific at *Midway.*

b. Allied Counteroffensive. In August 1942 General *Douglas MacArthur* started the Allied forces (chiefly American) on an "island-hopping" offensive on the road to Japan. In 1944 the American navy won a decisive victory at *Leyte Gulf* and American forces returned to the Philippines. In early 1945 they also captured *Iwo Jima* and *Okinawa.* From these islands American airmen launched destructive raids upon the Japanese homeland.

c. Atom Bomb and the Surrender of Japan. After Japan belittled the Allied demand to surrender or face "utter destruction," President Truman ordered the air force to use the newly developed atom bomb. Its use, Truman believed, would convince the Japanese military of the hopelessness of their situation, would save an estimated 1 million American casualties (and additional Japanese casualties) that would result from a seaborne invasion of Japan, and would hasten the end of the war.

In August 1945 the United States dropped a single atom bomb—the first to be used in war—on the Japanese city of *Hiroshima.* It killed or injured 130,000 people. Two days later Russia declared war against Japan and invaded Japanese-held Manchuria. The following day the United States dropped a second atom bomb, this time on *Nagasaki.* Defenseless against atomic bombings and without allies, Japan surrendered.

SIGNIFICANT FACTS DESCRIBING WORLD WAR II

1. Total War. The war was fought not only by armed forces at the battlefront but also by civilians in factories and homes. Even schoolchildren took part, collecting scrap metal, rubber, and newspapers; helping air-raid wardens; and assisting in war bond drives.

2. Global War. This most extensive war was fought on all major seas and in Africa, Asia, and Europe. It involved almost 60 nations, seven of them on the side of the Axis. To plan global military strategy, top Allied leaders held a series of conferences, such as the ones at Teheran, Yalta, and Potsdam.

576 / AMERICAN STUDIES

3. Scientific Progress. Scientists and engineers devised or adapted for war purposes such inventions as radar, guided missiles, jet-propelled planes, magnetic mines, and atom bombs. World War II witnessed the use of blood plasma, penicillin, and sulfa drugs to save lives.

4. Major Role of the Airplane. Fleets of airplanes attacked troop and naval units, destroyed railroads and industrial centers, and prepared the way for invasion. Control of the air was essential to offensive action on land and sea.

RESULTS OF WORLD WAR II

1. Economic. (*a*) The war—the most costly in history—exacted military expenditures of over $1100 billion and caused property damage of over $230 billion. (*b*) European and Asian nations, ravaged by military action, faced problems of economic recovery. (*c*) The Communist economic system spread from Russia to eastern and central Europe, and to several Asian nations.

2. Social. (*a*) The war—the most destructive in history—left over 22 million servicemen and civilians dead, and over 34 million wounded. For the United States alone, the dead and wounded totaled over 1 million. (*b*) Several million *refugees* and *displaced persons*, uprooted by the war, needed assistance to rebuild their shattered lives.

3. Political. (*a*) Germany, Italy, and Japan met complete military defeat, and their totalitarian systems were overthrown. (*b*) The United States and Russia emerged as the major world powers and soon came into a conflict called the *cold war*. (*c*) Russia acquired an empire of Communist satellite nations. (*d*) The Asian and African colonial peoples became intensely nationalistic and hastened the downfall of Western imperialism. (*e*) Great Britain and France declined as world powers and gradually relinquished their empires. (*f*) The atomic age brought problems of achieving international control of atomic energy and of missile delivery systems. (*g*) To preserve peace, the Allies formed a new international organization, the *United Nations*. (*h*) The United States joined the United Nations and otherwise actively assumed the responsibility of world leadership.

MULTIPLE-CHOICE QUESTIONS

1. The United States has at times pursued a policy of isolation and at other times a policy of international cooperation. The policy pursued at any given time depends *generally* upon the (1) need to serve what appears to be the national interest (2) desire to secure the support of developing nations (3) demands of the voters as expressed at the polls (4) willingness of Communist nations to remain peaceful.
2. Which factor encouraged the development of a policy of neutrality by the United States during the 1930's? (1) disillusionment with World War I and its results (2) a decline in the military preparedness of other nations (3) the belief that United States participation in World War I had little effect on the outcome (4) the economic prosperity of the period
3. The United States Senate rejected the Treaty of Versailles *mainly* because the treaty (1) contained the Covenant of the League of Nations (2) made Germany assume sole guilt for the war (3) required Germany to pay reparations (4) provided for the return of Alsace-Lorraine to France.

4. Republican leaders in the Senate opposed the unamended Treaty of Versailles because they (1) wanted Germany to pay reparations to the United States (2) considered the treaty too harsh on Germany (3) feared infringement upon American sovereignty (4) feared a revival of German militarism.

5. In which area was the League of Nations *most* successful? (1) improvement of health conditions (2) achievement of European disarmament (3) arbitration of the Italian-Ethiopian dispute (4) withdrawal of Japanese forces from Manchuria

6. United States neutrality legislation of the 1930's was based on the assumption that (1) the rights of neutrals had been established by the War of 1812 (2) isolation interfered with United States expansion in the Pacific (3) a show of force would prevent aggression against the United States (4) the United States could avoid being drawn into another World War by eliminating some of the causes for our involvement in World War I.

7. Our World War I allies claimed that they were unable to pay their war debts because the United States did *not* (1) join the League of Nations (2) sell them enough goods (3) lower its tariff rates (4) join the World Court.

8. The Kellogg-Briand Pact failed to accomplish its purpose because it (1) was not signed by Germany (2) was signed by too few nations (3) had no provisions for enforcement (4) was rejected by the League of Nations.

9. One similarity between the Embargo Act of 1807 and the Neutrality Act of 1937 is that both (1) distinguished clearly between aggressor and victim (2) showed United States determination to fight (3) abandoned substantially the principle of freedom of the seas (4) discouraged aggression in Europe.

10. During the 1930's, the leaders of Germany, Italy, and Japan promoted a warlike attitude among their peoples by (1) stressing the huge indemnities required of them by the Treaty of Versailles (2) playing upon nationalist feelings (3) condemning the League of Nations for refusing them membership (4) pointing to their loss of territory as a result of World War I.

11. Germany's rearmament, starting in 1935, was (1) essential to the policy of collective security (2) encouraged by France (3) in violation of the Treaty of Versailles (4) approved by the London Naval Conference.

12. The term "appeasement" is often used to describe the (1) Munich Pact (2) Destroyer-Naval Base Deal (3) Stimson Doctrine (4) Rome-Berlin-Tokyo Axis.

13. Hitler argued that Germany should annex the Sudetenland to (1) protect the German-speaking minority in that area (2) reduce French influence in Central Europe (3) gain control of additional munitions factories (4) prevent Communist seizure of the area.

14. The Non-Aggression Pact of 1939, preceding the outbreak of World War II, was between (1) Germany and Poland (2) Germany and the United States (3) Germany and Russia (4) Great Britain and the United States.

15. An international policy whereby nations agree to take joint measures against an aggressor nation is called (1) unilateral action (2) an offensive alliance (3) benevolent neutrality (4) collective security.

16. Which was an underlying cause of both World War I and World War II? (1) Japanese imperialism in Asia (2) Italy's demand for control of the Rhineland (3) German ambitions to dominate Europe (4) absence of alliances among nations

17. During the period 1939–1941, United States foreign policy can *best* be described as (1) consistently internationalist (2) aimed at avoiding war at all costs (3) moving steadily toward isolation (4) moving from isolation to active aid for the Allies.

18. In 1940 the United States leased naval bases from Great Britain to (1) cancel Great Britain's debts from World War I (2) build adequate defenses in the Western Hemisphere (3) give our investors markets for exports (4) secure sources of uranium.

19. The United States was referred to as the "arsenal of democracy" just before her entry into World War II because she (1) was one of the few nations then to maintain a democratic government (2) was a haven for refugees escaping from totalitarian governments (3) provided aid and supplies to nations fighting the Axis powers (4) trained leaders to take over Axis nations once they were defeated.
20. A widely adopted means of solving the manpower problem in industry during World War II was to (1) use forced labor (2) raise the immigration quotas (3) employ women (4) abolish relief payments.
21. The first city ever atom-bombed was (1) Munich (2) Tokyo (3) Hiroshima (4) Nagasaki.
22. Relations between the United States and its Allies during World War II indicate that the United States (1) was not interested in consulting with the Allies on basic strategy (2) resented Allied efforts to cooperate with the Soviet Union (3) supplied the Allies, including Russia, with much lend-lease military equipment (4) refused to grant aid to nations owing debts from World War I.
23. Which two countries were on our side in World War I and were our enemies in World War II? (1) Italy and Japan (2) Germany and Japan (3) Russia and Japan (4) Austria and France

IDENTIFICATION QUESTIONS: WHO AM I?

Neville Chamberlain	Dwight D. Eisenhower	Bernard Montgomery
Winston Churchill	Warren G. Harding	Franklin D. Roosevelt
James M. Cox	Henry Cabot Lodge, Sr.	Harry S. Truman
Charles de Gaulle	Douglas MacArthur	Woodrow Wilson

1. I became Prime Minister of Britain in 1940. I offered my people "blood, toil, tears, and sweat."
2. I commanded the Allied forces in the southwest Pacific. In 1944 I kept my pledge to return to the Philippines.
3. As chairman of the Senate Foreign Relations Committee, I led the fight for reservations to the Treaty of Versailles.
4. After the fall of France in 1940, I fled to England and established the "Free French" movement.
5. I delivered my "quarantine" speech to alert the American people to the danger of aggression.
6. As commander of the Anglo-American forces in Europe, I led the invasion of Normandy.
7. To shorten the war and save American lives, I ordered the use of the atom bomb against Japan.
8. As Prime Minister of Britain I made concessions to Hitler at the Munich Conference. I believed that my policy was preserving "peace in our time."
9. As Presidential candidate in 1920, I took no clear-cut stand regarding the League of Nations.

ESSAY QUESTIONS

1. (a) Describe *two* events or circumstances in the period 1919–1920 that kept the United States from membership in the League of Nations. (b) Give *two* arguments for and *two* arguments against the entrance of the United States into the League. (c) Explain *two* reasons why the League was unable to prevent war.
2. (a) Explain *one* reason why the United States adopted the policy of isolation early in its history. (b) Give *two* reasons for the change in sentiment between 1919 and 1941 regarding the policy of isolation. (c) Referring to these years, describe (1) *one* American

action illustrating isolation and (2) *one* American action illustrating international cooperation.

3. In the 1930's some Americans proposed that, in case of a foreign war, the United States maintain neutrality by cutting off all trade relations with the warring powers. (*a*) Show how this proposal developed out of our experience during the years 1914–1917. (*b*) State *two* provisions of the Neutrality Acts of 1935 and 1937. (*c*) Explain *one* reason why such neutrality legislation failed to keep the United States out of World War II.

4. The United States played a major role in the worldwide struggle against totalitarianism. (*a*) Discuss *two* reasons why the American people are opposed to totalitarianism. (*b*) Describe *three* factors that made it possible for the United States to be the "arsenal of democracy" during World War II. (*c*) After Hitler attacked the Soviet Union in 1941, should the United States have extended lend-lease aid to the Soviet Union? Give *one* argument to support your position.

5. State whether you agree or disagree with *each* of the following statements and give *two* facts to support your point of view: (*a*) Preparedness for war is the best guarantee of peace. (*b*) The United States was right in not joining the League of Nations. (*c*) Appeasement of dictators can preserve the peace. (*d*) The failure of the League proves that wars cannot be prevented by an international organization. (*e*) The causes of World War II were very different from those of World War I. (*f*) The United States decision to use the atom bomb against Japan was correct.

13. The United States Takes an Active Part in the United Nations

HOPES FOR A BETTER WORLD: FOUR FREEDOMS

In 1941 President Roosevelt said the United States looked forward to a world founded upon *Four Freedoms:* (*a*) freedom of speech, (*b*) freedom of religion, (*c*) freedom from want, and (*d*) freedom from fear. To achieve this goal, the Allied powers moved to create the United Nations.

STEPS TOWARD THE UNITED NATIONS

1. Atlantic Charter (1941). Roosevelt and Churchill, meeting on board ship in the Atlantic, issued a statement of principles, the *Atlantic Charter*. Remindful of Wilson's Fourteen Points, this document stated that Britain and the United States (*a*) desired no territorial gain, (*b*) respected the right of all peoples to choose their own form of government, (*c*) hoped that all men would live in freedom from fear and want, (*d*) believed that nations must abandon the use of force, and (*e*) would seek to establish a "system of general security," implying an international organization.

In 1942 the Allied nations met at Washington, pledged support for the Atlantic Charter, and adopted the name *United Nations* (UN).

2. Yalta Conference (February 1945). The Big Three—President Roosevelt, Prime Minister Churchill, and Premier Stalin—decided upon procedures for voting in the UN Security Council and called upon the United Nations to send delegates to San Francisco to prepare the final Charter.

3. San Francisco Conference (April–June 1945). Despite the unexpected death of President Roosevelt just before the conference, delegates representing 50 nations met as planned. They completed the UN Charter.

The United States became the first nation to ratify the Charter, as the Senate overwhelmingly approved American membership. Also, the United States provided the UN with headquarters, located in New York City.

PURPOSES OF THE UNITED NATIONS

The United Nations proposes to (1) maintain international peace and security, (2) use collective action so as to remove threats to peace and to suppress acts of aggression, (3) develop friendly relations among nations, (4) promote respect for human rights without distinction as to race, sex, language, or religion, and (5) encourage international cooperation in solving economic, social, cultural, and humanitarian problems.

ORGANIZATION OF THE UNITED NATIONS

1. General Assembly: The International Forum

a. Membership and Voting. The General Assembly consists of all UN member nations, now totaling about 150, each having one vote. General Assembly decisions on "important questions" require a two-thirds majority.

b. Powers. The General Assembly has the power to (1) discuss international problems fully and freely, (2) make recommendations to member nations, to the Economic and Social Council, to the Trusteeship Council, and to the Security Council, (3) elect members of other UN organs, (4) with the prior recommendation of the Security Council, suspend or expel any member nation persistently violating UN principles and admit any "peace-loving" nation to membership, (5) approve the UN budget and apportion expenses among the member nations, and (6) propose UN Charter amendments, which come into effect when ratified by two-thirds of the member nations, including all permanent members of the Security Council.

c. Sessions. The General Assembly meets in *regular* session annually, for about three months. If necessary, however, the Assembly may be summoned into *special* session.

2. Security Council: The Executive Agency

a. Membership. The Security Council consists of 15 members: (1) Five are *permanent:* the United States, Great Britain, France, Russia, and China. (Until 1971 China's seat was held by the Nationalist regime, which since 1949 controlled only the island of Taiwan. In 1971, as the United States and Communist China moved toward a better relationship, the General Assembly voted, with American support, to admit Communist China as representative of the Chinese people and, despite American opposition, to expel the Nationalist delegation as representative of Taiwan.) (2) Ten are *nonpermanent*, each elected for a two-year term by the General Assembly.

b. Voting. Decisions by the Security Council on important matters require the affirmative vote of nine members, including the five permanent members. Thus, by a negative vote, any one of the Big Five can defeat a Security Council

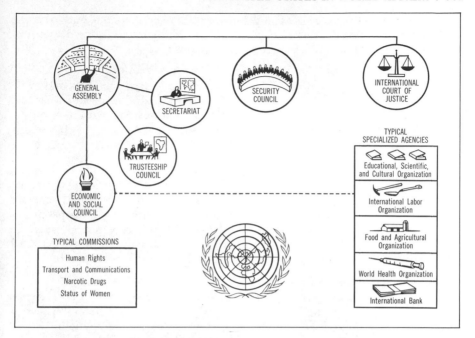

GENERAL
ASSEMBLY

SECRETARIAT

SECURITY
COUNCIL

INTERNATIONAL
COURT OF
JUSTICE

TRUSTEESHIP
COUNCIL

ECONOMIC
AND SOCIAL
COUNCIL

TYPICAL COMMISSIONS

Human Rights
Transport and Communications
Narcotic Drugs
Status of Women

TYPICAL
SPECIALIZED AGENCIES

Educational, Scientific,
and Cultural Organization

International Labor
Organization

Food and Agricultural
Organization

World Health Organization

International Bank

Organization of the United Nations

decision, that is, exercise its *veto power.* Abstention from voting by a permanent member is not considered a veto.

c. Powers. The Security Council bears primary responsibility for maintaining international peace and security. It has the power to (1) investigate disputes that endanger world peace, (2) make recommendations for peaceful settlement, and (3) if necessary, call upon UN member nations to take economic or military action against an aggressor nation.

d. Sessions. To be able to deal instantly with any international crisis, the Security Council functions *continuously.*

3. Secretariat: The Civil Service

a. Personnel and Duties. The Secretariat consists of the *Secretary General* and his staff. They are charged with primary loyalty to the United Nations. The Secretary General is appointed (usually for a five-year term) by the General Assembly upon the recommendation of the Security Council. The Secretary General selects and directs his staff, numbering several thousand employees, to perform UN clerical and administrative work. In addition, the Secretary General is authorized to (1) bring to the attention of the Security Council any matter threatening world peace, and (2) perform any other task entrusted to him by major UN organs. Such tasks have included the undertaking of special diplomatic missions and the directing of UN emergency military forces.

b. Persons Serving as Secretary General. (1) *Trygve Lie* of Norway (1946–1953), (2) *Dag Hammarskjold* of Sweden (1953–1961), (3) *U Thant* of Burma (1961–1971), (4) *Kurt Waldheim* of Austria (1972–   ).

4. International Court of Justice: The Court for Nations.
The International Court of Justice consists of 15 judges who decide cases by majority vote. The

Court has the power to (a) settle legal disputes between nations, and (b) grant UN organs advisory opinions on legal questions. Nations submitting disputes to the Court agree in advance to accept its decisions.

5. Trusteeship Council: For Protection of Colonial Peoples

a. Membership and Voting. The Trusteeship Council consists now of the five permanent Security Council members: Four do not administer any trust territories; the United States administers the sole remaining trust territory—certain Pacific islands. (A trust territory is a colonial area placed by the UN under the administration of a member nation.) The council's decisions require a simple majority.

b. Powers. The Trusteeship Council was established to supervise trusteeships so as to safeguard colonial peoples. It received power to (1) consider reports from the administering nations, (2) examine petitions from the peoples of the trust territories, (3) with consent of the administering nation, send an investigating committee, and (4) report to the General Assembly. As trust territories gained independence, the work of this council diminished.

6. Economic and Social Council (ECOSOC): For Humanity's Welfare

a. Membership and Voting. The Economic and Social Council consists of 54 members, each elected for a three-year term by the General Assembly. Decisions require a simple majority, each member nation having one vote.

b. Powers. The Economic and Social Council is concerned with improving economic, social, cultural, educational, and health conditions throughout the world. ECOSOC may conduct studies and make recommendations to UN member nations and to the General Assembly. Through ECOSOC's efforts, the UN hopes to eliminate the underlying causes of war.

c. ECOSOC Commissions and Committees. To further its objectives, ECOSOC organized (1) the *Commission on Human Rights*, which seeks to assure fundamental freedoms for all persons, regardless of race, sex, language, or religion, and (2) other commissions and committees concerned with such problems as control of narcotics, prevention of crime, and the status of women. ECOSOC also receives reports from the UN Children's Fund (UNICEF) and the High Commissioner for Refugees.

SPECIALIZED AGENCIES

The specialized agencies are independent organizations, some predating the United Nations, that came into existence by intergovernmental agreement. They include most (but not all) nations as members; they secure their funds chiefly by voluntary contributions from member nations; they directly serve only those nations that request assistance; and they coordinate their efforts with the UN through the Economic and Social Council.

The United States joined all the specialized agencies, actively participated in their work, and provided them with substantial funds. These agencies conduct some of the most important and yet least publicized activities of the UN.

1. United Nations Educational, Scientific, and Cultural Organization (UNESCO) seeks the worldwide exchange of information on education, science, and culture. UNESCO undertakes projects to raise educational standards and to combat ignorance and prejudice. UNESCO bases its work on the belief stated in its Charter: "Since wars begin in the minds of men, it is in the minds of men that the defenses of peace must be constructed."

2. International Labor Organization (ILO) endeavors to improve world labor conditions. ILO defines minimum labor standards and assists countries in formulating labor laws.

3. Food and Agriculture Organization (FAO) attempts to raise world food and nutrition levels. FAO provides information to improve methods of growing and distributing food.

4. World Health Organization (WHO) seeks to improve world health standards. WHO surveys health conditions, combats mass diseases and epidemics, and helps nations improve public health services.

5. International Bank for Reconstruction and Development (World Bank) aids world economic progress by providing loans for large-scale development projects, such as electric power plants, railroads, and highways.

6. Other specialized agencies include (*a*) *International Civil Aviation Organization* (ICAO)—to expand and improve civil aviation facilities and to standardize laws regarding use of air lanes, (*b*) *Universal Postal Union* (UPU)—to provide uniform mail procedures, and (*c*) *World Meteorological Organization* (WMO)—to coordinate data on weather and develop weather-forecasting services.

Major Actions Taken by the United Nations

UN ACTIONS PERTAINING TO SOCIAL AND ECONOMIC MATTERS

1. Children's Fund. In 1946 the General Assembly created the *United Nations International Children's Emergency Fund* (UNICEF). It provides food, vitamins, and medicines to millions of needy children; and it trains nurses to help mothers in child care. UNICEF's activities, now permanent, are financed by voluntary contributions of governments and individuals. (American youngsters raise funds for UNICEF by undertaking Halloween "trick or treat" collections and by selling UNICEF greeting cards.)

2. Declaration of Human Rights. In 1948 the General Assembly overwhelmingly approved the *Declaration of Human Rights*, drawn up by the Commission on Human Rights. The declaration states that all human beings are born free and equal, and are entitled to (*a*) *civil rights:* life; liberty; freedom of religion, speech, and assembly; and a voice in their government; (*b*) *legal rights:* freedom from arbitrary arrest and the right to a fair trial; (*c*) *economic rights:* employment, participation in labor unions, an adequate living standard, private property, and leisure time; and (*d*) *social rights:* education and a cultural life. Although these ideals will not soon be realized throughout the world, they provide a "standard of achievement for all peoples and all nations."

3. Genocide Convention. In 1948 the General Assembly adopted the *Genocide Convention*, drawn up by the Commission on Human Rights. The convention declares illegal the deliberate extermination of any human group (as the Nazis had attempted with Jews and with gypsies) and provides that violators be tried before an international court. The convention, ratified by 63 nations, represents an attempt to rally world opinion in favor of granting all people freedom from fear.

4. Technical Assistance. In 1949 the United Nations and several specialized agencies began the *Expanded Program of Technical Assistance.* This program coordinates efforts to improve social and economic conditions in over 140 underdeveloped territories and countries, chiefly in Africa, Asia, and Latin America. Several thousand technical experts have helped underdeveloped peoples increase food production, develop natural resources and industries, fight disease, and reduce illiteracy.

UN ACTIONS PERTAINING TO INTERNATIONAL DISPUTES

The United States Role. The United States has been involved significantly in UN efforts to settle international disputes. America has sought to protect its national interests, to reconcile its interests with those of other nations, to strengthen respect for international law and morality, and to promote the welfare of humanity. American influence, in the General Assembly and as a permanent member of the Security Council, has reflected (1) our leadership of the free-world nations, and (2) our tremendous financial, industrial, and military power. Although the United States has considerable influence, it does not control the UN because other permanent members can exercise the veto in the Security Council and because a decision by the General Assembly requires a two-thirds vote.

By similar reasoning the Soviet Union has great influence in but does not dominate the world organization. In cases where American and Soviet interests have clashed sharply, the UN has achieved only compromises or stalemates rather than clear-cut or final solutions. The American people, who expect clear-cut solutions based on principles of international morality *not* power politics, find such UN compromises of doubtful value and distasteful. In defense, the UN argues that such compromises lessen international tensions, gain time for further consideration, and eventually may lead to more permanent solutions.

Major International Disputes. In dealing with the world's trouble spots, the UN has compiled a mixed record:

1. Iran. In 1946 Iran complained that Russia had not withdrawn troops stationed on Iranian soil during World War II. Russia objected to Security Council discussion of the complaint but removed her troops.

2. Greece. In 1946 the Greek government charged that three Communist nations—Yugoslavia, Albania, and Bulgaria—were aiding rebel Communist guerrilla bands in northern Greece. The United Nations (a) established an investigating commission, which confirmed the Greek charges, and (b) requested the Communist nations to stop supporting the guerrilla bands. Following the split between Yugoslavia and Russia in 1948, Yugoslavia ceased aiding the Greek rebels and the rebellion collapsed. (For American efforts to help Greece, check the Index for the "Truman Doctrine.")

3. Palestine. Located in the eastern Mediterranean, Palestine had been given to Britain as a League of Nations mandate for the establishment of a Jewish homeland. As increasing numbers of Jews entered Palestine to escape persecution in Europe, they met hostility from the Palestinian Arabs. In 1947–1948 the General Assembly (a) conducted an investigation of the conflicting claims, and (b) approved the partition of Palestine into an Arab state and a Jewish state. The UN decision was defied by the Arab nations, which launched an armed attack on the infant Jewish state, Israel. The UN moved to halt the fighting, and *Ralph Bunche*, UN mediator, arranged a truce. (Check the Index for "Israel, emergence of.")

4. Indonesia. Following World War II, nationalists in the Dutch East Indies set up the Republic of Indonesia. In 1947 the Netherlands tried to win back Indonesia by force. The Security Council between 1947 and 1949 (a) arranged truces ending hostilities between Dutch and Indonesian forces, and (b) assisted in negotiations that led to Indonesia's independence.

5. Korea. At the end of World War II, the former Japanese colony of Korea was divided into Russian and American zones of occupation. In 1948 a UN commission to unify Korea held elections in United States-occupied South Korea but was denied admission into Russian-occupied North Korea.

In 1950, when the North Korean Communists invaded South Korea, the Security Council (with Russia absent) called upon the invaders to withdraw and, when that request was ignored, asked UN member nations to provide military aid to South Korea. The United States and 15 other nations sent troops, creating the first UN army. In early 1951, after Communist Chinese forces had entered the Korean War, the General Assembly declared Red China guilty of aggression. In mid-1951 the UN command began negotiations with the Communists and, in 1953, achieved a truce. (Check the Index for "Korea, since World War II.")

6. Kashmir. Since 1948 the United Nations (a) helped end hostilities between India and Pakistan over Kashmir, (b) secured agreement of both nations to a UN-supervised plebiscite, (c) was defied when India formally annexed, without any plebiscite, that portion of Kashmir held by Indian troops, and (d) declared India's action not binding upon the United Nations.

7. Hungary. In 1956 Russian troops suppressed a revolt of the Hungarian people against the Russian-dominated government of their country. The UN General Assembly overwhelmingly condemned Russia and demanded that Russia (a) cease her intervention in Hungarian affairs, (b) withdraw her military forces from Hungary, and (c) admit UN observers into the revolt-torn country. Russia rejected these demands. Check the Index for "Hungary."

8. Egypt. In 1956 Egypt was invaded (a) by Israel, which sought to stop border raids by Egyptian guerrillas and to end a shipping blockade by Egyptian guns at the Gulf of Aqaba, and (b) by Britain and France, which hoped to undo Egyptian nationalization of the Suez Canal.

The UN General Assembly condemned the invasion and passed resolutions for a cease-fire and withdrawal of the invading forces. The resolutions were heeded. To maintain peace in the area, the General Assembly requested member nations (excluding the Big Five) to volunteer troops for a *United Nations Emergency Force* (UNEF). (Check the Index for Sinai Campaign.)

9. Congo: 1960–1961

a. Background. In 1960 the Congo received independence from Belgium. The new African republic faced serious problems: rivalry between pro-Communist Premier *Patrice Lumumba* and pro-Western President *Joseph Kasavubu;* army mutinies; tribal conflicts; secession by mineral-rich Katanga province; and the continued presence of Belgian troops.

b. UN and the Congo Crisis. The Security Council (1) called upon Belgium to withdraw her troops, and (2) authorized Secretary General Hammarskjold to restore order in the Congo by means of a United Nations Emergency Force. Under Hammarskjold's direction, the UNEF helped prevent violence. Although Russia demanded that he support Lumumba in the Congolese power struggle, Hammarskjold remained neutral.

Meanwhile, Lumumba was removed from office, arrested by the Congo army, and slain by his political foes. Eventually, the Congo government passed into anti-Communist hands, Belgium withdrew her troops, and Katanga was brought back under central control.

c. Dispute Over Hammarskjold and the UN Congo Operation. (1) Russia Attacks Hammarskjold. Enraged by Lumumba's fall from power, Russia blamed Hammarskjold and demanded his resignation. Soviet Premier Khrushchev proposed that the duties of the Secretary General be taken over by a "troika," a three-man board of Western, Soviet, and neutralist representatives, each with veto power. (2) Hammarskjold Receives Support. With overwhelming support of the Western and most Afro-Asian nations, Hammarskjold refused to resign. He pointed out that the Soviet Union, by insisting upon the creation of a veto-dominated three-man board, could weaken the UN. (3) Hammarskjold Dies. After Hammarskjold died on a Congo peace mission, he received worldwide tribute for his devotion to the UN. Thereupon Russia ceased her demand for a three-member Secretary General and agreed to Burma's *U Thant* as Hammarskjold's successor.

10. Goa.
In 1961 India seized Goa, a tiny Portuguese colony on the Indian coast. At the UN, India was defended by most Afro-Asian nations and by Russia, which vetoed a Western resolution urging India to withdraw her troops and negotiate with Portugal. The UN took no other action.

11. Cyprus

a. Background. Cyprus, an island in the eastern Mediterranean some 50 miles south of Turkey, contains 650,000 people divided into two antagonistic ethnic groups: 80 percent Greek Cypriote and 20 percent Turkish Cypriote. Receiving independence from Britain in 1960, Cyprus adopted a constitution providing for a Greek Cypriote president and a Turkish Cypriote vice president, each with veto power over legislation. The first elected president of Cyprus was Archbishop *Makarios.*

b. UN and the First Cyprus Crisis. In 1963 Cyprus was torn by civil war between its Greek and Turkish Cypriote peoples. With Greece and Turkey each threatening to intervene militarily, the Security Council authorized a UN peace force to restore order on Cyprus. The UN force halted the conflict, but the Cyprus problem remained unsolved.

c. *UN and the Second Cyprus Crisis.* In 1974 Greek Cypriote forces, led by Greek officers who planned the union of Cyprus with Greece, overthrew the Makarios government. This coup, engineered by the military dictatorship in Greece, led to renewed civil war between Greek Cypriote and Turkish Cypriote communities, and then to an invasion of Cyprus by Turkish troops. The UN Security Council called for a Cyprus cease-fire to be policed by a UN peace force. Despite this and other cease-fire calls, the Turkish troops continued to advance, gaining control of 40 percent of the island. Thereafter, the fighting on Cyprus ceased but the problem of a satisfactory political solution remained.

12. Rhodesia (Zimbabwe). A British colony in Africa, mostly black-inhabited, Rhodesia exercised local self-government under a white-minority regime. For independence, Britain insisted that Rhodesia move toward rule by its black majority. Under Prime Minister *Ian Smith*, the Rhodesian government rejected Britain's demands and in 1965 declared the country independent. Britain labeled the breakaway regime "illegal," applied economic sanctions, and later secured a Security Council resolution requesting all UN members to apply economic sanctions. This resolution was derided by most African nations, which contended that sanctions would not topple the Smith regime and demanded that Britain use military force. In 1970 a Security Council resolution, condemning Britain for not using force against white-ruled Rhodesia, was vetoed by Britain and the United States.

In 1978 Prime Minister Smith and moderate black leaders inside Rhodesia reached an "internal agreement" calling for (1) black-majority rule based upon free elections open to all citizens and (2) various safeguards for the white minority. The 1979 elections attracted a voter turnout of 65 percent despite efforts to sabotage the voting by the leftist, Communist-supplied guerrillas of the *Patriotic Front*. The elections gave *Zimbabwe Rhodesia* a new government headed by a black prime minister, Bishop *Abel Muzorewa*. The Muzorewa government was labeled by Patriotic Front leaders as a "puppet regime" perpetuating white-minority rule, and it was condemned by the UN Security Council.

In late 1979, as Zimbabwe Rhodesia faced continued guerrilla warfare and the possibility of Russian and Cuban intervention, Britain convened the London Conference at Lancaster House to seek a peaceful settlement for Rhodesia. In attendance were Prime Minister Muzorewa, Ian Smith as spokesman for the Rhodesian whites, and *Joshua Nkomo* and *Robert Mugabe* as leaders of different groups constituting the Patriotic Front. After 14 weeks of hard negotiations the conference agreed to the following: (a) a democratic government with a Prime Minister responsible to a parliament, (b) a parliament of 100 members chosen in free elections open to all citizens and all political parties, (c) a guarantee of personal and individual rights, (d) political and property safeguards for the white minority, including 20 seats in parliament reserved for whites, (e) a cease-fire, and (f) appointment of a British governor with a 1300-troop Commonwealth force to assume temporary control of Rhodesia, enforce the cease-fire, and organize early 1980 elections. Thereafter, Britain would grant legal independence to Rhodesia.

Following the London Conference, economic sanctions against Rhodesia were lifted by Britain, the United States, most black African nations, and the UN Security Council.

The 1980 Elections. The campaign among blacks for the country's parliament was strongly contested and reflected tribal divisions. Robert Mugabe, leading the *Zimbabwe African National Union* (ZANU)-Patriotic Front, secured a clear majority of 57 seats. Joshua Nkomo gained 20 seats and Bishop Muzorewa took 3 seats. (Ian Smith at the head of the *Rhodesian Front* party received the 20 seats reserved for whites.) Despite some intimidation of voters, the results—according to the British election commissioner—broadly reflected the wishes of the people.

Robert Mugabe, during the years of guerrilla warfare, had received support from Communist China and was known as a radical Marxist-Leninist. Now, following his election victory, Mugabe adopted a moderate and conciliatory position. He urged blacks and whites to "remain calm," "work for unity," and "forget our grim past." He pledged to form a broadly based government and offered four cabinet posts to members of the Nkomo party and two cabinet posts to whites. Mugabe reassured the whites that his government would not seize their farmlands and other properties. Acknowledging that the country's economic structure was based on capitalism, he pledged to build on that foundation

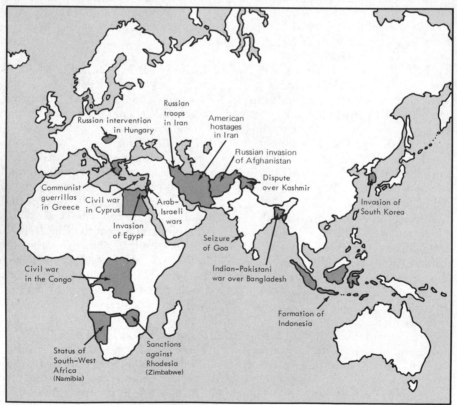

International Disputes Considered at the United Nations

to further prosperity. Although committed to improving conditions for blacks, Mugabe warned them that "change cannot occur overnight." Mugabe's conciliatory stance gave hope that his government would create a free, democratic, and prosperous Zimbabwe.

13. **South-West Africa (Namibia).** South Africa received this former German colony from the League of Nations as a mandate. Later South Africa refused to change the mandate into a UN trusteeship. South Africa's "apartheid" policies angered the Afro-Asian nations, which secured many UN condemnatory resolutions. In 1966 the General Assembly (a) declared South Africa's mandate over South-West Africa ended, (b) ordered the territory placed under UN control, and (c) created a committee to suggest ways for leading South-West Africa to freedom. South Africa declared that it would resist any UN interference in South-West Africa.

In 1973 the General Assembly declared the "authentic representative of the Namibian people" to be the *South-West Africa People's Organization* (SWAPO). With arms from Communist nations, SWAPO had conducted sporadic guerrilla warfare against South African control. More recently South Africa pledged independence for South-West Africa but rejected any role for SWAPO—a rejection supported by rival black groups in Namibia.

14. **Arab-Israeli War of 1967.** Following the outbreak of fighting, the Security Council passed several resolutions calling for a cease-fire. These resolutions, accepted by the victorious Israelis and eventually by the three vanquished Arab states, helped end the war. (Check the Index for "Arab-Israeli Wars; of 1967.")

Meanwhile, the Soviet Union vowed full support for the Arab cause and introduced a Security Council resolution (a) condemning Israel as the aggressor, and (b) demanding the withdrawal of Israeli forces to the 1949 armistice lines. The Soviet resolution was opposed by the United States as a "prescription for renewed hostilities," since it did not link the withdrawal of Israeli forces to steps for a durable peace. The Soviet resolution was overwhelmingly defeated in the Security Council and in the General Assembly. (The General Assembly, however, approved a resolution declaring invalid Israel's unification of Jerusalem.)

The Security Council later adopted *Resolution 242* calling for the (a) withdrawal of Israeli forces from the occupied territories, (b) right of every Middle Eastern state to live in peace within secure boundaries and free from acts of force, (c) free navigation of international waterways, and (d) just settlement of the refugee problem.

15. **Indian-Pakistani War (1971)**

a. Background. Pakistan consisted of two nonadjacent regions separated by 1000 miles of Indian territory. Aside from their Moslem religion, the people of the two regions had little in common. The West Pakistanis are mainly Punjabis, who speak Urdu and look westward to the Moslem Arabs; the former East Pakistanis are Bengalis, who speak Bengali and feel close to the Hindu Bengalis living in India. The West Pakistanis had controlled the central government, but in 1970 elections the Bengali *Awami League* gained a majority in the legislature. President *Yahya Khan* and Bengali leader Sheik *Mujibur Rahman* negotiated regarding East Pakistan's demand for autonomy but failed to agree. Thereupon the West Pakistani army, with great brutality, seized control of the East, killing many civilians and occupying the major cities. The Bengalis declared their region's independence and retained control mostly of rural areas.

India meanwhile voiced support for East Pakistan, received over 9 million Bengali refugees—creating a tremendous relief burden—and trained Bengali guerrilla fighters. India also gained international support by signing a 20-year treaty of friendship and cooperation with the Soviet Union. In late 1971 Indian military forces crossed into East Pakistan and in a two-week war defeated the West Pakistani army, making independence a reality for *Bangladesh*.

b. At the United Nations. Three Security Council resolutions, calling for a cease-fire and withdrawal of the invading forces, were vetoed by the Soviet Union. Thereupon the General Assembly voted overwhelmingly for a cease-fire and withdrawal of forces. India ignored this resolution, and its chief representative called the Assembly "not very realistic." With the war over, the Security Council passed a resolution requesting observance of the cease-fire and aid for the Bengali refugees in India. Meanwhile, the Pakistani representative denounced the UN as "a fraud and a farce."

16. Arab-Israeli War of 1973

a. The Security Council Cease-Fire. Despite the Egyptian and Syrian surprise attack, Israel did *not* request a Security Council meeting, asserting that the UN had never stopped any attack upon Israel and that, given the size of the Arab, Moslem, and Communist bloc, the Security Council could not achieve a "balanced discussion." The United States requested a Security Council meeting for a resolution simply to halt the hostilities, but with the Arab forces still maintaining their military initiative, the pro-Arab bloc insisted on including a demand that Israel unilaterally withdraw from the 1967-occupied territories. The Security Council remained unable to act. As the Israeli forces turned the tide of battle, the Soviet Union speeded diplomatic moves to protect its Arab "clients." The Soviet Union and the United States jointly secured adoption of an evenhanded Security Council resolution (1) calling for an immediate cease-fire, (2) reaffirming the 1967 request for an Israeli withdrawal coupled with the 1967 statement that every Mideast nation has the right to live in peace within secure boundaries, and (3)

"Mirror, Mirror, on the wall! Who's the most influential . . . ?" (*Renault in the Sacramento Bee, Cal.*)

urging negotiations for a "just and durable peace." The UN cease-fire was accepted by Israel, Egypt, and Syria. The Security Council also approved creation of a 7000-man UNEF force composed of troops of UN member nations (excluding the Big Five) to serve as a buffer between the opposing armies. (For details, check the Index for "Arab-Israeli Wars; of 1973.")

b. Subsequent General Assembly Votes

(1) *On the Palestine Liberation Organization (PLO).* In 1974 the General Assembly overwhelmingly voted to debate the "Palestine question," invited the *Palestine Liberation Organization* (PLO)—a coordinating Arab group—to attend as "representative of the Palestinian people," heard *Yasir Arafat* as PLO head demand establishment of a Palestinian state, and then voted for a resolution declaring the right of the Palestinian people to national independence.

Israel bitterly opposed the General Assembly actions. Israeli spokesmen called the PLO an organization of several thousand terrorists representing only themselves, assailed the demand for a Palestinian state as meaning the destruction of Israel, condemned the resolution for not affirming the right of Israel to exist, and concluded that General Assembly actions would deter progress toward a just and durable Middle East peace. Israel was supported in the General Assembly by few nations, the most important one being the United States.

(2) *On Zionism.* Simply stated, Zionism is the Jewish nationalist movement to reestablish and defend a Jewish homeland in Palestine.

In 1975 the General Assembly approved an Arab resolution condemning Zionism as "a form of racism and racial discrimination." In support were 72 nations—mainly Arab, Moslem, and Communist; in opposition were 35 nations—mainly the Western democracies; in abstention were 32 nations.

This resolution against Zionism was part of the Arab diplomatic offensive against Israel. The Israeli delegate at the UN condemned the resolution as reminiscent of Nazi anti-Semitism. *Daniel Moynihan*, the American delegate, expressed his country's outrage at the resolution, warning that the United States "will never acquiesce in this infamous act." UN Secretary General Waldheim deplored the resolution for worsening divisions among nations "at a time when the need for understanding . . . is more than ever necessary."

17. Iran. In 1979 militant Iranians in the capital city of Teheran seized the American embassy and took 50 staff members as hostages. For release of the hostages, the militants demanded that the United States return the deposed Shah to Iran to be punished for his "crimes." The United States refused and demanded the unconditional release of the hostages—a position supported

The small society (*Brickman in the Washington Star*)

unanimously by the UN Security Council and the World Court. To early 1980, however, the militants defied the UN and continued to hold the hostages. (For details, check the Index.)

18. Afghanistan. In 1979–1980 Soviet forces invaded Afghanistan to uphold a pro-Soviet government and to suppress a rebellion by Islamic guerrillas. The Soviets vetoed a UN Security Council resolution calling for "the withdrawal of all foreign troops"; thereafter the General Assembly, by a vote of 104 to 18, passed a similar resolution. The Soviets belittled the General Assembly action and their troops remained in Afghanistan. (For details, check the Index.)

EVALUATION OF THE UNITED NATIONS

1. Optimistic View: Effectiveness of the UN

a. Almost Universal Membership. The UN is the world's most representative body of nations. It mirrors the hopes and fears of humanity.

b. Availability of Forum. The UN provides a forum where any member nation may present its point of view on world problems.

c. Uniting for Peace Resolution. This resolution enables the General Assembly to deal with a threat to world peace if the Security Council fails to act because of a veto. It states that the General Assembly (1) if not in session, may be summoned into emergency session, and (2) may recommend, by a two-thirds vote, that UN members take collective action, including the use of armed force.

The Uniting for Peace resolution was invoked during the 1956 Egyptian and Hungarian crises.

d. Resolving International Problems. Through the UN, many international problems have been solved, brought closer to a solution, or at least kept from erupting into a major war. Examples of UN achievements include (1) independence for Indonesia, (2) the 1948 partition of Palestine, and (3) the 1956 withdrawal of invading forces from Egypt.

e. UN Military Forces. The UN has secured the military cooperation of a number of member nations. Examples are (1) the formation of a UN army to repel aggression against South Korea, and (2) the creation of UNEF units to preserve peace in the Middle East, the Congo, and Cyprus.

f. Economic and Social Progress. The Economic and Social Council and the specialized agencies have worked steadfastly toward eliminating some of the economic and social causes of war. The technical assistance program has improved conditions in many underdeveloped countries.

g. Colonial Independence. The Trusteeship Council has helped colonial peoples form independent nations, including Cameroon, Togo, Somalia, Tanganyika (now part of Tanzania), Rwanda, and Burundi.

h. Preventing International Anarchy. The UN keeps the world from reverting to total international anarchy. It serves as a bridge between the opposing sides in the cold war and enables the neutral nations to bring their influence to bear upon world problems.

2. Pessimistic View: Problems Besetting the UN

a. Blocs Within the UN. The UN consists of three blocs: (1) The *Western bloc* (about 50 nations) includes the United States, Western Europe, most of Latin America, and some British Commonwealth members. This bloc generally

U.N. PRESTIGE

TYRANNY OF THE MAJORITY

Bear market
(*Crawford. Reprinted by permission of Newspaper Enterprise Association*)

"Bear market" is an economics term used to denote values that are sharply falling. What is the cartoonist saying about UN prestige? According to the cartoonist, what has caused this trend in UN prestige? What other factors might be considered? How could the UN reverse this trend?

—but not always—supports American leadership. (2) The *Soviet Communist bloc* (about ten nations) consistently follows Russian policy. (3) The *Afro-Asian* or *Third World bloc* (about 90 nations) has grown tremendously with the admission of new UN members and now constitutes a UN majority. The Afro-Asian nations are opposed to colonialism, and most favor cold war neutrality.

The existence of blocs is a divisive force within the UN that tends to aggravate international friction.

b. Self-Serving Use of UN Organs and Specialized Agencies. UN members often consider international problems on the basis of individual or bloc interests, not on the basis of UN principles. Most Afro-Asian nations approved India's military seizure of Goa, although the UN Charter prohibits the use of force.

In the 1970's, Communist and Arab nations, with Third World support, "politicized" the work of UN specialized agencies. At the ILO, the Communist nations secured condemnation of the military regime in Chile for "denying trade union rights." Using a double standard, the ILO did not say a word about the denial of such rights in Communist and many Third World nations. At WHO the Arab nations secured rejection of a report by WHO experts that Israel had improved the health conditions of Arab peoples under Israeli control. At UNESCO, the Arab nations secured condemnation of Israel for archeological excavations in Jerusalem and achieved UNESCO expulsion of Israel. In 1976, by a technical maneuver, UNESCO readmitted Israel.

In a 1974 speech, the chief American representative to the United Nations deplored bloc voting and self-serving use of the UN by Communist, Arab, and other Third World nations. He referred specifically to the majority's decisions in the 1974 General Assembly to exclude South Africa entirely from the meeting and to curb the participation of Israel in the discussion of the "Palestine question." He warned that, by adopting unrealistic, one-sided positions and resolutions, the General Assembly was eroding support for the UN in the American Congress and among the American people. He further declared that "when the rule of the majority becomes the tyranny of the majority, the minority will cease to respect or obey it." The American representative urged the General Assembly to fulfill its true function: "to bridge the differences among its member states."

In 1975, at AFL-CIO and business prodding, the United States gave the required two-year notice of intent to withdraw from the ILO. The United States was particularly incensed that the ILO did not apply its labor standards equally to all nations, including Communist and Third World countries, and that the ILO accepted government delegates as worker representatives from countries that had no free labor unions. In 1977 the United States withdrew, thereby ending its ILO financial support (about 25 percent of ILO's budget) and expressing American displeasure with the "politicizing" of the UN and the specialized agencies.

(In 1980, as the ILO seemed to be abandoning its "politicizing" activities and returning to its original purpose of improving the condition of workers, the United States rejoined the organization.)

c. Veto Power. Russia has used the veto over 100 times, thereby limiting the effectiveness and decreasing the importance of the Security Council. The United States, Britain, and France have each used the veto only a handful of times.

The initial American vetoes were as follows: (1) In 1970 the United States vetoed a resolution that condemned Britain for not using force to end white rule in Rhodesia. (2) In 1972 the United States vetoed a resolution that condemned Israel for reprisal raids against Palestinian guerrillas in Lebanon without mentioning the provocation—the murder of 11 Israeli athletes at the Munich Olympic Games by Palestinian terrorists. (3) In 1973 the United States vetoed a resolution calling upon it to conclude a new "just and fair treaty" that would assure Panama "effective sovereignty" over the Panama Canal Zone, but making no mention of American efforts to achieve a new treaty and satisfy many Panamanian demands. (4) In 1974 the United States, together with Britain and France, vetoed a resolution to expel South Africa. While deploring South Africa's racial policies, the American spokesman asserted that "expulsion would set a shattering precedent that would greatly damage the United Nations structure."

d. Defiance of UN Resolutions. Some nations have defied UN resolutions, claiming that the issue involved was a domestic matter not subject to UN authority or insisting that they were protecting their national interests. Examples of defiance of the UN include (1) the 1948 Arab attack upon Israel, (2) Russia's refusal to permit UN-supervised elections in North Korea, (3) Russia's suppression of the Hungarian rebellion, (4) India's annexation of part of Kashmir, and (5) South Africa's refusal to recognize UN control of South-West Africa.

e. Lack of Military Power. The UN has no permanent military force of its own. It depends upon member nations to honor resolutions requesting armed forces. Only 16 nations—at that time constituting about one-fourth of the UN—heeded the call for troops to aid South Korea.

f. Financial Difficulties. The UN secures funds for its regular budget by assessing member nations according to ability to pay. In 1978 the United States was first, being assessed 25 percent of the UN regular budget, whereas the Soviet Union was second, being assessed 13 percent; in addition the United

States voluntarily contributed up to 45 percent of funds for UN special activities, whereas the Soviet Union voluntarily contributed only 1.5 percent.

The UN has been in financial straits because certain nations have been unable or unwilling to pay their regular assessments and to pay special assessments for UNEF forces. For example, the Soviet bloc and most Arab states refused to pay their share of UNEF Middle East expenses.

g. Bypassing the UN. The major nations have frequently resorted to direct diplomacy outside the UN. The United States, Russia, and Britain directly negotiated the nuclear test ban treaty. The United States and Russia directly concluded the SALT missile agreements. The UN loses prestige whenever nations ignore its facilities.

h. Limited Action Against International Terrorism. Extremist groups have employed terrorism—deliberate violence against innocent civilians—so as to further the extremists' political goals. Black revolutionaries in the United States hijacked American airplanes to Cuba and Algeria to escape from American authorities and sometimes to secure ransom and the release of other terrorists. Turkish extremists hijacked a Turkish airplane to Bulgaria and demanded that Turkey release three guerrillas sentenced to death for kidnapping and murder. Croatian separatists (opposed to Tito's Yugoslavia) hijacked a Swedish plane to Spain to secure the release of six Croatians imprisoned in Sweden for murder. South Moluccan terrorists in the Netherlands seized Dutch hostages to gain publicity and support for their goal of Moluccan independence from Indonesia.

Palestinian extremist groups, most notably *Al Fatah* and its *Black September* terrorists faction, seek to destroy Israel. They planted bombs to blow up planes of pro-Western nations flying passengers to Israel; also they hijacked pro-Western passenger planes to secure ransom or the release of captured Arab extremists. In recent years Palestinian guerrillas claimed responsibility for several particularly brutal massacres. In 1972 they employed three Japanese left-wing extremists who disembarked at the Israeli airport at Tel Aviv and with machine guns and hand grenades killed 25 persons (including 15 Puerto Ricans on a pilgrimage to

Civilization vs. barbarism—
which way for our world?
(*Crockett in the Washington Star*)

the Holy Land) and wounded 77 others. Later, Black September terrorists murdered 11 Israeli athletes at the Munich Olympic Games. In 1973 Black September terrorists coldbloodedly executed three diplomats—two Americans and a Belgian—in the Sudan. In 1974 Arab terrorists seized the school at the Israeli town of Ma'alot and murdered more than 20 children.

Secretary General Kurt Waldheim proposed that the General Assembly act to prevent international terrorism. His proposal was defeated in the General Assembly's Legal Committee by a coalition of Arab, Communist, and Third World nations. These nations claimed that terrorism was a legitimate weapon of peoples battling "alien regimes" to secure "self-determination."

In the mid-1970's, as terrorist attacks continued, many pro-Western nations toughened their stand against terrorists, enforced stringent airport security measures, and trained special commando units to combat airborne terrorism. In 1976 Israeli commandos flew to Entebbe airport in Uganda and rescued 102 Jewish hostages held by pro-Arab terrorists backed up by Ugandan troops. In 1977 West German commandos flew to Somalia and, with the cooperation of the Somali government, rescued 86 hostages, mainly West Germans, held by four Arabic-speaking terrorists. Thereafter the General Assembly approved a resolution requesting all member nations to combat air hijackings by strengthening airport security measures and by agreeing to prosecute or extradite hijackers. While some observers hailed this resolution as a significant UN move, others viewed it as a weak response, lacking power to diminish airborne terrorism.

3. Realistic View. The United Nations is not meant to be a world government; it is a loose confederation whose member states retain their sovereignty. The United Nations is only an instrument available for their use. Although the UN embodies humanity's highest hopes, its strength and influence will reflect the wishes of the world's peoples and governments.

MULTIPLE-CHOICE QUESTIONS

1. Which UN body provides a forum for expression by all UN members? (1) Security Council (2) Trusteeship Council (3) General Assembly (4) World Court
2. Each nation's voting strength in the General Assembly is according to (1) area (2) population (3) military strength (4) the principle of one vote per nation.
3. Which organ of the UN was given *primary* responsibility for investigating situations that threaten world peace? (1) the Economic and Social Council (2) the Secretariat (3) the Security Council (4) the Trusteeship Council
4. The nonpermanent members of the Security Council are selected by the (1) General Assembly (2) Economic and Social Council (3) five permanent members of the Council (4) Secretary General.
5. The Security Council has the power to (1) veto decisions of the General Assembly (2) cancel treaties made by member nations (3) recommend the use of force to stop aggression (4) elect the Secretary General.
6. The veto power in the UN is held by (1) each member of the Security Council (2) each member of the General Assembly (3) only the Soviet Union and the United States (4) the five permanent members of the Security Council.
7. The distribution of power within the Security Council is based on the principle that (1) neutral nations are an effective power bloc (2) important questions are settled by the International Court of Justice (3) agreement among the major nations

is necessary if the organization is to succeed   (4) large and small nations have equal influence in decisions about world problems.

8. One function of the Economic and Social Council is to   (1) settle boundary disputes   (2) promote respect for human rights   (3) direct the economies of underdeveloped nations   (4) regulate the use of atomic energy.

9. The specialized agency that seeks to promote cultural cooperation and understanding among nations is   (1) UNICEF   (2) Trusteeship Council   (3) WHO   (4) UNESCO.

10. A weakness of UNESCO in its efforts to foster world understanding is that it   (1) must report to ECOSOC   (2) is subject to vetoes by any of the Big Five   (3) cannot work within a country unless invited   (4) uses Communist personnel chiefly.

11. "Since wars begin in the minds of men" is a phrase used in the UNESCO Charter to emphasize the need for   (1) encouraging regional agreements on trade   (2) expanding educational opportunities   (3) controlling newspapers that stir up controversies   (4) stopping research on atomic weapons.

12. Which was an achievement of the UN?   (1) technical aid to underdeveloped regions   (2) release of Hungary from the control of the Soviet Union   (3) awarding of Kashmir to Pakistan   (4) establishment of UN control over South-West Africa

13. In 1950 the Security Council was able to pass a resolution calling upon the North Korean Communists to withdraw from South Korea because   (1) Russia approved the resolution   (2) Russia was absent from the meeting   (3) Russia was prohibited from voting since she was directly concerned with the issue   (4) the veto power had not yet gone into effect.

14. The General Assembly resolution urging Russia to cease her interference against the Hungarian revolt of 1956 was   (1) defeated by its failure to secure a majority   (2) defeated by the use of the veto   (3) heeded by Russia   (4) defied by Russia.

15. During the 1971 India-Pakistani war over Bangladesh   (1) India refused to heed a Security Council cease-fire resolution   (2) the United States vetoed a Security Council cease-fire resolution   (3) the General Assembly, with the Third World nations divided, was unable to approve any resolution   (4) India refused to heed a General Assembly cease-fire resolution.

16. In its success or failure to get member states to heed its requests, the UN closely resembles   (1) the United States under the Constitution   (2) the United States under the Articles of Confederation   (3) England in relation to the first English settlements in the New World   (4) a holding company in relation to its subsidiaries.

17. A *major* criticism of the voting procedure in the Security Council is that   (1) the Soviet Union has as much voting power as the United States   (2) a veto by any permanent member can prevent or delay action   (3) the permanent members have more votes than the nonpermanent members   (4) most member nations have no voting power in the Security Council.

18. Which is a reason why the UN General Assembly has become more involved in trying to meet international crises than its founders intended?   (1) The total membership of the Security Council changes annually.   (2) The Security Council has often been unable to take effective action.   (3) The Secretary General has lost all influence with the major powers.   (4) The major powers have more influence in the General Assembly than in the Security Council.

19. The UN finances its regular budget *chiefly* by   (1) charging admission to visitors   (2) assessing member nations   (3) placing a tax upon citizens of UN member nations   (4) selling UN stamps and souvenirs.

20. Which generalization is *best* supported by the record of UN actions?   (1) The big powers are abandoning their nationalistic policies.   (2) The spirit of nationalism is being replaced by a spirit of internationalism.   (3) All nations are ready to abandon their imperialistic policies.   (4) Crises in world trouble spots more often end in deadlocks than in permanent solutions.

21. When the American representative to the UN, in 1974, deplored the "tyranny of the majority," he was referring to (1) Russia's use of the veto (2) Communist China's insistence upon the ousting of Taiwan from the General Assembly (3) the actions of Third World nations in the General Assembly limiting the rights of any nation to which they were opposed (4) the policy of populous nations voting as a bloc.

22. The UN did not take action to stem international terrorism because terrorism (1) is declining (2) is better handled by nations acting individually (3) affects only Israel (4) is supported by many Asian, African, and Communist nations if employed for goals of which these nations approve.

23. Which problem has consistently troubled the United Nations? (1) member nations giving consideration only to their national interests (2) a steady decrease in membership of small nations (3) lack of a public forum where any nation may discuss world problems (4) fair distribution of its budgetary surpluses

ESSAY QUESTIONS

1. The UN represents an effort to solve the problems of international tension in an age of extreme danger. (a) Describe two ways in which the UN represents an improvement over the League of Nations. (b) Discuss two different ways in which the UN attempts to maintain world peace. (c) Show how the United States has cooperated with the UN in meeting two international crises. (d) Explain two limitations on the ability of the UN to meet world problems.

2. (a) State two functions of each of the following specialized agencies associated with the United Nations: (1) WHO (2) FAO (3) ILO (4) UNESCO. (b) Discuss two weaknesses that hinder the work of these specialized agencies.

3. At a discussion on the United Nations, the following arguments were given:

For the United Nations	*Against the United Nations*
a. The United Nations Charter has avoided the weaknesses of the Covenant of the League of Nations.	a. Since the United States pays about 25 percent of the cost of running the United Nations, our country might just as well "go it alone."
b. The war in Korea has tested the strength of the United Nations and proved that it can stop aggression.	b. The frequent use of the veto has made the United Nations helpless.
c. The UN serves as a safety valve where nations may talk out problems rather than resort to war.	c. By passing partisan and unrealistic resolutions which nations defy, the General Assembly has destroyed the prestige of the UN.

Agree or disagree with any two of the arguments above, giving two specific facts for each to support your point of view.

4. The United Nations has been the subject of considerable controversy. Giving two specific arguments to support your answer, discuss the extent to which you agree or disagree with each of the following statements. (a) The United Nations has successfully achieved its major aims. (b) The United States should withdraw from the United Nations. (c) The present "one-nation, one-vote" practice in the General Assembly should be replaced by a weighted system under which extra votes would be given to certain members on the basis of population and economic strength. (d) The specialized agencies of the United Nations have made significant contributions toward helping resolve economic and social problems. (e) In the future, historians will look back at the UN and judge it to have been as much a failure as was the League of Nations.

14. The United States Faces the Communist Challenge: The Cold War Era

AMERICAN LEADERSHIP IN WORLD AFFAIRS

From the mid-1930's, Americans had been moving away from isolation and toward large-scale global involvement and commitment. In 1941 our traditional policy of isolation received a fatal blow as the Japanese attacked Pearl Harbor and forced us actively into World War II. The American people finally realized that the United States had become a major world power and could not secure its national interests by a policy of isolation. American public opinion encouraged the government to pursue a new foreign policy: active American participation and leadership in world affairs.

OBJECTIVES OF AMERICAN FOREIGN POLICY IN THE COLD WAR ERA

(1) Safeguard United States national interests. (2) Avoid the outbreak of a nuclear world war. (3) Help other nations improve their social and economic conditions. (4) Promote democracy throughout the world. (5) Protect our friends and allies against Communist expansion.

COLD WAR

1. Origins. The "cold war" originated immediately after World War II as a struggle between the free world nations, led by the United States, and the Communist nations, led by the Soviet Union. The American people were alarmed by *(a)* the expressed Soviet aim of communizing the world, and *(b)* the expansion of Soviet power into Central Europe and Asia. President Truman began the American policy of keeping Russia from gaining control of any additional territories—a policy called *containment*.

2. Weapons. The cold war has been fought by means of *(a) propaganda*—in newspapers, on radio and television, in street demonstrations, and at the UN, *(b) diplomatic moves*, including international conferences and military alliances, *(c) scientific competition*, reflected in the development of nuclear weapons and missiles, and in the undertaking of space flights, *(d) economic competition*, especially aid to underdeveloped countries, *(e) espionage*, conducted by extensive spy rings, by intelligence ships, and by data-gathering vehicles in orbit around the earth, and *(f) subversion*, chiefly by local Communist groups that have sought to weaken and overthrow pro-Western governments by demonstrations, strikes, and guerrilla warfare.

The cold war also has been marked by localized military action but not by all-out war. The world has been living under an uneasy armed truce—an absence of total war but also an absence of genuine peace.

3. Today: A More Complex Situation. Although the cold war originated in a world generally divided into an American bloc and a Soviet bloc, this simple division no longer exists. Each bloc has experienced strains, and the cold war has become much more complex.

a. Free World. The free world nations have become less dependent militarily and economically upon the United States. Some free world nations have disagreed sharply with the United States on foreign policy. France, under President de Gaulle, began to oppose American influence in Europe. De Gaulle envisioned Europe as a French-led "third force" independent of the United States. Even Britain, our closest ally, diverged from American foreign policy by recognizing Communist China in 1950 and by trading with Communist Cuba.

b. Communist World. The Communist world has been troubled by disunity and discontent. Yugoslavia broke sharply with Stalinist Russia and adopted a program of national Communism. China has challenged Russia for world Communist leadership and has bitterly disagreed with Soviet foreign policy. (Check the Index for "China, Communist, and Soviet Union.")

TWO SUPERPOWERS: THE SOVIET UNION AND THE UNITED STATES

The Soviet Union and the United States emerged from World War II as the two superpowers. There were no others, for the war had destroyed the military and industrial might of the two major Axis powers—Germany and Japan; the war had bled the strength of and reduced to second-rate status two major Allied powers—France and Britain.

The Soviet Union and the United States are superpowers on the basis of their large populations—250 million Soviets and 210 million Americans, their strong and stable governments, their industrial leadership, their military power including the possession of nuclear weapons and missiles; and finally their technological progress.

A COMPARISON OF THE TWO SUPERPOWERS

1. Government: Dictatorial vs. Democratic

a. Political Parties

(1) *Soviet Union.* The Communist party is the only party permitted to exist. It selects all candidates for election to office and dominates the Soviet government.

(2) *United States.* Many political parties exist, the two major parties being the Democrats and the Republicans. The major and minor parties check upon each other, present candidates and issues to the people, and compete for support. No one party monopolizes the government.

b. Power Over the Country

(1) *Soviet Union.* Communist party leaders debate among themselves and decide upon Soviet policies, which are then presented to the nation as the not-to-be-challenged Communist position, or *party line.* The party takes a stand not only on political, military, and foreign affairs, but also on economic and cultural matters. It dominates every aspect of Soviet life.

(2) *United States.* National officials set American policies, but these are subject to public criticism. Public policies are influenced by leaders in such fields

as industry, agriculture, labor, race relations, education, and the information media. Because power is diffused, no one group or political party dominates the country.

c. Civil Liberties

(1) *Soviet Union*. Russian citizens lack many basic civil liberties and fear the *secret police*. Persons who speak against the government are regarded as criminals.

(2) *United States*. American citizens are guaranteed their civil liberties by the federal Constitution and by state constitutions. They can turn to the courts to protect their rights.

2. Economy: Communist vs. Capitalist

a. Industry

(1) *Soviet Union*. The government owns and operates all industry. The Communists transformed Russia from an agricultural nation into the world's second leading industrial nation through a series of *Five-Year Plans*. These emphasized capital goods to meet the demand of the state for heavy industry and military equipment. In recent years the Soviets have moved to overcome the poor quality and scarcity of consumer products.

(2) *United States*. Private entrepreneurs—individuals and corporations —own and operate most industry. Competition and the *profit motive* provide personal economic incentives. The government acts chiefly to prevent abuses. America, the world's leading industrial nation, exceeds Russia in output of capital goods and consumer products.

b. Labor

(1) *Soviet Union*. Almost all Russian workers belong to unions dominated by the Communist party. These unions spur the workers to greater productivity. However, they have no say in determining wages and no right to strike. Although the standard of living of Russian workers is higher than in Czarist times, it remains low by Western standards.

(2) *United States*. One-fourth of American workers belong to unions, which are free of government domination although subject to regulation. Unions bargain collectively with employers regarding wages and working conditions; they retain the right to strike. American workers enjoy a considerably higher living standard than Russian workers.

c. Agriculture

(1) *Soviet Union*. Russia employs one-third of its labor force in agriculture. Farmers must work on vast state-owned farms or in farm communities, called *collectives*. The peasants resent collectivization and concentrate upon their own small garden plots. Russian agriculture is also handicapped by crude farm equipment, outmoded production methods, and insufficient fertilizer. Russia periodically experiences serious food shortages.

(2) *United States*. The United States employs less than 5 percent of its labor force in agriculture. Farmers own their own lands or work on giant commercial farms. They utilize much machinery and fertilizer, and employ the latest farm

methods. They receive government aid to maintain soil fertility, achieve fair prices, and secure agricultural knowledge. American farmers produce crops large enough for domestic consumption and huge exports.

3. Culture: Regimentation vs. Freedom

a. Education

(1) *Soviet Union.* The central government controls education. All children receive compulsory schooling for at least eight years. Capable students are encouraged to study further, especially in mathematics and the sciences. Russia produces more engineers and scientists than does the United States. In the humanities, students are not trained to think for themselves but must accept the Communist party line.

(2) *United States.* The states and localities control education, although the federal government grants funds to expand school facilities, improve instruction, and aid capable students. Most children receive compulsory education to at least the age of sixteen. The United States turns out far more college graduates than does Russia. In the humanities, students are encouraged to pursue independent, nonregimented thinking.

b. Literature and Art

(1) *Soviet Union.* The Soviet regime encourages writers and artists, but it demands that they propagandize for communism. They must seek wide popular appeal, avoid experimentation, and praise the Soviet state. Many Soviet writers resent regimentation and represent a constant pressure upon the Communist party for greater freedom of expression.

(2) *United States.* The American government is prohibited constitutionally from interfering with free expression. American writers and artists produce works that represent their own taste and outlook on life. Their works may praise or criticize aspects of American culture and government.

BRIEF HISTORY OF SOVIET-AMERICAN RELATIONS

1. 1917–1941: Unfriendly. The Communists resented (*a*) American aid to anti-Communist forces following the Russian Revolution, and (*b*) America's refusal until 1933 to recognize the Soviet Union.

The United States resented (*a*) the Soviet withdrawal from World War I, enabling the Germans to concentrate their military forces on the western front, (*b*) Russian efforts to spread unrest and revolution in non-Communist countries by means of an organization called the *Comintern,* and (*c*) Russia's Nonaggression Pact of 1939 with Nazi Germany—an agreement that encouraged Germany to start World War II.

2. 1941–1945: Cooperative. During World War II, Russia and the United States found themselves fighting against a common enemy, Germany. To create amity with her democratic allies, Russia dissolved the Comintern. To assist Russia, the United States (*a*) provided her with $11 billion of lend-lease equipment, and (*b*) led the Western allies to open other European fronts by invading southern Italy and northern France. Also, Russia, the United States, and Britain coordinated military strategy and planned postwar arrangements at top-level conferences at *Teheran, Yalta,* and *Potsdam.*

3. Since 1945: Generally Unfriendly. As World War II ended, Russia reverted to her prewar attitude of hostility toward non-Communist countries, especially the United States. Soviet leaders declared that *(a)* "warmongers" in America were plotting against the Soviet Union, *(b)* the spread of communism was necessary for the security of the Soviet Union, and *(c)* communism inevitably must triumph over capitalism throughout the world. Stalin pursued a "hard line" toward the West, but his successors have urged *peaceful coexistence.* They have not, however, abandoned the Soviet goal of communizing the world.

American leaders *(a)* denied the warmongering charge, *(b)* held the expansion of Russian power a threat to the security of the free world, and *(c)* predicted victory for the American way of life in peaceful competition with communism.

4. Recently: A Search for Détente. In 1969 President Nixon declared that Soviet-American relations were ready to move from the confrontation of the cold war era to negotiation in an era of better understanding, or *détente.* His declaration received a positive response from the Soviet Union under Communist party chief Brezhnev. Détente recognized the basic differences between the two superpowers, but it also recognized their mutual interest in avoiding a nuclear war. Détente therefore meant an attempt by the two nations to avoid direct confrontations and to improve relations. After several years of détente, the two nations could point to some understandings—notably a 1971 Berlin agreement and two 1972 Salt I arms accords; but also to more disputes—notably the 1973 Middle East crises—that seemed identical with cold war confrontations.

With the Soviet invasion of Afghanistan (1979–1980) and the American response, many observers held that the era of détente was over.

Record of Communist Expansion Since 1939

Outright Annexations	Local Communist Parties Seize Control
By Russia 1. *Countries:* Estonia, Latvia, and Lithuania 2. *Territories:* from Czechoslovakia, Finland, Germany, Japan, Poland, and Rumania By China 1. *Country:* Tibet	1. *In Europe:* Albania, Bulgaria, Czechoslovakia, East Germany, Hungary, Poland, Rumania, and Yugoslavia 2. *In Asia:* China, North Korea, Laos, Cambodia, and Vietnam 3. *In America:* Cuba 4. *In Africa:* Mozambique and Angola

RUSSIA DOMINATES ITS EUROPEAN SATELLITES

1. Meaning of Satellites. The *satellites* are the Communist-dominated nations of East and Central Europe that, in most important matters, accept Russian authority. Communist satellites are Bulgaria, Czechoslovakia, East Germany, Hungary, Poland, and Rumania. Their relationship to Russia is similar to that of protectorates to a mother country.

Self-proclaimed *people's republics,* the satellite nations have governments that essentially imitate Russian domestic practices. *(a)* They are dictatorships, each controlled by its own Communist party. *(b)* They have nationalized industry, tried to collectivize agriculture, and proclaimed master economic plans. *(c)* They have denied many civil liberties and restricted free cultural expression. *(d)* In Poland and Hungary, both predominantly Roman Catholic, the governments have harassed the Catholic Church and at times arrested clergymen, most notably Hungary's *Cardinal Mindszenty*.

2. Establishment of Satellites. To help local Communist parties take over and maintain control, Russia *(a)* fostered Communist regimes in East and Central Europe as her armies pursued the retreating Germans during the closing year of World War II, *(b)* trained local Communists in revolutionary tactics and leadership, *(c)* provided military equipment and advisers for local Communist forces, *(d)* maintained Russian troops in East and Central Europe, and *(e)* violated a Yalta Conference agreement by thwarting free elections in Soviet-occupied nations.

3. Methods of Russian Control. *(a)* Russian specialists in political, economic, and military matters "advise" the satellite governments. *(b)* Russia tries to keep the satellite economies tied to her own by trade treaties. *(c)* Russian military forces are stationed in some satellite countries; they have also intervened to compel satellite conformity with Soviet policy. *(d)* Russian generals head a unified military command coordinating Soviet and satellite armed forces within an alliance, the *Warsaw Pact*.

IRON CURTAIN

As part of the cold war, the Communist regimes have kept their peoples from free contact with Western ideas. They have established restrictions on visitors, newspapers, magazines, books, and movies; they have jammed Western radio broadcasts, especially the *Voice of America* and *Radio Free Europe*. Speaking about this barrier between the Communist nations and the West, Winston Churchill used the term "iron curtain."

TROUBLE BEHIND THE IRON CURTAIN

1. Yugoslavia Since 1945. *Marshal Tito*, Communist ruler of Yugoslavia, defied Stalinist Russia and pursued nationalist policies. Tito was emboldened to act independently because Yugoslavia was not occupied by Russian troops and does not border Russia. Tito was denounced by the world Communist leadership for "a hateful policy in relation to the Soviet Union."

Stalinist Russia and the satellites sought to overthrow Tito by economic pressure, propaganda, and subversion within Yugoslavia. These efforts proved unsuccessful. Since Stalin's death, Russia and the satellites have somewhat repaired relations with Yugoslavia. Nevertheless, Yugoslavia remains free of Russian domination.

The Western democracies were cheered by Tito's independence of Russian control and his advocacy of *national communism*. The democracies hoped that other satellites would follow Tito's example. To enable Tito to resist Russian pressure, the democracies aided Yugoslavia with loans, food, trade treaties, diplomatic support, and military equipment. The West realizes that Yugoslavia is a Communist nation, but not a Russian satellite.

2. Power Struggle Following Stalin's Death in 1953. The death of Joseph Stalin signaled a bitter struggle for power among the top Russian Communists. *Nikita Khrushchev* became First Secretary of the Communist party and used that position to eliminate his chief rivals. One was executed; others were demoted to minor jobs. In 1958 Khrushchev assumed the Premiership, thus becoming the official head of the Soviet government.

The struggle for power after Stalin's death gave the world an unusual glimpse of the conflict that can exist within the Russian dictatorship—a conflict that is usually kept well hidden from the public.

3. Downgrading of Stalin (1956). Stalin had used every means of propaganda to encourage hero worship of himself as a great teacher, leader, and military genius. In 1956 Khrushchev began an all-out attack to downgrade Stalin in the eyes of the Soviet people. Khrushchev condemned Stalin for (a) purges of military and political leaders on false charges, (b) blunders in foreign affairs, (c) terror against innocent Soviet citizens, and (d) personal cowardice during World War II. After Khrushchev's denunciation of Stalin, the Communist party spread the new anti-Stalin line.

In the satellite nations, the anti-Stalin campaign strengthened the Titoist doctrine of national communism and helped set off upheavals, especially in Poland and Hungary.

4. Uprising in Poland (1956). The Polish people engaged in strikes and demonstrations (a) to achieve better living conditions, and (b) to end Russian domination. *Wladyslaw Gomulka*, who had been imprisoned as a Titoist, regained the leadership of the Polish Communist party and announced that Poland would seek her own road to socialism. Khrushchev was alarmed by Poland's trend toward independence, but Gomulka reassured him that Poland would remain Communist and allied with Russia. Khrushchev thereupon pledged not to interfere in Poland's internal affairs.

By this bloodless revolution, Poland under Gomulka achieved (a) a measure of independence in domestic matters, enabling Gomulka to end the forced collectivization of agriculture, and (b) expulsion of Russian agents from positions of authority over the Polish army, economy, and government.

5. Revolution in Hungary (1956). The Hungarian people revolted for (a) better living conditions, (b) the withdrawal of Soviet troops, and (c) full national independence. *Imre Nagy*, a Titoist, became head of the government, appointed some non-Communists to his cabinet, and demanded the removal of Soviet forces. Nagy announced Hungary's neutrality in the cold war and withdrawal from the Warsaw Pact.

Such anti-Russian moves were more than Khrushchev would permit. In spite of Nagy's appeal to the United Nations and a resolution by the General Assembly, Russian troops intervened and suppressed the Hungarian freedom fighters. Thousands of Hungarians were killed or deported to Siberia; others fled their native land. The Soviets smashed the Nagy government and replaced it with a puppet Hungarian regime under *Janos Kadar*.

Having trouble keeping them in orbit
(*Ellenwood in the Arizona Daily Star*)

6. Russian Split with Communist China. Check the Index.

7. Removal of Khrushchev (1964). In a surprise development, Khrushchev was removed, by collective action of the other top Communists, from his positions as First Secretary of the Communist party and as Premier. In *Pravda*, the Communist party newspaper, Khrushchev was denounced for "harebrained scheming, immature conclusions, and hasty decisions." Khrushchev was succeeded by *Leonid Brezhnev* as First Secretary and *Aleksei Kosygin* as Premier. Khrushchev's removal, according to Western observers, was caused by his worsening of the dispute with Communist China and his failure to improve the economy.

8. Invasion of Czechoslovakia (1968). *Alexander Dubcek* became head of the Czechoslovak Communist party and pledged a program of "liberalization." Dubcek lifted censorship of press, radio, and television, permitted non-Communists to form political groups, and said that Czechoslovakia would seek trade and loans from the West. To reassure Russia, Dubcek asserted that Czechoslovakia remained Communist and loyal to the Warsaw Pact.

Russian leaders, however, feared that the Czechoslovak reforms might spur similar movements in the other satellite nations. After Russian pressures failed to halt "liberalization," overwhelming Soviet forces, supported by troops of four Warsaw Pact nations—East Germany, Poland, Hungary, and Bulgaria—invaded and occupied Czechoslovakia. The Soviets allowed Dubcek to remain in office but at the price of enforcing Soviet demands for "normalization." Czechoslovakia reestablished censorship, banned non-Communist political organizations, removed officials disliked by the Russians, accepted Soviet advisers, and submitted to the stationing of Soviet troops in Czechoslovakia. In 1969 the Russians replaced Dubcek as head of the Czechoslovak Communist party by the more amenable *Gustav Husak*.

This invasion, condemned by Western and neutral nations, was also condemned by three Communist states—Yugoslavia, Rumania, and China—and by

"People of Czechoslovakia . . .
we have come to save you."
(*Gene Basset, Scripps-Howard Newspapers*)

West European Communist parties. These Communist groups rejected the Russian claim to have saved Czechoslovakia from "counterrevolutionary forces." They also rejected the Russian assertion that whenever a Communist nation endangers socialism at home or in other Communist countries, the Soviet Union has the duty to intervene with force—the *Brezhnev Doctrine*.

9. Unrest in Poland (1970–1971; 1976; 1979). In 1970–1971, Polish workers felt their earnings threatened by a new wage incentive system. When the government increased prices of food, fuel, and clothing, workers in coastal cities began riots and demonstrations. As the rioting spread to other cities, Wladyslaw Gomulka resigned as head of Poland's Communist party and was replaced by *Edward Gierek*. This change was approved by Russia, which feared that the Polish disturbances might infect the other satellite nations. The Gierek regime quieted discontent by shelving the wage incentive system and revoking the price increases, but it called for "law, order, and discipline."

In 1976 Polish workers again rioted to protest government increases in food prices—designed to offset internal inflationary costs and higher priced Western food imports. The government rescinded the higher prices, but it also sentenced some rioters to prison terms.

In 1978 Karol Cardinal Wojtyla of Poland was elected as Pope and took the name *John Paul II*. He is the first Polish pontiff in the history of the Roman Catholic Church. In 1979, as Pope, he visited his homeland, whose 35 million inhabitants are overwhelmingly Roman Catholic. Warmly and even emotionally received by huge crowds, the Pope spoke out for human rights, religious liberty, and Catholic Church interests; he condemned atheism and questioned Soviet domination of its East European satellites. The visit of this "Slavic Pope" heightened Polish nationalism—to the discomfort of the Soviet Union; it also intensified religious fervor and raised expectations of more personal freedom—to the discomfort of Poland's Communist rulers.

TROUBLE WITH WEST EUROPEAN COMMUNIST PARTIES: EUROCOMMUNISM

In 1976 at Moscow, delegates of most world Communist parties attended the

25th Congress of the Soviet party. *Enrico Berlinguer,* head of the Italian Communist party, expressed his party's policy differences with and independence of Moscow. Not mentioning Marx, Lenin, or international working class unity, Berlinguer voiced support for a multiparty democratic and nationalist system. *Georges Marchais,* head of the French Communist party, who boycotted the Congress, had previously denounced Soviet repression of domestic dissent and declared the "dictatorship of the proletariat" doctrine to be obsolete. At the Congress, the French delegate stated that his party would pursue "a socialism in the colors of France." Other West European Communist spokesmen have expressed similar independent views—all to the displeasure of Soviet leaders.

The ideological changes voiced by the major West European Communist parties have been (1) toward democracy—to behave as democratic parties, abide by the results of free multiparty elections, guarantee civil liberties, and renounce dictatorship and (2) toward nationalism—to remain independent of Russian domination, consider first the national interests of their respective countries, and participate loyally in West European defense and economic programs. Denounced by the Soviet Union, this new West European Communist ideology has become known by the term *Eurocommunism.*

15. The United States Promotes the Economic and Military Strength of the Free World

Foreign Aid

TRUMAN DOCTRINE

1. **Purpose.** In 1947 Greece, in economic chaos as a result of Axis occupation in World War II, was under attack from Communist guerrilla bands. Turkey was under pressure from Russia for concessions in the Dardanelles, the straits connecting the Black Sea and the Mediterranean. If successful, these Communist efforts would have expanded Russian influence into the eastern Mediterranean. President Truman therefore announced that "it must be the policy of the United States to support free peoples" against direct and indirect Communist aggression—the *Truman Doctrine.* Congress overwhelmingly approved economic and military aid for Greece and Turkey.

2. **Effects.** *(a)* With American economic aid, Greece revived her economy. With American military aid, Greece put down Communist guerrilla attacks. Also, Yugoslavia halted aid to the Greek guerrillas following Tito's split with Russia. *(b)* Bolstered by American economic and military aid, Turkey withstood Russian demands for control of the Dardanelles.

MARSHALL PLAN

1. **Reasons for Offer.** In 1947 Secretary of State *George C. Marshall* offered American economic aid to all European nations (including Russia and her satellites) to enable them to recover from the destruction of World War II. He said, "Our policy is directed not against any country or doctrine but against hunger, poverty, desperation, and chaos."

The United States wanted to help Europe to (a) improve European living standards, (b) end the need for continued American relief funds, (c) revive a mutually profitable trade between the United States and Europe, and (d) lessen the danger of communism in western Europe. (Especially in France and Italy, Communist parties commanded a considerable following.)

Also, American foreign policymakers feared that, if western Europe came under the domination of the Soviet Union, together they would (a) constitute an overwhelmingly powerful military and economic bloc and (b) irrevocably endanger American national interests throughout the world.

2. European Recovery Program (ERP). The Marshall Plan, officially the *European Recovery Program*, aided most non-Communist nations of Europe: Great Britain, France, Austria, Belgium, Denmark, Greece, Iceland, Ireland, Italy, Luxembourg, the Netherlands, Norway, Portugal, Sweden, Switzerland, Turkey, and West Germany. They cooperated with each other and with the United States to achieve "recovery, not relief." The United States provided $12.5 billion, most of which was spent in this country for foodstuffs, raw materials, and machinery.

3. Achievements. During its four years (1948–1951) the Marshall Plan helped strengthen Europe. It (a) promoted strong economic recovery, with many countries surpassing prewar levels of production, (b) furthered political stability, (c) reduced Communist influence, and (d) encouraged West European countries toward economic unity.

4. Russian Opposition. Russia condemned the Marshall Plan as an American scheme to gain economic and political control over Europe and acted to oppose the plan. (a) Russia and her European satellites refused America's offer of Marshall Plan aid. (b) Russia initiated her own economic aid program, the *Council of Mutual Economic Assistance* (COMECON). It competed with the Marshall Plan by bringing about closer economic relations between Russia and her satellites.

POINT FOUR PROGRAM

In his 1949 Inaugural Address, President Truman reaffirmed America's opposition to Russian expansion. As *Point Four* in America's effort to contain communism, Truman proposed a "bold new program" to give technical assistance to underdeveloped nations.

Under the Point Four Program, Congress annually has appropriated funds to assist developing nations in Latin America, the Middle East, Africa, and Asia. The United States has sent technical specialists to help increase agricultural and industrial output, encourage urban development, improve government administration, promote public health, and advance education.

EISENHOWER DOCTRINE

In 1957 President Eisenhower warned that, because of economic and political instability, the Middle East was vulnerable to Communist infiltration.

Eisenhower offered the Middle East nations (1) a program of economic and military aid, and (2) armed assistance, upon request, to repel open Communist aggression. The *Eisenhower Doctrine* was welcomed by Lebanon and Saudi Arabia but was denounced by Egypt and Syria as an American plot to dominate the Arab world. (Under the Eisenhower Doctrine, the United States in 1958 sent troops into Lebanon to protect that nation's government.)

PEACE CORPS

In 1961 President Kennedy inaugurated a new foreign aid agency, the *Peace Corps*. It enrolls idealistic volunteers who receive little pay, work in underdeveloped countries that request aid, and live with the native peoples. Peace Corps volunteers fill the gap between the highly skilled technical advisers of the Point Four Program and the relatively unskilled local labor. For example, they might follow up a Point Four malaria-control demonstration by remaining with the villagers and assisting in the day-by-day work.

Peace Corps volunteers have performed laudably in about 50 nations and have won friends for the United States.

AMERICAN FOREIGN AID: AN OVERVIEW

The United States continues to spend substantial sums for foreign aid— annually several billion dollars, which amount is 3 percent or less of our national budget. Currently, American military aid is administered by the Defense Department and economic aid by the State Department's *Agency for International Development (AID)*.

From 1945 to the present, the United States has extended over $220 billion in aid to some 140 countries. Of this total, 34 percent has been for military supplies and services, and 66 percent for economic and technical aid. One-third of American aid has been in the form of loans that are repayable; two-thirds has been in the form of grants that are outright gifts.

At first our foreign aid consisted chiefly of economic assistance for Europe, especially Britain, France, Italy, West Germany, and Greece. As Europe recovered from World War II, the United States extended economic and technical aid to the developing nations of the world. As a result of Communist aggression in Korea in 1950, the foreign aid program placed greater emphasis upon military aid for the Far East, especially South Korea, Japan, Taiwan, and South Vietnam. In the 1960's, the United States expanded the shipment of surplus agricultural produce to needy nations through its Food for Peace program and stepped up aid to Latin America through the Alliance for Progress. (Check the Index.)

CRITICISMS OF OUR FOREIGN AID PROGRAM

Most Americans agree that foreign aid furthers United States' national interests. Nevertheless, a minority opposes foreign aid, claiming that it (1) is a burden on the American taxpayer, (2) diverts funds needed for domestic purposes, (3) is characterized by inefficient administration, waste, and corruption, (4) creates competition for American manufacturers and farmers by building up foreign industry and agriculture, (5) has failed to win us friendship and support, especially among Third World nations, and (6) has failed to lessen the danger of communism. What do you think of these criticisms?

COMMUNIST ECONOMIC OFFENSIVE SINCE 1954

The Russians have boasted that communism will outstrip capitalism in peaceful economic competition. Since 1954 the Communist bloc has challenged the free world by offering aid to most underdeveloped nations, both neutral and pro-Western. Communist aid, chiefly loans and skilled personnel, has been accepted by more than 20 countries—notably Argentina, India, Indonesia, Iraq, Syria, and Egypt.

In recent years the Chinese Communists have offered aid to Latin American and Afro-Asian nations in competition with Russian aid programs.

To date American foreign aid remains far greater than that extended by the Communist nations.

West European Economic Unity

THE INNER SIX

The *Inner Six* West European nations—Belgium, France, Italy, Luxembourg, the Netherlands, and West Germany—having cooperated under the Marshall Plan, moved toward further economic unity.

1. European Coal and Steel Community. In 1952 the Inner Six agreed to (a) abolish tariffs on coal, iron, and steel, (b) establish a supranational (above any nation) *High Authority* to administer these resources in the interests of the entire community, and (c) grant the High Authority power to control prices, production, wages, and working conditions.

2. European Atomic Energy Community (Euratom). In 1957 the Inner Six agreed to form a supranational *European Atomic Energy Commission* to (a) coordinate atomic research, (b) pool nuclear materials, and (c) increase the production of electric power by atomic installations.

3. European Economic Community (EEC, or Common Market). In 1957 the Inner Six agreed to join in a tariff union. They established a supranational *European Economic Commission* to (a) provide for the gradual elimination of internal tariff barriers, and (b) establish a unified tariff system on goods to be imported from outside the tariff union area. European leaders envisioned the removal of man-made barriers to the movement of goods, capital, and labor —that is, a free-trade area or *Common Market*.

4. Objectives. Western European moves toward economic unity have aimed to (a) provide more coal, iron, steel, electric power, farm produce, and consumer goods at lower prices, (b) raise living standards, (c) reduce both domestic and foreign Communist threats, and (d) expand foreign trade.

AN ENLARGED COMMON MARKET (1973)

Britain twice applied for Common Market membership, but each application

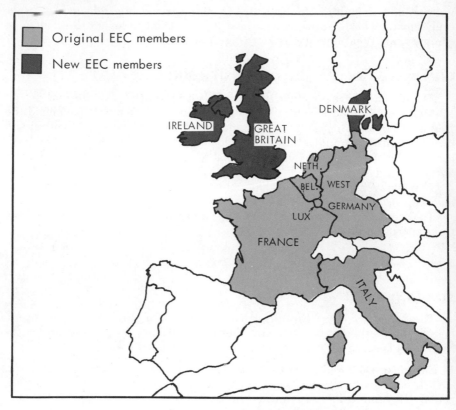

Original EEC members

New EEC members

DENMARK

IRELAND

GREAT BRITAIN

NETH.

BEL. WEST

LUX GERMANY

FRANCE

ITALY

The Enlarged Common Market

was vetoed by France under President de Gaulle. He viewed Britain's membership as a threat to his hopes for French leadership in Western Europe. With de
Gaulle's retirement, Britain again applied for membership and in 1971 was
accepted as follows: (1) to mid-1977 Britain and the six Common Market members would reciprocally reduce tariffs so as to achieve a customs union, and (2)
special protection would be provided for dairy products from New Zealand and
sugar from other British Commonwealth nations. Also, Britain's entry would be
accompanied by membership for Ireland and Denmark. (Norway was also offered membership, but the Norwegians voted narrowly to reject the offer.)

In 1973 Britain, Ireland, and Denmark officially joined, creating a nine-
member Common Market. They also joined the Coal and Steel Community and
the Atomic Energy Community. The nine nations have a combined population of
about 260 million and a gross national product (GNP) of over $1950 billion—sec-
ond only to the United States. Will the enlarged European Economic Community later move toward a common currency and a uniform foreign policy?

In 1979 Greece signed the necessary documents and within two years will
become the tenth member of the Common Market.

Military Alliances

NORTH ATLANTIC TREATY ORGANIZATION (NATO)

1. Free World Fears. In 1948 the free world nations were shocked by three Russian-inspired aggressions: (1) a coup d'etat in Czechoslovakia that eliminated democratic leaders—Foreign Minister Jan Masaryk was driven to suicide or murdered, and President Eduard Benes resigned—and gave the Communists complete control of the country, (2) pressure upon Finland to accept a mutual assistance pact with the Soviet Union which in effect compelled Finland to adhere to Russian foreign policy, and (3) a Russian attempt to drive the Western powers out of Berlin by a surface route blockade. Made fearful by these aggressive Russian moves, the free world nations formed the *North Atlantic Treaty Organization.*

2. Defensive Military Alliance. In 1949, 12 free world nations—Britain, France, Belgium, the Netherlands, Luxembourg, Denmark, Iceland, Italy, Norway, Portugal, Canada, and the United States—signed the *North Atlantic Pact.* They declared that they would (*a*) consider an attack on any one of them as an attack on all, and (*b*) come to the defense of the attacked member nation with armed force if necessary. The American Senate, by overwhelmingly ratifying the pact, again showed that the United States had abandoned its past isolationism.

NATO admitted the eastern Mediterranean countries of Greece and Turkey in 1952 and West Germany in 1955, bringing its membership to 15.

Europe Following World War II: Opposing Alliances in the Cold War

3. NATO Army. In 1950 the North Atlantic Pact nations further strengthened themselves against Communist aggression by authorizing "an integrated military force adequate for the defense of the freedom of Europe." The NATO army is headed by the *Supreme Allied Commander in Europe* (SACEUR), who has always been an American general. The first Supreme Commander was Dwight D. Eisenhower. NATO headquarters, located in Belgium, are known as the *Supreme Headquarters of the Allied Powers in Europe* (SHAPE).

To fulfill its obligations, the United States has assigned over 300,000 men —army, navy, and air force—to Europe as part of the NATO military establishment and has given billions of dollars in military equipment for NATO use. Other member nations also have assigned men and equipment to the NATO command. NATO's military strength, however, remains far less than that of Russia and its European satellites. Nevertheless, NATO hopes that its existence will deter the Communists from undertaking any aggression in Europe.

In 1979 the NATO members, viewing the military buildup of the Communist Warsaw Pact nations, agreed to increase their military defense spending and to accept the stationing in Western Europe of new American nuclear missiles capable of reaching deep into Russia.

4. Problems Facing NATO

a. Nuclear Fears. Many NATO members, vividly recalling World War II, are reluctant to equip West German personnel in NATO with nuclear weapons. They also are fearful that, in case of a Soviet-American conflict, Western Europe would suffer devastation as the nuclear battleground.

b. French Nationalism and Withdrawal From NATO. President Charles de Gaulle of France was a French nationalist, ambitious to achieve French leadership of Western Europe and resentful of American influence in NATO. In 1966 de Gaulle claimed that NATO was obsolete because (1) the development of missiles with nuclear warheads had made NATO defenses insignificant, and (2) the Soviet Union had adopted a policy of peaceful coexistence. Accordingly, de Gaulle withdrew all French forces from NATO and demanded the removal of all NATO troops, chiefly American and Canadian, from French soil. De Gaulle, however, pledged that France would remain a member of the North Atlantic Pact. De Gaulle's moves were deplored by the other NATO members, but they yielded to his demands. NATO troops left French soil, NATO bases in France were dismantled, and SHAPE headquarters were removed from near Paris to Belgium. French presidents after de Gaulle have kept his NATO policies.

c. Hostility Between Greece and Turkey. Although Greece and Turkey both joined NATO, the two countries have traditionally been enemies and in recent years have clashed bitterly over the island of Cyprus. In 1974 a Greek-backed coup, aimed at uniting Cyprus with Greece, failed and resulted in Turkish armies occupying 40 percent of the island. In Greece the military dictatorship that had planned the coup gave way to civilian and democratic rule. The new Greek regime, resenting the lack of NATO support for Greece, kept its NATO membership but withdrew its military forces from the NATO command.

In the course of the Cyprus dispute, Greece and Turkey both severely criticized the United States. Greece blamed the United States for not preventing the Turkish invasion of Cyprus. Turkey condemned the action of the United States Congress—cutting off military aid to Turkey because "substantial prog-

NATO—growing discord
(*Shanks in the Buffalo*
Evening News)

ress" had not been made toward a Cyprus settlement—and ordered American forces out of military installations and intelligence posts in Turkey. (These posts had enabled the United States and NATO to secure considerable information regarding Soviet military activities.)

In 1978 President Carter requested Congress to lift the three-year-old embargo. He pointed out that the embargo had not moved Turkey to make concessions regarding Cyprus, and he feared that Turkey might further weaken its ties to NATO. Congress narrowly approved an end to the ban.

d. American Disillusionment With NATO. For years American officials had been unhappy that the NATO powers, economically recovered from World War II, were questioning American leadership, obstructing unified foreign policies, and pursuing their own independent actions. In 1973 American disillusionment became intense as a result of the Arab-Israeli war. The major NATO members, yielding to Arab oil embargo threats, refused permission to the United States to use facilities on their soil for transporting military equipment to Israel. Their refusal compelled the United States to transport the equipment by a more difficult route. American officials, who held that support for Israel was essential to prevent Soviet domination of the Mideast, resented the lack of cooperation of NATO members and began to rethink the value of NATO.

e. Possibility of Communists in NATO Member Governments. NATO by the mid-1970's faced the possibility of Western Communists in the governments of member nations. This situation so far has not happened—but the problem surfaced as follows:

(1) *Portugal.* In 1974 an army coup ended over 40 years of conservative dictatorial rule but plunged Portugal into political chaos. For a time, the Portuguese Communist party—small and well-disciplined—seemed likely to seize complete control, but that threat disappeared with the suppression of a 1975 attempted leftist coup and with 1976 parliamentary elections, in which the Communists received less than 15 percent of the vote. The Socialists, the largest

party with 35 percent of the vote, formed a minority government committed to democracy, economic reform, and active NATO membership—policies supported by subsequent Portuguese governments.

(2) *Italy*. In 1976 parliamentary elections, the Christian Democrats remained the largest party with 39 percent of the popular vote, but the Italian Communists, the second largest party, received 35 percent of the popular vote—a substantial gain. The Christian Democrats formed a minority government, but their ability to secure a parliamentary majority depended upon tacit Communist cooperation. The Communists indicated that they would accept the arrangement for the time being but that their goal was full membership in an Italian coalition government. In that eventuality, Italian Communists might have access to confidential military data regarding NATO—which they now claim to support. Would Italian Communists refrain from transmitting such NATO data to Moscow?

In 1979 the Communists, having received no cabinet positions, caused the fall of the minority Christian Democratic government. After the 1979 elections, the Christian Democrats with minor-party support again formed a minority government. The Communists remained in opposition.

The United States meanwhile voiced concern that Communist entry into the government of a NATO member might have a devastating effect on NATO.

SOUTHEAST ASIA TREATY ORGANIZATION (SEATO)

1. Defensive Military Alliance (1954). Eight nations—the United States, Great Britain, France, Australia, New Zealand, Thailand, Pakistan, and the Philippines—established SEATO. Each member nation (a) agreed that armed aggression against any other member would "endanger its own peace and safety" and pledged to "meet the common danger in accordance with its constitutional processes," (b) recognized that civil wars might involve foreign aggression, and (c) offered to aid, upon request, the Southeast Asian states of Cambodia, Laos, and South Vietnam.

2. Weaknesses of SEATO. (a) SEATO lacked a unified armed force and military command. (b) SEATO's main strength came from its non-Asian members. (c) Four important Southeast Asian nations—India, Burma, Sri Lanka, and Indonesia—refused to join SEATO. These nations sought neutrality in the cold war. (d) France refrained from active participation in SEATO. (e) Displeased by lack of SEATO support in its conflicts with India, Pakistan in 1972 withdrew from SEATO.

3. End of SEATO (1976). Following the Communist triumphs in Indo-China, the active SEATO members agreed that in view of the "changing circumstances" in Southeast Asia, SEATO should be "phased out."

ADDITIONAL AMERICAN MILITARY ALLIANCES

The United States has military alliances with over 40 nations and maintains almost 400 major military bases overseas. In addition to NATO, the United States has entered into the following military commitments:

1. The Rio Inter-American Defense Treaty (1947) between the United States and the Latin American nations of the Organization of American States (OAS) provides for the common defense of the Western Hemisphere.

2. The Anzus Pact (1951) between Australia, New Zealand, and the United States provides that each nation (a) consider an attack upon any member as dangerous to its own safety, and (b) act to meet the common danger.

3. Bilateral Mutual Defense Treaties with Japan, the Philippines, and South Korea pledge the United States to consider an attack on any of these nations as a common danger and to assist the nation attacked.

Also, the United States maintains military bases in Spain.

COMMUNIST MILITARY ALLIANCES

1. Chinese-Soviet Treaty. In 1950 Soviet Russia and Communist China signed a 30-year treaty of "friendship, alliance, and mutual aid" providing for (a) mutual military aid in case of attack by Japan or by an ally of Japan (meaning the United States), and (b) consultation on all international matters of mutual concern.

Because the Soviet Union and China have been openly hostile toward each other since 1963, many observers doubt that this alliance is valid.

China recently stated that it would not renew this treaty beyond its 1980 expiration date.

2. Warsaw Pact. In 1955 Russia and its European satellites formed an alliance providing for a unified Communist military command under a Soviet general. This pact was designed as a counterweight to NATO.

MULTIPLE-CHOICE QUESTIONS

1. President Franklin D. Roosevelt stated: "We have learned that we must live as men, and not as ostriches, nor as dogs in the manger. We have learned to be citizens of the world, members of the human community." Which attitude does this statement reflect? (1) acceptance of an active role in world affairs (2) acceptance of responsibility for the failure of the United Nations (3) approval of a policy of appeasement toward aggressors (4) approval of our traditional foreign policy in world affairs
2. Which helps to explain why United States foreign policy today is very *different* from our foreign policy in the early 1800's? (1) Constitutional amendments have restricted the role of the President (2) Presidents are reluctant to act without direction from the Senate. (3) The United States has evolved from a newly independent nation into a world power. (4) The role of public opinion in determining foreign policy has decreased.
3. Which has been an aim of the United States policy of containment? (1) encouraging the people of Soviet Russia to revolt against communism (2) overthrowing the governments of the satellite nations in eastern Europe (3) encircling Soviet Russia with a belt of neutral nations (4) preventing the further spread of communism
4. All of the following are characteristics of a democracy *except* (1) majority rule and respect for minority rights (2) existence of the people for the state (3) responsible citizenship (4) government of, by, and for the people.
5. Russian leaders claim that the Soviet Union is democratic because (1) elections are held and citizens have the right to vote (2) party patronage is unknown (3) all workers are members of the Communist party (4) each citizen shares equally in goods produced.
6. Which of the following is true of Russia under Soviet rule? (1) Workers have the

right to strike.   (2) Writers are free to criticize the government.   (3) Agricultural shortages have been eliminated.   (4) Schools are provided for all children.

7. "We must somehow learn to live together in this world, to tolerate one another, or else we cannot survive." The author of this statement would *most* likely support a policy of   (1) nativism   (2) coexistence   (3) conformity   (4) isolation.

8. From events of the past two decades, which conclusion about communism may *best* be drawn?   (1) It has made no headway in Latin America.   (2) In different nations, communism is shaped by national needs and goals.   (3) Communist nations have moved closer to the Soviet Union.   (4) It has been weakened because of the Soviet Union's involvement in Vietnam.

9. Which group consists entirely of Russian satellites?   (1) Denmark, Poland, Turkey   (2) Czechoslovakia, Greece, Austria   (3) Bulgaria, East Germany, Poland   (4) Hungary, Israel, Rumania

10. Estonia, Latvia, and Lithuania are   (1) islands taken by Russia from Japan   (2) Russian satellite nations in the Balkans   (3) neutralist nations   (4) former independent nations now part of the Soviet Union.

11. Since the 1950's, the actions of most western European nations toward the United States have   (1) consistently supported our trade policy with Communist nations   (2) shown increasing independence of our policies   (3) required increasing amounts of United States economic aid   (4) supported our participation in the conflicts of Asia.

12. The Truman Doctrine was a   (1) proposal for the peaceful use of atomic energy   (2) program for general disarmament   (3) policy of extending aid to nations threatened by communism   (4) policy of giving technical aid to underdeveloped nations.

13. Under both Czarist and Communist rule, Russia's policy toward Turkey has been influenced by Russia's desire to gain control of   (1) the Red Sea   (2) Gibraltar   (3) the Suez Canal   (4) the Dardanelles.

14. Which could be appropriately cited as evidence of the success of the Marshall Plan?   (1) end of cold war tensions   (2) defection of Yugoslavia from communism   (3) failure of communism to hold its position in eastern Europe   (4) improvement of economic conditions in western Europe

15. The *primary* purpose of the Point Four Program was to help underdeveloped areas by   (1) furnishing technical aid   (2) providing food for starving people   (3) spreading information concerning the American way of life   (4) providing military aid to resist Communist aggression.

16. The Truman and Eisenhower Doctrines were *most* similar in that both were designed to   (1) reduce tariff barriers   (2) end the Korean War   (3) resist Communist aggression   (4) aid the same nations.

17. A *basic* purpose of the Peace Corps is to provide   (1) jobs for unemployed American youths   (2) scholarships for Americans to study in foreign countries   (3) aid to people in underdeveloped areas   (4) relief to Arab refugees in the Middle East.

18. Which has been a problem for the members of the European Common Market?   (1) conflict between national sovereignty and united action   (2) active opposition from the United States   (3) decline in living standards of western Europeans   (4) failure to remove tariff barriers within the union

19. In a sense, the United States has had a "common market" of its own because the original federal Constitution *prohibited* taxes on goods   (1) exported from the United States   (2) imported into the United States   (3) manufactured in the United States   (4) shipped from one state to another.

20. A *major* reason for creating the North Atlantic Treaty Organization (NATO) was to   (1) supervise the West German government   (2) protect member nations against Communist aggression   (3) distribute Point Four funds   (4) regulate world trade.

21. In which respect is our participation in NATO significant?   (1) It is our first

peacetime military alliance with any European nation. (2) It marks a return to the foreign policy of George Washington. (3) It nullifies the power of Congress to appropriate money for the armed forces. (4) It violates the UN Charter.

22. A country that was *not* a member of the Southeast Asia Treaty Organization is (1) Australia (2) Thailand (3) India (4) the Philippines.

MODIFIED TRUE-FALSE QUESTIONS

1. Soviet armed might in 1968 suppressed a Communist "liberalization" program in *Poland*.
2. The Point Four Program of the United States closely parallels the United Nations program of *technical assistance*.
3. British membership in the Common Market was approved on a third application. Previously, British membership had twice been vetoed by *Belgium*.
4. The European Communist country that first successfully resisted Russian domination was *Hungary*.
5. The Truman Doctrine was intended to keep Russian influence out of Turkey and *Egypt*.
6. The Communists seek to keep democratic ideas from their people by means of a barrier known as the *Warsaw Pact*.
7. The nation that remained a member of the North Atlantic Pact but set the precedent of withdrawing her military forces from the NATO army was *West Germany*.
8. Two NATO members, traditional enemies, who have clashed over Cyprus, are *Britain and Italy*.
9. The Peace Corps was originated by President *Eisenhower*.
10. During the 1973 Arab-Israeli war, American efforts to resupply Israel with military equipment *were not supported* by the major NATO nations.

ESSAY QUESTIONS

1. It is customary for totalitarian countries to attempt to disguise themselves as democracies. (*a*) Describe *three* democratic features of life in the United States that do *not* exist in the Soviet Union. (*b*) Discuss *two* devices used by the Soviet Union to give the impression that it is democratic. (*c*) Discuss *two* differences in economic and social life between the United States and the Soviet Union.
2. To win the cold war, the Western democracies must estimate as correctly as possible their own strengths and weaknesses as well as those of Communist Russia and her satellites. (*a*) Describe *one* strength and *one* weakness of the western democracies. (*b*) Describe *one* strength and *one* weakness of Communist Russia and her satellites. (*c*) Discuss *two* different ways by which the United States has attempted to win the cold war.
3. (*a*) Give *two* reasons why the United States has extended military and economic aid to foreign nations since the end of World War II. (*b*) Describe in detail *one* American foreign aid program. (*c*) Explain *one* criticism of American foreign aid. (*d*) Discuss *one* reason why the Communist bloc has undertaken its own foreign aid program.
4. For over 25 years, membership in NATO has been a cornerstone of American foreign policy. (*a*) Explain *one* reason why NATO was formed. (*b*) Discuss *two* disputes among NATO members, showing how *each* has weakened the organization. (*c*) In view of these disputes, does NATO retain any value as a military alliance today? Give *one* argument to support your opinion.

16. *The United States Deals With Problems Throughout the World*

Germany

ALLIED DECISIONS REGARDING GERMANY (1945)

At the Yalta and Potsdam Conferences and in other agreements, the United States, Britain, and Russia made major decisions concerning Germany.

1. Territory. The eastern provinces were detached from Germany with part occupied by Russia but most under Polish control (see map below). These territorial changes were meant to be temporary, pending a German peace treaty. Russia and Poland, however, considered these changes as permanent. (In 1975 the Western powers acquiesced to these boundaries by signing the Helsinki Pact. Check the Index.)

2. Occupation Zones. The rest of Germany was divided into four zones, Russia, Britain, the United States, and France each governing one zone. Berlin, lying 110 miles inside the Russian zone, was likewise divided into four sections, with each of the Big Four controlling one section. The three Western Allies were guaranteed access to Berlin by surface and air routes across the Russian zone. These divisions also were meant to be temporary.

3. Economy. The German economy was to be directed toward agriculture and peaceful industries. War industries were barred. Certain German factories and industrial equipment were to be dismantled and removed, chiefly to the Soviet Union, as partial reparation.

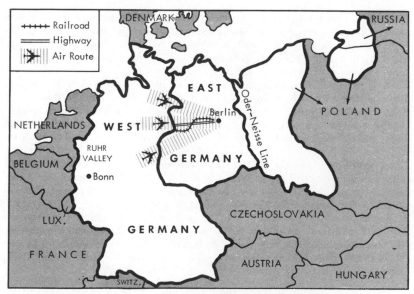

The map shows the railroad, highway, and air routes guaranteed to the Western Allies for access across the Russian zone to Berlin.

Germany Following World War II

Will we learn the lessons?
(*Partymiller in the Gazette
and Daily, York, Pa.*)

4. Disarmament. Germany was to be disarmed so as to render her unable to wage aggressive warfare again.

5. Education. German schools were to work for the "development of democratic ideas." The Allies recognized that reeducation of the German people would be a long and difficult task.

6. Denazification. Nazism was to be wiped out completely. All Nazi organizations, including the Nazi party, Storm Troopers, and the Gestapo (secret police), were dissolved. Active Nazis were not to be allowed to hold public office or other positions of influence. War criminals were to be brought to trial.

NAZI WAR CRIMES TRIALS

1. Nuremberg Trials. An *International Military Tribunal* met at Nuremberg (1945–1946) and tried Air Force Minister Hermann Goering and other top Nazi leaders. They were charged with crimes against humanity, violations of international law, and waging aggressive warfare. These trials, it was hoped, would serve to democratize Germany, expose the evils of Nazism, strengthen international law, and discourage future aggressors. The Tribunal found 19 of the 22 defendants guilty; it sentenced 12 to death and the others to prison.

2. In the American Zone. A special *United States Military Tribunal* tried the secondary Nazi leaders. *Alfred Krupp*, head of the Krupp munitions works, was sentenced to prison for exploiting slave labor and plundering Nazi-occupied countries. The United States later permitted West German *denazification courts* to try less important Nazis. These courts were quite lenient, and many former Nazis regained positions of influence.

3. In the Russian Zone. At first, the Communists severely punished Nazi war criminals. After a short time, the Communists abandoned denazification trials and treated former Nazis leniently in order to gain their support.

THE WEST AND RUSSIA DISAGREE ON GERMANY

After World War II, the West and Russia came into conflict over Germany. Western reunification plans that would swing Germany toward the West were rejected by Russia. Soviet reunification plans that would bring Germany into the Communist camp were rejected by the West.

RUSSIA PROVOKES A CRISIS: BERLIN BLOCKADE (1948–1949)

Under Stalin, Russia tried to drive the Western Allies out of Berlin by blockading the surface routes—roads, rails, and canals—between Berlin and the three western zones of Germany. To thwart this *Berlin Blockade*, the Allies resorted to an *airlift*. For almost a year, the airlift supplied more than 2 million West Berliners with food, medicine, and other necessities of life. The Soviets could not halt the airlift except by shooting down Allied planes, a course they were unwilling to take for fear of starting an all-out war. The Russians therefore abandoned the blockade.

DEVELOPMENTS IN WEST GERMANY

1. Establishment of the German Federal Republic. Unable to reach an agreement with Russia for German reunification, the three Western Allies in 1949 combined their zones to form the *Federal Republic of Germany* with its capital at *Bonn*. In 1955 West Germany was granted full sovereignty over domestic and foreign affairs (except for negotiations regarding German reunification and West Berlin) and was admitted to NATO.

West Germany's army, assigned to NATO, was limited to 12 divisions—a force of about 275,000. West Germany also was prohibited from manufacturing atomic, biological, or chemical weapons, guided missiles, or large warships.

2. Government of West Germany. The West German constitution provides for a democratic government with (*a*) a guarantee of civil liberties and free elections, (*b*) a two-house Parliament, and (*c*) a chancellor responsible to the Bundestag, the popularly elected lower house of Parliament.

Germany's two major parties are the *Christian Democrats* and the *Social Democrats*. Although they differ on details, both parties support welfare state measures, NATO membership, and a pro-Western foreign policy. The Christian Democrats for many years controlled the Bundestag and the government.

In 1969 elections, the Social Democrats in coalition with the minor Free Democratic party secured a narrow legislative majority. *Willy Brandt*, the Social Democratic leader, became chancellor. Brandt improved relations with East Germany, Poland, and Russia, and supported West European unity. In 1974 Brandt, accepting responsibility for failure to detect an East German Communist spy on his staff, resigned as chancellor. Brandt's successor, named by the Social Democratic party, was the former finance minister, *Helmut Schmidt*. Schmidt pledged to continue Brandt's foreign policy, emphasizing West European unity in partnership with the United States. In 1976 elections the Schmidt government retained a narrow Bundestag majority.

DEVELOPMENTS IN EAST GERMANY

1. Establishment of the German Democratic Republic. Russia in 1949 transformed its zone into the *German Democratic Republic* with its capital at *East*

Berlin. This East German state is a Russian satellite occupied by Soviet troops. In addition East Germany maintains its own army of over 100,000 troops and is a member of the Warsaw Pact.

2. Government of East Germany. A self-proclaimed "democratic republic," East Germany is in fact a typical Communist dictatorship with restrictions on civil liberties, a secret police, and only one political party. In 1953 East German riots against the satellite government were repressed by Soviet tanks and troops. Until the 1970's, the Western powers refused to recognize the East German regime.

For 25 years *Walter Ulbricht*, as head of the East German Communist party, exercised tight control over the country. In 1971 Ulbricht resigned because of ill health and old age, and was replaced by *Erich Honecker*.

COMPARISON OF THE TWO GERMANYS

1. Area. West Germany comprises 70 percent of the total area of postwar Germany as compared to 30 percent for East Germany.

2. Population. West Germany contains over 75 percent of the German people as compared to less than 25 percent for East Germany.

3. Industrialization. West Germany, the more industrial of the two Germanys, contains the industrial heart of Europe, the Ruhr Valley. The East German economy is more agricultural than that of West Germany.

4. Economic System. West Germany has a capitalist economy, typified by private enterprise, free labor unions, and limited government regulation of the economy. East Germany has a Communist economy, typified by government ownership of industry and collectivization of agriculture.

5. Economic Developments Since World War II. Aided by Marshall Plan funds, West Germany made a remarkable recovery from the devastation of World War II. Her cities, transportation system, and industry were all rebuilt. Today, West Germany is the leading industrial nation of Western Europe and enjoys a high standard of living.

In contrast, East Germany made a far slower recovery. For years, its cities—notably East Berlin—were not rebuilt, and its people suffered shortages of food and consumer goods. Seeking a better life, many East Germans fled to West Germany, chiefly through Berlin. To stop this flow, the Communists in 1961 built a barbed-wire and concrete barrier, the *Berlin Wall*. Having thus halted the flight of skilled workers and also having relaxed economic controls, East Germany in the 1960's experienced considerable economic growth, but its living standard remains lower than that of West Germany.

CONFLICTING PROPOSALS FOR GERMAN REUNIFICATION

1. Western Proposals. The Western nations proposed that the World War II Allies sign a German peace treaty that would (*a*) reunify Germany by UN-supervised elections in both East and West Germany, and (*b*) permit reunited Germany to join in any alliance, including NATO. Russia rejected these proposals because (*a*) free elections would probably result in a pro-Western government for all Germany, and *(b)* NATO membership for a reunited Germany would strengthen the military power of the West.

2. Russian Proposals. Russia proposed that *(a)* the Allies sign a peace treaty with the two Germanys, thereby enabling East Germany to retain its "socialist gains," *(b)* the East and West German governments negotiate with each other regarding reunification, and *(c)* a reunited Germany remain neutral in the cold war. The Western powers rejected these proposals because they would *(a)* perpetuate the East German satellite regime and *(b)* require West Germany to withdraw from NATO.

RUSSIA PROVOKES ANOTHER CRISIS OVER BERLIN (1958–1961)

1. Russian Proposals for Berlin. In 1958 Soviet Premier Khrushchev announced his determination to drive the Western powers out of West Berlin. If successful, Khrushchev probably expected that West Berlin *(a)* would be absorbed by East Germany, thereby closing down a "showcase" of democracy and capitalism behind the Iron Curtain, and *(b)* would no longer serve as an escape route for refugees fleeing from Communist eastern Europe. (In 1961 the Communists closed this escape route by building the Berlin Wall.)

2. Western Responses to the Soviet Challenge. The Western nations *(a)* stated their determination to remain in Berlin, *(b)* condemned the Berlin Wall, and *(c)* indicated willingness to negotiate over Berlin. Although negotiations failed, the Soviets did not act to drive out the Western powers.

STEPS TO REDUCE TENSIONS OVER BERLIN AND GERMANY (SINCE 1970)

1. West Germany Improves Relations With Communist East Europe (1970–1972). Chancellor Willy Brandt moved in 1970 to "normalize" West Germany's relations with the Communist nations of eastern Europe. Brandt traveled to Moscow and later to Warsaw, paying homage to the Soviet Unknown Soldier, the Polish Unknown Soldier, and the Jews who battled in the Warsaw Ghetto uprising—all victims of Nazi aggression in World War II. Brandt signed two separate treaties—with the Soviet Union and with Poland—by which (1) West Germany accepted the existing Soviet and Polish borders, including the *Oder-Neisse Line* as Poland's western boundary, thereby conceding sizable areas taken from prewar Germany (see map, page 620), and (2) the signatories renounced the use of force and agreed to strive for economic, scientific, and cultural cooperation. These treaties were hailed by Brandt as leading to a new era of peace for Europe, but they were opposed by many Germans for accepting the territorial losses to Poland and Russia. In 1972 the treaties secured a minimal approval in the Bundestag.

2. The Big Four Reach Another Berlin Agreement (1971). The Big Four powers reached a new Berlin agreement *(a)* providing for unimpeded road and rail traffic, and continued commercial and cultural ties, between West Berlin and West Germany, *(b)* permitting personal and business visits by West Berliners to East Germany, *(c)* accepting West German responsibility for, but limiting her political activity in, West Berlin, and *(d)* allowing Russia to open a consular office in West Berlin.

3. West Germany and East Germany "Normalize" Their Relations (1972). West Germany and East Germany signed a treaty that *(a)* confirmed the existence of two Germanys and established formal relations between them, *(b)* allowed additional visits by West Germans to relatives living in East Germany, *(c)* called for the two Germanys to cooperate in such areas as sports, environmental control, airlines, and technical knowledge, *(d)* proposed that both Germanys be admitted to the UN (which was done in 1973), and *(e)* left unanswered the question of German reunification.

4. Germany Remains Divided. After East Germany acceded to the 1971 Big Four agreement on Berlin, Britain and France opened diplomatic relations with the Communist regime. Other Western nations did likewise. In 1974 the United States became the last major Western power to establish formal diplomatic relations with East Germany.

Is Germany destined to remain permanently divided?

The Middle East

LOCATION AND IMPORTANCE

The Middle East consists of northeastern Africa and southwestern Asia. The region's importance lies in its (1) *vital waterways*—the Suez Canal and the Dardanelles, (2) *valuable oil resources*—in Saudi Arabia, Kuwait, Iraq, and Iran, and (3) *strategic location*—at the crossroads of Europe, Asia, and Africa, and on the southern flank of Russia (see map, page 626).

Israel and the Arab States

EMERGENCE OF ISRAEL

1. Jewish Claims to Palestine. *Theodor Herzl*, a journalist and Jewish intellectual, founded modern *Zionism*, the movement for restoring a Jewish homeland in Palestine. Zionists pointed out that the Jewish people *(a)* had lived in Palestine for over 1300 years during ancient times and *(b)* needed a refuge from anti-Semitic persecution. In 1917 the Zionist movement gained the support of the British government which issued the *Balfour Declaration*, viewing "with favor the establishment in Palestine of a national home for the Jewish people." To fulfill the Balfour Declaration, Britain in 1923 received the League of Nations mandate over Palestine.

By 1938 over 500,000 Jews had migrated to Palestine. They built modern cities, founded agricultural settlements, started industries, restored desert lands to fertility, reduced death from disease, and established schools.

2. Arab Opposition and a New British Policy. Opposition to Jewish immigration came from (*a*) Arab nationalists, who desired an Arab Palestine, (*b*) Arab ruling classes, who feared Western ideas of democracy, and (*c*) Arab peasants and nomads, who feared the loss of their traditional ways of living.

In 1939 just before the outbreak of World War II, Britain severely limited Jewish immigration to Palestine. By so appeasing the Arabs, the Zionists claimed, Britain was violating the Balfour Declaration.

During World War II, 6 million European Jews—men, women, and children—were savagely murdered by the Nazis. Of those who survived, many sought admission to Palestine. Britain, however, still kept the gates closed. Britain's policy was (*a*) defied by Palestinian Jews, who smuggled immigrants into the Holy Land, and (*b*) condemned by the United States. Britain rejected President Truman's repeated requests to ease immigration restrictions.

3. Palestine and the UN. In 1947 Britain turned the Palestine problem over to the UN General Assembly. It voted to (*a*) end the British mandate, (*b*) place Jerusalem under international control, and (*c*) partition Palestine into separate Arab and Jewish states.

Thereupon, in 1948 Israel proclaimed its independence under President *Chaim Weizmann* and Prime Minister *David Ben-Gurion.* The new Jewish state

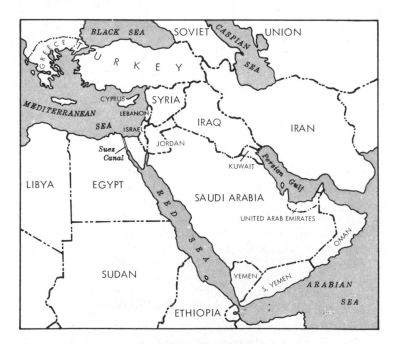

The Middle East Today

received immediate recognition from the United States. The Israeli republic is the Middle East's only modern democratic state.

4. Israel Maintains Its Existence

a. Israeli War for Independence (1948–1949). The Arab nations defied the UN decision for a Jewish state and attacked Israel. Despite their numerical superiority, the Arabs were driven back and lost some territory to the Israelis. In 1949 the Arab states accepted, as temporary, armistice agreements arranged by UN mediator *Ralph Bunche.*

(The Arab nations also defied the UN decision for a Palestinian Arab state. The areas proposed for such a state were seized—the Gaza Strip by Egypt and the land on the West Bank of the Jordan River by Jordan.)

b. Continued Arab Hostility (1949–1956). (1) The Arab League enforced an economic boycott against Israel and against Western companies doing business with Israel. (2) Under President Nasser, an Arab nationalist, Egypt barred Israeli ships from the Suez Canal. (3) Egyptian artillery on the Sinai Peninsula blockaded ships bound for Israel's port of *Elath* on the *Gulf of Aqaba* (see map, page 629). (4) Egypt allowed *fedayeen* (guerrilla) raids against Israeli border areas.

c. Sinai Campaign (1956). Israel feared Egypt's military buildup, which resulted chiefly from an arms deal in 1955 between Egypt and the Communist bloc. In 1956 Israel seized the initiative and invaded Egypt to wipe out fedayeen bases and end the Aqaba blockade. Israeli forces quickly scattered Nasser's armies and overran the Sinai Peninsula. (Britain and France also invaded Egypt to regain control of the Suez Canal. Check the Index.) The United Nations condemned the attacks, secured withdrawal of the invading forces, and stationed a *United Nations Emergency Force (UNEF)* in Egypt on the border with Israel and at the tip of the Sinai Peninsula. For ten years Israel was free from Egyptian fedayeen raids and free to use the Gulf of Aqaba.

SURVEY OF ARAB NATIONALISM (SINCE 1945)

1. Roots.
Arab peoples realized their common cultural background: Arabic language, Moslem religion, and the great Arab civilization of the Middle Ages.

2. Evidences of Arab Unity:

a. Arab League. Founded in 1945, the Arab League seeks to unify Arab policy on world issues, especially Arab efforts to destroy Israel.

b. Organization of Petroleum Exporting Countries (OPEC). Founded in 1960, OPEC consists of six non-Arab and seven Arab states—the major oil producer being Saudi Arabia. Dominated by its Arab members, OPEC's economic purpose is to increase its members' oil revenues. (For OPEC and the 1973 Arab-Israeli war, check the Index.)

c. Military Cooperation. In the 1973 Arab-Israeli war, the Arab states rushed to the aid of Syria and Egypt. (Check the Index.)

d. Palestine Liberation Organization (PLO). Because the PLO has been both a unifying and divisive force, it is discussed at greater length.

PALESTINE LIBERATION ORGANIZATION (PLO)

1. Background.
The Palestine Arab refugee problem arose out of the 1948–1949 war, when the Arab nations tried to destroy the newborn state of Israel. Mainly fearing for their safety, some 540,000 Arabs out of 700,000 in Israeli territory fled

to neighboring Arab nations. After the war, Israel proposed that the refugee problem be part of an overall settlement involving boundaries and diplomatic recognition, but the Arab nations rejected the Israeli proposal.

The Arab nations generally refused to assimilate the refugees into their societies. Many refugees were compelled to live in squalid camps dependent upon international charity for the necessities of life. This environment gave rise to various guerrilla groups committed to destroy Israel. In the mid-1960's, these groups formed an umbrella organization, the Palestine Liberation Organization (PLO). Eventually Yasir Arafat—leader of the largest guerrilla group Al Fatah—became head of the PLO.

2. Arab Support for the PLO. In 1974 the Arab nations, meeting at Rabat, Morocco, unanimously declared the PLO the "sole legitimate representative of the Palestinian people" and called for the creation of a Palestinian state. Also in 1974, the Arab nations secured a UN General Assembly invitation for the PLO to take part in its debate on the "Palestine question." (Check the Index for Palestine Liberation Organization.)

3. PLO as a Divisive Force in the Arab World. In 1970–1971 Palestinian guerrillas threatened the rule of King Hussein of Jordan, but his army drove them from Jordan. In the Lebanese civil war (1975–1976) leftist Palestinian guerrillas joined with leftist Lebanese Moslems to battle against rightist Lebanese Christian Arabs. Fearful of a hostile leftist regime in Lebanon, Syria sent its army into Lebanon, suppressed the leftist Palestinians and Lebanese Moslems, and enforced a cease-fire. (Check the Index for Lebanon, civil war in.)

SURVEY OF ARAB DISUNITY

1. Differences Among the Arab Nations. The Arab nations, in many ways, reveal great diversity. *(a)* Libya, Algeria, and Iraq are leftist, radical, and pro-Soviet; whereas Saudi Arabia, Jordan, and Tunisia are rightist, conservative, and generally pro-Western. *(b)* Saudi Arabia, Jordan, Morocco, and Kuwait are monarchies headed by hereditary rulers; most others are republics—in reality military dictatorships and one-party states.

2. Disputes in the Arab World: *(a) Yemen Civil War (1962–1970).* Egypt, then a leftist nation under Nasser, supported the Yemeni republican forces whereas Saudi Arabia aided the Yemeni royalists. In 1970 this civil war ended as royalist supporters accepted posts in the republican regime. *(b) Jordan vs. Palestinian Guerrillas (1970–1971).* King Hussein of Jordan thwarted the efforts of the Palestine guerrillas to overthrow his regime and drove them out of Jordan. They fled northward into Syria and Lebanon. *(c) Algeria vs. Morocco (since 1975).* These two nations have disputed control of phosphate-rich Western (Spanish) Sahara. *(d) Lebanon Civil War (1975–1976).* Check the Index.

ARAB-ISRAELI WAR (1967)

1. Background. Egypt entered into military alliances with Syria and Jordan, and the Arab states moved their armies toward their borders with Israel. Nasser secured removal of the UNEF and closed the Gulf of Aqaba to Israeli shipping. Meanwhile, Israel called up its military reserves. The opposing armies stood face to face, and eventually war started.

2. The War. In a six-day war, the Israelis routed the Arab forces and seized (1) from Egypt—the Gaza Strip and the entire Sinai Peninsula westward to the Suez Canal and southward to Sharm el Sheikh, opening the Gulf of Aqaba to Israeli shipping; (2) from Jordan—all territory on the West Bank of the Jordan River, including the Old City of Jerusalem; and (3) from Syria—the Golan Heights.

UN Security Council resolutions helped end the fighting. Israel urged direct negotiations to achieve a permanent peace settlement, but Egypt and Syria spoke of another round of fighting.

ARAB HOSTILITY AND DIPLOMACY (1967–1973)

1. No War But No Peace. Arab guerrilla groups gave Israel no peace. They increased terrorist raids against Israeli settlements and gunned Israeli commercial airplanes at airports in Greece and Switzerland. In 1972 Arab extremists employed Japanese leftists to massacre innocent civilians at the Tel Aviv airport; also Arab terrorists murdered 11 Israeli Olympic athletes at Munich. In response, Israel raided guerrilla bases in Syria and Lebanon. The main threat to Israel, however, was Egypt, whose leaders called for "fire and blood." Israel bested Egypt in artillery and airplane duels along the Suez Canal. Egypt increasingly became dependent upon Russia for military equipment and for over 20,000 military personnel, who manned missile sites and trained Egyptian forces.

2. Egypt Under Sadat. In 1970 Nasser died and his position was assumed by *Anwar al-Sadat.* The new Egyptian President directed his nation's foreign policy away from dependence on the Soviet Union. Although in 1971 he signed a

Israel and the Bordering Arab States

15-year Soviet-Egyptian treaty of friendship, cooperation, and military assistance, a year later he ordered Soviet military personnel to leave Egypt. The 20,000 Soviet troops, pilots, and military advisers were withdrawn. Soviet military equipment remained and the Soviets continued to supply Egypt with military spare parts.

Sadat, however, was determined to regain Egyptian territory lost to Israel in the 1967 war—if necessary by a new war.

ARAB-ISRAELI WAR (1973)

1. Military Front. By attacking on Yom Kippur, the most holy day of the Jewish religion and devoted to prayer, the Syrians and Egyptians gained an initial surprise advantage. Syrian forces advanced on the Golan Heights, and Egyptian forces crossed the Suez Canal eastward into the Sinai desert. Hastily mobilized, Israeli forces slowly reversed the tide of battle. The Israelis lost many planes to Russian-built SAM antiaircraft missiles but eventually achieved air supremacy. They advanced against the Syrians on the Golan Heights and crossed the Suez Canal westward into Egypt proper, trapping a 20,000-man Egyptian force in the Sinai desert. Against this military background, the three warring nations accepted the UN cease-fire calls.

2. Arab Unity Moves

a. Military Matters. To aid Syria and Egypt, the other Arab states sent troops and planes and pledged diplomatic and economic support.

b. Oil Embargo. The Arab states—especially Saudi Arabia, Kuwait, the Arabian peninsula sheikdoms, Iraq, Libya, and Algeria—possess the world's major known oil fields and have supplied significant amounts of the oil needs of industrialized nations: the United States, West European countries, and Japan. Since 1960 Arab and other oil-producing countries have been joined in the *Organization of Petroleum Exporting Countries (OPEC)* coordinating efforts to increase their oil revenues. With the outbreak of the 1973 Arab-Israeli war, the Arab states seized the opportunity to further their economic goal and, at the same time, use oil as a political weapon. They raised oil prices fourfold, reduced shipments to most West European nations and Japan, and totally embargoed oil shipments to the United States. As the diplomatic price for easing their cutoffs, the Arab states demanded that the oil-consuming nations voice support for the Arab position in the Mideast. Japan and most West European nations did so.

After the UN achieved a cease-fire, American Secretary of State Kissinger negotiated an Israeli-Egyptian troop-separation agreement that restored Egyptian control of both sides of the Suez Canal. Thereafter most oil-producing Arab states lifted the embargo against the United States, but they retained the higher price for oil.

3. Superpower Involvement. After the outbreak of the 1973 war, the United States acted unsuccessfully to halt the hostilities. The Soviet Union, in contrast, acted to spur hostilities, voicing support for Egypt and Syria, urging the other Arab states to join in the struggle, and pledging to "assist in every way" the Arab effort to retake the 1967 lost territories. As the war took a heavy toll of military equipment, the Soviets began airlifting massive amounts of additional supplies to Egypt and Syria. The United States thereupon acted to resupply Israel.

After the Israelis gained the military advantage, the Soviet Union and the

United States jointly sponsored a balanced UN resolution that achieved a Mideast cease-fire. A rumored Soviet plan to send Russian troops into the Mideast to bolster Egyptian forces led President Nixon to place the American military on a "precautionary alert." The danger of this possible confrontation was eased with the creation of the UNEF peacekeeping force—to serve as a buffer between the Israeli and Egyptian armies.

4. Observations

a. Israel "won" the war militarily but in other ways "lost." With its small population, Israel suffered heavy casualties, although they were only one-tenth those inflicted on the Arabs. With its limited resources, Israel incurred heavy war costs. Israel finally was more isolated diplomatically then ever before and retained but few friends among the world's nations.

b. Egypt experienced a tremendous upsurge of confidence as its armies demonstrated ability to master modern military equipment. Egypt also regained full control of the Suez Canal.

c. The United States increased its *leverage*—that is, its ability to influence Mideast affairs. While reaffirming its support for Israel's right to exist, the United States avoided an extreme partisan stand and gained increased respect among moderate Arabs. In particular Egypt resumed full diplomatic relations with the United States and sought American assistance for industrial and public works projects.

d. The Soviet Union demonstrated its ability to influence Mideast affairs. Its approval would seem necessary to assure any permanent Mideast settlement.

RECENT MIDDLE EAST DEVELOPMENTS

1. Rift in Egyptian-Soviet Relations. In 1976 Sadat, bitter that the Soviet Union had refused to replenish Egypt's weapons and to ease Egypt's debt repayment, moved to end the 1971 Soviet-Egyptian friendship treaty.

2. Entebbe Rescue Mission. In 1976 Palestinian guerrillas in Athens, Greece, hijacked an Air France plane coming in from Israel. After compelling the pilot to fly the plane to Entebbe airport in Uganda, the hijackers threatened death to over 100 Israeli hostages unless Israel released jailed Palestinian terrorists. While pretending to negotiate, Israel launched a daring 2500-mile air rescue mission. Israeli commandos landed at Entebbe airport on July 4; they wiped out the Palestinian hijackers and some 20 Ugandan soldiers assisting the hijackers and flew back all but four of the hostages and one of the commandos safely to Israel. For the Israelis, depressed by the 1973 Arab-Israeli war and its aftermath, "victory at Entebbe" brought a terrific boost in morale.

3. Developments in Lebanon

a. Civil War. In 1975–1976 Lebanon, a small Arab republic west of Syria and north of Israel, experienced civil war between rightist Arab Christian militia and leftist Arab Moslem forces supported by leftist Palestinian guerrillas. Syria —on unfriendly terms with leftist Iraq to its east—now feared the establishment of a hostile leftist regime in Lebanon. Syrian President *Hafez al-Assad* therefore sent his troops into Lebanon, giving battle to the leftist forces. Some 30,000 Syrian troops occupied most of Lebanon, enforced a cease-fire, and upheld a Lebanese government under a pro-Syrian Christian Arab, President *Elias Sarkis.* The

Lebanese civil war resulted in killing some 30,000 people and wounding many more, destroying the Lebanese economy, weakening the PLO, and strengthening the rightist Arab forces.

To expand their control, the Syrian occupation forces later launched sporadic attacks upon their former allies, the Christian Arabs centered mainly in southern Lebanon. These Syrian attacks perturbed Israel whose government viewed the Christian Arabs as friends and had aided the Christian Arab communities.

b. PLO Terrorism and the Israeli Invasion of Southern Lebanon. In early 1978 PLO terrorists belonging to Al Fatah came from southern Lebanon by boat and entered Israel. They killed more than 30 civilians and injured over 70 others before being suppressed by Israeli police and troops.

In response, Israel sent a force into southern Lebanon to deprive the PLO of this vantage area for attacks upon Israel. As the Palestinian guerrillas and refugees fled northward, the Israeli military established a "security belt" along Israel's border with southern Lebanon. The Israelis also strengthened the Christian Arab militia who were hostile to the PLO and friendly to Israel. At the UN the Security Council approved a resolution for Israel to withdraw from southern Lebanon and for a 4000-troop UNEF force to replace the Israelis and maintain peace in the area. Israel agreed, despite skepticism that the UNEF could prevent the return of PLO guerrillas to southern Lebanon.

4. The Sadat Visit to Israel. In late 1977, President Sadat informed the Egyptian parliament that, to further Mideast peace, he was ready to journey to Israel. Sadat thereupon received an official invitation from Israeli Prime Minister *Menachem Begin.* Sadat became the first Arab leader ever to visit Israel. He received a warm welcome from the Israeli people, worshipped in a mosque in Jerusalem, paid his respects at Yad Vashem—the Israeli memorial to the 6 million Holocaust victims of Nazi Germany, spoke with the leaders of the major Israeli political parties, and addressed the Knesset, the Israeli parliament.

In his speech, Sadat acknowledged that Israel's existence is a fact and stated that "we Arabs welcome you to live among us in peace and security." However, he reiterated Arab demands for the return of all lands occupied by Israel in the 1967 war and for the recognition of Palestinian rights to a homeland, but he significantly did *not* mention the PLO. In response, Prime Minister Begin praised Sadat for his courage and vision but reiterated Israeli demands for secure borders so as to protect the nation against the danger of destruction. In final statements the two leaders pledged "no more war."

The Sadat visit to Israel sharply divided the Arab world. Sadat's initiative was hailed overwhelmingly by the Egyptian people and was approved by the governments of Sudan, Tunisia, and Morocco. Sadat was denounced as a traitor to the Arab cause by the PLO and by the radical Arab states of Libya, Algeria, and Iraq. These states were known as "rejectionists" because they rejected any compromise that provided for the existence of Israel. Syria, while not fully joining the rejectionists, also condemned the Sadat visit.

For the United States, the Sadat initiative was hailed as a major step toward Mideast peace.

5. The Camp David (Maryland) Summit Conference (1978). In the months following the Sadat visit to Israel, the Egyptian-Israeli peace talks faltered, and the momentum for peace seemed lost. President Carter thereupon took bold action to revive the peace initiative by inviting President Sadat and Prime Minister Begin to meet with him at Camp David. For 13 days, the leaders conferred, with President Carter serving as mediator and urging flexibility and statesmanship. The Conference reached agreement upon two major documents:

a. "Framework for Peace in the Middle East" dealt with the West Bank of the Jordan River and the Gaza Strip. It provided: (1) Palestinians living in these areas will receive self-rule through an elected council. Thereafter the Israeli military government will end and Israeli troops will be partially withdrawn. These arrangements will prevail during a five-year transition period. (2) Within three years, Israel, Egypt, Jordan, and the elected Palestinian representatives will begin discussions on the "final status" of the areas. The negotiators will consider the "legitimate rights" of the Palestinians, including rules for admitting Arab refugees and also the need to assure the security of Israel. (3) This document is designed to provide a basis for peace between Israel and the three bordering Arab states of Jordan, Syria, and Lebanon.

b. "Framework for the Conclusion of a Peace Treaty Between Egypt and Israel" dealt with the Sinai Peninsula. It provided: (1) Israel agreed to return full sovereignty over the Sinai Peninsula to Egypt and, within three years, to withdraw all Israeli troops from the area. (2) Egypt agreed to demilitarize much of Sinai and to permit UN peacekeeping forces to be stationed in the Sinai along the Israeli border, along the Gulf of Aqaba, and in the Sharm el Sheikh area. (3) Israeli ships are guaranteed free passage through the Suez Canal and the Gulf of Aqaba. (4) Within three months, Egypt and Israel will negotiate a peace treaty and thereafter establish full diplomatic and economic relations.

The agreements evoked widely different responses. President Carter was jubilant, hailing the agreements as a major breakthrough on the road to Mideast peace. The Egyptian and Israeli peoples were pleased that the agreements had resolved many difficult issues. They realized, however, that the agreements had left unanswered several vital questions, notably the status of the Old City of Jerusalem and the future of the Jewish settlements in the West Bank. The PLO was bitter that its existence had been completely ignored. Syria and the "rejectionist" Arab states denounced the agreements and vowed opposition. The Soviet Union condemned the agreements as a new American "anti-Arab deal."

6. The Israeli-Egyptian Peace Treaty (1979). After lengthy negotiations and the personal involvement of President Carter, Israel and Egypt signed a formal peace treaty. It (*a*) reaffirmed generally the provisions of the Camp David "framework" regarding Israeli withdrawal from the Sinai, the stationing of a peacekeeping force, free passage through the Suez Canal and the Gulf of Aqaba for Israeli ships, and the establishment of normal relations between Israel and Egypt and (*b*) contained provisions for Israel to buy oil from the Sinai fields being returned to Egypt and for Israel and Egypt to hold negotiations regarding Palestinian self-rule in the West Bank and the Gaza Strip.

As part of the peace process, the United States agreed to (*a*) extend extensive economic and military aid and loans to both Israel and Egypt, (*b*) assist Israel in case of Egyptian violations of the peace treaty, (*c*) help meet Israel's oil needs for up to 15 years, and (*d*) take part in negotiations on Palestinian self-rule.

Although the peace treaty was welcomed by the Egyptian people, it received a hostile reception elsewhere in the Arab world. Most Arab nations—moderates as well as hard-liners—broke diplomatic relations with Egypt. Saudi Arabia ended economic aid to Egypt, and the Arab League moved its headquarters out of Cairo. Despite Egypt's isolation in the Arab world, President Sadat remained confident that his policies would bring genuine Middle East peace.

There are several alternatives.

In dealing with the bordering Arab states and with the Palestinians,
what alternatives (different policies) are available to Israel?

7. Negotiations on Palestinian Autonomy. Beginning in 1979, these negotiations were attended by Egypt, Israel, and the United States but were boycotted
by Palestinians of the West Bank and Gaza and by Jordan. The negotiations soon
revealed sharp disagreement. Egypt insisted that the Palestinians be granted full
local autonomy with the right, after five years, to establish an independent
Palestinian state. Israel declared a "united Jerusalem" to be its "eternal capital"
and asserted the right to establish additional Jewish settlements in "Judea and
Samaria"—the biblical names for the West Bank region. Israel rejected any
Palestinian state as a threat to its security and as a potential Soviet satellite nation
in the Middle East. Israel insisted upon maintaining its military forces in the
West Bank but offered the Palestinians local autonomy with the right after five
years to choose between Israeli and Jordanian citizenship. The United States
urged flexibility and compromise, asked the Palestinians to join the negotiations,
expressed concern for Palestinian rights and for the security of Israel, but
condemned new Jewish settlements in the West Bank as "harmful to the peace
process."

Iran: Another Middle East Trouble Spot

1. Background. Iran by religion is a Moslem state whose people are not Arabs
but are mainly Persians. The country nationalized its oil industry, which had
been developed originally by a British company. Iran is a major oil producer and
exporter, and is a member of OPEC.

Iran was a monarchy ruled by a Shah. The last Shah, who ruled from 1941 to
1979, was *Mohammed Riza Pahlevi.* He ruled autocratically, employed secret
police, and permitted no political opposition. The Shah, however, spurred
economic and social modernization, including land reform, literacy, and wom-
en's rights. He followed a pro-Western foreign policy and maintained a "special relationship" with the United States.

2. Upheaval and Unrest

a. Khomeini Seizes Control. By 1979 the Shah faced uncontrollable opposition by workers protesting low wages and inflation, by democratic and radical groups protesting autocratic rule, and by conservative religious groups protesting efforts to modernize the country. As the Shah fled Iran, the country came under the control of *Ayatollah* (holy man) *Ruhollah Khomeini.* This Moslem religious leader planned to transform Iran into an Islamic republic based on the principles of the 7th-century Moslem bible, the Koran. Supported by the clergy-dominated Revolutionary Council, Khomeini exercised dictatorial rule. In 1980 he permitted the Iranian voters to elect a civilian president. They chose *Abolhassan Bani-Sadr*, but his civilian regime's ability to govern was severely limited.

b. Problems Facing Iran. In addition to divided political authority, Iran faces many other problems: resentment of Marxist groups for being excluded from the government; resentment of moderate democratic groups against strict observance of the Koran and against Khomeini's dictatorial rule, which included a ban on broadcasts of music, a call for women to dress modestly in accordance with Islamic tradition, and a shutdown of opposition newspapers; revolts by ethnic minorities—Arabs to the south and Kurds in the north; assassinations; unemployment; inflation; and a sharp cut in oil production. A further problem arose when Iranian voters, despite opposition of ethnic minorities, approved an Islamic constitution that granted Ayatollah Khomeini dictatorial powers for life. *Ayatollah Shariat-Madari*, as leader of the ethnic Turks, Iran's largest minority, criticized the constitution for threatening minority rights, and his supporters seized control of Azerbaijan province.

3. Problems for the United States

a. Khomeini's Anti-American Attitude. The Ayatollah Khomeini spurred anti-American feeling and blamed the United States for Iran's problems. Iran canceled contracts, in the billions of dollars, for the purchase of American arms and other goods, and curtailed the shipment of oil to the United States— intensifying the American energy crisis. Khomeini halted the sale of Iranian oil to Israel and voiced support for the PLO. Iranian forces closed the American intelligence posts in northern Iran that had monitored Soviet missile tests.

b. American Hostages in Iran. In late 1979 President Carter allowed the Shah to enter the United States for surgery and postoperative treatment for cancer. Thereupon, in *Teheran*, capital of Iran, militants—supposedly students—occupied the American embassy and seized some 50 Americans as hostages. For release of the hostages, the "students" demanded that the United States deliver the Shah to Iran to be tried and punished for his "crimes." The militants, urged on by Khomeini, charged the Shah with massacring antigovernment demonstrators, torturing political prisoners, plundering the nation's wealth, eroding Iran's traditional Islamic values, and placing Iran under the control of Washington. As the United States refused to hand over the Shah, the Iranians escalated the campaign against the United States—charging that the American embassy in Teheran had been a "spy center" and threatening to place some hostages on trial for spying. Anti-American demonstrations in Iran spurred similar demonstrations in other Islamic nations, notably Pakistan and Libya. In general, however, the Islamic nations resisted Khomeini's efforts to fan a religious war against "the heathens."

The United States condemned the seizure of the American embassy and its staff as violations of international law and "blackmail." The United States demanded that the hostages be released unconditionally—a position supported by a unanimous vote of the UN Security Council, by a unanimous decision of the World Court, and by the members of NATO. The United States indicated that, after the release of the hostages, Iran could be offered a "world forum" to present its charges against the Shah. Meanwhile, President Carter exerted economic and social pressures against Iran by prohibiting American purchases of Iranian oil, freezing Iranian assets in the United States, and ordering the deportation of Iranian students illegally in the United States. Explaining that his primary concern was the safety of the hostages, President Carter nevertheless warned that he might be compelled to take other actions and ordered American warships into international waters near Iran.

In early 1980, although the Shah had left the United States, the American hostages were still in captivity. The United States therefore sought a UN Security Council resolution to embargo all shipments to Iran, except for food and medicine. The resolution received ten votes but was defeated by a Soviet veto. Deploring the veto, the United States asserted that it and its allies would proceed anyway to impose trade sanctions against Iran. Shortly afterward, the United States broke diplomatic relations with and embargoed American exports to Iran.

In April 1980 President Carter ordered a military mission to rescue the hostages, but at the last moment three helicopters malfunctioned and the President felt compelled to call off the mission. Although unsuccessful, President Carter's rescue effort was applauded by most Americans. However, the President was labeled a "criminal" by the Iranian militants, who announced plans to disperse the hostages to different cities in Iran so as to thwart any future rescue efforts.

The Far East

China

NATIONALISTS LOSE CHINA TO THE COMMUNISTS (1949)

1. Nationalist Weaknesses. Following World War II the Chiang Kai-shek regime lost public support in China because it *(a)* was a thinly veiled dictatorship marked by corruption and inefficiency, *(b)* wasted a considerable portion of the $2 billion in American loans and military supplies, *(c)* failed to earn the soldiers' loyalty and prevent army desertions, and *(d)* ignored the peasants' desire for land and the workers' demand for better living conditions. Chiang did not heed America's advice to improve conditions.

2. Communists Gain China. Chinese Communist armies, strengthened by equipment captured from the Japanese and supplies from the Soviet Union, defeated the Nationalists. In 1949 Communist armies drove Chiang Kai-shek to his only remaining stronghold, the island of Taiwan (Formosa). The Communists took control of all mainland China and rule its 800 million people.

At Peking, the capital city, the Communists proclaimed the *People's Republic of China* under the leadership of Premier *Chou En-lai* and Communist party head *Mao Tse-tung*.

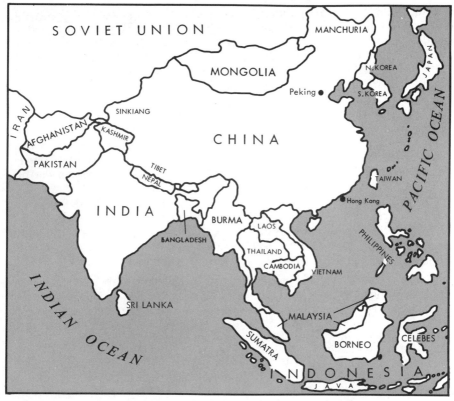

The Far East Today

UNFRIENDLY RELATIONS BETWEEN COMMUNIST CHINA AND THE UNITED STATES (TO 1971)

1. Communist China's Policies. The Communists harshly treated American officials, missionaries, and businessmen caught in China during the civil war. The Communists directly intervened in the Korean War and fought American troops. They sent military aid to the Communist forces in Vietnam. Communist China remained hostile toward the United States.

2. America's Policies. In opposition to Communist China, the United States *(a)* recognized the Nationalist government on Taiwan as the legal government of China, *(b)* refused to recognize the Peking regime, *(c)* opposed Communist China's admission to the UN, *(d)* maintained an embargo on trade with Communist China, *(e)* fought to prevent a Communist takeover in South Vietnam, and *(f)* signed mutual defense treaties with South Korea and Taiwan.

DISPUTE OVER TAIWAN (FORMOSA)

The United States viewed Taiwan as a vital Pacific military base, the Nationalist army as a dependable anti-Communist force, and the Nationalist government as an ally. Consequently, the United States extended economic and military aid to Taiwan and vowed to defend Nationalist-held territory.

Communist China was determined to annex the island and destroy the Nationalist government. The Chinese Communists warned the United States that nothing will deter them from "liberating" Taiwan.

CHINESE-SOVIET SPLIT: IN THE OPEN BY 1963

Despite their 1950 treaty of alliance, China and Russia gradually became hostile and by 1963 openly and bitterly disagreed as follows:

1. **Ideology.** *(a) Russia.* Khrushchev and his successor, Brezhnev, asserted that world communism can be achieved through *peaceful coexistence*. They claimed that people, impressed by Soviet achievements, will turn to communism. Meanwhile, Communist nations will subject the West to unremitting economic competition, propaganda, and subversion. However, Communists must make every effort to avoid nuclear war. A Communist paradise cannot be built upon millions of corpses. *(b) China.* Mao Tse-tung derided peaceful coexistence as a myth. If war does come, it will prove America to be a "paper tiger," will end capitalism, and will usher in a glorious Communist future.

2. **Russian Atomic Aid to China.** *(a) Russia.* The Soviets trained Chinese atomic scientists, sent Russian technicians to China, and provided China with a reactor to produce nuclear materials. When the ideological conflict became acute, Russia terminated her aid. *(b) China.* Peking at first complained that Soviet aid was not enough and then deplored its termination.

3. **Chinese-Soviet Borders.** *(a) Russia.* Soviet leaders contended that both Russia and China must respect the 19th-century treaties establishing the borders between them. These treaties provided for Russian annexation of sizable territories, including the Amur River Valley and the port of Vladivostok. *(b) China.* Chinese leaders argued that the treaties were imperialist-imposed and are not

Volleyball at the border (*Hesse in the St. Louis Globe-Democrat*)

valid now. In 1969 Chinese and Russian forces clashed at several border points, most notably north of Vladivostok.

4. World Communist Leadership. *(a) Russia.* As the oldest and most advanced Communist nation, Russia claimed the leadership of the Communist bloc. Khrushchev conceded that there are many roads to communism, including Tito's policies in Yugoslavia. The Soviets condemned Chinese appeals to nonwhite peoples as containing racial overtones. Russia retained the support of most Communist nations. *(b) China.* The most populous Communist nation, China claimed to be the true interpreter of Marxist-Leninist doctrine and the leader of the Communist world. The Chinese condemned the Yugoslavs as renegades. They also charged that Russia "sold out" the Communist movement in Latin America, Africa, and Asia.

CHINA DEVELOPS NUCLEAR WEAPONS: SINCE 1964

In 1964 China set off its first atomic bomb, in 1967 successfully exploded a hydrogen bomb, and in 1970 sent up its first earth satellite, indicating sufficient thrust power to launch ICBM's. China's progress in developing nuclear weapons and missiles created a major new world problem. In particular, it caused concern in two major Far Eastern nations—India and Japan, whose relations with China had not been friendly; in the Soviet Union, whose long border with China had been the scene of several armed clashes; and in the United States, whose leaders feared a possible Chinese missile attack.

RECENT DEVELOPMENTS

1. "Cultural Revolution" (1966–1969). *(a)* Reasons. Aged and ill, Mao Tse-tung wanted to assure that after his death China would continue his policies: (1) *within the country*, increased collectivization even over the opposition of the peasants, and (2) *in foreign affairs*, world revolution even at the risk of war. Mao did not want China to adopt "Soviet revisionism," by which he meant the use of profit as an economic incentive and the loss of revolutionary zeal in foreign affairs. Mao's opponents, holding important positions in the Communist party and the government, considered Mao's views inappropriate for building the nation. *(b)* Three Years of Turmoil. Mao moved to crush his opponents by a "great proletarian cultural revolution." He mobilized millions of youths into *Red Guard* groups which terrorized the opposition. The cultural revolution fragmented China's Communist party and undermined production, education, and transportation.

2. Stability and a New Foreign Policy. By 1970 China returned to stability: The Red Guards were disbanded and order was restored by realistic and increasingly powerful army leaders; and the government reflected control of moderate political leaders under Premier Chou En-lai. Thereupon, China turned from preoccupation with internal matters to a more active foreign role, especially steps to improve Chinese-American relations.

China arranged a visit by an American table tennis team. This visit, Premier Chou stated, "opened a new page in the relations of the Chinese and American people." President Nixon, who had made several overtures to "normalize" relations, relaxed our embargo on exporting nonstrategic goods to China. Thereafter, Chou En-lai invited President Nixon to visit China. Nixon accepted, expressing the hope that this "will become a journey for peace."

3. The Nixon Visit to China (1972). Accompanied by his national security adviser *Henry Kissinger,* President Nixon visited Communist China. Warmly received, Nixon spent a hectic week that included sightseeing, entertainment, banquets, a meeting with Mao Tse-tung, and numerous sessions with Chou En-lai. The visit concluded with the issuance of the Shanghai communiqué in which *(a)* the United States and China each stated its differences regarding Vietnam, Korea, and Taiwan, *(b)* the United States agreed that Taiwan is part of China, urged peaceful settlement of the Taiwan issue by the Chinese themselves, and agreed ultimately to withdraw all American forces from Taiwan (but did not renounce its mutual defense pact with Taiwan), and *(c)* the United States and China agreed to peaceful coexistence and to expand their contacts.

This historic visit, analysts believed, signified the following: *(a) for China—*realization that the major threat to its national interests comes from the Soviet Union rather than the United States and *(b) for the United States*—less fear that China threatens American interests in Eastern Asia.

Following the Nixon visit, China and the United States encouraged reciprocal visits by scholars, doctors, musicians, and sports figures and expanded trade. China placed large orders for American farm produce and bought some American jet airplanes.

4. Power Struggle Following the Deaths of China's Leaders (1976). With the deaths of Prime Minister Chou En-lai and, eight months later, of Chairman Mao Tse-tung, China experienced an open struggle for power between two Communist party factions labeled "radicals" and "moderates." The radicals favored strict adherence to Maoist theories of class warfare, no profit incentives, and "permanent revolution." The moderates stressed pragmatic goals of economic growth and political stability. The moderates attracted support of the industrial managers, government officials, and army leaders.

Hua Kuo-feng, an active party and government figure but little known to the Chinese people, was named Prime Minister. Hua was believed to be a middle-of-the-roader and therefore acceptable to both party factions. After Mao's death, Hua was also named as Communist Party Chairman. He then acted swiftly against four top radical leaders, the most notable one being Mao's widow, *Chiang Ching.* The radical leaders were purged from their party posts, placed under arrest, and charged with a plot to "usurp party and state power." Hua's action against the "gang of four" was acclaimed by huge demonstrations.

In foreign affairs, the new Chinese regime continued Chou En-lai's most recent policies. China rebuffed Soviet efforts to improve relations and indicated a strong desire to maintain and improve friendship with the United States.

5. Full Diplomatic Relations (1979). The United States and Communist China agreed to establish full diplomatic relations. For the United States, this agreement meant breaking diplomatic ties with Taiwan, withdrawing the American forces on that island, and giving the required one-year notice to end its mutual defense treaty with Taiwan. The United States, however, pledged to maintain cultural and economic ties with Taiwan, to sell Taiwan limited supplies of defensive arms, and to remain interested in the peaceful settlement of the

Taiwan issue. For Communist China, the agreement meant an implied promise—but no public statement—not to use force to gain control over Taiwan.

Teng Hsiao-ping, the senior Deputy Prime Minister of China, spurred the restoration of full diplomatic relations. A pragmatist and moderate, Teng wanted China to increase trade with and learn from the West so as to hasten China's modernization. Although twice purged during the Mao era, Teng bounced back and became most influential in post-Maoist China.

American skeptics and Taiwanese leaders denounced the Sino-American agreement. These people claimed that the United States would lose credibility as to its military defense pledges and its concern for human rights.

President Carter hailed the new Sino-American relationship—economically as furthering trade and politically as "simple reality" that "contributes to the cause of peace." Although the President stated that the normalization of Sino-American relations was not directed against any third nation, the Soviet Union indicated its concern over this development as potentially dangerous to its interests.

6. China vs. Vietnam: Hostility Between Communist Nations (By 1979). Check the Index for Vietnam.

Japan

TERRITORIAL LOSSES FOLLOWING WORLD WAR II

Following its surrender in 1945, Japan was stripped of its foreign territories. Japan lost Taiwan and Manchuria to China, and the Kuriles and the southern half of Sakhalin Island to Russia. The Ryukyu Islands, which contain Okinawa, were occupied by the United States. The Japanese-mandated Mariana, Marshall, and Caroline Islands in the Pacific were transferred to the United States as a UN trusteeship. Korea was divided into Russian and American zones pending independence.

JAPAN UNDER AMERICAN OCCUPATION (1945–1952)

General Douglas MacArthur, serving as Supreme Allied Commander in Japan, proceeded as follows:

1. New Constitution (1947). Under MacArthur's direction, Japan adopted a democratic constitution which *(a)* renounced the waging of war and the maintaining of offensive armed forces, *(b)* denied the Emperor's divine origin but retained him as a symbol of national unity, *(c)* contained a bill of rights guaranteeing civil liberties, separation of church and state, equality under the law (including equal rights for women), and *(d)* provided for a cabinet responsible to an elected two-house legislature, called the *Diet.*

2. Economic and Social Reforms. MacArthur promoted actions by which Japan *(a)* dissolved the huge business monopolies that had controlled much of Japan's economic life, *(b)* encouraged free labor unions with the right to strike, *(c)* provided farms for landless peasants, and (d) reformed education by removing ultranationalist teachers and textbooks and encouraging democratic learning.

3. War Crimes Trials. Japanese war leaders were tried before Allied courts on war crime charges: aggressive warfare and atrocities against prisoners. Some Japanese leaders were sentenced to prison; others were executed.

TREATY OF PEACE WITH JAPAN (1952)

Drawn up by the United States, the Japanese peace treaty was accepted by the major Allied nations except the Soviet Union. Russia refused to sign the treaty chiefly because it confirmed Japan's position as an ally of the United States. (In 1956 Russia signed a declaration of peace with Japan.) The 1952 treaty provided as follows:

1. Territory. Japan lost all its conquests but retained its four large home islands. (Japan consented to American administration of the Ryukyu Islands, including Okinawa, but retained the right to claim their return.)

2. Reparations. Japan was not required to pay reparations for war damages. However, Japan agreed to contribute goods and services to countries damaged by Japanese aggression in World War II.

3. Defense. Japan was recognized as an independent, sovereign nation possessing the right of military self-defense. In a separate pact, the United States and Japan agreed that American troops remain stationed in Japan.

AMERICAN FRIENDSHIP FOR JAPAN

1. Reasons. (a) American foreign policy experts hold that Japan must be kept from falling under Soviet control. Those two nations, in combination, would possess industrial, scientific, and military resources superior to the United States and, as potentially hostile, they would endanger American national interests. (b) Because of the reforms introduced in Japan during the American occupation, the United States considers Japan an Asian bulwark of democracy. (c) Japan's postwar government, democratically elected and controlled by the Liberal-Democratic party, has been stable, procapitalist, pro-American, and anti-Communist. Among Japanese voters, Communist influence has been small. (d) Japan represents a counterbalance to the growth of Communist power in Asia. (e) Japan is a valuable ally because of its industrial capacity, its productive labor force (drawn from a population of 117 million), and its strategic location off the Asian continent.

2. Evidences. The United States (a) treated Japan generously in the peace treaty, (b) extended economic and military aid, (c) kept American forces in Japan for the defense of Japan and other free world nations in East Asia, (d) developed close commercial and cultural ties, and (e) in 1972 returned the Ryukyu Islands, including Okinawa, to Japan. (In contrast the Soviet Union has refused to return four small northern islands seized at the end of World War II and repeatedly claimed by Japan.)

RECENT DEVELOPMENTS AND PROBLEMS

1. Limited Rearmament. In accordance with its constitution, Japan maintains only a small military force for "self-defense." These troops are insufficient to defend the nation. However, Japanese public opinion, strongly pacifist, remains unwilling to amend the constitution to permit more extensive rearmament. Meanwhile, the people are free of heavy military expenditures and depend on the United States to protect their homeland.

2. Economic Recovery. Under its free-enterprise economic system, postwar Japan achieved a remarkable economic growth rate. Industrial production had regained prewar levels by 1951 and has since then more than tripled. Japan ranks among the world's top manufacturers of automobiles, steel, synthetic fibers, electrical products, and cotton yarn; it is first in shipbuilding. Japan is the world's third greatest economic power and enjoys a standard of living approaching that of Western Europe. With limited farmland, petroleum, and mineral resources, however, Japan must "export or die."

3. Trade With the United States. Japan provides the second largest market for American exports and, in turn, finds the United States its best customer. Americans purchase Japanese textiles, toys, cameras, radios, and television sets. American manufacturers protest this competition and request adequate tariff protection, complaining that Japanese wages are lower than those paid American workers. To quiet these protests, Japan has, on several occasions, voluntarily limited its exports to the United States.

India

BRIEF SURVEY

1. Independence and Government. In 1947 India received independence from Britain. *Jawaharlal Nehru*, India's independence leader, became Prime Minister and promoted a democratic government. In 1975 Prime Minister *Indira Gandhi*, Nehru's daughter, moved India away from democracy by declaring a "state of emergency," arresting political opponents, and instituting press censorship. In 1977 elections, Mrs. Gandhi and her Congress party were decisively defeated, and she resigned as prime minister. The position of prime minister was taken by an advocate of democracy, *Morarji Desai*. In 1979 Desai lost his parliamentary majority and resigned. India experienced political instability that led to the dissolving of Parliament and the scheduling of new elections.

In the 1980 elections, Mrs. Gandhi emphasized her leadership qualities and avoided reference to her previous emergency dictatorial rule. The voters either chose not to remember or believed that she had learned a lesson and would not again resort to antidemocratic practices. Mrs. Gandhi achieved a remarkable triumph as her faction of the Congress party won over two-thirds of the seats in the legislature and she again became India's Prime Minister.

2. Mixed Economy. To raise the low living standards of its 640 million people,

India utilizes a "mixed economy" of private and public enterprise. To supplement private business, the government began *Five-Year Plans:* constructing irrigation projects, electric power plants, railroads, and steel mills; distributing land to the peasants; and fostering modern farming methods.

3. Foreign Policy of Neutrality. Nehru hoped to devote India's energies to domestic problems. Therefore, in the cold war, Nehru set a policy of nonalignment, or neutrality. Nehru's successors reaffirmed this policy.

CHINESE AGGRESSION AFFECTS INDIA (1959–1962)

Nehru's friendship for Communist China was shattered by Chinese actions in Tibet (India's northern neighbor) and on the Indian border.

1. Tibet. In 1959, after eight years of Chinese Communist occupation and rule, the Tibetan people revolted. The Chinese (a) suppressed the revolt, and (b) accused India of having aided the revolt, a charge that Nehru denied. Nehru condemned China's brutality in Tibet and granted asylum to thousands of Tibetan refugees, including their leader, the *Dalai Lama.*

2. Indian Border. For many years China had disputed its boundary with India. In 1959, following the Tibetan revolt, Communist Chinese troops crossed India's northern frontier, attacked Indian border patrols, and occupied large areas of territory claimed by India. In 1962 the Chinese renewed their attack and occupied additional territory. Declaring that India would resist Chinese aggression, Nehru secured military aid from Britain and the United States.

AMERICAN RELATIONS WITH INDIA

The United States hopes that India will side with the free world because India (1) in Nehru's words, is "firmly wedded to the democratic way of life," (2) has been menaced by China, and (3) needs American aid to raise the living standards of its people. India has received much American economic aid.

In 1959, during the India-China border dispute, President Eisenhower visited India and received a tremendous welcome. In 1962, when Chinese troops again attacked, President Kennedy airlifted weapons to India. In 1966 President Johnson authorized wheat shipments to prevent starvation in India. In 1971, however, President Nixon condemned India for sending its troops into East Pakistan and forcibly gaining independence for Bangladesh.

RUSSIAN RELATIONS WITH INDIA

Russia seeks to win India to the Soviet side or, at least, to keep it neutral in the cold war: (1) Russia granted loans for the development of India's heavy industry. (Russia's economic aid to India is far less, however, than that extended by the United States.) (2) In 1963, as the split between Russia and Communist China widened, Soviet leaders voiced support for India in its border dispute with China. (3) In 1966 Russia hosted an Indian-Pakistani conference at the Soviet city of Tashkent. India and Pakistan, having fought over Kashmir, agreed to observe a UN cease-fire, to restore diplomatic relations, and to settle disputes peacefully. (4) In 1971 Russia signed a treaty of friendship with India; thereafter, as the

Indian-Pakistani war started, Russia supported India by vetoing three Security Council resolutions for a cease-fire and the withdrawal of Indian forces.

Korea

KOREA AFTER WORLD WAR II

In 1945 Korea (a colony of Japan since 1910) was divided at the 38th parallel: the North occupied by Russian troops, the South by American troops. Russia and the United States failed to agree regarding Korean reunification, and Russia defied UN attempts to unify the country by free elections. In North Korea, the Russians established a Communist government led by the Korean Workers Communist party head *Kim Il-Sung*, and equipped a powerful army. In South Korea, UN-supervised elections established an independent anti-Communist government headed by President *Syngman Rhee.*

COMMUNIST AGGRESSION AGAINST SOUTH KOREA (1950–1953)

In June 1950, without warning, North Korean Communist forces crossed the 38th parallel and invaded South Korea. The UN Security Council, with Russia absent, promptly recommended that UN members furnish military assistance to South Korea. The UN army consisted chiefly of American and South Korean units, with contingents from 15 other anti-Communist nations. It was headed originally by General Douglas MacArthur.

At first, the UN forces retreated before the Communist assault. After reinforcements arrived, General MacArthur launched a counterattack that drove the North Korean armies back across the 38th parallel and deep into North Korea close to the Manchurian border. In November 1950 powerful Communist Chinese armies crossed into North Korea and attacked the UN forces, inflicting heavy losses and compelling MacArthur to retreat. By the summer of 1951 the battle line had become stabilized near the 38th parallel.

Meanwhile, the UN General Assembly voted (with opposition only from the Soviet bloc) to declare Communist China guilty of aggression in Korea and to recommend an embargo on the shipment of war goods to Communist China.

MacARTHUR-TRUMAN CONTROVERSY

In 1951 President Truman, as commander in chief of the American armed forces, dismissed General MacArthur for insubordination. Truman charged that the general had repeatedly disregarded instructions to refrain from making foreign policy statements that criticized government policies.

The two men had disagreed sharply. MacArthur advocated carrying the war into China, especially Manchuria. He urged that the United States fight an all-out war to win complete victory over communism in Asia. Truman feared that an invasion of Manchuria would lead to war with Russia. He held that the United States must fight a limited war in Asia so as not to leave western Europe, the key to American security, defenseless.

TRUCE IN KOREA (1953)

Meeting mainly at *Panmunjom*, UN and Communist negotiators took two years to agree upon truce terms. The conference was long deadlocked regarding the return, or *repatriation*, of prisoners. The UN claimed that many of its prisoners did not want to return to Communist rule; the Communists insisted upon compulsory repatriation. Finally, the conference agreed that all prisoners be given freedom of choice. (Eventually, two of every five prisoners held by the UN refused to return to Communist rule.)

The truce (1) was hailed by the UN as a victory against aggression, (2) was criticized by the South Korean government for failing to unify the country under anti-Communist leadership, and (3) was greeted by most Americans with relief. The Korean struggle cost the United States $18 billion, 103,000 wounded, and 33,000 killed.

KOREAN DEVELOPMENTS SINCE THE TRUCE

1. Continued American Interest. In support of South Korea, the United States extended considerable economic and military aid, kept 45,000 troops there, and signed a bilateral Mutual Defense Pact. In turn, South Korea sent a fighting force to aid the Americans in South Vietnam.

In 1977 President Carter, while reaffirming America's commitment to defend South Korea, announced plans for a phased withdrawal by 1982 of 33,000 American ground troops from South Korea. Carter's plans to withdraw these troops caused considerable anxiety among South Korean and Japanese leaders.

In 1979, as President Carter became aware of the increased strength of North Korea's armed forces, he suspended the withdrawal of the American troops.

2. Continued Communist Interest. In 1961 Soviet Russia signed a defense treaty pledging to assist North Korea "with all forces and by every means." Communist China also made a similar defense pledge to North Korea.

3. Renewed Communist Pressures (1967–1972)

a. Upon South Korea. North Korea sent a number of raiding parties into the South to commit sabotage and spread terror. In 1968 North Korean commandos slipped into the southern capital of Seoul to assassinate President Park, but they were captured before they could carry out their plans.

b. Upon the United States. In 1968 North Korean patrol boats seized the American intelligence ship *Pueblo*. The Communists claimed that the *Pueblo* had intruded into North Korean territorial waters on a hostile mission. The United States answered that the *Pueblo* had been in international waters. To secure the release of the *Pueblo* crew, the United States negotiated with the North Koreans. After almost a year, the chief American negotiator signed a document confessing intrusion into North Korean waters, while publicly repudiating the confession, and North Korea freed the *Pueblo* crew.

4. Governmental Changes in South Korea

a. Rhee Regime (1948–1960). In 1960 South Korea was swept by antigovernment riots protesting rigged elections, police terror, corruption, and autocratic rule. Syngman Rhee ended his 12-year presidency by resigning.

b. Park Regime (1961–1979). In 1961 General *Chung Hee Park*, leading a military junta (council), seized power. Four times thereafter Park was elected president. He improved economic conditions and maintained a pro-American foreign policy. In 1972 Park moved to "reform" South Korea's political structure. He imposed martial law, dissolved the National Assembly, prohibited political activities, and imposed press censorship. Under these conditions Park won a public referendum for a constitution enabling him to remain president for life, to dominate the other branches of government, and to rule dictatorially. Park became increasingly intolerant of dissent.

c. American Criticism of the Park Regime. The United States disapproved of Park's 1972 constitutional changes. Thereafter, the United States criticized the Park regime for its harsh treatment of dissidents, for its use—so it seemed—of campaign contributions and other means to influence American political leaders; and for its unwillingness to cooperate in the investigation of Korean agents presumed to have bribed American officials.

In 1979, after a visit by President Carter to South Korea, the United States—as part of its human rights campaign—asked the Park regime to release over 100 political prisoners held in South Korean jails.

d. Assassination of Park (1979). Jae Kyn Kim, head of Korea's Central Intelligence Agency, assassinated President Park. Kim's motives were not clearly known—possibly personal quarrels or possibly a policy rift, as Kim felt that Park's repression of opposition threatened the nation's stability. With Park's death South Korea was placed under martial law and faced political problems: What to do about Park's undemocratic constitution and how to select a successor to the presidency. The South Korean army was expected to play a major role in answering these questions.

The United States meanwhile warned North Korea not to "attempt to exploit the situation" in the South, placed American forces in South Korea on an alert, and sent an American aircraft carrier into South Korean waters.

Nations of Indo-China

INDO-CHINA UNDER FRENCH RULE

In the 19th century, France annexed Indo-China. This was an agricultural country in Southeast Asia with a predominantly Buddhist population. During World War II, while France was overrun by the Nazis, Indo-China was occupied by the Japanese. Indo-Chinese nationalists, opposed to both Japan and France, joined an independence movement called the *Vietminh*. Although this movement contained some non-Communist nationalists, it was controlled by Communists and led by Moscow-trained *Ho Chi Minh*.

COMMUNISTS SEEK CONTROL (1946–1954)

After the war, France promised partial independence to the three states of Indo-China: Laos, Cambodia, and Vietnam. The Vietminh rejected the French offer and gained popular support by appealing to (1) *nationalism*, with promises to drive out the French completely, and (2) *land hunger*, with promises to distribute land to the peasants. For eight years, civil war raged in Indo-China.

Finally, the tide of battle turned in favor of the Vietminh, who in 1954 won the crucial *Battle of Dien Bien Phu*.

GENEVA AGREEMENTS: TRUCE FOR INDO-CHINA (1954)

Britain, the Soviet Union, the United States, China, France, and the states of Indo-China sent representatives to Geneva to negotiate a settlement. The Geneva Agreements, not signed by the United States or South Vietnam, called for: (1) *Laos* and *Cambodia* to be independent and to observe neutrality in the cold war. (2) *Vietnam* to be divided at the 17th parallel: the North under a Communist government in *Hanoi*, the South under a French-sponsored anti-Communist government in *Saigon*. The people in both the North and the South were to vote by mid-1956 for a single all-Vietnam government.

DEVELOPMENTS IN VIETNAM (1955–1973)

1. Communist North Vietnam. Ho Chi Minh established a Communist dictatorship, increased the army's strength, eliminated most private enterprise, and received considerable Russian and Chinese aid. The Communists sought control of South Vietnam.

2. Anti-Communist South Vietnam. The Saigon government became fully independent of France, was strongly anti-Communist, and rejected plans for all-Vietnam elections. It argued that honest elections were impossible in the Communist north. To undermine the Saigon government, the Communist Vietcong waged guerrilla warfare throughout the south—terrorizing villagers and killing government supporters—and established Vietcong control over large rural areas. Saigon requested American aid. This was first granted by President Eisenhower and later expanded by President Kennedy. American leaders feared that a Communist takeover in South Vietnam might cause the bordering nations in Southeast Asia to fall to the Communists like a row of "falling dominoes."

3. Escalation of the War. In 1964 a limited number of American troops and military advisers were in South Vietnam, and American naval units patrolled the international waters of the Gulf of Tonkin. When North Vietnamese torpedo boats attacked American destroyers in the gulf, President Johnson ordered an air strike against North Vietnam's naval bases. The President's action received almost unanimous support from Congress in its vote for the *Gulf of Tonkin Resolution*. (In 1970 Congress repealed this resolution.)

In 1965, after American bases in South Vietnam had been attacked by Communist forces, President Johnson ordered continuous air strikes against North Vietnamese military targets. The United States increased its forces in South Vietnam, eventually to over 500,000 individuals. Also, four SEATO members—Australia, New Zealand, the Philippines, and Thailand—augmented the South Vietnamese and American forces.

The Communist nations increased their support for the Vietcong and Hanoi. Moscow provided additional military equipment. Peking assigned service troops to maintain transportation in the North.

4. Debate in America Regarding Vietnam. American public opinion divided sharply regarding Vietnam. *(a)* The "hawks" argued for increased military action to halt aggression and contain Communist expansion in Asia. Many hawks demanded that we drastically step up military pressures on Hanoi. *(b)* The "doves" urged the United States to seek peace by reducing its military activities in Vietnam. They argued that America was (1) lacking vital interests in Vietnam, (2) risking war with China, and (3) supporting a Saigon government that commanded no loyalty among the people. (This government was dominated, from 1967 to 1975, by the military leader who was elected as president, *Nguyen Van Thieu.*)

5. The Move to Peace Talks (1965–1968). President Johnson made several efforts to move the Vietnam conflict from the battlefield to the conference table—all unsuccessful. In 1968 President Johnson again halted the bombing, this time of most of North Vietnam, and Hanoi agreed to peace negotiations. The two nations began talks in Paris. Later the peace talks were expanded to include the Saigon government and the Vietcong.

6. Nixon Administration and Vietnam (1969–1974)

a. Diplomatic Stalemate Continues. President Nixon sought a Vietnam settlement that would free American prisoners of war and enable the South Vietnamese people to decide their own future by honest, internationally supervised elections. Communist leaders demanded complete withdrawal of American forces and replacement of the "puppet" Thieu government by a pro-Communist regime. The Paris talks remained deadlocked.

b. Vietnamization. Nixon spurred *Vietnamization,* that is, shifting the burden of fighting the war to South Vietnamese forces. By late 1972 he had withdrawn over 500,000 personnel, leaving there only 27,000 American troops. American casualty lists grew much shorter.

c. The War Spills Over Into the Other Indo-Chinese States

(1) *Cambodia.* In 1970 a new, rightist-leaning regime took control. It reaffirmed Cambodia's neutrality and demanded the withdrawal of North Vietnamese and Vietcong forces from bases in Cambodia. Instead, the Communist forces attacked Cambodian towns. Thereupon, President Nixon ordered American forces to join with South Vietnamese troops in a limited "incursion" into Cambodia to destroy the Communist bases.

(2) *Laos.* In 1970 North Vietnamese and local Communist Pathet Lao forces overran much of southern Laos. In 1971 South Vietnamese forces with American air support began a limited "incursion" into southern Laos to disrupt enemy supply routes.

Both incursions aroused much controversy in the United States again between the "hawks" and the "doves."

d. Secret Peace Talks. Since 1969 Washington and Hanoi had held, near Paris, a series of secret peace talks. The American negotiator was President Nixon's national security adviser, *Henry Kissinger;* the Hanoi negotiator was *Le Duc Tho.* In 1973, they reached an agreement.

7. The Paris Peace Agreement for Vietnam (1973)

a. Major Provisions

(1) *Military.* *(a)* The United States, North Vietnam, South Vietnam, and the Vietcong agree to a cease-fire. *(b)* The United States shall withdraw its remaining forces and dismantle its remaining military bases in South Vietnam. *(c)* Hanoi

and the Vietcong shall return all American prisoners of war and provide the fullest accounting for persons "missing in action" (MIA). *(d)* All foreign troops shall be withdrawn from Laos and Cambodia. *(e)* No more troops and no additional military supplies shall be introduced into South Vietnam.

(2) *Reunification.* *(a)* The reunification of Vietnam shall be achieved only by peaceful means. *(b)* Pending reunification, both North and South Vietnam shall respect the provisional military demarcation line at the 17th parallel.

(3) *Political Arrangements for South Vietnam.* *(a)* Saigon and the Vietcong shall each retain the areas under its control at the time of the cease-fire. *(b)* The South Vietnamese shall decide their political future through honest elections.

b. Observations. (1) The agreement was a compromise, with neither side gaining all its objectives. The United States did *not* secure *(a)* the withdrawal of an estimated 145,000 Hanoi troops out of the South and back to the North and *(b)* a cease-fire for Laos and Cambodia. Hanoi did *not* secure *(a)* the overthrow of the Thieu regime in Saigon and *(b)* the establishment of a Communist-dominated government in the South. (2) The Vietnamese War cost the United States over an 11-year period $140 billion, more than 300,000 wounded, and 46,000 killed. It was one of the costliest and most divisive wars in American history.

COMMUNIST FORCES TRIUMPH IN INDO-CHINA (1975)

1. In Cambodia (Kampuchea). The rightist-leaning government faced increasing military pressure from Communist forces—some North Vietnamese units and the local *Khmer Rouge.* The government forces, despite a Congress-imposed cutoff of American air support, withstood the Communist insurgents for more than a year. In 1975, the government forces collapsed. Communist troops occupied the capital city, Phnom Penh, and took control of the entire country.

The Khmer Rouge executed Cambodian leaders who had opposed them; forcibly drove urban residents out of the major cities into rural areas, which caused many deaths; and on charges of spying seized an American merchant vessel, the *Mayaguez.* When diplomatic efforts failed, President Ford ordered American forces to rescue the crew and vessel, which was done at a cost of almost 70 American casualties.

2. In Laos. The anti-Communist and Communist Pathet Lao forces reached a cease-fire agreement and established a coalition government. In 1975, following the Communist victories in Cambodia and South Vietnam, the Pathet Lao took full control of the country.

In 1976 reports out of Laos indicated that the Pathet Lao held 50,000 rightists and neutralists in harsh prison camps for punishment and "reeducation." Many inmates died from lack of food and medicine.

3. In South Vietnam. *(a)* The United States withdrew its remaining military forces but continued to give limited economic and military aid to the Thieu regime. *(b)* North Vietnam, in violation of the Paris truce agreement, increased its strength in the South to an estimated 400,000 soldiers. In 1975 the North Vietnamese and Vietcong mounted a major military offensive and gained full control of the South.

During this final phase of the Vietnam War, the United States proceeded as follows: (1) President Ford pledged that American forces would not return to

It makes a nice shield
(*Wright in the San Diego Union*)

Vietnam. (2) The United States helped evacuate thousands of South Vietnamese, many of whom had worked with the Americans and feared for their lives under Communist rule. Congress voted funds to assist some 120,000 Vietnamese refugees to come to the United States. (3) President Ford reassured our allies who, viewing the downfall of the pro-American governments in Cambodia and South Vietnam, were concerned regarding the direction of American foreign policy and the credibility of American defense treaties. The President warned any potential enemies that "we will stand up to them" and affirmed that "no allies or time-tested friends of the United States should worry or fear that our commitments to them will not be honored."

In 1976 reports out of South Vietnam indicated that the Communists held between 100,000 and 300,000 persons in labor camps where brutal conditions caused many deaths. Also in 1976 the Communists proclaimed the official reunification of the country as the *Socialist Republic of Vietnam.*

REFUGEES FROM INDO-CHINA (SINCE 1975)

Following the Communist takeovers, more than 1 million people fled from the three Indo-Chinese states and became refugees. They were driven by varied motives: (1) The earliest refugees were those Indo-Chinese closely identified with the overthrown anti-Communist regimes, who feared for their lives under Communist rule. (2) The ethnic Chinese, many of families who had lived in Vietnam for generations, were pressured to leave by the Hanoi regime. The Chinese had been merchants and moneylenders—capitalist enterprises; they were considered of doubtful loyalty by Hanoi; and they were disliked by the Vietnamese. Many Chinese were compelled to pay large sums to the Hanoi regime before being permitted to depart. (3) Cambodians fled political instability and renewed warfare as Vietnamese troops invaded Cambodia to oust a pro-Chinese regime and install a government subservient to Hanoi. (4) Other refugees fled harsh Communist rule, forced evacuation from cities into the rural areas, and the lack of food, clothing, and other essentials.

Some refugees fled overland to Thailand and China; others fled by sea and became known as the *boat people*. Fewer than half the boat people were estimated to have survived their unsafe vessels, the hazards of the sea, and pirate attacks and to have reached land in the Philippines, Malaysia, Indonesia, and southern Thailand. The refugees were not welcomed—and in many cases were forcibly driven out—by the Southeast Asian nations. These nations insisted that they lacked the facilities and resources to care for the refugees and were unwilling to absorb the refugees into their societies.

Refugees in large numbers were accepted by the United States and in lesser numbers by other Western nations—notably Canada, Australia, and France. Some 250,000 ethnic Chinese found temporary safety in Hong Kong and southern China.

The plight of the refugees led to a 1979 UN conference at which (1) Hanoi promised to stem the flow of refugees, (2) the UN promised—with funds mainly from Western nations and Japan—to care for the refugees in temporary transit camps, and (3) Western nations promised to accept additional refugees.

Vietnam meanwhile was viewed with grave mistrust by many Western powers, the Southeast Asian nations, and China.

VIETNAM VS. CHINA: HOSTILITY BETWEEN COMMUNIST NATIONS (BY 1979)

1. **Reasons.** By 1979 Vietnam had aroused the anger and hostility of Communist China. (*a*) Vietnam indicated its preference for the Soviet Union, which country China viewed as its major enemy. In 1978 Vietnam signed a 25-year friendship treaty with Russia, receiving pledges of economic aid and of "effective measures" in case of attack by a third party. Hanoi was cooperating with Moscow, so Peking believed, in encircling China with hostile states. (*b*) Vietnam moved to control all Indo-China. Whereas Laos yielded to Vietnamese dominance, Cambodia did not. Under *Pol Pot*, this Cambodian regime ruled with great brutality. It was pro-Chinese and received extensive Chinese military and economic aid. After a series of border skirmishes, Vietnam in late 1978 launched a full-scale invasion of Cambodia, overthrew the Pol Pot regime, and installed a puppet government. China resented the ousting of its ally and held that Moscow was using the Vietnamese in Asia as it had used the Cubans in Africa. (*c*) Vietnam harassed, exacted funds from, and expelled over 250,000 of its ethnic Chinese residents.

2. **The Limited War (1979).** After several border incidents, China announced that it would no longer tolerate "being pushed around" and would act to "teach Vietnam a lesson." Embarking upon a limited invasion, Chinese armies crossed the border into northern Vietnam and met strong resistance. Russia warned China to withdraw "before it is too late" and speeded military equipment to Vietnam but itself undertook no military moves. At the UN, Russia vetoed a Security Council resolution calling upon Vietnam to withdraw from Cambodia and upon China to withdraw from Vietnam. After four weeks of fighting, with heavy casualties on both sides, the Chinese withdrew. Thereafter, China and Vietnam engaged in peace talks but arrived at no meaningful understandings.

EFFECTS OF THE VIETNAMESE WAR
ON AMERICAN FOREIGN POLICY

1. The Nixon Doctrine (1969). President Nixon asserted that the United States would continue to play a major role in the Pacific but would seek to avoid involvement in another war like Vietnam. Consequently Nixon told our Asian friends that the United States would honor its treaty commitments, including military and economic aid, but would look to any Asian nation threatened by internal subversion or nonnuclear aggression to provide the armed forces for its own defense. The *Nixon Doctrine*, said the President, was an American policy that could "be sustained over the long run."

2. War-Powers Resolution (1973). In ordering American forces into combat in Vietnam, three successive Presidents—Kennedy, Johnson, and Nixon—had used the Presidential power of commander in chief but had not secured a Congressional declaration of war. In 1973 Congress moved to limit Presidential war-making powers by enacting, over President Nixon's veto, the *War-Powers Resolution*. It provided that (*a*) if the President commits American troops to combat abroad, he must present his reasons to Congress within 48 hours, (*b*) if the President expects ot keep American troops in combat abroad for more than 90 days, he must secure Congressional approval, (*c*) if the President does not secure Congressional approval, he must terminate the military action, and (*d*) Congress can order withdrawal of American forces from abroad, before 90 days, by adopting a concurrent resolution not subject to a Presidential veto.

Nixon condemned the resolution as "clearly unconstitutional" and declared that it would "seriously undermine this nation's ability to act decisively . . . in times of international crisis."

3. Other Effects. (*a*) *Thailand.* Now bordered by Communist Laos and Cambodia, and fearful that they might aid local guerrilla bands, Thailand in 1975 moved to reduce the American presence. The Thai government requested the United States to close American bases and withdraw American forces from her soil. The United States agreed. (*b*) *Angola.* After Portugal withdrew in 1975, Angola experienced civil war between pro-Western and pro-Communist groups. When the United States Congress became aware that the Ford administration was sending covert aid to the pro-Western forces, Congress voted overwhelmingly to prohibit such aid. Congress feared that such aid could lead America to involvement in another Vietnam-type situation.

Afghanistan

LAND AND PEOPLE

Located in central Asia, Afghanistan is a landlocked country of strategic importance. It is bordered on the north by the Soviet Union, on the west by Iran, on the south by Pakistan, and at its eastern tip by China (see map, page 637). Afghanistan contains some small fertile valleys interspersed among large deserts and extensive mountains. The Khyber Pass, 35 miles long, provides a major route through the Hindu Kush Mountains from Afghanistan into Pakistan. Afghanistan's natural resources remain largely untouched except for natural gas fields and coal deposits. Afghanistan is essentially a primitive, underdeveloped country.

The Afghan people, totaling 21 million, are devout Moslems. They belong to a number of different tribes and retain a strong sense of tribal identity and loyalty. They speak Persian or Persian-related languages. Few Afghans are urban dwellers; 90 percent live in rural areas, some working as livestock herders but most as farmers. Their per capita income is slightly above $100 per year, some 90 percent are illiterate, and the average life expectancy is 40 years.

PRO-SOVIET GOVERNMENT (1978)

By a 1978 revolution a pro-Marxist party seized control. It established an Afghan regime that signed a treaty of "friendship and cooperation" with the Soviet Union and accepted Soviet military and economic advisers. This pro-Soviet regime aroused strong opposition among the people for being "godless" and anti-Islamic, subservient to the Soviet Union, brutal in its treatment of political prisoners, and a threat to the traditional Afghan way of life. The Communist regime proved unable to suppress the rebellious Moslem tribal guerrilla bands, and by late 1979 it seemed likely to be overthrown.

SOVIET INVASION (1979–1980)

Thereupon the Soviet Union apparently sponsored a coup in Afghanistan, installing a new president—*Babrak Karmal*—in the capital city of Kabul and sending some 50,000 Soviet troops into the country to crush the rebellious tribal guerrillas. Russia claimed that its intervention had been requested by the Afghan authorities. The Soviet forces met with resistance from both the Afghan regular army and the guerrilla units.

This invasion—reminiscent of Soviet actions in 1956 in Hungary and in 1968 in Czechoslovakia—was protested by Western and many Third World nations. The United States condemned Russia for "blatant military interference," and President Carter warned of a serious deterioration of Soviet-American relations. China termed the invasion a threat to Chinese security and warned the Soviets to withdraw. Pakistan, which has housed many Afghan refugees, sponsored a letter signed by forty-three Third World and Western nations asking the UN Security Council to consider the situation in Afghanistan. The Security Council resolution, calling for the "unconditional withdrawal of all foreign troops from Afghanistan," received 13 out of 15 votes but was defeated by a Soviet veto. Thereupon, under the Uniting for Peace Resolution, the veto-free General Assembly considered the Soviet invasion of Afghanistan. By a vote of 104 to 18 (with 30 not voting), the General Assembly adopted a resolution strongly deploring the armed intervention in Afghanistan and calling for a withdrawal of all foreign troops. The General Assembly action was belittled by the Soviet Union.

THE CARTER DOCTRINE

In his 1980 State of the Union address, devoted mainly to foreign affairs, President Carter considered the implications of the Soviet invasion of Afghanistan. That invasion, the President held, threatened the Persian Gulf region, with its oil supplies essential to the Western democracies. Soviet forces now were within 300 miles of the Indian Ocean and close to the major waterway for transporting Persian Gulf oil, the *Strait of Hormuz*. The President therefore issued a warning that any attempt by outside forces "to gain control of the Persian Gulf region will be regarded as an assault" against the United States and "will be repelled by any means necessary, including military force." This warning became known as the *Carter Doctrine*.

American observers questioned the military capability of the United States to back up the Carter Doctrine and discussed its potential effect upon world peace. The Soviet Union meanwhile in its Communist party newspaper *Pravda* issued a high-level statement denying any Soviet designs on Middle East oil or warm-water ports on the Persian Gulf.

Latin America

GOOD NEIGHBOR POLICY AFTER WORLD WAR II

1. Rio Inter-American Defense Treaty. In 1947, at the Rio de Janeiro Conference, the American nations signed the *Rio treaty*. It provided that *(a)* an armed attack against any American state shall be considered an attack against all, and *(b)* the other American states shall assist the victim of attack. Faced with the danger of Russian aggression elsewhere, President Truman welcomed this treaty as an expression of hemispheric solidarity.

2. Organization of American States (OAS). In 1948 at Bogota, the American nations established the *Organization of American States*.

a. Purposes. The OAS charter obligates the signatory nations to pursue the following goals: (1) cooperation in economic, social, and legal matters, (2) peaceful settlement of disputes, (3) nonintervention in the internal affairs of any state except to preserve hemispheric peace and security, and (4) collective action against armed attack and against any situation threatening hemispheric peace.

b. Major Organs. (1) The *Inter-American Conference*, the supreme body, meets once every five years and determines general policy. (2) The *Council*, consisting of representatives of each member nation, is in permanent session as the executive body. (3) *Meetings of Consultation of Ministers of Foreign Affairs* are held as needed to consider urgent problems. (4) The *Inter-American Defense Board* coordinates hemispheric military defense. (5) The *Economic and Social Council*, the *Cultural Council*, and the *Council of Jurists* deal with special problems. (6) The *Pan-American Union* serves as the OAS secretariat.

c. Strengths. The OAS advances inter-American economic cooperation. It provides a forum for the American nations and makes possible hemispheric solidarity on international problems. Finally, by a two-thirds vote, the OAS may recommend action to protect its member nations.

d. Weaknesses. The OAS cannot be sure that its members will heed OAS recommendations. Further, the OAS operates on a limited budget and lacks a military force. Finally, many Latin American members resent the United States because of its economic wealth and military power, and complain that the United States dominates the OAS.

UNITED STATES NEGLECT OF LATIN AMERICA FOLLOWING WORLD WAR II

With the outbreak of the cold war, the United States concentrated its attention (1) upon Europe by such programs as the Truman Doctrine, the Marshall Plan, and NATO, and (2) upon the Far East by its defense of South Korea and its opposition to Communist China. Confident that the Good Neighbor Policy would assure solidarity in the Western Hemisphere, the United States tended to neglect Latin America and its very real problems.

BASIC FACTORS UNDERLYING LATIN AMERICAN UNREST

1. Social Factors

a. Population Explosion. Now totaling over 340 million, the population of Latin America is growing faster than that of any other area. By surpassing the growth of Latin America's economy, its population explosion hinders efforts to raise living standards.

b. Population Divisions. The whites, a large minority, are chiefly descendants of Spanish colonists. (In Brazil, most whites are of Portuguese descent.) The whites also include recent immigrants, such as Italians and Germans. Generally, the whites constitute the upper and middle classes. Usually, they own the large estates and occupy high positions in the dominant Roman Catholic Church, in the armed forces, and in the government. The rest of the population consists of a large minority of *mestizos* (people of mixed white and Indian ancestry) and smaller groups of Indians and blacks. These people make up the lower classes of city workers and peasants. These divisions in Latin America's population add overtones of race and nationality to economic problems.

c. Illiteracy. Latin America's rate of illiteracy is almost 25 percent. In the 20th century the trend has been away from Church control of education and toward free public schools. However, many children receive no education at all because they begin work at an early age and because there are not enough schools. In predominantly white countries, such as Argentina, Uruguay, Chile, and Costa Rica, illiteracy is low; in predominantly mestizo, Indian, and black countries, such as Bolivia, Guatemala, and Haiti, illiteracy is high.

2. Economic Factors

a. Poverty. Latin America is enmeshed in widespread poverty. The average income per person is very low, especially when compared to that of people in the United States. Great extremes exist between the rich and the poor. Two percent of the people possess 70 percent of the area's wealth. The Latin American masses are not content; they want to escape poverty and to secure more material goods. Their desire to advance economically, shared by peoples of most underdeveloped countries, is sometimes called the "revolution of rising expectations."

b. Agricultural Problems. Most Latin Americans earn their livelihood from agriculture. Yet only 10 percent of the population owns 90 percent of the arable land, much of which is organized into large estates. The *peons*—peasants who work the estates—are practically serfs, many being heavily indebted to the landowner. Reformers have demanded that the large estates be broken up and distributed to the peasants as small family-size farms. Land reform is not the only agricultural problem; others are primitive equipment, poor farming methods, and lack of fertilizer, irrigation, and electrification.

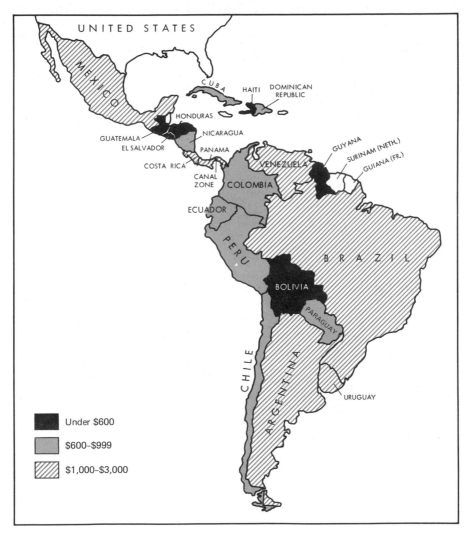

Latin America—Annual Per Capita Income

c. One-Product Economies. The wealth of Latin America lies in its mineral resources and agricultural produce: tin in Bolivia; copper in Chile; oil in Venezuela; coffee in Brazil, Colombia, Costa Rica, and Guatemala; bananas in Ecuador, Honduras, and Panama. Latin America exports these minerals and foodstuffs, and imports manufactured goods. Its major trading partner is the United States. Most Latin American countries face economic instability. Any change in the world price of their major export affects their entire economy.

d. Dependence on Foreign Investment. To develop its natural resources and industries, Latin America needs capital. However, the area lacks any significant middle class with funds to invest, and many wealthy Latin Americans, fearing revolution, have placed their capital in safe foreign banks. Therefore, Latin

Rocky soil
(*Hesse in the St. Louis
Globe-Democrat*)

America has looked for capital and technology to foreign, especially American, corporations. United States investments in Latin America total $33 billion.

3. Political Factors

a. Governmental Instability and Military Dictatorships. Latin American nations have democratic constitutions providing for elected executives and legislators. Nevertheless, many Latin American governments are dictatorships. The people lack any democratic tradition, since (1) Spanish colonial rule was autocratic, (2) the masses are poorly educated, (3) the democratically minded middle class is weak, and (4) military leaders have frequently seized the government. Many Latin American nations have been subject to frequent revolutions, but these have usually produced few economic and social improvements.

b. Doubts About Democracy. Latin Americans have had little experience with successful democratic government. Many consider the democratic system weak, corrupt, incapable of achieving basic reforms, and subject to manipulation by the wealthy and powerful.

COMMUNIST INFLUENCE IN LATIN AMERICA

To expand their influence among the discontented masses, Communist groups have demanded that workers receive better wages and that the peasants be given their own land. They have stirred up nationalism against "Yankee imperialism" and have urged seizure of foreign-owned properties. The Communists have achieved some following among labor unions, college students, and intellectuals.

The Communists have been encouraged by their (1) success under Castro in gaining control of Cuba, (2) use of Cuba to spread Communist influence into other Latin American countries and to stir up an independence movement in Puerto Rico, and (3) temporary ascendancy under Allende in Chile.

Although the number of Communists in Latin America remains small, some observers believe that, in the long run, communism poses a serious threat.

FACTORS OPPOSING COMMUNIST INFLUENCE

(1) Latin American upper classes—landowners, businessmen, military leaders, and government officials—feared the loss of their wealth and power. (2) Many Latin American governments outlawed the Communist party. Most do not maintain diplomatic relations with Communist Cuba. (3) The Roman Catholic Church has condemned communism as antireligious. (4) Many Latin Americans have strong cultural ties to Western nations, especially the United States, France, and Spain. (5) Left-of-center non-Communist groups, determined to achieve reform without totalitarianism, have shown strength. An example is the Democratic Action party in Venezuela. (6) The United States has moved to improve relations with Latin America. American interest was reawakened by developments in Cuba, Panama, and the Dominican Republic.

CUBA: FROM MILITARY DICTATORSHIP TO COMMUNISM

1. Batista Dictatorship (1952–1959). General *Fulgencio Batista* seized the Cuban government and set up a dictatorship. His regime was marked by corruption and terrorism. Beginning in 1956 Batista faced a rebellion led by *Fidel Castro*. Not then known as a Communist, Castro promised to restore democracy to Cuba. He gained support among students, peasants, businessmen, and professional people. Castro waged guerrilla warfare until Batista fled the country. In triumph, Castro entered Havana and became premier.

2. Castro Regime (Since 1959)

a. Denial of Democratic Rights. The Castro government adopted police state practices: suspending the writ of habeas corpus and other civil liberties, stifling press and radio criticism, refusing to hold free elections, and trying opponents before military courts without legal safeguards. Over 500,000 Cubans, including many former Castro supporters, fled to the United States and other Western Hemisphere nations.

b. Economic Changes. By an *Agrarian Reform Law*, Castro expropriated land from large plantations (chiefly American-owned) for use by the landless peasants within state-controlled cooperatives. Castro subsequently expropriated other properties owned by American corporations. In 1960 President Eisenhower responded by halting American imports of Cuban sugar and banning most American exports to Cuba. Its economy deteriorated, and Castro rationed gasoline, clothes, and food. Cuba required substantial Russian aid, estimated at $8 million a day, to bolster its faltering economy.

c. Anti-American Attitude. Castro inflamed anti-American sentiment among the Cuban people. He claimed the United States is imperialist, a supporter of counterrevolutionary forces, and the cause of Cuba's economic woes. Castro challenged America's right to retain its Cuban naval base at Guantanamo Bay. At the UN, the Castro regime repeatedly charged America with economic aggression and intrigue against Cuba. After denying such charges, President Eisenhower in 1961 broke diplomatic relations with Cuba, declaring that "there is a limit to what the United States in self-respect can endure."

d. Communist State. Castro granted key government positions to Communists. The government negotiated an economic pact with Russia, exchanging Cuban sugar for Russian manufactured goods, buying Russian machinery on credit, and securing Communist technicians. Castro also received Communist military equipment. In 1961 Castro publicly admitted being a "Marxist-Leninist." He announced plans to transform Cuba into a Communist state.

3. Bay of Pigs Invasion (1961). American-trained Cuban exiles launched a small-scale invasion of Cuba at the *Bay of Pigs.* Although easily crushed by Castro's military forces, the invasion sparked a bitter argument between Russia and the United States. Premier Khrushchev demanded that the United States halt its "aggression" against Cuba and warned that the Soviet Union would assist Castro. In reply, President Kennedy proclaimed American admiration for the Cuban invaders and warned Russia that the United States would "protect this hemisphere against external aggression."

4. OAS and Cuba (1962). The OAS nations approved resolutions *(a)* declaring communism incompatible with the principles of the inter-American system and *(b)* removing Cuba from the Inter-American Defense Board and from all other OAS organs.

5. Soviet Missile Bases in Cuba (1962)

a. Crisis. President Kennedy disclosed that Russia secretly was bringing offensive bombers and missiles into Cuba and building Cuban missile bases—a threat to the security of the Western Hemisphere. The President ordered a *quarantine* by American naval and air forces on shipments of offensive arms bound for Cuba. He demanded that Russia dismantle the Cuban missile bases and withdraw the bombers and missiles. This firm stand by the United States won the support of our NATO and OAS allies.

Russian proverbs
(*Alexander in the Philadelphia Evening Bulletin*)

At first, Russia called the American charges false and labeled the American quarantine "piracy." Then, after several suspenseful days, Khrushchev agreed to dismantle the missile bases and withdraw the offensive weapons. In turn, Kennedy agreed to lift the quarantine and pledged not to invade Cuba.

b. Reactions to the Settlement. (1) President Kennedy considered the settlement an honorable accord, not a victory. The President felt relieved that the Soviet offensive weapons were withdrawn in peace. However, the United States is aware that Cuba remains Communist, heavily armed with defensive weapons, and bolstered by Soviet military personnel. (2) Premier Khrushchev called the settlement an example of peaceful coexistence. He claimed that the American pledge not to invade Cuba ended the need for the missile bases.

6. Communist Cuban Troops in Africa: *(a) Angola.* In 1975 Cuba sent 15,000 troops to Angola, helping the pro-Soviet faction to gain control of the country. Resenting this intervention, the United States warned Cuba that "we cannot tolerate again a Cuban military adventure anywhere." *(b) Ethiopia.* In 1977, despite this warning, the Cuban troops in Africa moved to Ethiopia. They assisted the pro-Soviet Ethiopian military regime to battle a Somali rebellion. Thereafter President Carter warned the Soviet Union that its use of Cuban "proxy forces" in Africa endangers Soviet-American cooperation.

7. Soviet Combat Force in Cuba (1979). Check the Index for Cuba.

PANAMA SINCE 1964. Check the Index for "Panama Canal."

DOMINICAN REPUBLIC: FROM DICTATORSHIP TO UNREST

1. Trujillo Dictatorship (1930–1961). General *Rafael Trujillo* seized control of the Dominican Republic, ruled dictatorially, suppressed civil liberties, and employed terrorism. Trujillo used his power to become a partner in many Dominican business enterprises, thereby amassing a tremendous personal fortune. To improve the country, Trujillo built houses, hospitals, schools, and highways, and encouraged industry. In 1961 General Trujillo was assassinated by military leaders, supposedly to avenge personal slights.

2. Political Unrest (1961–1965). After Trujillo, the Dominican Republic was ruled by an elected government under left-of-center President *Juan Bosch.* Within seven months, military leaders deposed Bosch, charging him with being indifferent to a Communist threat. They established an army-backed civilian junta. In 1965 rebel groups overthrew the junta and planned to reinstate Bosch. Thereupon, the military leaders who had opposed Bosch organized a counter-revolution. The result was civil war.

3. United States and OAS Intervention. President Johnson sent American forces into the Dominican Republic—the first direct military intervention by the United States in Latin America in 30 years. Johnson's purposes were to protect American lives and to prevent a Communist takeover. Johnson asserted that "the American nations cannot, must not, and will not permit the establishment of another Communist government in the Western Hemisphere." This statement is sometimes referred to as the *Johnson Corollary* to the Monroe Doctrine.

In response to an American request, the OAS approved the establishment of an *Inter-American Peace Force.* Combining Latin American and United States troops, the OAS army halted the violence in the Dominican Republic.

Latin American and domestic critics argued that the Johnson administration had *(a)* exaggerated the danger of a Communist takeover, *(b)* allied the United States with reactionary military forces against forward-looking reformers, and *(c)* earned hemispheric ill-will by reviving American intervention in internal Latin American affairs. Administration spokesmen denied these charges, pointing out that the United States *(a)* could more easily prevent than cure a Communist takeover, *(b)* had respected the OAS charter, which permits intervention to preserve hemispheric security, and *(c)* had welcomed the acceptance of responsibility by the OAS.

4. Subsequent Developments. In OAS-supervised elections in 1966, *Joaquin Balaguer*, a right-of-center candidate, became president. Twice thereafter Balaguer was reelected. His regime helped improve the economy by attracting tourists and encouraging investments of foreign corporations. Nevertheless, the country faced economic problems, especially high unemployment and considerable inflation. In 1978 Balaguer was defeated in his bid for a fourth term by a left-of-center candidate, *Antonio Guzman.*

LATIN AMERICAN GRIEVANCES AGAINST THE UNITED STATES: A SUMMARY

1. Latin Americans complained that the United States *(a)* gave them too little foreign aid, *(b)* paid low prices for their exports of raw materials and foodstuffs while charging high prices for their imports of American manufactured goods, *(c)* dominated their economies through its investments, *(d)* supported such notorious Latin American dictators as Batista in Cuba and Trujillo in the Dominican Republic, and *(e)* intervened in internal matters, especially in 1965 in the Dominican Republic.

2. Americans replied that the United States *(a)* has limited resources and must distribute foreign aid according to needs throughout the world, *(b)* accepts prices as set by the economic laws of supply and demand, *(c)* through its investments, has developed the resources of Latin America, at the same time providing employment and paying taxes, *(d)* has had to deal with Latin American dictators, however repugnant, only because they represented official governments, and *(e)* intervened in the Dominican Republic to protect the Western Hemisphere from communism and subsequently received OAS approval for this action.

EFFORTS TO IMPROVE UNITED STATES-LATIN AMERICAN RELATIONS

1. Inter-American Development Bank (1959). The United States joined in founding and provided considerable capital for the *Inter-American Development Bank.* Its purpose is to finance long-term projects in Latin America.

2. Information Activities. The United States Information Agency endeavored to correct the distorted picture of the United States held by many Latin Americans. Congress voted funds for a student exchange program with Latin America.

3. Presidential Trips. Presidents Eisenhower, Kennedy, Johnson, and Nixon all visited Latin American nations and received friendly welcomes.

4. Alliance for Progress (1961). President Kennedy held that "those who make peaceful revolution impossible will make violent revolution inevitable." He proposed the *Alliance for Progress* to benefit the Latin American masses and thereby eliminate conditions that breed Castro-type revolutions.

a. Plans. The United States and the Latin American nations (Cuba excepted) adopted the following program: (1) Aid. The alliance nations agreed to a ten-year $20 billion aid program for Latin America. Of this sum, the United States was to provide more than half, chiefly as long-term, low-interest loans; the rest was to come from international agencies, western Europe, Japan, and private capital. (2) Trade. The alliance nations agreed to expand trade and to stabilize prices of Latin America's products, especially coffee and tin. (3) Reform. The alliance nations agreed to improve conditions for the Latin American masses by social and economic reforms: providing free schools for all children, reducing adult illiteracy, eradicating malaria, building public housing, breaking up large estates and giving land to the peasants, and distributing the tax burden fairly.

b. Mixed Record. The United States sharply increased aid to Latin America. American funds were used for distribution of food and for construction of schools, waterworks, power plants, housing, and highways. These efforts, however, proved to be only a small step toward solving Latin America's massive problems.

On the other hand, (1) Latin America did not significantly attract more private American capital, (2) most Latin American nations postponed land reforms, (3) the prices of many Latin American exports remained low, and (4) the GNP in Latin America increased somewhat, but only slightly more than the region's population.

In the United States and Latin America, the record of the Alliance for Progress caused considerable disillusionment. Nevertheless, the alliance received renewed pledges of Latin American support and of United States aid past 1971, the original terminal date.

5. Rockefeller Visits to Latin America (1969). Governor Nelson Rockefeller of New York undertook, for President Nixon, fact-finding tours of 20 Latin American republics. His visits were marred by a considerable number of anti-American demonstrations. Reporting that America had permitted its hemispheric relations

"The Apollo 11 rock samples are behind this glass—those are Nelson Rockefeller South American Trip rock samples." (*Mahood* © *Punch* [*Rothco*])

"to deteriorate badly," Rockefeller asserted that Latin America (a) is being swept by "forces of change": frustrations over low living standards, discontent with the Alliance for Progress, and anti-American nationalism, (b) faces the possibility of Castro-type Communist regimes, and (c) therefore needs American understanding and economic aid.

CHILE: FROM MARXIST TO MILITARY RULE

1. The Marxist-Leninist President (1970–1973)

Salvador Allende Gossens, supported by the Popular Unity coalition of Socialists, Communists, and other leftists, led in a three-man presidential race, winning a popular plurality of 36 percent. He was named president by the Chilean Congress even though his supporters were a minority. The Congress upheld the Chilean tradition of selecting the first-place finisher.

With socialism as his goal, Allende moved to seize the large estates and distribute the land to peasant cooperatives, to nationalize banks and other businesses, to raise workers' wages while freezing prices, and to expropriate copper mines and other properties, chiefly owned by American companies. Allende promised to compensate the American companies for their nationalized properties, but he added that Chile would deduct from such compensation undisclosed sums representing the "excess profits" of past years. Allende affirmed his belief in democracy and permitted non-Marxist parties to exist, but acted to weaken his opponents through legal means. (In 1974 the United States Central Intelligence Agency revealed that, as authorized by the National Security Council, it had conducted covert, or undercover, activities in Chile, providing funds to keep alive political parties and news media threatened by the Allende government.)

In foreign affairs, Chile resumed diplomatic relations with Castro's Cuba but also proclaimed a policy of cold war neutrality. Allende kept Chile in the OAS and promised to bar any foreign military bases in Chile that might threaten the United States.

By 1973 Allende was unable to govern Chile effectively and to end the economic chaos. He faced political problems: opposition from the parties controlling Congress and dissension among the parties in his Popular Unity coalition. Allende also faced economic problems. Chile suffered from shortages of foodstuffs and from a severe inflation. The middle and upper classes, constituting half of Chile's population, opposed Allende's expropriation of large estates and nationalization of small businesses. The Allende government was challenged by a series of strikes and demonstrations: by copper miners, truckers (mainly owners), small shopkeepers, doctors and other professionals, and city housewives— all protesting shortages, inflation, and government economic policies.

2. Military Rule (Since 1973).
In a swift military coup, marked by some bloodshed and the death of Allende, army leaders overthrew the Allende regime and replaced it by a military junta headed by General *Augusto Pinochet Ugarte* as president. The military thus broke a 46-year-old Chilean tradition of nonintervention in political affairs, believing it necessary to liberate Chile "from the Marxist yoke." (The CIA denied any direct role in this military coup.)

On the economic front, the junta acted to abolish food and price controls, to freeze workers' wages temporarily, and to return most small businesses to their former owners. The junta promised to restore lands, illegally expropriated, to their former owners and, while retaining Chilean ownership of the copper mines, to negotiate fairly with the American-owned copper companies regarding compensation for their former holdings. The junta also benefited from the halting of the strikes and demonstrations that had plagued Allende. By 1980 the junta, moving toward free-marketplace policies, had improved economic conditions—sharply curtailing inflation, attracting foreign investment, and although unemployment remained troublesome, achieving considerable economic growth.

On the political front, the junta proceeded to declare a state of seige, to outlaw the Marxist political parties that had supported Allende, to abolish the Workers Confederation, which was chiefly Communist-controlled, to recess Congress, to arrest suspected leftists, including large numbers of foreigners who had flocked to Allende's Chile, and to end diplomatic relations with Castro's Cuba. Thereafter, the junta made no move to restore Chile to civilian rule but maintained its military dictatorship.

In 1977 Chile was condemned for violating human rights by the UN Human Rights Commission and was criticized by President Carter. The Chilean military junta moved to improve its human rights record by releasing many political prisoners, abolishing its secret police, and, under certain conditions, granting labor unions the right to strike.

NICARAGUA: FROM DICTATORSHIP TO POLITICAL UNREST

1. The Somoza Regime (To 1979). The Somoza family for almost 50 years ruled Nicaragua as a military dictatorship. They manipulated elections, crushed political opposition, and employed terror against their enemies. The Somozas furthered economic growth by building roads, improving port facilities, and providing hydroelectric power. They invested in commercial, industrial, and agricultural enterprises and amassed a vast family fortune. In foreign policy, the Somoza regime was strongly pro-United States and anti-Communist.

General Anastasio Somoza Debayle, who became president in 1967, felt the full force of opposition to dictatorial rule from workers, business leaders, students, professionals, Catholic clergy, and radical Marxists. The opposition was centered in the *Sandinist National Liberation Front*—named after a reform leader, Augusto Sandino, reputedly killed in 1934 by orders of the Somoza regime. Although the Sandinist movement contained many moderates, it was dominated by leftist Marxist leaders. In the 1970's Sandinist guerrillas, some trained in Cuba and armed with Cuban weapons, mounted military attacks to topple the Somoza regime. Nicaragua experienced civil war with considerable destruction of property and loss of life.

2. Revolution and Unrest. In 1979 the United States, realizing that Somoza's power was fading and fearing "another Cuba" in the Western hemisphere, moved to shape Nicaraguan developments toward moderate, democratic policies. The United States proposal that an OAS peacekeeping force be sent to Nicaragua was rejected by the Latin American nations and by the Sandinist leaders. The United States thereafter sought to have the Sandinist movement give greater recognition to its moderate elements. After Somoza fled Nicaragua, the Sandinists named a five-member junta to govern the country. The new regime dissolved Congress, seized the Somoza estates and businesses, and pledged to rebuild the country. It requested humanitarian and economic aid of the United States—to which requests the Carter administration responded positively.

Nicaragua remains a matter of hemispheric concern. Will its government pursue a moderate program, or will it move to a leftist Marxist regime? What effect will the Nicaraguan revolution have on military rule in nearby Guatemala and El Salvador?

MULTIPLE-CHOICE QUESTIONS

1. A major problem in the establishment of peace immediately following World War II was the   (1) extreme difficulty in reconciling the goals of the victors   (2) refusal of the defeated powers to sign the terms of surrender   (3) policies of nonalignment adopted by the emerging nations   (4) international agreements that have weakened the role of the nation-state.

2. Which came first in postwar Germany?   (1) admission of West Germany to NATO   (2) Berlin blockade   (3) building of the Berlin Wall   (4) Potsdam Conference

3. Which was a result of both World War I and World War II?   (1) All of Germany was placed under occupation by Allied armies.   (2) The United States joined its allies in collecting reparations from Germany.   (3) Germany was forced to give up all her African colonies.   (4) Germany was forced to transfer territory to Poland.

4. At the Nuremberg trials, Nazi leaders were charged with   (1) losing the war   (2) destroying the German Republic   (3) inventing missiles   (4) committing crimes against humanity.

5. Khrushchev wanted to drive the Western powers from West Berlin because that city was   (1) traditionally Communist   (2) a valuable seaport   (3) NATO military headquarters   (4) a showcase of democracy and capitalism behind the Iron Curtain.

6. Western determination to remain in West Berlin was based upon   (1) the failure of the airlift of 1948–1949   (2) the friendship given to the Western powers by Berliners throughout the 20th century   (3) an effort to prevent the return of Nazism in West Berlin   (4) the belief that weakness here would encourage further Soviet aggression.

7. The Arab attack upon the newly proclaimed state of Israel in 1948   (1) was approved by the UN General Assembly   (2) was halted by a UN emergency force   (3) sought to destroy the new state   (4) sought to create a unified Arab nation.

8. Until the mid-1970's which Middle East nation received substantial military aid from the Communist bloc?   (1) Israel   (2) Saudi Arabia   (3) Egypt   (4) Turkey

9. Which represents the *major* goal of Israeli foreign policy?   (1) ending Communist influence in the Middle East   (2) destroying the Organization of Petroleum Exporting Countries (OPEC)   (3) gaining control of both sides of the Suez Canal   (4) assuring the physical and economic security of Israel

10. The waterway that has been a trouble spot in the relations between Egypt and Israel is the   (1) Mediterranean Sea   (2) Dead Sea   (3) Jordan River   (4) Gulf of Aqaba.

11. American foreign policy in the Middle East has sought   (1) a confrontation with the Soviet Union   (2) a compromise settlement of Arab-Israeli issues so as to end the recurrent crises   (3) peace in the area enforced by American marines   (4) an end to American investments in Arab countries.

12. Which is a *basic* cause of unrest throughout Asia?   (1) complete control by European powers   (2) lack of important natural resources   (3) manpower shortage   (4) low standard of living

13. Which nation in the Far East has achieved the greatest degree of industrial development?   (1) Burma   (2) India   (3) China   (4) Japan

14. The *most* important factor in determining United States policy toward Japan and Germany since World War II has been   (1) a need for their raw materials in the United States   (2) the power of the Communist nations   (3) a desire by the United States to fulfill prewar commitments   (4) the effort of the United States to win support in the United Nations.

15. Where does the government of Nationalist China maintain its headquarters? (1) Peking   (2) Taiwan   (3) Hong Kong   (4) Singapore

16. Which was a *major* point that created disunity between Communist China and Soviet Russia?   (1) Mao Tse-tung's rejection of Marxism   (2) Russia's criticism of India   (3) the downgrading of Lenin   (4) the borders between China and Russia.

17. Relations between India and China were strained by   (1) China's refusal to provide nuclear weapons to India   (2) India's efforts to spread Hinduism   (3) China's border attacks against India   (4) China's alliance with Sri Lanka.

18. In recent years, India   (1) agreed to divide Kashmir with Pakistan   (2) refused to recognize Communist China   (3) joined SEATO   (4) secured Russian support before waging war for the independence of Bangladesh.

19. Which event in Korea occurred *first*?   (1) North Korea's invasion of South Korea (2) the creation of a government for South Korea   (3) intervention of Chinese Communist troops in Korea   (4) division of Korea at the 38th parallel.

20. Which issue was the *chief* cause of delay in negotiating a truce in Korea?   (1) the UN resolution calling China an aggressor   (2) the boundary line between North and South Korea   (3) the exchange of war prisoners   (4) the North Korean seizure of the American intelligence ship *Pueblo*.

21. Which European country was directly involved in the civil war in Indo-China from 1946 to 1954?   (1) Great Britain   (2) France   (3) Italy   (4) the Netherlands

22. Which is the most accurate statement concerning United States involvement in the Vietnam conflict?   (1) Our involvement resulted from a declaration of war by Congress.   (2) Our European allies strongly urged large-scale involvement.   (3) Military preparedness of the United States encouraged involvement.   (4) Public opinion in the United States became divided over involvement.

23. The 1973 Paris Peace Agreement for Vietnam did *not* include which provision?   (1) withdrawal of all American troops from South Vietnam   (2) withdrawal of all Hanoi troops from South Vietnam   (3) return of all Americans held as prisoners of war   (4) Vietnam reunification by peaceful means only

24. As a result of United States military involvement in Southeast Asia, many members of Congress have attempted to   (1) delegate additional powers to the President   (2) place greater responsibility for foreign policy on the Secretary of State   (3) reassert the role of Congress in the formulation of foreign policy   (4) eliminate the requirement of a vote of Congress for a declaration of war.

25. If the "domino theory" regarding southeast Asia is correct, the fall of Cambodia to the Khmer Rouge should lead to increased pressures upon the government of   (1) Thailand   (2) the Philippines   (3) India   (4) Japan.

26. Which has been a *major* obstacle to economic development in Latin America?   (1) shortages of unskilled labor   (2) shortage of investment capital   (3) lack of markets   (4) insufficient natural resources

27. The term "revolution of rising expectations" refers to the   (1) desire of Communists to take over more of the world   (2) desire of people in developing nations to raise their standards of living   (3) demand of workers around the world for collective bargaining   (4) hope of the United States to achieve improved relations with Communist China.

28. By joining the Organization of American States, the United States   (1) achieved cooperation with Canada   (2) abandoned the Good Neighbor Policy   (3) achieved economic control over the Western Hemisphere   (4) reaffirmed its rejection of the Roosevelt Corollary to the Monroe Doctrine.

29. A unique feature of the Alliance for Progress is the degree to which it requires Latin American countries to (1) accept United States military bases (2) make trade concessions for products from the United States (3) provide evidence of basic reform programs (4) repress local Communist movements.
30. An important reason for the quarantine ordered by President Kennedy in the Cuban crisis of 1962 was to (1) protect refugees escaping from Cuba (2) protect the security of the United States (3) prevent a Cuban invasion of the Dominican Republic (4) prevent Communist China from shipping weapons to Cuba.
31. Since World War II, United States foreign policy toward Latin America has been characterized by (1) approval of Communist states (2) programs to increase economic and technical aid (3) frequent military intervention in political revolutions (4) attempts to secure guarantees of religious freedom.
32. The foreign policy of the United States toward the Western Hemisphere has been criticized by Latin Americans primarily on the grounds that it has (1) failed to keep foreign aggressors out of the hemisphere (2) placed economic gain above concern for people's welfare (3) resulted in Communist control of most of the area (4) prevented the development of natural resources in Latin America.

MATCHING QUESTIONS

For each office listed in Column A, select the *letter* preceding the name of the person in Column B who either once held or now holds that office.

Column A	*Column B*
1. Chairman of Communist party of China	a. Helmut Schmidt
2. Premier of Cuba	b. Menachem Begin
3. Prime Minister of India	c. Fidel Castro
4. President of Egypt	d. Chiang Kai-shek
5. President of North Vietnam	e. Ho Chi Minh
6. Negotiator of Vietnam peace agreement	f. Leonid Brezhnev
7. President of Nationalist China	g. Chou En-lai
8. Chancellor of West Germany	h. Hua Kuo-feng
9. Prime Minister of Israel	i. Anwar al-Sadat
10. President of South Korea	j. Jawaharlal Nehru
	k. Chung Hee Park
	l. Rafael Trujillo
	m. Henry Kissinger

CHRONOLOGY QUESTIONS

Harry Truman   John Kennedy   Richard Nixon
Dwight Eisenhower   Lyndon Johnson   Gerald Ford

For each of the following events in American foreign affairs, select the President in whose administration the event took place.

1. A quarantine was placed upon ships bound for Cuba with offensive weapons.
2. An army general was dismissed by the commander in chief on grounds of insubordination.
3. Congress overrode the President's veto and enacted the War Powers Resolution.
4. American troops were sent to aid Lebanon.
5. Air strikes were first ordered against North Vietnamese military targets.
6. Arab nations began a total embargo on oil shipments to the United States.
7. Great Britain was requested to ease restrictions on Jewish immigration into Palestine.
8. American troops were sent into the Dominican Republic.

9. The Khmer Rouge seized complete control of Cambodia.
10. An airlift was used to break Berlin blockade.
11. A Presidential visit to China was the beginning of an improvement in Sino-American relations.
12. The Alliance for Progress was inaugurated to improve conditions in Latin America.

ESSAY QUESTIONS

1. United States foreign policy is most often defined by what the policy makers say is our national interest. Throughout history our national interest has been influenced by and, at times, dictated by the actions of other nations. (a) For each of the following regions, describe one way in which the national interest of the United States has been involved: (1) Europe (2) Latin America (3) Middle East (4) Far East. (b) For one region, discuss to what extent a United States foreign policy decision has had a positive or negative effect on the United States national interest. You may discuss both positive and negative effects. (c) Discuss two reasons why the United States, since World War II, has increasingly used joint actions with other nations in attempting to solve international problems.
2. Discuss American foreign policy toward either Germany or Japan from 1930 to the present. Include in your answer the following topics: (a) one cause for ill-feeling, during the period from 1930 to 1941, between the United States and the country you have selected (b) a major aim of United States policy toward that country following World War II (c) two specific American attempts to carry out the aim given in your answer to part (b).
3. The United States has faced serious problems in its relations with Latin America during recent years. (a) Describe two developments affecting the relations between Cuba and the United States since 1898. (b) Show how policies of the United States since 1900 toward two Latin American countries other than Cuba have been criticized by Latin America. (c) Describe two policies of the United States during the 20th century that have gained favor in Latin America.
4. Agree or disagree with each of the following statements and give two reasons to support your opinion: (a) The dispute between the Soviet Union and Communist China has both ideological and nationalistic roots. (b) Germany will remain a divided nation for the foreseeable future. (c) The Middle East will have peace only after the Arab nations accept the existence of Israel. (d) The problems of Latin America were not caused and cannot be solved by the United States alone. (e) From its experiences in Vietnam, the United States should learn many lessons. (f) By the mid-1970's, the United States was turning away from the role of world policeman.
5. The following paragraph is a model representing events that led to war:

A long series of minor conflicts strained relations between A and B. Using all means available to them, molders of public opinion on each side aroused hostile feelings. The public on each side was only partially informed. As a result of limited information, each side increased its bitterness toward the other. An event took place which triggered strong emotional reactions and demands for war. Public officials were caught up in the excitement and gave in to demands for military action. War followed.

(a) Select any two wars and, using specific events, discuss the extent to which the model does or does not apply to each war chosen. (b) For one of the wars discussed in (a), discuss possible events or actions that might have prevented the war.

17. The United States Protects the National Interest Through Scientific Developments

Nuclear Energy

NUCLEAR ENERGY: FOR HUMANITY TO USE

1. Military Uses for Mass Destruction. The single atom bomb (A-bomb) dropped on Hiroshima in 1945 contained about two pounds of uranium and had the explosive power of 20,000 pounds of TNT. It killed or injured 130,000 people and destroyed 60 percent of the city. Subsequently, scientists developed the *hydrogen bomb* (H-bomb), which can generate up to several thousand times the explosive power of the Hiroshima bomb. A single hydrogen bomb can wipe out all life within a 60- to 100-mile radius.

The destructiveness of nuclear weapons results from their explosive blast, tremendous heat, and radioactivity, which can contaminate whole areas. Widespread fear exists that a nuclear war could mean the end of civilization.

2. Peaceful Uses for Mass Benefit. Atomic scientists devised methods to control nuclear reactions and utilize the tremendous heat to change water into steam. In turn, steam can be used to propel boats and to generate electricity. The United States possesses a fleet of atomic-powered surface ships and submarines, and a number of atomic-powered plants for the production of electricity. In many regions of the United States today, atomic power is competitive in cost with electricity generated by conventional fuels: natural gas, oil, and coal.

Atomic scientists also produced radioactive chemical substances called *isotopes*. These have significant uses (1) *in medicine*, to diagnose body ills, (2) *in agriculture*, to study plant growth and to preserve foods, and (3) *in industry*, to measure the flow of oil in pipelines and to uncover flaws in metal.

Within the United States, the *Atomic Energy Commission* (AEC) directed the development of peaceful and military uses of nuclear energy. In 1974 the AEC was abolished and its functions were assigned to two new agencies: the *Energy Research and Development Administration* (ERDA) to spur research on nuclear energy and new energy supplies; and the *Nuclear Regulatory Commission* (NRC) to regulate the use of nuclear materials.

3. Nations Possessing Nuclear Power. The United States led the way in developing nuclear energy, exploding the first atomic bomb in 1945. Other nations followed: Russia in 1949, Great Britain in 1952, France in 1960, Communist China in 1964, and India in 1974. A number of other nations, scientists believe, possess the technical know-how to become nuclear powers.

The United States and Russia—the two superpowers of today—each has more than enough nuclear weapons and delivery systems to inflict upon the other incredible death and destruction. In former times, nations were deterred somewhat from engaging in war because they were uncertain of victory due to a relatively equal "balance of power." In recent times, the two superpowers have been deterred somewhat from provoking each other into a major war because they realize that they live in the shadow of a nuclear "balance of terror."

FIRST EFFORT TO ACHIEVE INTERNATIONAL CONTROL: A FAILURE

1. United States Proposes the Baruch Plan. From 1946 to 1949 the United States held a monopoly over nuclear weapons. *Bernard Baruch*, the American representative to the *UN Atomic Energy Commission*, proposed international control of nuclear weapons according to the following generous plan: The United States would destroy its atom bombs and share its technical know-how with other nations on condition that an international authority (1) supervise the use of atomic energy for only peaceful purposes, and (2) have the power of unlimited inspection of atomic facilities without the restrictions of the Big Five veto in the UN Security Council.

2. Russia Rejects the Baruch Plan. Russia violently criticized the Baruch Plan, especially the proposals to eliminate the veto power and to provide unlimited inspection. In the Security Council in 1948, Russia vetoed the Baruch Plan and thereby halted the work of the UN Atomic Energy Commission. Unrestricted by any international controls, Russia exploded her own atom bomb in 1949, and ended the United States monopoly. Thereafter, both nations continued to develop and test nuclear weapons.

EFFORT TO HALT NUCLEAR BOMB TESTS: A PARTIAL SUCCESS

In the mid-1950's the people of the world became increasingly fearful of the rising level of radioactivity resulting from nuclear weapons testing. Their fears moved Russia, the United States, and Great Britain to seek agreement at Geneva (1958 to 1963) for halting nuclear tests.

1. Conflicting Proposals for Halting Nuclear Tests. Russia proposed the immediate cessation of nuclear tests without any provision for enforcement. The Western powers rejected an unpoliced ban. Instead, they proposed a test ban coupled with a system of inspection and control. Western statesmen feared that Russia could violate an unpoliced ban without the free world's knowledge. Russia vehemently rejected the Western proposal as a plot to establish, on Soviet territory, spy rings disguised as inspection stations.

In 1961 the United States proposed a treaty to ban nuclear tests that could be detected without on-site inspection, but to exclude underground blasts, since these could be confused with earthquakes and therefore could not be detected from far away. Two years later, the Russians agreed to this American proposal.

2. Limited Nuclear Test Ban Treaty (1963)

a. Provisions. The Big Three powers (1) agreed not to conduct nuclear tests in the atmosphere, in space, and under water (these tests can be detected, by air-sampling and monitoring devices, without on-site inspection), (2) excluded underground tests from the ban but agreed to continue negotiations on this matter, (3) invited all other nations to sign the treaty, and (4) provided an escape clause permitting each signatory to withdraw from the test ban if it feels that the treaty jeopardizes its national interests.

b. France and Communist China Abstain. Although about 100 nations joined the Big Three in signing this treaty, two key nations did not. (1) France. President de Gaulle insisted that France continue atmospheric testing and

Trying to close the gap
(*Bimrose, The Portland Oregonian*)

develop her own H-bomb. De Gaulle wanted to restore France to world prestige and end her dependence upon the nuclear strength of the United States. (2) Communist China. Chinese leaders denounced the treaty as an attempt by a few powers to monopolize nuclear weapons.

    c. The United States Senate Ratifies the Treaty. The Senate overwhelmingly ratified the treaty. American ratification was quickly followed by Russian and British ratification. President Kennedy warned that, although the treaty was a step toward peace, it did not eliminate the danger of war.

FURTHER EFFORTS TO HALT THE NUCLEAR ARMS RACE

1. Outlawing Nuclear Weapons in Outer Space. In 1966 the UN General Assembly approved a treaty on the peaceful uses of outer space. The treaty prohibited any nation from claiming sovereignty over the moon and forbade nations from placing weapons of mass destruction in outer space or on any heavenly body. In 1967 the treaty went into effect.

2. Outlawing the Spread of Nuclear Weapons. The *UN Disarmament Committee* sought a treaty to outlaw the spread, or *proliferation*, of nuclear weapons. The committee reasoned that as more nations gain nuclear weapons, the more difficult it will be to prevent their accidental or deliberate use. In 1968 the United States and Russia agreed upon a treaty which provided that the (*a*) nations without nuclear weapons agree not to develop such weapons and to accept an international system of inspection, (*b*) nuclear powers assist the other nations in developing peaceful uses of atomic energy, and (*c*) nuclear powers strive to halt the arms race.

    The *Nuclear Nonproliferation Treaty* was approved by the UN General Assembly. However, some nations without nuclear weapons, including Australia, India, Israel, Japan, and West Germany, expressed strong doubts. They were being asked to forgo atomic weapons, which could be vital to national defense. To gain support for the treaty, the United States, the Soviet Union, and

Britain each pledged to assist any signatory nation attacked by an aggressor using nuclear weapons. In 1970 the treaty went into effect.

Nuclear Proliferation: American Policy Toward Pakistan. In 1979 the United States ended its economic and military assistance to Pakistan after the Central Intelligence Agency reported that Pakistan secretly was building a plant to produce nuclear weapons. Pakistan denied the report but was unwilling to place its atomic facilities under international safeguards.

In 1980, however, as the Soviet invasion of Afghanistan placed Soviet troops at the Pakistani border, President Carter reaffirmed America's 1959 agreement to help Pakistan preserve its independence and offered Pakistan additional economic and military aid.

3. Outlawing Nuclear Weapons on the Seabed. In 1970 the UN General Assembly overwhelmingly approved a treaty prohibiting any nation from placing nuclear weapons on the seabed outside its 12-mile limit. In 1972 this treaty, signed by almost 100 nations, went into effect.

4. Strategic Arms Limitation Talks (SALT). Check the Index.

Missiles

TYPES OF MISSILES

Since World War II the United States and Russia have developed rocket-propelled missiles capable of delivering either conventional or nuclear warheads. The smallest are tactical missiles that have a short range and carry warheads of low explosive power. They can be used as battlefield artillery for close support of troops. The largest missiles, for offensive purposes, are the *intermediate-range ballistic missile* (IRBM) and the *intercontinental ballistic missile* (ICBM); and for defensive purposes the *antiballistic missile* (ABM).

1. Intermediate-Range Ballistic Missile (IRBM). These missiles soar into space and then descend to earth, hitting a target up to 2500 miles away from the launching site. The United States has produced several types of IRBM's. Our main reliance is on the *Polaris* and on its newer version, the *Poseidon*. Both missiles can be launched from a surface ship or from a submarine.

Patrolling Norwegian and Mediterranean waters, American missile-carrying submarines are close enough to the Soviet Union to expose Russia's major military targets to IRBM attack. Russia also has IRBM's for use (*a*) from land-based sites against our European allies, and (*b*) from missile-carrying submarines in the North Atlantic against major American targets.

2. Intercontinental Ballistic Missile (ICBM). These missiles soar into space, travel at a speed up to 20,000 miles per hour, and descend to earth, hitting a target over 6000 miles away from the launching site. The earliest ICBM's carried a single warhead. More recent models are capable of carrying multiple warheads, with each warhead aimed at a different target. These are named *multiple individually targetable reentry vehicles* (MIRV's).

The ICBM has been called the "ultimate weapon" because its speed and its nuclear explosive power make any defense against it extremely difficult. The United States relies chiefly on the solid-fueled *Minuteman*. Russia has ICBM's, which can be launched from sites in the Soviet Union against the United States. China is working to develop her own ICBM's.

3. Antiballistic Missile (ABM). These missiles are designed to destroy offensive missiles in space. When radar indicates that enemy missiles are en route, the ABM's are to be launched to explode in the path of the approaching missiles and destroy them by explosive force, heat, and radiation.

BEGINNING ABM DEFENSE SYSTEMS

1. In the Soviet Union. By 1967 the Russians had begun installing an ABM system around Moscow. Western observers surmised that Russian ABM's were meant for defense against American as well as Chinese missiles.

2. In the United States. In 1969 the Nixon administration proposed the *Safeguard* ABM system. Its purpose was to protect not our cities, but our ICBM launching sites against any Soviet or Chinese initial attack, or *first strike*, so as to preserve our retaliatory, or *second-strike*, capacity. Nixon won narrow Congressional approval for two ABM sites.

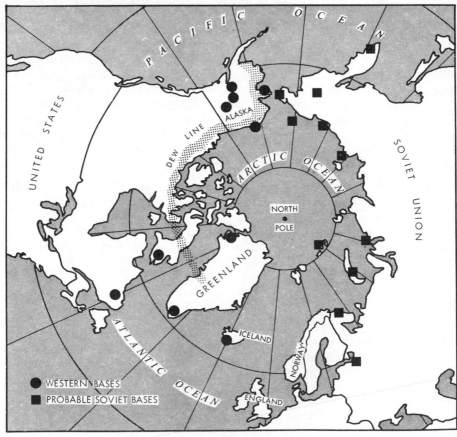

Western and Soviet Bases Facing the North Polar Region

TWO SALT I ACCORDS—SIGNED IN 1972

After almost three years of talks, American and Soviet negotiators completed two SALT I accords. Signed at Moscow by President Nixon and Communist party leader Brezhnev, the accords provided as follows:

1. The Treaty on ABM's. The United States and the Soviet Union (a) agreed to protect by ABM defense systems only two sites each—the national capital and one ICBM launching site, (b) accepted a ceiling of 100 ABM launchers for each site, (c) pledged not to build nationwide ABM defense systems, and (d) provided that the treaty be of unlimited duration but allowed each nation, upon six months' notice, to withdraw from the treaty if "extraordinary events . . . have jeopardized its supreme interests." (By a 1974 agreement, the number of ABM sites was reduced for each nation from two to one.)

Observations. This treaty (a) contained a withdrawal clause in apprehension of future Chinese developments and (b) reflected the belief that the United States and the Soviet Union each has the ability to absorb a "first strike" and to retaliate powerfully upon the other nation, thereby making the outbreak of a nuclear war between them improbable. This treaty was overwhelmingly ratified by the United States Senate.

2. The Interim Agreement on Offensive Missiles. The United States and the Soviet Union "froze" at the current level their offensive-missile systems: (a) for the United States—1054 land-launched ICBM's and 656 submarine-launched missiles, and (b) for the Soviet Union—1618 land-launched ICBM's and 710 submarine-launched missiles. This agreement was to last for five years.

Observations. This agreement (a) did *not* cover the number of warheads per missile, thereby giving the United States, with its advanced MIRV technology, the advantage of 5700 warheads as compared to 2500 for the Soviet Union, (b) did *not* cover the explosive power of each warhead, thereby giving the Soviet Union with its larger warheads a 3-to-1 lead in explosive power over the United States, (c) did *not* cover the number of long-range bombers capable of delivering nuclear bombs, thereby giving the United States a lead of 460 strategic bombers to 140 for the Soviet Union, (d) did *not* limit the construction of strategic bombers and did *not* prevent the replacement of existing missiles and submarines by more destructive models, and (e) did *not* provide for on-site inspection to prevent violations, although both nations pledged not to interfere with other methods of inspection.

Supporters of the interim agreement pointed out that it (a) reflects the opinion that both nations are roughly equal in offensive missile power, (b) may encourage a feeling of friendship and cooperation between the two nations, and therefore (c) may arrest the arms race.

Critics of the interim agreement pointed out that it (a) will not reduce the current offensive missile arsenals, (b) will shift the arms race from competition in missile numbers to competition in technology and in areas not covered by its provisions, and therefore (c) will make highly improbable any significant reduction in arms defense spending.

Although an executive agreement and therefore not requiring ratification, the offensive missiles accord was submitted by Nixon to both houses of Congress and received an overwhelming "concurrence."

THE SALT II TREATY—SIGNED IN 1979

After seven years, American and Soviet negotiators reached agreement on a treaty to replace the 1972 Interim Agreement on Offensive Missiles. The SALT II Treaty, signed at Vienna by President Carter and Soviet leader Brezhnev, was a highly technical 100-page document.

1. **Provisions.** *(a)* The United States and the Soviet Union each accepted, as of 1982, an overall ceiling of 2250 strategic nuclear-delivery vehicles. These included land-based intercontinental ballistic missiles (ICBM's), submarine-launched ballistic missiles (SLBM's), heavy bombers, and air-to-surface ballistic missiles (ASBM's) with a range of over 375 miles. Within the overall ceiling, the treaty imposed subceilings on these various missile types. It also set limits on the number of MIRV's, or warheads, per missile and the weight per missile. *(b)* The United States and the Soviet Union both agreed to test and deploy no more than one new type of ICBM. *(c)* The treaty placed no limits on Russia's *Backfire* bomber, which the Soviets insisted upon excluding from the treaty. The Soviets held the *Backfire* to be an intermediate-range plane, but Americans considered it to be a strategic long-range bomber. The Soviets pledged not to increase the current rate of *Backfire* production—about 30 per year. *(d)* The treaty limited, until 1982, America's air- or sea-launched cruise missile to a maximum range of 375 miles. (The cruise missile is a low-flying, pilotless vehicle that can be guided to its target.) *(e)* The treaty did not provide for on-site inspection to verify compliance with its terms. Both nations, however, agreed not to conceal missile activities and not to impede verification by "national technical means" (NTM)—such as satellites and intelligence listening posts. *(f)* The SALT II Treaty expires in 1985. Both nations agreed to work for further reductions and limitations in nuclear weapons as part of a SALT III Treaty.

2. **Arguments for the SALT II Treaty.** *(a)* It furthers the principle of equality in the two superpowers' strategic missile arsenals. *(b)* It requires the Soviets, by 1982, to dismantle over 10 percent of their strategic nuclear missile systems so as to conform to the 2250 ceiling. Also, by its various other ceilings, the treaty inhibits the growth of Soviet missile power, which without any treaty could expand greatly. *(c)* The restriction to 1982 on America's cruise missile is not vital since the United States could not produce longer-range cruise missiles within that time period. *(d)* President Carter claimed that the treaty "will lessen the danger of nuclear destruction while safeguarding our military security in a more stable, predictable, and peaceful world."

3. **Arguments Against the SALT II Treaty.** *(a)* Although the treaty limits both nations equally regarding overall nuclear-delivery vehicles, the Soviets have a major advantage in that their missiles are larger and more destructive than those of the United States. *(b)* By limiting new-type ICBM's to only one, the treaty severely handicaps American efforts to deploy varied mobile missile systems. These are needed since the existing, fixed, land-based *Minuteman* missiles are vulnerable to a surprise attack by increasingly accurate Soviet missiles. *(c)* The treaty places no limits on the Soviet *Backfire* bomber, which could be used for a one-way attack upon United States targets. *(d)* The United States will be unable to verify Soviet compliance with the treaty. The United States has lost its

intelligence listening posts in northern Iran, which were vital for monitoring Soviet military activities and missile tests. *(e)* By providing exceptions and permitting modernization of existing weapons, although limited, the treaty will not halt the nuclear arms race and will not permit any reduction in military spending. In fact, American military spending is expected to rise substantially.

4. Presidential Moves to Obtain Senate Ratification. The SALT II Treaty requires a two-thirds vote of the Senate for ratification. A number of Senators fear that the treaty confirms Soviet nuclear superiority over the United States. To quiet such fears, President Carter agreed to increase American military spending and to proceed with the *MX mobile missile system.* This system will move new, more powerful land-based missiles back and forth through 20-mile-long trenches so as to disguise their exact location from the Soviets. The MX system will be built in sparsely inhabited areas of Nevada and Utah, will cost some $30 billion, and will be fully operative by 1989.

5. A Complicating Factor: Soviet Combat Force in Cuba (1979). While the Senate Foreign Relations Committee was conducting hearings on the SALT II Treaty, American intelligence reports revealed the existence of a Soviet combat brigade, of up to 3000 men, in Cuba. Although President Carter held that this force posed no direct military threat to the United States, its presence in Cuba raised questions of Soviet motives and intentions. The Carter administration entered into negotiations with the Soviets, during which the Soviets insisted that the force was a "training center," not a combat unit, but pledged that they would "not change its function or status." President Carter announced a number of countermeasures: increased surveillance of Cuba, establishment of a full-time Caribbean military task force headquarters, and increased economic assistance for nations in the Caribbean region.

The President, however, urged the Senate to consider the SALT II Treaty on its own merits and to speed ratification. A number of Senators, however, argued that the Soviet combat force in Cuba was an additional reason for rejecting the SALT II Treaty.

6. A Second Complicating Factor: Soviet Invasion of Afghanistan (1979–1980). With the Soviet invasion of Afghanistan (check the Index), President Carter requested the Senate to delay consideration of the SALT II Treaty. A White House official explained that, while the President still held SALT II to be in the national interest, he concluded that the Soviet invasion in defiance of the UN Charter made consideration of SALT II at the present time "inappropriate."

The Carter administration, however, indicated that, as long as it believed the Soviet Union was abiding by the terms of the SALT II Treaty, the United States would do likewise.

Satellites and Other Space Vehicles

RUSSIA LAUNCHES ITS SPUTNIKS

The *International Geophysical Year* (1957–1958) was an international co-operative effort to increase humanity's knowledge of the physical environment.

As part of the program, the United States and Soviet Russia each announced plans to place into orbit around the earth data-gathering satellites. The Soviet Union was first to fulfill this promise. In 1957 Russian scientists orbited the first satellite, the 184-pound *Sputnik I*. Later in 1957 the Russians launched the 1120-pound *Sputnik II*.

EFFECT OF RUSSIA'S SATELLITES UPON THE UNITED STATES

Russia's initial lead in the space race greatly perturbed the American people. Why had the United States fallen behind? The following explanations were given: (1) As a dictatorship, Russia was able to concentrate all necessary resources toward achieving its goals regardless of the low standard of living of the people and their heavy tax burden. As a democracy, the United States had to heed the consumers' demands for goods and the taxpayers' demands for limiting government spending. (2) Soviet education, critics said, was ahead of that in the United States in science, mathematics, and technical subjects. (3) The Communists channeled their best students into science, mathematics, and engineering. In America many capable students selected nontechnical fields.

THE UNITED STATES SPEEDS UP ITS SPACE PROGRAM

(1) Congress approved additional funds for missile and satellite research, development, and production. (2) Congress passed the *National Defense Education Act* (1958) to improve education, especially in science and mathematics. (3) Congress established a new agency to direct the nonmilitary aspects of space exploration—the *National Aeronautics and Space Administration* (NASA).

INITIAL AMERICAN SPACE FLIGHTS

In 1958, from *Cape Canaveral*, Florida, the United States placed into orbit its first satellite, the 18-pound *Explorer I*. This achievement came some four months after the Russian launching of Sputnik I. Later in 1958 the United States placed into orbit the three-pound *Vanguard I* and the 18-pound *Explorer III*. Russian Premier Khrushchev gibed at the American satellites, calling them "grapefruits" in relation to the much larger Russian Sputniks.

Thereafter both Russia and America achieved considerable progress in space.

MAJOR SOVIET EFFORTS IN SPACE

1. **Unmanned Flights.** *(a) Around the Earth.* The Soviets have placed many satellites—of their *Cosmos* series—into orbit to test equipment for military and peaceful uses, to provide military communications, and to gather weather data. *(b) To the Moon.* The Soviets sent many *Luna* space vehicles to the moon, some reaching its surface and sending back pictures. In 1970 *Luna 17* landed on the moon, carrying a self-propelled vehicle, *Lunokhod I*. It roamed the lunar surface, analyzing lunar soil, and relayed the data back to earth. In 1972 *Luna 20* returned to earth with a cargo of moon rocks. *(c) To the Planets.* The Soviets sent several spaceships to the planets Mars and Venus and in 1975 achieved two soft landings on Venus. The more recent ships transmitted back scientific data such as the surface temperature and atmospheric composition of these planets.

What great discoveries lie ahead?
(*Palmer in the Springfield [Mo.] Leader and Press*)

2. Manned Flights. The Soviets achieved a number of space firsts. In 1961 *Vostok 1* orbited the earth once, carrying the world's first cosmonaut, *Yuri Gagarin.* In 1963 *Vostok 6* completed a 48-orbit flight carrying the first woman cosmonaut, *Valentina Tereshkova.* In 1964 *Voskhod 1* became history's first multipassenger space capsule. In 1965 a cosmonaut left *Voskhod 2* and achieved the first space walk. In 1971 the Soviets orbited *Salyut 1,* the first unmanned space station, and later sent a three-man team there to perform scientific tests. In 1979 a two-man Soviet team returned to earth after having lived in the *Salyut 6* space station for 175 days.

MAJOR AMERICAN EFFORTS IN SPACE

1. Unmanned Flights. (*a*) *Around the Earth.* The United States placed many satellites into orbit—the *Explorer* series to increase our scientific knowledge of space; *Transit* satellites to assist airplane and ship pilots in navigation; *Telstar, Early Bird,* and *Intelsat,* all privately financed satellites, to build a global telecommunications system; and the *Tiros* series to gather weather data. (*b*) *To the Moon.* The United States sent a number of spacecraft to the moon; some landed on the moon's surface and sent back thousands of photographs. (*c*) *To the Planets.* The United States sent to Mars and Venus a number of *Mariner* spaceships which sent back pictures and scientific data. In 1973 *Pioneer 10* ended a 21-month journey to Jupiter and provided photographs of that outer planet. Pioneer 10, carrying a pictorial plaque, was expected to escape from our solar system and travel into the Milky Way—where it might be seen by other intelligent beings, if any exist. In 1974 *Mariner 10* reached and photographed Mercury, the planet closest to our sun. In 1976 two *Viking* vehicles reached the vicinity of Mars and each placed a landing craft on that planet's surface. The

Viking landers sent back photographs of the terrain, data regarding the atmosphere, and analyses of the Martian soil. In 1979, after a six-and-a-half-year trip, *Pioneer 11* swept past and sent back data about the rings, moons, and atmosphere of the planet Saturn.

2. Manned Flights. At first behind, the United States eventually caught up with and then surpassed the Soviets in the number and complexity of manned flights. In 1962 the United States sent *Friendship 7* to circle the earth three times with America's first orbiting astronaut, *John Glenn*. Thereafter, the United States orbited numerous multipassenger space vehicles and American astronauts practiced spacewalking, then docking, or the joining together, of spacecraft in orbit, and finally guiding a lunar module or landing craft to leave and then return to the command, or "mother," ship.

In 1969, with the 11th flight of the *Project Apollo* series, the United States achieved an historic first. While *Michael Collins* orbited the moon in the "mother" ship *Columbia*, *Neil Armstrong* and *Edwin Aldrin* descended to the moon's surface in the lunar module *Eagle*. Armstrong, the first man to set foot on the moon, spoke the historic words, "That's one small step for a man, one giant leap for mankind." The two astronauts gathered rock samples, set up scientific experiments, stationed a plaque saying, "We came in peace for all mankind," and then ascended to the "mother" ship. The three men then returned safely to earth. Five subsequent Apollo flights repeated the moon-landing triumph.

In 1973 the United States placed into orbit its first space station, *Skylab*. Successive teams of American astronauts have lived in the space station, performing experiments and gathering data.

(In 1975 the *Apollo-Soyuz Test Project*—a joint American-Soviet space venture—took place successfully.)

3. Future Space Goals. President Nixon endorsed proposals for an unmanned "grand tour" of the outer, or more distant, planets by the late 1970's and for a manned landing on Mars by the mid-1980's. He asserted that in the making of space history "this nation means to play a major role." However, NASA has faced a cutback of federal funds and has slowed work on new space projects. As a result, many scientific and technical workers have been dismissed, and experienced space research and production teams have been broken up.

NASA nevertheless for the 1980's has been working on a *space shuttle*—a manned vehicle that can be placed into orbit and then can glide back safely to earth. Because it can be reused for many trips, the space shuttle will be less costly than previous single-use orbiting vehicles.

Should America maintain its efforts in the exploration of space?

18. American-Soviet Relations Follow a Fluctuating Pattern

Since World War II, relations between the United States and Russia have been generally unfriendly. Nevertheless, relations have varied from periods of great tension to periods of comparative calm.

1947–1953: PERIOD OF TENSION

While Stalin ruled, Russia pursued a "hard line" toward the free world, and the United States responded by its policy of containment. Evidences of tension were (1) Truman Doctrine (1947), (2) Berlin Blockade (1948–1949), (3) creation of NATO (1949), and (4) Korean War (1950–1953).

1954–1959: COMPARATIVE CALM

In the years after Stalin's death, Khrushchev espoused peaceful coexistence, and relations between Russia and the United States improved.

1. Summit Conference of 1955. President Eisenhower met at Geneva with the leaders of Great Britain, France, and Russia. They discussed East-West problems in a calm and friendly atmosphere but reached no settlements.

2. Scientific and Cultural Exchanges. In 1958 the United States and Russia inaugurated a scientific and cultural exchange program. Since then, reciprocal visits have been made by athletes, scholars, concert artists, orchestras, ballet groups, writers, and scientists.

3. Khrushchev's Visit to the United States. In 1959 Khrushchev visited the United States and received a friendly reception. Khrushchev showed great interest in many facets of American life. He met with President Eisenhower, and the two men initiated plans for another summit conference.

1960–1962: ANOTHER PERIOD OF TENSION

1. U-2 Incident and the Summit Conference of 1960. Two weeks before a new summit conference was to be held in Paris, the Soviets shot down, deep inside Russian territory, an unarmed American U-2 reconnaissance plane. The Soviets, who maintained an extensive espionage system in the West, had known of such U-2 flights but had not previously protested against them. In Paris, Khrushchev accused America of aggression, vilified Eisenhower, and demanded an apology. Eisenhower denied the charge of aggression and refused to apologize. The summit meeting was dead.

2. Building of the Berlin Wall (1961)

3. Cuban Missile Base Crisis (1962)

1963–1968: COMPARATIVE CALM

Following the peaceful settlement of the Cuban crisis and the deepening of the Soviet-Chinese split, Russian-American relations improved.

1. Limited Nuclear Test Ban Treaty. In 1963 the United States and Russia agreed to a ban on all but underground nuclear tests. This was the first agreement to emerge from 18 years of East-West disarmament negotiations.

2. Hot Line. In 1963 Russia and the United States established a "hot line," or emergency communications link, between Washington and Moscow to reduce the risk of war by blunder or miscalculation.

3. Wheat Sale. With Russia suffering from a poor grain harvest in 1963, the United States sold substantial quantities of wheat to the Soviet Union.

4. Consular Treaty. In 1964 the United States and Russia signed their first bilateral treaty. It *(a)* granted diplomatic immunity to consular officials and *(b)* required that consular officials be informed of and granted access to any of their country's citizens placed under arrest.

5. Nuclear Nonproliferation Treaty. In 1968 the United States and Russia agreed upon a treaty to outlaw the spread of nuclear weapons.

1969 TO 1980: COMPARATIVE CALM AND A SEARCH FOR DÉTENTE

Presidents Nixon, Ford, and Carter, and Soviet Communist party chief Brezhnev each voiced support for moving American-Soviet relations into a new era of détente. Secretary of State Kissinger defined détente as the "process of managing relations with a potentially hostile country in order to preserve peace while maintaining our vital interests." A Soviet expert on foreign policy explained that détente "sets limits on what each side can do without risking war and gets officials concerned—Soviet and American—talking with each other."

SUCCESS OF DÉTENTE

1. Four-Power Agreement on Berlin (1971)

2. Nixon's Journey to Moscow. In early 1972, despite Soviet-American tensions over Vietnam, President Nixon journeyed to Moscow to a summit meeting with Soviet Premier Kosygin and Communist party chief Brezhnev. Nixon received a restrained but correct welcome and his time was occupied chiefly with business-like negotiations. Nixon and the Soviet leaders signed a number of significant accords: *(a) on space*—to cooperate in 1975 in a joint Soviet-American docking and flight of manned spacecraft, *(b) on health*—to coordinate Soviet-American research on cancer, heart disease, and public health, *(c) on incidents at sea*—to set rules so that Soviet and American naval vessels operating near each other will avoid collisions, *(d) on environment and technology*—to cooperate in the study of pollution problems and in other scientific research, *(e) on trade*—to establish a joint commission to resolve trade problems so as to increase Soviet-American trade, and *(f) on nuclear arms*—to limit ABM sites and "freeze" current offensive-missile arsenals.

3. Strategic Arms Limitation Talks; Two SALT I Accords (1972)

4. Brezhnev's Visit to the United States. In 1973 Soviet Communist party chief Brezhnev visited the United States, projected a spirit of friendship, and spoke to the American people via television. He and President Nixon signed a number of accords: to make every effort to avoid a military confrontation, to expand air passenger service between the United States and the Soviet Union, to promote trade, to continue cultural and educational exchanges, and to cooperate in oceanography, transportation, and agricultural research.

5. Helsinki Pact (1975). Leaders of the United States, Canada, and 33 European

"Détente."
(*Drawing by Richter;* © *1974 The New Yorker Magazine, Inc.*)

nations met at Helsinki, Finland, to conclude the *Conference on Security and Cooperation in Europe.* They signed a charter containing two major provisions:

a. Accepting as inviolate the post–World War II boundaries in Europe. By this provision the Western powers held that they were being realistic—acknowledging a situation they could not alter peaceably. Russia was jubilant because this provision formally recognized Soviet territorial gains in Europe, the division of Germany into two nations, and Soviet domination of eastern Europe. This provision was hailed as a personal triumph for Soviet Communist party head Brezhnev.

b. Agreeing in principle to further human rights. By this provision the Soviet Union and the satellite Communist nations promised to ease the movement of individuals across frontiers, assist in the reunion of separated families, reduce restrictions on journalists, and increase East-West cultural exchanges. Western observers wondered, however, whether these promises would be kept.

DISILLUSIONMENT ABOUT DÉTENTE

1. United States. *(a)* Members of Congress protested the internal Soviet crackdown on dissident intellectuals and minority groups. Congressmembers pointed to the forced exile in 1974 of the Russian author and dissenter *Alexander Solzhenitsyn.* In his book *The Gulag Archipelago,* published only in the West, the famed Nobel Prize winner documented the history of Soviet prison camp tyranny and asserted that tyranny was an integral part of the Soviet system. Congressmembers also pointed to Soviet harassment of persons, chiefly Jews, seeking to leave the Soviet Union. Would-be emigrants, upon making their intentions known, were fired from their jobs, expelled from their living quarters, kept waiting for months and years enmeshed in bureaucratic red tape, and—if permitted to leave—required to pay exorbitant exit fees. In 1974 Congress approved a trade bill that permitted trade benefits for the Soviets on condition that they allow emigrants to leave the Soviet Union promptly and without harassment. *(b)* American foreign policy experts concluded that Soviet words and actions in the 1973 Arab-Israeli war were indistinguishable from the bitterest of cold war days. *(c)* American military leaders pointed out that Russia had accelerated its building of offensive nuclear weapons. Although permitted by the 1972 SALT I accord, these additional offensive nuclear weapons did not indicate peaceful intentions. *(d)* American critics of détente pointed out that the Soviet Union had provided the massive weapons used by Hanoi to triumph in South Vietnam and by the pro-Soviet faction and the Cubans to triumph in Angola. They further quoted Brezhnev's statement in 1976 that the Soviet Union sees détente as "the way to create more favorable conditions for peaceful socialist and Communist construction" and that détente does not "abolish or alter the laws of class struggle." American critics of détente claimed that it was a "one-way street" benefiting only the Soviet Union. *(e)* After taking office in 1977, President Carter announced that one aspect of his administration's foreign policy would be concern for human rights. Accordingly the United States charged Czechoslovakia with violating the Helsinki Pact provision on human rights by harassment of Czechoslovak dissidents. Some 300 writers, journalists, scientists, and former political figures had called for internal civil liberties and cultural freedom by signing and publicizing a document called *Charter 77*. The United States also stated that the Soviet Union would be in conflict with "accepted international standards of human rights" by continued efforts to silence the world-renowned dissident, atomic scientist, and 1975 Nobel Peace Prize winner *Andrei Sakharov*. (In 1980 the Soviet government, to silence Sakharov, removed him from Moscow and sentenced him to "internal exile" in a city closed to foreigners.) The President, however, explained to Moscow that his human rights campaign was not limited to Soviet-bloc nations but was global in scope, was not intended to threaten Soviet interests, was not designed to bring back the cold war—but was a reaffirmation of fundamental American values.

2. Soviet Union. *(a)* Soviet trade experts protested that the American Congress, despite administration promises, had long delayed a sweeping trade agreement. The Soviets wanted substantial American credits and loans with which to purchase American machinery and technology, pay for imports of American grain, and develop Siberian oil and gas resources. The Soviets also wanted the United States to tax Soviet imports at the lowest regular tariff rate—such treatment being known as "most-favored-nation" status. The Soviets resented the 1974 legislation passed by Congress which limited Export-Import Bank loans to Russia and tied trade benefits to the easing of Russian emigration policies. In early 1975 the Soviet Union canceled the 1972 Soviet-American trade accord. *(b)* Soviet political leaders objected to efforts by the American Congress to change Soviet policies regarding dissident intellectuals and minority groups. These policies, the Russians insisted, dealt with internal Soviet matters beyond the scope of American concern and would be maintained in the interests of the Communist state. The Soviets also expressed resentment against President Carter's human rights campaign as unwarranted interference with internal Soviet policies. At the 1977–1978 Belgrade Conference, held to review compliance with the Helsinki Pact, the Soviet Union warned the United States against raising human rights issues as dangerous to the cause of détente. With unanimous consent required for statements at Belgrade, the Soviet Union was able to compel the Conference to omit from its summary communiqué any mention of human rights. *(c)* Communist foreign policy experts complained that the United States was seeking to erode Soviet influence in the Arab Mideast.

An End to Détente? With the Soviet invasion of Afghanistan (1979–1980) and the American responses—delaying consideration of the SALT II Treaty, restricting grain and high-technology exports to the Soviet Union, offering increased military aid to Pakistan, and calling for a boycott of the summer Olympic Games at Moscow—observers believed that the two superpowers were abandoning détente and returning to the tensions of the cold war.

MULTIPLE-CHOICE QUESTIONS

1. The *least* important factor in explaining the destructiveness of nuclear weapons is their great (1) heat (2) radioactivity (3) blast (4) weight.
2. The Baruch Plan for international control of atomic energy did *not* propose (1) an international authority in which no nation would have the veto power (2) unlimited inspection (3) stockpiling of atomic bombs (4) sharing American atomic know-how with other nations.
3. The Baruch Plan never went into effect because of (1) the UN's lack of interest in the problem (2) American opposition to international control (3) a Russian veto in the UN Security Council (4) Britain's refusal to cooperate.
4. The *chief* factor that long blocked agreement between Russia and the United States on a nuclear test ban was the dispute regarding (1) admission of Red China to the test ban conference (2) the war in Vietnam (3) effective measures of inspection and control (4) the building of the Berlin Wall.
5. The limited nuclear test ban treaty permits testing (1) in the atmosphere (2) in space (3) below ground (4) underwater.
6. A leading European nation that refused to sign the limited nuclear test ban treaty was (1) Communist China (2) Czechoslovakia (3) France (4) Italy.
7. The "proliferation" of atomic weapons refers to their (1) spread to many nations (2) complexity (3) radiation (4) use to produce electricity.
8. In regard to the SALT I accords, which statement is *most* valid? (1) They did not provide for limiting ABM systems. (2) They called for on-site inspection to prevent violations. (3) They enabled the United States and Russia to significantly reduce their military defense spending. (4) They did not call for any reduction in existing offensive missile arsenals.
9. The SALT I accords are significant because they (1) provided an example of UN effectiveness (2) provided for joint American-Soviet space flights (3) are a first step toward limiting a nuclear missile arms race (4) ended the cold war.
10. In 1957 the first man-made satellite was placed into orbit around the earth by (1) a UN team of scientists (2) Russia (3) the United States (4) Great Britain.
11. Yuri Gagarin of the Soviet Union was the first man to (1) design a space vehicle (2) achieve a space flight (3) die on a space flight (4) take close-up photographs of the moon.
12. The chief object of Project Apollo was to (1) send space teams to the moon and back (2) gather data about Venus and Mars (3) establish a worldwide telecommunications system (4) improve the forecasting of weather.
13. "We came in peace for all mankind" was said (1) by President Carter and Soviet leader Brezhnev at their 1979 Vienna meeting (2) by American and Soviet negotiators at the SALT II meetings (3) on a plaque left on the moon by the two American astronauts who first set foot on the moon (4) by Alexander Solzhenitsyn, the Russian author and dissenter, who spoke for his family upon being exiled from Russia.

14. The "hot line" and the nuclear test ban treaty are indications that (1) the alliance systems headed by the Soviet Union and the United States are being strengthened (2) to some extent, cold war tensions between the United States and the Soviet Union could be eased (3) the United States is relying more heavily on its policy of containment (4) the great powers are seeking closer cooperation on the peaceful uses of space.

15. Détente is *best* explained as (1) an American policy of protection for intellectuals and minority groups (2) a Russian policy of seeking large loans and expanding trade (3) a policy of both the United States and the Soviet Union to reduce tensions and improve relations between the two countries. (4) a joint American-Soviet policy to impose peace terms upon the Middle East.

16. Which event indicated a Soviet "hard line" toward the West? (1) establishing the "hot line" communications link (2) signing the limited nuclear test ban treaty (3) placing missiles in Cuba (4) differing with China regarding peaceful coexistence

17. In recent years United States involvement in world crises has *most* clearly shown that (1) solutions to major international problems require the cooperation of the major world powers (2) isolation is the only way to assure the safety of the United States (3) international affairs have come to be dominated by the small nations (4) meaningful settlements can only come about through the UN.

18. Based on both world and United States history, which prediction would be easiest to defend? (1) Europe will have a single economic system by 1985. (2) Unsettled areas of Africa will provide space for the expanding population of North America. (3) Man's problems and the need to solve those problems will grow at an ever-increasing rate. (4) As more people become literate, conflict among nations will decrease.

ESSAY QUESTIONS

1. While we continue to develop the peaceful uses of atomic energy, we must find a way to deal with the problem of more and more countries possessing nuclear weapons. (a) Mention *one* military development in nuclear energy since 1945 *and one* development of nuclear energy for a peaceful use. (b) Name *two* international agreements regarding nuclear energy or missiles. Evaluate *each* agreement named as a means of reducing the possibility of nuclear warfare.

2. Science has taught us how to put the atom to work, but to make it work for good instead of evil is a problem in human relations. (a) Prove briefly that science has "put the atom to work." (b) Give *two* facts to show how the atom can "work for good instead of for evil." (c) Show why the major world problem today is not progress in science, but the relationship of human beings to each other.

3. Give *two* reasons for agreeing or disagreeing with *each* of the following statements: (a) It would have been better for mankind if nuclear energy had never been discovered. (b) The development of nuclear energy has increased the military security of the United States. (c) The SALT I accords were a major step toward world peace. (d) The space age will affect humanity as much as did the 16th-century age of discovery and exploration. (e) If detente is to succeed, the United States and the Soviet Union must place the goal of world peace ahead of all other national interests.

4. United States foreign policy since 1945 has had *three* specific goals: (a) defense of the United States against attack (b) the maintenance of world peace (c) the promotion of economic and social welfare abroad. Discuss *two* specific means used by the United States in an effort to accomplish *each* of these goals.

5. To answer this question, refer to the cartoon entitled "The course of human events" on page 682. (a) Briefly state the major idea or concept presented in this cartoon. (b) Name *two* foreign policy crises of the past and explain how *each* was solved. (c) Name *two* foreign policy crises of the present and indicate your ideas of what the solutions might be. (d) In your opinion what might be *one* foreign policy crisis in the near future? Give *one* reason to support your opinion.

THE DECLARATION
OF INDEPENDENCE

Unanimously Adopted by the Thirteen United States of America
Through Their Representatives Assembled in Congress, July 4, 1776

Introduction: An Address to Humanity*

When, in the course of human events, it becomes necessary for one people to dissolve the political bands which have connected them with another, and to assume, among the powers of the earth, the separate and equal station to which the laws of nature and of nature's God entitle them, a decent respect to the opinions of mankind requires that they should declare the causes which impel them to the separation.

Democratic Philosophy: Rights of Individuals
and the Purpose of Government

We hold these truths to be self-evident: That all men are created equal; that they are endowed by their Creator with certain unalienable rights; that among these are life, liberty, and the pursuit of happiness.

That to secure these rights, governments are instituted among men, deriving their just powers from the consent of the governed.

That whenever any form of government becomes destructive of these ends, it is the right of the people to alter or to abolish it, and to institute new government, laying its foundation on such principles and organizing its powers in such form as to them shall seem most likely to effect their safety and happiness. Prudence, indeed, will dictate that governments long established should not be changed for light and transient causes; and, accordingly, all experience hath shown that mankind are more disposed to suffer, while evils are sufferable, than to right themselves by abolishing the forms to which they are accustomed. But when a long train of abuses and usurpations, pursuing invariably the same object, evinces a design to reduce them under absolute despotism, it is their right, it is their duty, to throw off such government, and to provide new guards for their future security.

Grievances Against Great Britain:
Reasons for Separation

Such has been the patient sufferance of these colonies; and such is now the necessity which constrains them to alter their former systems of government. The history of the present King of Great Britain is a history of repeated injuries and usurpations, all having in direct object the establishment of an absolute tyranny over these states. To prove this, let facts be submitted to a candid world:

* The headings are not part of the Declaration of Independence but have been provided to assist the reader.

He has refused his assent to laws the most wholesome and necessary for the public good.

He has forbidden his governors to pass laws of immediate and pressing importance unless suspended in their operation till his assent should be obtained; and, when so suspended, he has utterly neglected to attend to them.

He has refused to pass other laws for the accommodation of large districts of people unless those people would relinquish the right of representation in the legislature, a right inestimable to them and formidable to tyrants only.

He has called together legislative bodies at places unusual, uncomfortable, and distant from the depository of their public records, for the sole purpose of fatiguing them into compliance with his measures.

He has dissolved representative houses repeatedly for opposing with manly firmness his invasions on the rights of the people.

He has refused for a long time, after such dissolutions, to cause others to be elected; whereby the legislative powers, incapable of annihilation, have returned to the people at large for their exercise; the state remaining, in the meantime, exposed to all the dangers of invasion from without and convulsions within.

He has endeavoured to prevent the population of these states; for that purpose obstructing the laws for naturalization of foreigners, refusing to pass others to encourage their migrations hither, and raising the conditions of new appropriations of lands.

He has obstructed the administration of justice by refusing his assent to laws for establishing judiciary powers.

He has made judges dependent on his will alone for the tenure of their offices and the amount and payment of their salaries.

He has erected a multitude of new offices, and sent hither swarms of officers to harass our people and eat out their substance.

He has kept among us, in times of peace, standing armies, without the consent of our legislatures.

He has affected to render the military independent of and superior to the civil power.

He has combined with others to subject us to a jurisdiction foreign to our constitution and unacknowledged by our laws; giving his assent to their acts of pretended legislation:

For quartering large bodies of armed troops among us;

For protecting them, by a mock trial, from punishment for any murders which they should commit on the inhabitants of these states;

For cutting off our trade with all parts of the world;

For imposing taxes on us without our consent;

For depriving us in many cases of the benefits of trial by jury;

For transporting us beyond seas to be tried for pretended offences;

For abolishing the free system of English laws in a neighbouring province, establishing therein an arbitrary government and enlarging its boundaries so as to render it at once an example and fit instrument for introducing the same absolute rule in these colonies;

For taking away our charters, abolishing our most valuable laws, and altering fundamentally the forms of our governments;

For suspending our own legislatures, and declaring themselves invested with power to legislate for us in all cases whatsoever.

He has abdicated government here by declaring us out of his protection and waging war against us.

He has plundered our seas, ravaged our coasts, burnt our towns, and destroyed the lives of our people.

He is, at this time, transporting large armies of foreign mercenaries to complete the works of death, desolation, and tyranny already begun with circumstances of cruelty and perfidy scarcely paralleled in the most barbarous ages, and totally unworthy the head of a civilized nation.

He has constrained our fellow citizens, taken captive on the high seas, to bear arms against their country, to become the executioners of their friends and brethren, or to fall themselves by their hands.

He has excited domestic insurrections among us, and has endeavoured to bring on the inhabitants of our frontiers the merciless Indian savages, whose known rule of warfare is an undistinguished destruction of all ages, sexes, and conditions.

In every stage of these oppressions we have petitioned for redress in the most humble terms. Our repeated petitions have been answered only by repeated injury. A prince whose character is thus marked by every act which may define a tyrant is unfit to be the ruler of a free people.

Nor have we been wanting in attentions to our British brethren. We have warned them from time to time of attempts by their legislature to extend an unwarrantable jurisdiction over us. We have reminded them of the circumstances of our emigration and settlement here. We have appealed to their native justice and magnanimity, and we have conjured them by the ties of our common kindred to disavow these usurpations, which would inevitably interrupt our connections and correspondence. They too have been deaf to the voice of justice and of consanguinity. We must therefore acquiesce in the necessity which denounces our separation, and hold them, as we hold the rest of mankind, enemies in war, in peace friends.

Conclusion: Dissolution of Bonds to Great Britain and Affirmation of Independence

We, therefore, the representatives of the United States of America, in General Congress assembled, appealing to the Supreme Judge of the world for the rectitude of our intentions, do, in the name and by authority of the good people of these colonies, solemnly publish and declare: that these united colonies are, and of right ought to be, free and independent states; that they are absolved from all allegiance to the British crown, and that all political connection between them and the state of Great Britain is, and ought to be, totally dissolved; and that, as free and independent states, they have full power to levy war, conclude peace, contract alliances, establish commerce, and to do all other acts and things which independent states may of right do.

And for the support of this Declaration, with a firm reliance on the protection of divine Providence, we mutually pledge to each other our lives, our fortunes, and our sacred honor.

Signed by John Hancock of Massachusetts as President of the Congress and by the Fifty-Five Other Representatives of the Thirteen United States of America

THE CONSTITUTION OF THE UNITED STATES

Preamble: Purposes of the Constitution*

We, the people of the United States, in order to form a more perfect Union, establish justice, insure domestic tranquillity, provide for the common defense, promote the general welfare, and secure the blessings of liberty to ourselves and our posterity, do ordain and establish this Constitution for the United States of America.

Article I. The Legislative Branch†

Section 1. The Bicameral Congress

All legislative powers herein granted shall be vested in a Congress of the United States, which shall consist of a Senate and House of Representatives.

Section 2. The House of Representatives

1. Representatives: Election and Term of Office. The House of Representatives shall be composed of members chosen every second year by the people of the several states, and the electors in each state shall have the qualifications requisite for electors of the most numerous branch of the state legislature.

2. Requirements Set for Representatives. No person shall be a Representative who shall not have attained to the age of twenty-five years, and been seven years a citizen of the United States, and who shall not, when elected, be an inhabitant of that state in which he shall be chosen.

3. Apportionment of Representatives Among the States. Representatives [*and direct taxes*] shall be apportioned among the several states which may be included within this Union, according to their respective numbers, [*which shall be determined by adding to the whole number of free persons, including those bound to service for a term of years, and excluding Indians not taxed, three-fifths of all other persons.*] The actual enumeration shall be made within three years after the first meeting of the Congress of the United States, and within every subsequent term of ten years, in such manner as they shall by law direct. The number of Representatives shall not exceed one for every 30,000, but each state shall have at least one Representative; [*and until such enumeration shall be made, the state of New Hampshire shall be entitled to choose three; Massachusetts, eight; Rhode Island and Providence Plantations, one; Connecticut, five; New York, six; New Jersey, four; Pennsylvania, eight; Delaware, one; Maryland, six; Virginia, ten; North Carolina, five; South Carolina, five; and Georgia, three.*]

---

* The headings—for the Articles, Sections, and clauses—are not part of the Constitution but have been added to assist the reader.

† Those portions of the Constitution no longer in effect are printed in italics and enclosed in brackets.

4. Filling House Vacancies. When vacancies happen in the representation from any state, the executive authority thereof shall issue writs of election to fill such vacancies.

5. Special Powers: Election of House Officers and Impeachment. The House of Representatives shall choose their Speaker and other officers; and shall have the sole power of impeachment.

Section 3. The Senate

1. Senators: Number, Election, and Term of Office. The Senate of the United States shall be composed of two Senators from each state, [*chosen by the legislature thereof,*] for six years, and each Senator shall have one vote.

2. Expiration of Terms of Senators; Filling Senate Vacancies. [*Immediately after they shall be assembled in consequence of the first election, they shall be divided as equally as may be into three classes. The seats of the Senators of the first class shall be vacated at the expiration of the second year, of the second class at the expiration of the fourth year, and of the third class at the expiration of the sixth year,*] so that one-third may be chosen every second year; [*and if vacancies happen by resignation, or otherwise, during the recess of the legislature of any state, the executive thereof may make temporary appointments until the next meeting of the legislature, which shall then fill such vacancies.*]

3. Requirements Set for Senators. No person shall be a Senator who shall not have attained to the age of thirty years, and been nine years a citizen of the United States, and who shall not, when elected, be an inhabitant of that state for which he shall be chosen.

4. Vice President as President of the Senate. The Vice President of the United States shall be president of the Senate, but shall have no vote, unless they be equally divided.

5. Other Senate Officers. The Senate shall choose their other officers, and also a president *pro tempore*, in the absence of the Vice President, or when he shall exercise the office of President of the United States.

6. The Senate as Jury in Impeachment Cases. The Senate shall have the sole power to try all impeachments. When sitting for that purpose, they shall be on oath or affirmation. When the President of the United States is tried, the Chief Justice shall preside; and no person shall be convicted without the concurrence of two-thirds of the members present.

7. Punishment in Cases of Impeachment. Judgment in cases of impeachment shall not extend further than to removal from office, and disqualification to hold and enjoy any office of honor, trust, or profit under the United States; but the party convicted shall nevertheless be liable and subject to indictment, trial, judgment, and punishment, according to law.

Section 4. Congressional Elections and Sessions

1. Regulations for Congressional Elections. The times, places, and manner of holding elections for Senators and Representatives shall be prescribed in each state by the legislature thereof; but the Congress may at any time by law make or alter such regulations, except as to the places of choosing Senators.

2. Sessions of Congress. The Congress shall assemble at least once in every year, [*and such meeting shall be on the first Monday in December,*] unless they shall by law appoint a different day.

Section 5. Organization and Rules of Each House of Congress

1. Control Over Members: Election Returns and Attendance. Each house shall be the judge of the elections, returns, and qualifications of its own members, and a majority of each shall constitute a quorum to do business; but a smaller number may adjourn from day to day, and may be authorized to compel the attendance of absent members, in such manner, and under such penalties, as each house may provide.

2. Rules of Procedure; Further Control Over Members. Each house may determine the rules of its proceedings, punish its members for disorderly behavior, and with the concurrence of two-thirds, expel a member.

3. Journal or Record of Proceedings. Each house shall keep a journal of its proceedings, and from time to time publish the same, excepting such parts as may in their judgment require secrecy; and the yeas and nays of the members of either house on any question shall, at the desire of one-fifth of those present, be entered on the journal.

4. Adjournment. Neither house, during the session of Congress, shall, without the consent of the other, adjourn for more than three days, nor to any other place than that in which the two houses shall be sitting.

Section 6. Congressional Privileges and Restrictions

1. Salaries and Special Privileges. The Senators and Representatives shall receive a compensation for their services, to be ascertained by law and paid out of the Treasury of the United States. They shall in all cases, except treason, felony, and breach of the peace, be privileged from arrest during their attendance at the session of their respective houses, and in going to and returning from the same; and for any speech or debate in either house, they shall not be questioned in any other place.

2. Restrictions. No Senator or Representative shall, during the time for which he was elected, be appointed to any civil office under the authority of the United States, which shall have been created, or the emoluments whereof shall have been increased, during such time; and no person holding any office under the United States shall be a member of either house during his continuance in office.

Section 7. Procedures for Passing Bills

1. Revenue Bills. All bills for raising revenue shall originate in the House of Representatives; but the Senate may propose or concur with amendments as on other bills.

2. Bills Subject to Presidential Approval or Veto. Every bill which shall have passed the House of Representatives and the Senate, shall, before it become a law, be presented to the President of the United States; if he approve, he shall sign it, but if not, he shall return it, with his objections to that house in which it shall have originated, who shall enter the objections at large on their journal, and proceed to reconsider it. If after such reconsideration two-thirds of that house shall agree to pass the bill, it shall be sent, together with the objections, to the other house, by which it shall likewise be reconsidered, and, if approved by two-thirds of that house, it shall become a law. But in all such cases the votes of both houses shall be determined by yeas and nays, and the names of the persons voting for and against the bill shall be entered on the journal of each house respectively. If any bill shall not be returned by the President within ten days (Sundays excepted) after it shall have been presented to him, the same shall be a law, in like manner as if he had signed it, unless the Congress by their adjournment prevent its return, in which case it shall not be a law.

3. Other Congressional Actions Subject to Presidential Approval or Veto. Every order, resolution, or vote to which the concurrence of the Senate and House of Representatives may be necessary (except on a question of adjournment) shall be presented to the President of the United States; and before the same shall take effect, shall be approved by him, or being disapproved by him, shall be repassed by two-thirds of the Senate and House of Representatives, according to the rules and limitations prescribed in the case of a bill.

Section 8. Powers Granted to Congress

1–17. Delegated or Enumerated Powers. The Congress shall have power

1. To lay and collect taxes, duties, imposts, and excises, to pay the debts and provide for the common defense and general welfare of the United States; but all duties, imposts, and excises shall be uniform throughout the United States;

2. To borrow money on the credit of the United States;

3. To regulate commerce with foreign nations, and among the several states, and with the Indian tribes;

4. To establish a uniform rule of naturalization, and uniform laws on the subject of bankruptcies throughout the United States;

5. To coin money, regulate the value thereof, and of foreign coin, and fix the standard of weights and measures;

6. To provide for the punishment of counterfeiting the securities and current coin of the United States;

7. To establish post offices and post roads;

8. To promote the progress of science and useful arts by securing for limited times to authors and inventors the exclusive right to their respective writings and discoveries;

9. To constitute tribunals inferior to the Supreme Court;

10. To define and punish piracies and felonies committed on the high seas and offenses against the law of nations;

11. To declare war, [*grant letters of marque and reprisal,*] and make rules concerning captures on land and water;

12. To raise and support armies, but no appropriation of money to that use shall be for a longer term than two years;

13. To provide and maintain a navy;

14. To make rules for the government and regulation of the land and naval forces;

15. To provide for calling forth the militia to execute the laws of the Union, suppress insurrections, and repel invasions;

16. To provide for organizing, arming, and disciplining the militia, and for governing such part of them as may be employed in the service of the United States, reserving to the states, respectively, the appointment of the officers, and the authority of training the militia according to the discipline prescribed by Congress;

17. To exercise exclusive legislation in all cases whatsoever, over such

district (not exceeding ten miles square) as may, by cession of particular states, and the acceptance of Congress, become the seat of government of the United States, and to exercise like authority over all places purchased by the consent of the legislature of the state in which the same shall be, for the erection of forts, magazines, arsenals, dock-yards, and other needful buildings;—and

18. Implied Powers: The Elastic Clause. To make all laws which shall be necessary and proper for carrying into execution the foregoing powers, and all other powers vested by this Constitution in the government of the United States, or in any department or officer thereof.

Section 9. Powers Denied to the Federal Government

1. May Not Interfere With the Slave Trade Prior to 1808. [*The migration or importation of such persons as any of the states now existing shall think proper to admit shall not be prohibited by the Congress prior to the year 1808; but a tax or duty may be imposed on such importation, not exceeding ten dollars for each person.*]

2. May Not Suspend the Writ of Habeas Corpus Except in Emergency. The privilege of the writ of habeas corpus shall not be suspended, unless when in cases of rebellion or invasion the public safety may require it.

3. May Not Enact a Bill of Attainder or an Ex Post Facto Law. No bill of attainder or ex post facto law shall be passed.

4. May Not Levy a Direct Tax Except in Proportion to Population. [*No capitation or other direct tax shall be laid, unless in proportion to the census or enumeration herein before directed to be taken.*]

5. May Not Levy an Export Tax. No tax or duty shall be laid on articles exported from any state.

6. May Not Favor the Ports of One State Over Those of Another. No preference shall be given by any regulation of commerce or revenue to the ports of one state over those of another: nor shall vessels bound to, or from, one state, be obliged to enter, clear, or pay duties in another.

7. May Not Spend Federal Funds Without Congressional Approval and Public Accounting. No money shall be drawn from the Treasury, but in consequence of appropriations made by law; and a regular statement and account of the receipts and expenditures of all public money shall be published from time to time.

8. May Not Grant Titles of Nobility. No title of nobility shall be granted by the United States; and no person holding any office of profit or trust under them, shall, without the consent of the Congress, accept of any present, emolument, office, or title, of any kind whatever, from any king, prince, or foreign state.

Section 10. Powers Denied to the States

1. Unconditional Denial of Various Powers. No state shall enter into any treaty, alliance, or confederation; grant letters of marque and reprisal; coin money; emit bills of credit; make anything but gold and silver coin a tender in payment of debts; pass any bill of attainder, ex post facto law, or law impairing the obligation of contracts, or grant any title of nobility.

2. Conditional Denial: May Not Levy Import and Export Taxes Without the Consent of Congress. No state shall, without the consent of the Congress, lay any imposts or duties on imports or exports, except what may be absolutely necessary for executing its inspection laws; and the net produce of all duties and imposts, laid by any state on imports or exports, shall be for the use of the Treasury of the United States; and all such laws shall be subject to the revision and control of the Congress.

3. Conditional Denial: May Not Prepare For and Wage War (Except in Emergency) Without the Consent of Congress. No state shall, without the consent of Congress, lay any duty of tonnage, keep troops, or ships of war in time of peace, enter into any agreement or compact with another state, or with a foreign power, or engage in war, unless actually invaded, or in such imminent danger as will not admit of delay.

Article II. The Executive Branch

Section 1. The President and the Presidential Office

1. Term of Office. The executive power shall be vested in a President of the United States of America. He shall hold his office during the term of four years, and together with the Vice President, chosen for the same term, be elected as follows:

2. Number of Presidential Electors per State. Each state shall appoint, in such manner as the legislature thereof may direct, a number of electors, equal to the whole number of Senators and Representatives to which the state may be entitled in the Congress; but no Senator or Representative, or person holding an office of trust or profit under the United States, shall be appointed an elector.

3. Election Procedures of the Electoral College and Congress. [*The electors shall meet in their respective states, and vote by ballot for two persons, of whom one at least shall not be an inhabitant of the same state with themselves. And they shall make a list of all the persons voted for, and of the number of votes for each; which list they shall sign and certify, and transmit sealed to the seat of the government of the United States, directed to the president of the Senate. The president of the Senate shall, in the presence of the Senate and House of Representatives, open all the certificates, and the votes shall then be counted. The persons having the greatest number of votes shall be the President, if such number be a majority of the whole number of electors appointed; and if there be more than one who have such majority, and have an equal number of votes, then the House of Representatives shall immediately choose by ballot one of them for President; and if no person have a majority, then from the five highest on the list the said House shall in like manner choose the President. But in choosing the President the votes shall be taken by states, the representation from each state having one vote. A quorum for this purpose shall consist of a member or members from two-thirds of the states, and a majority of all the states shall be necessary to a choice. In every case, after the choice of the President, the person having the greatest number of votes of the electors shall be the Vice President. But if there should remain two or more who have equal votes, the Senate shall choose from them by ballot the Vice President.*]

4. Nationwide Election Day. The Congress may determine the time of choosing the electors, and the day on which they shall give their votes; which day shall be the same throughout the United States.

5. Requirements Set for the President. No person except a natural-born citizen, [*or a citizen of the United States, at the time of the adoption of this Constitution,*] shall be eligible to the office of President; neither shall any person be eligible to that office who shall not have attained to the age of thirty-five years, and been fourteen years a resident within the United States.

6. Filling a Presidential Vacancy. In case of the removal of the President from office, or of his death, resignation, or inability to discharge the powers and duties of the said office, the same shall devolve on the Vice President, and the Congress may by law provide for the case of removal, death, resignation, or inability, both of the President and Vice President, declaring what officer shall then act as President, and such officer shall act accordingly, until the disability be removed, or a President shall be elected.

7. Salary of the President. The President shall, at stated times, receive for his services, a compensation, which shall neither be increased nor diminished during the period for which he shall have been elected, and he shall not receive within that period any other emolument from the United States, or any of them.

8. Presidential Oath of Office. Before he enter on the execution of his office, he shall take the following oath or affirmation:—"I do solemnly swear (or affirm) that I will faithfully execute the office of President of the United States, and will to the best of my ability, preserve, protect, and defend the Constitution of the United States."

Section 2. Powers of the President

1. Military, Executive, and Judicial Powers. The President shall be Commander in Chief of the Army and Navy of the United States, and of the militia of the several states, when called into the actual service of the United States; he may require the opinion, in writing, of the principal officer in each of the executive departments, upon any subject relating to the duties of their respective offices, and he shall have power to grant reprieves and pardons for offenses against the United States, except in cases of impeachment.

2. Treaty Making and Appointive Powers With the Consent of the Senate. He shall have power, by and with the advice and consent of the Senate, to make treaties, provided two-thirds of the Senators present concur; and he shall nominate, and by and with the advice and consent of the Senate, shall appoint ambassadors, other public ministers and consuls, judges of the Supreme Court, and all other officers of the United States, whose appointments are not herein otherwise provided for, and which shall be established by law; but the Congress may by law vest the appointment of such inferior officers, as they think proper, in the President alone, in the courts of law, or in the heads of departments.

3. Appointments During Recess of the Senate. The President shall have power to fill up all vacancies that may happen during the recess of the Senate, by granting commissions which shall expire at the end of their next session.

Section 3. Further Powers of the President: Legislative, Diplomatic, and Executive

He shall from time to time give to the Congress information of the state of the Union, and recommend to their consideration such measures as he shall judge necessary and expedient; he may, on extraordinary occasions, convene both houses, or either of them, and in case of disagreement between them, with respect to the time of adjournment, he may adjourn them to such time as he shall think proper; he shall receive ambassadors and other public ministers; he shall take care that the laws be faithfully executed, and shall commission all the officers of the United States.

Section 4. Impeachment of Civil Officers

The President, Vice President, and all civil officers of the United States, shall be removed from office on impeachment for, and conviction of, treason, bribery, or other high crimes and misdemeanors.

Article III. The Judicial Branch

Section 1. The Federal Courts: Supreme and Lower Courts; Tenure and Salary of Judges

The judicial power of the United States shall be vested in one Supreme Court, and in such inferior courts as the Congress may from time to time ordain and establish. The judges, both of the Supreme and inferior courts, shall hold their offices during good behavior, and shall, at stated times, receive for their services a compensation, which shall not be diminished during their continuance in office.

Section 2. Jurisdiction of the Federal Courts

1. **Cases Tried in Federal Courts.** The judicial power shall extend to all cases, in law and equity, arising under this Constitution, the laws of the United States, and treaties made or which shall be made, under their authority; to all cases affecting ambassadors, other public ministers and consuls; to all cases of admiralty and maritime jurisdiction; to controversies to which the United States shall be a party; to controversies between two or more states; [*between a state and citizens of another state;*] between citizens of different states; between citizens of the same state claiming lands under grants of different states, and between a state, or the citizens thereof, and foreign states, citizens, or subjects.

2. **Original and Appellate Jurisdiction of the Supreme Court.** In all cases affecting ambassadors, other public ministers and consuls, and those in which a state shall be a party, the Supreme Court shall have original jurisdiction. In all the other cases before mentioned, the Supreme Court shall have appellate jurisdiction, both as to law and fact, with such exceptions, and under such regulations as the Congress shall make.

3. **Rules Regarding Trials.** The trial of all crimes, except in cases of impeachment, shall be by jury; and such trial shall be held in the state where the said crimes shall have been committed; but when not committed within any state, the trial shall be at such place or places as the Congress may by law have directed.

Section 3. Treason

1. Definition of Treason; Requirements for Conviction. Treason against the United States shall consist only in levying war against them, or in adhering to their enemies, giving them aid and comfort. No person shall be convicted of treason unless on the testimony of two witnesses to the same overt act, or on confession in open court.

2. Punishment of Treason Limited to the Guilty Person. The Congress shall have power to declare the punishment of treason, but no attainder of treason shall work corruption of blood or forfeiture except during the life of the person attainted.

Article IV. Relations Among the States and With the Federal Government

Section 1. Relations Among States Regarding Official Acts

Full faith and credit shall be given in each state to the public acts, records, and judicial proceedings of every other state. And the Congress may by general laws prescribe the manner in which such acts, records, and proceedings shall be proved, and the effect thereof.

Section 2. Relations Among States Regarding Citizens and Fugitives

1. Exchange of Privileges of Citizenship. The citizens of each state shall be entitled to all privileges and immunities of citizens in the several states.

2. Extradition: Return of Fugitives From Justice. A person charged in any state with treason, felony, or other crime, who shall flee from justice, and be found in another state, shall on demand of the executive authority of the state from which he fled, be delivered up, to be removed to the state having jurisdiction of the crime.

3. Return of Fugitive Slaves and Indentured Servants. [*No person held in service or labor in one state, under the laws thereof, escaping into another, shall in consequence of any law or regulation therein, be discharged from such service or labor, but shall be delivered up on claim of the party to whom such service or labor may be due.*]

Section 3. New States and Territories

1. Admission of New States. New states may be admitted by the Congress into this Union; but no new state shall be formed or erected within the jurisdiction of any other state; nor any state be formed by the junction of two or more states, or parts of states, without the consent of the legislatures of the states concerned as well as of the Congress.

2. Regulations for Federal Territories and Properties. The Congress shall have power to dispose of and make all needful rules and regulations respecting the territory or other property belonging to the United States; and nothing in this Constitution shall be so construed as to prejudice any claims of the United States, or of any particular state.

Section 4. Federal Protection for the States

The United States shall guarantee to every state in this Union a republican form of government, and shall protect each of them against invasion; and on application of the legislature, or of the executive (when the legislature cannot be convened) against domestic violence.

Article V. Proposing and Ratifying Amendments to the Constitution

The Congress, whenever two-thirds of both houses shall deem it necessary, shall propose amendments to this Constitution, or, on the application of the legislatures of two-thirds of the several states, shall call a convention for proposing amendments, which, in either case shall be valid to all intents and purposes, as part of this Constitution, when ratified by the legislatures of three-fourths of the several states, or by conventions in three-fourths thereof, as the one or the other mode of ratification may be proposed by the Congress; provided that [*no amendments which may be made prior to the year 1808 shall in any manner affect the first and fourth clauses in the Ninth Section of the First Article; and that*] no state, without its consent, shall be deprived of its equal suffrage in the Senate.

Article VI. Miscellaneous Provisions

1. Acceptance of Previously Contracted Public Debts. All debts contracted and engagements entered into, before the adoption of this Constitution, shall be as valid against the United States under this Constitution, as under the Confederation.

2. The Constitution: Supreme Law of the Land. This Constitution, and the laws of the United States which shall be made in pursuance thereof, and all treaties made, or which shall be made, under the authority of the United States, shall be the supreme law of the land; and the judges in every state shall be bound thereby, anything in the constitution or laws of any state to the contrary notwithstanding.

3. Official Oath of Office; No Religious Test. The Senators and Representatives before mentioned, and the members of the several state legislatures, and all executive and judicial officers, both of the United States and of the several states, shall be bound by oath or affirmation, to support this Constitution; but no religious test shall ever be required as a qualification to any office or public trust under the United States.

Article VII. Ratification of the Constitution: Assent Required of Nine States

The ratification of the conventions of nine states shall be sufficient for the establishment of this Constitution between the states so ratifying the same.

Amendments to the Constitution

Amendment I (1791). Freedom of Religion, Speech, Press, Assembly, and Petition

Congress shall make no law respecting an establishment of religion, or prohibiting the free exercise thereof; or abridging the freedom of speech, or of the press; or the right of the people peaceably to assemble, and to petition the government for a redress of grievances.

Amendment II (1791). Right to a State Militia and to Bear Arms

A well-regulated militia, being necessary to the security of a free state, the right of the people to keep and bear arms shall not be infringed.

Amendment III (1791). Regulations for Quartering of Troops

No soldier shall, in time of peace, be quartered in any house, without the consent of the owner; nor in time of war, but in a manner to be prescribed by law.

Amendment IV (1791). No Unreasonable Searches and No Vague Search Warrants

The right of the people to be secure in their persons, houses, papers, and effects, against unreasonable searches and seizures, shall not be violated; and no warrants shall issue but upon probable cause, supported by oath or affirmation, and particularly describing the place to be searched, and the persons or things to be seized.

Amendment V (1791). Rights of Accused Persons; Protection of Private Property

No person shall be held to answer for a capital, or otherwise infamous, crime, unless on a presentment or indictment of a grand jury, except in cases arising in the land or naval forces, or in the militia, when in actual service in time of war or public danger; nor shall any person be subject for the same offense to be twice put in jeopardy of life or limb; nor shall be compelled, in any criminal case, to be a witness against himself; nor be deprived of life, liberty, or property, without due process of law; nor shall private property be taken for public use, without just compensation.

Amendment VI (1791). Further Rights of Accused Persons

In all criminal prosecutions, the accused shall enjoy the right to a speedy and public trial, by an impartial jury of the state and district wherein the crime shall have been committed, which district shall have been previously ascertained by law, and to be informed of the nature and cause of the accusation; to be confronted with the witnesses against him; to have compulsory process for obtaining witnesses in his favor, and to have the assistance of counsel for his defense.

Amendment VII (1791). Trial by Jury in Most Civil Cases

In suits at common law, where the value in controversy shall exceed twenty dollars, the right of trial by jury shall be preserved, and no fact tried by a jury shall be otherwise reexamined in any court of the United States than according to the rules of the common law.

Amendment VIII (1791). No Excessive Bail or Cruel Punishments

Excessive bail shall not be required, nor excessive fines imposed, nor cruel and unusual punishments inflicted.

Amendment IX (1791). Unlisted Rights Reserved to the People

The enumeration in the Constitution, of certain rights, shall not be construed to deny or disparage others retained by the people.

Amendment X (1791). Powers Reserved to the States or People

The powers not delegated to the United States by the Constitution, nor prohibited by it to the states, are reserved to the states respectively, or to the people.

Amendment XI (1798). No Suits in Federal Courts by Individuals Against a State

The judicial power of the United States shall not be construed to extend to any suit in law or equity, commenced or prosecuted against one of the United States, by citizens of another state, or by citizens or subjects of any foreign state.

Amendment XII (1804). Revised Procedures for Electing the President and Vice President

The electors shall meet in their respective states, and vote by ballot for President and Vice President, one of whom, at least, shall not be an inhabitant of the same state with themselves; they shall name in their ballots the person voted for as President, and in distinct ballots the person voted for as Vice President, and they shall make distinct lists of all persons voted for as President, and of all persons voted for as Vice President, and of the number of votes for each, which lists they shall sign and certify, and transmit, sealed, to the seat of government of the United States, directed to the President of the Senate; the President of the Senate shall, in the presence of the Senate and House of Representatives, open all the certificates and the votes shall then be counted; the person having the greatest number of votes for President shall be the President, if such number be a majority of the whole number of electors appointed; and if no person have such majority, then from the persons having the highest numbers not exceeding three on the list of those voted for as President, the House of Representatives shall choose immediately, by ballot, the President. But in choosing the President, the votes shall be taken by states, the representation from each state having one vote; a quorum for this purpose shall consist of a member or members from two-thirds of the states, and a majority of all the states shall be necessary to a choice. And if the House of Representatives shall not choose a President whenever the right of choice shall devolve upon them, [before the fourth day of March next following,] then the Vice President shall act as President, as in the case of the death or other constitutional disability of the President. The person having the greatest number of votes as Vice President shall be the Vice President, if such number be a majority of the whole number of electors appointed, and if no person have a majority, then, from the two highest numbers on the list, the Senate shall choose the Vice President; a quorum for the purpose shall consist of two-thirds of the whole number of Senators, and a majority of the whole number shall be necessary to a choice. But no person constitutionally ineligible to the office of President shall be eligible to that of Vice President of the United States.

Amendment XIII (1865). Abolition of Slavery

Section 1. No Slavery in the United States. Neither slavery nor involuntary servitude, except as a punishment for crime whereof the party shall have been duly convicted, shall exist within the United States, or any place subject to their jurisdiction.

Section 2. Enforcement. Congress shall have power to enforce this article by appropriate legislation.

Amendment XIV (1868). Protection of Civil Liberties Against State Infringement; Measures Against Former Confederate Leaders and Bondholders

Section 1. Definition of Citizenship; Due Process of Law and Equal Protection of the Laws. All persons born or naturalized in the United States and subject to the jurisdiction thereof, are citizens of the United States and of the state wherein they reside. No state shall make or enforce any law which shall abridge the privileges or immunities of citizens of the United States; nor shall any state deprive any person of life, liberty, or property, without due process of law; nor deny to any person within its jurisdiction the equal protection of the laws.

Section 2. Reduction of Representation of States Denying Vote to Citizens. Representatives shall be apportioned among the several states according to their respective numbers, counting the whole number of persons in each state, excluding Indians not taxed. But when the right to vote at any election for the choice of electors for President and Vice President of the United States, Representatives in Congress, the executive and judicial officers of a state, or the members of the legislature thereof, is denied to any of the male inhabitants of such state, being twenty-one years of age and citizens of the United States, or in any way abridged, except for participation in rebellion, or other crime, the basis of representation therein shall be reduced in the proportion which the number of such male citizens shall bear to the whole number of male citizens twenty-one years of age in such state.

Section 3. Exclusion of Former Confederate Leaders From Public Office. No person shall be a Senator or Representative in Congress, or elector of President and Vice President, or hold any office, civil or military, under the United States, or under any state, who, having previously taken an oath, as a member of Congress, or as an officer of the United States, or as a member of any state legislature, or as an executive or judicial officer of any state, to support the Constitution of the United States, shall have engaged in insurrection or rebellion against the same, or given aid or comfort to the enemies thereof. But Congress may, by vote of two-thirds of each house, remove such disability.

Section 4. No Repayment of the Confederate Debt. The validity of the public debt of the United States, authorized by law, including debts incurred for payment of pensions and bounties for services in suppressing insurrection or rebellion, shall not be questioned. But neither the United States nor any state shall assume or pay any debt or obligation incurred in aid of insurrection or rebellion against the United States, or any claim for the loss or emancipation of any slave; but all such debts, obligations, and claims shall be held illegal and void.

Section 5. Enforcement. The Congress shall have power to enforce, by appropriate legislation, the provisions of this article.

Amendment XV (1870). Right of Citizens to Vote

Section 1. Conditions Irrelevant to Suffrage. The right of citizens of the United States to vote shall not be denied or abridged by the United States or any state on account of race, color, or previous condition of servitude.

Section 2. Enforcement. The Congress shall have power to enforce this article by appropriate legislation.

Amendment XVI (1913). Power to Levy Income Taxes

The Congress shall have power to lay and collect taxes on incomes, from whatever source derived, without apportionment among the several states, and without regard to any census or enumeration.

Amendment XVII (1913). Direct Election of Senators

Section 1. Election by the People. The Senate of the United States shall be composed of two Senators from each state, elected by the people thereof, for six years; and each Senator shall have one vote. The electors in each state shall have the qualifications requisite for electors of the most numerous branch of the state legislatures.

Section 2. Regulations Regarding Vacancies and Temporary Appointments. When vacancies happen in the representation of any state in the Senate, the executive authority of such state shall issue writs of election to fill such vacancies: *Provided* that the legislature of any state may empower the executive thereof to make temporary appointments until the people fill the vacancies by election as the legislature may direct.

Section 3. Provisions Not Retroactive. [*This amendment shall not be so construed as to affect the election or term of any Senator chosen before it becomes valid as part of the Constitution.*]

Amendment XVIII (1919). National Prohibition

Section 1. No Manufacture, Sale, or Transportation of Intoxicating Liquors. [*After one year from the ratification of this article the manufacture, sale, or transportation of intoxicating liquors within, the importation thereof into, or the exportation thereof from, the United States and all territory subject to the jurisdiction thereof for beverage purposes is hereby prohibited.*]

Section 2. Enforcement. [*The Congress and the several states shall have concurrent power to enforce this article by appropriate legislation.*]

Section 3. Ratification Required Within Seven Years. [*This article shall be inoperative unless it shall have been ratified as an amendment to the Constitution by the legislatures of the several states, as provided in the Constitution, within seven years from the date of the submission hereof to the states by the Congress.*]

Amendment XIX (1920). Right of Women Citizens to Vote

Section 1. Woman Suffrage. The right of citizens of the United States to vote shall not be denied or abridged by the United States or by any state on account of sex.

Section 2. Enforcement. Congress shall have power to enforce this article by appropriate legislation.

Amendment XX (1933). Various Governmental Details, Especially No "Lame Duck" Congressmen

Section 1. Revised Dates for Terms of President, Vice President, and Congressmen. The terms of the President and Vice President shall end at noon on the 20th day of January, and the terms of Senators and Representatives at noon on the 3rd day of January, of the years in which such terms would have ended if this article had not been ratified; and the terms of their successors shall then begin.

Section 2. Revised Date for Sessions of Congress. The Congress shall assemble at least once in every year, and such meeting shall begin at noon on the 3rd day of January, unless they shall by law appoint a different day.

Section 3. Presidential Succession in Unusual Circumstances. If at the time fixed for the beginning of the term of the President, the President-elect shall have died, the Vice President-elect shall become President. If a President shall not have been chosen before the time fixed for the beginning of his term, or if the President-elect shall have failed to qualify, then the Vice President-elect shall act as President until a President shall have qualified; and the Congress may by law provide for the case wherein neither a President-elect nor a Vice President-elect shall have qualified, declaring who shall then act as President, or the manner in which one who is to act shall be selected, and such person shall act accordingly until a President or Vice President shall have qualified.

Section 4. Congress and Presidential Election in Unusual Circumstances. The Congress may by law provide for the case of the death of any of the persons from whom the House of Representatives may choose a President whenever the right of choice shall have devolved upon them, and for the case of the death of any of the persons from whom the Senate may choose a Vice President whenever the right of choice shall have devolved upon them.

Section 5. Effective Date of This Amendment. [*Sections 1 and 2 shall take effect on the 15th day of October following the ratification of this article.*]

Section 6. Ratification Required Within Seven Years. [*This article shall be inoperative unless it shall have been ratified as an amendment to the Constitution by the legislatures of three-fourths of the several states within seven years from the date of its submission.*]

Amendment XXI (1933). Repeal of Prohibition

Section 1. Repeal of Eighteenth Amendment. The eighteenth article of amendment to the Constitution of the United States is hereby repealed.

Section 2. Control of Liquor Left to the States. The transportation or importation into any state, territory, or possession of the United States for delivery or use therein of intoxicating liquors, in violation of the laws thereof, is hereby prohibited.

Section 3. Ratification Required Within Seven Years by State Conventions. [*This article shall be inoperative unless it shall have been ratified as an amendment to the Constitution by conventions in the several states, as provided in the Constitution, within seven years from the date of the submission hereof to the states by the Congress.*]

Amendment XXII (1951). Limitation on Presidential Terms

Section 1. No More Than Two Elected Terms as President. No person shall be elected to the office of the President more than twice, and no person who has held the office of President, or acted as President, for more than two years of a term to which some other person was elected President shall be elected to the office of the President more than once. [*But this Article shall not apply to any person holding the office of President when this Article was proposed by the Congress, and shall not prevent any person who may be holding the office of*

President, or acting as President, during the term within which this Article becomes operative from holding the office of President or acting as President during the remainder of such term.]

Section 2. Ratification Required Within Seven Years. [*This article shall be inoperative unless it shall have been ratified as an amendment to the Constitution by the legislatures of three-fourths of the several states within seven years from the date of its submission to the states by the Congress.*]

Amendment XXIII (1961). Presidential Electors for the District of Columbia

Section 1. Number of Electors. The District constituting the seat of Government of the United States shall appoint in such manner as the Congress may direct:

A number of electors of President and Vice President equal to the whole number of Senators and Representatives in Congress to which the District would be entitled if it were a State, but in no event more than the least populous State; they shall be in addition to those appointed by the States, but they shall be considered, for the purposes of the election of President and Vice President, to be electors appointed by a State; and they shall meet in the District and perform such duties as provided by the twelfth article of amendment.

Section 2. Enforcement. The Congress shall have power to enforce this article by appropriate legislation.

Amendment XXIV (1964). No Poll Tax in Federal Elections

Section 1. Citizens to Vote Without Payment of a Poll Tax. The right of citizens of the United States to vote in any primary or other election for President or Vice President, for electors for President or Vice President, or for Senator or Representative in Congress, shall not be denied or abridged by the United States or any state by reason of failure to pay any poll tax or other tax.

Section 2. Enforcement. The Congress shall have the power to enforce this article by appropriate legislation.

Amendment XXV (1967). Presidential Disability and Succession

Section 1. Filling a Presidential Vacancy. In case of the removal of the President from office or of his death or resignation, the Vice President shall become President.

Section 2. Filling a Vice Presidential Vacancy. Whenever there is a vacancy in the office of the Vice President, the President shall nominate a Vice President who shall take office upon confirmation by a majority vote of both houses of Congress.

Section 3. Presidential Disability: Vice President as Acting President. Whenever the President transmits to the President pro tempore of the Senate and the Speaker of the House of Representatives his written declaration that he is unable to discharge the powers and duties of his office, and until he transmits to them a written declaration to the contrary, such powers and duties shall be discharged by the Vice President as Acting President.

Section 4. Resumption of Power by the President. Whenever the Vice President and a majority of either the principal officers of the executive departments or of such other body as Congress may by law provide transmit to the President pro tempore of the Senate and the Speaker of the House of Representatives their written declaration that the President is unable to discharge the powers and duties of his office, the Vice President shall immediately assume the powers and duties of the office as Acting President.

Thereafter, when the President transmits to the President pro tempore of the Senate and the Speaker of the House of Representatives his written declaration that no inability exists, he shall resume the powers and duties of his office unless the Vice President and a majority of either the principal officers of the executive department or of such other body as Congress may by law provide transmit within four days to the President pro tempore of the Senate and the Speaker of the House of Representatives their written declaration that the President is unable to discharge the powers and duties of his office. Thereupon Congress shall decide the issue, assembling within forty-eight hours for that purpose if not in session. If the Congress, within twenty-one days after receipt of the latter written declaration, or, if Congress is not in session, within twenty-one days after Congress is required to assemble, determines by two-thirds vote of both houses that the President is unable to discharge the powers and duties of his office, the Vice President shall continue to discharge the same as Acting President; otherwise, the President shall resume the powers and duties of his office.

Amendment XXVI (1971). Right of Younger Citizens to Vote

Section 1. Voting Age Set at Eighteen. The right of citizens of the United States, who are eighteen years of age or older, to vote shall not be denied or abridged by the United States or any state on account of age.

Section 2. Enforcement. The Congress shall have the power to enforce this article by appropriate legislation.

Index